EVIDENCE

ASPEN CASEBOOK SERIES

EVIDENCE

Practice, Problems, and Rules
Third Edition

Arthur Best

Professor Emeritus of Law
University of Denver
Sturm College of Law

To contact Customer Service, e-mail customer.service@aspenpublishing.com, call 1-800-950-5259, or mail correspondence to:

    Aspen Publishing
    Attn: Order Department
    PO Box 990
    Frederick, MD 21705

Printed in the United States of America.

3 4 5 6 7 8 9 0

ISBN 978-1-5438-2448-3

Library of Congress Cataloging-in-Publication Data

Names: Best, Arthur, author.
Title: Evidence: practice, problems, and rules / Arthur Best, Professor
   Emeritus of Law, University of Denver, Sturm College of Law.
Description: Third edition. | Frederick, MD: Aspen Publishing, [2021] | Series:
   Aspen casebook series | Includes bibliographical references and index. |
   Summary: "This is a law school casebook on evidence" — Provided by
   publisher.
Identifiers: LCCN 2020042325 (print) | LCCN 2020042326 (ebook) | ISBN
   9781543824483 (hardcover) | ISBN 9781543824490 (ebook)
Subjects: LCSH: Evidence (Law)—United States. | LCGFT: Casebooks (Law)
Classification: LCC KF8935.B399 2020 (print) | LCC KF8935 (ebook) | DDC
   347.73/6—dc23
LC record available at https://lccn.loc.gov/2020042325
LC ebook record available at https://lccn.loc.gov/2020042326

About Aspen Publishing

Aspen Publishing is a leading provider of educational content and digital learning solutions to law schools in the U.S. and around the world. Aspen provides best-in-class solutions for legal education through authoritative textbooks, written by renowned authors, and breakthrough products such as Connected eBooks, Connected Quizzing, and PracticePerfect.

The Aspen Casebook Series (famously known among law faculty and students as the "red and black" casebooks) encompasses hundreds of highly regarded textbooks in more than eighty disciplines, from large enrollment courses, such as Torts and Contracts to emerging electives such as Sustainability and the Law of Policing. Study aids such as the *Examples & Explanations* and the *Emanuel Law Outlines* series, both highly popular collections, help law students master complex subject matter.

Major products, programs, and initiatives include:

- **Connected eBooks** are enhanced digital textbooks and study aids that come with a suite of online content and learning tools designed to maximize student success. Designed in collaboration with hundreds of faculty and students, the Connected eBook is a significant leap forward in the legal education learning tools available to students.
- **Connected Quizzing** is an easy-to-use formative assessment tool that tests law students' understanding and provides timely feedback to improve learning outcomes. Delivered through CasebookConnect.com, the learning platform already used by students to access their Aspen casebooks, Connected Quizzing is simple to implement and integrates seamlessly with law school course curricula.
- **PracticePerfect** is a visually engaging, interactive study aid to explain commonly encountered legal doctrines through easy-to-understand animated videos, illustrative examples, and numerous practice questions. Developed by a team of experts, PracticePerfect is the ideal study companion for today's law students.
- The **Aspen Learning Library** enables law schools to provide their students with access to the most popular study aids on the market across all of their courses. Available through an annual subscription, the online library consists of study aids in e-book, audio, and video formats with full text search, note-taking, and highlighting capabilities.
- Aspen's **Digital Bookshelf** is an institutional-level online education bookshelf, consolidating everything students and professors need to ensure success. This program ensures that every student has access to affordable course materials from day one.
- **Leading Edge** is a community centered on thinking differently about legal education and putting those thoughts into actionable strategies. At the core of the program is the Leading Edge Conference, an annual gathering of legal education thought leaders looking to pool ideas and identify promising directions of exploration.

To the memory of A. Leo Levin, the inspiring professor who introduced me to the field of Evidence, and to the many hundreds of students with whom I've had the honor of continuing that study.

SUMMARY OF CONTENTS

Contents   *xi*
Preface   *xxvii*
Acknowledgments   *xxix*
Using the Videos   *xxxi*

1. Relevance   1
2. Social Policy Relevancy Rules   45
3. Proof of Character   73
4. Habit and Sexual Conduct in the Context of Character   127
5. Hearsay: Foundations of the Doctrine   159
6. Opponents' Statements   199
7. Witnesses' Own Out-of-Court Statements   227
8. Hearsay Exceptions: Spontaneous and Personal Statements   259
9. Hearsay Exceptions: Recorded Statements   309
10. Hearsay: Unavailability Required Exceptions   359
11. Modifications of the Basic Hearsay Rules   383
12. Impeachment   447
13. Witnesses   513
14. Opinions   553
15. Privileges   607
16. Authentication and the Original Writing Rule   663
17. Presumptions and Judicial Notice   691

Table of Cases   *713*
Table of Authorities   *719*
Index   *723*

CONTENTS

Preface   xxvii
Acknowledgments   xxix
Using the Videos   xxxi

1   RELEVANCE   1

A. Introduction to Evidence Law   1

B. Introduction to Relevance   2
Topic Overview   2
Chapter Organization   3
Basic Structure for Analysis   3

C. Relevance and Admissibility, Defined and Distinguished   4
Rule 401. Test for Relevant Evidence   4
Rule 402. General Admissibility of Relevant Evidence   4
Rule 403. Excluding Relevant Evidence for Prejudice, Confusion,
    Waste of Time, or Other Reasons   5
Supreme Pork, Inc. v. Master Blaster, Inc.   6
Notes to *Supreme Pork, Inc. v. Master Blaster, Inc.*   10

D. Relevance and Substantive Legal Theory   12
Kaechele v. Kenyon Oil Company, Inc.   12
Notes to *Kaechele v. Kenyon Oil Company, Inc.*   15

**E. Recurring Relevance Patterns—Flight, Safety Record,
    and Destruction of Evidence   16**
United States v. Dillon   17
Notes to *United States v. Dillon*   19
Lovick v. Wil-Rich   20
Notes to *Lovick v. Wil-Rich*   23
Spino v. John S. Tilley Ladder Co.   23
Notes to *Spino v. John S. Tilley Ladder Co.*   27
Aloi v. Union Pacific Railroad Corp.   27
Notes to *Aloi v. Union Pacific Railroad Corp.*   31

F. **Conditional Relevance   32**

Rule 104. Preliminary Questions   32
Cox v. State   33
Notes to *Cox v. State*   35

G. **Discretion to Exclude Relevant Evidence   36**

Old Chief v. United States   37
Notes to *Old Chief v. United States*   43

H. **Summary   43**

2   SOCIAL POLICY RELEVANCY RULES   45

A. **Introduction   45**

Topic Overview   45
Chapter Organization   45

B. **Special Treatment for Subsequent Remedial Measures   46**

Rule 407. Subsequent Remedial Measures   46
Cyr v. J.I. Case Co.   47
Notes to *Cyr v. J.I. Case Co.   50*
Bethel v. Peters   52
Notes to *Bethel v. Peters   54*

C. **"Feasibility" Rationale for Admitting Subsequent Remedial Measures   55**

Flaminio v. Honda Motor Co., Ltd.   56
Kenny v. Southeastern Pennsylvania Transportation Authority   57
Notes to *Flaminio v. Honda Motor Co., Ltd.* and *Kenny v. Southeastern Pennsylvania Transportation Authority   58*

D. **Special Treatment for Compromises and Settlements   61**

Rule 408. Compromise Offers and Negotiations   61
Wal-Mart Stores, Inc. v. Londagin   62
Notes to *Wal-Mart Stores, Inc. v. Londagin   64*

E. **Bias Admission of Settlement Evidence   65**

Quirion v. Forcier   66
Notes to *Quirion v. Forcier   69*

F. **Postinjury Payments, Insurance, and Pleas   70**

Rule 409. Offers to Pay Medical and Similar Expenses   70
Rule 410. Pleas, Plea Discussions, and Related Statements   70
Rule 411. Liability Insurance   71

G. **Summary   71**

3 PROOF OF CHARACTER   73

A. Introduction   73

Topic Overview   73
Chapter Organization   74
Basic Structure for Analysis   75

B. Basic Rule Against Propensity Evidence   75

Rule 404. Character Evidence; Crimes or Other Acts   76
Boyd v. United States   76
Notes to *Boyd v. United States*   78
John A. Russell Corp. v. Bohlig   79
Notes to *John A. Russell Corp. v. Bohlig*   81
Rule 405. Methods of Proving Character   82

C. Permitted Propensity Inferences   83

Rule 404. Character Evidence; Crimes or Other Acts   83
City of Kennewick v. Day   84
Notes to *City of Kennewick v. Day*   86
State v. Gowan   88
Notes to *State v. Gowan*   91

D. Permitted Propensity Inferences About the Victim   92

Rule 404. Character Evidence; Crimes or Other Acts   92
Commonwealth v. Adjutant   93
Notes to *Commonwealth v. Adjutant*   96
United States v. Taken Alive   97
Notes to *United States v. Taken Alive*   100

E. Nonpropensity Use of Evidence That May Also Show Propensity   101

Rule 404. Character Evidence; Crimes or Other Acts   101
State v. Foxhoven   102
Notes to *State v. Foxhoven*   105
United States v. Queen   107
Notes to *United States v. Queen*   111
State v. Winebarger   112
Notes to *State v. Winebarger*   115
Leyva v. State   116
Notes to *Leyva v. State*   118
State v. Willett   119
Notes to *State v. Willett*   122

F. Summary   124

4   HABIT AND SEXUAL CONDUCT IN THE CONTEXT OF CHARACTER   127

A. Introduction   127

Topic Overview   127
Chapter Organization   128

B. Habit   128

Rule 406. Habit; Routine Practice   129
State v. Brown   130
Notes to *State v. Brown   132*
Aikman v. Kanda   132
Notes to *Aikman v. Kanda   135*
Gamerdinger v. Schaefer   136
Notes to *Gamerdinger v. Schaefer   138*

C. Alleged Victims of Sex Crimes   139

Rule 412. Sex-Offense Cases: The Victim's Sexual Behavior
    or Predisposition   139
Williams v. State   141
Notes to *Williams v. State   144*
State v. Jones   145
Notes to *State v. Jones   148*
Fells v. State   149
Notes to *Fells v. State   150*

D. Defendants Accused of Sex Crimes   151

Rule 413. Similar Crimes in Sexual-Assault Cases   152
United States v. Hollow Horn   152
Notes to *United States v. Hollow Horn   156*

E. Summary   157

5   HEARSAY: FOUNDATIONS OF THE DOCTRINE   159

A. Introduction   159

Topic Overview   159
Chapter Organization   160
Basic Structure for Analysis   160

B. Statements That Are Relevant Only if What They Assert Is True (Hearsay)   162

Rule 801. Definitions That Apply to This Article...   162
Rule 802. The Rule Against Hearsay   162
Vincelette v. Metropolitan Life Insurance Co.   163

Notes to *Vincelette v. Metropolitan Life Insurance Co.*   165
State v. Patterson   *166*
Notes to *State v. Patterson*   168
Schaffer v. State   *169*
Notes to *Schaffer v. State*   171
Biegas v. Quickway Carriers, Inc.   *172*
Notes to *Biegas v. Quickway Carriers, Inc.*   173

C. Statements That Are Relevant Regardless of Whether Their Assertions Are True (Not Hearsay)   **174**

United States v. Tenerelli   *175*
Notes to *United States v. Tenerelli*   177
Moen v. Thomas   *177*
Notes to *Moen v. Thomas*   180
Kenyon v. State   *181*
Note to *Kenyon v. State*   184
Field v. Trigg County Hospital, Inc.   *185*
Notes to *Field v. Trigg County Hospital, Inc.*   187
Hickey v. Settlemier   *188*
Notes to *Hickey v. Settlemier*   190
State v. Dullard   *191*
Note to *State v. Dullard*   196

D. Summary   **197**

6   OPPONENTS' STATEMENTS   199

A. Introduction   **199**
Topic Overview   199
Rule 801. Definitions That Apply to This Article; Exclusions from Hearsay   200
Chapter Organization   200

B. Party's Own Statement   **201**
United States v. Sprick   *201*
Notes to *United States v. Sprick*   203
Shields v. Reddo   *203*
Notes to *Shields v. Reddo*   204
Application of City of New York re Lincoln Square Slum Clearance Project   *205*
Notes to *Lincoln Square Slum Clearance Project*   205

C. Adoptive Statements   **207**
State v. Lambert   *207*
Notes to *State v. Lambert*   209

State v. Carlson   209
Notes to *State v. Carlson*   212

D. Authorized Speakers   213

Barnett v. Hidalgo   214
Notes to *Barnett v. Hidalgo*   216

E. Statements by a Party's Agent or Employee   216

B & K Rentals and Sales Co., Inc. v. Universal Leaf Tobacco Co.   217
Notes to *B & K Rentals and Sales Co., Inc. v. Universal Leaf Tobacco Co.*   220

F. Coconspirators' Statements   221

State v. Cornell   221
Notes to *State v. Cornell*   224

G. Summary   225

7 **WITNESSES' OWN OUT-OF-COURT STATEMENTS   227**

A. Introduction   227

Topic Overview   227
Rule 801. Definitions That Apply to This Article; Exclusions from
   Hearsay   228
Chapter Organization   228

B. Substantive and Nonsubstantive Use of a Witness's Prior Statements   229

C. Prior Inconsistent Statements by a Witness   229

United States v. Neadeau   230
United States v. Gajo   230
Notes to *United States v. Neadeau* and *United States v. Gajo*   233
United States v. Day   234
Notes to *United States v. Day*   237

D. Prior Consistent Statements by a Witness   238

Tome v. United States   239
Notes to *Tome v. United States*   243

E. Statements Identifying a Person Made After Perceiving the Person   245

United States v. Lewis   245
Notes to *United States v. Lewis*   248
State v. Shaw   249
Notes to *State v. Shaw*   251

F. "Subject to Cross-Examination" Requirement 252

Goforth v. State *252*
Notes to *Goforth v. State* 255

G. Summary 256

8 HEARSAY EXCEPTIONS: SPONTANEOUS AND PERSONAL STATEMENTS 259

A. Introduction 259

Topic Overview 259
Chapter Organization 260

B. Present Sense Impression and Excited Utterance 260

Rule 803. Exceptions to the Rule Against Hearsay—Regardless
   of Whether the Declarant Is Available as a Witness 260
Fischer v. State *261*
Notes to *Fischer v. State* 264
Pressey v. State *266*
Notes to *Pressey v. State* 268
State v. Flores *270*
Notes to *State v. Flores* 272
Graure v. United States *272*
Notes to *United States v. Graure* 274

C. Statement of Then-Existing Mental, Emotional, or Physical Condition 275

Rule 803. Exceptions to the Rule Against Hearsay—Regardless
   of Whether the Declarant Is Available as a Witness 275
Stoll v. State *276*
Notes to *Stoll v. State* 278
Schering Corp. v. Pfizer, Inc. *280*
Notes to *Schering Corp. v. Pfizer, Inc.* 283
State v. James *285*
Notes to *State v. James* 288
Camm v. State *289*
Notes to *Camm v. State* 291

D. Statements for Purposes of Medical Diagnosis or Treatment 292

Rule 803. Exceptions to the Rule Against Hearsay—Regardless
   of Whether the Declarant Is Available as a Witness 292
Hansen v. Heath *293*
Notes to *Hansen v. Heath* 295
Oldman v. State *296*
Notes to *Oldman v. State* 299

Colvard v. Commonwealth   *301*
Notes to *Colvard v. Commonwealth*   304

E. **Summary**   **306**

9   HEARSAY EXCEPTIONS: RECORDED STATEMENTS   309

A. **Introduction**   **309**

Topic Overview   309
Chapter Organization   310

B. **Recorded Recollection (and Present Recollection Refreshed)**   **310**

1. Recorded Recollection   310
   Rule 803. Exceptions to the Rule Against Hearsay—Regardless of Whether the Declarant Is Available as a Witness   311
   United States v. Jones   *311*
   Notes to *United States v. Jones*   313
   State v. Taylor   *314*
   Notes to *State v. Taylor*   317
   United States v. Dazey   *318*
   Notes to *United States v. Dazey*   320
2. Refreshing Present Recollection   321
   Rule 612. Writing Used to Refresh a Witness's Memory   322
   Germain v. State   *322*
   Notes to *Germain v. State*   326
   Rush v. Illinois-Central Railroad Co.   *326*
   Notes to *Rush v. Illinois-Central Railroad Co.*   330
   Rule 611. Mode and Order of Examining Witnesses and Presenting Evidence   330

C. **Records of Regularly Conducted Activity (Business Records)**   **333**

Rule 803. Exceptions to the Rule Against Hearsay—Regardless of Whether the Declarant Is Available as a Witness   334
United States v. Briscoe   *334*
Notes to *United States v. Briscoe*   336
Lust v. Sealy, Inc.   *336*
Notes to *Lust v. Sealy, Inc.*   338
United States v. Blechman   *339*
Notes to *United States v. Blechman*   342
Beneficial Maine, Inc. v. Carter   *343*
Notes to *Beneficial Maine, Inc. v. Carter*   347
People v. Ortega   *348*
Notes to *People v. Ortega*   349
Rule 803. Exceptions to the Rule Against Hearsay—Regardless of Whether the Declarant Is Available as a Witness   350

D. Public Records 350

Rule 803. Exceptions to the Rule Against Hearsay—Regardless of Whether
  the Declarant Is Available as a Witness 350
United States v. Midwest Fireworks Mfg. Co., Inc. 351
Notes to *United States v. Midwest Fireworks Mfg. Co., Inc.* 352
United States v. Dowdell 353
Notes to *United States v. Dowdell* 356

E. Summary 357

**10 HEARSAY: UNAVAILABILITY REQUIRED
EXCEPTIONS 359**

A. Introduction 359

Topic Overview 359
Chapter Organization 360

B. Former Testimony 360

Rule 804. Exceptions to the Rule Against Hearsay—When the
  Declarant Is Unavailable as a Witness 360
O'Banion v. Owens-Corning Fiberglas Corp. 361
Notes to *O'Banion v. Owens-Corning Fiberglas Corp.* 363
Rule 804. Exceptions to the Rule Against Hearsay—When the
  Declarant Is Unavailable as a Witness 364

C. Dying Declarations 365

Rule 804. Exceptions to the Rule Against Hearsay—When the
  Declarant Is Unavailable as a Witness 365
Grant v. State 365
Notes to *Grant v. State* 367

D. Statements Against Interest 368

Rule 804. Exceptions to the Rule Against Hearsay—When the
  Declarant Is Unavailable as a Witness 368
State v. Paredes 369
Notes to *State v. Paredes* 374

E. Statement by a Declarant Rendered Unavailable 375

Rule 804. Exceptions to the Rule Against Hearsay—When the
  Declarant Is Unavailable as a Witness 376
United States v. Gray 376
Notes to *United States v. Gray* 379

F. Summary 381

11 MODIFICATIONS OF THE BASIC HEARSAY RULES   383

A. Introduction   383

Topic Overview   383
Chapter Organization   384

B. Residual Exception   384

Rule 807. Residual Exception   385
Broderick v. King's Way Assembly of God Church   385
Notes to *Broderick v. King's Way Assembly of God Church*   388
People v. Katt   390
Notes to *People v. Katt*   394

C. Due Process Clause   395

State v. Cazares-Mendez   395
Notes to *State v. Cazares-Mendez*   402

D. Confrontation Clause   403

1. The Constitutional Issue and Its Treatment Prior to 2004   403
   United States Constitution, Sixth Amendment   404
2. New in 2004: The *Crawford* Analysis   404
   Davis v. Washington (*Hammon v. Indiana*)   405
   Notes to *Davis v. Washington*   410
   Giles v. California   411
   Notes to *Giles v. California*   414
3. Evolving Understanding of *Crawford*: Statements About Recent Criminal Conduct   414
   Michigan v. Bryant   415
   Notes to *Michigan v. Bryant*   421
   Ohio v. Clark   422
   Notes to *Ohio v. Clark*   426
4. Evolving Understanding of *Crawford*: Routine Documents in the Criminal Investigation Process   427
   Melendez-Diaz v. Massachusetts   427
   Notes to *Melendez-Diaz v. Massachusetts*   431
   Bullcoming v. New Mexico   431
   Notes to *Bullcoming v. New Mexico*   437
   Williams v. Illinois   437
   Notes to *Williams v. Illinois*   443

E. Summary   444

12 IMPEACHMENT 447

A. Introduction 447

Topic Overview 447
Rule 607. Who May Impeach a Witness 447
Chapter Organization 448

B. Reputation, Opinion, and Past Acts to Show Character for Truth Telling 449

Rule 608. A Witness's Character for Truthfulness or Untruthfulness 449
State v. Caldwell 450
Notes to *State v. Caldwell* 454
Rule 608. A Witness's Character for Truthfulness or Untruthfulness 456
People v. Segovia 456
Notes to *People v. Segovia* 460
State v. Guenther 461
Notes to *State v. Guenther* 465

C. Criminal Convictions to Show Character for Truth Telling 467

Rule 609. Impeachment by Evidence of a Criminal Conviction 467
State v. Hardy 470
State v. Williams 473
Notes to *State v. Hardy* and *State v. Williams* 475

D. Bias 478

United States v. Abel 478
Notes to *United States v. Abel* 483
Olden v. Kentucky 484
Notes to *Olden v. Kentucky* 487
Woolum v. Hillman 488
Notes to *Woolum v. Hillman* 492
Wrobleski v. de Lara 492
Notes to *Wrobleski v. de Lara* 496

E. Contradiction and Prior Inconsistent Statements 497

Rule 611. Mode and Order of Examining Witnesses and Presenting Evidence 498
Langness v. Fencil Urethane Systems, Inc. 499
Notes to *Langness v. Fencil Urethane Systems, Inc.* 501
McKee v. State 501
Notes to *McKee v. State* 503
Rule 613. Witness's Prior Statement 504
United States v. Schnapp 505
Notes to *United States v. Schnapp* 508

F. Impeaching Hearsay Declarants   509

Rule 806. Attacking and Supporting the Declarant's Credibility   509

G. Summary   510

13   WITNESSES   513

A. Introduction   513

Topic Overview   513
Chapter Organization   513

B. Personal Knowledge   514

Rule 602. Need for Personal Knowledge   514
State v. Long   514
Notes to *State v. Long*   516

C. Competency: Personal Traits   517

Rule 601. Competency to Testify in General   518
United States v. Allen   518
Notes to *United States v. Allen*   521
Rule 603. Oath or Affirmation to Testify Truthfully   522
Roark v. Commonwealth   523
Notes to *Roark v. Commonwealth*   528

D. Competency: Status   529

Dead Man's Statutes   529
Trammel v. United States   532
Notes to *Trammel v. United States*   537
Rule 605. Judge's Competency as a Witness   539
Rule 606. Juror's Competency as a Witness   539
Kendrick v. Pippin   540
Notes to *Kendrick v. Pippin*   544
Peña-Rodriguez v. Colorado   545
Notes to *Peña-Rodriguez v. Colorado*   549

E. Summary   551

14   OPINIONS   553

A. Introduction   553

Topic Overview   553
Basic Structure for Analysis   554
Chapter Organization   555

B. Science-Based Opinions **555**

Rule 702. Testimony by Expert Witnesses   555
Daubert v. Merrell Dow Pharmaceuticals, Inc.   556
Notes to *Daubert v. Merrell Dow Pharmaceuticals, Inc.*   561
Schafersman v. Agland Coop   563
Notes to *Schafersman v. Agland Coop*   568
United States v. Baines   570
Notes to *United States v. Baines*   573

C. Experience-Based Opinions **574**

Experience-Based Expertise: *Kumho Tire*   574
United States v. Walker   574
Notes to *United States v. Walker*   577
Rule 704. Opinion on an Ultimate Issue   577
State v. Torrez   578
Notes to *State v. Torrez*   582

D. Topics for Expert Testimony **583**

State v. Spigarolo   584
Hobgood v. State   585
Notes to *State v. Spigarolo* and *Hobgood v. State*   587
Specht v. Jensen   590
Notes to *Specht v. Jensen*   594

E. Inadmissible Evidence as a Basis for Expert Testimony **595**

Rule 703. Bases of an Expert's Opinion Testimony   595
Sphere Drake Insurance PLC v. Trisko   595
Notes to *Sphere Drake Insurance PLC v. Trisko*   598

F. Lay Opinion **600**

Rule 701. Opinion Testimony by Lay Witnesses   600
State v. Davis   601
Notes to *State v. Davis*   604

G. Summary **605**

15 PRIVILEGES 607

A. Introduction **607**

Topic Overview   607
Rule 501. Privilege in General   608
Chapter Organization   608

B. Lawyers and Clients   609

Wesp v. Everson   609
Notes to *Wesp v. Everson   615*
Upjohn Co. v. United States   617
Notes to *Upjohn Co. v. United States   622*
Rule 502. Attorney-Client Privilege and Work Product; Limitations on
    Waiver   623
Harp v. King   625
Notes to *Harp v. King   630*
In re Motion to Quash Bar Counsel Subpoena   632
Notes to *In re Motion to Quash Bar Counsel Subpoena   636*

C. Confidential Spousal Communications Privilege   636

State v. Christian   637
Notes to *State v. Christian   642*

D. Clergy-Penitent Communications   643

Varner v. Stovall   644
Notes to *Varner v. Stovall   647*

E. Mental Health Care Practitioners and Patients   649

Jaffee v. Redmond   649
Notes to *Jaffee v. Redmond   653*

F. Participants in Peer Review Processes   655

Lowy v. Peacehealth   655
Notes to *Lowy v. Peacehealth   659*

G. Summary   660

**16   AUTHENTICATION AND THE ORIGINAL
    WRITING RULE   663**

A. Introduction   663

Topic Overview   663
Chapter Organization   663

B. Authentication   664

Rule 901. Authenticating or Identifying Evidence   664
United States v. Newton   665
Notes to *United States v. Newton   667*
Tienda v. State   668
Notes to *Tienda v. State   672*
United States v. Johnson   673
Notes to *United States v. Johnson   675*

C. Original Writing Rule 676

Rule 1001. Definitions That Apply to This Article 676
Rule 1002. Requirement of the Original 676
Rule 1003. Admissibility of Duplicates 677
Rule 1004. Admissibility of Other Evidence of Content 677
United States v. Alexander 677
Notes to *United States v. Alexander* 681
United States v. Howard 682
Notes to *United States v. Howard* 684
Rule 1008. Functions of the Court and Jury 684
Seiler v. Lucasfilm, Ltd. 685
Notes to *Seiler v. Lucasfilm, Ltd.* 689

D. Summary 690

17 PRESUMPTIONS AND JUDICIAL NOTICE 691

A. Introduction 691

Topic Overview 691
Chapter Organization 691

B. Presumptions: Federal Treatment 692

Rule 301. Presumptions in Civil Cases Generally 692
Marr v. Bank of America, N.A. 692
Notes to *Marr v. Bank of America, N.A.* 696

C. Presumptions: Range of State Treatments 698

Rule 302. Applying State Law to Presumptions in Civil Cases 698
Counterexamples 698
Schultz v. Ford Motor Co. 701
Notes to *Schultz v. Ford Motor Co.* 705

D. Judicial Notice 706

Rule 201. Judicial Notice of Adjudicative Facts 706
Dippin' Dots, Inc. v. Frosty Bites Distribution, LLC 707
Notes to *Dippin' Dots, Inc. v. Frosty Bites Distribution, LLC* 710

E. Summary 711

Table of Cases 713
Table of Authorities 719
Index 723

This book offers basic coverage of the most important Evidence rules and doctrines. Its goal is to clear things up without dumbing them down. To that end, it provides a narrative introduction to each section, introduces each case with a brief description of the main problem that case analyzes, and uses charts and tables where that kind of exposition may be helpful. Many of the cases have interesting factual settings. This second edition improves some of the illustrative material and reflects recent developments related to the Confrontation Clause, limitations on testimony by jurors about their deliberations, and the use of a witness's prior consistent statements.

The book exposes students to rival approaches for many topics. This highlights the choices inherent in many of the Federal Rules of Evidence and some traditional doctrines. Along with providing a basic understanding of the main topics, the book covers intriguing frontier issues. Some of these are allowing extrinsic evidence of past false accusations for impeachment, the "near-miss" interpretation of the residual hearsay exception, treatment of innocent loss of memory for impeachment with prior inconsistent statements, and allowing character evidence about a defendant who introduces character evidence about a victim.

Why cases? The problem method has been very successful in many Evidence courses. But sometimes students can feel swamped by a full diet of hypothetical situations. In this book, cases are the new problems. By that, I mean they offer detailed factual settings for considering how evidence problems might be solved. Because the cases involve real people and real trials, they have inherent interest.

Any problems with that? Along with cases, this book presents about 80 problems. Each of them reinforces aspects of evidence that are clear-cut. And many require consideration of ambiguity in rules, or in the art of applying rules to diverse factual situations.

What's an interesting case? People are interested in different things. Where possible, this book's cases are recent and involve circumstances that current students may find engaging. For example, the multiple murders of a defendant's husbands provide the context for a case involving forfeiture of hearsay and Confrontation Clause claims. Authentication is presented in a case with many quotations from social media postings. An impeachment case involves a prosecutor using a defendant's photograph of himself holding a bag of drugs. Statements by an opposing party are introduced with a case in which a prosecutor sought to introduce a draft e-mail from a defendant's computer, which confessed a crime to a talk show host.

Why cover minority views? For some topics where treatment varies significantly among states, this book gives students examples of the range of choices. This allows students to compare, for example, the standard treatment of impeachment by proof of past convictions with choices that either allow that technique, essentially, always or never. Seeing the range can help students understand the majority choice better, can help them understand the values at stake in making a choice, and can prepare them to evaluate changes and developments during their future careers. Students may find it provocative to know that one state always treats evidence of subsequent remedial measures as relevant to negligence or product defect. Comparing the inclusion and exclusion of social interests in the hearsay exception for statements against interest can provoke a discussion of the common sense rationale for the majority rule.

Students who have used prior editions of this book have given it very favorable ratings in anonymous evaluations. Their enthusiasm, and their many suggestions, have shaped this edition. They have particularly appreciated the clear organization of the materials and the small introductions that help them dig into the cases.

The opinions have been edited with the goal of facilitating readability and understanding. Typographic choices used here may vary from those of the courts, and many citations have been omitted.

Evidence law is a great context for learning and reinforcing the skill of reading rules as a professional must read them, and of analyzing social problems and the judicial opinions that grapple with them. Teaching and learning from these materials has been lots of fun for my students and me, and I hope others will have the same experience.

Arthur Best
Denver, Colorado
November 2020

ACKNOWLEDGMENTS

I deeply appreciate the care and effort given by many students and colleagues who have helped in the production of this book. In particular, a large number of anonymous reviewers made many extremely helpful suggestions about various drafts of the first edition. Colleagues at Aspen Publishing were highly perceptive and thoughtful in helping the book's development—great thanks are due to Carol McGeehan and John Devins.

The video segments that accompany this book are based on scripts originally written by Prof. H. Patrick Furman of the University of Colorado School of Law and used by Continuing Legal Education in Colorado, Inc. in its programs. Permission to use these scripts as a basis for the video segments is gratefully acknowledged.

By integrating portions of the text with accompanying video, this book uses an innovative approach to demonstrate how Evidence law is applied in various trial scenarios. Videos that show parts of a hypothetical trial of a domestic violence case are visually keyed to specific parts of this text by this icon:

You will find these icons in various locations in the left-hand margin of the text. It is important to note that the particular short excerpts often include more than one aspect of Evidence law. This is because the videos represent how things work at a real trial, and testimony at a trial may not fit neatly into the various categories of Evidence law. To better understand the individual videos, therefore, it's a good idea to watch them all as a group at the start of the course. This will help you understand the context of each specific short section.

To access the website containing these videos, refer to the sticker on the inside front cover of your book for instructions. Visit www.CasebookConnect.com/Resources for more information.

EVIDENCE

CHAPTER 1

Relevance

A. Introduction to Evidence Law
B. Introduction to Relevance
C. Relevance and Admissibility, Defined and Distinguished
D. Relevance and Substantive Legal Theory
E. Recurring Relevance Patterns — Flight, Safety Record, and Destruction of Evidence
F. Conditional Relevance
G. Discretion to Exclude Relevant Evidence
H. Summary

A INTRODUCTION TO EVIDENCE LAW

Evidence rules and doctrines are the focus of this book, as part of an Evidence course that will help you develop expertise in the ways our legal system controls the flow of information in trials. Learning these rules and doctrines will not make a person a competent trial lawyer, just as knowing the rules for a sport will not make a person a good player. But learning evidence rules — distinct from trial skills — is a necessary beginning for lawyers who hope to do trial work. Knowing the rules also helps lawyers who do work outside the trial process, since lots of nontrial legal work takes place in the shadow of litigation.

Before considering this book's first topic, relevance, the overall structure of trials deserves to be briefly described. When a pending dispute does not lead to a settlement or a plea bargain, a trial takes place. Before the first day of trial, parties may make motions in limine, asking the judge to rule on the admissibility of evidence in advance. The trial judge can respond by ruling that the particular item of evidence will be admissible or excluded. The judge can also defer a ruling, usually because he or she believes that the context of other information produced at trial would likely affect the decision.

If there is no right to a jury trial, or if parties agree to forgo trial by jury, the judge will personally decide the case, in what is called a "bench trial." For jury trials, the first step is selecting a jury. Prospective jurors are questioned, during voir dire, about the possible connections to the case and about attributes that might make their service on the jury improper. Parties may reject some prospective jurors without giving a reason, using "peremptory" challenges. They can ask the judge to disqualify prospective jurors "for cause," as well.

Once a jury is selected, each party gives an opening statement, outlining its view of the case and the evidence that will be presented. Our system does not usually require a party to produce particular kinds of information or even to cover a precise list of topics. We rely on parties' self-interest in being persuasive to lead to the introduction of information adequate to resolve the dispute.

The plaintiff or prosecution presents its case first, with witnesses and physical evidence. Each witness is asked questions on direct examination. Then the opponent cross-examines the witness. Next, redirect examination takes place, followed sometimes by recross examination. In direct examination, questions are supposed to be open-ended and not "leading" (a leading question is one that suggests a desired answer). In cross-examination, the opponent of the witness is limited to questions about the credibility of the witness and about topics that were covered during direct examination.

Parties may object to questions or to the answers witnesses give. Judges rule on those objections immediately or after discussing the objections with the parties' lawyers outside the hearing of the jury.

When the plaintiff or prosecutor concludes the presentation of its case, the defendant ordinarily moves for dismissal or acquittal, claiming that no rational jurors could find that the plaintiff or prosecutor has met its burdens of production and persuasion. If that motion is rejected, the defendant puts on its case.

After all the evidence is presented, both sides present closing arguments, the judge instructs the jury, and a judgment is usually entered on a jury verdict. Where the judgment lacks supporting evidence of some fact that substantive law requires to be proved, reversal on appeal may be reasonably anticipated. But when the losing party's claim of error relates only to the admission or exclusion of evidence, reversal is rare. Appellate courts give deference to trial court discretion on most evidence decisions. And even if a trial court decision is outside the bounds of reasonable discretion, if the error was "harmless," the judgment will be affirmed. For these reasons, resolving evidence issues *at trial* is crucial, since the likelihood that they will affect the outcome of a case on appeal is low.

B   INTRODUCTION TO RELEVANCE

Topic Overview

Relevance, this chapter's topic, is a sensible starting point for studying evidence law because relevance is a fundamental requirement for admission of any evidence. Trials always involve efforts by parties to get the trier of fact (the judge or the jury) to believe that certain things are true. Usually, the plaintiff or prosecutor must persuade the fact finder that some events have happened or are likely to happen. Can parties introduce whatever evidence they can think of or can find? If parties had unlimited freedom to introduce evidence, trials might last forever. Also, trials might seem ridiculous. The legal system controls these risks with the concept of relevance. This limits the kinds of information a party can use to try to influence the fact finder's conclusions.

Chapter Organization

This chapter introduces the basic rules governing relevance. The rules are straightforward and establish a standard for relevance that is easy to meet. We apply the rules in the context of a party's factual and legal theories — the events a party wants a jury to believe actually happened and the substantive legal doctrines that control a case.

Even though human life is infinitely variable, there are some recurring situations in which courts have developed routine ways of deciding relevance questions. These include conduct such as fleeing in anticipation of arrest offered to show consciousness of guilt, the safety record of a place or a product offered to show how an injury may have occurred, and efforts to hide or destroy evidence offered to show that the hidden or destroyed evidence would have been harmful to the one who tampered with it.

This chapter covers two more important topics. Sometimes an item of information will be connected to something that matters in a case only if some other fact is established. This circumstance is called "conditional relevance." And finally, even when evidence satisfies the definition of relevance, a trial judge has discretion to deny admissibility if its probative value is substantially outweighed by certain risks (such as waste of time or unfair prejudice).

Basic Structure for Analysis

For the issues about relevance in this chapter and *also for all other evidence issues*,

STEPS FOR...

Analyzing Evidence Issues

To analyze evidence issues, we have to know two things:
- *What evidence* a party seeks to introduce, and
- *What purpose* the party claims the evidence will serve.

STEPS FOR ...

Relating Relevance to Admissibility

To decide on the admissibility of evidence, we consider:
- Whether the evidence is *relevant* for the purpose the party has specified, and
- Whether the judge may or must *exclude it even though* it is relevant.

there are two basic aspects we have to identify and keep in mind: precisely what evidence someone (the proponent) wants to be allowed to introduce and what purpose the proponent says the evidence will serve.

For relevance issues in particular, once we know what evidence a party is offering and the role that party claims the evidence should have in the trial, there are two broad categories of inquiry for deciding admissibility: We must consider whether the evidence is relevant and whether, even if it is relevant, there are reasons to bar its admission.

C. RELEVANCE AND ADMISSIBILITY, DEFINED AND DISTINGUISHED

Relevance describes a relationship between one fact and another fact. We say that the first fact is relevant to the second one if ordinary experience supports the belief that when the first fact is true, the second fact is more likely to be true than it would have been without information about that first fact. This idea is expressed in FRE 401,* defining relevant evidence.

Rule 401. Test for Relevant Evidence

Evidence is relevant if:

(a) it has any tendency to make a fact more or less probable than it would be without the evidence; and

(b) the fact is of consequence in determining the action.

Rule 402 provides that irrelevant evidence must always be kept out of trials, and that relevant evidence is admissible unless it is barred by other provisions of the rules or for other specified reasons.

Rule 402. General Admissibility of Relevant Evidence

Relevant evidence is admissible unless any of the following provides otherwise:

- the United States Constitution;
- a federal statute;

---

*At the end of 2011, "restyled" versions of all the Federal Rules of Evidence became effective. The restyled rules have improved formatting and clearer language, but were intended to preserve the meaning of the prior rules. Many state evidence rules currently use the form and language of earlier versions of the Federal Rules. The judicial opinions in this book usually refer to those earlier versions.

> ▪ these rules; or
> ▪ other rules prescribed by the Supreme Court.
>
> Irrelevant evidence is not admissible.

Note that Rule 402 acknowledges that even if an item of evidence is relevant, it must be excluded if the United States Constitution requires its exclusion. This is an example of extreme caution on the part of the rule drafters. The Constitution would trump the rules of evidence whether or not the rules of evidence said so.

Rule 403 specifies factors to be balanced in a trial court's discretion, to exclude evidence even though it is relevant.

Rule 403. Excluding Relevant Evidence for Prejudice, Confusion, Waste of Time, or Other Reasons

The court may exclude relevant evidence if its probative value is substantially outweighed by a danger of one or more of the following: unfair prejudice, confusing the issues, misleading the jury, undue delay, wasting time, or needlessly presenting cumulative evidence.

The definition in Rule 401 and the balancing test in Rule 403 both use general terms without specific reference to any particular types of evidence or any particular types of conclusions that parties might claim would be supported by types of evidence. This vagueness leaves lots of room for discretion on the part of trial judges and leads appellate courts to be deferential to trial court relevancy decisions.

▪   ▪   ▪

What's Relevant to What? — Supreme Pork. The plaintiff in this case wanted to prove that a company named PP&H did some bad construction work and that the bad work caused a fire. To support a conclusion about why a fire happened, it would have been great to have an eyewitness or a videotape showing a defendant lighting a match and using it to start something burning. But the plaintiff's proof was much less direct than that. The plaintiff's evidence showed that PP&H violated some building code provisions in part of the project that was not involved in the fire and that PP&H had once done work that caused a fire in a different building.

The trial court admitted this evidence. On appeal, the majority opinion explains the pro-admissibility stance represented in Rule 401. The dissent offers an analysis that recognizes the language of Rule 401 but would have applied it differently. Note the distinction the majority stresses between relevance and admissibility. Also, consider how an analysis of relevance may depend on the definition of the fact that the challenged evidence is claimed to show.

SUPREME PORK, INC. v. MASTER BLASTER, INC.

764 N.W.2d 474 (S.D. 2009)

GILBERTSON, C.J.

Master Blaster, Inc. (Master Blaster) appeals several evidentiary and legal rulings made at the jury trial in which it was found liable for damages caused to Supreme Pork, Inc. (Supreme Pork). We affirm.

In 1999, a small fire broke out in the pressure washer room of Supreme Pork's pig farrowing facility near Lake Benton, MN. The power washer sustained some damage but was completely repaired. In restoring the pressure washer room, Supreme Pork contracted with Master Blaster to add and install a second power washer. It was decided that the power washers' venting system needed to be redesigned and a new chimney installed. Master Blaster did not perform these services.

The parties disagree about the details of the subsequent conversation; however, it is undisputed that Master Blaster recommended Pipestone Plumbing and Heating (PP&H) for the venting and chimney work. Following this discussion, Master Blaster contacted PP&H. PP&H provided a price quote to Master Blaster. Master Blaster included the price of PP&H's quote, plus an additional fee, in Master Blaster's quote and bill to Supreme Pork.

On March 21, 2002, a second fire ignited above the ceiling of the pressure washer room, near the exhaust chimney. This fire did significant damage to Supreme Pork's facilities. Fire investigation experts were retained by a number of parties for post-fire causation analysis.

During the June 2007 trial, several of these experts testified about the cause of the fire and the surrounding circumstances. The trial court permitted testimony regarding . . . the existence of non-causal building code violations in the chimney installation [and] a different fire in 1999 which resulted from PP&H's installation. . . .

The trial court determined that PP&H served as Master Blaster's subcontractor/agent for this project, which, . . . made Master Blaster liable for PP&H's negligence. Master Blaster appeals these rulings.

ISSUES

. . . Whether the trial court erred when it admitted evidence of non-causal code violations on the same project and evidence regarding a 1999 fire at another facility.

For evidence to be admitted during trial, it first must be found to be relevant. . . .

Code Violations. During trial, the court allowed testimony regarding other building code violations in [parts of the exhaust system that did not cause the fire]. These violations were used to illustrate PP&H's lack of knowledge of building codes and safety requirements, resulting in the generally poor design and quality of workmanship. The trial court allowed Master Blaster to write limiting instructions for the jury explaining that these violations were not to be considered as a cause of the fire. The court read Master Blaster's instructions to the jury.

. . . The non-causal code violations were relevant, admissible, circumstantial evidence of PP&H's knowledge of safety standards at the time of installation. . . .

1999 Pipestone Fire. In 1999, a fire started in the pig barn of a veterinary clinic in Pipestone, MN. Investigators determined that the cause of this fire was the improper installation of the vent system for the building's power washer. This vent system was installed by PP&H. Chris Rallis, Supreme Pork's expert witness in this case, was hired by PP&H's insurance carrier to investigate the 1999 fire. He concluded PP&H's actions had caused the fire. . . .

After considering Master Blaster's motion in limine, the trial court concluded that the cause and timeframe of the Supreme Pork installation was similar enough to warrant inclusion. . . . Because of the almost identical nature of the incidents, this testimony was relevant to the foreseeability of harm, the risk of the danger with respect to the lack of safety measures, PP&H's lack of knowledge about installing exhaust chimneys in a manner that maintains the required clearances between combustibles and heat, and Master Blaster's lack of due care in selecting a subcontractor. . . .

Evidence of the 1999 fire also establishes that Master Blaster knew, at the time it subcontracted PP&H, that PP&H's power washer venting work had been the cause of fires, yet Master Blaster retained PP&H to do the work. . . . This knowledge was, therefore, relevant to the reasonableness of Master Blaster's recommendation to hire PP&H and its eventual subcontracting with them for the installation of flue vents. . . .

While this may be a closer call than the code violations, discussed above, we cannot conclude that the trial court abused its discretion.

Essentially, the dissent implies that the evidence of code violations and the 1999 fire were not admissible [because] these two pieces of evidence were irrelevant. . . . The dissent misconstrues the evidentiary rules, misapplies our standard of review, and errs in its conclusions.

Relevance vs. Admissibility. "Relevance" and "admissibility" are separate concepts, though our precedent has at times discussed them in a similar manner. This precedent is imprecise. The "relevance" of evidence must be determined before considering whether or not evidence is "admissible." Rule 401 presents the concept of "relevance." SDCL 19-12-1 (Rule 401) provides:

> "Relevant evidence" means evidence having any tendency to make the existence of any fact that is of consequence to the determination of the action more probable or less probable than it would be without the evidence.

After the relevance of evidence is determined, Rule 402 applies the concept of "admissibility" to that determination. "All relevant evidence is *admissible*. . . . Evidence which is not relevant is not *admissible*[ ]" (emphasis added). Other Rules further condition the "admissibility" of relevant evidence. *See* Rule 403 ("Although *relevant*, evidence may be excluded . . .") (emphasis added). . . .

Considered together, these Rules suggest that "relevant" evidence is either "admissible" or "inadmissible," depending on the applicability of the later Rules. However "irrelevant" evidence cannot be "admissible." Our cases have not always been clear on this distinction and occasionally merge these concepts.

Relevance. In its analysis, the dissent applies a particularly narrow interpretation of what evidence was "relevant" in this case. We disagree with the dissent's interpretation of relevant evidence under this Rule. The dissent suggests that the only evidence that is "relevant" in this case is that which relates to only one ultimate fact issue: the failure to affix attic shields to the attic floor. Quite simply, this narrow view of "relevancy" misinterprets Rule 401.

> Rule 401 uses a lenient standard for relevance. Any proffered item that would appear to alter the probabilities of a consequential fact is relevant, although it may be excluded because of other factors. To merely alter the probability of the existence of a fact, or 'make it more probable or less probable,' as the Advisory Committee notes, is not a stringent standard. Evidence, to be relevant to an inquiry, *need not conclusively prove the ultimate fact in issue,* but only have a tendency to make the existence of any fact that is of consequence to the determination of the action more probable or less probable than it would be without the evidence.
>
> To be admissible, evidence need only to alter the probabilities of a proposition; it need not sway the balance to any particular degree. This standard of relevance, adopted by most commentators, revisers and many courts is usually termed 'logical' relevance as opposed to the theory of 'legal' relevance championed by Wigmore, and adopted by some courts prior to the enactment of Rule 401. . . .
>
> The standard of logical relevance is more lenient, and permits evidence to be admitted even if it only slightly affects the trier's assessment of the probability of the matter to be proved. Even though each piece of evidence considered separately is less than conclusive, if when considered collectively with other evidence it tends to establish a *consequential fact,* such evidence is relevant. For purposes of Rule 401, that is enough.

2 Jack B. Weinstein & Margaret A. Berger, *Weinstein's Federal Evidence,* §401.04[2][c] (Joseph M. McLaughlin, ed., Matthew Bender 2d ed. 2008) (emphasis added). . . .

Master Blaster was the named defendant in this case; its negligence in hiring and recommending PP&H for the installation was another fact of consequence in the case. Though the negligent hiring issue was not directly put before the jury, Master Blaster's negligence in regard to the installation was considered by the jury. Master Blaster's knowledge of PP&H's involvement in the 1999 fire was a fact at least logically relevant to the theory that it was negligent in hiring PP&H

for this installation. We do not find that the trial court's rulings on the relevance issues were an abuse of discretion.

Admissibility. As recognized by the trial court, the relevance determination was not sufficient by itself to prove admissibility, in this case....

In relevant part, SDCL 19-12-3 (Rule 403) states: "evidence may be excluded if its probative value is substantially outweighed by the danger of unfair prejudice...."

Rule 403 is not simply a "more than, less than" comparison; the test is whether the probative value is substantially outweighed by the danger of unfair prejudice. "Once the evidence is found relevant, however, the balance tips emphatically in favor of admission unless the dangers set out in Rule 403 'substantially' outweigh probative value."

Furthermore, the Rule 403 test requires us to consider the probative value as the basis and measure the danger of prejudice against that probative value; not the other way around. While this distinction is subtle, the proper formulation reflects the burdens imposed by the Rule. The probative value is not required to "measure up" to the prejudicial value. Quite the opposite is true; the prejudicial value must be shown to substantially outweigh the probative value. "The party *objecting* to the admission of evidence *has the burden* of establishing that the trial concerns expressed in Rule 403 substantially outweigh probative value." State v. Mattson, 698 N.W.2d 538, 546 (S.D. 2005) (emphasis added).

Applying the abuse of discretion standard of review, we do not believe the trial court committed "'a fundamental error of judgment, a choice outside the range of permissible choices, a decision, which, on full consideration, is arbitrary or unreasonable.'" The trial court did not abuse its discretion when it determined that this evidence was admissible because it had purposes other than proving PP&H or Master Blaster's character, or that any prejudice which may have resulted from the admission of this evidence did not substantially outweigh the probative value....

Affirmed.

SABERS, Retired Justice (dissenting).

Because Master Blaster was not afforded a fair trial in this case, I dissent. The trial court abused its discretion by permitting the jury to consider two instances of other acts evidence, which were irrelevant to the claim asserted . . . and were substantially more prejudicial than probative. Therefore, this case should be remanded to provide Master Blaster with a fair trial on the merits of the negligence claim Supreme Pork lodged against it....

At trial, the issue was whether PP&H's failure to affix attic shields to the attic floor around the chimney vents and to cover the attic shields amounted to negligence for which Master Blaster could be held liable. Whether the alleged code violation of the eighteen-inch clearance caused the fire was not at issue. In fact, Supreme Pork openly agreed that this alleged violation was not the cause of the fire. Therefore, this alleged violation was irrelevant to the issue at hand because it was not a "fact . . . of consequence to the determination of the [negligence] action." SDCL 19-12-1 (Rule 401). . . .

Similarly, the evidence regarding the 1999 fire was not relevant to the instant action. The 1999 fire occurred shortly after construction of the building and was allegedly caused when the vent came in contact with the timbers in the building. The cause of the 1999 fire was not related to a failure to affix shields to the floor around the chimney vent. In fact, the 1999 fire occurred at an entirely separate location three years earlier under different circumstances. The facts surrounding the 1999 fire could not assist the trier of fact in determining whether the cause of the instant fire was as theorized by Supreme Pork. . . .

Even if this other act evidence were deemed relevant, it still should not have been admitted. [E]vidence must satisfy the threshold test of its probative value being substantially outweighed by its unfair prejudice. . . .

Supreme Pork contends that the other act evidence is admissible because it proves knowledge. However, no one can seriously argue that the probative value of this evidence outweighs the unfair prejudice it caused Master Blaster. "Prejudicial evidence is that which has *the capacity* to persuade the jury by illegitimate means which results in one party having an unfair advantage." Novak v. McEldowney, 655 N.W.2d 909, 913 (emphasis added). The admission of evidence relating to the unrelated alleged code violation and the unrelated 1999 fire certainly had the capacity, and most likely the actual effect, of persuading the jury by illegitimate means, thereby giving Supreme Pork an unfair advantage at the trial. . . .

Both instances of this evidence were far more prejudicial than probative even when considered alone. When considered together, their prejudice doubly exceeds any probative value. For all these reasons, this case should be reversed and remanded to provide Master Blaster with a fair trial.

NOTES TO SUPREME PORK, INC. v. MASTER BLASTER, INC.

1. *Relevant to What?* The dissent conceptualizes "the issue" at trial as the failure to install and cover attic shields. It seems to argue that evidence must have a direct link to that issue in order to be relevant. In contrast, the majority applies the relevance definition so that proof will be relevant if it supports a conclusion about a fact that could, in turn support a conclusion about a fact that could be determinative of the outcome of the case. To understand these different views, consider what a jury could conclude if it believed that PP&H had skimpy knowledge about building codes.

2. *Prohibited Rational Connections.* Because of specific policy concerns, some relevance rules exclude information that actually could have a rational relationship to facts that matter in trials. One of these rules prohibits proving character traits to support a finding of action consistent with that character

on a specific occasion. When the majority stressed that the evidence related to the state of PP&H's *knowledge,* it avoided the rules controlling character evidence because knowledge is different from character traits such as sloppiness or foolhardiness.

3. *Range of Inferences.* The dissent analyzed whether the admitted evidence might have had too much risk of unfair prejudice for its admission to have been proper. It referred to the concept of evidence "which has the capacity" to influence a jury improperly, and reasoned that the evidence in this case fit that definition. This required an unarticulated estimate of how jurors might think about the evidence. The majority applied a rule that speaks in terms of "evidence having any tendency" to alter the likely truth of a significant fact. Applying this concept also requires judgment about rational thought. For each of these inquiries — likely unfair prejudice and existence of a rational link between one fact and another — a court must decide what kind of thinking is common in our society and, on the other hand, what kind of thinking is too far-fetched to be acknowledged as part of our trial process.

4. *Motion in Limine.* A motion in limine is a request made to the trial judge prior to trial for a ruling on the admissibility of evidence. The trial judge can change that ruling as the trial develops. If the ruling remains in force, and the party disfavored by the in limine ruling loses the case, that party may base an appeal on that ruling.

QUESTION 1-1. Barbara Backseat was a passenger in a car, riding in its backseat. Frieda Frontseat was riding in the front seat of that same car. Tom Trucker drove his truck into the car. Backseat sued Trucker, claiming that he drove negligently and that she had suffered a back injury from the impact. At trial, Trucker admitted he had driven negligently, but denied that the collision had caused Backseat's injury. An expert witness testified for Trucker that the force of the collision was too slight to have caused an injury to Backseat. Backseat seeks to introduce evidence showing that the collision caused a bodily injury to Frontseat. Assuming Trucker makes appropriate objections, the best ruling by the trial judge would be that the evidence is:

> **GOOD TO REMEMBER**
>
> Relevance is a "yes/no" concept. There is no such thing as "a little bit relevant." Evidence is either relevant or not relevant.

A. Excluded because it is not relevant.
B. Excluded because it has only slight relevance.
C. Admitted because it has high relevance.
D. Excluded because it has low probative value, would require a lot of time to prove, and might be overvalued by the jury.

RELEVANCE AND SUBSTANTIVE LEGAL THEORY

The substantive legal doctrines that apply in a case provide the context for deciding relevance questions. In many instances, issues at trial will involve proving what happened on a specific occasion, as for example when a plaintiff suffered an injury or a victim was harmed by a criminal. In other instances, events that happened over a long period of time may matter, given the details of the substantive doctrines that govern a case.

■ ■ ■

Substantive Doctrines Can Control Relevance — **Kaechele.** The court considers whether it was proper to let a jury know that there had been lots of police activity at the defendant's place of business prior to the events that were the subject of the current case. The jurisdiction's tort law affected the trial court's relevance analysis. The opinion also considers the trial court's decision on unfair prejudice. Notice that the standard for review of a relevance decision is different from the standard for review of a decision about unfair prejudice.

KAECHELE v. KENYON OIL COMPANY, INC.

747 A.2d 167 (Me. 2000)

SAUFLEY, J.

Kenyon Oil Company, Inc., doing business as Xtra Mart, along with its insurers Warren Equities and the Groves Corporation, appeal from the judgment entered in the Superior Court on a jury verdict finding that the negligence of Xtra Mart was a cause of the injuries suffered by Albert Kaechele when he was assaulted at Xtra Mart by another customer. Xtra Mart argues that the trial court made . . . evidentiary errors. . . . We affirm the judgment.

Xtra Mart is a 24-hour convenience store located in Auburn. On the evening of May 4, 1994, Albert Kaechele went to the store to purchase a MegaBucks lottery ticket, and to visit his wife, May Kaechele, who was working as an Xtra Mart clerk. Also present in the store that evening were Darlene Mailey, who was also on duty as an Xtra Mart clerk; Valerie Rowe, an off-duty clerk; and Valerie Rowe's husband Armand Rowe, with their six-month-old daughter Tiffany.

Sometime around 7:45 P.M., Madrid Roddy entered the store and attempted to purchase cigarettes. May Kaechele refused to sell Roddy cigarettes without first examining his identification. Angry at the prospect of having to return home to get his license, Roddy yelled obscenities at May and Mailey and pounded the service counter. He continued for approximately fifteen minutes to object strenuously to the clerks' repeated requests for identification. Eventually, he left the store, slammed the door, and began pounding on the store's front window. Armand, fearful that Roddy might vandalize his vehicle, watched him from the door and suggested that Mailey or May call the police. No call was made at that time. Armand and Albert Kaechele eventually left the store, and a confrontation with Roddy ensued in the parking lot. Words were exchanged, and Roddy struck Kaechele, severely injuring his face. . . .

Kaechele filed suit to recover for his injuries, naming Roddy, Xtra Mart, Kenyon Oil Company, Inc., the Grove Corporation, and Warren Equities, Inc., as defendants. The complaint alleged that the negligence of Xtra Mart was a proximate cause of Kaechele's injuries. The jury found that both Kaechele and Xtra Mart were negligent, concluded that Xtra Mart was more negligent, and awarded Kaechele damages. The jury valued his damages at $210,000, but adjusted the award to $168,000 after taking into account Kaechele's own negligence. Xtra Mart moved for a judgment as a matter of law or for a new trial. The motion was denied, and this appeal followed.

Xtra Mart asserts that the trial court . . . erred in admitting evidence regarding Xtra Mart's previous calls to the Auburn Police Department. . . .

Xtra Mart argues that the evidence presented relating to previous calls from Xtra Mart to the Auburn Police Department was not relevant, and that to the extent it had any relevance, it should have been excluded on the basis of M.R. Evid. 403. We review a court's determination of relevance for errors of law as to the factual predicate; that is, as to the bare possibility that the evidence may have any tendency to make the "existence of a fact that is of consequence to the determination of the action" more or less probable. M.R. Evid. 401, Rich v. Fuller, 666 A.2d 71, 73 (Me. 1995). A fact may, however, be "of consequence" and yet of minimal value. The court's decision regarding the admissibility of relevant evidence therefore "blends imperceptibly into its discretion under Rule 403." Field & Murray, Maine Evidence §401.1 at 91. We review a decision to admit or exclude relevant evidence pursuant to Rule 403 for abuse of discretion because the determination "involves the weighing of probative value against considerations militating against admissibility." Rich, 666 A.2d at 73. Thus, once the bare fact of relevance is determined, we accord the trial judge significant discretion in determining its admissibility.

We first determine whether the challenged evidence was relevant to the determination of any fact before the jury. The trial court must undertake an analysis of relevance by first examining the precise cause of action presented by the plaintiff and the elements of proof necessary to the factfinder's decisions on those elements.

Kaechele's claim of negligence springs from Xtra Mart's duty to exercise reasonable care regarding the safety of its patrons. . . .

At trial, there was no real factual dispute regarding the place of the assault (on Xtra Mart's property), the results of the assault (relatively serious injuries to Kaechele's face), or the person who assaulted Kaechele (Roddy). The dispute for resolution by the jury centered on whether Xtra Mart anticipated, or should have anticipated, the assault....

A proprietor must guard its patrons against not only known dangers but also those which it "should reasonably anticipate." Therefore, whether Xtra Mart should have anticipated the assault must be analyzed from two perspectives: first, did Xtra Mart have notice that its facility generally presented a risk that third parties would assault its patrons; and second, did Xtra Mart know, or should it have anticipated, that Roddy would assault a patron on the evening in question. Generally, evidence of similar incidents in the past will be relevant on the issue of notice....

It was against this backdrop that the trial court was called upon to make its determination of the relevance of prior incidents at the Xtra Mart. After hearing from counsel, the court excluded evidence that it concluded had little probative value, including the specific details of a litany of reasons, unrelated to assaultive or dangerous behavior of third parties, that the police had previously been called to Xtra Mart. It concluded, however, that general evidence regarding the frequency of calls to Xtra Mart and evidence of prior assaults on the premises was relevant.

The evidence regarding prior calls to the police was presented by two members of the Auburn Police Department. The officers testified generally that Xtra Mart was the source of many calls, that they regularly responded to calls regarding violence at the store, that Xtra Mart was one of the most frequent sources of calls in the area, and that not all calls related directly to violence. The court did not err in concluding that the evidence was relevant under Rule 401 because it tended to show that: (1) Xtra Mart was on notice that this type of dangerous behavior was not uncommon at this Xtra Mart location [and] (2) Xtra Mart had sufficient notice of the risk over time that precautions of some type could have been instituted.... These inferences are directly probative on issues of Xtra Mart's notice of the general risk to patrons at its Auburn store.... The court did not err in concluding that the proffered evidence was relevant.

We turn then to Xtra Mart's claim that the prejudicial effect of the evidence substantially outweighed its probative value. Xtra Mart does not point to any particularly inflammatory information about prior incidents. Rather, it argues that the cumulative evidence of the numerous occasions on which police had been called to this location would tend to make the jury believe that it was a "hotbed of criminal activity or public nuisance." The court was careful to restrict the inquiry to avoid testimony regarding the specific outcomes of previous assaults, particularly one involving serious physical injury. The court did not exceed the bounds of its discretion when it concluded that the probative value of evidence related to prior police calls to this Xtra Mart, as limited by the court, was not substantially outweighed by any possible prejudice that could result from the admission of the evidence....

Judgment affirmed.

NOTES TO KAECHELE v. KENYON OIL COMPANY, INC.

1. *Legal Theory.* To establish that evidence has relevance, a party must relate the evidence to the legal doctrines that support a claim or a defense. In *Kaechele*, proof that there had been criminal conduct at the defendant's location was *not* introduced to show what happened on the day that the plaintiff was injured. Past criminal conduct was introduced to show that there had been past criminal conduct: Why did that fact have a role in the case?

2. *Standards for Review.* The *Kaechele* court stated that it would use an abuse of discretion standard for reviewing a trial court's Rule 403 ruling, but that it would review the decision regarding relevance (under Rule 401) under a different, less deferential standard. The United States Supreme Court has summarized its preferred terminology for standards of review: "For purposes of standard of review, decisions by judges are traditionally divided into three categories: denominated questions of law (reviewable de novo), questions of fact (reviewable for clear error), and matters of discretion (reviewable for 'abuse of discretion')." *See* Pierce v. Underwood, 487 U.S. 552, 558 (1988).

3. *Prejudice and Unfair Prejudice.* Unfair prejudice is one of the factors Rule 403 authorizes the trial court to weigh against the legitimate probative value of relevant evidence. There is an important difference between *prejudice* and *unfair prejudice*. All of the evidence one party introduces ought to be prejudicial to the interest of the opponent, or else the party would have been foolish to introduce it. Parties are allowed to seek to discredit their opponents. Unfair prejudice refers to an effect evidence might have in addition to some separate legitimate effect.

Evidence can cause unfair prejudice if a jury's reaction to it is likely to include two sets of ideas: a conclusion about some fact that matters in the case under the legal doctrines that describe the cause of action and a conclusion about some derogatory additional fact that does not have a legitimate relationship to the legal dispute. For example, in *Kaechele*, the evidence showing past criminal conduct at the defendant's store was relevant because the underlying legal theory of the plaintiff's case made it significant that customers had been at risk in the past. If the evidence the plaintiff sought to introduce had shown that individuals had threatened some danger to past customers while the individuals were helping the owner to figure out ways to sell spoiled meat and watered-down milk, there is a possibility that a jury might draw two conclusions from that evidence. One allowable conclusion would be that the location had a history of threats to customers' safety. The second, unfairly prejudicial, conclusion would be that the defendant company deserves to be punished because it was involved in bad conduct separate from the type of conduct that the plaintiff claimed had caused the plaintiff's injury.

QUESTION 1-2. In a criminal case, to prove that the defendant had stolen $25,000 from someone's safe, the prosecution sought to introduce evidence that after the date of the robbery the defendant had torn a picture off the wall of a hotel room and paid the hotel $900 for the damage. The prosecution argued that this conduct showed that the defendant possessed a disregard for the value of money, which could support an inference that the defendant did not acquire his money by giving value or substantial services in return, which in turn could support an inference that he probably acquired his money dishonestly, which in turn could support an inference that he committed the charged robbery. Does the picture-off-the-wall evidence pass Rule 401's test for the definition of relevant evidence?

Lp No

> **GOOD TO REMEMBER**
>
> "Unfair" is the important word in the phrase "unfair prejudice." Some prejudicial evidence causes unfair prejudice, but a lot of prejudicial evidence just properly hurts the party it's introduced against.

E RECURRING RELEVANCE PATTERNS — FLIGHT, SAFETY RECORD, AND DESTRUCTION OF EVIDENCE

Despite the infinite variety of human experience, there are lots of situations that come up again and again in trials. Specific rules (Rules 404 through 415) control relevance decisions in some of these circumstances. For some other recurring situations, there are no specific rules, but a trial judge's discretion may be controlled somewhat by a jurisdiction's precedents. Most jurisdictions have developed doctrines about: (1) proof that a person fled from police and the conclusion that the person committed a crime; (2) proof about the safety record of a defendant's product to support conclusions about the cause of a plaintiff's injury; and (3) proof that a person destroyed evidence and the conclusion that the evidence would have been damaging to him or her. A trial court's obligation to follow any standards set out in these opinions is moderated by the concepts of trial court discretion and limited appellate court review. On the other hand, these opinions do specify the factors trial courts should use in deciding these relevance questions.

■ ■ ■

When a Person Leaves Town, Is He Feeling Guilty? — **Dillon.** Dillon stood up his ex-wife and children on Christmas day. He left town and started using a phony name. The court uses a four-part test to decide whether it was fair to instruct the jury that it could infer Dillon's guilt from this information about "flight."

UNITED STATES v. DILLON

870 F.2d 1125 (6th Cir. 1989)

MERRITT, J.

Appellant Thomas J. Dillon was indicted for, and convicted of, various drug offenses.... He appeals[, arguing] that the District Court erred by admitting evidence of his flight and by giving the jury an instruction on flight....

The Fifth Circuit has devised a four-step analysis of flight evidence that, as many courts have recognized, allows an orderly inquiry into the inferences proposed by evidence of flight. According to this formulation, the probative value of flight evidence

> depends upon the degree of confidence with which four inferences can be drawn: (1) from the defendant's behavior to flight; (2) from flight to consciousness of guilt; (3) from consciousness of guilt to consciousness of guilt concerning the crime charged; and (4) from consciousness of guilt concerning the crime charged to actual guilt of the crime charged.

United States v. Myers, 550 F.2d 1036, 1049 (5th Cir.1977), *cert. denied* 439 U.S. 847, 99 S. Ct. 147, 58 L. Ed. 2d 149 (1978). All four inferences must be "reasonabl[y] support[ed]" by the evidence. *Myers,* 550 F.2d at 1050. In the present case, Dillon was charged with, and convicted of, supplying Edward Knezevich with cocaine between December 1982 and March 26, 1983. Knezevich obtained a pound of cocaine from Dillon on the latter date and sold it, through a pre-arranged deal, to Sheila Bezotsky. Bezotsky was cooperating with the FBI, and Knezevich was arrested when he delivered the cocaine to her. All those events took place in Columbus, where Dillon then lived.

Knezevich was eventually convicted for his role in this deal. After his conviction he was subpoenaed to testify before a Grand Jury. On December 19, 1984, Knezevich told Dillon that he would testify the next day before a Grand Jury, and that he intended to tell the truth about Dillon's role in the cocaine deal....

Dillon's ex-wife testified that Dillon did not keep his engagement to take custody of their children, on Christmas day. She also testified that, ever since that day and for the next two years, Dillon contacted her only by phone, and that she had no way of knowing whether he was in Columbus or not.

Dillon was arrested in Florida in June 1987. The FBI agent who arrested him testified that he was living there under an assumed name. There is no evidence that he denied to the FBI agent arresting him that he was Thomas Dillon. He was indicted on the present charges on July 30, 1987.

At trial, the government attempted to prove that Dillon had fled Columbus after learning about Knezevich's planned Grand Jury testimony, and that such a flight proved Dillon's awareness of his guilt of the crimes charged. Dillon preserved his appeal from the admission of evidence of flight by timely objections at trial. He seeks to persuade this Court that his departure from Columbus came at least two years after the alleged offense and well before the indictment was filed, so that he had "nothing to flee from." To accept this argument we would have to ignore the crucial fact that the government adduced evidence suggesting that Dillon fled Columbus within days after hearing from a co-conspirator that the co-conspirator was about to implicate Dillon in a big cocaine deal in Grand Jury testimony. The real question before us is whether the evidence, *including* Dillon's December 19 conversation with Knezevich, his unexplained failure to keep his Christmas plans with his children, and his subsequent phone rather than personal contacts with his ex-wife, are sufficiently probative of a guilty conscience to overcome the prejudice it entails. We conclude that the four *Myers* inferences are all adequately supported by the evidence introduced at Dillon's trial.

The first question is whether the evidence supports the inference that there has been a "flight" in the first place.... We believe that the evidence before Dillon's jury allowed a sound inference, not merely a speculative one, that he had fled. Dillon's ex-wife testified that, only six days after hearing from Knezevich about the latter's planned Grand Jury testimony, he broke an important family commitment and from then on contacted her by phone from an undisclosed location. He was arrested in Florida, where he was living under an assumed name. We do not believe it would be unreasonable for a jury to infer from these undisputed facts that Dillon fled Columbus soon after his conversation with Knezevich.

In this case, the second and third inferences — (2) that the defendant is afflicted with a guilty consciousness (3) of the crime charged — involve examination of two interrelated factors: immediacy and the defendant's knowledge that he is in trouble with the law. For flight evidence to be admissible, the timing of flight must itself indicate the sudden onset or the sudden *increase* of fear in the defendant's mind that he or she will face apprehension for, accusation of, or conviction of the crime charged. Flight immediately after the crime charged, of course, will tend to prove guilt of that crime. But the mental crisis that precipitates flight may fail to occur immediately after the crime, only to erupt much later, when the defendant learns that he or she is charged with the crime and sought for it.

. . . And it can occur long before the defendant learns of the charges: for instance, when flight occurs after the defendant is served, himself, with a subpoena to appear before a Grand Jury. *United States v. Grandmont*, 680 F.2d 867, 869-70 (1st Cir. 1982). Indeed, the "commencement of an investigation" may substitute for accusation as the precipitating event. *United States v. Beahm*, 664 F.2d at 420 (*dictum*).

Dillon argues that he departed Columbus a year and nine months after the crime at the earliest, that the indictment was issued after his arrest, and that nothing in the interim constitutes notice of the sort that courts have recognized as a substitute for immediacy-after-the-crime. This reasoning ignores the December 19 conversation with Knezevich and urges a wooden and literalistic reading of the case law. Common sense on this question is loud and clear: a guilty defendant is almost as unequivocally put on notice of his peril by a convicted co-conspirator who is on the verge of testifying before a Grand Jury about their common crime as he would be by hearing from someone that he is charged and sought. We see no flaws in an inference from such notice to the defendant's guilty consciousness of the crime charged.

Dillon raises no argument that the fourth *Myers* inference — from guilty consciousness to actual guilt — is unsupported by record evidence. We, therefore, hold that the District Court did not abuse its discretion in admitting evidence of flight at Dillon's trial. This conclusion forecloses any argument that the District Judge erred in deciding to give an instruction on flight to the jury. . . .

We conclude that the District Court properly allowed the government to introduce evidence of flight. . . . Accordingly, Dillon's judgment of conviction is affirmed.

NOTES TO UNITED STATES v. DILLON

1. *Class Bias?* The traditional flight instruction may reflect an idea — one should always cooperate with the police, and the legal system will treat one fairly — that is not equally shared by people in all social classes. In State v. Tibbetts, 749 N.E.2d 226 (Ohio 2001), a defendant fled from a murder scene and used a false name at a hospital. Are there reasons a person would act this way other than consciousness of guilt of a crime?

2. *Bible Study.* Compare some courts' references to the Old Testament in the context of inferring guilt from flight:

> It has long been held that proof of flight to elude capture or to prevent discovery is admissible because "flight is always some evidence of a sense of guilt." *Hord v. Commonwealth*, 13 S.W.2d 244, 246 (Ky. 1928). This common-law rule is based on the inference that the guilty run away but the innocent remain, which echoes more eloquent language from the Bible: "The wicked flee where no man pursueth; but the righteous are bold as a lion." *Proverbs* 28:1.

Kentucky Supreme Court, in Rodriguez v. Commonwealth, 107 S.W.3d 215, 219 (Ky. 2003).

> The author of Proverbs tells us, "The wicked flee when no man pursueth, but the righteous are bold as a lion." Over two thousand years later, in less majestic language, we noted that "[w]e have repeatedly held that flight is evidence of a circumstance from which an inference of guilt may be drawn." And this concept comports with common sense.

Texas Court of Criminal Appeals, in Ex parte Henderson, 246 S.W.3d 690, 697 (2007).

> In Alberty v. United States, 162 U.S. 499, 511, this Court said: ". . . it is not universally true that a man who is conscious that he has done a wrong, 'will pursue a certain course not in harmony with the conduct of a man who is conscious of having done an act which is innocent, right, and proper;' since it is a matter of common

knowledge that men who are entirely innocent do sometimes fly from the scene of a crime through fear of being apprehended as the guilty parties, or from an unwillingness to appear as witnesses. Nor is it true as an accepted axiom of criminal law that 'the wicked flee when no man pursueth, but the righteous are as bold as a lion.'" For the views of two Courts of Appeals see Vick v. United States, 216 F.2d 288, 233 (C.A. 5th Cir.) ("One motive is about as likely as another. Appellant may be guilty, but his conviction cannot rest upon mere conjecture and suspicion"); cf. Cooper v. United States, 94 U.S. App. D.C. 343, 218 F.2d 39, 41 ("After all, innocent people caught in a web of circumstances frequently become terror-stricken").

United States Supreme Court, in Wong Sun v. U.S., 371 U.S. 471, fn 10 (1963).

3. *Absence from Trial.* A defendant's choice to stay away from his or her trial presents a complicated problem with regard to inferences of guilt. As a factual matter, that conduct is different from fleeing to avoid arrest, since it takes place after the defendant has been arrested and charged. Since a defendant has no obligation to be present at trial, it may be unfair to highlight the choice to be absent and authorize a jury to infer guilt from that choice. *See* State v. Ingram, 951 A.2d 1000 (N.J. 2008) (instruction that defendant's absence could support a finding of consciousness of guilt was reversible error); Decker v. State, 971 A.2d 268 (Md. 2009) (allowing flight instruction where defendant left courthouse before start of his trial).

QUESTION 1-3. A member of the military was charged with rape, and he fled a military base on the day he was erroneously notified of failing a drug test, three weeks after notification of the rape charge. Should the trial court instruct the triers of fact that they could consider the accused's flight as evidence of the accused's consciousness of guilt of rape?

It's Happened Before or It's Never Happened Before: Do These Patterns Show Whether "It" Happened to a Plaintiff? — Lovick *and* Spino. Lovick v. Wil-Rich and Spino v. John S. Tilley Ladder Co. involve the possible links between a product's safety record and a plaintiff's injury. What can a record of past injuries show about the occurrence of a plaintiff's injury? And what can a good safety record, including a record of no injuries, show about a plaintiff's injury?

LOVICK v. WIL-RICH

588 N.W.2d 688 (Iowa 1999)

CADY, J.

. . . On May 20, 1993, Leo Lovick set out to cultivate a field preparatory to spring planting. He was an experienced farmer. The land was owned by Paul Rotgers[,] and Lovick was using his cultivator [manufactured by the defendant].

Lovick pulled the cultivator to the field with a tractor. The wings of the cultivator were in the upright, vertical position to accommodate its transportation. Once in the field, Lovick attempted to unfold or lower the wings into position to begin cultivation.

The wings of the cultivator folded and unfolded by the operation of two hydraulic cylinders, which also held the wings in its vertical position. Additionally, the wings were secured in the upright position by a metal pin manually inserted under each wing, near the rear of the implement. The pins were designed to hold the wing in the vertical position in the event of hydraulic or mechanical failure.

Lovick positioned himself under the left wing of the cultivator to remove the first pin. The wing immediately fell when the pin was removed. Lovick was severely injured. Later investigation revealed the wing fell when Lovick removed the pin because the linkage attaching the cylinder to the wing had broken. Consequently, the pin was the only device holding the wing in its upright position at the time it was removed.

Wil-Rich first introduced the vertical fold model cultivator into the market in 1971. Since that time it has manufactured approximately 35,000 units. The cultivator which injured Lovick was manufactured and sold by Wil-Rich in 1981. . . .

Lovick instituted a strict liability and negligence action against Wil-Rich. He sought compensatory and punitive damages. At trial, Lovick successfully introduced evidence that Deere & Company, a competitor of Wil-Rich, instituted a safety program in 1983 for its similarly designed cultivator after learning of instances of the wing falling on the operator. The Deere & Company program included efforts to locate the cultivator owners, and equip the existing cultivators with a wing safety latch and an upgraded warning label. Lovick also introduced evidence of the nine other accidents involving the wing of a Wil-Rich cultivator falling on an operator. . . .

The trial court submitted the case to the jury on the strict liability theory of defective design and the negligence claim of breach of a post-sale duty to warn. It also submitted punitive damages on the negligence claim. The jury returned a verdict in the amount of $2,057,000. The verdict included $500,000 in punitive damages and $400,000 in loss of consortium to Lovick's wife.

Wil-Rich appeals. It claims the trial court erred in . . . admitting evidence of other accidents. . . .

Evidence of other incidents is admissible for a variety of purposes, including: (1) the existence and nature of the defect; (2) causation; (3) notice; and (4) impeachment or rebuttal. Francis H. Hare, Jr., *Admissibility of Evidence Concerning Other Similar Incidents in a Defective Design Product Case: Courts Should Determine "Similarity" by Reference to the Defect Involved*, 21 Am. J. Trial Advoc. 491, 496 (1998). Although older cases often excluded evidence of prior incidences, the current trend is toward the inclusion of such evidence.

Our case law supports the inclusion of prior accident evidence to show the existence of a dangerous condition. Notwithstanding, a foundational showing must indicate the prior accidents occurred under substantially the same circumstances.[1]

We have considered the substantial similarity requirement in several cases involving products liability. Eickelberg v. Deere & Co., 276 N.W.2d 442, 445 (Iowa 1979) (holding other incidents not substantially similar to plaintiff's combine injury where plaintiff had been standing nearby and caught some clothing in one of the combine belts, while in one other incident a shield, present on the combine which injured plaintiff, had been removed, and in another incident the injured party was coming out from beneath the combine when the injury occurred); Sandry v. John Deere Co., 452 N.W.2d 616, 618 (Iowa App. 1989) (holding in strict liability action by mechanic whose hand was sucked into combine's rotating fan while completing repairs, evidence of three other accidents in which operators' hands contacted fan was properly admitted); Rattenborg by Rattenborg v. Montgomery Elevator Co., 438 N.W.2d 602, 606 (Iowa App. 1989) (holding evidence of two subsequent accidents involving escalator which injured mall customer admissible in action against escalator manufacturer, where injured customer's shoe had become lodged in escalator and the two subsequent incidents involved situations in which shoe became lodged in escalator). Identical circumstances are not required to prove substantial similarity. Where defendant has ample opportunity to show differences by cross-examination or by its own witnesses, the differences may go to the weight rather than the admissibility of the evidence.

Lovick offered evidence of nine prior accidents to prove the existence of a dangerous condition on his strict liability claim. Wil-Rich claims the district court erroneously admitted five of the nine prior accidents. It maintains the five accidents occurred under circumstances significantly different than those in Lovick's accident.

The first accident Wil-Rich claims was not substantially similar involved Roman John. He died when a Wil-Rich cultivator wing fell on him. The wing fell because a cylinder pivot pin connecting the clevis to the cylinder arm of the wing lift linkage was missing or had been removed. The second accident involved Roy Lipetzky. He also died as a result of a cultivator wing falling on him. In his case, a cylinder pivot pin was missing. The third accident involved Ryan Patton. He suffered injuries rendering him a paraplegic after a smaller cultivator wing fell on him. This accident occurred because the replacement cylinder was not properly charged. The fourth accident involved Leo Langenfeld. He was also injured by a Wil-Rich cultivator when the wing fell on him. He was tightening a newly installed shovel on the wing when his son pulled the lock pin. Finally, the fifth accident was described in a letter from an attorney and involved an individual

---

1. Generally, in negligence cases, evidence of prior incidences is admissible if there is a showing of substantial similarity and the occurrence was not too remote in time. Eickelberg v. Deere & Co., 276 N.W.2d 442, 445 (Iowa 1979). In strict liability cases the temporal element does not apply because knowledge or notice of a dangerous condition is not an issue in such actions. Id.

identified as Mr. Sedler. After removing the pin, the wing fell causing Sedler injuries.

While Wil-Rich attempts to distinguish the various origins of each incident resulting in the collapse of the cultivator wing, their commonality was the location of the wing lock bracket which caused the operator to come under the wing to remove the lock. The design defect therefore concerned the location of the lock rather than the technical events creating the possibility for the wing to fall. This evidence was clearly relevant and was highly probative on the issue of the existence of a dangerous condition. Further, we find no merit in Wil-Rich's argument that references to the fatalities or Patton's testimony from his wheel chair was unfairly prejudicial. Accordingly, we find no abuse of discretion by the admission of the evidence....

NOTES TO LOVICK v. WIL-RICH

1. *What Do Past Injuries Tend to Show?* The court noted that evidence of past injuries might be introduced to show any of four ideas: (1) the existence and nature of the defect; (2) causation; (3) notice; and (4) impeachment or rebuttal. Which of these was involved in *Lovick*?

2. *Relating Required Similarity to Purpose of Evidence.* Some courts hold that the degree of similarity between a plaintiff's injury and past injuries required to make information about past injuries relevant should vary according to whether the plaintiff's relevancy theory is that the past injuries show defect and causation, or the relevancy theory is that they show notice. When a plaintiff argues that a manufacturer should have investigated its product's safety because of past accidents, would differences in the details of those accidents and the details of the plaintiff's accident affect the strength of the conclusion that the defendant should have made inquiries that might have prevented the plaintiff's harm? *See* Ormsby v. Emil Frankel, Commissioner of Transportation, 768 A.2d 441 (Conn. 2001).

SPINO v. JOHN S. TILLEY LADDER CO.
696 A.2d 1169 (Pa. 1997)

NIGRO, J.

The issue before this Court is whether the trial court erred when it admitted "lack of prior claims" evidence. We conclude the Superior Court properly affirmed the trial court's decision to admit such evidence, and therefore, we affirm.

Appellants, Francis and Louise Spino ("the Spinos") purchased a type 3 ordinary household ladder in 1986 from a paint store. The ladder was manufactured by Appellee John S. Tilley Ladder Company ("Tilley") and was designed to accommodate ordinary household use restricted to a 200 pound weight bearing load. Francis Spino testified that he purchased the ladder for a painting project and later used the ladder for household projects. Louise Spino testified that she used the ladder two or three times a year to wash windows or hang curtains.

In November 1986, Louise Spino brought the ladder into her kitchen, placed a bucket of water on the ladder shelf and climbed the ladder. At trial, Mrs. Spino testified that while she reached her arm up in an attempt to clean the kitchen ceiling, she heard a cracking sound, the ladder shook, and the next thing she remembers she was on the floor. Mrs. Spino was then taken to the emergency room and underwent hospitalization and surgery to repair a fractured tibia and fibula. As a result, the Spinos instituted a product liability action against Appellees for Louise Spino's injuries and Francis Spino's loss of consortium. It was their assertion that the ladder leg cracked since it lacked an anti-split device. The Spinos initially asserted two theories of liability, common law negligence and strict liability pursuant to §402(A), Restatement (Second) of Torts. At the outset of trial, Appellants dismissed M.A. Buten and Son, Inc. from the case and abandoned any negligence claims, proceeding against Tilley on strict liability.

Prior to trial, the Spinos filed a Motion in Limine seeking preclusion of the admission of evidence provided by Tilley's President, Robert Howland. Mr. Howland was expected to testify that there had been no similar accidents or claims with respect to this particular product in his thirty years of employment with the company and neither he, nor anyone at the company, had ever been informed of a failure similar to the one alleged by the Spinos. . . .

The trial court denied the motion, finding that since this was a product design case, Mr. Howland's testimony constituted relevant rebuttal evidence to the Spinos' claim that the alleged defect was common to all type 3 household ladders manufactured by Tilley. Moreover, the trial court noted that "a sufficient proffer was made during the course of trial, in camera, to satisfy the Court of the reliability of Mr. Howland's testimony." After an in camera review, the trial judge found that Tilley maintained a chronological log of reported claims covering Tilley's ladder products, including the type 3 ladder. The court was satisfied that the log was an authentic business record and was "comprehensive in its recording of all reports and claims of problems which the Company had received from any source." None of the log entries reported a leg split of a type 3 ladder. . . .

At the conclusion of a three-day trial before the Honorable John W. Herron, the jury returned a verdict in favor of Tilley, finding there was no defect in the ladder which made it unsafe for its intended use. Following the verdict, the Spinos filed a Motion for Post-Trial Relief which the trial court denied. On appeal, the Superior Court affirmed, finding that Howland's "no prior claims" evidence was relevant as to the issue of causation[,] and the trial judge properly admitted such testimony. This Court granted the Spinos' Petition for Allowance of Appeal limited to the issue of whether the trial court erroneously allowed Tilley to introduce the "no prior claims" evidence of leg splitting. . . .

In a plaintiff's case-in-chief in a product liability action, our appellate courts have analyzed the admissibility of prior accidents testimony and have found such evidence relevant and admissible. In DiFrancesco v. Excam, Inc., 434 Pa. Super. 173, 185, 642 A.2d 529, 535 (1994), *appeal dismissed as improvidently granted* 543 Pa. 627, 674 A.2d 214 (1996), the Superior Court determined that evidence concerning other accidents involving the instrumentality that causes the present harm is relevant to show the product was unsafe, to prove causation, and/or to show that a defendant had actual or constructive knowledge of a condition that could cause harm. However, while such evidence may be admissible, the other accidents must be sufficiently similar to plaintiff's accident....

While our Court has yet to directly address the admissibility of evidence of prior claims in a defendant's case-in-chief in a product liability action, in Orlando v. Herco, Inc., 351 Pa. Super. 144, 505 A.2d 308 (1986), the Superior Court addressed a related evidentiary issue. In *Orlando*, plaintiff brought an action based upon breach of the implied warranty of merchantability, contending that he had become ill after consuming shrimp creole at the Hotel Hershey. The trial court allowed the hotel to present evidence that they received no other complaints from the twenty other guests who had consumed the shrimp creole that day. In affirming that decision, the Superior Court indicated that while it is not necessary to establish negligence in a breach of warranty claim, "it does not follow that evidence showing the absence of a defect is inadmissible merely because it tends to show that due care was exercised in the product's preparation or manufacture."

Courts of other jurisdictions have squarely considered the admissibility of no known prior claims testimony in defendant's case-in-chief, rendering decisions which we find instructive. In Espeaignnette v. Gene Tierney Company, Inc., 43 F.3d 1 (1st Cir. 1994), a worker who was injured using a wood saw machine brought a strict liability action against the manufacturer. The district court ... permitted the president of the company to testify that the company received no reports of similar accidents. The Court of Appeals for the First Circuit affirmed, finding that evidence of the absence of prior accidents tends to disprove causation and is both probative and relevant as to whether the product as designed was unreasonably dangerous. In that decision, the court stressed that such evidence would not be admitted unless the offering party first establishes that the lack of accidents was in regard to products substantially identical to the one at issue and used in a setting sufficiently similar to those surrounding the product at the time of the accident.

Similarly, in Jones v. Pak-Mor Manufacturing Company, 145 Ariz. 121, 700 P.2d 819 (1985), the Arizona Supreme Court held that in a product liability case involving a defective design claim, evidence of the existence or non-existence of prior claims is admissible provided that the offering party establishes the necessary predicate for the evidence. In reaching that conclusion, the Arizona Supreme Court recognized that evidence of a lack of prior accidents is no more than evidence that plaintiff was the first to be injured, creating the considerable risk of misleading the jury. As such, a defendant must create a proper foundation before such evidence is admitted, including that if there had been prior accidents, the defendant would have known about them.[8] Accordingly, the *Jones* court created a rule providing for the discretionary admission of such evidence in defective design cases. Moreover, the *Jones* rule promotes safety in that it provides manufacturers with an incentive to acquire, record and maintain information regarding the performance of their products.

The thrust of *Espeaignnette* and *Jones* is that lack of prior claims evidence may be admitted in a design defect product liability action if relevant to a contested issue of causation. We believe that the same reasoning should be applied in Pennsylvania, and, therefore, we hold that evidence of the non-existence of prior claims is admissible subject to the trial court's determination that the offering party has provided a sufficient foundation — that they would have known about the prior, substantially similar accidents involving the product at issue. Clearly, the determination of admissibility turns upon the facts and circumstances of the particular action. As such, the trial court must assess whether the offering party lays a proper foundation by establishing the accident occurred while others were using a product similar to that which caused plaintiff's injury.

Instantly, Tilley introduced Robert Howland's testimony to demonstrate that over 100,000 type 3 ladders have been put into the marketplace over the last one hundred years and there were no prior similar claims for this ladder model of which Tilley was aware. The trial court ruled the testimony admissible after it had conducted an in camera review of Tilley's claims log, finding the log both comprehensive and reflective of all reports, claims or problems involving its ladders. Having determined that Tilley maintained a reliable product problem log, the trial court was convinced that the ladder contained no variables which would diminish the requirement of substantial similarity. As such, the trial court had a sufficient factual basis and did not abuse its discretion in admitting the testimony at issue. . . .

This Court is fully cognizant of the danger of misleading a jury and the problems of prejudice in the inability of the opposing party to meet the evidence. However, there is little logic in allowing the admission of evidence of prior similar accidents but never admitting their absence. Clearly, had the Spinos discovered other accidents involving the type 3 household ladder, such evidence would be admissible subject to the trial court's discretion concerning similarity of both product and circumstances.

In adopting a rule allowing lack of prior claims evidence subject to the trial court's discretion, we are careful to note that while evidence of the absence of prior claims is admissible as relevant to the issue of causation, the evidence does not dictate an absolute finding that the product is not defective or unreasonably dangerous. . . .

---

8. The *Jones* Court noted that if the evidence is no more than testimony that no lawsuits have been filed, no claims have been made or that the defendant has never heard of any accidents, the trial judge should generally refuse such evidence since it has little probative value and has a high danger of prejudice. We agree with that assessment.

Opposing counsel can, and indeed should, soundly attack any prior claims testimony. We believe it is incumbent upon the party opposing the absence of prior claims testimony to attack such evidence through cross-examination, as well as request a cautionary or limiting instruction be provided.

As we find the trial court did not abuse its discretion in admitting Robert Howland's testimony concerning absence of prior claims, the Superior Court's decision is affirmed.

NOTES TO SPINO v. JOHN S. TILLEY LADDER CO.

1. *Comparing Good and Bad Safety Records.* The court examines two chains of inferences: (1) occurrence of prior accidents tends to show that a product defect *did cause* the plaintiff's injury, and (2) lack of prior accidents tends to show that a product defect *did not cause* the plaintiff's injury. Are the links in these two inferential chains of similar strength?

2. *"No News Is Good News" Sometimes but Not Always.* In footnote 8, the court says that it would require a trial court to exclude "no prior claims" evidence if it was merely testimony that the defendant had not heard of any problems. Is the defendant's evidence in this case different from that description?

QUESTION 1-4. Suppose that a type of tire made in a particular factory was associated with significantly more complaints from users than other types of tires made in that factory. Would evidence of this pattern be relevant to show that a failure of a tire of that type had been caused by a defect?

■ ■ ■

Finding Facts When a Party Destroys Evidence — Aloi. How should the legal system respond when someone who could anticipate litigation destroys information that would be relevant in the dispute? The *Aloi* court describes the most important issues in this setting: What benefit, if any, should the legal system provide to the victim of evidence destruction, and what should that victim be required to show in order to get that benefit?

ALOI v. UNION PACIFIC RAILROAD CORP.
129 P.3d 999 (Colo. 2006)

RICE, J.

Frank Aloi tripped over a loose rubber mat and was injured while working as a conductor for Union Pacific Railroad (UP). Aloi brought a personal injury action against UP. Prior to trial, UP destroyed documents relevant to the litigation. As a sanction for spoliation of evidence, the trial court instructed the jury it could draw an inference that the evidence contained in the destroyed documents would have been unfavorable to UP.... The jury returned a verdict for Aloi, and UP appealed. The court of appeals reversed the trial court's judgment and held that the trial court did not err in its decision to give an adverse inference instruction [but had acted erroneously in another way].... We granted certiorari....

On August 27, 1998, Union Pacific Railroad assigned Frank Aloi to conduct a train from North Platte, Nebraska[,] to Missouri Valley, Iowa. Before the train departed, Aloi tripped and fell while descending interior stairs on the locomotive. After examining the stairwell, Aloi discovered a loose rubber mat, which covered a vertical riser on a step.

After Aloi told the locomotive's engineer that he had tripped on the loose rubber mat, the engineer inspected the stairwell. Later that day, Aloi telephoned the UP manager of yard operations and reported that he had tripped on the stairs. Within a couple hours of receiving Aloi's phone call, the UP yard manager and a UP safety manager inspected the locomotive and took photographs. Later that day, the locomotive engineer completed an engineer's inspection form on which she documented the loose mat as a "tripping hazard."

The morning after Aloi returned from his shift, he filed a personal injury report with UP stating that he had tripped on a loose rubber riser and had sustained injuries. Within a week of the accident, Aloi's attorneys notified UP that Aloi would file a personal injury claim against the railroad.

During discovery, UP was unable to produce several documents that pertained to inspections and maintenance performed on the locomotive prior to Aloi's fall and documents that pertained to inspections and maintenance performed on the locomotive after Aloi's fall. Federal railroad and locomotive safety standards require carriers to make inspection reports and maintain the records for 92 days. Pursuant to this regulation, UP employs a 92-day document retention policy. When someone reports an accident, a UP claims agent should recover the relevant records before the 92-day period expires in order to prevent their destruction. Because of a failure that UP attributed to a change in personnel, the claims agent assigned to follow Aloi's accident did not collect the inspection reports or other maintenance records concerning the locomotive before the 92-day period expired. Consequently, UP destroyed the documents....

[UP] admitted negligence in failing to properly inspect and maintain the stairwell. UP, however, denied that its negligence caused Aloi's injuries and argued that, from a human factors perspective, Aloi's foot would not have contacted the riser and caused him to fall. The trial was limited to determining causation and damages.

On the morning trial began, UP ... argued that because it conceded negligence, the missing documents were not relevant to any issue at trial and evidence regarding the missing documents would only serve to prejudice UP. The trial court denied this motion.

[T]he trial court stated, "It's reasonable . . . to infer that destruction was willful and designed to impede, hinder and obstruct the ability of the plaintiff to prove the very issues that he has the burden of proving at trial."

. . . At the close of Aloi's case-in-chief, the trial court first read the following instruction to the jury:

> It is the duty of a party not to take action that will cause the destruction or loss of relevant evidence, hindering the other side from making its own examination and investigation of all potentially relevant evidence relating to whether that party's fault caused the incident in question. You are instructed you may infer, by reason of the Defendant's failure to produce these documents, that the evidence contained in such documents was unfavorable to Defendant. . . .

The jury returned a verdict in favor of Aloi and awarded six million dollars in damages. UP filed an appeal and argued, among other claims, that the trial court abused its discretion . . . by issuing the adverse inference instruction. . . .

The ability to provide the jury with an adverse inference instruction as a sanction for spoliation of evidence derives from the trial court's inherent powers. A trial court has broad discretion to permit the jury to draw an adverse inference from the loss or destruction of evidence. Accordingly, we will not overturn the trial court's imposition of an adverse inference unless the sanction is manifestly arbitrary, unreasonable, or unfair.

In determining whether the trial court abused its discretion, we must examine whether the rationales underlying the adverse inference supported giving the instruction as a sanction for spoliation. Colorado courts have recognized adverse inference instructions serve both a punitive and a remedial purpose. The punitive function serves to deter parties from destroying evidence in order to prevent its introduction at trial. The remedial function serves to restore the putative prejudiced party to the position it would have held had there been no spoliation. . . .

UP argues that the trial court should only have discretion to provide an adverse inference instruction where the proponent of the instruction demonstrates that the evidence was destroyed in bad faith. UP claims that because Aloi made no showing of bad faith destruction, the trial court abused its discretion by giving the instruction. In response, Aloi argues that the trial court's finding that UP destroyed evidence willfully justifies the instruction.

Courts in other jurisdictions are divided with regard to whether a trial court must find a party destroyed evidence in bad faith before it has discretion to impose an adverse inference instruction. Some courts have held that a trial court may only impose an adverse inference where there was bad faith because "[m]ere negligence . . . does not sustain an inference of consciousness of a weak case." *Vick v. Tex. Employment Comm'n,* 514 F.2d 734, 737 (5th Cir. 1975) (quoting McCormick, *Evidence* §273 at 660-61 (1972)).

In other jurisdictions, trial courts have the discretion to provide an adverse inference instruction under a wider range of circumstances without a showing of bad faith. *Glover v. BIC Corp.*, 6 F.3d 1318, 1329 (9th Cir. 1993) ("[A] trial court also has the broad discretionary power to permit a jury to draw an adverse inference from the destruction or spoliation against the party or witness responsible for that behavior.... [H]owever, a finding of 'bad faith' is not a prerequisite to this corrective procedure. Surely a finding of bad faith will suffice, but so will simple notice of 'potential relevance to the litigation.'") (internal citations omitted)[.] We discern no useful distinction between destroying evidence in bad faith and destroying evidence willfully....

The broader approach, which does not require a showing of bad faith, more closely serves the rationales behind the adverse inference instruction. With respect to the inference's remedial purpose, it does not matter whether a party destroyed evidence in bad faith or whether a party destroyed evidence willfully because, regardless of the destroying party's mental state, the opposing party will suffer the same prejudice. Likewise, the broader approach serves the inference's punitive purpose. Imposing an adverse inference where a party willfully destroys evidence will deter parties from destroying evidence that they know or should know will be relevant to litigation. Accordingly, providing the jury with an adverse inference instruction where the trial court finds that a party has willfully destroyed evidence serves the remedial and punitive rationales and therefore does not constitute an abuse of discretion.

In this case, because Aloi filed a personal injury report with the railroad the day after returning from his shift and informed UP that he intended to bring a personal injury action within a week of the accident, UP had notice that the locomotive inspection and repair documents would be relevant to litigation well before the 92-day document retention period expired. Accordingly, the trial court found that UP's failure to preserve the evidence was willful. Thus, we conclude it was not necessary for the trial court to find that UP destroyed evidence in bad faith; the trial court did not abuse its discretion by providing an adverse inference instruction where it found UP willfully destroyed evidence.

UP further argues that in the absence of bad faith the trial court should only have discretion to provide an adverse inference instruction where there is extrinsic evidence demonstrating that the destroyed evidence would have been unfavorable to the spoliator. In response, Aloi argues that the proponent of an adverse inference instruction need only demonstrate that the destroyed evidence would be relevant to a contested issue....

As a minimum threshold, we approve of the Fourth Circuit's approach: "To draw an adverse inference from the absence, loss or destruction of evidence, it would have to appear that the evidence would have been relevant to an issue at trial and otherwise would naturally have been introduced into evidence." *Vodusek v. Bayliner Marine Corp.*, 71 F.3d 148, 156 (4th Cir. 1995). We find that this approach accords with the rationales behind the adverse inference instruction. It serves the remedial function because it minimizes the prejudice suffered by the non-destroying party. This standard also serves the punitive function because it deters destruction by placing the risk that destroyed evidence may not have been detrimental on the party responsible for the destruction.

In this case, it appears the records of locomotive inspection and maintenance would have been relevant and otherwise introduced into evidence to demonstrate the condition of the locomotive stairwell. Additionally, the records may have provided more detailed information regarding the nature of the locomotive defect, the specific repair work performed, and other information helpful to determining whether the specific defect caused Aloi's injuries. Thus, because the rationales behind the adverse inference instruction support giving an instruction where a party destroys relevant documents which otherwise would have been introduced into evidence, the trial court did not abuse its discretion by providing the instruction based on the information available regarding the contents of the destroyed documents.

In sum, because the trial court found that UP acted willfully in destroying the documents and because it appears the documents would have been relevant and otherwise introduced into evidence, we hold that the trial court did not abuse its discretion by giving an adverse inference instruction. . . .

We affirm the court of appeals' holding that the trial court did not abuse its discretion by imposing an adverse inference instruction, [and remand the case to the court of appeals for consideration of issues the court of appeals had declined to consider].

NOTES TO ALOI v. UNION PACIFIC RAILROAD CORP.

1. *Strength of the Inference.* Spoliation of evidence can support a jury instruction allowing an inference, as in *Aloi*. It might also support a rebuttable presumption or some other stronger consequence. If, hypothetically, a defendant had destroyed *all* evidence of its misconduct, could proof of that spoliation satisfy a plaintiff's obligation to present a prima facie case?

The court in Kronisch v. United States, 150 F.3d 112, 128 (2d Cir. 1998), considered this question in a case involving an allegation that the CIA dosed an American citizen with LSD at a Paris bar, in an experiment to test the effects of mind-altering drugs on unsuspecting individuals. The court wrote:

> We do not suggest that the destruction of evidence, standing alone, is enough to allow a party who has produced no evidence — or utterly inadequate evidence — in support of a given claim to survive summary judgment on that claim. But at the margin, where the innocent party has produced some (not insubstantial) evidence in support of his claim, the intentional destruction of relevant evidence by the opposing party may push a claim that might not otherwise survive summary judgment over the line. In the absence of such a result, as noted above, the purposes of the adverse inference are eviscerated. . . .

2. *Missing Witnesses.* If one party has control over a potential witness, or better access to that witness than another party, and if the party with that relationship to the witness fails to call the witness, sometimes an inference is allowed that the individual's testimony would have been adverse to the party

who could have introduced it. For example, a tort plaintiff might be subject to such an inference if he or she failed to introduce testimony from a treating physician to substantiate the extent of physical injuries. In a civil case, it may be proper for a plaintiff's attorney to comment on the defendant's failure to testify, if the defendant was likely to have possessed relevant information.

3. *Tort Remedies.* About a dozen states recognize a tort remedy for spoliation of evidence, against prospective defendants (first-party spoliators) or others who had possession of evidence (third-party spoliators). The case for a tort remedy is strongest in the third-party cases. For example, a plaintiff might be injured by a defendant manufacturer's machine while on a third party's premises. If the premises' owner destroys the machine, the permissive inference approach would be unworkable, because the plaintiff's litigation would be against the machine manufacturer and not the premises' owner.

QUESTION 1-5. Sam Slipper was injured when he slipped and fell in a fast-food restaurant. The manager of the restaurant wrote an accident report and sent that document to the company's main office. A few weeks later, a fire caused by the company's negligence destroyed all the files in that office. The accident report was one of the destroyed documents. If Slipper sues the restaurant, and seeks an adverse inference instruction against the restaurant, the trial judge should:

A. Give the instruction, since the defendant willfully lost the document.
B. Give the instruction, since that will restore Slipper to the position he would have held if the fire had not occurred.
C. Deny the instruction, because the defendant did not destroy the report to prevent its introduction at trial.
D. Deny the instruction, since its contents may not have been relevant to Slipper's claims.

F   CONDITIONAL RELEVANCE

Sometimes a fact can have a relationship to the issues in a case only if some other facts are established. This circumstance is known as "conditional relevance." Rule 104(b) covers this situation.

Rule 104. Preliminary Questions

   (a) In General. The court must decide any preliminary question about whether a witness is qualified, a privilege exists, or evidence is admissible. In so deciding, the court is not bound by evidence rules, except those on privilege.

> **(b) Relevance that Depends on a Fact.** When the relevance of evidence depends on whether a fact exists, proof must be introduced sufficient to support a finding that the fact does exist. The court may admit the proposed evidence on the condition that the proof be introduced later.

Part (a) of this rule applies to all admissibility decisions, including typical relevance decisions, and gives the judge responsibility for them. Part (b) controls the treatment of evidence that depends for relevance on some additional evidence. The judge is allowed to admit that evidence either before or after the additional evidence is presented.

■　■　■

Webs of Connection — Cox. This case involves a number of individuals and the ways in which something one of them knew might have affected another one of them. The sad facts involve:

- Patrick Cox (defendant), accused of murdering James Leonard.
- James Leonard (murder victim), father of alleged molestation victim.
- Jamie Hammer (Patrick Cox's close friend), accused of molesting James Leonard's daughter.
- Helen Johnson (Jamie Hammer's mother).

COX v. STATE
696 N.E.2d 853 (Ind. 1998)

BOEHM, J.

In this direct appeal from a conviction for murder, Patrick E. Cox contends that . . . the trial court erred by admitting certain testimony, the relevance of which depended upon Cox's knowledge of the content of the testimony. . . .

We affirm.

In the early morning hours of September 22, 1995[,] James and Patricia Leonard were asleep in the ground floor bedroom of their home. At about 3:00 A.M. Patricia woke to look after the family dogs, returned to bed, switched on a bedroom television, and fell asleep. She was awakened by a single "loud pop sound," and quickly realized that James had been shot in the eye. James was rushed to the hospital but died three days later.

Bullet holes were found in the bedroom window and its screen, and a bullet casing was outside beneath the window. An officer who was called to the scene that night had a clear view of the inside of the bedroom from immediately outside the window. A firearms expert testified that the pattern of discoloration on the screen could have been produced only by a shot fired within six inches of the screen.

Police questioned Cox on the morning of the shooting. Cox denied any involvement in the crime and said he returned home from a nearby friend's house at about 1:00 A.M. However, later that morning one of Cox's friends told police that Cox had said that he had looked into the Leonards' window, fired a shot, and fled. . . . At trial, the firearms expert testified that [a gun found at Cox's house had] fired the deadly shot. In addition, Angela Bowling, a friend of Cox's, testified that she bought bullets for Cox at his request the night of the shooting and that she and a few other friends were with him at the home of Helen Johnson until Cox left between 3:30 and 4:00 A.M. Johnson was the mother of Cox's close friend, Jamie Hammer. Bowling said that Cox showed the bullets to the group and had a large object tucked into his trousers. The State contended that Cox killed Leonard as an act of retaliation because Hammer was in prison pending the resolution of charges filed against him by the Leonards for molesting their young daughter. The jury convicted Cox of murder but in a separate sentencing phase was unable to agree whether he should serve life in prison without parole. The trial court imposed life imprisonment and Cox appeals. . . .

At trial, Cox objected to testimony by David Puckett, a deputy prosecutor in Madison County. Puckett testified that four days before the murder he had represented the State of Indiana at a bond reduction hearing for Cox's close friend Jamie Hammer. He testified that: (1) he had informed the court at the hearing that three class B felony charges were to be filed against Hammer, in addition to a single pending charge, for alleged acts of child molestation of Leonard's daughter; (2) Helen Johnson, Hammer's mother, testified at the hearing; and (3) Hammer's bond was not reduced as a result of the hearing. Cox contends that this testimony was inadmissible because it could be relevant only if Cox knew what happened at the hearing and the State was unable to prove conclusively that Cox had that knowledge. The trial court admitted the evidence, concluding that because Hammer's mother knew about the denial of Hammer's bond reduction and the additional charges to be filed, "other persons in [Hammer's] circle reasonably are likely to know about it."

The admissibility of Puckett's testimony is governed by Indiana Evidence Rule 104(b), "Relevancy Conditioned on Fact," although neither party cites this rule. The Indiana Rule is identical to Federal Rule of Evidence 104(b). It provides: "When the relevancy of evidence depends upon the fulfillment of a condition of fact, the Court shall admit it upon, or subject to, the introduction of evidence sufficient to support a finding of the fulfillment of the condition." Here, the relevance of Puckett's testimony depends upon a condition of fact — whether Cox knew about what happened at the bond reduction hearing. If Cox knew of the latest developments in Hammer's case, then the information was relevant and extremely probative of the State's theory that Cox killed Leonard — the father of Hammer's victim — because of Hammer's plight. If Cox was ignorant of these developments, then Puckett's testimony would be irrelevant and unfairly prejudicial.

We have not yet had occasion to set out the standard for questions under Rule 104(b). Under its terms, the court may admit the evidence only after it makes a preliminary determination that there is sufficient evidence to support a finding that the conditional fact exists. As Weinstein commented, "[t]hese issues are, for the most part, simple factual questions to be decided on the basis of common sense, and the Rules [of Evidence] assume that the jury is as competent to decide them as the judge." 1 Weinstein's Federal Evidence §104.30[1], at 104-63 (2d ed. 1998). We adopt the prevailing federal standard that "the judge must determine only that a reasonable jury could make the requisite factual determination based on the evidence before it." The trial court is not required to weigh the credibility of the evidence or to make a finding. We will review the sufficiency of the evidence under 104(b) for an abuse of discretion. Here, the State introduced evidence that Cox spent almost every day at the Hammer house where Hammer's mother lived both before and after the bond reduction hearing and up to the time of the shooting. Hammer and Cox were close friends and Hammer's mother attended the hearing. This evidence is sufficient to support the inference that Cox had learned what transpired at the hearing. Accordingly, the trial court did not abuse its discretion by admitting the evidence.

Cox also contends that Puckett's testimony should have been excluded because its probative value was substantially outweighed by the danger of unfair prejudice. Ind. Evidence Rule 403. The thrust of Cox's contention is that the probative value of the evidence was diminished considerably because it was conditioned on Cox's knowledge of the events of the hearing. We disagree. If the fact upon which the evidence depends is too speculative, then the evidence will not be admitted under Rule 104(b). Once evidence passes the 104(b) hurdle, the court then separately determines admissibility under the other rules of evidence. The speculative component of evidence conditioned on the existence of a fact may then become part of the trial court's relevance inquiry. The trial court must determine whether the evidence is of no probative value or whether its probative value is substantially decreased by its speculative component and inadmissible under Rule 402 (relevance) or Rule 403 (balancing). This is a highly fact sensitive inquiry and accordingly is reviewed for abuse of discretion. Here, the court was well within its discretion in concluding that the evidence was both relevant and did not outweigh the danger of unfair prejudice. . . .

We affirm the trial court.

NOTES TO COX v. STATE

1. *Is All Relevance Conditional?* The prosecution claimed that the events at Jamie Hammer's bond reduction hearing were relevant to show that Patrick E. Cox had murdered James Leonard. How was the bond hearing's relevance conditioned on some other fact?

Most of the time, concluding that one fact sheds light on another fact involves assumptions about how the world works, or knowledge about context or background. Compare the chains of inferences in these examples:

A. To show that a parent had poor parenting skills, proof that the parent allowed a young child to play in a snowstorm wearing only a thin short-sleeved shirt.

B. To show that Patrick E. Cox had murdered James Leonard, proof that James Hammer's mother attended a bond hearing involving her son Jamie Hammer and learned that Mr. Leonard was causing additional charges to be filed against her son.

What information is necessary to link up the offered proof with the hoped-for conclusion in each situation?

2. *Conditional Relevance Risks.* If the proponent of evidence that is treated as conditionally relevant is unable to come up with proof of the "conditional fact," or if the proponent has some evidence about the conditional fact but the jury is not persuaded about that the conditional fact was true, will the jury likely rely on the conditionally relevant material in deciding the case? For example, if a defendant were accused of robbing a bank, and testimony was admitted to show that the defendant owned a black raincoat, that testimony might be conditionally relevant on the assumption that there would be proof showing that the robber had been wearing that type of coat. If the jury failed to conclude that the robber had been wearing a black raincoat, would there be any harm caused by the jury's having heard that the defendant owned a black raincoat?

> **GOOD TO REMEMBER**
>
> Conditional relevance is based on the common sense idea that people will only consider information that has a logical place in a narrative. If a jury hears information that never gets connected in a logical way to the questions the jury is trying to answer, the jury will likely ignore that information.

G DISCRETION TO EXCLUDE RELEVANT EVIDENCE

Rule 403 describes a process in which a trial court will balance the probative value of relevant evidence against certain dangers. But there are no units of measure for probative value or those dangers, and appellate courts give deference to the judgment involved in applying the balancing test. This makes it common for trial court rulings under Rule 403 to be affirmed on appeal. Nonetheless, it may be possible to articulate a framework for the Rule 403 analysis, and there may be some instances where a trial court's decision under Rule 403 could be outside the range of allowable discretion.

■   ■   ■

Balancing Probative Value and Unfair Prejudice — Old Chief. If an item of evidence has *some* probative value, it may be very difficult for an appellate court to rule that a trial judge's estimate of the magnitude of that value was wrong. A key to understanding *Old Chief* is its conclusion that the challenged evidence had *no* probative value greater than the probative value of other evidence that could have proved its same point. When two concepts are required to be balanced, and the value assigned to one of those concepts is zero, the outcome of the balance will be clear.

OLD CHIEF v. UNITED STATES
519 U.S. 172 (1997)

Justice SOUTER delivered the opinion of the Court.

Subject to certain limitations, 18 U.S.C. §922(g)(1) prohibits possession of a firearm by anyone with a prior felony conviction, which the government can prove by introducing a record of judgment or similar evidence identifying the previous offense. Fearing prejudice if the jury learns the nature of the earlier crime, defendants sometimes seek to avoid such an informative disclosure by offering to concede the fact of the prior conviction. The issue here is whether a district court abuses its discretion if it spurns such an offer and admits the full record of a prior judgment, when the name or nature of the prior offense raises the risk of a verdict tainted by improper considerations, and when the purpose of the evidence is solely to prove the element of prior conviction. We hold that it does.

In 1993, petitioner, Old Chief, was arrested after a fracas involving at least one gunshot. The ensuing federal charges included not only assault with a dangerous weapon and using a firearm in relation to a crime of violence but violation of 18 U.S.C. §922(g)(1). This statute makes it unlawful for anyone "who has been convicted in any court of, a crime punishable by imprisonment for a term exceeding one year" to "possess in or affecting commerce, any firearm. . . ." "[A] crime punishable by imprisonment for a term exceeding one year" is defined to exclude "any Federal or State offenses pertaining to antitrust violations, unfair trade practices, restraints of trade, or other similar offenses relating to the regulation of business practices" and "any State offense classified by the laws of the State as a misdemeanor and punishable by a term of imprisonment of two years or less." 18 U.S.C. §921(a)(20).

The earlier crime charged in the indictment against Old Chief was assault causing serious bodily injury. Before trial, he moved for an order requiring the government "to refrain from mentioning — by reading the Indictment, during jury selection, in opening statement, or closing argument — and to refrain from offering into evidence or soliciting any testimony from any witness regarding the prior criminal convictions of the Defendant, *except* to state that the Defendant has been convicted of a crime punishable by imprisonment exceeding one (1) year." App. 6. He said that revealing the name and nature of his prior assault conviction would unfairly tax the jury's capacity to hold the Government to its burden of proof beyond a reasonable doubt on current charges of assault, possession, and violence with a firearm, and he offered to "solve the problem here by stipulating, agreeing and requesting the Court to instruct the jury that he has been convicted of a crime punishable by imprisonment exceeding one (1) year[ ]." App. 7. He argued that the offer to stipulate to the fact of the prior conviction rendered evidence of the name and nature of the offense inadmissible under Rule 403 of the Federal Rules of Evidence, the danger being that unfair prejudice from that evidence would substantially outweigh its probative value. . . .

The Assistant United States Attorney refused to join in a stipulation, insisting on his right to prove his case his own way, and the District Court agreed, ruling orally that, "If he doesn't want to stipulate, he doesn't have to." At trial, over renewed objection, the Government introduced the order of judgment and commitment for Old Chief's prior conviction. This document disclosed that on December 18, 1988, he "did knowingly and unlawfully assault Rory Dean Fenner, said assault resulting in serious bodily injury," for which Old Chief was sentenced to five years' imprisonment. The jury found Old Chief guilty on all counts, and he appealed.

The Ninth Circuit addressed the point with brevity:

> "Regardless of the defendant's offer to stipulate, the government is entitled to prove a prior felony offense through introduction of probative evidence. Under Ninth Circuit law, a stipulation is not proof, and, thus, it has no place in the FRE 403 balancing process. . . .
>
> "Thus, we hold that the district court did not abuse its discretion by allowing the prosecution to introduce evidence of Old Chief's prior conviction to prove that element of the unlawful possession charge."

We granted Old Chief's petition for writ of certiorari because the Courts of Appeals have divided sharply in their treatment of defendants' efforts to exclude evidence of the names and natures of prior offenses in cases like this. . . . We now reverse the judgment of the Ninth Circuit.

As a threshold matter, there is Old Chief's erroneous argument that the name of his prior offense as contained in the record of conviction is irrelevant to the prior-conviction element, and for that reason inadmissible under Rule 402 of the Federal Rules of Evidence. Rule 401 defines relevant evidence as having "any tendency to make the existence of any fact that is of consequence to the determination of the action more probable or less probable than it would be without the evidence." To be sure, the fact that Old Chief's prior conviction was for assault resulting in serious bodily injury rather than, say, for theft was not itself an ultimate fact, as if the statute had specifically required proof of injurious assault. But its demonstration was a step on one evidentiary route to the ultimate fact, since it served to place Old Chief within a particular sub-class of offenders for whom firearms possession is outlawed by §922(g)(1). A documentary record of the conviction for that named offense was thus relevant evidence in making Old Chief's §922(g)(1) status more probable than it would have been without the evidence. . . .

The principal issue is the scope of a trial judge's discretion under Rule 403, which authorizes exclusion of relevant evidence when its "probative value is substantially outweighed by the danger of unfair prejudice, confusion of the issues, or misleading the jury, or by considerations of undue delay, waste of time, or needless presentation of cumulative evidence." Old Chief relies on the danger of unfair prejudice.

The term "unfair prejudice," as to a criminal defendant, speaks to the capacity of some concededly relevant evidence to lure the factfinder into declaring guilt on a ground different from proof specific to the offense charged. . . .

Such improper grounds certainly include the one that Old Chief points to here: generalizing a defendant's earlier bad act into bad character and taking that as raising the odds that he did the later bad act now charged (or, worse, as calling for preventive conviction even if he should happen to be innocent momentarily). As then-Judge Breyer put it, "Although . . . 'propensity evidence' is relevant, the risk that a jury will convict for crimes other than those charged — or that, uncertain of guilt, it will convict anyway because a bad person deserves punishment — creates a prejudicial effect that outweighs ordinary relevance." *United States v. Moccia*, 681 F.2d 61, 63 (C.A.1 1982). . . .

Rule of Evidence 404(b) reflects this common law tradition by addressing propensity reasoning directly: "Evidence of other crimes, wrongs, or acts is not admissible to prove the character of a person in order to show action in conformity therewith." There is, accordingly, no question that propensity would be an "improper basis" for conviction and that evidence of a prior conviction is subject to analysis under Rule 403 for relative probative value and for prejudicial risk of misuse as propensity evidence. . . .

As for the analytical method to be used in Rule 403 balancing, two basic possibilities present themselves. An item of evidence might be viewed as an island, with estimates of its own probative value and unfairly prejudicial risk the sole reference points in deciding whether the danger substantially outweighs the value and whether the evidence ought to be excluded. Or the question of admissibility might be seen as inviting further comparisons to take account of the full evidentiary context of the case as the court understands it when the ruling must be made. . . .

[A] reading of the companions to Rule 403, and of the commentaries that went with them to Congress, makes it clear that what counts as the Rule 403 "probative value" of an item of evidence, as distinct from its Rule 401 "relevance," may be calculated by comparing evidentiary alternatives. The Committee Notes to Rule 401 explicitly say that a party's concession is pertinent to the court's discretion to exclude evidence on the point conceded. Such a concession, according to the Notes, will sometimes "call for the exclusion of evidence offered to prove [the] point conceded by the opponent. . . ." . . . Thus the notes leave no question that when Rule 403 confers discretion by providing that evidence "may" be excluded, the discretionary judgment may be informed not only by assessing an evidentiary item's twin tendencies, but by placing the result of that assessment alongside similar assessments of evidentiary alternatives. . . .

In dealing with the specific problem raised by §922(g)(1) and its prior-conviction element, there can be no question that evidence of the name or nature of the prior offense generally carries a risk of unfair prejudice to the defendant. That risk will vary from case to case, for the reasons already given, but will be substantial whenever the official record offered by the government would be arresting enough to lure a juror into a sequence of bad character reasoning. Where a prior conviction was for a gun crime or one similar to other charges in a pending case the risk of unfair prejudice would be especially obvious, and Old Chief sensibly worried that the prejudicial effect of his prior assault conviction, significant enough with respect to the current gun charges alone, would take on added weight from the related assault charge against him. . . .

The District Court was also presented with alternative, relevant, admissible evidence of the prior conviction by Old Chief's offer to stipulate, evidence necessarily subject to the District Court's consideration on the motion to exclude the record offered by the Government. Although Old Chief's formal offer to stipulate was, strictly, to enter a formal agreement with the Government to be given to the jury, even without the Government's acceptance his proposal amounted to an offer to admit that the prior-conviction element was satisfied, and a defendant's admission is, of course, good evidence. . . .

Old Chief's proffered admission would, in fact, have been not merely relevant but seemingly conclusive evidence of the element. The statutory language in which the prior-conviction requirement is couched shows no congressional concern with the specific name or nature of the prior offense beyond what is necessary to place it within the broad category of qualifying felonies, and Old Chief clearly meant to admit that his felony did qualify, by stipulating "that the Government has proven one of the essential elements of the offense." As a consequence, although the name of the prior offense may have been technically relevant, it addressed no detail in the definition of the prior-conviction element that would not have been covered by the stipulation or admission. Logic, then, seems to side with Old Chief.

There is, however, one more question to be considered before deciding whether Old Chief's offer was to supply evidentiary value at least equivalent to what the Government's own evidence carried. In arguing that the stipulation or admission would not have carried equivalent value, the Government invokes the familiar, standard rule that the prosecution is entitled to prove its case by evidence of its own choice, or, more exactly, that a criminal defendant may not stipulate or admit his way out of the full evidentiary force of the case as the government chooses to present it. . . .

This is unquestionably true as a general matter. The "fair and legitimate weight" of conventional evidence showing individual thoughts and acts amounting to a crime reflects the fact that making a case with testimony and tangible things not only satisfies the formal definition of an offense, but tells a colorful story with descriptive richness. . . . This persuasive power of the concrete and particular is often essential to the capacity of jurors to satisfy the obligations that the law places on them. Jury duty is usually unsought and sometimes resisted, and it may be as difficult for one juror suddenly to face the findings that can send another human being to prison[ ] as it is for another to hold out conscientiously for acquittal. When a juror's duty does seem hard, the evidentiary account of what a defendant has thought and done can accomplish what no set of abstract statements ever could, not just to prove a fact but to establish its human significance, and so to implicate the law's moral underpinnings and a juror's obligation to sit in judgment. Thus, the prosecution may fairly seek to place its evidence before the jurors, as much to tell a story of guiltiness as to support an inference of guilt, to convince the jurors that a guilty verdict would be morally reasonable as much as to point to the discrete elements of a defendant's legal fault. . . .

But there is something even more to the prosecution's interest in resisting efforts to replace the evidence of its choice with admissions and stipulations, for beyond the power of conventional evidence to support allegations and give life to the moral underpinnings of law's claims, there lies the need for evidence in all its particularity to satisfy the jurors' expectations about what proper proof should be. Some such demands they bring with them to the courthouse, assuming, for example, that a charge of using a firearm to commit an offense will be proven by introducing a gun in evidence. A prosecutor who fails to produce one, or some good reason for his failure, has something to be concerned about. "If [jurors'] expectations are not satisfied, triers of fact may penalize the party who disappoints them by drawing a negative inference against that party." Saltzburg, *A Special Aspect of Relevance: Countering Negative Inferences Associated with the Absence of Evidence*, 66 Calif. L. Rev. 1011, 1019 (1978) (footnotes omitted). Expectations may also arise in jurors' minds simply from the experience of a trial itself. The use of witnesses to describe a train of events naturally related can raise the prospect of learning about every ingredient of that natural sequence the same way. If suddenly the prosecution presents some occurrence in the series differently, as by announcing a stipulation or admission, the effect may be like saying, "never mind what's behind the door," and jurors may well wonder what they are being kept from knowing. A party seemingly responsible for cloaking something has reason for apprehension, and the prosecution with its burden of proof may prudently demur at a defense request to interrupt the flow of evidence telling the story in the usual way.

In sum, the accepted rule that the prosecution is entitled to prove its case free from any defendant's option to stipulate the evidence away rests on good sense. A syllogism is not a story, and a naked proposition in a courtroom may be no match for the robust evidence that would be used to prove it. People who hear a story interrupted by gaps of abstraction may be puzzled at the missing chapters, and jurors asked to rest a momentous decision on the story's truth can feel put upon at being asked to take responsibility knowing that more could be said than they have heard. A convincing tale can be told with economy, but when economy becomes a break in the natural sequence of narrative evidence, an assurance that the missing link is really there is never more than second best.

This recognition that the prosecution with its burden of persuasion needs evidentiary depth to tell a continuous story has, however, virtually no application when the point at issue is a defendant's legal status, dependent on some judgment rendered wholly independently of the concrete events of later criminal behavior charged against him. As in this case, the choice of evidence for such an element is usually not between eventful narrative and abstract proposition, but between propositions of slightly varying abstraction, either a record saying that conviction for some crime occurred at a certain time or a statement admitting the same thing without naming the particular offense. . . . The issue is not whether concrete details of the prior crime should come to the jurors' attention but whether the name or general character of that crime is to be disclosed. Congress, however, has made it plain that distinctions among generic felonies do not count for this purpose; the fact of the qualifying conviction is alone what matters under the statute. . . . The most the jury needs to know is that the conviction admitted by the defendant falls within the class of crimes that Congress thought should bar a convict from possessing a gun, and this point may be made readily in a defendant's admission and underscored in the court's jury instructions. Finally, the most obvious reason that the general presumption that the prosecution may choose its evidence is so remote from application here is that proof of the defendant's status goes to an element entirely outside the natural sequence of what the defendant is charged with thinking and doing to commit the current offense. Proving status without telling exactly why that status was imposed leaves no gap in the story of a defendant's subsequent criminality, and its demonstration by stipulation or admission neither displaces a chapter from a continuous sequence of conventional evidence nor comes across as an officious substitution, to confuse or offend or provoke reproach.

Given these peculiarities of the element of felony-convict status and of admissions and the like when used to prove it, there is no cognizable difference between the evidentiary significance of an admission and of the legitimately probative component of the official record the prosecution would prefer to place in evidence. For purposes of the Rule 403 weighing of the probative against the prejudicial, the functions of the competing evidence are distinguishable only by the risk inherent in the one and wholly absent from the other. In this case, as in any other in which the prior conviction is for an offense likely to support conviction on some improper ground, the only reasonable conclusion was that the risk of unfair prejudice did substantially outweigh the discounted probative value of the record of conviction, and it was an abuse of discretion to admit the record when an admission was available. What we have said shows why this will be the general rule when proof of convict status is at issue, just as the prosecutor's choice will generally survive a Rule 403 analysis when a defendant seeks to force the substitution of an admission for evidence creating a coherent narrative of his thoughts and actions in perpetrating the offense for which he is being tried.

The judgment is reversed, and the case is remanded to the Ninth Circuit for further proceedings consistent with this opinion.

It is so ordered.

[Dissenting opinion by Justice O'CONNOR, with whom Chief Justice REHNQUIST, Justice SCALIA and Justice THOMAS joined, omitted]

NOTES TO OLD CHIEF v. UNITED STATES

1. *Measuring Probative Value.* Some courts attempt to apply a framework for determining the magnitude of probative value for particular items of evidence. For example, the Hawaii Supreme Court has stated:

> Probative value is a function not only of relevancy, but also of need for the evidence. Need assessment has perhaps three elements: (a) the centrality or relative importance of the fact to be inferred in the overall context of the lawsuit; (b) the degree to which the fact to be inferred is actually disputed; and (c) the availability and quality of other evidence tending to prove the same point.

Segment 11: offer of a stipulation

Walsh v. Chan, 908 P.2d 1198 (Hawaii 1995). How would this style of analysis apply to the challenged evidence in *Old Chief*?

2. *Measuring Unfair Prejudice.* The defendant's prior conviction was a possible source of unfair prejudice because it involved deplorable conduct. Additionally, the deplorable conduct it involved was similar to the conduct involved in one of current charges against the defendant. How does the similarity of the past crime and a crime charged in the current prosecution affect the risk of unfair prejudice? If the earlier conviction had involved something like embezzlement, how would that have affected the majority's analysis?

3. *Juror Expectations.* In line with Justice Souter's descriptions of the types of evidence jurors expect parties to present, some prosecutors now speculate that television shows about police science lead jurors to expect proof in criminal cases that is much more conclusive than the types of proof usually available. *See* Simon A. Cole and Rachel Dioso-Villa, *Investigating the 'CSI Effect' Effect: Media and Litigation Crisis in Criminal Law,* 61 Stan. L. Rev. 1335 (2009).

GOOD TO REMEMBER

Even though relevance is a binary concept — the link of relevance between two topics is either present or absent — probative value is measured in degrees. Evidence can be slightly probative or very probative.

QUESTION 1-6. In a prosecution for threatening a federal agent, the defendant was charged with having left the agent a voice-mail message saying, "Silver bullets are coming." Assume the prosecution sought to introduce testimony showing that the defendant had possessed some bullets that were silver in color. How would you analyze the probative value and possible unfair prejudice of that evidence?

H SUMMARY

Basic Relevance Definition in Rule 401. This chapter introduces the concept of relevance, which is a requirement that all evidence must meet in order to be admissible. Rule 401 provides a very pro-admissibility definition of relevance, since an item of evidence will be relevant if it could logically make any change in the likelihood that a significant fact is true.

Excluding Relevant Evidence under Rule 403. Since Rule 401 and its easy threshold might lead to trials lasting practically forever, there are provisions for excluding evidence that satisfies the requirements of Rule 401. Under Rule 403, evidence that is relevant can be excluded by the trial judge if its probative value is substantially outweighed by a risk of unfair prejudice or of other undesirable consequences such as confusion or waste of time.

Determining Relevance in Terms of Common Knowledge about How the World Works and in Terms of Substantive Legal Doctrines. When a trial judge decides whether information is relevant, the judge has to analyze it in terms of the judge's sense of how the world works. For example, in *Supreme Pork*, the trial judge was able to link information about past fire and building code violations to a crucial question, whether a particular company's employees had done work that caused a fire. In *Kaechele* the jurisdiction's legal rules about a retailer's obligations to protect its customers provided the context for determining whether certain evidence was relevant.

Recurring Relevance Situations: Flight, Safety History, and Destruction of Evidence. *Dillon*, *Lovick*, *Spino*, and *Aloi* represent examples of how the legal system treats certain recurring relevance questions. Fleeing when approached by the police may be relevant to consciousness of guilt. A past record of accidents or of safety may be relevant to determining what caused a particular injury. And destroying evidence may support a conclusion that the one who destroyed it would have been hurt by it in litigation.

Conditional Relevance. Sometimes a fact can have a logical role in a case only if some other fact is true. This situation is called "conditional relevance" and is treated in *Cox*.

Trial Judge Discretion to Balance Probative Value and Risks Such as Unfair Prejudice. Finally, the chapter considered whether there are any limits on the way a trial judge applies Rule 403. In *Old Chief*, a ruling that the probative value of some evidence was not substantially outweighed by the risk of unfair prejudice was reversed. It represents a rare instance where the probative value of the offered evidence was virtually zero, and where the likely prejudice associated with the evidence was high. Even though the *Old Chief* circumstances made it wrong for the trial judge to admit the evidence, the analysis in the case makes it clear that almost always trial judges will be affirmed in their judgment calls applying Rule 403, since evidence of such low probative value as the evidence in *Old Chief* is very rarely sought to be admitted.

CHAPTER 2

Social Policy Relevancy Rules

A. Introduction
B. Special Treatment for Subsequent Remedial Measures
C. "Feasibility" Rationale for Admitting Subsequent Remedial Measures
D. Special Treatment for Compromises and Settlements
E. Bias Admission of Settlement Evidence
F. Postinjury Payments, Insurance, and Pleas
G. Summary

A INTRODUCTION

Topic Overview

Some rules require the exclusion of information even though it actually does have logical relevance to the issues for which it might otherwise be introduced. These "relevant but inadmissible" rules express the common law's or the drafters' points of view on broad societal issues that are different from the usual truth-finding concerns of evidence law. Instead of allowing judges to apply the basic relevance rules (Rules 401, 402, and 403), for some topics these rules keep information out of trials even though the information might help the finder of fact make an accurate determination of disputed factual questions.

Chapter Organization

This chapter treats a number of the rules that apply exclusionary doctrines to evidence that would otherwise be relevant and likely to be admitted. They govern information about:

- remedial measures taken after injuries,
- settlements and statements made during settlement negotiations,
- pleas and plea discussions,
- payment of medical and similar expenses, and
- insurance.

Some other rules treated in later chapters also give special treatment to information that would likely be relevant in the absence of those special rules. These other rules cover "character" evidence and particular issues with regard to past conduct of individuals involved in alleged sexual misconduct.

B | SPECIAL TREATMENT FOR SUBSEQUENT REMEDIAL MEASURES

In situations where a person was injured and a defendant later repaired the thing or condition that had caused the injury, the victim is barred from introducing evidence of the repair as proof of negligent conduct. Rule 407 defines the particular type of evidence it covers and prohibits its use for certain specific purposes.

Rule 407. Subsequent Remedial Measures

When measures are taken that would have made an earlier injury or harm less likely to occur, evidence of the subsequent measures is not admissible to prove:

- negligence;
- culpable conduct;
- a defect in a product or its design; or
- a need for a warning or instruction.

But the court may admit this evidence for another purpose, such as impeachment or — if disputed — proving ownership, control, or the feasibility of precautionary measures.

The rule represents a choice to deprive trials of possibly relevant information to encourage people to learn from mistakes and to take corrective actions after injuries have occurred. The premise of the rule is that a person or company might decline to make improvements (for example, installing a railing on a staircase after a person fell, or changing the design of a product after an injury that might have been averted with a different design) if they anticipated that the injured person could use proof of that response to the injury in a lawsuit against them.

Because the rule excludes information that would otherwise be relevant and likely admissible, sometimes courts have tended to restrict its application. For example, some courts have refused to apply the rule in strict liability tort cases. When FRE 407 was originally adopted, it was ambiguous with regard to application in strict liability cases, but it has since been amended to provide express coverage in strict liability cases. (A number of state codes retain the language of the original federal rule.) Courts have limited the effect of Rule 407 in another way: when a remedial measure was made by anyone other than the defendant in a case, information about that action may be admitted. Also, it may sometimes be difficult to answer the threshold question of whether a defendant's actions after an injury actually were "subsequent remedial measures."

■ ■ ■

Justifying, but Avoiding, the Prohibition — Cyr. This opinion analyzes the policy justifications for keeping out information about a defendant's safety measures. Because the state version of Rule 407 that the court was applying was unclear about whether the prohibition should apply to strict liability cases, the court was required to consider the strengths and weaknesses of treating it that way. The opinion also considers the rationale for withdrawing the rule's constraint when an actor other than the defendant has performed a remedial measure. Finally, the opinion treats a probative value question: what can a subsequent remedial action tell a jury about the quality of an actor's conduct prior to the remedial action?

CYR v. J.I. CASE CO.

652 A.2d 685 (N.H. 1994)

JOHNSON, J.

This products liability case arose when a bulldozer backed into the plaintiff, Mark Cyr, and crushed his leg. Defendant J.I. Case Company (Case) manufactured the bulldozer and sold it to defendant Harold D. Smith & Sons, Inc. (Smith); Smith sold it to Cyr's employer, who used it on the construction site where Cyr was working when the accident happened. Cyr sued the defendants in strict liability and negligence. At trial, causation was a major issue, and the litigation focused on the bulldozer's lack of a back-up alarm and Cyr's failure to notice the vehicle's approach. The jury returned special verdicts for the defendants, and Cyr appealed, alleging the following [error] in the Superior Court's (Groff, J.) rulings: exclusion of evidence of subsequent modifications....

At trial, Cyr sought to admit evidence that, soon after the accident, Cyr's employer installed a back-up alarm on the 450C Case bulldozer that injured him and that, in 1987, Case made back-up alarms standard equipment on all

450C bulldozers. (Previously, such alarms were optional.) The trial court largely excluded this evidence, citing New Hampshire Rule of Evidence 407. Cyr first argues that Rule 407 does not apply to strict liability causes of action [because its coverage is limited to efforts to prove "culpable conduct"], and therefore, the evidence was admissible on his strict liability claims. We disagree. . . .

On its face, Rule 407 provides no clear answer to our question. Because the drafters of Rule 407 plainly intended it this way, we find little persuasive value in the parties' arguments concerning the meaning of the term "culpable conduct" in the rule.

More helpful is a look at the justifications for excluding subsequent modification evidence in negligence cases and an analysis of whether these reasons apply with sufficient force in strict liability cases. Two justifications for exclusion are generally given, the first being that such evidence is only minimally relevant to prove negligence. As expressed in Aldrich v. Railroad, 67 N.H. 250, 251, 29 A. 408, 409 (1892):

> Accidents may happen which human foresight cannot anticipate and which human wisdom cannot prevent. They may disclose the previously undiscoverable cause, and point out a way of preventing like accidents in the future. . . . Ordinary care is the standard of duty. Between reasonable and possible precaution the distance may be wide.

In other words, it does not necessarily follow that "because the world gets wiser as it gets older, therefore it was foolish before." Under New Hampshire's liberal definition of "relevance," however, see N.H. R. Ev. 401, this justification could not alone suffice to exclude subsequent modification evidence.

The controlling justification, rather, is a public policy concern that people may not "repair" their property after an accident if such measures could be used against them in a lawsuit. "Persons are loath to take precautions which may be used as evidence against them." Christie v. Company, 87 N.H. 236, 238, 177 A. 300, 302 (1935). In Aldrich v. Railroad, this court said:

> A person may have exercised all the care which the law required, and yet, in the light of his new experience, after an unexpected accident has occurred, and as a measure of extreme caution, he may adopt additional safeguards. The more careful a person is, the more regard he has for the lives of others, the more likely he would be to do so, and it would seem unjust that he could not do so without being liable to have such acts construed as an admission of prior negligence. We think such a rule puts an unfair interpretation upon human conduct, and virtually holds out an inducement for continued negligence.

Aldrich, 67 N.H. at 253, 29 A. at 410 (quotation omitted). Because this rationale is grounded in "common sense" notions of the relation between human motivation and the rules of evidence, it can be criticized as lacking any real proof to support it. This public policy concern, however, survives as the underlying basis for the rule in negligence cases.

Turning to the question at hand, we find that the public policy concern applies as well to strict liability causes of action as it does to negligence causes of action. "Although there are technical differences between negligence and strict liability, the end result — payment by a defendant — is the same. The defendant doesn't care under which theory he is sued. Therefore, to encourage defendants to take remedial measures, Rule 407 should apply in strict liability cases." Taylor & Gacioch, supra at 619 (analyzing cases).

Cyr relies on an Eighth Circuit case, Robbins v. Farmers Union Grain Terminal Ass'n, 552 F.2d 788, to support his position. This case, in turn, relies heavily on the reasoning of a California case, Ault v. International Harvester Co., 13 Cal. 3d 113, 528 P.2d 1148, 117 Cal. Rptr. 812 (Cal. 1974), see *Robbins*, 552 F.2d at 793 & n.10:

> The contemporary corporate mass producer of goods, the normal products liability defendant, manufactures tens of thousands of units of goods; it is manifestly unrealistic to suggest that such a producer will forego making improvements in its product, and risk innumerable additional lawsuits and the attendant adverse effect upon its public image, simply because evidence of adoption of such improvement may be admitted in an action founded on strict liability for recovery on an injury that preceded the improvement.

Ault, 528 P.2d at 1152. There are several problems with this analysis. First, it discounts the possible effect of an evidentiary exclusion rule on the thousands of small manufacturers doing business in this country, "whose long-term prospects become highly suspect when faced with the losses of a single short-term products liability suit." Note, Toups v. Sears, Roebuck & Co.: *Re-Assessing Admissibility of Subsequent Remedial Measures Evidence in a Products Liability Suit*, 48 La. L. Rev. 985, 998 (1988). Second, Rule 407 makes no distinction between small and mass producers. Third, even if mass producers were the only manufacturers affected by the rule, the California court's assumption about their likely behavior following an accident is open to attack. One commentator posits that corporate decision-makers might be more concerned with short-term profits than long-term, and thus avoid costly remedial measures. Fourth, the California rationale ignores the fact that mass producers are sued for both strict liability and negligence — often in the same case, as here. The threat of mass producers delaying remedial measures did not stand in the way of New Hampshire Rule of Evidence 407, which explicitly applies to negligence cases. Because the effect of the rule on a mass producer would be the same regardless of the theory of liability, it would be illogical to apply it in negligence cases but not in cases of strict liability. Accordingly, we conclude that Rule 407 applies to strict liability causes of action.

Cyr next argues that Rule 407 does not apply to evidence that his employer installed a back-up alarm on the bulldozer because his employer is not a defendant in this action. We agree. Weinstein and Berger explain:

> Because the controlling ground for excluding evidence has been the promotion of the policy of encouraging people to take safety precautions, remedial measures carried out by persons not party to the suit are not covered. Since the person taking the

remedial measures is not affected by having the evidence admitted as an admission of fault, the admissibility of the evidence should be governed by the general relevancy requirements of Rules 401-403 rather than Rule 407.

[2 J. Weinstein & M. Berger, Weinstein's Evidence], ¶ 407[01], at 407-11 to -12 [(1992)].

The trial judge in this case did in fact exclude all evidence of subsequent modifications by Cyr's employer under New Hampshire Rule of Evidence 403. . . . Because a trial court's rulings under Rule 403 are entitled to some deference, and because the evidence on remand could vary significantly from that which influenced the court's judgment at this trial, we express no opinion about the ruling. We do, however, emphasize the following points.

Although the evidence Cyr seeks to admit may meet the definition of relevant evidence, N.H. R. Ev. 401, its probative value should not be overestimated. . . . We also note that in weighing the possible prejudicial effect of the evidence, the public policy concerns of Rule 407 should not be considered because they do not apply to subsequent modifications by a non-defendant. Instead, potential confusion of the issues and misleading the jury may be the primary considerations.

Reversed and remanded.

NOTES TO CYR v. J.I. CASE CO.

1. *Limiting Rule 407's Impact.* *Ault*, discussed in *Cyr*, has been adopted in a number of states, although *Cyr* represents the majority position. Does it make sense for a jurisdiction to apply the prohibition in one type of personal injury case and to reject it in another type of case?

The *Cyr* court acknowledges two types of rationales for the usual exclusionary rule: low probative value and the social benefit of protecting makers of repairs from harming their litigation positions. How does the *Cyr* court treat those ideas in connection with nondefendant subsequent remedial measures, the changes made to the bulldozer by Cyr's employer?

2. *Counterexample.* Rhode Island applies the following rule:

> **Rhode Island Rules of Evidence**
>
> **Rule 407. Subsequent remedial measures.** When, after an event, measures are taken which, if taken previously, would have made the event less likely to occur, evidence of the subsequent measures is admissible.

How does this *minority* view differ from the current FRE? Does the logic of the *Cyr* opinion support or undermine Rhode Island's treatment of this issue?

The significance of Rhode Island's unusual rule may be slight, since most defendants who might be harmed by it would be able to avoid it by removing a case from a Rhode Island court to a federal court. In federal court, FRE 407 would apply.

QUESTION 2-1. Consider the following sequence of events, thinking about possible admission of evidence of the safety improvements in a lawsuit against Product Company, the manufacturer of a product that injured User:

- January 1, 2010 — Product Company designs and sells product.
- February 1, 2010 — Product Company changes design for safety.
- March 1, 2010 — User is injured by a unit made in January.
- April 1, 2010 — Product Company makes a second design change.
- May 1, 2010 — A retailer adds a safety device to unsold units.

Would proof of any of the February, April, and May design changes be admissible against the manufacturer to show that that Product Company's design was defective?

QUESTION 2-2. Which one of the following rationales for barring evidence of subsequent repairs to show negligence or product defect is the *least* sensible?

A. Proof that a defendant responded to an injury by making a repair or product improvement has no relevance to the quality of the defendant's conduct or product prior to the injury.

B. People might not make repairs after injuries if they anticipated that the fact of their having made repairs could be used against them at a trial.

C. While large manufacturers might make improvements regardless of evidence rules, small manufacturers or other low-volume enterprises might need the incentive of Rule 407 to encourage remedial action, and there is no principled way to separate the defendants who would respond to the incentive from the defendants who would be likely to make repairs regardless of the incentive.

D. Because this evidence has only low probative value, excluding it imposes a low cost on society; that cost is worth tolerating to encourage safety improvements.

■ ■ ■

GOOD TO REMEMBER

FRE 407 applies to negligence *and* strict liability claims, since its language refers to negligence *and* product defects and warning defects.

What Do "Subsequent" and "Remedial" Mean?—**Bethel.** Can an investigation after an accident be conceptualized as something that would have prevented the accident if it had been done prior to the accident? It's possible to think of this question as a paradox — can a postaccident report be written before an accident happens? On the other hand, a safety inspection or similar analysis can be done at any time. The

Bethel court analyzed this problem as crucial to determining whether a postaccident report is barred or admissible under Rule 407.

BETHEL v. PETERS

97 P.3d 822 (Alaska 2004)

FABE, J.

This appeal of a jury verdict in a tort suit against the City of Bethel presents the question whether recommendations for action contained in a post-accident report are excludable as subsequent remedial measures under Alaska Rule of Evidence 407. . . . Because the superior court did not err in its rulings, we affirm the judgment.

On July 14, 2000, Catherine Peters fell in the shower area of Bethel's city-owned senior center. She suffered multiple fractures of her right leg. She required surgery in Anchorage to place both internal and external hardware in her leg and for a bone graft. Her recovery involved several return trips to Anchorage to remove the external fixator apparatus and for follow-up exams. Her leg remains bent and her activity has been curtailed.

Following Peters's accident, Louise Charles, the City's director of senior services, prepared an "Accident/Incident Investigation Report," in which she recommended the installation of safety bars in the shower area. Safety bars were later installed. Peters sued the City in December 2000, alleging negligence in its maintenance of the shower.

The case was tried before a jury in August 2002. The thrust of Peters's theory of the case was that safety bars in the shower would have prevented the fall and that the City was therefore negligent in failing to install the safety bars before the accident. To this end, Peters introduced into evidence a redacted version of the accident report in which the section detailing the "corrective action taken" was blacked out. Peters's attorney also questioned Charles and senior center administrative assistant Bev Bell, asking each whether soon after the accident she thought safety bars should be installed, and whether she had thought of it before the accident. In response to a question about her pre-accident thoughts, Charles volunteered that safety bars had in fact been installed after the accident. In his closing argument, Peters's attorney argued that the City should have known before the accident that safety bars would make the shower area more safe. He mentioned the recommendations Louise Charles made in her report but never discussed the City's actual installation of the bars after Peters's fall.

. . . The jury found that the City was eighty-seven percent at fault for the accident . . . awarding $575,000 in noneconomic damages. The City appeals from the jury verdict, claiming that Alaska Rule of Evidence 407 should have barred the admittance of the accident report. . . .

Alaska Rule of Evidence 407 provides, in pertinent part: "When, after an event, measures are taken which, if taken previously, would have made the event less likely to occur, evidence of the subsequent measures is not admissible to prove negligence. . . ." The City claims that the rule should have barred the admission of the "Accident/Incident Investigation Report" completed by Louise Charles. The report includes sections headed "What Should Be Done?" and "Corrective Action Taken." The superior court allowed the introduction of the report with the "Corrective Action" section redacted. In the "What Should Be Done?" section, which remained intact in the admitted version of the report, Charles wrote that "[i]t would be helpful, to elders, if at least 3 more safety bars were installed on the walls in the sauna area and in the bathroom areas. Elders could then support themselves if necessary."

Evidence showing that the City followed Charles's recommendation and installed the safety bars is plainly barred by the rule. The City initially argues that the recommendation for safety bars in the report is this type of evidence and claims that the report "reveals the actual safety improvement later installed." But the redacted report only indicated that Charles suggested more safety bars. It did not reveal to the jury that the City followed her advice, and therefore was not excludable as evidence of the installation of the safety bars. Rule 407 excludes the challenged section of the report only if the recommendations themselves are covered by the rule.

Our previous cases applying this rule have concerned concrete fixes like placing barriers and flashing lights around a hole where an employee had been injured or salting and sanding an allegedly icy walkway after someone had fallen; we have never considered whether Rule 407 reaches a section of a post-accident report containing an investigation into an accident's causes or a recommendation for an improvement. Many courts applying analogous rules of evidence have held that the rule's scope is limited to improvements actually implemented. These courts rely in part on the rule's phrase "measures are taken," reasoning that "[r]emedial measures are those actions taken to remedy any flaws or failures." Under this reasoning, an investigation or recommendation is not a concrete action; a report on these activities "by itself . . . 'would' not 'have made the event less likely to occur.'" These courts therefore do not exclude reports of post-accident investigations and recommendations, often among "the best and most accurate sources of evidence and information" for injured parties.

Other courts disagree, holding that evidence of the parts of a report detailing investigatory findings and recommendations should be excluded as subsequent remedial measures. These latter courts rely on the sensible proposition that in many cases, "the investigation is the prerequisite to any remedial safety measure." They reason that admitting such post-accident evidence would discourage defendants from carefully investigating accidents and considering how to prevent them in the future; they would then be less equipped to make the safety improvements the rule is designed to promote. This broader interpretation of the rule's exclusionary scope may advance its goals, but it collides with another evidentiary policy, the principle of wide admission of relevant evidence, and with the language of the rule.

Under Rule 402, our "Rules of Evidence start from the proposition that all relevant evidence is admissible." Rules of exclusion like the one we consider today are merely exceptions to this general rule. Post-accident investigations and recommendations are often relevant to the issue of negligence and, by revealing facts about the causes of an accident and the defendant's concerns about it, may be particularly useful to factfinders. The general presumption in favor of admissibility strongly suggests, therefore, that such evidence should be admitted, despite any possible disincentive to safety improvements.

Between these two competing policies, the language of the rule favors admissibility. Rule 407 prohibits evidence of "measures" that have been "taken." We take "measures" to mean concrete actions, and to leave outside the rule's prohibition preliminary investigations and recommendations pointing toward those actions. Even if post-accident investigations and reports were considered "measures," the rule would not reach them. The rule excludes "subsequent measures" that would have reduced the likelihood of the accident if they had been "taken previously," meaning before the accident. "One cannot investigate an accident before it occurs, so an investigation and report . . . cannot be a measure that is excluded." The language of Rule 407 and the general presumption of admissibility laid down by Rule 402, along with persuasive authority from other courts, compel us to hold that evidence of post-accident investigations and recommendations are not automatically excluded as subsequent remedial measures.

Like all other evidence, investigations and recommendations are subject to the balancing test of Alaska Rule of Evidence 403, which provides that relevant evidence "may be excluded if its probative value is outweighed by the danger of unfair prejudice." The relation between admissible investigations and recommendations on the one hand and excluded measures on the other requires particular care in this balancing. If the jury is given evidence of the recommendations but not of the actual fix, there is a danger that jurors may draw the unfair inference that the recommendations were ignored. In deciding whether or not to admit recommendations, the trial court should carefully consider the likelihood of this inference and the prejudice it would cause. In this case, the superior court weighed relevance against prejudice and determined that Charles's report, redacted to exclude evidence of the remedial measures taken, was admissible. We find no error in its determination. . . .

For these reasons, the judgment of the superior court is AFFIRMED.

NOTES TO BETHEL v. PETERS

1. *The Power of Characterizations.* The court takes the position that one cannot investigate an accident before it occurs. But one can certainly investigate and evaluate the safety of something like a shower area at any time, either before or after the occurrence of an accident. Treating the report in this case as either a postaccident study or as simply a review of safety could control the issue of applicability of Rule 407. If either characterization could be legitimate, how should a court choose one?

2. *The Costs of Exclusionary Rules.* The court describes postaccident reports as among the best and most accurate sources of information about injury-causing events. Could a court interpret Rule 407 in a way that maximizes its exclusionary effect even if a court believed that the evidence the rule excludes could be highly probative?

3. *Unfair Prejudice.* A trial judge's application of FRE 403, balancing probative value and the risk of unfair prejudice, is necessarily speculative since the trial judge can only guess at a jury's reaction to particular facts. When the *Bethel* court reviewed the trial court's decision that FRE 403 allowed admission of the accident report, it suggested that in fact there was a risk that jurors might react unfairly to evidence of the accident report. What reaction did the *Bethel* court think jurors might have, and how could that reaction be unfairly prejudicial to the defendant?

QUESTION 2-3. Some states require the plaintiff in a products liability suit based on a claim of design defect to introduce evidence showing that an alternative safer design is practical. If a state that imposes this requirement precludes a plaintiff from showing that the defendant itself had adopted a safer design since the time of the plaintiff's injury, does that create a risk of jury misapprehension that could unfairly prejudice the plaintiff?

C "FEASIBILITY" RATIONALE FOR ADMITTING SUBSEQUENT REMEDIAL MEASURES

FRE 407 keeps out evidence of subsequent remedial measures *only* if that evidence is offered to prove negligence, culpable conduct, or a product or warning defect. If the proponent of subsequent remedial measures evidence can show that it could be relevant for some other purpose, the rule's prohibition is withdrawn. For example, a defendant might claim that it has no responsibility for an injury because it lacked control over the place where the injury occurred. In that situation, proof that the defendant had made a repair in the place would be admissible to show that the defendant in fact did have an association with that place. Another allowable use for this evidence is to impeach a witness's testimony.

The rule adds an important detail for one of the permissible uses of subsequent remedial measures evidence. A proponent may claim that the evidence is relevant to show that (1) because the defendant actually did adopt an improvement or safety measure, (2) that improvement or safety measure was *feasible*. That rationale is accepted only if the defendant has disputed ("controverted" in the original text of the federal rules) the feasibility of an improvement.

■ ■ ■

Distinguishing Between Justifying Past Conduct and Denying that Greater Safety Was Possible — Flaminio *and* Kenny. A defendant who wants to keep out evidence of subsequent remedial measures evidence must avoid controverting the feasibility of safety greater than the safety the defendant provided in the product it sold or the facilities it provided. In each of these cases, the defendant offered testimony about its past conduct. In *Flaminio,* the defendant claimed that it had made a considered design choice about a motorcycle. In *Kenny,* the defendant claimed that it had acted with "all" reasonable care. Do these claims amount to denying the feasibility of greater care?

FLAMINIO v. HONDA MOTOR CO., LTD.
733 F.2d 463 (7th. Cir. 1984)

POSNER, Circuit Judge.

. . . In 1978 a middle-aged man named Forrest Flaminio bought a "Gold Wing" motorcycle, a large and powerful touring motorcycle manufactured by the Honda Motor Company of Japan (Japanese Honda) and distributed in the United States by its wholly owned subsidiary, American Honda Motor Company (American Honda). The motorcycles are shipped from Japan partially assembled, but assembly is completed by the dealers to whom American Honda distributes the motorcycles rather than by American Honda itself. Three days after taking delivery, and shortly after a dinner at which he had one or two drinks, Flaminio was driving the motorcycle down a two-lane road at night when he came up behind a car traveling at about 40 miles per hour. He passed it at a speed of somewhere between 50 and 70 m.p.h. (the speed limit was 50), and as he did so felt a vibration in the front end of the motorcycle. He tried to look at the front wheel to see what was wrong. This was an awkward maneuver because his feet were up on the motorcycle's "highway pegs" (supplied and installed by the motorcycle dealer rather than by either of the defendants), so that he was leaning backward. By his own admission the effort in this position to see the front wheel probably brought him up off the seat. In any event the motorcycle began to wobble uncontrollably and then it shot off the road and crashed, inflicting injuries that have left Flaminio a paraplegic.

Joined by his wife, who is seeking to recover damages for loss of consortium, Flaminio sued Japanese Honda and American Honda, alleging that either the wobble was due to the defective design of the motorcycle, which should have been corrected, or the defendants should have warned users about the motorcycle's propensity to wobble. The jury exonerated Japanese Honda from all liability but found that American Honda had been negligent and that its negligence had been 30 percent responsible for the accident, and that Flaminio had also been negligent and that his negligence had been 70 percent responsible for the accident. Since under Wisconsin law, which the parties agree governs the substantive issues in this suit, a contributorily negligent plaintiff cannot recover any damages unless his negligence "was not greater than the negligence of the person against whom recovery is sought," judgment was entered for the defendants, and the plaintiffs have appealed.

The substantive issues on appeal relate to Japanese Honda's liability for the allegedly defective design that allowed the motorcycle to wobble. . . .

The issue [on appeal] with respect to the allegation of defective design is whether the district court erred in excluding evidence (consisting of two blueprints) that, the plaintiffs say, shows that after the accident Honda, in an effort to reduce wobble, made the struts ("front forks") that connect the Gold Wing's handlebars to its front wheel two millimeters thicker. . . . Flaminio argues that the blueprints were admissible under the exceptions [in FRE 407] for "proving . . . feasibility of precautionary measures, if controverted," and for impeaching the defendants' evidence. But the first of these exceptions is inapplicable because the defendants did not deny the feasibility of precautionary measures against wobble. Their argument was that there is a tradeoff between wobble and "weave," and that in designing the model on which Flaminio was injured Japanese Honda had decided that weave was the greater danger because it occurs at high speeds and because the Gold Wing model — what motorcycle buffs call a "hog" — was designed for high speeds. The feasibility, as distinct from the net advantages, of reducing the danger of wobble was not in issue. As for the second exception, if the defendants had testified that they would never have thickened the struts on the Gold Wing the blueprints would have been impeaching. But the defendants offered no such testimony. Although any evidence of subsequent remedial measures might be thought to contradict and so in a sense impeach a defendant's testimony that he was using due care at the time of the accident, if this counted as "impeachment" the exception would swallow the rule. . . .

The judgment for the defendants is affirmed.

KENNY v. SOUTHEASTERN PENNSYLVANIA TRANSPORTATION AUTHORITY

581 F.2d 351 (3d. Cir. 1978)

WEIS, J.

Whether a woman who is raped in the station of the Philadelphia transit system may recover damages from the carrier because of its lack of adequate protection is the issue in this diversity case. We conclude that a showing of deficient lighting on the station platform and insufficient attention to conditions by the only employee on the premises support a jury finding of carrier culpability. Accordingly, we reverse judgment n. o. v. in favor of the transit authority and reinstate the jury verdict. . . .

[The Southeastern Pennsylvania Transportation Authority,] SEPTA[,] has filed a cross appeal from the district court's dismissal of its motion for a new trial. Among the grounds asserted is that the trial court erred in allowing testimony that new lighting had been installed on the platform a few days after the attack. A SEPTA employee testified that lighting at the stations was checked on a daily basis. He produced records showing that about an hour after the rape one light bulb was replaced at a crossover between the two tracks, and the following night, three bulbs were installed. On the day before the incident, four bulbs had been replaced on the southbound platform.

On cross-examination, plaintiff's counsel elicited the fact that a new fluorescent fixture was installed four days after the attack. Defendant contends that this evidence of subsequent repairs was prejudicial. The trial judge, however, ruled that the testimony was admissible for impeachment purposes and also to show the feasibility of precautions. We conclude that the evidence was admissible.

As a general rule, evidence of remedial measures taken after the event is not admissible to prove culpable conduct. The reason for the exclusion is to encourage post-accident repairs or safety precautions in the interest of public safety. But when the defendant opens up the issue by claiming that all reasonable care was being exercised at the time, then the plaintiff may attack that contention by showing later repairs which are inconsistent with it.

In this case, the evidence did not show that a protective device of a nature not previously utilized was subsequently installed, but rather established the need for replacement of that which had previously been employed. As such, the testimony bore directly on the inference that since the lighting was checked on a daily basis, it was adequate at the time the incident occurred. The installation of a new fixture suggested that more than new light bulbs were necessary to maintain the level of lighting that apparently had once existed at the station. Moreover, the cross-examination tended to cast doubt on the thoroughness of the inspections made by the defendant. Hence, the evidence was admissible.

NOTES TO FLAMINIO v. HONDA MOTOR CO., LTD. AND KENNY v. SOUTHEASTERN PENNSYLVANIA TRANSPORTATION AUTHORITY

1. *Definitions of "Feasibility."* The *Flaminio* court describes the defendant as having determined that weave was a greater danger than wobble and as having selected a desirable trade-off between those two risks. If a court treated feasibility as meaning "capable of being used successfully," could a position like the defendant's be treated as a denial of feasibility? If feasible means just "possible," it is clear that Honda agreed that decreasing wobble was possible, and that therefore Honda had not controverted feasibility. If feasible means "possible in the context of producing a motorcycle with an acceptable balance of wobble and weave," could Honda be treated as having controverted feasibility?

2. *Pro-plaintiff Analysis of Defendant's Claims.* In *Kenny*, a witness for the defendant testified that prior to the victim's injury, lighting at stations was checked on a daily basis. The *Kenny* court treated this testimony as equal to a claim that "all reasonable care" was being exercised by the defendant. A defendant's claim of that breadth can easily be characterized as a denial of the feasibility of additional safety measures.

3. *Transcript.* In the case from which the following testimony is taken, the defendant's product was a large unit of industrial machinery that included a box for pressing large quantities of cotton into bales. The plaintiff was injured when the device actuated while he was inside the box. Should this testimony by the defendant's expert witness be treated as a denial of feasibility of the protective measures it describes?

Q. At the time of the manufacture and sale of this equipment was the technology available to you to hook up a device or wire to the doors-open button that would in turn be activated by a limit switch, the doors of the press which would in turn connect with the power to the motor that drives the boxes in this press and thereby keeping them from revolving when the doors were locked open?

A. Yes, I have heard such testimony and such a device could be provided.

Q. And do you know whether or not that would be a good device to put on to the press of this machine?

A. I don't know that I would classify it as good, bad, or indifferent. It could be done.

Q. A simple system of an electric eye that is used on the safety gate could be utilized as a back-up system to the doors-open switch, could it not?

A. To answer your question directly, yes, you can put one limit switch on top of another limit switch on top of another one until you might create a monster that is even more lethal.

Q. You think it would make it more lethal to back up a system with a switch that might —

A. To a point where a person depends on these sorts of devices instead of keeping themselves out of dangerous situation.

Should testimony like this be treated as opening the door to proof of subsequent remedial measures? This transcript is based on Hallmark v. Allied Products Corp., 646 P.2d 319 (Ariz. Ct. App. 1982).

4. *Illustration: Forbidden and Allowed Uses of Subsequent Remedial Measures Information.* Rule 407 excludes information about subsequent remedial measures *only* when it is introduced to show that a person acted negligently or that there is a basis for applying strict liability in a manufacturing, design or warning claim. The following chart shows the forbidden and allowed uses of this kind of information in its first two columns. The third column highlights why plaintiffs typically are highly interested in taking advantage of ways to avoid the Rule 407 prohibition. Once evidence of subsequent remedial measures is introduced for a permitted purpose, jurors may well think about it for both the permitted purpose and a forbidden purpose. The defendant will be entitled to an instruction that tells the jury to use the information for only the permitted purpose, but jurors may find it difficult to ignore the information when they evaluate the defendant's conduct or apply strict liability standards to the defendant's product.

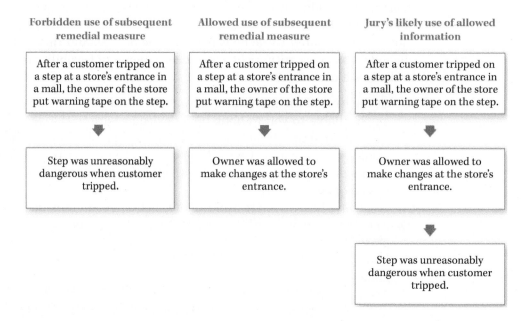

QUESTION 2-4. Inez Injured is the plaintiff in a products liability case. She knows that after she was injured by a unit of the defendant's product the defendant added a safety feature to the product. Injured would like to introduce evidence of that improvement to show that the design change was feasible. In direct examination, the defendant's president made each of the following statements. Which of these statements would provide the strongest basis for allowing the plaintiff to introduce evidence of the defendant company's design change?

   A. Ms. Injured got hurt because she misused our product.
   B. Our product complied with all relevant government regulations when we made it.
   C. Our product's design was the safest design anyone could come up with.
   D. Our product was safe when we designed it and sold it.

D   SPECIAL TREATMENT FOR COMPROMISES AND SETTLEMENTS

To encourage settlements of disputes, the common law and Federal Rule 408 prohibit proof of a settlement or of statements made in settlement negotiations if that proof is offered to show that the underlying claim was either valid or invalid. Keeping some information out of our trials seems worthwhile if it can encourage people to speak freely when trying to settle disputes. With regard to the rule's coverage of communications made in settlement talks, it's important to be aware that the rule only prevents testimony that someone said or wrote something in those talks. Something that a person mentions in the settlement context can still be proved if a party has a way to prove it that is different from showing that it was communicated during those negotiations. As is true for Rule 407 (about subsequent repairs), the prohibitions of Rule 408 are withdrawn if evidence related to settlements is offered for a purpose different from the purpose the rule prohibits.

The text of Rule 408 shows its coverage and the exceptions for which the rule's prohibition can be avoided. The specified exceptions are examples, so that in theory additional uses might be proper.

Rule 408. Compromise Offers and Negotiations

(a) Prohibited Uses. Evidence of the following is not admissible — on behalf of any party — either to prove or disprove the validity or amount of a disputed claim or to impeach by a prior inconsistent statement or a contradiction:

(1) furnishing, promising, or offering — or accepting, promising to accept, or offering to accept — a valuable consideration in order to compromise the claim; and

(2) conduct or a statement made during compromise negotiations about the claim — except when offered in a criminal case and when the negotiations related to a claim by a public office in the exercise of its regulatory, investigative, or enforcement authority.

(b) Exceptions. The court may admit this evidence for another purpose, such as proving a witness's bias or prejudice, negating a contention of undue delay, or proving an effort to obstruct a criminal investigation or prosecution.

■   ■   ■

Sometimes a Discussion Is Just a Discussion — Londagin. Rule 408 applies only when there was a dispute and an effort to reach a compromise in that dispute. *Londagin* focuses on how to decide whether an actor's conduct occurred in the context of a dispute.

WAL-MART STORES, INC. v. LONDAGIN

37 S.W.3d 620 (Ark. 2001)

THORNTON, J.

We have jurisdiction of this case . . . because the appeal requires us to construe Rule 408 of the Arkansas Rules of Evidence as it applies to the admissibility of evidence of an effort by Wal-Mart to satisfy a customer complaint during subsequent litigation by a third party seeking to recover damages arising out of the same transaction. The trial court ruled that Rule 408 did not require exclusion of the evidence, and the jury awarded damages. Wal-Mart brings this appeal contending that the trial court committed error in denying its motion to exclude this evidence. . . . We find no error and affirm.

The relevant facts are that on October 4, 1996, appellee, Laura Perkins, took her truck to the Wal-Mart Tire and Lube Express in Bentonville. Ms. Perkins requested that Wal-Mart change the oil in her truck and rotate the tires. When Ms. Perkins picked up her truck, she noticed that the tires had not been rotated. Wal-Mart moved the vehicle back inside and rotated the tires.

Later in the afternoon of October 4, 1996, Ms. Perkins was traveling on Highway 59 when the left front wheel came off of her truck, crossed the center line, and struck a vehicle owned and operated by appellee, Johnny Londagin, causing his vehicle to wreck. As a result of the wreck, Mr. Londagin sustained injuries. After the wreck, Ms. Perkins called Wal-Mart to report the accident. Wal-Mart sent representatives to the scene and provided Ms. Perkins with a rental car to continue her planned trip to Oklahoma. Wal-Mart then towed her truck back to their shop and had it repaired, all without cost to Ms. Perkins.

On January 13, 1998, appellee, Johnny Londagin and his wife, appellee, Sue Londagin, filed a complaint against Wal-Mart. The complaint sought damages for injuries sustained during the motor vehicle accident on October 4, 1996. The Londagins alleged that the accident was proximately caused by Wal-Mart's negligence and asserted that Wal-Mart failed to properly rotate Ms. Perkins's tires and failed to properly replace the lug nuts on the left front wheel of Ms. Perkins's truck. The complaint sought damages for personal injuries sustained by Mr. Londagin, including past and future medical expenses, pain and mental anguish, permanent disability, lost wages, and loss of enjoyment of life. The complaint also sought damages for loss of consortium on behalf of Mrs. Londagin.

On February 11, 1999, the Londagins amended their complaint to add Ms. Perkins as an additional defendant. . . .

On February 15, 2000, a jury trial was held. After the Londagins'[] case-in-chief, Ms. Perkins was granted a motion for directed verdict, and her case was dismissed. At the conclusion of the trial, the jury awarded Mr. Londagin

$125,000 in damages and awarded Mrs. Londagin $10,000 in damages. It is from this judgment that Wal-Mart appeals....

Wal-Mart argues that the trial court erred when it allowed the Londagins to introduce evidence of Wal-Mart's actions seeking to satisfy Ms. Perkins's complaint. The Londagins introduced evidence at trial that immediately after the accident, Wal-Mart employees came to the scene of the accident, provided a rental car for Ms. Perkins, and towed and repaired Ms. Perkins's truck. Wal-Mart argued in a motion in limine that introduction of such evidence would be in violation of Rule 408 of the Arkansas Rules of Evidence. The trial court denied Wal-Mart's motion and allowed the Londagins to present testimony as to the actions taken by Wal-Mart after the October 1996 accident....

We have strictly applied Rule 408. We have held that offers are inadmissible to prove a party's liability on the underlying claim. The rationale for Rule 408 is based upon the grounds of promotion of the public policy favoring the compromise and settlement of disputes. The purpose of Rule 408 is to promote complete candor between the parties to the settlement negotiations. However, we have held that Rule 408 is not a blanket prohibition against the admission of all evidence concerning offers to compromise. We have further held that Rule 408 requires the exclusion of statements made in compromise negotiations of a defendant with a third party. We have also held that offers to compromise or settle a disputed claim should be excluded from evidence even if no litigation has been commenced at the time of the compromise....

Our analysis of Rule 408 informs us that there are several elements that must be present in order to exclude evidence of compromise or offers to compromise. To invoke the Rule 408: (1) there must be a claim; (2) the purpose of offering the evidence must be to prove liability for, invalidity of, or amount of the claim; (3) valuable consideration must be furnished or offered to be furnished, or promised to be furnished, or valuable consideration must be accepted, offered, or promised to be accepted in an effort to compromise or attempt to compromise a claim; and (4) the claim must be disputed as to either validity or amount. The essential elements required to invoke Rule 408 protection have also been explained in McCormick's treatise on evidence. The treatise notes:

> to invoke the exclusionary rule, an actual dispute must exist, preferably some negotiations, and at least an apparent difference of view between the parties as to the validity or amount of the claim. An offer to pay an admitted claim is not privileged since there is no policy of encouraging compromises of undisputed claims, which should be paid in full.

See John W. Strong, McCormick on Evidence §266, at 183 (5th ed. 1999).

Our first inquiry is whether a claim existed between Wal-Mart and Ms. Perkins when Wal-Mart came to the accident scene and assisted Ms. Perkins on October 4, 1996. At trial, Ms. Perkins testified that immediately after the accident she phoned the Wal-Mart tire and lube express center from the scene and was "really upset." She informed Wal-Mart that "there's no way we can fix the truck as it is sitting." Ms. Perkins was informed that someone from Wal-Mart would come and assist her.

Jon Kuntz, a district manager for Wal-Mart tire and lube express, testified that he spoke with Ms. Perkins on the day of the accident. She described what had occurred, and he verified that Wal-Mart had worked on her truck prior to the accident. He informed Ms. Perkins that he would come to the accident scene and then secured a rental car for her. Finally, Mr. Kuntz testified that he participated in completion of the "first report of incident" form. That form states that it is to be filled out "when there is a customer injury as well as when settling a claim in the field." After reviewing the evidence, we conclude that when Ms. Perkins telephoned Wal-Mart, in a disgruntled state, alleging that her wheel had come off of her truck shortly after Wal-Mart had rotated the tires on her truck, and informed Wal-Mart of the accident, she expressed a claim against Wal-Mart.

It is clear that the Londagins were seeking to introduce evidence of Wal-Mart's actions to prove Wal-Mart's liability, thereby satisfying the second prong of our analysis. Additionally, because there was certainly a showing that Wal-Mart furnished valuable consideration to Ms. Perkins to satisfy her claim, the third element of Rule 408 is also present in this case.

The element remaining for analysis is whether Ms. Perkins's claim was disputed. The trial court concluded that the evidence did not demonstrate that Wal-Mart ever disputed the claim as to either validity or amount. The testimony showed that Ms. Perkins called Wal-Mart and notified it as to her claim. Wal-Mart responded to Ms. Perkins's claim by voluntarily bringing her a rental car, towing her truck, and repairing her truck. Wal-Mart towed and repaired Ms. Perkins's truck at no expense to Ms. Perkins, and according to her testimony, without her request that the services be performed. There is simply no showing that Wal-Mart disputed Ms. Perkins's claim, but rather the evidence supports the trial court's finding that Wal-Mart assumed responsibility for wholly paying the claim. The testimony established that Wal-Mart did not require Ms. Perkins to sign any paper work for the rental car or perform any act to authorize the repair of her truck. Moreover, Ms. Perkins testified that Mr. Kuntz apologized at the scene of the accident and assured her that "Wal-Mart would take care of everything." Based on the evidence, we cannot say that the trial court erred in finding that there was no dispute as to either validity or amount of Ms. Perkins's claim. We have held that evidentiary rulings are within the sound discretion of the trial court and will not be set aside absent an abuse of discretion. [W]e conclude that the trial court did not abuse its discretion in allowing the Londagins to introduce evidence of Wal-Mart's efforts to satisfy Ms. Perkins's claim.

NOTES TO WAL-MART STORES, INC. v. LONDAGIN

1. *Scope of Confidentiality.* When Rule 408 applies, it shields the communications and conduct it covers from disclosure in trials involving any of the

parties to the compromise. It also shields those communications from use in any trials involving strangers to the negotiation.

   2. *Dispute or Just Business?* Apparently the communications by Walmart's employee would have been treated as confidential if the employee had said something like, "We disagree that our workers did anything wrong, but we'd like to compromise and help you." The *Londagin* court's rigorous insistence that a dispute be present in order for Rule 408 to apply would protect against a party using the rule to shield communications that were really just part of an ongoing business relationship and were not meant to resolve a genuine dispute. That effort to limit the Rule's application to situations where applying it would advance the social policies behind the rule would make sense, but in the particular facts of *Londagin* it could lead to an unfortunate result. Managers of businesses like Walmart might instruct their employees to contradict and dispute customers often, even when justice and the businesses' self-interest would support a friendlier and less contentious approach to their customers.

QUESTION 2-5. Seller Company sued Buyer Company, claiming that Buyer Company owed Seller Company $10,000 as a result of a business transaction. Suppose that a Buyer Company employee made each of the following statements to a Seller Company employee. Which one is the most likely to be admissible to show that Buyer Company did owe money to Seller?

   A. I agree we owe you $10,000, but I need to know if you'd accept $8,000 instead.
   B. We don't owe you anything, but we'll pay you $4,000 if you'll accept that as payment in full.
   C. We definitely owe you some money, but you're wrong to say it's $10,000. The most we might owe you is $4,000, and that's an amount we're willing to pay.
   D. Your suggestion that we owe $10,000 is wrong because you never provided the services you said you'd provide, and even if you had, the amount would have been more like $4,000 than $10,000, so $4,000 is the most we'd consider paying.

BIAS ADMISSION OF SETTLEMENT EVIDENCE

Despite Rule 408's general prohibition against use of settlements or statements made in settlement negotiations, that information is properly admitted for purposes different from proving that an underlying claim was valid or invalid. For example, after parties have agreed to a settlement, if one party sues the other to enforce that agreement, proof of the agreement would be admitted. Other uses of the typically prohibited information are also legitimate, even though they ultimately would support one or another party's position on the validity of an underlying claim. The fact that some parties have settled claims can sometimes suggest that a witness in an ongoing case has a bias toward or against parties who have chosen not to make a settlement.

■ ■ ■

Using a Settlement to Prove Something Different from the Basic Conduct in Dispute — **Quirion.** The court considers whether information about a settlement could be used for a purpose different from showing the validity or invalidity of the underlying claim. A separate inquiry is whether Rule 403 (allowing exclusion of evidence because of the risk of unfair prejudice) can affect a trial court's decision to admit evidence of a settlement.

QUIRION v. FORCIER

632 A.2d 365 (Vt. 1993)

DOOLEY, J.

This is a medical malpractice action by Sandra Quirion, spouse of decedent Peter Quirion and administratrix of his estate, against Dr. R. Jackson Forcier and the Hitchcock Clinic, a part of Dartmouth Hitchcock Medical Center. After trial in the Orleans Superior Court, the jury brought in a defendants' verdict. On appeal, plaintiff claims that the trial court erred in allowing in evidence that plaintiff settled with three other doctors prior to trial. . . .

Decedent complained of chest pains from 1978 until his death in 1985, at thirty-three. During the period between 1982 and October 3, 1985, he was treated for this condition by Dr. James Holcomb, his primary physician; Dr. Richard Beloin, partner of Dr. Holcomb; and Dr. Alan Feltmarch, an emergency room physician at North Country Hospital. Each of these doctors practices in the area of decedent's residence in Newport, Vermont.

Decedent became dissatisfied with the lack of relief from the Newport-area doctors and, on the advice of a neighbor, consulted defendant Forcier in his office in Hanover, New Hampshire. Following a one-hour examination on October 3, 1985, defendant sent letters to decedent and Dr. Holcomb outlining his conclusions. The letter to Dr. Holcomb outlined the medical history, as conveyed by decedent, and the examination findings, and concluded, "I do not believe that Mr. Quirion's chest pain is related to coronary artery disease." The letter suggested that the pain might be related to "reflux esophagitis" and recommended certain tests. It also suggested that the symptoms might be brought on by anxiety. There was no follow-up to this letter by Dr. Holcomb. A little over a month later, decedent died of a heart attack, and an autopsy showed blockage of the coronary arteries.

Plaintiff sued the three Newport-area doctors, as well as defendants, and retained Dr. Alan Markowitz of Cleveland, Ohio[,] as her expert witness. Dr. Markowitz was deposed by counsel for each of the defendants in 1990. Thereafter, plaintiff settled with the Newport-area doctors, leaving only defendants Forcier and the Hitchcock Clinic in the case. Because Dr. Markowitz would not be available for trial, plaintiff conducted a second deposition of him by video, with cross-examination by counsel for defendants. This video deposition, with certain parts excised, became Dr. Markowitz's testimony at trial. Similarly, an expert witness for defendants, Dr. Thomas Ryan, testified at a videotaped deposition, and this deposition became his testimony at trial.

After two days of testimony, the jury found that defendants had not been negligent in their treatment of decedent. Plaintiff's appeal relates to . . . admissibility of the evidence of the settlement with the Newport-area doctors. . . .

During the video deposition of Dr. Markowitz, defendants' counsel asked questions related to plaintiff's settlement with the Newport-area doctors, attempting to show that Dr. Markowitz changed his testimony between the two depositions. According to defendants, in the first deposition Dr. Markowitz testified that the negligence of Doctors Holcomb, Beloin and Feltmarch was primarily responsible for decedent's death and that Dr. Forcier was largely blameless. In defendants' view, Dr. Markowitz changed his analysis with respect to Dr. Forcier after learning of the settlement and targeted him with responsibility. Defendants argue that the evidence of the settlements was necessary to show the reason for Dr. Markowitz's change of testimony.

Plaintiff moved in limine to exclude "any references to culpability on the part of former defendants Holcomb, Beloin and Feltmarch" as irrelevant to Dr. Forcier's negligence and specifically to exclude from the Markowitz testimony references to plaintiff's settlement with these doctors. The trial court denied these motions, and admitted the evidence at trial. As to the involvement of the other doctors, the court ruled that this would inevitably be part of the background and would go to the ability to diagnose decedent's condition from the symptoms. The court ruled that the fact of the settlement could be used in cross-examining Dr. Markowitz and was related to his credibility. It left to trial any further reasons to develop the settlement information. At trial, the court stated in its instructions to the jury that the fact of the settlements could be considered only as bearing on Dr. Markowitz's credibility and not on defendants' negligence. . . .

[P]laintiff relies primarily on Slayton v. Ford Motor Co., 140 Vt. 27, 29, 435 A.2d 946, 947 (1981), in which we held "that where there has been a liquidated settlement between one of several defendants and a plaintiff . . . the jury not be informed of such fact, or the sum paid, and that it be the function of the court . . . to find the amount by which such verdict should be reduced." We explained the rationale:

> If the jury is informed of either the fact or the amount of a settlement, there is a danger that it will draw improper inferences. A jury might conclude that the settling

defendant was the party primarily responsible for the injury, and that the remaining defendants should therefore be exonerated. . . . It might take the amount of the settlement as a measure of the plaintiff's damages. . . . It might consider one defendant's settlement to be an admission of negligence, and then impute this negligence to a nonsettling defendant. . . .

Id. at 29-30, 435 A.2d at 947 (citations omitted). In this case, the jury was informed of the settlements but not their amounts. Nevertheless, plaintiff alleges that one of the concerns in *Slayton*, that the jury would shift responsibility away from defendants to the doctors who settled, is exactly what occurred here.

Following the adoption of the Vermont Rules of Evidence, the holding of *Slayton* was explained in Sampson v. Karpinski, 147 Vt. 315, 515 A.2d 1066 (1986). There we held that the admissibility holding of *Slayton* is now controlled by Rule 408 of the Vermont Rules of Evidence, and further that the *Slayton* rule "is not absolute or unyielding." When failure to disclose the settlement to the jury has unfair and prejudicial results, "admission of sufficient evidence to alleviate that prejudice is within the sound discretion of the trial judge." Rule 408 prohibits the admission of settlement information "to prove liability for, the invalidity of, or the amount of the claim or any other claim" but allows the evidence to be admitted for another purpose, "such as proving bias or prejudice of a witness." In addition to the considerations discussed in *Slayton*, the trial judge may also consider the underlying policy of Rule 408 favoring voluntary settlements of disputes.

Defendants introduced the evidence of the settlements through plaintiff's expert in order to impeach his opinion because, they argued, he changed his testimony from virtually exonerating defendants, and blaming the Newport-area doctors, to blaming defendants. They offered the settlements as the motive for the changes of opinion. Thus, the settlement was used to show bias or prejudice of the expert witness, exactly one of the uses contemplated by Rule 408. . . .

We recognize that the fact that defendants had a legitimate reason for offering the settlement evidence does not end the inquiry. Because there is a substantial risk that the jury will use the evidence for an impermissible purpose, the evidence must pass the balancing test of Rule 403, weighing probative value against the "danger of unfair prejudice, confusion of the issues, or misleading the jury." In many of the reported opinions in which settlement evidence was excluded, the decision was grounded on Rule 403 considerations.

The trial court has broad discretion in ruling on 403 questions, and review here is only for abuse of discretion. . . . For a number of reasons, we do not believe that plaintiff has shown an abuse of discretion here.

[T]he risk of improper usage of the evidence by the jury is reduced somewhat by the requirement of *Sampson* that "the court must clearly instruct the jury to disregard the settlement when determining liability and damages," and the requirement of *Slayton* that the jury not be told the settlement amount. The jury was not told of the settlement amount in this case, and there was a clear instruction, agreed to by plaintiff. Consistent with the instruction, defendants' counsel stated in closing argument that the settlement was relevant to the credibility of Dr. Markowitz. . . .

[T]he evidence had substantial probative value in the context of this case. The trial was relatively short. Plaintiff's case on liability was built almost entirely on the testimony of Dr. Markowitz. Defendants had to attack the weight of the doctor's testimony in the minds of the jury, and the changes in testimony, combined with the motive shown by the settlement, were probative to do so.

Finally, it would be apparent to the jury that if plaintiff had a claim against defendants, she also had claims against the Newport-area doctors, whose involvement with decedent was much more extensive and who failed to diagnose his heart condition. The court could conclude in these circumstances that the risk of prejudice to both parties would be reduced by making the jury aware of the settlement rather than having it speculate on what happened to the other claims. . . .

NOTES TO QUIRION v. FORCIER

1. *Power of Limiting Instructions.* From the point of view of the plaintiff in a multi-party case, there are two problems with informing the jury that the plaintiff and some of the parties have settled. The jury may conclude that the settling defendants were really the ones mostly at fault. Also, the jury may guess that the plaintiff has already received enough compensation for the injury. Ordinarily evidence law assumes that juries will follow limiting instructions for circumstances like this, so that information that has value for one purpose need not be kept out just because of the risk of misuse.

2. *Impeachment.* Sometimes a person who participated in settlement talks may testify at a trial if the talks fail to lead to a settlement. In that situation, even if the person testifies in a way that contradicts something the person said in settlement talks, Rule 408 prevents the use of the settlement statement for impeachment. If an impeachment use of settlement talk statements were authorized (that is, treated the same way as use of settlement talks to show bias), probably people would be much more circumspect in those talks and settlements might be harder to achieve.

QUESTION 2-6. Carl Collector bought two "Picasso" prints from Alan Artdealer, the owner of an art gallery. Collector now believes that the prints are forgeries, and that Artdealer was aware of that when Artdealer sold them to Collector. Collector has found out that a year before Artdealer sold him the prints, Artdealer was sued by another of his customers who claimed that "Picasso" prints Artdealer had sold her were forgeries. Artdealer and that customer agreed on a settlement that required Artdealer to make a large payment to the customer. In a lawsuit by

GOOD TO REMEMBER

FRE 408 applies *only* when a party seeks to introduce information for one particular purpose: to show something about the validity of a claim that was in dispute.

Collector against Artdealer, if Artdealer's good faith is an issue, should Collector be permitted to introduce evidence of Artdealer's settlement with the earlier customer?

 ## F POSTINJURY PAYMENTS, INSURANCE, AND PLEAS

Some additional rules try to encourage certain socially desirable conduct by shielding information about it from admission at trials. They provide incentives for an array of actions: paying injury victims' medical expenses, making guilty pleas, and buying liability insurance. The focus in reading these rules (FRE 409, 410, and 411) should be on two aspects: precisely what information the rule generally keeps secret and the ways that the rule allows the information to be used in some selected circumstances.

Rule 409. Offers to Pay Medical and Similar Expenses

Evidence of furnishing, promising to pay, or offering to pay medical, hospital, or similar expenses resulting from an injury is not admissible to prove liability for the injury.

Rule 410. Pleas, Plea Discussions, and Related Statements

   (a) Prohibited Uses. In a civil or criminal case, evidence of the following is not admissible against the defendant who made the plea or participated in the plea discussions:

   (1) a guilty plea that was later withdrawn;

   (2) a nolo contendere plea;

   (3) a statement made during a proceeding on either of those pleas under Federal Rule of Criminal Procedure 11 or a comparable state procedure; or

   (4) a statement made during plea discussions with an attorney for the prosecuting authority if the discussions did not result in a guilty plea or they resulted in a later-withdrawn guilty plea.

   (b) Exceptions. The court may admit a statement described in Rule 410(a)(3) or (4):

   (1) in any proceeding in which another statement made during the same plea or plea discussions has been introduced, if in fairness the statements ought to be considered together; or

   (2) in a criminal proceeding for perjury or false statement, if the defendant made the statement under oath, on the record, and with counsel present.

> **Rule 411. Liability Insurance**
>
> Evidence that a person was or was not insured against liability is not admissible to prove whether the person acted negligently or otherwise wrongfully. But the court may admit this evidence for another purpose, such as proving a witness's bias or prejudice or proving agency, ownership, or control.

Segment 27: statements made during plea bargaining

Occasionally after an accidental injury, a potential defendant or a potential defendant's insurance company may pay for a victim's medical expenses. This may be motivated by a general sense of responsibility or fairness, or perhaps because quick medical care can reduce the extent of the victim's injury. These are both worthwhile motivations, and perhaps for this reason Rule 409 facilitates the payments. It prohibits introduction of evidence of this type of payment to prove liability for the injury. Note that the rule would permit introduction of this information for purposes different from proving liability for the injury.

Just as civil settlement agreements and negotiations receive special protection from disclosure, pleas and plea discussions in the criminal justice process are shielded from admissibility by Rule 410. The rule generally precludes admission of a guilty plea that is later permitted to be withdrawn, a plea of nolo contendere, and statements made in state and federal plea negotiations. Since plea bargaining is so central in our criminal justice system, it is understandable that an evidence rule might offer an incentive for that conduct.

With regard to liability insurance, some jurors might think that because a defendant had purchased insurance, that defendant was therefore likely to have acted negligently. Rule 411 protects against that assumption. It rejects the admission of evidence of insurance — or lack of insurance — on the issue of the quality of a person's conduct. Note, though, that insurance coverage may be proved if it is relevant to some other topic such as proof of ownership (of something that was insured) or control, or a witness's bias.

G   SUMMARY

To Achieve Social Policies, Evidence that Ordinarily Would Be Treated as Relevant Is Prohibited under Specialized Rules. A variety of social policy goals have led to the adoption of evidence rules that treat particular kinds of information as *not* relevant, even though a standard application of the Rule 401 relevance definition would produce the conclusion that the information passed the test in that Rule.

Subsequent Remedial Measures. Subsequent remedial measures, controlled by Rule 407, are one example of this kind of policy choice. When a plaintiff seeks to prove that a defendant acted negligently or sold a product with a defect, proof that the defendant had improved its conduct or its product after the plaintiff's injury would have a strong logical connection to the idea that the defendant's earlier conduct had been substandard. Evidence law keeps this kind of information out of trials, to encourage people to make repairs and improve their conduct. *Cyr* and *Bethel* explained the social policies behind this doctrine, and also illustrate how courts may sometimes try to limit its application.

Subsequent Remedial Measures Allowed When the Defendant Controverts Their Feasibility. The rule against introducing evidence of subsequent remedial measures to show negligent conduct is withdrawn if the defendant has claimed that a safer practice is not feasible. In *Flaminio* and *Kenny*, the courts decide whether to treat the defendants' claims as the kinds of denials of feasibility that entitle a plaintiff to introduce evidence of subsequent remedial measures.

Settlements and Statements in Settlement Negotiations. Another recurring circumstance in modern life is the settlement of disputes. To encourage that conduct, Rule 408 blocks the admissibility of evidence about settlements and statements made during settlement negotiations. In order for this rule to apply, a dispute must exist about an underlying claim of liability or about the amount of liability. *Londagin* involves a court's effort to define "dispute" in this context.

Limiting Rule 408 to Settlement Information Introduced to Prove Validity of an Underlying Claim. Rule 408 keeps evidence out only if it is offered for the specific purpose defined in the rule (the purpose of showing liability on the underlying claim involved in the settlement or settlement negotiations). *Quirion* illustrates one way in which a party might persuasively claim that evidence of a settlement matters in a case in a way different from showing that the settled claim was valid. The occurrence of the settlement was linked to possible bias on the part of an expert witness, which is a use different from establishing whether the conduct that was involved in the basic dispute had complied with legal standards.

Additional Social Policy Exclusionary Rules. Finally, with structures parallel to the structures of Rules 407 and 408, the Chapter notes that similar rules constrain the use of evidence of payments of medical expenses after an injury, possession of insurance, and pleas and plea bargains and statements related to pleas and plea bargains.

CHAPTER 3

Proof of Character

A. Introduction
B. Basic Rule Against Propensity Evidence
C. Permitted Propensity Inferences
D. Permitted Propensity Inferences about the Victim
E. Nonpropensity Use of Evidence that May also Show Propensity
F. Summary

A INTRODUCTION

Topic Overview

Evidence law is ambivalent about information that shows a person's character, personality, or essential traits. The starting point is a simple idea. Knowing that a person has a particular type of personality could help someone decide how that person probably acted at a particular time, but evidence law places significant limitations on that inference. It restricts the introduction of evidence if the *only* use of that evidence would be to reach a conclusion about a person's character or personality traits in order to use that conclusion to infer how that person actually acted on a specific occasion. Rule 404(a) generally prohibits introducing evidence about a person's character to show that the person acted in conformity with that character on a specific occasion. This forbidden use is sometimes called the "propensity inference," since it involves inferring (1) that a person's character gives that person a propensity to act in a certain way and (2) that the person did in fact act consistently with that propensity on a specific occasion.

Ambivalence shows up, however, because the scope of Rule 404(a) is shaped by a number of exceptions. These exceptions allow use of character evidence to show that a person did act in conformity with his or her character on a specific occasion. Also, Rule 404(b) provides examples of situations in which evidence that could support a conclusion about a person's propensity to act in a certain way may nonetheless be admissible. It can be admitted if a juror can use it in connection with an issue in a case without reaching a conclusion based on the person's possible propensity to act in a certain way. The following table highlights the uneasy combination of a general prohibition and a large number of exceptions to that prohibition. It highlights the discrepancy between the law's claimed aversion to the propensity inference and the many situations in which the law allows that inference. This chapter and the next chapter examine details of the general rule and the exceptions.

IS EVIDENCE ABOUT A PERSON'S CHARACTER ADMISSIBLE TO SHOW THAT THE PERSON ACTED IN CONFORMITY WITH IT?

NO	YES (subject to Rule 403 balancing)
General rule prohibits proof about a person's character to show that the person acted in conformity with it.	*About a criminal defendant* if introduced by the defendant or by prosecution to rebut it
	About an alleged victim if introduced by a criminal defendant or by prosecution to rebut
	When a criminal defendant introduces evidence about an alleged victim's character trait, evidence *about the defendant's same character trait* introduced by the prosecution
	About civil or criminal defendant accused of sexual assault or child molestation
	About alleged homicide victim to rebut any evidence that victim was the first aggressor
	About any witness's credibility

Chapter Organization

This chapter begins with a description of the general rule prohibiting propensity inferences from proof about a person's character, and with some explanations of the policy reasons that support the prohibition. It next considers the major exceptions to the prohibition: certain allowed information about a criminal defendant's character, certain allowed information about a victim's character (in criminal cases), and certain allowed information about a person's past conduct when there is a logical chain of inferences from that conduct to a disputed issue in a case that does not require a conclusion about character.

Basic Structure for Analysis

For issues about character evidence, there are two key analytical steps. We first make certain that a "character" evidence problem is present by determining if the only way the jury could make use of the offered information is by using it to reach a conclusion about the type of person some person is, on the way to drawing a conclusion that because the person has that character the person probably acted in conformity with that character at a particular time. The second step in analysis is to see whether the proposed use of the evidence is covered by any of the many exceptions to the prohibition against the propensity inference.

B BASIC RULE AGAINST PROPENSITY EVIDENCE

A number of concerns support the general rule against the propensity inference. Establishing exactly what character traits a person has is difficult, because character traits may be hard to define and the complexities of a person's psyche might be infinite. And even if it was easy to know what "type" of person someone is, reasoning from that idea to a conclusion about exactly how that person acted on a particular occasion would also be hard. For example, sometimes people who are aggressive act in violent ways, and sometimes they don't. Finally, in many cases where parties might want to introduce evidence of someone's character, the character they would be interested in showing the jury is bad character. To support an inference that someone acted wrongly at the time involved in a particular controversy, they would like to be allowed to show that the person has a generally unsavory nature or that the person has acted badly at other times in the past. This carries the risk that a jury will decide what a person did based on feelings about the person instead of on information more directly linked to his or her actions.

The text of Rule 404(a) provides a clear statement of the law's starting point for character evidence. It incorporates the propensity inference and prohibits the use of evidence that depends on that inference for its relevance.

STEPS FOR...

Analyzing Character Evidence Issues

To analyze character evidence issues, we use two inquiries:

- For the trier of fact to use the evidence to decide how a person acted, would the trier of fact *necessarily* have to draw a conclusion about that person's character traits?
- If using the evidence would require a conclusion about character to decide how a person acted, is that use allowed by any exception to the general antipropensity rule?

Rule 404. Character Evidence; Crimes or Other Acts

(a) Character Evidence.
(1) *Prohibited Uses.* Evidence of a person's character or character trait is not admissible to prove that on a particular occasion the person acted in accordance with the character or trait.

■   ■   ■

Can We Let the Jury Know the Defendant Is a Bad Person? — Boyd. In April, 1890, Boyd, Standley, and Davis encountered four other men: Dansby, Butler, Martin Byrd, and Joseph Byrd. Evidence at a trial tended to show that Boyd shot Dansby. Other evidence was admitted to show that about three weeks earlier, Boyd and Standley committed some robberies. The Supreme Court analyzed whether it was proper to let the jury know that the defendants accused of murder might also have committed robberies at an earlier time.

How could the robberies be relevant to the murder? The Court describes one theory asserted by the prosecution and rejects it. Consider how the Court's rhetoric — using words like "wretches" and "depraved" — may indicate the strength of the Court's belief in the principle it applied to reverse the conviction.

BOYD v. UNITED STATES

142 U.S. 450 (1892)

Mr. Justice HARLAN delivered the opinion of the Court.

The plaintiffs in error were jointly indicted in the Court below for the crime of murder, alleged to have been committed on the 6th day of April, 1890, at the Choctaw Nation, in the Indian country, within the western district of Arkansas....

The defendants were found guilty of murder as charged in the first count. A motion for a new trial having been overruled, the defendants were condemned to suffer the punishment of death.

The proof was conflicting upon many points, but there was evidence tending to show the following facts: In the night of April 6, 1890, the defendants, Boyd and Standley, with John Davis, *alias* Myers, came to a ferry, on Cache creek, in the Indian country, a short distance from Martin Byrd's, at whose house, at the time, were John Dansby, the deceased, Joseph Byrd, a brother of Martin Byrd, and Richard Butler. The defendants and Davis, or one of them, called to the ferryman, Martin Byrd, to come and set them over the creek. Byrd protested that he did not like to do work of that kind after dark, but finally consented to get the key of the boat, and take them across the creek. He went to his house, avowedly to obtain the key; and, after remaining away some time, returned, accompanied by Dansby, Joseph Byrd, and Richard Butler, each with weapons. When Martin Byrd reached the ferry-boat, and was about to unlock the chain by which it was held fast — Boyd being at the time in the rear end of the boat while Davis and Standley were sitting upon the bank of the creek — Davis said to him, "Lay down that chain, and throw out your rusty change." Upon Byrd saying, "Don't you want to cross?" Davis, holding his pistol upon Byrd, replied, with an oath, "No, it's your money we're after." Dansby started towards Byrd, and was shot in the back by Boyd. . . . Dansby lived a few days only, and died at Martin Byrd's house, from the wounds inflicted upon him on the above occasion. . . .

The principal assignments of error relate to the admission, against the objection of the defendants, of evidence as to several robberies committed prior to the day when Dansby was shot, and which . . . had no necessary connection with, and did not in the slightest degree elucidate, the issue before the jury, namely, whether the defendants murdered John Dansby on the occasion of the conflict at the ferry. This evidence tended to show, and, for the purposes of the present discussion, it may be admitted that it did show, that in the night of March 15, 1890, Standley, under the name of Henry Eckles, robbed Richard C. Brinson and Samuel R. Mode [and] that in the afternoon of March 17, 1890, he and Boyd robbed Robert Hall. . . . In relation to these matters the witnesses went into details as fully as if the defendants had been upon trial for the robberies they were, respectively, charged by the evidence with having committed. The admissibility of this evidence was attempted to be sustained in part upon the ground that Martin Byrd and his crowd, having the right to arrest the parties guilty of the robberies, were entitled to show that the robberies had been in fact committed by the defendants. [T]here is nothing to show that he or his associates had ever heard, before the meeting at the ferry, of the robberies of Brinson, Mode, [and Hall]. . . .

[W]e are constrained to hold that the evidence as to the Brinson, Mode, and Hall robberies was inadmissible. . . . Whether Standley robbed Brinson and Mode, and whether he and Boyd robbed Hall, were matters wholly apart from the inquiry as to the murder of Dansby. They were collateral to the issue to be tried. . . . Those robberies may have been committed by the defendants in March, and yet they may have been innocent of the murder of Dansby in April. Proof of them only tended to prejudice the defendants with the jurors, to draw their minds away from the real issue, and to produce the impression that they were wretches whose lives were of no value to the community, and who were not entitled to the full benefit of the rules prescribed by law for the trial of human beings charged with crime involving the punishment of death. Upon a careful scrutiny of the record we are constrained to hold that, in at least the particulars to which we have adverted, those rules were not observed at the trial below. However depraved in character, and however full of crime their past lives may have been, the defendants were entitled to be tried upon competent evidence, and only for the offence [sic] charged.

The judgment is reversed and the cause remanded, with directions to grant a new trial.

NOTES TO BOYD v. UNITED STATES

1. *Relevance of Past Bad Acts.* Given the pro-admissibility definition of relevance in the Federal Rules, it would be difficult to argue that information about a person's past bad acts has no relevance to a person's conduct at a particular later time. The Court's statement in *Boyd* that the robberies were "wholly apart" from the charged murder may be based on a more demanding relevance standard than the one now specified in the Federal Rules. But the Court offers an additional basis for its conclusion. Letting the jury know about the past robberies would violate the idea that a defendant may be tried only for a particular charged crime. This concept is the fundamental basis for prohibiting the propensity inference. We avoid giving a jury a chance to convict a defendant on the basis of the defendant's general antisocial nature or past antisocial conduct, and we do that even if the defendant is a person whose life is of "no value to the community."

2. *Alternative Basis for Admissibility.* Evidence that would be barred by the rule against the propensity inference may properly be admitted if it is relevant in some way that doesn't involve the propensity chain of inferences. *Boyd* illustrates this notion.

The prosecution claimed that information about the past robberies was properly admitted because Byrd and his "crowd" had a right to attempt to arrest Boyd for his role in those past robberies. That theory is different from the propensity theory. Unfortunately for the prosecution, there was no showing that Byrd knew about the past robberies, so Byrd was not entitled to claim any privilege to make an arrest. The Court does not consider another reason to reject this arrest rationale: Byrd's possible right to arrest Boyd does not have any logical connection to the controverted questions in the case.

Segment 1:
past bad acts
testimony

QUESTION 3-1. If you ran a restaurant and needed to hire a chef who would be punctual and reliable in other ways, would you consider an applicant's past record as a chef at other restaurants? If past conduct like that would affect your decision about hiring, discuss whether you would be in favor of changing our antipropensity inference rule so that juries in criminal trials could know more about the past conduct of defendants.

■   ■   ■

Depending on Context, Information May Have a "Character" or a "Noncharacter" Logical Use in a Case — John A. Russell Corp. When does evidence involve the propensity inference? Rule 404(a) prohibits the introduction of evidence when its relevance depends on the jury's reaching a conclusion about a person's character in order to reach another conclusion about how that person acted at a specific time. *John A. Russell* involves an effort to use evidence that James Bohlig was dishonest in previous employment to show that he had been dishonest while later working for a different employer. To determine if this involves the propensity inference, consider how dishonesty at one time might be related to dishonesty at another time. If the logical link between the past dishonesty and the claimed future dishonesty requires an intermediate conclusion about the actor's traits such as honesty or dishonesty, then the propensity inference is the basis of the claimed relevancy, and the evidence would be barred by Rule 404(a).

JOHN A. RUSSELL CORP. v. BOHLIG

739 A.2d 1212 (Vt. 1999)

JOHNSON, J.

Former employee James Bohlig appeals from a jury verdict on his counterclaim for breach of an employment contract by his former employer, the John A. Russell Corporation. Mr. Bohlig contends that the court erred by . . . admitting evidence of his character in violation of V.R.E. 404, 405 and 608. We agree . . . and thus reverse and remand for a new trial on the counterclaim.

In May 1989, Mr. Bohlig was hired as executive vice president and chief operating officer by the John A. Russell Corporation, a general contracting company in Rutland, Vermont. The parties entered into an employment contract for a term of three years on May 16, 1989. Shortly after starting his job, Mr. Bohlig began renovating his house in Shrewsbury using employees and equipment of the Corporation with the permission of the Corporation. The cost of the renovations eventually exceeded $600,000. . . .

Subsequently, the Corporation brought suit against Mr. Bohlig for breach of the employment contract, alleging inappropriate self-dealing, breach of fiduciary responsibility, and breach of employment obligations arising from the contract. At trial, the Corporation maintained that Mr. Bohlig was dishonest to the Corporation in representing the scope of his home renovations and his ability to pay for the renovations. . . .

Mr. Bohlig's . . . claim for severance pay and benefits was based upon paragraph 4 of the contract, which states:

Termination: Employer may terminate this contract after twenty four (24) months or any renewal period hereof, upon twelve (12) months written notice, (or pay and other benefits for a twelve month period in lieu of said notice). Employer may terminate this Contract without said twelve month notice and with no further obligation (other than wages and benefits earned but not paid) only in the following instances:

1) for Employee's dishonesty in the performance of his duties or wanton disregard of his duties;

. . . At trial, Mr. Bohlig maintained that, under paragraph 4, he was entitled to twelve months' severance pay and benefits because he did not get twelve
months' notice. The Corporation contended that, under paragraph 4, it . . . was
not obligated to give Mr. Bohlig notice or severance pay because he was terminated for "dishonesty in the performance of his duties."

The jury rendered a verdict in favor of the Corporation for $218,413.20. It ren-
dered a verdict for Mr. Bohlig for $2,828.25. . . . Mr. Bohlig does not appeal from the
verdict for the Corporation. He appeals from the verdict on his counterclaim. . . .
We reach the following [issue]: whether the court erred in admitting certain evidence of Mr. Bohlig's character. . . . .

Mr. Bohlig claims . . . that the court violated V.R.E. 404, 405 and 608 by admitting evidence that Mr. Bohlig was terminated from his previous employment
for dishonesty involving his expense accounts. He contends that this is character evidence improperly admitted to prove he acted dishonestly in his employment with the Corporation in this case. The general rule in V.R.E. 404(a) is that
"evidence of a person's character or a trait of his character is not admissible for
the purpose of proving that he acted in conformity therewith on a particular
occasion." . . . In addition, V.R.E. 404(b) allows evidence of specific instances of
conduct for purposes other than "to prove the character of a person in order to
show that he acted in conformity therewith," and V.R.E. 405(b) allows evidence
of specific instances of conduct to prove character if the character of the person
is an essential element [of the claim or] the defense. . . .

The Corporation first asserts that the evidence — that Mr. Bohlig was terminated from his previous employment for dishonesty — was admissible under
V.R.E. 404(b) to provide the context in which the Corporation hired Mr. Bohlig.
In criminal cases, we have upheld the admission of evidence of other misconduct that is part of the context of a crime charged where it is so interwoven with
the crime charged it cannot be separated without skewing the narrative. Thus,
evidence of other misconduct may be admissible if excluding the evidence would
leave gaps in the narrative detracting from its credibility. This rule is not applicable here, however, because the circumstances of Mr. Bohlig's termination by
a previous employer is not interwoven with the breach of contract alleged in
this case and can be excluded without affecting the narrative on the breach of
contract at all. Indeed, Mr. Russell admitted at trial that Mr. Bohlig's previous
termination had nothing to do with the termination of the contract in this case.

The Corporation next contends that the evidence was admissible to prove
an essential element of the defense, Mr. Bohlig's dishonesty. See V.R.E. 405(b)
(where character of person is an essential element of claim or defense, proof may
be made by specific instances of conduct). The defense was that the Corporation
terminated Mr. Bohlig for "dishonesty in the performance of his duties." Evidence
of Mr. Bohlig's dishonesty with another employer was circumstantial evidence
of a dishonest disposition, rather than evidence of dishonesty on the occasion in

question. Because dishonesty on some other occasion is not an element of the Corporation's defense, this evidence was not admissible under V.R.E. 405(b)....

The Corporation contends that Mr. Bohlig failed to show that the error in admitting this evidence was prejudicial. We disagree. Of the three methods of proving character, "evidence of specific instances of conduct is the most convincing." Advisory Committee Note to F.R.E. 405. It also "possesses the greatest capacity to arouse prejudice." Id. This type of character evidence can undermine accurate fact finding because of the tendency of juries to give it too much weight....

Here, the Corporation was required to prove that it terminated Mr. Bohlig for dishonesty in the performance of his duties on this occasion. It was highly prejudicial to admit evidence that he was terminated from his previous position for dishonesty and had substantial potential for influencing the jury that Mr. Bohlig acted in conformity therewith on this occasion.... We conclude that the error was not harmless. Because Mr. Bohlig has shown error affecting all theories of recovery, we must remand for a new trial.

NOTES TO JOHN A. RUSSELL CORP. v. BOHLIG

1. *Overlaps Between Character Evidence and Direct Evidence of Conduct.* The court states that the evidence of Mr. Bohlig's dishonesty in the past "was circumstantial evidence of a dishonest disposition, rather than evidence of dishonesty on the occasion in question." Could evidence of a dishonest disposition also have some tendency to show that Mr. Bohlig had been dishonest on a particular occasion? It could support a finding of dishonesty only if a juror thought that a person who was once dishonest is more likely, because of that fact, to have been dishonest on another occasion. Even though most people would accept that inference, the rules of evidence reject it.

2. *Character as a Relevant Fact Itself.* "Character" may sometimes have relevance in a way different from supporting a conclusion about how a person might have acted in accordance with his or her character. For example, if the contract had entitled the defendant to fire Mr. Bohlig for being a "dishonest type of person," rather than for "dishonesty in the performance of his duties," that would have changed the court's analysis. If Mr. Bohlig's character, or nature, was relevant to the contract dispute, then proof about that character would have been relevant and admissible.

3. *Style of Proof.* The court held that character evidence was wrongly admitted. In evaluating whether the error was significantly prejudicial, the court pointed out that the type of evidence used in the case was evidence of specific past bad acts that the jury could rely on to reach a general conclusion about Mr. Bohlig's character. In all character evidence cases, there are two separate inquiries: (1) whether proof related to character is acceptable, and (2) if it is, what kinds of proof are acceptable. Rule 405 controls the style of proof.

Under Rule 405, proof in the form of reputation and opinion testimony is allowed in all cases where proof of character is permitted. Another kind of proof that could help a jury reach a conclusion about a person's character, proof about specific conduct a person had exhibited, can be used only in a specific and relatively rare kind of case. Proof of specific acts to show character is permitted only if the person's character is an essential element of a charge, claim, or defense.

Rule 405. Methods of Proving Character

   (a) By Reputation or Opinion. When evidence of a person's character or character trait is admissible, it may be proved by testimony about the person's reputation or by testimony in the form of an opinion. On cross-examination of the character witness, the court may allow an inquiry into relevant specific instances of the person's conduct.

   (b) By Specific Instances of Conduct. When a person's character or character trait is an essential element of a charge, claim, or defense, the character or trait may also be proved by relevant specific instances of the person's conduct.

---

4. *Character as an Essential Element.* The substantive law of a case controls whether character is an essential element of any party's claim or defense. For example, when a criminal defendant raises an entrapment defense, the defendant must prove that he or she is generally law-abiding. That proof would *not* be introduced to show that because the defendant is generally law-abiding he or she acted in a particular way (that would entail the prohibited propensity inference). It would be introduced to show simply that he or she is generally law-abiding. That would be an instance of proof about character to show character. Proving character to show character is outside the prohibition of Rule 404(a)(1), and it is explicitly recognized in Rule 405(b).

Negligent entrustment tort cases are another example where a person's character is an issue in itself and not something that is relevant only to show how the person acted at a particular time. Defamation cases may also involve character as an ultimate issue rather than as a stepping-stone to conclusions about something else — for example, if a defamation plaintiff alleges that a defendant falsely said that the plaintiff is a person with no respect for private property.

GOOD TO REMEMBER

FRE 404 defines many situations when character evidence is allowed. FRE 405 controls how a party is allowed to prove it, when it is allowed.

GOOD TO REMEMBER

The focus of Rule 404 is on information that a jury would use to reach a conclusion about a person's character in order to conclude that the person once acted in a way that is consistent with that character. There is a big difference between proving character and proving conduct.

QUESTION 3-2. In a contracts case, Buyer seeks damages from Seller, claiming that Seller delivered substandard merchandise. Buyer seeks to introduce evidence showing that in the past, Seller has published false advertisements, failed to pay debts owed to other companies, and infringed on rivals' patents. Information of this type would support a finding that Seller is unscrupulous and likes to cheat. These are character traits. The information certainly increases the likelihood that Buyer's claim is correct (that Seller really did deliver bad merchandise). Since Buyer must prove that Seller delivered bad merchandise, can Buyer describe the information about Seller's past conduct as an essential element of Buyer's case?

C   PERMITTED PROPENSITY INFERENCES

There are two main reasons for prohibiting the propensity inference. First, its logic is weak. Second, the information it is usually based on may carry the risk of unfair prejudice against the person whose character is proved. These concerns may help to understand some of the exceptions to the prohibition that have developed under common law and under modern rules. These exceptions mostly grant criminal defendants the right to introduce character evidence about themselves. In these situations, the problems with the propensity inference are reduced. Allowing evidence of weak probative value gives defendants every possible chance to protect themselves against wrongful conviction. And the risk of unfair prejudice disappears when the defendant, rather than the prosecution, seeks to bring the information into the trial. Rule 404(a)(2)(A) withdraws the ban against propensity evidence when a defendant wants to introduce evidence about his or her own pertinent character trait.

Rule 404. Character Evidence; Crimes or Other Acts

    (a) Character Evidence.
      (1) *Prohibited Uses. . . .*
      (2) *Exceptions for a Defendant or Victim in a Criminal Case.* The following exceptions apply in a criminal case:
        (A) a defendant may offer evidence of the defendant's pertinent trait, and if the evidence is admitted, the prosecutor may offer evidence to rebut it. . . .

■   ■   ■

Defining Pertinent Traits — **City of Kennewick v. Day.** When a criminal defendant seeks to introduce evidence under the exception to the prohibition against character evidence, the evidence must relate to a "pertinent trait." Deciding what traits are pertinent can sometimes require a clear understanding of the precise charged crime.

CITY OF KENNEWICK v. DAY

11 P.3d 304 (Wash. 2000)

MADSEN, J.

Doug R. Day was convicted by a Benton County District Court jury of possession of . . . drug paraphernalia. . . . The trial court excluded testimony regarding Day's reputation for sobriety from drugs and alcohol, finding this was not evidence of a "pertinent trait of character" under ER 404(a)(1). We hold that the trial court abused its discretion by refusing to admit the proffered testimony and, accordingly, reverse and remand for a new trial.

On November 4, 1996, Day was stopped for investigation of driving under the influence after maneuvering his truck around a police barrier set up to facilitate an accident investigation. The officer who stopped Day immediately suspected he was intoxicated. Day claimed he had not been drinking, but was unwilling to take a field sobriety test or a portable "BAC DataMaster" test. Day was arrested and his truck was searched.

In the center armrest console, between the front seats, the officer found a small amount of marijuana and a marijuana pipe. Day immediately claimed the items were not his, that he had never seen them before, and that he had just picked up his truck from a repair shop. Day's postarrest BAC reading was .04, so he was only charged with negligent driving in the first degree. The arresting officer also cited Day for possession of . . . drug paraphernalia under the Kennewick Municipal Code.

A trial was held in Benton County District Court. With respect to the drug-related charges, Day asserted the defense of "unwitting possession," claiming he was unaware that the marijuana and marijuana pipe were in his car prior to the officer finding them. In support of his defense, Day offered the testimony of Don Simmonson. Simmonson, the owner of an auto repair shop, testified that Day's vehicle had been in his shop undergoing major modifications for approximately four months up until a "couple" of days prior to Day's arrest. He also testified that one of the employees who worked on Day's vehicle was fired for suspected drug use outside of work, and Simmonson recounted a prior incident in which a customer complained about finding drug paraphernalia in a car after it was picked up from his shop. Defense counsel proceeded to ask Simmonson if he was aware of Day's reputation in the community for sobriety, as to both drugs and alcohol. The court sustained the prosecutor's objection to this question.

The trial court excluded Day's proffered character evidence stating that "it's not an issue of character, it's an issue of conduct and past conduct is not necessarily admissible to show present conduct." . . .

The jury acquitted Day of negligent driving, but found him guilty of possession of... drug paraphernalia. Day appealed to the Benton County Superior Court. The superior court reversed Day's conviction, finding the district court erred in precluding Day from presenting testimony regarding his reputation for sobriety.

The City moved for discretionary review of the superior court's ruling. In an unpublished opinion, the Court of Appeals, Division Three, reversed the superior court, reinstating Day's convictions. Day petitioned this Court for review and review was granted, limited to the issue of whether the trial court erroneously precluded Day from presenting evidence of his reputation for sobriety from drugs and alcohol. . . .

The admissibility of character evidence offered by a criminal defendant, as to his or her own character, is governed by [a state rule]:

> (a) Character Evidence Generally. Evidence of a person's character or a trait of character is not admissible for the purpose of proving action in conformity therewith on a particular occasion, except:
>
> (1) *Character of Accused.* Evidence of a *pertinent* trait of character offered by an accused, or by the prosecution to rebut the same[.]

(Emphasis added).

Through the use of character evidence, "the defendant generally seeks to have the jury conclude that one of such character would not have committed the crime charged." *State v. Kelly,* 102 Wn. 2d 188, 195, 685 P.2d 564 (1984). Although the concept of character is "amorphous," *id.,* it is generally thought to include traits such as "honesty, temperance, [and] peacefulness." 1 *McCormick on Evidence* §195 *(Character and Habit),* at 686 (John W. Strong, ed., 5th ed. 1999).

We have held that the term "pertinent," as used in [our rule] is synonymous with "relevant." *State v. Eakins,* 127 Wn. 2d 490, 495, 902 P.2d 1236 (1995). Thus, "a pertinent character trait is one that tends to make the existence of any material fact more or less probable than it would be without evidence of that trait." *Eakins,* 127 Wn. 2d at 495-96; *Quinto v. City & Borough of Juneau,* 664 P.2d 630 (Alaska Ct. App. 1983) (reputation for sobriety is pertinent to charge of driving while intoxicated), *rev'd,* 684 P.2d 127 (Alaska 1984); *State v. Rabe,* 5 Haw. App. 251, 687 P.2d 554 (1984) (reputation for abstinence from drugs is pertinent to charge of promotion of prison contraband). . . .

The crime of possession of drug paraphernalia is defined by Kennewick Municipal Code (KMC) 9.32.020(5):

> It is unlawful for any person to use, or to possess with the intent to use, drug paraphernalia to . . . inject, ingest, inhale, or otherwise induce into the human body a controlled substance . . . or to deliver, possess with the intent to deliver, or manufacture with the intent to deliver, drug paraphernalia, knowing, or under circumstances where one reasonably should know, that it will be used to . . . inject, ingest, inhale, or otherwise introduce into the human body a controlled substance. . . .

... The City fails to recognize that "use or intent to use" is an element of the charged offense. Day persuasively argues that because the charge requires the City to prove he used or intended to use paraphernalia to ingest marijuana, his reputation for sobriety from drugs and alcohol is "pertinent" to the element of intent....

[T]he question is whether evidence of Day's reputation for sobriety from drugs and alcohol makes it less probable that he used or intended to use the marijuana pipe to smoke marijuana. Considering that the threshold for relevance is extremely low under ER 401, we must answer in the affirmative. *See* ER 401 (relevant evidence is ... "evidence having *any* tendency to make the existence of *any* fact that is of consequence ... more probable or less probable") (emphasis added). We believe that a jury could conclude that a person who does not use drugs (by reputation at least) is less likely to use a marijuana pipe to smoke marijuana.

More than mere possession was at issue here. The City was required to prove intent to use the paraphernalia. By failing to recognize this point, the trial court based its decision to exclude Day's proffered character evidence "on an erroneous view of the law." This was an abuse of discretion....

[I]t appears the trial court excluded Day's reputation evidence based on its misapprehension of the legal issues. The judge did not recognize that sobriety from drugs is a character trait or that "intent to use" is an element of possession of drug paraphernalia.... Since the trial court made its determination based on an incomplete analysis of the law, its decision was based on untenable grounds and constituted an abuse of discretion.

Day's reputation for sobriety from drugs and alcohol is "pertinent" to the charge of possession of drug paraphernalia because "intent to use" is an element of the offense.... Day presented evidence tending to establish that the marijuana and marijuana pipe were placed in his truck while it was being repaired. Defendant's presentation of third party testimony regarding his reputation for abstention from the use of drugs was important to his defense.

We believe a reasonable probability exists that "the outcome of the trial could have been materially affected had this evidence been admitted. . . ." *Eakins*, 127 Wn. 2d at 503 (citing *State v. Kelly*, 102 Wn. 2d 188, 193, 685 P.2d 564 (1984)).

Accordingly, we *reverse* and *remand* for a new trial.

NOTES TO CITY OF KENNEWICK v. DAY

1. *Identifying the Propensity Inference.* The evidence the defendant sought to introduce was relevant only if the jury used the propensity inference — the defendant wanted the jury to believe (1) he had a reputation for sobriety with regard to illegal drugs, and that (2) therefore he had the personality trait of sobriety with regard to illegal drugs, and that (3) therefore he did not have an intent to use illegal drugs at the time they were found in his possession. This "action in conformity with character" inference is the kind of inference generally prohibited by Rule 404(a)(1) but allowed under the pro-defendant exception in Rule 404(a)(2)(A).

2. *Defining "Pertinent" Traits.* A character trait need not be very specific or detailed in order to be "pertinent." For example, sobriety is a fairly specific trait, and there is a clear link between it and the likelihood of possessing drug paraphernalia with intent to use it. In contrast, the trait of being law-abiding is very general, and it is usually treated as pertinent in criminal cases. But a court may exclude evidence of a trait when there may be a significant discrepancy between that trait and a charged offense. For example, the character trait of truthfulness might be irrelevant in a trial for unlawful possession of firearms.

Segment 24: opinion-based character testimony

3. *Context for Reputation.* When proof of character is introduced in the form of testimony about a defendant's reputation, courts must consider the basis of the witness's knowledge of that reputation. For example, if the witness knows only what a few people think of the defendant, the feelings of those people probably would not be treated as being the defendant's "reputation." On the other hand, a court would likely admit evidence of reputation gleaned from knowledge of what "a lot" or "most" of the people in a neighborhood seem to think. At common law, reputation evidence was typically described as being what a community thought about a person. Modern cases recognize that there can be many different communities, such as one's workplace or a sports league. *See* State v. Tucker, 968 A.2d 543 (Me. 2009) for a range of examples.

4. *Defendant's Option.* Rule 404 treats prosecutors differently from criminal defendants. In a case like *Day*, if the defendant had a reputation for using illegal drugs, the prosecution would be barred from introducing evidence about that reputation *unless* the defendant introduced character evidence himself. The prosecution's ability to use character evidence is controlled by the defendant's trial strategy because allowing defendants to use the propensity inference originated as a "mercy rule" meant to decrease the risk of wrongful convictions.

■ ■ ■

GOOD TO REMEMBER

The defendant's ability to use information about character is an exception to the general prohibition against use of character to prove action in conformity with that character. Evidence law gives defendants the right to bring this supposedly low-quality evidence into a trial, but it also lets prosecutors use that kind of evidence once a defendant has decided to use it.

"Opening the Door" for Character Evidence — **State v. Gowan.** This case explains the rationale for the "mercy rule" that allows a defendant to introduce evidence of his or her pertinent good character. But that opportunity carries a risk for a defendant: the defendant's character witness can be cross-examined, and the introduction of character evidence entitles the prosecution to introduce contradicting evidence about the defendant's character. *Gowan* considers when it is fair to treat the defendant

as having introduced character evidence, which is significant because it controls the prosecution's opportunity to respond.

STATE v. GOWAN

13 P.3d 376 (Mont. 2000)

HUNT, J.

Defendant, Richard Lance Gowan (Gowan), appeals from a jury verdict in the Eleventh Judicial District Court, Flathead County, finding him guilty of two counts of criminal sale of dangerous drugs. We reverse and remand for a new trial.

The dispositive issue on appeal can be restated as follows:

Did the District Court err in holding that a defense witness'[s] gratuitous statement, offered in response to the State's cross-examination, opened the door for rebuttal character evidence? . . .

A jury trial was held on March 2-3, 1998. After opening statements, the parties again met with the District Court to discuss the admissibility of Gowan's prior perjury conviction and what evidence, if any, would be admissible should Gowan choose to testify. The District Court ruled that while direct evidence of a prior conviction was not admissible, the State would be permitted to ask Gowan, in the event he testified, only if he had lied under oath in the past. Once again, the District Court clarified that the State was not to make references to Gowan's prior convictions.

At trial, Gowan called his girl friend, Kris McPherson (McPherson), as a witness. She was not designated as a character witness and on direct-examination McPherson offered no character testimony. On cross-examination, however, the following transpired:

[Prosecutor]

Q. Why didn't you tell him to go to the police, instead of selling drugs, to get the title to your car?

[McPherson]

A. Because I didn't tell him to sell drugs to get the title to the car. I actually told him the guy's melon —

(court reporter stops proceedings)

A. Sorry. And then it wasn't until after everything had went down that I found out — I never knew Paul's last name. I'm in the car business, so I deal with all the car dealers in town. He had just told me about some car from Paul, paid him in full, and he hadn't got a title yet. And I couldn't believe he'd do that, but he's a very honest and trusting person.

Q. Who's honest and trusting?

A. Lance.

Q. Lance is honest?

A. Yes. He trusted Mr. Southwick with the title.

Q. What do you base that comment on, him being honest? Come on, Ms. McPherson.

A. I don't know what you're getting at, Mr. Corrigan.

Q. Lance isn't honest.

[Defense Counsel]

Musick: Objection, your honor.

After argument of counsels, the District Court ruled that in light of our decision in State v. Austad (1982), 197 Mont. 70, 641 P.2d 1373, and under Rules 404(a)(1) and 405(a), M.R.Evid., that McPherson had offered character evidence. Therefore, the District Court concluded that McPherson had opened the door to character evidence, even though her testimony was in response to cross-examination. The State was allowed to inquire if McPherson was aware that Gowan had been convicted of perjury. The State also made references to Gowan being on probation and being sued for failure to deliver a title.

The jury found Gowan guilty of both counts of criminal sale of dangerous drugs. . . .

. . . Gowan now appeals his conviction to this Court.

Did the District Court err in holding that a defense witness'[s] gratuitous statement, offered in response to the State's cross-examination[,] opened the door for rebuttal character evidence? . . .

Generally, a defendant's character or character trait is not admissible in criminal cases to prove that the defendant acted in conformity with that trait. Rule 404(a), M.R.Evid. "The inquiry is not rejected because character is irrelevant; on the contrary, it is said to weigh too much with the jury and to so overpersuade [sic] them as to prejudge one with a bad general record and deny him a fair opportunity to defend against a particular charge." Michelson v. United States (1948), 335 U.S. 469, 475-76, 93 L. Ed. 168, 69 S. Ct. 213. In other words, persons of bad character are more likely to commit crimes than are persons of good character, but the law fears that a defendant will be convicted merely because he is an unsavory person.

The various justifications for this general rule are reducible to three: (1) the strong tendency to believe a defendant is guilty of the offense charged merely because he is a likely person to do such acts because of his distasteful propensities; (2) the deep tendency of human nature to condemn, not because a defendant is guilty of the offense charged, but because he is a bad person who has escaped punishment from past transgressions and may as well be punished now that he is caught; and (3) the overwhelming burden of requiring a defendant to not only defend against the offense charged but also allegations of bad conduct from his whole past. 1A Wigmore, Evidence § 58.2, at 1215 (Tiller rev. 1983). Or put simply, character evidence is excluded to prevent undue prejudice, confusion of issues, and unfair surprise.

Justice Jackson rightfully described the law regarding proof of a criminal defendant's character as "archaic, paradoxical and full of compromises and compensations by which an irrational advantage to one side is offset by a poorly reasoned counterprivilege to the other." *Michelson*, 335 U.S. at 486. It extends "helpful but illogical options to a defendant" but then balances these with "equally illogical conditions to keep the advantage from becoming an unfair and unreasonable one." *Michelson*, 335 U.S. at 478-79. Even saying that the defendant placed his character at issue is misleading. The defendant's character does not become an element of the offense. Rather, the defendant is attempting to prove his innocence through circumstantial evidence. Likewise, the State attempts to establish that the defendant's bad propensities make his guilt of the charged crime more probable.

Because character evidence is relevant in resolving probabilities of guilt, however, the law allows a defendant to introduce evidence of his good character. Rule 404(a)(1), M.R. Evid. "He may introduce affirmative testimony that the general estimate of his character is so favorable that the jury may infer that he would not be likely to commit the offense charged." *Michelson*, 335 U.S. at 476. But in doing so, he may be opening the door to irresponsible gossip, innuendo and smear.

Once the door is opened, the State may introduce rebuttal evidence of its version of the defendant's true character. Rule 404(a)(1), M.R. Evid. The State may accomplish this by either cross-examining the defendant's character witness or by calling rebuttal witnesses of its own. Rule 405(a), M.R. Evid. In establishing bad character, the State may enter evidence of both reputation and opinion. "It is not the man that he is, but the name that he has which is put in issue." *Michelson*, 335 U.S. at 479. For these reasons, only the defendant is allowed to make the precarious decision to put character at issue.

We have held that a defendant put his character at issue by answering a question on cross-examination with an unnecessary, self-serving statement which he knew to be untrue, intended to place him in a better light with the jury. In that situation, the door is open for the prosecution to rebut this gratuitous character testimony by the defendant. *Austad*, 197 Mont. at 90, 641 P.2d at 1384. We concluded that "the Rules of Evidence were not intended to muzzle the State against [a] defendant's deliberate attempts to mislead jury members by lying to them in answering specific question." *Austad*, 197 Mont. at 90, 641 P.2d at 1384. The case at bar, however, involves statements that the defendant had no control over.

Here, Gowan's witness offered no character testimony on direct-examination. On cross-examination, however, this defense witness gave a non-responsive answer which contained a gratuitous good character statement about Gowan. She said "but he's a very honest and trusting person." The State should have requested that the witness confine her answers to the questions asked, and requested that her statement be stricken from the record. Instead the State pounced on this opportunity to introduce evidence of bad character. The District Court, relying on our decision in *Austad*, concluded that this opened the door for the State to pursue rebuttal character evidence. We disagree.

The facts here are distinguishable from those of *Austad*. In *Austad*, the defendant opened the door with his own statements. Something he had total control over. He attempted to enter testimony of his good character and he paid the price. Gowan, conversely, had no control over what his witness said while being cross-examined by the State. The State cannot elect to convert a defense witness, who has neither been called as a character witness nor testified of good character on direct-examination, into a character witness. Because of the deep tendency of human nature to give evidence of bad character much weight in assigning guilt, only the accused are allowed to open that door.

Since only a defendant can open the door to rebuttal character evidence, the District Court erred in holding that a defense witness could in a statement made during cross-examination. Something Gowan had no control over. Because this issue is dispositive, we need not address the other issues Gowan raises.

Gowan's conviction is reversed and his case is remanded for a new trial.

[Dissenting opinion omitted.]

NOTES TO STATE v. GOWAN

1. *Cross-examining a Character Witness.* The trial judge in *Gowan* ruled wrongly that the defendant had introduced character evidence about himself. Once the trial judge ruled that Kris McPherson had introduced character evidence on behalf of the defendant, the prosecution was entitled to respond to that character evidence. The cross-examiner asked if she was aware that the defendant had been convicted of perjury. This questioning is allowed by Rule 405. Note that the rule allows only inquiry on cross-examination. It does not allow proof separate from what the cross-examined witness might say.

2. *Inquiry but No Extrinsic Proof.* Asking a reputation witness if he or she has heard of a reputation contrary to the reputation about which he or she has testified is permitted. Similarly, a witness who has given an opinion about someone's character may be asked if he or she knows certain facts about that person that might contradict the opinion the witness has stated.

To allow the jury to form a conclusion about a person's character, the rules allow the jury to hear about the person's reputation or to hear someone's opinion of the person's character. They prohibit extrinsic evidence about the person's past conduct, even though that might be the surest basis for knowing what kind of character the person has. This choice to use mediocre evidence for proof of character reflects the law's basic concerns that the inferences involved in character proof are weak, and that allowing more concrete proof about past conduct might lead to lengthy and distracting testimony that seeks to resolve disputes about what actually had happened.

QUESTION 3-3. Assume that a defendant might offer each of the following items of testimony personally in his or her case. Would any of them entitle the prosecution to respond with its own character evidence about the defendant?

A. "I did not commit the robbery."
B. "I would never do something like the charged crime."
C. "I'm too law-abiding to have committed the charged crime."

D   PERMITTED PROPENSITY INFERENCES ABOUT THE VICTIM

In many criminal cases involving a violent encounter between a victim and an assailant, the defendant will admit having inflicted an injury but will assert that the victim was the first aggressor and that therefore the defendant was entitled to inflict an injury in self-defense. The Federal Rules allow the defendant to use the propensity inference to introduce information about the victim's character to support a finding that the victim acted consistently with that character when the victim interacted with the defendant. Defendants use this rule to show that the victim was a violent person and to suggest to the jury that this fact increases the likelihood that the victim acted first.

Rule 404.   Character Evidence; Crimes or Other Acts

(a) Character Evidence.
(1) *Prohibited Uses.* [propensity inference generally barred]
(2) *Exceptions for a Defendant or Victim in a Criminal Case.* The following exceptions apply in a criminal case:

. . .

(B) subject to the limitations in Rule 412, a defendant may offer evidence of an alleged victim's pertinent trait, and if the evidence is admitted, the prosecutor may:
(i) offer evidence to rebut it; and
(ii) offer evidence of the defendant's same trait; and
(C) in a homicide case, the prosecutor may offer evidence of the alleged victim's trait of peacefulness to rebut evidence that the victim was the first aggressor.

The Rule is straightforward, but some of its features deserve special attention.

- The defendant's ability to present information about the victim's character is withdrawn for cases involving sex crimes. That is the significance of the reference to Rule 412.
- When a defendant introduces evidence of the victim's pertinent character trait, the prosecution may respond.
  - The prosecution may counter the defendant's evidence about the victim's character with contrary evidence about the victim's character. For example, the defendant might introduce evidence showing that

the victim was a violent person. The rule allows the prosecution to respond by offering evidence that the victim was a peaceful person.

☐   The rule allows a second mode of response that can be used, of course, in federal courts, but is prohibited in most of the states that have adopted evidence rules similar to the Federal Rules. Under Rule 404(a)(2)(B)(ii), the prosecution may introduce evidence showing that the *defendant* has the same character trait that the defendant claimed the victim had. If a defendant had shown that the victim was a violent kind of person, the prosecution in federal court would be allowed to introduce evidence showing that the defendant is a violent kind of person.

■   Finally, when a defendant in a homicide case introduces *any kind of evidence* to support the claim that the victim was the initial aggressor, the prosecution is permitted to use character evidence about the victim to rebut that claim.

■   ■   ■

Relating a Victim's Character to a Defendant's Self-Defense Claim: Commonwealth v. Adjutant. This case presents a sad instance of the category of cases in which a defendant may be permitted to introduce evidence about a victim's character. Note that the court describes two possible ways in which a victim's character might be relevant. Consider how the theory of relevance controls whether or not the jury would be asked to accept the logic of the propensity inference.

The opinion offers two rationales for the legal system's willingness to permit defendants to rely on the propensity inference. When courts allow many exceptions to the prohibition against the propensity inference, the unspoken question is whether the overall prohibition still makes sense. In order to maintain the general prohibition while recognizing exceptions to it, a court would have to believe that the reasons for permitting the propensity inference in particular kinds of instances do not undermine the justification for generally prohibiting the propensity inference.

COMMONWEALTH v. ADJUTANT

824 N.E.2d 1 (Mass. 2005)

CORDY, J.

Following a jury trial, Rhonda Adjutant, a woman employed by an escort service, was found guilty of voluntary manslaughter for killing Stephen Whiting, a client of the service. In this appeal, Adjutant argues that evidence of Whiting's violent reputation and past conduct, even though unknown to her at the time of the killing, should have been admitted at her trial because it was relevant to her claim that Whiting was the "first aggressor" in the altercation that resulted in his death, and that she acted in self-defense. . . .

The evidence at trial was as follows. Adjutant worked as an escort for Newbury Cosmopolitan International Escort Service (Newbury). In the early morning of September 25, 1999, Whiting telephoned Newbury and requested an escort. The Newbury dispatcher told Whiting that he could receive a full body massage and one hour of an escort's company for $175. Whiting agreed to these terms, and arrangements were made for Adjutant to visit Whiting's home in Revere. Shortly thereafter, Adjutant was dropped off there by a driver and the dispatcher's boy friend (drivers). Whiting met her outside his building and accompanied her to his basement apartment.

Once inside, Whiting paid Adjutant, who then telephoned Newbury to report that she had received payment. Adjutant testified that during and after the call Whiting snorted two lines of cocaine. Adjutant then offered to begin a massage. Whiting replied that he wanted intercourse and believed that he had paid for it. Adjutant denied that she was sent to have intercourse with him, and telephoned the Newbury dispatcher on her cellular telephone to inform her that Whiting wanted more than a massage. Adjutant then handed the phone to Whiting, and the dispatcher reminded him of the original terms. Whiting demanded a total refund, which neither the dispatcher nor Adjutant offered. . . .

There was conflicting testimony as to when the defendant and the victim armed themselves for their fatal confrontation. Adjutant testified that when she attempted to leave, Whiting pushed her onto his bed and retrieved a crowbar from the kitchen, at which point Adjutant picked up a knife that was lying on the bedside table, next to a plate of cocaine. The dispatcher, on the other hand, testified that while she was talking to Whiting, he said that Adjutant had a knife, and that when Adjutant then got back on the telephone with her, Adjutant said that Whiting was picking up a crowbar.

In any event, after arming himself, Whiting first slammed the crowbar on a counter and then swung it at Adjutant, striking her in the leg. She responded by nicking him in the face with the knife, drawing blood. . . .

Within minutes, Adjutant's drivers returned to the scene, heard her screams, and kicked in the door to the apartment. According to Adjutant, the moment one of the drivers kicked in the door, Whiting advanced on her with the crowbar raised, at which point she stabbed him in the neck, inflicting the fatal wound. . . .

Adjutant maintained at trial that all her actions were defensive and intended to help her escape the apartment. The jury's main task was determining whether Adjutant acted in self-defense. That inquiry required the jury to . . . decide who moved first to attack the other during the last moments of the standoff. . . .

During the trial, Adjutant's counsel sought to cross-examine Whiting's neighbors about his previous violent behavior and reputation for violence. The judge sustained the prosecutor's objections to these questions and also barred testimony about Whiting's behavior while intoxicated [or under the influence of drugs], ruling that Whiting's violent past or reputation for violence was only relevant if Adjutant had been aware of them at the time of the stabbing.

At the conclusion of the trial, the jury convicted Adjutant of voluntary manslaughter. She appealed and the Appeals Court affirmed the conviction. We granted her application for further appellate review limited to whether the trial judge erred in concluding that she had no discretion to admit Adjutant's proffered evidence and consequently excluding it.

In almost every American jurisdiction, evidence of a victim's violent character may be admitted to support an accused's claim of self-defense under two distinct theories. First, it may be admitted to prove that at the time of the assault the defendant was reasonably apprehensive for his safety, and used a degree of force that was reasonable in light of the victim's violent tendencies. Because such evidence is relevant to the defendant's state of mind (the subjective reasonableness of his apprehension and actions), a predicate to its admissibility is the defendant's prior knowledge of it. Second, it may be admitted as tending to prove that the victim and not the defendant was likely to have been the "first aggressor," where there is a dispute as to who initiated the attack. Under the first theory, the evidence is not admitted for the purpose of showing that the victim acted in conformance with his character for violence; under the second theory, it is. . . .

Under Rules 404 and 405 of the Federal Rules of Evidence, all Federal courts now permit the introduction of evidence of the victim's violent character to support a defendant's self-defense claim that the victim was the first aggressor. Similarly, appellate courts in forty-five of the forty-eight State jurisdictions that have considered the issue have decided that some form of such evidence is properly admissible on the first aggressor issue, regardless whether the victim's violent character was known to the defendant at the time of the assault. . . .

The basis of the overwhelming trend toward admitting some form of this evidence can be found in the view that evidence reflecting the victim's propensity for violence has substantial probative value and will help the jury identify the first aggressor when the circumstances of the altercation are in dispute. In the words of Professor Wigmore, "When the issue of self-defense is made in a trial for homicide, and thus a controversy arises *whether the deceased was the aggressor,* one's persuasion will be more or less affected by the character of the deceased; it may throw much light on the probabilities of the deceased's action." 1 J. Wigmore, Evidence §63, at 467 (3d ed. 1940).

There can be no doubt that at least some of the proffered evidence in this case was relevant to Adjutant's self-defense claim. Whether Whiting was a violent man, prone to aggression when intoxicated or under the influence of drugs, "throws light" on the crucial question at the heart of Adjutant's self-defense claim — who attacked first in the final moments before the fatal stabbing. The evidence, if admitted, would have supported the inference that Whiting, with a history of violent and aggressive behavior while intoxicated, probably acted in conformity with that history by attacking Adjutant, and that the defendant's story of self-defense was truthful.

[Admitting evidence of the victim's character] on the first aggressor issue reflects the principle that "in criminal cases there is to be greater latitude in admitting exculpatory evidence than in determining whether prejudicial potentialities in proof offered to show guilt should result in its exclusion." *Matter of Robert S.,* 52 N.Y.2d 1046, 1053, 438 N.Y.S.2d 509, 420 N.E.2d 390 (1981) (Fuchsberg, J., dissenting), citing 1 J. Wigmore, Evidence § 194 (3d ed. 1940) (criticizing New York rule excluding victim's specific acts of violence to show propensity). . . .

Notwithstanding our usual hesitation to allow the admission of character evidence to prove conduct, we are persuaded that some form of evidence tending to show the victim's violent character should be admissible for the limited purpose of supporting the defendant's self-defense claim that the victim was the first aggressor . . . .

The judgment against the defendant is reversed, the verdict is set aside, and the case is remanded to the Superior Court for a new trial and further proceedings consistent with this opinion.

NOTES TO COMMONWEALTH v. ADJUTANT

1. *Reasonable Fear and Rule 404.* A defendant may claim that harming a victim was justified, in self-defense, because of the defendant's reasonable fear of the victim. In this circumstance, proof about what the defendant had heard about the victim's character traits related to violence would be admissible even without any particular language in Rule 404. This use of information about character would not be to support a propensity inference. It would involve only a claim that the defendant had believed that the victim possessed those traits.

2. *Victim's Character and the Propensity Inference.* A second rationale for admitting information about a victim's character is precisely to allow the propensity inference. The victim's character may be proved (through reputation or opinion testimony) to support an inference that the victim acted in accordance with that character at the time the defendant injured the victim.

QUESTION 3-4. A defendant who is on trial for murder asserts that the victim attacked him and that the defendant's conduct that killed the victim was legitimate self-defense. If the defendant sought to introduce evidence showing the following facts, under the Federal Rules which evidence should be kept out?

A. The defendant did not know it at the time of the killing, but the victim had a reputation for acting violently.

B. The defendant did not know it at the time of the killing, but the victim had a reputation for stealing other people's property.

C. The defendant did not know it at the time of the killing, but a neighbor of the victim had the opinion that the victim was an aggressive person.

D. The defendant did not know it at the time of the killing, but the victim had killed a person in a fight a year earlier.

Prosecution Options When a Defendant Introduces Evidence about the Victim's Character — Taken Alive. This case highlights a controversial issue about the propensity inference and the actions of victims. When a defendant chooses to introduce evidence about a victim's character, should that choice justify admitting any other character evidence? In all jurisdictions, when a defendant introduces evidence about a victim's character, the prosecution may respond with contradictory evidence about the *victim's* character. But there are rival views about another possible prosecution response, the introduction of evidence about the *defendant's* character. The trial court in *Taken Alive* believed that the defendant's right to introduce evidence about the victim's character should be balanced with permission for the prosecution to introduce evidence about the defendant's character.

The trial court in *Taken Alive* misapplied the Federal Rules that were in effect at the time of the trial. Since that time, Rule 404 has been amended to reflect the concerns that motivated that trial judge's ruling. The following table offers a context for this dispute.

WHEN A *DEFENDANT* INTRODUCES EVIDENCE ABOUT A *VICTIM'S* AGGRESSIVE CHARACTER, WHAT MAY THE PROSECUTION SHOW?
(by type of evidence and jurisdiction)

	Most States	**Former Federal Rule (at time of *Taken Alive*)**	**Current Federal Rule (consistent with trial court's concerns in *Taken Alive*)**
Victim's Peaceful Character	YES	YES	YES
Defendant's Aggressive Character	NO	NO	YES

UNITED STATES v. TAKEN ALIVE
262 F.3d 711 (8th Cir. 2001)

BRIGHT, J.

A jury convicted Ralph Emeron Taken Alive, II of violating 18 U.S.C. § 111, which makes it unlawful to assault, resist, or impede a federal officer engaged in his official duties. Thereafter, the district court sentenced him to a term of imprisonment. Taken Alive appeals his conviction, arguing that the district court abused its discretion in refusing to admit evidence of the federal police officer's character under Fed. R. Evid. 404(a)(2) and 405. Evidence of the police officer's character was crucial to Taken Alive's self-defense case. The exclusion of that evidence prejudiced Taken Alive and, thus, was not harmless error. We reverse and remand.

On the evening of December 16, 1999, Bureau of Indian Affairs (BIA) Officer Yellow responded to a report of an altercation at a bar in McLaughlin, South Dakota, which is on the Standing Rock Sioux Indian Reservation. When he arrived at the bar, Officer Yellow learned that Taken Alive was intoxicated, had been in an argument with other bar patrons, and had just left the bar. After a brief search, Officer Yellow saw Taken Alive walking on a nearby street. Officer Yellow stopped Taken Alive and, after a brief conversation, arrested him "for detox" (sic) and directed Taken Alive to take a seat in the police car.

Officer Yellow testified that he took Taken Alive to the passenger side, rear door of the patrol car, and that, as he opened the rear door, Taken Alive pulled free, grabbed Officer Yellow by the throat, and pushed him up against the side of the patrol car. Officer Yellow felt he was losing consciousness and so he started punching Taken Alive. Taken Alive released his grip on Officer Yellow's neck but the fighting continued. Taken Alive broke free from Officer Yellow and ran toward his father's house. Officer Yellow chased Taken Alive and caught up to him on the porch of Taken Alive's father's house. After a brief struggle, Officer Yellow handcuffed Taken Alive and took him into custody.

Taken Alive testified to a different version of the events surrounding his arrest. Taken Alive testified that after Officer Yellow arrested him, Officer Yellow grabbed his arm and twisted it behind his back, even though Taken Alive offered no resistance. Then, as Taken Alive was getting into the patrol car, Officer Yellow slammed the car door on his head, and Taken Alive fell to the ground. Officer Yellow started hitting him with some unknown object and Taken Alive tried to defend himself. Taken Alive also tried to flee; he pulled Officer Yellow's jacket over the Officer's head and then ran toward his father's house. Officer Yellow caught Taken Alive at the house, knocked Taken Alive to the ground, and hit him with a baton. Then Officer Yellow handcuffed Taken Alive.

On May 19, 2000, the district court granted Taken Alive's motion in limine to exclude 404(b) evidence of Taken Alive's four prior incidents involving the assault of law enforcement officers. The district court ruled that the government failed to notify Taken Alive as required by Rule 404(b). Four days later, the government made a motion in limine to exclude hearsay testimony about Officer Yellow's use of excessive force. Taken Alive objected and the district court reserved ruling until trial.

At trial, Taken Alive argued that he acted in self-defense. As part of his defense, Taken Alive tried to present character evidence about Officer Yellow's aggressive and violent tendencies under Fed. R. Evid. 404(a)(2) and 405(a). . . . The district court rejected defense counsel's proposed proof and excluded the evidence under Fed. R. Evid. 403, finding it highly prejudicial. The district court reasoned that it would be unfair and misleading to allow the jury to think that Taken Alive had never been violent toward law enforcement officers while at the same time indicating that Officer Yellow is a violent person. The district court, nonetheless, granted Taken Alive a self-defense jury instruction.

The jury found Taken Alive guilty of assaulting, resisting, or impeding a federal officer in violation of 18 U.S.C. § 111. . . . Taken Alive timely appealed. . . .

Taken Alive argues that the district court should have admitted the character evidence concerning Officer Yellow's reputation for aggression and violence. Taken Alive offered two witnesses who would testify about Officer Yellow's reputation for aggression and violence. Initially, the court rejected the tender of aggressive character evidence against the officer, stating:

> Well, I'm also going to exclude it under Rule 403. Even though it may be relevant, I think it should be excluded because its probative value is substantially outweighed by the danger of unfair prejudice, confusion of the issues, or misleading the jury. I have previously ruled, although it is not a final ruling, but I have ruled on a motion in limine that the government is not going to be going into these other assaults by the defendant. He clearly has a terrible record of violence toward police officers, I know that. The jury doesn't, but I know that. And it would be an unfair picture and very misleading to allow the jury to think that this defendant has never been a violent person toward law enforcement officers, which is not true, and then to indicate that the sergeant is a violent person. And, again, we would be wasting time getting into all these mini trials. Then the government is going to be calling witnesses to testify that, no, the officer is not violent, he doesn't have anything on his record and this is going to wind up as a trial of the officer instead of a trial of whether or not the defendant impeded or assaulted a federal officer, or whether he acted in self-defense.
>
> So, for the moment, at least, I'm not going to allow the character evidence to be admitted. Now, if you wish to make an offer of proof at some point, you probably want to do that, and we can do that after the jury leaves or something of that nature.

Thereafter, during the trial, Taken Alive made an offer of proof that two witnesses would testify as to Officer Yellow's aggressiveness, quarrelsomeness, and violence in the performance of his duties as an officer. The district court rejected this offer of proof, stating:

> Okay. And those offers of proof will both be rejected. That type of evidence would normally be admitted under 404(a)(2), particularly where personally the defendant had some knowledge of this reputation. However, in this case in view of what has transpired with regard to the Court keeping out any evidence as to the previous record of the defendant, at least four other instances in which he's been involved in assaulting police officers in connection with either being arrested or in custody, it would be unfair to the government. And for all those reasons which I've previously stated the evidence will not be admitted because of Rule 403.

The district court excluded this evidence, in essence, for being "unfair" to the government, particularly since the government had been banned from proving Taken Alive's prior assaults on police. Taken Alive's claim relies on the character evidence regarding Officer Yellow's reputation for aggression and violence to support Taken Alive's testimony that he acted in self-defense. When a defendant raises a self-defense claim, reputation evidence of the victim's violent character is relevant to show the victim as the proposed aggressor. A victim's use of unlawful force may justify the defendant's reciprocal use of force. Because there were no eyewitnesses to the initial confrontation between Taken Alive and Officer Yellow, the reputation-character evidence relating to Officer Yellow becomes very important and material to prove Taken Alive's self-defense claim.

Relevant character evidence may be excluded if its probative value is substantially outweighed by the danger of unfair prejudice. Fed. R. Evid. 403. However, evidence is not unfairly prejudicial merely because it hurts a party's case. In this case, the district court determined that because it had previously granted Taken Alive's motion in limine to exclude Taken Alive's prior assaults on law enforcement officers, that it was now necessary to exclude the proffered character evidence regarding Officer Yellow's reputation for aggressiveness and violence. The district court reasoned that to permit such evidence would be "unfair" to the government. Rule 403, however, is concerned with "unfair prejudice"; that is, evidence that has an "undue tendency to suggest [a] decision on an improper basis, commonly, though not necessarily, an emotional one." Rule 403, Adv. Comm. Notes. In this case, there's the rub. There is a difference between evidence that is unfair in that it hurts a party's case and evidence that is unfairly prejudicial. The district court erred in its evaluation of the evidentiary rules.

The district court's evidentiary ruling affected Taken Alive's substantial rights in presenting his self-defense case. Therefore, the district court prejudicially erred in excluding Taken Alive's proposed adverse character evidence against Officer Yellow. We reverse the conviction and remand for a new trial.

NOTES TO UNITED STATES v. TAKEN ALIVE

1. *Current Federal Rule.* Rule 404(a)(2)(B)(ii) contains a provision that was not in effect at the time of the trial in *Taken Alive.* That provision states that if a defendant introduces evidence about a victim's character trait, the prosecution may introduce evidence to show that the accused has that same character trait. How does that change relate to the position taken by the trial court in *Taken Alive*? Would you recommend that states incorporate this change in their own versions of the evidence rules?

Segment 26: self-defense character evidence

2. *Evolving Confidence in the Propensity Inference.* The exceptions to the prohibition of propensity evidence originated at common law to protect "good" people from criminal conviction, and perhaps to protect juries from regret over rendering a guilty verdict against a defendant who they later find out had "good" character. These rationales are consistent with a belief that the propensity inference itself has only weak probative value in determining how a person acted at any particular time. The exception for proof of a victim's character in a self-defense circumstance may also be rationalized as an effort to protect defendants from being wrongly convicted, even though the propensity inference is weak.

Under the current federal rule when a defendant uses character evidence about an alleged victim, the prosecution is allowed to use the propensity inference against the defendant (by introducing evidence about the defendant's character). The rationale for this must be that the prosecution should be allowed to use weakly probative evidence whenever the law gives that ability to a defendant, or that the propensity inference is not really so weak, after all.

E   NONPROPENSITY USE OF EVIDENCE THAT MAY ALSO SHOW PROPENSITY

Rule 404 prohibits the use of character evidence when its *only* relevance is to show that a person acted in conformity with his or her character. It states the prohibition twice. The first presentation of the antipropensity rule is in Rule 404(a)(1). Then Rule 404(b)(1) offers what is essentially a repetition of the rule first set out in Rule 404(a)(1). But sometimes evidence that could lead a jury to reach a conclusion about a person's character may be relevant in a way that does not require the jury to make the forbidden propensity inference.

Rule 404(b)(2) recognizes that evidence of this type is outside the ban established in Rules 404(a)(1) and 404(b)(1). Rule 404(b)(2) offers examples of evidence that could be relevant in ways that are different from establishing a person's character and then supporting an inference that a person with a particular character acted in conformity with that character. The rule also requires prosecutors to give notice to defendants before seeking to introduce this kind of evidence.

Rule 404. Character Evidence; Crimes or Other Acts

(b) Crimes, Wrongs, or Other Acts.

(1) *Prohibited Uses.* Evidence of a crime, wrong, or other act is not admissible to prove a person's character in order to show that on a particular occasion the person acted in accordance with the character.

(2) *Permitted Uses; Notice in a Criminal Case.* This evidence may be admissible for another purpose, such as proving motive, opportunity, intent, preparation, plan, knowledge, identity, absence of mistake, or lack of accident. On request by a defendant in a criminal case, the prosecutor must:

(A) provide reasonable notice of the general nature of any such evidence that the prosecutor intends to offer at trial; and

(B) do so before trial — or during trial if the court, for good cause, excuses lack of pretrial notice.

■   ■   ■

Similarities Between a Past Crime and a Charged Crime—Foxhoven. Using evidence that might support a character inference to show "identity" is one of the "permitted uses" in Rule 404(b)(2). Using a person's past conduct to link that person to some other conduct might or might not require a jury to reach a conclusion about the person's character. When there is a logical way to use the past conduct in the case *without necessarily* thinking about the person's character, information about the past conduct is properly admitted.

This rationale is used often when there is proof that a defendant committed a past crime with particular characteristics that match up with the crime for which the defendant is currently charged. Writing about this circumstance, the famous scholar Charles McCormick stated: "Much more is demanded than the mere repeated commission of crimes of the same class. . . . The pattern and characteristics of the crimes must be so unusual and distinctive as to be like a signature."[*] In *Foxhoven* the past crimes and charged crimes involved actual *signatures*, not just characteristics *like* signatures.

STATE v. FOXHOVEN

163 P.3d 786 (Wash. 2006)

ALEXANDER, C.J.

In 2004, petitioners Lawrence Michael Foxhoven and Anthony Sanderson were each found guilty of several counts of malicious mischief for etching graffiti on the windows of several businesses. The graffiti included three different "tags,"[1] two of which police concluded were used by petitioners. At their joint trial, the judge admitted evidence that each petitioner had used one of the tags on previous occasions. Petitioners claim that evidence was improperly admitted under Evidence Rule (ER) 404(b), which excludes evidence of prior bad acts when that evidence is used for the purpose of proving conformity with those actions on a different occasion. We conclude that the evidence was admissible to prove modus operandi in order to corroborate or establish the identity of the persons responsible for the graffiti vandalism charged. We, therefore, affirm the convictions.

In October 2001, graffiti was etched with acid into the windows of a number of businesses in downtown Bellingham. The graffiti consisted of three different tags: "HYMN," "GRAVE," and "SERIES." Investigating officers determined that petitioner Sanderson is associated with the tag "HYMN" and petitioner Foxhoven with the tag "SERIES." Foxhoven, Sanderson, and a third person who was associated with the tag "GRAVE" were each charged in Whatcom County Superior Court with several counts of malicious mischief for the graffiti. The third person pleaded guilty to several counts of malicious mischief, but petitioners proceeded to a joint trial before a jury.

---

[*]1 *McCormick on Evidence* (5th ed. 1999) §190, p. 663.

1. A "tag" is a moniker or pseudonym used by a graffiti artist in his or her graffiti. . . .

Before trial, Foxhoven and Sanderson each moved to exclude any evidence of prior bad acts under ER 404(b). Foxhoven specifically objected to the admission of (1) his criminal history of graffiti from California and (2) photographs seized from Foxhoven's home that depicted graffiti involving the "SERIES" tag. Sanderson objected to the admission of (1) his prior arrests for graffiti, (2) drawings of the "HYMN" tag seized from his home, (3) photos of him painting the "HYMN" tag, and (4) photos of graffiti involving the "HYMN" tag that were seized from his home. . . . In his order, the judge made the following findings of fact:

> The State alleges that each vandal had adopted a distinctive tag (pseudonym) and vandalized property with that unique tag again and again for years until it had become their vandalism identity. The State alleges that part of the overarching scheme or plan of such vandals is to gain notoriety in the graffiti subculture by placing their adopted vandal names on the property of others. . . .
> The "probative value" of evidence tending to show that each defendant is committed to a culture that explicitly encourages vandalism and that each defendant marks his crime with his unique signature is extremely high. . . .
> There is no "unfair prejudice." The other acts for which evidence will be admitted are not marginally related or emotionally inflammatory. . . .

The challenged evidence was admitted in trial, with [a] limiting jury instruction, . . . Foxhoven was found guilty of 4 counts of first degree malicious mischief and 11 counts of second degree malicious mischief; Sanderson was found guilty of 2 counts of first degree malicious mischief and 5 counts of second degree malicious mischief. . . .

The petitioners appealed separately to Division One of the Court of Appeals, each claiming primarily that the evidence described above was improperly admitted under ER 404(b). The Court of Appeals . . . affirmed the trial court. . . .

ER 404(b) prohibits a court from admitting "[e]vidence of other crimes, wrongs, or acts . . . to prove the character of a person in order to show action in conformity therewith." This prohibition encompasses not only prior bad acts and unpopular behavior but *any* evidence offered to "show the character of a person to prove the person acted in conformity" with that character at the time of a crime. The State is incorrect when it asserts that the drawings of tags and most of the photographs fall outside the scope of ER 404(b) because they do not show criminal conduct or bad acts. In our judgment, all of the evidence at issue here is prohibited by ER 404(b) if offered to prove character.

ER 404(b) evidence, may, however, be admissible for another purpose, such as proof of motive, plan, or identity. ER 404(b) is not designed "to deprive the State of relevant evidence necessary to establish an essential element of its case," but rather to prevent the State from suggesting that a defendant is guilty because he or she is a criminal-type person who would be likely to commit the crime charged. In this case, the challenged evidence was offered and admitted "to show a 'common scheme or plan' or to establish [identity via] a particular 'modus operandi.'"

Before admitting ER 404(b) evidence, a trial court "must (1) find by a preponderance of the evidence that the misconduct occurred, (2) identify the purpose for which the evidence is sought to be introduced, (3) determine whether the evidence is relevant to prove an element of the crime charged, and (4) weigh the probative value against the prejudicial effect." . . .

Petitioners are challenging the third requirement: relevance. . . .

This court has previously held: When evidence of other bad acts is introduced to show identity by establishing a unique modus operandi, the evidence is relevant to the current charge "only if the method employed in the commission of both crimes is 'so unique' that proof that an accused committed one of the crimes creates a high probability that he also committed the other crimes with which he is charged." A prior act "is not admissible for this purpose merely because it is similar, but only if it bears such a high degree of similarity as to mark it as the handiwork of the accused." *State v. Coe*, 101 Wn. 2d 772, 777, 684 P.2d 668 (1984). The modus operandi "'must be so unusual and distinctive as to be like a signature.'" *Coe*, 101 Wn. 2d at 777 (quoting Edward W. Cleary, *McCormick's Handbook of the Law of Evidence* §190, at 449 (2d ed. 1972)). The more distinctive the defendant's prior acts, "the higher the probability that the defendant committed the crime, and thus the greater the relevance." When there are few or no dissimilarities between prior acts and the crime charged, this adds to the strength of the similarities.

Petitioners argue that their prior tagging was too dissimilar from the vandalism in this case to constitute a modus operandi. Indeed, the evidence depicting prior tagging by petitioners involved different mediums on a wide variety of buildings, vehicles, and papers, and showed the use of various styles and fonts. Although some of the graffiti was very similar, virtually the only consistency throughout the tagging evidence was the use of the particular tags "HYMN" and "SERIES."

However, there is a great deal of evidence in this case showing that tags are not mere words; they are akin to signatures. Officer Don Almer, who investigates most of the graffiti in Bellingham, testified that the graffiti world is its own subculture, "a social network and framework that has its own norms, its own . . . societal kind of operations." Within that subculture, a tag is a person's identity. Officer Almer explained:

> Basically a tag is a fingerprint. . . . [A] graffiti vandal [is] not going to use [his or her] real name . . . just because of the negative connotation associated with tagging and the likelihood of facing arrest or imprisonment or incarceration, things like that.
>
> . . . [W]hat they do is come up with an identity, a moniker. What they do is they pick a word that . . . they like that has some specific meaning to them. . . . But they pick something that is their identity. They assume this identity. . . .

Detective Rodney Hardin, a Seattle Police Department detective assigned to the graffiti unit, testified that, in his experience, taggers do not take on another's identity by stealing or "biting" their tag. Officer Almer agreed and testified that petitioner Sanderson had told him, "You don't do that. People will throw down with you if that happens." . . .

Given this evidence, we agree with the Court of Appeals that the trial court did not abuse its discretion in admitting the challenged ER 404(b) evidence. The fact that there were differences in font, style, medium, and canvas used for the graffiti goes to the *weight* that the jury should attach to the evidence of the prior acts; they do not render the evidence inadmissible. The degree of similarity petitioners would require is necessary only when a criminal has not signed his or her name. In those cases, we look at all the circumstances of a crime and the perpetrator's acts to try to distinguish a type of signature. Here, the equivalent of a signature was in fact provided: a tag. Where a signature is provided, the signature alone is sufficiently distinctive to be admissible under the modus operandi exception to ER 404(b)....

We conclude that the trial court did not abuse its discretion in admitting this evidence.... In sum, if a tag like the "mark of Zorro"[3] is left at the crime scene and there is evidence that the person charged with the crime made that mark at other crime scenes, it is admissible. Accordingly, we affirm the Court of Appeals' decision upholding petitioners' convictions.

NOTES TO STATE v. FOXHOVEN

1. *Relevance of Past Acts.* In cases involving the use of character-type evidence for a noncharacter purpose, it's very important to identify the rationale claimed to support admission. The prosecutor here sought to introduce evidence about past vandalism. That evidence could support a conclusion that the defendant had various bad character traits, such as low respect for property. The claimed relevance here, though, involved something different from proving bad character. The prosecution claimed that the past acts "prove modus operandi in order to corroborate or establish the identity of the persons responsible for the graffiti vandalism."

2. *Noncharacter Use of Evidence That Could Show Character.* If a person charged with a crime is known to have used a distinctive "signature" while committing past crimes, such as the "mark of Zorro" or the tag "SERIES," and the new crime was committed by someone who used the mark of Zorro or SERIES at the crime scene, Rule 404(b)(2) allows evidence of the past crimes to be admitted. The theory is that the evidence can support a finding about the identity of the wrongdoer in the new crime without requiring the jury to draw any conclusions about the defendant's character. The jury can use the information about the old crimes just to conclude that the defendant is a person who commits crimes and uses a distinctive mark while doing that. Linking the defendant to a new crime that uses the mark is based on thinking about the mark, not on thinking about the actor's personality traits.

---

3. The Oregon Supreme Court has noted, "A classic example to illustrate the concept of *modus operandi* having a signature quality is the 'mark of Zorro.'" *State v. Pinnell*, 311 Or. 98, 806 P.2d 110, 118 n.18 (1991).

3. *Did the Past Acts Actually Happen?* Proof that the past acts really happened was very clear in *Foxhoven*. In cases where there might be doubt about the occurrence of past acts, admission can be based on evidence that could support a jury conclusion that the acts did take place. This is true even in a criminal case where the prosecution is required to prove its overall case by a beyond-a-reasonable-doubt standard.

4. *Comparing Character and Noncharacter Uses of Evidence.* The following chart shows some differences between character and noncharacter uses of evidence. Suppose a defendant is accused of robbing a bank using a sophisticated electronic device to avoid detection. Suppose also that the defendant was once convicted of robbing a convenience store. The left-hand column illustrates a forbidden use of the convenience store information. That information could support a conclusion about guilt of the bank robbery only if the jury reasoned in the way that the left-hand column shows.

But if the defendant had once been convicted of robbing a store using a sophisticated electronic device, the right-hand column shows that a jury could

Forbidden Use of Character Evidence	Allowed Use of Evidence that Could Support a Finding about Character
Information showing defendant once robbed a convenience store.	Information showing defendant once robbed a convenience store using a sophisticated electronic device to avoid detection.
Belief that defendant is disrespectful of property and legal rules.	Belief that defendant knows how to use a sophisticated electronic device to avoid detection.
Conclusion that defendant committed a bank robbery using a sophisticated electronic device to avoid detection.	Conclusion that defendant committed a bank robbery using a sophisticated electronic device to avoid detection.
	Belief that defendant is disrespectful of property and legal rules.

reason from that information to a belief about guilt of the bank robbery *without* thinking about the defendant's character in general. Having knowledge about an unusual subject is different from having a character trait (since character traits are general aspects of personality, such as disrespect for property or propensity for violence or greediness).

The last box in the right-hand column acknowledges that the jury might *also* conclude that the defendant has a certain character trait (disrespectful of property), but the jury would not need to reach that conclusion in order to link the information about the defendant's past to a conclusion about the defendant's connection to the charged bank robbery.

Segment 3: testimony showing past conduct similar to charged conduct

QUESTION 3-5. Late one night outside a bar in a neighborhood with a high crime rate, Frank First left the bar and was accosted by a man and a woman. They told First that the man had a gun. The woman grabbed First's wallet, took all the money out of it, and gave the wallet back. The man and woman then ran away. Robert Robber was convicted of this crime.

Two years later, late one night outside the same bar, Sam Second was accosted by a man and a woman. They said that the woman had a gun. The man snatched Second's wallet, took all the money out of it, and gave the wallet back. The man and woman then ran away.

If Robert Robber is charged with robbing Second, should the trial court admit evidence showing that Robber robbed First?

Can Past Conduct with a Particular Purpose Prove an Actor's Intent in Later Similar Circumstances?—**Queen.** Intent is almost always proved by circumstantial evidence. Sometimes when there is ambiguity about a person's intent on a particular occasion, evidence will be admitted about the person's intent on similar past occasions. *Queen* considers how much similarity should be required when this theory is used to avoid the general antipropensity exclusionary rule. The case explains various rationales for the antipropensity rule and considers how they affect use of past acts for the purpose of showing intent.

UNITED STATES v. QUEEN
132 F.3d 991 (4th Cir. 1997)

NIEMEYER, Circuit Judge.

The primary issue raised in this appeal is whether evidence of the defendant's prior acts of witness tampering were properly admitted under Federal Rule of Evidence 404(b) to prove the element of intent in a later prosecution for a separate act of witness tampering. . . .

[Queen's] indictment alleged that during the period from February 1994 to March 1995 Queen had illegally attempted to dissuade a witness named Feronica Isaacs from testifying in the drug trafficking trial of Stephen Hester and others.

Before trial, the government notified Queen that it intended to introduce evidence at trial indicating that Queen had tampered with witnesses in 1986. In response, Queen filed a motion in limine to exclude that evidence under Federal Rules of Evidence 404(b) and 403. At a pretrial hearing on the motion, the government presented two witnesses whom it intended to have testify to the 1986 conduct. According to one witness, before Queen's 1986 trial for armed robbery, Queen threatened to shoot him if he testified against Queen at trial, and according to the other, before the same trial Queen had threatened to "deal with" him for his role in alerting the authorities to Queen's involvement in the armed robbery. The district court denied the motion in limine. . . .

At trial, in addition to introducing evidence of Queen's prior acts of witness tampering, the government introduced evidence of a conspiracy between Queen and Hester to tamper with witnesses before and during Hester's trial. . . . In instructing the jury, the district court told the jury not to consider Queen's prior acts evidence for any purpose other than to infer intent as to the charged crime.

The jury returned a verdict of guilty on both counts charged, and the court sentenced Queen to 174 months imprisonment. . . .

As his principal argument on appeal, Queen contends that the district court abused its discretion in admitting the evidence that he had twice intimidated witnesses before his 1986 armed robbery trial. . . .

Because [Rule 404(b)] recognizes the admissibility of prior crimes, wrongs, or acts, with only the one stated exception, it is understood to be a rule of inclusion, authorizing evidence of prior acts for purposes other than character, such as "motive, opportunity, intent, preparation, plan, knowledge, identity, or absence of mistake or accident." Fed. R. Evid. 404(b).[3] . . .

The principal danger that Rule 404(b) targets is addressed by the language of the rule itself—that defendants not be convicted simply for possessing bad character. This danger is compounded by the idea that juries might face defendants whom the government has brought forth merely because it has "rounded up the usual suspects" who have a history of prior bad acts.

---

3. Indeed, this circuit has found prior act evidence admissible for a wide range of reasons unrelated to character. See, e.g., United States v. Sanchez, 118 F.3d 192, 195 (4th Cir. 1997) (holding prior drug deals admissible to prove knowledge of the drug trade); Aramony, 88 F.3d at 1378 (holding evidence of defendant's previous sexual advances towards women admissible to show motive in fraudulent scheme to use company funds for personal relationships); United States v. Ford, 88 F.3d 1350, 1362 (4th Cir.), cert. denied, 136 L. Ed. 2d 388, 117 S. Ct. 496 (1996) (holding prior arrest in connection with an undercover drug buy admissible to show intent to distribute narcotics); United States v. Hayden, 85 F.3d 153, 159 (4th Cir. 1996) (holding evidence of prior witness intimidation admissible to show criminal intent and guilty conscience); United States v. Morsley, 64 F.3d 907, 911-912 (4th Cir. 1995) (holding prior act testimony admissible to establish the identity behind an alias); United States v. Tanner, 61 F.3d 231, 237 (4th Cir. 1995) (holding prior acts of illegal drug distribution admissible to show modus operandi, knowledge, and absence of mistake); United States v. Boyd, 53 F.3d 631, 636-37 (4th Cir. 1995) (holding evidence of prior drug use admissible to show motive and the nature of the defendant's relationship with co-conspirators); United States v. Bengali, 11 F.3d 1207, 1213 (4th Cir. 1993) (admitting testimony of defendant's prior extortionate acts to show motive, intent, and plan); Russell, 971 F.2d at 1106-07 (holding evidence of defendant's extramarital affairs and discharge from the Marine Corps admissible to show motive in the murder of defendant's wife).

There are two other dangers that Rule 404(b) addresses. First, it protects against juries trying defendants for prior acts rather than charged acts, and guards against juries becoming confused by the purpose of the admitted acts and using the acts improperly in arriving at a verdict. And second, it protects against the "trial by ambush" that would occur if one were confronted at trial not only with acts alleged in the indictment but also with prior acts from the span of one's entire lifetime. Such a trial would be nearly impossible to prepare for effectively. . . .

Even though Rule 404(b) recognizes the existence of these dangers and seeks to minimize their risk, it also recognizes that "extrinsic acts evidence may be critical to the establishment of the truth as to a disputed issue, especially when that issue involves the actor's state of mind and the only means of ascertaining that mental state is by drawing inferences from conduct." Huddleston v. United States, 485 U.S. 681, 685, 99 L. Ed. 2d 771, 108 S. Ct. 1496 (1988). Once an act is assumed to be done, "the prior doing of other similar acts . . . is useful as reducing the possibility that the act in question was done with innocent intent. The argument is based purely on the doctrine of chances, and it is the mere repetition of instances . . . that satisfies our logical demand." Wigmore on Evidence, §302, at 245 (Chadbourn rev. 1979) (footnote omitted). But in order for repeated actions to have probative value, the earlier actions must be similar in nature to the charged acts. This similarity may be demonstrated through physical similarity of the acts or through the "defendant's indulging himself in the same state of mind in the perpetration of both the extrinsic offense and charged offenses." United States v. Beechum, 582 F.2d 898, 911 (5th Cir. 1978). The more similar the extrinsic act or state of mind is to the act involved in committing the charged offense, the more relevance it acquires toward proving the element of intent. Furthermore, when only a defendant's similar acts are introduced, the concern that a defendant is being tried merely for having a bad character is somewhat allayed. The similarity of the acts not only provides a logical nexus between the extrinsic act and the charged act, but also provides a cognizable divide between the kinds of evidence that are introduced to show a particular intent and those that are introduced only to show a much more generalized intent (and therefore propensity to commit crime in general).

Thus, when the mental state of a defendant is at issue, similar acts that do not strongly implicate the dangers that Rule 404(b) was designed to protect against may be admitted as evidence relevant to and probative of intent. For example, in cases where identity is not at issue, the fear that the defendant is on trial for being a "usual suspect" diminishes. In cases where the trial judge has given a limiting instruction on the use of Rule 404(b), the fear that the jury may improperly use the evidence subsides. . . .

These observations about the purposes of Rule 404(b) suggest further qualifications to [a test we have articulated in the past]. Thus, we hold that evidence of prior acts becomes admissible under Rules 404(b) and 403 if it meets the following criteria: (1) The evidence must be relevant to an issue, such as an element of an offense, and must not be offered to establish the general character of the defendant. In this regard, the more similar the prior act is (in terms of physical similarity or mental state) to the act being proved, the more relevant it becomes. (2) The act must be necessary in the sense that it is probative of an essential claim or an element of the offense. (3) The evidence must be reliable. And (4) the evidence's probative value must not be substantially outweighed by confusion or unfair prejudice in the sense that it tends to subordinate reason to emotion in the factfinding process....

Turning now to the case before us, the evidence of Queen's prior acts in witness tampering was specifically offered to prove the intent element essential to proving witness tampering under 18 U.S.C. §1512(b)(1); it was not offered to prove Queen's character as a bad actor or a criminal. Indeed, the high degree of similarity between the prior acts and the act with which Queen was charged supports the finding that the acts were relevant to intent. Moreover, the district court wisely instructed the jury that it could only consider the prior-act evidence to infer the element of intent. Because we believe that the jury could reasonably have taken the similar prior acts as evidence tending to make it less probable that Queen's intent in visiting Isaacs was for an innocent purpose, the evidence was relevant....

Having affirmed, therefore, that the prior act testimony was relevant, we move on to consider whether the district court properly determined that the evidence met the other prongs of our four-part test, that is, whether it was necessary, reliable, and properly balanced under Rule 403.

Evidence is necessary where, considered in the "light of other evidence available to the government," United States v. DiZenzo, 500 F.2d 263, 266 (4th Cir. 1974), it is an "essential part of the crimes on trial, or where it furnishes part of the context of the crime." United States v. Mark, 943 F.2d 444, 448 (4th Cir. 1991) (internal citation and quotation marks omitted). In this case, the government presented the prior-act evidence in order to prove intent, which is an essential element of the crime charged. Because the government's case for intent rested solely on the testimony of Isaacs and one other witness, the similar prior-act evidence was important in making the case that Queen possessed the requisite intent to tamper with witnesses. The evidence was, therefore, "necessary."

There was also sufficient evidence that the witnesses testifying to the prior acts were reliable. Both were cross-examined prior to trial and both had testified to Queen's threats against them before the earlier trial. Queen argues that the witnesses' reliability was damaged because the two witnesses were testifying pursuant to agreements for favorable treatment in their cases. We have noted, however, that while a defendant may always impugn witnesses' credibility on the basis of bias, "there is the countervailing consideration that self-exposure to a perjury charge is unlikely. The plea bargainer's position frequently makes him extremely reluctant to commit another crime or crimes and thus lay himself open to greater punishment." United States v. Hadaway, 681 F.2d 214, 218 (4th Cir. 1982).

Finally, in weighing the evidence under Rule 403, the district court concluded that while it was prejudicial, it was only prejudicial because it was so highly probative. There is no suggestion that the prior testimony would invoke emotion in place of reason as a decisionmaking mechanism. . . .

For the foregoing reasons, we conclude that the district court properly applied both Rule 404(b) and Rule 403 and did not abuse its discretion in admitting the evidence of Queen's prior acts.

[Affirmed.]

NOTES TO UNITED STATES v. QUEEN

1. *Significance of Similarity Between Past Act and Charged Act.* The court states that if the defendant's past conduct is similar to the charged conduct, that decreases the risk that a jury would use the past conduct merely to reach a conclusion about the person's character, and increases the likelihood that the past conduct does actually show what the person's intent was on the occasion of the charged crime. Might the similarity between the past conduct and the charged conduct lead the jury to conclude something like "once a witness tamperer, always a witness tamperer"?

2. *Past Unlawful Acts Not Resulting in Conviction.* Where a person's past conduct has not resulted in conviction of a crime, how should that affect a trial court's decision on whether to admit information about that conduct? The 1986 tampering in *Queen* apparently was never the subject of a conviction. Note that the court recognized possible flaws in the testimony that sought to establish that prior tampering, but held that it provided an adequate basis for concluding that it had, in fact, occurred.

GOOD TO REMEMBER

The list of situations in FRE 404(b)(2) when evidence that could support a finding about character is nevertheless admissible is just a list of examples. They share the attribute that in each situation a jury could use information about the defendant to evaluate the defendant's guilt *without using it to decide anything about the defendant's character or personality.*

3. *Additional Consequences from Admission of "Intent" Evidence.* The defendant in *Queen* offered to stipulate that *if* the jury found that he had had conversations with Feronica Isaacs, he had done so with the intent to commit witness tampering. The prosecution declined to accept that stipulation and therefore offered its proof of intent. The jury was instructed to use the evidence of the other acts only on the issue of intent. That instruction is the only control our system uses to prevent the jury from using information about other acts, admitted to show intent, for purposes additional to considering intent. There is no way to know if the jury used the past acts as part of its consideration of whether the defendant actually had had conversations with Isaacs.

Discretion in Deciding Whether Past Conduct Can Show Relevant Knowledge in Addition to Character Traits — **Winebarger.** This case may illustrate the attractiveness of evidence of past acts to some trial judges and, consequently, to appellate courts as well. The defendant shot and killed his son-in-law and claimed it was an accident. But he had a history of being a truculent person who brandished firearms when he was angry. How might that history relate to whether he shot the victim on purpose or accidentally?

STATE v. WINEBARGER

617 S.E.2d 467 (W. Va. 2005)

PER CURIAM.

This is an appeal by Dewey Daniel Winebarger (hereinafter "Appellant") from a jury determination in the Circuit Court of McDowell County finding the Appellant guilty of voluntary manslaughter of his son-in-law, Mr. Kenny Price (hereinafter "decedent" or "Mr. Price"). On appeal, the Appellant contends that the lower court erred in admitting certain testimony concerning allegations of the Appellant's prior utilization of weapons. Upon thorough review of the arguments, briefs, record, and applicable precedent, this Court affirms the determinations of the lower court.

The Appellant and his wife, Regina, own several small businesses in McDowell County, West Virginia, including a service station, rental property, and a bar and grill. For personal protection when transporting monetary deposits or traveling on rural roads, the Appellant occasionally carried a handgun. On the evening of December 23, 2001, the Appellant and his wife had loaned automobiles to their daughter and her husband, the decedent Mr. Price. The Appellant had previously instructed that the vehicles were not to be taken to a particular location known as Joe's Bar. While driving home that evening from a Christmas party in Bluefield, West Virginia, the Appellant and his wife noticed that their vehicles were parked outside Joe's Bar. They took the cars home, leaving their daughter and son-in-law to find other transportation back to their own home.

When Mr. Price left the bar and obtained transportation, he stopped at the Appellant's home, and an argument ensued between the Appellant and Mr. Price regarding the utilization of the Appellant's vehicles. The Appellant maintained that Mr. Price was intoxicated and became violent and aggressive during the altercation. The Appellant contends that he attempted to use his .22 caliber derringer to fire a warning shot into the air. The bullet struck Mr. Price in the neck and fatally wounded him.

The Appellant was indicted for first degree murder and was ultimately found guilty of voluntary manslaughter and sentenced to ten years. Although the Appellant's petition for appeal to this Court contained multiple assignments of error, this Court accepted this appeal on only two grounds, both dealing specifically with the introduction of Rule 404(b) evidence against the Appellant.....

The Appellant contends that the lower court erred by permitting the State to introduce evidence that the Appellant had brandished a weapon on other occasions five to fifteen years prior to the date in question. The State maintained that such evidence was introduced to show "the defendant's experience in carrying, handling and brandishing handguns that he used in arguments to gain the upper hand and have his way. This evidence tends to show the absence of mistake or accident...."

In response to the Appellant's contentions, the State maintains that the Appellant alleged that the incident in which his son-in-law was killed was essentially an accident and that evidence of prior acquaintance with the use of firearms was therefore appropriate. Furthermore, the State emphasizes that the lower court properly required the State to provide a detailed written notice of its intention to utilize Rule 404(b) evidence and the specific purposes for which the evidence would be offered. The lower court ... ruled that the State could use evidence of three of the five incidents initially offered by the State as tending to prove the absence of mistake or accident and intent. The lower court also provided the jury with an appropriate limiting instruction on two separate occasions.

This Court has provided considerable guidance regarding the method of determination of the issue of admissibility of Rule 404(b) evidence. In [State v. McGinnis, 193 W. Va. 147, 455 S.E.2d 516 (1994)], this Court specifically outlined the prerequisites to admission of Rule 404(b) evidence....

Syllabus point one of *McGinnis* addresses the usage of the offered evidence and provides as follows:

> When offering evidence under Rule 404(b) of the West Virginia Rules of Evidence, the prosecution is required to identify the specific purpose for which the evidence is being offered and the jury must be instructed to limit its consideration of the evidence to only that purpose. It is not sufficient for the prosecution or the trial court merely to cite or mention the litany of possible uses listed in Rule 404(b). The specific and precise purpose for which the evidence is offered must clearly be shown from the record and that purpose alone must be told to the jury in the trial court's instruction.

In evaluating issues of admissibility of evidence, this Court has also consistently emphasized the extent of discretion vested in the trial court....

[W]e find that the lower court performed a rigorous and diligent in camera evaluation of the evidence offered by the State and correctly determined that the events actually occurred. The lower court dismissed the jury, explaining that certain matters required attention outside the presence of the jury, and proceeded to hear the testimony of Mr. Blevins, Mr. Rhodes, and Mr. Hunley [who allegedly were involved in past gun-related misconduct by the defendant]. Mr. Blevins explained that he, Mr. Rhodes, and the Appellant's son, Jonathan Winebarger, were arguing outside a bar in a parking lot. While Mr. Blevins did not recall the reason for the argument, he did distinctly recall that the Appellant pointed a handgun at him and told him "to get down the road...." Mr. Blevins

also indicated that the Appellant had brandished a gun during another altercation in a bar-related disagreement. Mr. Rhodes also testified about the incidents which Mr. Blevins described. The Appellant's son, Jonathan Winebarger,
also corroborated the incidents at the bail hearing and the McGinnis hearing.
Mr. Hunley testified that the Appellant had pulled a handgun partially out of his
pocket and threatened him with it when Mr. Hunley was involved in an altercation with Jonathan Winebarger outside the Winebargers' tavern.

Further, the lower court correctly found that the evidence was admissible
for a legitimate purpose, to demonstrate the Appellant's intent and the absence
of accident or mistake, and thereafter adequately instructed the jury regarding
those limited purposes. The lower court instructed the jury as follows:

> Ladies and Gentlemen of the Jury, before you hear testimony from this witness,
> I need to give you a cautionary instruction.
>
> The State of West Virginia is now going to present evidence of other crimes or
> wrongs or acts, and you are instructed that these other crimes, wrongs or acts are
> not admissible to prove the character of a person in order to show that he acted in
> conformity therewith; however, the evidence you are about to hear is used for the
> purpose of showing absence of mistake or accident and, also, to show intent.

The law of this state is also quite clear on the issue of remoteness of Rule
404(b) evidence. . . . This Court has explained that the issue of remoteness goes
to the weight to be given to such evidence and does not necessarily render it
inadmissible. . . .

Based upon the foregoing, we find no abuse of discretion in the lower court's
decision to admit the Rule 404(b) evidence in question. While this Court is hesi-
tant to give blanket approval to the admission of Rule 404(b) evidence occurring
fifteen years prior to the charged incident in all cases, the circumstances of this
case are such that admission was warranted. The evidence admitted in this case
involved substantially similar conduct, similar circumstances, and similar prov-
ocations to the offense charged. Reviewing the evidence in a light most favorable to the party offering the evidence, as required by *McGinnis*, we affirm the
decision of the lower court that such evidence was not too remote to be properly
utilized by the State.

Acknowledging the extensive discretion vested in the trial court, we find no
abuse of discretion in the lower court's finding that the probative value of the
Rule 404(b) evidence regarding the Appellant's prior threatening use of firearms
was not substantially outweighed by the danger of unfair prejudice. . . .

Some degree of prejudice is inherent in Rule 404(b) evidence and cannot be
completely eliminated. Rule 403 addresses a situation in which the probative
value of the evidence is substantially outweighed by the danger of unfair prejudice. The Fifth Circuit Court of Appeals explained this concept as follows in
Ballou v. Henri Studios, Inc., 656 F.2d 1147 (5th Cir. 1981):

> As this court has consistently held, "'unfair prejudice' as used in Rule 403 is not
> to be equated with testimony simply adverse to the opposing party. Virtually all

evidence is prejudicial or it isn't material. The prejudice must be 'unfair.'" Dollar v. Long Manufacturing, N.C., Inc., 561 F.2d 613, 618 (5th Cir. 1977), cert. denied, 435 U.S. 996, 98 S. Ct. 1648, 56 L. Ed. 2d 85 (1978). Unfair prejudice within the context of Rule 403 "means an undue tendency to suggest [a] decision on an improper basis, commonly, though not necessarily, an emotional one." Notes of the Advisory Committee on Proposed Federal Rules of Evidence, 28 U.S.C.A. Rule 403 at 102.

. . . Having thoroughly reviewed arguments of counsel, briefs, the record, applicable rules, and applicable precedent, we affirm the lower court in all respects.

NOTES TO STATE v. WINEBARGER

1. *Specificity of Rationale.* Admission of the controversial evidence was affirmed on the ground that it could properly show "intent and absence of accident or mistake." According to the court, the defendant's case rested on a claim that he attempted to use his gun to fire a warning shot into the air. Does evidence that the defendant had in the past brandished a weapon in arguments without shooting it support a conclusion that this shooting was likely intentional?

2. *Deferential Appellate Review.* Various factors might weaken the probative value of the past acts in *Winebarger*: They had never been adjudicated prior to this case, and they had taken place a long time before the charged crime. Also, none of the past acts had involved a shooting. This increased the risk that jurors might use information about them to establish the defendant's character rather than something more specific. Nonetheless, the appellate court deferred to the trial court's "extensive discretion" in affirming its action.

3. *Past Acts for Which a Person Was Tried and Acquitted.* In Dowling v. United States, 493 U.S. 342 (1990), the Supreme Court held that it is constitutionally acceptable to admit evidence of a prior act to show a common plan or intent, even if the defendant was acquitted of the criminal charges arising out of the prior act. It held that this does not violate due process or subject the defendant to double jeopardy.

■   ■   ■

Past Acts That Are "Part" of Charged Acts—Leyva. The list of allowable purposes for other acts evidence in Rule 404(b)(2) is illustrative, not exhaustive. ("This evidence may be admissible for another purpose, such as proving motive, opportunity, intent, preparation, plan, knowledge, identity, absence of mistake, or lack of accident"). *Leyva* shows courts' willingness to admit evidence of uncharged misconduct when it is "part and parcel" of the actions of a defendant that have a clear relationship to a charged crime.

LEYVA v. STATE

165 P.3d 446 (Wyo. 2007)

BURKE, J.

Mr. Leyva appeals his conviction on two felony counts, one for burglary and one for third offense illegal possession of a controlled substance. We affirm....

On September 8, 2005, Rawlins police received a phone call from Kelly King, who reported that a television set had been taken from his apartment. When officers arrived at the apartment complex, they observed a parked vehicle with a television set in the front passenger seat. At the officers' request, Mr. King's son identified the television as the one taken from his father's apartment. Soon thereafter, the officers saw two individuals getting into the vehicle. The individuals turned out to be Erin Setright, who owned the vehicle, and Mr. Leyva. Ms. Setright told the officers that Mr. Leyva had the television set with him when he asked her for a ride.

The officers detained Mr. Leyva on suspicion of stealing the television set. Then, after learning of an outstanding warrant, they placed Mr. Leyva under arrest. Their pat down search of Mr. Leyva revealed, among other items, a knife, a brass pipe with marijuana residue, and a plastic bag containing a minimal amount of methamphetamine residue. Mr. Leyva told the police that he had borrowed the television set from Mr. King. He also claimed that he had borrowed the pants he was wearing from Mr. King. The brass pipe was not his, he said, and must have been in the pocket when he borrowed the pants that morning. The knife was his, he admitted, but with the inconsistent explanation that he had put the knife in the pocket of the pants the night before.

Mr. Leyva was charged with two felony counts, one for burglary involving the television set, and one for possession of a controlled substance (methamphetamine), third offense....

During the trial, Mr. Leyva objected to the State's evidence that he was in possession of a brass pipe containing marijuana residue at the time of his arrest. The district court admitted the evidence. The jury subsequently returned a verdict of guilty on both charges.... Mr. Leyva filed this timely appeal....

When Mr. Leyva was arrested, he was in possession of a brass pipe containing marijuana residue. This evidence, he says, was introduced by the State for the sole purpose of proving that he had the character to possess drugs, and to show that he acted in conformity with that character. He contends that this evidence was inadmissible under W.R.E. 404(b)....

We agree with Mr. Leyva that evidence that he was in possession of a brass pipe containing marijuana residue is evidence of "other crimes, wrongs, or acts" under W.R.E. 404(b). Those terms are not defined in the rules, but we have previously said that "wrongs" include "any sort of conduct that is likely to reflect adversely on the person in the eyes of the jury," and "other acts" include "any conduct, good or bad, that tends to show the character of the person involved." When the crime charged is illegal possession of methamphetamine, evidence that the defendant was also in possession of marijuana is exactly the kind of uncharged misconduct evidence to which W.R.E. 404(b) is meant to apply. Such evidence tends to show the character of the accused, increases the likelihood that the jury will render a guilty verdict on an improper basis, and should not be admitted unless the requirements of W.R.E. 404(b) are met.

The State maintains that the evidence was not subject to W.R.E. 404(b) because it was "part and parcel" of the events surrounding and following Mr. Leyva's arrest. Mr. Leyva told the police officers that he had borrowed the television set and the pants from Mr. King. Explaining the items in the pockets of the pants, Mr. Leyva gave inconsistent accounts of when he had borrowed the pants, saying he had put the knife in the pocket the evening before, but that the pipe must have been in the pocket when he borrowed the pants that morning. These inconsistent statements cast doubt on Mr. Leyva's veracity, in the State's view, and made it more likely that he had stolen the television, as the State asserted, and less likely that he had borrowed it from Mr. King, as Mr. Leyva had told the police. The State said it would be difficult or impossible to relate the inconsistent statements to the jury without reference to the knife and the pipe, because the inconsistent statements were made about those very items. Evidence of the knife and the pipe was admissible, the State asserted, because it was necessary to "give the jury the whole story and enhance the natural development of the facts of the case."

While the State uses the term "part and parcel" of the crimes charged, this Court has more often termed evidence of this type "intrinsic" evidence. We have said that evidence of other crimes, wrongs, or acts is intrinsic when it "and the evidence of the crime charged are inextricably intertwined or both acts are part of a single criminal episode or the other acts were necessary preliminaries to the crime charged."

Intrinsic evidence is still subject to W.R.E. 404(b)... See ... Ross v. State, 930 P.2d 965, 969-70 (Wyo. 1996) (Evidence "which does not constitute a portion of [the] crimes charged but has a natural, necessary, or logical connection to the crime" must be analyzed for admissibility under W.R.E. 404(b).).

Evidence of "other crimes, wrongs, or acts," intrinsic or not, may improperly invite the jury to convict a defendant because of other misdeeds, not because of his guilt of the crime charged. Such evidence should be admitted only when it has some proper purpose, is relevant, and is more probative than prejudicial. As detailed in the discussion below, this is the result W.R.E. 404(b) is designed to accomplish. For that reason, placing intrinsic evidence beyond the reach of W.R.E. 404(b) would be "unwise and wrong."

Evidence that Mr. Leyva was in possession of a pipe with marijuana residue was analyzed by the district court ... under W.R.E. 404(b).

We have said that a district court must consider four criteria in applying W.R.E. 404(b) to uncharged misconduct evidence: (1) Is the evidence offered for a proper purpose? (2) Is the evidence relevant? (3) Is the probative value of the evidence substantially outweighed by its potential for unfair prejudice? (4) Upon request, should the jury be given a limiting instruction? No request for a limiting instruction was made, so we will review the district court's application of the first three criteria. If the district court applied these criteria and had a legitimate basis for its ruling, we will uphold the decision.

Evidence of other crimes, wrongs, or acts is admissible if it serves a proper purpose, and is excluded only if its sole purpose is to prove that a defendant has a disposition to commit crimes. W.R.E. 404(b) lists several purposes, other than proof of character, for which evidence may be admitted: proof of motive, opportunity, intent, preparation, plan, knowledge, identity, or absence of mistake or accident. The list of allowable purposes identified in W.R.E. 404(b) is exemplary, not exhaustive.

We have previously recognized that evidence of uncharged misconduct is admissible if it "forms part of the history of the event or serves to enhance the natural development of the facts." We have referred to this as the "course of conduct" purpose. Other jurisdictions applying this concept have called it the "same transaction" purpose or the "complete story" purpose.

The State asserted that the evidence at issue was intrinsic because it was needed to "give the jury the whole story and enhance the natural development of the facts of the case." While that does not mean the evidence was beyond the reach of W.R.E. 404(b), it does show that the State had a proper "course of conduct" or "complete story" purpose for admitting the evidence. In its ruling, the district court did not explicitly use the terms "course of conduct," but it plainly agreed with the State that the evidence was offered for that proper purpose. The record provides a legitimate basis for the district court's conclusion.

The district court expressly found that the evidence was relevant, and that the evidence was more probative than prejudicial. The State had emphasized the relevance and probative value of the evidence because it was part of Mr. Leyva's inconsistent stories about borrowing the pants, making it more likely that the television was stolen and less likely that it was borrowed. The district court agreed. As stated above, a trial court's rulings on the admissibility of evidence are entitled to considerable deference. The record reflects that the district court considered the required criteria, had legitimate bases for its conclusions, and did not abuse its discretion in admitting the evidence at trial. . . .

The district court did not abuse its discretion in admitting uncharged misconduct evidence. Rather, the district court properly analyzed the evidence under W.R.E. 404(b), had a legitimate basis for admitting the evidence, and under the circumstances, fulfilled the mandatory requirements for admitting evidence under W.R.E. 404(b). We affirm the district court's decisions in all respects.

NOTES TO LEYVA v. STATE

1. *Relevance of Inconsistent Statements to Police.* Telling a lie to a police officer may be similar to fleeing the scene of a crime as an indicator of a guilty conscience. In this case, the alleged lies involved a knife and a marijuana pipe. The state's theory for admission might require a jury to consider those lies only

with regard to their inconsistency with the truth, but jurors might be particularly influenced by the fact that they involved drug use in a case where drug possession was one of the charged crimes.

2. *Comparing Doctrinal Frameworks.* The *Leyva* court described a four-part doctrinal framework for considering other acts evidence. It stated that a trial court must consider whether the evidence:

- is offered for a proper purpose,
- is relevant,
- has potential for too much unfair prejudice, and
- should be accompanied by a limiting instruction.

In United States v. Queen, the Fourth Circuit used a different test, considering whether the evidence:

- is relevant other than to establish the general character of the defendant,
- is probative of an essential claim or an element of the offense,
- is reliable, and
- has potential for too much unfair prejudice.

The terms of these frameworks are not identical, but their overall effect might be similar. Would *Leyva* likely have been decided the same way if the *Queen* elements had been used for analysis?

■   ■   ■

Past Drug Sales as Context for Alleged Drug Sales — Willett. To show that the defendant possessed narcotics with intent to deliver them to others, the prosecution was allowed to introduce testimony showing she had sold drugs in the past. As is typical, admission of the evidence was affirmed on appeal. This elicited a concurring opinion expressing frustration with the consequences of modern evidence rules.

STATE v. WILLETT

674 S.E.2d 602 (W. Va. 2009)

PER CURIAM.

Gloria Jean Willett, defendant below and appellant herein (hereinafter referred to as "Mrs. Willett"), appeals from an order of the Circuit Court of Raleigh County denying her motion for a new trial. Mrs. Willett was sentenced to prison after being convicted by a jury on four counts of drug possession with intent to deliver. She was also convicted of one count of conspiracy to commit a felony. In this Court. Mrs. Willett assigns error to the trial court's ruling that permitted the jury to hear evidence of collateral crimes under Rule 404(b) of the West Virginia Rules of evidence. After a careful review of the briefs and the record submitted on appeal, and having listened to the oral arguments of the parties, we affirm. . . .

The sole issue presented for resolution is whether the circuit court properly admitted testimony presented by [Alan] Reed under Rule 404(b). . . . Mr. Reed's testimony involved prior criminal drug sales by Mrs. Willett. Insofar as Mrs. Willett was charged with possession of drugs with intent to deliver, Mr. Reed's testimony involved "other crimes" by Mrs. Willett. . . .

When looking at the evidence in its totality, we are satisfied that the trial court properly admitted Mr. Reed's testimony under Rule 404(b). Even though Mr. Reed was unable to give any specific dates regarding his drug transactions with Mrs. Willett, that matter is tempered by the fact that there was testimony by Mrs. Willett that her brother gave the police a statement that corroborated Mr. Reed's accusations against her. Consequently, we find no clear error in the trial court's determination that there was sufficient evidence to show that the other bad acts actually transpired. We further find that the trial court properly deemed the evidence admissible for a legitimate purpose under the Rule 404(b) analysis. It was used to demonstrate Mrs. Willett's motive, planning, and intent. . . .

Mr. Reed's testimony about the uncharged drug transactions was integrally connected to the criminal activity charged in the indictment. Evidence of the prior drug sales was necessary to place Mrs. Willett's possession of such a large amount of narcotic prescription pills in context and to complete the story of the charged crimes. . . .

The circuit court's order denying Mrs. Willett's motion for a new trial is affirmed.

KETCHUM, J., concurring:

I concur with the majority's opinion. Reading the record in the light most favorable to the prosecution, the trial judge did not abuse his discretion in allowing the jury to hear evidence of the defendant's uncharged "bad acts" admitted under Rule 404(b) of the West Virginia Rules of Evidence.

I feel compelled to write separately because I believe that the use of "bad acts" evidence under Rule 404(b) in criminal trials is now routinely used to convince the jury that they should convict the defendant because he or she is not a nice person.

Modification of Rule 404(b) Is Needed to Protect the Innocent. We all know the axiom that "[i]n the trial of a criminal offense, the presumption of innocence existing in favor of a defendant continues through every stage of the trial until a finding of guilty by the jury." Syllabus Point 11, State v. Pietranton, 140 W. Va. 444, 84 S.E.2d 774 (1954). But the real world truth is that, when a jury hears evidence that a defendant has committed some bad acts beyond those in the indictment, the jury dispenses with any notions that the defendant is innocent and reviews the evidence from the perspective that the defendant is a "bad person." It is undeniable that a jury will be more inclined to convict once they hear that a defendant may have engaged in other "bad acts" — even if the defendant was never charged or convicted for that other conduct. . . .

Rule 404(b) was originally designed to keep such fundamentally unfair evidence of uncharged misconduct away from the jury, allowing the jury to focus on the proper question: does the evidence show the defendant committed the crime with which he or she is currently charged? However, since I took the bench two months ago, "bad acts" evidence has been raised as an error in virtually every criminal appeal presented to our Court. It is obvious that prosecutors are using "bad acts" evidence to prejudice defendants and to divert jurors' attention from the evidence surrounding the charged crime. This abusive use of uncharged "bad acts" evidence by prosecutors will, in the future, lead to the conviction of an innocent person. Of this, I am convinced. I therefore propose a change to Rule 404(b) in criminal cases.

The Correct Rule: State v. Miller (1915). . . . As we said in Syllabus Point 2 of State v. Miller, 75 W. Va. 591, 84 S.E. 383 (1915):

> It is error to admit evidence, in such a case, tending to prove bad character or degradation on the part of the accused, over his objection and in the absence of evidence adduced by him to establish good character on his part. . . .

The Shift Away from the Correct Rule. When I first started practicing law in 1967, prosecutors rarely if ever tried to convict a defendant using evidence of "uncharged misconduct" and "other bad acts." Courts were exceptionally restrictive, and rarely allowed the use of collateral crimes to be admitted. The defendant was tried for the crime charged in the warrant or the indictment. The common-law rule of evidence on "other bad acts" in West Virginia was a clear rule of exclusion: the evidence could not be admitted, except for a few narrow exceptions.

It was axiomatic that when a person was placed on trial for the commission of a particular crime, if the person was going to be convicted, then the person was going to be convicted based upon evidence showing the person's guilt of the specific offense charged in the indictment. Nothing more, nothing less. . . .

The Academics Take Over. In 1975, Congress adopted the Federal Rules of Evidence. "The philosophy of the Federal Rules, and it qualifies as revolutionary, is that any relevant evidence, by which it is meant anything that gives promise of being helpful to the trier of facts, is admissible if it is not rendered incompetent, for policy-based reasons, by a dwindling number of exclusionary rules[.]" Jon R. Waltz, "Judicial Discretion in the Admission of Evidence Under the Federal Rules of Evidence," 79 N.W.U. L. Rev. 1097, 1120 (1984). . . .

With a few variations, this Court adopted most of the Federal Rules into the West Virginia Rules of Evidence in 1985.

Because of the potentially decisive impact of uncharged misconduct, and its countervailing prejudicial character, defense attorneys vigorously contest the use of uncharged misconduct evidence. Consequently, Rule 404(b) disputes are the most frequently litigated evidentiary issue in appellate courts. In an unscientific search of West Virginia cases, I found at least 78 published criminal cases in the last 20 years where the admission of other bad acts under W. Va. R.E. Rule 404(b) was disputed on appeal.

In many cases, I believe that Rule 404(b) is being applied inconsistently. It appears that prosecutors and trial courts often search for a convenient "pigeonhole" to admit proof of other bad acts, then perform a perfunctory balance of the probative value against its prejudicial effect before admitting the other bad acts evidence. [O]n appeal this Court has rarely found that the trial court abused its discretion in admitting the other bad acts evidence. If the Court does find the trial court abused its discretion, then this Court will often then hold that the admission of the other bad acts evidence in a criminal case was "harmless error."

An Equitable Solution. . . . . I realize that I will never convince our Court to revert back to the correct rule set out in State v. Miller, *supra*, in 1915. I therefore propose that Rule 404(b) be amended, either directly or through this Court's jurisprudence, to eliminate the "harmless error" safety net that prosecutors, trial courts, and this Court have relied upon to uphold convictions based upon the admission of uncharged misconduct. I am not advocating for the abrogation of the harmless error rule, only its elimination from our Rule 404(b) jurisprudence.

When a trial court has abused its discretion and admitted irrelevant or prejudicial bad acts evidence, I would hold that reversal and remand for a proper trial should be automatic, no matter how much evidence is otherwise presented. Removing Rule 404(b) errors from the protection of the harmless error rule would force prosecutors and trial judges to limit the evidence to relevant evidence pertaining to the specific charge in the indictment. It would force prosecutors and trial judges to make more careful, consistent and hopefully more equitable decisions about the admission of uncharged misconduct in criminal trials.

I otherwise respectfully concur with the majority's decision.

NOTES TO STATE v. WILLETT

1. *Volume of Appellate Litigation.* The concurrence notes that there have been many appellate decisions considering admission of past acts evidence. This may show that the law is vague and difficult to apply. Or it may reflect the fact that appeals are frequent in criminal cases and that asserting error on 404(b) issues is simple to do.

2. *Rules vs. Standards.* The concurrence seeks "more careful, consistent and hopefully more equitable" 404(b) decisions. Would making the consequence

of a wrong decision more drastic improve the quality of those decisions in general, or would it put pressure on judges to rule against the prosecution more often?

QUESTION 3-6. On September 27, 2011, Alan and Maggie Smallman were at a pool hall, drinking beer and playing pool. Brad Largeguy, Maggie's ex-husband, stopped in to chat with a friend. Alan Smallman and Largeguy had a history of animosity between them because Maggie had started dating Smallman while she was still married to Largeguy. Smallman approached Largeguy to ask him a question. Largeguy indicated he did not want to talk to Smallman. Later, Largeguy and Smallman got into an argument outside the pool hall. Largeguy claims he turned to leave and Smallman hit him in the back of the head. Largeguy hit Smallman three times, and Smallman called 911. Smallman sought medical treatment and was diagnosed with a sprained jaw, a minor concussion, and a probable broken nose.

Largeguy was charged with assault causing bodily injury. Witnesses are available who could testify to the following facts:

- In February 2004, Largeguy pushed Smallman outside a bar and told Smallman that the only thing keeping Largeguy from beating Smallman up was the fact that Largeguy is a lawyer and Smallman was not worth his license to practice law.
- In May 2004, at a country club golf course, Largeguy shook his fist at Smallman and said he would be waiting for him.
- In May 2004, Largeguy told a waiter at a restaurant that he should have thrown Smallman off the balcony the other day at the golf course.
- In the summer of 2004, Smallman was walking his dog in front of the old high school, and Largeguy pushed Smallman down and said some obscene things to him.
- In June of 2009, Largeguy approached Smallman while he and his son were sitting in his car in front of a store. Largeguy threatened Smallman, punched him, and then asked Smallman's son whether he was "going to grow up to be a jerk like his dad." In exchange for dropping an assault charge, Largeguy agreed to abide by a no-contact order for one year and to undergo an anger management evaluation.
- In February 2010, at a wrestling meet, Largeguy and Smallman were both in the concession lunch line, and Largeguy blew up at Smallman and cursed at him.
- In January 2011, Largeguy spit at Smallman outside of a high school and said to Smallman, "come on, let's do something."

How might the prosecution and Largeguy argue that any of these incidents should or should not be introduced into evidence, either to prove Largeguy's intent or to refute a claim by Largeguy that he had acted in self-defense?

F SUMMARY

Barring the Propensity Inference. Evidence law prohibits introduction of evidence about a person's character traits if it is sought to be introduced to support an inference that because the person has those traits the person likely acted in conformity with those traits at a particular time. Rule 404 incorporates this idea. *Boyd* and *John A. Russell Corp.* described reasons for rejecting this propensity inference and also introduced the idea that sometimes evidence that supports a finding about a person's character can be relevant in a way different from supporting a propensity inference.

Allowing the Propensity Inference. The propensity inference is associated with a number of dangers. It would invite a jury to draw conclusions on very vague information. It also carries the risk that negative information about a person, introduced to show the person's character, might be used by a jury just to conclude that the person is evil and deserves punishment regardless of the facts about the crime for which the defendant is charged. Despite these dangers, when a criminal defendant seeks to use the propensity inference, evidence law allows it under certain controls.

The Defendant's Propensity, Introduced by the Defendant. A criminal defendant may introduce evidence of his or her pertinent character traits to support an inference that because he or she has those traits he or she would not have committed a charged crime, as in *City of Kennewick*. When a defendant puts on character evidence, the prosecution is permitted to respond with character evidence about that same trait. *Gowan* deals with this prosecution prerogative, although it involves a question about what kind of evidence constitutes a defendant's opening the door to this kind of prosecution response.

A Victim's Propensity, Introduced by the Defendant. Also in line with the law's interest in offering criminal defendants substantial opportunities to respond to prosecution evidence, defendants are permitted to introduce evidence of the character traits of an alleged victim, as in *Adjutant*. This opportunity does *not* apply to character evidence related to sexual conduct, but it applies to the character trait of aggressiveness, usually when a defendant asserts the defense of self-defense. The prosecution may respond with (1) its own character evidence about the victim and, (2) under the Federal Rules, with character evidence about the defendant's possession of whatever trait the defendant has tried to prove that the victim possessed. *Taken Alive* highlighted this second prosecution response.

Style of Proof. When character evidence is allowed to support a propensity inference, the form must be evidence of reputation or a witness's opinion. Proof of specific past acts (which might seem the best way to develop an impression of someone's character) is forbidden.

Evidence That Could Show Character May Be Introduced with a Noncharacter Rationale. Evidence that might show character, such as a defendant's past crimes, can sometimes be introduced if it could support a jury's conclusion in a current case in a way that is different from a jury using the past acts to draw a conclusion about the defendant's character. This is common, for example when a defendant's past acts and a current charged crime have strong similarities like a signature (as in *Foxhoven*) or when past acts suggest a mental state like intent that was likely present in the past acts and therefore in current charged acts (as in *Queen*). Defendants are also subject to juries finding out about noncharged offenses when those offenses are "part and parcel" of a charged crime (as in *Leyva*), or when small similarities are treated by a trial judge as equivalent to a signature (as was criticized in the concurrence in *Willett*).

CHAPTER 4

Habit and Sexual Conduct in the Context of Character

A. Introduction
B. Habit
C. Alleged Victims of Sex Crimes
D. Defendants Accused of Sex Crimes
E. Summary

A INTRODUCTION

Topic Overview

Applying Rules 404(a) and 404(b) can be problematic. A judge must decide whether particular past conduct has relevance only because it supports a character inference, and sometimes must estimate the strength of a non-character chain of inferences. Responding to these difficulties, for some recurring situations the rules attempt to simplify the process and make results more predictable.

Rule 406 recognizes a distinction between *character* and *habit*. The concept of "habit" provides a contrast to character. A pattern of past conduct might support an inference based on character, and therefore would be covered by the antipropensity rule. On the other hand, a pattern of conduct might represent merely a habit — something less integral to a person's way of life than character — and therefore would be outside the control of Rule 404.

Character traits related to *sexual conduct* also receive particularized treatment in the rules. The inferences from a person's past sexual conduct to whether a specific sexual act was consensual or whether the act even occurred has been problematic. Rule 412 limits the availability of this inference for the conduct of the alleged *victim* of prohibited sexual conduct. Three other rules, 413, 414, and 415, take the opposite approach for evidence of this kind related to the conduct of the alleged *perpetrator* of prohibited sexual conduct. They make past prohibited sexual conduct generally admissible to show similar conduct on another occasion.

Chapter Organization

This chapter begins with the topic of special treatment for evidence about habits. It explores the relationship between a person's habits and a person's character traits. It also considers how broadly or narrowly the term "habit" may be understood by courts in this context. The chapter then covers special treatment for information about people's sexual conduct, contrasting current treatment of alleged victims and alleged perpetrators.

B   HABIT

The general antipropensity rule forbids introduction of evidence that shows a person's character traits to support a conclusion that the person acted in conformity with those traits on a specific occasion. But evidence about a person's habit or an organization's usual way of operating is admissible to support a conclusion that the person or organization acted in conformity with that habit or routine on a specific occasion.

The following chart shows the chain of inferences for the prohibited propensity inference and compares that logic with the more straightforward link that allowable habit evidence supports. The initial information for habit is narrowly defined, in contrast to the nearly infinite kinds of information that could support a conclusion about character. To go from a belief that a person has a habit to a belief that the person acted in accordance with the habit, a trier of fact would never have to think about the person's personality or character traits. That, too, is different from the logic that would be involved in a propensity line of reasoning.

Rule 406 expressly allows the inference from habit to conduct on a specific occasion. It rejects two aspects of earlier evidence law doctrine. At common law this kind of evidence was sometimes limited to situations where it was corroborated or where it involved an event with no eyewitnesses. The Federal Rule rejects those limitations.

Forbidden Propensity Inference	Allowed Habit Inference
Information about a person's conduct and personality	Particularized information about a single kind of response a person makes repeatedly to a certain kind of stimulus

Conclusion about the person's character

Conclusion that the person acted on a **specific** occasion in a way that is consistent with his or her character

Conclusion that at a particular time the person made the response he or she repeatedly makes to a certain kind of stimulus

---

Rule 406. Habit; Routine Practice

Evidence of a person's habit or an organization's routine practice may be admitted to prove that on a particular occasion the person or organization acted in accordance with the habit or routine practice. The court may admit this evidence regardless of whether it is corroborated or whether there was an eyewitness.

Carrying a Gun, Being Violent When Angry: Habits or Traits?— **Brown.** Information about how a person ordinarily acts might support a jury's inferences about that person's character and then could lead to inferences from that character to conduct on a specific occasion. That use of information would be prohibited by the antipropensity rule. Habit evidence avoids this bar because, in theory, it can allow a jury to make an inference about conduct on a specific occasion without necessarily drawing a conclusion about the person's character traits. *Brown* considers this distinction between character evidence and habit evidence in the context of murder.

STATE v. BROWN

543 S.E.2d 552 (S.C. 2001)

MOORE, J.

Appellant was convicted of murder for shooting to death his twenty-five-year-old grandnephew Shane Hammond (Victim). Appellant admitted killing Victim but claimed self-defense. He appeals on the ground he was prejudiced by the improper admission of bad character evidence. We affirm.

Victim was living in appellant's home. The State put up evidence that the day before the killing, appellant and Victim argued over rent money. Two eyewitnesses, Jack Williams and Kelly Williams, testified they saw appellant hit Victim on the head several times with a blunt tool, lacerating Victim's scalp. Appellant was holding a gun in his other hand at the time. Victim was unarmed and simply tried to fend off the attack by covering his head.

The next day, Victim returned to the house to retrieve his belongings. Appellant's wife, Erlene Brown, testified that when Victim arrived, he went into the kitchen. Mrs. Brown went down the hall to the bedroom to get Victim's things. She saw her husband in the hallway with a billy club behind his back and she said to him, "Don't do anything, don't say anything. [Victim's] just come to get his clothes, you know, and he's leaving and I'm getting his clothes for him."

... Appellant testified he was in his bedroom when Victim entered the house. He went down the hall to the kitchen and told Victim to leave. When appellant turned around, Victim "blind sided" him. Appellant testified he thought Victim was going to kill him and that he was fighting for his life.

During the fight, appellant found his gun on the kitchen floor where he claimed it had fallen from the top of the refrigerator. He shot Victim as Victim was charging into him. Victim continued attacking and, as they tussled over the gun, appellant shot again, killing Victim.

The trial judge submitted murder and voluntary manslaughter to the jury and gave a charge on self-defense. Appellant was convicted of murder and sentenced to forty years.

Appellant contends the trial judge erroneously admitted character evidence that was unfairly prejudicial. . . .

During Mrs. Brown's testimony, she was asked why she fled during the fight. She responded, "I know the moods of my husband and I knew I had to get out." The Solicitor asked what mood appellant was in that night and Mrs. Brown stated that he had become "very angry and agitated." The Solicitor then asked, "What happens when he becomes angry and agitated?" Over appellant's objection, Mrs. Brown stated, "He gets violent." Appellant contends this testimony impermissibly attacked his character. He claims he was prejudiced because the Solicitor argued this violent propensity indicated appellant was the aggressor in the fight with Victim.

Character evidence is not admissible to prove the accused possesses a criminal character or has a propensity to commit the crime with which he is charged. Rule 404(a), SCRE, states the general rule that "evidence of a person's character or a trait of character is not admissible for the purpose of proving action in conformity therewith on a particular occasion."

The State argues, however, that the evidence appellant reacts violently was admissible as evidence of habit under Rule 406, SCRE, which provides in pertinent part:

Evidence of habit of a person . . . is relevant to prove that the conduct of the person . . . on a particular occasion was in conformity with the habit. . . .

Federal courts have recognized the tension between Rule 406 (habit) and Rule 404 (character) and noted the difficulty in distinguishing between admissible evidence of habit and inadmissible character evidence. As indicated in the advisory committee's note to Federal Rule of Evidence 406, which is identical to our Rule 406, the distinguishing feature of habit is its degree of specificity. Habit has been described as conduct that is "situation-specific" or "specific, particularized conduct capable of almost identical repetition." Becker v. ARCO Chem. Co., 207 F.3d 176, 204 (3d Cir. 2000). This Court has defined the term "character," on the other hand, as "a generalized description of a person's disposition or a general trait such as honesty, temperance, or peacefulness."

In this case, Mrs. Brown's testimony identified no specific conduct but simply indicated appellant's general propensity to become violent. We find this evidence inadmissible as evidence of habit under Rule 406. Cf. Perrin v. Anderson, 784 F.2d 1040 (10th Cir. 1986) (evidence of specific violent incidents admissible as habit evidence where party invariably reacted with extreme violence to any contact with uniformed police officer).

[Discussion of harmless error issues omitted]

In questioning appellant's grandson, Billy, the Solicitor asked if Billy had seen appellant with a gun on the night of the shooting. Billy answered, "I didn't see it that night but I knew [appellant] always carried it on him." When asked what he meant by that, Billy testified over appellant's objection, "He usually had [the gun] in his belt or he kept it in his right pocket or usually just somewhere near him all the time." Similarly, Mrs. Brown testified, again over appellant's objection, that she did not see the gun that night but "the gun either is in his pocket, tucked in his belt right there, or either on the bed beside him." When asked, "Does it ever leave him?" she answered, "no."

Appellant contends this testimony was erroneously admitted as habit evidence. He claims he was unfairly prejudiced by its admission because, while he admitted shooting Victim in self-defense, he denied carrying a gun down the hall into the kitchen and accosting Victim.

We find this evidence was properly admitted as habit evidence. Unlike the testimony regarding appellant's general predisposition to violence, this evidence describes a pattern of specific, particularized conduct. Under Rule 406, this evidence was properly admitted to show appellant acted in conformity with this pattern of behavior on the night in question. See United States v. Yazzie, 188 F.3d 1178 (10th Cir. 1999) (reflexive action of placing gun in waistband admissible as habit evidence because uniformity of behavior established habitual nature). . . .

Affirmed.

NOTES TO STATE v. BROWN

1. *Jury Use of Habit and Character Evidence.* The rules treat habit and character differently mainly because of the ways in which a jury would likely use each type of evidence. Using information about a habit does not involve suppositions about character traits, and — most importantly — it does not require consideration of the many different ways that a person's character traits might become manifest in different situations. These differences between character and habit, of course, are strongest when a "habit" is straightforward, easy to describe, and really is conduct that an actor repeats without variation.

2. *Specificity of Habit.* The Brown court characterized the testimony that the defendant "gets violent" when angry and agitated as outside the definition of habit because it did not describe particular conduct. But the court acknowledged a Tenth Circuit case in which a party's habit was reacting with violence to encounters with police. This suggests that there may be lots of variation in the specificity courts require for proof of habit. For example, in Whittemore v. Lockheed Aircraft Corp., 65 Cal. App. 2d 737, 151 P.2d 670 (1944), evidence that the alleged pilot of a crashed aircraft was the pilot on four previous flights was treated as admissible habit evidence. Also, in Chomicki v. Wittekind, 128 Wis. 2d 188, 381 N.W.2d 561 (App. 1985), testimony of four tenants that a landlord had made sexual advances to them was held sufficient to establish habit.

> **GOOD TO REMEMBER**
>
> Habit is different from character because it's uncomplicated and specific. Those attributes can help in deciding whether information a party offers should be called "habit" or "character" information.

■ ■ ■

Volition, Complexity, and Habit — Aikman. This court uses a mathematical analysis as part of its treatment of whether certain conduct can properly be called a habit. It also considers whether conduct that is complex and volitional can be habitual.

AIKMAN v. KANDA

975 A.2d 152 (D.C. 2009)

THOMPSON, J.

Appellant Evelyn Aikman appeals from the trial court's denial of her motion for a new trial in her medical malpractice action against Dr. Louis Kanda and his (former) practice group, Cardiovascular & Thoracic Surgery Associates, P.C. We affirm the trial court's ruling.

In October 2001, Aikman was admitted to the Washington Hospital Center for surgery to repair her mitral valve (the valve between the heart's left atrium and left ventricle). Dr. Kanda, a cardiac surgeon, performed the open-heart operation on October 3, 2001. Following the surgery, Aikman was slow to recover from the anesthesia, and, when she did awaken, she manifested weakness in her extremities. A brain scan performed the day after the surgery revealed that Aikman had suffered an embolic stroke, a stroke that is caused by small particles traveling through the bloodstream to the brain. Aikman was left with permanent physical injuries, including loss of the use of her legs and diminished use of her left hand, and emotional injuries. On September 24, 2004, Aikman sued Dr. Kanda and his professional association, contending that her injuries resulted from air that accumulated in her heart while it was open during the surgery and that traveled to her brain afterwards, and alleging negligence. Specifically, Aikman claimed that Dr. Kanda either failed to employ procedures to remove air from her heart (so-called "air drill" procedures) before completing the surgery, or performed the air drill inadequately.

After the jury returned a verdict in favor of Dr. Kanda on all counts, Aikman filed a motion for a new trial. . . . The trial judge, the Honorable Neal Kravitz, denied the motion. This appeal followed. . . .

Over objections by Aikman's counsel, Dr. Kanda testified about the air drill procedures that he routinely performs after completing a mitral valve repair. Aikman's . . . contention on appeal is that Judge Kravitz erred in permitting Dr. Kanda to do so, entitling Aikman to reversal of the judgment and a new trial. Aikman's argument is actually twofold. First, she contends that Dr. Kanda's testimony about his routine practice of air removal following open-heart surgery amounted to inadmissible character testimony (i.e., testimony that Dr. Kanda's character was to be careful), rather than habit testimony. Second, Aikman argues that even if Dr. Kanda's testimony could fairly be regarded as habit testimony, habit testimony should not be allowed in a medical negligence action. For the reasons that follow, we reject both arguments.

Habit evidence "denotes a person's regular response to a repeated situation to the point where 'the doing of the habitual act may become semi-automatic. . . .'" Smith v. United States, 583 A.2d 975, 980 n.9 (D.C. 1990) (quoting McCormick on Evidence §195 at 575 (3d ed. 1984)) (emphasis in Smith). The proponent of habit evidence bears the burden of "proffer[ing] instances sufficient in number to warrant a finding that the habit or routine existed in fact." Id. at 980 (quoting Wilson v. Volkswagen of America, Inc., 561 F.2d 494, 511-12 (4th Cir. 1977)) ("[w]hile precise standards for measuring the 'extent to which instances must be multiplied and consistency of behavior maintained in order to support an inference of habit or pattern of conduct cannot be formulated,' it is obvious that no finding [of habit] is supportable . . . which fails to examine critically the 'ratio of reactions to situations'"). The "offering party must establish the degree of specificity and frequency of uniform response that ensures more than a mere 'tendency' to act in a given manner, but rather, conduct that is 'semi-automatic' in nature." Smith,

583 A.2d at 981 (quoting Simplex Inc. v. Diversified Energy Sys., Inc., 847 F.2d 1290, 1293 (7th Cir. 1988)).

Aikman contends that Dr. Kanda's testimony was not habit testimony because the performance of a complex surgical procedure is not "semi-automatic in nature." However, as Judge Kravitz explained in denying Aikman's motion for a new trial, Dr. Kanda established that he had performed more than 500 mitral valve operations, and he testified that the air drill "is an integral part of the procedure. So, I do it every time." In addition, Dr. Kanda described his air drill routine step by step, and in great detail, and described his specific responses to various triggers and developments that occur over the course of the procedure. Given Dr. Kanda's very specific testimony, we cannot agree that Dr. Kanda's account amounted to character evidence rather than habit evidence. "[C]haracter evidence is a generalized description of a person's disposition.... Habit evidence, on the other hand, is more specific because it denotes a person's regular response to a repeated situation...." Smith, supra, 583 A.2d at 980. In addition, in light of the high ("100 percent") "ratio of reactions to situations" that Dr. Kanda described and the specificity of his account of his routine, we cannot conclude that Judge Kravitz erred in determining that, for Dr. Kanda, the air drill was semi-automatic in nature.

Aikman also argues that a complex surgical procedure "cannot be so free from volition as to regard it as habit." Judge Kravitz reasoned that "[t]he volitional aspect of the de-airing procedures ... went to the weight of the evidence of Dr. Kanda's habit but did not require its exclusion." Judge Kravitz's analysis on this point is consistent with this court's observation that the volitional nature of habitual conduct is relevant to its probative force, not its admissibility. See Smith, supra, 583 A.2d at 982 ("the probative force of habit evidence is in inverse proportion to the extent the habit involves volitional activity") (internal citation and punctuation omitted).

Judge Kravitz reasonably determined that the defense satisfied the foundational requirements for the admission of Dr. Kanda's testimony as habit evidence. That does not end the analysis, however, because, as we recognized in Smith, "courts should be cautious in permitting admission of habit or pattern of conduct evidence" because of the "danger that it may afford a basis for improper inferences, cause confusion, or operate unfairly to prejudice a party." Smith, 583 A.2d at 980 (quoting Wilson, supra, 561 F.2d at 511). Here, we are satisfied that Judge Kravitz took steps to assure that the jury would not be confused by Dr. Kanda's testimony. Before Dr. Kanda responded to defense counsel's request that he "take the ladies and gentlemen of the jury through a mitral valve procedure," Judge Kravitz interjected that the response should describe "not specifically what you did when you were operating on the plaintiff [regarding which Dr. Kanda had just testified that he had no specific recollection], but I think what he's asking you is what is your routine in terms of performing a mitral valve repair surgery. Do you understand that?"

Finally, we discern no reason why, as a general rule, habit evidence should be any less admissible in medical negligence actions than in other types of cases.

Courts in many jurisdictions have allowed evidence of a medical practitioner's routine practice as evidence relevant to what the practitioner did on a particular occasion.[15] As some courts have reasoned, habit evidence may not be properly admissible where the physician's routine varies according to the condition of the patient. But, as we read the testimony in this case, the air drill procedures that Dr. Kanda described as part of his routine are proper during any mitral valve repair operation. It was not error to allow the jury to hear his account of his routine during mitral valve surgery. The jury could still have discredited Dr. Kanda's testimony that he performed his air drill routine "100 percent" of the time, including in Aikman's case.

For the foregoing reasons, we affirm the judgment of the trial court and the order denying the motion for a new trial.

NOTES TO AIKMAN v. KANDA

1. *High Ratio of Reactions to Situations.* The appellate court notes that the proponent of habit evidence characterized the ratio of reactions to situations as 100 percent (which would be a 1:1 ratio), but it also praised the trial court for having told the jury it would be hearing the defendant's description of his general practices and not a description of what he actually did in operating on the plaintiff. Can a jury make a rational distinction between these two types of descriptions?

2. *Habit of Due Care.* No court would admit testimony such as, "I perform operations with reasonable care all the time" as habit evidence. Yet courts will frequently admit evidence equivalent to "typically careful" as long as it describes specific repeated conduct.

3. *Post-injury Habit.* Can proof of a habit that includes evidence of a defendant's conduct after a plaintiff's injury sensibly support a finding that the habit existed when the plaintiff was harmed? In Dawkins v. Sawicki, 22 A.3d 1142 (R.I. 2011), the court wrote:

---

15. *See, e.g., Rivera v. Anilesh,* 8 N.Y.3d 627, 838 N.Y.S.2d 478, 869 N.E.2d 654, 657-58 (2007) (holding that the record supported the admissibility of the dentist's "deliberate and repetitive practice" with respect to administering injections of anesthesia, in light of the testimony indicating that the dentist "performed this procedure in the same manner thousands of times," and because there was "no evidence suggesting that [the dentist's] pre-extraction injection procedure would vary from patient to patient depending on the particular medical circumstances or physical condition of the patient"); *Hoffart v. Hodge,* 9 Neb. App. 161, 609 N.W.2d 397, 404 (2000) (recognizing that while physician's testimony about his routine of advising his patients about mammogram failure rates was self-serving, that fact went to the weight and credibility of the testimony rather than its admissibility, and observing that for a physician who has treated thousands of patients, "substantially decreas[ing] the likelihood that the doctor will recall a specific conversation with a specific patient," evidence of habit "may be the only vehicle available for a doctor to prove that he or she acted in a particular way on a particular occasion")....

The plaintiff takes issue with the time frame for which defendant established his routines, namely that the routine practice evidence must have occurred before . . . he treated plaintiff. We disagree. There was adequate testimony that during the approximately ten years he was an emergency room physician, defendant had treated thousands of patients, and therefore was able to describe his routines at the time he treated plaintiff.

If the condition of a physical thing at one time can be relevant to how that thing was at an earlier time, would that idea support an inference that conduct after a particular time would show how a person acted before that time?

■   ■   ■

"Habit" of Negligence—Gamerdinger. The court refers to evidence of the defendant's "habit of being negligent." That description is far afield from typical black letter definitions of habits as patterns of specific acts repeated with little variation in response to similar stimuli. Nonetheless, the appellate court held that the evidence should have been admitted. Consider whether this result can be supported as consistent with underlying principles of habit evidence, despite the court's broad description of the nature of the evidence.

GAMERDINGER v. SCHAEFER

603 N.W.3d 950 (Iowa 1999)

SNELL, J.

In this personal injury action the district court granted a new trial on plaintiffs' motion. Defendants appealed and plaintiffs cross-appealed. We now affirm the granting of a new trial for reasons raised in plaintiffs' cross-appeal.

Plaintiffs, Sharri and Thomas Gamerdinger, filed suit against defendants, Patrick Schaefer and Deere & Company, for damages the Gamerdingers sustained as a result of a collision at Deere's plant between a motorized cart driven by Sharri Gamerdinger and a forklift truck driven by Patrick K. Schaefer. Sharri Gamerdinger claimed she sustained personal injuries as a result of the accident; Thomas Gamerdinger brought a claim for loss of consortium.

Following a jury trial, a verdict was returned in which fifty percent of the fault for the accident was attributed to Sherri Gamerdinger, twenty percent to Schaefer, and thirty percent to Deere. . . .

Gamerdinger moved for a new trial, arguing in part that the jury verdict was inconsistent in that it awarded medical expenses but failed to confer corresponding amounts for pain and suffering and loss of function. The district court agreed and suggested additur of $40,000. Both parties objected to the amount proposed so the court sustained the motion for a new trial. . . .

On cross-appeal, plaintiffs raise . . . evidentiary issues that we find dispositive. For this reason we do not address . . . other matters.

Gamerdinger asserted that she was injured when Schaefer negligently operated his forklift truck and ran into her motorized cart. She sought to introduce evidence of Schaefer's habit of being negligent in operating the forklift.

Iowa Rule of Evidence 406 is implicated here. It states:

> Evidence of the habit of a person or of the routine practice of an organization, whether corroborated or not and regardless of the presence of eyewitnesses, is relevant to prove that the conduct of the person or organization on a particular occasion was in conformity with the habit or routine practice.

Prior to the beginning of evidence, the trial court granted defendants' motion in limine concerning the safety of Schaefer's previous operation of the forklift. The court ruled that it would not allow this evidence unless defendants made it an issue by averring that Schaefer was a safe driver. The matter surfaced again at trial via direct examination of Schaefer by defendants, cross-examination, redirect and recross-examination. Plaintiffs' request for rebuttal testimony was denied, the court saying:

> My ruling that I made in connection with the motion in limine remains unchanged. There weren't any significant developments during the course of the trial during defendants' presentation of evidence that would give me cause to change that. . . . Mr. Anderson, I feel, was quite careful to avoid getting into those areas. I find that he didn't open those areas up, and the ruling that I had previously made in connection with defendants' motion in limine should remain unchanged, so your proffer in that regard, Mr. Fransdal, is denied.

At trial, plaintiffs developed testimony of Tim Davison, who retired from Deere in May of 1995, after more than twenty-nine years of service. For the last seven years of his employment, he unloaded tires from trucks in the loading dock area. He worked with defendant Schaefer for five and one-half to six of those years.

Davison observed Sharri Gamerdinger approaching the scene of the accident on her food cart. She was going about as fast as a person can walk. She was going no faster than food carts usually traveled as they went about their business in the Wheel Building. As she approached the dock area, Davison observed Schaefer back his forklift truck out of the semi trailer he was unloading and collide with the left side of her food cart. Defendant sounded no horn prior to exiting the trailer, and did not look either way or stop prior to backing the vehicle out of the trailer.

Following the testimony of Tim Davison, plaintiffs made an offer of proof related to the habit and custom of Schaefer in the operation of his forklift truck. According to Davison, defendant's driving habits were erratic in that he did not always know what was going on around him. Davison had testified before the jury that it was the forklift driver's responsibility to look in the mirror, behind, to the left, and to the right in backing the forklift out of a trailer. In the offer of proof, Davison said Schaefer had a long-standing problem in not following this procedure. Defendant's laxity in this respect was so problematic Davison felt compelled to talk to Schaeffer's supervisor, Ron Mills, one or two times per month, for the five and one-half to six years that the men worked together. Davison indicated that improvements in Schaefer's driving occurred temporarily after he spoke with Mills, but the improvements never lasted.

Another offer of proof was made by plaintiffs with regard to testimony from Jerry Linsey, a long-time employee of Deere. Linsey retired from Deere in April of 1997, after more than thirty years of service. He drove a yard tractor around the Wheel Building for the last five to eight years of his employment. Linsey testified that Schaefer had a custom or habit of not looking to see if there were any pedestrians in the way or coming through the area when backing out of a trailer with a load of tires. He indicated that this occurred daily. Linsey said that he talked to Ron Mills about Schaefer's inattentiveness on fourteen or fifteen occasions. He also notified another supervisor, Bill Holmes, but the complaints never seemed to make a difference in Schaefer's driving habits.

A habit is a person's regular practice of responding to a particular kind of situation with a specific kind of conduct. 1 McCormick on Evidence §195, at 686-87 (5th ed. 1999). Evidence of habits that come within this definition has greater probative value than does evidence of general traits of character. Furthermore, the potential for prejudice is substantially less. Id. The basis for admissibility of habit and custom is the inference that if a person has acted a certain way with regularity in the past, it is probable the person acted in conformity with that pattern on the occasion in question.

We have held that the trial court has wide discretion in ruling on the admissibility of evidence. The trial court's decisions will not be disturbed unless there is a clear and prejudicial abuse of discretion. . . .

Plaintiffs' offers of proof sought to establish defendant's past custom and habit in operating the forklift truck. Both witnesses testified about Schaefer's habit of not watching for pedestrians and other vehicles as he unloaded trailers with his forklift. They further testified that Schaefer hit or nearly hit numerous other objects as a result of his failure to watch where he was going. Plaintiffs' witnesses Davison and Linsey also stated that their repeated complaints to supervisors at Deere did not remedy Schaefer's driving habits. . . .

We find that this evidence was relevant and probative as to the likelihood of Schaefer's being negligent in operating his forklift truck. It also may bear on the jury's assessment of the percentage of fault attributable to Schaefer by his conduct. The evidence clearly comes within the purview of Iowa Rule of Evidence 406 and should have been admitted. . . . We hold the trial court erred in not so ruling on the admissibility of this evidence proffered at trial.

NOTES TO GAMERDINGER v. SCHAEFER

1. *Required Consistency.* Some testimony portrayed Mr. Schaefer's driving as "erratic" and marked by frequent improvements that "never lasted." Do these

descriptions take away from the consistency that is usually required for treating a pattern of conduct as habit?

2. *Business Habits.* Rule 406 covers the habits of individuals and the routines of businesses. In a minority approach, Massachusetts rejects the category of individual habit evidence but recognizes habit and custom evidence for businesses. Applying the distinction can be difficult. Palinkas v. Bennett, 416 Mass. 273, 620 N.E.2d 775 (1993), affirmed a trial court's admission of a defendant's doctor's habit with regard to discharging premature infants from the hospital, noting that "often the line between a personal habit and a business habit is not a bright one."

QUESTION 4-1. Tom Tenant was hurt while trying to get into his car in a parking lot at an apartment house where he lived. He sought damages from Oscar Owner, the owner of the apartment house, claiming that Owner had failed to maintain the pavement in the parking lot properly, and that bad maintenance of the pavement had caused Tenant to move awkwardly while he approached the door of his car. To support this claim, Tenant seeks to introduce evidence showing that Owner allowed trash to collect in the lobby, Owner had failed to remove graffiti from the building's front door, and that fire extinguishers required by law to be present in the building's hallways were sometimes missing. Should a trial judge allow Tenant's evidence as evidence of Owner's habit of poor building maintenance?

 ALLEGED VICTIMS OF SEX CRIMES

In rape prosecutions, it once was common to permit a defendant to introduce evidence showing that the alleged victim was "unchaste," which was usually defined as having had sexual relations outside of marriage. This information was treated as relevant to determining whether the woman consented to the sex act, on the theory that a woman who had consented to sexual conduct outside of marriage on one occasion would likely have done so on another occasion. Prior sex outside of marriage was also treated as relevant to the woman's honesty as a witness, on the theory that the immorality of nonmarital sex would indicate lack of respect for other moral standards such as truth telling under oath.

Rule 412, sometimes called the "rape shield" rule, restricts the use of evidence about the past sexual conduct of an alleged victim of a sex crime.

Rule 412. Sex-Offense Cases: The Victim's Sexual Behavior or Predisposition

    (a) Prohibited Uses. The following evidence is not admissible in a civil or criminal proceeding involving alleged sexual misconduct:

        (1) evidence offered to prove that a victim engaged in other sexual behavior; or

(2) evidence offered to prove a victim's sexual predisposition.

(b) Exceptions.

(1) *Criminal Cases.* The court may admit the following evidence in a criminal case:

(A) evidence of specific instances of a victim's sexual behavior, if offered to prove that someone other than the defendant was the source of semen, injury, or other physical evidence;

(B) evidence of specific instances of a victim's sexual behavior with respect to the person accused of the sexual misconduct, if offered by the defendant to prove consent or if offered by the prosecutor; and

(C) evidence whose exclusion would violate the defendant's constitutional rights.

(2) *Civil Cases.* In a civil case, the court may admit evidence offered to prove a victim's sexual behavior or sexual predisposition if its probative value substantially outweighs the danger of harm to any victim and of unfair prejudice to any party. The court may admit evidence of a victim's reputation only if the victim has placed it in controversy.

(c) Procedure to Determine Admissibility.

(1) *Motion.* If a party intends to offer evidence under Rule 412(b), the party must:

(A) file a motion that specifically describes the evidence and states the purpose for which it is to be offered;

(B) do so at least 14 days before trial unless the court, for good cause, sets a different time;

(C) serve the motion on all parties; and

(D) notify the victim or, when appropriate, the victim's guardian or representative.

(2) *Hearing.* Before admitting evidence under this rule, the court must conduct an in camera hearing and give the victim and parties a right to attend and be heard. Unless the court orders otherwise, the motion, related materials, and the record of the hearing must be and remain sealed.

(d) Definition of "Victim." In this rule, "victim" includes an alleged victim.

◾   ◾   ◾

Past Prostitution and Consent to Sex on a Specific Occasion — **Williams.** The controversial evidence in this case was proof that the alleged victim had worked in the past as a prostitute, offered to show that she was working as a prostitute when she encountered Williams. This case treats that evidence under Rule 412. In the absence of Rule 412 this evidence might have been treated under Rule 404(b)(2) if the defendant claimed it showed something like "plan" or "absence of mistake." Consider how the position Rule 412 takes on relevance compares with the position many courts take on relevance when they apply Rule 404(b)(2) to admit evidence of a person's past acts for noncharacter purposes.

WILLIAMS v. STATE
681 N.E.2d 195 (Ind. 1997)

BOEHM, J.

A jury convicted defendant Adrian Williams of attempted criminal deviate conduct, a Class A felony, and criminal confinement, a Class B felony. A majority of the Court of Appeals reversed the convictions on the grounds that the trial court erred in excluding certain evidence. Because we conclude that the evidence was properly excluded and no other reversible error occurred, we now grant transfer, vacate the opinion of the Court of Appeals, and reinstate the convictions.

This appeal raises the following [issue]: . . . Did the trial court err by excluding evidence of the victim's past sexual conduct pursuant to Indiana Evidence Rule 412? . . .

During the early morning hours on January 9, 1993, the victim was working as a topless dancer at a nightclub in downtown Indianapolis. The following is her version of the events of that night. When she finished work at approximately 2:45 a.m., she walked out into the parking lot and asked two strangers, Williams and co-defendant Antoine Edmondson, for a ride home. The two men agreed and she got into the car. Williams did not drive the car directly to the victim's home. Instead, he told her that "they had to make a stop." He drove into an alley behind a different club where Edmondson exited the car. The victim then attempted to run away but Edmondson grabbed her arms and pulled her into the back seat of the car. As the victim struggled with Edmondson in the car, Williams drove to a public park and stopped the car in a dark area of its parking lot.

The two then ordered the victim to engage in sexual acts with them simultaneously. Edmondson pulled a gun out of his pocket and placed it on the arm rest of the front seat. He then removed the victim's shoe and sock and pulled her right pants leg off. The victim managed to grab the gun, open the car door, and run away. As she ran, she fired the gun behind her and, although she apparently had never fired a weapon before, shot Edmondson in the jaw. Williams and Edmondson were subsequently arrested and each was charged with two counts of attempted criminal deviate conduct, criminal confinement, and carrying a handgun without a license. The two men were tried together. . . .

The trial court . . . properly excluded testimony [by a friend of the victim] that on prior occasions the victim had committed acts of prostitution in exchange for money or cocaine. Williams claims this testimony supports his defense that the victim consented and accompanied the men because they had promised to obtain drugs for her. The trial court excluded the friend's testimony regarding the victim's prior alleged acts of prostitution because evidence of a victim's past sexual conduct is not admissible except as provided in Indiana's Rape Shield Rule, Indiana Evidence Rule 412. Rule 412 provides that in prosecutions for a sex crime, evidence of a victim's or witness' past sexual conduct is inadmissible, except in the following circumstances: 1) evidence of the victim's or witness' past sexual conduct with the defendant; 2) evidence that shows that some person other than the defendant committed the act upon which the prosecution is founded; 3) evidence that the victim's pregnancy at the time of trial was not caused by the defendant; or 4) evidence of a conviction for a crime offered for impeachment under Rule 609. Otherwise stated, past incidents of consent, except in these limited circumstances, are not permitted to imply consent on the date in question.

None of the exceptions to Rule 412's general prohibition of inquiry into the victim's sexual history apply here. The evidence offered here was of the classic sort precluded by the Rape Shield Rule: purported incidents with other men at other times offered simply to show that the victim had consented in the past in the hope the inference will be drawn that she consented here. Rule 412 was enacted to prevent just this kind of generalized inquiry into the reputation or past sexual conduct of the victim in order to avoid embarrassing the victim and subjecting the victim to possible public denigration. The Rule reflects a policy first embodied in Indiana's Rape Shield Act, Indiana Code §35-37-4-4, that inquiry into a victim's prior sexual activity is sufficiently problematic that it should not be permitted to become a focus of the defense. Rule 412 is intended to prevent the victim from being put on trial, to protect the victim against surprise, harassment, and unnecessary invasion of privacy, and, importantly, to remove obstacles to reporting sex crimes.

Balanced against these considerations is the defendant's right to present relevant evidence. For this reason, Rule 412 permits evidence of the defendant's past experience with the victim, but does not permit a defendant to base his defense of consent on the victim's past sexual experiences with third persons. The allegation of prostitution does not affect this calculus. We agree with the Fourth Circuit's view that it is "intolerable to suggest that because the victim is a prostitute, she automatically is assumed to have consented with anyone at any time." United States v. Saunders, 943 F.2d 388, 392 (4th Cir. 1991), cert. denied, 502 U.S. 1105, 112 S. Ct. 1199, 117 L. Ed. 2d 439 (1992). Moreover, even when evidence does fall within one of Rule 412's exceptions and is admissible, it is still subject to Evidence Rules 401 and 403. In this case, the evidence would shift the jury's attention away from the defendants' actions to the past acts of the victim. Any probative value is "substantially outweighed by the danger of unfair prejudice." Evid. R. 403. Thus, the trial court properly excluded the evidence.

Williams contends that the trial court's application of Indiana's Rape Shield Rule violates his Sixth Amendment right to present witnesses. Indiana's Rape

Shield Rule has repeatedly been held facially constitutional. However, "the constitutionality of such a law as applied to preclude particular exculpatory evidence remains subject to examination on a case by case basis." Tague v. Richards, 3 F.3d 1133, 1137 (7th Cir. 1993) (citation omitted). Many jurisdictions acknowledge that a rape shield statute or rule serves to emphasize the general irrelevance of a victim's sexual history. Although there are instances where the application of the Rape Shield Rule may violate a defendant's Sixth Amendment right, this is not one of them. For example, admission of such evidence may be constitutionally required where the evidence is offered not to show the victim's consent but to establish some other point such as that an injury could have been inflicted by someone other than the defendant. It may also be required when the trial court restricts a defendant from giving his own account of the events at issue. And the Sixth Amendment may be implicated when a defendant establishes that the victim engaged in a similar pattern of sexual acts. People v. Sandoval, 135 Ill. 2d 159, 552 N.E.2d 726, 738, 142 Ill. Dec. 135 (Ill. 1990) (prior pattern exception applies to the admission of certain evidence which reveals activity marked by characteristics tending to show an individual's unique "signature").

In this case, there was no restriction on the ability of the defense to present evidence of the incident. The trial court allowed both defendants to testify that the victim agreed to perform sex acts in exchange for money. The jury was informed through testimony of the defendants and the victim that the victim voluntarily entered a car with two strange men at 2 A.M. in the parking lot of a topless club. Whatever her initial motive, at some point, according to her, she clearly communicated her lack of consent to proceeding as the men directed. Whatever her sexual past, if the jury accepted that story, conviction was proper. As noted above, the excluded evidence did not serve to explain any physical evidence. Under these facts, exclusion of the victim's past sexual experiences with third persons is not unconstitutional. We do not agree that an alleged prostitute's prior sexual history becomes fair game simply by reason of her prior actions, or that there is any constitutional right to present evidence of past consensual sex with other persons for that reason alone. Accordingly, Williams' constitutional right to present witnesses was not violated.

. . . The reasoning of the Court of Appeals would permit evidence of the victim's past sexual conduct to support the theory that the victim consented to the sex acts on the night in question for the same reason as she had allegedly consented in the past. Similar reasoning would subject any complaining victim with an allegedly promiscuous past to unfettered examination of sexual history. That is precisely what Evidence Rule 412 prevents. Where a specific rule — Evidence Rule 412 — makes the past sexual conduct of a victim or witness inadmissible, except under specified circumstances, a party cannot circumvent the requirements of Rule 412(b) by relying on the general doctrines of Rule 404(b). We conclude that the trial court properly excluded evidence of the victim's prior drug history and past sexual conduct pursuant to Indiana's Evidence Rules.

NOTES TO WILLIAMS v. STATE

1. *"Automatic" Assumptions.* The *Williams* court relies on the Fourth Circuit's statement that it would be intolerable to automatically assume that a person who is a prostitute would have consented to sex acts at any time. Admitting evidence of past sexual conduct would not, of course, *automatically* require a conclusion about conduct at another time. But these courts' willingness to use such an extreme description of the consequences of admitting this type of evidence underscores how powerful it sometimes seems.

2. *Counterexample.* Tennessee applies the following rule:

> **Tennessee Rules of Evidence Rule 412(c)(4)(iii)**
>
> [Evidence of an alleged victim's sexual conduct with persons other than the defendant may be admitted] to prove consent if the evidence is of a pattern of sexual behavior so distinctive and so closely resembling the defendant's version of the alleged encounter with the victim that it tends to prove that the victim consented to the act charged or behaved in such a manner as to lead the defendant reasonably to believe that the victim consented.

How would *Williams* have been decided under this rule?

3. *Sanctions.* If a defendant is responsible for bringing to the jury's attention evidence that is barred by a rape shield rule or statute, a mistrial could be declared. Additionally, the defense lawyer might be sanctioned for contempt. Upholding a criminal contempt order and a fine of $2,000 imposed on a defense lawyer, In re Jasdeep Pannu, 5 A.3d 918 (Vt. 2010), is a state supreme court ruling that stresses the policies behind the rape shield law, such as protecting victims from unnecessary indignities and emotional trauma and increasing the number of rapes actually reported.

QUESTION 4-2. A defendant who is accused of rape and seeks to establish that the alleged victim had consented to sexual intercourse is barred from introducing evidence that the victim had a reputation for promiscuous behavior. The most sensible justification for this position is:

A. A person's past promiscuous conduct has no relationship to that person's conduct on any particular future occasion.

B. Inferring conduct on a particular occasion from a person's character traits is highly uncertain.

> **GOOD TO REMEMBER**
>
> FRE 412 and state rape shield statutes treat information about the character of a victim of a sex crime differently from the way FRE 404 treats information about the character of a victim of any other crime.

C. Keeping this kind of information out of trials minimizes what would otherwise be a significant obstacle to prosecuting sex crimes, since victims might decline to participate in prosecutions if that put them at risk of public scrutiny of their past conduct.

■   ■   ■

Recent Conduct and the Rape Shield Concept—**Jones.** How can a rape shield statute apply to conduct at what the court called a "sex party"? The court relied on the statute's use of the word "past" to resolve the issue of admissibility of evidence of an alleged victim's conduct hours before an alleged rape. The opinion offers a valuable analysis of constitutional limitations on evidence rulings that impair a criminal defendant's defense.

STATE v. JONES

230 P.3d 576 (Wash. 2010)

OWENS, J.

This case allows us to consider whether a trial court can bar a criminal defendant from testifying about sexual conduct contemporaneous with an alleged criminal act. The defendant argues that the trial court violated his Sixth Amendment right to present a defense when it effectively barred him from testifying about his version of the events during an alleged rape. We hold that the trial court erred by (1) preventing the defendant from testifying about the events in question and (2) improperly applying the rape shield statute (RCW 9A.44.020(2)). Since this error was not harmless beyond a reasonable doubt, we reverse and remand for a new trial.

K.D.[1] claimed that her uncle, Christopher Jones, put his hands around her neck and forcibly raped her. Jones was then charged in Benton County Superior Court with first degree rape of K.D. The jury found Jones not guilty of first degree rape but could not reach agreement on the lesser offense of second degree rape. The prosecutor then amended the charge to second degree rape and alleged the aggravating circumstance of use of a position of trust to facilitate the commission of the crime.

A second trial commenced, and in an offer of proof, Jones's attorney argued that Jones wished to testify that on the night of the incident K.D. used alcohol and cocaine and engaged in consensual sex not only with Jones but also with two other men. More specifically, Jones was prepared to testify that Jones and K.D. went to the King City Truck Stop where they met two men and one woman

---

1. K.D. was 17 years of age at the time of the alleged rape. We use initials to protect her identity

and that during a nine-hour alcohol- and cocaine-fueled sex party the two women danced for money and engaged in consensual sexual intercourse with all three males. The court found that evidence of the sex party was offered for the purpose of attacking the victim's credibility and was barred by the rape shield statute. The court therefore ruled that Jones could not testify to these claims or cross-examine K.D. about them, despite Jones's protests that the ruling prevented him from exercising his right to confrontation and his right to present a defense....

The jury found Jones guilty of second degree rape with the aggravating circumstance of use of a position of trust to facilitate the commission of the crime.

Jones appealed to the Court of Appeals, Division Three, which affirmed the conviction but remanded for resentencing based on another issue that is not before this court. We granted review....

I. The Trial Court Violated the Sixth Amendment When It Refused to Let Jones Testify about the Sex Party. Jones argues that the trial court improperly refused to let him testify or cross-examine witnesses about the events on the night of the alleged sexual encounter. . . . Jones argues that this ruling violated his Sixth Amendment right to present a defense. We agree.

"The right of an accused in a criminal trial to due process is, in essence, the right to a fair opportunity to defend against the State's accusations." *Chambers v. Mississippi,* 410 U.S. 284, 294, 93 S. Ct. 1038, 35 L. Ed. 2d 297 (1973). A defendant's right to an opportunity to be heard in his defense, including the rights to examine witnesses against him and to offer testimony, is basic in our system of jurisprudence. *Id.* "The right to confront and cross-examine adverse witnesses is [also] guaranteed by both the federal and state constitutions." *State v. Darden,* 145 Wash. 2d 612, 620, 41 P.3d 1189 (2002) (citing *Washington v. Texas,* 388 U.S. 14, 23, 87 S. Ct. 1920, 18 L. Ed. 2d 1019 (1967)).

These rights are not absolute, of course. Evidence that a defendant seeks to introduce "must be of at least minimal relevance." *Id.* at 622, 41 P.3d 1189. Defendants have a right to present only relevant evidence, with no constitutional right to present *irrelevant* evidence. *State v. Gregory,* 158 Wash. 2d 759, 786 n.6, 147 P.3d 1201 (2006). "[I]f relevant, the burden is on the State to show the evidence is so prejudicial as to disrupt the fairness of the fact-finding process at trial." *Darden,* 145 Wash. 2d at 622, 41 P.3d 1189. The State's interest in excluding prejudicial evidence must also "be balanced against the defendant's need for the information sought," and relevant information can be withheld only "if the State's interest outweighs the defendant's need." *Id.* We must remember that "the integrity of the truthfinding process and [a] defendant's right to a fair trial" are important considerations. *State v. Hudlow,* 99 Wash. 2d 1, 14, 659 P.2d 514 (1983). We have therefore noted that for evidence of *high* probative value "it appears no state interest can be compelling enough to preclude its introduction consistent with the Sixth Amendment and Const. art. 1, §22." *Id.* at 16, 659 P.2d 514. In *Hudlow,* we made a clear distinction between evidence of the general promiscuity of a rape victim and evidence that, if excluded, would deprive defendants of the ability to testify to their versions of the incident. In that case, evidence of past general promiscuity could be excluded, but the clear implication was that evidence of high probative value could not be restricted regardless of how compelling the State's interest may be if doing so would deprive the defendants of the ability to testify to their versions of the incident.

Jones was prepared to testify that K.D. consented to sex during an all-night drug-induced sex party. The trial court refused to let Jones present this testimony or cross-examine K.D. about the testimony. This is not marginally relevant evidence that a court should balance against the State's interest in excluding the evidence. Instead, it is evidence of extremely high probative value; it is Jones's entire defense. Jones's evidence, if believed, would prove consent and would provide a defense to the charge of second degree rape. Since no State interest can possibly be compelling enough to preclude the introduction of evidence of high probative value, the trial court violated the Sixth Amendment when it barred such evidence. . . .

II. The Rape Shield Statute Did Not Apply. The trial court ruled that the sex party evidence was offered for the purpose of attacking the victim's credibility and was barred by the rape shield statute. The trial court erred, as the rape shield statute did not apply to the case at hand, and even if it did apply, the rape shield statute cannot be used to bar evidence of high probative value.

The rape shield statute provides:

> Evidence of the victim's past sexual behavior including but not limited to the victim's marital history, divorce history, or general reputation for promiscuity, non-chastity, or sexual mores contrary to community standards is inadmissible on the issue of credibility and is inadmissible to prove the victim's consent except as provided in subsection (3) of this section, but when the perpetrator and the victim have engaged in sexual intercourse with each other in the past, and when the past behavior is material to the issue of consent, evidence concerning the past behavior between the perpetrator and the victim may be admissible on the issue of consent to the offense.

RCW 9A.44.020(2).

The rape shield statute does not apply in this case. The Court of Appeals correctly stated that "[n]o Washington case has defined the phrase 'past sexual behavior' for purposes of the rape-shield statute." It also correctly noted that Division Three had previously questioned whether flirtatious behavior on the evening of a rape counted as past sexual conduct and held that such behavior was not barred by the rape shield statute. *Id.* (citing *State v. Sheets,* 128 Wash. App. 149, 156–58, 115 P.3d 1004 (2005)). A quick reading of the rape shield statute, however, shows that it applies only to *past* sexual behavior. When interpreting a statute, we must first look to its language. *Cerrillo v. Esparza,* 158 Wash. 2d 194, 201, 142 P.3d 155 (2006). . . . The language of the statute states unequivocally that evidence of the victim's "past sexual behavior" is "inadmissible to prove the victim's consent." Any reading of the statute that conflates "past" with "present" sexual conduct is tortured. The statute was not designed to prevent defendants from testifying as to their version of events but was instead created to erase the misogynistic and antiquated notion that a woman's past sexual behavior somehow affected her credibility.

Jones's evidence refers not to past sexual conduct but to conduct on the night of the alleged rape. He wanted to testify that K.D. was not raped, but that she consumed alcohol and cocaine and consented to sex with three men during an all-night sex party. If we bar this evidence because of the rape shield statute, we are effectively reading the word "past" out of the statute. There is no indication that this is what the legislature intended. . . .

The rape shield statute cannot be a separate basis for excluding this evidence as it does not apply to this case. Furthermore, even if the rape shield statute *did* apply, the sex party testimony is of extremely high probative value and cannot be barred without violating the Sixth Amendment. . . .

We reverse the Court of Appeals and remand for a new trial. The trial court improperly applied the rape shield law, violating Jones's Sixth Amendment right to present a defense. This error was not harmless beyond a reasonable doubt, as a reasonable jury could have found differently if it heard the proffered evidence. . . .

NOTES TO STATE v. JONES

1. *Rationale for Rape Shield Rules.* The *Jones* court states that the rape shield law was adopted to eliminate the misogynistic view that a woman's past sexual conduct can affect her credibility. It did not refer to another significant rationale for rape shield provisions: the probative value of sexual conduct on one occasion is now generally thought to be low with respect to establishing the details of sexual conduct on other occasions. This second rationale may make the result in *Jones* more difficult to justify.

2. *Defendant's Need for Evidence.* In analyzing whether excluding evidence of the party would impair the defendant's case more significantly than the Constitution allows, the court noted that the challenged evidence was Jones's entire defense. This suggests that if other evidence that might have established the likelihood of consent had been available, the constitutional analysis of excluding information about the party might have produced a different result. This is an instance where the weakness of a party's case can increase the likelihood that low-quality evidence will be required to be admitted.

■ ■ ■

Conduct Ambiguously Related to Sexual Acts — Fells. The trial court and the intermediate appellate court disagreed on whether the alleged victim's HIV-positive status was information within the scope of the rape shield statute's coverage. Because the defendant had not complied with that statute's notice provisions, evidence on that topic would be barred if the statute governed.

FELLS v. STATE

207 S.W.3d 498 (Ark. 2005)

DICKEY, J.

Korey Fells was convicted in the Pulaski County Circuit Court of the rape of S.H. and sentenced to a term of eighteen years. On appeal, Fells argues that the trial court erred in . . . refusing to allow the defense to present evidence that the rape victim had tested positive for the human immunodeficiency virus (HIV). . . . We affirm.

S.H., the rape victim, testified that on February 3, 2002, Super Bowl Sunday, she was standing in the entrance to the Shorter Gardens housing project when Fells drove up and beckoned to her. When S.H. approached his car, he rolled down his window and asked if he knew her. The two then talked for about twenty to thirty minutes. S.H. mentioned that she was hungry, and he offered to drive her to a gas station so that she could get something to eat. Fells complimented S.H. on her physical appearance, and he portrayed himself as a trustworthy friend in whom she could confide. On the way to the gas station, he asked S.H. if she wanted to drive with him so that they could watch the Super Bowl on his car's television and S.H. could finish talking about her problems. S.H. agreed. He drove several miles and parked in an area with which S.H. was unfamiliar. While they drove, S.H. told Fells that she was pregnant and had suffered complications from her pregnancy earlier that day. She also told him that there were warrants out for her arrest and that she had few friends and nowhere to go. Fells parked his car, and the two sat in the backseat so that they could watch the Super Bowl. He then began to grope S.H. When she protested, he threatened to leave her to find her own way home. S.H. testified that she then feared for her life and the life of her unborn child, and she submitted. Shortly thereafter, police officers approached the vehicle. Fells told the police that everything was fine, but S.H. said that she had been raped. He then told the officers S.H.'s name and that she had warrants out for her arrest. S.H. left with the police, and Fells was eventually charged with rape.

Just before trial, the State moved *in limine* to prevent Fells from questioning S.H. regarding her HIV-positive status. The court granted the State's motion. . . .

The jury found Fells guilty of rape, and the trial court entered judgment on September 17, 2003.

The court of appeals reversed Fells's conviction, holding that Fells should have been able to present evidence that S.H. was HIV-positive. . . . We now affirm the trial court and reverse the court of appeals. . . .

Fells . . . argues that the trial court erred in refusing to allow him to present evidence that the rape victim, S.H., was HIV-positive. He contends that this evidence was admissible because it showed that S.H. had a motive to lie about being raped. According to Fells, because it is a crime for a person to knowingly expose another to HIV, S.H. "knew that if she did not say she was raped, it would be consensual sex and she'd be charged with a crime."

Under Arkansas's rape-shield statute, Ark. Code Ann. §16–42–101 (Repl. 1999), evidence of a victim's prior sexual conduct may be introduced at trial only after the proponent of the evidence has first filed a written motion explaining its relevance, and after the court has held a hearing and determined that the evidence is more probative than prejudicial. Although Fells admits that he did not comply with the required procedures, he argues that the information was not subject to the rape-shield law because it did not address any prior sexual activity, merely the fact that S.H. was HIV-positive.

The issue of whether a victim's HIV status falls under the purview of the rape-shield statute is one of first impression. We hold that the HIV status of a rape victim is protected under Arkansas's rape-shield statute. The statute prohibits the use of past sexual behavior to embarrass and degrade victims; its purpose is to shield rape victims from public humiliation. While it is possible to contract HIV through blood transfusions or other means, the public generally views it as a sexually-transmitted disease. In the minds of the jurors, evidence that S.H. was HIV-positive would be tantamount to evidence of her prior sexual behavior.

One should not conclude, as the dissent suggests, that a defendant can never present evidence of a rape victim's HIV status when that evidence is relevant to a defense at trial.

On the contrary, the rape-shield statute specifically contemplates the admission of such evidence, *once the required procedures have been followed and the trial court has determined that the evidence is more probative than prejudicial*. Fells did not comply with the rape-shield statute's procedures: he never filed the required motion, and he never gave the trial court the opportunity to hold a hearing and determine if the probative value of the HIV evidence was outweighed by its highly prejudicial effect. Had he done so, it is possible that the trial court would have allowed the evidence to be admitted. Because HIV status is protected under the rape-shield statute, however, Fells's failure to follow the required procedures means that the evidence was properly excluded. . . .

Trial court affirmed; Court of Appeals reversed.

[Dissenting opinions omitted.]

NOTES TO FELLS v. STATE

1. *Defining Sexual Behavior.* In applying rape shield provisions, courts have had to decide whether to characterize a variety of kinds of conduct as sexual behavior. For example, the Iowa Supreme Court has concluded that posing in the nude for photographs does not constitute a prior sexual act for rape shield purposes. *See* State v. Zaehringer, 280 N.W.2d 416 (Iowa 1979). That same court

applied the rape shield statute to require exclusion of evidence that an alleged victim went skinny-dipping in a river with a friend and declined to kiss him in the water. The court supported its conclusion by stating:

> To say it was not sexual behavior would be to say a circumstance where the complaining witness was thwarted in her attempt to meet someone for an amorous rendezvous was not sexual behavior. Such a result would be contrary to the purpose of the rape-shield law, which is to protect the victim's privacy, encourage the reporting and prosecution of sex offenses, and prevent the parties from delving into distractive, irrelevant matters.

State v. Alberts, 722 N.W.2d 402 (Iowa 2006).

2. Balancing Tests. The *Fells* majority states that the implication of its holding is not severe to defendants, since applying the rape shield statute would not necessarily require exclusion of the type of evidence at stake in *Fells*. The majority notes that once the statute does apply, evidence may still be admitted if its probative value outweighs the risk of prejudice. This balancing test, however, is different from the usual balancing test under Rule 403. Under the test in Rule 403, relevant evidence must be admitted if probative value and risk of prejudice are equal, or if the probative value is only somewhat less than the risk of prejudice.

3. False Claims of Rape. Would evidence that an alleged victim in the past made a false claim of rape involve proof about the alleged victim's past sexual conduct? In one analysis, it does not. It would be introduced to prove only that despite what the victim claimed, the victim had *not* been involved in sexual conduct. On the other hand, establishing that the victim had been truthful about the past rape would definitely involve information about the victim and the victim's past involvement in sexual conduct. Courts generally allow information of this type to be admitted, so long as the falsity of the prior claim has been established (with degrees of proof that vary among jurisdictions) outside the hearing of the jury.

D   DEFENDANTS ACCUSED OF SEX CRIMES

The Federal Rules of Evidence contain three rules specifically authorizing the use of the propensity inference against defendants in criminal and civil cases involving sex crimes. Rule 413 allows introduction of evidence of a defendant's past sexual assaults in a sexual assault case. Rule 414 is parallel to Rule 413, but applies to child molestation cases. And Rule 415 applies the provisions of Rules 413 and 414 to civil cases. Congress added these rules to the original Federal Rules of Evidence. This contrasts with the ordinary process in which changes to the rules are developed through a process supervised by the Supreme Court and then become effective unless rejected by Congress.

> **Rule 413. Similar Crimes in Sexual-Assault Cases**
>
> **(a) Permitted Uses.** In a criminal case in which a defendant is accused of a sexual assault, the court may admit evidence that the defendant committed any other sexual assault. The evidence may be considered on any matter to which it is relevant.
>
> **(b) Disclosure to the Defendant.** If the prosecutor intends to offer this evidence, the prosecutor must disclose it to the defendant, including witnesses' statements or a summary of the expected testimony. The prosecutor must do so at least 15 days before trial or at a later time that the court allows for good cause.
>
> **(c) Effect on Other Rules.** This rule does not limit the admission or consideration of evidence under any other rule.
>
> **(d) Definition of "Sexual Assault."** In this rule and Rule 415, "sexual assault" means a crime under federal law or under state law (as "state" is defined in 18 U.S.C. §513) involving:
>
> **(1)** any conduct prohibited by 18 U.S.C. chapter 109A;
>
> **(2)** contact, without consent, between any part of the defendant's body — or an object — and another person's genitals or anus;
>
> **(3)** contact, without consent, between the defendant's genitals or anus and any part of another person's body;
>
> **(4)** deriving sexual pleasure or gratification from inflicting death, bodily injury, or physical pain on another person; or
>
> **(5)** an attempt or conspiracy to engage in conduct described in subparagraphs (1)–(4).

Distinctions Between Past Sexual Wrongdoing and Charged Sexual Wrongdoing—Hollow Horn. This case involves sexual assaults against children. The past conduct the prosecution wanted to prove, however, was a sexual assault against an adult, so the court applies Rule 413, about prior sexual assaults, instead of Rule 414 which applies to child molestation. Consider whether the past conduct would likely have qualified for admission under Rule 404, if Rules 413 and 414 were not part of the structure of the Federal Rules.

UNITED STATES v. HOLLOW HORN

523 F.3d 882 (8th Cir. 2008)

SMITH, J.

Following a jury trial, Maurice Hollow Horn was convicted of two counts of abusive sexual contact, in violation of 18 U.S.C. §§1153, 2244(a)(1), 2241(c), and 2246(3). The district court denied Hollow Horn's motion for new trial and sentenced him to concurrent terms of 34 months' imprisonment. Hollow Horn appeals. We affirm. . . .

At trial, the evidence established that in July 1999, several girls attended the 10th birthday party for Hollow Horn's daughter, Maurisa. The girls included R.R.A., who is Maurisa's first cousin (and Hollow Horn's niece) and H.C., who is Maurisa's second cousin (and the daughter of Hollow Horn's first cousin, Laudine). The party began at Hollow Horn's home. The adults also set up a tent outside of Maurisa's grandmother's home a few hundred yards away, so that the girls could have a sleep-over. . . . R.R.A. — who was 7 years old at the time — became scared, left the tent, and went into her grandmother's house to sleep on the couch. The other four girls spent the night in the tent.

R.R.A. testified that as she began to doze off on the couch, Hollow Horn (her uncle) entered the room wearing only his underwear and sat down on the couch near her feet. R.R.A. testified that Hollow Horn removed her covers and touched her vagina, rubbing it in an "up and down" motion with his hand over her panties but underneath the long shirt that she was wearing. Hollow Horn continued this rubbing for a couple of seconds before R.R.A. kicked him in the side, causing him to stop. Hollow Horn then placed the covers back on R.R.A., told her to be quiet and go back to sleep, and walked out of the room. . . .

H.C., who was 10 years old at the time of the party, testified that she was asleep inside the tent with the three other girls, when she was awakened by someone rubbing her breasts in a circular motion. H.C. testified that she opened her eyes when she felt someone lift up her nightgown, exposing her stomach, and she saw Hollow Horn trying to remove her panties. At that point, but before her panties were removed, H.C. told Hollow Horn to stop, and he complied. . . .

After an offer of proof by the government, the district court, over Hollow Horn's objection, allowed H.C.'s mother, Laudine, to testify pursuant to Federal Rule of Evidence 413. Laudine testified that Hollow Horn raped her at a New Year's Eve party on the night of December 31, 1987 or early morning of January 1, 1988, when Laudine was 20 years old. Laudine testified that she became intoxicated at the party and passed out. When she came to, she found her pants at her ankles, her shirt pulled up, and Hollow Horn — her first cousin — having sex with her. Laudine testified that she told Hollow Horn to get off of her, and he moved back, pulled up his pants, and watched as she got dressed. . . . The police took a report from Laudine and transported her to the hospital for an examination. After Laudine's police report was filed, a tribal prosecution was commenced, but Laudine subsequently withdrew the complaint due to pressure from her mother. In withdrawing the complaint, Laudine did not recant her allegation. Nevertheless, after the complaint was withdrawn, Hollow Horn was not prosecuted for the alleged rape. Laudine further testified that she would not have consented to sex with Hollow Horn. . . .

The jury subsequently found Hollow Horn guilty on both counts of abusive sexual contact — one count each relating to his contact with R.R.A. and H.C. . . . Subsequently, the district court sentenced Hollow Horn to 34 months' imprisonment on each count, with the sentences to run concurrently. . . .

On appeal, Hollow Horn argues that the district court erred in admitting Laudine's testimony regarding his alleged rape of her. The district court admitted the evidence under Rules 413 and 403 and gave a limiting instruction to the jury. We review these evidentiary rulings by the district court for abuse of discretion.

"Evidence of prior bad acts is generally not admissible to prove a defendant's character or propensity to commit crime." *Gabe,* 237 F.3d at 959 (citing Fed. R. Evid. 404(b)). Congress, however, modified this rule in sex offense cases when it adopted Rules 413 and 414 of the Federal Rules of Evidence. In sexual assault and child molestation cases, "evidence that the defendant committed a prior similar offense 'may be considered for its bearing on any matter to which it is relevant,' including the defendant's propensity to commit such offenses." *Id.* If the evidence of the defendant's prior sexual offense is relevant, "the evidence is admissible unless its probative value is 'substantially outweighed' by one or more of the factors enumerated in Rule 403, including 'the danger of unfair prejudice.'" *Gabe,* 237 F.3d at 959 (citing *United States v. LeCompte,* 131 F.3d 767, 769 (8th Cir. 1997)).

Federal Rule of Evidence 413(a) states: "In a criminal case in which the defendant is accused of an offense of sexual assault, evidence of the defendant's commission of another offense or offenses of sexual assault is admissible, and may be considered for its bearing on any matter to which it is relevant." The definition of an "offense of sexual assault" for purposes of Rule 413, includes, among other things: "contact, without consent, between any part of the defendant's body . . . and the genitals or anus of another person," as well as "an attempt . . . to engage in [such] conduct. . . . " Fed. R. Evid. 413(d). Laudine's testimony qualifies as Rule 413 evidence because it is evidence that Hollow Horn committed another offense of sexual assault. Hollow Horn was charged with abusive sexual contact, which undeniably meets the definition of an offense of sexual assault. But, as discussed above, to be admissible, the Rule 413 evidence must also be relevant and its probative value must not be substantially outweighed by the danger of unfair prejudice.

The district court found that Hollow Horn's alleged rape of Laudine was relevant, and that its probative value outweighed the danger of unfair prejudice.[8] Hollow Horn's alleged rape of Laudine occurred approximately 11 and a half years prior to the date of Hollow Horn's alleged abusive sexual contact with R.R.A. and H.C., and the alleged rape was of a 20 year old, not a child. Nonetheless, we agree with the district court that the evidence was relevant and probative. Both

---

8. In ruling on the admissibility of the Rule 413 evidence, the district court first made a record of the proposed evidence out of the presence of the jury, and then made a clear record of the factors it weighed in reaching its determination. These factors included: (1) Rule 413 did not contain a time limitation; (2) the Rule is intended to be interpreted broadly; (3) the probative value of the evidence was not overcome by its prejudice; and (4) the similarity between the circumstances of assault upon the testifying witness and the alleged assaults upon the present victims, and the factual similarities of the Defendant's actions in the separate assaults. The method employed by the district court was procedurally sound and created a clear record for appellate review.

offenses involved sexual assaults of defenseless victims. The instant charges involve Hollow Horn's alleged sexual assault of sleeping minor victims, and the earlier alleged rape also involved an unconscious victim. Furthermore, Hollow Horn was related to all three alleged victims. Additionally, in all three instances, the accusers testified that once they realized what Hollow Horn was doing, they took action, either verbally or physically, to make him stop, and he did so. Thus, the district court did not abuse its discretion in ruling that the Rule 413 evidence was relevant.

We must next decide whether the probative value of Laudine's testimony was "substantially outweighed by its potential for unfair prejudice." Laudine's testimony was undoubtedly prejudicial to Hollow Horn as evidence admitted under Rule 413 is very likely to be. Rule 403, however, "is concerned only with 'unfair prejudice, that is, an undue tendency to suggest decision on an improper basis.'" *Gabe,* 237 F.3d at 960 (quoting *United States v. Yellow,* 18 F.3d 1438, 1442 (8th Cir. 1994)). Laudine's testimony is prejudicial to Hollow Horn for the same reason it is probative — it tends to prove his propensity to commit sexual assaults on vulnerable female members of his family when presented with an opportunity to do so undetected. *See Gabe,* 237 F.3d at 960 (finding witness's testimony that defendant sexually molested her 20 years earlier admissible under Rule 414, stating that the "testimony is prejudicial ... for the same reason it is probative — it tends to prove his propensity to molest young children in his family when presented with an opportunity to do so undetected"). Because this specific type of propensity evidence is admissible under Rule 413, Hollow Horn has not shown that its prejudice was *unfair. See id.* (ruling that because Rule 414 evidence is admissible to prove propensity, the resulting prejudice from the admission of the Rule 414 evidence was not "*unfair* prejudice").

Although the prior sexual assault alleged against Hollow Horn was over 11 years prior to the alleged sexual offenses at issue here, "Congress expressly rejected imposing any time limit on prior sex offense evidence," when it enacted Rule 413. *Id.* (citing 140 CONG. REC. H8968–01, H8992 (daily ed. Aug. 21, 1994) (statement by Rep. Molinari) ("No time limit is imposed on the uncharged offenses for which evidence may be admitted; as a practical matter, evidence of other sex offenses by the defendant is often probative and properly admitted, notwithstanding very substantial lapses of time in relation to the charged offense or offenses.")). Further, we have previously held that a district court did not abuse its discretion in admitting Rule 414 evidence despite a 20–year lapse in time between the prior act and the current one. *See Gabe,* 237 F.3d at 960 (finding no abuse of discretion in district court's allowance under Rule 414 of witness's testimony that defendant, who was on trial for child molestation offenses, had molested her 20 years earlier). Additionally, despite the passage of time in this case, the district court also found Laudine's testimony to be credible.

"There is a strong legislative judgment that evidence of prior sexual offenses should ordinarily be admissible." Moreover, the district court gave a limiting instruction thereby decreasing the danger that Hollow Horn was *unfairly* prejudiced by Laudine's testimony.[9] *See id.* ("Limiting instructions decrease the danger of unfair prejudice"). For all of these reasons, we hold that the district court did not abuse its discretion in allowing Laudine's testimony....

Accordingly, we affirm the judgment of the district court.

NOTES TO UNITED STATES v. HOLLOW HORN

1. *Equal Protection Clause.* Special rules governing past sexual conduct can be constitutional, even though they treat individuals who have committed sex crimes differently from those who have committed other kinds of crimes. The rules do not burden a fundamental right or affect members of a protected class. They therefore need satisfy only a rational relationship test, which could be satisfied by findings that recidivism is particularly common in sex crimes or that the need for evidence of low probative value is particularly high in sex crime cases.

2. *Propensity, not Motive or Intent.* Rules 413 and 414 are explicitly intended to allow a propensity inference from a defendant's past conduct. This contrasts with the position of Rule 404 that generally prohibits the propensity inference, and allows proof of past bad acts only when they logically support inferences different from propensity.

3. *"Lustful Disposition" Doctrine.* Some states have authorized the propensity inference in sex crime cases under a "lustful disposition" doctrine, but may interpret it more narrowly than is the case under Rules 413 and 414. For example, in Mitchell v. State, 539 So. 2d 1366 (Miss. 1989), the court held that evidence of past acts of sexual relations between a defendant and a victim were admissible to show the "lustful, lascivious disposition of the defendant toward that particular victim," but that past acts by the defendant with individuals other than the victim could not be shown.

> **GOOD TO REMEMBER**
>
> FRE 413 requires almost automatic admission of evidence that a defendant accused of a sex crime has in the past committed acts of sexual misconduct.

---

9. After Laudine's direct examination at trial, but prior to her cross-examination, the district court instructed the jury, stating:

> Ladies and gentlemen of the jury, ... this is evidence that is received for a limited purpose only. Congress passed a rule that said that in cases of alleged sexual assaults that evidence of other alleged sexual assaults may be admissible in evidence.
>
> It's — it doesn't mean that the Defendant is guilty of the crimes for which he's on charge here. But the jury can give this evidence plus the cross-examination, of course, as much weight as you want to give it. And so that's the purpose of this evidence.
>
> Normally, as I said before, the fact that you were speeding five years ago doesn't mean that you were speeding yesterday or something of that nature, okay?

QUESTION 4-3. Fred First is accused of shooting a child. According to the prosecution, in 2011 he traveled to a city far from his home, entered a day-care center, and asked the manager for money. When she was slow to respond, First allegedly shot a child who was nearby. To show that First is the person who committed the shooting in the day-care center, the prosecution seeks to introduce evidence that in 2005 First ended a three-year relationship with a woman and shot her child during an argument about the dissolution of their relationship. He was convicted of attempted murder for that shooting.

Sam Second is accused of attempted rape. According to the prosecution, in 2011 he traveled to a city far from his home, entered a day-care center and asked the manager for money. When she was slow to respond, Second allegedly attempted to rape the manager. To show that Second is the person who committed the attempted rape in the day-care center, the prosecution seeks to introduce evidence that in 2005 Second ended a three-year relationship with a woman and attempted to rape her during an argument about the dissolution of their relationship. He was convicted of attempted rape for that conduct.

In each of these cases, should the judge admit the evidence of the defendant's past conduct?

E SUMMARY

Habit Evidence Is Admissible, Even Though Character Evidence Is Usually Forbidden. A habit is a kind of conduct that a person does almost automatically, in a typical response to a particular stimulus. Evidence law allows evidence that would support a finding that a person has a habit to be introduced to show that the person acted in accordance with that habit on a particular occasion. This is different from the way evidence law typically treats character evidence. The difference is justified because habits are specific, so there are fewer problems with vague interpretations of what a person's character might be and how any particular character might be related to particular conduct. *Brown, Aikman,* and *Gamerdinger* explain differences between character evidence and habit evidence. They also consider how to distinguish between conduct that shows only character and information about conduct that can support a finding that a person has a habit.

Evidence About an Alleged Sex Crime Victim's Past Sexual Conduct to Show Character Traits Related to Sexuality Is Usually Forbidden. Rape shield statutes and FRE 412 impose strict limits on the admissibility of evidence about an alleged victim's past sexual conduct. *Williams* shows how past work as a prostitute, which might be thought to support a finding that the individual was likely to consent to sexual acts, must be excluded if offered for that purpose. *Jones* and *Fells* examined how very recent conduct or conduct with only an ambiguous relationship to sexual acts may be treated under these rules and statutes.

Evidence About an Alleged Sex Crime Perpetrator's Past Sexual Conduct to Support the Propensity Inference Is Admissible under FRE 413, 414, and 415. These rules expressly permit the usually forbidden propensity inference to be used against defendants in sex crime cases: Past sexual misconduct may be introduced to support a conclusion that the individual acted on the occasion of a charged offense as he or she had acted on a previous occasion involving sexual misconduct. *Hollow Horn* shows how only slight similarity between the past and charged acts may be required.

CHAPTER 5

Hearsay: Foundations of the Doctrine

A. Introduction
B. Statements That Are Relevant Only If What They Assert Is True (Hearsay)
C. Statements That Are Relevant Regardless of Whether Their Assertions Are True (Not Hearsay)
D. Summary

A | INTRODUCTION

Topic Overview

The hearsay doctrine is based on a simple idea: The best way to find out something a person knows is to talk to that person directly. For example, assume that someone called Watcher once saw a car accident. If you asked Watcher what had happened, Watcher might say something like, "The sporty car was going really fast." Because you were talking directly with Watcher, you could ask Watcher additional questions to find out: (1) how Watcher saw the events, (2) whether Watcher has a good memory, (3) what Watcher means by words like "sporty" or "fast," and (4) whether Watcher seemed to be lying or trying to communicate honestly. In your conversation with Watcher, you could check on Watcher's *perception* of the events he thought he saw, his *memory* of those events, the ambiguity in his *narration* of the facts he thought he remembered, and his apparent *honesty*.

Another way to find out what a person knows about a topic would be to talk to somebody else who had once talked about it with that person. For example, if Watcher once told someone named Friend about the accident and then you spoke with Friend about it, Friend would be able to say to you something like, "Watcher once told me 'the sporty car was going really fast.'" Unfortunately, Friend might not know how Watcher had seen the events. And asking Friend about Watcher's memory would not be as helpful as having a way to evaluate it yourself. Also, if there is ambiguity in words like "sporty" and "fast," Friend might not know exactly what Watcher had meant to convey by using them. Finally, Friend's opinion of Watcher's honesty might not be as useful as the sense you might get of truthfulness by observing Watcher yourself. If the only person you talk to is Friend, you won't be able to evaluate Watcher's *perception* of the events he thought he saw, Watcher's *memory* of those events, the ambiguity in Watcher's *narration* of the facts he thought he remembered, and Watcher's apparent *honesty*. This is why a conversation with Friend is worse than a conversation with Watcher, if you want to know what Watcher knows. The hearsay rule is based on this comparison: First-hand information is better than second-hand information.

When a party wants to bring someone's out-of-court words into a trial to support a finding that those words are an accurate description of some out-of-court event, the out-of-court words are called "hearsay." Hearsay is inadmissible (unless an exception to the general hearsay prohibition applies).

Chapter Organization

This chapter begins with the basic hearsay concept, applied to identifying what kinds of statements are hearsay. A hearsay statement is an assertion made out of court, introduced in court for a purpose that requires a finder of fact to rely on the truthfulness of the out-of-court assertion. In this chapter, the first cases evaluate different kinds of communications to determine if the offered evidence fits the definition of hearsay. In the next group of cases, out-of-court statements may have relevance regardless of whether they are true. Statements of this kind are outside the definition of hearsay.

Basic Structure for Analysis

Using the hearsay doctrine involves several analytical steps. Some of them are covered in this chapter; some are covered in Chapters 6 through 10. The following chart gives an overview of the entire doctrine and puts this chapter's initial coverage into context.

WHEN DOES THE HEARSAY RULE KEEP EVIDENCE OUT OR ALLOW IT IN?

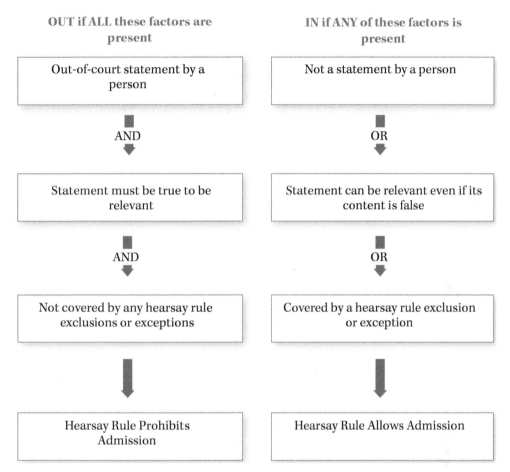

OUT if ALL these factors are present	IN if ANY of these factors is present
Out-of-court statement by a person	Not a statement by a person
AND	OR
Statement must be true to be relevant	Statement can be relevant even if its content is false
AND	OR
Not covered by any hearsay rule exclusions or exceptions	Covered by a hearsay rule exclusion or exception
Hearsay Rule Prohibits Admission	Hearsay Rule Allows Admission

The chart shows that the first consideration is whether the evidence is anything different from an out-of-court statement by a person. This is important because the hearsay rule applies only to out-of-court statements by people.

If the evidence is a statement by a person made out of court, then the next inquiry is whether it is being introduced for the truth of what it asserts. Another way of describing this is to consider whether the statement would have relevance even if it was false.

If the statement is being introduced for the truth of its assertions, it is hearsay, and the next step in the analysis is to determine whether any of the exemptions or exclusions that take away what would otherwise be the hearsay doctrine's prohibition against introducing the evidence.

FIRST STEPS FOR...

Analyzing Hearsay

To analyze hearsay issues, we have to know two things:
- *Is the evidence an out-of-court statement by a person?*
- *Is it being introduced for a purpose that depends on the truth of the statement's assertion?*

STATEMENTS THAT ARE RELEVANT ONLY IF WHAT THEY ASSERT IS TRUE (HEARSAY)

A statement is hearsay only if it was made out of court and is introduced to prove that what it asserted was true. Rule 801 sets out a definition of hearsay. Rule 802 states that hearsay is not admissible (unless a statute or other rules make it admissible).

Rule 801. Definitions That Apply to This Article . . .

(a) **Statement.** "Statement" means a person's oral assertion, written assertion, or nonverbal conduct, if the person intended it as an assertion.

(b) **Declarant.** "Declarant" means the person who made the statement.

(c) **Hearsay.** "Hearsay" means a statement that:

(1) the declarant does not make while testifying at the current trial or hearing; and

(2) a party offers in evidence to prove the truth of the matter asserted in the statement.

. . .

Rule 802. The Rule Against Hearsay

Hearsay is not admissible unless any of the following provides otherwise:

- a federal statute;
- these rules; or
- other rules prescribed by the Supreme Court.

■   ■   ■

"It's True That He Said It" versus "What He Said Is True" — **Vincelette.** The key to working well with the hearsay concept is to be clear about two things: exactly what statement a party is trying to introduce and the identity of the person who made the statement. Hearsay problems always involve a statement and the declarant of the statement. In *Vincelette* the court applies the definition of hearsay to a statement a hotel worker made about a guest.

The out-of-court statement would be hearsay if its proponent wanted to have it admitted as proof of what it asserted. It would be nonhearsay if it could have relevance in the case just because someone said it, regardless of whether it was true or false. As often happens in hearsay situations, the proponent of the statement sought to justify its admission by claiming that it could be relevant even if its meaning had not been true.

VINCELETTE v. METROPOLITAN LIFE INSURANCE CO.

968 P.2d 275 (Mont. 1998)

TERRY N. TRIEWEILER, J.

The plaintiff, Darlene M. Vincelette, commenced this action in the District Court for the Thirteenth Judicial District in Yellowstone County to recover damages for personal injuries sustained while a guest of the defendant, Billings Sheraton Hotel. Following a jury trial, a verdict was returned for the hotel. Darlene appeals from the judgment entered pursuant to that verdict and from the denial of her motion for a new trial. We reverse the judgment of the District Court and remand for further proceedings....

Around midnight on March 19 or 20, 1989, Darlene Vincelette fell while entering the Billings Sheraton Hotel. She and her companion had passed through the outer doors leading to the hotel lobby and were crossing over a carpeted entryway. Darlene took a step backward to allow her companion to open one of the inner doors. As she did so, she fell and injured her back.

Darlene asserts that the cause of the fall was either a defect in the carpeting or negligent maintenance of the carpeting. The hotel denied any defect or negligence. It alleged that Darlene was intoxicated and that her condition was the cause of her fall.

Darlene moved the District Court prior to trial for an order excluding testimony from hotel employees that they had been told Darlene was drunk. The District Court did not rule on the motion.

At trial, one of the hotel's maintenance engineers was allowed to testify that he had received a radio call from another hotel employee, who stated that Darlene was drunk. Plaintiff's counsel moved to strike the testimony as hearsay, but the motion was denied. The declarant was never identified nor produced as a witness....

Did the District Court abuse its discretion when it allowed a witness to testify about out-of-court statements made by an unidentified declarant?...

Darlene alleged that the cause of her fall was the condition of the hotel carpeting, caused by improper maintenance. As a defense, the hotel asserted that there was nothing wrong with the carpeting but that Darlene's intoxication was the cause of her fall. Prior to trial, Darlene filed a motion in limine to exclude testimony from hotel employees that they were told the plaintiff was drunk. The District Court did not rule on the motion, but stated that it would make a decision at trial, once a foundation for the testimony existed.

At trial, Darlene called Larry Vandenbosch, a maintenance engineer on duty at the hotel the night of her accident, as an adverse witness. On direct examination, Mr. Vandenbosch testified that he received a report by radio that a woman had fallen in the entryway. He then went to investigate, but the entryway and lobby were empty when he arrived. He further testified that upon his arrival he examined the entryway carpeting.

On cross-examination, counsel for the hotel asked Vandenbosch what "information" the radio caller gave him. Vandenbosch then testified that he was told a woman had fallen in the entryway and that she was drunk. He could not remember who placed the radio call, and the unidentified caller did not testify at trial.

Darlene moved to strike the statement that she was drunk on the basis that it was hearsay. The District Court allowed the statement on the basis that it was not offered for the truth of the matter asserted, but "merely to reflect what was said to him and therefore it's not hearsay."

Following the ruling, the hotel again elicited testimony from Vandenbosch that he had been told Darlene was drunk. Then, in closing argument, counsel for the hotel repeated the testimony.

On appeal, Darlene contends the out-of-court statement was offered to show that her fall resulted from intoxication rather than a defect in the carpeting. The hotel contends that the testimony was not hearsay because it was not offered to prove the truth of the matter asserted[ ] but to show its effect on the witness's state of mind and to show why he went to the entryway to investigate.

Hearsay is a statement, other than one made by the declarant while testifying at the trial, offered in evidence to prove the truth of the matter asserted. See Rule 801(c), M. R. Evid. Hearsay is not admissible except as provided by the rules of evidence. See Rule 802, M. R. Evid. A statement does not fit within the definition of hearsay when it is not offered to prove the truth of the matter asserted, but to show the resulting effect on the witness's state of mind. See Moats Trucking Co. v. Gallatin Dairies (1988), 231 Mont. 474, 479, 753 P.2d 883, 886.

In *Moats*, the plaintiff trucking firm brought an action for breach of contract and breach of the covenant of good faith and fair dealing when the defendant dairy company terminated a hauling contract with forty-eight days' notice. The district court allowed one of the defendant's employees to explain why notice was not given immediately when the decision was made to terminate the contract by relating an out-of-court conversation with another employee, who expressed concern that the plaintiff would terminate services immediately upon being advised that its contract was being terminated. The district court held that the out-of-court conversation was not admitted to prove that the plaintiff would actually have terminated services immediately, but to show the effect that it had on the state of mind of the defendant's employee. Prior to allowing the testimony, the district court cautioned the jury that the party's testimony was admitted only for the purpose of showing that the statements were made, not for proving that they were true. We affirmed the ruling of the district court on that basis.

Here, there is no similar purpose for admitting an out-of-court statement about Darlene's intoxication. The testimony that a woman had fallen, offered on direct examination, served to show why Vandenbosch went to the entryway and examined the carpeting. The specific statement that the woman was drunk had no bearing on his decision to investigate. The statement served no other purpose than to prove that Darlene fell because she was drunk. . . .

[T]he hotel's argument that Vandenbosch's testimony was not offered to prove the truth of what was asserted is belied by the fact that the hotel's defense was based on its contention that Darlene was intoxicated. The evidence the hotel sought to present, suggesting that Darlene was drunk, was an out-of-court statement offered to prove the truth of what was asserted, and was inadmissible hearsay pursuant to Rules 801(c) and 802, M. R. Evid. We conclude that the District Court erred when it allowed the hearsay testimony.

For error to be the basis for a new trial, it must affect the substantial rights of the appellant. Because of the inflammatory nature of the evidence, and Darlene's complete inability to test its reliability by cross-examination, we conclude that the evidence did affect Darlene's substantial rights and was prejudicial. For this reason, we reverse the judgment of the District Court and remand for a new trial.

NOTES TO VINCELETTE v. METROPOLITAN LIFE INSURANCE CO.

1. *Basic Hearsay Analysis.* The out-of-court statement in this case is something like "woman is drunk." The declarant was an unidentified hotel employee (who said those words over the hotel's radio system to Larry Vandenbosch). The plaintiff argued that the defendant introduced those words to support a finding that the woman had been drunk. The defendant argued that it introduced those words only to show that Mr. Vandenbosch had heard them and that they motivated him to go to the entryway to investigate.

The ability to cross-examine the declarant about the declarant's perception, memory, narration or ambiguity of speech, and honesty would matter greatly if the out-of-court words are being used to support a finding that the plaintiff had been drunk. For example, it would be helpful to know that the declarant meant by the word "drunk." But losing the ability to clarify perception, memory, narration, and honesty would not matter at all if the words were being introduced just to show that Mr. Vandenbosch heard them and reacted to them.

2. *Statements Relevant Even If False.* Depending on the substantive law of a case, sometimes an out-of-court statement can be relevant even if its contents were false. In that situation, there is no harm in admitting the statement even though there is no way to explore the declarant's perception, memory, narration, and honesty. The *Moats* case that the *Vincelette* court distinguished is an example of an instance where the truth or falsity of some out-of-court words had no bearing on the relevance of those words.

QUESTION 5-1. To show that that there was a dangerous spill on the floor of a store, a plaintiff seeks to introduce testimony that a shopper had said to the store manager, "There's a dangerous spill on the floor near the display of peaches." Does the testimony contain hearsay? How do the basic rationales for the hearsay doctrine apply in your analysis?

■   ■   ■

Nonverbal Statements — **Patterson.** A declarant can make a statement with words or with conduct meant to convey an assertion. In *Patterson*, the majority presents a strange analysis of whether a composite sketch produced with the participation of an eyewitness to a crime should be treated as an assertion made by that eyewitness. Note that the majority opinion fails to respond to the concurrence. This is probably because the concurrence's understanding of hearsay is better than the majority's.

STATE v. PATTERSON

420 S.E.2d 98 (N.C. 1992)

MITCHELL, J.

The defendant was indicted for robbery with a firearm in violation of N.C.G.S. §14-87. He was tried at the 21 August 1989 Criminal Session of Superior Court, Guilford County. The jury found the defendant guilty of robbery with a firearm, and the trial court entered judgment imposing a sentence of life imprisonment. The Court of Appeals found no error in the defendant's trial. On 7 November 1991, this Court entered its order allowing the defendant's petition for discretionary review....

[The defendant] contends that the trial court erred by admitting composite drawings of the perpetrators of the robbery in question, prepared with the participation of eyewitnesses to that crime and according to those witnesses' descriptions of the perpetrators. The defendant argues that those drawings or pictures were inadmissible because they were hearsay....

... Under our Rules of Evidence, "[h]earsay is not admissible except as provided by statute or by these rules." N.C.G.S. §8C-1, Rule 802 (1988). "Hearsay" is defined as "a *statement*, other than one made by the declarant while testifying at the trial or hearing, offered in evidence to prove the truth of the matter asserted." N.C.G.S. §8C-1, Rule 801(c) (1988) (emphasis added). In this context, a "statement" is "(1) an oral or written assertion or (2) nonverbal conduct of a person, if it is intended by him as an assertion." N.C.G.S. §8C-1, Rule 801(a) (1988)....

The composite sketches or pictures in question here were created by Special Investigator J.A. Armfield using an "Identi-kit" procedure during consultations with four witnesses the day after the robbery. At trial, Armfield testified that the kit had hundreds of different facial features which he could place on clear plastic plates to construct a composite picture. He explained:

> [T]he composite process is performed by creating an original face, and then asking the individuals what's wrong with it[ ]. . . . [A]t this point we begin changing the features of the face until the individual is satisfied that what we have is as close as we can get to the person they are trying to identify.

The State contends that no out-of-court statements of the witnesses themselves were introduced through the testimony of Special Investigator Armfield. The State argues that the composite pictures did not constitute "statements" and, therefore, were not hearsay under our Rules. The State reasons in support of this argument that the composite pictures are akin to a photograph, in that they are produced by mechanical procedures essentially re-creating a picture and not producing a "statement" or an "assertion" within the meaning of our Rules of Evidence. We agree.

Other appellate courts have had the opportunity to consider whether composite pictures fall within the definition of a "statement" under their jurisdictions' versions of Rule 801(a). Since North Carolina's Rule 801(a) mirrors the language of the versions applied in those jurisdictions, we find such cases instructive on questions of whether such composite pictures are statements under our version of Rule 801(a).

In United States v. Moskowitz, 581 F.2d 14 (2d Cir. 1978), the United States Court of Appeals for the Second Circuit considered whether the trial court should have excluded a sketch of the defendant made by a police artist the day after the robbery in question. The court held that the composite drawing introduced against the defendant was not a "statement" under Federal Rule 801(a). It explained that "[t]he sketch itself, as distinguished from [the witnesses'] statements about it, need not fit an exception to the rule against hearsay because it is not a 'statement' and therefore can no more be 'hearsay' than a photograph identified by a witness." . . .

We recognize that some courts have expressed a contrary view and have deemed such composite pictures to be hearsay. . . . However, we . . . conclude that a composite picture of a perpetrator prepared by police pursuant to the directions of a witness to a crime does not constitute a "statement" under North Carolina Rule of Evidence 801(a). Such a composite picture is the functional equivalent of a photograph in that it merely reflects the perpetrator's likeness, albeit as recorded by the witness's eyes rather than the witness's camera. No assertion or statement is involved. Therefore, a composite picture is not "hearsay" as defined by Rule 801(c), and Rule 802 does not apply to bar the admission of a composite picture into evidence. . . .

Justice FRYE concurring in result.

I respectfully disagree with the Court's holding that the composite pictures in this case are not hearsay. I believe they are hearsay and, not falling within any recognized exception to the hearsay rule, should have been excluded as substantive evidence. I agree with the Court, however, that the admission of the composite pictures in this case did not prejudice defendant. I therefore concur in the result reached by the Court. . . .

Put simply, it seems clear that had the police artist repeated the statements made to him by the eyewitnesses, these statements would be classified as hearsay. How, then, can the product of these statements — the composite pictures — be somehow transformed into nonhearsay? I don't believe it can and thus am unable to join the Court's opinion. I therefore concur only in the result reached by the Court.

NOTES TO STATE v. PATTERSON

1. *Information from Animals and Machines.* The hearsay rule has absolutely no application to a witness's testimony describing a bloodhound's conduct, the readings on a thermometer, or other information from animals and machines. How does the text of Rule 801 make this clear?

2. *Using the Hearsay Rule's Rationale to Identify Hearsay.* The hearsay rule is ordinarily justified by considering whether cross-examining a declarant to learn about the declarant's perception, memory, use of language, and probable honesty would be helpful, considering the purpose for which the declarant's words are introduced. That analysis can test the majority position that the composite sketch is properly compared to a photograph. Even if it were possible, there would be no benefit to asking a photograph how well it had seen what its image represents, or what it meant by a particular pattern of lines or shadings. Asking an eyewitness what he or she meant by selecting one pattern of hairline instead of another, or how he or she had observed what he or she was describing to the artist, on the other hand, might produce worthwhile information for assessing the accuracy of the eyewitness's information.

3. *Things Are Not Statements.* In this article about a baseball controversy, the hearsay analysis is wrong.

> In the manager's office in the Mets' clubhouse, Davey Johnson opened the lower right-hand drawer of his desk. "Here they are," he said. As the drawer moved, eight National League baseballs rolled around. Some were cleaner than others. Some were slightly smudged with dirt or grass stains. But on each ball, the white cowhide was scuffed, as if sandpapered, in the area where the red stitches widen.
>
> "They're all scuffed in the same spot," Johnson was saying now. "All in the middle of the ball on top of the ball. I don't think that's an accident."
>
> What the Mets' manager does think is that Mike Scott of the Astros is using a foreign substance, perhaps a small piece of hidden sandpaper, to scuff the ball when he rubs it up, thereby helping it to break sharper than it should. . . .
>
> While it's possible that the Mets might have scuffed the balls themselves, their manager was willing to take a lie-detector test to show that nobody in the Mets' organization had tampered with the baseballs. But when Hal Lanier, the Astros' manager, was asked if he would take a lie-detector test, he never answered directly.
>
> "In a court of law, those scuffed balls the Mets have would all be hearsay," Lanier said. . . .

Dave Anderson, *Scuffed in the Same Spot*, N.Y. Times, Oct. 14, 1986, §A, at 29.

If this scuffing controversy ever mattered in a trial, the balls would not be hearsay because they are not a statement. Words by Davey Johnson, spoken out of court, saying something like, "I saw scuffed baseballs," would be hearsay if introduced to show that he had actually seen them.

4. *Surveillance Videos.* The hearsay rule bar would allow admission of a videotape taken by a surveillance camera, if the tape were introduced to prove that what it depicted had actually happened. The proponent would have to accompany the video with evidence sufficient to support a conclusion that it actually did show what it purported to show. This evidence would likely be testimony from someone who operated the surveillance system and knew about custody of the recording between the time it was made and the time of trial.

GOOD TO REMEMBER

The hearsay rule applies only to statements by people.

QUESTION 5-2. Victim was attacked and badly beaten. In the hospital, a friend said to Victim, "Blink your eyes three times if it's true that the ones who did this to you drove away in a pickup truck," and Victim blinked his eyes three times. To show that the assailants had used a pickup truck, would testimony describing what happened in the hospital be defined as hearsay?

■   ■   ■

Implied Quotation — **Schaffer.** Can testimony that does not quote or repeat an out-of-court statement ever be treated as testimony that contains hearsay? In criminal trials, a recurring circumstance involves prosecution witnesses who respond to questions such as, "After you spoke to the eyewitnesses, what did you do?" by saying things such as, "I went around the neighborhood looking for a man wearing an Oakland Raiders sweatshirt and a red hat." If the prosecution's witness had said, "The eyewitnesses told me to look for a man with a Raiders shirt and a red hat," all courts would identify that as testimony containing hearsay. Testimony that just lets jurors infer what was said out of court sometimes gets different treatment. *Schaffer* shows how a court can treat testimony of this type as testimony that reports a statement.

SCHAFFER v. STATE

777 S.W.2d 111 (Tex. Crim. App. 1989)

McCormick, P.J.

A jury found appellant, Michael Lee Schaffer, guilty of possessing peyote, a controlled substance. The trial court assessed punishment at ten years' confinement. The Corpus Christi Court of Appeals reversed appellant's conviction finding that the trial court improperly allowed the State to introduce hearsay evidence before the jury. We granted the State's petition for discretionary review to examine the Court of [Appeals'] holding and now affirm.

A McAllen police officer arrested appellant in a stolen van which contained approximately 1,700 grams of bagged and loose peyote buttons. Appellant testified at trial. He admitted to being inside the stolen van and to knowing that the van contained the controlled substance. Appellant's defense, however, was that he was acting as a police informer. He named "Jimmy Seals" as the Abilene police officer with whom he had worked for two years previous to his arrest. He further testified that during those two years he had provided authorities information leading to the arrests and convictions of several drug dealers.

Apparently surprised, the prosecutor asked Manuel A. Segovia, a narcotics investigator for the Hidalgo County Sheriff's Office who had testified earlier on behalf of the State, to phone Officer Seals. Thereafter, in rebuttal to appellant's testimony, Officer Segovia testified as follows:

"**Q.** Officer Segovia, when was the first time you heard the name of a person by the name of Jimmy Seals?"
"**A.** This morning."
"**Q.** And who, if anybody, informed you of that name?"
"**A.** You did, sir."
"**Q.** And were you able to contact Officer Seals?"
"**A.** Yes, sir."
"**Q.** And when was this?"
"**A.** This morning."
"**Q.** And did you have occasion to talk to him?"
"**A.** Yes, sir, I did."
"**Q.** Without telling us what he told you, Officer Segovia, would you, at this time, ask the State to drop charges against Mr. Schaffer?"
"**A.** No, sir."

Neither the State nor appellant subpoenaed Officer Seals for trial. Appellant testified that he had talked with Seals about testifying but that the Officer did not know if he would be able to come on such short notice. Seals did not testify at trial.

At trial and upon appeal, appellant asserted that the State had elicited hearsay testimony before the jury when it received a negative answer from Officer Segovia in response to its question of whether the Officer would request that the State drop charges against appellant after talking with Officer Seals. The trial court overruled appellant's hearsay objection but the Corpus Christi Court of Appeals reversed the conviction, holding:

"While this form of question and answer does not produce hearsay in the classic or textbook sense, it is nevertheless designed to circumvent the hearsay rule and present the jury with information from unsworn, out-of-court sources. It should be called 'backdoor' hearsay and should be subject to the same rules and limitations as the more common form."

We agree with the Court of Appeals and hold that the trial court should have sustained appellant's hearsay objection.

The State in its petition for discretionary review insists that there is no valid reason to label Officer's Segovia's testimony as hearsay. The State offers Tex. R. Crim. Evid. 801(d) as instructive of what constitutes hearsay: "'Hearsay' is a statement, other than one made by the declarant while testifying at the trial or hearing, offered in evidence to prove the truth of the matter asserted." By inference, the State suggests that since no out-of-court "statement" was received into evidence, no hearsay violation occurred. We disagree....

[W]here there is an inescapable conclusion that a piece of evidence is being offered to prove statements made outside the courtroom, a party may not circumvent the hearsay prohibition through artful questioning designed to elicit hearsay indirectly. In short, "statement" as defined in Tex. R. Civ. Evid. 801(a) (now see Tex. R. Crim. Evid. 801(a)) necessarily includes proof of the statement whether the proof is direct or indirect.

In the case before us, the State did indirectly that which it could not do directly — Officer Segovia's testimony informed the jury that Seals told him that appellant was not an informant. To regard the testimony in any other manner is disingenuous — a jury is not likely to make legal distinctions between a flat-out narrative ("Seals told me that appellant is not an informant") and an oblique narrative ("Without telling us what [Officer Seals] told you . . . would you ask the State to drop the charges"). There is no doubt that the State's sole intent in pursuing this line of questioning was to convey to the jury that Seals had told Segovia that appellant was not an informant. There is no other reason to question Segovia (who had already testified at trial on other matters) other than to destroy appellant's defense that he was working with authorities....

We therefore hold that the trial court improperly allowed the State to introduce hearsay testimony before the jury....

[W]e hold that introduction of the hearsay has affected "a substantial right" of appellant mandating reversal of his conviction.... Therefore, the opinion of the Court of Appeals reversing appellant's conviction is affirmed.

[Dissenting opinion omitted.]

NOTES TO SCHAFFER v. STATE

1. *Implied Quotation.* The purposes of the hearsay rule would be thwarted if out-of-court statements could be brought to the attention of a jury in the indirect way that was attempted by the prosecution in *Schaffer*. If the meaning of a witness's testimony necessarily entails information from out-of-court statements, courts and litigants should be alert to the possibility that the testimony is equivalent to a direct quotation of those out-of-court words.

2. *Quoting Statements to Explain Police Actions.* In many cases, a police officer will testify that individuals said things that led the police to go to a location or to make an arrest. Courts sometimes allow these quotations without much analysis, on the basis that the out-of-court words explain the conduct of the police. One state supreme court has attempted to limit this practice, stating that hearsay statements associated with actions by police officers may be introduced only "where the taking of action by the police is an issue in the case and where it tends to explain the action that was taken as a result of the hearsay information." Gordon v. Commonwealth, 916 S.W.2d 176, 179 (Ky. 1995). Where explaining to the jury why police did something does have relevance, some courts suggest that the testifying officer should be restricted to using explanations like "on information received" rather than explanations that quote what an out-of-court speaker may have said.

■　■　■

Segment 6: out-of-court statement to show a reason for action

Statements Quoting Statements — **Biegas.** Some statements quote other statements. When that happens, and we have one statement included in another, the concept of "hearsay within hearsay," or multiple hearsay, can arise. In *Biegas* it is important to identify all the statements and to assign a declarant to each one.

BIEGAS v. QUICKWAY CARRIERS, INC.

573 F.3d 365 (6th Cir. 2009)

MOORE, J.

In this diversity personal-injury case, Plaintiff-Appellant Terri Biegas ("the Estate"), personal representative of the estate of Richard Biegas ("Biegas"), appeals the district court's grant of partial summary judgment in favor of Defendants-Appellees Quickway Carriers, Inc., and Quickway Distribution Services, Inc. (collectively, "Quickway") . . . and now seeks a new trial. . . .

At around 9:30 P.M. on July 13, 2005, [Richard] Biegas was struck and killed by a passing tractor-trailer as he stood outside of his dump truck during an emergency stop along eastbound I-96 near Livonia, Michigan. Minutes before the accident, Biegas, who owned a concrete-removal company, was driving home from a job with his employee, Nick Cohen, who rode in the passenger seat. Attached to Biegas's red dump truck was a flatbed trailer which was loaded with a backhoe that Biegas had used earlier that day. [The backhoe] struck the overpass at Wayne Road, which has a clearance of fourteen feet. Biegas immediately pulled over and stopped on the shoulder of the highway to the right of the white fog line to check for any damage to his equipment, trailing traffic, or the overpass. . . .

Cohen testified at his deposition that he and Biegas stepped out of the truck on their respective sides and walked to the back of the trailer. . . . Although he did not see the tractor-trailer strike Biegas, Cohen saw Biegas's torso fall to the ground near the rear of the backhoe trailer. Cohen ran around the side of the backhoe trailer, finding Biegas's dead body near the rear driver's side tire of the backhoe trailer. . . .

The Estate argues that the district court abused its discretion by permitting the introduction of . . . Cohen's statement to [Lonnie Dailey, the driver of the tractor-trailer,] that Cohen had told Biegas prior to the accident to "get out of the road, he was going to get hit." The district court admitted the statements, ruling that they fell within the excited-utterance exception to the hearsay rule. We review evidentiary rulings by the district court, including determinations of whether testimony is inadmissible hearsay, for abuse of discretion. Whether a statement is hearsay is a question of law, which we review de novo.

The first question is whether the [statement at issue is] hearsay. Hearsay is an out-of-court statement offered to prove the truth of the matter asserted. Fed. R. Evid. 801(c). . . .

Turning to Cohen's statement to Dailey that he had told Biegas before the accident to "get out of the road, he was going to get hit," this consists of two statements: (1) the out-of-court statement by Cohen to Biegas and (2) the out-of-court statement by Cohen to Dailey recounting his earlier statement to Biegas. We consider each layer in turn.

The first layer — Cohen's statement to Biegas to "get out of the road" — is not hearsay because it was not offered for its truth content. This statement was not offered to prove that Biegas was in fact standing in the travel lane at the time of the accident, but rather to show that Biegas had been put on notice that he was in imminent danger and should have been aware of the risk he faced. A statement that is not offered to prove the truth of the matter asserted but to show its effect on the listener is not hearsay. Cohen's statement was offered for its probable effect on Biegas in the moments before the accident. Under Quickway's theory of the case, Biegas was so upset at the time that he ignored Cohen's warning and continued to walk in the travel lane where he was struck by Dailey's tractor-trailer.

The second layer — Cohen's statement to Dailey recounting his earlier statement — is hearsay. This statement was offered for its truth content — to prove that Cohen had in fact told Biegas earlier to "get out of the road." Accordingly, we consider whether the district court correctly ruled that the excited-utterance exception applies to this statement. [Discussion of the exception omitted.]

For the reasons explained above, we . . . affirm the district court's evidentiary rulings [and remand for new trial based on other grounds].

NOTES TO BIEGAS v. QUICKWAY CARRIERS, INC.

1. *Self-Quotation as Hearsay.* The *Biegas* court does not make it clear whether Cohen's out-of-court words were quoted at the trial by Cohen or someone else, perhaps Dailey. The analysis would be the same whichever way the out-of-court words were introduced. If Cohen testified at the trial, he would have

said something like, "I said to Dailey, 'I said, "get out of the road" to Biegas.'" This would be an instance of a declarant of an out-of-court statement also testifying at a trial. When a declarant testifies in court that he or she once said something out of court, that quotation fits within the definition of hearsay, since it is a statement that "the declarant does not make while testifying at the current trial or hearing."

An example with only one out-of-court statement can illustrate this idea. A worker might testify, "I told my boss, 'I checked the gate.'" That witness might also testify, "I checked the gate." To prove that the worker examined the gate, the first example is hearsay, but the second example is not. We would prefer to have the worker testify about what he or she remembers doing, instead of what he or she remembers saying. If there is some doubt about exactly what the worker did, it may be helpful to be able to cross-examine the worker about what he or she did. It may be less helpful to cross-examine about what he or she said to a boss at an earlier time out of court.

2. *"Truth Content" and Layers.* The *Biegas* court uses some helpful terminology. It summarizes the essential definitional aspect of applying the hearsay definition by referring to the "truth content" of statements. This is another way of saying that a statement will be hearsay if, given its claimed relevance at a trial, the statement's truth is an essential aspect of why the words are relevant.

> ### GOOD TO REMEMBER
>
> When an out-of-court statement describes another statement, be sure to identify each statement and link it with both a declarant and the fact it is being introduced to prove.

The court's other helpful terminology is identifying each out-of-court statement as a "layer" of hearsay. Some courts use the word "level" for the same idea. Either label is fine, and either one can help in the essential task of specifying each and every out-of-court statement and associating each one with its declarant.

QUESTION 5-3. A disputed issue at a trial is whether a store manager named Alan Able had instructed an employee named Bruce Baker to clean up a spill on the floor of the store. The store's owner seeks to introduce testimony that Able once said to another worker, "Right before that man slipped, I told Baker to clean up the spill." Would this testimony be hearsay?

C   STATEMENTS THAT ARE RELEVANT REGARDLESS OF WHETHER THEIR ASSERTIONS ARE TRUE (NOT HEARSAY)

Sometimes an out-of-court statement has relevance regardless of its truth or falsity. In those situations, there are no concerns about the truthfulness of the person who made the statement, or whether that person perceived something clearly, remembered it well, or used words that might fail to communicate what he or she believed. When the fact that someone made a statement matters in a case whether the statement was true or not, the statement is outside the definition of hearsay.

■ ■ ■

Words that Are Part of a Crime — Tenerelli. Drug sales usually involve someone's offer to buy drugs and another person's delivery of the drugs. The statement, "I want to buy drugs" might be considered hearsay, since the meaning of that statement might need to be true in order to establish that the speaker really is a prospective customer. A much more common treatment of statements of this kind is to characterize them as nonhearsay. The terms of art "verbal act" and "legally operative words" are sometimes used to explain that whatever the speaker may have thought, the words help explain a sequence of events.

UNITED STATES v. TENERELLI
614 F.3d 764 (6th Cir. 2010)

CLEVENGER, J.

Anthony Tenerelli appeals from his convictions of conspiracy to distribute and possess with intent to distribute methamphetamine . . . aiding and abetting possession with intent to distribute methamphetamine . . . and felon in possession of a firearm. . . . Mr. Tenerelli primarily argues that the district court erred . . . by allowing testimony regarding statements and actions attributed to a confidential reliable informant ("CRI").

On August 16, 2006, Deputy Doug Wood, a narcotics investigator with the Ramsey County Sheriff's Department, used a CRI to arrange a methamphetamine purchase from Mr. Tenerelli. Deputy Wood observed the CRI dial Mr. Tenerelli's phone number and listened to the CRI's request to purchase methamphetamine, but could not hear the other side of the conversation. After the phone call concluded, Deputy Wood drove the CRI to a local home improvement store, searched the CRI for contraband and money, gave the CRI money to use for the methamphetamine purchase, and dropped the CRI off in front of the store. . . . The CRI returned to Deputy Wood's unmarked car with one-quarter ounce of methamphetamine. . . .

Mr. Tenerelli was arrested and indicted for drug and weapon possession crimes in the District of Minnesota. . . .

At trial, Deputy Wood and two other officers testified about the controlled buy. . . .

Mr. Tenerelli challenges that the district court erred by allowing Deputy Wood to make certain statements about the controlled drug buy. Specifically,

Mr. Tenerelli argues that Deputy Wood's statements describing what he observed when the CRI dialed Mr. Tenerelli's telephone number and ordered methamphetamine from the person who answered are inadmissible hearsay. The government counters that Deputy Wood's statements were not offered for the truth, but were instead just describing verbal acts that he witnessed. . . .

Hearsay is defined as "a statement, other than one made by the declarant while testifying at the trial or hearing, offered in evidence to prove the truth of the matter asserted." Fed. R. Evid. 801(c). "The hearsay rule excludes out-of-court assertions used to prove the truth of the facts asserted in them. Verbal acts, however, are not hearsay because they are not assertions and not adduced to prove the truth of the matter." *Mueller v. Abdnor,* 972 F.2d 931, 937 (8th Cir. 1992).

Deputy Wood testified:

Q. On August 16, 2006, did you make any request of the CRI to contact Anthony Tenerelli?

A. Yes, I did.

Q. And were you present when that occurred?

A. Yes, I was.

Q. What did you observe the CRI do[,] without getting into what was said?

A. She dialed his phone number.

Q. Okay. You observed this?

A. Yes, I observed that.

Q. And there was — then what did she do in regard to the call? Was she speaking?

A. Yes. . . .

Q. What was the intention behind the phone call by the CRI to Mr. Tenerelli?

A. She ordered methamphetamine.

Q. That was the act that she did?

A. Yes.

Mr. Tenerelli does not point to any particular statement made by Deputy Wood as hearsay. Instead, Mr. Tenerelli broadly alleges that the effect of the testimony was to elicit an implied assertion of what the CRI told Deputy Wood about aspects of the purchase that were not witnessed by the officers. Notably, Deputy Wood was cross-examined extensively about his observations of the controlled buy.

We agree with the district court that Deputy Wood's statements regarding what he observed during the controlled buy are not hearsay; no statements of the CRI were offered for the underlying truth. Instead, Deputy Wood testified about the fact that the order occurred, a verbal act of which Deputy Wood had personal knowledge. *See United States v. Roach,* 164 F.3d 403, 410 (8th Cir. 1998) ("testimony that [a person] had asked her to sell drugs involved a verbal act; the government offered the statement not to prove its truth, but that it had been made") (citing Fed. R. Evid. 801(c) advisory committee's note on 1972 proposed rule and *United States v. Robinson,* 774 F.2d 261, 273 (8th Cir. 1985)). . . . We find no reversible error in the admission of Deputy Wood's testimony. . . .

Accordingly, we affirm Mr. Tenerelli's convictions. . . .

NOTES TO UNITED STATES v. TENERELLI

1. *Verbal Acts and Hearsay Dangers.* Knowing that someone made a statement like "I want to buy drugs" can explain the significance of later conduct by someone else, such as the delivery of drugs. When the statement is used in that way, even if the speaker had been lying about the speaker's interest in buying drugs, or if the speaker's understanding of words like buy and drugs was different from a typical understanding of those words, the fact that the alleged seller had heard those words and then delivered drugs would help a jury interpret the alleged seller's conduct.

2. *Distinguishing "It's True That Someone Spoke" from "What Someone Said Was True."* There is a difference between proving that it is true that a person spoke and proving that the ideas a person conveyed were true. With regard to establishing that a person actually said some words, there is nothing special about the event of speaking that would distinguish it from any other acts that parties are allowed to prove. Just like a party is allowed to introduce evidence showing that it was raining on a particular day or that a traffic light was broken, a party is allowed to introduce evidence to support a conclusion that a person said some words.

3. *Give Me Your Money or I'll Kill You.* The hearsay rule permits a witness in a robbery trial to testify that the defendant said to the alleged victim, out of court, "Give me your money or I will kill you." This is because none of the testimonial dangers that support the hearsay prohibition matter in circumstances where the law applies an objective test and ultimately applies legal consequences to the act of saying particular words.

■ ■ ■

Words with Legal Power — Moen. This is a sad story of a family dispute that went on for a number of years even after this decision was rendered, even including an action against the family's lawyer for malpractice. It offers additional examples of words that have relevance in a trial, regardless of the truth of what they may assert.

MOEN v. THOMAS

627 N.W.2d 146 (N.D. 2001)

NEUMANN, J.

Laurie Thomas, Kisten Thomas, and Tessa Thomas have appealed from a judgment which quieted title in certain property in the Jay V. Thomas Family Trust, ordered the trust was entitled to exclusive possession of the property, and awarded damages for the use and occupation of the property. We conclude the trial court did not err in admitting testimony of an oral year-to-year lease and in finding the parties had a year-to-year lease which could be terminated at the end of a yearly term by the trustees. We therefore affirm the judgment. Laurie was married to Jerry Thomas and they had two daughters, Kisten and Tessa. Jerry's father, Jay, owned a ranch in Williams County. During the marriage, Jerry and Laurie lived on the Thomas family ranch and worked the ranch with Jay.

Jay died on October 19, 1995. Under the terms of Jay's will, Jerry received the surface of the ranch headquarters and some additional ranch land. Under Article VII of the will, Jerry also received an option to purchase or lease other ranch land. . . .

The will was admitted to probate in November 1995, and Jay's daughter, Donna Sneva, was appointed personal representative. Jerry exercised his option under the will to purchase the machinery and livestock from the estate, but advised the other heirs at a December 1995 family meeting that he was declining the first option to purchase the land. Jerry orally stated, however, that he intended to exercise his right to lease the property. In late 1995 Jerry tendered, and the personal representative accepted, rent for 1996 at $3.00 per acre.

The family ultimately decided to place the property in trust to administer the surface and mineral interests of the estate. Attorney Fred Rathert, who had drafted Jay's will and represented the personal representative in probating the estate, drafted the trust agreement which was signed by the family members, including Jerry, on December 3, 1996. . . .

. . . LaRae Thomas, Carol Moen, and Donna Sneva [family members and co-trustees] testified that Jerry told the family he did not want to be bound to a seven-year lease, but preferred to continue renting the property on an oral year-to-year lease. They testified it was at Jerry's request that no written seven-year lease was executed, and the family agreed to an oral year-to-year lease. In late 1996 Jerry tendered rent for 1997 to the trustees.

Jerry died in a ranching accident on May 12, 1997. Laurie continued in possession of the property, and discussed with the trustees her desire to rent some of the property. In the fall of 1997 the trustees informed Laurie they would not lease the land to her in 1998. In December 1997 Laurie tendered a check for rent for 1998 to the trustees. They returned the check, notifying her in an accompanying letter that she did not have a valid lease for 1998.

When Laurie remained in possession, the trustees brought this action against Laurie, Kisten, and Tessa (hereafter collectively "Laurie") to quiet title to the property, to recover possession, and seeking damages for the value of use and possession of the property after December 31, 1997. Laurie answered and counterclaimed, alleging the seven-year lease and option to purchase under the will was in effect and survived Jerry's death. Laurie also alleged fraud and breach of fiduciary duty by the trustees.

Following a bench trial, the trial court found Jerry had a year-to-year lease which terminated at the end of 1997. The court quieted title in favor of the trust, ordered possession of the land be turned over to the trustees, and awarded damages of $19,000 for use and occupation of the property. The court also dismissed the counterclaim. Laurie appealed from the judgment.

Laurie argues the trial court erred in allowing Donna Sneva, LaRae Thomas, and Carol Moen to testify that Jerry stated to them and other family members he did not want to be bound to a seven-year lease and that, at his request, they agreed to an oral year-to-year lease. Laurie asserts this testimony was hearsay and should not have been admitted.

Rule 801(c), N.D. R. Ev., defines hearsay as "a statement, other than one made by the declarant while testifying at the trial or hearing, offered in evidence to prove the truth of the matter asserted." If an out-of-court statement is not offered to prove its truth, it is not hearsay. A statement offered to prove it was made is not hearsay.

We have held that statements offered to prove an oral contract existed are not hearsay, because they are not offered to prove the truth of the matter asserted. Statements about the terms of, or assent to, an oral contract fall within the category of non-hearsay designated as "verbal acts" or "verbal conduct." The utterance of the words is, in itself, an operative fact which gives rise to legal consequences. Because it is the outward manifestations of assent which govern, not the parties' secret intentions, it is the mere fact of utterance which is relevant in determining whether there was an oral agreement. It makes no difference whether Jerry was being truthful when he said he did not want to be bound to a seven-year lease and agreed to an oral year-to-year lease, because it is his outward manifestations which determine whether a contract existed.

The underlying rationale for the rule is explained in ... Creaghe v. Iowa Home Mut. Cas. Co., 323 F.2d 981, 984 (10th Cir. 1963):

> "The hearsay rule does not exclude relevant testimony as to what the contracting parties said with respect to the making or the terms of an oral agreement. The presence or absence of such words and statements of themselves are part of the issues in the case. This use of such testimony does not require a reliance by the jury or the judge upon the competency of the person who originally made the statements for the truth of their content. Neither the truth of the statements nor their accuracy are then involved. In the case at bar we are not concerned with whether the insured was truthful or not when he told the agent he wanted the policy cancelled and that he did not need it any more. It is enough for the issues here presented to determine only whether or not he made such statements to the agent. The fact that these statements were made was testified to by the agent, and his competency and truthfulness as to this testimony was subject to testing through cross-examination by counsel for appellant, and this was done at considerable length."

We conclude the trial court did not err in admitting testimony about Jerry's statements because the testimony did not constitute hearsay under N.D.R.Ev. 801(c).

We have reviewed the remaining issues raised by Laurie on appeal and find them to be without merit. The judgment is affirmed.

NOTES TO *MOEN* v. THOMAS

1. *Objective Standards in Contract Law.* The result in cases like *Moen* is compelled by an aspect of contract law—that objective manifestations count—when a party could reasonably believe them. That doctrine explains why understanding what a speaker "really" thought doesn't matter and therefore why the hearsay rule may properly be withdrawn.

2. *Donative Intent.* Consider the possible hearsay issue in this extract from an appellate opinion involving a dispute about ownership of shares in a family business:

> In the fall of 1968, Sol sold one of the four shares, previously given to him by Jack, to Wolff and Kopolow for $25,000. Sol used a portion, at least, of this money to take a vacation trip to Hawaii. Subsequently, Jack learned of Sol's stock transfer to Wolff and Kopolow. Jack, who was greatly upset by this news, then confronted Sol and told him that he "had no right to sell the family stock to an outsider." As heretofore stated, a heated discussion ensued. During the course of this discussion Sol told his brother Jack that he had not sold the share, rather he had borrowed the $25,000 using the share as collateral. The following day Sol, who was still very upset, confronted Jack at the latter's house. Sol had with him the certificates for the three remaining shares. The men resumed their argument. During the course of which Sol told Jack[,] "Here's your stock, shove them up your. . . ." Sol then threw the stock on Jack's desk and ran out of Jack's home. Jack has retained possession of the three shares since the above incident.
>
> . . . Defendants argue that the evidence is less than clear and convincing that Sol intended to make a present gift. . . . We do not agree. Considering the fact that Sol delivered the certificates to Jack and the language Sol used at the time of delivery demonstrates, in our view, that Sol had the intention to transfer ownership and title to the stock to his brother.

See Schultz v. Schultz, 1981 Mo. App. LEXIS 3291.

QUESTION 5-4. An issue at a trial was whether people had been inside a room in a university laboratory during a particular evening. The following items of testimony could help to establish that the people were present. Which one of them would be hearsay?

> ### GOOD TO REMEMBER
>
> If legal rules mean that when particular words are spoken the law applies particular consequences, hearsay problems disappear. We don't care what the speaker had in mind if the law says that the mere existence of the words changes reality.

A. A maintenance worker would testify that he walked past the room that evening and heard someone inside the room say, "It's really hot in here."

B. A maintenance worker would testify that he walked past the room that evening and heard someone inside the room say, "I've been in this room for two hours already."

C. A maintenance worker would testify that in the lobby of the building that evening a laboratory worker said to him, "I spent about two hours in the lab tonight."

■　■　■

Words That Make an Impression on a Person Who Hears Them — **Kenyon.** There are many circumstances where words that are spoken may have an effect on someone who hears them, regardless of whether those words are true. *Kenyon* is an example of a recurring circumstance that meets this definition. It also involves two levels of out-of-court statements, so it requires a careful analysis.

KENYON v. STATE

986 P.2d 849 (Wyo. 1999)

MACY, J.

Appellant Robert Kenyon appeals from the judgment and sentence which was entered after he was convicted of grand larceny.

We reverse and remand.

Kenyon presents the following [issue] for our review:

Whether the district court abused its discretion when it denied the appellant the opportunity to introduce statements made to him by his fiancee regarding consent to use the vehicle. . . .

Kenyon and his fiancee, Kelly Crossfield, went on a trip around the United States during the summer of 1997. They were returning to their home in Oregon when their van broke down in Kansas. Kenyon and Crossfield could not afford to repair the van, so they placed it in storage and hitchhiked to Denver, Colorado. They planned to stay with Crossfield's sister, who lived in Denver, but she did not have room for them. Kenyon and Crossfield continued hitchhiking and eventually ended up in Cheyenne.

In early September 1997, Kenyon and Crossfield entered the Southside Furniture store. Kenyon spoke with James Sanchez, who was a store employee, and told him that he and Crossfield were hungry and did not have a place to stay. Sanchez gave Kenyon and Crossfield some money and told them that they could stay in a trailer which was parked next to the house he shared with his fiancee. Sanchez asked the couple to do some odd jobs in exchange for being allowed to use the trailer. . . .

On September 28, 1997, Sanchez allowed Kenyon to use [his] truck to go to his worksite. Crossfield accompanied Kenyon in the truck. A police officer stopped

Kenyon for speeding and discovered that Kenyon's driver's license had been suspended. The officer took Kenyon and Crossfield to Sanchez's home and explained the situation to Sanchez. Sanchez was upset because Kenyon had been driving his truck without a valid driver's license, and he told Kenyon that he could not use his truck any longer.

Shortly thereafter, Crossfield spoke with her children, who were living in California with their father. The children told her about a family emergency. On September 30, 1997, Crossfield and Kenyon took Sanchez's truck and went to California to retrieve Crossfield's children. Sanchez reported to the police that his truck had been stolen.

Kenyon and Crossfield were arrested in Oregon on October 12, 1997. Kenyon pleaded guilty in Oregon to one count of unauthorized use of a motor vehicle. He was subsequently extradited to Wyoming and charged with grand larceny. The trial court held a jury trial on May 11, 1998, and the jury found Kenyon guilty of the crime. The trial court entered a judgment and sentence which was consistent with the jury's verdict, and Kenyon appealed to the Wyoming Supreme Court.

Kenyon maintains that the trial court abused its discretion when it refused to allow him to testify that Crossfield told him Sanchez had given them permission to use the truck. We agree with Kenyon. . . .

Kenyon was tried for the crime of grand larceny as proscribed by Wyo. Stat. Ann. §6-3-402(a) and (c)(i) (LEXIS 1999). That statute states:

> (a) A person who steals, takes and carries, leads or drives away property of another with intent to deprive the owner or lawful possessor is guilty of larceny. . . .

Kenyon testified on his own behalf at the trial. He was the only defense witness. The defense attorney sought to elicit testimony from Kenyon that, before they left Cheyenne, Crossfield told him Sanchez had given them permission to use his truck. The following exchange occurred at the trial:

Q. (BY [DEFENSE ATTORNEY]) Okay. In any event, there was a family emergency. You decided to leave. What actions did you take?

A. At that time I didn't take any actions. I wasn't sure exactly what to do. I forget what the date was. It was in the morning. We were going to pull the last of the garbage out to the dump with [Sanchez's] trailer. Went over there, found out it didn't have a license plate, so that was off. [Sanchez] was at work. I don't know if [Sanchez's fiancee] had went to work or not. [Crossfield] and I had the pickup truck. And I was in the trailer, [Crossfield] was doing something in the house. I don't know what. She come out. She said are you ready? I said to do what? She said well, let's go get the girls. She said that she had spoke with [Sanchez], that it was all right —

[PROSECUTOR]: Objection, Your Honor, irrelevant, relevance, hearsay.

THE COURT: It is technically hearsay, but it isn't offered for the truth of the matter, so go ahead.

[KENYON]: She asked me if I was ready. I said for what. And she said that she had spoke with [Sanchez], and that it was all right for us to use the truck to go and get her girls.

[PROSECUTOR]: May I have a continuing objection to conversation with [Sanchez] along these lines if it's not offered for the truth?

THE COURT: I misspoke. I'm sorry.

[DEFENSE ATTORNEY]: I'll move on.

THE COURT: The jury will be instructed that the testimony that—who did you speak to? What was her name?

[KENYON]: My fiancee is Kelly Crossfield.

THE COURT: She told you you had permission?

[KENYON]: Yes, sir.

THE COURT: I see. That will be stricken. Ladies and gentlemen, the fact that his fiancee told him he had permission will be totally disregarded by you. That's not admissible. I shouldn't have let it come before you.

[DEFENSE ATTORNEY]: Your Honor, I'd offer that as effect on the—

THE COURT: If you wish to argue, we can go over here.

The trial court conducted a bench conference to consider the admissibility of the proffered testimony. During the bench conference, the defense attorney argued that Crossfield's out-of-court statement was admissible . . . to show its effect on the listener—himself—and not to prove the truth of the matter asserted. His defense counsel stated:

> I would further add, Your Honor, that it also falls under the exception, the common-law hearsay exception, effect on the hearer, what he thought of it. It's basic evidentiary law we learned in law school. . . .
>
> . . . Now, the effect that it had on Mr. Kenyon is that he apparently had consent. . . . He has to be able to testify he . . . apparently [had] consent. He thought he had. That's why he took this vehicle. . . .

Kenyon claims that the trial court erred by excluding Crossfield's statement because the statement was not offered to prove the truth of the matter asserted—that Sanchez had, in fact, given Crossfield permission to use the truck—but, rather, was offered to show its effect on him. He argues that the testimony would have bolstered his defense that he did not harbor the criminal intent to permanently deprive Sanchez of his truck.

. . . In Armstrong v. State, 826 P.2d 1106, 1119 (Wyo. 1992), this Court recognized that, when an out-of-court statement is not offered to prove the truth of the matter asserted but is, instead, offered for the purpose of showing its effect on the mental or emotional state of the person hearing it, it is not hearsay. Such out-of-court statements are admissible.

The Arkansas Supreme Court quoted from McCormick on Evidence to explain the general principle that an out-of-court statement offered to show its effect on the hearer is not hearsay. Cole v. State, 323 Ark. 8, 913 S.W.2d 255, 257 (Ark. 1996).

"Some Out-of-Court Utterances Which Are Not Hearsay.

". . . Utterances and writings offered to show effect on hearer or reader. When it is proved that D made a statement to X, with the purpose of showing the probable state of mind thereby induced in X, such as being put on notice or having knowledge, or motive, or to show the information which X had as bearing on the reasonableness or good faith or voluntariness of the subsequent conduct of X, or anxiety, the evidence is not subject to attack as hearsay . . . " McCormick on Evidence, §249, pp. 733-34 (3d Ed. 1984).

Id. Similarly, an Arizona Court of Appeals explained: "'Words offered to prove the effect on the hearer are admissible when they are offered to show their effect on one whose conduct is at issue.'" State v. Rivers, 190 Ariz. 56, 945 P.2d 367, 371 (Ariz. Ct. App. 1997) (quoting State v. Hernandez, 170 Ariz. 301, 823 P.2d 1309, 1314 (Ariz. Ct. App. 1991)). The general principle that an out-of-court statement offered to show its effect on the hearer is generally admissible because it is not hearsay is widely recognized.

The traditional credibility concerns associated with hearsay statements are not relevant when an out-of-court statement is offered to show its effect on the listener rather than to prove the truth of the matter asserted. "Testimony of out-of-court statements used other than to establish the truth of the matter asserted does not rest for its value on the credibility of the out-of-court declarant but, rather, on the credibility of the witness, who was present in court and subject to cross-examination." People v. Shoultz, 289 Ill. App. 3d 392, 682 N.E.2d 446, 449, 224 Ill. Dec. 885 (Ill. App. 3d 1997). . . .

In keeping with the general principle, we conclude that the trial court in this case abused its discretion when it refused to allow Kenyon to testify concerning Crossfield's out-of-court statement that Sanchez had given them permission to use the truck. The statement was not offered to prove the truth of the matter asserted. Crossfield's statement was offered, instead, to show its effect on Kenyon's intent and subsequent conduct. . . .

The heart of Kenyon's defense was that he did not have the requisite criminal intent to be convicted of grand larceny. Taking the entire record into consideration, we conclude that there is a reasonable probability that the verdict would have been more favorable to Kenyon if the trial court had admitted Crossfield's out-of-court statement. The trial court's refusal to allow Kenyon to testify about Crossfield's out-of-court statement affected Kenyon's substantial rights, and he is, therefore, entitled to have his conviction reversed. . . .

NOTE TO KENYON v. STATE

1. *What We Learned in Law School.* When the attorney at trial referred to "basic evidentiary law we learned in law school," apparently he or she failed to refresh the judge's recollection of that part of the course. How could the attorney have persuaded the judge to allow the evidence in, by referring to the existence or nonexistence of the risks that usually justify excluding hearsay?

QUESTION 5-5. In a negligence case, a plaintiff who had fallen in a store might need to prove that there had been a dangerous condition in a store *and* that the operator of the store had known about the condition for a long enough time to fix it. If the plaintiff sought to have a witness testify that an hour before the fall, a customer in the store had said to the manager, "There is some slippery stuff on the floor here," would that testimony be hearsay with regard to either of the two propositions the plaintiff needed to establish?

■   ■   ■

Difficulty in Determining If Words Are Relevant Just Because They Were Said or Because of the Truth of What They Assert — Field. When out-of-court words are relevant just because someone said them or someone heard them, the dangers of hearsay will disappear. That makes it very important to characterize out-of-court words as relevant either (1) because they are an accurate report of something the declarant knew or (2) because someone said them or someone heard them. Words spoken over the phone to the defendant doctor in *Field* might have been relevant in either of these two ways, so the choice about how to characterize them is crucial.

FIELD v. TRIGG COUNTY HOSPITAL, INC.

386 F.3d 729 (6th Cir. 2004)

COLE, J.

Plaintiffs-Appellants, Tina and Norman Field, appeal the district court's denial of their motion for a new trial after a jury returned a verdict in favor of Defendant-Appellee, Dr. William B. Anderson, following a trial for medical malpractice in federal court based on diversity jurisdiction. Plaintiffs contend that they are entitled to a new trial because the district court improperly admitted prejudicial hearsay evidence when it permitted Dr. Anderson to testify about the statements made by two unnamed, undisclosed physicians with whom he allegedly consulted concerning Tina Field's medical care....

At approximately 9:20 P.M. on September 1, 1998, Tina Field sought treatment at the Trigg County Hospital emergency room, in Cadiz, Kentucky, immediately after being bitten twice in her right foot by a copperhead snake. Defendant–Appellee, William B. Anderson, was the physician on call when Field arrived at the hospital....

When she arrived at the emergency room, Tina Field reported that she felt sick to her stomach, faint, dizzy, and numb, and Dr. Anderson noted significant swelling in her right foot and that the foot was warm. Dr. Anderson determined that Field had a "wet" copperhead snake bite, which meant that there had been envenomation. His plan was to monitor her, administer intravenous fluids and a tetanus shot, and look for any progression of the bite's severity. Dr. Anderson checked on Field periodically during the night, but did not give her any antivenin. When Dr. Anderson next saw her, at 9:00 A.M. on September 2, Field had swelling above her right knee, and her right foot was becoming cold and had a bluish color to it.

At 5:00 P.M. on September 2, Field complained of pain in her right big toe and coldness in her right foot. At this point, Nurse Stephen P'Poole checked Field's right foot for a pulse, but did not feel one. As a result, P'Poole called Dr. Anderson. At no time after 5:00 P.M. did Tina Field have a pulse in her right foot.

Three hours later, at 8:10 P.M., Dr. Anderson made his first call for assistance. He phoned an attending emergency room physician at the Vanderbilt University Medical Center, who then referred him to a Vanderbilt toxicologist.... According to Dr. Anderson, the Vanderbilt emergency room physician and toxicologist told him that he was "doing everything appropriately," that "they would be doing the same thing," and that the main treatment is to elevate and monitor the leg....

[Tina Field's condition did not improve. She was treated later by other doctors and was required to undergo a partial leg amputation.]

... The relevant testimony was as follows:

Defendant's Counsel: Dr. Anderson, when you talked to the physicians at Vanderbilt, did they tell you anything or did you get any information from them?
Anderson: Yeah, both the ER doctor and the toxicologist that I talked to said essentially the same thing.... As far as the leg goes, they said that they never administer antivenin to copperhead snake bites and certainly would not, you know, this, you know, far, you know, into the course. They felt like, you know, that we were doing everything appropriately, you know, keeping the leg, you know, elevated, you know, that you would normally expect for the swelling to progress over 24 to 48 hours and then she would start to, you know, show some improvement, you know from there. So that, you know, the ER doctor said that and he said he would get a toxicologist to talk to me, too, to, you know, to get, you know, this person's opinion.... And then in a little while the toxicologist called back and again I presented the, you know, the whole history to her and, you know, she said eventually, you know, the same thing ... [that] the leg was doing what would be expected with a copperhead snake bite, that she does not administer antivenin, you know, to copperhead snake bites and, and that the main treatment is keeping it elevation, you know, keeping it elevated, monitoring and giving supportive treatment and that they would be doing the same thing. She did say that she would be willing to take, you know, if the patient and the family wanted to come up there, but she felt like they would not do anything different.

Defendant contends that the statements of the Vanderbilt physicians — admitted through Dr. Anderson's testimony — were not hearsay because they were not used to prove the truth of the matter asserted (the matter asserted being that Dr. Anderson was "doing everything appropriately" and that "they would not do anything different."). Defendant contends that the statements were elicited to prove simply that Dr. Anderson provided proper care by "consulting with other physicians who were better versed in the field of toxicology." As a preliminary matter, that argument fails because the qualifications—indeed, the very identities—of the Vanderbilt physicians are not even known. But more importantly, the argument is simply not credible. The fact that a conversation took place between Dr. Anderson and the Vanderbilt physicians is not hearsay, and the simple fact that a consultation took place could have been elicited easily by Defendant's counsel without revealing the substance of the Vanderbilt physicians' responses. . . . Therefore, the only possible purpose for taking the additional step of telling the jury what was allegedly said by the Vanderbilt physicians was to expose the jury to the substance of those statements and persuade the jury of their truth—namely, that Dr. Anderson was "doing everything appropriately." The statements were hearsay because they went well beyond conveying that Dr. Anderson sought out a consultation to the entirely self-serving purpose of exposing the jury to the approving words of two purported experts from a purportedly esteemed medical institution.

[Discussion of exception for statements for purpose of medical diagnosis or treatment omitted.]

Finally, we do not find, as Defendant urges us to, that the district court's jury instruction concerning the statements was curative. The court's instruction was as follows:

> **The Court:** You just heard about a telephone conversation with Vanderbilt. It's permissible for you to hear that, to hear the doctor's testimony as to the statements that he heard over the telephone. That's proper for you to consider that. That's not proper to consider whether—the information received is not proof of the validity of the advice given, but it is proper for you to consider the testimony that there was a conversation with these people at Vanderbilt. That's a matter for you to consider. Thank you.

Given the instruction's patently jumbled and confusing nature, we are certain that no juror would have properly understood it to prohibit his or her consideration of the substance of the Vanderbilt physicians' statements. . . .

For the foregoing reasons, we vacate the jury's verdict and remand this case to the district court for a new trial. . . . .

NOTES TO FIELD v. TRIGG COUNTY HOSPITAL, INC.

1. *Value of Cross-Examination.* If the Vanderbilt doctors had testified in court about whether Dr. Anderson's treatment was proper, what kinds of questions might the plaintiff's lawyer asked them? Applying the hearsay rule to their out-of-court statements represents the legal system's judgment that those cross-examination questions would have been highly important. Bearing in

mind the situation the Vanderbilt doctors were assessing, which aspects of their statements — the perceptions on which the declarants based them, the declarants' memories of those perceptions, the clarity or ambiguity of the declarants' words, and the honesty of the declarants — would probably be the most important?

2. *Clarity of Limiting Instruction.* The appellate court is highly critical of the limiting instruction, even though that instruction read literally did tell the jury that the information in that call was not proof of its validity. The way the judge communicated this to the jury was certainly confusing. It may be that the appellate court felt particularly free to discount the limiting instruction because it had already ruled that the testimony had no valid purpose. Where testimony has both a valid purpose and a risk of wrong use by a jury, limiting instructions are usually accepted even though there can be doubt about their power. In this instance, since there was no need at all for the testimony, the court may have been particularly willing to demand that the limiting instruction have great clarity.

■   ■   ■

Saying Defamatory Words (and Saying Someone Said Defamatory Words) — Hickey. In defamation cases, the plaintiff must prove that the defendant actually made (or "published") the allegedly defamatory out-of-court statement. The defamation plaintiff, of course, will not allege that the defamatory statement was true. This explains the nonapplicability of the hearsay rule in this circumstance. *Hickey* illustrates this, but also offers an opportunity to analyze multiple levels of out-of-court statements.

HICKEY v. SETTLEMIER

864 P.2d 372 (Ore. 1993)

IN BANC. PETERSON, J.

This action for defamation involves statements allegedly made by defendant to the reporter and camera crew of a national television program, "20/20." The trial court granted defendant's motion for summary judgment. . . . Our consideration of the case involves . . . whether a television reporter's account, contained in a videotape of the "20/20" program, attributing to defendant certain statements, is admissible over a hearsay objection to establish publication of the allegedly defamatory statement. . . .

Defendant, who is plaintiff's neighbor, was interviewed by the nationally televised program "20/20" in connection with a segment that "20/20" was producing that focused on "pet bandits." The record in this case contains a videotape of the program that shows defendant making certain statements and an ABC reporter saying:

"[M]ore than 300 people in central Oregon have complained that their pets were stolen and delivered to [plaintiff's] operation. Many want [plaintiff's facility] closed down, including [plaintiff's] own godmother, [defendant], who lives next door. *She says there's no doubt in her mind that he's mistreating animals and dealing in stolen pets.*" (Emphasis added.)

In her deposition, which was offered in connection with her motion for summary judgment, defendant denied making any statement to the effect that plaintiff mistreats animals or deals in stolen pets. . . .

Defendant moved for summary judgment and offered sworn deposition testimony that she did not make the allegedly defamatory statements . . . concerning mistreatment of animals and dealing in stolen pets. Relying on the videotape, the Court of Appeals concluded that publication was a question of fact. The Court of Appeals, therefore, must have determined that the videotape was admissible to prove that defendant made the statements. . . .

. . . Plaintiff offered the videotape as evidence that the statements were made. The videotape shows . . . the reporter stating, "[Defendant] says there's no doubt in her mind that [plaintiff is] is mistreating animals and dealing in stolen pets." The reporter's statement is relevant . . . and, because the statement only appears in the record on the videotape, it presents a potential hearsay problem under OEC 801(3).

Some statements are themselves significant legal facts, that is, the substantive law attaches certain consequences to utterances so that the mere making of the statement becomes an issue in the case. Utley v. City of Independence, 240 Or. 384, 393, 402 P.2d 91 (1965). Such statements made out-of-court are not offered for the truth of what they state and, therefore, are not hearsay. Instead, they are classified as verbal acts.

Defamation is one example of a verbal act. The making of the defamatory statement is itself of legal significance. Therefore, when an allegedly defamatory out-of-court statement is offered, it is not being offered to prove its truth, but that it was made. Indeed, it is legally significant because of its alleged untruth. Therefore, the allegedly defamatory statements made directly by defendant on the videotape are not hearsay.

Defendant denied making the statement attributed to her by the reporter. . . . In the absence of the reporter's comment attributing those statements to defendant, there was no evidence of publication of [the allegedly defamatory statement] by defendant. The question, then, is whether the reporter's statement is hearsay.

When statements made to a television reporter are sought to be proven by offering a videotape of the broadcast, as in the instant case, a problem of multiple hearsay is presented. OEC 805 states that multiple hearsay is admissible provided that each level of hearsay satisfies an exception to the hearsay rule. The videotape is being offered to prove what the reporter heard defendant say. That is the first level of hearsay, because this brings into play the perception, recollection, narration, and sincerity of the reporter. If defendant's words are also being offered for their truth, a second level of hearsay exists, because this brings into play the perception, recollection, narration, and sincerity of defendant.

The statement made by the reporter on the tape is hearsay within the definition of OEC 801(3), because it is being offered to prove its truth (that defendant said that plaintiff was "mistreating animals and dealing in stolen pets"). Defendant's alleged statement within the reporter's statement is not hearsay, because it is a verbal act. The requirement of OEC 805 applies to nonhearsay statements within hearsay. Therefore, in order for the reporter's account to be admissible, the reporter's statement must come within an exception to the hearsay rule under OEC 803 or 804.

Analytically, a television videotape is analogous to a newspaper article. The facts of this case are similar to the facts in Bevan v. Garrett, 284 Or. 293, 586 P.2d 1119 (1978). Bevan involved a defamation claim against a person who allegedly defamed the plaintiff in statements made to a newspaper reporter, statements that were reported in the newspaper. The defendant moved for summary judgment. . . . He supported his motion with an affidavit in which he denied making the allegedly defamatory statements to the reporter. The plaintiff filed no affidavit in opposition to the defendant's affidavit denying publication. The trial court granted summary judgment, and the plaintiff appealed, arguing that he could rely on the allegations of his complaint to prove publication.

This court affirmed the granting of summary judgment stating that, in opposing summary judgment, a party could not rely simply on the allegations of the complaint. . . . Although the foregoing is the specific holding in the case, it is implicit in the *Bevan* decision that, by itself, a newspaper article is hearsay, and not admissible to prove publication by a defendant. Had the article been admissible to prove publication, the court's discussion of a party's inability to simply rely on the party's pleadings would have been beside the point.

What was true of the newspaper article in *Bevan* is true of the videotape in the case at bar. The reporter's hearsay statement on the videotape is not within any hearsay exception and is, therefore, inadmissible to establish publication by defendant. . . .

The effect of the inadmissibility of a portion of the videotape is that plaintiff has not set forth specific facts showing that there is a genuine issue of material fact concerning publication of the statement concerning mistreatment of animals and dealing in stolen pets, the first of three allegations made by plaintiff. Even so, we affirm the decision of the Court of Appeals ordering a new trial [because issues of fact did exist with regard to other allegations by the plaintiff].

NOTES TO HICKEY v. SETTLEMIER

1. *Videotape as a Declarant.* The videotape is not a layer of hearsay, nor is the videotape a statement made by a declarant. Although the court may not be perfectly clear about this, statements as that term is defined in Rule 801 were made by the reporter and the defendant, not by a videotape.

2. Media Defendants. If ABC had been a defendant and the plaintiff's theory sought to impose defamation liability on ABC for the information it disseminated in its broadcast, there would be no hearsay issues associated with introduction of the videotape. The tape would, in this variation of the real case, be introduced to show what ABC had broadcast, not to show that any information in it was true.

■   ■   ■

Unintended Assertions (Inferred at Trial) — **Dullard.** If an out-of-court speaker said, "This ship looks seaworthy to me," a quotation of that statement by a witness at a trial would be hearsay if it was offered to show that the ship had been seaworthy. Courts have been troubled by an analogous situation. Suppose a retired ship captain looked at a ship and then got on it to take a voyage. If there was a trial where the seaworthiness of the ship was an issue, could a witness testify that he or she saw the retired captain look at the ship and then get on board? The relevance of the testimony about the captain's conduct depends on treating the conduct as a manifestation of the captain's beliefs about the ship. That is, proof of the conduct is relevant because it allows the jury to draw an unintended inference from the captain's actions. When the captain manifests beliefs by saying them out loud, the hearsay rule applies. When the captain manifests beliefs by acting on them, many courts reject a hearsay analysis and allow a party to have a witness describe the conduct.

Dullard considers a related problem: how to treat unintended implications from someone's *statements*. In the sea captain example, the issue is how to treat unintended implications of someone's *conduct*. In *Dullard,* instead of asking what to do when someone's *conduct* can support an inference on a topic the person did not mean to communicate about, the court must decide whether to invoke the hearsay prohibition when prosecutors seek to introduce some out-of-court *words* to support an idea the out-of-court declarant did not mean to assert. The decision may show some ambiguity in the Federal Rules treatment of the issue.

STATE v. DULLARD

668 N.W.2d 585 (Iowa 2003)

CADY, J.

... Police officers from the city of Des Moines police department went to a home in a residential neighborhood of Des Moines in response to a report of a methamphetamine lab located at the house. The officers knocked on the front door of the house, and Brett Dullard eventually opened the door. The officers believed Dullard lived in the home with his mother. Dullard's mother arrived at the home a short time later, and gave permission for the officers to search the residence, as well as a detached garage. . . .

The search of the garage revealed potential methamphetamine precursors and numerous materials commonly used to manufacture methamphetamine. . . .

The police also found a small spiral notebook in a wooden desk located in the garage. It contained a handwritten note from an unidentified person. The note read as follows:

> B - I had to go inside to pee + calm my nerves somewhat down.
>   When I came out to go get Brian I looked over to the street North of here + there sat a black + white w/the dude out of his car facing our own direction — no one else was with him. . . .

Dullard was charged with possession of ephedrine or pseudoephedrine with intent to use it as a precursor and with possession of ether with the intent to use it as a precursor. At trial, the State, among other evidence, introduced some of the items seized during the search. . . .

The handwritten note was also introduced into evidence over Dullard's hearsay objection. The State argued the note was not offered to prove the truth of the matters it asserted but to connect Dullard to the items in the garage. . . . The State argued the note was written to Dullard based on the first letter of his first name.

The jury found Dullard guilty of possession of ephedrine or pseudoephedrine with intent to use it as a precursor. . . .

Dullard appealed and claimed . . . the district court admitted the handwritten note into evidence in violation of the rule against hearsay. . . .

The court of appeals reversed the conviction after concluding the trial court erred in admitting the handwritten note into evidence. . . . We granted further review. . . .

Hearsay "is a statement, other than one made by the declarant while testifying at the trial . . . offered in evidence to prove the truth of the matter asserted." Iowa R. Evid. 5.801(c). Hearsay is not admissible unless it is exempt from the rule or falls within one of the exceptions. . . .

A statement is defined under our rules of evidence as "(1) an oral or written assertion or (2) nonverbal conduct of a person, if it is intended by the person as an assertion." Iowa R. Evid. 5.801(a). The term assertion is not similarly defined in the Iowa or federal rules of evidence. Nevertheless, it is generally recognized to be a statement of fact or belief. . . .

The court of appeals . . . found the note contained an implied proposition by the writer that Dullard possessed the methamphetamine materials. Under this approach, the court of appeals determined the note was hearsay because it was offered to show the declarant's belief in this implied proposition, and the declarant was not available at trial to be cross-examined about the proposition. Thus, the resolution of this issue requires us to examine the concept of implied assertions and the extent to which they constitute statements under our definition of hearsay within rule 5.801(c). . . .

The implied assertion issue arises in this case because the words written by the out-of-court declarant are not offered to prove the truth of the words. In fact, the words themselves have no real relevance to the case. Instead, the hand-written note is offered solely to show the declarant's belief, implied from the words and the message conveyed, in a fact the State seeks to prove — Dullard's knowledge and possession of drug lab materials. Thus, the question is whether this implied belief of the declarant is a statement under our definition of hearsay under rule of evidence 5.801(*c*).

The starting point for the common law approach to implied assertions inevitably begins with the celebrated and durable case of *Wright v. Tatham*, 112 Eng. Rep. 488 (Ex. Ch. 1837). The case involved an action to set aside a will based on the incompetency of the testator. At trial, the proponents of the will offered several letters written to the testator by various individuals concerning a variety of business and social subjects. The purpose of the letters was to show the absent declarants must have believed the testator was able to engage in intelligent discourse on the various topics discussed in the letters. This belief, therefore, constituted evidence of the testator's competency.

In the course of holding that the statements contained in the letters were hearsay, the court in *Wright*, through the scholarship of Baron Parkes' opinion, utilized the now-famous example of a sea captain, who, after carefully inspecting his ship, embarked on an ocean voyage with his family, an action offered as proof of the seaworthiness of the ship. Baron Parke used the illustration to show that such nonverbal conduct would nevertheless constitute hearsay because its value as evidence depended on the belief of the actor. This illustration was important in the court's analysis because the main problem sought to be avoided by the rule against hearsay — an inability to cross-examine the declarant — is the same whether or not the assertion is implied from a verbal statement or implied from nonverbal conduct. Thus, assertions that are relevant only as implying a statement or opinion of the absent declarant on the matter at issue constitute hearsay in the same way the actual statement or opinion of the absent declarant would be inadmissible hearsay.

This approach became the prevailing common law view, but did not escape criticism and debate over the years from legal scholars and some courts. Two central arguments surfaced to support a competing approach that advocated a separation between implied assertions and expressed assertions so that implied assertions would be removed from the rule against hearsay. One legal scholar summarized these arguments:

> First, when a person acts in a way consistent with a belief but without intending by his act to communicate that belief, one of the principal reasons for the hearsay rule — to exclude declarations whose veracity cannot be tested by cross-examination — does not apply, because the declarant's sincerity is not then involved. In the second place, the underlying belief is in some cases self-verifying: There is frequently a guarantee of the trustworthiness of the inference to be drawn ... because the actor has based his actions on the correctness of his belief, i.e., his actions speak louder than words.

4 Jack B. Weinstein et al., *Weinstein's Evidence* ¶ 801(a)[01], at 801-61 to 801-62 (1st ed. 1990) (citation omitted).

Once the proposition is accepted that the lack of intent to assert frees conduct from the hearsay rule, the opponents of the common law rule concluded that an unintended implication of a verbal assertion should similarly fall outside the hearsay rule. As with conduct, the opponents argue, the lack of intent to assert an implied assertion from speech also makes unintended implied assertions much less vulnerable than expressed assertions to the problem sought to be avoided by the hearsay rule. In particular, the opponents point out that there is a reduced risk of mendacity in implied assertions when the declarant has no real intention of asserting a fact sought to be proved. Consequently, the critics of the common law approach claim implied assertions should not be treated as express assertions because of lack of opportunity for cross-examination to test the veracity of the implied assertion would have no significant impact.

Federal rule of evidence 801(a) appears to support the departure from the common law, evidenced more by the advisory committee note accompanying the rule than the language of the rule itself. Although the rule does not expressly address the subject of implied assertions, the advisory committee note states:

> The definition of "statement" assumes importance because the term is used in the definition of hearsay in subdivision (c). The effect of the definition of "statement" is to exclude from the operation of the hearsay rule all evidence of conduct, verbal or nonverbal, not intended as an assertion. The key to the definition is that nothing is an assertion unless intended to be one.
>
> It can scarcely be doubted that an assertion made in words is intended by the declarant to be an assertion. Hence verbal assertions readily fall into the category of "statement." Whether nonverbal conduct should be regarded as a statement for purposes of defining hearsay requires further consideration. Some nonverbal conduct, such as the act of pointing to identify a suspect in a lineup, is clearly the equivalent of words, assertive in nature, and to be regarded as a statement. Other nonverbal conduct, however, may be offered as evidence that the person acted as he did because of his belief in the existence of the condition sought to be proved, from which belief the existence of the condition may be inferred. This sequence is, arguably, in effect an assertion of the existence of the condition and hence properly includable within the hearsay concept. . . . Admittedly, evidence of this character is untested with respect to the perception, memory, and narration (or their equivalents) of the actor, but the Advisory Committee is of the view that these dangers are minimal in the absence of an intent to assert and do not justify the loss of the evidence on hearsay grounds. No class of evidence is free of the possibility of fabrication, but the likelihood is less with nonverbal than with assertive verbal conduct. The situations giving rise to the nonverbal conduct are such as virtually to eliminate questions of sincerity. Motivation, the nature of the conduct, and the presence or absence of reliance will bear heavily upon the weight to be given the evidence. Similar considerations govern nonassertive verbal conduct and verbal conduct which is assertive but offered as a basis for inferring something other than the matter asserted, also excluded from the definition of hearsay by the language of subdivision (c).

Fed. R. Evid. 801(a) advisory committee note.

The thrust of the advisory committee note is that the same considerations that justify the specific exclusion of nonverbal conduct not intended as an assertion from the definition of a statement under rule 801(a) — the minimal dangers resulting from the inability to cross-examine the declarant — support, by analogy, the similar exclusion of nonassertive verbal conduct, as well as assertive verbal conduct offered as a basis for inferring something other than the asserted matter....

The circumstances of this case, as well as other cases, can make it tempting to minimize hearsay dangers when a declaration is assertive but offered as a basis for inferring a belief of the declarant that most likely was not a significant aspect of the communication process at the time the declaration was made. Absent unusual circumstances, the unknown declarant likely would not have thought about communicating the implied belief at issue, and this lack of intent arguably justifies excluding the assertion from the hearsay rule. Nevertheless, we are not convinced that the absence of intent necessarily makes the underlying belief more reliable, especially when the belief is derived from verbal conduct as opposed to nonverbal conduct.

Four dangers are generally identified to justify the exclusion of out-of-court statements under the hearsay rule: erroneous memory, faulty perception, ambiguity, and insincerity or misrepresentation. Yet, the distinction drawn between intended and unintended conduct or speech only implicates the danger of insincerity, based on the assumption that a person who lacks an intent to assert something also lacks an intent to misrepresent. The other "hearsay dangers," however, remain viable, giving rise to the need for cross-examination. Moreover, even the danger of insincerity may continue to be present in those instances where the reliability of the direct assertion may be questioned. If the expressed assertion is insincere, such as a fabricated story, the implied assertion derived from the expressed assertion will similarly be unreliable. Implied assertions can be no more reliable than the predicate expressed assertion.

The consequence of the committee's approach is to admit into evidence a declarant's belief in the existence of a fact the evidence is offered to prove, without cross-examination, just as if the declarant had explicitly stated the belief. Yet, if the declarant of the written note in this case had intended to declare his or her belief that Dullard had knowledge and possession of drug lab materials, the note would unquestionably constitute hearsay. Implied assertions from speech intended as communication clearly come within the definition of a statement under rule 5.801(*a*)(1). Unlike the committee, however, we do not believe indirect or unintentional assertions in speech are reliable enough to avoid the hearsay rule.[5] We think the best approach is to evaluate the relevant assertion in the context of the purpose for which the evidence is offered.

---

5. We do not consider whether conduct or actions that may be associated with oral or written assertions could be used to support the admission of unintentional implied assertions under Iowa Rule of Evidence 5.801(*a*)(2).

We recognize this approach will have a tendency to make most implied assertions hearsay. However, we view this in a favorable manner because it means the evidence will be judged for its admission at trial based on accepted exceptions or exclusions to the hearsay rule. It also establishes a better, more straightforward rule for litigants and trial courts to understand and apply. . . .

[With regard to hearsay exemptions or exceptions, the Court found that there was insufficient foundation for any of them to apply.]

We conclude the judgment and sentence of the district court must be reversed based on the error in admitting the hearsay evidence. The case shall be remanded for a new trial.

NOTE TO STATE v. DULLARD

1. *Implied Assertions and Probative Value.* The aspect of implied assertions that causes the Federal Rules to treat them as nonhearsay may affect their probative value. For example, to show that a store had been brightly lit on a particular occasion, the out-of-court statement "yesterday the store was brightly lit" would be hearsay. The statement "yesterday my eyes hurt when I was in the store" would not be hearsay. The second statement is saved from being defined as hearsay because its connection to brightness is somewhat remote. But the aspect of the statement that saves it from being called hearsay may decrease its probative value. A statement such as "yesterday I didn't like being in the store" would not be hearsay on the topic of the brightness of the store's lighting, but it would have no probative value on that point (and therefore would not even be relevant).

> **GOOD TO REMEMBER**
>
> Treating unintended assertions as hearsay is a *minority* position, rejected by the Federal Rules. Its logic, however, is compelling to many scholars and to some state courts.

QUESTION 5-6. In a products liability case, the plaintiff claims that a large piece of farm machinery was designed so that its operator could easily suffer muscle fatigue and distraction while operating it. Consider how the following evidence would be treated by the *Dullard* court and by a court applying the Federal Rules. In each example, to show that Frank Farmer, an experienced farmer, considered the machine safe to operate, the defendant seeks to show that after he had tested the machine for about two weeks:

- Farmer bought one.
- Farmer said to a friend, "I'd like to buy one of those."
- Farmer said to a friend, "That machine seems safe to me."

QUESTION 5-7. Carl Clerk was shot to death at a convenience store he owned. Dan Defendant was tried for the murder. According to the prosecution, Defendant killed Clerk because Clerk owed Defendant $800 and Clerk had not paid that debt. The prosecution has admissible evidence to show that about a week before the murder, Defendant told some of his friends that he was angry about an $800 debt that somebody owed him and that he was going to try hard to collect that money.

The prosecution would like to introduce testimony by Clerk's wife that several days before the murder, Clerk said to her, "Can you lend me $800?" to support its contention that Clerk was the person from whom Defendant was going to seek to collect a debt.

Should the trial court characterize "can you lend me $800?" as hearsay?

D SUMMARY

Hearsay Policy Foundation. When a person knows something, the best way to find out what the person knows is to talk directly with that person. That way, you can check on how that person knows it, how the person remembers it, what the person means by their words, and whether the person seems to be honest. If you can only find out what the person knows by having somebody else tell you what that first person once said, you lose the opportunity to evaluate the first person's perception, memory, narration, and sincerity. These ideas are the basis for the hearsay rule.

The hearsay rule prohibits introduction of an out-of-court statement whenever the relevance of the statement depends on the truth of what the statement conveyed. If the out-of-court statement can be relevant to some issue, regardless of whether it was true or not, then the hearsay rule has no effect. (If the statement can matter in the current trial, even if it was false when it was said, then there is no problem with our inability to know what the speaker had seen, had remembered, or had meant to convey.) As in *Vincelette*, careful analysis of a hearsay problem requires identification of the declarant, identification of the words of the out-of-court statement, and a careful description of how the out-of-court statement is relevant.

Identifying Statements. Sometimes there can be doubt about whether someone has made a statement out of court or about whether a witness has quoted an out-of-court statement. *Patterson* considered this for information conveyed out of court by a person who helped a police officer construct a drawing of a criminal suspect. *Schaffer* presented a common circumstance in which a witness only indirectly quoted what a person had said out of court.

Levels of Hearsay. When a witness quotes an out-of-court statement, usually there is only one declarant, the person who the witness is quoting. But sometimes a statement made out of court may itself contain an additional statement, made either by the out-of-court speaker or by someone else. As in *Biegas*, each statement must be considered individually, must be linked with its declarant, and must be analyzed to see whether it can be relevant just because it was said or whether its relevance depends on its being true.

Relevant Even If False. Assuming there is adequate proof that a statement was made out of court (it's true that the statement was made), there are many situations in which the truth of that statement (the statement was true) has no bearing on its role in a case. This describes words that are part of a crime, as in *Tenerelli*. Relevant whether or not true is a concept that applies as well to words that have legal effect, as in *Moen*. And sometimes proving that some words were said can matter because they may have had an effect on the person who heard them, regardless of whether they were true. This describes words that give their hearer a reason to believe an owner granted permission to do something, as in *Kenyon*. This same possibility was explored in *Field*. A very clear example of words being relevant even if untrue occurs in defamation cases. The plaintiff will introduce out-of-court words to prove that they were spoken, as part of the plaintiff's prima facie case. The plaintiff, as in *Hickey*, will actually argue that the words were false and that therefore they are actionable.

Unintended Assertions. If a jury could infer an out-of-court person's knowledge or ideas from learning about something that person did, the jury would really be relying on that person's past perceptions and memory. That could bring up the dangers that the hearsay rule is meant to protect against. And if out-of-court words are used in the same way, to support an inference that the speaker knew something, once more it could be argued that hearsay dangers are present. Under the Federal Rules, unintended assertions are outside the definition of hearsay. The *Dullard* opinion, from a state court, rejects the federal position on this issue and offers a setting for comparing the two approaches.

CHAPTER 6

Opponents' Statements

A. Introduction
B. Party's Own Statement
C. Adoptive Statements
D. Authorized Speakers
E. Statements by a Party's Agent or Employee
F. Coconspirators' Statements
G. Summary

 INTRODUCTION

Topic Overview

At common law and under the Federal Rules, despite the general prohibition against hearsay evidence, many out-of-court statements may be admitted as proof of what they assert. Exceptions to the hearsay exclusion allow admission of a wide variety of statements. Additionally, the Federal Rules have exemptions from the definition of hearsay for two classes of out-of-court statements offered for their truth. This chapter examines the most common of these exemptions: opponents' statements (sometimes called "admissions"), which are a party's own statements offered against that party.

"Anything you say may be used against you" sums up the treatment of opponents' statements. The rules allow any statement a party ever made to be introduced against the party to prove the truth of what it asserted. The proponent must satisfy only two conditions. First, the statement must be a statement made by a party. Second, the statement must be introduced against that party (under this rationale, your opponent gets to introduce your out-of-court words, but you don't). Opponents' statements were called admissions in early versions of the Federal Rules and continue to have that name in many state codes.

In addition to a party's own words, the concept of opponents' statements also covers some other types of statements associated with a party. There are five types of opponents' statements: a party's own statement; a statement a party adopts; a statement made by a party's spokesperson; a statement made by a party's agent or employee; and a statement made by an alleged conspirator's coconspirator. Each of these can be admitted to prove the truth of what it asserts, so long as the party's opponent is the one seeking to introduce it.

Rule 801(d)(2) defines an opposing party's statement as excluded from the definition of hearsay. The subparts of the rule, 802(d)(2)(A) through 801(d)(2)(E), define various types of statements that are considered a party's statements.

Rule 801. Definitions That Apply to This Article; Exclusions from Hearsay

. . .

(d) Statements That Are Not Hearsay. A statement that meets the following conditions is not hearsay:

. . .

(2) *An Opposing Party's Statement.* The statement is offered against an opposing party and:

(A) was made by the party in an individual or representative capacity;

(B) is one the party manifested that it adopted or believed to be true;

(C) was made by a person whom the party authorized to make a statement on the subject;

(D) was made by the party's agent or employee on a matter within the scope of that relationship and while it existed; or

(E) was made by the party's coconspirator during and in furtherance of the conspiracy.

The statement must be considered but does not by itself establish the declarant's authority under (C); the existence or scope of the relationship under (D); or the existence of the conspiracy or participation in it under (E).

Chapter Organization

This chapter covers the five kinds of opponents' statements that are detailed in the Federal Rules, in the order in which they appear in FRE 801(d)(2). Cases and notes explain how each variety of statement is usually treated, and also offer some descriptions of the reasons why these statements are exempted from the usual hearsay prohibition.

B PARTY'S OWN STATEMENT

A party's own statement is outside the definition of hearsay if an opponent of the party seeks to introduce it. Note that the party's statement might have been either advantageous or disadvantageous to the party at the time he or she made it. Obviously, the statement will be disadvantageous to the party in the context of the current trial, or the opponent would not seek to introduce it.

■ ■ ■

"I Did a Wrong Thing" — **Sprick.** The sad story in this case provides a compelling example of a party's own words, admissible as an opponent's statement. As in all cases involving out-of-court statements, the main ideas to keep in mind are precise identification of the out-of-court words, the declarant of those words, and the purpose for which a party seeks to introduce them.

UNITED STATES v. SPRICK
233 F.3d 845 (5th Cir. 2000)

WIENER, J.

In this prosecution for bank fraud, mail fraud, and money laundering, Defendant-Appellant Michael Arlan Sprick appeals the jury's verdict of guilty on one of six bank fraud counts, six of six mail fraud counts, and seven money laundering counts — one related to the bank fraud count of conviction and six related to the mail fraud counts of conviction. He contends [among other claims] that the district court erred in . . . admitting evidence of a failed e-mail transmission in violation of Federal Rule of Evidence 403.

We conclude that the district court did not abuse its discretion in admitting evidence of the failed e-mail transmission. . . .

In the mid-1980s, Sprick went into business as a financial advisor. His principal clients were three elderly widows: Mrs. Maurita Johnson, who entrusted him with $1,090,000; Mrs. Corrine Parker, who entrusted him with $800,000; and Mrs. Annie Hallford, who entrusted him with $70,000. Each entrusted funds to Sprick in the expectation that he would manage them for her benefit. To each victim it was a given that Sprick would not spend her funds to support his lavish lifestyle or otherwise for his personal benefit. Yet Sprick did just that, spending his investors' money on, among other things, a luxurious personal residence in Odessa, Texas. . . .

During a search of Sprick's home, the contents of his computer were examined and a failed e-mail transmission was discovered. That e-mail was addressed to a radio personality known as "Delilah," but it was returned as undeliverable because the wrong e-mail destination had been used. Over defense counsel's objection grounded in Federal Rule of Evidence 403, the failed e-mail was admitted into evidence. Its message was:

> ... I was successful in business earning in excess of $200K per year, but that never seemed good enough for her. ... I built one of the biggest houses in Odessa for her. She wanted for nothing in material matters. ... I am in the financial services industry and deal with large amounts of money. I misappropriated, (or as another listener of your show mentioned the same earlier, and you straightened him out to admit stole), a large amount of money. Nobody was hurt because of their resources, but that does not excuse, and I am not trying to justify my actions, what and why I did what I did.
>
> Delilah, today my attorney got a fax from the assistant attorney general of the United States. They are wanting me to admit what I did and face 3-4 years in a federal prison. I know I am guilty. I did a wrong thing because of the right reason ... love.

This message was presented to the jury several times, including once when the entire e-mail was read aloud and again when only a portion, reproduced on a large illustration, was placed within the jury's view. The trial judge issued a cautionary instruction, stating in relevant part that "it is pretty clear that ... this e-mail was written at a time when the Government was only considering ... charges of bank fraud. It was not written at a time when the Government was considering a mail fraud charge."

Sprick contends that the evidence of the failed e-mail should not have been admitted at trial because its "probative value [was] substantially outweighed by the danger of unfair prejudice." Clearly, the e-mail is probative, as it is tantamount to a confession by Sprick that he had knowingly committed bank fraud, one of the offenses for which he was charged. There is also no question that the contents of this e-mail, in which he admits guilt, are prejudicial to his case. The question under Rule 403, however, is not whether the evidence is prejudicial vel non but whether it is unfairly prejudicial.

The e-mail did not influence the jury in its assessment of Sprick's guilt in any improper way; rather, its effect corresponds with the purpose for its admission, namely its bearing on Sprick's guilt. Moreover, the jury was properly instructed on the limited purposes for which it could consider the e-mail; namely, to determine Sprick's guilt on the bank fraud charges under consideration at the time of the attempted transmission of the e-mail and not his guilt on the later-added counts of mail fraud and money laundering. Thus, the e-mail had no unfairly prejudicial effect. Given the incontrovertible probative nature of this evidence, the e-mail would have to be unfairly prejudicial in the extreme for Rule 403 to be violated. As that is not the case, the district court acted within its discretion in admitting the evidence and in issuing its instructions to the jury.

... We therefore reject Sprick's complaints about the evidentiary rulings of the district court. ...

NOTES TO UNITED STATES v. SPRICK

1. *Is the Opponents' Statements Exemption Necessary?* Mr. Sprick's words stated that he had committed a crime, and they were introduced to prove that he had committed a charged crime. This fits the standard definition of hearsay. If evidence law had not developed special treatment for opponents' statements, the trial court would have been required to exclude the text of the e-mail. Under the Federal Rules, the hearsay rule never blocks a party's admission of an opponent's out-of-court words.

2. *Exemption or Exception?* To be faithful to the drafting of the Federal Rules, one would say that Mr. Sprick's words were not hearsay (because Rule 801(d)(2)(A) defines them as outside the scope of hearsay). Many practitioners know this but prefer to think of opponents' statements as an exception to the hearsay exclusionary rule. Either way, the words are admissible. The Federal Rules do exempt them from the definition of hearsay. The alternate conception — not reflected in the rules — would be to think of them as hearsay since they are out-of-court words admitted to prove the truth of what they assert, but to consider them admissible due to an exception to the hearsay exclusionary rule.

■   ■   ■

Why Treat an Opponent's Statements as Nonhearsay? — Shields. This brief excerpt announces a basic rationale for admitting an opponent's out-of-court statements. The court refers both to an 1849 case and to the fact that our trial system is adversarial.

SHIELDS v. REDDO

443 N.W.2d 145 (Mich. 1989)

GRIFFIN, J.

The rationale for admitting a party-opponent statement, despite the hearsay rule, "rests not upon any notion that the circumstances in which it was made furnish the trier means of evaluating it fairly, but upon the adversary theory of litigation. A party can hardly object that he had no opportunity to cross-examine himself or that he is unworthy of credence save when speaking under sanction of an oath." Morgan, Basic Problems of Evidence 266.

To put it more colloquially, the admissibility of a party-opponent statement springs from a sense of fundamental fairness captured in the phrase, "You said it; you're stuck with it." The hearsay rule operates to prevent a party from being "stuck" with what others have said without an opportunity to challenge them directly before the trier of fact. However, there is no reason, given the adversarial nature of our system, to extend the rule's protection to a party's own statements. In the more elegant words of nineteenth century jurisprudence: "[T]he general rule is — and it has few exceptions — that a man's acts, conduct, and declarations, wherever made, provided they be voluntary, are admissible against him, as it is fair to presume they correspond with the truth; and it is his fault if they do not." Truby v. Seybert, 12 Pa. 101, 104 (1849).

NOTES TO SHIELDS v. REDDO

1. *Multiple Justifications for Admitting Opponents' Statements.* The opinion describes two types of reasons in support of treating opponents' statements as an exception to the usual hearsay exclusion rule. One idea is that cross-examination, often not available in hearsay situations, will always be available when the declarant is a party. The other idea is that, for some unspecified reason, people should be required to stand by their own statements.

2. *The "Against the Party" Requirement.* A party's own words are admissible for their truth under the opponents' statements rationale only if offered against the party. If the words are reliable enough for admission when offered by an opponent, why wouldn't they be reliable enough when introduced by the party who once said them? First, when a party's own words are offered against that party, if there are reasons why those words may have conveyed a mistaken or wrong meaning, the party is likely to know about that and have the ability to explain it to the trier of fact. An opponent of a party would have a harder time knowing how to correct past out-of-court statements made by the party, if that party were allowed generally to introduce them. Second, allowing a party the general freedom to introduce evidence of his or her own past statements might present too strong a temptation for false reports of past statements.

■   ■   ■

Opponent's Motive When Making a Statement — Lincoln Square Slum Clearance Project. This case makes explicit one important aspect of the rules concerning opponents' statements: A party's words can be introduced by the party's opponent regardless of whether the words were favorable or unfavorable to the party when the party said them. The dispute in this case involved how much a property owner should be paid for property that was condemned for the building of Lincoln Center in New York City.

APPLICATION OF CITY OF NEW YORK RE LINCOLN SQUARE SLUM CLEARANCE PROJECT

194 N.Y.S.2d 259 (Sup. Ct. 1959)

HECHT, J.

At first blush, it seems unconscionable to award $2,403,000 for a property which the owner declared under oath to be worth only $1,100,000 a year before, in an effort to get its taxes reduced. Mature reflection, however, indicates that such a conclusory statement has no great probative value in determining value in condemnation.

The owner does not qualify as an expert. My experience in tax certiorari cases shows that the City pays little attention to the owner's claim of value. Where a reduction is granted without trial, it is done on the basis of income, sales of comparable properties, definite facts as to the structural value, etc. And if the reduction is granted as the result of trial, it is on the basis of the foregoing factors as developed by expert or other competent testimony.

We are dealing here with a constitutional mandate that the owner receive "just compensation" for the property taken. When the court determines what such just compensation is . . . it cannot constitutionally deprive the owner of that just compensation because the latter was greedy enough to try to pay less than its fair share of taxes.

Therefore, while one owner's claim of value is relevant as an admission, it is not sufficient in this case to outweigh the more competent and convincing proof of value.

NOTES TO LINCOLN SQUARE SLUM CLEARANCE PROJECT

1. *No Such Thing as "Admission Against Interest."* Opponents' statements are sometimes called "admissions," and some lawyers and some courts occasionally use a strange version of that term: "admission against interest." Under the Federal Rules, that expression has no meaning. An opponent's statement (formerly called an admission) can be any statement a party ever made, if it is introduced by the party's opponent. (A hearsay exception for "statement against interest" is among the set of exceptions that can be used only if the declarant is unavailable. It is covered in Chapter 10.)

2. *Effect of Opponents' Statement Rule.* The rules allow a party's opponent to introduce evidence of the party's statements. This means that the trier of fact may consider the statements. The trier of fact can conclude that the party's words were accurate, but the trier of fact can also decide that they were false. In litigation, an opponent's statement is not usually conclusive evidence of what it asserts.

3. *Counterexample.* In Minnesota, a statute rejects the idea that a person ought to be responsible for all the statements he or she makes, allowing an opportunity for a particular class of statements to be excluded even though they otherwise might meet the definition of admissions:

Minn. Stat. Ann §602.01 (2011). Certain statements presumed to be fraudulent.

Any statement secured from an injured person at any time within 30 days after such injuries were sustained shall be presumably fraudulent in the trial of any action for damages for injuries sustained by such person or for the death of such person as the result of such injuries. No statement can be used as evidence in any court unless the party so obtaining the statement shall give to such injured person a copy thereof within 30 days after the same was made.

Statements covered by this statute would likely be statements obtained by investigators, such as investigators for insurance companies, who are preparing to defend suits that might be brought in the aftermath of an injury.

GOOD TO REMEMBER

A party can introduce an opponent's statement against the opponent without any hearsay obstacle. It doesn't matter whether the statement was helpful or hurtful to the opponent when the opponent made it.

QUESTION 6-1. Harry Homeowner hired Connie Contractor to remodel Homeowner's kitchen. After the job was done, Homeowner sued Contractor, claiming that Contractor's work had caused the kitchen ceiling to sag down about five inches at one end of the kitchen. Contractor contends that the ceiling was sagging before Contractor worked on the kitchen. Discuss the admissibility of the following evidence in terms of hearsay and the opponents' statements exemption from the hearsay definition:

A. To show that the ceiling was sagging before Contractor worked on the kitchen, Contractor seeks to testify: "I told Homeowner before I started the work that the ceiling was sagging down."

B. To show that the ceiling was fine before Contractor worked on the kitchen, Homeowner seeks to testify: "The day he started the job, Contractor told me that the ceiling was in fine condition."

C. To show that the ceiling was fine before Contractor worked on the kitchen, Homeowner seeks to testify: "The day Contractor started the job, my neighbor, Nan Neighbor, mentioned to me that the one good thing about my kitchen was its perfect ceiling."

ADOPTIVE STATEMENTS

Adoptive statements are among the numerous types of opponents' statements included in Rule 801(d)(2). A statement will be an opponent's adoptive statement if the party "manifested" adoption of the statement or belief in it.

■ ■ ■

Silence as a Statement — Lambert. Characterizing one person's statement as a second person's statement because that second person adopted it has a powerful effect. As Lambert shows, someone else's words will be admitted against a party once the court determines that there were circumstances supporting a conclusion that the party agreed with or "adopted" those words.

STATE v. LAMBERT

705 A.2d 957 (R.I. 1997)

LEDERBERG, J.

This case came before the Supreme Court on the appeal of the defendant, Michael Lambert (Lambert or defendant), from a judgment of conviction of murder in the second degree and of committing a crime of violence while armed with a firearm. For the following reasons, we sustain the convictions. A summary of the facts pertinent to this appeal follows.

At about 6:30 P.M. on Thanksgiving Day, November 24, 1994, Lambert, two months before turning eighteen, and William Page (Page), aged eighteen, were walking in downtown Providence near the I-95 on-ramp at Francis Street. Lambert was throwing rocks as the pair approached the train tracks that run under the overpass. Sylvester Gardiner (Gardiner), a homeless man who was living under the highway, apparently shouted at the teenagers, and a confrontation between Gardiner and the youths ensued. Lambert testified at trial that Page approached Gardiner and pulled out a BB gun that looked like a bullet-firing pistol. Lambert further testified that after having forced Gardiner to lie on the ground, Page directed Lambert to find a rope with which Page then hog-tied the victim. Although acknowledging that the gun actually belonged to him rather than Page, Lambert claimed that he was unaware that Page had it with him that night. Page's statements to the police about what transpired that night differed significantly from Lambert's, but it is undisputed that Gardiner was the victim of a savage and brutal beating that resulted in his death. In their statements to the police both youths admitted delivering at least some of the blows that fell upon Gardiner....

On March 3, 1995, Lambert and Page were charged by indictment with the murder of Gardiner. Lambert's ... trial in January 1996 resulted in a jury verdict of second-degree murder and of committing a crime of violence while armed. Lambert's motion for a new trial was heard and denied on February 1, 1996, and on April 4, 1996, the trial justice sentenced Lambert to a term of life imprisonment on the murder count and an additional ten-year sentence, to run consecutively, on the count of committing a crime of violence while armed with a firearm.

Lambert filed a timely notice of appeal with this Court in which he [argued that] the trial justice improperly allowed a witness to testify at the trial regarding certain out-of-court statements made by Page. . . .

During the course of Lambert's trial, the state presented a young witness named Joanna Rodrigues (Rodrigues), who testified regarding a conversation that took place among herself, Lambert, Page, and a few other friends at an abandoned downtown warehouse. According to Rodrigues, Page told the other youths that he and Lambert had "beat up the old guy that used to live under the bridge [because] they didn't like him." Rodrigues also testified that Lambert said he had hit the victim in the head with a gun and that they said "that one hit him in the face with the tube. It came out through his neck, and they hit him in the face with a gun a couple of times." Lambert's counsel objected to Rodrigues's testimony concerning both Page's statements and those that Rodrigues ambiguously attributed to Lambert and Page collectively. The trial justice overruled Lambert's objections on the ground that the statements were adoptive admissions and were therefore properly admissible under Rule 801(d)(2)(B) of the Rhode Island Rules of Evidence.

When an incriminating or accusatory statement is made during a conversation that took place in the presence and hearing of an accused, and the statement is not denied by him or her under circumstances in which the repudiation of an untrue statement would be expected, the statement and the fact that the accused failed to deny it are admissible as an admission of the statement's truth and the accused's adoption of it as his own. State v. Lerner, 112 R.I. 62, 83-84, 308 A.2d 324, 338 (1973). Although we promulgated the Rhode Island Rules of Evidence in 1987, the test first set forth in Lerner continues to govern the admissibility of adoptive admissions pursuant to Rule 801(d)(2)(B). In order to admit testimony regarding an out-of-court statement as an adoptive admission, the trial justice should consider:

> "(1) [whether] the statement was incriminatory or accusatory in nature;
> "(2) [whether] it was one to which an innocent person in the situation of the defendant would reply;
> "(3) [whether] it was made within the presence and hearing of the defendant;
> "(4) [whether the defendant] understood the meaning of the statement; and
> "(5) [whether the defendant] had an opportunity to deny or reply to the statement."

In this case, the trial justice was careful to evaluate Rodrigues's testimony in accordance with these standards, and he was satisfied that each of the requisite factors was applicable to Page's statements at the warehouse. It is clear that Lambert participated in this conversation and had the opportunity to deny Page's assertions. Not only did Lambert fail to deny them, he in fact expanded upon them with his own statements. Rodrigues testified that after Page's initial statement, Lambert provided further details, telling the group that "they beat [him up and] hit him in the head with a gun, couple of times in his face." Consequently, we hold that the trial justice correctly applied the Lerner test, and therefore, the out-of-court statements were properly admitted....

For the foregoing reasons, we deny and dismiss the defendant's appeal and affirm the judgment of the Superior Court, to which the record in this case may be returned.

NOTES TO STATE v. LAMBERT

1. *Typical Conduct of Innocent People.* The multipart test the *Lambert* court uses to determine if a statement should be treated as a party's adoptive admission includes an inquiry about whether an innocent person in the situation would have replied after hearing it. The court seems to treat that inquiry without directing attention to the social setting in which Page made his statements, and Lambert failed to deny them.

2. *Words that Usually Elicit Responses.* Does a statement have to accuse someone who hears it in order to be the type of statement that would be corrected by the hearer if it seemed false to that person? Consider the following statements. If they were untrue, they would usually elicit a contradiction.

A. "Here's an envelope with all the money that I owe you."
B. "Here is a list of the prices we'll all charge our customers, so that even though they'll think there's competition, we've really fixed the prices."

■ ■ ■

Who Decides If a Person's Silence Is the Person's Statement? — Carlson. This case applies a state rule that is the equivalent of Federal Rule 801(d)(2)(B). When there is ambiguity about whether a person has adopted a statement made by someone else, that factual question could be decided by the judge or the jury; *Carlson* explains why an initial determination by the judge makes sense.

STATE v. CARLSON

808 P.2d 1002 (Ore. 1991)

UNIS, J.

Defendant appeals from his convictions for unlawful possession of a controlled substance, methamphetamine, and endangering the welfare of a minor. The Court of Appeals affirmed without opinion. We affirm the decision of the Court of Appeals and the judgment of the Lane County Circuit Court.

On August 3, 1988, Officer Lewis was dispatched to an apartment in response to a report of a domestic dispute between defendant and his wife, Lisa. . . .

. . . Lewis noticed what appeared to be needle marks on defendant's arms. Without first advising defendant of his constitutional rights, Lewis asked defendant about the needle marks. Defendant initially responded, "Yeah, I got a few tracks," and then said that the marks were injuries that he had received from working on a car. Lisa, who was present during the exchange and close enough to hear what was being said, broke in by yelling: "You liar, you got them from shooting up in the bedroom with all your stupid friends." Defendant "hung his head and shook his head back and forth."

. . . At trial, over defendant's timely hearsay objection, the court also permitted Lewis to testify about Lisa's statement, "You liar, you got [the marks on your arms] from shooting up in the bedroom [where the methamphetamine was found] with all your stupid friends" and defendant's nonverbal reaction thereto. . . .

The state first contends that Lewis' testimony about Lisa's accusatory statement ("[y]ou liar, you got [the marks on your arms] from shooting up in the bedroom [where the methamphetamine was found] with all your stupid friends") and defendant's nonverbal reaction thereto ("hung his head and shook his head back and forth") was properly admitted in evidence as an "adoptive admission" under OEC 801(4)(b)(B). Defendant responds that Lewis' testimony is inadmissible hearsay. He argues, in essence, that his head shaking manifested his rejection, rather than his adoption, of his wife's accusation. . . .

When a party unambiguously manifests, by words or conduct, an adoption of or belief in the truth of another's statement, little difficulty arises in the application of OEC 801(4)(b)(B). When it is claimed, however, that a party-litigant has manifested an adoption or a belief by nonverbal conduct and the conduct is susceptible of more than one interpretation, the analysis is more complex. In that circumstance, the court must examine the totality of the circumstances surrounding the hearsay declaration and the party's nonverbal behavior to determine whether the party intended to adopt, agree with or approve the contents of the declaration.

The proponent of evidence under OEC 801(4)(b)(B) has the burden, after appropriate objection has been raised, of establishing the factual precondition of intent to adopt, agree, or approve. Whether a party intended to adopt, agree with or approve another person's statement is a preliminary question of fact to be determined by the trial judge under OEC 104:

"(1) Preliminary questions concerning the qualification of a person to be a witness, the existence of a privilege or the admissibility of evidence shall be determined by the court, subject to the provisions of subsection (2) of this section. In making its determination, the court is not bound by the rules of evidence except those with respect to privileges.

"(2) When the relevancy of evidence depends upon the fulfillment of a condition of fact, the court shall admit it upon, or subject to, the introduction of evidence sufficient to support a finding of the fulfillment of the condition."

A threshold question in this case is whether the intent to adopt, agree or approve is a preliminary question of fact for the trial judge to decide under OEC 104(1) or a question of conditional relevancy under OEC 104(2). . . .

For reasons that follow, we hold that whether the party intended to adopt, agree with or approve of the contents of the statement of another, a precondition to the admissibility of evidence offered under OEC 801(4)(b)(B), is a preliminary question of fact for the trial judge under OEC 104(1).

. . . The objection to admissibility, based on the rule against hearsay, furthers an important legal policy of preventing the trier of fact from considering the possible truthfulness of out-of-court statements, unless the statements have sufficient guarantees of trustworthiness. The purpose of the hearsay rule is to guard against the risks of misperception, misrecollection, misstatement, and insincerity, which are associated with statements of persons made out of court. Safeguards in the trial procedure, such as the immediate cross-examination of the witness and the opportunity of the trier of fact to observe the demeanor of the witness who swears or affirms under the penalty of perjury to tell the truth, are designed to reduce those risks.

There are several difficulties with leaving the question of intent to adopt, agree or approve to the jury as a question of conditional relevancy under OEC 104(2). If the OEC 104(2) conditional relevancy standard is employed, the legal policy underlying the hearsay rule would be furthered incompletely, if at all. The jury passing on the admission by conduct will have to hear not only evidence about the conduct and the surrounding circumstances, but also the out-of-court statement, as necessary predicates for understanding what the party allegedly adopted. For example, in the present case, the wife's accusatory statement, to which defendant's nonverbal conduct is a response, would have to be admitted to give meaning to defendant's conduct, and the accusation is relevant to prove the truth of the accusation even though it may not be admissible for that purpose. A juror could (a) overlook the question of intent to adopt, agree or approve, and consider the truth of the matter asserted in the out-of-court statement, (b) use the out-of-court statement before considering and resolving the preliminary question of intent to adopt, agree or approve, or (c) consider the hearsay statement regardless of what conclusion is reached on the preliminary question of adoption or belief. If the evidence is inadmissible, i.e., the jury does not find the preliminary fact (intent to adopt, agree or approve) to exist, preventing jury contamination may prove impossible. Additionally, a general verdict would not indicate the jury's resolution of whether intent to adopt existed. A record for appellate review would require a special set of preliminary jury findings.

In short, we believe that judicial intervention is required to prevent improper use of evidence. The preliminary question of intent to adopt, agree or approve, therefore, should be left to the trial judge under OEC 104(1).

In the present case, the preliminary question of fact for resolution by the trial judge under OEC 104(1) was whether the proponent of the evidence, the state, had established by a preponderance of the evidence (more likely than not) that defendant's nonverbal reaction to his wife's accusatory statement manifested defendant's intention to adopt, agree with or approve of the statement.

In the face of his wife's accusatory statement, defendant "hung his head and shook his head back and forth." Although the record discloses that Lewis twice demonstrated defendant's nonverbal reaction, it does not disclose whether defendant's shaking his head back and forth was positive or negative in character. Defendant essentially testified that he had not intended to adopt, agree with or approve of his wife's remarks and that he did not see any benefit in arguing with an irrational, mentally ill and angry woman.

Various factual hypotheses are suggested by defendant's ambiguous, nonverbal reaction. Head shaking back and forth generally means a negative reply. Village of New Hope v. Duplessie, 304 Minn. 417, 231 N.W.2d 548, 552 (1975) (quoting Bill v. Farm Bureau Ins. Co., 254 Iowa 1215, 119 N.W.2d 768, 773 (1963). "[T]he lateral motion might . . . mean merely bewilderment or confusion, an 'I don't know' answer," id., a reluctance to engage in, or to continue, a dispute with his wife, a decision to stand mute in a situation that was intimidating by the presence of a police officer, or, as the state asserts in this case on appeal, an expression of dismay or resignation that his wife told the police the truth about how defendant obtained the needle marks on his arms.

We view the record consistent with the trial court's ruling on a preliminary question of fact under OEC 104(1), accepting reasonable inferences and reasonable credibility choices that the trial judge could have made. In the circumstances of this case, defendant's nonverbal reaction is so ambiguous that it cannot reasonably be deemed sufficient to establish that any particular interpretation, consistent with the trial judge's ruling, is more probably correct. We hold, therefore, that there was insufficient evidence to support a finding by a preponderance of the evidence that defendant intended to adopt, agree with or approve the contents of his wife's accusatory statement. Accordingly, we hold that evidence of his wife's hearsay statement and defendant's nonverbal reaction thereto was not admissible under OEC 801(4)(b)(B). . . .

[Because the evidence was admissible on another theory, the] decision of the Court of Appeals and the judgment of the circuit court are affirmed.

> ## GOOD TO REMEMBER
>
> The judge, not the jury, decides if the circumstances make it reasonable to treat someone as having adopted another person's statement.

Segment 21: contrasting conditional relevance with other admissibility issues

NOTES TO STATE v. CARLSON

1. *Admissibility, Not Relevance.* The court rejects the conditional relevance approach for the question of whether the defendant adopted his wife's accusatory statement. It supports that conclusion by analyzing the possibility

that juries might not give proper effect to the policies that support the hearsay rule. That analysis underscores the difference between considerations of admissibility and relevance.

  2. *Constitutional Issues.* Since the time *Carlson* was decided, the constitutional law aspects of the use of hearsay evidence against criminal defendants have changed. This would not affect the court's analysis of the adoptive admission issue and it would not affect use of the defendant's own statement (if he made one) against him. Because of the involvement of a police officer in the conversation, if the prosecution sought to introduce the defendant's wife's statements without characterizing them as having been adopted by the defendant, the Confrontation Clause might bar their admission. These constitutional issues are covered in Chapter 10.

QUESTION 6-2. Paula Patient is suing Doris Doctor, who was her doctor, for medical malpractice. Patient claims Doctor was inattentive while asking about her medical history and that this inattention led to an injury. Patient wrote a letter to Doctor saying, "I'm switching to another doctor right away, because I think you don't do careful work. For instance, you never even asked me whether I have allergies to drugs and you never asked me any questions to clarify things when I was telling you about my medical history." Doctor never replied to this letter. May Patient introduce the letter to show that Doctor never asked her whether she had drug allergies?

D   AUTHORIZED SPEAKERS

Statements by a party's authorized spokesperson can fall within the definition of opponents' statements, if the spokesperson was authorized to speak on the statement's topic. A lawyer is a classic example of a person authorized by a party to speak. A public relations officer of a company would similarly have authority to make statements on many subjects.

■   ■   ■

  Speakers Who Are Authorized but Not Controlled — Barnett. In some states, in order to begin a medical malpractice case a plaintiff must file an affidavit from a medical expert evaluating the legitimacy of the plaintiff's claim. When a plaintiff hires an independent professional to give an opinion, the professional is authorized to speak for the plaintiff. But the professional is not controlled by the plaintiff and is authorized to say what he or she thinks is correct, not just to say specific things on behalf of the plaintiff. The *Barnett* court considers the concept of authorized speaker in the context of these aspects of an expert professional's role.

BARNETT v. HIDALGO

732 N.W.2d 472 (Mich. 2007)

MARKMAN, J.

. . . In this medical malpractice case, the decedent, James Otha Barnett, III, died from a rare blood disorder after undergoing gall bladder surgery performed by defendant Dr. Renato Albaran, a general surgeon at defendant Crittenton Hospital. . . .

As the personal representative of the estate of her deceased husband, plaintiff Wapeka Barnett filed a medical malpractice action against [Dr. Albaran and two other doctors who had treated Mr. Barnett, Dr. Muskesh Shah and Dr. Cesar Hidalgo]. Plaintiff's affidavits of merit were signed by a general surgeon, Dr. Scott Graham; a neurologist, Dr. Eric Wassermann; and a hematologist, Dr. Rachel Borson. Graham's affidavit of merit stated that Albaran failed to take sufficient precautions to prevent a postsurgical infection before he discharged Barnett. Wassermann's affidavit of merit stated that Hidalgo misdiagnosed Barnett's condition as a stroke and failed to take proper precautions when Barnett was transferred to a different medical facility for the MRI testing. Finally, Borson's affidavit of merit stated that Shah should have performed further testing, should have stabilized Barnett before discharging him from the hospital, and should have diagnosed TTP and initiated treatment. . . .

At trial, the testimony of plaintiff's three experts differed from their statements in their depositions and affidavits of merit. . . .

At the outset of trial, plaintiff moved to exclude the admission of her experts' affidavits of merit for any purpose. . . . The trial court admitted plaintiff's affidavits of merit as substantive evidence . . . and permitted defense counsel to cross-examine plaintiff's experts regarding the differences between the affidavits of merit and their trial testimony. The jury found in favor of defendants, and plaintiff filed a motion for a new trial, which the trial court denied.

Plaintiff appealed by right, claiming that she was entitled to a new trial because the admission of the affidavits of merit as substantive . . . evidence . . . denied her a fair trial. The Court of Appeals agreed and reversed the trial court's judgment. [T]he Court held that the affidavits of merit constituted inadmissible hearsay that could not be used as substantive evidence . . . . We granted applications by Albaran and Hidalgo for leave to appeal. . . .

Affidavits of merit are required to accompany a complaint alleging medical malpractice. MCL 600.2912d(1) provides:

> Subject to subsection (2), the plaintiff in an action alleging medical malpractice or, if the plaintiff is represented by an attorney, the plaintiff's attorney shall file with the complaint an affidavit of merit signed by a health professional who the plaintiff's attorney reasonably believes meets the requirements for an expert witness under section 2169. The affidavit of merit shall certify that the health professional has reviewed the notice and all medical records supplied to him or her by the plaintiff's attorney concerning the allegations contained in the notice and shall contain a *statement* of each of the following:

(a) The applicable standard of practice or care.

(b) The health professional's opinion that the applicable standard of practice or care was breached by the health professional or health facility receiving the notice.

(c) The actions that should have been taken or omitted by the health professional or health facility in order to have complied with the applicable standard of practice or care.

(d) The manner in which the breach of the standard of practice or care was the proximate cause of the injury alleged in the notice. [Emphasis added.]

We disagree with the Court of Appeals that Borson's affidavit of merit constitutes inadmissible hearsay. . . .

In order for plaintiff to demonstrate that she has a valid malpractice claim and as a precondition to initiating her action, plaintiff was required to file an affidavit of merit in support of her complaint. As part of the pleadings, an affidavit of merit is generally admissible as an adoptive admission; by filing the affidavit of merit with the court, plaintiff manifests "an adoption or belief in its truth." MRE 801(d)(2)(B). In the instant case, from among the universe of potential experts, plaintiff hired experts of her own choosing to prepare the affidavits of merit, she was fully cognizant of the experts' statements made in the affidavits, she voluntarily chose to submit those particular affidavits in support of her complaint, and she summoned the same experts as witnesses at trial. These steps each reflect an acceptance of the contents of the affidavits of merit sufficient, in our judgment, to constitute an adoption or belief in their truth.

Moreover, an affidavit of merit satisfies the requirements of MRE 801(d)(2)(C). An independent expert who is not withdrawn before trial is essentially authorized by the plaintiff to make statements regarding the subjects listed by MCL 600.2912d(1)(a) through (d). Therefore, consistent with the actual language of MRE 801(d)(2)(C), an affidavit of merit is "a statement by a person authorized by the party to make a statement concerning the subject. . . . " In the instant case, although plaintiff had no right to control the content of the independent experts' statements, she hired the experts and invested them with the authority to prepare affidavits of merit on her behalf. Subsequently, with full knowledge of the contents of these affidavits and with a belief that they demonstrated the validity of her claims, plaintiff submitted the affidavits of merit in support of her complaint. Plaintiff called the same experts as witnesses at trial and failed to amend the affidavits of merit to reflect any change in opinion. Plaintiff cannot now reasonably deny that she authorized the experts to make statements concerning the subject of the affidavits.

While it is true that plaintiffs have a statutory obligation to submit affidavits of merit in support of their complaints before having the benefit of discovery, we cannot conclude that the nature of this obligation relieves them altogether of accountability for the substance of these statements. The purpose of the affidavits of merit is to deter frivolous medical malpractice claims by verifying through the opinion of a qualified health professional that the claims are valid. The purpose of the statutory obligation to submit affidavits of merit would be defeated, or at least significantly undermined, if there were to be no accountability—including potentially adverse consequences—for statements made on the basis of information available at the time the affidavits of merit were submitted. When confronted with admissions made in their affidavits of merit, the plaintiffs may reasonably point out to the fact-finder that they had access to a more limited factual development before discovery and explain the basis for any changes in opinion.

We conclude on the basis of MRE 801(d)(2)(B) and (C) . . . that the affidavits of merit were admissible as substantive evidence because they constitute admissions by a party opponent. . . . Accordingly, we reverse the Court of Appeals judgment.

NOTES TO BARNETT v. HIDALGO

1. *Distinguishing Judicial Admissions from Admissions.* A party's pleadings and a party's responses to requests for admissions are controlling in the cases in which they are filed. They are "judicial admissions." They limit the issues at trial and they require that facts that are admitted be treated as true. These effects are, in general, limited to the trial in which the pleadings and responses to requests for admission are filed. In considering whether judicial admissions such as pleadings may meet the definition of Rule 801(d)(2)(C), complications may arise. For example, pleading in the alternative is allowed in civil cases, and even inconsistent claims may be permitted. This makes treating any particular statement as an admission problematic.

2. *Proving Authorization.* The text of Rule 801(d)(2) makes clear that some "bootstrapping" is allowed—a court is allowed to consider the contents of a statement in deciding whether that statement was made by someone authorized to make it. The rule's only limitation on bootstrapping is its provision that a decision on admissibility must be based on more than just the content of the offered statement.

 ## E   STATEMENTS BY A PARTY'S AGENT OR EMPLOYEE

The Federal Rules treatment of statements by a party's employees recognizes what had been a developing trend in common law. While some early decisions had taken the position that only employees authorized to speak on subjects could make statements that would be treated as admissions, other courts had been willing to characterize more employees' statements as opponents' statements admissible against employers.

■ ■ ■

If a Boss Benefits from a Worker's Work, Should the Boss Be Burdened by the Worker's Words? — B & K Rentals and Sales. This case presents the main justifications for treating a worker's words as admissible against his or her employer. It also offers an example of multiple-level hearsay statements.

B & K RENTALS AND SALES CO., INC. v. UNIVERSAL LEAF TOBACCO CO.

596 A.2d 640 (Md. 1991)

CHASANOW, J.

Universal Leaf Tobacco Co. (Universal), through its subsidiary, Winstead Co., Inc., owned and operated a tobacco warehouse. B & K Rentals and Sales Co., Inc. (B & K) leased a portion of the warehouse to store equipment used in its business of renting scaffolding and seating for public gatherings. A fire broke out at the warehouse destroying most of B & K's equipment. Contending that the negligence of Universal and its employees caused the fire, B & K brought an action for damages against Universal in the Circuit Court for Anne Arundel County.

On the day of the fire, two of Universal's employees, Walter Johnson (Johnson) and Leonard Grimes (Grimes), were present and working within the tobacco warehouse. Johnson was killed by the fire. The parties dispute B & K's ability to locate Grimes at the time of trial. Consequently, they also dispute his availability as a witness. Nonetheless, B & K neither deposed nor subpoenaed Grimes. Rather, B & K called Lieutenant Kenneth J. Klasmeier (Lt. Klasmeier), a fire investigator with the Anne Arundel County Fire Department, as an expert witness for the purpose of testifying as to the cause of the fire.

Lt. Klasmeier had investigated the fire in progress and had received a written report from Lieutenant James Stallings (Lt. Stallings), who is also a fire investigator with the Anne Arundel Fire Department, regarding the origin and cause of the fire. Pursuant to his investigation and report, Lt. Stallings had interviewed various people, including Grimes, at the scene of the fire. Grimes told Lt. Stallings that: 1) Johnson and he were the only two people working at the warehouse at the time of the fire; 2) Grimes had lit an acetylene torch for Johnson a couple of hours before the fire; 3) Johnson was using the torch to burn strings caught in the jack wheels of a wooden dolly; 4) Grimes heard a popping noise and saw smoke coming from the area where Johnson had just finished burning the string from the jack wheels; and 5) Grimes believed the cause of the fire was related to Johnson's use of the acetylene torch.

Lt. Klasmeier . . . was permitted to testify that in his opinion "the cause and origin would have been the actions of Johnson using an acetylene torch to burn strings off of wheels inside the warehouse." Lt. Klasmeier was permitted to so testify despite his admission that he would not have been able to formulate such an opinion absent Grimes' statements. The . . . jury returned a verdict for B & K for $123,252.00. Universal moved the court for judgment notwithstanding the verdict on the grounds that the expert opinion of Lt. Klasmeier was improperly admitted into evidence. . . . The trial court granted the motion. . . . B & K then appealed. . . .

In addressing the admissibility of Lt. Klasmeier's testimony, the Court of Special Appeals quite properly reasoned that "[i]f, in fact, the predominant basis for the opinion is information that the law deems unreliable, the opinion loses much, if not all, of its probative value, for it then essentially regurgitates the underlying untrustworthy information." By Lt. Klasmeier's own admission, Grimes' statements furnished the predominant basis for his opinion. Therefore, the decisive question addressed by the intermediate appellate court, and the question upon which this Court granted certiorari, was whether each of Grimes' statements to Lt. Stallings constituted admissions by Universal.

Although it is clear that Grimes was Universal's agent, he had no express authority to speak for Universal. B & K argued below and now urges this Court to adopt the principle embodied in Federal Rule of Evidence 801(d)(2)(D) that a statement made by an agent of a party opponent which concerns a matter within the scope of the agency or employment and is made during the existence of that relationship constitutes an admission of the party opponent. While recognizing and discussing the sound rationale behind liberalizing the admission of an agent's statement, the Court of Special Appeals concluded that Grimes' statements were not admissible under existing Maryland law. We take this opportunity to re-examine the development of our case law on vicarious admissions and to join the substantial majority of states adopting the principle embodied in F.R.E. 801(d)(2)(D).

Traditionally, an agent was required to have "speaking authority" before his statement was considered an admission of the principal. See Brown v. Hebb, 167 Md. 535, 547, 175 A. 602, 607 (1934), where we quote the Restatement of Agency, §286 (1933): "Statements of an agent to a third person are admissible in evidence to prove the truth of facts asserted in them as though made by the principal, if the agent was authorized to make the statement or was authorized to make, on the principal's behalf, true statements concerning the subject matter." . . .

[T]he application of this traditional test of agency law as an evidentiary standard "frequently caused courts to exclude the agent's highly probative statement on the theory that the employer had not authorized the agent to make damaging remarks about him." 4 J. Weinstein & M. Berger, Weinstein's Evidence, §801(d)(2)(D)[01] at 219 (1988).

. . . We now . . . adopt the standard embodied in F.R.E. 801(d)(2)(D). Statements by agents concerning a matter within the scope of the agent's employment and made during the existence of the agency relationship should be admissible without the necessity of proving that the agent had authority to speak or that the statements were part of the res gestae.

This change in our law will place Maryland in accord with the clear majority of states that have adopted the principle embodied in F.R.E. 801(d)(2)(D) either by statute, rule, or decision. . . . Weinstein summarizes the underlying policy considerations that have prompted the widespread adoption of F.R.E. 801(d)(2)(D):

"Often, of course, particularly in tort cases, the agent was the only one who knew what happened.

... Rule 801(d)(2)(D) adopts the approach pioneered by Model Code Rule 508(a) and endorsed by Uniform Rule 63(9)(a) which, as a general proposition, makes statements made by agents within the scope of their employment admissible. . . . Once agency, and the making of the statement while the relationship continues, are established, the statement is exempt from the hearsay rule so long as it relates to a matter within the scope of the agency. '[T]he authority to do an act would conclusively imply authority to speak narratively about the act, if the utterance was made before the termination of the agency.'

*** The arguments for broadening the traditional narrow formulation were well stated by Professor Brooks, the Reporter for the New Jersey Committee which endorsed adoption of Uniform Rule 63(9)(a) for that state: 'The argument for the Rule is, first, one of necessity. Unless it is adopted many valid admissions which would help in the effective disposition of litigation would be lost. . . . To continue the restriction on this exception would be to immunize all principals from statements made by their working agents and employees who transact their business. . . . '" (Emphasis added, footnotes omitted).

4 Weinstein's Evidence, §801(d)(2)(D)[01] at 219-25.

Principles of fairness would also justify the adoption of the rule embraced by F.R.E. 801(d)(2)(D). As stated in the Official Comments to La. Code Evid. 801(D)(3)(a): "[I]t may be said that, in accord with principles of substantive law, one who undertakes to create an agency relationship should generally be made to reap the deleterious as well as the beneficial effects of what the agent sows." Hearsay is inadmissible primarily because of the lack of cross-examination to test for flawed perception, memory, or sincerity. When an employer entrusts responsibility for a job to an employee, it relies on the latter's perceptions, abilities, and judgments and consequently can be vicariously liable for any resulting deficiencies. It seems unfair to allow an employer to challenge an agent's relevant statements as hearsay merely because the employer has not had an opportunity to impugn through cross-examination the agent's perception, memory, or sincerity. Therefore, just as an employer is vicariously liable for the acts of its employees within the scope of employment, so too should the employer be vicariously liable for the statements of its employees concerning those acts.

The seeming unfairness of allowing an employer to reap the benefits of its employee's labor, yet remain immune from a statement by the latter about his assigned tasks, led to a number of pre-rules decisions rejecting the traditional limit. For example, the United States District Court for the District of Columbia rejected the traditional common law rule and admitted a truck driver's statement after an accident.

"To say, in these circumstances, that the owner of a motor truck may constitute a person his agent for the purpose of the operation of such truck over public streets and highways, and to say at the same time that such operator is no longer the agent of such owner when an accident occurs, for the purpose of truthfully relating the facts concerning the occurrence to an investigating police officer on the scene shortly thereafter, seems to me to erect an untenable fiction, neither contemplated by the parties nor sanctioned by public policy. It is almost like saying that [an admission] in the instant case could only have been made had the truck been operated by an officer or the board of directors of the Corporation owning the truck; and trucks are not operated that way. To exclude the statement of the driver of the truck as to the speed of the truck at the time of the collision . . . would be to deny an agency which I believe inherently exists regardless of whether the statement is made at the moment of the impact, or some minutes later to an investigating officer, or other authorized person."

Martin v. Savage Truck Line, 121 F. Supp. 417, 419 (D.D.C. 1954). . . .

Applying the 801(d)(2)(D) standard to Grimes' statements, we find adequate evidence, independent of the statements themselves, to support the conclusions that 1) Grimes was Universal's agent; 2) Grimes' statements concerned activities undertaken in the warehouse that were within the scope of his employment; and 3) Grimes' statements were made during his employment. Therefore, Grimes' statements should not be excluded as inadmissible hearsay. Likewise, neither the reports nor the lieutenants' testimony would be properly excluded on this ground. We reverse the holding of the Court of Special Appeals. . . .

NOTES TO B & K RENTALS AND SALES CO., INC. v. UNIVERSAL LEAF TOBACCO CO.

1. *Multiple Rationales.* The court refers to a variety of arguments in support of treating a worker's statements as admissible against the worker's employer. One is "necessity," meaning that workers' statements are often highly useful in litigation. Others are based on symmetry, suggesting that if an employer benefits from having a worker work, the law should also expose the employer to losses from that worker's work-related statements.

2. *Internal Communications.* The opposing party statement characterization can apply to statements workers make to people outside an enterprise. It can also apply to statements that workers make to each other; for example, internal communications such as e-mails that are easily subject to discovery and are thus likely to be available as evidence at trials.

> **GOOD TO REMEMBER**
>
> Under the modern view, a worker's job does not have to involve communications in order for the worker's statements to be introduced against his or her employer, as long as the statements refer to topics within the scope of the employment.

3. *Levels of Hearsay.* The testifying witness in this case, Lt. Klasmeier, actually learned of Grimes's statements by reading a report by another inspector, Lt. Stallings. In a portion of the opinion omitted from this version, the court recognized that the report was itself an out-of-court statement. Thus, there were two levels of

hearsay: Grimes's words to the writer of the report were an out-of-court statement, and the report was an out-of-court statement by the report writer. The report was admissible under an exception to the hearsay rule for "business records."

QUESTION 6-3. Wally Writer, a magazine writer, was invited to lunch at a cafeteria operated by XYZ Company for its workers and their guests. Writer slipped and fell in the cafeteria, and he was injured. Later that day, Nancy Counter, an accountant who was a full-time XYZ employee, said, "I saw Writer slip on some grease that was on the floor." If Writer seeks damages from XYZ, may Writer introduce testimony quoting Counter's statement to show that there was grease on the floor?

F   COCONSPIRATORS' STATEMENTS

Collegiality and the Duration of a Conspiracy — State v. Cornell. Statements by a coconspirator are treated as admissions by another coconspirator if they meet a variety of requirements. State v. Cornell examines the elements the proponent must satisfy to have a statement characterized as an admission of this type.

STATE v. CORNELL

842 P.2d 394 (Ore. 1992)

UNIS, J.

Defendant appeals from convictions on two counts of felony murder for the homicide of John Ruffner, allegedly committed during the course of robbing him and burglarizing his residence. Defendant was originally indicted with Mark Allen Pinnell in October 1985 for one count of aggravated murder and two counts of felony murder. In January 1988, defendant and Pinnell were indicted on five counts of aggravated murder. Defendant's motion for a separate trial was allowed in March 1988. In that trial, defendant was acquitted of aggravated murder and convicted on both counts of felony murder, which were merged for purposes of sentencing. The Court of Appeals affirmed the judgment of the trial court. We allowed review to consider defendant's challenge of the introduction of evidence of statements of a coconspirator under OEC 801(4)(b)(E).

We take the following statement of facts from the Court of Appeals' opinion:

"Defendant and Pinnell got the victim's name and phone number from the Swing N Sway magazine, where people advertise for sexual contacts. They drove to the victim's residence in a car borrowed from Dixie Timmons, Pinnell's ex-wife. They were accompanied by a woman named Velma Varzali. She stayed in the car when defendant and Pinnell went into the victim's residence. Several hours later the two men returned to the car and loaded it with personal property taken from the residence. Later that same day, defendant wrote checks on the victim's account and used his credit cards.

"The next day, the victim's body was discovered on the bathroom floor of his apartment. His feet and hands were tied behind his back with an electric appliance cord and there was a cord around his neck. Evidence at trial described this type of restraint as 'hog-tying.' The victim died of asphyxiation, because of the cord around his neck and the wad of toilet paper stuffed in his mouth. [The victim had been struck on the right side of his head, which caused a tear of his ear.] The apartment had been ransacked and several items of property taken, including the victim's wallet and checkbook.

"When defendant and Pinnell were arrested a few days later at Timmons' house, defendant had the victim's checkbook and credit cards and was wearing two rings taken from the victim. The police also seized several items of the victim's property that were at Timmons' house.

"During trial, the state introduced evidence that defendant and Pinnell had assaulted and robbed Randy Brown about 10 days before they killed Ruffner. The state's theory for admission of the evidence was that the facts of the Brown assault were so similar to the Ruffner homicide that it was relevant to identify the two men as the perpetrators of that killing."

The trial court, over defendant's objection, allowed the state to introduce, through the testimony of other witnesses, eleven statements made by Pinnell. The Court of Appeals held that the trial court did not err in admitting the statements as statements of a coconspirator under OEC 801(4)(b)(E). . . . We affirm.

When "offered against a party," OEC 801(4)(b)(E) treats as "not hearsay" "[a] statement by a coconspirator of a party during and in furtherance of the conspiracy." OEC 801(4)(b)(E) requires that the party seeking to introduce a statement by a coconspirator must establish, as foundational requirements: (1) that there was a conspiracy in which both the accused and the declarant were members; (2) that the declarant made his or her statement "during the course" of the conspiracy; and (3) that the statement was made "in furtherance of the conspiracy." Whether the foundational requirements are met is a preliminary question of fact to be determined by the trial court under OEC 104(1), and each requirement is to be established by a preponderance of the evidence.

In the present case, the statements at issue — Pinnell's statements — were offered by the state against a party (defendant). Thus, in order to admit Pinnell's statements under OEC 801(4)(b)(E), the trial court was required to find by a preponderance of the evidence (1) that there was a conspiracy with respect to the Ruffner and Brown crimes and that both defendant and the declarant (Pinnell) were members of that conspiracy, (2) that Pinnell's statements were made "during the course" of the conspiracy, and (3) that Pinnell's statements were made "in furtherance of the conspiracy." The trial court found that the foundational requirements were met and admitted Pinnell's statements under OEC 801(4)(b)(E). . . .

EXISTENCE OF CONSPIRACY AND MEMBERSHIP REQUIREMENT

The substantive law defines a conspiracy. ORS 161.450(1) states that a criminal conspiracy exists if, "with the intent that conduct constituting a crime punishable as a felony or a Class A misdemeanor be performed, [a] person agrees with one or more [other] persons to engage in or cause the performance of such conduct." Although the substantive law defines a criminal conspiracy, the Oregon Evidence Code states the evidentiary principles concerning the admissibility of coconspirator statements. A person need not be charged with or found guilty of criminal conspiracy or of the underlying crime in order to be a coconspirator under OEC 801(4)(b)(E). Because there usually is no formal agreement to begin a conspiracy, the very existence of a conspiracy usually must be inferred from the facts surrounding the statements.

Based on the facts in the record, summarized above, and accepting reasonable inferences and reasonable credibility choices that the trial judge could have made, we conclude that there was sufficient evidence to support the trial judge's finding, by a preponderance of the evidence, that a conspiracy existed with respect to the Ruffner and Brown crimes and that defendant and Pinnell were members of that conspiracy.

"DURING THE COURSE" OF THE CONSPIRACY REQUIREMENT

For the purpose of applying the coconspirator exemption in OEC 801(4)(b) (E), the duration of a conspiracy is not limited by the commission of the elements of the underlying crime. Conduct before or after the commission of the elements of the underlying crime are part of a conspiracy, if the conduct is either in planning, preparing for, or committing the crime, or in eluding detection for, disposing of, or protecting the fruits of the crime. Here, the alleged conspiracy included robbing the victims. At a minimum, a conspiracy to rob continues until the articles stolen are removed from the scene of the crime and are disposed of in some manner.

In this case, the challenged statements by Pinnell were made before or shortly after one of the robberies and before the stolen articles had been disposed of. There was sufficient evidence to support the trial judge's finding, by a preponderance of the evidence, that Pinnell's statements were made "during the course" of the conspiracy.

"IN FURTHERANCE OF THE CONSPIRACY" REQUIREMENT

Pinnell's statements must also have been made "in furtherance of the conspiracy." This requirement goes beyond the temporal requirement that the statement be made "during the course" of the conspiracy and focuses on whether the statement was intended in some way to advance the objectives of the conspiracy. A statement in furtherance of a conspiracy must have been meant to advance the objectives of the conspiracy in some way, i.e., it must be made in furtherance of planning, preparing, or committing the crime, or in furtherance of eluding detection for, disposing of, or protecting the fruits of the crime. Whether this prerequisite is met is determined in the context in which the particular statement is made. When a statement is made in the presence of a coconspirator, a statement that would not otherwise be in furtherance of the conspiracy may be in furtherance of the conspiracy if the statement demonstrates a desire to encourage a coconspirator to carry out the conspiracy or to develop camaraderie in order to ensure the success of the continuing conspiracy.

In this case, defendant challenges the introduction of a coconspirator's statement, related by Varzali, that "I went for the ear, but ol' [defendant] had got there first." If this statement had been made to the police or out of the presence of defendant, it might be difficult to see how it could be in furtherance of the conspiracy. Here, however, the statement was made in defendant's presence, and the record reflects that defendant was "really quiet" and "very upset." Although the alleged crime had been completed just prior to the statement, defendant and the coconspirator were fleeing from the scene with the stolen articles; the conspiracy was continuing. In these circumstances, a trier of fact would be entitled to infer that the coconspirator's statements were made to encourage defendant, a coconspirator, to carry out the conspiracy or to develop camaraderie with defendant in order to ensure the success of the continuing conspiracy. There was, therefore, sufficient evidence to support the trial judge's finding, by a preponderance of the evidence, that the statement was made in furtherance of the conspiracy.

We have examined the other statements made by Pinnell and, accepting reasonable inferences and reasonable credibility choices that the trial judge could have made, we find that there was sufficient evidence to support the trial judge's finding, by a preponderance of the evidence, that each statement was made during the course of and in furtherance of the conspiracy.

We conclude that the eleven statements made by Pinnell were admissible as statements of a coconspirator under OEC 801(4)(b)(E)....

The decision of the Court of Appeals and the judgment of the circuit court are affirmed.

NOTES TO STATE v. CORNELL

1. *Purpose of the "In Furtherance" Requirement.* Just as a statement by an agent or employee must relate to a "matter within the scope of that relationship" in order to be admissible against the principal or employer, a coconspirator's statement must be "in furtherance" of the conspiracy to be treated as an admission. The requirement may be understood as seeking to ensure the reliability of statements, on the theory that statements on unimportant topics may not be made carefully and are not likely to be corrected if wrong. The application of this requirement in State v. Cornell exemplifies a pro-admissibility interpretation of the range of comments that might be characterized as serving the goals of a conspiracy.

2. *Preponderance Standard.* In determining the admissibility of statements under the coconspirator admission rule, the trial court must be persuaded by a preponderance of evidence that the elements are present. The judge, not the jury, determines admissibility.

QUESTION 6-4. Tom Talker gave an interview to Rachel Reporter, a newspaper reporter, and told Reporter that five years earlier he and a friend of his, Frank Friend, devised a scheme to steal money from a credit card company. He told Reporter that they had transferred $200,000 from that company into fake bank accounts and then spent the money on a vacation. Reporter published an article about what Talker had said. The credit card company has been unable to find Talker, but it has sued Friend, seeking $200,000 it claims he stole from it. The company seeks to have Reporter testify about what Talker told her. This testimony is:

A. Not admissible as a coconspirator's statement because this lawsuit is a civil case.

B. Admissible as a coconspirator's statement because someone in Talker's position is unlikely to have made the statement unless it was true.

C. Not admissible as a coconspirator's statement because the statement was not in furtherance of the conspiracy.

D. Admissible as a coconspirator's statement unless the only proof that Friend and Talker committed the crime together is Talker's statement.

G SUMMARY

General Rule. Out-of-court statements made by a party's opponent are excepted from the definition of hearsay. This means that even if they are offered to prove the truth of what they assert, the hearsay prohibition does not apply. Statements made by a party's opponent may be introduced by that party against the opponent to prove the truth of what they assert.

A Party's Own Statements. The first and most common kind of statement by a party opponent is that party's own statement. A party's own statements are admissible against the party, regardless of whether they were favorable to the party or unfavorable to the party at the time the party made them. *Sprick*, *Shields*, and *Lincoln Square Slum Clearance Project* illustrate this basic kind of opposing party's statement, and offer some rationales for allowing their admission for the truth of what they assert.

Adoptive Statements. Another kind of statement by a party opponent is an adoptive statement. By adoptive statement, the law means a statement made by someone else that a party opponent has agreed with or accepted. We know that a party opponent has agreed with a statement or accepted it based on all of the circumstances in which the statement was made and the party opponent had an opportunity to reject it, correct it, or accept it, as in *Lambert* and *Carlson*.

Statements by an Authorized Speaker. When a person hires someone to make statements on his or her behalf, or otherwise authorizes someone to make statements for himself or herself, those statements are referred to as "statements by authorized speakers," as in *Barnett*. These statements are covered by the opponents' statements rule.

Employees' Statements. Many times in litigation, a party seeks to introduce statements made by employees of the defendant. These statements made by employees are usually treated as opponents' statements, and they are admissible for the truth of what they assert. This makes sense, bearing in mind a requirement of the rule that the statement must have been made during the course of employment, and the statement must relate to the subject matter of that employment. This aspect of the rule is illustrated and explained in *B & K Rentals and Sales*.

Coconspirators' Statements. Finally, a statement by a party's coconspirator is treated as that party's own statement and can be introduced against that party. The sometimes liberal interpretation of the issue of whether a statement was made in furtherance of the conspiracy is demonstrated in State v. Cornell. The general treatment of these statements is parallel to the treatment of adoptive statements and statements by a party's employee or agent.

CHAPTER 7

Witnesses' Own Out-of-Court Statements

A. Introduction
B. Substantive and Nonsubstantive Use of a Witness's Prior Statements
C. Prior Inconsistent Statements by a Witness
D. Prior Consistent Statements by a Witness
E. Statements Identifying a Person Made after Perceiving the Person
F. "Subject to Cross-Examination" Requirement
G. Summary

A INTRODUCTION

Topic Overview

The Federal Rules treat a witness's own out-of-court statements as hearsay if they are introduced to prove the truth of what they assert, even though the witness is present in court and even though the witness could be cross-examined about the statement. The definition of hearsay in Rule 801(c) makes this clear. It says "'Hearsay' means a statement that . . . the declarant does not make while testifying at the current trial or hearing. . . . " When a witness gives testimony that includes self-quotation (for example, "Last year, out of court, I said there was an oil slick on the pond, introduced to prove that there was an oil slick on the pond"), the words the witness quotes at the trial are a statement the witness did *not* make at the current trial.

The main justification for treating self-quotation as hearsay depends on the idea that the timing of cross-examination is very important. If there were problems with a speaker's perception, memory, choice of words, or honesty, probing for those testimonial infirmities at the time a person first makes a statement may be the most effective to ferret out possible errors. Discovering those flaws may be harder some time later, in court, if the person repeats an out-of-court statement. So, if cross-examination the first time the person makes the statement is not possible (because a statement was made out of court), the rules generally treat the statement as hearsay. This strict analysis supports categorizing a witness's own past statements as hearsay when the witness repeats them in court.

Despite this general position, Rule 801(d)(1) exempts three types of a witness's out-of-court statements from the hearsay definition, if certain conditions are met. These statements are prior inconsistent statements, prior consistent statements, and statements identifying a person.

Rule 801. Definitions That Apply to This Article; Exclusions from Hearsay

. . .

(d) Statements That Are Not Hearsay. A statement that meets the following conditions is not hearsay:

(1) *A Declarant-Witness's Prior Statement.* The declarant testifies and is subject to cross-examination about a prior statement, and the statement:

(A) is inconsistent with the declarant's testimony and was given under penalty of perjury at a trial, hearing, or other proceeding or in a deposition;

(B) is consistent with the declarant's testimony and is offered:

(i) to rebut an express or implied charge that the declarant recently fabricated it or acted from a recent improper influence or motive in so testifying; or

(ii) to rehabilitate the declarant's credibility as a witness when attacked on another ground; or

(C) identifies a person as someone the declarant perceived earlier.

. . .

Chapter Organization

This chapter examines the three kinds of declarant-witness's prior statements, in the order in which Rule 801(d)(1) presents them. Note that for each of these kinds of statements, there is a requirement that the declarant must testify and be subject to cross-examination. The chapter concludes with consideration of how parties can satisfy the requirement of "subject to cross-examination."

B SUBSTANTIVE AND NONSUBSTANTIVE USE OF A WITNESS'S PRIOR STATEMENTS

If an out-of-court statement is hearsay, it may not be admitted as proof of what it asserts. On the other hand, when the rules exclude a witness's prior statement from the definition of hearsay, the statement may be relied on for substantive purposes, for proof of whatever it asserts. But even if substantive use is forbidden, a statement might be available for a nonsubstantive use. The distinction between substantive and nonsubstantive uses is important for Rule 801(d)'s treatment of prior consistent and prior inconsistent statements.

A nonsubstantive use of a witness's past statements involves impeachment (impeachment is covered in detail in Chapter 12). To persuade a finder of fact that a witness has given inaccurate testimony, the opponent may show that the witness once said something inconsistent with the witness's in-court testimony. When a past statement is introduced only to cast doubt on the accuracy of testimony, the jury is forbidden to rely on the past statement as proof of what it asserts. The jury is allowed to consider the past statement only as a basis for evaluating whether the testimony is accurate. This limits the jury's use of the statement to a nonsubstantive purpose.

Example. Dan Defendant was charged with bank robbery. Investigators talked to Walter Walker, who had walked by the bank at the time of the robbery. Walker told investigators he saw the defendant robbing the bank. At the defendant's trial, if Walker testified that he had seen the defendant rob the bank, that might be an adequate basis to support a conviction.

The distinction between substantive and impeachment-only use of out-of-court statements would be illustrated if Walker testified differently at the trial. If Walker for some reason testified that he had been near the bank at the time of the robbery but that he had been unable to see who robbed the bank, and if no other witness testified about the defendant, then the defendant might be entitled to acquittal. This would depend on how the prosecution might be allowed to use Walker's out-of-court statement to investigators. If the statement was admissible only to undermine the credibility of Walker's testimony, the defendant would be entitled to acquittal because the totality of the prosecution's case would be discredited testimony about Walker's not having seen the robber: Discredited testimony about not seeing a robber is different from evidence that Walker had seen the defendant. If the statement could be used substantively, it might possibly be an adequate basis for a conviction.

C PRIOR INCONSISTENT STATEMENTS BY A WITNESS

If three conditions are satisfied, a witness's prior inconsistent statement may be introduced for substantive purposes. The proponent must show that the statement contradicts a witness's in-court testimony, that it was given under oath in a proceeding, and that the witness is available for cross-examination.

■   ■   ■

How Inconsistent Must the Prior Statement Be?—Neadeau *and* Gajo. Rule 801(d)(1)(A) applies only when an out-of-court statement by a witness is inconsistent with that witness's testimony in a current trial. *Neadeau* presents an extreme example in which establishing inconsistency is impossible. *Gajo* considers a much more complex problem: whether a witness's testimony that he or she has no memory of an event should be treated as inconsistent with an early statement describing the event.

UNITED STATES v. NEADEAU

639 F.3d 453 (8th Cir. 2011)

MARSHALL, J.

A jury convicted Marcus Neadeau of conspiring to distribute (and possess with the intent to distribute) at least 50 grams of crack cocaine.... Neadeau appeals his conviction, arguing that the district court abused its discretion by admitting at trial the detention-hearing testimony of Vanessa Sagataw—Neadeau's wife and later co-defendant....

The district court stumbled a bit on the evidentiary issue, but the error was harmless. Sagataw testified for her husband at his detention hearing. She was later indicted and tried with him. In the face of her Fifth Amendment-based decision not to testify at trial, the United States offered her detention-hearing testimony as a prior inconsistent statement. The court admitted it on this basis.

Sagataw's earlier testimony, however, was not a prior inconsistent statement because it was missing an essential ingredient: she did not testify inconsistently at trial.... She did not testify there at all. Sagataw's detention-hearing testimony thus does not qualify as this kind of non-hearsay....

... This marginal error was harmless....

Affirmed.

UNITED STATES v. GAJO

290 F.3d 922 (7th Cir. 2002)

FLAUM, J.

A jury convicted Defendant—Appellant Bogdan Gajo of [various arson and mail fraud crimes]. Gajo appeals his conviction, challenging two evidentiary rulings related to the admission of tape recorded statements and a witness's grand jury testimony. For the reasons stated herein, we affirm.

Gajo owned a business called Cragin Sausage, which sold specialty ethnic foods, beverages and cigarettes. On January 16, 1996, the building where Cragin

Sausage was located caught fire and burned moderately. The fire was concentrated in the rear kitchen and storage area of Cragin Sausage. After the fire was safely extinguished, Daniel Cullen, who worked in the Fire Department's Office of Fire Investigation, examined the property and concluded that the fire was deliberately set. . . . Approximately one week after the fire, Gajo submitted an insurance claim for the damage at Cragin Sausage. . . .

During the arson investigation, government agents examined Cragin Sausage's outgoing telephone records, which led them to an individual named Jay Smith. Agents questioned Smith, who ultimately agreed to cooperate with the government. Smith recounted that in December 1995, a former coworker named Edward Baumgart approached Smith at his place of employment (the Banks Grill) and introduced him to Gajo. According to Smith, Baumgart told him that "Gajo needed a building burned down." Smith also stated that although Gajo spoke almost exclusively in Polish, Gajo told him in English that burning down Cragin Sausage "was urgent." Gajo and Baumgart offered Smith $4,000 to set fire to Cragin Sausage, but Smith declined. . . .

At trial, Smith described his meeting with Baumgart and Gajo at the Banks Grill. During Smith's cross-examination, defense counsel established that Smith could not remember if Gajo said anything to him in English. Smith made this admission despite testifying on direct that Gajo said in English that burning down Cragin Sausage was urgent. The government addressed the issue on redirect, but Smith still could not recall Gajo's precise words. The government, over defense counsel's objection, then moved to admit Smith's grand jury testimony as substantive evidence. The district court ruled that Smith's lack of memory as to what Gajo said at the Banks Grill meeting was inconsistent with his grand jury testimony and admitted the transcripts. The portions of the grand jury testimony read to the jury revealed that Gajo directly solicited Smith's assistance, that Gajo asked him in English to help find someone to "torch" his business for the "insurance money," and that Gajo told Smith it was important that somebody burn down Cragin Sausage. The jury convicted Gajo, and Gajo appeals.

In this appeal, Gajo . . . submits that the district court abused its discretion when it admitted as substantive evidence a transcript of Smith's grand jury testimony. During Smith's cross-examination, Smith admitted that he could not remember whether Gajo spoke to him in English during the Banks Grill meeting. This cast some doubt on Smith's direct testimony that Gajo had told him in English that burning down Cragin Sausage was urgent.[4] In response,

---

4. The direct examination between Smith and the prosecutor proceeded as follows:

Q. Did Mr. Gajo himself speak English to you?
A. If he did — yes.
Q. Do you recall what he said?
A. It was urgent.
Q. What was urgent?
A. To get this building burned.
Q. When he said that it was urgent, was he speaking Polish?
A. No, English.

the government moved to admit Smith's grand jury testimony, arguing that it was inconsistent with Smith's trial testimony. Before the grand jury, Smith had testified that Gajo told him in English that burning Cragin Sausage was "really important," that Gajo had to "have this done," and that Gajo needed the building burned for "insurance money." The district court admitted this portion of the grand jury testimony, ruling that although the court could not determine if Smith was lying on the stand, his lack of memory could be considered an inconsistent statement under Rule 801. Gajo now challenges this decision.

Federal Rule of Evidence 801(d)(1) provides that a statement is not hearsay if "the declarant testifies at the trial or hearing and is subject to cross-examination concerning the statement, and the statement is (A) inconsistent with the declarant's testimony, and was given under oath subject to the penalty of perjury at a trial, hearing, or other proceeding, or in a deposition." Because a trial witness's grand jury testimony is not hearsay and is admissible as substantive evidence when it is inconsistent with his trial testimony, the issue we must address is whether a lack of memory at trial qualifies as an inconsistent statement. In United States v. DiCaro, 772 F.2d 1314 (7th Cir. 1985), and United States v. Williams, 737 F.2d 594 (7th Cir. 1984), we addressed this issue and suggested that memory loss is an appropriate justification for admitting prior grand jury testimony. Each case, however, involved a "turncoat" witness who effectively lied on the stand to avoid testifying at trial. Indeed, in *DiCaro*, we identified an underlying concern in both cases that "a recalcitrant witness might defraud both the parties and the court by feigning a lack of memory." Gajo attempts to seize this language and narrow the applicability of Rule 801(d)(1)(A) to situations involving a witness whose lack of memory is attributable to recalcitrance or other improper motives.

We first note that no court has addressed the precise issue presented by this appeal. To be sure, many circuits — including this one in *Williams* and *DiCaro* — have held that in the context of the recalcitrant witness, a lack of memory is inconsistent with the description of specific details before the grand jury. In contrast, only one court has suggested that a prior statement should not be admitted under Rule 801(d)(1)(A) if a witness genuinely cannot remember crucial facts related to the prior statement.

[W]e decline to adopt Gajo's narrow reading of Rule 801(d)(1)(A). Beyond the difficulty in administering such a rule, nothing in *DiCaro* or *Williams* suggests that the holdings in those cases should be limited to the turncoat witness. Indeed, *Williams* instructs that the term "inconsistent" in Rule 801(d)(1)(A) should not be confined to "statements [that are] diametrically opposed or logically incompatible," and that inconsistency "may be found in evasive answers, . . . silence, or changes in positions." [S]ee also United States v. Distler, 671 F.2d 954, 958 (6th Cir. 1981) ("when a witness remembers events incompletely, or with some equivocation at trial, it is not improper to admit a prior statement that otherwise complies with the limitations of Rule 801(d)(1), if that prior statement indicates that at an earlier time the witness remembered the events about which he testifies with more certainty or in more detail"). Moreover, we believe that the district court is in a better position to evaluate the "multitude of factors" that help determine whether a witness's trial testimony is truly inconsistent with his or her prior grand jury testimony.

Here, the trial judge found that Smith's trial testimony (where he could not remember what Gajo said to him in English) was inconsistent with his grand jury testimony (where Smith specifically recounted what Gajo said). The trial judge also ruled that this was the only inconsistency and limited the introduction of the grand jury testimony accordingly. We believe this was the appropriate course of action. In some cases, a witness's genuine lack of memory may be inconsistent with his prior testimony, which naturally occurred closer in time to the actual events described. Because we believe the trial judge is in the best position to make that determination, we find that the district court did not abuse its discretion in admitting limited portions of Smith's grand jury testimony.

The district court did not abuse its discretion in admitting . . . Smith's prior grand jury testimony. As a result, we affirm Gajo's conviction.

NOTES TO UNITED STATES v. NEADEAU AND UNITED STATES v. GAJO

1. *Controlling Use of Prior Inconsistent Statements.* Rule 801(d)(1)(A) sets up some significant controls over the substantive use of prior inconsistent statements. As *Neadeau* illustrates, the declarant must testify at the current trial. The requirement of inconsistency imposes another limitation. Inconsistent could mean something like "showing that the witness has likely lied," or it might just mean "different from the witness's testimony." *Gajo* moves in the direction of requiring only a difference, not a difference that suggests false testimony.

2. *Prior Partly Inconsistent Statements.* If a witness's prior statement is partly consistent and partly inconsistent with the witness's testimony, a trial court ought to exclude the statement if the inconsistency is slight. If the inconsistency is significant, the trial court might require that only the inconsistent portion be introduced. This approach would need to be correlated with Rule 106, the "completeness" rule, which allows otherwise inadmissible parts of documents or statements to be introduced if they will allow full understanding of portions that are otherwise properly admitted.

■ ■ ■

Where Did the Witness Make the Prior Statement? — Day. There can be many different settings in which a person may make a sworn statement. A crucial issue in applying Rule 801(d)(1)(A) is to define which of these circumstances should satisfy the rule's "given under penalty of perjury at a trial, hearing, or other proceeding" requirement. *Day* provides a clear description of that requirement's legislative history.

UNITED STATES v. DAY

789 F.2d 1217 (6th Cir. 1986)

KRUPANSKY, J.

Defendants-appellants Delmer E. Day (Day) and Johnny A. Pack (Pack) appealed their jury convictions for preparing false income tax returns....

In substance, Clarence M. Moore (Moore) was charged with willfully preparing and subscribing his own false individual tax returns and willfully aiding and assisting in the preparation of false partnership tax returns for the tax years 1977 and 1978. Pack was charged with willfully preparing and subscribing his own false tax returns for the years 1977 and 1978. . . . Day was charged with willfully aiding and assisting in the preparation of false income tax returns for Moore [and Pack]....

Both Moore and Day testified at trial. Pack did not appear as a witness. Moore was examined and cross-examined exhaustively. During the cross examination of Moore, the government made a cursory ineffective attempt to impeach his testimony by reference to a certain recorded statement given by him during a pretrial interview conducted by Revenue Agent John Bright (Bright) and Special Agent John G. Doble (Doble) on December 15, 1980. During its rebuttal, the government moved to introduce certain highly prejudicial and incriminating excerpts from the recorded interview as substantive evidence. The court permitted the jury to listen to the offered testimony over defense objections.

Pack and Day were convicted of the crimes as charged in the indictment. Moore was acquitted on all counts. Pack and Day filed a timely appeal assigning as error the admission of Moore's highly prejudicial statement as substantive evidence against the defendants during rebuttal.

As previously noted, Moore had been interviewed on December 15, 1980 by Bright and Doble. Prior to the commencement of the interview, Doble assured Moore that he was not the target of any pending criminal investigation. He also advised Moore of his constitutional right to remain silent; that any statements he would make could be used against him in a later proceeding; that he had a right to have an attorney present and that he could terminate the interview at will to seek the advice and assistance of legal counsel. Upon these assurances, Moore taped what was characterized in the record as a sworn statement in which he cast himself as an uneducated country boy who left school upon entering the third grade and who had labored his way through the trials of life until he was misled by Pack and Day, both of whom had counseled and advised him in his business and financial affairs including the manner in which to accumulate the necessary cash monies with which to purchase Pack's partnership interest in the Company without legal implications. He characterized Day as a "damn crook" and identified Pack as the primary perpetrator of the check conversion scheme [related to the tax evasion charges].

His statements were not only extremely prejudicial to both Pack and Day but contradicted his own testimony given during his appearance as a witness at trial.

On appeal, Pack and Day charged error to the trial court in permitting the admission of Moore's recorded statement as substantive evidence characterizing it as inadmissible hearsay. The district court justified the admission of Moore's recorded interview as a . . . prior inconsistent statement given by the declarant Moore during the course of an "other proceeding" and admissible pursuant to Fed. R. Evid. 801(d)(1)(A). . . .

The precise qualifying language of the . . . rule mandates that the declarant's inconsistent statement be given "under oath *subject to the penalty of perjury* at a trial, hearing, or other proceeding, or in a deposition." Although Moore's statement was characterized as a sworn statement, the evidence failed to disclose whether Doble had legal authority to administer an oath that would invoke the penalty of perjury upon a showing that the declarant perjured himself. The proponent of a hearsay statement bears the burden of proving each element of a given hearsay exception or exclusion. It was therefore incumbent upon the government, as proponent of Moore's tape recorded declaration, to prove by affirmative evidence that the individual administering the oath had legal authority to invoke the penalty of perjury. Because the record is devoid of any evidence that Doble had been invested with the legal authority to officially administer an oath that would and could subject Moore to the penalty of perjury at a trial, this court cannot conclude, as a matter of law, that Moore's statement was given under oath and was in fact subject to the penalty of perjury.

The government's position, to be viable, must also qualify the interview conducted by Bright and Doble as an "other proceeding" defined in the above rule. The legislative history of 801(d)(1)(A) discloses that Congress intended to qualify only those prior inconsistent statements that were highly reliable and firmly anchored in the probability of truth as admissible substantive evidence. In seeking to limit the admissibility of prior inconsistent statements for substantive purposes, Congress determined that statements given under oath at a "formal proceeding" were inherently more reliable than statements given in the absence of such formalities.[2]

---

2. An explanation of the legislative history attendant to the evolution of Rule 801(d)(1)(A) is helpful in understanding the legislative intent embodied into the enactment of the Rule in its final form. Prior to the promulgation of the Federal Rules of Evidence, inconsistent statements of a witness made before trial were inadmissible as substantive evidence and were legally functional only for the limited purpose of impeaching the witness' credibility. Rule 801(d)(1)(A), in its present form, was the product of a compromise negotiated in the Joint House and Senate Conference Committee which recognized as substantive evidence only those prior inconsistent statements of a declarant which were given under oath subject to the penalty of perjury at a trial, hearing or other proceeding, or in a deposition.

The Rule as initially proposed by the Supreme Court rejected the traditional view and would have permitted the admission of all prior inconsistent statements made by a declarant as substantive evidence. The House Subcommittee on Criminal Justice, however, amended the Supreme Court proposal to include inconsistent statements "given under oath and subject to the penalty of perjury at a trial or hearing or in a deposition or before a grand jury." The House Committee on the Judiciary struck the reference to grand jury proceedings and imposed the contemporaneous opportunity for cross-examination of the declarant as a condition for qualifying the prior statements as admissible substantive evidence. The House Committee on the Judiciary stated:

Several circuits have already incorporated the congressional intent into decisions that have refused to admit statements given under informal circumstances tantamount to a station house interrogation setting which later prove inconsistent with a declarant's trial testimony and have denied their admissibility as substantive evidence pursuant to 801(d)(1)(A). *See, e.g., United States v. Livingston*, 213 U.S. App. D.C. 18, 661 F.2d 239 (D.C. Cir. 1981) (sworn statement given to postal inspector investigating robbery); *United States v. Ragghianti*, 560 F.2d 1376 (9th Cir. 1977) (prior statement obtained by FBI in criminal investigation); *Martin v. United States*, 528 F.2d 1157 (4th Cir. 1975) (statements made to federal agents investigating firebombing). . . .

Mindful of the congressional intent to ensure the reliability and truthfulness of any prior inconsistent statement as a condition of its admissibility as substantive evidence at trial, this court must evaluate the reliability and truthfulness of the Moore statement by examining the totality of the circumstances that pervaded the Moore interview.

Apart from the fatal infirmity of the controversial Moore recording, namely, the complete absence of affirmative proof that it was given under an oath that invoked the penalty of perjury, the statement fails to satisfy the criteria imposed by Congress to qualify it as prior inconsistent statement given during the course of an "other proceeding" because the circumstances surrounding the recording of the statement militate against reliability and truthfulness.

Initially, it is interesting to note that agents Bright and Doble characterized their meeting with Moore as an interview and not a formal proceeding. Although the statement was purportedly a sworn attestation, the evidence failed to disclose that it was given "under oath subject to the penalty of perjury." Moreover, Moore's motivation, mirrored in the tone and content of the statement, disclaims its reliability and truthfulness. . . .

Accordingly, for the reasons articulated herein, this Court concludes that Moore's statement is fatally flawed because it was not given "under an oath subject to the penalty of perjury" and because the statement was given under circumstances more aptly described as a station house interrogation than an "other proceeding" which would, as contemplated by 801(d)(1)(A) of the Federal

---

The rationale for the committee's decision is that (1) unlike in most other situations involving unsworn or oral statements, there can be no dispute as to whether the prior statement was made; and (2) the context of a formal proceeding, an oath, and the opportunity for cross-examination provide firm additional assurances of the reliability of the prior statement.

The House Judiciary Committee's proposal was ultimately adopted by the House of Representatives.

The Senate rejected the House Rule and adopted the original Supreme Court rule. Thereafter, Representatives of the House and Senate conferred and arrived at a compromise. The Joint Conference Committee eliminated the contemporaneous cross-examination requirement that had been incorporated into the House proposal and provided that, to qualify as substantive evidence, a prior inconsistent statement had to be "given under oath subject to the penalty of perjury at a trial, hearing or other proceeding, or in a deposition." The Conference Committee note specifically stated that "the rule as adopted covers statements before a grand jury." The Conference Committee version was promulgated as law by both the House and the Senate.

Rules of Evidence, ensure and inspire the reliability and truthfulness of the statements. To permit it to be considered as substantive evidence by the jury constituted prejudicial error as against all defendants.

NOTES TO UNITED STATES v. DAY

1. *Categories of Prior Inconsistent Statements.* The legislative history shows consideration of different descriptions of prior inconsistent statements that could be admitted for substantive use:

- all of them,
- statements made subject to penalties for perjury, and
- statements made subject to cross-examination.

What factors differentiate these different categories of statements?

2. *Counterexamples.* The following Colorado statute and New Jersey rule differ from Rule 801(d)(10)(A). Consider the choices they incorporate and how those choices might be supported.

> ### GOOD TO REMEMBER
>
> Statements someone makes in testimony before a grand jury can be covered by Rule 801(d)(1)(A) even though there is no cross-examination in a grand jury proceeding. The rule's requirement of cross-examination applies to the trial at which the prior statement might be introduced, not to the proceeding at which the witness made the prior statement.

Colorado Revised Statutes, §16-10-201 — Inconsistent statement of witness — competency of evidence.

(1) Where a witness in a criminal trial has made a previous statement inconsistent with his testimony at the trial, the previous inconsistent statement may be shown by any otherwise competent evidence and is admissible not only for the purpose of impeaching the testimony of the witness, but also for the purpose of establishing a fact to which his testimony and the inconsistent statement relate, if:

(a) The witness, while testifying, was given an opportunity to explain or deny the statement or the witness is still available to give further testimony in the trial; and

(b) The previous inconsistent statement purports to relate to a matter within the witness's own knowledge.

New Jersey R. Evid. 803. The following statements are not excluded by the hearsay rule:

(a) Prior statements of witnesses. A statement previously made by a person who is a witness at a trial or hearing, provided it would have been admissible if made by the declarant while testifying and the statement:

(1) is inconsistent with the witness' testimony at the trial or hearing and is offered in compliance with [a rule requiring that the witness be given a chance to explain the inconsistency]. However, when the statement is offered by the party calling the witness, it is admissible only if, in addition to the foregoing requirements, it (A) is contained in a sound recording or in a writing made or signed by the witness in circumstances establishing its reliability or (B) was given under oath subject to the penalty of perjury at a trial or other judicial, quasi-judicial, legislative, administrative or grand jury proceeding, or in a deposition. . . .

QUESTION 7-1. In a vehicular homicide case, a prosecution witness testifies that Defendant drove a white car. What would happen under the Federal Rules, the Colorado statute, and the New Jersey rule if:

    A. Prosecution seeks to introduce evidence that while testifying at another trial about the same incident, the witness said Defendant drove a black car.

    B. Defendant seeks to introduce evidence that while testifying at another trial about the same incident, the witness said Defendant drove a black car.

    C. Prosecution seeks to introduce evidence that while having dinner once with a friend, the witness said Defendant drove a black car.

    D. Defendant seeks to introduce evidence that while having dinner once with a friend, the witness said Defendant drove a black car.

QUESTION 7-2. In a vehicular injury tort case, plaintiff's witness testifies that Defendant drove a white car. What would happen under the Federal Rules, the Colorado statute, and the New Jersey rule if the Plaintiff were to introduce evidence that while testifying at another trial about the same incident the witness said Defendant drove a black car?

D. PRIOR CONSISTENT STATEMENTS BY A WITNESS

A witness's prior out-of-court statement that is consistent with the witness's testimony can sometimes be admissible with substantive weight. Rule 801(d)(1)(B) defines two categories of prior consistent statements and excludes them from the definition of hearsay. They are statements that rebut charges that the declarant's statement was recently fabricated or influenced by a recent improper motive, and statements that rehabilitate the declarant's credibility when it has been attacked on some other basis. This means that a jury will be allowed to rely on these kinds of prior statements by a witness to find facts, and that when a judge considers whether there was adequate evidence to support a verdict, the judge can consider them in that analysis.

■   ■   ■

Prior to What?—Tome. Rule 801(d)(1)(B)(i) gives substantive treatment to a witness's prior consistent statements if they are introduced in response to claims that the witness's testimony was affected by certain specified events. The rule is silent about whether, to be covered by this rule, a statement just had to be made before the witness's testimony or whether it must have been made before both the witness's testimony and the occurrence of the event that was a basis for challenging the witness's testimony. *Tome* answers this question.

TOME v. UNITED STATES

513 U.S. 150 (1995)

KENNEDY J.

Delivered the opinion of the Court, [except as to a part omitted here related to a reviewing court's appropriate use of legislative history.]

Various Federal Courts of Appeals are divided over the evidence question presented by this case. At issue is the interpretation of a provision in the Federal Rules of Evidence bearing upon the admissibility of statements, made by a declarant who testifies as a witness, that are consistent with the testimony and are offered to rebut a charge of a "recent fabrication or improper influence or motive." Fed. Rule Evid. 801(d)(1)(B). The question is whether out-of-court consistent statements made after the alleged fabrication, or after the alleged improper influence or motive arose, are admissible under the Rule.

Petitioner Tome was charged in a one-count indictment with the felony of sexual abuse of a child, his own daughter, aged four at the time of the alleged crime. The case having arisen on the Navajo Indian Reservation, Tome was tried by a jury in the United States District Court for the District of New Mexico, where he was found guilty. . . .

Tome and the child's mother had been divorced in 1988. A tribal court awarded joint custody of the daughter, A.T., to both parents, but Tome had primary physical custody. In 1989 the mother was unsuccessful in petitioning the tribal court for primary custody of A.T., but was awarded custody for the summer of 1990. Neither parent attended a further custody hearing in August 1990. On August 27, 1990, the mother contacted Colorado authorities with allegations that Tome had committed sexual abuse against A.T.

The prosecution's theory was that Tome committed sexual assaults upon the child while she was in his custody and that the crime was disclosed when the child was spending vacation time with her mother. The defense argued that the allegations were concocted so the child would not be returned to her father. At trial A.T., then 6 1/2 years old, was the Government's first witness. For the most part, her direct testimony consisted of one- and two-word answers to a series of leading questions. Cross-examination took place over two trial days. The defense asked A.T. 348 questions. On the first day A.T. answered all the questions posed to her on general, background subjects.

The next day there was no testimony, and the prosecutor met with A.T. When cross-examination of A.T. resumed, she was questioned about those conversations but was reluctant to discuss them. Defense counsel then began questioning her about the allegations of abuse, and it appears she was reluctant at many points to answer. As the trial judge noted, however, some of the defense questions were imprecise or unclear. The judge expressed his concerns with the examination of A.T., observing there were lapses of as much as 40-55 seconds between some questions and the answers and that on the second day of examination the witness seemed to be losing concentration. The trial judge stated, "We have a very difficult situation here."

After A.T. testified, the Government produced six witnesses who testified about a total of seven statements made by A.T. describing the alleged sexual assaults. . . .

A.T.'s out-of-court statements, recounted by the six witnesses, were offered by the Government under Rule 801(d)(1)(B). The trial court admitted all of the statements over defense counsel's objection, accepting the Government's argument that they rebutted the implicit charge that A.T.'s testimony was motivated by a desire to live with her mother. . . . Following trial, Tome was convicted and sentenced to 12 years' imprisonment.

On appeal, the Court of Appeals for the Tenth Circuit affirmed, adopting the Government's argument that all of A.T.'s out-of-court statements were admissible under Rule 801(d)(1)(B) even though they had been made after A.T.'s alleged motive to fabricate arose. The court reasoned that "the pre-motive requirement is a function of the relevancy rules, not the hearsay rules" and that as a "function of relevance, the pre-motive rule is clearly too broad . . . because it is simply not true that an individual with a motive to lie always will do so." "Rather, the relevance of the prior consistent statement is more accurately determined by evaluating the strength of the motive to lie, the circumstances in which the statement is made, and the declarant's demonstrated propensity to lie." The court recognized that some Circuits require that the consistent statements, to be admissible under the Rule, must be made before the motive or influence arose, but cited the Ninth Circuit's decision in *United States* v. *Miller*, 874 F.2d 1255, 1272 (1989), in support of its balancing approach. Applying this balancing test to A.T.'s first statement to her babysitter, the Court of Appeals determined that although A.T. might have had "some motive to lie, we do not believe that it is a particularly strong one." The court held that the District Judge had not abused his discretion in admitting A.T.'s out-of-court statements. It did not analyze the probative quality of A.T.'s six other out-of-court statements, nor did it reach the admissibility of the statements under any other rule of evidence.

We granted certiorari, and now reverse.

The prevailing common-law rule for more than a century before adoption of the Federal Rules of Evidence was that a prior consistent statement introduced to rebut a charge of recent fabrication or improper influence or motive was admissible if the statement had been made before the alleged fabrication, influence, or motive came into being, but it was inadmissible if made afterwards....

Rule 801 defines prior consistent statements as nonhearsay only if they are offered to rebut a charge of "recent fabrication or improper influence or motive." Noting the "troublesome" logic of treating a witness'[s] prior consistent statements as hearsay at all (because the declarant is present in court and subject to cross-examination), the Advisory Committee decided to treat those consistent statements, once the preconditions of the Rule were satisfied, as nonhearsay and admissible as substantive evidence, not just to rebut an attack on the witness' credibility. A consistent statement meeting the requirements of the Rule is thus placed in the same category as a declarant's inconsistent statement made under oath in another proceeding, or prior identification testimony, or admissions by a party opponent.

The Rules do not accord this weighty, nonhearsay status to all prior consistent statements. To the contrary, admissibility under the Rules is confined to those statements offered to rebut a charge of "recent fabrication or improper influence or motive," the same phrase used by the Advisory Committee in its description of the "traditional" common law of evidence, which was the background against which the Rules were drafted. Prior consistent statements may not be admitted to counter all forms of impeachment or to bolster the witness merely because she has been discredited. In the present context, the question is whether A.T.'s out-of-court statements rebutted the alleged link between her desire to be with her mother and her testimony, not whether they suggested that A.T.'s in-court testimony was true. The Rule speaks of a party rebutting an alleged motive, not bolstering the veracity of the story told.

This limitation is instructive, not only to establish the preconditions of admissibility but also to reinforce the significance of the requirement that the consistent statements must have been made before the alleged influence, or motive to fabricate, arose. That is to say, the forms of impeachment within the Rule's coverage are the ones in which the temporal requirement makes the most sense. Impeachment by charging that the testimony is a recent fabrication or results from an improper influence or motive is, as a general matter, capable of direct and forceful refutation through introduction of out-of-court consistent statements that predate the alleged fabrication, influence, or motive. A consistent statement that predates the motive is a square rebuttal of the charge that the testimony was contrived as a consequence of that motive. By contrast, prior consistent statements carry little rebuttal force when most other types of impeachment are involved.

There may arise instances when out-of-court statements that postdate the alleged fabrication have some probative force in rebutting a charge of fabrication or improper influence or motive, but those statements refute the charged fabrication in a less direct and forceful way. Evidence that a witness made consistent statements after the alleged motive to fabricate arose may suggest in some degree that the in-court testimony is truthful, and thus suggest in some degree that that testimony did not result from some improper influence; but if the drafters of Rule 801(d)(1)(B) intended to countenance rebuttal along that indirect inferential chain, the purpose of confining the types of impeachment that open the door to rebuttal by introducing consistent statements becomes unclear. If consistent statements are admissible without reference to the timeframe we find imbedded in the Rule, there appears no sound reason not to admit consistent statements to rebut other forms of impeachment as well. Whatever objections can be leveled against limiting the Rule to this designated form of impeachment and confining the rebuttal to those statements made before the fabrication or improper influence or motive arose, it is clear to us that the drafters of Rule 801(d)(1)(B) were relying upon the common-law temporal requirement.

The underlying theory of the Government's position is that an out-of-court consistent statement, whenever it was made, tends to bolster the testimony of a witness and so tends also to rebut an express or implied charge that the testimony has been the product of an improper influence. Congress could have adopted that rule with ease, providing, for instance, that "a witness' prior consistent statements are admissible whenever relevant to assess the witness' truthfulness or accuracy." The theory would be that, in a broad sense, any prior statement by a witness concerning the disputed issues at trial would have some relevance in assessing the accuracy or truthfulness of the witness' in-court testimony on the same subject. The narrow Rule enacted by Congress, however, cannot be understood to incorporate the Government's theory.

. . .

The case before us illustrates some of the important considerations supporting the Rule as we interpret it, especially in criminal cases. If the Rule were to permit the introduction of prior statements as substantive evidence to rebut every implicit charge that a witness' in-court testimony results from recent fabrication or improper influence or motive, the whole emphasis of the trial could shift to the out-of-court statements, not the in-court ones. The present case illustrates the point. In response to a rather weak charge that A.T.'s testimony was a fabrication created so the child could remain with her mother, the Government was permitted to present a parade of sympathetic and credible witnesses who did no more than recount A.T.'s detailed out-of-court statements to them. Although those statements might have been probative on the question whether the alleged conduct had occurred, they shed but minimal light on whether A.T. had the charged motive to fabricate. At closing argument before the jury, the Government placed great reliance on the prior statements for substantive purposes but did not once seek to use them to rebut the impact of the alleged motive.

We are aware that in some cases it may be difficult to ascertain when a particular fabrication, influence, or motive arose. Yet, as the Government concedes, a majority of common-law courts were performing this task for well over a century, and the Government has presented us with no evidence that those courts, or the judicial circuits that adhere to the rule today, have been unable to make the determination. Even under the Government's hypothesis, moreover, the thing to be rebutted must be identified, so the date of its origin cannot be that much more difficult to ascertain. By contrast, as the Advisory Committee commented, the Government's approach, which would require the trial court to weigh all of the circumstances surrounding a statement that suggest its probativeness against the court's assessment of the strength of the alleged motive, would entail more of a burden, with no guidance to attorneys in preparing a case or to appellate courts in reviewing a judgment. . . .

[Concurring and dissenting opinions omitted]

NOTES TO TOME v. UNITED STATES

1. *Proving the Timing of an Improper Motive.* The *Tome* adoption of a pre-motive requirement for use of prior consistent statements necessarily requires courts to determine when a witness's motive to lie might have arisen. This might present highly difficult factual issues, for example, if a witness and a party to a case had been lifelong friends.

2. *Prior Consistent Statements to Refute Attacks on a Witness's Credibility Different from Claims of Recent Improper Influence or Motive.* Rule 801(d)(1)(B)(ii) applies non-hearsay status to prior consistent statements that are introduced in response to impeachment efforts other than the kind of impeachment effort covered by Rule 801(d)(1)(B)(i) and elaborated in *Tome.* For example, an opponent might attack a witness's testimony by attempting to show that the witness's current memory had become inaccurate due to the passage of time since the event the witness has described in testimony. Showing that the witness had given a similar description of the event earlier could respond to that challenge.

3. *Distinguishing Substantive and Nonsubstantive Use of Prior Consistent Statements.* Rule 801(d)(1)(B)(ii) protects the trial process from a confusing conceptual problem. In theory, a prior consistent statement might be introduced not for substantive purposes but just for a non-substantive rehabilitation purpose, to shore up the believability of in-court testimony. But that analysis would likely be confusing to jurors. For example, a witness who testifies, "It was raining that day," might also have said at an earlier time that it had been raining that day. If the jury is allowed to hear the earlier statement, and is told it may rely on it substantively, the jury might conclude that there was rain that day. The jury's conclusion might legitimately be based on the in-court

GOOD TO REMEMBER

All prior statements that are the same as a witness's in-court testimony might logically refute a claim that the in-court testimony was motivated by a recent improper influence, but *Tome* requires a showing that the prior statements were made at a time before the witness allegedly had a motive to lie *if they are introduced in response to an improper motive or influence challenge.*

testimony or on the out-of-court statement. If, however, the jury was instructed it could *not* rely on the out-of-court statement substantively but could just rely on it to help evaluate the in-court testimony, the jury might still conclude that there had been rain and we would have no way to know exactly how the jury used the out-of-court statement in reaching its conclusion. As one court has commented, "[T]he line between substantive use of prior statements and their use to buttress credibility on rehabilitation is one which lawyers and judges draw but which may well be meaningless to jurors." *See* United States v. Simonelli, 237 F.3d 19 (1st Cir. 2001). The coverage of Rule 801(d)(1)(B)(ii) avoids this confusion by giving substantive non-hearsay treatment to many prior consistent statements.

QUESTION 7-3. Alan Anderson and Barbara Bell got married in 2004. In 2011, Barbara sought a divorce from Alan. After mediation failed, a trial was held. Barbara's sister, Carol Bell, testified that she saw Alan punch Barbara in 2008 at a small party. To discredit Carol's testimony, Alan's lawyer showed during cross-examination that Carol and Barbara had a very close relationship as sisters and that Carol would usually do whatever she could to help Barbara when Barbara needed help. Barbara would like to have Carol testify that, about a year after the party, Carol told Carol's and Barbara's mother that Alan had punched Barbara at that party. Testimony about what Carol told her mother would most likely be:

A. Admissible as a prior inconsistent statement.

B. Admissible as a prior consistent statement if Carol is under oath and subject to cross-examination.

C. Admissible as a prior consistent statement because it refutes a claim of recent improper influence or motive for Carol's testimony.

D. Inadmissible as a prior consistent statement.

QUESTION 7-4. Sal Slipper and Gowith were shopping at Goodfood grocery store on August 1, 2018. Slipper slipped on grease on the floor near a display of rotisserie chickens. Slipper fell and was badly injured. On August 2, 2018 Gowith told the store manager that because of bad lighting it was impossible to see the grease before Slipper slipped on it.

Slipper sued Goodfood. At the trial, Gowith testifies it was impossible to see the grease before Slipper slipped on it.

A. In Gowith's direct testimony, may Gowith say that on August 2, 2018 Gowith told the manager it was impossible to see the grease (to show that it was impossible to see the grease)?

B. Assume that after Gowith testifies, Goodfood introduces testimony showing that there was good lighting near the chickens. May Gowith (on re-direct examination) testify that on August 2, 2018 Gowith told the manager it was impossible to see the grease?

C. Assume that in cross-examination, Gowith admits that he and Slipper had recently agreed to go on a cruise together, paid for by Slipper, if Slipper wins this lawsuit. May Gowith (on re-direct examination) testify that that on August 2, 2018 Gowith told the manager it was impossible to see the grease?

D. Assume that in cross-examination, Gowith cannot remember the size of the display or its location in the store. May Gowith (on re-direct examination) testify that on August 2, 2018 Gowith told the manager it was impossible to see the grease?

E. Assume that in cross-examination, Gowith states that he and Slipper have been close friends for 40 years. May Gowith (on re-direct examination) testify that on August 2, 2018 Gowith told the manager it was impossible to see the grease?

Segment 22: prior consistent and inconsistent statements

E STATEMENTS IDENTIFYING A PERSON MADE AFTER PERCEIVING THE PERSON

This exemption from the hearsay definition has very common application in criminal cases. It allows a witness who has made this type of statement to repeat it from the witness stand. Also, if someone heard the declarant make the statement, that person can quote it at a trial, so long as the declarant is present and can be cross-examined.

■ ■ ■

Pointing to a Marshal Instead of the Defendant — Lewis. This case illustrates the typical use of "statements of identification of a person" exemption, and also provides a policy justification for it.

UNITED STATES v. LEWIS

565 F.2d 1248 (2d Cir. 1977)

FEINBERG, J.

After a jury trial in the United States District Court for the Eastern District of New York before Thomas C. Platt, J., appellant Frank Tillman Lewis was convicted of armed bank robbery and conspiracy to commit that crime. For these offenses, Lewis received consecutive sentences of 25 years and five years, respectively. . . .

There is no claim that the evidence on the bank robbery conviction was insufficient, and the jury could have found the following: On the morning of January 3, 1977, appellant and an accomplice robbed the Barclay's Bank at 2215 Church Avenue in Brooklyn. The robbers operated in style. They were driven to the vicinity of the bank in a chauffeured white Cadillac limousine, and went in pretending to be customers. In short order, both men drew guns and threatened those inside the bank. Appellant threw a woman customer to the ground and fired two shots from his gun. His accomplice disarmed a bank guard and collected about $11,800 from the cash drawers and the employees. The two men then went around the corner to the waiting limousine.

Twelve days later, the FBI arrested appellant at a New York hotel. After the agents identified themselves, appellant came to the door of his hotel room, shielding himself with a woman. The agents arrested appellant and gave him his *Miranda* warnings. Thereafter, the agents discovered in the room both the gun that was taken from the bank guard and a gun that had fired a bullet in the bank.

At trial, the case against appellant was overwhelming. The guns were, of course, strong evidence of guilt. In addition, a bank customer (Norma Sharpe) had identified appellant from photographs after the robbery, and she so testified. The driver of the limousine service testified that he drove appellant to and from the vicinity of the bank on January 3. Also, the jury was told of appellant's admission, when arrested, that he was guilty. In short, the jury's verdict was amply justified.

In his thorough brief and argument, appellant's counsel maintains that the district judge committed a number of errors of law. The most substantial arguments on appeal stem from Norma Sharpe's pre-trial identification of appellant from a display of photographs. At trial, Mrs. Sharpe was unable to identify appellant in the courtroom and mistakenly picked out a Deputy United States Marshal instead. When Mrs. Sharpe was then shown the photographic display, she testified that she had previously identified one of the bank robbers from the group of pictures, and she then picked out the photograph she had earlier selected. This picture, which was of appellant, was then admitted into evidence. After Mrs. Sharpe's testimony, FBI Agent Leo Farrell testified as to the way in which he had prepared the photographic spread. He also confirmed that Mrs. Sharpe had selected appellant's picture shortly after the bank robbery. . . .

Appellant . . . argues that the identification testimony should have been excluded as hearsay, and is not permitted by the new Federal Rules of Evidence. Appellant directs our attention to Rule 801(d), which contains various definitions. . . . Appellant argues that Agent Farrell's testimony should have been excluded because "identification of a person made after perceiving him" contemplates only corporeal, not photographic, identification; and because it was improper to allow Farrell to testify in the absence of an in-court identification by Mrs. Sharpe. Appellant also claims that Mrs. Sharpe's testimony about her prior identification after she erroneously identified someone else in court amounted to testimony about a prior inconsistent statement not made under oath, rendering it improper under subsection (A), which overrides subsection (C).

Subsection (C) of Rule 801(d)(1), the focal point of appellant's arguments, appeared in its present form in the Rules as promulgated by the Supreme Court in November 1972. However, the Senate deleted the subsection before the Rules were approved by Congress in December 1974. Not long thereafter, the subsection was resurrected in an amendment to Rule 801, effective October 31, 1975. . . . The controversy over, and the rationale of, subsection (C) are both admirably summarized in 4 Weinstein's Evidence, 801-3*ff.*, P. 801(d)(1)(C)(01). We agree with the observation there made that

> Congress has recognized, as do most trial judges, that identification in the courtroom is a formality that offers little in the way of reliability and much in the way of suggestibility. The experienced trial judge gives much greater credence to the out-of-court identification.

Id. at 801-803. This court recently pointed out that "the purpose of the rule was to permit the introduction of identifications made by a witness when memory was fresher and there had been less opportunity for influence to be exerted upon him." *United States v. Marchand*, 564 F.2d 983, 996 (2d Cir. 1977).

With these considerations in mind, we turn to appellant's specific contentions. The legislative history makes clear that Congress intended "nonsuggestive . . . photographic," as well as lineup, identifications to be covered by subsection (C). . . . We can see no sound principle for construing "identification of a person" to exclude identification by a photograph. True, there are dangers peculiar to photographic identification and these, like the dangers of a lineup or even those of an on-the-spot identification, must be taken into account in assessing reliability. But they do not justify a limiting construction of subsection (C).

Appellant's second argument on this point is that the failure of Mrs. Sharpe to identify appellant in court made inadmissible Agent Farrell's evidence that she had identified appellant a month or two earlier. Appellant may be confusing this situation with that posed by the failure or refusal of the identifying witness to recall in court the earlier identification, which is discussed in Judge Weinstein's treatise from which appellant's brief extensively quotes. In that situation, testimony like Agent Farrell's might well raise questions concerning the adequacy of cross-examination and the right to confront the original identifying witness. In this case, however, Mrs. Sharpe did recall her prior identification and so testified. Even before the new Rule, we approved of admitting evidence of prior identification, albeit corporeal, by the declarant's "own testimony and also by that of others corroborating his version of the details." If appellant is suggesting that under the new Rule testimony like Agent Farrell's may only be used to bolster an accurate in-court identification, we disagree. It seems clear both from the text and the legislative history of the amended Rule that testimony concerning extra-judicial identifications is admissible regardless of whether there has been an accurate in-court identification. The Senate Report recognizes the possibility that there may be a "discrepancy . . . between the witness's in-court and out-of-court testimony," and the House Report praises the amended Rule as a means of ensuring that "delays in the criminal justice system do not lead to cases falling through because the witness can no longer recall the identity of the person he saw commit the crime." The occurrence of the very contingency foreseen by the Congress will obviously not serve, of itself, to bar the Farrell testimony.

Appellant's final point seems to be that subsection (C) does not apply at all when the identifier has made an erroneous in-court identification because the prior identification is inconsistent with it and was not given under oath, as required by subsection (A). The Government responds that since appellant's appearance had changed significantly by the time of trial, there was no inconsistency. More significantly, even though Rule 801(d)(1) embraces subsection (C), the latter is not limited by the earlier subsections. Subsection (C) represents a legislative decision to admit statements of identification provided the declarant "testifies at . . . trial . . . and is subject to cross-examination concerning the statement." These conditions were met here, and we do not think that subsection (C) is rendered inoperative by Mrs. Sharpe's misidentification in court.

NOTES TO UNITED STATES v. LEWIS

1. *Significance of Rule 801(d)(1)(C).* Compare the following two items of testimony, with regard to hearsay issues:

A. "Last year, I heard X tell a police officer that he had seen the robber use a black truck," offered to prove that the robber used a black truck.

B. "Last year, I heard X tell a police officer that Dan Defendant was the man in a lineup who had committed the robbery," offered to prove that Dan Defendant had committed a robbery.

Rule 801(d)(1)(C) requires that "B" be treated differently from "A." The different treatment is usually supported by the rationale given by the *Lewis* court.

2. *Differing Results Under Multiple Rules.* The court considers the defendant's argument that although the controversial statement might be admissible under one provision of the rules, it should be excluded because it fails to satisfy the requirements of another provision of the rules. In general, avoiding the hearsay bar with *any* rule is a complete answer to the hearsay problem.

■ ■ ■

Elaborating the Definition of "Someone the Declarant Perceived Earlier"—Shaw. The current language of Rule 801(d)(1)(C) refers to "someone the declarant perceived earlier." A literal reading of that phrase would extend its coverage to all statements about someone's identity, so long as the statements were made after the declarant had once observed that person. *Shaw* interprets the rule more narrowly.

STATE v. SHAW

705 N.W.2d 620 (S.D. 2005)

GILBERTSON, J.

James Shaw (Shaw) appeals his conviction for attempted first degree murder and aggravated assault. We affirm.

In the summer of 1999, Shaw was employed as a cook at the Crazy Horse monument in Custer County, South Dakota. The victim, J.W.H., was a minor at the time and was also employed at the monument. Both J.W.H. and Shaw were permitted to live on site in trailer houses. J.W.H. lived in a trailer along with two roommates, Joseph White Hat (White Hat) and another minor, K.D. Shaw had one roommate, Derek Pond (Pond). All the roommates either worked together or were acquainted with each other from their employment at the monument. Trouble between J.W.H. and his roommates arose when J.W.H. was accused of taking their food and borrowing compact discs without permission. Shaw also accused J.W.H. of stealing beer from his refrigerator.

In the evening hours of July 11, 1999, the co-workers put a fund together to purchase beer for a party. Shaw and Pond left in Pond's small pickup and returned with three or four cases of beer. [Later on a fight took place among several people, J.W.H. was badly injured, and Shaw was charged with attempting to murder him.] . . .

Shaw argues that the statements given by J.W.H. to police during an interview ten days after the assault meet the requirements of SDCL 19-16-2(3). Shaw further argues these statements should have been admitted as substantive evidence of White Hat's role in the assault and attempted murder, and to support the defense's theory that Shaw was a bystander and lacked the requisite intent for the attempted murder charge.

SDCL 19-16-2(3) provides in relevant part: "A statement is not hearsay if the declarant testifies at the trial or hearing and is subject to cross-examination concerning the statement, and the statement is: (3) [o]ne of identification of a person made after perceiving him." SDCL 19-16-2(3) closely patterns Federal Rule of Evidence 801(d)(1)(C). The legislative history of FRE 801(d)(1)(C) is therefore instructive for our rule version of the non-hearsay rule under SDCL 19-16-2(3). In addition, decisions by Federal courts concerning the application of the Federal Rules of Evidence provide analytical assistance in the interpretation of our state rules of evidence.

The legislative history of FRE 801(d)(1)(C) makes it clear the rule is intended to apply to out-of-court identification procedures such as line-ups, show-ups and displays of photographs, that must comport with the due process standard of the Fifth and Fourteenth Amendments to the United States Constitution in order to be admissible under the rule. The rationale for the rule is that courtroom identification can be very suggestive as the defendant is known to be present and generally sits in a specific location in the courtroom, while out-of-court identifications are generally more reliable. In addition, an early out-of-court identification provides fairness to the defendant by ensuring accuracy of the identification before witnesses' memories fade.

Few cases have addressed the issue of when an out-of-court statement of identification meets the requirements of FRE 801(d)(1)(C) such that it is not hearsay and may be admitted as substantive evidence. In *United States v. Thomas,* 41 M.J. 732 (N.M. Ct. Crim. App. 1994), the Government sought to introduce out-of-court statements made by a witness outside the context of a line-up, show-up, or photographic identification procedure as not-hearsay statements of identification under Military Rule of Evid, 801(d)(1)(C). Military Rule of Evid, 801(d)(1)(C) is taken verbatim from FRE 801(d)(1)(C). The U.S. Navy — Marine Corps Court of Criminal Appeals held that the Government's attempt to bolster a witness's testimony by such an out-of-court statement was not permitted under the rule, as the intent of the rule was to make it clear that *nonsuggestive line-ups, show-ups, and photographic arrays and other identification procedures are not hearsay and therefore admissible.* That court held that Mil. R. Evid, 801(d)(1)(C), or FRE 801(d)(1)(C), did not apply to prior consistent statements of a witness not conducted at such an identification procedure, and introduced merely to bolster the witness' in-court testimony.

The court in *United States v. Kaquatosh,* 242 F. Supp. 2d 562, 565 (E.D. Wis. 2003), used similar rationale for not admitting out-of-court statements made to a police officer during an interview under FRE 801(d)(1)(C). The language of FRE 801(d)(1)(C) "made after perceiving him," refers to a witness recognizing the defendant after a subsequent observation and identifying the defendant. This requires the witness to make the statement of identification after observing or perceiving the defendant in person for a second time at a hearing, line-up or show-up, or from a likeness in a photo array, after the initial observation of the defendant at the time of the incident in question. *Id.* Out-of-court statements made during a police interview are more properly characterized as accusatory statements rather than statements of identification for purposes of FRE 801(d)(1)(C).

Only the Third Circuit Court of Appeals and District of Columbia Circuit Court of Appeals have affirmed the admission of such accusatory or interview statements under FRE 801(d)(1)(C). *See United States v. Lopez,* 271 F.3d 472, 485 (3rd Cir. 2001); *United States v. Davis,* 337 U.S. App. D.C. 36, 181 F.3rd 147, 149 (D.C. Cir. 1999); and *United States v. Brink,* 39 F.3d 419, 426 (3rd Cir. 1994). However, these courts did not provide rationale other than to state that the evidence was admissible without further explanation. *See, e.g., Lopez,* 271 F.3d at 485 (stating "[c]ertainly the purpose of the Rule seems to be fulfilled here[.]").

We find the *Thomas* and *Kaquatosh* decisions persuasive. SDCL 19-16-2(3) applies only to statements of identification made at an identification procedure conducted by police such as a photographic array, show-up or line-up. A line-up or other identification procedure to "identify" suspects involved in the assault did not occur in this case. The trial court did not err when it held that J.W.H.'s statements made in a police interview did not qualify as not-hearsay statements of identification within the meaning of SDCL 19-16-2(3), and therefore were not admissible as substantive evidence. . . .

We affirm Shaw's convictions on the aggravated assault and attempted first degree murder charges.

NOTES TO STATE v. SHAW

1. *Prodefendant Rationale.* The court suggests that this rule is favorable to defendants. The narrow interpretation that the court applies would be more beneficial to defendants than a broader one, but surely a defendant would prefer to be tried without any Rule 801(d)(1)(C) at all.

2. *Relating Interpretation to Rationale.* The *Shaw* court's analysis is supported by the rationale for the rule. If identification statements are particularly reliable when they are made under circumstances controlled by constitutional requirements about investigatory identifications, when that attribute is missing, the coverage of the rule could sensibly be withdrawn.

GOOD TO REMEMBER

Despite the general language of FRE 801(d)(1)(C), it is usually applied to the particular circumstances of identifications made in somewhat formal settings such as police lineups.

Segment 10: statement identifying previously perceived person

QUESTION 7-4. Bob Bandana was tried for attempted robbery. At trial, Carl Customer testified that he went to a convenience store one evening and noticed four or five men standing around a truck. One of them was wearing a red bandana on his face, and it appeared he had a gun under his sleeve. The man approached him and demanded money while the others pounded on his car. Customer said that he did not have any money and called the police on his cell phone, prompting the men to get in the truck and flee. The police arrived about ten minutes later. They drove Customer to a nearby street, where he saw the red truck and several individuals. They had been detained by other police officers. The police asked Customer if he could identify any individuals involved in the robbery attempt. He identified the man who demanded money from him, and he identified others he recognized. Customer stated in his testimony that he could not currently recall whether Bandana was one of the offenders.

A police officer, Frank First, apprehended the men in the red truck near the convenience store. He testified that he presented each man to Customer individually for purposes of identification. First could not see whom Customer identified because another officer, Steve Second, stood next to Customer and pointed a bright light toward First and the man being identified. Rather, Officer Second conveyed the information from Customer to Officer First through hand signals. If Officer First seeks to testify that Officer Second made a signal indicating that Customer had identified Bandana as an individual involved in the robbery, should the trial court allow that testimony?

"SUBJECT TO CROSS-EXAMINATION" REQUIREMENT

The treatment in Rule 801(d)(1) of prior inconsistent statements, prior consistent statements, and statements that identify a person applies *only* if the person who made the out-of-court statement testifies and is subject to cross-examination. If a witness is physically present at trial but is difficult to cross-examine because of recalcitrance or mental problems, applying the "subject to cross-examination" requirement can be difficult.

■   ■   ■

"I Can't Remember Probably Half My Life"—Goforth. The *Goforth* court analyzes whether a witness who had suffered a memory-impairing injury was subject to cross-examination. The issue arose in the context of the Confrontation Clause rather than Rule 801(d)(1), but the analysis would likely apply in any circumstance where admissibility of evidence hinges on the opponent's ability to cross-examine a witness. The Confrontation Clause, covered in Chapter 10, applies only in criminal cases.

GOFORTH v. STATE

70 So. 3d 174 (Miss. 2011)

WALLER, J.

Amanda Goforth, a former high-school teacher, was indicted on five counts of sexual battery involving one of her former students [referred to as Jane Doe in this opinion]. She was convicted on two counts and acquitted on the remaining three. Because we find that Goforth was not afforded a constitutionally adequate opportunity to confront one of the witnesses against her, we reverse. . . .

A written statement signed by Chase Rigdon, dated November 23, 2009, was admitted and read before the jury at trial. In the statement, Rigdon said that he had accompanied Doe to Goforth's house one Friday night and that Goforth had been drinking. He said [he observed and participated in sexual acts among himself, Doe, and Goforth].

The State called Rigdon as a witness at trial. A January 2010 automobile accident had substantially impaired his physical and mental conditions. He was confined to a wheelchair, and he testified that he could not remember anything that had occurred two years prior to the wreck. "I can't remember probably half my life," Rigdon said. He did not recall having known Doe or Goforth prior to the wreck. He could not remember going to Goforth's house, speaking to any officers about the alleged incident, or writing out a statement. He recognized his signature at the bottom of the statement, but he could only "guess" that the statement itself had been written by him.

Following Rigdon's testimony, Deputy Hollingsworth testified that he was present when Rigdon provided the statement. The State then sought to admit Rigdon's statement under [a hearsay exception]. Goforth objected on the basis that Rigdon was unavailable as a witness, that she had a constitutional right to cross-examine the witnesses against her. . . . The trial court ruled that Rigdon was available to testify. . . .

Goforth argues that the Confrontation Clauses in both the federal and state constitutions were violated because she was not able to confront Rigdon about his prior statement. His complete memory loss, she contends, rendered him essentially unavailable for cross-examination. . . .

We begin by noting that, even if Rigdon's statement was admissible under the "recorded recollection" hearsay exception of Rule 803(5), it is still subject to scrutiny under the Confrontation Clause. . . .

In [United States v. Owens, 484 U.S. 554 (1988)], the Supreme Court addressed whether a Confrontation Clause violation can be based upon a witness's loss of memory. In that case, a prison correction counselor had sustained severe memory impairment after being beaten with a metal pipe. When the counselor first spoke with the FBI, he was unable to remember his attacker's name. Weeks later, in a second interview with an FBI agent, he was able to describe the attack, name his attacker, and identify his attacker from a photo line-up. At trial, the counselor recounted what he had been doing just prior to the attack, described feeling blows to his head, and recalled seeing blood on the floor. He also vividly remembered identifying the defendant as his assailant during the second interview. On cross-examination, however, he acknowledged that he could not remember seeing his assailant at the time of the assault. And, even though he had received numerous visitors during his hospital stay, the counselor could not remember any of them except one, nor could he recall if any of those visitors had suggested that the defendant was his attacker. Defense counsel unsuccessfully sought to refresh the counselor's recollection with hospital records, which showed that he had, at one point, attributed the assault to someone other than the defendant. The Supreme Court held that no Confrontation Clause violation had occurred. "'[T]he Confrontation Clause guarantees only 'an opportunity for effective cross-examination, not cross-examination that is effective in whatever way, and to whatever extent, the defense might wish.'" (quoting Kentucky v. Stincer, 482 U.S. 730, 739, 107 S. Ct. 2658, 2664, 96 L. Ed. 2d 631 (1987)). The Court explained that the opportunity for cross-examination "is not denied when a witness testifies as to his current belief but is unable to recollect the reason for that belief." It is sufficient, rather, "that the defendant has the opportunity to bring out such matters as the witness's bias, his lack of care and attentiveness, his poor eyesight, and even (what is often a prime objective of cross-examination . . .) the very fact that he has a bad memory." The Court reasoned that there are "realistic weapons" to attack a witness's statement when memory loss is asserted. In that particular case, for example, the defendant had emphasized the counselor's memory loss, and had argued that the counselor's identification of the defendant had been the result of a suggestion made by one of his hospital visitors. The Court noted that these weapons may not always be successful, "but successful cross-examination is not the constitutional guarantee."

Several years later, the Supreme Court in *Crawford* [v. Washington, 541 U.S. 36 (2004),] held that the Confrontation Clause requires that pretrial, testimonial statements made by a witness who is absent at trial are admissible only if the witness is unavailable and the accused had a prior opportunity for cross-examination. In footnote nine of its opinion, the Supreme Court reiterated that "when the declarant appears for cross-examination at trial, the Confrontation Clause places no constraints at all on the use of his prior testimonial statements."

In the wake of *Owens* and *Crawford*, many courts have found that a declarant's appearance and subjection to cross-examination at trial are all that is necessary to satisfy the Confrontation Clause, even if his or her memory is faulty....

If the Confrontation Clause requires solely that the declarant be physically present and subject to cross-examination, its demands were satisfied in this case. Without question, Rigdon physically appeared at trial and was subject to cross-examination. But the United States Court of Appeals for the Seventh Circuit has noted that, according to *Crawford*, physical appearance alone is not necessarily dispositive. Cookson v. Schwartz, 556 F.3d 647, 651 (7th Cir. 2009).

In *Cookson*, Cookson argued that a certain witness was not "available" for Confrontation Clause purposes because the witness could not remember having made the prior statements to police. The State argued that no Confrontation Clause problem existed, because the witness had appeared at trial and Cookson had been able to cross-examine her. The State pointed specifically to the familiar language in *Crawford* that "when the declarant appears for cross-examination at trial, the Confrontation Clause places no constraints at all on the use of his prior testimonial statements." But the Seventh Circuit said that this language was not dispositive. It pointed out that the Supreme Court elaborated on that statement just two sentences later: "[T]he Clause does not bar admission of a statement so long as the declarant is present at trial to defend or explain it." After comparing the facts in *Cookson* to those in *Owens* and United States. v. Keeter, 130 F.3d 297 (7th Cir. 1997), the court concluded that Cookson had been afforded a constitutionally adequate opportunity to examine the witnesses against him. It noted that, unlike the witnesses in *Owens* and *Keeter*, the witness in Cookson had been able to remember the underlying events described in her prior statements.

We find the Seventh Circuit's interpretation of footnote nine in *Crawford* to be insightful and persuasive. According to it, a fair reading of footnote nine is that the Confrontation Clause does not bar admission of a prior testimonial statement if the declarant appears for cross-examination at trial to defend or explain his or her statement. Importantly, the pertinent language does not require the record to actually show that the defendant did in fact defend or explain the statement. The language, rather, focuses on "presence and ability to act."

We find that Rigdon, though physically present at trial, did not have the requisite, minimal ability or capacity to act. Significantly, no one here disputes that Rigdon's total loss of memory was genuine. The trial judge, in fact, stated that "[i]t is obvious to the Court that [Ridgon] suffers physical disabilities, and also a mental impairment in that he does not have recollection of matters that has [sic] occurred within his lifetime." Nothing in the record indicates that Rigdon's memory loss was feigned. He had no recollection of the underlying events surrounding his statement, and he could not even remember having known Goforth or Doe. It was, in his mind, as if the alleged events had never occurred. Additionally, he could not recall ever having spoken to police. The most he could do was verify his signature and "guess" that he had provided the written statement above it. This total lack of memory deprived Goforth any opportunity to inquire about potential bias or the circumstances surrounding Rigdon's statement. In sum, Goforth simply had no opportunity to cross-examine Ridgon about his statement.

The case before us . . . is distinguishable from . . . *Owens*. . . . Though the declarant in *Owens* could not remember the underlying events surrounding his prior testimonial statement, he vividly recalled identifying the defendant when he had spoken to authorities. The defendant in that case also was able to cast doubt upon the identification and asserted that it had been based upon a suggestion by one of the individuals who had visited the defendant while he had been hospitalized. . . .

We find that, under the Mississippi Constitution, Goforth did not have a constitutionally adequate opportunity to cross-examine Rigdon at trial or beforehand. . . .

Goforth's state constitutional right to confront the witnesses against her was violated. We find that this violation constitutes reversible error. We further find that Goforth's constitutional right to be free from double jeopardy precludes any future prosecution on these same charges or for any same crimes that occurred during the period of time set forth in the indictment. Therefore, we reverse Goforth's conviction and render judgment on her behalf, discharging her.

NOTES TO GOFORTH v. STATE

1. *Context for "Available" for Cross-Examination*. *Goforth* considers a witness's availability for cross-examination in the context of the Confrontation Clause, not the specific context of introduction of prior statements under Rule 801(d)(1). It is reasonable to assume that resolution of the availability for cross-examination issue would be the same in both contexts. Also, where Rule 801(d)(1) is invoked in a criminal case, the Confrontation Clause would apply.

2. *Voluntary Refusal to Testify*. Where a person who has given a statement in the past voluntarily refuses to answer questions at a trial, Rule 801(d)(1) does not allow introduction of the person's past statements, because he or she should

be treated as not available for cross-examination. The person might be subject to contempt sanctions, if, for example, he or she refused to testify even after being granted immunity, but a witness who refuses to answer questions cannot reasonably be considered available for cross-examination.

G SUMMARY

Substantive and Nonsubstantive Use of Prior Statements. The rule covered in this chapter excludes certain prior statements of witnesses from being defined as hearsay. This means that they are admissible for the truth of what they assert. Another way to describe this treatment is that the prior statements may be used substantively.

For some prior statements, nonsubstantive use may be available. This means that there can be proof that the statement was made, but the trier of fact is prohibited from relying on it as proof of what it asserts. When a prior statement is admitted only for nonsubstantive use, it is usually a statement that is inconsistent with a witness's testimony. The trier of fact can use it to assess the accuracy or the in-court testimony. This is an impeachment use of the prior statement, and is different from a substantive use.

Prior Inconsistent Statements. If a witness has made a statement prior to testifying that is inconsistent with the witness's testimony, that prior statement may be introduced to prove the truth of what it asserts, provided certain requirements are met. The proponent must establish that the statement was made at some other proceeding or in a deposition, and that it was made under penalty of perjury. Additionally, the witness must be available for cross-examination about the statement. These elements are illustrated in *Neadeau, Gajo,* and *Day.*

Prior Consistent Statements. If a witness made statements out of court that are consistent with testimony the witness later gives at a trial, the prior consistent statements may be admitted for substantive use when they could logically refute impeachment efforts. When the opponent of the witness's testimony has claimed that the witness recently fabricated the information or testified about it as a result of improper influence, a prior consistent statement is admissible if it was made before the existence of the alleged improper influence or before the time when any other motive to lie had developed. When the opponent challenges a witness's testimony on any other basis (poor memory, for example), prior consistent statements that would counter that challenge may be admitted for substantive use.

Statements Identifying a Person Previously Seen. If a witness has once identified a person as someone the witness had previously seen, that out-of-court statement is admissible as substantive evidence, as described in *Lewis.*

The declarant must be subject to cross-examination about the statement. The majority interpretation of the rule, discussed in *Shaw*, makes it available only where the out-of-court statement was made in some formal context such as a police lineup, where procedural controls are present and there is a high likelihood that the report of the statement will be accurate.

"Subject to Cross-Examination" Requirement. The three kinds of statements covered by Rule 801(d)(1) are all admissible only if the declarant testifies at the current trial and is subject to cross-examination. As explained in *Goforth*, a witness who is willing to answer questions on cross-examination is typically treated as available for cross-examination even if the witness's memory has been severely impaired. In an extreme case, where a witness has no memory of any aspects of the topic on which his or her prior statement was made, a ruling that the witness is not available for cross-examination is proper.

CHAPTER 8

Hearsay Exceptions: Spontaneous and Personal Statements

A. Introduction
B. Present Sense Impression and Excited Utterance
C. Statement of Then-Existing Mental, Emotional, or Physical Condition
D. Statements for Purposes of Medical Diagnosis or Treatment
E. Summary

A INTRODUCTION

Topic Overview

The hearsay prohibition recognizes that for many statements, a fair search for truth requires that the opposing party have an opportunity to cross-examine the speaker in order to explore issues related to the speaker's perception, memory, use of language, and honesty. Against this background, however, our legal system has concluded that it is reasonable to use certain out-of-court statements to prove the truth of what they assert.

There can be many reasons for withdrawing the hearsay prohibition. There may be something about the nature of the statements that makes them more reliable than typical out-of-court statements. Alternatively, some classes of statements may seem to be extremely valuable — too good to be kept out by the hearsay rule. For all of the kinds of statements covered by exceptions to the hearsay exclusionary rule, their typical value exceeds the risks associated with the opponent's loss of ability to cross-examine the speaker.

The Federal Rules contain 28 specific exceptions, organized in two categories: exceptions that can be used only if the declarant is unavailable and exceptions that can be used regardless of the declarant's availability. This book covers the most important exceptions, beginning with some of the "availability immaterial" exceptions. This chapter examines some exceptions for statements that are likely to be reasonably reliable because the circumstances in which declarants make the statements decrease the risk of intentional falsehood and increase the chance that the contents of the statements are accurate.

Chapter Organization

This chapter examines the most significant "declarant available or unavailable" exceptions to the hearsay exclusionary rule. These exceptions are enumerated in FRE 803. This chapter studies them in the order in which they appear in that rule.

- Present sense impression (a statement about something the declarant has observed, made during the observation or close in time to the observation).
- Excited utterance (a statement about something that has startled the declarant, made while the declarant is under the stress of that experience).
- Statement of then-existing mental, emotional, or physical condition (statements about the speaker's perceptions of the speaker's mind or body).
- Statements for medical diagnosis or treatment (statements about someone's health, for diagnosis or treatment).

B   PRESENT SENSE IMPRESSION AND EXCITED UTTERANCE

One justification for creating an exception to the hearsay prohibition for some statements would be that declarants make the statements in circumstances where intentional lying would be difficult. Another justification would be that the circumstances reduce memory problems. The "present sense impression" and "excited utterance" exceptions may fit both of these rationales.

Rule 803. Exceptions to the Rule Against Hearsay — Regardless of Whether the Declarant Is Available as a Witness

The following are not excluded by the rule against hearsay, regardless of whether the declarant is available as a witness:

> **(1)** *Present Sense Impression.* A statement describing or explaining an event or condition, made while or immediately after the declarant perceived it.
>
> **(2)** *Excited Utterance.* A statement relating to a startling event or condition, made while the declarant was under the stress of excitement that it caused.
>
> . . .

■ ■ ■

Can a Police Officer's Statements Made During an Encounter with a Suspect Be Present Sense Impressions? — Fischer. Note the difference between the literal meaning of the present sense impression exception and the more narrow construction the court applies. The court's description of the history and rationale of the exception supports a policy-based analysis.

FISCHER v. STATE

252 S.W.3d 375 (Tex. Crim. App. 2008)

Cochran, J.

This case presents a novel question in Texas evidentiary law: Are a law enforcement officer's factual observations of a DWI suspect, contemporaneously dictated on his patrol-car videotape, admissible as a present sense impression exception to the hearsay rule under Tex. R. Evid. 803(1)?. . .

At about 1:40 A.M. on May 29, 2004, DPS Trooper Martinez turned on his dashboard-mounted video camera and announced, on tape, that he was pulling over a driver who wasn't wearing a seatbelt. After the driver, appellant, parked his truck in his apartment complex parking lot, Trooper Martinez approached appellant and began questioning him. All of that questioning was recorded through Trooper Martinez's body microphone and captured on camera.

Trooper Martinez. . . told appellant, "I'm going to conduct a small exam of your eyes." He directed appellant to stand outside the range of the video camera and administered a horizontal gaze nystagmus (HGN) test.

After the HGN test was completed, Trooper Martinez again left appellant and returned to his patrol car and recorded the following observations:

Subject has equal pupil size, equal tracking, has a lack of smooth pursuit in both eyes, and has distinct nystagmus at maximum deviation in both eyes. Subject also has onset of nystagmus prior to forty-five degrees in both eyes.

Trooper Martinez also dictated into his microphone: (1) he stated that he had seen a "wine opener" in appellant's truck; (2) he repeated that there was a strong odor of alcohol on appellant's breath; and (3) he again noted that appellant had glassy, bloodshot eyes and "slurred speech.". . .

After appellant was charged with DWI, he filed a motion to suppress the audio portion of the patrol-car videotape, claiming that it contained Trooper Martinez's "bolstering, self-serving statements about what he was allegedly doing and seeing." It was "a highly prejudicial and inflammatory narrative" of what Trooper Martinez would have the viewer believe was taking place. The trial judge denied appellant's motion and concluded that the audio narrative was admissible as a "present sense impression.". . .

The court of appeals concluded that the trial court had erred. . . .

The hearsay doctrine, codified in Rules 801 and 802 of the Texas Rules of Evidence, is designed to exclude out-of-court statements offered for the truth of the matter asserted that pose any of the four "hearsay dangers" of faulty perception, faulty memory, accidental miscommunication, or insincerity. The numerous exceptions to the hearsay rule set out in Rules 803 and 804[8] are based upon the rationale that some hearsay statements contain such strong independent, circumstantial guarantees of trustworthiness that the risk of the four hearsay dangers is minimal while the probative value of such evidence is high. The twenty-four hearsay exceptions listed in Texas Rule 803 may be roughly categorized into (1) unreflective statements, (2) reliable documents, and (3) reputation evidence. The rationale for all of the exceptions is that, over time, experience has shown that these types of statements are generally reliable and trustworthy.

The first set of hearsay exceptions, unreflective statements, are "street corner" utterances made by ordinary people before any thoughts of litigation have crystallized. . . . In most instances, the speaker was not thinking at all; the statement was made without any reflection, thought process, or motive to fabricate or exaggerate.

One of those "unreflective statements" exceptions to the hearsay rule is defined in Rule 803(1), the present sense impression. . . .

Texas was the first jurisdiction to recognize this exception by name, and its leading case, *Houston Oxygen Co. v. Davis,* is cited in the advisory committee's note to Federal Rule 803(1). The facts in that case are typical of those that support the exception. At trial, the passenger of a car going down the highway testified that he saw another car pass theirs going "sixty to sixty-five miles" an hour and that it was "bouncing up and down in the back and zig zagging." The passenger then testified that the driver of the car turned to him and said that "they must have been drunk, that we would find them somewhere on the road wrecked if they kept that rate of speed up." Sure enough, five miles down the road the speeding car hit another vehicle and caused the plaintiff's injuries. The Texas Supreme Court held that the passenger's recitation of what the driver said to him at the time the speeding car passed them was admissible as a present sense

---

8. Additional exemptions from the operation of the hearsay rule are set out in Rule 801 which simply defines those matters — such as party admissions, prior consistent statements, etc. — out of the rule itself.

impression because "[i]t is sufficiently spontaneous to save it from the suspicion of being manufactured evidence. There was no time for a calculated statement."

The rationale for the exception is that the contemporaneity of the statement with the event that it describes eliminates all danger of faulty memory and virtually all danger of insincerity. This Court has previously explained that rationale:

> If a person observes some situation or happening which is not at all startling or shocking in its nature, nor actually producing excitement in the observer, the observer may yet have occasion to comment on what he sees (or learns from other senses) *at the very time that he is receiving the impression.* Such a comment, as to a situation then before the declarant, does not have the safeguard of impulse, emotion, or excitement, but there are other safeguards. In the first place, the report at the moment of the thing then seen, heard, etc., is safe from any error from defect of *memory* of the declarant. Secondly, there is little or no *time* for calculated misstatement, and thirdly, the statement will usually be made to another (the witness who reports it) who would have equal opportunities to observe and hence to check a misstatement. Consequently, it is believed that such comments, strictly limited to reports of *present* sense-impressions, have such exceptional reliability as to warrant their inclusion within the hearsay exception for Spontaneous Declarations. . . .

The State's first ground for review claims that the court of appeals in this case held that Rule 803(8)(B), which explicitly excludes investigative reports by law enforcement from the public records exception to the hearsay rule, "trumps" Rule 803(1) and disallows any out-of-court factual observations by police officers. The court of appeals did not say this. Of course police officers, like the rest of humanity, may make spontaneous, unreflective, contemporaneous present sense impression statements that qualify for admission under Rule 803(1). . . .

Although Rule 803(8)(B) does not "trump" Rule 803(1), the basis for exclusion of police reports and investigative recordings is exactly the same under both rules. The recorded factual observations made by police officers investigating a suspected crime are not the type of "non-reflective" street-corner statements of objective observers that the present sense impression exception is designed to allow. Courts admit present sense impression statements precisely because they are non-narrative, off-hand comments made without any thought of potential litigation by a neutral and detached observer without any motive to fabricate, falsify, or otherwise exaggerate his observations.

Conversely, on-the-scene observations and narrations of a police officer conducting a roadside investigation into a suspected DWI offense are fraught with the thought of a future prosecution: the police officer is gathering evidence to use in deciding whether to arrest and charge someone with a crime. Calculation and criminal litigation shimmer in the air; the officer is gathering evidence, he is not making an off-hand, non-reflective observation about the world as it passes by. Similarly, factual observations, narrations, opinions, and conclusions made by a citizen or bystander that might be intended by the declarant to be made with an eye toward future litigation or evidentiary use are inadmissible under the rule. . . .

Throughout this incident, Trooper Martinez was professionally and politely "engaged in the competitive enterprise of ferreting out crime." One applauds him for that worthy endeavor, but the adversarial nature of this on-the-scene investigation of a potential crime is entirely at odds with the unreflective, instinctive comments of a "street-corner" speaker who was not thinking about the legal consequences of his statements.

The State argues that "[h]earsay may be admissible under one hearsay exception even if it is inadmissible under another hearsay exception." That is correct. . . . Here, however, the rationale for excluding Trooper Martinez's recorded oral narrative of his on-the-scene investigation as a present sense impression under Rule 803(1) is precisely the same as the rationale for excluding that evidence under Rule 803(8)(B): the presumed unreliability of law enforcement observations in an adversarial, investigative setting. Thus, Rule 803(1) cannot be used "as a 'back door' to admit evidence explicitly inadmissible under Rule 803(8)(B).". . .

In sum, most of the statements made by Trooper Martinez on the videotape constituted a calculated narrative in an adversarial, investigative setting. These particular statements may be entirely reliable ones, but the setting is one that human experience and the law recognizes is brimming with the potential for exaggeration or misstatement.

We therefore agree with the court of appeals which had held that Trooper Martinez's recorded investigation narrative did not qualify for admission as a present sense impression under Rule 803(1). At trial, Trooper Martinez may testify to exactly what he saw and heard during his investigative detention of appellant, and his words might be the very same as those he used during his on-the-scene narrative, but they must be given under oath and subject to cross-examination.

We affirm the judgment of the court of appeals.

NOTES TO FISCHER v. STATE

1. *Passage of Time and Reflection.* The New Jersey Supreme Court has considered whether the present sense impression definition could cover an eyewitness's description of a robbery that had happened ten minutes earlier. It stated:

> Case law from other jurisdictions suggests that a delay measured in minutes will take a statement outside of the present sense impression hearsay exception. *See, e.g., United States v. Manfre,* 368 F.3d 832, 840 (8th Cir. 2004) (noting that declarant's "intervening walk or drive" between observing event and making statement negated finding of present sense impression); *United States v. Cain,* 587 F.2d 678, 681 (5th Cir.) (finding that witness's out-of-court statement, likely made minutes after observation, did not qualify as "immediately thereafter"), *cert. denied,* 440 U.S. 975 (1979); *Hilyer v. Howat Concrete Co.,* 578 F.2d 422, 425-26, 426 N. 7 (D.C. Cir. 1978) (holding that witness's statement to officer fifteen minutes after accident "hardly qualifies as 'immediately' after the accident"); *Young v. Commonwealth,* 50 S.W.3d 148, 165-66 (Ky. 2001) (concluding that statement to officer seven minutes after observing shooting was not "immediately thereafter"). *But see United States v. Blakey,* 607 F.2d 779, 785-86 (7th Cir. 1979) (determining that tape-recorded

telephone statement made by witness "between several and 23 minutes" after event qualified as present sense impression); *Miller v. Crown Amusements, Inc.,* 821 F. Supp. 703, 706-07 (S.D. Ga. 1993) (finding that declarant's statements within ten minutes of accident were present sense impressions); *State v. Odom,* 316 N.C. 306, 341 S.E.2d 332, 335–36 (1986) (holding that witness's statement to officer ten minutes after observing abduction was present sense impression).

Segment 13: statement by stressed child to doctor

When considering whether a statement is a present sense impression, it is not hairsplitting to recognize a distinction between a matter of seconds, however many they may be, and an interval of as much as ten minutes separating a recollection from the observation. For purposes of a *present* sense impression, a declarant's statement that "the blue sports car is going through the red light" or that "the blue sports car just went through the red light" (seconds ago) is different from a declarant's statement that "the blue sports car went through the red light ten minutes ago."

In the Interest of J.A., 949 A.2d 790, 798 (N.J. 2008).

2. *Corroboration.* In many present sense impression circumstances, the declarant will describe something to another person who is in a position to see it or otherwise confirm the accuracy of the declarant's words. Where this kind of corroboration is lacking (for example, when a declarant talks to someone on the phone and describes something to that person), some courts would reject use of the present sense impression exception.

QUESTION 8-1. Maxdata and Fastinfo are providers of Web site software and services to automobile manufacturers. Maxdata sued Fastinfo, claiming that Fastinfo had committed the tort of tortious interference with a prospective business relationship by misrepresenting to Ford Motor Company the scope of a license that Fastinfo had from Maxdata.

At trial, Maxdata sought to introduce into evidence an e-mail sent by a Maxdata employee to several other Maxdata employees. The e-mail was sent at 5:59 P.M. on Wednesday, June 25, 2008. The subject line reads, "Update from Randy on his meetings in Detroit today." It stated:

> "Just a quick update from my conversation with Randy this afternoon. . . . he is going to send out more complete notes later today or tomorrow. . . . Lunch with Chuck Sullivan—cordial lunch. Chuck likes Maxdata. . . inherited decision from a subsidiary to move in a different direction. . . i.e., Fastinfo. . . the ship has set sail—feedback he has gotten is that there is little to no IP risk given the approach they are taken. Chuck was told that Fastinfo has a license to our broadest patent portfolio (not true). Randy does not feel Chuck fully understands the complexity of the issue or perhaps is not worried given what he's been told internally."

Should a court allow the introduction of this e-mail as part of Maxdata's proof that Fastinfo had mischaracterized the scope of its license to use Maxdata patents?

■   ■   ■

Was Calm Excited? — **Pressey.** The court considers the excited utterance exception and whether the declarant — Anthony Calm — was under the influence of an exciting event when he made the out-of-court statement. The case also involves a common complication: Exactly what event should be considered the exciting or startling event associated with a particular statement? This is important, because to satisfy the terms of the excited utterance exception, the subject matter of the statement must relate to the event that caused the speaker to be excited. As *Pressey* illustrates, the present sense impression exception and the excited utterance exception are closely related. In some instances, each could apply to a single out-of-court statement.

PRESSEY v. STATE

25 A.3d 756 (Del. 2011)

HOLLAND, J.

Following a jury trial in the Superior Court, the defendant-appellant, Jamour Pressey ("Pressey"), was convicted of Robbery in the First Degree and Resisting Arrest. In this direct appeal, Pressey contends that the trial judge abused her discretion in admitting a victim's prior out-of-court statement under the excited utterance exception to the hearsay rule. . . .

The crime at issue occurred when seventeen-year-old Anthony Calm ("Calm") was walking to his house in Wilmington. When Calm was approximately one-half of a block away from his house, three men approached him. All three men were wearing black-and-white checkered scarves and pointing guns at Calm. The men robbed Calm of his cell phone, house key, school identification card, and cash. Two of the men then walked away. The third man stayed and robbed Calm of the coat, pants, and boots that he was wearing. That man then directed Calm to sit on a nearby step. Calm complied.

As soon as the third man was out of sight, Calm ran home. Because the men had stolen his house key, Calm began banging on the front door. After approximately two minutes, Calm's sister answered the door. Calm told his sister and mother that he had been robbed. Calm's mother, Kimberly Wallace, recalled that Calm was "scared," "hysterical," and "crying."

Wallace left the house in search of the perpetrators. After Wallace drove two blocks, she encountered Wilmington Police Detective Michael Ballard and Wilmington Police Officer Brian Vettori in their vehicle. Wallace "frantically" informed them of the robbery and then continued to drive in search of the robbers. Ballard and Vettori followed.

Wallace then observed a man walking down the street. Wallace exited her car and told Ballard and Vettori that the man was one of the robbers. Ballard, who was wearing a tactical vest, exited his vehicle and yelled, "Stop, police!" but the man fled. Ballard chased the man on foot, and Vettori followed in his car.

When the man stopped running, Vettori exited his vehicle and ordered the man to the ground at gunpoint. The man that Ballard and Vettori took into custody was Pressey. . . .

Wallace returned to the house and then drove Calm to the scene of the arrest to identify the assailant. While Wallace was searching for the perpetrators, Calm put on a t-shirt and sweatpants because the robber had left him in only his boxers and socks. . . .

During the prosecutor's direct examination of [Kimberly Wallace, Calm's mother], defense counsel objected: "[T]hey are going to ask [Wallace] whether [Calm] identified Pressey as the person who robbed him. . . . I think that's clearly hearsay." The trial judge ruled from the bench as follows:

> Under. . . Delaware [R]ule[ ] of [E]vidence 803, an excited utterance [is a] statement related to a startling event or condition made while the declarant was under the stress of excitement caused by the event or condition.
>
> . . . Therefore, if the State can lay a foundation that this was indeed an excited utterance, whether or not the questions were asked of [Calm] is irrelevant. And if you can lay that foundation I am going to admit the statements as excited utterances.

Immediately thereafter, Wallace testified that Calm was "scared," "still crying," and "slouched down" and that he "didn't want to get out of the car" when he identified Pressey as one of the robbers. The trial judge ruled that the prosecutor had laid a sufficient foundation. Wallace then testified that Calm identified Pressey as one of the robbers. . . .

Pressey argues that the trial judge abused her discretion in admitting Calm's prior out-of-court statement under the excited utterance exception to the hearsay rule. . . .

[T]hree foundational requirements must be satisfied to admit a statement under the excited utterance exception: "(1) the excitement of the declarant must have been precipitated by an event; (2) the statement being offered as evidence must have been made during the time period while the excitement of the event was continuing; and (3) the statement must be related to the startling event." Pressey acknowledges that the prosecutor laid a proper foundation to satisfy the first and third requirements. Pressey argues that the prosecutor did not satisfy the second requirement because Calm's statement was not made during the time period while the excitement of the event was continuing. Pressey argues that "the act of Wallace forcing Calm to return to the scene was a superseding event that cause[d] Calm to be excited, not the prior robbery."

In *Culp v. State*, [766 A.2d 486 (Del. 2001)], we explained that although "the amount of time that has elapsed from the occurrence of the event or condition is a factor to consider in the analysis, it is not solely determinative." We noted that "[i]t is generally recognized that the more time that has passed, the less likely it is the declarant was under the stress of excitement caused by the event." We also observed, however, that "[w]here the declarant is continuously under the influence of the event, a statement made later in time from the event may be just as reliable as one made closer to the time of the event."

In *Culp* this Court compared D.R.E. 803(1) with D.R.E. 803(2) and pointed out that D.R.E. 803(1) contains an express contemporaneity requirement that must be satisfied for a statement to be admitted as a present sense impression. We also noted that D.R.E. 803(2) does not mandate that a statement be made within a certain amount of time following the startling event to be admissible, but that the rule explicitly requires the declarant to be under the "stress of excitement" caused by the startling event or condition at the time of the statement's making. Additionally we stated "[i]t is the making of the statement under these circumstances that furnishes the underlying reliability of a statement admitted pursuant to Rule 803(2)."

In *Culp*, we held that a D.R.E. 803(2) analysis must focus on the condition of the declarant at the time the statement was made and includes a careful consideration of all the factors present. We. . . have applied those principles in several other cases. For example, we held in *Evans v. State* that the trial judge correctly admitted two out-of-court statements of a gunshot victim under the excited utterance exception, even though the statements occurred approximately four and nine hours later, because the declarant made those statements while under the stress of excitement caused by the event.

In this case, Wallace testified that Calm was "scared," "still crying," and "slouched down" and that he "didn't want to get out of the car" when he identified Pressey as one of the robbers. [Police officer Brian] Vettori testified that Calm "was seated in the back seat of the car," "appeared to be nervous," was "shaking," and "[h]is voice was shaky." The record reflects that Calm's identification of Pressey as one of the robbers satisfied all three of the foundational requirements to qualify as an "excited utterance" under D.R.E. 803(2). The record does not establish that "the act of Wallace forcing Calm to return to the scene was a superseding event that cause[d] Calm to be excited, not the prior robbery." Accordingly, Pressey has not shown that the trial judge abused her discretion in admitting Calm's statement into evidence under the excited utterance exception to the hearsay rule.

The judgments of the Superior Court are affirmed.

NOTES TO PRESSEY v. STATE

1. *Continuous or Rekindled Excitement.* The trial judge must find the facts associated with each element of the excited utterance exception in order to rule that the exception covers a particular statement. If the judge had believed that Calm's emotional state at the time he identified the defendant had been stimulated both by the robbery and by his mother's conduct in bringing Calm back to the scene of the crime, it would likely have been correct to rule that the excited utterance exception applied to his statements.

2. *Counterexamples: Timing of Present Sense Impression and Excited Utterance Statements.* The *Pressey* court refers to cases in which excited

utterances were made fairly long after the events that made the speakers excited. The terminology of Federal Rule 803(1) that defines present sense impressions requires that the statement be made "while or immediately after the declarant perceived" the subject of the statement. Consider why the following two variations on that rule might have seemed sensible to their drafters:

> **Ohio R. Evid. 803(1).** Present sense impression. A statement describing or explaining an event or condition made while the declarant was perceiving the event or condition, or immediately thereafter unless circumstances indicate lack of trustworthiness.
>
> **Colo. R. Evid. 803(1).** Spontaneous Present Sense Impression. A spontaneous statement describing or explaining an event or condition made while the declarant was perceiving the event or condition.

3. *Comparing the Present Sense Impression and Excited Utterance Exceptions under the Federal Rules.* This table highlights the small but significant differences between the present sense impression and excited utterance exceptions.

	KIND OF EVENT OR CONDITION	STATEMENT CONTENTS	STATEMENT TIMING
Present Sense Impression	Any	Describes or explains event	Made while or immediately after the declarant perceived the event or condition
Excited Utterance	Startling	Relates to event	Made while the declarant was under stress from the event or condition

■   ■   ■

Segment 7: foundation for excited utterance

Can "Excited" Mean Just "Reacting"?—**Flores.** The court considers whether application of the excited utterance exception should require a showing that the declarant was in a frenzied or hyperactive state when he or she made an assertion. The case also illustrates how the excited utterance and present sense impression exceptions may overlap.

STATE v. FLORES

226 P.3d 641 (N.M. 2010)

DANIELS, J.

Defendant Joseph Flores brings this direct appeal from his first-degree murder conviction for fatally stabbing his former lover, Vernon Green, twenty-one times with a Phillips screwdriver. We . . . determine that the trial court did not abuse its discretion by admitting . . . testimony of Green's mother regarding Green's spontaneous verbal identification of Defendant when he unexpectedly saw Defendant in Carlsbad. . . . Finding no error, we affirm his conviction and life sentence. . . .

Approximately two weeks before the stabbing, Green left Defendant and moved to Carlsbad to live with his parents. . . .

Green's mother testified that while she was driving Green to work several days before the stabbing, Defendant pulled alongside their car at a stop light in Carlsbad. She testified that Green looked over at Defendant and spontaneously stated, "There's Joseph," while appearing to be "very agitated" and "scared." She immediately looked over at the man her son was referring to and later identified Defendant in court as the man she had seen driving the adjacent car. When the light changed to green, Defendant turned his car and drove away without making contact. . . .

Rule 11–803(B) NMRA provides for the admissibility over a hearsay objection of "[a] statement relating to a startling event or condition made while the declarant was under the stress of excitement caused by the event or condition." . . .

Defendant argues that the excited utterance exception does not apply here because there was insufficient excitement in the victim's voice when he spontaneously uttered "There's Joseph" upon seeing Defendant driving along next to him. Defendant's argument both disregards the reasoning underlying the excited utterance exception and takes an overly narrow view of the word "excited."

As we have recently emphasized, "[t]he theory underlying the excited utterance exception is that the exciting event induced the declarant's surprise, shock, or nervous excitement which temporarily stills capacity for conscious fabrication and makes it unlikely that the speaker would relate other than the truth." Accordingly, to constitute an excited utterance, "the declaration should be spontaneous, made before there is time for fabrication, and made under the stress of the moment."

There is nothing in the case law nor in the ordinary meaning of "excited" which restricts the meaning of the word to any narrow requirement of a frenzied or hyperactive state. *The American Heritage Dictionary of the English Language* 620 (4th ed. 2000) defines "excited" as "[b]eing in a state of excitement; emotionally aroused; stirred" and defines "excite" as "1. To stir to activity. 2. To call forth (a reaction or emotion, for example); elicit: *odd noises that excited our curiosity. . . .*"

We apply the excited utterance analysis to a particular fact situation through an examination of the totality of the circumstances, including how much time passed between the startling event and the statement, and whether, in that time, the declarant had an opportunity for reflection and fabrication; how much pain, confusion, nervousness, or emotional strife the declarant was experiencing at the time of the statement; whether the statement was self-serving[; and whether the statement was] made in response to an inquiry.

In this case, the totality of the circumstances surrounding Green's declaration indicates that he was making an utterance in direct and immediate response to a surprising event that triggered an emotional response. Shortly before the stabbing, Green moved over eight hundred miles to Carlsbad. The evidence at trial indicated that he did so because he had left a troubled relationship with Defendant. It is a reasonable inference that Green was startled to see that Defendant had tracked him down from Nevada to New Mexico. Green's appearance to his mother as "very agitated" and "scared" upon seeing Defendant further indicates that he responded emotionally when making his immediate and spontaneous utterance, "There's Joseph." The testimony established a textbook case for application of the excited utterance exception, and Green's hearsay statement to his mother identifying Defendant as the driver of the nearby car was admissible on that ground alone.

The testimony was equally admissible under the present sense impression exception. A present sense impression is a "statement describing or explaining an event or condition made while the declarant was perceiving the event or condition, or immediately thereafter." As the advisory committee notes to the Federal Rules of Evidence observe, "[i]n considerable measure the [excited utterance and present sense impression exceptions] overlap, though based on somewhat different theories. The most significant practical difference will lie in the time lapse allowable between the event and statement." Fed. R. Evid. 803(1)-(2) advisory committee's notes. The theory underlying the present sense impression exception is that "substantial contemporaneity of event and statement negate the likelihood of deliberate or conscious misrepresentation." *Id.*

Both excited utterances and present sense impressions were among the theories subsumed within the pre-rules res gestae cluster of exceptions. As their textual elements indicate, they differ in that an excited utterance requires a reasonable inference that emotional stress has contributed to the making of the statement, while present sense impression requires instead that the statement be substantially contemporaneous with the event it is describing or explaining.

The disputed testimony in this case presents no timeliness issue whatsoever. Green uttered, "There's Joseph," at the very moment he was looking at Defendant in the car next to him and his mother. *Cf. State v. Massengill,* 62 P.3d 354 (N.M. 2003) (concluding that four or more hours between an event and a statement describing that event are not "sufficiently contemporaneous"). There was virtually no time for Green to decide to misrepresent to his mother that Defendant was driving along the streets of Carlsbad, presumably so Defendant could be falsely accused of killing Green several days in the future. . . .

We conclude that, under these circumstances, the statement by Green to his mother contemporaneously identifying Defendant as the driver of the neighboring car as Defendant was clearly admissible under the present sense impression exception to the hearsay rule....

We hold that Defendant's conviction was supported by sufficient evidence and that the trial court did not abuse its discretion in making the various evidentiary rulings challenged by Defendant. We therefore affirm Defendant's conviction and sentence.

NOTES TO STATE v. FLORES

1. *Res Gestae.* The excited utterance and present sense impression exceptions have developed from a common law concept of "res gestae," which was typically defined as applying to statements that were inherent in a situation. The two newer categories are meant to be more clearly defined.

2. *Textbook Case.* The court describes the declarant's statement as a textbook case of an excited utterance. The circumstances of the statement highlight strengths and weaknesses of the doctrine. There is a low likelihood that the declarant would have articulated a lie in response to seeing the person in a car next to his, but on the other hand the sudden onset of strong emotions might preclude careful narration or any kind of double-checking by the declarant to confirm the accuracy of what he believed he had just perceived.

■   ■   ■

Can Answers Be Excited Utterances? — Graure. The Graure court considers another circumstance in which a declarant's emotional state can be evaluated. It treats a common issue in application of the excited utterance exception, whether a conversation — as opposed to a monologue — can include statements that qualify as excited utterances.

GRAURE v. UNITED STATES

18 A.3d 743 (D.C. 2011)

Thompson, J.

A jury convicted appellant Vasile Graure of three counts of assault with intent to kill while armed (AWIKWA), four counts of assault with a deadly weapon (ADW), mayhem while armed, two counts of second-degree burglary while armed, arson, and felony destruction of property, all in connection with a fire at the Good Guys strip club located in the 2300 block of Wisconsin Avenue, N.W., on the evening of November 3, 2007. In this appeal, Graure contends,... that the trial court erred when it... admitted the out-of-court statements made by a club employee who was engulfed in flames during the fire....

We. . . . turn to appellant's argument that the trial court erred in admitting Djordjevic's statements to Lazorchack and Talebnejad — i.e., his statements that he "saw that man coming back with a [gas] can" and "tr[ying] to burn" the club, and that he (Djordjevic) "tried to stop him" — over defense objections that the statements were. . . inadmissible hearsay. . . . We conclude that the court did not err when it admitted the statements as. . . excited utterances.

"A spontaneous or excited utterance is a well-recognized exception to the hearsay rule." *Johnson v. United States,* 980 A.2d 1174, 1185 (D.C. 2009). Three factors must be established before a statement may be admitted into evidence as an excited utterance:

> (1) The presence of a serious occurrence or startling event which causes a state of nervous excitement or physical shock in the declarant; (2) a declaration made within a reasonably short period of time after the occurrence so as to assure the declarant has not reflected upon the event and possibly invented a statement; and (3) the presence of circumstances that in their totality suggest the spontaneity and sincerity of the remark.

Id. . . . Here, the trial court did not err in finding that Djordjevic's statements qualified as excited utterances. As the trial judge noted, the evidence established that Djordjevic made the statements to his co-workers "within moments" of emerging from the back door of the club, having been "completely burned," when smoke was still rising from his body and his skin "was rolled off." At the time, "everybody" standing in the area behind the club was in "[c]onfusion" and "shock" and "sort of a little bit bewildered." The scenario was "overwhelming." Djordjevic in particular was "screaming" and "shouting," was "very frantic" and "very nervous," and was "just in shock."

Appellant argues that Djordjevic's statements do not qualify as excited utterances because Djordjevic himself was "composed enough" to tell Lazorchack to "stay calm," and because "the situation had calmed considerably" by the time Djordjevic spoke to his colleagues. However, ample evidence — of Djordjevic's physical condition, demeanor, and tone of voice — supported a finding that Djordjevic was in a state of "nervous excitement [and] physical shock" at the time he spoke. *Johnson,* 980 A.2d at 1185. Djordjevic's condition, rather than calming, was growing worse as time passed: a police officer who arrived on the scene testified that Djordjevic "had that thousand mile stare" and, when the officer asked him questions, had no "reaction at all, not in the eyes, no body movement, no body motion, anything."[13] While most of the testimony indicated that Djordjevic's statements were made several minutes after he had succeeded in extinguishing the flames on his body, this court has accepted as excited utterances statements made after the elapse of considerably longer periods between the startling event and the out-of-court statements. *See, e.g., Reyes — Contreras*

---

13. The officer testified that "it was something like out of a Road Runner cartoon where Wiley Coyote was just blown up by the Road Runner with dynamite just standing there charred and not responsive to anything."

v. United States, 719 A.2d 503, 505–06 (D.C. 1998) (excited utterance admitted when statements were made thirty minutes after startling event when victim was crying and upset); *Smith v. United States,* 666 A.2d 1216, 1223 (D.C. 1995) (excited utterance admitted when it was made no more than fifteen minutes after the startling event).

We also reject appellant's arguments that Djordjevic's statements should have been excluded because they were "in response to questioning" from his co-workers who had "management responsibilities" and for whom "it was part of their job to get information," and because Lazorchack had already called 911 and had shouted to a uniformed man (who may have been a Secret Service officer assigned to the nearby Vice-Presidential mansion) before she prompted the statements from Djordjevic by asking, "[H]ow did this happen [?]" The critical factor is whether "the nature of the questions required deliberative and thoughtful answers." *Reyes v. United States,* 933 A.2d 785, 791 (D.C. 2007). "[R]esponses to preliminary investigative questions, made while the declarant is still under the spell of the startling event, may qualify as spontaneous utterances because the questions are asked to ascertain the nature of the emergency and do not provide an opportunity for the declarant to reflect on the event or to premeditate a response." *Id.* The trial court did not err in finding that this was the case here. . . .

Affirmed.

> **GOOD TO REMEMBER**
>
> The main requirement for the excited utterance exception — that the speaker must be under stress — might cause a speaker to make mistakes in narration or be confused about the events that have happened. Nevertheless, the exception is widely used and widely respected.

NOTES TO UNITED STATES v. GRAURE

1. *Nature of Questioning.* The trial judge decides personally whether a statement fits the requirements of the excited utterance. In cases where a declarant has responded to questions, the judge will consider whether the statements interrupted the spontaneity and excitement that the exception requires. To do that, the judge would bear in mind the rationale for the rule and estimate whether the questioning likely stimulated reflective responses.

QUESTION 8-2. This scenario includes some out-of-court statements by an alleged victim of child sexual abuse. How should the excited utterance exception apply to those statements?

> Adam, a six-year old, was brought by his mother to Dr. Alan Anderson, because he was suffering from nightmares and deteriorating health. The doctor thought that sexual abuse might have occurred. He conduced a rectal examination on Adam and found swelling, inflammation, and several fissures. He suspected physical trauma, but when he asked Adam about this, Adam responded, "Oh, no, no, no. . . no problems." Dr. Anderson decided that Adam should be seen by an expert, and he recommended that Elizabeth take him to XYZ Child Center. When informed of Dr. Anderson's suspicions, Adam's mother asked Adam if he had been abused. He again said no.

Adam and his mother left the doctor's office at about noon. While they were driving from place to place, the mother again asked Adam if he had been molested and listed several people, including Bob Bailey, who might have done so. Adam denied having been abused and replied "no" to every name. Eventually, Adam and his mother headed toward Adam's grandparents' home. They arrived there at about 7:00 or 7:30 that evening. In the car on the way, the mother again asked Adam if he had been molested. This time, he told her "yes" and began to scream. The screams were not words, and he did not say who molested him. This conversation occurred more than seven hours after the initial medical examination.

At his grandmother's home, Adam told his grandmother that Bob Bailey had molested him.

The next day, Adam's mother took him to XYZ Center, where he spoke with therapist Cal Carter. During that first session, Adam agreed that he had been sexually abused, but he did not say who had done it. Later, Adam told Carter he "really didn't like it" when Bailey raped him.

C STATEMENT OF THEN-EXISTING MENTAL, EMOTIONAL, OR PHYSICAL CONDITION

Statements a person makes about his or her current mental or physical feelings or condition are covered by this exception to the hearsay exclusion. Memory problems are absent from statements covered by this exception because the exception requires that the statement be about "then-existing" feelings or condition. With regard to the accuracy of the declarant's perception, some would argue that a person's knowledge of his or her own mental or physical feelings would always be accurate.

Rule 803. Exceptions to the Rule Against Hearsay — Regardless of Whether the Declarant Is Available as a Witness

The following are not excluded by the rule against hearsay, regardless of whether the declarant is available as a witness:

. . .

(3) *Then-Existing Mental, Emotional, or Physical Condition.* A statement of the declarant's then-existing state of mind (such as motive, intent, or plan) or emotional, sensory, or physical condition (such as mental feeling, pain, or bodily health), but not including a statement of memory or belief to prove the fact remembered or believed unless it relates to the validity or terms of the declarant's will.

. . .

■ ■ ■

Murder Victim's Statements of Fear—Stoll. Many criminal cases deal with statements a victim made before being harmed that express fear of a particular person or express a prediction that a particular person will harm the victim. The relevance of statements like these controls application of the state-of-mind exception.

STOLL v. STATE
762 So. 2d 870 (Fla. 2000)

PER CURIAM.

We have on appeal the judgment and sentence of the trial court imposing the death penalty upon Michael Stoll. We have jurisdiction. See art. V, §3(b)(1), Fla. Const.

Stoll was found guilty of premeditated murder in the first degree and was sentenced to death on June 9, 1998, for the murder of his wife, Julie Stoll, on November 3, 1994. The primary witness for the State was Christopher Stewart, who lived with the Stolls and worked for Stoll. At the time that the murder was committed, Stewart was nineteen years old and Stoll was thirty-three years old.

At trial, Stewart testified in graphic detail about the plans leading up to the murder, as well as about the details of the murder itself. Stewart testified that he was the one who actually killed Julie Stoll, but that he did so at the personal direction of Stoll, who planned the murder and was present when Julie Stoll was killed.

Stoll himself testified at trial and denied directing or assisting Stewart in the killing of his wife, although he did admit to "participating after the fact." In addition, Stoll discussed a prior domestic violence charge brought by his wife, and he testified that he and his wife had an argument concerning that charge only days before the murder.

The jury found Stoll guilty of premeditated murder in the first degree and thereafter returned an advisory sentence of death, with a vote of seven to five.

After weighing the aggravating factors against the mitigating factors, the trial court found that the mitigating circumstances did not outweigh the aggravating circumstances and thereafter imposed a sentence of death.

On appeal, Stoll raises. . . issues regarding the guilt phase of the trial. We agree that reversal is required because of [error in] permitting the State to call Dana Martin as a rebuttal witness. . . .

. . . During its case-in-chief, the State called Martin, a longtime friend of Julie Stoll. Martin testified that as soon as she heard that Julie Stoll was dead, she went to the Stolls' house. As she began to explain why she went to the Stolls' house, defense counsel objected and the trial court sustained the objection as to allowing Martin to testify as to hearsay. Thereafter, in rebuttal, the State again called Martin, and again, defense counsel objected on the basis of hearsay. The trial court overruled this objection whereupon Martin testified that:

Julie made me promise her in August [1994] when she came to my house one Saturday morning and was upset and shaken and crying, and they had been fighting all night the night before, that if anything ever happened to her I would go to the police and tell them that Michael did it or had it done. That he had threatened to kill her more than once and she. . . she knew he would do it.

Martin also revealed that one month before that incident, she noticed that Julie Stoll was bruised and that Julie Stoll had told Martin that "Michael did it. And that [Julie] was afraid that he was going to kill her."

In response to Stoll's argument that Martin's testimony concerning what Julie Stoll told her constituted inadmissible hearsay, the State contends that these statements fell within. . . the state-of-mind exception, section 90.803(3). . . .

[W]e reject the State's argument that Martin's statement, in whole or in part, was admissible under the state of mind exception to the hearsay rule, section 90.803(3). First, the portion of Martin's testimony that Julie Stoll told Martin that Stoll "had threatened to kill her more than once" is hearsay within hearsay. In other words, Martin testified to what Julie Stoll told her that Michael Stoll had stated. This part of Martin's testimony is clearly inadmissible because no exceptions to the hearsay rule apply. See Hill v. State, 549 So. 2d 179, 181 (Fla. 1989) (finding that where testimony combines two hearsay statements, the testimony is considered hearsay within hearsay and inadmissible unless both statements conform to a hearsay exception).

The remainder of the statement allegedly made by Julie Stoll to Martin concerning her fears that her husband was going to kill her are solely expressions of Julie Stoll's state of mind. In particular, Martin testified: "Julie made me promise her. . . that if anything happened to her [Julie Stoll] I would go to the police and tell them that Michael did it or had done it." She also testified that Stoll had threatened to kill Julie Stoll and that Julie Stoll "knew he would do it" and that Julie was "afraid that [Stoll] was going to kill her."

The victim's hearsay statements in a homicide case that the victim was afraid of the defendant generally are not admissible under the state of mind exception because the victim's state of mind is not a material issue in a murder case. As we recently stated in Woods v. State, 733 So. 2d 980, 987 (Fla. 1999), "[A] homicide victim's state of mind prior to the fatal event generally is neither at issue nor probative of any material issue raised in the murder prosecution." Likewise, a victim's statements cannot be used to prove the defendant's state of mind.

There are, however, certain circumstances where the victim-declarant's state of mind may become an issue in the case. First, the state of mind of the victim-declarant may be relevant to an element of the crime. In Peede v. State, 474 So. 2d 808, 816 (Fla. 1985), for example, the defendant was charged with kidnapping and it was necessary for the State to prove that the victim had been forcibly abducted against her will. We held that the trial court did not abuse its discretion in admitting the victim's statements to her daughter just prior to her disappearance because they demonstrated "the declarant's state of mind at that time was not to voluntarily accompany the defendant outside of Miami or to North Carolina." Id.

We have also found that the victim's state of mind may become relevant to an issue in the case where the defendant claims: (1) self-defense; (2) that the victim committed suicide; or (3) that the death was accidental. See Woods, 733 So. 2d at 987-88. In addition, the state of mind of the victim may become an issue to rebut a defense raised by the defendant. See State v. Bradford, 658 So. 2d 572, 574–75 (Fla. 5th DCA 1995). In Bradford, the Fifth District held that the victim's statements of fear of the defendant may become admissible to "rebut the defendant's theory that the victim willingly let him inside her car and that is how his fingerprint got in her car." Id. at 575. The court added, however, that "if the defendant does not put forth the theory that the victim willingly let him in her car, then her state of mind would not be at issue."

In this case, Stoll did not raise a claim of self-defense, suicide, or accidental death. Nonetheless, the State maintains that Martin's testimony was relevant to rebut. . . Stoll's trial testimony that he thought he had a happy marriage until just days before Julie Stoll's death. . . and. . . Stoll's claim that someone else committed the murder. . . .

Martin's statements regarding Julie Stoll's state of mind, however, do not rebut what Stoll thought about his marriage, nor do they properly impeach his statement that someone else committed the murder. First, the State's theory was that someone else — Chris Stewart — committed the murder, but that it was at Stoll's direction. Second, admitting Martin's otherwise inadmissible statement regarding Julie Stoll's state of mind to impeach Stoll's contention that someone else committed the murder would contradict our pronouncements in *Woods*, 733 So. 2d at 987, that a victim's state of mind is generally not a material issue in a murder case, except under very limited circumstances. Accordingly, we reject the State's argument that the victim's state-of-mind statements should have been admissible under the state of mind exception to the hearsay rule, as rebuttal evidence, or to impeach Stoll. Because Martin's testimony concerning what Julie Stoll told her is hearsay and not otherwise admissible under any exception to that rule, we conclude that the trial court erred by permitting the State to call Martin as a rebuttal witness. . . .

As the foregoing clearly reveals, by introducing the inadmissible hearsay statements allegedly made by Julie Stoll to Martin. . . the State was provided with an additional and powerful witness who could neither be impeached nor cross-examined — Julie Stoll. Based on this fact, along with consideration of the other evidence in this case, we conclude that the State has not demonstrated beyond a reasonable doubt that the errors "did not contribute to the verdict or, alternatively stated, that there is no reasonable possibility that the error contributed to the conviction." Accordingly, we reverse Stoll's conviction and vacate the sentence imposed, and we remand this case for a new trial. . . .

NOTES TO STOLL v. STATE

1. *Relevance.* A statement by a murder victim about someone who is later charged with the murder is likely to have great effect on jurors, if the statement

expresses fear of the defendant or a suggestion that the defendant is likely to kill the declarant. For this reason, courts pay close attention to the claimed relevance of these statements. While the state-of-mind exception can protect these statements from the hearsay obstacle, their relevance must be established. The *Stoll* court makes this clear by comparing a kidnapping charge with a murder charge. Because the victim's state of mind is an element in establishing that the victim's liberty was taken against the victim's will, the victim's state of mind is relevant. But murder in general does not involve any necessary finding about the victim's state of mind.

2. *Extortion and State of Mind.* In an extortion case, the prosecution must prove that the defendant put the victim in fear. Statements by the victim that express fear would be relevant on that point and would be covered by the state-of-mind exception. If an alleged victim's statement expressed fear of the defendant and also described conduct by the defendant, the portion that described the defendant's conduct might be kept out of the trial. If narrowing the report at trial of the victim's remarks is not possible, a limiting instruction would be proper, to tell the jury to consider the remarks only on the topic of the victim's fear.

QUESTION 8-3. Defendant is charged with killing Victim by strangling Victim. Defendant's only defense is that Defendant was away from the scene of the killing at the time it took place. Would the prosecution be able to introduce each of these items of testimony?

A. Testimony that about a month before Victim was killed, Victim said, "Last year Defendant tried to kill me."

B. Testimony that about a month before Victim was killed, Victim said, "I am afraid of Defendant."

C. Testimony that a friend of Victim's had said, one month before Victim was killed, "Defendant tried to kill Victim last year."

■　■　■

Segment 18:
state of mind
hearsay
exception

Surveys and Statements of Belief to Show Belief—Schering. When an expert witness describes a survey, hearsay problems arise. A survey is essentially a compilation of a large number of out-of-court statements by the survey's respondents. Dealing with surveys, courts have to apply the exception's limitation that blocks the use of a "statement of memory to prove the fact remembered."

SCHERING CORP. v. PFIZER, INC.
189 F.3d 218 (2d Cir. 1999)

SOTOMAYOR, J.

This appeal invites us to revisit an increasingly important issue in the law of evidence, and one that has confused many courts. Today we clarify the circumstances under which scientifically conducted surveys may be admitted into evidence over a hearsay objection. . . .

Schering is a pharmaceutical corporation that produces Claritin, a leading prescription antihistamine. . . . The first generation of antihistamines, introduced in the 1940s, caused drowsiness in a high percentage of users, and modern over-the-counter antihistamines have this same effect. Claritin, by contrast, is a new, second-generation prescription antihistamine, launched in 1993, which causes no more sedation than placebos in clinical tests. This feature has been important to Claritin's market success.

UCB is a European pharmaceutical company that has developed a competing second-generation prescription antihistamine called "Zyrtec." Because of UCB's limited presence in the United States, UCB licensed Pfizer, a Delaware corporation, to co-promote the product domestically. Regulations promulgated by the United States Food and Drug Administration ("FDA") required Pfizer to perform several controlled clinical tests on Zyrtec before the drug could be registered for domestic use, however, and these tests revealed that Zyrtec causes approximately twice as much sedation as a placebo. . . .

In early 1996, Pfizer and UCB began selling Zyrtec in the United States. To promote the product, Pfizer used a method that is common in the pharmaceutical industry: it employed a team of approximately 1200 sales representatives to visit physicians across the nation and emphasize the product's qualities in one-on-one informational meetings called "detailings." . . .

Suspicious that Zyrtec representatives might be misrepresenting the product's somnolence levels in the detailings, Schering [attempted to uncover facts that would show that such misrepresentations were being made]. In February 1996, Schering thus filed suit against Pfizer for violating Section 43(a)(2) of the Lanham Act, by false advertising. On April 4, 1996, this dispute ended in a settlement agreement (the "Settlement Agreement"), under which Pfizer and UCB agreed not to permit their sales representatives to state "either 'expressly' that Zyrtec was 'low-sedating' or 'expressly or by implication' that Zyrtec was 'nonsedating' or 'essentially nonsedating.'" These restrictions applied to all forms of advertising, including "verbal statements made to doctors. . . .

On October 5, 1998, Schering brought suit in the United States District Court for the Southern District of New York seeking a preliminary injunction against alleged ongoing and pervasive breaches of the Settlement Agreement and Section 43(a)(2) of the Lanham Act. In the course of discovery, Schering learned that soon after receiving Schering's original letter of complaint, Pfizer had commissioned Market Measures Inc. ("MMI") to perform a "FasTape Survey," a common type of market survey that probes the main messages conveyed in an advertising campaign, "to understand the key messages and competitive claims concerning the sedation side effect pertaining to Zyrtec." This survey involved a random sample of 74 physicians, who were allegedly representative of a panel of over 20,000 doctors prescribing antihistamines nationwide. . . . They were then asked: "In one or two sentences, what was the main message of the presentation?" The FasTape Survey stated that "Zyrtec representatives appear to be focusing almost equally on the drug's indications. . . and efficacy, *followed by its low/no sedation.*" (Emphasis added). . . .

During discovery, Schering also learned that Pfizer had commissioned Scott-Levin, another well-known market research company, to conduct a survey to identify the main messages being conveyed in the detailings. This survey, unlike the others, asked only about messages concerning nonsedation and did not poll for messages concerning low sedation. . . . Because Schering was unable to obtain the entire survey, Schering commissioned its own Scott-Levin survey, which polled approximately 150 physicians per month from March through August of 1998. The survey results suggested that on average, approximately 16% of the Zyrtec agents were communicating a message that Zyrtec was nonsedating.

At the hearing on the preliminary injunction motion, Schering sought to introduce. . . the FasTape Survey and the Scott-Levin Survey. . . . Pfizer responded with a motion arguing that all of this evidence contained hearsay and was thus inadmissible under Rule 802 of the Federal Rules of Evidence. The district court agreed and issued a written opinion refusing to admit Schering's surveys for any purpose.

The only other significant evidence that Schering offered in support of its motion was a series of manuals used by Pfizer to train its sales representatives. These manuals contained some instructions to call Zyrtec "low sedating.". . . The district court found this evidence insufficient to warrant a preliminary injunction and denied Schering's motion. This appeal followed. . . .

In the first half of this century, surveys were generally regarded as inherently untrustworthy because they contained hearsay, or out-of-court statements offered to prove the truth of the matters asserted. *See, e.g., Dupont Cellophane Co. v. Waxed Prods.,* 6 F. Supp. 859, 884 (E.D.N.Y. 1934), *modified,* 85 F.2d 75 (2d Cir. 1938) (refusing to admit survey because court could not "see how plaintiff could even test the facts, as it had no opportunity for cross-examination of those who were supposed to have answered the questions"). Schering argues, however, that "the modern view is that the hearsay objection is without merit and that any technical deficiencies in survey methodology go to [a survey's] weight as evidence, not to its admissibility.". . .

A review of the case law suggests that there are, in fact, two ongoing controversies that tend to complicate the question of whether survey evidence should be admitted in a particular case. First, there is a dispute over the proper consequence of a finding of methodological error in a survey. While some courts in this Circuit believe such flaws are proper grounds for exclusion, others view methodological errors as affecting only the weight of the evidence.

The second dispute reflected in the case law involves the proper rationale for allowing admissible surveys into evidence. As Judge Feinberg explained in *Zippo* [*Manufacturing Co. v. Rogers Imports, Inc.*, 216 F. Supp. 670 (S.D.N.Y. 1963)]:

> Some cases hold that surveys are not hearsay at all; other cases hold that surveys are hearsay but are admissible because they are within the recognized exception to the hearsay rule for statements of present state of mind, attitude, or belief.

. . . Because the Federal Rules of Evidence govern the admissibility of all evidence over a hearsay objection, the question of survey admissibility is ultimately a question of statutory interpretation. [C]areful attention to the possible statutory grounds for admitting hearsay can help harmonize most of the case law. Whether the district court was correct to exclude the. . . surveys in this case thus merits detailed discussion, with particular attention to the types of statements contained in the surveys, the purposes for which they were offered and the various possible grounds for their admission.

One of the two most common bases for admitting survey evidence is Rule 803(3), which creates an exception to the hearsay rule for statements that express a declarant's state of mind at the time of the utterance. . . . The great majority of surveys admitted in this Circuit, including those used in Lanham Act cases to establish actual confusion or secondary meaning, fall into this category: they poll individuals about their presently-existing states of mind to establish facts about the group's mental impressions.

It is important for district courts to recognize surveys of this type because their qualification for a traditional hearsay exception obviates the need to examine methodology before overruling a hearsay objection. Regardless of the basis cited for admitting these surveys, errors in methodology thus properly go only to the weight of the evidence — subject, of course, to Rule 403's more general prohibition against evidence that is less probative than prejudicial or confusing. The "modern view" urged by Schering is thus fully applicable to these kinds of surveys.

Schering argues that both the FasTape and Scott Levin surveys fall into this category because they asked physicians to relate the "main messages" conveyed by Zyrtec agents in the detailings. The surveys thereby asked physicians to relate not only what was said in the meetings but the impressions with which they were left. Such impressions are classic states of mind and, as such, fall under Rule 803(3).

The district court did not address directly whether these surveys polled for then-existing states of mind. Instead, the court appears to have viewed evidence of these states as irrelevant to the present litigation. The court explained:

> The Court does not fully concur with Schering's suggestion that the Court need not conclude that the surveys report "what exact words were spoken." While it may not need to know the exact words spoken, the Court must know the exact substance of what was said by the representatives to the physicians, *because it is that substance that violates, or does not violate, the settlement agreement.* To determine that

substance requires an effort to determine, as closely as possible, the exact words that were spoken.

(emphasis added) (citation omitted). We disagree.

The Settlement Agreement states in relevant part that:

> Pfizer and UCB Pharma hereby agree that, in connection with their advertising and promotion of ZYRTEC in the United States, they will not claim *or allow those acting on their behalf to claim,* either expressly *or by **implication*** that:
>   (1) ZYRTEC and/or its active ingredient cetirizine is nonsedating or essentially nonsedating...

(emphasis added). The Settlement Agreement thus prohibits not only explicit but also implicit falsehoods. In this sense, the agreement is reminiscent of the Act upon which it was based — i.e., the Lanham Act — which prohibits advertisements that are not only literally but also impliedly false. . . .

Cases in the Lanham Act context demonstrate, moreover, that the mental impressions with which an audience is left can be relevant, and sometimes even necessary, to establish what a defendant is implying in a challenged representation. *See, e.g., Coca-Cola Co. v. Tropicana Prods., Inc.,* 690 F.2d 312, 317 ("When a merchandising statement or representation is literally or explicitly false, the court may grant relief without reference to the advertisement's impact on the buying public. When[, however,] the challenged advertisement is implicitly rather than explicitly false, its tendency to violate the Lanham Act by misleading, confusing or deceiving *should be tested by public reaction.*" (emphasis added) (citations omitted)). . . .

These considerations persuade us that the FasTape and Scott Levin surveys are relevant to show ongoing violations of both the Settlement Agreement and the Lanham Act, on a theory that Zyrtec agents were making statements that regardless of their veracity, left the physicians with false impressions. Although statements by out-of-court declarants — e.g., the surveyed physicians — relating such impressions are hearsay where, as here, they are offered to establish the existence of the impressions themselves, see Fed. R. Evid. 801(c), these declarations are independently admissible under Rule 803(3) as expressions of the declarant physicians' then-existing states of mind. The district court should have thus admitted the FastTape and Scott Levin surveys for the limited purpose of establishing a pattern of implied falsehood.

This ruling concerning admissibility in no way suggests that the district court should give these surveys any particular weight on remand . . . .

NOTES TO SCHERING CORP. v. PFIZER, INC.

1. *Memory to Show Fact Remembered.* There is an important distinction between "it's true that a person has a belief" and "a person has a belief that is true." The text of Rule 803(3) distinguishes between a statement introduced to show a declarant's belief (treating belief as a state of mind) and a statement introduced

to show that because a declarant had a belief, the facts the declarant believed were true. For example, an out-of-court statement "last week, the truck ran a stop sign" would be hearsay if it was introduced to show that the truck ran the stop sign. An out-of-court statement "I believe that last week the truck ran a stop sign" is also hearsay if it is introduced to show that the truck ran the stop sign.

2. *Relevance of Mere Beliefs.* When is a person's belief relevant, regardless of whether the belief is true? The court refers to lawsuits involving "actual confusion," a concept used in trademark law to describe the situation when the brand name a defendant uses leads consumers who intend to buy the plaintiff's product to buy the defendant's product instead, thinking that it is a product made by the plaintiff. In a case where showing what buyers thought about a product was relevant, would surveys that reported their beliefs fit within Rule 803(3)? In *Schering* the court states that the physicians' impressions were relevant, because the settlement agreement prohibits conduct that could give physicians certain impressions. The court's analysis would not support use of the state-of-mind exception to introduce the survey results to show what the representatives had said. On the other hand, the court treats the existence of the respondent's mental impressions as proof that the defendant had violated its agreement.

QUESTION 8-4. Pat Prisoner, serving a life sentence in a state prison, suffers from gender dysphoria (emotional distress over a marked incongruence between one's experienced/expressed gender and one's assigned gender). Since being incarcerated in 2010, Prisoner has sought but not received any treatment for this condition. Prisoner has filed a pro se lawsuit, pursuant to 42 U.S.C. §1983, against the prison warden, alleging denial of adequate medical care in violation of the Eighth Amendment of the United States Constitution. Prisoner seeks a range of relief.

Under the Eighth Amendment, to establish a violation when a prisoner's health is at issue, an inmate must prove that the official responsible for the inmate's care has intentionally ignored a serious medical need or been deliberately indifferent to it.

Several years ago, when considering whether to provide Prisoner with the requested treatment, the warden had the prison's staff conduct a survey of prisons in a large number of states, to determine what procedures and treatment options they provided to individuals with gender dysphoria. Responses to the survey were submitted by prisons in about 20 states. The responses indicated that in about 80 percent of prisons, no treatment was provided to those inmates.

The defendant warden seeks to introduce the survey to prove that "no treatment" is the approach many prisons take to conditions like Prisoner's, and to show that the process by which the defendant chose to follow that course did not manifest "deliberate indifference" to Prisoner's health.

GOOD TO REMEMBER

Relevance concepts control the usefulness of the mental state exception. If someone's having a belief is relevant, the person's statement about the belief is admissible under the mental state exception. If the truth of the belief is what is relevant, the exception does *not* apply.

Discuss the hearsay issues, if any, in the warden's effort to introduce the survey results for these two purposes.

■ ■ ■

Planning to Be Someplace with Somebody — James. Rule 803(3) explicitly covers a person's statement of a plan. But defining "plan" may be difficult. *James* confronts a recurring situation: Sometimes a person's plan involves the conduct of people in addition to the person who makes a statement about a plan. The opinion discusses the classic *Hillmon* case that considered this issue in the nineteenth century.

STATE v. JAMES

717 N.E.2d 1052 (N.Y. 1999)

LEVINE, J.

Defendant was convicted after a jury trial of two counts of perjury in the first degree (Penal Law §210.15). The conviction was premised on defendant's denial, during a Grand Jury investigation, that he had been present at an October 20, 1990 meeting at which information pertaining to an upcoming New York City Transit Police Department promotional examination was illegally revealed to defendant and other potential examinees. . . .

On appeal, defendant's principal arguments for reversal focus on the claimed errors of the trial court in admitting in evidence against him the recordings of. . . telephone conversations. . . .

On Friday, October 19, 1990, Lieutenant Gordon [an author of some questions on the examination] telephoned both defendant and Lizette Lebron [an officer who worked with defendant]. On Saturday, October 20, at about 10 P.M. he again called Lebron and, as previously noted, that conversation was recorded. First, Gordon reminded her of the meeting which had been set up in the previous telephone conversation, to which Lebron replied that he had not told her the time when it was to take place. Gordon then stated "I got Sam and Dave they're coming to my house around, between 11:00 and 12:00 o'clock tonight. . . [f]or what. . . I told you yesterday." Lebron asked for confirmation that the purpose of the meeting that night was "[s]o you're just going to tell me what to study and I'll study it?" Gordon replied affirmatively. Lebron testified that "Sam" referred to defendant and "Dave" was David Tarquini, both of whom were planning to take the sergeant's promotional exam.

The October 20 recorded conversation between Gordon and Lebron concerning the intended meeting of all of them at Gordon's home later that evening "to tell [them] what to study" was admitted into evidence against defendant under the state of mind exception to the hearsay rule. It was offered in this perjury prosecution of defendant to prove, contrary to defendant's Grand Jury testimony, that the planned meeting of defendant, Lebron and other officers to discuss the promotional exam questions, did in fact take place.

The seminal precedent on the admissibility of Gordon's October 20 statement is the celebrated 1892 decision of the United States Supreme Court in *Mutual Life Ins. Co. v. Hillmon* (145 U.S. 285). Because the issue is an important one of first impression in our Court, and because we disagree with the defendant's reading of *Hillmon*, a recital at length of the facts, issues and the holding in the case is necessary.

The plaintiff in *Hillmon* was the wife of John W. Hillmon, suing the insurers on three recently purchased policies covering his life. Her evidence of Hillmon's death was that in early March 1879 he left Wichita with a friend named Brown looking for land to purchase for use as a cattle ranch. Two weeks later, while encamped in Crooked Creek, Kansas, Hillmon was killed by the accidental discharge of Brown's gun. He was buried in a neighboring town. The defendant insurance companies introduced evidence that the body was not that of Hillmon, but of Frederick Walters, who had disappeared at the same time. The body was exhumed and Walters' relatives identified it as his.

At issue in the *Hillmon* case was the admissibility of two letters Walters wrote in early March 1879, to his sister and fiance, in which he related his intention to accompany "a certain Mr. Hillmon," and "a man by the name of Hillmon" on a trip from Wichita. In Walters' letter to his fiance he told her that Hillmon's purpose was "to start a sheep ranch, and as he promised me more wages than I could make at anything else I concluded to take it." The defendant insurers sought to introduce the letters in support of their defense that Hillmon induced Walters to accompany him to some remote place where he would be killed in order to provide a corpse on which to base Mrs. Hillmon's fraudulent claim to the proceeds of the policies insuring her husband's life.

The *Hillmon* trial court excluded the letters on the ground that they were hearsay. A jury found in favor of Hillmon's wife. The United States Supreme Court reversed and ruled that upon retrial, the letters would be admissible under the state of mind exception to the hearsay rule. The Court held that a declarant's extra-judicial statement of intention can be admitted into evidence under that exception "whenever the intention is of itself a distinct and material fact in a chain of circumstances" (145 U.S., at 295). In support of the admissibility of Walters' declarations, Justice Gray, writing for the Court, pointed to factors in the case of the kind that Wigmore and other scholars identify as justifying most common-law hearsay exceptions, i.e., "a circumstantial probability of trustworthiness, and a necessity, for the evidence" because of the unavailability of the declarant (5 Wigmore, *op. cit.*, §1420, at 251). Justice Gray wrote: "Letters from [Walters] to his family and his betrothed were *the natural, if not the only attainable, evidence of his intention*" (145 U.S., at 295 [emphasis supplied]). The Court also emphasized that trustworthiness was bolstered because the letters were "written by [Walters] *at the very time* and *under circumstances precluding a suspicion of misrepresentation*" (*id.*, at 295 [emphasis supplied]).

Because Walters was unavailable to testify to accompanying Hillmon on his search for suitable ranch land, and because of the foregoing salient indicia of trustworthiness of Walters' declarations of his intent to do so, the court ruled that his letters were of sufficient probative value on the insurers' defense theory to be admissible "as evidence that. . . [Walters] had the intention of going [away from Wichita], *and of going with Hillmon* which *made it more probable* both that he did go and *that he went with Hillmon,* than if there had been no proof of such intention" (*id.,* at 296 [emphasis supplied]). . . .

Defendant argues that this case differs from *Hillmon* in several major respects. According to defendant, the October 20 statement is being offered not at all to prove the future intent and subsequent act of Gordon, the declarant, but solely to prove the future intent and subsequent act of defendant, a non-declarant. Defendant would read *Hillmon* to support admissibility of a statement of future intent to prove only the solitary acts of the declarant. He claims that using Gordon's statement to prove his acts expands *Hillmon* "far beyond its logical and intended limits." Additionally, defendant contends that here the declaration implicitly asserts and is being used to prove not just future intent and subsequent acts, but also acts prior to the declaration — Gordon's implied assertion that defendant had previously agreed to meet at his home.

In our view these criticisms misconstrue the probative value of Gordon's October 20 statement in defendant's perjury trial and misread *Hillmon.* Gordon's statement of his future intent and his subsequent actions with the prospective examinees taken upon that intent were highly relevant to the perjury prosecution of defendant. Defendant was charged with false testimony before a Grand Jury inquiring into his *joint* action with Gordon and Lebron at their meeting at Gordon's home regarding the forthcoming promotional examination. Gordon's intent to hold that meeting and to reveal the examination questions supplied the materiality element of the questions defendant falsely answered. Without proof of Gordon's plan and his joint action upon it with the recipients of the illegal disclosures, defendant's answers to the questions posed before the Grand Jury would be meaningless to a trial jury. . . .

The Supreme Court in *Hillmon* ruled that Walters' declarations of intent to leave Wichita were "competent" not only to permit a trier of fact to infer that he went away (the limited application of the *Hillmon* doctrine advocated by defendant) but also to permit the inference, so the Court explicitly stated, "that he went with Hillmon" (*Mutual Life Ins. Co. v. Hillmon, supra,* 145 U.S., at 296). Indeed, excision of Walters' declarations of intention to leave *with Hillmon* would have rendered his letters irrelevant to the insurers' defense that the body held out as Hillmon was really Walters.

The very same analytical infirmities identified and objected to by defendant in admitting Gordon's October 20 statement under the state of mind exception were present in *Hillmon.* Just as here, where Gordon's October 20 statement implies the existence of a prior discussion and agreement concerning the meeting that night, in *Hillmon,* Walters' statement of intention to accompany Hillmon implied that a prior discussion had taken place in which they had agreed to embark together on a trip to search for suitable ranch land.

Thus, *Hillmon* does fully support the admissibility under the state of mind hearsay exception of Gordon's October 20 pre-meeting statement as proof of the joint or cooperative action of Gordon, defendant and others. Indeed, even early commentators who expressed concern that *Hillmon* would be expanded to support admissibility of declarations of memory of past events (essentially destroying the hearsay rule) did not read *Hillmon* in the narrow manner that defendant advocates here.

Defendant argues alternatively that we should not adopt the entire *Hillmon* doctrine, but limit its application to make a statement of future intent admissible solely to prove the individual act of the declarant.... Jurisdiction after jurisdiction of State and Federal courts have determined to follow the lead of *Hillmon* . . . in admitting against criminal defendants (upon establishment of an appropriate foundation) the statements of a declarant's intention to perform acts entailing the participation jointly or cooperatively of the nondeclarant accused. We also adopt that rule....

[A]s with other hearsay exceptions, statements of intent to engage in future conduct with another person largely obviate the dangers of a declarant's faulty memory or perception, two of the four testimonial infirmities (along with insincerity and ambiguity) which the hearsay rule requires to be tested through cross-examination. This is generally sufficient to justify an exception, when there is independent evidence of reliability.

It is not difficult to fashion foundational safeguards appropriate to ensure against both the dangers of unreliability common to most hearsay exceptions and those peculiar to this one. Thus, before a statement of intent to engage in joint or cooperative activity is admissible against the named nondeclarant, it must be shown that (1) the declarant is unavailable; (2) the statement of the declarant's intent unambiguously contemplates some *future* action by the declarant, either jointly with the nondeclarant defendant or which requires the defendant's cooperation for its accomplishment; (3) to the extent that the declaration expressly or impliedly refers to a prior understanding or arrangement with the nondeclarant defendant, it must be inferable under the circumstances that the understanding or arrangement occurred in the recent past and that the declarant was a party to it or had competent knowledge of it; and (4) there is independent evidence of reliability, i.e., a showing of circumstances which all but rule out a motive to falsify.

[Each required showing was satisfied in this case.]

Thus, the trial court properly admitted Gordon's October 20 statement under the state of mind exception to the hearsay rule.

NOTES TO STATE v. JAMES

1. *Probative Value of Plans.* On the issue of whether a declarant did go to the movies on a particular day, compare the probative value of these two statements: (1) "I went to the movies yesterday" and (2) "I plan to go to the movies tomorrow." The second one is admissible under Rule 803(3) even though its

probative value on the issue is lower than the probative value of the statement about a past event.

2. *Jury's Discounting Ability.* The ways in which people may fail to carry out their plans are well known. For that reason, allowing a jury to hear that a person possessed a plan may not entail large risks of overuse of the information. In comparison, a jury's ability to discount a statement about a declarant's past actions may be less. That discount would require a full understanding of the reasons for the hearsay rule and the significance of the testimonial infirmities.

■   ■   ■

Planning for Someone Else to Act — **Camm.** A murder victim told a friend that she expected her husband to come home at a particular time. The court distinguishes that from a statement like "I plan to be home and meet my husband there," but its main analysis involves a narrow interpretation of the *Hillmon* case. To support its result, the *Camm* court relies in part on its state's rules advisory committee's comments about the proper scope of plans.

CAMM v. STATE
908 N.E.2d 215 (Ind. 2009)

DICKSON, J.

The defendant, David R. Camm, appeals his three convictions and sentence of life imprisonment without parole for murdering his wife and two children. . . .

The defense also presented testimony that supported the defendant's alibi that he had been playing basketball at the time of the killings. . . .

[The defendant contends] that the trial court erred in allowing his wife's friend, Cindy Mattingly, to testify concerning an out-of-court statement made by his wife. On the day of the murders, the two women spoke during their daughters' dance class. And "during a normal, every day-type conversation about how busy life was, and in response to [her friend's] statement as to when she expected her husband home," the defendant's wife told the friend that "she was expecting her husband home between 7:00 and 7:30, around that time." This testimony was received at trial over the defendant's hearsay objection.

. . . In deciding whether to admit an out-of-court statement, a trial court must answer two preliminary questions: Is the statement hearsay, and, if so, does an exception apply? As to the first question, the State, defendant, and trial court agreed that the wife's statement is hearsay. What divided the parties was whether the statement properly fell within a hearsay exception. Supporting the trial court's decision, the State insists that Evidence Rule 803(3) allowed the friend's testimony as a state-of-mind declaration. The defendant, on the other hand, argues that his wife's statement of belief as to his future actions, when offered to prove those actions, falls outside Rule 803(3)'s purview. . . .

Regarding this theory, such declarations may be admitted not only as proof of the declarant's then-existing state of mind, but also as circumstantial evidence of the *declarant's future conduct. See Mutual Life Ins. Co. v. Hillmon,* 145 U.S. 285, 12 S. Ct. 909, 36 L. Ed. 706 (1892). A jury may infer from the declarant's past state of mind that the declarant held the same mental state at a future time and acted on it. Courts permit this sub-category of evidence because it lacks many of the dangers traditionally associated with hearsay: a jury's connecting a declarant's expressed mental state to their actions requires inferring only that one generally does what they intend, with no need to appraise memory, perception, or testimonial qualities. This Court's cases have repeatedly permitted such use under Rule 803(3). *See, e.g., Taylor v. State,* 659 N.E.2d 535, 543 (Ind. 1995); *Carter v. State,* 501 N.E.2d 439, 441–42 (Ind. 1986) (co-defendant's statement, during a conversation about drugs, that he would "check with [the defendant] to see if it was available," explained the declarant's later phone call to the defendant (citing *Hillmon*)); *Dunaway v. State,* 440 N.E.2d 682, 686 (Ind. 1982) ("The statements indicate a fearful state of mind which would circumstantially explain her later action of attempting to hit defendant.").

But the wife did not say, "*I* plan to be home between 7:00 and 7:30 P.M." Rather, her statement more directly relayed a belief about the *defendant's* future act of returning home. . . .

When admitted as circumstantial proof of the fact believed, as here, the evidence ceased to be a statement of the declarant's state of mind but rather was a statement of her expectation of the defendant's actions, and one which lacked a foundation about the basis for that expectation. The relevance of the wife's expectation necessarily depended on her accurate perception and memory: she could not know the defendant's plans without perceiving and remembering some past fact — something the defendant (or some other person) said or did to indicate that he would arrive home at that time. The wife's statement is thus no more reliable than any other classic form of hearsay, and this unreliability erodes the basis for admitting state-of-mind declarations in the first place. *See* 2 McCormick on Evidence §275 (6th ed. 2006) ("The danger of unreliability is greatly increased when the action sought to be proved is not one that the declarant could have performed alone, but rather is one that required the cooperation of another person.").

Indeed, had the wife's statement explicitly related the basis for her knowledge of the defendant's intent (e.g., that the defendant had phoned her), arguably making the statement more reliable, a trial court could not admit that additional fact because it would be a statement of memory or belief, offered to prove the fact believed. *See, e.g., United States v. Cohen,* 631 F.2d 1223, 1225 (5th Cir. 1980) ("[T]he state-of-mind exception does not permit the witness to relate any of the declarant's statements as to why he held the particular state of mind, or what he might have believed that would have induced the state of mind."). The logic that compels excluding explicit references applies even more forcefully to implication: It necessarily depends on the wife's accurate knowledge of some past fact about the defendant, without which her statement amounted to irrelevant speculation, and which was impossible for the defendant to cross-examine.

These concerns were highlighted in the Committee Notes accompanying Indiana's own Rule 803(3),[5] and several states, either by rule or through case law, disallow the use of state-of-mind declarations to prove a third party's conduct. We agree, and hold that, while state-of-mind declarations are admissible under Rule 803(3) when offered to prove or explain acts or conduct of the declarant, they are not admissible when offered to prove a third party's conduct. Because the wife's statement expressed a belief about the defendant's future plans, and was used as evidence of what the defendant in fact did, the admission of the wife's hearsay statement was an abuse of discretion.

And while the State suggests that the statement is probative of whether the defendant's wife actually arrived home at those times, this rationale finds little support in this case. The wife's being at home at 7:30 P.M. was not contested — yet even if relevant for that narrow purpose, common sense shows too high a risk that the jury would misuse the statement to infer the defendant's act. We hold that it was error to admit the friend's testimony that she heard the defendant's wife state the time she was expecting her husband home. . . .

In view of conflicting evidence concerning the defendant's alibi, we cannot conclude that the error in admitting this evidence was harmless.

We reverse the defendant's convictions and remand for new trial or other proceedings consistent with this opinion.

NOTES TO CAMM v. STATE

1. *Rival Approaches.* Courts have developed a number of responses to the ambiguity in Rule 803(3) regarding a declarant's plans that involve other people. *Camm* represents the narrow approach that rejects use of such a statement to show what another person did. *James* represents a pro-admissibility stance, allowing the statement as proof of what a nondeclarant did, so long as there are circumstances associated with the statement that minimize the likelihood of a false statement. The *Camm* and *James* courts' different outcomes are reflected by their different descriptions of the landmark *Hillmon* case.

Some courts allow admission of these statements to show the subsequent conduct of the declarant and of the nondeclarant if independent evidence exists to corroborate the hearsay statement as to the nondeclarant. For example, in

---

5. The Committee concluded that

[The question] [w]hether statements of intent by one person should be admitted to prove that another person did an act has always been controversial. The usual context is a statement by a crime victim that the victim is going out to meet the defendant, offered to prove that the victim in fact met the defendant. *The committee fails to see the connection, because the victim has no control over what the defendant does, and therefore the victim's intent cannot influence the defendant.* . . .

United States v. Best, 219 F.3d 192 (2d Cir. 2000), the court approved admission of a hearsay statement when independent evidence connected the declarant's statement about a future act with a nondeclarant's later actions.

QUESTION 8-5.   To prove that Runner participated in a marathon race in August 2011, which one or ones of the following statements would likely be admissible?

A. Runner said in September 2011, "I ran the marathon last month."
B. Runner said in July 2011, "I will run the marathon next month."
C. Runner's friend said in September 2011, "Runner ran the marathon last month."
D. Runner's friend said in July 2011, "Runner will run the marathon next month."

STATEMENTS FOR PURPOSES OF MEDICAL DIAGNOSIS OR TREATMENT

Statements made for medical diagnosis or treatment are covered by Rule 803(4). This exception is supported by the idea that a person who seeks medical care will ordinarily have a motivation to speak accurately. The reference to *diagnosis* in this rule makes it clear that its coverage extends beyond the context of medical *treatment*. Even if a doctor's only role in connection with a patient is to provide a diagnosis, statements in that setting are within the rule's definition.

Rule 803. Exceptions to the Rule Against Hearsay — Regardless of Whether the Declarant Is Available as a Witness

The following are not excluded by the rule against hearsay, regardless of whether the declarant is available as a witness:

. . .

(4) *Statement Made for Medical Diagnosis or Treatment.* A statement that:

(A) is made for — and is reasonably pertinent to — medical diagnosis or treatment; and

(B) describes medical history; past or present symptoms or sensations; their inception; or their general cause.

. . .

■   ■   ■

"Doctor, Right Before the Car Crash I Lost Consciousness" — **Hansen.** This opinion stresses the main elements of Rule 803(4) and also considers whether the self-serving nature of a statement a person might make when seeking medical treatment should be a factor in applying the rule.

HANSEN v. HEATH

852 P.2d 977 (Utah 1993)

HALL, C. J.

Plaintiff Gail Hansen appeals a jury verdict of no cause in her action to recover for injuries sustained in an automobile accident involving James Woo.[1]

On July 15, 1988, Hansen was injured when Woo's vehicle struck her vehicle from behind. At the time of the accident, Woo, then 78 years old, was returning from a doctor appointment at the Veteran's Administration Hospital ("VA"), where he was receiving on-going treatment for shortness of breath associated with lung and heart disease. Woo's medical records revealed that on the day of the accident, his condition was improving and he was sent home with no restrictions on driving.

At the accident scene, paramedics examined Woo and later noted in their report that Woo had possibly suffered a syncopal episode. A syncopal episode occurs when a person suddenly loses consciousness without warning. It appears that Woo did not volunteer any information to the paramedics concerning any loss of consciousness. Instead, the paramedics reached that conclusion independently.

Shortly after the accident, Woo was transported to the VA, where he told his treating physician that he had suddenly lost consciousness without warning and that he remembered nothing about the accident until a woman was pulling him from his car after the collision. Woo's physician diagnosed his condition as "syncope and CHF (coronary heart failure)." Woo was admitted to the hospital for six days and received treatment for the syncopal episode.

Hansen filed a complaint on February 3, 1989, alleging that Woo negligently caused the accident that injured her. Woo responded and set forth the affirmative defense that he had suddenly and without prior warning lost consciousness at the time of the accident and was therefore not liable for Hansen's injuries. Woo died six months after the complaint was filed. He was never deposed.

Prior to trial, Hansen filed a motion to strike and a motion in limine to exclude Woo's statement to his treating physician that he blacked out prior to the accident. Hansen claimed that because Woo was no longer alive, the statement was inadmissible hearsay under Utah Rule of Evidence 802 and did not qualify as an exception to the hearsay rule.

The trial court denied Hansen's motions. The court permitted Heath's expert, Dr. Freedman, to testify regarding not only the medical record that included

---

1. Woo died while this action was pending and is represented here by John Heath, the personal representative of Woo's estate. We will refer to Heath as the party defendant and to Woo personally when necessary.

Woo's actual statement, but several other subsequent medical records indicating the syncope diagnosis. Freedman also testified that Woo's medical records and actions were consistent with a blackout, which was most likely caused by a condition known as "ventricular tachycardia," meaning a rapid heartbeat.

The jury returned a verdict for Heath, finding that Woo had suffered a blackout that absolved him of liability for the accident. Hansen now appeals. . . .

At trial, Heath presented the medical record containing Woo's statement to his treating physician following the accident. The medical record states in pertinent part, "Patient states he was driving, suddenly lost consciousness [without] warning. Remembers nothing until a lady was pulling him from his car." This testimony strongly supported Heath's assertion that Woo suffered a syncopal episode that absolved him of liability for the accident. The jury evidently believed that to be the case and returned a verdict for Heath. Hansen claims on appeal that the trial court erred in admitting Woo's statement and that the error was prejudicial.

Hansen asserts that Woo's statement constitutes inadmissible hearsay that does not qualify for any of the exceptions to the hearsay rule. Utah Rule of Evidence 802 forbids the admission of hearsay evidence, and rules 803 and 804 provide exceptions to the hearsay rule. Heath claims that Woo's statement is admissible under the hearsay exception found in rule 803(4). . . .

To qualify as an exception to the prohibition against the use of hearsay testimony at trial, a statement to a physician must satisfy two elements: (1) the statement must be made with an intent to facilitate medical diagnosis or treatment, and (2) the statement must in fact be reasonably pertinent to diagnosis or treatment. If the statement meets both qualifications, it is admissible because of the "patient's strong motivation to be truthful" when discussing his or her medical condition with a doctor. Such statements carry a "guarantee of trustworthiness" entitling them to an exception from the mandates of the hearsay rule.

In admitting Woo's statement contained in the medical record, the trial court relied on rule 803(4). The court reasoned:

> The Court is going to permit the medical records. The Court agrees with [Heath's] view of Rule 803. There's a built-in safeguard. A patient has an interest in having their [sic] medical needs treated. And trying to mislead or make incorrect statements to a physician, I think, is not the motive that you'd expect the patient to give the doctor. So, I think there's a reasonable safeguard as to that statement.

We agree with the trial court's ruling and the reasoning supporting it. Woo made the declaration to his treating physician immediately after being transported from the accident scene to the VA. His physician transcribed the statement in her own handwriting. The statement reflected Woo's medical condition at the time of the accident, something a concerned patient would undoubtedly want to share with his or her doctor. Hence, it was made with intent to facilitate medical diagnosis and treatment. Furthermore, losing consciousness suddenly would undoubtedly prompt medical attention, and any information concerning the episode is reasonably pertinent to diagnosis and treatment. We therefore find ample record evidence that the statement was made for the purpose of medical diagnosis and treatment, and we will not disturb the trial court's ruling on the matter.

Hansen also suggests that Woo's statement is inherently untrustworthy because it is self-serving and because Woo could have contrived his "story" about passing out before the accident while in the ambulance on the way to the VA. Although the declaration was ultimately exculpatory, it also expressed a past or present symptom, which is admissible under rule 803(4). A statement that qualifies for a hearsay exception should not be stricken merely because it is self-serving unless there is substantial doubt about its trustworthiness.[15]

At the time of the accident, Woo was 78 years old, was ailing, and had difficulty expressing himself in English. It is doubtful that he knew that, as a matter of law, unconsciousness could absolve him of liability, much less that he had the wherewithal to fabricate a story while in the back of an ambulance. Woo's statement engenders no inherent lack of trustworthiness; on the contrary, we believe the trial court was correct in ruling that it is a reliable declaration, qualifying for exemption from the hearsay rule under section 803(4). . . .

We see no error on the part of the trial court in admitting Woo's statement. . . . Consequently, we affirm the jury verdict for Heath.

NOTES TO HANSEN v. HEATH

1. *Levels of Hearsay in Medical Records.* As is typical in medical records, there were two levels of hearsay involved in the introduction of Mr. Woo's statement. One level was the out-of-court oral statement by Mr. Woo. The second level was the out-of-court written statement by medical personnel, in the hospital records, quoting Mr. Woo. (There would have been only one level of hearsay if a witness had testified about having heard Mr. Woo's words.) In a portion of the opinion deleted from this version, the hospital's records were treated as covered by the hearsay exception for "business records."

2. *Various Providers and Recipients of Information.* If Mr. Woo had made his statement to a receptionist at the hospital, rather than to a physician, the statement's admissibility would likely have been the same, as long as it seemed to the trial court that he had a reasonable belief that making the statement was a part of the process of obtaining treatment.

When parents or others with a close relationship to a patient provide information, the rule's coverage extends to them, since the rule does not expressly provide that the declarant must be the patient.

---

15. See 29 Am. Jur. 2d Evidence §621 (1967) (noting that the real concern regarding self-serving statements is their untrustworthy nature. However, "since the real objection to self-serving statements is their hearsay character, and since even hearsay is admissible under exceptions to the general rule of exclusion, declarations may be admitted in evidence under some circumstances even though they are self-serving." Id. §622, at 675-76 (citations omitted)); see also Shell Oil Co., 119 N.E.2d at 231 (implicitly rejecting claim that a self-serving statement is barred by the hearsay rule if it otherwise qualifies for an exception to the rule). Hence, if a statement is reliable and admissible under an exception to the hearsay rule, its self-serving nature is irrelevant.

3. *General Cause of Symptoms.* A patient's statement that he was hit by a car is clearly covered by this rule. But if a patient said he was hit by a car that was running a red light, that statement would very likely be outside the rule's coverage (on the basis of the commonsense basis for the rule and also the rule's use of the word "general").

4. *Counterexample.* New Hampshire's version of Rule 803(4) covers topics on which the Federal Rule of Evidence 803(4) is silent. Does the additional language suggest that the New Hampshire rule could produce results different from results under the federal rule?

> **N.H. R. Evid. 803(4): Statements for Purposes of Medical Diagnosis or Treatment.**
>
> Statements made for purposes of medical diagnosis or treatment and describing medical history, or past or present symptoms, pain, or sensations, or the inception or general character of the cause or external source thereof insofar as reasonably pertinent to diagnosis or treatment, regardless of to whom the statements are made, or when the statements are made, if the court, in its discretion, affirmatively finds that the proffered statements were made under circumstances indicating their trustworthiness.

■   ■   ■

Telling a Doctor the Name of an Assailant — Oldman. Relying on a leading case, United States v. Renville, the *Oldman* court considers whether a patient's statement to a physician naming a person who had assaulted the patient should be treated as a statement for the purpose of medical diagnosis or treatment.

OLDMAN v. STATE

998 P.2d 957 (Wyo. 2000)

THOMAS, J.

The primary claim of error presented by Steven Charles Oldman (Oldman), who was convicted of [aggravated assault and battery] is that an emergency room physician should not have been permitted to testify about statements made to him by the victim with respect to the identity of her assailant. . . . We hold that the hearsay statements recounted by the emergency physician were admissible in evidence under W.R.E. 803(2) and 803(4), and no error was committed in admitting that testimony. . . .

GOOD TO REMEMBER

Applying this rule only to statements that have information pertinent to medical treatment makes sense two ways: (1) the speaker is likely to be careful about it because its accuracy will affect his or her health care, and (2) the person to whom the statement is given will also be attentive and may seek clarifications if the topic matters to health.

At the time of the material events in this case, Oldman was living in Riverton. The victim also lived in Riverton in an apartment with two of her four children. The victim and Oldman had lived together off and on for some ten to twelve years. They had four children together, and although never formally married, they held themselves out as husband and wife. The victim was six-months pregnant bearing the couple's fifth child. On the afternoon of April 2, 1995, the victim's neighbor heard a male voice yelling and screaming in the victim's apartment. Again at about 3:00 A.M. the next day, the neighbor heard a male yelling, and that was followed by the sound of a woman or a child crying. The neighbor called 911, and reported what he had overheard. He then heard a voice outside in the alley, and looking out his window, he saw a man walking away. He did not see the man's face, but the neighbor described him as having the same build, hair color, and skin tone as Oldman.

Two Riverton police officers were dispatched to the apartment in response to the neighbor's call. Before they arrived at the apartment, the dispatcher informed the officers that a badly beaten woman had arrived at the police station. The woman told the dispatcher that she had just left the apartment where the officers had been sent. The officers returned to the station, and they found the victim badly beaten, bleeding, crying, and hysterical. . . .

. . . The officers called an ambulance which took the victim to the hospital. The attending physician, who saw the victim in the emergency room, noted a black and blue eye; facial bruising; and a "significant number of human bite marks" on her back, arm, thigh, hands, and feet. Although the physician did not ask, the victim told him that her husband had beaten her and bitten her.

Oldman was charged with the crime of aggravated assault. . . . He was tried before a jury on August 14, 1995. The victim did not appear, but. . . the attending physician in the emergency room. . . testified about the statements she made. . . identifying Oldman as her assailant. Oldman objected to the testimony of the attending physician as hearsay, but the trial court overruled the objection, invoking W.R.E. 803(4). Oldman was found guilty by the jury, and, on October 10, 1995, the district court pronounced a sentence of seven to ten years in the Wyoming State Penitentiary. Oldman has appealed from the Judgment and Sentence.

In support of his first claim of error, Oldman contends that the trial court should not have allowed the emergency room physician to testify about the statements the victim made to him during the course of the medical treatment. The State argues that both W.R.E. 803(2) and 803(4) justify the testimony of the physician about the victim's statements. The trial court ruled that the testimony was admissible as an exception to the hearsay rule under W.R.E. 803(4). . . . We hold that the testimony was admissible under either paragraph of W.R.E. 803. . . .

Pursuant to W.R.E. 803(4), "statements made for purposes of medical diagnosis or treatment and describing medical history, or past or present symptoms, pain, or sensations, or the inception or general character of the cause or external source thereof insofar as reasonably pertinent to diagnosis or treatment" can be received in evidence. According to the same treatise, this exception finds its basis in "the likelihood that the patient believes that the effectiveness of the treatment depends on the accuracy of the information provided to the doctor...." John W. Strong, *McCormick on Evidence*, (5th ed. 1999) §277 at 233.

Statements that have the effect of attributing fault or causation generally are not admissible in evidence under W.R.E. 803(4) because they are not relevant to diagnosis or treatment. We have, however, recognized this exception to the hearsay rule when the statement is perceived as necessary for diagnosis or treatment. The United States Court of Appeals for the Eighth Circuit first articulated a two-part test for invoking this exception in *United States v. Iron Shell*, 633 F.2d 77, 84 (8th Cir. 1980), *cert. denied*, 450 U.S. 1001, 68 L. Ed. 2d 203, 101 S. Ct. 1709 (1981). The test was clarified in *United States v. Renville*, 779 F.2d 430, 436 (8th Cir. 1985), in which the court said:

> First, the declarant's motive in making the statement must be consistent with the purposes of promoting treatment [or diagnosis]; and second, the content of the statement must be such as is reasonably relied on by a physician in treatment or diagnosis.

The first prong of the *Renville* test demands that "the declarant's motive in making the statement must be consistent with the purposes of promoting treatment [or diagnosis.]" Identity rarely is germane to the promotion of treatment or diagnosis, but we, as well as other courts, have recognized that such statements can be relevant to treatment in instances of child abuse. The rationale for relevance in such instances is that "the physician must be attentive to treating the emotional and psychological injuries which accompany this crime."

In [*Blake v. State*, 933 P.2d 474 (Wyo. 1997)], we extended this exception to a sixteen-year-old victim of domestic sexual abuse. The United States Court of Appeals for the Tenth Circuit has applied it in a sexual assault case. *United States v. Joe*, 8 F.3d 1488, 1494-95 (10th Cir. 1993), *cert. denied*, 510 U.S. 1184 (1994). In *Joe*, the statement of the victim to an attending physician was that her estranged husband had raped her. The United States Court of Appeals for the Tenth Circuit ruled that the statement was admissible under F.R.E. 803(4), reasoning:

> All victims of domestic sexual abuse suffer emotional and psychological injuries, the exact nature and extent of which depend on the identity of the abuser. The physician generally must know who the abuser was in order to render proper treatment because the physician's treatment will necessarily differ when the abuser is a member of the victim's family or household. In the domestic sexual abuse case, for example, the treating physician may recommend special therapy or counseling and instruct the victim to remove herself from the dangerous environment by leaving the home and seeking shelter elsewhere. In short, the domestic sexual abuser's

identity is admissible under Rule 803(4) where the abuser has such an intimate relationship with the victim that the abuser's identity becomes "reasonably pertinent" to the victim's proper treatment.

Joe, 8 F.3d at 1494-95 (footnote omitted). There is no logical reason for not applying this rationale to non-sexual, traumatic abuse within a family or household, since sexual abuse is simply a particular kind of physical abuse. We hold that the victim's statements to the emergency room physician were consistent with the purpose of promoting diagnosis and treatment.

In its second prong, the *Renville* test requires that "the content of the statements must be such as is reasonably relied on by a physician in treatment or diagnosis." *Renville,* 779 F.2d at 436. In most cases, to treat or diagnose a physician would have no need to know who was responsible for the injury. In a case such as this, however, the identity of the assailant is highly relevant in order for the physician to prescribe an appropriate course of treatment. There are two reasons that justify this holding. First, the victim's injuries included numerous human bites. It was important for the emergency room physician to know the source of the bites in order to treat the victim properly for any infectious condition related to the assailant. Second, the victim had been so brutally abused by the named assailant that the hospital reasonably could rely on her statement in order to deny access to the hospital by the assailant. This would prevent further abuse or injury which could impede her recovery both physically and psychologically. The identity of the assailant in this case was relevant to the effort of the emergency room physician to treat the abuse as an underlying cause, rather than simply the injuries that were inflicted on this occasion. We hold that the trial court properly admitted the testimony of the examining physician as an exception to the hearsay rule under W.R.E. 803(4).

[The excited utterance exception also applied to the victim's statements to the emergency room physician.]

The Judgment and Sentence of the trial court is affirmed.

NOTES TO OLDMAN v. STATE

1. ***Statements to Mental Health Practitioners.*** When people obtain mental health care, the number of words they speak to the practitioner and the topics of those words may be significantly different from communications to practitioners in other fields. The Texas Court of Criminal Appeals explored this in Taylor v. State, 268 S.W.3d 571 (Tex. Crim. App. 2008):

> The effectiveness of on-going treatment, and especially of mental-health treatment, we have no doubt, will at least sometimes depend, in some particulars, upon the patient's veracity. When that is the case, and so long as the patient can be made to understand that dependency, there is little reason to question his motive to be truthful in the interest of improving his own mental health.
>
> Still, we recognize that reclining on a therapist's or psychiatrist's couch is not quite the same as sitting in the emergency room in the immediate aftermath of an

injury or on the physician's cold examination table in the interest of diagnosing and curing some exigent disease or ailment. In the latter contexts, it seems only natural to presume that adults, and even children of a sufficient age or apparent maturity, will have an implicit awareness that the doctor's questions are designed to elicit accurate information and that veracity will serve their best interest. This explains the almost universal tendency of courts under these circumstances to assay the record, not for evidence of such an awareness, but for any evidence that would *negate* such an awareness, even while recognizing that the burden is on the proponent of the hearsay to show that the Rule 803(4) exception applies.

In the therapist's office, however, this tacit presumption is far less compelling. It is not always so readily apparent (indeed, it may not always be *accurate*) in the mental-health context that truth-telling is vital. Not even an older, more mature child (maybe not even an adult) will necessarily recognize and appreciate the necessity (assuming there is a necessity) always to tell a mental-health provider the truth in order to assure the efficacy of treatment. In this context we think it is incumbent upon the proponent of the hearsay exception to make the record reflect both 1) that truth-telling was a vital component of the particular course of therapy or treatment involved, and 2) that it is readily apparent that the child-declarant was aware that this was the case. Otherwise, the justification for admitting the out-of-court statement over a valid hearsay objection is simply too tenuous.

. . . By the express terms of Rule 803(4), . . . the proponent of hearsay evidence must show that the particular statement proffered is also "pertinent to . . . treatment," — that is to say, that it was reasonable for the therapist to rely on the particular information contained in the statement in treating the declarant. This includes showing that a statement from a child-declarant revealing the identity of the perpetrator of sexual abuse is pertinent. In *Renville*, the Eighth Circuit made it clear that this information might be pertinent because it is important for a physician to discover the extent of the child's "emotional and psychological injuries" — particularly when the perpetrator might be a family or household member and it is important to remove the child from the abusive environment.

It is far less obvious how that information will necessarily be pertinent, long after the fact of the abuse, in an on-going course of mental-health treatment or therapy. At that point, knowing who is at fault for the emotional or psychological trauma may not be critical to every treatment plan, especially if the perpetrator was not a family or household member.

The court held that when a party seeks to introduce a hearsay statement in which a patient told a mental health care practitioner the identity of an abuser, the proponent must show that it was important to the efficacy of the treatment for the declarant to disclose the identity of the perpetrator and that the declarant understood that importance.

QUESTION 8-6. The *Oldman* court provides a broad description of the aspects of a patient's well-being for which a doctor is responsible. Suppose a patient being treated for very severe injuries sustained in a car accident said to an emergency room physician, "My wallet should have about three thousand dollars in it. If the money's missing, the only one who could have taken it is Peter Passenger, who was riding in the car with me." In a later prosecution of Passenger for theft of money from the patient's wallet, could the patient's words be admitted under Rule 803(4) on the theory that having adequate money to pay for care is part of medical treatment for severe injuries?

■   ■   ■

Segment 12: statements for medical treatment or diagnosis

Patients' Incentives for Accurate Health Care Statements—Colvard. This case presents another view on applying the medical statements exception to statements identifying a wrongdoer. The *Colvard* court reconsiders its earlier reliance on *Renville.*

COLVARD v. COMMONWEALTH

309 S.W.3d 239 (Ky. 2010)

VENTERS, J.

Appellant, Fred Colvard, was convicted by a Jefferson Circuit Court jury of one count of first-degree sodomy, two counts of first-degree rape, one count of first-degree burglary, and of being a second-degree persistent felony offender (PFO II). For these crimes, Appellant was sentenced to life imprisonment. Appellant now appeals to this Court as a matter of right. Ky. Const. §110.

Among other things, Appellant argues on appeal that certain testimony from medical personnel was improperly admitted through the hearsay exception under KRE 803(4). . . .

On March 2, 2006, Appellant allegedly sexually assaulted two girls, D.J. and D.Y., in their bedroom. D.J. and D.Y. were six and seven years old, respectively, at the time of the events. Appellant knew the children because not only did he live in the same apartment complex as them, but just a few months before, he was engaged to marry their grandmother. . . . .

When D.J. and D.Y. told their mother that they had just been sexually assaulted by Appellant, she immediately reported it to the authorities. The girls were then medically examined and interviewed by several medical professionals. The medical examinations turned up no DNA or other physical evidence connecting Appellant to the crime. However, the examinations were not inconsistent with the girls' allegation of sexual assault.

A jury trial was conducted and the jury found Appellant guilty of two counts of first-degree rape, one count of first-degree sodomy, and one count of first-degree burglary. . . . .

Jennifer Polk, Dr. Cole Condra, and Dr. Lisa Pfitzer are medical personnel who testified at trial that the victims identified Colvard as the perpetrator of the crimes committed against them. Because the testimony of each of these medical personnel implicates KRE 803(4) and the ongoing viability of the extension of that rule created in *Edwards v. Commonwealth,* 833 S.W.2d 842 (Ky. 1992), we consider Colvard's allegations of error as it relates to these medical witnesses together.

A. Jennifer Polk. Polk, an EMT who responded to the emergency call, was called by the Commonwealth to testify about the events of March 2, 2006. Over Colvard's objection, Polk was allowed to testify that the first child to whom she spoke said that "Fred from number seven [Appellant]... stuck his 'dick' in her."...

B. Dr. Condra. Appellant argues that Dr. Condra improperly gave testimony about statements D.J. made to the triage nurse at the hospital. Dr. Condra testified from notes made by the nurse on March 2, 2006, when the children were initially admitted into the hospital for evaluation. Among other things, Dr. Condra testified that D.J. told the triage nurse that Appellant sexually abused her....

C. Dr. Pfitzer. ... Dr. Pfitzer testified that she saw the children as a result of sexual abuse allegations made against "a neighbor" named "Fred" and that the allegations involved vaginal and anal penetration. Dr. Pfitzer also testified that D.J.'s mother reported that D.J. told her that "Fred was f***ing us."

[T]he testimony of these medical personnel implicates KRE 803(4), the medical diagnosis exception to the hearsay rule.... However, the general rule is that the identity of the perpetrator is not relevant to treatment or diagnosis.

However, in *Edwards,* this Court recognized an exception to the identification rule in cases where a family or household member is the perpetrator of sexual abuse against a minor of that household. In *Edwards,* we relied on *United States v. Renville,* 779 F.2d 430 (8th Cir. 1985), as persuasive authority for the family, or household member, exception to the general rule. Therein, we acknowledged:

> In *Renville,* the Court made this exception to the general rule that physicians rarely have reason to rely on statements of identity because of two important aspects involved in the case: (1) the physician was not merely diagnosing and treating the child/patient for physical injuries but psychological injuries as well, and (2) the abuser was a *family,* household member.
>
> The physician in that case testified that he was treating the child for her emotional and physical trauma. He also said that the identity of the abuser was extremely important to him in helping the child work through her problems. The identity was also particularly important if the abuser lived with the child, because the abuse would likely continue as long as the child remained in the household with the abuser.
>
> . . .
>
> Upon reconsideration of the plain language of KRE 803(4) and its underlying purpose, we have come to the view that the identification exception we adopted in *Edwards* [was] based upon an ill-advised and unsound extension of a traditional exception to the hearsay rule....

We know that an ill or injured person seeking to be healed or cured is ordinarily highly motivated to give truthful information to the physician or medical provider treating that illness or injury. The essential element that lends credence to the statement is that the patient, the "declarant" in hearsay law parlance, believes that the doctor must have that information to render effective treatment. The doctor's actual need, use, or reliance upon the declarant's information is less meaningful than the declarant's belief that the information is essential to effective treatment. The declarant's belief makes the out-of-court statement inherently trustworthy.

As expressed in *Willingham v. Crooke*, 412 F.3d 553, 561–562 (4th Cir. 2005):

> Rule 803(4) of the Federal Rules of Evidence [the federal counterpart of KRE 803(4)] allows the admission of hearsay statements "made for purposes of medical diagnosis or treatment and describing... present symptoms, pain, or sensations, or the inception or general character of the cause or external source thereof insofar as reasonably pertinent to diagnosis or treatment." This exception to the hearsay rule is premised on the notion that a declarant seeking treatment "has a selfish motive to be truthful" because "the effectiveness of medical treatment depends upon the accuracy of the information provided." 5 Jack B. Weinstein & Margaret A. Berger, *Weinstein's Federal Evidence* §803.06[1] (Joseph M. McLaughlin, ed., 2d ed. 2004); *see Morgan v. Foretich*, 846 F.2d 941, 949 (4th Cir. 1988). Admissibility of a statement pursuant to Rule 803(4) is governed by a two-part test: "(1) the declarant's motive in making the statement must be consistent with the purposes of promoting treatment; and, (2) the content of the statement must be such as is reasonably relied on by a physician in treatment or diagnosis." *Morgan*, 846 F.2d at 949.

(internal quotation marks & footnote omitted).

Hence, we except from the hearsay rule statements made by a patient to medical personnel for the purpose of medical treatment or diagnosis. In the *Edwards* case, we enlarged that exception to include statements of a patient identifying the perpetrator of sexual abuse when that perpetrator is a member of the family or household of the victim, not because the utterance of the statement was motivated by the victim's desire for effective treatment, but because the medical professional might use that information to protect the victim from further abuse by a member of the victims family or household. In so doing, we failed to recognize that it is the patient's desire for treatment, not the doctor's duty to treat, that gives credibility to the patient's out-of-court statement. There is no inherent trustworthiness to be found in a hearsay statement identifying the perpetrator when that statement did not arise from the patient's desire for effective medical treatment....

The *Renville* rule has also received... scholarly criticism. *State v. Jones*, 625 So. 2d 821, 825 (Fla. 1993), for example, sets forth learned authorities which criticize the rule and the reasonings therefor:

> However, the trend to adopt a *Renville*-type analysis also has been harshly criticized. As the Maryland Court of Special Appeals noted in a scholarly opinion:
> > In stretching outward their list of a physician's responsibilities and in pushing forward with their definition of "medical treatment and diagnosis," the expansionists have left behind, abandoned and forgotten, the state of mind of the declarant.... Physical self-survival dictates revealing even embarrassing truth to avoid the risk of the wrong medicine or the needless operation. Presupposing a declarant conscious

of the probable consequences of his assertions, the imperative to speak truthfully is not nearly so strong when the anticipated result is a social disposition. The temptation to influence the result may, indeed, run in quite the opposite direction. Truthful answers as to the identity of its abuser may well wrench a child from the reassuring presence of its mother or father or both. It is highly unlikely that there operates in an infant declarant a compelling desire to bring about such a result.

Moreover, many commentators have expressed concern that in the course of laudable efforts to combat child abuse, prosecutors, courts, and others have occasionally overreached. See, e.g., Michael H. Graham, *The Confrontation Clause, the Hearsay Rule, and Child Sexual Abuse Prosecutions: The State of the Relationship,* 72 Minn. L. Rev. 523, 529 N. 26 (1988) ("The successful prosecution of child sexual abuse cases should not be permitted to distort the hearsay exception for statements for medical diagnosis or treatment. Almost anything is relevant to the diagnosis or treatment of psychological well being, and far too many untrustworthy statements are relevant to preventing repetition of the abuse."); Robert P. Mosteller, *Child Sexual Abuse and Statements for the Purpose of Medical Diagnosis or Treatment,* 67 N.C. L. Rev. 257, 258 (1989) (Applications of medical diagnosis or treatment exception in child abuse cases "have tended to expose the thinness of the justification for extending the exception to statements made without any view toward treatment.")

As reflected by the foregoing discussion, we have carefully considered the *Renville* rule, its merits and demerits, and now conclude that our adoption of the rule was an unwise departure from the traditional hearsay rule that has served our system of justice well for many generations. One cannot reasonably conclude that the statements identifying the perpetrator, such as those at issue in this case, were made by young children "for the purpose of medical treatment or diagnosis." The *Renville* rule is inconsistent with the plain language of KRE 803(4), and, as the above authorities explain, the reliability of a child's identification of the perpetrator of the abuse to a medical professional contains the same tangible risks of unreliability generally inherent in all hearsay testimony. Accordingly, *Edwards...* and other cases applying the exception to the hearsay rule are overruled. ...

Based upon the above discussion, we conclude that it was error for the trial court to have permitted Polk, Dr. Condra, and Dr. Pfitzer to testify under the *Renville* construction of the medical treatment exception to the hearsay rule. Moreover, because the testimony served to bolster the children's testimony and the Commonwealth's theory of the case, the testimony was highly prejudicial. ...

For the reasons stated herein, the judgment of the Jefferson Circuit Court is reversed, and the cause is remanded for additional proceedings consistent with this opinion.

NOTES TO COLVARD v. COMMONWEALTH

1. *Alternative Hearsay Treatment for Statements by Vulnerable Individuals.* In a child abuse prosecution, if the medical statements exception is not applicable, other exceptions may cover the victim's statements, depending on circumstances. In particular, the excited utterance exception may be available.

2. *Child Hearsay Statutes.* Most states have adopted statutes that facilitate the admission of statements by victims in child abuse cases. The following statute is an example.

Colorado Child Hearsay Statute
Colorado Revised Statutes 13-25-129

Statements of child victim of unlawful sexual offense against a child or of child abuse — hearsay exception

(1) An out-of-court statement made by a child, as child is defined under the statutes which are the subject of the action, describing any act of sexual contact, intrusion, or penetration, . . . performed with, by, on, or in the presence of the child declarant, not otherwise admissible by a statute or court rule which provides an exception to the objection of hearsay, is admissible in evidence in any criminal, delinquency, or civil proceedings in which a child is a victim of an unlawful sexual offense, . . . or in which a child is the subject of a proceeding alleging that a child is neglected or dependent, . . . and an out-of-court statement by a child, as child is defined under the statutes which are the subject of the action, describing any act of child abuse . . . to which the child declarant was subjected or which the child declarant witnessed, not otherwise admissible by a statute or court rule which provides an exception to the objection of hearsay, is admissible in evidence in any criminal, delinquency, or civil proceedings in which a child is a victim of child abuse or the subject of a proceeding alleging that a child is neglected or dependent . . . if:

(a) The court finds in a hearing conducted outside the presence of the jury that the time, content, and circumstances of the statement provide sufficient safeguards of reliability; and

(b) The child either:

(I) Testifies at the proceedings; or

(II) Is unavailable as a witness and there is corroborative evidence of the act which is the subject of the statement.

(2) If a statement is admitted pursuant to this section, the court shall instruct the jury in the final written instructions that during the proceeding the jury heard evidence repeating a child's out-of-court statement and that it is for the jury to determine the weight and credit to be given the statement and that, in making the determination, the jury shall consider the age and maturity of the child, the nature of the statement, the circumstances under which the statement was made, and any other relevant factor.

(3) The proponent of the statement shall give the adverse party reasonable notice of his intention to offer the statement and the particulars of the statement.

How would this statute apply to statements like the ones in *Colvard?*

3. *Special Hearsay Treatment for the Elderly?* Consider the following statute (based on one formerly in effect in Florida — *see* Conner v. State, 748 So. 2d 950 (Fla. 2000)). How might the reasons that support the enactment of child hearsay statutes apply or not apply to it? What significant differences are there between this statute and the Colorado child hearsay statute?

> Unless the source of information or the method or circumstances by which the statement is reported indicates a lack of trustworthiness, an out-of-court statement made by an elderly person or disabled adult, describing any act of abuse or neglect, any act of exploitation, the offense of battery or aggravated battery or assault or aggravated assault or sexual battery, or any other violent act on the declarant elderly person or disabled adult, not otherwise admissible, is admissible in evidence in any civil or criminal proceeding if:
>
> 1. The court finds in a hearing conducted outside the presence of the jury that the time, content, and circumstances of the statement provide sufficient safeguards of reliability. In making its determination, the court may consider the mental and physical age and maturity of the elderly person or disabled adult, the nature and duration of the abuse or offense, the relationship of the victim to the offender, the reliability of the assertion, the reliability of the elderly person or disabled adult, and any other factor deemed appropriate; and
> 2. The elderly person or disabled adult either:
>   a. Testifies; or
>   b. Is unavailable as a witness, provided that there is corroborative evidence of the abuse or offense.

E   SUMMARY

For statements that are marked by spontaneity or the personal nature of the statement's topic, hearsay exceptions may be applicable. These exceptions may be used regardless of the availability of the declarant.

Present Sense Impression. The present sense impression exception covers statements that describe or explain something, if the declarant makes the statement while observing that event or condition or immediately after observing it. The rationale for this exception is that when a person describes something while seeing it or right after seeing it, the likelihood that bad memory has impaired the accuracy of the statement is very low. Also, the risk of intentional falsehood may sometimes be decreased in this situation. Contemporaneous narration may not give the speaker enough time to formulate a lie. Also, some present sense impressions are probably made in the presence of additional individuals who also perceive the event that the speaker is describing. This is another factor that could cut down on intentional falsehoods. These policy ideas are applied in *Fischer* (to deny application of the exception).

Excited Utterance. The excited utterance exception comes into play when the declarant has experienced a startling event or condition. Anything the declarant says that relates to the startling event or condition is covered by the excited utterance exception, so long as the declarant makes the statement while still under the stress of the excitement brought about by the event or condition. *Pressey, Flores,* and *Graure* concern important details of this exception, such as the need to link a declarant's excitement to the event the declarant describes, the degree of excitement needed for the exception's application, and whether ability to respond to questions contradicts a finding that the speaker was under stress.

Statement of Then-Existing Mental, Emotional, or Physical Condition. This exception covers statements a declarant makes about the declarant's own mental, emotional, or physical condition. The rationale for this exception is that perception and memory flaws are rare when the topic of a statement is how the speaker feels at the time the speaker is speaking.

This exception covers a statement about speaker's beliefs, to prove that the speaker has those beliefs. It does not cover statements about a speaker's beliefs to prove that the substance of those beliefs actually is true. This requires careful analysis of relevance in cases where the mental state exception is invoked, as in *Stoll*. For example, in murder cases statements by a victim may implicate the defendant. If proving that the victim was afraid of the defendant has relevance, a statement about fear would be admissible to prove that the victim had that feeling. But a statement such as "I think the defendant may harm me some day" is not likely to be relevant. And because a statement of that kind has strong prejudicial power, courts will ordinarily be careful in considering whether or not the hearsay rule blocks the statement's admission.

When people are respondents in survey research, their statements are covered by this exception. As seen in *Schering*, use of the exception for statements made to survey investigators requires a careful distinction between proving that a speaker has a belief and using proof of that belief as proof of the fact the speaker believes. The exception covers only use of the statement to prove the existence of a belief.

The mental state of having a plan is covered by this exception. So, a statement that the declarant has an intention to do something will be admissible to prove that the declarant possessed that intention. It will also be admissible as proof (although not conclusive proof) that the declarant actually did do a planned act. Controversially, some courts extend the coverage of this exception to statements in which the declarant states a plan to do something with another person, as in

James. To prove that the other person did the described act, the rationale that supports the mental state exception needs to be stretched very far (a result that the *Camm* court rejected).

Statements for Purposes of Medical Diagnosis or Treatment. When people speak to health care providers, they ordinarily have a very strong incentive to speak the truth. For that reason, this exception withdraws the hearsay prohibition from these medical diagnosis or treatment statements, as in *Hansen.* The declarant can be the patient or someone who is communicating on behalf of the patient. The most significant issues with this exception involve defining what subjects are legitimately related to medical treatment or diagnosis. Specifically, victims of injury may describe the source of their injury. If knowing the source is significant for treatment, then the naming of the source would properly be covered by this exception. Some courts have held that in assault cases, the name of the assailant is significant for medical care, defining medical care broadly to encompass protecting the victim from further injury. *Oldman* and *Colvard* present the range of views on this issue.

CHAPTER 9

Hearsay Exceptions: Recorded Statements

A. Introduction
B. Recorded Recollection (and Present Recollection Refreshed)
C. Records of Regularly Conducted Activity (Business Records)
D. Public Records
E. Summary

A INTRODUCTION

Topic Overview

What does it take for the common law or rules drafters to relax the prohibition against hearsay? It's clear from the hearsay exceptions covered in the previous chapter that there needs to be some reason to think that a kind of statement will be free to some extent from one or more of the shortcomings usually associated with hearsay. Since admitting hearsay for substantive purposes comes at a cost — the opponent has no chance to examine the declarant's perception, memory, narration, or sincerity — the exceptions may describe situations where those losses will be relatively small. But hearsay exceptions are not based on a belief that *all* of these problems will be minimal for particular kinds of statements. And they are not based on an idea that every statement that fits the terms of an exception will present only minimal risks. The exceptions have developed for statements that minimize some of the risks some of the time. This pattern is seen in the exceptions covered in this chapter.

This chapter's exceptions involve statements that are recorded ("recorded" can mean preserved in any form, such as writing or electronic data storage). For "recorded recollection" statements — personal records of information a person knows at the time he or she makes the record — memory problems will be slight. And the details of this exception require that the declarant be present in court, so issues of ambiguous language can be probed. For records that businesses and governments maintain, reliability may be expected because those enterprises rely on them and might find errors if mistakes were made in creating them. Also, the people within the enterprise who make the records have an incentive to be accurate, in order to continue their employment.

Evidence law recognizes a style of testimony known as "present recollection refreshed." This is sometimes confused with the admission of out-of-court statements under the recorded recollection exception. In this chapter, present recollection refreshed and some related doctrines are covered in the context of the recorded recollection exception.

Chapter Organization

This chapter examines three important hearsay exceptions enumerated in FRE 803 in the order in which they appear in that rule. The introduction to Rule 803 states that its exceptions may be used regardless of the availability of the declarant. This is true for the exceptions that apply to records of regularly conducted activities and public records. It is not entirely true for the exception for recorded recollection, since the declarant of that type of statement must be present at trial in order for the exception to be used.

- Recorded recollection (a statement about something the declarant once knew, accurately recorded while the knowledge was fresh, if the declarant no longer remembers it well enough to give full testimony).
  - □ Present recollection refreshed is a nonhearsay technique for stimulating a witness's memory. Because it has some overlaps with the recorded recollection hearsay exception, it's presented here.
- Records of a regularly conducted activity (sometimes called "business records," these records are made by people with knowledge in the regular course of the operations of the activity).
- Public records (these are an analogue to the records of a regularly conducted activity, for public records; some limitations are part of this exception to reflect the role of government in criminal trials).

B RECORDED RECOLLECTION (AND PRESENT RECOLLECTION REFRESHED)

1. Recorded Recollection

Sometimes a person who knows something makes a record of it. The exception for "recorded recollection" covers these records when the proponent of the record (which is an out-of-court statement) shows three things: first, that the declarant made or adopted it about something when the declarant knew it, second, that the record was an accurate recording of what the declarant knew, and third, that the declarant no longer recalls it well enough to testify about it. The exception is codified among the exceptions that may be used regardless of the availability of the declarant, but the rule applies only to statements made or adopted by someone who is a witness at the trial (and is therefore "available").

Rule 803. Exceptions to the Rule Against Hearsay — Regardless of Whether the Declarant Is Available as a Witness

The following are not excluded by the rule against hearsay, regardless of whether the declarant is available as a witness:

. . .

(5) *Recorded Recollection.* A record that:

(A) is on a matter the witness once knew about but now cannot recall well enough to testify fully and accurately;

(B) was made or adopted by the witness when the matter was fresh in the witness's memory; and

(C) accurately reflects the witness's knowledge.

If admitted, the record may be read into evidence but may be received as an exhibit only if offered by an adverse party.

. . .

■   ■   ■

Is a Videotaped Interrogation a Recorded Recollection? — Jones. The court describes the prosecution's compliance with the requirements of Rule 803(5) as lackluster. To take advantage of the recorded recollection exception, the proponent must establish specified elements. The trial court was apparently generous to the proponent in deciding that the elements were satisfied, and it might be said that the standard of review used by the Eleventh Circuit was generous to the trial court. It may be that unspoken assumptions about the truthfulness of the witness affected both courts in their applications of the rule.

UNITED STATES v. JONES

601 F.3d 1247 (11th Cir. 2010)

MARTIN, J.

Deon Monroe Jones ("Mr. Jones") appeals his convictions and sentences. . . .

In the early morning of June 1, 2004, David Buskirk ("Mr. Buskirk") was shot with a .38 caliber bullet outside his home in Savannah, Georgia. Detective Robert

Von Lowenfeldt ("Detective Von Lowenfeldt") led the investigation into Mr. Buskirk's shooting, and, over the course of his investigation, identified Mr. Jones as a prime suspect....

On June 23, 2004, Detective Von Lowenfeldt conducted a videotaped interview of sixteen-year-old Kelly Bigham ("Ms. Bigham"). In their conversation, Ms. Bigham informed the detective that she had sold a .38 revolver to Mr. Jones. She described how she and Mr. Jones drove to a nice area of town, where Mr. Jones shot a white man. After the interview, Ms. Bigham directed Detective Von Lowenfeldt to the street on which Mr. Buskirk lived, and she demonstrated how Mr. Jones got out of the car, fired at the man, and got back into the car....

[Mr. Jones was charged with a variety of offenses connected to the shooting, and was convicted.] At sentencing, the district court merged Count One with Two and Count Three with Four. Evaluating the 18 U.S.C. §3553(a) factors, the district court noted the seriousness of the offense, Mr. Jones's "sinister nature" and criminal history, the need to provide just punishment for the offense, his lack of remorse, and the great risk he posed to society. Having stated these reasons, the district court varied from the Sentencing Guidelines' applicable sentencing range of 130 to 162 months and sentenced Mr. Jones to 200 months imprisonment. Mr. Jones timely appealed....

... Mr. Jones argues that the district court erred when it admitted a videotaped interview of Ms. Bigham as past recollection recorded. Prior to trial, the government informed Mr. Jones and the district court of its intent to offer the video as evidence, pursuant to Rules 804(b)(1) (former testimony) and 804(b)(3) (statement against interest) of the Federal Rules of Evidence.

At trial, the district court permitted the jury to view the full video of Ms. Bigham's custodial interrogation as part of the government's case-in-chief. The district court admitted the video not under the government's original theory that the hearsay exceptions for unavailable declarants applied, but rather as past recollection recorded, pursuant to Rule 803(5). During deliberation, the jury sent the court a note, requesting a second viewing of the video. Over Mr. Jones's objection, the district court allowed the video to be played for the jury a second time.

Mr. Jones argues that by admitting the video as past recollection recorded, the district court erred in its application of the Federal Rules of Evidence....

Federal Rule of Evidence 803(5) sets out the predicates for admission of past recollections recorded. For one thing, the Rule requires the proponent to demonstrate that the witness-declarant's memory has faded so that he is no longer able "to testify fully and accurately."

At trial [in late 2007], the government elicited a handful of responses from Ms. Bigham that indicated she lacked "clear and distinct recollection in [her] response to the question[s]" regarding the subject matter of her interview with Detective Von Lowenfeldt. *NLRB v. Hudson Pulp & Paper Corp.*, 273 F.2d 660, 665 (5th Cir. 1960). She could not remember that she sold Mr. Jones the .38 revolver "in the end of April of 2004." She also could not recall Mr. Jones making any statements about the gun. After showing Ms. Bigham the video outside the presence of the jury, the government inquired into whether Ms. Bigham's memory had been refreshed. In response to a question about whether she remembered "more about the things you did with Deon Jones than you did before we watched the video," she responded, "I remember what was just said." When pressed further, she responded that she could recall "some" of the relevant events. Before the court showed Ms. Bigham the video, Mr. Jones conceded to its use for the purpose of refreshing recollection. Based on this record, we do not find that the district court clearly abused its discretion in concluding that Ms. Bigham lacked sufficient memory to testify to the subject matter of the video.

Rule 803(5) also requires that the witness verify the contents of the past statement. "The witness must be able now to assert that the record accurately represented his knowledge and recollection at the time. The usual phrase requires the witness to affirm that he knew it to be true at the time."

Here, Ms. Bigham arguably verified the contents of the video through her testimony at trial. First, she testified that it was easier to remember the events described in the videotape at the time of the interrogation than on the date of the trial. When the government asked whether the things said were true and accurate to the best of her knowledge, Ms. Bigham responded, "If that was what was said then, that's what I remember then, what was just in the video." Further, Ms. Bigham also testified that she repeated the contents of her interview in juvenile court, and she agreed that "the things that [she] [said] to the detective at that time [were] true and accurate to the best of [her] knowledge." Finally, as to whether the video was an accurate record of her statements to Detective Von Lowenfeldt, Ms. Bigham acknowledged, at a minimum, "that's me talking" on the video.

The government's efforts to demonstrate compliance with Rule 803(5)'s prerequisites were lackluster, at best. However, we review application of the Federal Rules of Evidence for abuse of discretion. "In applying this standard, we will affirm a district court's evidentiary ruling unless the district court has made a clear error of judgment or has applied an incorrect legal standard." *Conroy v. Abraham Chevrolet-Tampa, Inc.*, 375 F.3d 1228, 1232 (11th Cir. 2004) We conclude that on the facts presented here, admission of the video as past recollection recorded was not a clear error of judgment on the part of the district judge.

[Convictions on some counts were affirmed and convictions on other accounts were reversed.]

NOTES TO UNITED STATES v. JONES

1. *Affirmance at Trial.* The court states that in order for a recorded recollection to be admitted, the declarant must assert that the record accurately represented his knowledge and recollection at the time. Rule 803(5) does not explicitly impose this requirement, but many courts do so. If a witness testifies that he or she does not know if a record actually does reflect what he or she knew when he or she made the record, many courts would hold that Rule 803(5) would not allow use of the recorded recollection.

2. *Accuracy of Recording.* Because the record in this case was a video, the likelihood of inaccurate recording is much less than in situations where a declarant speaks and someone, such as an investigator, makes notes. In addition to the reduction of possible inaccuracy, the video makes it difficult for a declarant to claim that the "record" fails to convey what he or she knew at the time the record was made.

QUESTION 9-1. Sarah Surgeon was charged with 28 counts of health care fraud arising from her medical office billing practices. Before trial, Surgeon prepared notes that she intended to use at trial to assist her while testifying. As Surgeon prepared to take the stand for her direct testimony, her attorney presented the notes to the government, and explained that Surgeon would refer to them while testifying. The government objected to her use of them. How should the trial court rule?

■ ■ ■

Records Created by More Than One Person — Taylor. This opinion, from one of the states that has not adopted rules parallel to the Federal Rules of Evidence, highlights the concern some courts apply to the detailed requirements for the recorded recollection exception.

STATE v. TAYLOR

598 N.E.2d 693 (N.Y. 1992)

HANCOCK, Jr., J.

Defendant was tried before a jury on one indictment and convicted of separate crimes involving two different victims: i.e., rape and sodomy of Clara B. and attempted rape and sexual abuse of Elizabeth G. In defendant's appeal of the Appellate Division's affirmance of his convictions, we address . . . whether the trial court erred in admitting — under the hearsay exception for a past recollection recorded — a police officer's phone message with a license plate number allegedly belonging to defendant's car. . . . For the reasons stated hereinafter, we hold that admission of the phone message as a past recollection recorded was improper. . . .

On February 24, 1987, a man forced his way into Clara B.'s apartment in the Bronx and raped and sodomized her at gunpoint. On March 2, 1987, a man sexually abused and attempted to rape Elizabeth G. at knifepoint in her apartment, also in the Bronx. Detective Thomas Connelly arrested defendant on March 13, and each victim identified him as her attacker at the police station in separate lineups. A Grand Jury subsequently indicted defendant for these and other crimes.

At trial each complainant again identified defendant and the prosecution adduced other evidence linking him to the scene of each crime. Defendant testified and denied any involvement in either crime. After defendant was found guilty but before sentencing he pleaded guilty to other rapes and attempted rape charges with the understanding that the sentences for these charges would be concurrent with and no longer than the sentences to be imposed for the trial convictions.

The Appellate Division affirmed defendant's convictions, holding that the phone message with the license plate number was admissible as a past recollection recorded because the observer and transcriber each testified "regarding the accuracy of their respective roles." . . . A Judge of this Court granted defendant leave to appeal.

Faye Lopez — the daughter of one of Ms. B.'s neighbors — testified that on March 10, 1987, approximately two weeks after Ms. B. was attacked, she was at her mother's apartment. She and her mother saw and heard a man knocking at Ms. B.'s door. The man was asking for "Cindy", the fake name which Clara B. testified she had given the rapist. When no one answered, the man left and got into a car. Ms. Lopez testified that she saw the license plate number, wrote it down "with [her] mother", and then called the police and gave them the number. Her mother, however, testified that it was she who got the plate number while her daughter was calling the police. Ms. Lopez tried unsuccessfully to reach Detective Connelly at the Bronx precinct. She talked instead to Detective Valentin who took the message, including the number of the license plate. The next day, Detective Connelly received the phone message containing the license number "567-TBP". A computer check revealed that a vehicle with a similar plate number "5967-TBP" was registered to defendant. Two days later — linked to the crime scene as the owner of the car — defendant was arrested.

A year later when the case came to trial, Ms. Lopez had lost the piece of paper on which she had written the license plate information. She could not remember it. She testified, however, that to the best of her recollection, the license plate number she gave to Detective Valentin was the one she saw on the car. Detective Valentin testified that he recognized the message to be in his handwriting, but that he could not recall taking the message or writing it down. He stated, however, that it was his habit to take messages as accurately as he possibly could. Based on the combined testimony of Detective Valentin and Ms. Lopez, the trial court, over objection, admitted the memorandum containing the license information under the hearsay exception for a past recollection recorded. . . .

We address . . . the question of the admissibility of the phone message containing the license plate number of defendant's car under the doctrine of past recollection recorded. Under this doctrine — which has a long history of acceptance in New York — a memorandum made of a fact known or an event observed in the past of which the witness lacks sufficient present recollection may be received in evidence as a supplement to the witness's oral testimony. The requirements for admission of a memorandum of a past recollection are generally stated to be that the witness observed the matter recorded, the recollection was fairly fresh when recorded or adopted, the witness can presently testify that the record correctly represented his knowledge and recollection when made, and the witness lacks sufficient present recollection of the recorded information.

The rationale for the doctrine is that the recorded information is essential to further the truth-seeking function of the trial proceeding and that when the conditions for admission have been met, there is sufficient assurance of the accuracy of the recordation and its trustworthiness. As we stated in *Halsey v Sinsebaugh* (15 NY 485): "To exclude such a record, when shown to have been honestly made, would be to reject the best and frequently the only means of arriving at truth." When such a memorandum is admitted, it is not independent evidence of the facts contained therein, but is supplementary to the testimony of the witness. The witness' testimony and the writing's contents are to be taken together and treated in combination as if the witness had testified to the contents of the writing based on present knowledge. Admission of the memorandum is a matter for the exercise of the court's discretion in determining whether the proponent has made a sufficient showing of the accuracy of the recording and its reliability.

The above requirements are most easily met where the witness testifies about a memorandum in which the witness personally recorded information based on his or her observations. Memoranda have also been admitted based on the observations of one person which were transcribed by another where from their combined testimony the court could be satisfied that what was written was an accurate transcription of what was observed or then known. There are limits, however, to the admission of such jointly established records of past recollection. In *Peck v Valentine* (94 NY 569), the Court held that admission of a "memorandum not in its nature original evidence of the facts recorded, and *not verified* by the party who made the original and knew the facts, would open the door to mistake, uncertainty and fraud."

In this case, the requirement that the memorandum must have been made or adopted while the recollection was fairly fresh, poses no obstacle to admission. The testimony of Ms. Lopez and Detective Valentin established that her transmission of the message containing the plate number and his receipt and recording of it all occurred immediately after Ms. Lopez's observation. Nor does the requirement of the witness' inability to recall the memorandum's contents present a problem. Ms. Lopez testified that she could not remember the number. Thus, the critical question remaining is whether the proof adequately assured that the phone message transcribed by Detective Valentin correctly represented the information observed and transmitted by Ms. Lopez.

Reduced to its essentials, the testimony of Ms. Lopez and Detective Valentin comes to this. Ms. Lopez stated she transmitted to Detective Valentin what she believed to be her accurate observation of the license plate number. Detective Valentin had no recollection of that transmission or of having made the memorandum. Thus, he could not state that what he wrote down was what he had been told. He could state only that because the memorandum was in his handwriting he must have taken the message and that it was his habit to take messages as accurately as possible. There is no proof that Detective Valentin read back the plate number to Ms. Lopez for her verification or that she had any knowledge that he had received and recorded her message accurately.

Thus, there can be no more than supposition on the critical question of whether what was observed and sent corresponded with what was heard by the recorder and written down. Without *some verification* by the observer-sender that what was recorded accurately reflected her observations when made, the record of those observations should not have been received against defendant as substantive incriminating evidence. Contrary to the dissent, this is not an "unnecessarily rigid formula for admissibility." It is rather the application of the basic and sensible rule of evidence that before a record of observations made in the past by someone other than the observer can be received in evidence, there should be some showing that the recording was accurately made. We conclude that these facts taken together show that the memorandum lacked sufficient assurances of accuracy and trustworthiness. It was error, therefore, to admit the license plate number as a memorandum of Ms. Lopez's past recollection. . . .

Accordingly, the Appellate Division order should be reversed and the case remitted to Supreme Court for further proceedings in accordance with this opinion.

[Dissenting opinion omitted.]

NOTES TO STATE v. TAYLOR

1. *Common Law vs. Codified Law.* New York State has not adopted a code of evidence. Its requirement of "verification" may serve the same purpose as Rule 803(5)'s "accurately reflects the witness's knowledge" language.

2. *Mental Gymnastics.* For the recorded recollection exception to apply, a witness must have *forgotten* the substance of what his or her memorandum shows but must *remember* details about how he or she created it. In many instances, truthful testimony that describes the making of a record may be difficult to obtain, since making a record may be commonplace and therefore not particularly memorable.

■ ■ ■

How Bad Must the Declarant's Memory Be at Trial? — **Dazey.** This opinion offers another context for considering the requirement in Rule 803(5) that the declarant must be unable to testify fully and accurately about the subject covered in the record he or she had made. Also, a record that satisfies Rule 803(5) will be read to jurors, but the proponent is barred from introducing the record as an exhibit. The court considers the significance of that provision.

UNITED STATES v. DAZEY

403 F.3d 1147 (10th Cir. 2005)

McCONNELL, J.

Robert Gerald Craft, Roy Mathew, Dennis Dean Dazey, and Diane Lenore Griffith were convicted of conspiracy to commit wire fraud. The defendants were also convicted of a number of substantive counts of wire fraud, securities fraud, and/or money laundering. On appeal, each defendant challenges the sufficiency of evidence for conviction, as well as raising several procedural and evidentiary issues. . . .

The four defendants were implicated in a fraudulent investment company called Wealth-Mart. Wealth-Mart styled itself as an investment fund with a highly lucrative international "bank debenture" investment program that traded in secret overseas markets in accordance with Christian and humanitarian investment principles. . . . Not a penny of the funds investors entrusted to Wealth-Mart's care was invested overseas, and most of it was never returned. . . .

Wealth-Mart put on three investment seminars at a luxurious ranch in Colorado. The defendants chartered airplanes and buses to transport themselves and investors to the seminars. Dr. Craft presided at the seminars, made speeches, mingled with the potential investors, and in general attempted to create the aura of an elite gathering of international financial insiders. Dr. Craft presented Mr. Dazey to the audience, under the alias "Wooly West," as Wealth-Mart's international trader. Wooly West addressed the seminar participants on international financial topics and touted his financial connections. . . .

Inevitably, investors began complaining when hefty checks representing the results of Wooly West's savvy trading failed to arrive in the mail. . . .

Wealth-Mart's activities eventually came to the attention of the authorities . . . . After a three-week trial, the jury convicted [the defendants]. . . .

At trial, the government offered testimony from several people who attended Wealth-Mart's Colorado seminars. Some of these investors took notes. The government offered, as exhibits, the seminar notes of three such investors. The district court admitted the notes over defense counsel's objection. On appeal, Appellants Craft and Dazey contend that the district court erred in admitting the notes. We review a district court's evidentiary rulings for abuse of discretion, and our review of decisions to admit evidence over hearsay objections is especially deferential.

Appellants claim the notes are inadmissible hearsay. Hearsay is an out-of-court statement offered to prove the truth of the matter asserted. The government argues that the notes are not hearsay, because they were offered to prove only the content of the seminar speeches and not the truth of what was said. This is true in part, but the notes are still hearsay insofar as the notes are in effect an out-of-court assertion that Dr. Craft and Mr. Dazey said certain things at the seminars. The notes were offered to prove the truth of that assertion, and therefore they fit the definition of hearsay.

Federal Rule of Evidence 803(5) provides an exception to the hearsay rule for a witness' recorded recollection. . . .

When defense counsel objected to admission of the notes, the district court asked[,] "Why is this not a past recollection recorded?" Defense counsel responded, "We don't think the foundation has been established for that." The district judge himself then asked the witness, "Did you make these notes contemporaneously with the events that occurred?" The witness responded affirmatively, and the judge permitted the witness to continue testifying about the notes and also admitted the notes as an exhibit.

On appeal, the appellants acknowledge that the judge and the government laid a partial foundation for admission of the notes under Rule 803(5), but they claim that the witnesses' inability to testify fully and accurately from memory was never established. The government concedes that neither the prosecutor nor the court specifically asked the witnesses whether their memory was sufficient to testify fully without the notes, but the government contends that the witnesses' lack of memory is "[i]mplicit in the context of their testimony."

Unfortunately, it is difficult to discern from the record exactly how much the witnesses remembered about what they heard at the seminars. The government's examination generally takes the form of a running commentary on the notes. The prosecutor points to a particular phrase in the notes and asks what it means, and the witness explains the notation and elaborates on what Dr. Craft or Mr. Dazey said on that topic. It is clear that the witnesses retained some independent memory of what was said, and none of the witnesses actually stated that he or she could not recollect any particular aspect of the seminars. In similar situations, courts have held that it is error for the district court to admit evidence under Rule 803(5) without a showing that the witness lacks sufficient memory to testify fully.

Even if the district court erred in admitting the notes without a proper foundation, such an error does not require reversal of the appellants' convictions if it is harmless. A decision to admit evidence is harmless unless a substantial right of a party is affected. Fed. R. Evid. 103(a). An error affecting a substantial right is one which had a "substantial influence" on the trial's outcome or which creates a "grave doubt" as to whether it had such effect.

We are convinced that the district court's decision to admit the notes did not have a substantial influence on the outcome of the trial. In so concluding, we acknowledge that the content of the pitch delivered by Mr. Dazey and Dr. Craft at the seminars was an important part of the government's case against Mr. Dazey . . . . The notes supported this claim, because the witnesses jotted down some of the dizzying stream of financial jargon that Mr. Dazey presented to the audience. Nevertheless, there was a sufficient supply of properly admitted evidence about what Mr. Dazey said at the seminars to make the additional evidence contained in the notes immaterial. . . .

Appellants also point out that the district court should not have admitted the notes into evidence as exhibits. Under Rule 803(5), even if the proper foundation had been laid to admit the notes as a past recollection recorded, the notes should have been read into evidence and not received as an exhibit. The only rationale discernible to us for requiring that notes be read aloud into the record rather than received into evidence is so that the "past recollection recorded" evidence is treated on par with the oral testimony presented at trial. Otherwise, the jury might, in its deliberations, tend to privilege the notes that it gets to take into the jury room over the oral testimony that might already be half-forgotten. In this case, the likelihood that the jury overemphasized the notes, simply because they were admitted as exhibits rather than read aloud at trial, was vanishingly small. The notes themselves, without the accompanying testimony of the note-takers, are fairly inscrutable. Some of the handwriting is illegible, and even where the words are discernible, they mostly form sentence fragments whose meaning is less than obvious. Moreover, this is not a case where the jury was sitting in the jury room with nothing but the erroneously admitted notes in front of them. During the trial, the court admitted hundreds of documents as exhibits. The government's exhibits fill twenty three-ring binders. It is difficult to imagine that the jury, awash as it was in a flood of documentary exhibits, improperly focused on a few pages of difficult to discern notes at the expense of the rest of the evidence presented at trial. . . .

For the foregoing reasons, all Appellants' convictions . . . are affirmed.

NOTES TO UNITED STATES v. DAZEY

1. *Identifying Hearsay.* The government's argument that the notes were not hearsay "because they were offered to prove only the content of the seminar speeches and not the truth of what was said" offers an opportunity to review the issue of identifying hearsay statements. In this instance, it can be helpful to identify each statement and associate a declarant with each statement. Suppose a note said the words "humanitarian principles." The court treated such a statement as the equivalent of "Wooly West said the company uses humanitarian principles." Analyzed this way, one declarant is Wooly West saying "humanitarian principles." Another declarant is a seminar audience member saying "Wooly West said the words 'humanitarian principles.'" West's words do not need to be true to be relevant. And they are an opponent's statement, which would be another way to legitimize their admission. But the seminar audience member's words fit into the case only if they are used as a basis for concluding that the event they describe really did happen (that West really did say the identified words). That makes the audience member's words hearsay.

2. *Recorded Recollection — Read to the Jury, Not Given to the Jury.* When the recorded recollection exception applies, the record will be read (or played) to the jury. This is different from giving the record to the jury as an exhibit. As the court explains, the record is intended to substitute for the memory the declarant might have had if the trial had occurred closer to the time that the declarant made his or her record. Since the record is conceptually the equivalent of live

testimony, the rule allows it to be given to the jury only if the opponent of the testimony chooses that option. Otherwise, the jury perceives the record more or less the way it would have perceived testimony in court from the declarant had the declarant's memory been better.

QUESTION 9-2. Pedestrian was hit by a car while he was trying to cross a street in the summer of 2007. Three years later, Pedestrian wrote an e-mail to a friend describing how the injury happened. Pedestrian has sued the driver of the car that hit Pedestrian. In 2012, Pedestrian testifies at the trial and has forgotten some important details about the accident. If Pedestrian seeks to introduce the e-mail as part of Pedestrian's effort to prove how the accident occurred, which aspect of the requirements for using the recorded recollection exception is likely to be the most difficult for Pedestrian to satisfy?

A. Pedestrian doesn't remember enough about the accident to testify fully and accurately.

B. Pedestrian once knew the details of the accident.

C. Pedestrian's memory of the accident was fresh when Pedestrian wrote the e-mail.

D. Pedestrian is present at trial and available for cross-examination.

2. Refreshing Present Recollection

When a witness seems not to have a full memory of the topic of his or her testimony, the questioner is allowed to show something to the witness to stimulate the witness's memory. The witness might be shown anything (for example, a document the witness had once written, a document someone else had written, a picture, or an object). Because the witness is testifying from current memory, and because whatever the witness looked at is not introduced as evidence, hearsay problems are absent.

FRE 612 requires that when a party uses a document to refresh a witness's recollection, the adverse party is allowed to see the document, and may be allowed to introduce parts of it as evidence. This can facilitate cross-examination. It can also allow the court to determine whether the witness really has experienced a refreshing of memory or whether, on the other hand, the witness is just quoting the otherwise inadmissible document.

Rule 612. Writing Used to Refresh a Witness's Memory

(a) **Scope.** This rule gives an adverse party certain options when a witness uses a writing to refresh memory:

(1) while testifying; or

(2) before testifying, if the court decides that justice requires the party to have those options.

(b) **Adverse Party's Options; Deleting Unrelated Matter.** Unless 18 U.S.C. §3500 provides otherwise in a criminal case, an adverse party is entitled to have the writing produced at the hearing, to inspect it, to cross-examine the witness about it, and to introduce in evidence any portion that relates to the witness's testimony. If the producing party claims that the writing includes unrelated matter, the court must examine the writing in camera, delete any unrelated portion, and order that the rest be delivered to the adverse party. Any portion deleted over objection must be preserved for the record.

(c) **Failure to Produce or Deliver the Writing.** If a writing is not produced or is not delivered as ordered, the court may issue any appropriate order. But if the prosecution does not comply in a criminal case, the court must strike the witness's testimony or — if justice so requires — declare a mistrial.

■ ■ ■

Refreshing Memory Without Hearsay Statements — Germain. The practice of attempting to refresh a witness's recollection is illustrated in *Germain*. The concepts of Rule 612 are not discussed because the document in question was available to both parties and because the trial court prohibited the effort to refresh the witness's memory. The opinion quotes some prominent authorities on the details of how "present recollection revived" or "present memory refreshed" differs from the concept of "past recollection recorded."

GERMAIN v. STATE

769 A.2d 931 (Md. 2001)

CATHELL, J.

Petitioner, Jean Bernard Germain, was convicted by a jury in the Circuit Court for Anne Arundel County of attempted second degree murder, first degree assault, reckless endangerment, and carrying a weapon with intent to injure. Petitioner appealed to the Court of Special Appeals. In an unreported opinion filed June 12, 2000, the Court of Special Appeals affirmed his conviction. Petitioner presents one question to this Court, for which we granted certiorari:

> Did the Court of Special Appeals err in not reversing Petitioner's conviction on the ground that the trial court precluded Petitioner from using a key State witness's Pre-Sentence Investigation (PSI) for any reason including to refresh the witness's recollection, on the ground that PSIs are confidential and privileged? . . .

Petitioner and Mr. John Campbell (Campbell), two individuals incarcerated in the State of Maryland, shared cell 205 in D building, Bravo Wing of the Maryland House of Corrections Annex located in Jessup, Maryland. . . .

At approximately 11:25 P.M. on August 1, 1998, after being cell-mates for approximately two weeks, a fight broke out between the two inmates. The issue at petitioner's trial for this assault was not whether the assault occurred but whether petitioner was acting in self-defense. . . .

[D]efense counsel's theory of the case was that petitioner was acting in self-defense by warding off an unwanted, forced sexual assault upon him by Campbell, who petitioner believed to be a homosexual, a convicted sex offender, and a HIV positive individual. On cross-examination, Campbell denied being a homosexual and stated that if he made any sexual advances toward petitioner while they were cell-mates, that he did not remember making them. He further testified on cross-examination that, although he remembered pleading guilty to two second degree sex offenses and he was serving a forty-year sentence, he did not recall the specifics of the charges. . . . On recross-examination, defense counsel again tried to elicit the specifics behind Campbell's convictions for two second degree and one third degree sexual offense. . . .

Q: Mr. Campbell, the victim of your sexual offense was an 11-year-old boy; is that correct?

. . .

A: I don't remember nothing.

Q: You don't recall pleading guilty to sodomizing an 11-year-old boy.

A: I remember pleading guilty to second degree sex offense. That's all I remember.

. . .

Shortly thereafter, the following discussion took place at a bench conference:

Mr. Paone: Your Honor, defense counsel has just shown me a copy of what appears to be a PSI for the [witness]. I can only assume he is going to cross-examine him about the contents of that PSI. I am going to object before we get into it.

The Court: What —

Mr. Gunning: Initially I am going to use it to refresh his recollection.

Mr. Paone: A PSI is confidential.

The Court: How —

Mr. Gunning: That doesn't mean I can't use it to refresh his recollection.

The Court: This report is for official Court use only. It is saying here it is confidential and protected. Where did you get this?

Mr. Gunning: Through subpoena....

The Court: I think it is confidential. It says this report — public inspection —

. . . The record indicates that at this point the bench conference ended.

The question before us is simply whether the trial court erred in refusing to permit petitioner's defense counsel to use Campbell's PSI to attempt to refresh his recollection on the sole basis that PSIs are confidential. It is helpful to our analysis to review the nature of PSIs and their role in the criminal justice process. A "pre-sentence investigation" is an "[i]nvestigation of the relevant background of a convicted offender, usually conducted by a probation officer attached to a court, designed to act as a sentencing guide for the sentencing judge."

Because a PSI is a tool generally utilized by a sentencing judge, the circumstances, which present themselves in the case *sub judice,* are unusual....

In the posture of the case at bar, when the trial court denied defendant the use of the PSI, it was not proposed that it be admitted into evidence. It was merely to be used for recollection refreshing purposes. Generally . . . there are no limitations on the nature of the relevant documents that may be used in the refreshing of a witness's recollection. Such documents are not being admitted into evidence.

. . . When faced with defense counsel's assertion that he was entitled to use the generally confidential PSI to refresh Campbell's recollection, the trial court repeatedly relied solely on the document's status as "confidential" and "for official Court use only." The trial court failed to recognize that the confidentiality requirement . . . would not apply to showing it to the subject for whom it was prepared, a person who had the right to see it. Additionally, the trial court failed to perceive any difference in respect to its use in official court proceedings to refresh a witness's recollection, and making it available for "public inspection." In other words, the trial court erroneously concluded that it had no authority to allow the disclosure of the contents of the PSI because such information was always confidential. That is simply incorrect. The trial court's failure to permit defendant to utilize the PSI to refresh a witness's recollection was reversible error.

Whether a witness's recollection may be refreshed by a writing or by other means depends on the particular facts and circumstances of the individual case. As we said in *Oken v. State,* 327 Md. 628, 612 A.2d 258 (1992), *cert. denied,* 507 U.S. 931, 113 S. Ct. 1312, 122 L. Ed. 2d 700 (1993):

> While it is true that in many circumstances, an examining attorney must first establish that a witness's memory is exhausted before refreshing the recollection of that witness, *see* 6 L. McLain, *Maryland Evidence* §612.1 (and cases cited therein), laying such a foundation is not an absolute prerequisite. Instead, the question of whether a witness's recollection may be refreshed by a writing or some other object depends upon the particular circumstances.... C. McCormick, *Evidence* §9 at 33-34 (4th ed. 1992) ("The witness may believe that she remembers completely but on looking at the memorandum she would be caused to recall additional facts. As the

Chinese proverb has it, 'The palest ink is clearer than the best memory.' On the other hand, there is the ever-present danger that a suggestible witness may think that she remembers a fact because she reads it. It seems eminently a matter for discretion, rather than rule.") . . .

Id. at 672-74, 612 A.2d at 279-80 (alterations in original);.

We also recognize the large amount of freedom that an attorney has when choosing an object with which a witness's recollection can be refreshed. It is important to note the distinction between the admission of a memorandum into evidence as past recorded recollection and a memorandum or other item used only to revive present recollection. The limitations and concerns present for past recollection recorded have little bearing on present recollection revived. As the Court of Special Appeals has said:

> When dealing with an instance of Past Recollection Recorded, the reason for the rigorous standards of admissibility is quite clear. Those standards exist to test the competence of the report or document in question. Since the piece of paper itself, in effect, speaks to the jury, the piece of paper must pass muster in terms of its evidentiary competence.
>
> Not so with Present Recollection Revived! By marked contrast to Past Recollection Recorded, no such testimonial competence is demanded of a mere stimulus to present recollection, for the stimulus itself is never evidence. Notwithstanding the surface similarity between the two phenomena, the difference between them could not be more basic. *It is the difference between evidence and non-evidence.* Of such mere stimuli or memory-prods, McCormick says, at 18, "[T]he cardinal rule is that they are not evidence, but only aids in the giving of evidence." When we are dealing with an instance of Present Recollection Revived, the only source of evidence is the testimony of the witness himself. The stimulus may have jogged the witness's dormant memory, but the stimulus itself is not received in evidence. . . .

Judge Learned Hand noted in *United States v. Rappy,* 157 F.2d 964 (2d Cir. 1946), that:

> When a party uses an earlier statement of his own witness to refresh the witness' memory, the only evidence recognized as such is the testimony so refreshed; and the party may not put the statement in evidence, although the other side may do so, and apparently the jury may call for it, sua sponte. . . . Anything may in fact revive a memory: a song, a scent, a photograph, and allusion, even a past statement known to be false.

Id. at 967 (footnote omitted). . . .

We hold that the Court of Special Appeals erred in not reversing petitioner's conviction on the ground that the trial court should not have precluded petitioner from using a key State witness's PSI to refresh that witness's recollection. The confidentiality of a PSI is primarily directed to protect against "public inspection." It is not absolute. Accordingly, we reverse the decision of the Court of Special Appeals and remand with instructions to reverse the judgment of the Circuit Court for Anne Arundel County and remand the case to that court for a new trial.

NOTES TO GERMAIN v. STATE

1. *Extent of Disclosure of a Writing Used to Refresh Memory.* The confidentiality of the presentence investigation report would have been preserved if the trial court had allowed the defendant's lawyer to follow typical procedures for refreshing recollection. Only the defendant, the defendant's lawyer, and the prosecution would have been required to read the document. Most importantly, the contents of the document would not have been read to the jury.

2. *False Claim of Lack of Memory.* If Campbell had been shown the presentence investigation report, Campbell might have read it and then stated that it did not improve his memory of his past crime. In that circumstance, the defense would have had to consider other methods of proving Campbell's past conduct.

3. *Distinguishing Refreshed Recollection from Recorded Recollection.* The document the defendant attempted to use to refresh Campbell's recollection was not made or adopted by Campbell. That fact has no bearing on use of the document as a means of refreshing recollection, but it prevents application of the recorded recollection exception.

■   ■   ■

Refreshing Memory with a Witness's Own Statements — Rush. Two witnesses are involved in this case, Moore and Lockett. In terms of present recollection refreshed, the examination of one of these witnesses was done properly, and the examination of the other involved a significant error. The court also analyzes the application of the past recollection recorded exception to the testimony by the second of these witnesses.

RUSH v. ILLINOIS-CENTRAL RAILROAD CO.

399 F.3d 705 (6th Cir. 2005)

ECONOMUS, J.

This appeal arises from a diversity action brought by the plaintiff-appellant, Annette Rush, following her nine-year-old son's fall from a railcar owned and operated by the defendant-appellee, Illinois Central Railroad Company ("CN-IC"). The plaintiff-appellant [argues on appeal that] the district court erroneously admitted into evidence at trial the prior statements of two witnesses. . . .

Nine-years-old Johnathan Rush ("Rush") and several friends — Quan Reed ("Reed") (age 11), Doyle Lockett ("Lockett") (age 10), Darrell Moore ("D. Moore") (age 9), and Justin Moore ("Moore") (age 8), . . . began playing near a CN-IC train. At some point during these activities, Rush fell under the train and sustained injuries that ultimately required a below-the-knee amputation of his left leg.

Within several hours of the accident, Tom Martin ("Martin"), a Risk Manager and Railroad Police Officer for CN-IC, interviewed Lockett, D. Moore and Moore as to the earlier day's events. Each interviewee purportedly informed Martin that Rush fell while attempting to jump onto a moving train. Martin audio-recorded these statements and later transcribed the interviews (hereinafter the "interview transcript").

Annette Rush, as the natural mother and next of kin of Johnathan Rush, filed a diversity action against CN-IC in the United States District Court for the Western District of Tennessee alleging common law negligence. . . .

The plaintiff-appellant contends that the district court erroneously permitted defense counsel to cross-examine Lockett and Moore with the interview transcripts. CN-IC counters that it utilized the interview transcripts to refresh the witnesses' memory pursuant to Rule 612 of the Federal Rules of Evidence.

Rule 612 of the Federal Rules of Evidence authorizes a party to refresh a witness's memory with a writing so long as the "adverse party is entitled to have the writing produced at the hearing, to inspect it, to cross-examine the witness thereon, and to introduce in evidence those portions which relate to the testimony of the witness." Fed. R. Evid. 612. The propriety of permitting a witness to refresh his memory from a writing prepared by another largely lies within the sound discretion of the trial court.

> Proper foundation requires that the witness's recollection to be exhausted, and that the time, place and person to whom the statement was given be identified. When the court is satisfied that the memorandum on its face reflects the witness's statement or one the witness acknowledges, and in his discretion the court is further satisfied that it may be of help in refreshing the person's memory, the witness should be allowed to refer to the document.

United States v. Shoupe, 548 F.2d 636, 641 (6th Cir. 1977). Upon establishing the proper foundation, "counsel will typically offer the witness the writing to inspect, and will show a copy of the writing to the opposing parties." 4 Jack B. Weinstein & Margaret A. Berger, Weinstein's Federal Evidence §612.03[4][a][i] (Joseph M. McLaughlin ed., 2d ed. 2004). "The best practice is for the trial court to have the witness silently read the writing and then to state whether the writing has refreshed his or her recollection." *Id.*

The plaintiff-appellant's assertion that defense counsel improperly utilized the interview transcript to refresh Moore's recollection warrants little attention. Moore repeatedly testified that he did not remember meeting with Martin following the accident. Having exhausted Moore's memory during cross-examination, defense counsel presented Moore with the interview transcript. After Moore silently read the writing, the district court posed the following questions:[12]

---

12. See Fed. R. Evid. 614(b) ("The court may interrogate witnesses, whether called by itself or by a party.").

Q: Now Justin, having — having looked at it, having read it, do you recall now whether or not you had a conversation and made any statements to anyone about this accident?

A: No, ma'am, because —

Q: Okay. Now you — that — that statement that he just handed you doesn't refresh your recollection about whether or not you gave an interview to Sergeant Halfacre and Mr. Martin.

A: No, ma'am, because back then we didn't call him Johnathan, I didn't know his name back then, his real name.

Defense counsel promptly concluded the cross-examination.

No evidentiary error occurred during the attempt to refresh Moore's memory. Defense counsel established a proper foundation by repeatedly inquiring whether Moore recalled meeting with Martin following the accident. *See Shoupe,* 548 F.2d at 641-42 (finding that counsel established a proper foundation under Rule 612 where counsel "properly used leading questions to establish the time, place and person to whom [the witness] had allegedly made his prior, unsworn statements"). The subsequent procedures employed by the district court were consistent with the well-established mandates of Rule 612. Indeed, the district court intervened in the cross-examination to ensure that the inadmissible contents of the writing were not presented to the jury. Furthermore, defense counsel terminated the cross-examination when it appeared that the transcript failed to refresh Moore's memory. We therefore find no evidentiary error arising from the attempt to refresh Moore's memory with the interview transcript.

We reach a different conclusion regarding the attempts to refresh Lockett's memory of the post-accident interview. As with the cross-examination of Moore, defense counsel attempted to exhaust Lockett's memory by posing leading questions regarding the time, date and place of the post-accident interview. Lockett repeatedly responded that he did not remember meeting with Martin. Defense counsel, however, did not attempt to immediately refresh Lockett's memory of the meeting with the interview transcript. Instead, defense counsel posed the following question:

> Okay. Do you remember that you told, in the presence of your aunt, that you told Mr. Martin and Sergeant Halfacre of the Memphis Police Department that you were playing around the train yard when Johnathan got hurt, and that you saw Johnathan running alongside the train to get on, do you remember telling them that?

While we have authorized the use of leading questions to establish a witness's lack of memory as to a particular event, we have cautioned that the trial court may abuse its discretion when otherwise inadmissible evidence is introduced to the jury through the guise of refreshing a witness's recollection. *See Shoupe,* 548 F.2d at 641 ("[W]e find no precedent sanctioning the recitation in the presence of the jury of extended unsworn remarks. . . . "). Rule 103(c) of the Federal Rules of Evidence provides that a jury trial shall be conducted "to prevent inadmissible evidence from being suggested to the jury by any means, such as . . . asking questions in the hearing of the jury." FED. R. EVID. 103(c). The Advisory Committee's Note to Rule 103(c) indicates that the rule "proceeds on the supposition that a ruling which excludes evidence in a jury case is likely to be a pointless procedure if the excluded evidence nevertheless comes to the attention of the jury." FED. R. EVID. 103(c), advisory committee notes. Defense counsel's question demonstrated that he failed to understand the impropriety of attempting to refresh Lockett's recollection by incorporating into his question the otherwise inadmissible contents of the writing — i.e, that "Johnathan was running alongside the train to get on."

Lockett's subsequent testimony exacerbated the potential evidentiary error caused by defense counsel's improper question. After silently reading the interview transcript, Lockett testified that his memory was refreshed and that the writing accurately reflected his prior statements. He then read aloud from the interview transcript whereby the jury heard his prior statement that "Johnathan was running alongside the train trying to get on." However, Rule 612 requires a witness whose memory has been refreshed to testify from his present recollection, rather than to merely restate the contents of the writing.

It is the witness's present refreshed recollection — as opposed to the contents of the writing used to refresh memory — that is the substantive evidence of the matter at issue. While defense counsel ostensibly utilized the writing to refresh Lockett's present recollection of the interview, the query posed following Lockett's silent review of the writing targeted only whether the interview transcript accurately recounted Lockett's prior, out-of court statements. ("Is that correct what you said on the afternoon of this accident, November the 10th of 1996, is that correct?"). Remarkably, defense counsel did not enquire whether the interview transcript refreshed Lockett's recollection of the matter at issue; namely, the post-accident interview. Defense counsel instead instructed Lockett to read, in the presence of the jury, the prior, unsworn statements contained in the interview transcript. We thus reach the inescapable conclusion that defense counsel impermissibly utilized the "guise of refreshing recollect," *Shoupe,* 548 F.2d at 642, to place before the jury Lockett's prior, out-of-court statements regarding the manner in which Rush fell from the CN-IC train.

It follows that defense counsel's attempt to use Lockett's out of court statements as substantive evidence of the manner in which the accident occurred is governed by the rules of evidence addressing the use of hearsay. . . . CN-IC contends on appeal that Lockett's prior, out of court statements were admissible pursuant to the recorded recollection hearsay exception of Rule 803(5).

CN-IC misplaces its reliance on the recollection recorded exception to the hearsay rule. Rule 803(5) allows a document to be read to the jury as a past recollection recorded if "(1) the witness once had knowledge about the facts in the document; (2) the witness now has insufficient memory to testify about the matters in the document; and (3) the document was recorded at a time when the matters were fresh in the witness's mind and the document correctly reflects the witness's knowledge of the matters." *United States v. Smith,* 197 F.3d 225, 231 (6th Cir. 1999). Under CN-IC's application of the recorded recollection exception, the interview transcript served to stand in the place of Lockett's "insufficient memory" of the accident. However, Lockett provided detailed and lengthy testimony at trial regarding the events prior to, during, and immediately following the accident. It therefore would be erroneous to conclude that Lockett had "insufficient memory to testify about the matters" in the interview transcript. . . . Accordingly, the past recollection recorded exception to the hearsay rule is wholly inapplicable to Lockett's prior statements regarding the accident. . . .

[The error was harmless, and] the judgment of the district court is affirmed.

NOTES TO RUSH v. ILLINOIS-CENTRAL RAILROAD CO.

1. *Leading Questions.* A leading question suggests its answer. For that reason, Rule 611 restricts their use.

Rule 611. Mode and Order of Examining Witnesses and Presenting Evidence

. . .

(c) **Leading Questions.** Leading questions should not be used on direct examination except as necessary to develop the witness's testimony. Ordinarily, the court should allow leading questions:

(1) on cross-examination; and

(2) when a party calls a hostile witness, an adverse party, or a witness identified with an adverse party.

The leading questions the court discusses were asked during cross-examination, but the court points out that a leading question can serve the purpose of conveying information to the jury. When the information may be something relatively inconsequential, such as the occurrence of an interview, that aspect of leading questions is not likely to bring inadmissible information to the jury's attention. But a leading question that quotes an out-of-court statement that would otherwise be excluded would have exactly that improper effect.

2. *Insufficient Memory about What?* To support introduction of a declarant's recorded recollection, the proponent must show that the declarant has a poor memory of the topic of the recorded recollection. That is different from a poor memory of the occasion of making the recorded recollection.

3. *A Witness's Out-of-Court Words: The Range of Uses, Risks, and Responses to Risks. Rush* considered the use of a witness's own out-of-court words for refreshing the witness's present recollection. This is a common kind of effort, although it raises identifiable risks. A treatise quoted in the *Germain* opinion stated that "a witness's recollection may be refreshed by a writing or some other object." When a lawyer attempts to refresh a witness's recollection by having him

or her look at an object or, as another example, smell some perfume, there are no hearsay problems because no out-of-court statement is involved. In contrast, most cases of present recollection refreshed involve having the witness look at a writing. And this use of out-of-court statements does require thinking about hearsay.

If a document is covered by a hearsay exception, it generally is admissible. If a document is within the recorded recollection exception, its information will be read to the jury. But when a party attempts to refresh a witness's recollection with a document that is outside the coverage of hearsay exceptions, the risk arises that the witness will be a conduit for that inadmissible hearsay. The witness may read the document, claim to have a refreshed memory, and then say out loud whatever the document said.

In *Rush*, the court required a detailed foundation. This does not make sense technically, since the out-of-court words ought not to be heard by the jury, and since even an object (for example, a rock) could have been used to stimulate memory. But some courts do require detailed foundations for the use of writings to stimulate memory. They may do this because there is some chance that a jury will eventually learn about the contents of the document, or because of confusion between recorded recollection, prior inconsistent statements for impeachment, and the use of documents to stimulate recall.

4. *Comparing Uses of a Witness's Past Statements.* A witness's past statements can have a variety of uses at trial. Some of these uses implicate hearsay issues and some do not.

To substitute for testimony. When a witness has insufficient memory to testify on a topic, some past statements may bring the witness's past knowledge into the trial for substantive use.

- *Recorded recollection.* A witness's out-of-court statement may be a record that satisfies the definition of the recorded recollection hearsay exception.

To supplement testimony. When a witness has testified on a topic, some past statements can be additional sources of information that the factfinder may rely on in reaching a verdict.

- *Prior inconsistent statement for substantive use.* A witness's out-of-court statement may be admissible as a prior inconsistent statement outside the definition of hearsay, if it satisfies the requirements of FRE 801(d)(1)(A). Recall that for substantive use of a witness's prior statement that is inconsistent with the witness's testimony, the earlier statement must have been made under oath at a proceeding.
- *Prior consistent statement for substantive use.* A witness's out-of-court statement may be admissible as a prior consistent statement outside the definition of hearsay, if it satisfies the requirements of FRE 801(d)(1)(B).

To scrutinize testimony. Some of a witness's prior statements may be used only for impeaching the witness, to scrutinize the believability of the witness's testimony. In this use, their contents are forbidden to be used as a basis for a finding of fact, but may be used by the factfinder to discredit a proposition that a witness's testimony has supported.

■ *Prior inconsistent statement for impeachment use.* When a witness has made a prior inconsistent statement that fails to satisfy the requirement of FRE 801(d)(1)(A) for substantive nonhearsay use, that statement can still be used at trial. Its use is limited to impeachment.

To stimulate testimony. One other use is available for a witness's past statements. They can be used to stimulate testimony through the present recollection refreshed procedure.

■ *Witness's recorded statement.* A witness's out-of-court statement that fails to satisfy the requirements of the recorded recollection exception can be shown to the witness, in an attempt to stimulate the witness's present recollection of something. (Using something different from a writing is another method of attempting to refresh present recollection. It does not involve the witness's past statements, but bearing this procedure in mind can help understand the use of statements for the same memory-refreshing purpose.)

The following charts show some important aspects of using a witness's past statement to *substitute for, supplement, scrutinize,* and *stimulate* testimony.

PAST STATEMENTS BY A WITNESS, TO SUBSTITUTE FOR, SUPPLEMENT, SCRUTINIZE, OR STIMULATE TESTIMONY

Function of Prior Statement by Witness	Does Witness testify about topic?	Technique for using past statement	Foundation for past statement	Can jury rely on Witness's testimony?	Can jury rely on Witness's past statement?
Substitute *Recorded Recollection—Rule 803(5)*	No. Witness does not remember topic.	Proponent or Witness reads document aloud.	See Rule 803(5).	No, since Witness has no memory of topic.	Yes.
Supplement *Prior Statement, Inconsistent or Consistent, Eligible for Substantive Use—Rule 801(d) (1)(A) and (B).*	Yes.	Proponent introduces past statement.	See Rule 801(d)(1)(A) or 801(d)(1)(B).	Yes.	Yes.
Scrutinize *Prior Inconsistent Statement NOT Eligible for Substantive Use.*	Yes.	Witness has opportunity to explain past statement.	See Rule 613(b).	Yes (if jury chooses to believe it).	No (jury may use it only to reject Witness's testimony).

Function of Prior Statement by Witness	Does Witness testify about topic?	Technique for using past statement	Foundation for past statement	Can jury rely on Witness's testimony?	Can jury rely on Witness's past statement?
Stimulate *Present Recollection Refreshed with Document.*	Yes, after Witness states that his or her memory has been refreshed.	Witness reads past statement silently.	Compliance with Rule 612. (*Rush* court required additional foundation, not specified in Rules.)	Yes.	No.

QUESTION 9-3. A large appliance store suffered severe fire damage, and Owner is currently on trial for arson, accused of starting the fire. One of the prosecution's witnesses has testified that late one night he saw Owner near the store shortly before the fire started and that he saw Owner carrying large cans of the type that can contain gasoline. When asked where he was standing when he saw Owner and where Owner was in relation to the store building, the prosecution witness said he could not remember where he and Owner were. The prosecution would like to show the witness a photograph of the store building and its surrounding parking lots, to refresh the witness's recollection. The photograph was taken on a sunny morning after the fire. Because the store was remodeled after the fire, the photograph does not depict the store exactly as it was prior to the fire. Should the trial judge allow the prosecution to show its witness this photograph?

GOOD TO REMEMBER

A party can use anything, such as a writing, a photograph, a song, or a scent, to attempt to refresh a witness's recollection. In the abstract, no foundation requirements should apply to the thing shown to the witness, but where the thing is a writing, courts can be more demanding.

C RECORDS OF REGULARLY CONDUCTED ACTIVITY (BUSINESS RECORDS)

The records that a business ordinarily keeps are likely to be accurate, because employees have an incentive to record true information (to stay employed), and businesses have an incentive to maintain information carefully (to stay in business). Also, errors in records may be discovered and corrected in some instances, particularly if a business uses the records in its relationships with customers or others with whom it conducts transactions.

The "business records" exception applies to records maintained by businesses or individuals so long as they are associated with a "regularly conducted activity."

Rule 803. Exceptions to the Rule Against Hearsay — Regardless of Whether the Declarant Is Available as a Witness

The following are not excluded by the rule against hearsay, regardless of whether the declarant is available as a witness:

. . .

(6) *Records of a Regularly Conducted Activity.* A record of an act, event, condition, opinion, or diagnosis if:

  (A) the record was made at or near the time by — or from information transmitted by — someone with knowledge;

  (B) the record was kept in the course of a regularly conducted activity of a business, organization, occupation, or calling, whether or not for profit;

  (C) making the record was a regular practice of that activity;

  (D) all these conditions are shown by the testimony of the custodian or another qualified witness, or by a certification that complies with Rule 902(11) or (12) or with a statute permitting certification; and

  (E) the opponent does not show that the source of information or the method or circumstances of preparation indicate a lack of trustworthiness.

■   ■   ■

Records of a Customer's Actions — Briscoe. A telephone company's records of what numbers are called from a particular phone represent a standard example of records that fit the definition of Rule 803(6). Consider how the facts of this case relate to the reasons that records businesses use in their ordinary work are usually covered by a hearsay exception.

UNITED STATES v. BRISCOE

896 F.2d 1476 (7th Cir. 1990)

COFFEY, J.

This is the consolidated appeal of fourteen individuals who, based on their involvement in a heroin importation and distribution conspiracy, were convicted of various offenses under the federal narcotics laws. On appeal, they raise a number of arguments challenging their convictions and/or sentences. We affirm.

This case arises out of an extensive heroin network centered in Chicago, Illinois. Between 1984 and 1986 this drug enterprise imported approximately three kilograms of heroin having an estimated street value of over one million dollars into the United States from Pakistan, India and Nigeria. . . .

Defendants Orija, Erinle, Duale and Smith challenge the admission of computerized telephone records under Fed. R. Evid. 803(6). The telephone records listed the telephone numbers, the names of the subscribers placing calls to, as well as the subscribers receiving calls from, the three telephone numbers that were the subjects of the DEA wiretap investigation, the date, time and length of the call. The defendants allege that the trial court abused its discretion in admitting the telephone records because the government failed to present sufficient foundational evidence to establish that the computer records were accurate compilations of the telephone call data associated with the three "wiretapped" telephones.

It is well established that computer data compilations are admissible as business records under Fed. R. Evid. 803(6) if a proper foundation as to the reliability of the records is established. A proper foundation is established if the government demonstrates that the business records, in this case, the computerized telephone records, "are kept in the course of regularly conducted business activity, and [that it] was the regular practice of that business activity to make records, as shown by the testimony of the custodian or other qualified witness." "Business records are reliable to the extent they are compiled consistently and conscientiously."

At trial, the government presented the testimony of Merny Miller, the keeper of the records at Illinois Bell Telephone Company. Miller testified that the telephone records proffered by the government were Automatic Message Accounting Interrogation sheets which are compilations of call data entered into a computer when an Illinois Bell subscriber places a telephone call prepared for billing purposes. According to Miller, it was the regular business practice of Illinois Bell to assemble and maintain the records of the subscriber's telephone calls.[13] Moreover, Miller also stated that the computer assembling the call data scanned itself for error every fifteen seconds. Finally, defense counsel were given an opportunity to, and did in fact, cross-examine Miller on all of the information concerning the telephone records presented at trial. In light of these facts, we are convinced that the government's foundation evidence established the reliability of Illinois Bell's computerized telephone records.

Despite the government's extensive foundation evidence, as well as the defendants' opportunity to cross-examine Miller, the defendants argue that the foundation for the computer records is deficient because the government failed to establish that the computers were tested for internal programming errors on a monthly basis as were the computers in *United States v. Weatherspoon*, 581 F.2d 595, 598 (7th Cir. 1978). Although the government did, in fact, present such evidence in *Weatherspoon*, that case in no way requires that such a showing be made in every case as a prerequisite to the admission of computer records. As long as

---

13. We note that the fact that the actual computer printouts presented at trial were prepared specifically for this case, thus not in the regular course of Illinois Bell's business, does not preclude their admission under Rule 803(6). It is sufficient that the data compiled in the printouts was entered into the computer contemporaneous with the placing of each telephone call and maintained in the regular course of business. *See United States v. Sanders*, 749 F.2d 195, 198 (5th Cir. 1984). As the Sixth Circuit aptly stated: "It would restrict the admissibility of computerized records too severely to hold that the computer product as well as the input upon which it is based, must be produced at or within a reasonable time after each act or transaction to which it relates." *United States v. Russo*, 480 F.2d 1228, 1240 (6th Cir. 1973), *cert. denied*, 414 U.S. 1157, 39 L. Ed. 2d 109, 94 S. Ct. 915 (1974).

the government provides sufficient facts to warrant a finding that the records are trustworthy and the opposing party is afforded an opportunity to inquire into the accuracy thereof and how the records were maintained and produced, a proper foundation has been established. From our review of the testimony, we are convinced that the government's foundation in this case complies with this standard and hold that the trial court's admission of the telephone records was not an abuse of discretion.

NOTES TO UNITED STATES v. BRISCOE

1. *Computers.* One of the main rationales for the business records exception is that workers have an incentive to be accurate at work in order to keep their jobs. This rationale does not apply to records a computer makes. However, another important rationale for the business records exception is the likelihood in most business settings that errors will be discovered in records when the business relies on those records to deal with its customers or take other actions. That rationale applies regardless of the involvement of human beings.

2. *Hearsay?* A court could plausibly reject the characterization of these records as hearsay, since there may not have been any human declarant. Certainly the human beings who used phones to call other phones were not intending to assert anything about the numbers they were calling. Nonetheless, the easy application of the business records exception is likely to tempt courts to avoid this analysis by calling the records hearsay and applying the exception.

■   ■   ■

Records to Create Evidence of Freedom from Liability — Lust. The "regular practice" element of Rule 803(6) is important in this case. The required finding that there is not a "lack of trustworthiness" might also have been a basis for the court's analysis.

LUST v. SEALY, INC.

383 F.3d 580 (7th Cir. 2004)

Posner, J.

Tracey Lust sued her employer, Sealy, the mattress manufacturer, for sex discrimination in violation of Title VII. A jury returned a verdict in her favor, awarding her $100,000 in compensatory damages and $1 million in punitive damages. Pursuant to 42 U.S.C. §1981a(b)(3)(D), which places a ceiling of $300,000 on the total damages that may be awarded in an employment discrimination case against the largest employers (a category that includes Sealy), the judge reduced the total damages award to $300,000, to which she added $1,500 in back pay (which is not within the statutory meaning of "damages," 42 U.S.C. §1981a(b)(2)).

Sealy attacks the judgment on a variety of grounds. . . .

Sealy . . . complains about the exclusion of three memos that [Al Boulden, one of Lust's supervisors,] wrote when Lust complained to him that she was being passed over for discriminatory reasons. In the memos he said that he hadn't promoted her because of deficiencies in her interpersonal skills and — inconsistently — that he was planning to promote her soon. A memo normally is hearsay, being offered to prove the truth of a statement made out of court; and unlike some other forms of hearsay, the argument for excluding it from evidence unless it falls within one of the exceptions to the hearsay rule is compelling. There is no more facile a method of creating favorable evidence than writing a self-exculpatory note. Such notes have no warrants of reliability and allowing them to be placed in evidence would operate merely as a subsidy to the forest-products industry.

Even when contemporaneous with the events narrated in them, they fall outside the spontaneity exceptions in Fed. R. Evid. 803(1)-(3). The rationale for these exceptions is that spontaneous utterances, especially in emotional circumstances, are unlikely to be fabricated, because fabrication requires an opportunity for conscious reflection. As with much of the folk psychology of evidence, it is difficult to take this rationale entirely seriously, since people are entirely capable of spontaneous lies in emotional circumstances. "Old and new studies agree that less than one second is required to fabricate a lie." Douglas D. McFarland, "Present Sense Impressions Cannot Live in the Past," 28 *Fla. St. U.L. Rev.* 907, 916 (2001). It is time the law began paying attention to such studies. But that is a story for another day, since in any event the rationale of the spontaneity exceptions is not engaged by this case. Boulden was hardly under emotional pressure when he was writing these memos, and their length, lucidity, and self-congratulatory tone all refute any inference of spontaneity.

Sealy argues that the memos were alternatively admissible as "records of regularly conducted activities." Fed. R. Evid. 803(6). They were business records in the literal sense, or perhaps *a* literal sense, of being documents created for a business purpose — namely to create evidence of nonliability! They were not the kind of business record to which the business-records exception to the hearsay rule refers, as is apparent from the requirement that it be "the regular practice of that business activity to make" the record. Because a business depends on the accuracy of its recordkeeping, its records, although of course not sworn, are likely to be at least reasonably accurate, or at least not contrived for the purpose of making the business look better if it is sued. Boulden's memos were not created as a part of the regular recordkeeping processes of the Sealy mattress company. Those processes include the making of personnel records, but Sealy does not contend that memos that Boulden makes of conversations with employees become part of the employee's personnel record. Their only purpose was to create evidence for use in Lust's anticipated lawsuit, and that purpose disqualifies them from admission as business records. . . .

To summarize, the judgment is affirmed except with respect to the award of punitive damages, as to which Sealy is entitled to a new trial unless the plaintiff accepts a remittitur of the excess of those damages over $150,000 [since punitive damages set at the ceiling amount would fail to reflect post-misconduct remedial efforts and thus would eliminate incentives for employers to make such efforts].

NOTES TO LUST v. SEALY, INC.

1. *Accident Reports.* If an enterprise has the routine practice of collecting reports about accidents, how should the business records exception apply? Is it likely that these reports are meant "to create evidence of nonliability"? In a case where a customer of a fast-food restaurant allegedly slipped on grease in the restaurant's parking lot, the Eighth Circuit held that an accident report prepared by the restaurant's employees was outside the coverage of the business records exception. This reflects a traditional skepticism about the truthfulness of accident reports:

> In addition, the incident report was inadmissible as a business record under Fed. R. Evid. 803(6) because it had been prepared in anticipation of litigation. [T]he incident report lacks reliability or trustworthiness because it was not made in the ordinary course of business but instead with the knowledge that the incident could result in litigation. Here, the incident report shows on its face that it was prepared in anticipation of litigation and not in the ordinary course of Hardee's usual restaurant business operations. The directions on the incident report form instructed the person completing the form to "get COMPLETE information," "phone report within 30 minutes of incident, if serious," and "forward written report same day." Other directions on the form noted that "this form is to be used for reporting all types of incidents — Premises or Product Liability, Fire, Theft and Property Damage" and specifically instructed the person completing the form to distribute the white copy "to your local claims office," the pink copy to the "Risk Management Dept.," and the yellow copy to the "Area Director of Operations."

Scheerer v. Hardee's Food Systems, Inc., 92 F.3d 72 (8th Cir. 1996). The statement that accident reports are outside the course of normal operations requires a very limited view of the normal operations of large enterprises. But the implication that accident reports may be biased could well be legitimate.

QUESTION 9-4. From 2002 to 2011, Sam Seller maintained business diaries in which he made handwritten entries related to two companies he owned. The diaries included contact log pages with preprinted spaces for writing notes about phone conversations. During 2008 and 2009, Seller kept notes on four conversations with Bob Buyer regarding false documents Buyer asked Seller to provide. The false documents would assert that Seller's products had been obtained in any ways that conformed with federal statutes. Seller made notes only about "highlights" of conversations and about topics he considered important.

In a criminal trial, Buyer is being prosecuted for knowingly obtaining products that had been produced in violation of certain federal statutes. The prosecution seeks to introduce Seller's business diaries as proof that Buyer asked for false documents from Seller. The prosecution seeks to support admission of the diaries with the business records exception. Buyer argues that the business records exception should not apply, because (1) the diaries show only infrequent entries, not regular entries, and (2) the diaries refer to illegal conduct that cannot be treated as part of the ordinary course of business. How should the trial court rule?

■   ■   ■

Information from Declarants Outside the Business — Blechman. Many business records include information from multiple sources. In the simplest cases, all who contribute to the record are employees of the enterprise. When a stranger or volunteer is involved, the analysis must reflect that fact.

UNITED STATES v. BLECHMAN
657 F.3d 1052 (10th Cir. 2011)

EBEL, J.

In January 2009, Defendant-Appellant Robert Andrew Blechman and a codefendant, Itsik ("Issac") Yass, were tried together in the District of Kansas on charges of mail fraud, aggravated identity theft, and conspiracy to commit mail fraud and aggravated identity theft. Evidence introduced at trial showed that Yass operated a business that he used to temporarily halt home foreclosures by "attaching" foreclosure properties to fraudulent bankruptcy cases in order to take advantage of the Bankruptcy Code's automatic stay provision. Several different pieces of evidence connected Blechman to Yass's scheme, including e-mails sent from "rablechman@aol.com" to Yass. . . . After a two-week trial, the jury found Blechman and Yass guilty of all of the counts charged against them. . . .

Early in the trial, the Government sought to introduce an AOL account record, Exhibit 1–BBB, through Patricia Johnson, an investigator with AOL. The purpose of the exhibit was to "show[ ] that an individual using the screen name 'Rablechman' who listed a name and address of 'Robert Blechman, 10736 Jefferson Blvd., Culver City, CA 90230' established an account with AOL." (Aple. Br. . . . stating that the purpose of the exhibit was "to link the email address 'rablechman@aol.com' to Blechman"). Exhibit 1–BBB consisted of three pages. The first page showed that someone using the screen name "rablechman" logged on to AOL on December 5, 2008, from a Cox Communications IP address. The second page indicated that the screen name "rablechman" was associated with a free AOL account. This page also featured a description of free AOL accounts, which read, in part, "Registration information is recorded but not verified. Fictitious names and addresses are common." The third page contained registration information for the account corresponding to the screen name "rablechman." This page showed that the account was created on May 20, 1998, and that the account was registered to Robert Blechman in Culver City, California.

Johnson testified that Exhibit 1–BBB was an AOL record kept in the regular course of business, made at or near the time of the information recorded, and made by a person with knowledge of AOL's business. She also testified that AOL regularly records the activity reflected in Exhibit 1–BBB and creates reports of that activity. When questioned by defense counsel, however, Johnson admitted that AOL did not verify who originally input the "subscriber information" contained on the third page of the exhibit and that it could have been "anybody in the world who could access a computer." For this reason, Blechman objected to admission of Exhibit 1–BBB on hearsay grounds. But the district court overruled the objection, concluding that the exhibit fell within the business records exception to the hearsay rule set forth in Federal Rule of Evidence 803(6).

On appeal, Blechman argues that the district court erred in admitting Exhibit 1–BBB (the AOL record) . . . under Federal Rule of Evidence 803(6), the business records exception to the hearsay rule. He contends that because the critical, user-identifying information in all of these records was input by a third party over the Internet and was not verified by AOL . . . the exhibits contained inadmissible double hearsay and should have been excluded. Further, he argues that he was harmed by admission of the exhibits because they constituted the primary evidence linking him to Yass's scheme. . . .

The Federal Rules of Evidence define "hearsay" as "a statement, other than one made by the declarant while testifying at the trial or hearing, offered in evidence to prove the truth of the matter asserted." Hearsay is generally inadmissible unless it falls within a specific exception to the hearsay rule.

In this case, it is undisputed that the AOL record [was] offered to prove the truth of the matters asserted in these documents—namely, that Blechman was the registered owner of the "rablechman@aol.com" e-mail address. . . . Accordingly, the records constitute hearsay.

Nevertheless, the district court admitted the records under the business records exception to the hearsay rule, which provides that certain records of regularly conducted business activity are admissible for their truth even though they contain hearsay. Fed. R. Evid. 803(6). To satisfy the business records exception, a record

> must (1) have been prepared in the normal course of business; (2) have been made at or near the time of the events recorded; (3) be based on the personal knowledge of the entrant or of a person who had a business duty to transmit the information to the entrant; and (4) indicate the sources, methods and circumstances by which the record was made were trustworthy.

United States v. Ary, 518 F.3d 775, 786 (10th Cir. 2008). Blechman argues that Exhibit 1–BBB [does] not meet these requirements because the records feature "double" or "layered" hearsay in the form of unverified user-input information.

"Double hearsay in the context of a business record exists when the record is prepared by an employee with information supplied by another person." If the person who provides the information is an outsider to the business who is not under a business duty to provide accurate information, then the reliability rationale that underlies the business records exception ordinarily does not apply. *See . . . United States v. Snyder,* 787 F.2d 1429, 1433–34 (10th Cir. 1986) ("The business records exception is based on a presumption of accuracy, accorded because the information is part of a regularly conducted activity, kept by those trained in the habits of precision, and customarily checked for correctness, and because of the accuracy demanded in the conduct of the nation's business. The reason underlying the business records exception fails, however, if any of the participants is outside the pattern of regularity of activity." (citation and internal quotation marks omitted)). Accordingly, the general rule is that "[a]ny information provided by . . . an outsider to the business preparing the record[ ] must itself fall within a hearsay exception to be admissible." Fed. R. Evid. 805 ("Hearsay included within hearsay is not excluded under the hearsay rule if each part of the combined statements conforms with an exception to the hearsay rule provided in these rules.").

This Court, however, has recognized one exception to the general rule: information provided by an outsider that is included in a business record may come in under the business records exception "[i]f the business entity has adequate verification or other assurance of accuracy of the information provided by the outside person." *United States v. McIntyre,* 997 F.2d 687, 700 (10th Cir. 1993); *see also United States v. Cestnik,* 36 F.3d 904, 908 (10th Cir. 1994). In the context of identity information provided by an outsider, we have identified "two ways to demonstrate this 'guarantee[ ] of trustworthiness': (1) proof that the business has a policy of verifying [the accuracy of information provided by someone outside the business]; or (2) proof that the business possesses 'a sufficient self-interest in the accuracy of the [record]' to justify an inference of trustworthiness." *Cestnik,* 36 F.3d at 908 (some alterations in original) (quoting *McIntyre,* 997 F.2d at 700).

Applying these principles, we conclude that the district court erred in admitting Exhibit 1–BBB. . . . It is undisputed that the crucial information in the AOL . . . records — specifically, the information concerning the identity of the user of the "rablechman" AOL account . . . — was provided by a third party over the Internet, not by an employee of AOL. . . . Thus, the Government was required to demonstrate the trustworthiness of the information in one of the two ways mentioned above. *See United States v. Samaniego,* 187 F.3d 1222, 1224 (10th Cir. 1999) ("The obligation of establishing the applicability of a hearsay exception for these records falls upon the government as the proponent of the evidence.").

But the record makes clear that [AOL did not make] a meaningful attempt to verify the identity of the person who submitted the information. . . . Patricia Johnson, the AOL investigator, admitted that AOL did not verify who input the "subscriber information" contained on the third page of Exhibit 1–BBB and that it could have been "anybody in the world who could access a computer." Moreover,

Exhibit 1–BBB states in no uncertain terms that AOL made no effort to verify the identity of the individual who registered the "rablechman" account: "Registration information is recorded but not verified. Fictitious names and addresses are common." (Gov't Ex. 1–BBB–AOL account information for "rablechman"). . . . Furthermore, nothing in the record suggests — and the Government does not argue — that . . . AOL . . . "had a sufficiently compelling self-interest in ensuring the accuracy of information filled out by [their] customers to justify an inference of reliability." *Cestnik,* 36 F.3d at 908. If anything, the record reveals that AOL [was] uninterested in the accuracy of the user-input information. For these reasons, the district court improperly admitted Exhibit 1–BBB . . . under the business records exception to the hearsay rule. . . .

In light of all of [other] properly admitted evidence linking Blechman to the "rablechman@aol.com" e-mail address, we conclude that the Government has met its burden of demonstrating that the district court's erroneous admission of Exhibit 1–BBB was harmless to Blechman. . . .

For the foregoing reasons, we affirm Blechman's convictions for mail fraud and conspiracy to commit mail fraud.

NOTES TO UNITED STATES v. BLECHMAN

1. *Rationale for the Exception.* If AOL did attempt to verify information from users, or if AOL's business required it to have accurate knowledge about those who use its e-mail services, the analysis would have been different because the underlying rationales for the exception would have applied.

2. *Johnson v. Lutz.* A classic case, Johnson v. Lutz, was described by the First Circuit in United States v. Vigneau, 187 F.3d 70 (1st Cir. 1999), in a case involving business records that contained information from an outsider:

> The difficulty is that despite its language, the business records exception does not embrace statements contained within a business record that were made by one who is not a part of the business if the embraced statements are offered for their truth. The classic case is Johnson v. Lutz, 253 N.Y. 124, 170 N.E. 517 (N.Y. 1930), which excluded an unredacted police report incorporating the statement of a bystander (even though the police officer recorded it in the regular course of business) because the informant was not part of that business. The Advisory Committee Notes to Rule 803(6) cite Johnson v. Lutz and make clear that the rule is intended to incorporate its holding.
>
> Johnson v. Lutz is not a technical formality but follows directly from the very rationale for the business records exception. When a clerk records the receipt of an order over the telephone, the regularity of the procedure, coupled with business incentives to keep accurate records, provide reasonable assurance that the record thus made reflects the clerk's original entry. Thus the business record, although an out-of-court statement and therefore hearsay, is admitted without calling the clerk to prove that the clerk received an order.
>
> But no such safeguards of regularity or business checks automatically assure the truth of a statement to the business by a stranger to it, such as that made by the bystander to the police officer or that made by the money sender who gave

the form containing his name, address, and telephone number to Western Union. Accordingly, the Johnson v. Lutz gloss excludes this "outsider" information, where offered for its truth, unless some other hearsay exception applies to the outsider's own statement. This gloss on the business records exception, which the Federal Rules elsewhere call the "hearsay within hearsay" problem, Fed. R. Evid. 805, is well-settled in this circuit. Other circuits are in accord. . . .

The hearsay rule is an ancient and, even to most lawyers, a counter-intuitive restriction now riddled with many exceptions. However, the drafters chose to retain the hearsay rule, and any trial lawyer who has tried to cross-examine a witness whose story depends on the hearsay statements of others understands why. . . .

■   ■   ■

Integrating Outsiders' Information in the Operation of a Business— Beneficial Maine. The business record exception is so widely used and ordinarily so easy to satisfy that some enterprises may have become complacent about its availability. Beneficial Maine apparently describes this pattern.

BENEFICIAL MAINE, INC. v. CARTER
25 A.3d 96 (Me. 2011)

SAUFLEY, C.J.

Timothy G. and Kathleen A. Carter appeal from a summary judgment entered in the District Court . . . in favor of Beneficial Maine Inc. on its foreclosure complaint. The Carters challenge the foundation presented by Beneficial to support the admissibility of its mortgage records pursuant to the business records exception to the hearsay rule. *See* M.R. Evid. 803(6). . . .

On November 4, 2009, Beneficial filed a complaint for foreclosure against the Carters in the District Court. Beneficial alleged that the Carters had defaulted in payment on their promissory note to Beneficial. . . .

After the parties were unable to resolve the case through mediation, Beneficial moved for summary judgment and submitted a statement of material facts. In support of its statement of material facts, Beneficial referred to [an affidavit] from Shana Richmond, Vice President of Administrative Services for HSBC Consumer Lending Mortgage Servicing, described in the affidavit as Beneficial's "servicer." Beneficial cited to Richmond's affidavit, with its attached exhibits, as the sole evidentiary support for its allegations of its ownership of the note and mortgage, the Carters' obligation on the note, the Carters' default, and the amount that the Carters owed. Richmond's affidavit states the following as the foundation for her factual assertions:

The Bank [Beneficial] is the holder of the note and mortgage. . . . I have access to the records relating to the mortgage transactions with respect to said note and mortgage. My knowledge as to the facts set forth in this affidavit is derived from my personal knowledge of this account and of the records of this account, which are kept in the ordinary course of business by the Bank and which were made at or near the time of the transactions by, or from information transmitted by, a person with knowledge of the facts set forth in said records. These records are kept in the ordinary course of business, pursuant to the company's regular practice of making such records. The exhibits attached hereto are true copies of the original documents.

The Carters objected to the admissibility of the Richmond affidavit and the attached exhibits on the grounds that they constituted hearsay and that Beneficial had not established a foundation for application of the business records exception. The court entered summary judgment in the bank's favor on its foreclosure complaint. The Carters appealed. . . .

Beneficial attempted to support its statement of material facts with the affidavit of Shana Richmond, an individual who was not Beneficial's employee. The cursory reference in Richmond's affidavit to her knowledge of the critical issues — how Beneficial created, maintained, and produced the records — prompts us to clarify the foundation of knowledge that a nonemployee must possess to be a "qualified witness" to lay the foundation for a business record, M.R. Evid. 803(6), in an affidavit to support summary judgment in a foreclosure action. . . .

In the past, we have reviewed courts' consideration of business records on summary judgment for an abuse of discretion. Since these cases were decided, however, we have clarified that, when we review a *trial* ruling regarding the admissibility of a business record, we review foundational findings for clear error and the ultimate determination of the record's admissibility for abuse of discretion. *See Bank of Am., N.A. v. Barr*, 2010 ME 124, ¶ 17, 9 A.3d 816, 820.

Because we review the summary judgment record de novo in the light most favorable to the nonprevailing party, and because the evidence relied on at summary judgment must be of a quality that would be admissible at trial, we follow our bifurcated standard of review from *Barr* to determine (1) whether competent undisputed evidence, properly referenced in the statements of material facts, supports the foundational facts required for admissibility of the asserted business records; and (2) if those facts are supported, whether the court abused its discretion in considering the evidence. If necessary foundational elements for admission of a business record are not supported by competent undisputed evidence in the summary judgment record, that business record may not be considered on summary judgment

If we conclude that specific documents presented in support of summary judgment lacked the necessary foundation to be admissible as business records or that the court abused its discretion in considering them, we review de novo whether, in the absence of those records, there are sufficient undisputed facts to entitle the moving party to judgment as a matter of law. Beneficial's records, offered through the affidavit of HSBC's employee, constitute the only evidence in the summary judgment record concerning the contract and the breach. If those records cannot be considered, Beneficial will have failed to meet its burden on summary judgment to provide undisputed facts upon which it is entitled to judgment as a matter of law. Accordingly, the outcome of this appeal turns on the admissibility of the business records.

Hearsay, defined as "a statement, other than one made by the declarant while testifying at the trial or hearing, offered in evidence to prove the truth of the matter asserted," M. R. Evid. 801(c), is inadmissible except as provided by law or by the Maine Rules of Evidence. Pursuant to the Maine Rules of Evidence, a business's record of acts or events is admissible as an exception to the hearsay rule if the necessary foundation is established "by the testimony of the custodian or other qualified witness." M.R. Evid. 803(6). This requirement is tied to the purpose underlying the business records exception to the hearsay rule: to allow the consideration of a business record, without requiring firsthand testimony regarding the recorded facts, by supplying a witness whose knowledge of business practices for production and retention of the record is sufficient to ensure the reliability and trustworthiness of the record.

The affiant whose statements are offered to establish the admissibility of a business record on summary judgment need not be an employee of the record's creator. For instance, if the records were received and integrated into another business's records and were relied upon in that business's day-to-day operations, an employee of the receiving business may be a qualified witness. In such instances, records will be admissible pursuant to the business records exception to the hearsay rule, if the foundational evidence from the receiving entity's employee is adequate to demonstrate that the employee had sufficient knowledge of both businesses' regular practices to demonstrate the reliability and trustworthiness of the information.

Such an affiant must demonstrate knowledge that

- the producer of the record at issue employed regular business practices for creating and maintaining the records that were sufficiently accepted by the receiving business to allow reliance on the records by the receiving business;
- the producer of the record at issue employed regular business practices for transmitting them to the receiving business;
- by manual or electronic processes, the receiving business integrated the records into its own records and maintained them through regular business processes;
- the record at issue was, in fact, among the receiving business's own records; and
- the receiving business relied on these records in its day-to-day operations.

The affiant must have firsthand knowledge, based on the affiant's supervision of or participation in day-to-day business operations of the receiving business, that the records were among those created, maintained, and transmitted through regular business practices. An affiant so qualified must aver the following standard foundational elements, some of which may already have been established through proof of the witness's qualifications:

(1) the record was made at or near the time of the events reflected in the record by, or from information transmitted by, a person with personal knowledge of the events recorded therein;

(2) the record was kept in the course of a regularly conducted business;

(3) it was the regular practice of the business to make records of the type involved; and

(4) no lack of trustworthiness is indicated from the source of information from which the record was made or the method or circumstances under which the record was prepared.

In the matter before us, Richmond was not an employee of Beneficial itself but of Beneficial's "servicer," HSBC. Although Richmond's affidavit states that the records were kept by Beneficial in the ordinary course of business from information supplied at or near the time of the recorded events by a person with knowledge of those events, it does not provide any basis for Richmond's personal knowledge of Beneficial's practices. Richmond does not purport to be the custodian of the records, nor does she explain the source of her understanding of Beneficial's "daily operation" or show the "firsthand nature of [her] knowledge." *Murphy,* 2011 ME 59, ¶ 10, 19 A.3d at 820. Her affidavit indicates only that she has personal knowledge of "this account and of the records of this account" and that she has "access to the records." The affidavit provides no elaboration on the nature of HSBC's role as Beneficial's "servicer," or of HSBC's responsibilities and activities with regard to Beneficial's accounts.

Although it is possible that an employee of HSBC — perhaps even Richmond herself — may have personal knowledge of both entities' practices for creating, maintaining, and transmitting the records, the affidavit does not report the basis for Richmond's knowledge of (1) Beneficial's practices for creating, maintaining, and transmitting the records at issue; (2) HSBC's practices in obtaining and maintaining the bank's records for HSBC's own use; or (3) HSBC's integration of the bank's records into HSBC's own records. Richmond did not, therefore, establish that she was a "custodian or other qualified witness" who could provide trustworthy and reliable information about the regularity of the creation, transmission, and retention of the records offered. M.R. Evid. 803(6). Because Richmond's affidavit could not establish the foundation for the records' admissibility, the court could not properly consider those records on summary judgment.

Beneficial presented no other evidence regarding the mortgage . . . to support its motion for summary judgment. Because of the deficiencies in the affidavit, Beneficial has failed to demonstrate on summary judgment that the Carters were obligated by, and defaulted on, the mortgage note, and that Beneficial is entitled to judgment as a matter of law. Accordingly, we vacate the summary judgment entered in favor of Beneficial. Having reached this conclusion, we do not address the Carters' additional argument regarding the adequacy of the notice of default and the right to cure.

Summary judgment vacated. Remanded for further proceedings.

NOTES TO BENEFICIAL MAINE, INC. v. CARTER

1. *Recipients' Incentives.* When a business receives information from another business and puts it in its files, it may have an incentive to require accuracy from the submitting business. On the other hand, its operations may not be affected by the accuracy of the information it receives. This idea is inherent in the court's statement that there must be a showing that "the receiving business relied on those records."

QUESTION 9-5. In June of 2010, Vince Johnson, had a checking account with Mutual Federal Savings Bank. The account could be accessed through an automatic teller machine (ATM) with a card and a four-digit personal identification number (PIN). After receiving notification of several overdrafts, Johnson called Glenda Thomas, the bank's branch manager to inquire as to the nature of the overdraft. After meeting with Johnson, Thomas investigated his account and discovered that on June 10 Johnson had reported his card as missing and the bank had placed a hold on his account. She also found two ATM withdrawals of $100 and $50 and three attempted ATM withdrawals of $50, $20, and $10, all made on June 9 one after the other. Johnson had told her he did not make these withdrawals. Later, Thomas viewed the bank's videotape of ATM transactions and verified that Johnson was not the person at the ATM at the time of the withdrawals. At a June 15 meeting, Thomas told Johnson of the videotape and said that before he could view the tape, or be reimbursed, the bank required him to complete an "affidavit of forgery." Johnson completed the affidavit, saying that he did not (1) withdraw the funds; (2) authorize their withdrawal; or (3) benefit from their withdrawal. The bank reimbursed Johnson $100 (the amount of withdrawals less $50) and refunded him $60 in overdraft charges. The bank retained that affidavit. In a criminal prosecution of someone accused of using Johnson's card, should Johnson's affidavit be admissible to prove that he did not authorize use of his card?

> **GOOD TO REMEMBER**
>
> When a business record contains information provided by someone outside the business, that information is admissible for its truth only if it is covered by an additional hearsay exception (such as the excited utterance exception, for example) or if there is a reason to believe that the business that saved the information had evaluated it or typically relied on it.

■ ■ ■

Information Relevant to the Business That Makes a Record? — Ortega. Hospital records may often contain entries that present multiple levels of hearsay. A patient's words, for example, can be one level. But when a medical worker makes notes of those words, the worker is an additional declarant. Ortega is focused on this latter level of hearsay, the statement by the medical worker declarant.

PEOPLE v. ORTEGA

942 N.E.2d 210 (N.Y. 2010)

LIPPMAN, C.J.

The . . . issue presented . . . is whether certain statements appearing in medical records were properly admitted at trial as relevant to diagnosis and treatment under the business records exception to the hearsay rule. . . .

Complainant, a 25-year-old man, encountered defendant outside a bodega in Washington Heights at about 4:30 A.M. on July 14, 2007. Although complainant initially asked defendant to purchase marijuana for him, complainant testified that defendant and another man escorted him, at gunpoint, to a nearby building where they forced him to smoke crack cocaine from a glass pipe. The men also allegedly forced him to give them the PIN numbers to his bank cards. Subject to threats that he or his family would be hurt if he did not cooperate, complainant was allegedly forced to withdraw money from his bank accounts on several occasions over the course of the morning. Complainant was allegedly taken back to the nearby building and was again forced to smoke crack between the additional trips to obtain cash.

Complainant was eventually able to escape his captors shortly after noon that day. When he returned home, he was shaking, crying and incoherent. Complainant was taken to the hospital, where he told medical staff that he "was forced to smoke [a] white substance from [a] pipe." Later that night, defendant was arrested after being pulled over for an unrelated traffic offense. He was in possession of a small amount of crack, as well as complainant's bank cards, identification cards and cell phone.

Defendant's version of events differed significantly from complainant's. Defendant essentially testified that complainant voluntarily smoked crack with him and that complainant withdrew the money from his bank accounts of his own volition. Defendant also explained that complainant had willingly handed over his personal property and left it in defendant's possession.

Defendant was convicted of two counts of criminal possession of stolen property in the fourth degree. The Appellate Division affirmed, finding that even if the court should have redacted the statements at issue from complainant's hospital records, any error was harmless. A Judge of this Court granted defendant leave to appeal, and we now affirm.

Under the business records exception to the hearsay rule,

> "[a]ny writing or record . . . made as a memorandum or record of any act, transaction, occurrence or event, shall be admissible in evidence in proof of that act, transaction, occurrence or event, if the judge finds that it was made in the regular course of any business and that it was the regular course of such business to make it, at the time of the act, transaction, occurrence or event, or within a reasonable time thereafter" (CPLR 4518 [a]). . . .

Generally, business records are deemed trustworthy both because they reflect routine business operations and because the person making the particular entry has the responsibility to keep accurate records that can be relied upon for business purposes (*see Williams v. Alexander,* 309 N.Y. 283, 286, 129 N.E.2d 417 [1955]). Hospital records, in particular, are trustworthy as they are "designed to be 'relied upon in affairs of life and death'" (*Williams,* 309 N.Y. at 288, 129 N.E.2d 417, quoting 6 Wigmore, Evidence §1707, at 36 [3d ed. 1940]) and as they reflect the condition of a patient who has the clear motivation to report accurately. Hospital records fall within the business records exception when they "reflect[ ] acts, occurrences or events that relate to diagnosis, prognosis or treatment or are otherwise helpful to an understanding of the medical or surgical aspects of . . . [the particular patient's] hospitalization" (*Williams,* 309 N.Y. at 287, 129 N.E.2d 417 [internal quotation marks and citations omitted]). Where details of how a particular injury occurred are not useful for purposes of medical diagnosis or treatment, they are not considered to have been recorded in the regular course of the hospital's business.

For example, in *Williams,* plaintiff was struck by a car, but the parties disagreed over how the accident happened. Plaintiff's statement to a physician that he was hit after a car that had been stopped at an intersection was propelled into him by another vehicle was deemed inadmissible. The statement concerned the manner in which the accident occurred and was irrelevant to diagnosis or treatment.

We noted in *Williams* that, in certain situations, how the patient was injured "may be helpful to an understanding of the medical aspects of his [or her] case." . . .

[T]he statement that complainant was "forced to" smoke a white, powdery substance was relevant to complainant's diagnosis and treatment. As the trial judge reasoned, under such a scenario, complainant would not have been in control over either the amount or the nature of the substance he ingested. In addition, treatment of a patient who is the victim of coercion may differ from a patient who has intentionally taken drugs. The references to complainant being "forced to" consume crack were admissible under the business records exception to the hearsay rule. . . .

Accordingly . . . the order of the Appellate Division should be affirmed.

NOTES TO PEOPLE v. ORTEGA

1. *First Level of Hearsay.* The *Ortega* court ignores the first level of hearsay, the statements by the crime victim. This may be because New York state has yet to recognize a hearsay exception for statements for the purpose of medical treatment, so that glossing over that level of hearsay may have helped the court reach its result.

2. *Omissions in Records.* Suppose a standard medical history form used at a hospital had a space for recording a patient's allergies. If that space was blank in a form, and an issue arose about whether a patient had informed the hospital about allergies or had failed to give that information, introducing evidence of the blank place in the form could raise a hearsay problem. (Some would say, to the contrary, that a blank space is not an assertion.) The following rule solves this problem.

> **Rule 803. Exceptions to the Rule Against Hearsay — Regardless of Whether the Declarant Is Available as a Witness**
>
> The following are not excluded by the rule against hearsay, regardless of whether the declarant is available as a witness:
>
> . . .
>
> **(7)** *Absence of a Record of a Regularly Conducted Activity.* Evidence that a matter is not included in a record described in paragraph (6) if:
>
> **(A)** the evidence is admitted to prove that the matter did not occur or exist;
>
> **(B)** a record was regularly kept for a matter of that kind; and
>
> **(C)** the opponent does not show that the source of information or the method or circumstances of preparation indicate a lack of trustworthiness.

D PUBLIC RECORDS

Records maintained by units of government, public records, are covered by an exception grounded in the same rationale as Rule 803(6), the exception for records of a regularly conducted activity. The public records exception, however, has special provisions that limit its application in criminal cases.

> **Rule 803. Exceptions to the Rule Against Hearsay — Regardless of Whether the Declarant Is Available as a Witness**
>
> The following are not excluded by the rule against hearsay, regardless of whether the declarant is available as a witness:
>
> . . .
>
> **(8)** *Public Records.* A record or statement of a public office if:
>
> **(A)** it sets out:
>
> **(i)** the office's activities;
>
> **(ii)** a matter observed while under a legal duty to report, but not including, in a criminal case, a matter observed by law-enforcement personnel; or
>
> **(iii)** in a civil case or against the government in a criminal case, factual findings from a legally authorized investigation; and
>
> **(B)** the opponent does not show that the source of information or other circumstances indicate a lack of trustworthiness.

What Does "Factual Finding" Mean?—Midwest Fireworks Mfg. Co., Inc. This opinion refers to Rule 803(8)(C) of the original Federal Rules. In the restyled rules (shown above), that provision is 803(8)(A)(iii). The court considers concepts that are found in the restyled rule's part (A) and the restyled rule's part (B).

UNITED STATES v. MIDWEST FIREWORKS MFG. CO., INC.

248 F.3d 563 (2001)

SILER, J.

This action arises out of defendants' sale of certain fireworks the Consumer Products Safety Commission ("CPSC") determined to be hazardous under the Federal Hazardous Substances Act ("FHSA"), 15 U.S.C. §1191 *et seq.* (2000), and the regulations promulgated thereunder. Defendants challenge the permanent injunction issued by the district court prohibiting them from selling over seventy-nine types of fireworks.... We affirm.

Four years prior to the initiation of this action, the CPSC, in conjunction with the United States Customs Service, began testing various fireworks sold by defendants due to a concern that defendants were importing and distributing hazardous products which failed to comply with federal law. Based on the laboratory tests performed, the CPSC determined that over seventy fireworks devices being imported and/or sold by defendants violated FHSA and CPSC regulations. Most of these violations involved devices containing pyrotechnic powder in excess of the amount permitted under 16 C.F.R. §1500.17. Pyrotechnic powder in a firework creates a "report charge" or "audible effect" when ignited. This regulation limits "fireworks devices" that are "intended to produce audible effects" to a charge of "2 grains of pyrotechnic composition" or less. 16 C.F.R. §1500.17(a)(3). Two grains of this powder must weigh no more than 130 milligrams. *See* 27 C.F.R. §55.11 (2001).

The CPSC sent "letters of advice" on these devices, outlining the violations and describing the procedures to be followed if defendants disagreed with the CPSC's findings. When the defendants refused to comply with these "letters of advice," the CPSC sought a temporary restraining order ("TRO") banning the defendants from selling seventy-nine different types of fireworks. Two hearings were held by the district court in 1999, whereby the CPSC introduced numerous exhibits demonstrating that defendants possessed banned hazardous substances. From the bench, the district court issued a permanent injunction prohibiting defendants from selling these hazardous fireworks. An amended order followed on January 28, 2000 as the previous permanent injunction and judgment did not fully reflect the district court's bench rulings....

Over somewhat general objections by the defendants, the district court admitted the CPSC's Exhibits 1-90, 105-115 under Fed. R. Evid. 803(6), the business records exception, and Fed. R. Evid. 803(8), the public records exception, during the injunction hearings. Each exhibit contained the following records: (1) a sample collection report which includes reports prepared by the CPSC investigator collecting the fireworks sample; (2) a laboratory test report which includes reports of laboratory test results prepared by CPSC technicians and reviewed by the director of the laboratory; (3) a compliance assessment worksheet prepared by the responsible CPSC compliance officer determining if the device violates the regulations based on the laboratory test reports; and (4) a letter of advice from the CPSC to defendants notifying them of their violative product and requesting a written response including a plan for corrective action.

Without deciding whether these exhibits were admissible under the business records exception, the court finds that the exhibits were public records admissible under Fed. R. Evid. 803(8) because the exhibits were compiled by a public agency and included "factual findings resulting from an investigation made pursuant to authority granted by law. . . . " Fed. R. Evid. 803(8)(C).* . . .

"Opinions, conclusions, and evaluations, as well as facts, fall within the Rule 803(8)(C) exception[,]" and enjoy a presumption of admissibility. *Bank of Lexington & Trust Co. v. Vining-Sparks Sec., Inc.*, 959 F.2d 606, 616 (6th Cir. 1992). This presumption is further bolstered by testimony that the CPSC technicians compiling the exhibits annually perform 4,000 to 5,000 pyrotechnic overload tests. Only four of defendants' 101 devices studied by the CPSC appear to have been tested in an atypical manner. Even if the CPSC's conclusions on these four devices were erroneous, the reports involving the ninety-seven other devices indicate that defendants' fireworks violate federal regulations.

The CPSC regularly prepares reports of violative fireworks irrespective of whether enforcement of those determinations results in litigation. Fed. R. Evid. 803(8) was designed to permit the admission of these types of exhibits into evidence even if the person with knowledge of the underlying facts is not present. Admitting the records under the 803(8) exception is a practical necessity that must be afforded to government officers "who have made in the course of their duties thousands of similar written hearsay statements concerning events coming within their jurisdictions." *Wong Wing Foo v. McGrath*, 196 F.2d 120, 123 (9th Cir. 1952); Fed. R. Evid. 803(8) advisory committee's note.

Hence, the district court did not abuse its discretion in admitting Exhibits 1-90, 105-115 as they were admissible under the public records exception of Fed. R. Evid. 803(8). . . .

The district court did not err in issuing a permanent injunction ordering defendants to destroy or re-export all fireworks devices deemed hazardous substances under 16 C.F.R. §1500.17(a)(3). . . .

Affirmed.

NOTES TO UNITED STATES v. MIDWEST FIREWORKS MFG. CO., INC.

1. *Facts and Opinions.* Sometimes a government report may contain opinions as well as facts, such as the statements in the Midwest Fireworks

---

* In the Restyled Rules, this concept is in 803(8)(A)(iii). — Ed.

reports that particular devices violated regulations. These blends of information and analysis are admissible under Rule 808(8)(A)(iii). *See* Beech Aircraft Corp. v. Rainey, 488 U.S. 153, 109 S. Ct. 439, 102 L. Ed. 2d 445 (1988).

2. *Trustworthiness.* To apply the trustworthiness factor, courts often use a four-factor test, examining: (1) the timeliness of the investigation; (2) the special skill or experience of the official; (3) the level at which the investigation was conducted; and (4) whether the report was made with any improper motive.

■ ■ ■

What Does "Matter Observed by Law Enforcement Personnel" Mean? — Dowdell. While the Rule 803(8) exception generally allows the admission of public records, a provision construed in *Dowdell* withdraws that treatment for certain law enforcement records in criminal cases. In the restyled rules, as shown above, this provision is 803(8)(A)(ii). In the original rules (used in *Dowdell*), it was 803(8)(B). *Dowdell* interprets the "law-enforcement" limitation on use of this hearsay exception.

UNITED STATES v. DOWDELL

595 Fed.3d 50 (1st Cir. 2010)

HOWARD, J.

Following a three-day jury trial, Defendant Darryl Dowdell was convicted of distribution of cocaine base and sentenced as a career offender to 198 months' imprisonment. Dowdell appeals the conviction, alleging . . . that the trial court abused its discretion on various evidentiary rulings. . . .

In the summer of 2001, several Massachusetts authorities launched a coordinated effort with the federal Drug Enforcement Administration (DEA) to investigate drug trafficking in the area of a housing project in Roxbury. The investigation involved a task force of undercover officers who made controlled purchases of cocaine and crack cocaine from dealers operating in the project. One of these officers was Boston Housing Authority investigator Joao Monteiro. . . .

On July 6, 2001, Monteiro observed Dowdell standing on the sidewalk with a man named Robert White, whom Monteiro recognized from previous encounters. Dowdell was wearing dark pants and a black shirt. He and White were counting cash. Monteiro signaled to White that he wished to purchase crack cocaine, and White went to talk to Dowdell. White then approached Monteiro's car and got into the passenger seat. White told Monteiro that Dowdell, at this point identified only as "the dark-skinned brother" in the dark shirt, was a trustworthy dealer. After purchasing 1.1 grams of crack cocaine for $230, Monteiro asked White whether "the dude in black" was the person to see for future purchases if White were unavailable. White replied affirmatively and informed Monteiro that Dowdell went by the name "Smoke." . . .

Monteiro returned for [another] buy on July 16. . . . When he arrived, he saw Dowdell standing in a small group, wearing blue jeans and a blue checkered shirt. Monteiro again asked for White, who was unavailable. Monteiro asked for directions and drove away, making it appear that he was going off to search for White. After waiting long enough to give the impression that the search was unsuccessful, he returned to the project looking for Dowdell. He found Dowdell on the sidewalk, still wearing a blue checkered shirt. Monteiro called out "Yo, Smoke, can I holler at you." Dowdell approached Monteiro's car, and the two of them proceeded to have a conversation through the passenger-side window. Continuing to address Dowdell as "Smoke," Monteiro asked for about $200 worth of crack cocaine. Dowdell left briefly to meet with another individual and then returned with six bags of crack cocaine, worth approximately $100. Seven more bags would eventually follow. The total weight of the thirteen bags was approximately 2.3 grams. . . .

Later that day, Dowdell was arrested on an outstanding warrant unrelated to his transactions with Monteiro. He was brought to a Boston police station where a booking photo was taken. In the photo, Dowdell was wearing a blue checkered shirt, as Monteiro had described earlier in the day. Later, around four hours after completing the buy from Dowdell, Monteiro was shown the photograph and identified the depicted individual as "Smoke." Monteiro reported that the individual in the photograph was the same person from whom he had purchased drugs that day and whom he had seen standing on the corner with White ten days beforehand. . . .

At trial, Dowdell's primary argument was misidentification. He claimed that he was not the "Smoke" referred to in surveillance recordings and that the video footage was inconclusive as to whether a man with a blue checkered shirt was actually involved. In order to corroborate Monteiro's identification of Dowdell as Smoke, the government introduced, . . . the booking sheet from the July 16 arrest. . . .

The booking sheet contained both the photograph of Dowdell in the blue checkered shirt on which Monteiro had based his identification, as well as a textual description of Dowdell's clothing as including a "blue plaid shirt." Dowdell argued that the document was inadmissible because a provision of Federal Rule of Evidence 803(8), the so-called "law-enforcement exception," forbids the introduction of police reports against criminal defendants. The government countered that a booking sheet should not run afoul of the exception because it contained merely "rote, routine administrative information." The district court concluded that the document was admissible. . . .

Normally, an otherwise hearsay public record is admissible so long as it sets forth "matters observed pursuant to duty imposed by law as to which matters there was a duty to report." Fed. R. Evid. 803(8)(B).[*] However, under what is sometimes called the "law-enforcement exception," Rule 803(8)(B) retains the hearsay

---

[*] In the Restyled Rules, this provision is 803(8)(A)(ii). — Ed.

prohibition in criminal cases for any "matters observed by police officers and other law enforcement personnel." We have interpreted this rule to mean that, as a general matter, "police reports are inadmissible in a criminal case when offered by the prosecution." *United States v. Arias-Santana,* 964 F.2d 1262, 1264 (1st Cir. 1992). The Rule on its face seems equally applicable to the observations contained in a booking sheet. Nevertheless, the district court held that the law enforcement exception was not meant to encompass routine, non-adversarial documents, and on that basis found the booking sheet admissible. Although our review of rulings admitting or excluding evidence is typically for abuse of discretion, our review of the district court's interpretation of a rule of evidence is de novo.

We have yet to consider whether the law enforcement exception applies to an ostensibly objective, non-adversarial document such as a booking sheet. On two previous occasions, however, we have at least hinted that it should not. First, in *United States v. Union Nacional de Trabajadores,* 576 F.2d 388 (1st Cir. 1978), we held admissible a copy of a U.S. marshal's return despite its genesis at the hands of law enforcement personnel. We reasoned that

> [t]here is nothing to indicate that Congress meant to cut back upon the common law rule respecting sheriff's returns. A sheriff or marshal reporting the service of process is not reporting in the capacity of a police observer at the scene of a crime, nor is he ordinarily connected with the case in a law enforcement capacity. The "adversarial" circumstances which might render a law enforcement officer's observations unreliable are unlikely, therefore, to be present.

Then, in *United States v. Trenkler,* 61 F.3d 45 (1st Cir. 1995), we cited *United States v. Brown,* 9 F.3d 907, 911-12 (11th Cir. 1993), in dicta for the proposition that "Rule 803(8) does not necessarily prohibit the use of police records prepared in a routine non-adversarial setting that do not result from subjective investigation and evaluation."

Drawing a line at routine, non-adversarial documents would best comport with the purpose for which Congress originally approved the exception. The Rule's enactment history indicates that "the reason for this exclusion is that observations by police officers at the scene of the crime or the apprehension of the defendant are not as reliable as observations by public officials in other cases because of the adversarial nature of the confrontation between the police and the defendant in criminal cases." S. Rep. No. 1277, 93d Con., 2d Sess., reprinted in (1974) U.S.C.C.A.N. 7051, 7064. Congress was generally "concerned about prosecutors attempting to prove their cases in chief simply by putting into evidence police officers' reports of their contemporaneous observations of crime."

Recognizing this intent, those circuits to have considered the issue have all found that the limitation in Rule 803(8)(B) does not exclude routine observations that are inherently non-adversarial. *See, e.g., United States v. Harris,* 557 F.3d 938, 941 (8th Cir. 2009) (admitting testimony regarding the contents of a probation file because while the rule "does prohibit the admission of records that contain opinions or conclusions resulting from criminal investigations, it does not bar the admission of records concerning routine and unambiguous factual matters"); *United States v. Quezada,* 754 F.2d 1190, 1193-94 (5th Cir. 1985) (admitting an INS form indicating arrest and deportation because officials' only motivation was to "mechanically register an unambiguous factual matter").

Dowdell argues that this construction violates the Rule's plain language, which seems to bar categorically the prosecution's introduction of any and all documents prepared by the police. This much may be true. Yet, the alternative would violate the rule's plain purpose, and "[i]t is a well-established canon of statutory construction that a court should go beyond the literal language of a statute if reliance on that language would defeat the plain purpose of the statute." *Bob Jones Univ. v. United States,* 461 U.S. 574, 586, 103 S. Ct. 2017, 76 L. Ed. 2d 157 (1983). Given the clear intent that undergirded the passage of Rule 803(8), we decline to give it a literal, unqualified meaning. Instead, we join the other circuits in concluding that ministerial, non-adversarial information is admissible under Rule 803(8)(B), notwithstanding its documentation at the hands of law enforcement personnel.

With this interpretation of Rule 803(8)(B) in place, we now must consider whether a booking sheet would violate it. In an unpublished decision, a panel of the Fifth Circuit answered this precise question in the negative, summarily finding that "booking information [i]s taken in a routine, nonadversarial setting." *United States v. Haughton,* 235 Fed. Appx. 254, 255 (5th Cir. 2007). We agree. The rote recitation of biographical information in a booking sheet ordinarily does not implicate the same potential perception biases that a subjective narrative of an investigation or an alleged offense might. A booking sheet does not recount the work that led to an arrest so much as the mere fact that an arrest occurred. As a result, unlike the investigative reports that lie at the heart of the law enforcement exception, booking sheets raise little concern that suspicion of guilt will function as proof of guilt. We think that a police booking sheet is in this respect analogous to the INS warrant that was the subject of the Fifth Circuit's analysis in *Quezada.* The *Quezada* court upheld the admissibility of the warrant, which recounted the defendant's prior arrest and deportation, "[d]ue to the lack of any motivation on the part of the recording official to do other than mechanically register an unambiguous factual matter." The same reasoning applies here. . . .

The appellant's conviction and sentence are affirmed.

NOTES TO UNITED STATES v. DOWDELL

1. *Confrontation Clause.* When out-of-court statements are offered against a criminal defendant, the Confrontation Clause must be considered in addition to hearsay issues. A statement might be covered by a hearsay exception but still be inadmissible because of the Confrontation Clause. These issues are considered in Chapter 11.

2. *Statements Used Against the Government.* For investigative reports, the rule allows use "against the government in a criminal case," while for "a matter observed by law-enforcement personnel" the rule bars all use in a criminal case. This distinction is hard to justify, and many courts have allowed both kinds of statements to be used against the government in criminal cases.

QUESTION 9-6. Law enforcement personnel at a large airport met each day to discuss any problems that had been observed in person or on video by officers throughout the airport. A daily log was prepared that summarized this information. A customer at a store at the airport was hurt when someone attempted to rob the cashier. The customer sought damages in a civil suit, suing the store operator for failing to have adequate precautions against crime. To show that there was little reason to anticipate crime, the store operator seeks to introduce copies of many of the law enforcement daily logs, to show that robberies were rare. How would the hearsay exception for public records apply to those documents?

E SUMMARY

Segment 9:
public records
and police
reports

Recorded Recollection. The hearsay exception for recorded recollection statements covers any kind of record a person has made of something that person once knew. The proponent of the statement must show that at trial the declarant lacks adequate memory of the information to testify about it fully and accurately. The out-of-court statement can be admitted as a substitute for the live testimony the declarant would have given if the declarant's memory had been better. It can be read to the jury, although it is usually not made an exhibit in the case. Besides showing that the declarant has a weak memory of the information at the time of trial, the proponent must show that the declarant made the record when its information was fresh in the declarant's memory, and that the record accurately reflects that knowledge.

Present Recollection Refreshed. A party questioning a witness may seek to stimulate the witness's recollection of things the witness once knew but seems to have forgotten by showing the witness a document — or anything else — that might plausibly reawaken the witness's recollections. Theoretically this procedure does not involve the hearsay doctrine because any out-of-court statement that might be shown to the witness would not be introduced into evidence. And if the witness is shown an object, then another reason why the hearsay rule has no bearing on the process is that an object is not a statement. When a witness does see a document in the effort to refresh the witness's recollection, courts may supervise the process closely, to try to avoid a situation where the witness claims his or her memory has been refreshed but the witness in fact just repeats what he or she has just read in the document. When a document used to refresh recollection was prepared by the witness, some courts seem to require a foundation that is similar to the foundation required to classify a document as recorded recollection.

Records of Regularly Conducted Activity (Business Records). When an enterprise keeps records, they are likely to be accurate. Employees want to keep their jobs. Enterprises are run by managers who want the enterprises to be successful. Customers or others who interact with the enterprise might notice errors in their records. All these reasons justify confidence in "business records," or records of a regularly conducted activity. Sometimes circumstances may suggest that a business record lacks reliability. In those cases, the exception is withdrawn.

An enterprise may sometimes keep information from outsiders in its records. If the enterprise has a basis for evaluating the truthfulness of that kind of information, or if the enterprise relies on it for its own work, the business records rationale can apply to that type of statement. But if the business does not evaluate the statement or does not rely on it for its own operations, the business record rationale should not apply to support substantive use of the outsider's statement. In a case of that kind, the business record can serve as proof that the outsider made the statement, but for the outsider's statement to avoid the hearsay bar some other exception would be needed.

Public Records. A hearsay exception for public records is a specialized application of the more general business records exception. It has much of the same underlying rationale. The details of this exception limit the use of public records in criminal cases.

CHAPTER 10

Hearsay: Unavailability Required Exceptions

A. Introduction
B. Former Testimony
C. Dying Declarations
D. Statements Against Interest
E. Statement by a Declarant Rendered Unavailable
F. Summary

A INTRODUCTION

Topic Overview

Rule 804 defines five hearsay exceptions that may be used only if the declarant is "unavailable." This requirement is a contrast with Rule 803. The exceptions in Rule 803, a much larger group, may be used whether the witness is available or unavailable. The unavailability condition for the Rule 804 exceptions suggests that the drafters intended them to be used less often than the exceptions for which availability or unavailability of the declarant does not matter. They must involve statements where the balance of need and reliability is slightly different from that balance for the exceptions grouped in Rule 803.

A declarant's unavailability can be established in a variety of ways, from the most obvious proof—death—to other circumstances such as application of a privilege that excuses a witness from testifying.

The most important exceptions in Rule 804 allow admission of the following types of hearsay statements, when there is a showing that the declarant is unavailable: former testimony, dying declarations, statements against interest, and statements introduced against someone who has wrongfully made the declarant unavailable.

Chapter Organization

This chapter examines four important hearsay exceptions enumerated in FRE 804 in the order in which they appear in that rule.

- Former testimony (testimony given at a different trial, subject to a requirement related to cross-examination at the time it was given)
- Statement under belief of imminent death (the "dying declaration" exceptions covers statements about the cause of death in homicide and civil trials)
- Statement against interest (statements that were contrary to the declarant's pecuniary, proprietary, and penal interests at the time the declarant made them)
- Statement offered against a party that wrongfully caused the declarant's unavailability (statements made by a declarant whose unavailability was caused or acquiesced in by a party against whom the statement is introduced)

The details of the unavailability requirement (which applies to each of these exceptions) are covered in the notes to the chapter's first case.

B FORMER TESTIMONY

When a person testifies at a trial, there is an accurate record of what he or she says, and there is usually an opportunity for cross-examination that can clarify ambiguities, bring out related information, and probe the credibility of the witness. Since these factors can reduce the risks that the hearsay rule is meant to protect against, it's understandable that a hearsay exception covers former testimony. FRE 804(b)(1) provides the exception with variations, depending on whether the out-of-court former testimony is sought to be introduced in a civil or a criminal case.

Rule 804. Exceptions to the Rule Against Hearsay — When the Declarant Is Unavailable as a Witness

. . .

　　(b) The Exceptions. The following are not excluded by the rule against hearsay if the declarant is unavailable as a witness:

> **(1)** Former Testimony. Testimony that:
>
>   **(A)** was given as a witness at a trial, hearing, or lawful deposition, whether given during the current proceeding or a different one; and
>
>   **(B)** is now offered against a party who had — or, in a civil case, whose predecessor in interest had — an opportunity and similar motive to develop it by direct, cross-, or redirect examination.

■ ■ ■

What's a Predecessor, What's an Interest? — O'Banion. The former testimony exception allows testimony from an earlier proceeding to be introduced against a party who was able to develop that testimony adequately in that prior proceeding. In civil cases, the exception also admits past testimony against a party if that party's "predecessor in interest" had an opportunity to develop that testimony. *O'Banion* reinforces the significance of the unavailability requirement and also takes a position on how "predecessor in interest" should be understood in the context of this rule.

O'BANION v. OWENS-CORNING FIBERGLAS CORP.

968 F.2d 1011 (10th Cir. 1992)

SAFFELS, J.

This is a products liability and negligence action brought under Oklahoma law. Plaintiff-appellants alleged that Stanley O'Banion suffered from asbestos-related disease as a result of exposure to the defendant-appellees' asbestos-containing products. Plaintiff Stanley John O'Banion worked from 1962 through 1980 as a plumber and pipefitter. Following a one week trial, beginning on June 21, and ending on June 29, 1990, a verdict for the defendants was rendered....

[On appeal, plaintiff-appellants] contend that the district court erred in admitting trial testimony given by an expert during another asbestos-related case arising out of the Western District of Texas. Appellants contend admission of the testimony was erroneous because the conditions of Fed. R. Evid. 804(b)(1) were not met. Thus, the appellants contend, this testimony should have been excluded under the hearsay rule.

... Appellants contend that the district court abused its discretion in admitting the former trial testimony of Dr. Hans Weill who testified on the issue of the state of the art in another case. This issue was first addressed in the court's Master Order in which the court denied both parties' request to admit the former testimony of witnesses in other personal injury cases unless this evidence could qualify as an admission against interest, the parties stipulate to its admission or it qualifies under Fed. R. Evid. 804(b)(1).

Subsequently, the trial court addressed this issue at a final pretrial conference, in which the court clarified its previous ruling for purposes of this case, and several other cases. At this conference the trial judge stated:

> "there has been possibly a misinterpretation of the application of that order. In any case in which Baron & Budd appeared, that testimony would be admissible even in the Iola cases (plaintiffs' counsel in this case). The feeling of the court was that you have a compatibility of interest, commonalty of interest, you have reliability of representation; and that was the intent of the court's previous order, and that's not just in the two cases in which Iola acts as local counsel."

Thus, the court concluded that testimony given at other trials could be offered against the parties in the present trial, if during the previous trial, the opposing party was represented by counsel of similar capabilities. The court further opined:

> "there was a commonalty of position and you have represented them as local counsel here, you have worked together with them and there would be a presumption that the interests of your clients would be well represented in those cases and that was the import of the order that the court had previously entered."

Id. Nowhere in the record does there appear to be consideration of the unavailability of the declarant expert witness.

We conclude that the court abused its discretion in admitting this former testimony into evidence under Rule 804(b)(1) without a finding of unavailability. One of the express requirements of this hearsay exception is that the witness be unavailable. Fed. R. Evid. 804(b)(1). Rule 804(a) defines "unavailability." Unavailability includes those instances wherein the declarant is: privileged, refuses to testify, testifies to a lack of memory of the subject matter of the declarant's statement, unavailable because of death, or then existing physical or mental illness or infirmity. Unavailability also involves those instances wherein the declarant is "absent from the hearing and the proponent of his statement has been unable to procure the declarant's attendance . . . by process or other reasonable means." Fed. R. Evid. 804(a)(5).

In the record before the court, there does not appear to be any showing of unavailability. Rather, the primary concern seems to be the expense to the defendants in view of the large number of cases involved. While we are sympathetic to the plight of the defendants in defending themselves in numerous actions, we cannot overlook the express requirements of Rule 804(b)(1). Like the court in Dykes v. Raymark Industries, Inc., 801 F.2d 810, 817 (6th Cir. 1986), cert. denied,

481 U.S. 1038 (1987), recognized, the potential risk in admitting expert testimony without an adequate opportunity to conduct cross-examination may create too heavy an aura of authoritativeness.

However, notwithstanding our conclusion that the district court abused its discretion, we do not find the district court's ruling to have been prejudicial to the plaintiffs in this case. In this respect, appellants have not offered any explanation as to how their interests were compromised, nor does the record reflect that the appellants offered the district court an opportunity to consider why the cross examination of the expert witness in the former trial was inadequate. Without such development, the district court is unable to determine what lines of questioning have been inadequately addressed during the cross-examination of the former testimony.

Furthermore, a careful review of the former testimony of Dr. Weill, reveals that his cross-examination was conducted in a very thorough manner. Plaintiffs' predecessor in interest had an opportunity and similar motive to develop Dr. Weill's testimony during cross-examination and to challenge Dr. Weill's opinion on the state of the art as it relates to pipefitters. Accordingly, we conclude admission of the former testimony did not constitute reversible error.

NOTES TO O'BANION v. OWENS-CORNING FIBERGLAS CORP.

1. *Predecessor in Interest.* Apparently, Dr. Weill had been cross-examined in another plaintiff's case by a lawyer who had sometimes been associated with Mr. O'Banion's lawyer in the litigation of similar cases. Rule 804(b)(1)(B) uses the expression "predecessor in interest" in connection with the rule's application to civil cases. Courts have frequently construed that expression in a nontechnical way, avoiding its ordinary legal meaning.

2. *Narrower Availability in Criminal Cases.* The former testimony exception admits former testimony in criminal cases only if the party against whom it is offered had an opportunity and similar motive to develop the testimony when it was first given. This is narrower than the "predecessor in interest" category that is available in civil cases.

3. *"Unavailability."* If a declarant who was a witness at an earlier trial could testify at the current trial, it would make sense to provide an incentive for fresh testimony delivered by that person in front of the jury in the current trial. In *O'Banion*, the appellate court noted that unavailability was not established, although the court's harmless error analysis meant that this mistake would not support reversal or an order for a new trial. Rule 804(a) describes a number of ways in which the proponent of a hearsay statement may establish that the declarant is unavailable.

Rule 804. Exceptions to the Rule Against Hearsay — When the Declarant Is Unavailable as a Witness

(a) Criteria for Being Unavailable. A declarant is considered to be unavailable as a witness if the declarant:

(1) is exempted from testifying about the subject matter of the declarant's statement because the court rules that a privilege applies;

(2) refuses to testify about the subject matter despite a court order to do so;

(3) testifies to not remembering the subject matter;

(4) cannot be present or testify at the trial or hearing because of death or a then-existing infirmity, physical illness, or mental illness; or

(5) is absent from the trial or hearing and the statement's proponent has not been able, by process or other reasonable means, to procure:

(A) the declarant's attendance, in the case of a hearsay exception under Rule 804(b)(1) or (6); or

(B) the declarant's attendance or testimony, in the case of a hearsay exception under Rule 804(b)(2), (3), or (4).

But this subdivision (a) does not apply if the statement's proponent procured or wrongfully caused the declarant's unavailability as a witness in order to prevent the declarant from attending or testifying.

QUESTION 10-1. Paul Patient was treated by Dr. Max Medic, and later sued Medic for large damages, claiming that Medic's treatment was negligent. Medic's defense involved testimony from 12 experts. Patient's lawyer cross-examined most of the experts thoroughly, but used only brief cross-examination for Dr. Twelve, one of the experts. Patient's lawyer made that choice because she thought Twelve seemed unpersuasive and that giving Twelve's testimony greater attention might harm Patient's overall factual theory about Medic's conduct. The trial ended in a mistrial. In a second trial of the case, if Twelve is unavailable and Medic seeks to introduce Twelve's testimony under the former testimony exception, the evidence should be:

> **GOOD TO REMEMBER**
>
> To use the former testimony exception, the declarant must be unavailable.

A. Admitted because Patient had an opportunity to cross-examine Twelve.

B. Admitted because Patient had an opportunity to cross-examine Twelve and had a motive to do so that was similar to Patient's motive in the second trial.

C. Excluded because Patient chose not to conduct a thorough cross-examination of Twelve in the first trial.

D. Excluded because the number of experts Medic used in the first trial shows that Medic has little need for the testimony of any single one of them.

DYING DECLARATIONS

FRE 804(b)(2) is the hearsay exception for a "statement under the belief of imminent death." This exception, often called the dying declaration exception, has deep historical roots. The common law adopted it on the basis of the idea that a person who believes he or she is about to die will be reluctant to speak untruthfully because lying could cause adverse consequences in the afterlife. A nonreligious view might suggest that the stress of fearing death could impair accuracy and that for some people the best time of all to tell a lie with no fear of retribution is the time when death is approaching. The federal version of this exception limits its coverage to statements on specified topics. At common law the exception applied only in homicide cases. The federal rule adds all civil cases to the situations in which the exception may be used.

Rule 804. Exceptions to the Rule Against Hearsay — When the Declarant Is Unavailable as a Witness

. . .

(b) The Exceptions. The following are not excluded by the rule against hearsay if the declarant is unavailable as a witness:

. . .

(2) *Statement Under the Belief of Imminent Death.* In a prosecution for homicide or in a civil case, a statement that the declarant, while believing the declarant's death to be imminent, made about its cause or circumstances.

■　■　■

Last Words — Grant. Evidence law gives special treatment to a person's last words, if they touch on the topic of why the person is dying. This treatment extends to words a person thinks are likely to be his or her last words even if it turns out that the anticipated death does not occur. *Grant* explains the required elements of the exception.

GRANT v. STATE

161 S.W.3d 785 (Ark. 2004)

DICKEY, C. J.

Appellant Abraham Grant was found guilty by a Phillips County Circuit Court jury of capital murder and first-degree battery. He was sentenced to life in prison without parole for the capital murder conviction and five years for first-degree battery, with the sentences to run concurrently. On appeal Grant contends that the trial court erred in admitting into evidence statements made by the victim, Ms. Rosetta Pittman, under the dying declaration exception to the hearsay rule. . . .

On June 20, 2001, appellant Abraham Grant entered an apartment in Helena, Arkansas, that belonged to his mother-in-law, Ms. Rosetta Pittman. As he entered through the open front door, he began shooting at the occupants of the residence. Ms. Pittman suffered gunshot wounds to her hand, chest, and neck. Ms. Pittman's niece, Louise Perry, was shot in the hand as well. The first officer to arrive on the scene, Captain David Lovell of the Helena Police Department, testified that upon entering the home, he noticed a trail of blood in the front room leading to the back of the apartment. Lovell followed the blood trail and found Ms. Pittman lying in a large puddle of blood at the back door. Lovell testified that Ms. Pittman was upset and crying, and she had blood coming from her mouth, but he managed to calm her down and asked what happened. Ms. Pittman told the officer, "Abraham Grant shot me, and he ran out the back door." Captain Lovell reported that Ms. Pittman began losing consciousness and that he could only understand what she was saying when he got really close to her. While the officer could not testify that Ms. Pittman knew she was dying, he reported that Ms. Pittman knew that she had lost a lot of blood and that she was "in real bad shape."

At trial, Grant moved to exclude any statements by Ms. Pittman as hearsay. At the pretrial hearing, the State called Officer Lovell to testify. The trial court determined that Ms. Pittman's statement was a dying declaration, and could be admitted into evidence. . . .

For his sole point on appeal, Grant asserts that Ms. Pittman's statements were inadmissible hearsay and not dying declarations. In Arkansas, hearsay is defined as a statement other than one made by the declarant while testifying at trial or hearing, offered in evidence to prove the truth of the matter asserted. Ark. R. Evid. 801(c). Hearsay is inadmissible except as provided by law or by the rules of evidence. Ark. R. Evid. 802. Rule 804 of the Arkansas Rules of Evidence provides hearsay exceptions that apply when the declarant of a statement is unavailable. One of these exceptions to the hearsay rule is a statement under belief of impending death, commonly referred to as a "dying declaration." A dying declaration is defined as a statement made by a declarant while believing that his death was imminent, concerning the cause or circumstances of what he believed to be his impending death. Ark. R. Evid. 804(b)(2). Dying declarations are deemed inherently trustworthy. The principal consideration upon which such statements are admitted is that one who realizes that death is inevitable in consequence of the injury inflicted speaks with solemnity and will not resort to fabrication in order to unjustly punish another. We have held that a sense of imminent death need not be shown by the declarant's express words alone, but can be supplied by inferences fairly drawn from his condition.

In the case at bar, this court must decide whether Ms. Pittman's statement "Abraham Grant shot me, and he ran out the back door" was made while she believed her death was imminent. Grant asserts that inferring Ms. Pittman knew she was dying would require great speculation, and, therefore, the statement is not a dying declaration. We disagree.

In the instant case, the victim had been shot multiple times; she knew that she was lying in a large puddle of blood; she wasn't trying to move; she was sobbing, and she was passing in and out of consciousness. The trial court found that there was enough proof to show a fear of imminent death. Clearly, the evidence showed Ms. Pittman's condition was grave and that she was no doubt aware of the severity of her injuries. Based on the facts of this case, we cannot say that the trial court abused its discretion in determining that Ms. Pittman's statement was a dying declaration. Accordingly, we affirm the trial court's ruling. . . .

NOTES TO GRANT v. STATE

1. *Surviving Declarants.* Note that in a civil case the rule will apply to a statement by a declarant who failed to die. In the criminal setting, however, the rule applies only where the charge is homicide.

2. *Overlap with Excited Utterance Exception.* It is likely that the circumstances surrounding a statement that might fit the dying declaration exception would also support use of the excited utterance exception. The topics that each of these rules cover are also similar ("relating to a startling event" and an impending death's "cause or circumstances").

3. *Facts Supporting Application of the Rule.* In a case where the trial judge believes there is adequate basis for applying the dying declaration exception, the judge should not explain the requirements of that exception to the jury or invite the jury to disregard the out-of-court words if the jury concludes that the speaker did not anticipate death at the time the speaker spoke. A party against whom a dying declaration is introduced may, of course, argue that the statement should be ignored or valued only lightly based on facts about how certain the declarant was that death was imminent.

4. *Counterexample.* The following rule differs from the federal rule in the breadth of its coverage.

Hawaii R. Ev. 804(b)(2)

(2) Statement under belief of impending death. A statement made by a declarant while believing that the declarant's death was imminent, concerning the cause or circumstances of what the declarant believed to be the declarant's impending death.

GOOD TO REMEMBER

The dying declaration exception applies in *all civil* cases but applies in the *criminal* context only in *homicide* cases.

QUESTION 10-2. Decedent committed suicide and left a note explaining that she was taking her own life because she had been the victim of a sexual attack at a fraternity house operated by the defendant. Assuming that a jurisdiction's tort law might allow damages against the fraternity for a claim of this nature, should Rule 804(b)(2) allow admission of the decedent's letter?

D STATEMENTS AGAINST INTEREST

The statement against interest exception is based on the idea that a person will ordinarily say things that could harm his or her important interests only if the statement is true. At common law, this exception applied only to statements related to the declarant's monetary or property interests. FRE 804(b)(3) applies to statements that could harm a person financially, hurt the person's property rights, or put the person at risk of suffering criminal penalties (pecuniary, proprietary, and penal interests).

Rule 804. Exceptions to the Rule Against Hearsay — When the Declarant Is Unavailable as a Witness

. . .

(b) The Exceptions. The following are not excluded by the rule against hearsay if the declarant is unavailable as a witness:

. . .

(3) Statement Against Interest. A statement that:

(A) a reasonable person in the declarant's position would have made only if the person believed it to be true because, when made, it was so contrary to the declarant's proprietary or pecuniary interest or had so great a tendency to invalidate the declarant's claim against someone else or to expose the declarant to civil or criminal liability; and

(B) is supported by corroborating circumstances that clearly indicate its trustworthiness, if it is offered in a criminal case as one that tends to expose the declarant to criminal liability.

■   ■   ■

Implied or Partial Adverseness to a Speaker's Interest — Paredes. *Paredes* involves statements that may have been against the declarant's penal interest. It shows a range of complex issues on the topic, such as how to treat statements that only imply something negative about the speaker, or statements that combine negative information with neutral information, and how the roles of the judge and the jury should be defined for use of this exception.

STATE v. PAREDES

775 N.W.2d 554 (Iowa 2009)

APPEL, J.

Edwin Paredes appeals his conviction for child endangerment resulting in serious injury. The charges arose after his infant child was diagnosed with shaken-baby syndrome. Paredes claims that the district court erred in excluding hearsay statements made by the child's mother that she "may have" caused the baby's injuries. The court of appeals affirmed Paredes' conviction. For the reasons expressed below, we vacate the decision of the court of appeals, reverse the judgment of the district court, and remand the case for a new trial.

Paredes and Cassidy Millard are the parents of a young infant. At the time of the events relevant to this proceeding, Paredes was twenty-four years old, Millard was sixteen years old, and the baby was two months old. . . .

After being seen by a physician on Saturday, April 23, 2005 for what appeared to be a routine ear infection, the baby's condition deteriorated. On Sunday, after consulting with the child's physician, Millard called for an ambulance to take the infant to a local hospital. . . .

At the hospital, medical personnel diagnosed the baby with shaken-baby syndrome. . . . Based on the onset of . . . seizures, medical personnel determined that the injury occurred sometime between late Friday and early Saturday morning. As mandatory reporters, hospital staff contacted the Iowa Department of Human Services (DHS) to report the suspected abuse.

On Sunday evening, Chad Bollweg of DHS and Coralville Police Detective Robbie Swank met with Paredes and Millard. Both denied any knowledge of how the child was injured. They did admit, however, that they were the child's only caregivers during the period in question, except for a brief fifteen-minute period when Paredes' sister cared for the baby.

On Monday, Bollweg and another social worker, Vicky Leau, met with the couple. Leau informed the parents that all future visits with the child would have to be supervised. Upon hearing this, Paredes declared that supervised visits would not be necessary — he caused the injuries. Leau wondered whether Paredes "was just saying that so that Cassidy could be unsupervised and spend more time at the hospital." Millard commented that Paredes should not say something simply for her sake. . . .

On May 1, Millard called a social worker, Susan Gail, with whom she had prior contact. Because of the nature of the call, Gail memorialized the contents of the conversation. According to Gail's memorandum, Millard told her that Millard's child had shaken-baby syndrome. When Gail asked Millard what had happened, Millard responded:

> . . . She told me she knows Edwin would not hurt the baby and hinted around that maybe she did it, but didn't remember. I asked about the day that it happened. I asked her if the baby was crying. She told me that he cried all the time, he was colicky [sic]. She said that she just yelled at him to "shut up", but never hit him. She then said that she had started spanking him lately, but that it did not hurt him since he had on a big diaper.

The Gail memorandum further states:

> Cassidy was afraid that if she told that she might have done it, she would go to prison when she is 18. I told her that she needed to talk to her attorney. . . .
>
> Cassidy told me that she has been crying for a week because she does not want her boyfriend to take the fall for this. She said that he is not that kind of guy, not violent. She said that Edwin didn't even take care of the baby that much. She kept saying, "if I did it."

At this point, Gail continued to talk to Millard as if she did do it and was not contradicted. Gail again advised Millard to contact her attorney. . . .

On the day of trial, the State filed a motion in limine to exclude Gail's testimony regarding her conversation with Millard as impermissible hearsay. . . .

In a ruling on the record, the district court held that the statements made by Millard in the memorandum . . . did not meet the hearsay exception for statements against interest under Iowa Rule of Evidence 5.804(b)(3). . . .

Paredes was convicted at trial. On appeal, the court of appeals affirmed his conviction. . . . We granted further review. . . .

In this case, Paredes claims that the trial court should have admitted the various statements made by Millard to Gail as statements against interest under rule 5.804(b)(3) [identical to FRE 804(b)(3) prior to restyling]. Paredes claims that admissible statements made by Millard include: her statement that she had begun spanking her two-month-old baby, her statement that Paredes did not hurt the baby and her hinting that maybe she was responsible, her statement that she did not want Paredes to take the fall, her questions and comments about criminal penalties, and her silence or lack of contradiction when Gail spoke to her as if she were the perpetrator.

Paredes further asserts that the statements were sufficiently corroborated under the totality of facts and circumstances to require their admission into evidence. . . .

The State counters that Millard's statements were not sufficiently inculpatory that a reasonable person in her position would not have made them unless they were true. . . .

In determining whether a statement is admissible under rule 5.804(b)(3) several questions arise.

The first question under rule 5.804(b)(3) is the scope of the term "statement." There are several possible approaches. The term could broadly refer to an entire narrative. Conversely, the term narrowly could mean only individual factual assertions. Or, the term could mean individual factual assertions along with collateral material necessary to understand the context in which the factual assertions are made.

The United States Supreme Court confronted the meaning of the term "statement" in Williamson v. United States, 512 U.S. 594 (1994). Prior to *Williamson*, federal courts were divided on the question of the admissibility of collateral, noninculpatory statements contained in a confessional narrative. In *Williamson*, Justice O'Connor wrote for the majority that each individual statement within a narrative must be evaluated to determine whether it was admissible under the rule. Justice O'Connor noted that "reasonable people, even reasonable people who are not especially honest, tend not to make self-inculpatory statements unless they believe them to be true." On the other hand, she noted that trustworthy statements against interest can be interspersed in a narrative with other statements that do not have the same level of credibility.

Because of this inherent tension, we adopt the middle-ground approach. We hold that only inculpatory statements and the collateral material necessary to provide context to the statements are admissible under our rule of evidence. When presented with a writing or narrative testimony, the district court must sift through it and admit the wheat and discard the chaff as suggested by Justice O'Connor in *Williamson*.

The second question presented under the rule is whether the statement is sufficiently inculpatory as to amount to a statement against penal interest. Under our rule, a statement against penal interest must have "so far tended" to inculpate the accused "that a reasonable person in the declarant's position would not have made the statement unless believing it to be true." Iowa R. Evid. 5.804(b)(3). This requirement is designed to establish a threshold level of trustworthiness of the underlying statement.

Although not expressly required, this adversity requirement implicitly demands that the person knew or at least believed that the statement was against penal interest at the time it was made. Otherwise, the rationale of the exception, namely, that a reasonable declarant would not make a statement against interest unless true, would be undermined.

The threshold adversity requirement also poses a question of degree. Some cases indicate that a statement does not come within the rule unless the statement squarely and unequivocally implicates the declarant in criminal activity or is tantamount to a confession. The rationale in these cases being that some statements are simply so vague or equivocal that they do not really amount to statements against interest.

Others cases suggest a lower standard. These cases tend to emphasize the "so far tended" language in the rule which suggests that incriminating statements which amount to less than a full confession may be admissible. Most commentators also believe that statements that fall short of a confession are the kinds of statements that should be admitted under the rule.

Given the broad and general language of the rule, especially the "so far tended" clause, we conclude that a statement need not amount to a full confession in order to be admissible as a statement against penal interest.

There also is a question regarding the proper result when there are potentially conflicting motivations for making the incriminating statements. For example, a father may claim that he alone possessed drugs, a statement that, if believed, would exonerate his son. . . .

We conclude that the use of the term "tended" in the rule suggests that it is not necessary that the statement be an explicit admission. We also conclude that the presence of conflicting motivations is ordinarily a question for the jury to consider.

The third question presented under this rule is the scope of the corroboration requirement when the statement against interest is being offered to exculpate the accused. [C]ourts have struggled over the meaning of corroboration contained in the last sentence of rule 5.804(b)(3). The corroboration rule must require something more than the inherent trustworthiness associated with a declaration against interest. Otherwise, the additional sentence would be written out of the rule. But what exactly is required? . . .

Given the broad, general language of the last sentence of the rule . . . , the best approach to determining whether a statement is adequately corroborated appears to be a multifactored test in which all evidence bearing on the trustworthiness of the underlying statement may be considered. . . .

A second major issue under the corroboration requirement is the amount or level of corroboration required. What amount of evidence is sufficient to provide corroboration clearly indicating trustworthiness? While the term "clearly" is a relatively strong term, the word "indicating," particularly in the law of evidence, is comparatively weak. Considering the language alone, it seems reasonable to conclude that there may be facts or circumstances that clearly indicate trustworthiness, even though a reasonable jury might conclude otherwise. . . .

We do not adopt a hard and fast rule regarding corroboration. Instead, we conclude that each statement against interest must be evaluated in context. Clearly, specious assertions . . . by persons completely unconnected with the time and place of the abduction and murder, lack corroboration and should be excluded. On the other hand, if a declarant is tied to the time and place of the crime and the statement has substantial plausibility, the corroboration requirement has been met.

Applying these principles to this case, we conclude that Millard did make statements against interest under rule 5.804(b)(3). She stated that Paredes "did not do it," that he "would not hurt the baby," that she "does not want her boyfriend to take the fall" for the child's injuries, that Paredes "is not that kind of guy, not violent," and that he "did not take care of the baby that much." Considered in isolation, these statements merely exculpate Paredes, but they are plainly self-inculpatory when considered in context. Except for a brief fifteen-minute interval when the baby was cared for by Paredes' sister, Millard and Paredes were the infant's only caregivers when the injuries were inflicted. As a result, by making statements tending to exculpate Paredes, Millard was indirectly implicating herself as the person who caused the injuries. These statements were not hypothetical when evaluated in the proper context.

In addition, Millard made statements that were directly inculpatory. She stated that the baby had been crying, that she yelled at him to "shut up," and that she had "started spanking him lately," which she claimed did not hurt him since he wore a diaper. Yelling "shut up" at a crying two-month-old shows obvious lack of self-control. Further, spanking a two-month-old child for crying, even with a diaper on, is an admission of inappropriate behavior that could give rise to an inference that Millard was the person who injured the child....

Finally, Millard asked Gail what would happen to her if it was discovered that she did hurt the baby. Although she at no time directly admitted that she was responsible for the injuries, an inquiry about potential sanctions tends to suggest that she may have been responsible....

We further note that Gail herself considered the statements significant. Twice during the conversation she admonished Millard that she needed to consult with her attorney.... It is clear that Gail and her supervisors recognized the potential criminal implications of the conversation. As a result, we conclude that the above statements amount to statements against interest under Iowa Rule of Evidence 5.804(b)(3)....

Even though Millard's express statements are sufficiently inculpatory to qualify as [statements] against interest under Iowa Rule of Evidence 5.804(b)(3), they are not admissible to exculpate Paredes unless corroborating circumstances indicate their trustworthiness. We have previously held that it is not necessary to demonstrate corroborating evidence of the statements themselves. Rather, as noted above, we conclude that the focus is on whether the circumstances under which the statements were made are sufficiently trustworthy to allow a jury to make the ultimate determination concerning their truth.

We conclude that there are sufficient corroborating circumstances to allow admission of Millard's inculpatory statements. First, Millard chose to make these statements to someone she trusted, a person who was not directly involved in the case. On its face, it appears that Millard was seeking advice from Gail and not trying to manipulate the system. Second, Millard's statements to Gail find at least some support in the record — Millard was a caregiver to the infant at the relevant time, her statements are consistent with Paredes' recantation of his confession, and her statements are to some extent corroborated by the testimony of Paredes' sister.

... Under the record presented here, we conclude that a reasonable jury could find Millard's statements truthful. As such, the district court erred by refusing to admit her statements under Iowa Rule of Evidence 5.804(b)(3)....

We hold that the court of appeals erred when it affirmed Paredes' conviction on the ground that Paredes failed to show that Millard was unavailable to testify at trial. We further hold that Millard's statements constitute statements against interest that were erroneously excluded from evidence in Paredes' trial. Under all the facts and circumstances, we conclude that the error was not harmless. As a result, the decision of the court of appeals is vacated, the judgment of the district court is reversed, and the matter is remanded to the district court.

NOTES TO STATE v. PAREDES

1. *Different from Statement by a Party Opponent (Admissions).* The exception for statements against interest is different from the provision for statements by a party-opponent in Rule 801(d)(2). Anyone can make a "statement against interest," not just a party or someone with a connection to a party. And a declarant's statement against interest may be introduced by any party in a case.

2. *When Is Corroboration Required?* FRE 804(b)(3) requires that a statement against penal interest be corroborated if it is offered in a criminal case. In an earlier version, this corroboration requirement applied only if the statement was sought to be introduced by a criminal defendant. It did not apply if the prosecution sought to use the exception. The state rule analyzed in *Paredes* was modeled after the earlier version of the federal rules.

3. *Role of the Jury.* The court states that, with regard to the corroboration requirement, a reasonable jury could find that the declarant's statement was true. This may represent a mistaken allocation of decision making between the court and the jury. Since corroboration is a required element of the definition of the exception, it is the court's obligation to determine whether that factor is present. If it is absent, then the exception has no application and the out-of-court statement should be excluded. If the out-of-court statement merits admission only if there is corroboration, it would be problematic to allow a jury to hear the statement and then to decide if corroboration was present. A jury that heard the statement and then, by hypothesis, decided that there was only weak corroboration might still be influenced by it.

4. *Multiple Levels of Hearsay.* Although it did not matter in the context of the *Paredes* appeal, there were two levels of hearsay involved in the case: Millar's spoken words to Gail, and Gail's written document that described Millar's words and conduct. The document would probably have been treated as admissible under the public records exception or the present sense impression exception.

5. *Criteria for Corroboration.* Factors courts consider for corroboration can include the declarant's apparent motive to misrepresent, the declarant's character, spontaneity, the timing of the statement, and the relationship between the declarant and the person to whom the declarant made the statement.

6. *Counterexample.* Some states recognize more kinds of statements than FRE 804(b)(3) does for the statement against interest exception. See, for example, Wisconsin's definition of the exception:

> **Wis. St. Ann. 908.045. Statement against interest.**
>
> A statement which was at the time of its making so far contrary to the declarant's pecuniary or proprietary interest, or so far tended to subject the declarant to civil or criminal liability or to render invalid a claim by the declarant against another or to make the declarant an object of hatred, ridicule, or disgrace, that a reasonable person in the declarant's position would not have made the statement unless the person believed it to be true. . . .

QUESTION 10-3. A defendant was accused of murdering an alleged drug dealer named Alvarez. The defendant sought to introduce a tape-recorded statement by Geraldo Lucia in which Lucia described having conducted illegal drug transactions with Alvarez, to show that Lucia as well as others might have had a motive to kill Alvarez. The recording contained a conversation between Lucia and Alvarez's attorney. Lucia described transactions with Alvarez. The lawyer told Lucia, "I will do everything I can to not hurt you" and that Alvarez and the lawyer didn't "have any interest [in] getting you [Lucia] in trouble." Alvarez's attorney also said that law enforcement personnel "can't just charge you [Lucia] with a crime," but that if they did, the prosecution would not "get very far if it's just you [Lucia] saying, 'Yeah, you know, I, I was once involved in [a] marijuana deal.'" Should Lucia's statements be admissible under Rule 804(b)(3)?

GOOD TO REMEMBER

The exceptions for "statement against interest" and "statement by an opponent" have major differences.

A statement by an opponent must be introduced *against the opponent* who made it. It need not have been adverse to the declarant when the declarant made it.

A statement against interest can be introduced *against anyone.* It had to be against the declarant's interest when the declarant made it.

E STATEMENT BY A DECLARANT RENDERED UNAVAILABLE

For most hearsay exceptions, there is a reason to believe that the covered statements have some indicia of reliability. Rule 804(b)(6) allows admission of statements made under any circumstances with any amount of likely accuracy, if they are introduced against someone who sought to prevent the declarant from being a witness. Even though this exception applies to statements regardless of their apparent reliability, it does relate to the overall goal of improving the truth-finding process at trials.

Rule 804. Exceptions to the Rule Against Hearsay — When the Declarant Is Unavailable as a Witness

. . .

(b) The Exceptions. The following are not excluded by the rule against hearsay if the declarant is unavailable as a witness:

. . .

(6) Statement Offered Against a Party That Wrongfully Caused the Declarant's Unavailability. A statement offered against a party that wrongfully caused — or acquiesced in wrongfully causing — the declarant's unavailability as a witness, and did so intending that result.

■ ■ ■

Deterring Threats and Harm to Witnesses — Gray. After allegedly killing two different husbands and collecting life insurance benefits, the defendant was prosecuted in federal court for mail and wire fraud. The *Gray* court deals with an ambiguity in FRE 804(b)(6). If the defendant in a trial participated in rendering a person unavailable to testify, what motive for causing that unavailability does the rule require the proponent of the hearsay to establish?

UNITED STATES v. GRAY

405 F.3d 227 (4th Cir. 2005)

SHEDD, J.

A grand jury indicted Josephine Gray on five counts of mail fraud and three counts of wire fraud relating to her receipt of insurance proceeds following the deaths of her second husband and a former paramour. Gray was convicted on all counts, and the district court sentenced her to 40 years' imprisonment, three years of supervised release, restitution in the amount of $170,000, and a special assessment of $800. Gray now challenges her conviction, arguing that . . . district court improperly admitted . . . hearsay evidence. . . .

Wilma Jean Wilson met Gray in the late summer of 2000, and the two became friends. They spoke over the telephone, and Wilson sometimes visited Gray's house. During one of those visits, Gray was busy cleaning a cluttered room and Wilson offered to help. As they were talking, Gray stopped cleaning and left the room briefly; when she returned, she brought newspaper articles describing her prior arrests. In fact, those articles reported that Gray had killed her former husbands. Wilson asked if the reports were true, and Gray replied that she was going to tell Wilson something she had never told anyone before and she did not want Wilson to say anything about it. In an emotionless, matter-of-fact manner, Gray then told Wilson that "she had killed both her husbands and another gentleman."

Gray told Wilson that she had killed her first husband, Norman Stribbling, because she was tired of being abused by him. . . .

Gray had been having an affair with Robert Gray while she was still married to Stribbling. In August 1975, the couple bought a house in Gaithersburg, Maryland — using most of the proceeds from Stribbling's insurance policy as a down payment — and three months later they married. . . .

Robert Gray left the Gaithersburg house in August 1990, telling family members that his wife was trying to kill him and that she was having an affair with [Clarence] Goode, who had been living with the Grays. So convinced was Robert Gray that his wife intended him harm that he removed her as his beneficiary under two . . . insurance policies. He asked relatives and friends for help in avoiding a possible assault by Gray or Goode.

In late August 1990, Robert Gray brought criminal charges against Gray, alleging that Gray had assaulted him at his workplace by swinging at him with a club and lunging at him with a knife. Robert Gray also brought charges against Goode, alleging that Goode had threatened him with a 9-millimeter handgun. Robert Gray appeared in court on October 5, 1990, but the case against Gray and Goode was continued. . . . One week before the November 16, 1990 trial date, Robert Gray was discovered dead in his new apartment, shot once in the chest and once in the neck with a .45 caliber handgun.

Gray told police investigators that she was not involved in her husband's death and that she did not own a .45 caliber handgun. Other witnesses testified, however, that they had seen Gray in possession of a .45 caliber handgun, and police investigators retrieved a .45 caliber bullet from her purse. Gray also offered an alibi that other witnesses at trial discredited.

As a result of Robert Gray's death, Minnesota Mutual paid approximately $51,625 to Perpetual Savings Bank — the named beneficiary — to cover the mortgage on the Gaithersburg house. Once the mortgage was satisfied, Gray sold the house for a significant profit. The total benefit under Robert Gray's policy exceeded the mortgage pay-off amount, so Minnesota Mutual expected to pay the excess benefit to Robert Gray's spouse. Because Gray's whereabouts were unknown to Minnesota Mutual, that benefit was not processed for about ten years. . . .

The district court . . . admitted into evidence several out-of-court statements made by Robert Gray during the three months preceding his murder: Robert Gray's criminal complaint alleging that Goode had tossed a 9-millimeter handgun on the table at his house to provoke an argument; Robert Gray's criminal complaint alleging that Gray had tried to stab him with a knife and attack him with a club; [s]tatements made by Robert Gray to Darnell Gray and a police detective, claiming that Gray and Goode had assaulted him in October 1990; and [s]tatements made by Robert Gray to Rodney Gray claiming that Goode had pulled a gun on him outside a restaurant in September or October 1990.

Although out-of-court statements ordinarily may not be admitted to prove the truth of the matters asserted, the doctrine of forfeiture by wrongdoing allows such statements to be admitted where the defendant's own misconduct rendered the declarant unavailable as a witness at trial. The Supreme Court applied this doctrine in *Reynolds v. United States*, 98 U.S. 145, 25 L. Ed. 244 (1878), stating that "the Constitution gives the accused the right to a trial at which he should be confronted with the witnesses against him; but if a witness is absent by [the accused's] own wrongful procurement, he cannot complain if competent evidence is admitted to supply the place of that which he has kept away." *Id.* at 158. By 1996, every circuit to address the issue had recognized this doctrine.[7]

Fed. R. Evid. 804(b)(6), which took effect in 1997, codifies the common-law doctrine of forfeiture by wrongdoing as an exception to the general rule barring admission of hearsay evidence. Fed. R. Evid. 804(b)(6) advisory committee note. Under Rule 804(b)(6), "[a] statement offered against a party that has engaged or acquiesced in wrong-doing that was intended to, and did procure the unavailability of the declarant as a witness" is admissible at trial. In order to apply the forfeiture-by-wrongdoing exception, the district court must find, by the preponderance of the evidence that (1) the defendant engaged or acquiesced in wrongdoing (2) that was intended to render the declarant unavailable as a witness and (3) that did, in fact, render the declarant unavailable as a witness. The district court need not hold an independent evidentiary hearing if the requisite findings may be made based upon evidence presented in the course of the trial.

Gray contends that Rule 804(b)(6) should not apply in this case because she did not intend to procure Robert Gray's unavailability as a witness at *this* trial . . . . The text of Rule 804(b)(6) requires only that the defendant intend to render the declarant unavailable "as a witness." The text does not require that the declarant would otherwise be a witness at any *particular* trial, nor does it limit the subject matter of admissible statements to events distinct from the events at issue in the trial in which the statements are offered. Thus, we conclude that Rule 804(b)(6) applies *whenever* the defendant's wrongdoing was intended to, and did, render the declarant unavailable as a witness against the defendant, without regard to the nature of the charges at the trial in which the declarant's statements are offered. . . .

Our interpretation of Rule 804(b)(6) advances the clear purpose of the forfeiture-by-wrongdoing exception. The advisory committee noted its specific goal to implement a "prophylactic rule to deal with abhorrent behavior which strikes at the heart of the system of justice itself." Fed. R. Evid. 804(b)(6) advisory committee note (internal quotations omitted). More generally, federal courts have

---

7. The Supreme Court recently confirmed the continuing vitality of the forfeiture-by-wrongdoing doctrine. *See Crawford v. Washington*, 541 U.S. 36, 124 S. Ct. 1354, 1370, 158 L. Ed. 2d 177 (2004).

recognized that the forfeiture-by-wrongdoing exception is necessary to prevent wrongdoers from profiting by their misconduct. *See Reynolds*, 98 U.S. at 158-59 (holding that a criminal defendant waives his right to confront a witness whose absence his own misconduct procured and stating that this rule "has its foundation in the maxim that no one shall be permitted to take advantage of his own wrong")....

[O]ur interpretation of Rule 804(b)(6) ensures that a defendant will not be permitted to avoid the evidentiary impact of statements made by his victim, whether or not he suspected that the victim would be a witness at the trial in which the evidence is offered against him. A defendant who wrongfully and intentionally renders a declarant unavailable as a witness in any proceeding forfeits the right to exclude, on hearsay grounds, the declarant's statements at that proceeding and any subsequent proceeding. *See United States v. Aguiar*, 975 F.2d 45, 47 (2d Cir. 1992) (affirming the district court's admission of hearsay testimony to prove witness tampering as well as an underlying drug conspiracy, and stating that "[a] defendant who procures a witness's absence waives the right of confrontation for all purposes with regard to that witness").[9]

Having rejected Gray's interpretation of Rule 804(b)(6), we need only determine whether the district court properly applied the Rule in admitting Robert Gray's out-of-court statements. Those statements were admissible only if the district court properly found, by a preponderance of the evidence, that (1) Gray engaged in some wrongdoing (2) that was intended to procure Robert Gray's unavailability as a witness and (3) that did, in fact, procure his unavailability as a witness. The district court in this case found that Robert Gray "was killed prior to the court date on November 15 and 16, and after the defendant was well aware of his status as a witness, justifies the inference that . . . the killing was motivated . . . to prevent [Robert Gray] from being available . . . at court proceedings." These findings are supported by the evidence and are sufficient to warrant application of the Rule 804(b)(6). Accordingly, the district court did not abuse its discretion in admitting testimony concerning out-of-court statements made by Robert Gray....

We affirm Gray's conviction for mail fraud and wire fraud. The evidence was sufficient to prove all the elements of each offense, and the district court's evidentiary rulings were correct....

NOTES TO UNITED STATES v. GRAY

1. *Ways to Render a Declarant Unavailable.* In addition to killing a declarant, other conduct may render a declarant unavailable. For example, in a case where a defendant's spouse asserted a privilege and refused to testify

---

9. We emphasize that the intent requirement in Rule 804(b)(6) continues to limit application of the forfeiture-by-wrongdoing exception to those cases in which the defendant intended, at least in part, to render the declarant unavailable as a witness against him. Absent such intent, Rule 804(b)(6) has no application.

against him, a court was justified in finding that the defendant's pattern of violence and violations of a no-contact order amounted to procuring the spouse's unavailability as a witness. *See* United States v. Montague, 421 F.3d 1099 (10th Cir. 2005).

2. Relationship Between Hearsay Claims and Confrontation Clause Claims. Admission of an out-of-court statement might be barred for either of two reasons: (1) it is hearsay, or (2) its introduction would violate the Confrontation Clause. In federal courts, showing that a defendant has caused the unavailability of a declarant as a witness requires a finding that the declarant's statements are covered by the Rule 804(b)(6) hearsay exception. It also requires a finding that the defendant has forfeited his or her rights under the Confrontation Clause issue.

These same two conclusions would be required in a state that has adopted a state version of FRE 804(b)(6). However, in a state that has not adopted a version of Rule 804(b)(6), even if a showing that a defendant had caused the unavailability of a witness means that the defendant has lost his or her confrontation rights, ordinary hearsay rules would still apply and might require exclusion of the unavailable declarant's statement.

In a federal court, when a statement's admission against a party is proper under the Confrontation Clause because that party caused the declarant's unavailability as a witness, hearsay objections will be satisfied by Rule 804(b)(6). In some state courts, a hearsay objection might still be valid. See, for example, this rule:

Cal. Evid. Code §1350. Unavailable declarant; hearsay rule

(a) In a criminal proceeding charging a serious felony, evidence of a statement made by a declarant is not made inadmissible by the hearsay rule if the declarant is unavailable as a witness, and all of the following are true:

(1) There is clear and convincing evidence that the declarant's unavailability was knowingly caused by, aided by, or solicited by the party against whom the statement is offered for the purpose of preventing the arrest or prosecution of the party and is the result of the death by homicide or the kidnapping of the declarant.

(2) There is no evidence that the unavailability of the declarant was caused by, aided by, solicited by, or procured on behalf of, the party who is offering the statement.

(3) The statement has been memorialized in a tape recording made by a law enforcement official, or in a written statement prepared by a law enforcement official and signed by the declarant and notarized in the presence of the law enforcement official, prior to the death or kidnapping of the declarant.

(4) The statement was made under circumstances which indicate its trustworthiness and was not the result of promise, inducement, threat, or coercion.

(5) The statement is relevant to the issues to be tried.

(6) The statement is corroborated by other evidence which tends to connect the party against whom the statement is offered with the commission of the serious felony with which the party is charged. The corroboration is not sufficient if it merely shows the commission of the offense or the circumstances thereof.

. . .

QUESTION 10-4. Defendant is on trial for arson. About a year before the trial, Defendant killed a former friend of his, Friend, in a fight about a gambling debt. The prosecution seeks to introduce an out-of-court statement that Friend once made to his spouse. Friend's spouse will testify that Friend said that Defendant told Friend he had set the fire. Should the trial court admit this testimony by Friend's spouse, as part of the prosecution's proof that Defendant set the fire?

F   SUMMARY

Unavailability Required. Rule 804 enumerates a number of hearsay exceptions that can be used only if the proponent shows that the declarant is unavailable. The most important exceptions in this group are the ones for former testimony, dying declarations, statements against interest, and statements introduced against someone who has rendered the declarant unavailable. The unavailability requirement is likely to be significant for former testimony and statements against interest. For dying declarations the declarant will almost always be unavailable. For statements by someone whose unavailability has been procured, the declarant will of course be unavailable.

Former Testimony. The former testimony exception allows introduction of statements given at a prior trial by a witness at that trial who is not available to testify at the current trial. In criminal cases, the statements can be admitted only if the defendant against whom the former testimony is sought to be introduced had an opportunity to cross-examine the witness at the prior trial. In civil trials, former testimony can similarly be introduced if the party against whom it is offered had an opportunity to cross-examine the witness at the prior trial. But in civil trials there is an additional avenue for admissibility. Former testimony may be used even if the party against whom it is offered never had a chance to cross-examine the witness at the prior trial so long as a predecessor in interest of the party did have that opportunity. "Predecessor in interest" is a technical term, but courts interpreting this exception have tended to give it a very broad meaning.

Dying Declarations. This exception covers statements made by a person who anticipates imminent death about the cause or circumstances of the death. For historical reasons, this exception applies in homicide cases, but not other criminal cases. It also, in the modern FRE 804(b)(2) version, applies in civil cases of any kind.

Statements Against Interest. The commonsense idea that people are only likely to say things that could harm their interests if those statements are true is the basis for this hearsay exception. Originally limited to statements against the declarant's pecuniary and proprietary interests, the exception in the modern federal rules covers statements against pecuniary, proprietary, and penal interests (the interest a person has in avoiding criminal liability). If this exception is sought to be used in a criminal case, there must be corroborating circumstances that clearly indicate the trustworthiness of the statement.

Statement by a Declarant Rendered Unavailable. If there is a showing that the person against whom an out-of court statement is introduced had a role in rendering the declarant unavailable as a witness, this exception removes the hearsay bar from any statement the declarant made under any circumstances at any time.

CHAPTER 11

Modifications of the Basic Hearsay Rules

A. Introduction
B. Residual Exception
C. Due Process Clause
D. Confrontation Clause
E. Summary

A INTRODUCTION

Topic Overview

The hearsay rules have a straightforward framework: definition of hearsay, categorization of some out-of-court statements as "not hearsay," and the enumeration of a large number of specific exceptions to the hearsay bar. These rules create a fairly clear map of the hearsay doctrine and its boundaries. However, there are some ways in which hearsay outside the definitions of the exceptions may be admitted. Also, there are circumstances where it would violate the Constitution to admit hearsay even though it fits within recognized exceptions to the general hearsay rule.

The Federal Rules and most parallel state codes incorporate a "catchall" or "residual" exception. This provision allows admission of out-of-court statements that fail to satisfy any of the enumerated hearsay exceptions or exclusions but that have aspects that make it desirable to allow their admission.

The Constitution imposes some significant modifications of the hearsay rules. In some rare cases, due process requires the admission of out-of-court statements that the hearsay doctrine would ordinarily bar. And in criminal cases, the Confrontation Clause sometimes requires exclusion of out-of-court statements that would otherwise be admissible under various provisions of the hearsay rules.

Chapter Organization

This chapter begins by examining the residual exception, with the particular attributes it requires a statement to have in order to avoid the hearsay bar. It also covers an important analytical question: When a statement is nearly covered by a particular exception but fails to earn admissibility under that exception, should the "near-miss" help or hurt that statement's chance for admissibility under the residual exception?

The Constitution is the next focus. Even if evidence doctrines such as the hearsay rule would keep some evidence out of a trial, occasionally that result would violate the due process clause. Identifying those situations is difficult, and is necessarily highly dependent on the overall array of evidence in a case.

The Confrontation Clause is the final topic in the chapter. The ways in which this part of the Constitution may prohibit the admission of hearsay were fairly clear until 2004. In that year, the Supreme Court decided a case that changed the analysis. While the law is still in flux, this chapter examines current Confrontation Clause jurisprudence in three settings: (1) the basic outlines of the new doctrines announced in 2004, (2) application of the doctrines to statements to law enforcement actors about recent criminal conduct, and (3) application of the doctrines to routine documents in the criminal investigation process.

B RESIDUAL EXCEPTION

In addition to the enumerated exclusions and exceptions that are part of the Federal Rules treatment of hearsay, Rule 807 allows admission of hearsay statements that would not otherwise be admissible, so long as they satisfy a variety of criteria. This rule, called the residual exception, was originally codified as two rules, 803(24) and 804(b)(5). They provided the same opportunity for admission separately for statements whose declarants were unavailable and statements whose declarants were either available or unavailable.

Applying the residual or "catchall" exception involves numerous evaluations within the discretion of a trial court. For example, the proponent of hearsay under the rule must persuade the trial judge that the statement "has sufficient guarantees of trustworthiness," and also that it is more probative on its point than other reasonably obtainable evidence.

Rule 807. Residual Exception

    (a) In General. Under the following conditions, a hearsay statement is not excluded by the rule against hearsay even if the statement is not admissible under a hearsay exception in Rule 803 or 804:

    (1) the statement is supported by sufficient guarantees of trustworthiness — after considering the totality of circumstances under which it was made and evidence, if any, corroborating the statement; and

    (2) it is more probative on the point for which it is offered than any other evidence that the proponent can obtain through reasonable efforts.

    (b) Notice. The statement is admissible only if the proponent gives an adverse party reasonable notice of the intent to offer the statement, including its substance and the declarant's name — so that the party has a fair opportunity to meet it. The notice must be provided in writing before the trial or hearing — or in any form during the trial or hearing if the court, for good cause, excuses a lack of earlier notice.

■ ■ ■

Is the Statement Trustworthy, and Did the Declarant Really Say It? — **Broderick.** This civil case involves a state's residual exception that is similar to Federal Rule 807. The court concentrates its attention on guarantees of trustworthiness. The opinion also provides a helpful reminder of the difference between proof that a statement was made and use of a statement as proof that its information is true.

BRODERICK v. KING'S WAY ASSEMBLY OF GOD CHURCH

808 P.2d 1211 (Alaska 1991)

BURKE, J.

    Judith Broderick appeals from the superior court's grant of summary judgment in favor of the defendants in Broderick's damage action against Shirley Gilman and King's Way Assembly of God Church for the alleged sexual abuse of Broderick's daughter. We reverse.

    In 1983 Judith Broderick and Gene Jansen, then married, attended King's Way Assembly of God Church. While attending church services, they left their three-year-old daughter, J.S.J., in the church's "tiny tots" program, under the care of Sue McNiece. In mid-1983 Shirley Gilman replaced McNiece. Gilman generally had at least one assistant when she supervised the program.

Shortly after Gilman replaced McNiece, Broderick observed behavioral changes in J.S.J. She noted that J.S.J. no longer wanted to attend "tiny tots" and would scream, kick and cry as they approached the church and the classroom. Broderick noted red rashes on J.S.J.'s elbows and behind her knees. Broderick also observed that J.S.J. was reluctant to take her panties off in front of Broderick and that J.S.J. complained that her genitals hurt when she bathed and used the toilet.

[J.S.J. told Broderick "the mean lady at the church" hurt "her wee-wee." At the church, J.S.J. saw Gilman and said, "That's the lady who hurt me."] . . .

On October 23, 1987, Judith Broderick filed a complaint on behalf of J.S.J. alleging that Shirley Gilman sexually abused J.S.J. while the child was entrusted to the care of the King's Way "tiny tots" program. The complaint further alleged that King's Way was also liable under theories including negligent supervision and hiring and *respondeat superior.*

[The trial court granted summary judgment motions by Gilman and King's Way.] . . .

Our sole task in this appeal is to determine whether Broderick offered evidence sufficient to raise a triable issue as to: (1) whether J.S.J. was abused while at church, and (2) if so, whether she was abused by Gilman.

[The court found that the plaintiff's evidence presented a triable issue with regard to the occurrence of abuse.]

The only evidence in the record establishing Shirley Gilman's identity as the abuser of J.S.J. comes from third-party accounts of J.S.J.'s identification of Gilman. Such accounts fall squarely within Evidence Rule 801, which defines hearsay as "a statement, other than one made by the declarant while testifying at the trial or hearing, offered in evidence to prove the truth of the matter asserted." Alaska R. Evid. 801(c). Unless the hearsay comes within the ambit of some exception provided by a statute or a rule prescribed by this court, it is inadmissible as evidence. Alaska R. Evid. 802.

[A]bsent an applicable exception to Rule 802, the hearsay nature of the only evidence presently in the record that links Shirley Gilman to the abuse of J.S.J. would be fatal to Broderick's case. Under the facts of this case, however, Broderick's account of J.S.J.'s identification of Gilman falls under the residual exceptions to the hearsay rule found in Rule 803(23) and Rule 804(b)(5).

Evidence Rule 803(23) provides:

> A statement not specifically covered by any of the foregoing exceptions but having equivalent circumstantial guarantees of trustworthiness, [is admissible] if the court determines that (a) the statement is offered as evidence of a material fact; (b) the statement is more probative on the point for which it is offered than any other evidence which the proponent can procure through reasonable efforts; and (c) the general purposes of these rules and the interest of justice will best be served by admission of the statement into evidence. However, a statement may not

be admitted under this exception unless the proponent of it makes known to the adverse party sufficiently in advance of the trial or hearing to provide the adverse party with a fair opportunity to prepare to meet it, his intention to offer the statement and the particulars of it, including the name and address of the declarant.

Alaska R. Evid. 803(23). We emphasize that this residual hearsay exception is intended to be used "sparingly" and only after rigorous application of the requirements of the section to the facts under consideration. Commentary, Alaska R. Evid. 803(23). We conclude, in light of all the facts in this particular case, that the hearsay accounts of J.S.J.'s identification of her abuser meet these requirements.

Rule 803(23) entails five requirements for admissibility: (1) the statement which is the subject of the hearsay testimony must have circumstantial guarantees of trustworthiness equivalent to that possessed by the specific hearsay exceptions; (2) the statement must concern a material fact; (3) it must be more probative than any other evidence which the proponent can reasonably procure; (4) admission must best serve the general purposes of the evidence rules and the interest of justice; and (5) the opponent must have appropriate notice that the hearsay will be offered.

Turning to the first requirement, we must assess whether the circumstances surrounding the identification of Gilman suggest trustworthiness to the same degree as the circumstances giving rise to the established hearsay exceptions. Because the twenty-two situations specified as exceptions under Rule 803 vary greatly in their circumstantial indicia of trustworthiness, this standard is necessarily inexact. In this situation, several factors support the conclusion that J.S.J.'s statements of identification are trustworthy enough to justify their admission in hearsay form.

First, the record indicates that the identifications were spontaneous, made without undue suggestions by someone else. At the time that J.S.J. first told her mother of the abuse, Broderick asked her who did it. Although Broderick did suggest a number of individuals — such as J.S.J.'s father, her grandparents and Broderick's boyfriend — the girl named a perpetrator that Broderick did not suggest: "[t]he mean lady at the church." When Broderick . . . took J.S.J. to the church, the girl reacted to Gilman's presence immediately upon seeing the woman. She then told them that Gilman was "the mean lady — that's the lady who hurt my wee-wee."

J.S.J.'s age at the time of the identifications is also a factor suggesting trustworthiness. The girl was three and a half years old when she identified Gilman as her abuser. As the Eighth Circuit noted under similar circumstances, "a declarant's young age is a factor that may substantially lessen the degree of skepticism with which we view their motives." *United States v. Renville,* 779 F.2d 430, 441 (8th Cir. 1985) (involving eleven-year-old sexual abuse victim). . . . By the same token, no evidence exists in the record to suggest that J.S.J. would have a motive to lie in identifying Gilman as her abuser, even assuming that she had the capability to do so.

J.S.J.'s use of "childish terminology" also gives her identification of Gilman "the ring of verity." *United States v. Nick,* 604 F.2d 1199, 1204 (9th Cir. 1979). J.S.J. told Broderick . . . that Gilman was the "mean lady" — the "bad lady" — who had hurt her "wee wee." . . . She also indicated to Broderick that the mean lady had touched her "heart," meaning her breast.

J.S.J.'s consistency in linking the "mean lady" at the church to the abuse is another factor suggesting trustworthiness. Although consistency may sometimes suggest rehearsal, the facts in this case militate in favor of reliability. J.S.J. referred to the "mean lady" at the church the first time she discussed the fact that she had been abused. Subsequent to that initial revelation, J.S.J. identified the "mean lady" at the church as her abuser in statements to her mother, to her mother's boyfriend, and to a child psychologist.

The fact that the witnesses to J.S.J.'s statements . . . may be unreliable or motivated by selfish interests is irrelevant to evaluation of the reliability of the statements themselves, which is what concerns us here. Noting that the circumstantial guarantees of trustworthiness under the residual exception must be "equivalent" to the guarantees underpinning the specific exceptions, the Seventh Circuit has concluded: "The specific exceptions to the hearsay rule are not justified by any circumstantial guarantee that the witness who reports the statement will do so accurately and truthfully. That witness can be cross-examined and his credibility thus tested in the same way as that of any other witness." *Huff v. White Motor Corp.*, 609 F.2d 286, 293 (7th Cir. 1979). We agree and reiterate that credibility of witnesses is "exclusively within the province" of the trier of fact.

The remainder of the requirements of Rule 803(23) are easily satisfied. J.S.J.'s statements are offered to prove a material fact and there is nothing more probative in a child abuse case than the victim's personal statements regarding the incident. Admission in this case serves the interest of justice by giving a jury the opportunity to resolve issues of fact surrounding these grave charges. Notice clearly is not a problem. We conclude, in light of the above, that J.S.J.'s statements are admissible for purposes of proving the identity of her abuser. . . .

The orders granting summary judgment to Gilman and King's Way are vacated and the case is remanded for proceedings consistent with this opinion.

NOTES TO BRODERICK v. KING'S WAY ASSEMBLY OF GOD CHURCH

1. *Equivalent Circumstantial Guarantees of Trustworthiness.* The "equivalent guarantees of trustworthiness" requirement might mean equivalent to the overall amount of trustworthiness that all of the exceptions in Rules 803 and 804 embody or it might mean equivalent to the amount of trustworthiness found in any single one of those exceptions. The *Broderick* court's analysis is representative of most courts' treatments of this part of the analysis.

The *Broderick* court refers to spontaneity, the age of the declarant, and style of language to support its finding of likely trustworthiness. Of these factors, only spontaneity can be found in the enumerated exceptions (for excited utterances and, perhaps, present sense impressions). This suggests that the court was interested in considering a wide range of factors to assess whether the out-of-court statement was likely a truthful one.

The court describes this as an inexact standard. Its opinion describes the guarantees it finds in the declarant's statements but does not link those to guarantees in the enumerated exceptions. Could the court have made such comparisons convincingly?

2. *Repetition.* With regard to trustworthiness, the court considers the declarant's consistent repetition of the contents of her initial statement. This is different from the typical treatment of prior consistent statements that a witness may have made after a motive to lie had arisen.

3. *Distinguishing "True that the Declarant Said It" from "What the Declarant Said Was True."* Doubt about whether an offered out-of-court statement was ever actually made should not be relevant in considering its admissibility. The jury can decide the factual question of whether the statement really was made the same way it can decide any other factual question. It can hear testimony about whether the statement was made, for example. On the other hand, the likely accuracy of an out-of-court statement may be difficult for a jury to evaluate. This second concern is the fundamental reason for the hearsay bar.

QUESTION 11-1. A prosecutor is considering bringing charges against Cal Cardman for defrauding various banks and credit card companies. The prosecutor believes that Cardman posed as a business owner to obtain electronic devices with which he processed false charges to stolen credit cards.

The prosecutor has records from 44 banks regarding 270 credit card customers containing, among other things, customers' statements that their credit cards were stolen. The banks' fraud investigators have provided the records.

There are two types of records. Some are letters and affidavits from the cardholders stating that their cards had been lost, stolen, or not received, and that their account bills contained unauthorized charges. Others are computer printouts from banks reporting phone calls made by cardholders to bank personnel in which the cardholders informed the bank that their credit cards were lost, stolen, or had never been received. The cardholders relayed this information orally to the bank personnel, who in turn entered the statements directly into the bank's computer.

A fraud investigator for one of the banks with 22 years of experience can testify that he has participated in over 1,000 fraud investigations and that he can remember only three or four instances in which the cardholder was lying about not making the charges.

Segment 20:
residual
exception

The prosecutor would like to introduce the letters, affidavits, and computer records to show that the customers had not made the charges for which they were billed. Discuss the applicability of Rule 807 to this evidence.

	Statements Almost Covered by an Enumerated Exception — **Katt.** When an item of evidence meets most of the requirements of an enumerated exception but is a "near miss," courts have differed about whether the evidence should be eligible for consideration under the residual exception. *Katt* explains the controversy in the context of a child's hearsay statement.

PEOPLE v. KATT

662 N.W.2d 12 (Mich. 2003)

Kelly, J.

The issue in this case is whether the trial court properly admitted under MRE 803(24) the victim's hearsay statement made to a social worker that defendant sexually abused her. The statement did not qualify for admission under MRE 803A, the tender-years rule.

A jury convicted defendant of three counts of first-degree criminal sexual conduct, sexual penetration of a victim under thirteen years of age (CSC I). M.C.L. §750.520b(1)(a). The Court of Appeals affirmed the convictions.

Before trial, the prosecutor moved to admit the testimony of Angela Bowman, a child-protective-services specialist with the Family Independence Agency (FIA). During the hearing, Bowman testified that she had visited DD at his elementary school after the FIA received an anonymous report that the children's mother was physically abusing them.

In the course of their conversation, Bowman asked DD to name the members of his household. He named defendant as a relative and spontaneously told Bowman that defendant was doing "nasty stuff" to him. . . .

Bowman related the details of . . . specific instances of defendant's abuse as DD had revealed them to her.

The prosecution conceded that DD's statement to Bowman was not admissible under the tender-years exception to the hearsay rule, MRE 803A, because it was his second statement about the abuse. Defendant argued that MRE 803A "covers the field," meaning that, if a statement falls in the category of a tender-years statement and is inadmissible under MRE 803A, it cannot be admitted under MRE 803(24).

The trial court rejected defendant's argument and admitted the evidence under MRE 803(24). In ruling that DD's statements satisfied the requirements of MRE 803(24), the court stated:

> [I]n the Court's opinion there are several indicia of trustworthiness in the statements given by [DD] to Miss Bowman. First is the spontaneity of [DD's] first statements to Miss Bowman. . . . Now, Miss Bowman's qualifications to interview children

were obvious from the record. She is aware of how to . . . interview children. She testified that she avoided leading questions and avoided other pitfalls of questioning
young children. And the Court finds that she was totally aware how to get truthful
information from [DD]. The Court finds that the record and the dynamics of this
exchange between Miss Bowman and [DD] provided a form [sic] that an accurate
statement would be uttered by [DD]. . . .

[T]he Court of Appeals affirmed the trial court's admission of the evidence.

The Michigan Rules of Evidence contain [a provision, MRE 803(24), similar
to Federal Rule 807]. . . .

The residual exceptions are designed to be used as safety valves in the hearsay rules. They will allow evidence to be admitted that is not "specifically covered" by any of the categorical hearsay exceptions under circumstances dictated
by the rules. Differing interpretations of the words "specifically covered" have
sparked the current debate over the admissibility of evidence that is factually
similar to a categorical hearsay exception, but not admissible under it.

"The Near Miss theory . . . states that a piece of hearsay evidence may be
offered only under the exception that most nearly describes it. If it is excluded
under that exception, it may not be offered under the residual exceptions." *In re
Japanese Electronic Products Antitrust Litigation*, 723 F.2d 238, 302 (C.A.3 1983),
rev'd on other grounds *Matsushita Electric Industrial Co., Ltd. v. Zenith Radio
Corp.*, 475 U.S. 574, 580, 106 S. Ct. 1348, 89 L. Ed. 2d 538 (1986). Judge Easterbrook
gave a concise statement of the rationale behind the near-miss theory in his concurring opinion in *United States v. Dent*, 984 F.2d 1453, 1465-1466 (C.A.7 1993):

> [The residual exception] reads more naturally if we understand the introductory
> clause to mean that evidence of a kind specifically addressed ("covered") by one of
> the [categorical exceptions] must satisfy the conditions laid down for its admission,
> and that other kinds of evidence not covered (because the drafters could not be
> exhaustive) are admissible if the evidence is approximately as reliable as evidence
> that would be admissible under the [categorical exceptions]. . . .

The great majority of courts have rejected the near-miss theory by interpreting the residual exception to omit as "specifically covered" *only those hearsay
statements admissible under a categorical exception*. A statement not admissible
under the categorical exceptions would not be "specifically covered" by those
exceptions, and thus could be a candidate for admissibility under the residual
exceptions. . . .

In our view, the arguments in favor of the near-miss theory are unpersuasive
and do not conform to the language of the rule. *Random House Webster's College
Dictionary* (1995) defines "cover" as "8. to deal with or provide for; address: *The
rules cover working conditions*." (Emphasis in original.) Therefore, a rule concerning the same subject matter as a piece of evidence, or from a similar source,
arguably could be said to "cover" that evidence.

If the rule applied to all evidence not "covered" by other exceptions, the
near-miss theory would be more persuasive. However, the rule modifies the term

"covered" with the adjective "specifically." Hence, more than simple "coverage" is required. Black's Law Dictionary (7th ed.) defines "specific" as "1. Of, relating to, or designating a particular or defined thing; explicit. . . . 2. Of or relating to a particular named thing. . . . 3. *Conformable to specific requirements. . . .* " (Emphasis added.)

Reading the words "specifically covered" together and giving each its normally understood meaning, we conclude that to be "specifically covered" requires *more* than to be "covered." Since "specific" can mean "conformable to specific requirements" and "cover" can mean "addressing" or "dealing with," we understand that a statement is only "specifically covered" by a categorical exception when it is *conformable to all the requirements of that categorical exception.* To hold otherwise would read "specifically" out of the rule. . . .

We stress that this interpretation of the residual exceptions does not subvert the purpose of the hearsay rules. Each of the categorical exceptions requires a quantum of trustworthiness and each reflects instances in which courts have historically recognized that the required trustworthiness is present. The residual exceptions require *equivalent* guarantees of trustworthiness. Thus, if a near-miss statement is deficient in one or more requirements of a categorical exception, those deficiencies must be made up by alternate indicia of trustworthiness. To be admitted, residual hearsay must reach the same quantum of reliability as categorical hearsay; simply, it must do so in different ways.

Thus, we affirm that the residual exceptions may be used to admit statements that are similar to, but not admissible under, the categorical hearsay exceptions. . . .

We now turn to the facts of this case. In order to invoke MRE 803(24), the proffered statement must "not [be] specifically covered by any of the foregoing exceptions" of MRE 803. MRE 803(24). As described above, we interpret "specifically covered" to mean "admissible." Defendant does not assert that DD's statement would be admissible under any of the MRE 803 categorical exceptions. Therefore, the statement is a proper candidate for admissibility under MRE 803(24). . . .

In aggregate, the trial court found that these circumstances justified the admission of DD's statement under MRE 803(24). The spontaneity of the interview, lack of motive to lie, and Ms. Bowman's interviewing methods combine to give the statement circumstantial guarantees of trustworthiness equivalent to the categorical exceptions. The unavailability of DD's first statement, the timing of the interview, and Ms. Bowman's careful conduct in eliciting information make this statement the most probative evidence of defendant's abusive acts. Having found that DD's statement met the first three requirements of MRE 803(24), the court concluded that admission would not endanger the interests of justice and ruled the statement admissible.

We agree with the Court of Appeals and hold that (1) the trial court properly analyzed DD's statement under MRE 803(24), and (2) there was sufficient evidence to support the trial court's findings. Consequently, we conclude that the trial court did not abuse its discretion in admitting the statement under MRE 803(24), even though the statement was not admissible under MRE 803A.

The trial court properly admitted DD's statement to Ms. Bowman under MRE 803(24), although it did not qualify for admission under MRE 803A. All the elements of MRE 803(24) were satisfied. Accordingly, there was no abuse of discretion and we affirm the decision of the Court of Appeals.

YOUNG, J., dissenting.

. . . The approach advanced by the majority subverts our historical prohibition against the admission of hearsay evidence. In the majority view, evidence that is clearly inadmissible under one of the enumerated hearsay exceptions gets a second chance at admissibility under the residual exception if, among other factors, "the interests of justice", MRE 803(24)(C), would be served by its admission. The criterion, particularly when coupled with the deferential abuse of discretion standard for appellate review, essentially renders the general prohibition against hearsay, and the development of what hearsay is excepted and not excepted, hollow and meaningless.

Against the nearly four hundred-year-old historical development of our hearsay rules, it is clear that the drafters of the rules did not intend a wholesale trampling of the enumerated hearsay exceptions when the federal residual hearsay exceptions were enacted. The advisory committee noted that the residual exceptions "do not contemplate an unfettered exercise of judicial discretion, but they do provide for treating *new and presently unanticipated situations* which demonstrate a trustworthiness within the spirit of the specifically stated exceptions."

In this case, DD's statement to Angela Bowman was not a *"new and presently unanticipated situation."* In fact, evidence of second and subsequent corroborative statements are specifically contemplated and explicitly rejected by the clear language of MRE 803(A) "[i]f the declarant made more than one corroborative statement about the incident, *only the first is admissible* under this rule." (Emphasis added.) . . .

The majority treats the residual hearsay exception as if it read "A statement not specifically *admissible* under any of the foregoing exceptions" rather than "specifically covered." Clearly, the plain language of the rule does not support such a reading.

This Court made deliberate choices in deciding what varieties of hearsay would be admissible and reflected those choices in the words of the hearsay exceptions. The line-drawing efforts reflected in the enumerated hearsay exceptions are rendered purposeless if hearsay that does not meet the textual requirements of a specific hearsay exception is alternatively admitted under the residual exception. . . .

While the alternative construction proffered by my colleagues in the majority is a principled one, I believe my construction best harmonizes with the actual text of the evidentiary rule as well as our general and historical prohibition against the admission of hearsay evidence. The clear language of the residual hearsay exception precludes admissibility where the evidence does not meet the specific textual requirements of an enumerated hearsay exception.

I urge this Court to consider repealing MRE 803(24) and MRE 804(b)(5).

NOTES TO PEOPLE v. KATT

1. *"Tender Years" Exception.* Michigan's child hearsay provision, which would not have allowed admission of the declarant's statements in *Katt*, provides a hearsay exception for statements that meet the following specifications:

> A statement describing an incident that included a sexual act performed with or on the declarant by the defendant or an accomplice is admissible to the extent that it corroborates testimony given by the declarant during the same proceeding, provided:
>
> (1) the declarant was under the age of ten when the statement was made;
>
> (2) the statement is shown to have been spontaneous and without indication of manufacture;
>
> (3) either the declarant made the statement immediately after the incident or any delay is excusable as having been caused by fear or other equally effective circumstance; and
>
> (4) the statement is introduced through the testimony of someone other than the declarant.
>
> If the declarant made more than one corroborative statement about the incident, only the first is admissible under this rule.
>
> A statement may not be admitted under this rule unless the proponent of the statement makes known to the adverse party the intent to offer the statement, and the particulars of the statement, sufficiently in advance of the trial or hearing to provide the adverse party with a fair opportunity to prepare to meet the statement.
>
> This rule applies in criminal and delinquency proceedings only.

QUESTION 11-2. Rob Runner was running outdoors at about 4:00 in the morning at a large outdoor shopping mall that was designed to look like an urban neighborhood. A tall sculpture composed of many large metal cubes had recently been installed there. Runner was found unconscious next to a large segment of the sculpture that had fallen down.

Runner has sued Mallco, the operator of the mall, for damages, claiming that Mallco violated a duty of reasonable care by installing a dangerous sculpture. Runner has no memory of the event, but he will present an expert's testimony that the sculpture segment hit Runner as it was falling. This expert testimony will be based on an examination of the segment and an analysis of Runner's injury. Runner will also seek to introduce testimony by Hal Helper, a city social worker, to show that the sculpture part hit Runner. (Mallco will contend that Runner carelessly tripped on the sculpture part after it had fallen to the ground.)

Helper would testify that he works with homeless people who spend time at the mall. About a week after Runner's injury, Helper talked with Oliver Oldman, a homeless person, at the mall. Oldman told Helper, "I saw that statute fall apart and hit that runner guy about a week ago — I didn't try to get help or check on him because I think fitness freaks like him deserve to be dead." Oldman is not available to testify.

Mallco will object to Helper's testimony on hearsay grounds. Discuss how the trial court should rule on the objection.

DUE PROCESS CLAUSE

The residual exception can allow the admission of hearsay that would otherwise be excluded under the basic structure of hearsay rules and doctrine. Its power is derived from the choices made by the drafters of the hearsay rules. Another way in which evidence that would otherwise be kept out by the hearsay ban may be required to be admitted is based on the United States Constitution. The Due Process Clause guarantees defendants a trial that is "in accord with traditional and fundamental standards of due process."* In a small number of cases, applying evidence rules to exclude evidence may violate that right. Determining when an evidence rule may properly exclude information and when the exclusion of that information would violate the Constitution is, understandably, a somewhat vague inquiry. This aspect of constitutional and evidence law is considered here in the context of the hearsay rule, but the due process right can apply when rules of any type have the effect of excluding evidence.

■ ■ ■

When Does the Constitution Trump a Hearsay Exception's Explicit Definition? — Cazares-Mendez. This case involves a state's version of the hearsay exception for statements against interest. The substance of the state exception was identical to the provision in the Federal Rules. It required a proponent to show various factors, including the declarant's unavailability. The opinion considers whether the Constitution might require admission of evidence that met most but not all of the requirements of the statement against interest exception.

STATE v. CAZARES-MENDEZ
256 P.3d 104 (Or. 2011)

BALMER, J.

Defendants José Guadalupe Cazares-Mendez and Jorge Reyes-Sanchez were convicted of aggravated murder in the death of Jessie Valero. During their separate trials, the court refused to allow them to present hearsay evidence from four different witnesses that another person, Tiffany Scherer, had stated that she had committed the murder. The Court of Appeals held that the trial court had erred in excluding the hearsay testimony. This court allowed the state's petitions for review. On review, we agree with the Court of Appeals and remand both cases for a new trial. . . .

---

* Chambers v. Mississippi, 410 U.S. 284, 302 (1973).

The victim, Jessie Valero, was found dead in her Hillsboro apartment on the morning of March 17, 2005. She had died from approximately 29 stab wounds. The apartment contained a red bicycle that Valero did not own, and the contents of her jewelry box had been emptied on the bed....

Both Reyes-Sanchez and Cazares-Mendez ... were indicted for two counts of aggravated murder, three counts of murder, one count of first-degree robbery, and one count of first-degree burglary. Reyes-Sanchez was tried first, beginning in January 2007. Cazares-Mendez was tried shortly afterward, beginning in late February 2007.

During their respective trials, both defendants attempted to offer evidence that another person, Tiffany Scherer, had confessed to the crime. Specifically, they offered testimony that Scherer had admitted committing the murder to four different witnesses on four separate occasions. Because the testimony was hearsay, both defendants attempted to introduce the evidence under exceptions to the hearsay rule. Defendant Cazares-Mendez sought to introduce the evidence under the "statement against penal interest" exception, OEC 804(3)(c). Defendant Reyes-Sanchez sought to introduce the evidence under the residual hearsay exception of OEC 803(28)(a).... What follows is a summary of the testimony of the four witnesses as presented through defendants' offers of proof.

Connie Torres had known Scherer for five years and considered her a friend; she also had known Scherer's mother for 10–15 years. Torres also had known Valero. Approximately one week after Valero's death had been reported in the news, Torres found Scherer sitting under a friend's truck (the truck had a very high clearance), listening to music and rocking back and forth, "acting like a little kid." Torres coaxed Scherer out, at which point Scherer broke down and confessed that she had stabbed a woman, although Scherer did not identify the person she had stabbed. Scherer stated that she and the woman had been arguing and then started fighting, at which point Scherer stabbed her.... Afterward, Scherer stated, she had attempted to make it look like a burglary....

Naomi Rivera was a friend of both Scherer and defendant Cazares-Mendez.... At some point after Rivera learned that Valero had been killed, Scherer told Rivera that she had stabbed a "bitch" who had been "coming at" Scherer....

Jessica Callahan was using methamphetamine when she met Scherer sometime around March 2005.... When they met in March, Callahan testified, Scherer stated that she was hiding from the police because she had stabbed a lady after the lady had "jumped" her....

Lisa Ann Smith had known Scherer for all of Scherer's life; she also had known Scherer's mother for years....

Smith did not know Valero, but she learned of her death in the newspaper. A couple of months afterward, on hearing rumors that Scherer had been involved in causing the victim's death, Smith asked Scherer if she had killed Valero. Scherer stated that she had been at a bar with Valero and that she and Valero went back to Valero's place. Scherer indicated that she had stabbed Valero about 22 times. Scherer also told Smith that she had later sent someone back to rob the place....

Scherer testified in both trials in connection with defendants' offers of proof. She admitted that she was using methamphetamine during the period when the crime occurred. She also admitted knowing Torres, Rivera, and Smith. She denied knowing Callahan or Valero. She denied stabbing Valero, and she denied telling any of the witnesses that she had stabbed Valero. . . .

The trial court refused to allow either defendant to put on the hearsay testimony that Scherer had admitted killing Valero. . . .

[D]efendant Cazares-Mendez contended that the witnesses' testimony as to the statements by Scherer met almost all of the requirements of the "statement against penal interest" exception, OEC 804(3)(c). . . .

Cazares-Mendez asserted that there were corroborating circumstances that clearly indicated the trustworthiness of the witnesses' testimony: Scherer had confessed to four separate witnesses that she had murdered a woman by stabbing her, to one witness that Valero was the victim, and to two witnesses that she had sent someone back to steal from the crime scene. Defendant admitted that one requirement of OEC 804(3)(c) was not met, because the declarant, Scherer, was available to testify as a witness (and had done so). Defendant asserted, however, that the Due Process Clause of the Fourteenth Amendment to the United States Constitution superseded the unavailability requirement, because it was an "artificial" restriction that was not rational under the circumstances. See *Chambers v. Mississippi*, 410 U.S. 284 (1973) (violation of due process to use state evidentiary rule to exclude hearsay testimony that another person had admitted committing the crime, when there was considerable evidence of reliability of statements). The state countered that, in any event, the proffered evidence lacked the required trustworthiness.

The trial court agreed with the state, concluding that the "corroborating circumstances" did not clearly indicate the trustworthiness of the statements attributed to Scherer. . . .

In his trial, defendant Reyes-Sanchez asserted that the testimony should be admitted under the residual hearsay exception, OEC 803(28). . . .

As in *Cazares-Mendez*, and largely for the same reasons, the state asserted that the testimony lacked the required circumstantial guarantees of trustworthiness.

Again, the trial court agreed with the state. The court began by noting that the testimony did not meet the requirements of the statement against penal interest exception, OEC 804(3)(c), because Scherer was available. The court then elaborated on its conclusion that the "statement against penal interest" exception did not apply, building from there to the conclusion that the residual hearsay exception did not apply either:

> . . . "But, you know, these statements do not have the indicia of reliability such that they would qualify under [OEC 803(28)]. They — even if the statements were made, there's no trustworthiness that they're not the product of Tiffany Scherer — even if they were made, that they're not the product of Tiffany Scherer's drug-induced hallucinations. Because in all the situations here, she was acting in the manner

that — that basically was indicative of somebody [who] was under the influence and in at least two or maybe three of the occasions it's clear that that was what her state was. . . .

At the conclusion of each trial, each defendant was convicted on all counts. The jury declined to impose the death penalty, and defendants each were sentenced to life in prison without the possibility of parole.

Both defendants appealed to the Court of Appeals, which reversed in both cases. The court ruled first in *Cazares-Mendez.* As in the trial court, defendant Cazares-Mendez asserted that the testimony met all the requirements of the "statement against penal interest" exception to the hearsay rule, OEC 804(3)(c), except the unavailability requirement. Defendant contended, however, that it would violate due process under the United States Constitution to prohibit him from presenting trustworthy evidence merely because the declarant, Scherer, was available.

The Court of Appeals agreed. The court first held that the corroboration requirement of OEC 804(3)(c) was "a screening device designed to frustrate fabrication either by declarants seeking to falsely exculpate a criminal defendant or by witnesses who, by way of hearsay, falsely ascribe inculpatory statements to purported declarants." The Court of Appeals concluded that corroborating circumstances did clearly indicate the trustworthiness of the statements attributed to Scherer, for five reasons. First, Scherer had confessed to stabbing a female victim to death on four separate occasions to four different witnesses. Second, neither Scherer nor the witnesses had any motivation to lie; Scherer had no reason to falsely claim to have killed Valero, and three of the four witnesses had no reason to falsely implicate Scherer in the murder. Third, Scherer's statements to the witnesses were essentially consistent, and in some places included details that were peculiar to this murder. In particular, the court noted that Valero had been stabbed 29 times: Smith testified that Scherer had stated that she had stabbed the victim 22 times, while both Torres and Rivera . . . described Scherer as stating that she had stabbed a woman repeatedly. Furthermore, Valero had epilepsy, and Scherer had told Smith that Valero had had a seizure. Finally, the crime scene showed evidence of a burglary, and both Torres and Smith reported that Scherer had stated that she had attempted to cover up the murder by making it look like a burglary or robbery.

Nevertheless, although the court concluded that the testimony met the trustworthiness requirement of OEC 804(3)(c), the court recognized that the rule did not apply, because the declarant, Scherer, was available to testify. That did not end the matter, however. In *Chambers,* the United States Supreme Court held that a state court had violated a criminal defendant's due process rights when (among other things) it refused to allow three witnesses to testify that another person had admitted committing the crime to them. The Supreme Court had concluded that the statements had "'considerable assurance of their reliability,'" because the declarant had made them to close acquaintances near the time of the crime, because the confessions were corroborated by other evidence, and because the multiple confessions effectively corroborated each other. The Court of Appeals concluded that the testimony in *Cazares-Mendez* met the requirements of *Chambers,* and so the trial court had erred in excluding it. . . .

In *Reyes-Sanchez,* the Court of Appeals wrote a briefer opinion, relying significantly on its opinion in *Cazares-Mendez.* . . .

As noted, defendant Reyes-Sanchez contends that the hearsay testimony in his case is admissible under the residual hearsay exception, OEC 803(28)(a). The state argues, however, that OEC 803(28)(a) does not apply on the facts of this case. [W]e agree with the state on that point. [Oregon accepts the "near-miss" argument; because the offered statements were against penal interest, their failure to qualify for admission under that exception barred reliance on the residual exception.]

Having rejected defendant Reyes-Sanchez's argument that the evidence was admissible under OEC 803(28)(a), we must consider his alternative argument on review — that the hearsay statements should have been admitted for the reasons articulated by the Court of Appeals.

As we previously noted, the Court of Appeals in *Reyes-Sanchez* relied on its substantive conclusion in *Cazares-Mendez* that the evidence was admissible under the statement against penal interest exception of OEC 804(3)(c) as modified by application of the Due Process Clause of the United States Constitution. In light of its holding in *Cazares-Mendez* that the evidence was admissible, the Court of Appeals determined that the trial court's exclusion of the evidence in *Reyes-Sanchez* constituted plain error. . . .

On review, the state does not challenge the Court of Appeals' application of the plain error rule. The only remaining issue in *Reyes-Sanchez,* then, is the substantive one presented in *Cazares-Mendez*: whether the hearsay statements in fact were admissible under OEC 804(3)(c), as modified by the requirements of due process. We turn to that question. . . .

Defendant Cazares-Mendez asserts that the trustworthiness of the hearsay testimony that he proffered is clearly indicated by corroborating circumstances. We agree. In this case, the jury could find that Scherer confessed on four separate occasions to four different witnesses. All of the statements were identical at their core, in that Scherer had admitted to stabbing to death a female victim. (To Smith, Scherer admitted stabbing Valero in particular.) Those confessions were against Scherer's interest, in that they could expose her to criminal liability. Scherer was not under any pressure to confess, and she obtained no benefit from doing so. The statements were made shortly after the murder, and (with the exception of the statements to Smith) were spontaneous. Furthermore, several of the statements included additional, corroborating details about the crime: three of the witnesses reported Scherer as stating that she had stabbed the victim repeatedly (the victim was stabbed about 29 times); two witnesses reported Scherer as stating that she had attempted to make the murder appear to be a robbery or burglary, with one witness testifying that Scherer stated she had sent someone back to rob the place; and one witness testified that Scherer had described Valero as suffering a seizure during the attack, when Valero in fact had epilepsy.

All those considerations were relevant to determining the trustworthiness of Scherer's hearsay statements. The state itself concedes as much. Yet the trial court in *Cazares-Mendez* seemingly failed to give weight to any of them. . . . The trial court erred as a matter of law in failing to evaluate those considerations in determining whether the hearsay statements were trustworthy.

We conclude, as did the Court of Appeals, that those corroborating circumstances clearly indicate the trustworthiness of the hearsay statements offered by defendant Cazares-Mendez. Accordingly, that aspect of OEC 804(3)(c) was met in this case.

It is undisputed, however, that the hearsay statements at issue are not admissible under OEC 804(3)(c), because the declarant, Scherer, was available to testify. As did the Court of Appeals, we now turn to the question whether due process nevertheless required the trial court to admit the testimony.

The key case in that regard is *Chambers*. Briefly, the facts of that case were as follows. The defendant was charged with having murdered a police officer. The defendant asserted that another man was the killer. Not only had the other suspect admitted to three friends in private conversations that he had killed the officer, but he had also signed a written confession, although he later repudiated it. The defendant called the other suspect to the stand and introduced the confession, but the state elicited from the suspect that he had repudiated the confession, and the trial court, based on state law, refused to allow the defendant to cross-examine the suspect as an adverse witness. The defendant also sought to introduce the testimony of the three witnesses to whom the suspect had confessed, but the trial court excluded the testimony as inadmissible hearsay — state law did not recognize a hearsay exception for statements against penal interest.

The United States Supreme Court concluded that the defendant had been denied "a trial in accord with traditional and fundamental standards of due process." Besides concluding that the trial court had erred in refusing to allow the defendant to cross-examine the other suspect, the Court also held that, under the circumstances, due process required the trial court to admit the hearsay testimony by the three witnesses. The Court explained that the testimony of the three witnesses was offered "under circumstances that provided considerable assurance of their reliability." Specifically:

> "First, each of [the other suspect's] confessions was made spontaneously to a close acquaintance shortly after the murder had occurred. Second, each one was corroborated by some other [independent] evidence in the case. . . . The sheer number of independent confessions provided additional corroboration for each. Third, whatever may be the parameters of the penal-interest rationale, each confession here was in a very real sense self-incriminatory and unquestionably against interest. [The other suspect] stood to benefit nothing by disclosing his role in the shooting to any of his three friends, and he must have been aware of the possibility that disclosure would lead to criminal prosecution. . . . Finally, if there was any question about the truthfulness of the extrajudicial statements, [the other suspect] was present in the courtroom and was under oath. He could have been cross-examined by the State, and his demeanor and responses weighed by the jury."

Because the hearsay statements were trustworthy and were central to the defendant's defense, the Court concluded, due process required that the testimony be admitted:

> "Although perhaps no rule of evidence has been more respected or more frequently applied in jury trials than that applicable to the exclusion of hearsay, exceptions tailored to allow the introduction of evidence which in fact, is likely to be trustworthy have long existed. *The testimony rejected by the trial court here bore persuasive assurances of trustworthiness,* and thus was well within the basic rationale of the exception for declarations against interest. That testimony also was critical to [the defendant's] defense. In these circumstances, *where constitutional rights directly affecting the ascertainment of guilt are implicated, the hearsay rule may not be applied mechanistically to defeat the ends of justice."* (emphasis added).

Chambers remains good law. The United States Supreme Court recently reaffirmed the holding of *Chambers* in *Holmes v. South Carolina,* 547 U.S. 319, 325–26, 126 S. Ct. 1727, 164 L. Ed. 2d 503 (2006), where the Court unanimously concluded that the trial court erred in preventing a defendant from introducing hearsay testimony that another person had admitted committing the crime. Other courts have recently relied on *Chambers* to conclude that state laws restricting the introduction of trustworthy hearsay evidence violated due process, where the evidence was that another person had committed the crime.

We have already concluded that the "corroborating circumstances clearly indicate the trustworthiness" of the hearsay statements at issue here. We see no meaningful distinction between that standard and *Chambers'* requirement that the hearsay statements have "persuasive assurances of trustworthiness." Nor does the state assert that any difference exists.

The state contends, however, that due process is not violated here, because the unavailability requirement of OEC 804(3)(c) reflects a rational and reasonable policy preference for live testimony by the declarant, rather than hearsay testimony by witnesses. As the United States Supreme Court has explained, a criminal defendant's right to a "meaningful opportunity to present a complete defense" is violated by "evidence rules that infring[e] upon a weighty interest of the accused and are arbitrary or disproportionate to the purposes they are designed to serve." *Holmes,* 547 U.S. at 324. *Holmes* cited *Chambers* as an example of such an arbitrary or disproportionate rule. The state contends that OEC 804(3)(c)'s requirement that the declarant be unavailable is not arbitrary or disproportionate; it instead reflects a sensible preference that the declarant, when available, should be called to the stand and directly examined in the presence of the jury, rather than permit a defendant to present less reliable hearsay testimony.

Defendant Cazares-Mendez asserts — and we agree — that, where the unavailability requirement is used, as here, to exclude otherwise trustworthy evidence that, if believed, shows that a person other than defendant committed the crime, that requirement is arbitrary and disproportionate to the purpose that the evidentiary rule is designed to serve. As defendant correctly points out, the unavailability of a declarant who has allegedly confessed to the crime would not make her hearsay testimony *more* reliable — it would make it *less* reliable. If the hearsay declarant is available, as here, the declarant can take the stand and clarify or refute the confession that he or she allegedly made. If the declarant is unavailable, however, no such opportunity exists. Indeed, the unavailability of the declarant actually would help witnesses concoct falsified "confessions" by absent third parties, because they would know that the missing declarant will not be around to deny their claims. Accordingly, we conclude that the Due Process Clause, as interpreted in *Chambers* and similar cases, required the trial court to disregard the "unavailability" requirement of OEC 804(3)(c) and permit the testimony of Torres, Rivera, Callahan, and Smith. . . .

In summary, we conclude that courts evaluating "trustworthiness" under the hearsay exceptions should not consider the credibility of the witnesses testifying to the hearsay statements, but rather should focus on whether the declarant's statements are sufficiently corroborated. We conclude in both *Cazares-Mendez* and *Reyes-Sanchez* that the hearsay statements met the requirements for admission as statements against penal interest under OEC 804(3)(c), but for the fact that the declarant was available to testify. Further, we conclude that barring the admission of hearsay statements that another person had confessed to the crimes with which defendants were charged on the ground that the declarant was available to testify was, on the facts here, a violation of each defendant's rights under the Due Process Clause.

The decisions of the Court of Appeals are affirmed. The . . . matters are remanded to the circuit court for further proceedings.

NOTES TO STATE v. CAZARES-MENDEZ

1. *Applying Due Process Outside the Hearsay Context.* The principle illustrated in *Cazares-Mendez* has been applied in a wide range of circumstances. The United States Supreme Court has treated as arbitrary and therefore impermissible:

- prohibiting testimony by any witness who has been subject to hypnosis (Rock v. Arkansas, 483 U.S. 44 (1987))
- prohibiting a defendant from attempting to show that his confession was unreliable because of the circumstances under which it was obtained (Crane v. Kentucky, 476 U.S. 683 (1986))
- prohibiting evidence of a third party's commission of a crime for which the defendant is charged unless the prosecution's case is weak (Holmes v. South Carolina, 547 U.S. 319 (2006))

2. *The Unavailability Requirement for Some Hearsay Exceptions.* Requiring a showing of the declarant's unavailability as a condition for use of some hearsay exceptions makes those exceptions somewhat less available for use

than they would be if they ignored the declarant's status as available or unavailable. Limiting their use in this way may reflect a belief at common law or during the drafting process that the statements covered by these exceptions are relatively unreliable. Another rationale would be that given their relative unreliability, it makes sense to have a rule structure that makes it the most likely that an available declarant will actually testify. The *Cazares-Mendez* court takes the position that when the declarant of a statement against penal interest is unavailable, that fact decreases the likely reliability of the declarant's statement. While this may be true, the drafters of the rule the court applied must have believed the opposite.

QUESTION 11-3. Defendant, charged with burglarizing a store, has introduced testimony from four witnesses. They all testified that they had been at a movie with Defendant for the entire time period in which the prosecution claims that the crime occurred. Defendant sought to have his mother testify that a month before the trial a friend of hers had told her that she had seen Defendant at the time of the crime at the movie theater. The trial court sustained a hearsay objection to Defendant's mother's testimony about what her friend said.

If Defendant is found guilty and claims on appeal that exclusion of his mother's testimony was a violation of his due process rights, which of the following arguments would be strongest in support of the trial court's action?

A. The friend's statement is hearsay, and no exclusion or enumerated exception would allow its admission.

B. The evidence was not critical to Defendant's case because Defendant had ample evidence from other sources to establish the same point.

C. The friend's statement is hearsay, no exclusion or enumerated exception would allow its admission, and it is outside the proper coverage of the residual exception.

D. The friend's statement is not trustworthy, because Defendant's mother has a motive to lie about it.

D CONFRONTATION CLAUSE

1. The Constitutional Issue and Its Treatment Prior to 2004

Criminal defendants have claimed that the Sixth Amendment's Confrontation Clause should be applied to prevent the use of hearsay at their trials.

United States Constitution, Sixth Amendment

In all criminal prosecutions, the accused shall enjoy the right to a speedy and public trial, by an impartial jury of the State and district wherein the crime shall have been committed, which district shall have been previously ascertained by law, and to be informed of the nature and cause of the accusation; **to be confronted with the witnesses against him**; to have compulsory process for obtaining witnesses in his favor, and to have the Assistance of Counsel for his defence. (Emphasis added.)

Hearsay statements are made by declarants who are out of court, and the Confrontation Clause guarantees a defendant the right to "be confronted with the witnesses against him." How can a defendant "confront" an absent declarant? The Supreme Court's answer to this question, from 1980 to 2004, was provided by Ohio v. Roberts, 448 U.S. 56 (1980). In *Roberts*, the Court held that the meaning of the Confrontation Clause was to provide accuracy in the fact-finding process. Hearsay could be used, therefore, if a declarant was unavailable and the hearsay evidence was either covered by a "firmly rooted" hearsay exception or had "particularized guarantees of trustworthiness."

2. New in 2004: The *Crawford* Analysis

In 2004, the Supreme Court adopted a new Confrontation Clause analysis in Crawford v. Washington.* The Court's opinion reasoned that the 1603 trial of Sir Walter Raleigh was the main influence that led to adoption of the Confrontation Clause. In that trial, evidence against Raleigh included a letter from Raleigh's alleged coconspirator in treason and testimony that coconspirator had given in a proceeding in which Raleigh did not participate. This process was characterized as "trial by affidavit." With this background, the Court held that admission of hearsay violates the Constitution in a criminal case if the hearsay is "testimonial," as was the affidavit in the Sir Walter Raleigh case. Prior to *Crawford*, hearsay rules and the Confrontation Clause were almost identical — if an out-of-court statement was admissible under typical hearsay rules, its admission was acceptable under the Confrontation Clause. After *Crawford*, even if an out-of-court statement satisfied a hearsay exception, its admission would violate the Confrontation Clause if the statement was "testimonial" (unless the declarant testified or had earlier been cross-examined by the defendant).

The Court did not offer a full definition of "testimonial" in *Crawford*. At one point, it wrote: "An accuser who makes a formal statement to government officers bears testimony in a sense that a person who makes a casual remark to an

---

* 541 U.S. 36 (2004).

acquaintance does not." Developing a fuller understanding of "testimonial" has been difficult, as a series of later cases shows.

■   ■   ■

Initial Elaborations of Crawford — Davis *and* Hammon. These companion cases focus on the motivation of the speaker in the speaker's statements to law enforcement personnel. In particular, the speaker's grammar choice in using either the present tense or the past tense may affect the outcome.

DAVIS v. WASHINGTON (HAMMON v. INDIANA)

126 S. Ct. 2266 (2006)

Justice SCALIA delivered the opinion of the Court.

These cases require us to determine when statements made to law enforcement personnel during a 911 call or at a crime scene are "testimonial" and thus subject to the requirements of the Sixth Amendment's Confrontation Clause.

The relevant statements in *Davis v. Washington* were made to a 911 emergency operator. . . . When the operator answered the initial call, the connection terminated before anyone spoke. She reversed the call, and Michelle McCottry answered. In the ensuing conversation, the operator ascertained that McCottry was involved in a domestic disturbance with her former boyfriend Adrian Davis, the petitioner in this case:

"**911 Operator:** Hello."
"**Complainant:** Hello."
"**911 Operator:** What's going on?"
"**Complainant:** He's here jumpin' on me again."
"**911 Operator:** Okay. Listen to me carefully. Are you in a house or an apartment?"
"**Complainant:** I'm in a house."
"**911 Operator:** Are there any weapons?"
"**Complainant:** No. He's usin' his fists."
"**911 Operator:** Okay. Has he been drinking?"
"**Complainant:** No."
"**911 Operator:** Okay, sweetie. I've got help started. . . . Do you know his last name?"
"**Complainant:** It's Davis."
"**911 Operator:** Davis? Okay, what's his first name?"
"**Complainant:** Adran . . ."

As the conversation continued, the operator learned that Davis had "just r[un] out the door" after hitting McCottry, and that he was leaving in a car with someone else. McCottry started talking, but the operator cut her off, saying, "Stop talking and answer my questions." She then gathered more information about Davis (including his birthday), and learned that Davis had told McCottry that his purpose in coming to the house was "to get his stuff," since McCottry was moving. . . .

The State charged Davis with felony violation of a domestic no-contact order. "The State's only witnesses were the two police officers who responded to the 911 call. Both officers testified that McCottry exhibited injuries that appeared to be recent, but neither officer could testify as to the cause of the injuries." [154 Wash. 2d 291 (2005) (en banc).] McCottry presumably could have testified as to whether Davis was her assailant, but she did not appear. Over Davis's objection, based on the Confrontation Clause of the Sixth Amendment, the trial court admitted the recording of her exchange with the 911 operator, and the jury convicted him. The Supreme Court of Washington, with one dissenting justice, . . . affirmed, concluding that the portion of the 911 conversation in which McCottry identified Davis was not testimonial, and that if other portions of the conversation were testimonial, admitting them was harmless beyond a reasonable doubt.

In *Hammon v. Indiana,* police responded late on the night of February 26, 2003, to a "reported domestic disturbance" at the home of Hershel and Amy Hammon. 829 N.E.2d 444, 446 (Ind. 2005). They found Amy alone on the front porch, appearing "'somewhat frightened,'" "but she told them that "'nothing was the matter,'" *Id.* She gave them permission to enter the house, where an officer saw "a gas heating unit in the corner of the living room" that had "flames coming out of the . . . partial glass front. There were pieces of glass on the ground in front of it and there was flame emitting from the front of the heating unit."

Hershel, meanwhile, was in the kitchen. He told the police "that he and his wife had 'been in an argument' but 'everything was fine now' and the argument 'never became physical.'" "By this point Amy had come back inside. One of the officers remained with Hershel; the other went to the living room to talk with Amy, and "again asked [her] what had occurred." *Ibid.* Hershel made several attempts to participate in Amy's conversation with the police, but was rebuffed. The officer later testified that Hershel "became angry when I insisted that [he] stay separated from Mrs. Hammon so that we can investigate what had happened." After hearing Amy's account, the officer "had her fill out and sign a battery affidavit." Amy handwrote the following: "Broke our Furnace & shoved me down on the floor into the broken glass. Hit me in the chest and threw me down. Broke our lamps & phone. Tore up my van where I couldn't leave the house. Attacked my daughter."

The State charged Hershel with domestic battery and with violating his probation. Amy was subpoenaed, but she did not appear at his subsequent bench trial. The State called the officer who had questioned Amy, and asked him to recount what Amy told him and to authenticate the affidavit. Hershel's counsel repeatedly objected to the admission of this evidence. . . . Nonetheless, the trial court admitted the affidavit as a "present sense impression," and Amy's statements as "excited utterances" that "are expressly permitted in these kinds of cases even if the declarant is not available to testify." . . .

The trial judge found Hershel guilty on both charges. . . . The Indiana Supreme Court . . . affirmed, concluding that Amy's statement was admissible for state-law purposes as an excited utterance . . . and that Amy's oral statement was not "testimonial." . . . It also concluded that, although the affidavit was testimonial and thus wrongly admitted, it was harmless beyond a reasonable doubt, largely because the trial was to the bench.

The Confrontation Clause of the Sixth Amendment provides: "In all criminal prosecutions, the accused shall enjoy the right . . . to be confronted with the witnesses against him." In *Crawford v. Washington,* 541 U.S. 36, 53-54 (2004), we held that this provision bars "admission of testimonial statements of a witness who did not appear at trial unless he was unavailable to testify, and the defendant had had a prior opportunity for cross-examination." A critical portion of this holding, and the portion central to resolution of the two cases now before us, is the phrase "testimonial statements." Only statements of this sort cause the declarant to be a "witness" within the meaning of the Confrontation Clause. It is the testimonial character of the statement that separates it from other hearsay that, while subject to traditional limitations upon hearsay evidence, is not subject to the Confrontation Clause.

Our opinion in *Crawford* set forth "[v]arious formulations" of the core class of "'testimonial'" statements, but found it unnecessary to endorse any of them, because "some statements qualify under any definition." Among those, we said, were "[s]tatements taken by police officers in the course of interrogations." The questioning that generated the deponent's statement in *Crawford*—which was made and recorded while she was in police custody, after having been given *Miranda* warnings as a possible suspect herself—"qualifies under any conceivable definition" of an "'interrogation.'" We therefore did not define that term, except to say that "[w]e use [it] . . . in its colloquial, rather than any technical legal, sense," and that "one can imagine various definitions . . . , and we need not select among them in this case." The character of the statements in the present cases is not as clear, and these cases require us to determine more precisely which police interrogations produce testimony.

Without attempting to produce an exhaustive classification of all conceivable statements—or even all conceivable statements in response to police interrogation—as either testimonial or nontestimonial, it suffices to decide the present cases to hold as follows: Statements are nontestimonial when made in the course of police interrogation under circumstances objectively indicating that the primary purpose of the interrogation is to enable police assistance to meet an ongoing emergency. They are testimonial when the circumstances objectively indicate that there is no such ongoing emergency, and that the primary purpose of the interrogation is to establish or prove past events potentially relevant to later criminal prosecution.[1]

---

1. Our holding refers to interrogations because, as explained below, the statements in the cases presently before us are the products of interrogations—which in some circumstances tend to generate testimonial responses. This is not to imply, however, that statements made in the absence of any interrogation are necessarily nontestimonial. The Framers were no more willing to exempt from cross-examination volunteered testimony or answers to open-ended questions than they were to exempt answers to detailed interrogation. . . . And of course even when interrogation exists, it is in the final analysis the declarant's statements, not the interrogator's questions, that the Confrontation Clause requires us to evaluate.

In *Crawford,* it sufficed for resolution of the case before us to determine that "even if the Sixth Amendment is not solely concerned with testimonial hearsay, that is its primary object, and interrogations by law enforcement officers fall squarely within that class." Moreover, as we have just described, the facts of that case spared us the need to define what we meant by "interrogations." The *Davis* case today does not permit us this luxury of indecision. The inquiries of a police operator in the course of a 911 call are an interrogation in one sense, but not in a sense that "qualifies under any conceivable definition." We must decide, therefore, whether the Confrontation Clause applies only to testimonial hearsay; and, if so, whether the recording of a 911 call qualifies.

The answer to the first question was suggested in *Crawford,* even if not explicitly held:

> "The text of the Confrontation Clause reflects this focus [on testimonial hearsay]. It applies to 'witnesses' against the accused — in other words, those who 'bear testimony.' 1 N. Webster, An American Dictionary of the English Language (1828). 'Testimony,' in turn, is typically 'a solemn declaration or affirmation made for the purpose of establishing or proving some fact.' *Ibid.* An accuser who makes a formal statement to government officers bears testimony in a sense that a person who makes a casual remark to an acquaintance does not."

A limitation so clearly reflected in the text of the constitutional provision must fairly be said to mark out not merely its "core," but its perimeter. . . .

The question before us in *Davis,* then, is whether, objectively considered, the interrogation that took place in the course of the 911 call produced testimonial statements. When we said in *Crawford* that "interrogations by law enforcement officers fall squarely within [the] class" of testimonial hearsay, we had immediately in mind (for that was the case before us) interrogations solely directed at establishing the facts of a past crime, in order to identify (or provide evidence to convict) the perpetrator. The product of such interrogation, whether reduced to a writing signed by the declarant or embedded in the memory (and perhaps notes) of the interrogating officer, is testimonial. It is, in the terms of the 1828 American dictionary quoted in *Crawford,* "'[a] solemn declaration or affirmation made for the purpose of establishing or proving some fact.'" . . . A 911 call, on the other hand, and at least the initial interrogation conducted in connection with a 911 call, is ordinarily not designed primarily to "establis[h] or prov[e]" some past fact, but to describe current circumstances requiring police assistance.

The difference between the interrogation in *Davis* and the one in *Crawford* is apparent on the face of things. In *Davis,* McCottry was speaking about events *as they were actually happening.* . . . Sylvia Crawford's interrogation, on the other hand, took place hours after the events she described had occurred. Moreover, any reasonable listener would recognize that McCottry (unlike Sylvia Crawford) was facing an ongoing emergency. Although one *might* call 911 to provide a narrative report of a crime absent any imminent danger, McCottry's call was plainly a call for help against bona fide physical threat. Third, the nature of what was asked and answered in *Davis*, again viewed objectively, was such that the elicited statements were necessary to be able to *resolve* the present emergency, rather than simply to learn (as in *Crawford*) what had happened in the past. That is true even of the operator's effort to establish the identity of the assailant, so that the dispatched officers might know whether they would be encountering a violent felon. And finally, the difference in the level of formality between the two interviews is striking. Crawford was responding calmly, at the station house, to a series of questions, with the officer-interrogator taping and making notes of her answers; McCottry's frantic answers were provided over the phone, in an environment that was not tranquil, or even (as far as any reasonable 911 operator could make out) safe.

We conclude from all this that the circumstances of McCottry's interrogation objectively indicate its primary purpose was to enable police assistance to meet an ongoing emergency. She simply was not acting as a *witness;* she was not *testifying.* What she said was not "a weaker substitute for live testimony" at trial, *United States v. Inadi,* 475 U.S. 387, 394 (1986), like Lord Cobham's statements in *Raleigh's Case,* 2 How. St. Tr. 1 (1603), or . . . Sylvia Crawford's statement in *Crawford.* In each of those cases, the *ex parte* actors and the evidentiary products of the *ex parte* communication aligned perfectly with their courtroom analogues. McCottry's emergency statement does not. No "witness" goes into court to proclaim an emergency and seek help. . . .

Determining the testimonial or nontestimonial character of the statements that were the product of the interrogation in *Hammon* is a much easier task, since they were not much different from the statements we found to be testimonial in *Crawford.* It is entirely clear from the circumstances that the interrogation was part of an investigation into possibly criminal past conduct. . . . There was no emergency in progress; the interrogating officer testified that he had heard no arguments or crashing and saw no one throw or break anything. When the officers first arrived, Amy told them that things were fine, and there was no immediate threat to her person. When the officer questioned Amy for the second time, and elicited the challenged statements, he was not seeking to determine (as in *Davis*) "what is happening," but rather "what happened." Objectively viewed, the primary, if not indeed the sole, purpose of the interrogation was to investigate a possible crime — which is, of course, precisely what the officer *should* have done.

It is true that the *Crawford* interrogation was more formal. It followed a *Miranda* warning, was tape-recorded, and took place at the station house. While these features certainly strengthened the statements' testimonial aspect — made it more objectively apparent, that is, that the purpose of the exercise was to nail down the truth about past criminal events — none was essential to the point. It was formal enough that Amy's interrogation was conducted in a separate room, away from her husband (who tried to intervene), with the officer receiving her replies for use in his "investigat[ion]." What we called the "striking resemblance" of the *Crawford* statement to civil-law *ex parte* examinations, is shared by Amy's statement here. Both declarants were actively separated from the defendant — officers forcibly prevented Hershel from participating in the interrogation. Both statements deliberately recounted, in response to police questioning, how potentially criminal past events began and progressed. And both took place some time after the events described were over. Such statements under official interrogation are an obvious substitute for live testimony, because they do precisely *what a witness does* on direct examination; they are inherently testimonial. . . .

We affirm the judgment of the Supreme Court of Washington. We reverse the judgment of the Supreme Court of Indiana, and remand the case to that Court for proceedings not inconsistent with this opinion.

NOTES TO DAVIS v. WASHINGTON

1. *Testimonial and Nontestimonial Aspects of Single Statements.* A person reporting an emergency and seeking help might additionally provide information in response to questions that relate more to investigation than to providing assistance. Trial courts can exclude any parts of a statement that are testimonial without being required to exclude the entire statement.

2. *Domestic Violence and Suppression of Testimony.* Violent spouses may intimidate their victims to suppress their testimony. The protections of the Confrontation Clause are forfeited in this circumstance, as will be seen in the next case, *Giles*. Courts usually use a preponderance of the evidence standard to determine whether a defendant has procured the unavailability of a witness's testimony. They may consider hearsay evidence, including the unavailable witness's out-of-court statements, in making that determination.

■   ■   ■

> **GOOD TO REMEMBER**
>
> When the Confrontation Clause applies, the out-of-court statement may be introduced only if the declarant is unavailable and the defendant against whom the hearsay is sought to be introduced had an opportunity to cross-examine the declarant about the statement on an earlier occasion.

Narrow Application of Forfeiture — Giles. Domestic abuse cases frequently involve Confrontation Clause issues because victims who have been abused sometimes refuse to testify against those who have abused them. *Crawford, Davis*, and *Hammon* involved that troubling pattern. Tragically, sometimes domestic abuse leads to murder. In that circumstance, the question arises whether the killer should lose the protection of the Confrontation Clause.

Rule 804(b)(6), "Statement Offered Against a Party That Wrongfully Caused the Declarant's Unavailability," controls the question of whether the hearsay rules preclude admission of such statements. The Confrontation Clause's effect on such statements is a matter of constitutional law, not evidence rules. *Giles* presents a highly controversial context for the Court majority's strong allegiance to its pro-defendant understanding of the Confrontation Clause.

GILES v. CALIFORNIA

554 U.S. 353 (2008)

Justice SCALIA delivered the opinion of the Court.

We consider whether a defendant forfeits his Sixth Amendment right to confront a witness against him when a judge determines that a wrongful act by the defendant made the witness unavailable to testify at trial.

On September 29, 2002, petitioner Dwayne Giles shot his ex-girlfriend, Brenda Avie, outside the garage of his grandmother's house. No witness saw the shooting, but Giles' niece heard what transpired from inside the house. She heard Giles and Avie speaking in conversational tones. Avie then yelled "Granny" several times and a series of gunshots sounded. Giles' niece and grandmother ran outside and saw Giles standing near Avie with a gun in his hand. Avie, who had not been carrying a weapon, had been shot six times. One wound was consistent with Avie's holding her hand up at the time she was shot, another was consistent with her having turned to her side, and a third was consistent with her having been shot while lying on the ground. Giles fled the scene after the shooting. He was apprehended by police about two weeks later and charged with murder.

At trial, Giles testified that he had acted in self-defense. Giles described Avie as jealous, and said he knew that she had once shot a man, that he had seen her threaten people with a knife, and that she had vandalized his home and car on prior occasions. He said that on the day of the shooting, Avie came to his grandmother's house and threatened to kill him and his new girlfriend, who had been at the house earlier. . . . He said that Avie charged at him, and that he was afraid she had something in her hand. According to Giles, he closed his eyes and fired several shots, but did not intend to kill Avie.

Prosecutors sought to introduce statements that Avie had made to a police officer responding to a domestic-violence report about three weeks before the shooting. Avie, who was crying when she spoke, told the officer that Giles had accused her of having an affair, and that after the two began to argue, Giles grabbed her by the shirt, lifted her off the floor, and began to choke her. According to Avie, when she broke free and fell to the floor, Giles punched her in the face and head, and after she broke free again, he opened a folding knife, held it about three feet away from her, and threatened to kill her if he found her cheating on him. Over Giles' objection, the trial court admitted these statements into evidence under a provision of California law that permits admission of out-of-court statements describing the infliction or threat of physical injury on a declarant when the declarant is unavailable to testify at trial and the prior statements are deemed trustworthy.

A jury convicted Giles of first-degree murder. He appealed. While his appeal was pending, this Court decided in Crawford v. Washington that the Confrontation Clause requires that a defendant have the opportunity to confront the witnesses who give testimony against him, except in cases where an exception to the confrontation right was recognized at the time of the founding. The California Court of Appeal held that the admission of Avie's unconfronted statements at Giles' trial did not violate the Confrontation Clause as construed by *Crawford* because *Crawford* recognized a doctrine of forfeiture by wrongdoing. It concluded that Giles had forfeited his right to confront Avie because he had committed the murder for which he was on trial, and because his intentional criminal act made Avie unavailable to testify. The California Supreme Court affirmed on the same ground. We granted certiorari. . . .

We have previously acknowledged that two forms of testimonial statements were admitted at common law even though they were unconfronted. The first of these were declarations made by a speaker who was both on the brink of death and aware that he was dying. Avie did not make the unconfronted statements admitted at Giles' trial when she was dying, so her statements do not fall within this historic exception.

A second common-law doctrine, which we will refer to as forfeiture by wrongdoing, permitted the introduction of statements of a witness who was "detained" or "kept away" by the "means or procurement" of the defendant. The doctrine has roots in the 1666 decision in Lord Morley's Case, at which judges concluded that a witness's having been "detained by the means or procurement of the prisoner," provided a basis to read testimony previously given at a coroner's inquest. . . .

The terms used to define the scope of the forfeiture rule suggest that the exception applied only when the defendant engaged in conduct designed to prevent the witness from testifying. . . .

Cases and treatises of the time indicate that a purpose-based definition of these terms governed. . . .

An 1858 treatise made the purpose requirement more explicit still, stating that the forfeiture rule applied when a witness "had been kept out of the way by the prisoner, or by some one on the prisoner's behalf, in order to prevent him from giving evidence against him." E. Powell, The Practice of the Law of Evidence 166 (1st ed. 1858) (emphasis added). The wrongful-procurement exception was invoked in a manner consistent with this definition. We are aware of no case in which the exception was invoked although the defendant had not engaged in conduct designed to prevent a witness from testifying, such as offering a bribe.

The manner in which the rule was applied makes plain that unconfronted testimony would not be admitted without a showing that the defendant intended to prevent a witness from testifying. In cases where the evidence suggested that the defendant had caused a person to be absent, but had not done so to prevent the person from testifying — as in the typical murder case involving accusatorial statements by the victim — the testimony was excluded unless it was confronted or fell within the dying-declaration exception. Prosecutors do not appear to have even argued that the judge could admit the unconfronted statements because the defendant committed the murder for which he was on trial....

In 1997, this Court approved a Federal Rule of Evidence, entitled "Forfeiture by wrongdoing," which applies only when the defendant "engaged or acquiesced in wrongdoing that was intended to, and did, procure the unavailability of the declarant as a witness." Fed. Rule Evid. 804(b)(6). We have described this as a rule "which codifies the forfeiture doctrine." Davis v. Washington. Every commentator we are aware of has concluded the requirement of intent "means that the exception applies only if the defendant has in mind the particular purpose of making the witness unavailable." ...

The dissent [points] out that a forfeiture rule which ignores *Crawford* would be particularly helpful to women in abusive relationships — or at least particularly helpful in punishing their abusers. Not as helpful as the dissent suggests, since only testimonial statements are excluded by the Confrontation Clause. Statements to friends and neighbors about abuse and intimidation, and statements to physicians in the course of receiving treatment would be excluded, if at all, only by hearsay rules, which are free to adopt the dissent's version of forfeiture by wrongdoing. In any event, we are puzzled by the dissent's decision to devote its peroration to domestic abuse cases. Is the suggestion that we should have one Confrontation Clause (the one the Framers adopted and *Crawford* described) for all other crimes, but a special, improvised, Confrontation Clause for those crimes that are frequently directed against women? Domestic violence is an intolerable offense that legislatures may choose to combat through many means — from increasing criminal penalties to adding resources for investigation and prosecution to funding awareness and prevention campaigns. But for that serious crime, as for others, abridging the constitutional rights of criminal defendants is not in the State's arsenal.

The domestic-violence context is, however, relevant for a separate reason. Acts of domestic violence often are intended to dissuade a victim from resorting to outside help, and include conduct designed to prevent testimony to police officers or cooperation in criminal prosecutions. Where such an abusive relationship culminates in murder, the evidence may support a finding that the crime expressed the intent to isolate the victim and to stop her from reporting abuse to the authorities or cooperating with a criminal prosecution — rendering her prior statements admissible under the forfeiture doctrine. Earlier abuse, or threats of abuse, intended to dissuade the victim from resorting to outside help would be highly relevant to this inquiry, as would evidence of ongoing criminal proceedings at which the victim would have been expected to testify. This is not, as the dissent charges, nothing more than "knowledge-based intent." (Emphasis deleted.)

The state courts in this case did not consider the intent of the defendant because they found that irrelevant to application of the forfeiture doctrine. This view of the law was error, but the court is free to consider evidence of the defendant's intent on remand....

We decline to approve an exception to the Confrontation Clause unheard of at the time of the founding or for 200 years thereafter. The judgment of the California Supreme Court is vacated, and the case is remanded for further proceedings not inconsistent with this opinion.

It is so ordered.

[Some concurring and dissenting opinions omitted]

NOTES TO GILES v. CALIFORNIA

1. *Distinguishing Constitutional and Hearsay Doctrines.* Compare two hearsay statements in a murder case: First, the victim made a testimonial statement covered by the excited utterance exception, and the defendant intentionally caused the victim's unavailability at trial. Second, the victim wrote an accusatory letter about the defendant to a police officer, and the defendant intentionally caused the victim's unavailability at trial. When a defendant intentionally causes a declarant's absence from a trial and therefore loses his or her Confrontation Clause protection from admission of hearsay statements by that declarant, should all hearsay statements by the declarant be admitted, or should the declarant's hearsay statements still be subject to a standard hearsay analysis?

2. *"Intent" to Prevent Testimony.* In a concurrence, Justice Souter wrote:

"[The requisite] element of intention would normally be satisfied by the intent inferred on the part of the domestic abuser in the classic abusive relationship, which is meant to isolate the victim from outside help, including the aid of law enforcement and the judicial process. If the evidence for admissibility shows a continuing relationship of this sort, it would make no sense to suggest that the oppressing defendant miraculously abandoned the dynamics of abuse the instant before he killed his victim, say in a fit of anger."

This position did not accrue the support of a majority of the court. It might allow application of the forfeiture rule in a trial for murder of a domestic abuse victim even if the abuser was thinking about something other than preventing the victim from being a witness when the abuser harmed the victim.

3. Evolving Understanding of *Crawford*: Statements About Recent Criminal Conduct

What Is a Continuing Emergency? — Bryant. Should the Confrontation Clause apply to statements made to police by a dying crime victim? The majority opinion seems open to a range of ways to treat the Confrontation Clause that might decrease the number of statements to which it applies. The opinion was written by Justice Sotomayor, who was not a member of the court that decided *Crawford*. The opinion's possible limitation of the reach of the Confrontation

Clause may point somewhat in the direction of pre-2004 results, in terms of case outcomes if not in terms of doctrine.

MICHIGAN v. BRYANT

131 S. Ct. 1143 (2011)

Justice SOTOMAYOR delivered the opinion of the Court.

At respondent Richard Bryant's trial, the court admitted statements that the victim, Anthony Covington, made to police officers who discovered him mortally wounded in a gas station parking lot. A jury convicted Bryant of, *inter alia,* second-degree murder. On appeal, the Supreme Court of Michigan held that the Sixth Amendment's Confrontation Clause, as explained in our decisions in *Crawford v. Washington* and *Davis v. Washington* rendered Covington's statements inadmissible testimonial hearsay, and the court reversed Bryant's conviction. We granted the State's petition for a writ of certiorari to consider whether the Confrontation Clause barred the admission at trial of Covington's statements to the police. . . .

Around 3:25 A.M. on April 29, 2001, Detroit, Michigan police officers responded to a radio dispatch indicating that a man had been shot. At the scene, they found the victim, Anthony Covington, lying on the ground next to his car in a gas station parking lot. Covington had a gunshot wound to his abdomen, appeared to be in great pain, and spoke with difficulty.

The police asked him "what had happened, who had shot him, and where the shooting had occurred." Covington stated that "Rick" shot him at around 3 A.M. He also indicated that he had a conversation with Bryant, whom he recognized based on his voice, through the back door of Bryant's house. Covington explained that when he turned to leave, he was shot through the door and then drove to the gas station, where police found him.

Covington's conversation with the police ended within 5 to 10 minutes when emergency medical services arrived. Covington was transported to a hospital and died within hours. . . .

At trial, which occurred prior to our decisions in *Crawford* and *Davis,* the police officers who spoke with Covington at the gas station testified about what Covington had told them. The jury returned a guilty verdict on charges of second-degree murder, being a felon in possession of a firearm, and possession of a firearm during the commission of a felony. . . .

[W]e confront for the first time circumstances in which the "ongoing emergency" discussed in *Davis* extends beyond an initial victim to a potential threat to the responding police and the public at large. This new context requires us to provide additional clarification with regard to what *Davis* meant by "the primary purpose of the interrogation is to enable police assistance to meet an ongoing emergency." . . .

As our recent Confrontation Clause cases have explained, the existence of an "ongoing emergency" at the time of an encounter between an individual and the police is among the most important circumstances informing the "primary purpose" of an interrogation. The existence of an ongoing emergency is relevant to determining the primary purpose of the interrogation because an emergency focuses the participants on something other than "prov[ing] past events potentially relevant to later criminal prosecution." Rather, it focuses them on "end[ing] a threatening situation." Implicit in *Davis* is the idea that because the prospect of fabrication in statements given for the primary purpose of resolving that emergency is presumably significantly diminished, the Confrontation Clause does not require such statements to be subject to the crucible of cross-examination.

This logic is not unlike that justifying the excited utterance exception in hearsay law. Statements "relating to a startling event or condition made while the declarant was under the stress of excitement caused by the event or condition," Fed. Rule Evid. 803(2), are considered reliable because the declarant, in the excitement, presumably cannot form a falsehood. An ongoing emergency has a similar effect of focusing an individual's attention on responding to the emergency.

Following our precedents, the court below correctly began its analysis with the circumstances in which Covington interacted with the police. But in doing so, the court construed *Davis* to have decided more than it did and thus employed an unduly narrow understanding of "ongoing emergency" that *Davis* does not require.

[T]he Michigan Supreme Court failed to appreciate that whether an emergency exists and is ongoing is a highly context-dependent inquiry. *Davis* and *Hammon* involved domestic violence, a known and identified perpetrator, and, in *Hammon,* a neutralized threat. Because *Davis* and *Hammon* were domestic violence cases, we focused only on the threat to the victims and assessed the ongoing emergency from the perspective of whether there was a continuing threat *to them.*

Domestic violence cases like *Davis* and *Hammon* often have a narrower zone of potential victims than cases involving threats to public safety. An assessment of whether an emergency that threatens the police and public is ongoing cannot narrowly focus on whether the threat solely to the first victim has been neutralized because the threat to the first responders and public may continue.

The Michigan Supreme Court also did not appreciate that the duration and scope of an emergency may depend in part on the type of weapon employed. The court relied on *Davis* and *Hammon,* in which the assailants used their fists, as controlling the scope of the emergency here, which involved the use of a gun. The problem with that reasoning is clear when considered in light of the assault on Amy Hammon. Hershel Hammon was armed only with his fists when he attacked his wife, so removing Amy to a separate room was sufficient to end the emergency. If Hershel had been reported to be armed with a gun, however, separation by a single household wall might not have been sufficient to end the emergency.

The Michigan Supreme Court's failure to focus on the context-dependent nature of our *Davis* decision also led it to conclude that the medical condition of a declarant is irrelevant. But *Davis* and *Hammon* did not present medical emergencies, despite some injuries to the victims. Thus, we have not previously considered, much less ruled out, the relevance of a victim's severe injuries to the primary purpose inquiry.

. . . The medical condition of the victim is important to the primary purpose inquiry to the extent that it sheds light on the ability of the victim to have any purpose at all in responding to police questions and on the likelihood that any purpose formed would necessarily be a testimonial one. The victim's medical state also provides important context for first responders to judge the existence and magnitude of a continuing threat to the victim, themselves, and the public. . . .

Finally, our discussion . . . should not be taken to imply that the existence *vel non* of an ongoing emergency is dispositive of the testimonial inquiry. As *Davis* made clear, whether an ongoing emergency exists is simply one factor — albeit an important factor — that informs the ultimate inquiry regarding the "primary purpose" of an interrogation. Another factor . . . is the importance of *informality* in an encounter between a victim and police. . . . As we explain further below, the questioning in this case occurred in an exposed, public area, prior to the arrival of emergency medical services, and in a disorganized fashion. All of those facts make this case distinguishable from the formal station-house interrogation in *Crawford.*

In addition to the circumstances in which an encounter occurs, the statements and actions of both the declarant and interrogators provide objective evidence of the primary purpose of the interrogation. . . .

As we suggested in *Davis,* when a court must determine whether the Confrontation Clause bars the admission of a statement at trial, it should determine the "primary purpose of the interrogation" by objectively evaluating the statements and actions of the parties to the encounter, in light of the circumstances in which the interrogation occurs. The existence of an emergency or the parties' perception that an emergency is ongoing is among the most important circumstances that courts must take into account in determining whether an interrogation is testimonial because statements made to assist police in addressing an ongoing emergency presumably lack the testimonial purpose that would subject them to the requirement of confrontation. As the context of this case brings into sharp relief, the existence and duration of an emergency depend on the type and scope of danger posed to the victim, the police, and the public.

Applying this analysis to the facts of this case is more difficult than in *Davis* because we do not have the luxury of reviewing a transcript of the conversation between the victim and the police officers. . . .

As explained above, the scope of an emergency in terms of its threat to individuals other than the initial assailant and victim will often depend on the type of dispute involved. Nothing Covington said to the police indicated that the cause of the shooting was a purely private dispute or that the threat from the shooter had ended. The record reveals little about the motive for the shooting.

The police officers who spoke with Covington at the gas station testified that Covington did not tell them what words Covington and Rick had exchanged prior to the shooting. What Covington did tell the officers was that he fled Bryant's back porch, indicating that he perceived an ongoing threat. The police did not know, and Covington did not tell them, whether the threat was limited to him. The potential scope of the dispute and therefore the emergency in this case thus stretches more broadly than those at issue in *Davis* and *Hammon* and encompasses a threat potentially to the police and the public.

This is also the first of our post-*Crawford* Confrontation Clause cases to involve a gun. The physical separation that was sufficient to end the emergency in *Hammon* was not necessarily sufficient to end the threat in this case; Covington was shot through the back door of Bryant's house. Bryant's argument that there was no ongoing emergency because "[n]o shots were being fired," surely construes ongoing emergency too narrowly. An emergency does not last only for the time between when the assailant pulls the trigger and the bullet hits the victim. If an out-of-sight sniper pauses between shots, no one would say that the emergency ceases during the pause. That is an extreme example and not the situation here, but it serves to highlight the implausibility, at least as to certain weapons, of construing the emergency to last only precisely as long as the violent act itself, as some have construed our opinion in *Davis*. . . .

This is not to suggest that the emergency continued until Bryant was arrested in California a year after the shooting. We need not decide precisely when the emergency ended because Covington's encounter with the police and all of the statements he made during that interaction occurred within the first few minutes of the police officers' arrival and well before they secured the scene of the shooting — the shooter's last known location.

We reiterate, moreover, that the existence *vel non* of an ongoing emergency is not the touchstone of the testimonial inquiry; rather, the ultimate inquiry is whether the "primary purpose of the interrogation [was] to enable police assistance to meet [the] ongoing emergency." We turn now to that inquiry, as informed by the circumstances of the ongoing emergency just described. The circumstances of the encounter provide important context for understanding Covington's statements to the police. When the police arrived at Covington's side, their first question to him was "What happened?" Covington's response was either "Rick shot me" or "I was shot," followed very quickly by an identification of "Rick" as the shooter. In response to further questions, Covington explained that the shooting occurred through the back door of Bryant's house and provided a physical description of the shooter. When he made the statements, Covington was lying in a gas station parking lot bleeding from a mortal gunshot wound to his abdomen. His answers to the police officers' questions were punctuated with questions about when emergency medical services would arrive. He was obviously in considerable pain and had difficulty breathing and talking. From this description of his condition and report of his statements, we cannot say that a person in Covington's situation would have had a "primary purpose" "to establish or prove past events potentially relevant to later criminal prosecution."

For their part, the police responded to a call that a man had been shot. As discussed above, they did not know why, where, or when the shooting had occurred. Nor did they know the location of the shooter or anything else about the circumstances in which the crime occurred. The questions they asked — "what had happened, who had shot him, and where the shooting occurred," — were the exact type of questions necessary to allow the police to "'assess the situation, the threat to their own safety, and possible danger to the potential victim'" "and to the public, including to allow them to ascertain "whether they would be encountering a violent felon." In other words, they solicited the information necessary to enable them "to meet an ongoing emergency." . . .

Finally, we consider the informality of the situation and the interrogation. This situation is more similar, though not identical, to the informal, harried 911 call in *Davis* than to the structured, station-house interview in *Crawford*. As the officers' trial testimony reflects, the situation was fluid and somewhat confused: the officers arrived at different times; apparently each, upon arrival, asked Covington "what happened?"; and, contrary to the dissent's portrayal, they did not conduct a structured interrogation. The informality suggests that the interrogators' primary purpose was simply to address what they perceived to be an ongoing emergency, and the circumstances lacked any formality that would have alerted Covington to or focused him on the possible future prosecutorial use of his statements.

Because the circumstances of the encounter as well as the statements and actions of Covington and the police objectively indicate that the "primary purpose of the interrogation" was "to enable police assistance to meet an ongoing emergency," Covington's identification and description of the shooter and the location of the shooting were not testimonial hearsay. The Confrontation Clause did not bar their admission at Bryant's trial. . . .

For the foregoing reasons, we hold that Covington's statements were not testimonial and that their admission at Bryant's trial did not violate the Confrontation Clause. We leave for the Michigan courts to decide on remand whether the statements' admission was otherwise permitted by state hearsay rules. The judgment of the Supreme Court of Michigan is vacated, and the case is remanded for further proceedings not inconsistent with this opinion. *It is so ordered.*

Justice THOMAS, concurring in the judgment.

I agree with the Court that the admission of Covington's out-of-court statements did not violate the Confrontation Clause, but I reach this conclusion because Covington's questioning by police lacked sufficient formality and solemnity for his statements to be considered "testimonial." . . .

Justice SCALIA, dissenting.

Today's tale — a story of five officers conducting successive examinations of a dying man with the primary purpose, not of obtaining and preserving his testimony regarding his killer, but of protecting him, them, and others from a murderer somewhere on the loose — is so transparently false that professing to believe it demeans this institution. . . . Instead of clarifying the law, the Court makes itself the obfuscator of last resort. Because I continue to adhere to the Confrontation Clause that the People adopted, as described in *Crawford v. Washington,* I dissent. . . .

Crawford and *Davis* did not address whose perspective matters — the declarant's, the interrogator's, or both — when assessing "the primary purpose of [an] interrogation." In those cases the statements were testimonial from any perspective. I think the same is true here, but because the Court picks a perspective so will I. . . . For an out-of-court statement to qualify as testimonial, the declarant must intend the statement to be a solemn declaration rather than an unconsidered or offhand remark; and he must make the statement with the understanding that it may be used to invoke the coercive machinery of the State against the accused. That is what distinguishes a narrative told to a friend over dinner from a statement to the police. The hidden purpose of an interrogator cannot substitute for the declarant's intentional solemnity or his understanding of how his words may be used. . . .

The only virtue of the Court's approach (if it can be misnamed a virtue) is that it leaves judges free to reach the "fairest" result under the totality of the circumstances. If the dastardly police trick a declarant into giving an incriminating statement against a sympathetic defendant, a court can focus on the police's intent and declare the statement testimonial. If the defendant "deserves" to go to jail, then a court can focus on whatever perspective is necessary to declare damning hearsay nontestimonial. And when all else fails, a court can mix-and-match perspectives to reach its desired outcome. . . .

According to today's opinion, the *Davis* inquiry into whether a declarant spoke to end an ongoing emergency or rather to "prove past events potentially relevant to later criminal prosecution," is *not* aimed at answering whether the declarant acted as a witness. Instead, the *Davis* inquiry probes the *reliability* of a declarant's statements, "[i]mplicit[ly]" importing the excited-utterances hearsay exception into the Constitution. A statement during an ongoing emergency is sufficiently reliable, the Court says, "because the prospect of fabrication . . . is presumably significantly diminished," so it "does not [need] to be subject to the crucible of cross-examination." . . .

We tried that approach to the Confrontation Clause for nearly 25 years before *Crawford* rejected it as an unworkable standard unmoored from the text and the historical roots of the Confrontation Clause. . . .

The Court attempts to fit its resurrected interest in reliability into the *Crawford* framework, but the result is incoherent. Reliability, the Court tells us, is a good indicator of whether "a statement is . . . an out-of-court substitute for trial testimony." That is patently false. Reliability tells us *nothing* about whether a statement is testimonial. Testimonial and nontestimonial statements alike come in varying degrees of reliability. An eyewitness's statements to the police after a fender-bender, for example, are both reliable and testimonial. Statements to the police from one driver attempting to blame the other would be similarly testimonial but rarely reliable. . . .

For all I know, Bryant has received his just deserts. But he surely has not received them pursuant to the procedures that our Constitution requires. And what has been taken away from him has been taken away from us all.

NOTES TO MICHIGAN v. BRYANT

1. *Reliability.* The majority opinion states, "Implicit in *Davis* is the idea that because the prospect of fabrication in statements given for the primary purpose of resolving that emergency is presumably significantly diminished, the Confrontation Clause does not require such statements to be subject to the crucible of cross-examination." This reference to reliability may be a hint of a return to the reliability focus of *Roberts.*

2. *History.* In *Crawford*, Justice Scalia wrote that dying declarations might be admissible even if made in a testimonial setting, because the dying declarations exception was recognized at the time the Bill of Rights was adopted.

QUESTION 11-4. Joseph Boyfriend was prosecuted for assaulting Irma Injured. Injured testified at his trial, and identified herself as the speaker in a recording of a 911 phone call. She refused to testify about anything else, claiming a Fifth Amendment privilege. Consider whether the Confrontation Clause would permit introduction of the recording as proof that Boyfriend had attacked Injured. A transcript of the call includes these statements:

Caller: "I'm using my neighbor's phone. I'm in her apartment. I live at [street address and apartment number]. My boyfriend just beat me up. I need a cruiser."

911 operator: "What's his name?"

Caller: "Joseph Boyfriend."

911 Operator: "Joseph?"

Caller: "Yup. Joseph Boyfriend."

911 Operator: "Boyfriend?"

Caller: "Yup."

911 Operator: "OK. Is he still in your apartment?"

Caller: "He's still there, he's packing his stuff now. I'm in the downstairs apartment, my neighbor's apartment"

911 Operator: "Do you need an ambulance?"

Caller: "Umm . . . please. And I, I need you to send the cops now, before he leaves."

911 Operator: "OK. We'll send someone out. OK?"

Caller: "Yup."

■   ■   ■

Continuing to Narrow Application of the Confrontation Clause: Declarant's Youth, Interrogator's Semi-Official Status, and Anticipated Crime as a Continuing Emergency — Clark. Can statements by a child be testimonial? If an interrogator is not a police officer or prosecutor, can the Confrontation Clause apply? Does fear of future injury to someone currently in a safe place constitute an ongoing emergency? All of these questions arise when a statement, unlike one made to police by an adult, is made by a three-year-old to a teacher.

OHIO v. CLARK

135 U.S. 2173 (2015)

Justice ALITO delivered the opinion of the Court....

Darius Clark, who went by the nickname "Dee," lived in Cleveland, Ohio, with his girlfriend, T.T., and her two children: L.P., a 3-year-old boy, and A.T., an 18-month-old girl. Clark was also T.T.'s pimp, and he would regularly send her on trips to Washington, D.C., to work as a prostitute. In March 2010, T.T. went on one such trip, and she left the children in Clark's care.

The next day, Clark took L.P. to preschool. In the lunchroom, one of L.P.'s teachers, Ramona Whitley, observed that L.P.'s left eye appeared bloodshot. She asked him "[w]hat happened," and he initially said nothing. Eventually, however, he told the teacher that he "fell." When they moved into the brighter lights of a classroom, Whitley noticed "[r]ed marks, like whips of some sort," on L.P.'s face. She notified the lead teacher, Debra Jones, who asked L.P., "Who did this? What happened to you?" According to Jones, L.P. "seemed kind of bewildered" and "said something like, Dee, Dee." Jones asked L.P. whether Dee is "big or little," to which L.P. responded that "Dee is big." Jones then brought L.P. to her supervisor, who lifted the boy's shirt, revealing more injuries. Whitley called a child abuse hotline to alert authorities about the suspected abuse.

When Clark later arrived at the school, he denied responsibility for the injuries and quickly left with L.P. The next day, a social worker found the children at Clark's mother's house and took them to a hospital, where a physician discovered additional injuries suggesting child abuse. L.P. had a black eye, belt marks on his back and stomach, and bruises all over his body. A.T. had two black eyes, a swollen hand, and a large burn on her cheek, and two pigtails had been ripped out at the roots of her hair.

A grand jury indicted Clark on five counts of felonious assault (four related to A.T. and one related to L.P.), two counts of endangering children (one for each child), and two counts of domestic violence (one for each child). At trial, the State introduced L.P.'s statements to his teachers as evidence of Clark's guilt, but L.P. did not testify.... [U]nder Ohio Rule of Evidence 807, which allows the admission of reliable hearsay by child abuse victims, the court ruled that L.P.'s statements to his teachers bore sufficient guarantees of trustworthiness to be admitted as evidence.

Clark moved to exclude testimony about L.P.'s out-of-court statements under the Confrontation Clause. The trial court denied the motion, ruling that L.P.'s responses were not testimonial statements covered by the Sixth Amendment. The jury found Clark guilty on all counts except for one assault count related to A.T., and it sentenced him to 28 years' imprisonment. Clark appealed his conviction, and a state appellate court reversed on the ground that the introduction of L.P.'s out-of-court statements violated the Confrontation Clause.

In a 4-to-3 decision, the Supreme Court of Ohio affirmed. . . . We granted certiorari . . . and we now reverse.

The Sixth Amendment's Confrontation Clause, which is binding on the States through the Fourteenth Amendment, provides: "In all criminal prosecutions, the accused shall enjoy the right . . . to be confronted with the witnesses against him." In *Ohio v. Roberts* (1980), we interpreted the Clause to permit the admission of out-of-court statements by an unavailable witness, so long as the statements bore "adequate 'indicia of reliability.'" Such indicia are present, we held, if "the evidence falls within a firmly rooted hearsay exception" or bears "particularized guarantees of trustworthiness."

In *Crawford v. Washington* (2004), we adopted a different approach. We explained that "witnesses," under the Confrontation Clause, are those "who bear testimony," and we defined "testimony" as "a solemn declaration or affirmation made for the purpose of establishing or proving some fact." . . .

Our more recent cases have labored to flesh out what it means for a statement to be "testimonial." In *Davis v. Washington* and *Hammon v. Indiana*, which we decided together, we dealt with statements given to law enforcement officers by the victims of domestic abuse. The victim in *Davis* made statements to a 911 emergency operator during and shortly after her boyfriend's violent attack. In *Hammon*, the victim, after being isolated from her abusive husband, made statements to police that were memorialized in a "'battery affidavit.'"

We held that the statements in *Hammon* were testimonial, while the statements in *Davis* were not. Announcing what has come to be known as the "primary purpose" test, we explained: "Statements are nontestimonial when made in the course of police interrogation under circumstances objectively indicating that the primary purpose of the interrogation is to enable police assistance to meet an ongoing emergency. They are testimonial when the circumstances objectively indicate that there is no such ongoing emergency, and that the primary purpose of the interrogation is to establish or prove past events potentially relevant to later criminal prosecution." . . . In the end, the question is whether, in light of all the circumstances, viewed objectively, the "primary purpose" of the conversation was to "creat[e] an out-of-court substitute for trial testimony." . . .

In this case, we consider statements made to preschool teachers, not the police. We are therefore presented with the question we have repeatedly reserved: whether statements to persons other than law enforcement officers are subject to the Confrontation Clause. Because at least some statements to individuals who are not law enforcement officers could conceivably raise confrontation concerns, we decline to adopt a categorical rule excluding them from the Sixth

Amendment's reach. Nevertheless, such statements are much less likely to be testimonial than statements to law enforcement officers. And considering all the relevant circumstances here, L.P.'s statements clearly were not made with the primary purpose of creating evidence for Clark's prosecution. Thus, their introduction at trial did not violate the Confrontation Clause.

L.P.'s statements occurred in the context of an ongoing emergency involving suspected child abuse. When L.P.'s teachers noticed his injuries, they rightly became worried that the 3-year-old was the victim of serious violence. Because the teachers needed to know whether it was safe to release L.P. to his guardian at the end of the day, they needed to determine who might be abusing the child. Thus, the immediate concern was to protect a vulnerable child who needed help. Our holding in [*Michigan v. Bryant*] is instructive. As in *Bryant*, the emergency in this case was ongoing, and the circumstances were not entirely clear. L.P.'s teachers were not sure who had abused him or how best to secure his safety. Nor were they sure whether any other children might be at risk. As a result, their questions and L.P.'s answers were primarily aimed at identifying and ending the threat. Though not as harried, the conversation here was also similar to the 911 call in *Davis*. The teachers' questions were meant to identify the abuser in order to protect the victim from future attacks. . . .

There is no indication that the primary purpose of the conversation was to gather evidence for Clark's prosecution. On the contrary, it is clear that the first objective was to protect L.P. At no point did the teachers inform L.P. that his answers would be used to arrest or punish his abuser. L.P. never hinted that he intended his statements to be used by the police or prosecutors. And the conversation between L.P. and his teachers was informal and spontaneous. The teachers asked L.P. about his injuries immediately upon discovering them, in the informal setting of a preschool lunchroom and classroom, and they did so precisely as any concerned citizen would talk to a child who might be the victim of abuse. This was nothing like the formalized station-house questioning in *Crawford* or the police interrogation and battery affidavit in *Hammon*.

L.P.'s age fortifies our conclusion that the statements in question were not testimonial. Statements by very young children will rarely, if ever, implicate the Confrontation Clause. Few preschool students understand the details of our criminal justice system. Rather, "[r]esearch on children's understanding of the legal system finds that" young children "have little understanding of prosecution." . . . Thus, it is extremely unlikely that a 3-year-old child in L.P.'s position would intend his statements to be a substitute for trial testimony. On the contrary, a young child in these circumstances would simply want the abuse to end, would want to protect other victims, or would have no discernible purpose at all. . . .

Finally, although we decline to adopt a rule that statements to individuals who are not law enforcement officers are categorically outside the Sixth Amendment, the fact that L.P. was speaking to his teachers remains highly relevant. Courts must evaluate challenged statements in context, and part of that context is the questioner's identity. Statements made to someone who is not principally charged with uncovering and prosecuting criminal behavior are significantly less likely to be testimonial than statements given to law enforcement officers. It is common sense that the relationship between a student and his teacher is very different from that between a citizen and the police. We do not ignore that reality. In light of these circumstances, the Sixth Amendment did not prohibit the State from introducing L.P.'s statements at trial.

Clark's efforts to avoid this conclusion are all off-base. He emphasizes Ohio's mandatory reporting obligations, in an attempt to equate L.P.'s teachers with the police and their caring questions with official interrogations. But the comparison is inapt. The teachers' pressing concern was to protect L.P. and remove him from harm's way. Like all good teachers, they undoubtedly would have acted with the same purpose whether or not they had a state-law duty to report abuse. And mandatory reporting statutes alone cannot convert a conversation between a concerned teacher and her student into a law enforcement mission aimed primarily at gathering evidence for a prosecution. . . .

We reverse the judgment of the Supreme Court of Ohio and remand the case for further proceedings not inconsistent with this opinion.

Justice SCALIA, with whom Justice GINSBURG joins, concurring in the judgment. I agree with the Court's holding. . . . The statements here would not be testimonial under the usual test applicable to informal police interrogation. . . .

I write separately, however, to protest the Court's shoveling of fresh dirt upon the Sixth Amendment right of confrontation so recently rescued from the grave in *Crawford v. Washington*. For several decades before that case, we had been allowing hearsay statements to be admitted against a criminal defendant if they bore "'indicia of reliability.'" *Ohio v. Roberts*. Prosecutors, past and present, love that flabby test. *Crawford* sought to bring our application of the Confrontation Clause back to its original meaning, which was to exclude unconfronted statements made by *witnesses — i.e.,* statements that were *testimonial*. We defined testimony as a "'solemn declaration or affirmation made for the purpose of establishing or proving some fact,'" — in the context of the Confrontation Clause, a fact "potentially relevant to later criminal prosecution," *Davis v. Washington*.

Crawford remains the law. But when else has the categorical overruling, the thorough repudiation, of an earlier line of cases been described as nothing more than "adopt[ing] a different approach," *ante*, as though *Crawford* is only a matter of twiddle-dum twiddle-dee preference, and the old, pre-*Crawford* "approach" remains available? . . . A suspicious mind (or even one that is merely not naïve) might regard this distortion as the first step in an attempt to smuggle longstanding hearsay exceptions back into the Confrontation Clause — In other words, an attempt to return to *Ohio v. Roberts*.

But the good news is that there are evidently not the votes to return to that halcyon era for prosecutors; and that dicta, even calculated dicta, are nothing but dicta. They are enough, however, combined with the peculiar phenomenon of a Supreme Court opinion's aggressive hostility to precedent that it purports to be applying, to prevent my joining the writing for the Court. I concur only in the judgment.

Justice THOMAS, concurring in the judgment. I agree with the Court that Ohio mandatory reporters are not agents of law enforcement, that statements made to private persons or by very young children will rarely implicate the Confrontation Clause, and that the admission of the statements at issue here did not implicate that constitutional provision. I nonetheless cannot join the majority's analysis. . . . I would use the same test for statements to private persons that I have employed for statements to agents of law enforcement, assessing whether those statements bear sufficient indicia of solemnity to qualify as testimonial. . . .

NOTES TO OHIO v. CLARK

1. *Composition of the Court.* Of the nine members of the Court who joined in the *Crawford* opinion and a concurring opinion in 2004, only five were serving on the Court that decided *Clark* in 2015 (and Michigan v. Bryant in 2011). This change in composition may partly explain the outcome in *Clark* (and *Bryant*) and in the cases in the next section concerning routine criminal prosecution documents.

SUPREME COURT MEMBERSHIP: 2003–2004 AND 2010–2015 (SHADING INDICATES SERVICE IN BOTH PERIODS)

2003–2004	2010–2015
	Alito
Breyer	Breyer
Ginsburg	Ginsburg
	Kagan
Kennedy	Kennedy
O'Connor	
Rehnquist	
	Roberts
Scalia	Scalia
	Sotomayor
Souter	
Stevens	
Thomas	Thomas

QUESTION 11-5. The mother of a four-year old child suspected that the youngster had been sexually abused by a neighbor. She reported that belief to the police, and an interview with the child was arranged. The interview took place at a state social services office and was conducted by a social worker. A police

officer was present during the interview and consulted with the social worker at one point to suggest some inquiries. If the neighbor is charged with abusing the child, what issues would arise if the prosecution sought to introduce statements the child made during the interview for the truth of what they assert?

4. Evolving Understanding of *Crawford*: Routine Documents in the Criminal Investigation Process

Segment 8:
Confrontation
Clause

Are Crime Lab Reports Testimonial? — Melendez-Diaz. Does it make sense to apply the Confrontation Clause to the large number of documents that police crime labs produce in their ordinary work? The majority considered this a simple question in terms of the *Crawford* doctrines, but the dissenters argued for a narrower understanding of the Confrontation Clause's protections.

MELENDEZ-DIAZ v. MASSACHUSETTS

557 U.S. 305 (2009)

Justice SCALIA delivered the opinion of the Court.

The Massachusetts courts in this case admitted into evidence affidavits reporting the results of forensic analysis which showed that material seized by the police and connected to the defendant was cocaine. The question presented is whether those affidavits are "testimonial," rendering the affiants "witnesses" subject to the defendant's right of confrontation under the Sixth Amendment. . . .

Melendez-Diaz was charged with distributing cocaine and with trafficking in cocaine in an amount between 14 and 28 grams. At trial, the prosecution placed into evidence the bags seized. . . . It also submitted three "certificates of analysis" showing the results of the forensic analysis performed on the seized substances. The certificates reported the weight of the seized bags and stated that the bags "[h]a[ve] been examined with the following results: The substance was found to contain: Cocaine." The certificates were sworn to before a notary public by analysts at the State Laboratory Institute of the Massachusetts Department of Public Health, as required under Massachusetts law.

Petitioner objected to the admission of the certificates, asserting that our Confrontation Clause decision in Crawford v. Washington required the analysts to testify in person. The objection was overruled, and the certificates were admitted pursuant to state law as "prima facie evidence of the composition, quality, and the net weight of the narcotic . . . analyzed."

The jury found Melendez-Diaz guilty. He appealed, contending, among other things, that admission of the certificates violated his Sixth Amendment right to be confronted with the witnesses against him. The Appeals Court of Massachusetts rejected the claim. . . . The Supreme Judicial Court denied review. We granted certiorari. . . .

There is little doubt that the documents at issue in this case fall within the "core class of testimonial statements" [described in *Crawford*]. . . . The documents at issue here, while denominated by Massachusetts law "certificates," are quite plainly affidavits: "declaration[s] of facts written down and sworn to by the declarant before an officer authorized to administer oaths." Black's Law Dictionary 62 (8th ed. 2004). . . . The fact in question is that the substance found in the possession of Melendez-Diaz and his codefendants was, as the prosecution claimed, cocaine — the precise testimony the analysts would be expected to provide if called at trial. The "certificates" are functionally identical to live, in-court testimony, doing "precisely what a witness does on direct examination." Davis v. Washington, 547 U.S. 813, 830, 126 S. Ct. 2266, 165 L. Ed. 2d 224 (2006) (emphasis deleted).

[U]nder Massachusetts law the sole purpose of the affidavits was to provide "prima facie evidence of the composition, quality, and the net weight" of the analyzed substance. We can safely assume that the analysts were aware of the affidavits' evidentiary purpose, since that purpose — as stated in the relevant state-law provision — was reprinted on the affidavits themselves.

In short, under our decision in *Crawford* the analysts' affidavits were testimonial statements, and the analysts were "witnesses" for purposes of the Sixth Amendment. Absent a showing that the analysts were unavailable to testify at trial and that petitioner had a prior opportunity to cross-examine them, petitioner was entitled to "'be confronted with'" the analysts at trial. . . .

We turn now to the various legal arguments raised by respondent and the dissent. . . .

Respondent claims that there is a difference, for Confrontation Clause purposes, between testimony recounting historical events, which is "prone to distortion or manipulation," and the testimony at issue here, which is the "resul[t] of neutral, scientific testing." Relatedly, respondent and the dissent argue that confrontation of forensic analysts would be of little value because "one would not reasonably expect a laboratory professional . . . to feel quite differently about the results of his scientific test by having to look at the defendant."

This argument is little more than an invitation to return to our overruled decision in [Ohio v.] Roberts, 448 U.S. 56 [1980], which held that evidence with "particularized guarantees of trustworthiness" was admissible notwithstanding the Confrontation Clause. What we said in *Crawford* in response to that argument remains true:

> "To be sure, the Clause's ultimate goal is to ensure reliability of evidence, but it is a procedural rather than a substantive guarantee. It commands, not that evidence be reliable, but that reliability be assessed in a particular manner: by testing in the crucible of cross-examination. . . . Dispensing with confrontation because testimony is obviously reliable is akin to dispensing with jury trial because a defendant is obviously guilty. This is not what the Sixth Amendment prescribes."

Respondent and the dissent may be right that there are other ways — and in some cases better ways — to challenge or verify the results of a forensic test. But the Constitution guarantees one way: confrontation. We do not have license to suspend the Confrontation Clause when a preferable trial strategy is available.

Nor is it evident that what respondent calls "neutral scientific testing" is as neutral or as reliable as respondent suggests. Forensic evidence is not uniquely immune from the risk of manipulation. According to a recent study conducted under the auspices of the National Academy of Sciences, "[t]he majority of [laboratories producing forensic evidence] are administered by law enforcement agencies, such as police departments, where the laboratory administrator reports to the head of the agency." . . . A forensic analyst responding to a request from a law enforcement official may feel pressure — or have an incentive — to alter the evidence in a manner favorable to the prosecution. . . .

Respondent argues that the analysts' affidavits are admissible without confrontation because they are "akin to the types of official and business records admissible at common law." But the affidavits do not qualify as traditional official or business records, and even if they did, their authors would be subject to confrontation nonetheless.

Documents kept in the regular course of business may ordinarily be admitted at trial despite their hearsay status. See Fed. Rule Evid. 803(6). But that is not the case if the regularly conducted business activity is the production of evidence for use at trial. Our decision in Palmer v. Hoffman, 318 U.S. 109 (1943), made that distinction clear. There we held that an accident report provided by an employee of a railroad company did not qualify as a business record because, although kept in the regular course of the railroad's operations, it was "calculated for use essentially in the court, not in the business." The analysts' certificates — like police reports generated by law enforcement officials — do not qualify as business or public records for precisely the same reason. . . .

Respondent also misunderstands the relationship between the business-and-official-records hearsay exceptions and the Confrontation Clause. As we stated in *Crawford*: "Most of the hearsay exceptions covered statements that by their nature were not testimonial — for example, business records or statements in furtherance of a conspiracy." Business and public records are generally admissible absent confrontation not because they qualify under an exception to the hearsay rules, but because — having been created for the administration of an entity's affairs and not for the purpose of establishing or proving some fact at trial — they are not testimonial. Whether or not they qualify as business or official records, the analysts' statements here — prepared specifically for use at petitioner's trial — were testimony against petitioner, and the analysts were subject to confrontation under the Sixth Amendment. . . .

This case involves little more than the application of our holding in Crawford v. Washington. The Sixth Amendment does not permit the prosecution to prove its case via ex parte out-of-court affidavits, and the admission of such evidence against Melendez-Diaz was error. We therefore reverse the judgment of the Appeals Court of Massachusetts and remand the case for further proceedings not inconsistent with this opinion.

It is so ordered.

Justice THOMAS, concurring. [opinion omitted]

Justice KENNEDY, with whom The Chief Justice, Justice BREYER, and Justice ALITO join, dissenting.

The Court sweeps away an accepted rule governing the admission of scientific evidence. Until today, scientific analysis could be introduced into evidence without testimony from the "analyst" who produced it. This rule has been established for at least 90 years. . . .

It is remarkable that the Court so confidently disregards a century of jurisprudence. We learn now that we have misinterpreted the Confrontation Clause — hardly an arcane or seldom-used provision of the Constitution — for the first 218 years of its existence. The immediate systemic concern is that the Court makes no attempt to acknowledge the real differences between laboratory analysts who perform scientific tests and other, more conventional witnesses — "witnesses" being the word the Framers used in the Confrontation Clause.

Crawford and *Davis* dealt with ordinary witnesses — women who had seen, and in two cases been the victim of, the crime in question. Those cases stand for the proposition that formal statements made by a conventional witness — one who has personal knowledge of some aspect of the defendant's guilt — may not be admitted without the witness appearing at trial to meet the accused face to face. But *Crawford* and *Davis* do not say — indeed, could not have said, because the facts were not before the Court — that anyone who makes a testimonial statement is a witness for purposes of the Confrontation Clause, even when that person has, in fact, witnessed nothing to give them personal knowledge of the defendant's guilt.

Because *Crawford* and *Davis* concerned typical witnesses, the Court should have done the sensible thing and limited its holding to witnesses as so defined. . . .

The Court today expands the Clause to include laboratory analysts, but analysts differ from ordinary witnesses in at least three significant ways. First, a conventional witness recalls events observed in the past, while an analyst's report contains near-contemporaneous observations of the test. An observation recorded at the time it is made is unlike the usual act of testifying. A typical witness must recall a previous event that he or she perceived just once, and thus may have misperceived or misremembered. But an analyst making a contemporaneous observation need not rely on memory; he or she instead reports the observations at the time they are made. We gave this consideration substantial weight in *Davis*. There, the "primary purpose" of the victim's 911 call was "to enable police assistance to meet an ongoing emergency[ ]" rather than "to establish or prove past events potentially relevant to later criminal prosecution." The Court cites no authority for its holding that an observation recorded at the time it is made is an act of "witness[ing]" for purposes of the Confrontation Clause.

Second, an analyst observes neither the crime nor any human action related to it. Often, the analyst does not know the defendant's identity, much less have personal knowledge of an aspect of the defendant's guilt. The analyst's distance from the crime and the defendant, in both space and time, suggests the analyst is not a witness against the defendant in the conventional sense.

Third, a conventional witness responds to questions under interrogation. But laboratory tests are conducted according to scientific protocols; they are not dependent upon or controlled by interrogation of any sort. . . . There is no indication that the analysts here — who work for the State Laboratory Institute, a division of the Massachusetts Department of Public Health — were adversarial to petitioner. Nor is there any evidence that adversarial officials played a role in formulating the analysts' certificates.

Rather than acknowledge that it expands the Confrontation Clause beyond conventional witnesses, the Court relies on our recent opinions in *Crawford* and *Davis*. The Court assumes, with little analysis, that *Crawford* and *Davis* extended the Clause to any person who makes a "testimonial" statement. But the Court's confident tone cannot disguise the thinness of these two reeds. Neither *Crawford* nor *Davis* considered whether the Clause extends to persons far removed from the crime who have no connection to the defendant. Instead, those cases concerned conventional witnesses. . . .

Laboratory analysts who conduct routine scientific tests are not the kind of conventional witnesses to whom the Confrontation Clause refers. The judgment of the Appeals Court of Massachusetts should be affirmed.

NOTES TO MELENDEZ-DIAZ v. MASSACHUSETTS

1. *"Witnesses Against."* Compare the majority and dissent interpretations of the concept "witnesses against."

2. *Statements Not Specifically about a Particular Person.* Under the majority's analysis, would an affidavit stating that a blood-alcohol measuring device had been calibrated properly prior to its use by a police officer be testimonial?

■ ■ ■

Did Melendez-Diaz *Mean What It Said?* — Bullcoming. Not long after it had decided *Melendez-Diaz*, the Court granted certiorari in *Bullcoming*, where a crime lab report was not titled "affidavit."

BULLCOMING v. NEW MEXICO
131 S. Ct. 2705 (2011)

Justice GINSBURG delivered the opinion of the Court [except as to a portion on the burden the holding might place on law enforcement, omitted here]

In *Melendez-Diaz v. Massachusetts,* 557 U.S. ——, 129 S. Ct. 2527, 174 L. Ed. 2d 314 (2009), this Court held that a forensic laboratory report stating that a suspect substance was cocaine ranked as testimonial for purposes of the Sixth Amendment's Confrontation Clause. The report had been created specifically to serve as evidence in a criminal proceeding. Absent stipulation, the Court ruled, the prosecution may not introduce such a report without offering a live witness competent to testify to the truth of the statements made in the report.

In the case before us, petitioner Donald Bullcoming was arrested on charges of driving while intoxicated (DWI). Principal evidence against Bullcoming was a forensic laboratory report certifying that Bullcoming's blood-alcohol concentration was well above the threshold for aggravated DWI. At trial, the prosecution did not call as a witness the analyst who signed the certification. Instead, the State called another analyst who was familiar with the laboratory's testing procedures, but had neither participated in nor observed the test on Bullcoming's blood sample. The New Mexico Supreme Court determined that, although the blood-alcohol analysis was "testimonial," the Confrontation Clause did not require the certifying analyst's in-court testimony. Instead, New Mexico's high court held, live testimony of another analyst satisfied the constitutional requirements.

The question presented is whether the Confrontation Clause permits the prosecution to introduce a forensic laboratory report containing a testimonial certification — made for the purpose of proving a particular fact — through the in-court testimony of a scientist who did not sign the certification or perform or observe the test reported in the certification. We hold that surrogate testimony of that order does not meet the constitutional requirement. The accused's right is to be confronted with the analyst who made the certification, unless that analyst is unavailable at trial, and the accused had an opportunity, pretrial, to cross-examine that particular scientist.

In August 2005, a vehicle driven by petitioner Donald Bullcoming rearended a pick-up truck at an intersection in Farmington, New Mexico. When the truckdriver exited his vehicle and approached Bullcoming to exchange insurance information, he noticed that Bullcoming's eyes were bloodshot. Smelling alcohol on Bullcoming's breath, the truckdriver told his wife to call the police. Bullcoming left the scene before the police arrived, but was soon apprehended by an officer who observed his performance of field sobriety tests. Upon failing the tests, Bullcoming was arrested for driving a vehicle while "under the influence of intoxicating liquor" (DWI), in violation of N.M. Stat. Ann. §66-8-102 (2004).

Because Bullcoming refused to take a breath test, the police obtained a warrant authorizing a blood-alcohol analysis. Pursuant to the warrant, a sample of Bullcoming's blood was drawn at a local hospital. To determine Bullcoming's blood-alcohol concentration (BAC), the police sent the sample to the New Mexico Department of Health, Scientific Laboratory Division (SLD). In a standard SLD form titled "Report of Blood Alcohol Analysis," participants in the testing were identified, and the forensic analyst certified his finding.

SLD's report contained in the top block "information . . . filled in by [the] arresting officer." This information included the "reason [the] suspect [was] stopped" (the officer checked "Accident"), and the date ("8.14.05") and time ("18:25 PM") the blood sample was drawn. The arresting officer also affirmed that he had arrested Bullcoming and witnessed the blood draw. The next two blocks contained certifications by the nurse who drew Bullcoming's blood and the SLD intake employee who received the blood sample sent to the laboratory.

Following these segments, the report presented the "certificate of analyst," completed and signed by Curtis Caylor, the SLD forensic analyst assigned to test Bullcoming's blood sample. Caylor recorded that the BAC in Bullcoming's sample was 0.21 grams per hundred milliliters, an inordinately high level. Caylor also affirmed that "[t]he seal of th[e] sample was received intact and broken in the laboratory," that "the statements in [the analyst's block of the report] are correct," and that he had "followed the procedures set out on the reverse of th[e] report." Those "procedures" instructed analysts, *inter alia,* to "retai[n] the sample container and the raw data from the analysis," and to "not[e] any circumstance or condition which might affect the integrity of the sample or otherwise affect the validity of the analysis." Finally, in a block headed "certificate of reviewer," the SLD examiner who reviewed Caylor's analysis certified that Caylor was qualified to conduct the BAC test, and that the "established procedure" for handling and analyzing Bullcoming's sample "ha[d] been followed."

SLD analysts use gas chromatograph machines to determine BAC levels. Operation of the machines requires specialized knowledge and training. Several steps are involved in the gas chromatograph process, and human error can occur at each step.

Caylor's report that Bullcoming's BAC was 0.21 supported a prosecution for aggravated DWI, the threshold for which is a BAC of 0.16 grams per hundred milliliters, §66-8-102(D)(1). The State accordingly charged Bullcoming with this more serious crime.

The case was tried to a jury in November 2005, after our decision in *Crawford v. Washington,* but before *Melendez-Diaz.* On the day of trial, the State announced that it would not be calling SLD analyst Curtis Caylor as a witness because he had "very recently [been] put on unpaid leave" for a reason not revealed. A startled defense counsel objected. The prosecution, she complained, had never disclosed, until trial commenced, that the witness "out there . . . [was] not the analyst [of Bullcoming's sample]." Counsel stated that, "had [she] known that the analyst [who tested Bullcoming's blood] was not available," her opening, indeed, her entire defense "may very well have been dramatically different." The State, however, proposed to introduce Caylor's finding as a "business record" during the testimony of Gerasimos Razatos, an SLD scientist who had neither observed nor reviewed Caylor's analysis.

Bullcoming's counsel opposed the State's proposal. Without Caylor's testimony, defense counsel maintained, introduction of the analyst's finding would violate Bullcoming's Sixth Amendment right "to be confronted with the witnesses against him." The trial court overruled the objection, and admitted the

SLD report as a business record.[3] The jury convicted Bullcoming of aggravated DWI, and the New Mexico Court of Appeals upheld the conviction, concluding that "the blood alcohol report in the present case was non-testimonial and prepared routinely with guarantees of trustworthiness."

While Bullcoming's appeal was pending before the New Mexico Supreme Court, this Court decided *Melendez-Diaz*....

In light of *Melendez-Diaz*, the New Mexico Supreme Court acknowledged that the blood-alcohol report introduced at Bullcoming's trial qualified as testimonial evidence.... Nevertheless, for two reasons, the court held that admission of the report did not violate the Confrontation Clause.

First, the court said certifying analyst Caylor "was a mere scrivener," who "simply transcribed the results generated by the gas chromatograph machine." Second, SLD analyst Razatos, although he did not participate in testing Bullcoming's blood, "qualified as an expert witness with respect to the gas chromatograph machine." "Razatos provided live, in-court testimony," the court stated, "and, thus, was available for cross-examination regarding the operation of the . . . machine, the results of [Bullcoming's] BAC test, and the SLD's established laboratory procedures." Razatos' testimony was crucial, the court explained, because Bullcoming could not cross-examine the machine or the written report. But "[Bullcoming's] right of confrontation was preserved," the court concluded, because Razatos was a qualified analyst, able to serve as a surrogate for Caylor.

We granted certiorari to address this question: Does the Confrontation Clause permit the prosecution to introduce a forensic laboratory report containing a testimonial certification, made in order to prove a fact at a criminal trial, through the in-court testimony of an analyst who did not sign the certification or personally perform or observe the performance of the test reported in the certification. Our answer is in line with controlling precedent: As a rule, if an out-of-court statement is testimonial in nature, it may not be introduced against the accused at trial unless the witness who made the statement is unavailable and the accused has had a prior opportunity to confront that witness. Because the New Mexico Supreme Court permitted the testimonial statement of one witness, *i.e.*, Caylor, to enter into evidence through the in-court testimony of a second person, *i.e.*, Razatos, we reverse that court's judgment.

The Sixth Amendment's Confrontation Clause confers upon the accused "[i]n all criminal prosecutions, . . . the right . . . to be confronted with the witnesses against him." In a pathmarking 2004 decision, *Crawford v. Washington*, we overruled *Ohio v. Roberts*, 448 U.S. 56 (1980), which had interpreted the Confrontation Clause to allow admission of absent witnesses' testimonial statements based on a judicial determination of reliability. Rejecting *Roberts* "'amorphous notions of 'reliability,'" "*Crawford* held that fidelity to the Confrontation Clause permitted admission of "[t]estimonial statements of witnesses absent

---

3. The trial judge noted that, when he started out in law practice, "there were no breath tests or blood tests. They just brought in the cop, and the cop said, 'Yeah, he was drunk.'"

from trial . . . only where the declarant is unavailable, and only where the defendant has had a prior opportunity to cross-examine." . . .

The State in the instant case never asserted that the analyst who signed the certification, Curtis Caylor, was unavailable. The record showed only that Caylor was placed on unpaid leave for an undisclosed reason. Nor did Bullcoming have an opportunity to cross-examine Caylor. *Crawford* and *Melendez-Diaz,* therefore, weigh heavily in Bullcoming's favor. The New Mexico Supreme Court, however, although recognizing that the SLD report was testimonial for purposes of the Confrontation Clause, considered SLD analyst Razatos an adequate substitute for Caylor. We explain first why Razatos' appearance did not meet the Confrontation Clause requirement. We next address the State's argument that the SLD report ranks as "nontestimonial," and therefore "[was] not subject to the Confrontation Clause" in the first place.

The New Mexico Supreme Court held surrogate testimony adequate to satisfy the Confrontation Clause in this case because analyst Caylor "simply transcribed the resul[t] generated by the gas chromatograph machine," presenting no interpretation and exercising no independent judgment. . . .

Caylor certified that he received Bullcoming's blood sample intact with the seal unbroken, that he checked to make sure that the forensic report number and the sample number "correspond[ed]," and that he performed on Bullcoming's sample a particular test, adhering to a precise protocol. He further represented, by leaving the "[r]emarks" section of the report blank, that no "circumstance or condition . . . affect[ed] the integrity of the sample or . . . the validity of the analysis." These representations, relating to past events and human actions not revealed in raw, machine-produced data, are met for cross-examination. . . .

The New Mexico Supreme Court stated that the number registered by the gas chromatograph machine called for no interpretation or exercise of independent judgment on Caylor's part. We have already explained that Caylor certified to more than a machine-generated number. In any event, the comparative reliability of an analyst's testimonial report drawn from machine-produced data does not overcome the Sixth Amendment bar. . . .

Recognizing that admission of the blood-alcohol analysis depended on "live, in-court testimony [by] a qualified analyst," the New Mexico Supreme Court believed that Razatos could substitute for Caylor because Razatos "qualified as an expert witness with respect to the gas chromatograph machine and the SLD's laboratory procedures." But surrogate testimony of the kind Razatos was equipped to give could not convey what Caylor knew or observed about the events his certification concerned, *i.e.,* the particular test and testing process he employed. Nor could such surrogate testimony expose any lapses or lies on the certifying analyst's part. . . .

More fundamentally, as this Court stressed in *Crawford,* "[t]he text of the Sixth Amendment does not suggest any open-ended exceptions from the confrontation requirement to be developed by the courts." . . . Accordingly, the Clause does not tolerate dispensing with confrontation simply because the court believes that questioning one witness about another's testimonial statements provides a fair enough opportunity for cross-examination. . . .

In short, when the State elected to introduce Caylor's certification, Caylor became a witness Bullcoming had the right to confront. Our precedent cannot sensibly be read any other way. . . .

For the reasons stated, the judgment of the New Mexico Supreme Court is reversed, and the case is remanded for further proceedings not inconsistent with this opinion. *It is so ordered.*

Justice SOTOMAYOR, concurring in part.

I agree with the Court that the trial court erred by admitting the blood alcohol concentration (BAC) report. I write separately first to highlight why I view the report at issue to be testimonial — specifically because its "primary purpose" is evidentiary — and second to emphasize the limited reach of the Court's opinion. . . .

Although this case is materially indistinguishable from the facts we considered in *Melendez-Diaz,* I highlight some of the factual circumstances that this case does *not* present.

First, this is not a case in which the State suggested an alternate purpose, much less an alternate *primary* purpose, for the BAC report. For example, the State has not claimed that the report was necessary to provide Bullcoming with medical treatment. . . .

Second, this is not a case in which the person testifying is a supervisor, reviewer, or someone else with a personal, albeit limited, connection to the scientific test at issue. . . .

Third, this is not a case in which an expert witness was asked for his independent opinion about underlying testimonial reports that were not themselves admitted into evidence. . . .

Finally, this is not a case in which the State introduced only machine-generated results, such as a printout from a gas chromatograph. . . . Thus, we do not decide whether, as the New Mexico Supreme Court suggests, a State could introduce (assuming an adequate chain of custody foundation) raw data generated by a machine in conjunction with the testimony of an expert witness.

This case does not present, and thus the Court's opinion does not address, any of these factual scenarios.

As in *Melendez-Diaz,* the primary purpose of the BAC report is clearly to serve as evidence. It is therefore testimonial, and the trial court erred in allowing the State to introduce it into evidence via Razatos' testimony. I respectfully concur.

Justice KENNEDY, with whom The Chief Justice, Justice BREYER, and Justice ALITO join, dissenting.

. . . Seven years after its initiation, it bears remembering that the *Crawford* approach was not preordained. This Court's missteps have produced an interpretation of the word "witness" at odds with its meaning elsewhere in the

Constitution, including elsewhere in the Sixth Amendment, and at odds with the sound administration of justice. It is time to return to solid ground. A proper place to begin that return is to decline to extend *Melendez-Diaz* to bar the reliable, commonsense evidentiary framework the State sought to follow in this case.

NOTES TO BULLCOMING v. NEW MEXICO

1. *Counting Votes.* The Court's grant of certiorari in *Bullcoming* was surprising to some, and might have been an occasion for reversing or limiting *Melendez-Diaz*. How does *Bullcoming* change or advance our Confrontation Clause jurisprudence?

2. *Costs of Prosecution.* Justice Ginsburg's footnote 3 seems somewhat approving of the simpler style of prosecution that had been recalled by the trial judge. The majority and other dissenting opinions highlighted the use of empirical data in constitutional decision making. The dissent (in a passage not included here) not only anticipated new empirical studies, but also anticipated their findings ("New and more rigorous empirical studies further detailing the unfortunate effects of *Melendez-Diaz* are sure to be forthcoming").

■ ■ ■

Did Melendez-Diaz *and* Bullcoming *Mean What They Said?* — Williams. Information from a crime lab report was made available to the jury through the testimony of an expert who relied on that report to form an opinion. For five justices, this was allowable under the Confrontation Clause. The rationale presented varies from the rationales in the two prior similar cases, and may call into question the continued viability of the "testimonial" concept as the primary means of identifying circumstances where the Confrontation Clause applies.

WILLIAMS v. ILLINOIS

132 S. Ct. 2221 (2012)

Justice ALITO announced the judgment of the Court and delivered an opinion, in which the Chief Justice, Justice KENNEDY, and Justice BREYER join.

In this case, we decide whether Crawford v. Washington precludes an expert witness from . . . expressing an opinion based on facts about a case that have been made known to the expert but about which the expert is not competent to testify. . . .

In petitioner's bench trial for rape, the prosecution called [Sandra Lambatos,] an expert who testified that a DNA profile produced by an outside laboratory, Cellmark, matched a profile produced by the state police lab using a sample of petitioner's blood. On direct examination, the expert testified that Cellmark was an accredited laboratory and that Cellmark provided the police with a DNA profile. The expert also explained the notations on documents admitted as business records, stating that, according to the records, vaginal swabs taken from the victim were sent to and received back from Cellmark. The expert made no other statement that was offered for the purpose of identifying the sample of biological material used in deriving the profile or for the purpose of establishing how Cellmark handled or tested the sample. . . . Nevertheless, petitioner contends that the expert's testimony violated the Confrontation Clause as interpreted in *Crawford*. . . .

We now conclude that this form of expert testimony does not violate the Confrontation Clause because that provision has no application to out-of-court statements that are not offered to prove the truth of the matter asserted.* . . .

As a second, independent basis for our decision, we also conclude that even if the report produced by Cellmark had been admitted into evidence, there would have been no Confrontation Clause violation. The Cellmark report is very different from the sort of extrajudicial statements, such as affidavits, depositions, prior testimony, and confessions, that the Confrontation Clause was originally understood to reach. The report was produced before any suspect was identified. The report was sought not for the purpose of obtaining evidence to be used against petitioner, who was not even under suspicion at the time, but for the purpose of finding a rapist who was on the loose. And the profile that Cellmark provided was not inherently inculpatory. . . .

The abuses that the Court has identified as prompting the adoption of the Confrontation Clause shared the following two characteristics: (a) they involved out-of-court statements having the primary purpose of accusing a targeted individual of engaging in criminal conduct and (b) they involved formalized statements such as affidavits, depositions, prior testimony, or confessions. In all but one of the post-*Crawford* cases in which a Confrontation Clause violation has been found, both of these characteristics were present. . . .

In *Hammon*, the one case in which an informal statement was held to violate the Confrontation Clause, we considered statements elicited in the course of police interrogation. We held that a statement does not fall within the ambit of the Clause when it is made "under circumstances objectively indicating that the primary purpose of the interrogation is to enable police assistance to meet an ongoing emergency." In *Bryant*, another police-interrogation case, we explained that a person who makes a statement to resolve an ongoing emergency is not acting like a trial witness because the declarant's purpose is not to provide a solemn declaration for use at trial, but to bring an end to an ongoing threat. We noted that "the prospect of fabrication . . . is presumably significantly diminished" when

---

* Five justices disagreed with this position and believed that the expert's testimony used statements made by Cellmark employees for the truth of what they asserted. — Ed.

a statement is made under such circumstances, and that reliability is a salient characteristic of a statement that falls outside the reach of the Confrontation Clause. We emphasized that if a statement is not made for "the primary purpose of creating an out-of-court substitute for trial testimony," its admissibility "is the concern of state and federal rules of evidence, not the Confrontation Clause."

In *Melendez-Diaz* and *Bullcoming*, the Court held that the particular forensic reports at issue qualified as testimonial statements, but the Court did not hold that all forensic reports fall into the same category. Introduction of the reports in those cases ran afoul of the Confrontation Clause because they were the equivalent of affidavits made for the purpose of proving the guilt of a particular criminal defendant at trial. There was nothing resembling an ongoing emergency, as the suspects in both cases had already been captured, and the tests in question were relatively simple and can generally be performed by a single analyst. In addition, the technicians who prepared the reports must have realized that their contents (which reported an elevated blood-alcohol level and the presence of an illegal drug) would be incriminating. . . .

Here, the primary purpose of the Cellmark report, viewed objectively, was not to accuse petitioner or to create evidence for use at trial. When the [Illinois State Police] lab sent the sample to Cellmark, its primary purpose was to catch a dangerous rapist who was still at large, not to obtain evidence for use against petitioner, who was neither in custody nor under suspicion at that time. Similarly, no one at Cellmark could have possibly known that the profile that it produced would turn out to inculpate petitioner — or for that matter, anyone else whose DNA profile was in a law enforcement database. . . .

It is also significant that in many labs, numerous technicians work on each DNA profile. When the work of a lab is divided up in such a way, it is likely that the sole purpose of each technician is simply to perform his or her task in accordance with accepted procedures.

Finally, the knowledge that defects in a DNA profile may often be detected from the profile itself provides a further safeguard. In this case, for example, Lambatos testified that she would have been able to tell from the profile if the sample used by Cellmark had been degraded prior to testing. . . . At the time of the testing, petitioner had not yet been identified as a suspect, and there is no suggestion that anyone at Cellmark had a sample of his DNA to swap in by malice or mistake. And given the complexity of the DNA molecule, it is inconceivable that shoddy lab work would somehow produce a DNA profile that just so happened to have the precise genetic makeup of petitioner, who just so happened to be picked out of a lineup by the victim. The prospect is beyond fanciful.

In short, the use at trial of a DNA report prepared by a modern, accredited laboratory "bears little if any resemblance to the historical practices that the Confrontation Clause aimed to eliminate." *Bryant*, (Thomas, J., concurring). . . .

For the two independent reasons explained above, we conclude that there was no Confrontation Clause violation in this case. Accordingly, the judgment of the Supreme Court of Illinois is Affirmed.

Justice BREYER, concurring.

. . . I adhere to the dissenting view set forth in *Melendez-Diaz* and *Bullcoming*, under which the Cellmark report would not be considered "testimonial" and barred by the Confrontation Clause. That view understands . . . the word "testimonial" as having outer limits and *Crawford* as describing a constitutional heartland. And that view would leave the States with constitutional leeway to maintain traditional expert testimony rules as well as hearsay exceptions where there are strong reasons for doing so and *Crawford's* basic rationale does not apply. . . .

Justice THOMAS, concurring in the judgment.

I agree with the plurality that the disclosure of Cellmark's out-of-court statements through the expert testimony of Sandra Lambatos did not violate the Confrontation Clause. I reach this conclusion, however, solely because Cellmark's statements lacked the requisite "formality and solemnity" to be considered "'testimonial'" for purposes of the Confrontation Clause. . . .

Having concluded that the statements at issue here were introduced for their truth, I turn to whether they were "testimonial" for purposes of the Confrontation Clause. In *Crawford*, the Court explained that "[t]he text of the Confrontation Clause . . . applies to 'witnesses' against the accused — in other words, those who 'bear testimony.'" Id., at 51, 124 S. Ct. 1354 (quoting 2 N. Webster, An American Dictionary of the English Language (1828)). "'Testimony,'" in turn, is "'[a] solemn declaration or affirmation made for the purpose of establishing or proving some fact.'" . . .

Applying these principles, I conclude that Cellmark's report is not a statement by a "witnes[s]" within the meaning of the Confrontation Clause. The Cellmark report lacks the solemnity of an affidavit or deposition, for it is neither a sworn nor a certified declaration of fact. Nowhere does the report attest that its statements accurately reflect the DNA testing processes used or the results obtained. The report is signed by two "reviewers," but they neither purport to have performed the DNA testing nor certify the accuracy of those who did. And, although the report was produced at the request of law enforcement, it was not the product of any sort of formalized dialogue resembling custodial interrogation. . . .

Justice KAGAN, with whom Justice SCALIA, Justice GINSBURG, and Justice SOTOMAYOR join, dissenting.

. . . Under our Confrontation Clause precedents, this is an open-and-shut case. The State of Illinois prosecuted Sandy Williams for rape based in part on a DNA profile created in Cellmark's laboratory. Yet the State did not give Williams a chance to question the analyst who produced that evidence. Instead, the prosecution introduced the results of Cellmark's testing through an expert witness who had no idea how they were generated. That approach . . . deprived Williams of his Sixth Amendment right to "confron[t] . . . the witnesses against him." . . .

The plurality . . . argues . . . that the Cellmark report falls outside the Confrontation Clause's ambit because it is nontestimonial. The plurality tries out a number of supporting theories, but all in vain: Each one either conflicts with this Court's precedents or misconstrues this case's facts. Justice Thomas rejects the plurality's views for similar reasons as I do, thus bringing to five the number of Justices who repudiate the plurality's understanding of what statements count as testimonial. Justice Thomas, however, offers a rationale of his own for deciding that the Cellmark report is nontestimonial. I think his essay works no better. When all is said and done, the Cellmark report is a testimonial statement.

[W]e just last year treated as testimonial a forensic report prepared by a "modern, accredited laboratory"; indeed, we declared that the report at issue "fell within the core class of testimonial statements" implicating the Confrontation Clause. . . . So the plurality must explain: What could support a distinction between the laboratory analysis there and the DNA test in this case?

As its first stab, the plurality states that the Cellmark report was "not prepared for the primary purpose of accusing a targeted individual." Where that test comes from is anyone's guess. Justice Thomas rightly shows that it derives neither from the text nor from the history of the Confrontation Clause. And it has no basis in our precedents. . . . None of our cases has ever suggested that, in addition, the statement must be meant to accuse a previously identified individual; indeed, in *Melendez-Diaz*, we rejected a related argument that laboratory "analysts are not subject to confrontation because they are not 'accusatory' witnesses."

Nor does the plurality give any good reason for adopting an "accusation" test. . . . But surely the typical problem with laboratory analyses—and the typical focus of cross-examination—has to do with careless or incompetent work, rather than with personal vendettas. And as to that predominant concern, it makes not a whit of difference whether, at the time of the laboratory test, the police already have a suspect.

The plurality next attempts to invoke our precedents holding statements nontestimonial when made "to respond to an 'ongoing emergency,'" "rather than to create evidence for trial; here, the plurality insists, the Cellmark report's purpose was "to catch a dangerous rapist who was still at large." But that is to stretch both our "ongoing emergency" test and the facts of this case beyond all recognition. We have previously invoked that test to allow statements by a woman who was being assaulted and a man who had just been shot. In doing so, we stressed the "informal [and] harried" nature of the statements, that they were made as, or "minutes" after the events they described "actually happen[ed]," by "frantic" victims of criminal attacks, ibid., to officers trying to figure out "what had . . . occurred" and what threats remained. On their face, the decisions have nothing to say about laboratory analysts conducting routine tests far away from a crime scene. And this case presents a peculiarly inapt set of facts for extending those precedents. Lambatos testified at trial that "all reports in this case were prepared for this criminal investigation . . . [a]nd for the purpose of the eventual litigation—in other words, for the purpose of producing evidence, not enabling emergency responders. And that testimony fits the relevant timeline. The police did not send the swabs to Cellmark until November 2008—nine months after L.J.'s rape—and did not receive the results for another four months. That is hardly the typical emergency response.

Finally, the plurality offers a host of reasons for why reports like this one are reliable. . . . But once again: Been there, done that. In *Melendez-Diaz*, this Court rejected identical arguments, noting extensive documentation of "[s]erious deficiencies . . . in the forensic evidence used in criminal trials." Scientific testing is "technical," to be sure, but it is only as reliable as the people who perform it. That is why a defendant may wish to ask the analyst a variety of questions: How much experience do you have? Have you ever made mistakes in the past? Did you test the right sample? Use the right procedures? Contaminate the sample in any way? Indeed, as scientific evidence plays a larger and larger role in criminal prosecutions, those inquiries will often be the most important in the case.

And *Melendez-Diaz* made yet a more fundamental point in response to claims of the über alles reliability of scientific evidence: It is not up to us to decide, ex ante, what evidence is trustworthy and what is not. That is because the Confrontation Clause prescribes its own "procedure for determining the reliability of testimony in criminal trials." *Crawford*. That procedure is cross-examination. And "[d]ispensing with [it] because testimony is obviously reliable is akin to dispensing with jury trial because a defendant is obviously guilty." Id.

. . . The plurality can find no reason consistent with our precedents for treating the Cellmark report as nontestimonial. That is because the report is, in every conceivable respect, a statement meant to serve as evidence in a potential criminal trial. And that simple fact should be sufficient to resolve the question.

Justice Thomas's unique method of defining testimonial statements fares no better. On his view, the Confrontation Clause "regulates only the use of statements bearing 'indicia of solemnity.'" And Cellmark's report, he concludes, does not qualify because it is "neither a sworn nor a certified declaration of fact." But Justice Thomas's approach grants constitutional significance to minutia, in a way that can only undermine the Confrontation Clause's protections.

To see the point, start with precedent, because the Court rejected this same kind of argument, as applied to this same kind of document, at around this same time just last year. In *Bullcoming*, the State asserted that the forensic report at issue was nontestimonial because—unlike the report in *Melendez-Diaz*—it was not sworn before a notary public. We responded that applying the Confrontation Clause only to a sworn forensic report "would make the right to confrontation easily erasable"—next time, the laboratory could file the selfsame report without the oath. We then held . . . that "[i]n all material respects," the forensic report in *Bullcoming* matched the one in *Melendez-Diaz*. First, a law enforcement officer provided evidence to a state laboratory assisting in police investigations. Second, the analyst tested the evidence and "prepared a certificate concerning the result[s]." Third, the certificate was "formalized in a signed document . . . headed a 'report.'" That was enough.

Now compare that checklist of "material" features to the report in this case. The only differences are that Cellmark is a private laboratory under contract with the State (which no one thinks relevant), and that the report is not labeled a "certificate." That amounts to (maybe) a nickel's worth of difference: The similarities in form, function, and purpose dwarf the distinctions. Each report is an official and signed record of laboratory test results, meant to establish a certain set of facts in legal proceedings. Neither looks any more "formal" than the other; neither is any more formal than the other. . . .

Before today's decision, a prosecutor wishing to admit the results of forensic testing had to produce the technician responsible for the analysis. That was the result of not one, but two decisions this Court issued in the last three years. But that clear rule is clear no longer. . . . What comes out of four Justices' desire to limit *Melendez-Diaz* and *Bullcoming* in whatever way possible, combined with one Justice's one-justice view of those holdings, is — to be frank — who knows what. Those decisions apparently no longer mean all that they say. Yet no one can tell in what way or to what extent they are altered because no proposed limitation commands the support of a majority.

. . . I respectfully dissent.

NOTES TO WILLIAMS v. ILLINOIS

1. *Defendants' Subpoena Power.* In many cases where the prosecution seeks to introduce a hearsay statement, the defendant might be able to subpoena the declarant and thus secure live testimony to replace or supplement the declarant's hearsay statement. For the strongest proponents of the *Crawford* analysis of the Confrontation Clause, this ability to subpoena witnesses is beside the point, if the Confrontation Clause requires the prosecution to make the declarant available.

2. *Does It Matter?* In a portion of Justice Kagan's opinion not included above, she wrote that in an earlier case, California prosecuted a man named John Kocak for rape. The state presented preliminary hearing testimony from an analyst at Cellmark Diagnostics Laboratory. The analyst had compared DNA from a bloody sweatshirt found at the crime scene to two other samples. One of the samples was from Kocak and the other was from the victim. The analyst's report stated that the DNA found on the sweatshirt belonged to Kocak. After undergoing cross-examination, the analyst realized she had made an error. She took the stand again and admitted that the report listed the victim's control sample as coming from Kocak. The DNA on the sweatshirt matched the victim, not Kocak. The analyst testified, "I'm a little hysterical right now, but I think . . . the two names should be switched."

QUESTION 11-6. Dr. Ellen Examiner, a physician employed in a state's Office of Medical Examiner, conducted an autopsy of an apparent crime victim and wrote a report of her findings. If she is not available to testify about her findings at a criminal trial of someone accused of killing the victim, how would the Confrontation Clause affect admissibility of her report? Assume that a statute in her state contains this provision:

> The Chief Medical Examiner shall be responsible to the Director of the Division of Health in all matters except that the Chief Medical Examiner shall operate with independent authority for the purposes of: (1) the performance of death investigations; (2) the establishment of cause and manner of death; and (3) the formulation of conclusions, opinions, or testimony in judicial proceedings."

E SUMMARY

The "residual exception" in the Federal Rules of Evidence and most state codes allows the admission of hearsay even if it is not covered by a specifically enumerated exception, under certain circumstances. And the Due Process Clause can sometimes require the admission of hearsay (and other evidence as well) if its exclusion would too seriously undermine the fairness of a criminal defendant's trial. An opposite modification of the basic hearsay rules takes place when the Confrontation Clause applies. In those situations, even though a hearsay statement could qualify for admission according to hearsay doctrines, the Constitution requires that it be excluded.

Residual Exception. The residual, or "catchall," exception may be used to admit hearsay that is not eligible for admission under any of the other hearsay provisions, if it has circumstantial guarantees of trustworthiness that are equivalent to those in the enumerated exceptions, if it is more probative on the point for which it is offered than other evidence that can be obtained with reasonable means, and if justice will be served by its admission.

The circumstantial guarantee of trustworthiness refers to the likelihood that the out-of-court statement's information is accurate. It does not refer to the quality of proof supporting a finding that the statement was actually made.

When a statement almost fits the terms of an enumerated exception but fails to satisfy those terms fully, it is sometimes called a "near-miss." A minority of jurisdictions reject the use of the residual exception for near-miss statements, but most allow it.

Due Process. A state may not reject evidence on any theory that is "arbitrary." For example, the Due Process Clause requires the admission of evidence even if the hearsay rule would ordinarily require its exclusion, if the evidence (1) has persuasive assurances of trustworthiness and (2) is critical for the defendant's defense. This same due process requirement applies to evidence rules other than hearsay rules that might have the same effect of excluding crucial and trustworthy evidence.

Confrontation Clause. The Confrontation Clause guarantees that a criminal defendant may confront those who are witnesses against him or her. As applied until 2004, this provision meant that admission of hearsay statements was a violation of a defendant's constitutional rights *unless* the hearsay was either covered by a hearsay exception that was "firmly rooted" or had "particularized guarantees of trustworthiness." In 2004, the Supreme Court changed this jurisprudence in Crawford v. Washington, holding that hearsay statements must be excluded if they are "testimonial" (unless the declarant is unavailable and the defendant had a prior opportunity to cross-examine the declarant about the statement). Under this new regime, hearsay statements that are not testimonial may be admitted if the ordinary hearsay rules would allow that result.

Defining "testimonial," and thus defining the reach of the Confrontation Clause, has been complicated in the years since *Crawford*. Formal statements to law enforcement authorities are definitely testimonial. Statements that are in the past tense and describe past criminal conduct are testimonial, too, unless their primary purpose was to help to resolve an ongoing emergency.

The definition of "ongoing emergency" has turned out to be flexible. The presence in society of a criminal with a firearm may support a finding of ongoing emergency even if the criminal is absent and some time has passed since he or she committed the crime. Also, suspicion that a child has suffered abuse at home may support a finding of ongoing emergency.

The Supreme Court has applied its new Confrontation Clause jurisprudence to statements made by employees of crime labs about whether a substance was an illegal drug, the amount of alcohol in a blood sample, and whether a DNA sample matched some other DNA sample. At first, the doctrine seemed clear, and statements knowingly made for the purpose of assisting in criminal prosecutions were within the coverage of the Confrontation Clause. The most recent Supreme Court decision, however, rejected that result for a crime lab worker's statement presented within an expert witness's testimony, in an array of opinions that offered a variety of rationales for the result.

CHAPTER 12

Impeachment

A. Introduction

B. Reputation, Opinion, and Past Acts to Show Character for Truth Telling

C. Criminal Convictions to Show Character for Truth Telling

D. Bias

E. Contradiction and Prior Inconsistent Statements

F. Impeaching Hearsay Declarants

G. Summary

 A **INTRODUCTION**

Topic Overview

To attempt to persuade the trier of fact that a witness testified falsely, a party may use a variety of impeachment techniques. Rule 607 introduces this concept and makes clear that any party may impeach a witness. This means that even a party who calls a witness may attempt to impeach that witness.

Rule 607. Who May Impeach a Witness

Any party, including the party that called the witness, may attack the witness's credibility.

A number of impeachment techniques, using various types of proof, allow the opponent of a witness to suggest that the witness has a character trait of untruthfulness and that the witness acted in conformity with that trait while testifying. These techniques are based on the propensity inference, which is allowed in the context of impeachment even though it is rejected in other circumstances. Consistent with evidence law's general ambivalence about character evidence, there are detailed rules for using it for impeachment. Information about a witness's past convictions that shed light on truthfulness may be used fairly freely, but there are significant limits on proof of a witness's past bad acts that have not led to convictions.

There are also methods of impeachment that do not involve an attempt to show that a witness characteristically lies. An opponent may show that a witness is subject to some form of bias that could cause the witness to give false testimony. An opponent may introduce evidence that contradicts elements of a witness's testimony, to suggest that errors about those elements call into question the rest of the witness's testimony. Finally, an opponent may show that the witness has made prior statements that are inconsistent with the witness's testimony.

After a witness has been impeached, the party who has introduced that witness's testimony is entitled to rehabilitate that witness's testimony. Character evidence is permitted, as is evidence that would refute a showing of bias or factual error or that would explain an apparent inconsistency between trial testimony and prior statements.

When information from an out-of-court statement is brought into a trial, the declarant of that statement is subject to impeachment with the same techniques that could have been used if the declarant had testified.

Chapter Organization

This chapter begins with the character-based propensity inference techniques of impeachment. The opponent of a witness may attempt to persuade the trier of fact that the witness testified falsely because the witness has the character trait of untruthfulness. These character inferences may be based on evidence about past bad acts the witness has done, or on the witness's convictions of certain kinds of crimes.

Bias is the next topic covered. Although the Federal Rules make no explicit reference to impeachment by a showing of bias, this technique is recognized as derived from common law experience. In extreme circumstances, the Due Process Clause may require admission of bias evidence that otherwise might be excluded.

The chapter next considers impeaching a witness by introduction of evidence that contradicts the witness's testimony or by using past statements the witness has personally made, to highlight the differences between the witness's testimony and those prior statements.

The chapter concludes with consideration of how these impeachment techniques apply to the declarant of an out-of-court statement that has been admitted as proof of what it asserts.

REPUTATION, OPINION, AND PAST ACTS TO SHOW CHARACTER FOR TRUTH TELLING

A witness's credibility may be attacked or supported with evidence about that witness's character traits of truthfulness or untruthfulness, under Rule 608. This propensity inference is directly contrary to the general prohibition of the propensity inference in Rule 404, but one of that rule's exceptions is Rule 404(a)(3), stating that "[e]vidence of a witness's character may be admitted under Rules 607, 608, and 609."

Rule 608. A Witness's Character for Truthfulness or Untruthfulness

   (a) Reputation or Opinion Evidence. A witness's credibility may be attacked or supported by testimony about the witness's reputation for having a character for truthfulness or untruthfulness, or by testimony in the form of an opinion about that character. But evidence of truthful character is admissible only after the witness's character for truthfulness has been attacked.

   . . .

The rule allows evidence in the form of reputation or opinion. For example, suppose "Witness Two" testifies about the character of "Witness One" for truthfulness. In that situation, Witness Two may testify only about Witness One's reputation for truthfulness or untruthfulness, or about Witness Two's own opinion about Witness One's character for truthfulness or untruthfulness.

If a witness (for example, "Witness One") has acted in the past in ways that might indicate bad character for truth telling, the opponent of the witness is entitled to ask about those past acts when cross-examining that witness ("Witness One") or cross-examining another witness who has testified about the first witness's character for truth telling.

Evidence meant to show that a witness is characteristically truthful may be introduced only if that witness's character for truthfulness has been attacked.

■   ■   ■

How Can a Witness Know Another Witness's Reputation? — Caldwell. Rule 608 allows reputation and opinion evidence, but it does not define the required basis for either of these types of information. *Caldwell* describes standards for reputation testimony and applies them to testimony by three different witnesses.

STATE v. CALDWELL

529 N.W.2d 282 (Iowa 1995)

McGIVERIN, J.

This case involves the interpretation of one of the foundational requirements for the admission of reputation testimony under the Iowa rules of evidence and Iowa case law — the requirement that the testimony be derived from comments made by "a general cross-section of the community." More specifically, we must determine whether this representativeness requirement is concerned with the variety of the nature of the comments made or with the variety of the sources of the comments made.

Focusing on the nature of the comments, the district court concluded that negative comments about a police officer, a witness for the State, are comments from a limited class. As a result, the district court refused to admit before the jury any of defendant's three character witnesses' proposed testimony concerning the police officer.

Upon defendant's appeal, we conclude that the district court erred by focusing on the nature of the comments and abused its discretion in excluding the offered reputation testimony of one of defendant's character witnesses, whose testimony was derived from a variety of sources in the officer's work community. Because we also conclude that the defendant was prejudiced by the exclusion of this testimony, we reverse the district court's judgment in part and affirm in part, and remand for a new trial.

[The defendant was accused of possession of a controlled substance and violation of a state law requiring tax stamps for illegal drugs. The state's main evidence was testimony by a police officer, Mark Meyer, that he had seen the defendant take a bag out of a pocket and throw it away. A bag as described by Officer Meyer was found and was determined to contain illegal drugs.]

A jury trial was held. The defendant called three witnesses to testify concerning officer Mark Meyer's alleged reputation for untruthfulness, but the district court refused to admit each of the witnesses' proposed reputation testimony before the jury.

The jury returned verdicts of guilty on both charges. . . .

Defendant appealed, contending that the district court abused its discretion by refusing to allow three of defendant's witnesses to testify concerning officer Mark Meyer's alleged reputation for untruthfulness.

Admissibility of Reputation Evidence. At trial the defendant offered three witnesses' testimony regarding officer Mark Meyer's alleged reputation for untruthfulness in an effort to impeach his credibility pursuant to Iowa Rule of Evidence 608(a). Defendant apparently sought to challenge the credibility of officer Mark Meyer's testimony that defendant threw the baggie containing cocaine base against the fence during the chase. The State timely objected to each witnesses' [sic] testimony, generally arguing that the defendant had not laid the proper foundation for reputation testimony. The defendant then made an offer of proof by a voir dire of each witness outside the presence of the jury.

After hearing the testimony, the court sustained the State's objections, primarily on the basis that each of the witnesses' testimony was based on comments made by persons who had had an adverse contact with officer Mark Meyer in connection with his police duties and thus failed to satisfy the foundational requirement that reputation testimony be based upon the comments of a general cross-section of the community. We conclude that the district court erred by focusing on the nature of the comments rather than the source of the comments and abused its discretion by disallowing the testimony of one of defendant's reputation witnesses, Ray Dial.

A. Foundational Requirements for Reputation Testimony. In order to properly introduce reputation testimony bearing on the credibility of a witness, strict foundational requirements must be met. Several evidentiary facts must be established before a witness may testify as to what the witness has heard concerning another witness' reputation for truthfulness or untruthfulness. These required facts include:

> (1) The background, occupation, residence, etc., of the character witness, (2) [The witness'] familiarity and ability to identify the party whose general reputation was the subject of comment, (3) Whether there have in fact been comments concerning the party's reputation for [truthfulness or untruthfulness], (4) The exact place of these comments, (5) The generality of these comments, many or few in number, (6) Whether from a limited group or class as opposed to a general cross-section of the community, (7) When and how long a period of time the comments have been made.

State v. Hobbs, 172 N.W.2d 268, 272 (Iowa 1969).

The foundational requirement at issue in this case is number (6): whether the witness' reputation testimony is based on comments from a limited group or class, which is not acceptable, or from a general cross-section of the community, which is acceptable.

B. Meaning of "General Cross-Section of the Community." We have previously had the opportunity to more precisely define the terms in the phrase "general cross-section of the community" in State v. Buckner, 214 N.W.2d 164 (Iowa 1974). Regarding the term "community," we recognized that in modern times one's reputation may be better known where a person works than where a person resides. We then stated: "Comments need not always come from a cross-section of an entire city or town. It is sufficient that they come from a cross-section of those persons among whom the individual lives and acts."

We then implicitly defined the phrase "cross-section of persons." We noted that the purpose of this requirement is to foster two qualities necessary for the hearsay exception — reliability and trustworthiness. *Buckner*, 214 N.W.2d at 169; see also 5 Wigmore, Evidence §1610, at 582 (Chadbourn rev. 1974) (stating that the hearsay exception allowing reputation evidence is justified by the circumstantial probability of trustworthiness derived from comments made by those who have a general interest in the subject). We then ruled that this purpose is served if the reputation testimony is based on comments from a representative number of persons who know of the reputation for truthfulness or untruthfulness of the target of the testimony through association with that person in that person's work. As a result, we held that the court would have acted well within its discretion in allowing the Buckner defendant's employer to testify as to the Buckner defendant's reputation for honesty because that testimony was based on comments from a representative number of persons who knew of and associated with him through work.

Representativeness of comments heard by defendant's reputation witnesses. During the defendant's offer of proof outside the presence of the jury, each of the defendant's three witnesses testified as to the comments forming the basis of their proposed reputation testimony.

Defendant's first character witness was Phillip Glenn Caldwell, Sr., the defendant's father. Caldwell testified that, as a twenty-one year resident of Waterloo, he had heard comments from a couple of families who had "had some dealings with [officer Mark Meyer]" and other comments from a few young people who had "had some problems." Caldwell characterized the comments as being made by people with whom he worked, attended church, or did business.

Defendant's second witness, Elisha Culpepper, was a twenty-three year old student attending a university in Davenport, Iowa but who had grown up in Waterloo. Culpepper told the court that he had heard comments regarding officer Mark Meyer's deceitfulness from at least four persons. One comment was made by a person just before that person went to jail and another comment was made by a person who had had an "altercation with [officer Mark Meyer]." All of the comments were made by Culpepper's friends or by persons whom Culpepper knew by "just hanging around."

Defendant's final character witness was Ray Dial, a teacher in his fifteenth year with the Waterloo Community School District and a member of several community organizations. Dial testified that he could recall five or six specific remarks from students and other members of the community. One of these specific remarks came from a student whose boyfriend had had a problem with the officer and another came from a family whose complaint had stemmed from "an incident" involving officer Meyer. Each of these five or six remarks involved an allegation that officer Mark Meyer had tried to get someone arrested for drugs.

Dial also told the court that besides such specific comments, he had also heard several other members of the community remark that the officer "lied about stuff." Dial stated that "all of the comments that [he had] heard [had] come to [him] from people who either directly had a problem with [officer Mark Meyer] or [had] an interest in it because of a friendship or a family relation." Dial also stated that he had received the majority of this information through his role on related committees where he received complaints about police officers and that he had heard the information from a "pretty good chunk of all [of] Waterloo . . . whether black, white, young, old, male or female."

Regarding each of the witnesses' testimony, the trial court determined that it was derived from a limited class which was not representative of officer Mark Meyer's work community. In making these determinations, however, the trial court, agreeing with the State, focused on the nature of the comments. Specifically, the trial court ruled that the comments were derived from a limited class because they were made by persons who had had a bad experience with officer Mark Meyer in connection with his official duties.

As we have described, however, the foundational requirement that comments come from "a general cross-section" of the community is concerned with the variety of persons making the comments rather than with the persons' reasons for making the comments. This is especially true with reputation testimony because the comments will usually be based upon either a good or a bad experience, depending on whether the testimony is for truthfulness or untruthfulness. For example, had the offered reputation testimony involved a police officer's reputation for honesty and had such testimony been based on comments made by a representative number of the officers working with the target officer, the fact that each officer's comment had been based upon a good experience with that officer would not be grounds for excluding the testimony. Thus, the trial court's grounds for sustaining the State's foundational objections to each of the witnesses' testimony are clearly untenable.

Looking at the appropriate inquiry, we think the summaries of the witnesses' testimony demonstrate that only Dial's testimony is derived from comments made by a representative number of the people among whom officer Mark Meyer is known and works. Both Caldwell's and Culpepper's testimony was supported only by a few remarks made by their friends. On the other hand, Dial's testimony was based on comments made by numerous persons with various backgrounds and connections to the community, including school activities, religious functions, and community organizations. Accordingly, we conclude that Dial's testimony was based on comments from a general cross-section of officer Mark Meyer's work community, but that Caldwell's and Culpepper's testimony was derived from comments from a narrow, nonrepresentative group.

Disposition. Having concluded that Caldwell's and Culpepper's testimony falls short of meeting the foundational requirement that reputation testimony be based on comments from a representative number of persons in the relevant community, we find no abuse of discretion and affirm the trial court's exclusion of their testimony.

However, we find an abuse of discretion and disagree with the trial court's refusal to admit the reputation testimony offered by Ray Dial because his testimony did fulfill the "general cross-section" foundational requirement.

[Remand for new trial was required.]

NOTES TO STATE v. CALDWELL

1. *Reputation in Two Contexts: Truth Telling under Rule 608 and Defendants' and Victims' Character under Rules 404 and 405.* The court applies a set of requirements that are not explicit in Rule 608. In another circumstance where evidence of character is permitted, evidence of defendants' and victims' character under Rules 404 and 405, there is a parallel omission of foundation requirements. The same foundation requirements should apply in both settings.

2. *Bad Character for Truthfulness Is Always Relevant.* Rule 608 allows evidence of a witness's bad character for truthfulness whenever a witness testifies. This means that a prosecutor, for example, may introduce negative character information about any witness who testifies for a defendant. In contrast, when character evidence might be admissible to show kinds of conduct different from truth telling — as in the many instances set out in Rule 404 — it is usually the defendant who controls whether character evidence may be used. In most situations, if the defendant refrains from introducing character evidence, the prosecution will not be allowed to use it either.

3. *Hearsay and Reputation.* Rule 803(21) provides a hearsay exception that correlates with Rule 608. It defines the exception as: "*Reputation Concerning Character.* A reputation among a person's associates or in the community concerning the person's character."

QUESTION 12-1. Carl Camper was tried for crimes associated with destruction of property at a trailer campground. He testified in his own defense and was cross-examined vigorously with regard to his truthfulness. Later in the trial, Camper sought to introduce testimony by Frank Friend, a friend of Camper's, to show that Camper had a reputation for honesty in that campground. Consider whether the following questions and answers would support admission of Friend's testimony about Camper's reputation for honesty:

Q: Did you see Camper interact in the campground?
A: Yes.
Q: With other individuals in the campground?
A: Yes.
Q: All right. And did any of those people discuss his reputation with you?
A: No.
Q: Did you discuss with any of your neighbors Camper's reputation within the community?
A: Yes.

Q: All right. And what was that?

A: That Camper's a good guy. He . . . He — Camper was helpful — very helpful to a lot of people.

Court: You know . . . he might be a good guy; and he can be helpful. Did you ever speak, when you were speaking to any of the neighbors in the campground, about Camper besides being helpful? Did you ever talk to them about whether he was truthful and honest?

A: Yeah. Yeah; He's friendly, in talking to new people that would come into the campground.

Court: You talked with other people in the campground?

A: Yeah.

Court: And you talked about his reputation for truthfulness and honesty?

A: Talking about . . . You . . . Well, yeah; as far as being a good person.

Court: Did you ask any of the other people that were there in the campground what it — what they thought of Camper's reputation for truthfulness and honesty?

A: As far as asking about Camper, no; I . . . Camper was the first person I met in the campground.

Q: Did anybody ever mention to you whether Camper was truthful or not?

A: No; not — not saying it like that. It's . . . Camper was a good person. I mean, that — talking to other people, and . . . I take that as a . . . you know, truthful, honest person — good . . .

Q: People would tell you that Camper was a good guy?

A: Yeah.

■   ■   ■

Shoplifting and Truthfulness — Segovia. For a jury to develop an idea about how truthful a witness is, it might be helpful for the jury to learn about specific actions that witness had done that could be consistent with truthfulness or untruthfulness. The rules prohibit this approach. They bar extrinsic evidence about a witness's specific acts. However, the rules allow *inquiry* about a witness's specific acts during cross-examination of that witness or of someone who has given reputation or opinion testimony about that witness's truthfulness.

As Rule 608 states, a cross-examiner may ask about acts that are probative of truthfulness (remember that acts related to someone's typical truthfulness are also, by logic, probative about that person's typical degree of untruthfulness as well). The past acts must relate to truth telling. *Segovia* considers these aspects of the rule while reviewing the rulings of a trial judge who made multiple errors.

> **Rule 608. A Witness's Character for Truthfulness or Untruthfulness**
>
> . . .
>
> **(b) Specific Instances of Conduct.** Except for a criminal conviction under Rule 609, extrinsic evidence is not admissible to prove specific instances of a witness's conduct in order to attack or support the witness's character for truthfulness. But the court may, on cross-examination, allow them to be inquired into if they are probative of the character for truthfulness or untruthfulness of:
>
> > **(1)** the witness; or
> >
> > **(2)** another witness whose character the witness being cross-examined has testified about.
>
> By testifying on another matter, a witness does not waive any privilege against self-incrimination for testimony that relates only to the witness's character for truthfulness.

PEOPLE v. SEGOVIA

196 P.3d 1126 (Colo. 2008)

RICE, J.

In this original proceeding brought pursuant to C.A.R. 21, the defendant in a criminal case seeks review of the trial court's denial of his motion to dismiss on double jeopardy grounds. We issued a rule to show cause to the trial court and now make that rule absolute, holding that the trial court erred in finding evidence of a prior instance of shoplifting inadmissible pursuant to CRE 608(b). Based on what occurred during the trial, there was no manifest necessity to declare a mistrial. Accordingly, the Double Jeopardy Clause prohibits retrial of the defendant.

Facts and Procedural History. Petitioner, Jose Palma Segovia (Palma),[1] is charged with sexual assault on a child. He was brought to trial on February 4, 2008, where the prosecution's chief witness was the thirteen-year-old victim, T.L. Palma contended that T.L.'s allegations were fabricated, and was prepared to offer videotapes and call witnesses to support his theory of the case. After T.L. testified, she was cross-examined by defense counsel. The following exchange occurred:

[Defense counsel]: Now, you have promised the Judge to tell the truth to this jury, haven't you?

[Witness]: Yes.

[Defense counsel]: And in order to tell the truth to the jury, that requires you to be honest, correct?

---

1. Defense counsel and the court of appeals referred to Petitioner as Mr. Palma, rather than Mr. Segovia.

[Witness]: Yes.

[Defense counsel]: Okay. And — but you're not always honest, are you?

[Witness]: What do you mean?

[Defense counsel]: Well, I mean in mid-July, around July 15th of 2007, at your mother's store in Avon, you and Josh stole $100 from your mother's store, didn't you?

[Witness]: No.

At this point, the prosecutor objected and defense counsel asserted CRE 608(b) as grounds to allow the question.

Outside the presence of the jury, the trial court and the attorneys addressed the objection. The trial court ruled that the question about shoplifting was a prior bad act that was inadmissible pursuant to CRE 404(b) and was not properly noticed to the court and prosecutor. Additionally, the court held that defense counsel was attempting to attack T.L.'s truthfulness by extrinsic evidence, which was impermissible. The court also concluded the shoplifting incident would go to truthfulness only if counsel established "she was untruthful with regard to that issue when questioned by someone on that topic." Furthermore, the court held that the prosecution had not bolstered T.L.'s credibility on direct examination, so the witness's truthfulness was not at issue. Finally, the court concluded the error could not be corrected and *sua sponte* declared a mistrial.

Palma filed a motion to dismiss the charge on double jeopardy grounds. The trial court denied the motion and scheduled a second trial. Palma seeks review of that ruling.

An original proceeding is appropriate to prevent an excess of jurisdiction by a lower court where no other remedy would be adequate. Because Palma may otherwise be forced to endure a second trial in violation of his constitutional rights, we exercise our original jurisdiction....

1. CRE 404(b) or CRE 608(b). At the outset, we clarify some confusion in the trial court's ruling because it is not entirely clear under what rule the trial court found the question objectionable. The trial court merged its analysis of the evidence under two evidentiary rules: it found the substance of the shoplifting question objectionable pursuant to CRE 404(b) and found the method of proof objectionable pursuant to CRE 608(b). We first explain why the shoplifting question was properly at issue under rule 608(b), rather than rule 404(b).

Both rule 404(b) and rule 608(b) permit admission of evidence that would otherwise be considered inadmissible character evidence for limited purposes. Rule 404(b) prohibits the use of evidence to show a person acted in conformity with a certain character, but does not preclude use of that evidence for other purposes, such as proof of motive, opportunity, intent, plan, or absence of mistake. Rule 404(b) does not address the use of evidence for impeachment. In contrast, rule 608(b) governs evidence used to impeach a witness's credibility. Thus, evidence of specific acts used solely for impeachment is governed by rule 608(b), rather than rule 404(b).

Here, defense counsel asked T.L. about the shoplifting act in order to impeach her credibility. This purpose is made apparent by counsel's foundational question: "But you're not always honest, are you?" The evidence was not offered for any of the purposes listed in rule 404(b), so the trial court erred when it applied that rule to the evidence.

2. CRE 608(b). We next consider whether defense counsel's question was admissible under rule 608(b), starting with whether the question was the correct method of impeachment. Specific instances of conduct intended to impeach the credibility of a witness may not be proved by extrinsic evidence, but may be inquired into on cross-examination of a witness. CRE 608(b). The rule provides:

> Specific instances of the conduct of a witness, for the purpose of attacking or supporting the witness' character for truthfulness other than conviction of crime as provided in [section] 13–90–101 may not be proved by extrinsic evidence. They may, however, in the discretion of the court, if probative of truthfulness or untruthfulness, be inquired into on cross-examination of the witness (1) concerning the witness' character for truthfulness or untruthfulness. . . .

CRE 608(b). Extrinsic evidence is evidence not contained in the source before the court, but which is available from other sources. Thus, where a witness is testifying, her answer to any question is intrinsic evidence, while the admission of any documents or calling of other witnesses constitutes extrinsic evidence. Here, defense counsel inquired about an act of shoplifting during cross-examination, which is intrinsic evidence that complies with rule 608(b). Therefore, the trial court erred in concluding that asking the question on cross-examination was extrinsic evidence.

Because the question was not extrinsic evidence, we next consider whether an act of shoplifting is proper impeachment evidence under rule 608(b). If a witness takes the stand and testifies, she puts her credibility in issue. Thus, the opposing party is entitled to impeach the witness's credibility. Under rule 608(b), a witness may be asked about specific instances of conduct that are probative of a witness's character for truthfulness or untruthfulness. The rule does not explain how to determine if an act is probative of truthfulness, and there is no committee comment on the rule to guide our inquiry.

Colorado courts have held that the following instances of conduct are probative of the witness's truthfulness: providing false information to a police officer, intentionally failing to file tax returns, and misrepresenting financial information to obtain a loan. In contrast, Colorado courts have excluded acts of violence, instances of drug use, and bigamy, because those acts are not probative of truthfulness.

This court has never considered whether an act of shoplifting is probative of truthfulness or untruthfulness pursuant to rule 608(b). . . . We take this opportunity to decide whether shoplifting, an act that involves dishonesty, is probative of truthfulness.

To aid our analysis, we conducted a fifty-state and federal survey, which revealed the law is not well-settled. A majority of federal courts and some state courts have held that acts of theft are not probative of truthfulness or do not involve dishonesty. In contrast, a number of courts have concluded that theft is probative of truthfulness or dishonesty.

These cases can be grouped into three categories, based on their view of the definition of truthfulness or dishonesty: broad, middle, and narrow. The broad approach would allow testimony of any indication of weak or bad character as probative of veracity. This approach improperly subjects a witness to questioning about almost any event in her past. Almost no modern decisions adopt this view.

In contrast, the narrow approach requires the act to have an element of false statement or deception, limiting the inquiry to acts such as perjury, false statement, criminal fraud, embezzlement, or false pretense. A majority of federal courts take this view.

The middle view incorporates the narrow view but also suggests that conduct seeking personal advantage by taking from others in violation of their rights reflects on dishonesty or truthfulness. In our view, the middle approach strikes the appropriate balance, as it acknowledges that some acts that do not involve false statement or misrepresentation are nonetheless probative of truthfulness. Therefore, we decline to follow the courts that have reasoned that only acts that have an affirmative element of misrepresentation or false statement are probative of truthfulness, because these holdings create an unduly narrow category of acts that reflect on one's character for truthfulness.

We are most persuaded by those courts that have taken the middle approach and have concluded theft is probative of truthfulness or dishonesty. "Dishonest" is a synonym for "untruthful." *Webster's New College Dictionary* 1568 (2005). It is illogical to conclude that an act which involves dishonesty is at the same time an act that is not probative of truthfulness. Moreover, common experience informs us that a person who takes the property of another for her own benefit is acting in an untruthful or dishonest way. *See Gordon v. United States*, 383 F.2d 936, 940 (D.C. Cir. 1967) ("[A]cts of . . . stealing, for example, are universally regarded as conduct which reflects adversely on a man's honesty and integrity."). Such behavior reflects on one's truthfulness because a person who stole from another may be more inclined to obtain an advantage for herself by giving false testimony. Therefore, we hold that shoplifting is a specific instance of conduct that is probative of truthfulness pursuant to CRE 608(b). . . .

We note that a prior act of shoplifting does not always mean a witness will testify untruthfully. This is especially true where there are facts that lessen the blame attached to the act, e.g., the act is committed at a young age, as a result of peer pressure, or involves property of minimal value. However, such considerations generally go to the weight given the evidence by the jury, rather than to its admissibility.

Additionally, our holding does not restrict admissibility considerations under CRE 403 and other applicable evidentiary rules. Therefore, a trial court could exercise its discretion to exclude an act of shoplifting if it found the act inadmissible for other reasons. . . .

Because the trial court erroneously determined CRE 404(b) applied to the evidence and incorrectly interpreted CRE 608(b), we hold that the trial court abused its discretion in finding defense counsel's question improper. . . .

III. Conclusion. We conclude it was proper for defense counsel to inquire, on cross-examination, about the witness's prior act of shoplifting, and therefore the trial court was not justified in declaring a mistrial. Without manifest necessity to declare a mistrial, double jeopardy bars retrial of Palma. We make the rule absolute and order the trial court to dismiss the charge.

[Dissenting opinion omitted.]

NOTES TO PEOPLE v. SEGOVIA

1. ***Judges Make Mistakes.*** Can you identify the judge's mistakes in each of these four sentences the *Segovia* court used to describe the judge's rationale and rulings?

- The trial court ruled that the question about shoplifting was a prior bad act that was inadmissible pursuant to CRE 404(b) and was not properly noticed to the court and prosecutor.
- Additionally, the court held that defense counsel was attempting to attack T.L.'s truthfulness by extrinsic evidence, which was impermissible.
- The court also concluded the shoplifting incident would go to truthfulness only if counsel established "she was untruthful with regard to that issue when questioned by someone on that topic."
- Furthermore, the court held that the prosecution had not bolstered T.L.'s credibility on direct examination, so the witness's truthfulness was not at issue.

2. *"Taking the Answer."* When a cross-examiner asks a witness about some past conduct by the witness, the witness's answer is the only evidence allowed about that conduct. If, for example, the witness denies having done whatever was asked about, the questioner is prohibited from introducing proof about it.

3. ***Counterexample.*** Compare the Federal Rules position on inquiry about past acts with the following state rule.

> **GOOD TO REMEMBER**
>
> Past acts related to truthfulness can be asked about but cannot be proved. This reflects evidence law's belief that a lot of character evidence has only small probative value. Since its value is low, protecting trials from including large amounts of it may make sense.

> **Texas Rules of Evidence: Rule 608. Evidence of Character and Conduct of a Witness**
>
>   **(b) Specific Instances of Conduct.** Specific instances of the conduct of a witness, for the purpose of attacking or supporting the witness' credibility, other than conviction of crime as provided in Rule 609, may not be inquired into on cross-examination of the witness nor proved by extrinsic evidence.

QUESTION 12-2. In a trial in a federal district court, Nancy Narrator testified on behalf of a criminal defendant, supporting the defendant's alibi. May the prosecution ask Narrator each of the following questions, or offer extrinsic proof that the conduct they describe actually occurred?

- Last year, didn't you write a check to ABC Health Club that was returned for insufficient funds, and hadn't you bounced checks to that business twice before?
- Isn't it true that you tried to hire someone to kill your husband six years ago?
- Didn't you serve alcohol to underage high school students at a Christmas party two years ago?

■ ■ ■

Extrinsic Proof of Specific Past Lies? — Guenther. Rule 608 prohibits the introduction of extrinsic proof about past conduct of a witness in order to support an inference that the witness has poor character for truth telling (or has the character trait of deceitfulness). This means that ordinarily when the opponent of a witness knows that the witness has told lies in the past, the opponent is limited to asking about those lies. The *Guenther* court considers whether this doctrine should be changed when the specific past conduct involves the making of false accusations.

STATE v. GUENTHER

854 A.2d 308 (N.J. 2004)

ALBIN, J.

Defendant Kenneth Guenther was convicted of sexual assault and other crimes related to the abuse of his stepdaughter. At trial, he was denied the opportunity to present evidence of a prior false accusation of sexual abuse that his stepdaughter made against a neighbor. N.J.R.E. 608 embodies the common law rule that generally forbids admission of specific instances of conduct to attack a witness's character for truthfulness. We must decide, pursuant to N.J.R.E. 608, whether the credibility of a witness who has accused a defendant of sexual abuse may be impeached by evidence that she made a prior false criminal accusation....

Defendant asks us to make an exception to the general prohibition on the use of specific conduct evidence to allow him to establish D.F.'s character for lack of truthfulness. Defendant argues for the admission of D.F.'s prior false criminal accusation for the purpose of drawing the inference that a witness who has falsely accused once will do so again. [Constitutional claims omitted.]

New Jersey's Rules of Evidence generally prohibit evidence of "a person's character or a trait of his character" offered to prove that the person acted in conformity with that trait on a particular occasion. N.J.R.E. 404(a). The general prohibition on the use of character evidence, however, is subject to a number of exceptions. See N.J.R.E. 404(a)(1) to (3)....

[O]ur rules permit evidence in the form of opinion, reputation, or a prior criminal conviction to attack a witness's credibility by establishing the witness's character for untruthfulness. N.J.R.E. 608, 609. A party may introduce such evidence for the purpose of asking a jury to draw an inference that a witness with a reputation for untruthfulness is capable of lying on the stand. However, evidence of specific instances of conduct — other than a prior conviction — to prove the character trait of untruthfulness is prohibited. N.J.R.E. 608. For example, we do not allow a party to attack a witness's general credibility through the introduction of specific evidence that the witness falsely completed a licensing application.

The general principle embodied in N.J.R.E. 608 and 405(a) originated in the common law. Accordingly, we must examine the rationale for the common law rule barring the use of specific conduct evidence to challenge a witness's credibility for truthfulness. We must determine whether that rule has continuing vitality when applied to evidence of a victim-witness's prior false accusation.

Several centuries ago, courts began to prohibit the use of prior instances of conduct to attack the credibility of a witness for two essential reasons: to prevent unfairness to the witness and to avoid confusion of the issues before the jury. Those reasons remain the present justification for the exclusion of specific conduct evidence. The use of prior instances of misconduct to impeach credibility was considered to be unfair to the witness because "it would be practically impossible for the witness to have ready at the trial competent persons who would demonstrate the falsity of allegations that might range over the whole scope of his life." Thus, the rule was designed to prevent unfair foraging into the witness's past, as well as unfair surprise.

The second rationale for the bar on specific conduct evidence was the concern that such wide-ranging collateral attacks on the general credibility of a witness would cause confusion of the true issues in the case. Courts were reluctant to permit testimony on minor points that would invite more tangential testimony relating to the witness's character for truthfulness, needlessly protracting the trial "with relatively little profit." Modern courts continue to cite that rationale — the avoidance of "minitrials" on collateral matters that "tend to distract and confuse the jury" — as the primary justification for the exclusion of prior acts evidence. It was not a lack of relevance that gave rise to the rule prohibiting evidence of prior instances of untruthful conduct to impeach the witness's credibility, but the "auxiliary policies" regarding unfairness to the witness, confusion of issues, and undue consumption of time.

When those "auxiliary policies" do not apply, the rationale for the exclusion of such evidence no longer exists. An example is the long-standing rule allowing the admission of a prior criminal conviction as a method of undermining the general credibility of a witness. . . . However, we prohibit the use of specific instances of conduct to prove a character trait for pragmatic reasons associated with the efficient and orderly presentation of a trial. . . .

Various courts across the nation have addressed the issue whether a defendant may impeach the credibility of a witness-accuser by showing that the witness made a prior false criminal accusation. Notwithstanding the common law bar, in sexual crime cases many courts have permitted cross-examination of a witness-accuser who has falsely alleged a sexual crime on a previous occasion. A number of courts also permit the introduction of extrinsic evidence to prove the point. . . .

We conclude that in limited circumstances and under very strict controls a defendant has the right to show that a victim-witness has made a prior false criminal accusation for the purpose of challenging that witness's credibility. Although our Confrontation Clause jurisprudence informs our decision, we do not decide this issue on constitutional grounds, but rather by making a narrow exception to N.J.R.E. 608 consistent with the rationale of that rule.

A witness's propensity for making false criminal allegations is admissible if presented in the proper form. For instance, under our evidence rules, a witness may testify in the form of an opinion that the victim has a reputation for lying, and the defendant may argue from such testimony that the victim is, therefore, not worthy of belief. N.J.R.E. 608. Moreover, a criminal conviction may be used to impeach the witness for the purpose of drawing an inference that the witness's testimony is not as trustworthy as that of a person with a blameless past. See N.J.R.E. 608, 609. Both examples are permissible attacks on the general credibility of a witness; neither imposes the burden of a mini-trial.

That a victim-witness uttered a prior false accusation may be no less relevant, or powerful as an impeachment tool[ ] than opinion testimony that the witness has a reputation for lying. Moreover, a prior criminal conviction for criminal mischief or aggravated assault probably has far less bearing on the trustworthiness of a victim's testimony than a prior false accusation, but there is no question concerning the admissibility of the prior conviction. Yet, proving a prior false accusation — unlike presenting reputation testimony or evidence of a prior conviction — if not strictly regulated, could cause the very type of side-show trial that N.J.R.E. 608 was intended to prevent. We are confident, however, that trial courts, with proper guidance and limitations, can decide appropriately when the admission of prior false accusation evidence is central to deciding a case that hinges on the credibility of a victim-witness. Trial courts are well qualified to determine when such evidence will create the prospect of a mini-trial and when the probative value of that evidence is outweighed by the risk of undue prejudice, confusion of the issues, or waste of time. In certain cases, we believe that the interests of justice require that we relax the strictures against specific conduct evidence in N.J.R.E. 608. The weight of authority from other jurisdictions generally favors that approach, though we chart a path consistent with our own jurisprudence and values.

We see no reason why prior false accusation evidence should be limited to cases in which the witness is the victim of a sexual crime. We, therefore, part from those jurisdictions that have modified their evidence rules, whether on constitutional or non-constitutional grounds, only in sexual crime cases. We are not aware of any empirically-based evidence that sexual crime victim-witnesses are more likely to have made prior false criminal allegations than other crime victims. Limiting such evidence to sexual crime cases would only appeal to stereotypes that we have long since banished from our jurisprudence.

We now must determine the circumstances that will justify the admission of prior false accusation evidence. First, we limit our holding to a criminal case that involves the impeachment of a victim-witness whose credibility was the central issue in the case. The trial in this case essentially was reduced to a credibility contest between the victim and defendant. Second, the introduction of the prior false accusation evidence cannot become the tail wagging the dog; that is, proof of the false accusation cannot become such a diversion that it overshadows the trial of the charges itself. On the one extreme, we will have the witness who admits the false accusation on cross-examination, averting the need for extrinsic evidence. At the other extreme, we will have the witness who claims that the prior accusation is true, in which case only a complete trial of that issue will determine the truth or falsity of the accusation. In keeping with the historical rationale for the common law rule now codified in N.J.R.E. 608, we disfavor using the trial of charged offenses as the forum for an extended mini-trial for the collateral determination of a prior criminal accusation.

In deciding whether to permit the impeachment of a victim-witness who allegedly made a prior false accusation, trial courts must first conduct an admissibility hearing pursuant to N.J.R.E. 104. At that hearing, the court must determine by a preponderance of the evidence whether the defendant has proven that a prior accusation charging criminal conduct was made by the victim and whether that accusation was false. That standard strikes the right balance, placing an initial burden on the defendant to justify the use of such evidence while not setting an exceedingly high threshold for its admission. We note that the admission of this type of specific conduct evidence is an exception to N.J.R.E. 608 and should be limited only to those circumstances in which the prior accusation has been shown to be false. Among the factors to be considered in deciding the issue of admissibility are:

1. whether the credibility of the victim-witness is the central issue in the case;
2. the similarity of the prior false criminal accusation to the crime charged;
3. the proximity of the prior false accusation to the allegation that is the basis of the crime charged;
4. the number of witnesses, the items of extrinsic evidence, and the amount of time required for presentation of the issue at trial; and
5. whether the probative value of the false accusation evidence will be outweighed by undue prejudice, confusion of the issues, and waste of time.

If the court, pursuant to its gate-keeping role, determines that evidence of the prior false accusation is admissible, the court has the discretion to limit the number of witnesses who will testify concerning the matter at trial. The court must ensure that testimony on the subject does not become a second trial, eclipsing the trial of the crimes charged. . . .

In this case, we are not creating a new rule of evidence, but merely carving out a narrow exception to the common law rule embodied in N.J.R.E. 608 for the purpose of permitting the jury to consider relevant evidence — in clearly defined circumstances — that may affect its estimation of the credibility of a key witness. . . .

We, therefore, affirm the judgment of the Appellate Division and remand . . . to the trial court for proceedings consistent with this opinion.

NOTES TO STATE v. GUENTHER

1. *What Kinds of False Allegations in What Kinds of Cases?* As the *Guenther* court states, some courts allow evidence of past false charges only in cases involving sex crimes. The *Guenther* court refused to limit the admissibility of past false charges to sex crime cases. And for all cases where past false charges are sought to be shown, the *Guenther* court did not require that the past false charges be the same type of charges as those involved in the current charged crime (New Jersey's version of Rule 608 has been amended to reflect the *Guenther* holding). A similar result in the Missouri Supreme Court, in State v. Long, 140 S.W.3d 27 (Mo., 2004) elicited this dissent:

I first take issue with the majority's expansive and unprecedented holding that the prior false allegations sought to be introduced need not be similar to the charged offense. Instead, as the majority explains, "[t]he relevance of prior false allegations is not premised upon the subject matter of the prior false allegation . . . [and] . . . the fundamental requirement for admitting extrinsic evidence of a prior false allegation is essentially a showing of legal relevance by balancing the probative value of the knowingly made prior false allegation with the potential prejudice." As the majority acknowledges, however, "[i]n cases involving rape or sexual assault, most states require trial courts to make a preliminary determination . . . that (1) the prosecuting witness made another allegation of rape or sexual assault [that was false]." In fact, *every* state that has allowed extrinsic evidence of false allegations in sexual assault cases requires that the prior false allegation be the same as or at least similar to the charged offense.

In effect, these states already have undertaken the majority's legal relevance/balancing approach by determining, categorically, and as a matter of law, that in cases of sexual assault, the probative value of knowingly made false allegations outweighs the potential prejudice only where the false allegations are the same or similar to the charged offense. Conversely, where the false allegations are not the same or similar to the charged offense, the probative value of the false allegations never outweighs the potential prejudice. This is the better rule. It is a bright line that is easier to apply, and it is more in keeping with the general rule, as cited by the majority, that bars extrinsic evidence of prior, specific acts of misconduct so to conserve judicial resources by avoiding mini-trials on collateral issues. Theoretically, under the majority rule, even the false report of a property loss to collect insurance proceeds or the willful failure to pay a tax is admissible in a sexual assault case. This is the unfortunate result of painting with too broad a brush.

2. *Rape Shield Rules and Proof of Past Charges Related to Sexual Conduct.* If an alleged victim has in the past made charges about having been the victim of prohibited sexual acts, the *Guenther* decision will require that alleged victim be involved in a judicial hearing about whether the acts he or she charged in the past really did take place. The question arises whether the prospect of such a hearing might conflict with the policies that support rape shield evidence rules. The Indiana Supreme Court has stated, in State v. Walton, 715 N.E.2d 824 (Ind. 1999):

> Rule 412 is designed only to preclude evidence of a complaining witness's prior sexual conduct. Evidence of prior false accusations of rape made by a complaining witness does not constitute "prior sexual conduct" for rape shield purposes. In presenting such evidence, the defendant is not probing the complaining witness's sexual history. Rather, the defendant seeks to prove for impeachment purposes that the complaining witness has previously made false accusations of rape. Viewed in this light, such evidence is more properly understood as verbal conduct, not sexual conduct. To the extent a defendant offers evidence of prior false accusations of rape to impeach the credibility of the witness, we hold that its admission does not run afoul of the Rape Shield Rule.

QUESTION 12-3. Paul Patient has sued Max Medic, a doctor, for malpractice. Patient testifies that he told Medic he was allergic to penicillin, but Medic prescribed a drug for him that contained penicillin, which caused him to suffer a severe allergic reaction. Which, if any, of the following responses may Medic make?

A. Introduce testimony by an office assistant who used to work for Medic stating that Patient once lied to her about his insurance coverage.

B. Introduce testimony by a neighbor of Patient's, who has been involved with Patient in various neighborhood organizations, that in his opinion Patient is not trustworthy.

C. Introduce testimony by another neighbor of Patient's that, to his knowledge many people in the neighborhood consider Patient untrustworthy.

D. Introduce evidence showing that Patient once falsely accused his next-door neighbor of stealing mail from his mailbox.

C   CRIMINAL CONVICTIONS TO SHOW CHARACTER FOR TRUTH TELLING

The rules set up a detailed array of provisions governing evidence showing that a witness has been convicted of a crime. Rule 609 allows this kind of extrinsic evidence in certain circumstances.

Rule 609.   Impeachment by Evidence of a Criminal Conviction

(a) In General. The following rules apply to attacking a witness's character for truthfulness by evidence of a criminal conviction:

(1) for a crime that, in the convicting jurisdiction, was punishable by death or by imprisonment for more than one year, the evidence:

(A) must be admitted, subject to Rule 403, in a civil case or in a criminal case in which the witness is not a defendant; and

(B) must be admitted in a criminal case in which the witness is a defendant, if the probative value of the evidence outweighs its prejudicial effect to that defendant; and

(2) for any crime regardless of the punishment, the evidence must be admitted if the court can readily determine that establishing the elements of the crime required proving — or the witness's admitting — a dishonest act or false statement.

(b) Limit on Using the Evidence After 10 Years. This subdivision (b) applies if more than 10 years have passed since the witness's conviction or release from confinement for it, whichever is later. Evidence of the conviction is admissible only if:

(1) its probative value, supported by specific facts and circumstances, substantially outweighs its prejudicial effect; and

(2) the proponent gives an adverse party reasonable written notice of the intent to use it so that the party has a fair opportunity to contest its use.

(c) Effect of a Pardon, Annulment, or Certificate of Rehabilitation. Evidence of a conviction is not admissible if:

(1) the conviction has been the subject of a pardon, annulment, certificate of rehabilitation, or other equivalent procedure based on a finding that the person has been rehabilitated, and the person has not been convicted of a later crime punishable by death or by imprisonment for more than one year; or

(2) the conviction has been the subject of a pardon, annulment, or other equivalent procedure based on a finding of innocence.

(d) Juvenile Adjudications. Evidence of a juvenile adjudication is admissible under this rule only if:

(1) it is offered in a criminal case;

(2) the adjudication was of a witness other than the defendant;

(3) an adult's conviction for that offense would be admissible to attack the adult's credibility; and

(4) admitting the evidence is necessary to fairly determine guilt or innocence.

(e) Pendency of an Appeal. A conviction that satisfies this rule is admissible even if an appeal is pending. Evidence of the pendency is also admissible.

Note that in applying this rule, important aspects include: (1) whether the witness to be discredited is a criminal defendant or any other witness; (2) whether the crime involved truth telling or was some other kind of crime; and (3) whether the crime occurred more than ten years before the testimony.

Rule 609(a) describes three combinations of witnesses and kinds of past convictions:

- Truth-telling crime and any witness
- Non-truth-telling crime and a criminal defendant witness
- Non-truth-telling crime and a witness other than a criminal defendant

Rule 609(b) describes a possible attribute of any conviction:

- More than ten years' old

For each of these four circumstances, a particular balancing test is specified for the trial judge to apply in considering admissibility of a conviction. The tests involve different relationships between probative value and risk of prejudice. One of the tests is the Rule 403 test, which allows exclusion of evidence only if the risk of prejudice substantially outweighs the probative value of the evidence. Under this test, evidence could be admitted even if its probative value is exceeded by the risk of prejudice, so long as the probative value was not *substantially* outweighed by the risk of prejudice. All of the balancing tests and the evidence to which they apply are shown in this table:

APPLICATION OF BALANCING TESTS IN RULE 609(a)(1) AND (2) SHOULD EVIDENCE BE LET IN OR KEPT OUT?

Balance of Probative Value and Prejudice	Type of Crime and Witness			
	Truth-telling crime (any witness)	Non-truth-telling crime (witness other than criminal defendant)	Non-truth-telling crime (criminal defendant witness)	Any crime more than ten years old
Substantially less probative than prejudicial	In	Out	Out	Out
Less probative than prejudicial	In	In	Out	Out
More probative than prejudicial	In	In	In	Out
Substantially more probative than prejudicial	In	In	In	In

■　■　■

Drug Dealing and Truthfulness — Hardy *and* Williams. Rule 609 allows extrinsic evidence of a witness's past bad acts for the purpose of establishing the witness's character with regard to truth telling, if the acts led to a criminal conviction. The fact of the conviction is admissible evidence. Treating convictions differently from other evidence of past acts makes sense: there is no risk of wasting time or distracting the jury with a "mini-trial" about the past act when the witness has actually been convicted of having done it.

Rule 609 reflects the fact that some kinds of crimes have elements that require a showing of a dishonest act or a false statement while other kinds of crimes do not. For crimes where conviction did not require proof of a dishonest act or false statement, the rule allows admission if a particular balancing test is met. To apply that balancing test, a court must determine how much probative value a particular conviction has on the topic of the witness's character for truth telling. *Hardy* and *Williams* each consider whether drug-dealing offenses shed light on truth telling. They apply different conceptual frameworks and reach different results.

STATE v. HARDY

946 P.2d 1175 (Wash. 1997)

Sanders, J.

Patrick Hardy appeals a second degree robbery conviction, asserting a prior drug conviction was improperly admitted into evidence contrary to ER 609(a)(1). The Court of Appeals affirmed, but we reverse. As held in State v. Jones, 101 Wash. 2d 113 (1984) . . . prior drug convictions "have little to do with a defendant's credibility as a witness. . . . "

At trial complaining witness Shamsa Wilkins testified that as she stood on a downtown Seattle street corner at 4:30 in the morning, Hardy approached her, spoke with her for a few minutes, and then robbed her of her jewelry. Wilkins testified Hardy remained for a few minutes trying to strike up a friendly relationship but she refused. . . .

Hardy took the stand and testified to a different version of events. He claimed Wilkins was in a push and shove match with her female friend and he had simply helped out by picking up loose jewelry from the ground. He did not deny he left the scene with the jewelry in his pocket, but such would not constitute robbery.

Before trial the State moved to introduce Hardy's prior felony drug conviction for impeachment purposes should he choose to testify. Defense counsel objected claiming the prior drug conviction was not only irrelevant to Hardy's credibility but very prejudicial as well. The court stated on the record "the impeachment value of the prior crime is almost nil" and as a drug crime it would be particularly prejudicial given the anti-drug "fever." The court, nevertheless, admitted the prior conviction as an unnamed felony, reasoning "the jury should be entitled to know that there is some prior conviction." Responding to the court's ruling, Hardy's counsel elicited the unnamed prior conviction on direct. The jury convicted Hardy. Hardy appealed to the Court of Appeals, but for naught.

The appellate court affirmed, reasoning all prior drug convictions are relevant to the defendant's credibility because drug convictions necessarily show secrecy and deceit. . . . We reverse on the admissibility of the prior drug conviction under ER 609(a)(1). . . .

Evidence of prior felony convictions is generally inadmissible against a defendant because it is not relevant to the question of guilt yet very prejudicial, as it may lead the jury to believe the defendant has a propensity to commit crimes. ER 609 represents a narrow exception to this rule against admitting evidence of prior convictions.

> For the purpose of attacking the credibility of a witness in a criminal or civil case, evidence that the witness has been convicted of a crime shall be admitted if elicited from the witness or established by public record during examination of the witness but only if the crime (1) was punishable by death or imprisonment in excess of 1 year under the law under which the witness was convicted, and the court determines that the probative value of admitting this evidence outweighs the prejudice to the

party against whom the evidence is offered, or (2) involved dishonesty or false statement, regardless of the punishment.

Drug convictions are not crimes of "dishonesty or false statement" like perjury or criminal fraud and thus ER 609(a)(2) does not apply. Rather the inquiry focuses on ER 609(a)(1), which allows admittance of prior felony convictions only if "the probative value of admitting this evidence outweighs the prejudice to the party against whom the evidence is offered. . . . " State v. Jones, 101 Wash. 2d 113 (1984) is dispositive.

ER 609(a)(1) requires the prior conviction have "probative value." When assessing probative value it is critical to understand "the sole purpose of impeachment evidence [under ER 609(a)(1)] is to enlighten the jury with respect to the defendant's credibility as a witness." *Jones*.[5] Credibility in this context refers to truthfulness. Prior convictions are therefore only "probative" under ER 609(a)(1) to the extent they are probative of the witness's truthfulness.

State v. Begin, 59 Wash. App. 755 (1990)[,] declared all prior felonies "'are evidence of non-law-abiding character'" and thus "probative" under ER 609(a)(1). However, the proper inquiry under ER 609(a)(1) is not whether the prior conviction shows a "non-law-abiding character" but whether it shows the witness is not truthful. To the extent *Begin* suggests all criminal convictions go to truthfulness or that every criminal act is evidence of an untruthful personality it is disapproved. "Simply because a defendant has committed a crime in the past does not mean the defendant will lie when testifying." To the contrary, we have held "few prior offenses that do not involve crimes of dishonesty or false statement are likely to be probative of a witness' veracity." We again affirm that position and caution [that] prior convictions not involving dishonesty or false statements are not probative of the witness's veracity until the party seeking admission thereof shows the opposite by demonstrating the prior conviction disproves the veracity of the witness.

Jones held "the trial court must state, for the record, the factors which favor admission or exclusion of prior conviction evidence." The court must consider such factors to assess whether probative value outweighs prejudice. It is imperative the court state, on the record, how the proffered evidence is probative of veracity to allow appellate review.

Some of the *Jones* and *Alexis* factors may also be useful to assess probative value.[8] For example, factor one focuses attention on the nature of the prior crime while factors two (remoteness) and four (age and circumstances) may indicate an otherwise probative conviction is less probative because it is chronologically remote.

---

5. *See also State v. Alexis*, 95 Wash. 2d 15 (1980).

8. The *Jones/Alexis* factors include: (1) the type and nature of the prior crime; (2) the remoteness of the prior conviction; (3) the similarity of the prior crime to the current charge; (4) the age and circumstances of the defendant when previously convicted; (5) whether the defendant testified at the previous trial; and (6) the length of defendant's criminal record. *Jones*, 101 Wash. 2d at 121-22.

The Court of Appeals relied upon State v. Thompson, 95 Wash. 2d 888, 892, 632 P.2d 50 (1981)[,] for the proposition that prior drug convictions, by their nature, are always probative of veracity. State v. Hardy, 83 Wash. App. at 175-76 (quoting *Thompson*, 95 Wash. 2d at 892) (a drug seller lives a life of "secrecy and dissembling" and thus prior drug convictions go to veracity). But we rejected that aspect of *Thompson* in *Jones* wherein we stated a prior "felony conviction . . . for possession of drugs . . . has little to do with a defendant's credibility as a witness." *Jones*, 101 Wash. 2d at 122.[9]

We find nothing inherent in ordinary drug convictions to suggest the person convicted is untruthful and conclude prior drug convictions, in general, are not probative of a witness's veracity under ER 609(a)(1). Numerous sister jurisdictions are in accord.[10]

If the prior conviction is probative of veracity under ER 609(a)(1) the court must still assess prejudicial effect. "Prior conviction evidence is inherently prejudicial" when the defendant is the witness because it tends to shift the jury focus "from the merits of the charge to the defendant's general propensity for criminality." *Jones*. Several studies confirm the prejudice. One commentator observed[:] "if the jury learns that a defendant previously has been convicted of a crime, the probability of conviction increases dramatically." Alan D. Hornstein, Between Rock and a Hard Place: The Right to Testify and Impeachment by Prior Conviction, 42 Vill. L. Rev. 1 (1997). The threat of admitting inherently prejudicial prior convictions places the accused in a catch-22 where he must either forego testifying in his defense or testify and risk portrayal as a criminal. Forcing the accused to such a Hobson's choice is not favored.

Additionally, the trial court must assess whether even greater prejudice may result from the particular nature of the prior conviction. Several of the *Jones* . . . factors help identify particularly prejudicial scenarios. For example, factor three points out the more similar the prior crime to the one presently charged, the greater the prejudice. Likewise, factor six highlights the fact that the longer the record the greater the prejudicial prospect the jury will use such as evidence to infer guilt.

---

9. We agree with State v. Wilson, 83 Wash. App. 546, 553, 922 P.2d 188 (1996), review denied, 130 Wash. 2d 1024, 930 P.2d 1231 (1997), wherein the court noted *Thompson* was no longer controlling:

> We question the underlying premise expressed here that all those convicted of delivery crimes participate in a web of lies and deceit. Common experience belies this assumption. Otherwise, police "buy-bust" operations targeted at street sales would need to be more elaborate than the usual "You looking?" and brief negotiations that characterize most transactions. The possibility of dissembling and secrecy certainly exists, especially at higher levels of the delivery hierarchy, but for the street seller, such secrecy is most likely a means to avoid detection and arrest rather than part of the crime itself.

10. See State v. Geyer, 194 Conn. 1, 480 A.2d 489, 497 (1984); People v. Siebert, 72 Ill. App. 3d 895, 390 N.E.2d 1322, 1328, 28 Ill. Dec. 732 (1979), cert. denied, 444 U.S. 1081, 100 S. Ct. 1033, 62 L. Ed. 2d 764 (1980); Commonwealth v. Roucoulet, 22 Mass. App. Ct. 603, 496 N.E.2d 166 (1986); State v. Zaehringer, 325 N.W.2d 754, 757 (Iowa 1982); Peterson v. State, 518 So. 2d 632, 637 (Miss. 1987). We also note some jurisdictions have held the reverse. See, e.g., United States v. Ortiz, 553 F.2d 782, 784 (2d Cir.), cert. denied, 434 U.S. 897, 98 S. Ct. 277, 54 L. Ed. 2d 183 (1977). However, these cases "typically do not examine the impact on veracity at any length, if at all." State v. Zaehringer, 325 N.W.2d 754, 757 (Iowa 1982).

Prior convictions are inadmissible under ER 609(a)(1) until the party seeking admission affirmatively demonstrates (1) the prior conviction bears on the witness's veracity and (2) the probative value outweighs the prejudice.

With the burden on the party seeking admission the trial court must conduct an on-the-record analysis of probative value versus prejudicial effect. Such requires an articulation of exactly how the prior conviction is probative of the witness's truthfulness.

The trial court attempted to lessen the prejudice by admitting the prior conviction under ER 609(a)(1) as an unnamed felony. But unnaming a felony "is not a substitute for the balancing process required" under ER 609(a)(1). State v. Rivers, 129 Wash. 2d 697, 706, 921 P.2d 495 (1996). If the balance merits admission, it is anomalous to unname the felony as it is generally the nature of the prior felony which renders it probative of veracity. Courts should not admit unnamed felonies under ER 609(a)(1) unless they can articulate how unnaming the felony still renders it probative of veracity. . . .

The trial court erred when it admitted Hardy's prior drug conviction as neither the State nor the trial court articulated how it was probative of Hardy's veracity. The trial court even concluded on the record "the impeachment value of the prior crime is almost nil."

. . . We conclude there was at least a reasonable probability that this improper impeachment affected the jury's determination. Accordingly, reversal is the remedy.

STATE v. WILLIAMS

771 N.W.2d 514 (Minn. 2009)

DIETZEN, J.

In March 2007 appellant Antoine Delany Williams was convicted of first-degree assault, second-degree assault, and possession of a firearm by a felon. . . . Appellant argues that the district court erred . . . in ruling that the State could impeach him with his prior convictions. . . .

On the afternoon of September 14, 2006, Minneapolis police responded to a 911 call of a shooting in South Minneapolis. The responding officer found Bennie Hodges lying on his stomach with blood on his pants near the buttocks area. . . .

Appellant was charged with first-degree assault. . . .

Appellant argues that the district court abused its discretion when it ruled that the State could impeach him with two prior drug-related felony convictions if he chose to testify. Appellant contends that these convictions bear little relevance to his truthfulness and that their probative value is outweighed by their potential prejudice. . . .

Minnesota Rule of Evidence 609(a)(1) sets forth two requirements for the admissibility of prior convictions as impeachment evidence. First, the earlier crime must be punishable by more than one year of incarceration; second, the prejudicial effect of the prior conviction evidence must not outweigh its probative value. *Id.* In *State v. Jones*, 271 N.W.2d 534, 537–38 (Minn. 1978), we set forth five factors to be considered in determining whether the probative value of impeachment evidence outweighs its prejudicial effect. Those factors are: (1) the impeachment value of the prior crime; (2) the date of the conviction and the defendant's subsequent history; (3) the similarity of the past crime with the charged crime; (4) the importance of defendant's testimony; and (5) the centrality of the credibility issue. Appellant's prior convictions were punishable by more than one year of incarceration. Thus, the question here is whether the probative value of the evidence of those convictions outweighs its prejudicial effect. Appellant argues that it does not. Specifically, appellant argues that the district court misapplied the *Jones* factors in considering the admissibility of his prior convictions and that these errors were harmful. We review his arguments in turn.

Appellant argues that the first factor, which considers the impeachment value of the prior crime, favors the exclusion of the evidence. In *State v. Brouillette*, 286 N.W.2d 702, 707 (Minn. 1979), we observed that impeachment by prior crime aids the jury by permitting it to see the "whole person" of the testifying witness and therefore to better judge the truth of his testimony. Subsequently, in *State v. Gassler*, 505 N.W.2d at 67, we observed that the fact that "a prior conviction did not directly involve truth or falsity does not mean it has no impeachment value." Consequently, we affirmed the district court's application of the "whole person" test under *Brouillette*.

Here, the district court applied the "whole person" test and determined that the first *Jones* factor "slightly favored" admissibility of the prior convictions because the prior convictions would help the jury see appellant's "whole person." We conclude that the district court did not abuse its discretion when it made this determination.

Appellant contends that even if the "whole person" test favors admissibility here, its use should be reconsidered because district courts will admit prior conviction evidence merely because it may enlighten the jury about the defendant's past, without regard for any prejudice the evidence might create for the defendant. Essentially, appellant asks us to abrogate the "whole person" test and convert the first *Jones* factor into a balancing test between prejudicial impact and probative value. We decline the invitation for two reasons. First, appellant provides no persuasive reason to abrogate the "whole person" test. The underlying rationale of the "whole person" test is that it allows the jury to see the "whole person" of the testifying witness to better evaluate the truth or falsity of the testimony. We believe that the rationale for the test expressed in *Brouillette* is sound and see no reason to change the test. Second, Rule 609 requires that the court determine that "the probative value of [impeachment] evidence outweighs its prejudicial effect" before admitting such evidence. Thus, the rule already provides the necessary safeguards requested by appellant.

Appellant next argues that the second *Jones* factor weighed neither for nor against the admissibility of the State's impeachment evidence. The district court concluded that "the recency of the [prior convictions], as well as the recency of one [prior conviction] to the other favors admissibility of those two prior offenses." On this record, Williams' prior convictions showed a pattern of lawlessness and occurred less than two years prior to trial. *See State v. Ihnot,* 575 N.W.2d 581, 586 (Minn. 1998) (concluding that two felony convictions within two years, together with another felony conviction from eight years prior constituted a "pattern of lawlessness" favoring admissibility under the second *Jones* factor). Thus, the court did not abuse its discretion in finding that this factor favored admissibility.

Appellant further argues that the third *Jones* factor weighed against admission because of the risk that the jury would associate his prior nonviolent drug-related convictions with the charged crimes and convict him based on "negative character evidence." The district court concluded that the prior convictions are "dissimilar to the crimes charged, which favors admissibility."

We have stated "if the prior conviction is similar to the charged crime, there is a heightened danger that the jury will use the evidence not only for impeachment purposes, but also substantively." *Gassler,* 505 N.W.2d at 67. Here, appellant's prior drug-related convictions were dissimilar to the instant offense in that they did not involve violence. Accordingly, we see no abuse of discretion with regard to the court's finding that this factor favored admissibility.

Appellant further argues that the fourth factor, which considers the importance of his testimony at trial, favors exclusion. He argues that admitting the prior convictions essentially precluded him from testifying at trial and thereby violated his due process right to explain his conduct to the jury.

In *Gassler,* we concluded that when the defendant's version of events was presented to the jury through the testimony of other witnesses, and no offer of proof was made as to any additional testimony the defendant would have added if he had taken the stand, the district court was within its discretion to conclude that the fourth factor favored admissibility. Here, the district court concluded that appellant was able to present his theory of the case through another witness. . . . Thus, we conclude that the court did not abuse its discretion in finding that the fourth *Jones* factor weighed in favor of admissibility. Consequently, the district court did not violate appellant's due process rights.

Finally, appellant argues that his credibility was not a central issue at trial. The district court concluded that the fifth *Jones* factor favored admissibility, on the ground that the identity of the perpetrator was a central issue at trial in which appellant's testimony would have contradicted the other witnesses. The record supports the district court. Thus, we conclude that the district court did not abuse its discretion in finding that the fifth *Jones* factor favored admissibility.

We conclude that the district court did not abuse its discretion in determining that appellant's prior convictions were admissible for impeachment purposes. . . .

Affirmed.

NOTES TO STATE v. HARDY AND STATE v. WILLIAMS

1. *Comparing Factors.* The *Hardy* and *Williams* courts each apply a multi-factor test for admissibility of the criminal defendant's past conviction. Are there significant differences between the tests, and would any differences likely affect outcomes?

The *"Jones"* test in *Hardy* considers:

- The type and nature of the prior crime.
- The remoteness of the prior conviction.
- The similarity of the prior crime to the current charge.
- The length of defendant's criminal record.
- The age and circumstances of the defendant when previously convicted.
- Whether the defendant testified at the previous trial.

The test in *Williams*, coincidentally also called the *"Jones"* test, uses these factors:

- The impeachment value of the prior crime.
- The date of the conviction.
- The similarity of the past crime with the charged crime.
- The defendant's subsequent history.
- The importance of defendant's testimony.
- The centrality of the credibility issue.

Segment 25: impeachment with past instances of untruthfulness

2. *Defendants' Strategy and Limitations on Appeal.* When a defendant knows that if he or she testifies, past convictions may be permitted to be a subject of cross-examination, the defendant might (1) decline to testify; (2) testify and have his or her lawyer reveal the convictions during direct examination, in an effort to avoid the appearance of having tried to hide them from the jury; or (3) testify and wait to see how the trial judge rules on admissibility of the past convictions in the context of all the evidence at trial, if the prosecution seeks to introduce them.

In *Hardy*, the defendant chose the second of these three strategies, and was permitted to base an appeal on the court's ruling. In federal court, a defendant who chooses the first strategy, declining to testify, will not be permitted to base an appeal on the judge's ruling. *See* Luce v. United States, 469 U.S. 38 (1984), holding that "any possible harm flowing from a district court's *in limine* ruling permitting impeachment by a prior conviction is wholly speculative." A defendant in federal court who chose the second strategy, as in *Hardy*, would also be barred from appeal. *See* Ohler v. United States, 529 U.S. 753 (2000).

3. *Counterexamples.* Some states treat impeachment by conviction differently than Federal Rule 609 does. For example, Hawaii and Colorado, in opposite ways, reject the position of that rule.

> ## GOOD TO REMEMBER
>
> The probative value of a conviction for the purposes of Rule 609 is considered in terms of what it shows about a witness's truth telling, not what it shows about someone's conduct out of court.

Hawaii Rule of Evidence 609 — Impeachment by evidence of conviction of crime.

(a) General rule. For the purpose of attacking the credibility of a witness, evidence that the witness has been convicted of a crime is inadmissible except when the crime is one involving dishonesty. However, in a criminal case where the defendant takes the stand, the defendant shall not be questioned or evidence introduced as to whether the defendant has been convicted of a crime, for the sole purpose of attacking credibility, unless the defendant has oneself introduced testimony for the purpose of establishing the defendant's credibility as a witness, in which case the defendant shall be treated as any other witness as provided in this rule.

(b) Effect of pardon. Evidence of a conviction is not admissible under this rule if the conviction has been the subject of a pardon.

(c) Juvenile convictions. Evidence of juvenile convictions is admissible to the same extent as are criminal convictions under subsection (a) of this rule.

(d) Pendency of appeal. The pendency of an appeal therefrom does not render evidence of a conviction inadmissible. Evidence of the pendency of an appeal is admissible.

Colorado — C.R.S. §13-90-101

. . . In every case the credibility of the witness may be drawn in question, as now provided by law, but the conviction of any person for any felony may be shown for the purpose of affecting the credibility of such witness. The fact of such conviction may be proved like any other fact, not of record, either by the witness himself, who shall be compelled to testify thereto, or by any other person cognizant of such conviction as impeaching testimony or by any other competent testimony. Evidence of a previous conviction of a felony where the witness testifying was convicted five years prior to the time when the witness testifies shall not be admissible in evidence in any civil action.

QUESTION 12-4. Dan Defendant is on trial for arson and attempted murder. He is accused of setting fire to a store early one morning while workers were inside the store getting ready to open for the day's business. Dan has testified, "I didn't do it." The prosecution has proof of each of the following facts. What use can the prosecution make of each item of information?

- Nine years ago Defendant was convicted of aggravated assault and sentenced to two years in jail.
- Four years ago Defendant was convicted of fraud and sentenced to two years in jail.

■ At a state university last year, Defendant falsely claimed to be a resident of the state to get a lower tuition rate.

Suppose Defendant does not testify, and a friend of Defendant's testifies, "Defendant has a reputation for being gentle and for trying to make things better for people." What use could the prosecution make of each of the items of information for which it has proof?

D BIAS

Showing that a witness has a reason to be biased in favor of one party is a method of impeachment that is not treated specifically in the Federal Rules, but it has been recognized as an aspect of the common law of evidence that continues to apply under the rules. When a witness has a personal connection to a party in a case or has a strong preference for a particular outcome for any reason, the witness may shape his or her testimony to favor that party or outcome, either consciously or unconsciously.

■ ■ ■

Prison and the Book-of-the-Month Club — Abel. Kurt Ehle testified for the prosecution, against the defendant, John Abel. Then Robert Mills testified that Ehle had once told him he was planning to testify falsely in order to get favorable treatment from the government. Would proof that Mills and the defendant were fellow members of a secret prison organization help the jury evaluate Mills's testimony about Ehle's supposed conversation with him?

UNITED STATES v. ABEL

469 U.S. 45 (1984)

Justice REHNQUIST delivered the opinion of the Court.

A divided panel of the Court of Appeals for the Ninth Circuit reversed respondent's conviction for bank robbery. The Court of Appeals held that the District Court improperly admitted testimony which impeached one of respondent's witnesses. We hold that the District Court did not err, and we reverse.

Respondent John Abel and two cohorts were indicted for robbing a savings and loan in Bellflower, Cal., in violation of 18 U.S.C. §§2113(a) and (d). The cohorts elected to plead guilty, but respondent went to trial. One of the cohorts, Kurt Ehle, agreed to testify against respondent and identify him as a participant in the robbery.

Respondent informed the District Court at a pretrial conference that he would seek to counter Ehle's testimony with that of Robert Mills. Mills was not a participant in the robbery but was friendly with respondent and with Ehle, and had spent time with both in prison. Mills planned to testify that after the robbery Ehle had admitted to Mills that Ehle intended to implicate respondent falsely, in order to receive favorable treatment from the Government. The prosecutor in turn disclosed that he intended to discredit Mills' testimony by calling Ehle back to the stand and eliciting from Ehle the fact that respondent, Mills, and Ehle were all members of the "Aryan Brotherhood," a secret prison gang that required its members always to deny the existence of the organization and to commit perjury, theft, and murder on each member's behalf.

Defense counsel objected to Ehle's proffered rebuttal testimony as too prejudicial to respondent. After a lengthy discussion in chambers the District Court decided to permit the prosecutor to cross-examine Mills about the gang, and if Mills denied knowledge of the gang, to introduce Ehle's rebuttal testimony concerning the tenets of the gang and Mills' and respondent's membership in it. The District Court held that the probative value of Ehle's rebuttal testimony outweighed its prejudicial effect, but that respondent might be entitled to a limiting instruction if his counsel would submit one to the court.

At trial Ehle implicated respondent as a participant in the robbery. Mills, called by respondent, testified that Ehle told him in prison that Ehle planned to implicate respondent falsely. When the prosecutor sought to cross-examine Mills concerning membership in the prison gang, the District Court conferred again with counsel outside of the jury's presence, and ordered the prosecutor not to use the term "Aryan Brotherhood" because it was unduly prejudicial. Accordingly, the prosecutor asked Mills if he and respondent were members of a "secret type of prison organization" which had a creed requiring members to deny its existence and lie for each other. When Mills denied knowledge of such an organization the prosecutor recalled Ehle.

Ehle testified that respondent, Mills, and he were indeed members of a secret prison organization whose tenets required its members to deny its existence and "lie, cheat, steal [and] kill" to protect each other. The District Court sustained a defense objection to a question concerning the punishment for violating the organization's rules. Ehle then further described the organization and testified that "in view of the fact of how close Abel and Mills were" it would have been "suicide" for Ehle to have told Mills what Mills attributed to him. Respondent's counsel did not request a limiting instruction and none was given.

The jury convicted respondent. On his appeal a divided panel of the Court of Appeals reversed. The Court of Appeals held that Ehle's rebuttal testimony was admitted not just to show that respondent's and Mills' membership in the same group might cause Mills to color his testimony; the court held that the contested evidence was also admitted to show that because Mills belonged to a perjurious organization, he must be lying on the stand. This suggestion of perjury, based upon a group tenet, was impermissible. . . .

We hold that the evidence showing Mills' and respondent's membership in the prison gang was sufficiently probative of Mills' possible bias towards respondent to warrant its admission into evidence. Thus it was within the District Court's discretion to admit Ehle's testimony, and the Court of Appeals was wrong in concluding otherwise.

Both parties correctly assume, as did the District Court and the Court of Appeals, that the question is governed by the Federal Rules of Evidence. But the Rules do not by their terms deal with impeachment for "bias," although they do expressly treat impeachment by character evidence and conduct, Rule 608, by evidence of conviction of a crime, Rule 609, and by showing of religious beliefs or opinion, Rule 610. Neither party has suggested what significance we should attribute to this fact. Although we are nominally the promulgators of the Rules, and should in theory need only to consult our collective memories to analyze the situation properly, we are in truth merely a conduit when we deal with an undertaking as substantial as the preparation of the Federal Rules of Evidence. In the case of these Rules, too, it must be remembered that Congress extensively reviewed our submission, and considerably revised it.

Before the present Rules were promulgated, the admissibility of evidence in the federal courts was governed in part by statutes or Rules, and in part by case law. . . . This Court had held in *Alford v. United States,* 282 U.S. 687 (1931), that a trial court must allow some cross-examination of a witness to show bias. This holding was in accord with the overwhelming weight of authority in the state courts as reflected in Wigmore's classic treatise on the law of evidence. . . .

With this state of unanimity confronting the drafters of the Federal Rules of Evidence, we think it unlikely that they intended to scuttle entirely the evidentiary availability of cross-examination for bias. One commentator, recognizing the omission of any express treatment of impeachment for bias, prejudice, or corruption, observes that the Rules "clearly contemplate the use of the above-mentioned grounds of impeachment." E. Cleary, McCormick on Evidence §40, p. 85 (3d ed. 1984). Other commentators, without mentioning the omission, treat bias as a permissible and established basis of impeachment under the Rules.

We think this conclusion is obviously correct. Rule 401 defines as "relevant evidence" evidence having any tendency to make the existence of any fact that is of consequence to the determination of the action more probable or less probable than it would be without the evidence. Rule 402 provides that all relevant evidence is admissible, except as otherwise provided by the United States Constitution, by Act of Congress, or by applicable rule. A successful showing of bias on the part of a witness would have a tendency to make the facts to which he testified less probable in the eyes of the jury than it would be without such testimony.

The correctness of the conclusion that the Rules contemplate impeachment by showing of bias is confirmed by the references to bias in the Advisory Committee Notes to Rules 608 and 610, and by the provisions allowing any party to attack credibility in Rule 607, and allowing cross-examination on "matters affecting the credibility of the witness" in Rule 611(b). The Courts of Appeals have upheld use of extrinsic evidence to show bias both before and after the adoption of the Federal Rules of Evidence....

Ehle's testimony about the prison gang certainly made the existence of Mills' bias towards respondent more probable. Thus it was relevant to support that inference. Bias is a term used in the "common law of evidence" to describe the relationship between a party and a witness which might lead the witness to slant, unconsciously or otherwise, his testimony in favor of or against a party. Bias may be induced by a witness'[s] like, dislike, or fear of a party, or by the witness'[s] self-interest. Proof of bias is almost always relevant because the jury, as finder of fact and weigher of credibility, has historically been entitled to assess all evidence which might bear on the accuracy and truth of a witness'[s] testimony. The "common law of evidence" allowed the showing of bias by extrinsic evidence, while requiring the cross-examiner to "take the answer of the witness" with respect to less favored forms of impeachment.

Mills' and respondent's membership in the Aryan Brotherhood supported the inference that Mills' testimony was slanted or perhaps fabricated in respondent's favor. A witness'[s] and a party's common membership in an organization, even without proof that the witness or party has personally adopted its tenets, is certainly probative of bias....

Respondent argues that even if the evidence of membership in the prison gang were relevant to show bias, the District Court erred in permitting a full description of the gang and its odious tenets. Respondent contends that the District Court abused its discretion under Federal Rule of Evidence 403, because the prejudicial effect of the contested evidence outweighed its probative value. In other words, testimony about the gang inflamed the jury against respondent, and the chance that he would be convicted by his mere association with the organization outweighed any probative value the testimony may have had on Mills' bias.

Respondent specifically contends that the District Court should not have permitted Ehle's precise description of the gang as a lying and murderous group. Respondent suggests that the District Court should have cut off the testimony after the prosecutor had elicited that Mills knew respondent and both may have belonged to an organization together. This argument ignores the fact that the *type* of organization in which a witness and a party share membership may be relevant to show bias. If the organization is a loosely knit group having nothing to do with the subject matter of the litigation, the inference of bias arising from common membership may be small or nonexistent. If the prosecutor had elicited that both respondent and Mills belonged to the Book of the Month Club, the jury probably would not have inferred bias even if the District Court had admitted the testimony. The attributes of the Aryan Brotherhood — a secret prison sect sworn to perjury and self-protection — bore directly not only on the *fact* of bias but also on the *source* and *strength* of Mills' bias. The tenets of this group showed that Mills had a powerful motive to slant his testimony towards respondent, or even commit perjury outright.

A district court is accorded a wide discretion in determining the admissibility of evidence under the Federal Rules. Assessing the probative value of common membership in any particular group, and weighing any factors counseling against admissibility is a matter first for the district court's sound judgment under Rules 401 and 403 and ultimately, if the evidence is admitted, for the trier of fact.

Before admitting Ehle's rebuttal testimony, the District Court gave heed to the extensive arguments of counsel, both in chambers and at the bench. In an attempt to avoid undue prejudice to respondent the court ordered that the name "Aryan Brotherhood" not be used. The court also offered to give a limiting instruction concerning the testimony, and it sustained defense objections to the prosecutor's questions concerning the punishment meted out to unfaithful members. These precautions did not prevent *all* prejudice to respondent from Ehle's testimony, but they did, in our opinion, ensure that the admission of this highly probative evidence did not *unduly* prejudice respondent. We hold there was no abuse of discretion under Rule 403 in admitting Ehle's testimony as to membership and tenets.

Respondent makes an additional argument based on Rule 608(b). That Rule allows a cross-examiner to impeach a witness by asking him about specific instances of past conduct, other than crimes covered by Rule 609, which are probative of his veracity or "character for truthfulness or untruthfulness." The Rule limits the inquiry to cross-examination of the witness, however, and prohibits the cross-examiner from introducing extrinsic evidence of the witness' past conduct.

Respondent claims that the prosecutor cross-examined Mills about the gang not to show bias but to offer Mills' membership in the gang as past conduct bearing on his veracity. This was error under Rule 608(b), respondent contends, because the mere fact of Mills' membership, without more, was not sufficiently probative of Mills' character for truthfulness. Respondent cites a second error under the same Rule, contending that Ehle's rebuttal testimony concerning the gang was extrinsic evidence offered to impugn Mills' veracity, and extrinsic evidence is barred by Rule 608(b). . . .

It seems clear to us that the proffered testimony with respect to Mills' membership in the Aryan Brotherhood sufficed to show potential bias in favor of respondent; because of the tenets of the organization described, it might also impeach his veracity directly. But there is no rule of evidence which provides that testimony admissible for one purpose and inadmissible for another purpose is thereby rendered inadmissible; quite the contrary is the case. It would be a strange rule of law which held that relevant, competent evidence which tended to show bias on the part of a witness was nonetheless inadmissible because it also tended to show that the witness was a liar.

We intimate no view as to whether the evidence of Mills' membership in an organization having the tenets ascribed to the Aryan Brotherhood would be a specific instance of Mills' conduct which could not be proved against him by extrinsic evidence except as otherwise provided in Rule 608(b). It was enough that such evidence could properly be found admissible to show bias.

The judgment of the Court of Appeals is *Reversed.*

NOTES TO UNITED STATES v. ABEL

1. *Sources of Bias.* In the absence of specific rules defining types of bias, litigants must rely on common sense and judges' ideas about human motivation to argue that particular circumstances could influence a witness's testimony. How would you argue for admissibility of evidence showing the following facts about a witness?

- Witness dislikes individuals with a particular ethnicity or race shared either by the defendant or another actor involved in the events that are the basis for charges against the defendant. *See* United States v. Rahman, 189 F.3d 88 (2d. Cir. 1999).
- Witness once had a sexual relationship with the party for whom she testified. *See* Orkin Exterminating Co. v. McIntosy, 452 S.E.2d 159 (Ga. Ct. App. 1994).
- Prosecution witness in criminal case has a pending civil suit against the defendant arising out of the charged crime. *See* State v. Whitman, 429 A.2d 203 (Me. 1981).

Segment 23:
proof of bias

2. *Extrinsic Evidence.* Bias may always be proved with extrinsic evidence. This effort is subject to the ordinary requirements of relevance and possible control by the various balances in FRE 403. While impeachment by past bad acts is hemmed in by the rule that the questioner must accept the witness's response, there is no parallel limitation for proof of bias.

QUESTION 12-5. Late one night, a group of five young men were in a playground at a public park. An argument developed, and one of the men, Victor Victim, was stabbed. The wound was fatal. Sam Second, who was present among the group arguing in the playground, was tried for this murder. Witnesses against him were three other individuals who had been present that night: Theodore Third, Frank Fourth, and Fred Fifth. Second appeared at the trial dressed in a conservative suit. The parents and grandparents of Victim had money delivered to Third, Fourth, and Fifth, in exchange for promises by them that they would use the money to buy similar conservative suits to wear when they testified. Should the defendant be allowed to introduce testimony proving that Victim's family had paid for those witnesses' suits?

■   ■   ■

Balancing Jurors' Supposed Racial Biases and a Witness's Romantic Bias — **Olden.** The relevance aspect of an attempt to impeach a witness by showing that the witness has a bias is decided by the trial judge, in a decision that ordinarily receives substantial deference from appellate courts. *Olden* considers whether there can be some circumstances where a judge's decision to reject bias evidence might violate a defendant's due process rights.

OLDEN v. KENTUCKY

488 U.S. 277 (1988)

PER CURIAM.

Petitioner James Olden and his friend Charlie Ray Harris, both of whom are black, were indicted for kidnaping, rape, and forcible sodomy. The victim of the alleged crimes, Starla Matthews, a young white woman, gave the following account at trial: She and a friend, Regina Patton, had driven to Princeton, Kentucky, to exchange Christmas gifts with Bill Russell, petitioner's half brother. After meeting Russell at a local car wash and exchanging presents with him, Matthews and Patton stopped in J.R.'s, a "boot-legging joint" serving a predominantly black clientele, to use the restroom. Matthews consumed several glasses of beer. As the bar became more crowded, she became increasingly nervous because she and Patton were the only white people there. When Patton refused to leave, Matthews sat at a separate table, hoping to demonstrate to her friend that she was upset. As time passed, however, Matthews lost track of Patton and became somewhat intoxicated. When petitioner told her that Patton had departed and had been in a car accident, she left the bar with petitioner and Harris to find out what had happened. She was driven in Harris' car to another location, where, threatening her with a knife, petitioner raped and sodomized her. Harris assisted by holding her arms. Later, she was driven to a dump, where two other men joined the group. There, petitioner raped her once again. At her request, the men then dropped her off in the vicinity of Bill Russell's house.

On cross-examination, petitioner's counsel focused on a number of inconsistencies in Matthews' various accounts of the alleged crime. Matthews originally told the police that she had been raped by four men. Later, she claimed that she had been raped by only petitioner and Harris. At trial, she contended that petitioner was the sole rapist. Further, while Matthews testified at trial that petitioner had threatened her with a knife, she had not previously alleged that petitioner had been armed.

Russell, who also appeared as a State's witness, testified that on the evening in question he heard a noise outside his home and, when he went out to investigate, saw Matthews get out of Harris' car. Matthews immediately told Russell that she had just been raped by petitioner and Harris.

Petitioner and Harris asserted a defense of consent. According to their testimony, Matthews propositioned petitioner as he was about to leave the bar, and the two engaged in sexual acts behind the tavern. Afterwards, on Matthews' suggestion, Matthews, petitioner, and Harris left in Harris' car in search of cocaine. When they discovered that the seller was not at home, Matthews asked Harris to drive to a local dump so that she and petitioner could have sex once again.

Harris complied. Later that evening, they picked up two other men, Richard Hickey and Chris Taylor, and drove to an establishment called The Alley. Harris, Taylor, and Hickey went in, leaving petitioner and Matthews in the car. When Hickey and Harris returned, the men gave Hickey a ride to a store and then dropped Matthews off, at her request, in the vicinity of Bill Russell's home.

Taylor and Hickey testified for the defense and corroborated the defendants' account of the evening. While both acknowledged that they joined the group later than the time when the alleged rape occurred, both testified that Matthews did not appear upset. Hickey further testified that Matthews had approached him earlier in the evening at J.R.'s and told him that she was looking for a black man with whom to have sex. An independent witness also appeared for the defense and testified that he had seen Matthews, Harris, and petitioner at a store called Big O's on the evening in question, that a policeman was in the store at the time, and that Matthews, who appeared alert, made no attempt to signal for assistance.

Although Matthews and Russell were both married to and living with other people at the time of the incident, they were apparently involved in an extramarital relationship. By the time of trial the two were living together, having separated from their respective spouses. Petitioner's theory of the case was that Matthews concocted the rape story to protect her relationship with Russell, who would have grown suspicious upon seeing her disembark from Harris' car. In order to demonstrate Matthews' motive to lie, it was crucial, petitioner contended, that he be allowed to introduce evidence of Matthews' and Russell's current cohabitation. Over petitioner's vehement objections, the trial court nonetheless granted the prosecutor's motion *in limine* to keep all evidence of Matthews' and Russell's living arrangement from the jury. Moreover, when the defense attempted to cross-examine Matthews about her living arrangements, after she had claimed during direct examination that she was living with her mother, the trial court sustained the prosecutor's objection.

Based on the evidence admitted at trial, the jury acquitted Harris of being either a principal or an accomplice to any of the charged offenses. Petitioner was likewise acquitted of kidnaping and rape. However, in a somewhat puzzling turn of events, the jury convicted petitioner alone of forcible sodomy. He was sentenced to 10 years' imprisonment.

Petitioner appealed, asserting, *inter alia,* that the trial court's refusal to allow him to impeach Matthews' testimony by introducing evidence supporting a motive to lie deprived him of his Sixth Amendment right to confront witnesses against him. The Kentucky Court of Appeals upheld the conviction. The court specifically held that evidence that Matthews and Russell were living together at the time of trial was not barred by the State's rape shield law. Moreover, it acknowledged that the evidence in question was relevant to petitioner's theory of the case. But it held, nonetheless, that the evidence was properly excluded as "its probative value [was] outweighed by its possibility for prejudice." By way of explanation, the court stated: "[T]here were the undisputed facts of race; Matthews was white and Russell was black. For the trial court to have admitted into evidence testimony that Matthews and Russell were living together at the time of the trial may have created extreme prejudice against Matthews." Judge Clayton, who dissented but did not address the evidentiary issue, would have reversed petitioner's conviction both because he believed the jury's verdicts were "manifestly inconsistent," and because he found Matthews' testimony too incredible to provide evidence sufficient to uphold the verdict.

The Kentucky Court of Appeals failed to accord proper weight to petitioner's Sixth Amendment right "to be confronted with the witnesses against him." That right, incorporated in the Fourteenth Amendment and therefore available in state proceedings, *Pointer v. Texas,* 380 U.S. 400 (1965), includes the right to conduct reasonable cross-examination. *Davis v. Alaska,* 415 U.S. 308, 315-316 (1974).

In *Davis v. Alaska,* we observed that, subject to "the broad discretion of a trial judge to preclude repetitive and unduly harassing interrogation . . . , the cross-examiner has traditionally been allowed to impeach, *i.e.,* discredit, the witness." We emphasized that "the exposure of a witness'[s] motivation in testifying is a proper and important function of the constitutionally protected right of cross-examination." Recently, in *Delaware v. Van Arsdall,* 475 U.S. 673 (1986), we reaffirmed *Davis,* and held that "a criminal defendant states a violation of the Confrontation Clause by showing that he was prohibited from engaging in otherwise appropriate cross-examination designed to show a prototypical form of bias on the part of the witness, and thereby 'to expose to the jury the facts from which jurors . . . could appropriately draw inferences relating to the reliability of the witness.'"

In the instant case, petitioner has consistently asserted that he and Matthews engaged in consensual sexual acts and that Matthews — out of fear of jeopardizing her relationship with Russell — lied when she told Russell she had been raped and has continued to lie since. It is plain to us that "[a] reasonable jury might have received a significantly different impression of [the witness's] credibility had [defense counsel] been permitted to pursue his proposed line of cross-examination." *Delaware v. Van Arsdall, supra,* 475 U.S., at 680.

The Kentucky Court of Appeals did not dispute, and indeed acknowledged, the relevance of the impeachment evidence. Nonetheless, without acknowledging the significance of, or even adverting to, petitioner's constitutional right to confrontation, the court held that petitioner's right to effective cross-examination was outweighed by the danger that revealing Matthews' interracial relationship would prejudice the jury against her. While a trial court may, of course, impose reasonable limits on defense counsel's inquiry into the potential bias of a prosecution witness, to take account of such factors as "harassment, prejudice, confusion of the issues, the witness' safety, or interrogation that [would be] repetitive or only marginally relevant," *Delaware v. Van Arsdall, supra,* at 679, the limitation here was beyond reason. Speculation as to the effect of jurors' racial biases cannot justify exclusion of cross-examination with such strong potential to demonstrate the falsity of Matthews' testimony.

In *Delaware v. Van Arsdall, supra,* we held that "the constitutionally improper denial of a defendant's opportunity to impeach a witness for bias, like other Confrontation Clause errors, is subject to *Chapman* [*v. California,* 386 U.S. 18 (1967)] harmless-error analysis." . . .

Here, Matthews' testimony was central, indeed crucial, to the prosecution's case. Her story, which was directly contradicted by that of petitioner and Harris, was corroborated only by the largely derivative testimony of Russell, whose impartiality would also have been somewhat impugned by revelation of his relationship with Matthews. Finally, as demonstrated graphically by the jury's verdicts, which cannot be squared with the State's theory of the alleged crime . . . the State's case against petitioner was far from overwhelming. In sum, considering the relevant *Van Arsdall* factors within the context of this case, we find it impossible to conclude "beyond a reasonable doubt" that the restriction on petitioner's right to confrontation was harmless.

The . . . judgment of the Kentucky Court of Appeals is reversed, and the case is remanded for further proceedings not inconsistent with this opinion.

[Dissenting opinion omitted.]

NOTES TO OLDEN v. KENTUCKY

1. *High Standard.* Relevance rulings and rulings that apply doctrines like the hearsay exclusion may operate to keep evidence out of a trial that a defendant claims is important. When will such a result be unconstitutional? The *Olden* decision characterizes the trial court's action as "beyond reason," in determining its unconstitutionality and *then* evaluates its consequences in a harmless error analysis. These two concepts preserve a great deal of discretion for trial courts.

2. *Rape Shield Limitations.* The state courts concluded that the state's rape shield statute did not bar introduction of the challenged evidence. The federal rule on this topic (Rule 412) might exclude this evidence, but it would have to yield to an application of *Olden.*

■ ■ ■

Financial Interest in the Outcome of a Case—Woolum. When parties present testimony from expert witnesses, their opponents often seek to show that the experts have financial incentives to shape their testimony, in spite of their claimed independence. *Woolum* considers an issue that occurs in many medical malpractice cases where an expert and a defendant practitioner happen both to have insurance coverage provided by the same insurer.

WOOLUM v. HILLMAN

329 S.W.3d 283 (Ky. 2010)

NOBLE, J.

Appellees, Lisa Ann and Aaron Hillman, received a judgment in Bell Circuit Court in their wrongful death action for the death of their stillborn child against Appellant Dr. Jerry Woolum and his medical practice. Appellant challenges the judgment. . . .

Appellees filed their wrongful death action against Appellant in Bell Circuit Court. Their theory of the case was that Appellant committed medical malpractice by postponing delivery after Hillman had been diagnosed with pregnancy-induced hypertension. Appellant countered that the cause of death was a genetic disease, trophoblasts, which affected the placenta and which was untreatable by Appellant. . . .

[Appellant's] primary argument is that testimony about a defense witness's commonality of insurance with the defendant (Appellant) was impermissibly admitted at trial. . . .

Appellant filed a pretrial motion in limine to exclude evidence that Appellant and his expert witness, Dr. Butcher, shared a malpractice insurance carrier. Appellees sought to admit the evidence to demonstrate the expert witness's bias in favor of Appellant. Appellees argued that Dr. Butcher was biased by their commonality of insurance because he believed that a judgment against his insurance company could adversely affect his own premiums.

In making this claim, Appellees relied on Dr. Butcher's deposition testimony. When previously deposed, Dr. Butcher had described how several malpractice claims against his former liability insurer had driven up his premiums and eventually drove the insurer into bankruptcy, effectively forcing him out of practice in Mississippi. Regarding his new practice in Kentucky, he had stated that doctors were now leaving the Commonwealth because of malpractice claims resulting in increased premiums.

After an extensive hearing, the court denied the motion in limine. The morning before the expert was to testify, the court returned to the matter and again denied the motion in limine and then permitted evidence of the common insurance coverage to be introduced at trial.

It is well-recognized that evidence of a defendant's insurance is inadmissible to imply liability. As provided in KRE 411, "Evidence that a person was or was not insured against liability is not admissible upon the issue whether the person acted negligently or otherwise wrongfully." Under this rule, a doctor's malpractice insurance may not be introduced to suggest that, because he would not bear the burden of any damage to a patient, he was more likely to be negligent in his treatment. The rule is not, however, a complete bar on evidence of liability insurance. The remainder of KRE 411 explicitly instructs, "This rule does not require the exclusion of evidence of insurance against liability when offered for another purpose, such as proof of agency, ownership, or control, or *bias or prejudice of a witness.*" (Emphasis added.)

Evidence of commonality of insurance was thus clearly not barred by KRE 411 when offered to prove a witness's bias. That was the purpose for which it was offered and that is the purpose for which the trial court allowed it. While the weight of such evidence is debatable, and is indeed case-specific as will be discussed below, it must certainly pass the relaxed test for relevance under KRE 401. A juror might reasonably find it more likely that the expert would be biased in favor of Appellant having the same insurance coverage than if they did not. *See* KRE 401.

Yet this does not end the inquiry as to admissibility of such evidence. "Although relevant, evidence may be excluded if its probative value is substantially outweighed by the danger of undue prejudice. . . . " KRE 403. The very existence of KRE 411 demonstrates a concern that proof of a defendant's liability insurance inherently creates the danger of undue prejudice. There is always the danger that a jury will show less sympathy to an insured defendant, inappropriately resulting in a verdict for the plaintiff. The question presented in this case is whether that danger in admitting Appellant's and his expert's shared insurance coverage substantially outweighed its probative value.

The only bright-line solution to this problem has been developed by the Supreme Court of Ohio, which employs versions of Rules 403 and 411 identical to Kentucky's. That court has conclusively held that "in a medical malpractice action, evidence of a commonality of insurance interests between a defendant and an expert witness is sufficiently probative of the expert's bias as to clearly outweigh any potential prejudice evidence of insurance might cause." *Ede v. Atrium S. OB–GYN*, 71 Ohio St. 3d 124, 642 N.E. 2d 365, 368 (1994). . . .

Ohio's formation of a bright-line rule rests on two vital principles: the general inclusionary thrust of the Rules of Evidence and the preference for allowing evidence for bias. These are core principles of Kentucky's evidence law also. *See Baker v. Kammerer*, 187 S.W.3d 292, 296 (Ky. 2006) (noting significance of "the general inclusionary thrust of the Rules of Evidence and the more particular preference to allow evidence of bias"). Nevertheless, this Court finds a bright line rule on admissibility of common insurance to be incompatible with KRE 403.

Ohio's approach disregards the role of judicial discretion under Rule 403, which is the same in both Ohio and Kentucky. The dissent in *Ede* noted this and correctly emphasized the role of judicial discretion in balancing probative value against prejudicial effect:

> In applying Evid. R. 403, a trial court must have broad discretion because of the practical problems inherent in the balancing of tangible and indefinable factors, such as unfair prejudice and probative value. The task of assessing potential prejudice is one for which a trial judge, in light of his familiarity with all the evidence in a particular case, is well suited. Unlike reviewing judges who must look at a cold record, a trial judge is in a superior position to evaluate the impact of the evidence because he sees the mannerisms and reactions of the jurors, witnesses, parties, and attorneys.

The *Ede* dissent echoes this Court's own implementation of judicial discretion in a similar insurance-bias case, *Baker v. Kammerer*. In *Baker*, the plaintiff attempted to reveal a defense witness's employment with the defendant's insurance company. This Court "recognize[d] the trial court's inherent discretion over evidentiary questions such as this one," and then stated:

> Because a multitude of factors may be considered by a trial judge addressing such an issue, judges are free to consider a spectrum of potential remedies. In an appropriate case, a judge might reasonably conclude that insurance evidence should be freely admitted. Another judge might choose a middle ground, allowing the identification of a witness as an agent of the defendant, but refusing to allow the disclosure that a defendant is insured. Likewise, applying the balancing test of KRE 403 might lead to the conclusion that certain insurance evidence is inadmissible.

We concluded by rejecting a "rigid, *per se* exclusion of any evidence of insurance" in favor of "the flexible, case-by-case approach required by KRE 403."

Appellant principally bases his argument on the Court of Appeals' decision in *Wallace v. Leedhanachoke*, 949 S.W.2d 624 (Ky. App. 1996). In *Wallace,* the expert and the defendant shared an insurance company, but the plaintiff could not supply the trial court with any hint of bias stemming from that relationship. The trial court excluded evidence of the shared insurance because any bias inherent therein was too remote and speculative to outweigh its prejudicial effect. The court stated it was "not prepared to adopt a *per se* rule either permitting or prohibiting this line of cross-examination," and affirmed the trial court's exercise of discretion.

Appellant urges this Court to adopt and directly apply *Wallace* to hold that evidence of insurance should have been excluded in this case as well. While willing to adopt the well-reasoned analysis in *Wallace,* this Court disagrees with Appellant that its disposition controls the outcome here. Although the facts of both cases are indeed similar, *Wallace* does not provide a per se rule that evidence of shared insurance should be excluded. On the contrary, it vests the trial judge with broad discretion to evaluate the proof of bias on a case-by-case basis.

When the trial court in this case addressed the matter a second time, the morning before the evidence was introduced, it listed several factors that swayed it toward admitting the commonality of insurance evidence. Those factors, paraphrased, were as follows:

(1) Dr. Butcher unequivocally stated in his deposition that he is of the belief and opinion that malpractice cases result in, and have a direct link to, rate increases;

(2) Dr. Butcher left one state because he believed there was collusion between judges and lawyers in malpractice cases;

(3) Dr. Butcher's comments were so severe during his deposition that defense counsel felt the need to rein him in and caution him;

(4) Dr. Butcher has established a general hostility to medical negligence cases;

(5) Dr. Woolum and Dr. Butcher have more than simply the casual connection of having the same insurance company, as they had worked side by side for twenty years in the same community hospital.

In factoring these considerations into its estimation of probative value, the trial court properly exercised its discretion under KRE 403. Admittedly, as Appellant contends, these factors indicate bias on their own, isolated from the issue of common insurance. Notwithstanding this independent impeachment value, these factors also develop a link between the shared insurance and Dr. Butcher's bias against this malpractice claim. They demonstrate that Dr. Butcher is no average, passive policyholder, but instead a practitioner very concerned with the affairs of his insurer.

Based on these factors, the court made the following finding about Dr. Butcher upon first considering the issue:

> I wish it could be avoided, but I think they can get in under the bias exception. If they're both insured — I mean he's clearly got a perceived financial stake in the outcome of this trial if they're insured by the [same insurance company] — based on his testimony in his deposition. He obviously believes that lawsuits are the — are what are pushing his premiums up. It's obvious perceived bias. . . .

"As noted above, dual concerns — the general inclusionary thrust of the Rules of Evidence and the more particular preference to allow evidence of bias — weigh heavily in favor of admissibility." *Baker,* 187 S.W.3d at 294. A situation such as *Wallace,* where there is absolutely no evidence linking common insurance to witness bias, is the exception, not the rule. "Absent unusual circumstances wherein the evidence would be . . . minimally probative, the principal question is the scope of the evidence of bias to be allowed," not its "initial admissibility." In this case, the scope of such evidence consisted of only two questions. The trial court appropriately exercised its discretion by including this evidence of bias.

It is important to note that Dr. Butcher's trial testimony about his insurance carrier and his belief in the effect of the litigation on his premiums is immaterial to the analysis of whether such questioning should have been permitted. The questioning proceeded as follows:

Q: Now, you and Dr. Woolum share the same insurance carrier, correct?
A: He has the same one that I have.
Q: And what happens in this case to Dr. Woolum you believe will have some impact or may have some impact on your insurance premium, don't you, sir?
A: No.

With his denial of any impact, all questioning about their common insurance ceased. . . .

As a result of the strong connection between common insurance and witness bias, it was not an abuse of discretion to admit the evidence. . . .

For the aforementioned reasons, the decision of the Court of Appeals is hereby affirmed.

NOTES TO WOOLUM v. HILLMAN

1. *Applying Discretion.* A Mississippi opinion used arithmetic to calculate, based on the number of physicians covered by a particular insurer and the state's statutory ceiling on medical malpractice recoveries, that a judgment for the plaintiff could have had a financial impact on an insured expert witness in the amount of $136. Excluding information about this financial impact, offered to show bias, was within the trial court's discretion. *See* James v. Tucker, 997 So. 2d 908 (Miss. 2008).

2. *Substantial Connection Test.* Some courts use a "substantial connection" to admit insurance evidence where a witness has a significant connection with a defendant's insurer (requiring a connection greater than merely being insured by that insurer). For example, in Yoho v. Thompson, 548 S.E.2d 584 (S.C. 2001), evidence that an expert maintained an employment relationship with a defendant's insurer was admissible), and in Bonser v. Shainholtz, 3 P.3d 422, 426 (Colo. 2000), evidence was admissible that an expert was a founder of a trust that insured the defendant, because the trust had only 1,500 members and an adverse verdict could substantially affect the expert's premiums).

■   ■   ■

Are You a Doctor or a Professional Witness?—Wrobleski. The opponent of an expert witness is ordinarily allowed to ask what payment the witness will receive for his or her testimony. *Wrobleski* reviews additional methods that opponents may use to demonstrate the bias of an expert. It also considers whether fuller information about the expert's finances should be an allowable topic for cross-examination.

WROBLESKI v. de LARA

727 A.2d 930 (1999)

WILNER, J.

This is a medical malpractice case. Linda Wrobleski claimed that Nora de Lara negligently damaged Ms. Wrobleski's small intestine during a laparoscopic procedure performed by Dr. de Lara on June 6, 1994. . . . A jury in the Circuit Court for Baltimore City found no negligence on Dr. de Lara's part, and from the judgment entered upon that verdict, Ms. Wrobleski appealed. The Court of Special Appeals affirmed. We granted *certiorari* to consider whether the trial court erred in allowing defense counsel to question one of Ms. Wrobleski's medical expert witnesses as to how much money the witness had earned in 1995 from testifying as an expert. We agree with the Court of Special Appeals that there was no error in permitting the question.

The facts underlying the claim of negligence are not especially important in terms of the single issue before us. . . .

The two medical experts who testified for Ms. Wrobleski — Drs. Battle and Lilling — asserted that Dr. de Lara was negligent, although for somewhat different reasons. The three medical experts who testified for Dr. de Lara concluded that there was no negligence — that Dr. de Lara's conduct was within the appropriate standard of care and that the perforation was not the result of negligence on her part. The issue of negligence, in other words, involved a classic disagreement among the experts.

When Dr. Battle — the first expert — was called, defense counsel elicited, without objection, that the witness had testified some 50 to 60 times for medical malpractice plaintiffs, that about 25 of those appearances had been for clients of Mr. Ellin, who served as Ms. Wrobleski's attorney, and that, in the preceding twelve months, Dr. Battle had earned between $30,000 and $50,000 from testifying as an expert, which amounted to about 15% of his income. Most of those earnings, he said, were derived from Mr. Ellin's cases. Dr. Battle stated that about 80% of his appearances had been on behalf of plaintiffs. To blunt the unfavorable implications from that testimony, Mr. Ellin brought out that, in about half of the cases Dr. Battle reviewed for him, the doctor opined that there was no malpractice and that, to the best of Dr. Battle's knowledge, Mr. Ellin did not take those cases.

What provoked this appeal was a similar effort directed at Dr. Lilling. It appears that, during Dr. Lilling's pretrial deposition, the doctor disclosed how much he had been paid by Mr. Ellin for his services in the Wrobleski case and stated that the total amount he earned from testifying as an expert witness was less than 20% of his total income, but he refused to reveal the total amount of income he received from testifying as a witness. At trial, counsel asked Dr. Lilling whether he was prepared to tell the jury how much he made in 1995 from testifying as an expert, and the witness again refused. The basis of his reticence seemed to be his belief that, having stated that less than 20% of his income was derived from his services as a witness, disclosure of the amount of that income would be tantamount to revealing his gross income, which he said was none of counsel's business. Ms. Wrobleski objected to questioning Dr. Lilling about the total income he received from testifying. She had no objection to questioning the witness as to income earned from Mr. Ellin but asserted that any inquiry beyond that was irrelevant. The court overruled the objection but did not require Dr. Lilling to answer the question. Once again, the question was put whether the witness was willing to disclose the information, and once again the witness declined. He did reveal that he had earned $27,000 from Mr. Ellin's cases in 1995.

Relying principally on an intermediate appellate decision from Pennsylvania, Ms. Wrobleski asserts that allowance of the unanswered question was error. She attributes the unfavorable jury verdict to that question, contending that the only reason the jury could have for ignoring her injuries was its belief that Dr. Lilling was trying to hide something from it. In light of the other evidence in the case, that causal connection is tenuous at best, but we shall accept it for purposes of this appeal. . . .

Exposure of potential bias based on self-interest is often attempted through cross-examination directed at how much the witness is being paid for his or her services in the case at bar, the frequency with which the witness testifies in similar kinds of cases, whether the witness customarily appears for a particular type of party (usually plaintiff or defendant), whether the witness is frequently employed by a particular party or attorney and, if so, how much income the witness derives from that employment, and, as in this case, the amount or the percentage of the witness's total income that is derived from lawyer referrals or testimony in lawsuits. Some forms of inquiry seek to uncover a specific and enduring relationship between the witness and the party or attorney, from which a direct bias may be inferred. Others are directed at exposing the more subtle problem of the professional "hired gun," who earns a significant portion of his or her livelihood from testifying and, rather than having a tie to a specific party or attorney, may have a general economic interest in producing favorable results for the employer of the moment. . . .

The amount of money that a witness is paid for testifying in the particular case is unquestionably disclosable on cross-examination. The dispute, on grounds of relevance, arises from questions seeking information on amounts earned from testifying generally, which necessarily includes amounts earned from testifying in other litigation. . . .

Only a few courts have dealt directly with the issue before us, and there seems to be some split of authority. A slight majority of the courts that have considered the issue have allowed expert witnesses to be questioned about income earned from their forensic activities and have rejected the various arguments mounted by Ms. Wrobleski in this case. The clearest example is *Trower v. Jones,* 121 Ill. 2d 211 (1988). *Trower* also was a medical malpractice case in which defense counsel was allowed to cross-examine the plaintiff's medical expert as to (1) the frequency with which he testified for plaintiffs rather than defendants, and (2) the annual income derived from services related to testifying as an expert witness. In earlier cases, the Illinois Supreme Court had generally curtailed (or blessed the curtailing of) that kind of inquiry but because, in the court's view, both the difficulty and the importance of thorough cross-examination of expert witnesses had markedly increased in the intervening years, it determined that a more liberal rule was required. . . .

> "Adding to the importance of effective cross-examination is the proliferation of expert 'locator' services which, as a practical matter, can help the litigants of either side of most any case find an expert who will help advocate the desired position. As this case helps illustrate, many experts today spend so much of their time testifying throughout the country that they might be deemed not only experts in their field but also experts in the art of being a persuasive witness and in the art of handling cross-examination."

As does Ms. Wrobleski here, the plaintiff in *Trower* argued that inquiry regarding an expert witness's financial interest should be limited to the remuneration received for testifying (1) in the particular case, (2) for a particular party, or (3) for a particular party's attorney. [T]he court rejected those limitations, noting that "[a] favorable verdict may well help [the witness] establish a 'track record' which, to a professional witness, can be all-important in determining not only the frequency with which [the witness] is asked to testify but also the price which [the witness] can demand for such testimony." The court found wanting the additional arguments that allowing such an inquiry would inject collateral issues into the trial, such as the reasonableness of the fees charged by the witness, and that it would complicate the discovery process by creating conflicts between the need to discover impeachment evidence and various evidentiary privileges, such as the physician-patient privilege. Both of those problems, it held, could be controlled by the trial court and did not suffice to keep relevant information from the jury.

The Fifth Circuit Court of Appeals took a somewhat similar position in *Collins v. Wayne Corp.,* 621 F.2d 777 (5th Cir. 1980). The witness there was an accident reconstruction expert called by the plaintiffs in a crash-worthiness product liability case, who was asked about fees received for testifying in earlier cases. Finding no error, alternatively to finding that no proper objection had been made, the court observed that "[a] showing of a pattern of compensation in past cases raises an inference of the possibility that the witness has slanted his testimony in those cases so he would be hired to testify in future cases." [Survey of cases in additional jurisdictions omitted.]

[T]wo basic principles are fixed as part of Maryland law and the law generally: the scope of cross-examination of expert witnesses is largely within the control and discretion of the trial judge, but wide discretion must be allowed in permitting cross-examination as to bias and interest. The normal and appropriate function of cross-examination into the compensation an expert witness earns, either for services rendered in the case at bar or from forensic activities generally, is to expose bias — any personal interest the witness may have in arriving at the stated opinion. It is not the function, or at least not the *proper* function, of such cross-examination to embarrass witnesses or to invade unnecessarily their legitimate privacy, and thus to discourage them from testifying and thereby make it more difficult for parties to obtain needed expert testimony.

For the reasons noted above, summarized and applied by the Illinois court in *Trower,* we believe that it is generally appropriate for a party to inquire whether a witness offered as an expert in a particular field earns a significant portion or amount of income from applying that expertise in a forensic setting and is thus in the nature of a "professional witness." If there is a reasonable basis for a conclusion that the witness may be a "professional witness," the party may inquire both into the amount of income earned in the recent past from services as an expert witness and into the approximate portion of the witness's total income derived from such services. The trier of fact may find either or both to be significant in determining the witness's credibility. We hasten to add, however, two important caveats. First, we do not intend by our decision today to authorize the harassment of expert witnesses through a wholesale rummaging of their personal and financial records under the guise of seeking impeachment evidence. The allowance of the permitted inquiry, both at the discovery and trial stages, should be tightly controlled by the trial court and limited to its purpose, and not permitted to expand into an unnecessary exposure of matters and data that are personal to the witness and have no real relevance to the credibility of his or her testimony. Second, the fact that an expert witness devotes a significant amount of time to forensic activities or earns a significant portion of income from those activities does not mean that the testimony given by the witness is not honest, accurate, and credible. It is simply a factor that is proper for the trier of fact to know about and consider.

Judgment of Court of Special Appeals affirmed, with costs.

> **GOOD TO REMEMBER**
>
> Bias may always be proved with independent evidence. The impeaching party can use that in addition to intrinsic evidence derived during cross-examination.

NOTES TO WROBLESKI v. de LARA

1. *Mutual Assured Destruction.* When plaintiffs' experts and defendants' experts are all paid to testify, the advantage to showing their financial interests may be small.

2. *Legislation about "Professional Witnesses."* The concern addressed in *Wrobleski* has been addressed by some legislatures. Instead of allowing the opponent of an expert witness to impeach the witness with evidence of the degree to which the witness's career is focused on giving expert testimony, they adopt per se rules controlling whether a professional may serve as an expert witness. See, for example:

> **Kansas Stat. Ann., Article 34, 60-3412**
>
> In any medical malpractice liability action . . . in which the standard of care given by a practitioner of the healing arts is at issue, no person shall qualify as an expert witness on such issue unless at least 50% of such person's professional time within the two-year period preceding the incident giving rise to the action is devoted to actual clinical practice in the same profession in which the defendant is licensed.

> **Michigan Comp. L. Ann, Chapter 600, Sec. 2169.**
>
> (1) In an action alleging medical malpractice, a person shall not give expert testimony on the appropriate standard of practice or care unless the person is licensed as a health professional in this state or another state and meets the following criteria:

. . .
(b) . . . during the year immediately preceding the date of the occurrence that is the basis for the claim or action, [the person] devoted a majority of his or her professional time to either or both of the following:

(i) The active clinical practice of the same health profession in which the party against whom or on whose behalf the testimony is offered is licensed and, if that party is a specialist, the active clinical practice of that specialty.

(ii) The instruction of students in an accredited health professional school or accredited residency or clinical research program in the same health profession in which the party against whom or on whose behalf the testimony is offered is licensed and, if that party is a specialist, an accredited health professional school or accredited residency or clinical research program in the same specialty.

QUESTION 12-6. Tom Talker testified for Bob Buyer at a civil trial, in a claim by Buyer against Sally Seller. To show bias, which of the following facts would Seller likely be barred from showing?

A. Talker and Buyer are old friends.
B. Talker and Buyer are second cousins.
C. Talker and Buyer are business partners.
D. Talker and Buyer are both natives of San Francisco.

E   CONTRADICTION AND PRIOR INCONSISTENT STATEMENTS

When a witness gives testimony about a topic relevant in a case, an opposing party is likely to introduce testimony from other witnesses to contradict the first witness's information. The jury will decide what really happened, and in doing so will implicitly conclude that some of the witnesses gave testimony that was accurate and that some gave testimony that was wrong. Note that a witness might give "wrong" testimony and yet be an honest person who intended to be truthful. Introduction of contradictory information is a form of impeachment that is allowed on any topic that is *relevant* at trial.

A recurring circumstance in impeachment comes up when a witness testifies about an *irrelevant* topic. If a witness provides irrelevant information in response to a question that did not ask about that topic, the opponent may ask the trial judge to strike that part of the witness's answer from the record and to instruct the jury to ignore it. If it is obvious that a lawyer's question would elicit irrelevant information, the question itself is subject to an objection.

Despite these possible controls on witnesses' giving irrelevant information to the jury, if a witness does include irrelevant information in his or her testimony and the opponent has evidence that could contradict what the witness said, the law must decide what options to offer the opponent. If the topic is "collateral," meaning that it has no relevance to the disputed issues in the case, the opponent is forbidden to introduce extrinsic evidence about it but may ask the witness questions about it on cross-examination. Showing the jury that a witness was incorrect about *anything* in his or her testimony might help the jury decide if the witness was accurate in the significant parts of the testimony. On the other hand, if a topic has low importance, a mistake about it might have only low probative value about the witness's general accuracy. Furthermore, taking time to establish whether the witness was right or wrong in testimony that had low or no relevance might distract the jury from the issues that really are relevant at the trial.

Another common form of impeachment is informing a jury that a witness has made a statement prior to testifying that is inconsistent with the witness's testimony. The Federal Rules liberalize one important aspect of this type of impeachment: the requirement that the questioner alert the witness to the statement the witness allegedly made prior to trial. Some courts, however, have been unenthusiastic about that change.

Rule 611. Mode and Order of Examining Witnesses and Presenting Evidence

(a) **Control by the Court; Purposes.** The court should exercise reasonable control over the mode and order of examining witnesses and presenting evidence so as to:

(1) make those procedures effective for determining the truth;

(2) avoid wasting time; and

(3) protect witnesses from harassment or undue embarrassment.

(b) **Scope of Cross-Examination.** Cross-examination should not go beyond the subject matter of the direct examination and matters affecting the witness's credibility. The court may allow inquiry into additional matters as if on direct examination.

. . .

■   ■   ■

False Statements about Nonrelevant Topics — Langness. Rule 611 ordinarily limits the scope of cross-examination to topics that were brought up during direct examination and topics that relate to credibility. What about topics that are not relevant? A common law doctrine not specifically included in the rules prohibits the introduction of extrinsic evidence about "collateral" matters. The same notion should be used to prohibit cross-examination questioning about them. *Langness* illustrates an effort to cross-examine on a topic that does not relate to the issues at stake in the case and does not relate to credibility.

LANGNESS v. FENCIL URETHANE SYSTEMS, INC.

667 N.W.2d 596 (N.D. 2003)

MARING, J.

Duane Langness appealed from a judgment entered upon a jury verdict dismissing his action against Fencil Urethane Systems, Inc. for negligent application of epoxy primer and exposure to toxic chemicals. . . .

[Among other points,] Langness argues the trial court erred in allowing Fencil to impeach him on a collateral matter. On cross-examination of Langness, the following colloquy occurred:

Q. [Mr. Bakke:] I have some questions for you also. First of all, is this your first lawsuit that you have been involved in?

Mr. Hagen: I object. I don't know what relevance it has.

Mr. Bakke: Goes to bias and credibility.

The Court: Okay. Overruled.

The Witness: In what type of lawsuit?

Q. (Mr. Bakke Continuing) In any type of lawsuit?

The Court: Well, let's be more specific, Counsel.

Q. (Mr. Bakke Continuing) Any civil lawsuit?

A. Yes, I had one in, maybe, '68, '70, '69.

Q. Okay. Is that the one involving The Bowler?

A. Yes.

Q. In Fargo?

A. Yes.

Q. And you sued someone?

A. Yes.

Q. You sued The Bowler?

A. Yes, I did.

Q. As a result of an altercation that occurred?

A. That is correct.

Q. Okay. And is that the only civil lawsuit you have been involved in?

A. Yes, it is.

Q. And that's what you testified to in your deposition, is that correct?

A. Yes.

Q. And you stick with that answer?

A. Yes, I do.

Q. And you understand when you gave that deposition testimony you were under oath to tell the truth?

A. Yes.

Q. You've lived in Cass County for quite some time, is that correct?

A. Since 1957.

Q. Do you remember a lawsuit you were involved in, a civil lawsuit, by The Foreign Publishing Company versus Duane Langness?

A. No, I don't.

Mr. Hagen: Your Honor, I object. We're on some pretty remote collateral matters. He's trying to pick something out 20, 30 years ago and then trying to make a liar out of him. Clearly, it's improper.

Mr. Bakke: Your Honor, this is impeachment.

The Court: I guess he said he didn't recall. I'm going to let you proceed a little bit further. We're talking about something that's how old here?

Mr. Bakke: 1990, Your Honor.

The Court: Okay. For now, the objection is overruled. Proceed.

Thereafter, Fencil's counsel asked Langness about his involvement in several other lawsuits.

Langness argues his involvement in unrelated litigation was irrelevant and could not be brought up on cross-examination under N.D. R. Ev. 608(b). Fencil responds Langness did not object on the grounds of improper character evidence or past conduct under N.D. R. Ev. 608(b) and is precluded from raising that argument on appeal.

Evidence sought to be introduced through cross-examination must be relevant to be admissible. The scope of cross-examination for impeachment purposes is within the trial court's discretion. In *State v. Tucker,* 58 N.D. 82, 224 N.W. 878, 887 (1929), this Court recognized a witness may not be questioned about wholly irrelevant matters merely for the purpose of contradicting those matters with other extrinsic evidence, and if irrelevant questions are asked and answered, the answer cannot be contradicted by the cross-examiner:

> Witnesses may often be questioned, on cross-examination, as to matters collateral to the issue for the purpose of testing their credibility. But it is a well-settled rule that witnesses cannot be interrogated as to matters wholly irrelevant, merely for the purpose of contradicting them by other evidence. Hence, if irrelevant questions are asked and answered, the answer cannot be contradicted by the cross-examiner. If a party inquires of a witness as to immaterial matters, he must take the answer, and cannot raise an issue thereon by introducing evidence to contradict it.

Because we remand for further proceedings, we need not decide whether Langness has properly preserved this issue for review, or whether the court abused its discretion in allowing this line of questioning. On remand, however, Fencil must establish that questions about prior lawsuits are relevant and tied to matters at issue in this lawsuit. . . .

We reverse the judgment and remand for proceedings consistent with this opinion.

NOTES TO LANGNESS v. FENCIL URETHANE SYSTEMS, INC.

1. *Barring Inquiry and Barring Extrinsic Evidence.* The rule prohibiting extrinsic evidence on collateral topics is taken seriously and enforced fairly strictly by trial courts. The related issue — barring even inquiry about collateral topics — seems to receive less attention. The costs in terms of juror distraction and time are small when unimportant or irrelevant questions are asked and answered, compared with the costs associated with allowing additional proof from other witnesses.

2. *"Scope of Direct" vs. "Wide-Open" Rules.* To define what topics are permissible on cross-examination, jurisdictions use either the "scope of direct" or the "wide-open" rule. The language of Rule 611 incorporates each of these ideas, with a preference for the scope of direct position. The rule's basic requirement that cross-examination cover only topics raised in direct examination favors allowing the party who presents various witnesses to shape the content of the narrative presented to the jury. The opponent will be able to present a counternarrative when the opponent presents its case. To some extent this rule may avoid jury confusion. The rule authorizes the trial judge, though, to allow questioning on any topic in the judge's discretion.

Segment 5: scope of cross-examination

■   ■   ■

Prosecutor's Jackpot? A Photo of the Defendant with Illegal Drugs — McKee. The prosecutors in this drug case discovered an almost irresistibly tempting item of evidence: a photograph of the defendant apparently showing off his possession of drugs. Unfortunately, the photo had a date that was different from the dates connected with his charged offenses. The *McKee* court considers whether introduction of the photograph was proper, treating it as extrinsic evidence to contradict the defendant's testimony. The court does not give clear consideration to another topic: whether intrinsic questioning on the topic of the photograph was proper.

McKEE v. STATE

917 P.2d 940 (Nev. 1996)

Per Curiam.

This is an appeal from a judgment of conviction of one count of possession of a controlled substance, and one count of trafficking in a controlled substance–level III. On appeal, appellant Rockwood Lee McKee (McKee) contends that . . . he is entitled to a new trial since the prosecutor engaged in misconduct. We hold that . . . the prosecutor engaged in misconduct that materially prejudiced McKee's defense.

We therefore reverse the district court's judgment of conviction, and remand the matter to the district court.

In July 1994, McKee was living in Las Vegas, Nevada, where he worked as a carpenter. Prior to moving to Las Vegas, McKee lived in Southern California. While in Southern California, McKee performed several carpentry jobs for Verna Lovely (Lovely). On July 10, 1994, Lovely called McKee and asked him to drive her to Boise, Idaho, so that she could visit a friend. In return for his efforts, Lovely offered to fly McKee to Los Angeles and give him enough money to fix his truck. McKee agreed, and flew to Los Angeles.

After arriving in Los Angeles, McKee made some repairs to Lovely's vehicle. Because it was getting late, McKee purchased some methamphetamine to help him stay awake during the trip. McKee hid the drug in his sock. At about 1:00 A.M. on July 13, 1994, the couple began their trip. When they arrived in Truckee, California, some minor repairs were made to the car, and Lovely began driving. However, Lovely became fatigued before they arrived in Reno, so McKee took over the driving. Later that day, at about 9:00 P.M., Nevada Highway Patrol Trooper Charles Stamey (Stamey) observed Lovely's car traveling at a high rate of speed near Winnemucca, Nevada. After Stamey stopped the car, the couple informed the trooper that Lovely was the owner of the vehicle. Even though McKee was driving, Stamey asked to see Lovely's license and registration. As she was looking for her license, Stamey observed a telephone pager, a cellular telephone, a large road atlas, a pit bull dog in the back seat, the smell of air freshener, and a two-inch hole in the passenger side door. . . .

Concluding that he had probable cause, Trooper Stamey conducted a search of the car. Stamey's search produced the following: a loaded nine millimeter semi-automatic pistol; a brown bag containing 451.27 grams of methamphetamine; a salt container with a false bottom in which Stamey found a baggy containing methamphetamine; a set of scales capable of weighing up to 1,000 grams; a white envelope containing 4.8 grams of marijuana; and a pink paper bag containing three grams of methamphetamine. Stamey arrested McKee and Lovely. While searching McKee's person, Stamey found a baggy containing 0.83 grams of methamphetamine in McKee's sock.

A jury trial was held on September 21, 22, and 23, 1994, after which a jury found McKee guilty of trafficking in a controlled substance–level III, and possession of a controlled substance. On January 11, 1995, the district court sentenced McKee to serve twenty-five years in the Nevada State Prison and to pay a $500,000.00 fine for trafficking in a controlled substance–level III, and to serve four years in the Nevada State Prison for possession of a controlled substance. On January 27, 1995, McKee filed a timely notice of appeal. . . .

In the course of cross-examining McKee, the prosecution asked McKee if he had used drugs on July 12, 1994. McKee answered, "No." The prosecution then produced a photograph of McKee, dated July 12, 1994, in which McKee was shown holding a straw and a baggy in his right hand. McKee then admitted that he had used drugs on July 12, 1994. McKee's counsel objected to the use of the photograph.

It is error to allow the State to impeach a defendant's credibility with extrinsic evidence relating to a collateral matter. See NRS 50.085(3).[1] In Rowbottom v. State, 105 Nev. 472, 779 P.2d 934 (1989), Rowbottom was charged with first-degree murder. At one point, Rowbottom testified to the close relationship he had with his sisters. On cross-examination, the prosecution inquired into his relationship with his sisters. Rowbottom's mother was then called as a witness. During the prosecution's cross-examination of the mother, the mother testified about Rowbottom's past sexual misconduct with his sisters. In concluding that this impeachment was improper, we stated:

> Had the prosecution wished to rebut [Rowbottom's] testimony and impeach Rowbottom's credibility with specific instances of conduct it could have done so by inquiring about Rowbottom's alleged prior misconduct during his cross-examination. If Rowbottom denied having committed the act, the prosecution could not, however, prove specific instances of conduct by extrinsic evidence, i.e., Rowbottom's mother's testimony.

In the instant case, the district court erred in allowing the prosecutor to impeach McKee with the photograph. Initially, we conclude that whether McKee was using methamphetamine on July 12, 1994, several days before his arrest, is an issue collateral to whether he was trafficking in a controlled substance on the night in question. Impeachment on a collateral matter is clearly not allowed. In addition, the photograph used to impeach McKee's testimony is extrinsic evidence. As we noted in Rowbottom, under NRS 50.085(3), the prosecution is allowed to inquire into specific instances of conduct on cross-examination [ ] but must accept the witness' answer. The prosecution is not allowed to prove up the conduct through extrinsic evidence. Unfortunately, that is exactly what happened here. The prosecution asked McKee if he used drugs on July 12, 1994, McKee said, "No"; then the prosecution proved through extrinsic evidence that he did. In so doing, the prosecutor violated the rules of impeachment under NRS 50.085(3).

. . . The district court's judgment of conviction is hereby reversed, and the case is remanded to the district court for a new trial.

NOTES TO McKEE v. STATE

1. *Defining Collateral.* The court does not define "collateral" when it uses that characterization to describe the evidence of July 12 drug use. Would

---

1. NRS 50.085(3) states:

Specific instances of conduct of a witness, for the purpose of attacking or supporting his credibility, other than conviction of crime, may not be proved by extrinsic evidence. They may, however, if relevant to truthfulness, be inquired into on cross-examination of the witness himself or on cross-examination of a witness who testifies to an opinion of his character for truthfulness or untruthfulness, subject to the general limitations upon relevant evidence and the limitations upon interrogations and subject to the provisions of NRS 50.090.

evidence that the defendant had used drugs on July 12 have been admissible as part of the prosecution's affirmative case to show guilt of the charged crimes? One common definition of "collateral" is that a topic is collateral if it lacks relevance to a charge, claim, or defense.

2. *Distinguishing Inquiry from Extrinsic Proof.* The *McKee* court apparently would have allowed the prosecution to inquire into the collateral topic on cross-examination. What limitations would be associated with this technique? The difference between permitting inquiry and permitting extrinsic evidence is illustrated in this case by the prosecution's use of the photo in addition to the prosecution's use of questions.

■   ■   ■

Telling Two Different Stories—Schnapp. Showing that a witness's in-court testimony contradicts something the witness has said out of court can have a powerful effect on the credibility of the testimony. Because this pattern of information is common, a rule imposes certain controls on it. Rule 613 requires that the witness be given a chance to explain or deny the statement. At common law this opportunity had to occur before extrinsic evidence of the statement was introduced. The Federal Rule abolishes that requirement, but as *Schnapp* shows, some courts prefer the common law approach.

Rule 613. Witness's Prior Statement

(a) Showing or Disclosing the Statement During Examination. When examining a witness about the witness's prior statement, a party need not show it or disclose its contents to the witness. But the party must, on request, show it or disclose its contents to an adverse party's attorney.

(b) Extrinsic Evidence of a Prior Inconsistent Statement. Extrinsic evidence of a witness's prior inconsistent statement is admissible only if the witness is given an opportunity to explain or deny the statement and an adverse party is given an opportunity to examine the witness about it, or if justice so requires. This subdivision (b) does not apply to an opposing party's statement under Rule 801(d)(2).

UNITED STATES v. SCHNAPP

322 F.3d 564 (8th Cir. 2003)

McMILLIAN, J.

Christopher Schnapp ("defendant") appeals from a final judgment entered in the United States District Court for the Eastern District of Missouri upon a jury verdict finding him guilty of one count of arson in violation of 18 U.S.C. §844(i). For reversal, defendant argues that the district court (1) abused its discretion in disallowing his testimony regarding a prior inconsistent statement allegedly made by one of the government's witnesses....

On April 9, 1998, at approximately 11 P.M., a fire broke out at the St. Clair One-Stop Convenience Store ("the One Stop" or "the store"), which was owned by defendant's parents and operated by defendant and his wife....

Jim Schuhmacher, an investigator with the Franklin County prosecuting attorney's office, had been called to the scene shortly after the fire started. He entered the One Stop building on several occasions after the fire. Based upon his inspections of the building and interviews of defendant and [a store employee], he concluded that the fire was not ignited by natural gas coming from the furnace, smouldering cigarette butts in the trash, a faulty gas line, the electrical systems, flammable liquids spilled or poured on the floor, or any other accidental cause. He testified that, in his opinion, "the fire's origin was the furnace storage room area located at floor level and was deliberately introduced by a human being."

Bill Buxton, a part owner of a firm called Pyr-Tech, Inc. ("Pyr-Tech"), was hired to conduct a fire cause-and-origin investigation by the company that had insured the One Stop building, Secura Insurance Co. ("Secura"). Giving reasons similar to Schuhmacher's, Buxton testified that, in his opinion, the fire had been deliberately set using ordinary combustible items such as cardboard boxes, beer cases, and paper bags at floor level....

At the time of the fire, the One Stop was having financial difficulties....

[A]ccording to the government's theory of the case, defendant deliberately set the fire at the One Stop as a desperate attempt to get the business out of its dire financial circumstances.

The defense cross-examined the government's witnesses. Schuhmacher, on cross-examination, admitted that, on or about April 10, 1998, he removed a fluorescent light fixture and a junction box from the ceiling of the furnace room of the One Stop building. He testified, however, that he could not remember why he had done so. Schuhmacher also admitted that, before taking his job with the prosecutor's office, he was employed as a fire investigator with Pyr-Tech, the company that was partly owned by Buxton and was hired by Secura to investigate the cause and origin of the One Stop fire. Schuhmacher had worked directly under Buxton while employed at Pyr-Tech and had remained friendly with Buxton over the years. Buxton and Schuhmacher had talked on the telephone before Buxton inspected the One Stop building on April 14, 1998, and

Schuhmacher accompanied him on that inspection. Neither Schuhmacher nor Buxton mentioned their relationship with one another in their respective written reports regarding the cause and origin of the fire. Some of the government witnesses conceded, on cross-examination, that there was evidence of electrical arcing at the scene of the fire. . . .

During defendant's testimony, defense counsel asked defendant if he and Schuhmacher had gone into the One Stop building together shortly after the fire was extinguished. Defendant answered that they had. At that point, the government asked to approach the bench. In a sidebar conference, counsel for the government stated that he believed defense counsel was about to ask defendant about statements made to him by Schuhmacher just after the fire. The government objected to this anticipated testimony on hearsay grounds. Defense counsel responded that the statements would not be offered for their truth but rather as prior inconsistent statements, to impeach Schuhmacher's testimony at trial regarding the cause of the fire. The district court noted that defense counsel had not questioned Schuhmacher about the alleged prior inconsistent statement despite having the opportunity to do so when cross-examining Schuhmacher during the government's case-in-chief. . . . The district court then sustained the government's hearsay objection. . . .

The jury thereafter found defendant guilty. Defendant was sentenced to 60 months imprisonment, 3 years supervised release, a $100 assessment, and restitution in the amount of $247,098.98. He appealed.

Defendant argues on appeal that the district court abused its discretion in disallowing his testimony regarding the statement Schuhmacher allegedly made to him on the night of the fire. Defendant would have testified that Schuhmacher, upon inspecting the building's interior right after the fire, stated the opinion that the fire had started in the *ceiling* of the furnace room. According to defendant, this testimony would have supported the argument that Schuhmacher *changed* his opinion after discussing the matter with Buxton — his longtime mentor and friend, who was hired by the insurance company. After talking with Buxton, Schuhmacher began asserting that the fire appeared to have started on the *floor* of the furnace room. This evidence also would have explained why both Schuhmacher and Buxton completely failed to disclose in their written reports their longstanding relationship with one another and Schuhmacher's former employment with Pyr-Tech. It further would have explained why, on April 10th, Schuhmacher removed a fluorescent light fixture and a junction box from the ceiling of the furnace room despite his claim that he had ruled out the electrical systems as a source of the fire. Defendant argues that the district court abused its discretion in disallowing this evidence, notwithstanding Fed. R. Evid. 613(b). . . .

Defendant argues that the testimony in question should have been admitted because Schuhmacher was available to be recalled by the government on rebuttal. Defendant admits that defense counsel should have, on cross-examination during the government's case-in-chief, asked Schuhmacher about the statement he allegedly made to defendant right after the fire. Nevertheless, defendant argues, the government would not have been, and clearly was not, surprised by the prospect of defendant testifying about that statement as he had already done so in a deposition. Defendant also suggests that the interests of justice required full disclosure to the jury of Schuhmacher's lack of credibility, a "major issue in the case," which could have swayed the jury's ultimate finding of guilt. Defendant explains:

> It is painfully obvious that Schuhmacher wanted his finding to agree fully with those of the insurance company's origin and cause expert so he lied and said he'd not done any investigation, even though he clearly was in the building on the 9th and the 10th. It is clear, however, that, after meeting Buxton, his mentor, on April 14 and hearing [Buxton's] opinion on the origin (the floor) of the fire, Schuhmacher "fell into line" and abandoned the ceiling theory. His report so reflects this. . . . [T]he proffered testimony [i.e., that, on April 9th, Schuhmacher said he thought the fire started in the ceiling] . . . would have shown the jury [that Schuhmacher] is the kind of witness who would change his conclusions to conform with those of a more seasoned mentor.

Brief for Appellant at 33-34.

In response, the government argues that no abuse of discretion occurred in light of defense counsel's failure to ask Schuhmacher about his alleged statement on April 9th, despite ample opportunity to do so on cross-examination. The government also argues that the defense was really attempting to present Schuhmacher's statement for the truth of the statement, notwithstanding the claim that it was being offered for impeachment purposes. The government further suggests that the defense could have called Schuhmacher to the stand, asked him about the alleged statement, then called defendant. Having failed to lay a proper foundation under Fed. R. Evid. 613(b), the government concludes, defendant should not now be afforded a new trial. For the reasons stated below, we agree.

. . . Rule 613(b) provides that extrinsic evidence of a prior inconsistent statement by a witness is not admissible unless: (1) the witness is afforded an opportunity to explain or deny the statement and the opposing party is afforded an opportunity to interrogate the witness about the statement or (2) the interests of justice otherwise require. The rule, on its face, does not require that the witness be cross-examined about the alleged prior inconsistent statement *before* that statement may be presented as impeachment evidence. Indeed, the advisory committee's notes explain:

> The familiar foundation requirement that an impeaching statement first be shown to the witness before it can be proved by extrinsic evidence is preserved but with some modifications. . . . The traditional insistence that the attention of the witness be directed to the statement on cross-examination is relaxed in favor of simply providing the witness an opportunity to explain and the opposite party an opportunity to examine on the statement, *with no specification of any particular time or sequence.*

Fed. R. Evid. 613(b) advisory committee's notes (emphasis added). In fact, the latter part of the rule, referring to the interests of justice, indicates that such evidence may, under appropriate circumstances, be admitted even if the witness is never afforded an opportunity to explain or deny the alleged statement.

In *United States v. Sutton,* 41 F.3d 1257, 1260 (8th Cir. 1994), *cert. denied,* 514 U.S. 1072 (1995), as in the present case, testimony regarding a witness's prior inconsistent statement was disallowed by the trial judge "because [the witness] was not given the opportunity to explain or deny having made a prior inconsistent statement while he was on the stand, which is normally the proper foundation for impeachment under Fed. R. Evid. 613(b)." On appeal, the defendant argued that, under Rule 613(b), the trial court should have admitted the testimony regarding the witness's prior inconsistent statement because the witness was available to be recalled to deny or explain the statement. We rejected the defendant's argument, explaining that such a procedure "is not mandatory, but is optional at the trial judge's discretion."[6]

In the present case, the district court had the option to allow defendant to testify regarding Schuhmacher's alleged prior inconsistent statement, and then permit the government to recall Schuhmacher to explain or deny the alleged statement. However, as the district court noted, defense counsel could have asked Schuhmacher to explain or deny the alleged statement while Schuhmacher was on the stand as a witness during the government's case-in-chief, but failed to do so. Upon careful review, we cannot say that the district court's decision to disallow defendant's testimony regarding Schuhmacher's alleged prior inconsistent statement rises to the level of an abuse of discretion. . . .

For the reasons stated, the judgment of the district court is affirmed.

NOTES TO UNITED STATES v. SCHNAPP

1. *Queen's Case.* The origin of Rule 613 is the rule in Queen Caroline's Case, 2 Br. & B. 284, 129 Eng. Rep. 976 (1820), known as "Queen's Case." The rule in Queen's case states:

> If it be intended to bring the credit of a witness into question by proof of anything he may have said or declared touching the cause, the witness is first asked, upon cross-examination, whether or not he has said or declared that which is intended to be proved.

2. *Persistence of the Common Law Approach.* The common law requirement that the opportunity to explain the introduction of extrinsic evidence of a prior inconsistent statement apparently has strong appeal to many courts,

---

6. Therefore, because this court cited *Sutton,* 41 F.3d at 1260, for the proposition that "Rule 613(b) allows impeachment by a prior inconsistent statement only when a witness is first provided an opportunity to explain the statement," *United States v. Dierling,* 131 F.3d 722, 733 (8th Cir. 1997), *cert. denied,* 523 U.S. 1066, 118 S. Ct. 1401, 140 L. Ed. 2d 659 (1998), we read that statement in the context of *Sutton's* reference to what is "normally the proper foundation for impeachment under Fed. R. Evid. 613(b)." 41 F.3d at 1260. In other words, impeachment of a witness by a prior inconsistent statement is *normally* allowed only when the witness is first provided an opportunity to explain or deny the statement.

despite the Advisory Committee explanation of reasons to reject it. Sometimes courts may misunderstand Rule 613. The *Schnapp* court's treatment of its statement in an earlier opinion that "Rule 613(b) allows impeachment by a prior inconsistent statement only when a witness is first provided an opportunity to explain the statement" (see footnote 6) may highlight this problem.

F IMPEACHING HEARSAY DECLARANTS

When an out-of-court statement is admitted as proof of what it asserts, the credibility of the person who made that statement is subject to challenge. Rule 806 expresses this simply, but its details may raise some complications.

Rule 806. Attacking and Supporting the Declarant's Credibility

When a hearsay statement — or a statement described in Rule 801(d)(2)(C), (D), or (E) — has been admitted in evidence, the declarant's credibility may be attacked, and then supported, by any evidence that would be admissible for those purposes if the declarant had testified as a witness. The court may admit evidence of the declarant's inconsistent statement or conduct, regardless of when it occurred or whether the declarant had an opportunity to explain or deny it. If the party against whom the statement was admitted calls the declarant as a witness, the party may examine the declarant on the statement as if on cross-examination.

The rule applies to out-of-court statements defined as hearsay and also to some out-of-court statements admissible for their truth but exempted from the definition of hearsay (statements by an opponent's authorized declarant, agent or employee, or coconspirator). It allows the party against whom the statement is admitted to respond with typical impeachment measures. For example, if there is evidence that a declarant had a bias related to the case, evidence of that bias is admitted. If the declarant had been convicted of a crime, evidence of that crime can be admitted, subject to the controls of Rule 609.

If the declarant is not in court, the detailed requirements for use of a prior inconsistent statement cannot be met, since there is no way to direct the declarant's attention to the statement and offer a chance for the declarant to explain it, as Rule 613 requires. That is why Rule 806 refers specifically to this situation and allows use of a prior inconsistent statement without requiring compliance with the Rule 613 procedure.

There is another way in which the basic plan of Rule 806 (that is, treat the declarant exactly as one would treat a witness) cannot be carried out. If a witness has committed some past act related to truth telling, Rule 608 allows a cross-examiner to inquire about it on cross-examination. The rule expressly prohibits introduction of extrinsic proof about the act. When a declarant has committed this type of past act, there is no way to ask the declarant about it, if the declarant is not in court. Some courts have responded to this dilemma by refusing to permit this type of impeachment under Rule 806. Others have worked around the rule by allowing the party against whom the out-of-court statement was introduced to ask some other witness about the declarant's supposed bad act. *See*, generally, United States v. Saada, 212 F.3d 210 (3d Cir. 2000).

QUESTION 12-7. Last year, Lou Landowner invited Pat Plaintiff to Landowner's land to camp and to swim in a pond there. Plaintiff spent ten days there, camping and swimming. But Plaintiff then became ill.

Plaintiff has sued Landowner for damages associated with his illness. Plaintiff claims that toxic chemicals in the pond made him sick and that Landowner knew the chemicals were in the pond. The state's tort law requires a landowner to warn a social guest about hidden dangers known to the landowner. Landowner admits he gave no warning but claims he was ignorant of the presence of the chemicals.

To prove that Landowner knew that chemicals were in the pond, Plaintiff seeks to introduce testimony by Bob Barman. Barman works as a bartender in a bar near Landowner's land. Barman would testify that a frequent customer at the bar, Harry Handyman, had often spoken to him about Landowner. Handyman is not available to testify.

Barman would testify that a year or two before Pat Plaintiff's visit to Landowner's land, Handyman said (1) that Landowner had recently paid Handyman to dump large containers of chemicals into Landowner's pond, (2) that Landowner told Handyman the chemicals were toxic, and (3) that Landowner told Handyman dumping them was illegal.

Assume that Barman's testimony is admitted for some substantive purpose, and assume that witnesses are available who could testify to the following items of information. Discuss what use, if any, Landowner could make of each of those items of information in response to Barman's testimony.

- **A.** Handyman had a reputation in his hometown for being a liar.
- **B.** Handyman was convicted of tax evasion in 2004.
- **C.** Handyman once said, "Landowner is one of the most ethical people I know."
- **D.** Plaintiff owes Barman a large sum of money.

G SUMMARY

The process of impeachment involves a variety of techniques to suggest to the trier of the fact that a witness has testified falsely. Some of these techniques are based on suggesting that the witness has lied on purpose; others merely call into question the accuracy of what the witness has said.

The Propensity Inference and Character in General. One permitted style of impeachment is to introduce evidence suggesting that the witness has a character trait of untruthfulness. This is allowed by introducing evidence that the witness has a reputation for untruthfulness. It is also possible to introduce testimony by someone who has a well-founded opinion about the witness's truthfulness. But most often, this type of character-based impeachment relies on evidence about reputation.

If the witness who is sought to be impeached has done things in the past that suggest an untruthful character, it is permissible to ask that witness about those past acts. In this situation, the questioner is allowed only to ask about those acts. No matter what the witness replies, there is a prohibition against introducing extrinsic evidence of those acts.

In one specific situation, some courts have relaxed the prohibition against extrinsic evidence of past acts to show untruthfulness. These cases involve a witness's past false accusations of sexual crimes.

Establishing a Propensity for Untruthfulness with Proof of Past Convictions. Past convictions may be proved by extrinsic evidence, for the purpose of impeachment. The rules governing this process are detailed. Admissibility of a conviction varies according to whether or not the witness to be impeached is a criminal defendant and according to the specific nature of the past crime for which there was a conviction.

If the conviction involves a crime for which the prosecution was acquired to prove untruthfulness, the conviction is automatically admissible (unless it is more than ten years old).

If the crime did not involve truth telling, its treatment changes according to whether the witness sought to be impeached is or is not a criminal defendant. If the witness is someone other than a criminal defendant, proof of the non-truth-telling crime is admissible unless its probative value is substantially less than the risk of prejudice. If the witness is a criminal defendant, proof of a non-truth-telling crime is admissible only if its probative value exceeds the risk of unfair prejudice.

For all convictions, if more than ten years have passed from the date of conviction or release of confinement related to the conviction, the evidence must stay out unless a trial court finds that it is substantially more probative than prejudicial.

When a crime does not involve truth telling, in order for a trial court to carry out any of the required balancing tests, the trial court must determine the extent of the crime's probative value regard to truth telling. Jurisdictions vary on this issue. Some treat virtually all felonies as having significant probative value with regard to truth telling. Others are more skeptical and limit the number of crimes in that category. Drug convictions are a prime example of this controversy.

Bias. If a witness has some connection with parties in a case, any party who seeks to impeach that witness will be allowed to introduce proof about that connection. Typical examples of connections that show bias would be joint membership in a club, family relationships, romantic relationships, or a business or financial stake in the outcome of the case.

Contradiction and Prior Inconsistent Statements. If a witness has testified and provided information that has relevance to the issues in the case, the opponent will always be entitled to introduce contrary evidence that supports another view of the facts related to those issues. When a witness has testified about nonrelevant material, a cross-examiner is allowed to ask questions about that topic. If the topic has no relevance, however, it is called "collateral." Extrinsic evidence about collateral topics is prohibited.

If a witness has said something in the past that contradicts what the witness has said at trial, proof of the prior inconsistent statement is always allowed. The only control imposed by evidence law is that the attention of the witness must be directed to the prior statement so that the witness can have an opportunity to explain the apparent inconsistency. The federal rules have eliminated a common law requirement that the opportunity to explain should be provided before introduction of evidence of the prior statement. However, some courts continue to apply that constraint as a matter of discretion.

Impeaching a Hearsay Declarant. Essentially all of the techniques that may be used to impeach a witness are available to use for impeaching a hearsay declarant. In the case of a prior inconsistent statement, however, there is no need to offer an opportunity for explanation, since the person who might have been able to offer an explanation will likely not be in court. The law is unsettled with regard to impeaching a hearsay declarant by asking about past acts that did not lead to convictions. The reason this complication arises is that the declarant is likely absent from the trial and therefore cannot be asked about those past acts.

CHAPTER 13

Witnesses

A. Introduction
B. Personal Knowledge
C. Competency: Personal Traits
D. Competency: Status
E. Summary

 ## A INTRODUCTION

Topic Overview

In contrast to rules about the substance and form of admissible testimony, a number of evidence concepts deal primarily with the personal attributes of witnesses. Rules in Article VI of the Federal Rules, "Witnesses," require that a witness must be competent as defined in Rule 601, a witness must have personal knowledge of the subject of his or her testimony as required in Rule 602, and must swear or affirm that he or she will testify truthfully.

Even if a person does have personal knowledge and does swear to tell the truth, that person may still be rejected as a witness because of his or her status. For example, a person who makes a claim against another person's estate may be barred from testifying about transactions with the decedent.

If a person is a spouse of a criminal defendant, the person may be treated as incompetent to testify. If a person is a judge or juror, Rules 605 and 606 impose significant limitations on that person's ability to give testimony.

Chapter Organization

This chapter begins with coverage of the personal knowledge requirement, examining its frequent overlap with hearsay issues. Then, with regard to competency, the chapter explores the law's particular treatment of children and witnesses who have undergone hypnosis. The chapter also includes an unusual case considering the application of competency concepts to witnesses with multiple personalities.

Sometimes a person's status affects his or her ability to be a witness. Issues of this type are the remaining focus of the chapter. "Dead Man's" statutes that control a person's ability to testify about transactions with a person whose estate the person has sued are an important kind of competency limitation. The chapter concludes with attention to the circumstances under which incompetency applies to spouses of a defendant, to judges, and to jurors.

B   PERSONAL KNOWLEDGE

Rule 602 prohibits testimony by a witness who lacks personal knowledge of the subject of the testimony. This requirement is a specific instance of the general requirement that all evidence must be relevant. Information from a person who does not personally know what he or she says happened or what he or she says someone else said might well be irrelevant to establishing what happened or what was said.

Rule 602. Need for Personal Knowledge

A witness may testify to a matter only if evidence is introduced sufficient to support a finding that the witness has personal knowledge of the matter. Evidence to prove personal knowledge may consist of the witness's own testimony. This rule does not apply to a witness's expert testimony under Rule 703.

■ ■ ■

How Do You Know Who Burned Your Trailer? — Long. This opinion shows that a witness might have personal knowledge of an event or might have personal knowledge of words someone said. It also indicates that proof of a witness's personal knowledge can come from that witness's testimony on the subject.

STATE v. LONG
656 A.2d 1228 (Maine 1995)

CLIFFORD, J.

Justin Long appeals from convictions of arson, and conspiracy to commit arson, following a jury trial in the Superior Court. Long contends that the court improperly excluded certain exculpatory testimonial evidence. Our review of the record reveals no error or abuse of discretion in the court's evidentiary rulings. Accordingly, we affirm the judgments.

At some point prior to September 18, 1992, David LaFlamme was subpoenaed to testify before a grand jury considering charges against Brett Bodman. LaFlamme refused to testify and informed Bodman's mother that the state might be looking for Bodman. Between September 18 and September 24, 1992, the trailer owned by LaFlamme was painted with "narc," "rat," vulgarities, and sexual obscenities about LaFlamme's girlfriend. On September 24, the trailer was burned down.[1]

Long and David Oakes were charged with setting the fire based on statements they made during conversations they had with law enforcement officers. Long and Oakes talked about setting someone up to take the blame for the fire and that they would not be personally involved in setting the fire because they had engaged someone else to do it. After the fire, both men referred to a fire that had occurred and mentioned the name "Frank" in conjunction with it.

On September 25, Frank Achorn, an acquaintance of Long and Oakes, was arrested on charges unrelated to this case. Achorn had singed hair, eyebrows, and wrists, and pink blotches on both hands. Achorn testified that he did not set the fire and that neither Long nor Oakes asked him to set the fire.

At some point after the fire, LaFlamme spoke with Bodman, who allegedly admitted that he was responsible for setting the fire. At trial, LaFlamme testified as follows:

Q: While you were incarcerated, did you have an opportunity to talk with Mr. Bodman?

A: Yes.

Q: And when was that, if you recall?

A: I don't remember the date exactly, but it was after — it was after the fire, and —

The State objected and argued that Bodman's statement was hearsay and that it could come in as a statement against interest only if corroborating circumstances existed. Long argued that the corroborative evidence was that Bodman had a motive to act against LaFlamme, Bodman voluntarily made the statement, and there was no collusion between the two. Long also argued that the statement was exculpatory because Bodman admitted responsibility for the crime with which Long was charged. The court ruled the evidence inadmissible. After the ruling, the direct examination of LaFlamme was resumed:

Q: Do you know who is responsible for the fire at your trailer?

State: Objection, Your Honor.

Court: Basis.

---

1. During the latter half of 1992, LaFlamme was incarcerated on cocaine trafficking charges.

State: To foundation, for this person being able to say from personal knowledge that he knows who did the fire.

Court: The objection is sustained.

Q: I have no other questions.

The jury returned verdicts of guilty against Long.

On appeal, Long contends that the court erred in excluding LaFlamme's testimony about who set the fire....

Long first contends that the court improperly precluded LaFlamme from testifying that he knew who set fire to his trailer because an adequate foundation for LaFlamme's personal knowledge was established. A witness may testify only to those matters about which he has personal knowledge. M.R. Evid. 602. Personal knowledge refers to that which the witness "has perceived through the physical senses." P. Murray, *Maine Evidence* §602.1 at 6-9 (3d ed. 1992). A straightforward application of the rule shows, contrary to Long's contention, that LaFlamme did not perceive through his physical senses that Bodman set the fire. LaFlamme's "knowledge" of who burned down his trailer was based solely on what he was told by Bodman.

Although a witness may testify from personal knowledge that a statement was made, testimony about the content of such a statement raises hearsay problems. "If a witness personally hears another make a statement, he is qualified to testify under Rule 602 that such statement was made. He may not, however, testify as to the contents of the out-of-court statement if such statement is offered to prove the truth of the matter asserted and falls within no exception to the hearsay rule." *State v. Duquette,* 475 A.2d 1145, 1147 n.1 (Me. 1984). Long contends that Bodman's statements to LaFlamme were admissible pursuant to M.R. Evid. 804(b)(3) as a statement against interest. [The court rejected that contention because Long failed to show that Bowman was unavailable.]

Judgments affirmed.

NOTES TO STATE v. LONG

1. *Intrinsic Evidence Supporting Personal Knowledge.* In many instances no special attention is needed to establish the personal knowledge requirement. For example, it would be satisfied if an eyewitness to a crime testified, "I saw the defendant use a wrench to hit the bank teller in the head." In contrast, testimony like "I saw the defendant use a 15 percent solution of chloroform, on a handkerchief, to knock out the bank teller" would need to be accompanied by more testimony from the eyewitness or someone else in order to satisfy the personal knowledge requirement.

2. *Judge and Jury Roles.* A witness's knowledge of what a witness testifies about presents an issue analogous to conditional relevance under FRE 104(b). If a judge believes there is adequate evidence on which a jury could conclude that a witness did have personal knowledge of the topic of his or her testimony, the

Segment 1: personal knowledge requirement

judge should rule that Rule 602 has been satisfied. If the jury decides that the witness lacked personal knowledge, the jury will very likely ignore the witness's testimony.

QUESTION 13-1. Tom Treasurer served a national nonprofit organization as its treasurer and office manager. He has been indicted for fraud and theft, accused of writing checks on the organization's account and then depositing them in his own checking account and keeping the proceeds. He claims in defense that he used the money that was credited to his account to pay the organization's bills, and that routing the organization's money through his own account allowed him to pay the organization's creditors more quickly than if he had just written checks from the organization to each creditor.

Treasurer seeks to establish that he paid some of the organization's bills with money from his own checking account by having his wife, Theresa Treasurer, testify that it was his practice to pay the organization's bills from that account. Which of the following foundation facts would support admission of her testimony?

A. Tom Treasurer often explained to her that he was using his checking account to pay the organization's bills.

B. Theresa Treasurer saw her husband working at home on many occasions and saw him going through stacks of bills that were not bills for their own household's expenses.

C. Theresa Treasurer has confidence in her husband and knows he would not have taken money from the organization and then failed to use it to pay the organization's bills.

D. Theresa Treasurer once participated in a telephone call her husband made to the bank in which an employee of the bank said that many checks issued from Tom Treasurer's account were made out to companies that had business dealings with the organization.

C   COMPETENCY: PERSONAL TRAITS

"Competent" means eligible to testify. Rule 601 recognizes a requirement that a witness be competent in order to testify. Actual practice deviates from the rule's statement that every person is competent, as courts have developed techniques for dealing with particular situations, such as testimony by children or individuals who have been hypnotized or suffer from mental illness.

> ### Rule 601. Competency to Testify in General
>
> Every person is competent to be a witness unless these rules provide other-wise. But in a civil case, state law governs the witness's competency regarding a claim or defense for which state law supplies the rule of decision.

■ ■ ■

What Does "Every Person Is Competent" Mean?—**Allen.** United States v. Allen presents issues related to the competency of a child witness. A federal statute described in *Allen* and excerpted after *Allen* also contrasts with Rule 601.

UNITED STATES v. ALLEN
127 F.3d 1292 (10th Cir. 1997)

BRORBY, J.

Allen J. appeals his adjudication of juvenile delinquency in the United States District Court for the District of New Mexico. In a non-jury trial . . . the district court adjudged Allen J. a juvenile delinquent pursuant to the Federal Juvenile Delinquency Act, after finding he had committed Aggravated Sexual Abuse . . . by knowingly using force to engage in a sex act with a juvenile. . . .

The only issue Allen J. raises on appeal is whether the trial court erred in finding the victim competent to testify.

Because district courts have the advantage of direct observation of witnesses, this court defers to their determinations regarding the competency of witnesses to testify. District courts have "broad discretion in determining the competency of a witness to testify, and [their] decisions will not be reversed in the absence of an abuse of discretion."

The competency of witnesses to testify in federal criminal trials is governed by Fed. R. Evid. 601. Rule 601 establishes a presumption "every person is competent to be a witness." This means there is no minimum or baseline mental capacity requirements witnesses must demonstrate before testifying. Indeed, the drafters of Rule 601 considered mental capacity not to be a question of competence, but to be a question "particularly suited to the [trier of fact] as one of weight and credibility."

In addition to the general presumption of competency found in Rule 601, there is a specific statutory presumption children[1] are competent to testify. 18

---

1. The statute applies only to children who have been "[a] victim of a crime of physical abuse, sexual abuse, or exploitation" or who have witnessed a crime committed against another. 18 U.S.C. §3509(a)(2)(A). This victim qualifies.

U.S.C. §3509(c)(2). The statutory scheme places a heavy burden on a party seeking to have a child declared incompetent to testify. A court may only conduct a competency examination of a child witness upon submission of a written motion by a party offering *compelling* proof of incompetency. 18 U.S.C. §3509(c)(3), (4). Even if this hurdle is met and a competency examination is held, the purpose of the examination is only to determine if the child is capable of "understanding and answering simple questions." Therefore, Allen J. has a difficult standard to meet in this case. He must demonstrate the district court abused its discretion in allowing the testimony of a child victim — a decision the rules strongly favor....

Allen J. states the test for determining the competency of a child witness is found in *United States v. Spoonhunter*, 476 F.2d 1050 (10th Cir. 1973). In *Spoonhunter*, this Circuit applied the test for determining the competency of a child witness established by the Supreme Court in *Wheeler v. United States*, 159 U.S. 523 (1895). In that case, the Court held competency "depends on the capacity and intelligence of the child, [the child's] appreciation of the difference between truth and falsehood, as well as of [the child's] duty to tell the former." This determination was to be left primarily in the hands of the trial courts. The Court, however, warned trial courts to take care when excluding witnesses, in order to avoid "staying the hand of justice."

Both *Wheeler* and *Spoonhunter*, however, pre-date the enactment of Fed. R. Evid. 601 and 18 U.S.C. §3509.[2] For this reason, the *Wheeler* test this court has relied upon for years no longer completely states the applicable standard for determining the competency of a child witness, although it may inform any examinations taking place pursuant to 18 U.S.C. §3509(c) and may help explain the type of evidence necessary to demonstrate a compelling reason for such an examination.

Allen J. argues the district court "erred in finding [the victim] competent to testify because the court never determined [the victim] understood the difference between the truth and falsehood, and the consequences of falsehood, and what was required by the oath," as required by *Spoonhunter*. Upon enactment of §3509, the rules changed. Now children are presumed competent and the party seeking to prevent a child from testifying has the burden of providing a compelling reason for questioning the child's competence.

We agree with the district court's conclusion that the evidence offered by Allen J. in his Motion to Examine Child Witness for Competence did not constitute a "compelling reason" to hold a §3509(c) competency examination. To counter the presumption favoring competency, Allen J. asserted the victim suffers mild mental retardation, possibly due to Fetal Alcohol Syndrome, which caused her to repeat first grade. As the district court correctly pointed out, even if the victim only had the mental development of a much younger child, she would still be competent to testify. The evidence offered by Allen J. did not begin to show the victim had such severe problems she could not "understand

---

2. Rule 601 was enacted in 1975, and §3509 was enacted in 1990.

and answer simple questions" 18 U.S.C. §3509(c)(8), or "understand the difference between truth and falsehood, and the consequences of falsehood, and what was required by the oath," *Spoonhunter*, 476 F.2d at 1054.

When the victim was called to testify, the court asked her a series of questions seeking to confirm she understood the importance of the oath. These questions included: "Do you understand what it is to tell the truth?" and "Do you know the difference between the truth and a lie?" The victim did not respond to the judge's questioning. The court then asked the prosecutor to try questioning the witness. The prosecutor began with simple questions ("What is your last name?", "How old are you?", and "Where do you live?"), which the victim answered. After about thirty questions along these lines, almost all of which the victim was able to answer correctly, the prosecutor shifted to questions relating to the difference between the truth and lies. Among other questions, the prosecutor asked the victim if she understood she had promised to tell the truth in court, to which the victim responded affirmatively. After this series of questions, which established the victim knew the difference between a truth and a lie, knew she was to tell the truth in court, and knew she would be punished if she told a lie, the court directed the prosecutor to proceed to the heart of her case.[3] Defense counsel objected repeatedly throughout this process and throughout the remainder of the victim's testimony.

Allen J. essentially bases his appeal on several instances in the victim's testimony where she had difficulty answering questions. The victim did not respond to the trial judge's questioning. She gave wrong answers to some of counsel's questions (*e.g.*, she said she was eleven, when she was thirteen), and she gave nonsensical answers to others (*e.g.*, she answered "true" to the question "is it good or bad to tell a lie?"). In addition, she apparently paused for long periods of time before answering some questions.

Any inconsistencies in the victim's story or problems with her testimony, however, raise questions of credibility, not competence. Allen J.'s argument boils down to an attack on credibility couched in terms of competence. The credibility of a witness is a question to be determined by the trier of fact, not this court.

Over one hundred years ago, the Supreme Court held it was proper for a five-year-old to give critical testimony in a capital case. Since that time, the trend in the law has been to grant trial courts even greater leeway in deciding if a witness is competent to testify.

---

3. This initial questioning of the victim, during which the court satisfied itself the victim understood the need to be truthful in her statements, was not a competency examination pursuant to 18 U.S.C. §3509(c). Fed. R. Evid. 603 requires every witness to declare he or she will testify truthfully. In addition to confirming for the court the victim understood the oath, the initial questioning of the victim also served "to awaken the witness' conscience and impress the witness'[s] mind with the duty to [testify truthfully]," as required by Rule 603. The type of questions asked by the prosecutor along this line, and the answers given by the victim, were comparable to examinations approved in *Spoonhunter*, 476 F.2d at 1054, and *Wheeler*, 159 U.S. at 524. For this reason, to the extent Allen J.'s argument may be construed to be an appeal based on Rule 603, we find the district court did not err and fully complied with the requirements of Rule 603.

We find nothing in the record demonstrating the district court abused its discretion in permitting the victim in this case to testify. The decision of the district court is, therefore, affirmed.

NOTES TO UNITED STATES v. ALLEN

1. *Relating Rule 601 to the Federal Child Competency Statute.* The statute described in *Allen*, shown below, establishes procedures for competency examinations and claims that it does not abrogate Rule 601. It seems to incorporate a philosophy different from Rule 601's statement that "every person" is competent.

Child Competency Statute: 18 U.S.C. §3509

(c) Competency examinations.

(1) Effect of Federal Rules of Evidence. Nothing in this subsection shall be construed to abrogate Rule 601 of the Federal Rules of Evidence.

(2) Presumption. A child is presumed to be competent.

(3) Requirement of written motion. A competency examination regarding a child witness may be conducted by the court only upon written motion and offer of proof of incompetency by a party.

(4) Requirement of compelling reasons. A competency examination regarding a child may be conducted only if the court determines, on the record, that compelling reasons exist. A child's age alone is not a compelling reason.

(5) Persons permitted to be present. The only persons who may be permitted to be present at a competency examination are

(A) the judge;

(B) the attorney for the Government;

(C) the attorney for the defendant;

(D) a court reporter; and

(E) persons whose presence, in the opinion of the court, is necessary to the welfare and well-being of the child, including the child's attorney, guardian ad litem, or adult attendant.

(6) Not before jury. A competency examination regarding a child witness shall be conducted out of the sight and hearing of a jury.

(7) Direct examination of child. Examination of a child related to competency shall normally be conducted by the court on the basis of questions submitted by the attorney for the Government and the attorney for the defendant including a party acting as an attorney pro se. The court may permit an attorney but not a party acting as an attorney pro se to examine a child directly on competency if the court is satisfied that the child will not suffer emotional trauma as a result of the examination.

> **(8) Appropriate questions.** The questions asked at the competency examination of a child shall be appropriate to the age and developmental level of the child, shall not be related to the issues at trial, and shall focus on determining the child's ability to understand and answer simple questions.
>
> **(9) Psychological and psychiatric examinations.** Psychological and psychiatric examinations to assess the competency of a child witness shall not be ordered without a showing of compelling need.

2. Required Oath or Affirmation. Barring some children from testifying can be based on a judge's application of a rule that requires all witnesses to swear or affirm that they will testify truthfully.

Rule 603. Oath or Affirmation to Testify Truthfully

Before testifying, a witness must give an oath or affirmation to testify truthfully. It must be in a form designed to impress that duty on the witness's conscience.

A trial court might decide that a child lacks the ability to satisfy the requirements of this rule, and use that conclusion as the basis for a decision to bar the child's testimony.

3. Impaired Witnesses. A witness whose low intelligence may weaken the reliability of his or her testimony is permitted to testify, with the likelihood that jurors will take the witness's attributes into account when they consider the testimony. A similar approach has been applied to witnesses who testify while intoxicated or under the influence of drugs. *See* State v. Cruz, 181 P.3d 196 (Ariz. 2008).

4. Probable Effect of Treating Everyone as Competent. The position of Rule 601, that everyone is competent, can be justified in two ways. First, in every instance where a person of weak intelligence or weak mental state might testify, the jury can be expected to identify those weaknesses and react accordingly. Second, in many instances a party would have no incentive to introduce testimony by an "incompetent" witness.

GOOD TO REMEMBER

Despite the statement in Rule 601 that everyone is competent, allowing competency inquiries reflects a consensus that it would harm the judicial system and produce unfair results if children with no understanding of past events or of the concepts of truth and falsity were allowed to be witnesses.

QUESTION 13-2. An 11-year-old child named Yolanda Youngster was present in an apartment when a young child named Vin Victim was killed. Youngster has an IQ that is significantly lower than average and may suffer from fetal alcohol syndrome. Additionally, Youngster has committed many disciplinary infractions in her school and from time to time has been suspended from school. At a trial of a defendant accused of killing Victim, the prosecution sought to introduce testimony by Youngster. The trial judge asked Youngster whether Youngster knew the difference between the truth and a lie. Youngster replied, "Sometimes," and then said, "A lie is different from the truth." The judge asked Youngster if Youngster and the judge were inside or outside, and Youngster replied, "Inside." The judge asked, "If I told you we were outside now, would that be the truth?" and Youngster replied, "No." Should the judge allow Youngster to testify?

■　■　■

After Hypnosis, Can a Person Be a Reliable Witness? — Roark. Sometimes a crime victim may be subjected to hypnosis and may discuss the crime with the hypnotist. Should a person who has been hypnotized be allowed to act as a witness at a trial? *Roark* describes and evaluates four responses to this issue that various jurisdictions have developed.

ROARK v. COMMONWEALTH

90 S.W.3d 24 (Ky. 2002)

Cooper, J.

Appellant Franklin Roark, Jr., was convicted by a Campbell Circuit Court jury of burglary in the second degree, robbery in the first degree, and sexual abuse in the first degree.... He appeals to this Court as a matter of right....

On December 19, 1997, [the victim, N.T., was] at home alone, clothed only in a robe and underwear, when she was attacked from behind by a male intruder. The intruder placed a knife against N.T.'s throat and told her to remain quiet. He then forced her to the floor and covered her head with his overcoat. N.T. lay still for a few minutes, then removed the overcoat from her face, intending to flee from the residence. However, the intruder was standing only a few feet away. She was able to observe the intruder for approximately five seconds before he exclaimed, "Now I am going to kill you," then attacked [her sexually].

The first police officer to arrive at N.T.'s residence on December 19th was Tom Lake. N.T. described the intruder to Officer Lake as a white male, 25 to 30 years old, five feet six inches to five feet seven inches tall, weighing approximate 155 pounds, and having light-colored hair. She did not mention whether his hair was thick or thin and specifically could not recall whether he had any facial hair....

Several days after the December 19th incident, N.T. was shown two photo lineups.... She was unable to identify her assailant from any of these photographs.

... In March 1998, N.T., on her own initiative and without further suggestion from the police, was hypnotized by Jill Brunner, a "certified hypnotherapist" and an acquaintance of N.T.'s husband. The hypnosis was conducted in the presence of N.T.'s husband and was audiotaped. During the hypnosis, N.T. described her assailant in various ways, *i.e.,* white male, between 25 and 30 years old, between 22 and 24 years old, 150 to 155 pounds, about 140 pounds, between five feet six inches and five feet eight inches tall, and similar in appearance to one of her neighbors. She also described him for the first time as bald and having a full beard. N.T. delivered the audio recording of the hypnotism session to the police and examined another photo lineup but to no avail.

On October 28, 1998, Appellant's residence was searched by police in regard to an unrelated investigation. During the search, the police found [items that had been stolen from N.T.'s] bedroom on December 19, 1997. On November 10, 1998, N.T. was shown another photo lineup, including, for the first time, a photograph of Appellant. She immediately identified Appellant as the person who had assaulted and robbed her on December 19, 1997. She was also presented with audiotapes of different male voices speaking words that had been spoken to her by her assailant. She immediately identified Appellant's voice as that of the assailant. . . .

The trial judge overruled Appellant's pretrial motion to suppress N.T.'s photograph and voice identifications of him as the perpetrator. . . . The trial judge also found that the . . . fact that N.T. was subjected to hypnosis prior to her photo and voice identifications were simply part of the "totality of circumstances" to be considered in determining the validity of the identification. . . .

At trial, N.T. described the person who attacked her on December 19, 1997, as a white male, between 25 and 30 years old, weighing approximately 155 pounds, and being five feet six inches to five feet seven inches tall. She also made an in-court identification of Appellant as being that person. Appellant is a white male, 43 years old, five feet five inches tall, weighing 160 pounds, with light hair, and balding. An acquaintance of Appellant testified that Appellant had a full beard during November and December 1997. . . .

Perhaps no issue in the law of evidence has been more hotly debated over the past twenty-five years than the admissibility of testimony by a witness who has been previously subjected to hypnotism. Surprisingly, this case represents our first major encounter with the issue. Our only previous decision on the subject, *Rowland v. Commonwealth,* 901 S.W.2d 871 (Ky. 1995), turned not on the reliability of hypnotically induced, refreshed or enhanced recollection but on the fact that the witness's recollection of the crucial events in that case was essentially the same after her hypnosis as before. Here, however, N.T.'s posthypnotic recollection of her assailant's appearance differed substantially from her prehypnotic recollection in that none of her previous descriptions included the facts that he was bald and had a full beard. . . .

Three aspects of hypnosis have raised substantial doubts concerning the reliability of posthypnotic testimony: (1) During hypnosis, the subject is highly susceptible to suggestions made by the hypnotist and, in fact, one of the primary medical usages of hypnotism is to alleviate pain by the power of hypnotic suggestion. (2) During hypnosis, the subject rarely admits an inability to recall and will confabulate to fill in missing details in an effort to please the hypnotist. Typically, as with recollection implanted by suggestion, neither the subject nor the hypnotist is able to later distinguish between confabulation and true recollection. (3) After hypnosis, the subject becomes "memory hardened," *i.e.*, convinced that his/her "recollections" are accurate, an overconfidence that substantially impairs any possibility of effective cross-examination, Charles A. Wright and Victor J. Gold, 27 *Fed. Prac. & Proc. Evid.* §6011, at notes 33-36, 60 (West 1990), thus implicating a criminal defendant's constitutional right of confrontation. . . .

> ***1. Per Se *Admissible*.*** Early judicial decisions refused to admit any evidence purportedly induced, refreshed or enhanced by hypnosis. The first reported case approving the admission of such evidence at trial was *Harding v. State,* 246 A.2d 302 (Md. 1968). There, the recollection of a victim of a sexual assault was "refreshed" during hypnosis induced by a police-employed hypnotist. The defendant was already under arrest and the victim knew that the primary purpose of her hypnosis was to provide evidence against him. The victim subsequently insisted that she was testifying from her own independent recollection[,] and the hypnotist denied that the victim's recollection had been tainted by any suggestions made by him during the hypnosis. The evidence was held *per se* admissible, *i.e.*, subject only to whatever weight and credibility a jury chose to give to it. . . . Most pre-1980 judicial decisions followed the *Harding* rule of *per se* admissibility. However, in the face of growing scientific skepticism about the accuracy of hypnotically induced, refreshed or enhanced recollections, *Harding*, itself, was overruled by the same court that had produced it. Only four state court jurisdictions presently follow the rule of *per se* admissibility.

> ***2. Per Se *Inadmissible*.*** Most state jurisdictions currently adhere to a modified form of the *per se* inadmissible rule first adopted in *State v. Mack,* 292 N.W.2d 764 (Minn. 1980). After examining the then-current scientific literature on the subject, *Mack* held that because hypnotically induced, refreshed or enhanced recollection was regarded as unreliable in the relevant scientific community, *i.e.*, psychology and psychiatry, it was inadmissible as evidence under the "scientific acceptance" test enunciated in *Frye v. United States,* 293 F. 1013 (D.C. Cir. 1923). . . . Most states that follow *Mack* exclude evidence of facts only remembered after hypnosis but admit evidence of facts remembered *and related* before hypnosis. The burden is on the proponent of the evidence to prove that the recollection predated the hypnosis. At present, twenty-six states adhere to some form of the *per se* inadmissible rule.

This apparent trend, however, must be viewed in light of two major post-*Mack* decisions by the United States Supreme Court. In *Rock v. Arkansas,* 483 U.S. 44, 107 S. Ct. 2704, 97 L. Ed. 2d 37 (1987), that Court held that the right of a defendant to testify in his/her own defense cannot be precluded even if the testimony has been induced, refreshed or enhanced by hypnosis — and suggested that the same might be true with respect to an "arbitrary" rule that precludes a criminal defendant from presenting the testimony of other witnesses in support of his/her defense. "This rule operates to the detriment of any defendant who undergoes hypnosis, without regard to the reasons for it, the circumstances under which it took place, or any independent verification [corroboration] of the information it produced." Although the Court ultimately opted for no position with respect to the admissibility of testimony of a previously hypnotized witness other than the defendant, the same logic would seem to apply as well to the *per se* exclusion of the testimony of any witness, including the victim of the crime, *e.g.,* N.T.

Virtually every jurisdiction that has adopted the per se inadmissible rule has, like *Mack*, arrived at its ultimate conclusion by application of the *Frye* test. That test, however, was abrogated for Federal Courts under Federal Rule of Evidence (FRE) 702 and replaced by the more liberal *Daubert* test, *Daubert v. Merrell Dow Pharmaceuticals, Inc.,* 509 U.S. 579 (1993), under which acceptance within the relevant scientific community is only one factor to be considered in determining the reliability of scientific evidence. . . . Of course, that does not mean that a different result will be obtained but only that a different test will be applied. Note that both the *Frye* and *Daubert* tests are primarily tests of admissibility, *i.e.,* posthypnosis evidence is admissible if posthypnotic recollection is determined to be scientifically reliable. Another view, however, is that the issue is not so much one of scientific reliability as one of the competency of the witness to give accurate testimony. Professors Wright and Gold espouse this view, and three state courts, California, Illinois and Missouri[,] have held that the memory of a person subjected to hypnosis is so tainted thereby that he/she is incompetent to testify.

3. Procedural Safeguards. A third approach with respect to the use of hypnotically induced, refreshed or enhanced recollection is that such evidence is admissible if certain safeguards were applied to the conduct of the hypnotism session. In *State v. Hurd,* 86 N.J. 525, 432 A.2d 86 (1981), it was held that posthypnosis evidence is admissible if the following procedural safeguards were followed:

(1) The person conducting the hypnosis was a trained psychologist or psychiatrist;

(2) The professional conducting the session was independent of the parties;

(3) Information given to the hypnotist prior to the session was recorded;

(4) Before the hypnosis was induced, the hypnotist obtained a detailed description of the event from the subject;

(5) All contacts between the hypnotist and the subject were recorded;

(6) No one except the hypnotist and the subject were present during the hypnotism.

Six states currently follow the "procedural safeguards" rule of admissibility, five by judicial decision and one by statute. . . .

4. Totality of Circumstances. A fourth theory that currently has support in nine state courts [*see, e.g., People v. Romero,* 745 P.2d 1003 (Colo. 1987)] and a growing number of federal courts is a hybrid that neither automatically admits nor excludes posthypnosis evidence but determines admissibility on a case-by-case basis from the "totality of the circumstances." An illustrative list of those circumstances could include: (1) whether the purpose of the hypnosis was therapeutic or investigative, the latter tending to indicate pressure on the subject to remember; (2) whether procedural safeguards were employed with respect to the hypnotic session; (3) whether independent corroborating evidence exists to substantiate the witness's refreshed recollection; (4) whether, as in *Rowland v. Commonwealth, supra,* the witness's posthypnotic recollection was substantially the same as the witness's prehypnotic recollection as actually related; (5) the likelihood that the witness's memory has been tainted by outside influences (as in *Harding v. State, supra,* where the sexual assault victim identified after hypnosis the person who was already accused of assaulting her), or not [as in cases] where the subject described matters unknown to the hypnotist); and (6) whether, under Evidence Rule 403, the probative value of the evidence is substantially outweighed by its prejudicial effect. Ordinarily, admissibility will be determined at an *in limine* hearing at which the proponent of the evidence must prove its reliability by a preponderance of the evidence. . . .

. . . Professors Wright and Gold also discern fewer flaws with this approach than with the other three approaches.

> While each of the three other approaches focus on important issues, they do so to the exclusion of other important considerations. For example, the per se competent approach is most concerned with the potential loss of valuable evidence and the effect a rule of incompetence might have on the investigatory use of hypnosis. But that approach could in some circumstances permit the admission of clearly unreliable testimony. On the other hand, the per se incompetent approach is preoccupied with the dangers of hypnosis. As a result, application of that approach could exclude valuable testimony which may be just as reliable as testimony from witnesses who have not undergone hypnosis. Finally, the *Hurd* approach unduly focuses on a limited number of procedural safeguards. Thus, testimony may be disallowed even where other circumstances suggest it is reliable and testimony may be permitted even where other circumstances suggest it is unreliable.

[Wright and Gold, *supra,* §6011, following note 223.]

We agree and conclude that the "totality of circumstances" approach is the soundest approach thus far developed for evaluating the admissibility of evidence that is the product of an hypnotically induced, refreshed or enhanced recollection. Applying that test to the facts of this case, at least three circumstances militate against the admission of N.T.'s posthypnotic identification and testimony. (1) The purpose of the hypnosis was investigative, not therapeutic, and N.T. was under substantial pressure, albeit primarily self-imposed, to identify her assailant. (2) N.T.'s posthypnotic recollection of her assailant's appearance was not substantially the same as her prehypnotic recollection. (3) No procedural safeguards were employed with respect to the conduct of the hypnotism, specifically, (a) the hypnotist was neither a psychologist nor a psychiatrist, but a "certified hypnotherapist" who admittedly was not qualified to perform a forensic hypnotism suitable for a criminal investigation; (b) the hypnotist was not independent, but was an acquaintance of N.T.'s family; (c) no information given to the hypnotist prior to the hypnotism was recorded; (d) the hypnotist did not obtain a detailed description of the event from N.T. before conducting the hypnotism; (e) all contacts between the hypnotist and N.T. were not recorded; and (f) another person, N.T.'s husband, was present during the entire hypnotism.

At least two circumstances militate in favor of admission of N.T.'s posthypnotic identification and testimony. (1) There is little likelihood that N.T.'s memory was tainted by suggestion or confabulation. Appellant had not been identified as a suspect at the time the hypnotism took place; thus, the fact that he was bald and had a full beard was unknown to the hypnotist. (2) N.T.'s subsequent identification of Appellant as the perpetrator was corroborated by independent evidence that Appellant was in possession of property stolen from N.T.'s residence on the occasion of the assault. The first of these two circumstances diminishes the significance of the first and third circumstances militating against admission, *i.e.*, investigative purpose and no procedural safeguards; and the second of these two circumstances diminishes the significance of the second circumstance militating against admission, *i.e.*, differences between prehypnotic and posthypnotic recollections.

Thus, we conclude that the trial judge's admission of N.T.'s posthypnotic identification and testimony in this case was neither clearly erroneous, nor an abuse of discretion. . . .

Accordingly, the judgment of conviction and sentences imposed by the Campbell Circuit Court are affirmed.

NOTES TO ROARK v. COMMONWEALTH

1. *Scientific Acceptance.* The per se exclusion has been justified in the context of jurisdictions' doctrines on the admissibility of scientific evidence, discussed in the next chapter. Those doctrines are usually applied to control testimony by expert witnesses based on their application of scientific principles to facts.

2. *Legitimacy of Exclusion.* The *Roark* court explains that in addition to relying on doctrines about scientific evidence, courts may base an exclusion decision on general competency grounds. In taking the competency approach, in the face of a rule that states everyone is competent, a trial court might support that action by referring to Rule 602, requiring personal knowledge.

QUESTION 13-3. Sandra Slavik and Ruth Kay Wall suffer from multiple personality disorder, now known as dissociative identity disorder (DID). They testified in suits they brought against personnel of a mental health care facility, claiming that they had been the victims of sexual abuse by those personnel. Both Slavik and Wall dissociate and manifest alternative identities, commonly known as alters. Slavik calls herself "Mary," and her alters include "Elizabeth," "Kate," and "Amelia." Wall's alters include "Kay," "Michael," "Daniel," "the Silent One," "the Destroyer," and "the Little Girls." When the alters spoke, the women were dissociating.

The trial court decided that Slavik and Wall were competent to testify while in a dissociative state. The court did not do a preliminary competency determination on each of the alters, but Slavik's and Wall's counsel and defense counsel questioned the alters about their ability to tell the truth. Some of the alters who testified were only three or four years old.

Segment 4: attacking witness competency

Experts testified that persons with DID can be highly suggestible. To the extent that inaccurate information is "recalled" during dissociative episodes, the person's belief in the memory's validity is increased.

Discuss whether the trial court's ruling on competency was proper.

D   COMPETENCY: STATUS

The oldest and now-rejected competency doctrines prohibited anyone from testifying in a case in which he or she had an interest. One rationale for this doctrine was the idea that anyone who had an interest in a case would have a powerful incentive to lie, and the state should not put a person in a position where the person would be forced to violate either that strong aspect of human nature or, on the other hand, moral and religious principles. Currently "spousal incompetency" is an important status-based incompetency, as are rules concerning judges, jurors, and claimants against estates.

Dead Man's Statutes. Statutes known as Dead Man's statutes are in force in many states. They apply in suits against estates to bar testimony by a claimant against the estate that would describe any assertions made by the estate's decedent. The theory of these statutes is that lying about what a dead person said is easy and may seem relatively risk-free to a potential perjurer. Opponents of these statutes point out that anyone can lie about anything, and that denying plaintiffs the opportunity to introduce important testimony about their claims may be just as unfair as opening estates to the risk of false claims.

The following three statutes represent a range of treatments of this problem. They vary in terms of admissibility of testimony about a decedent's statements, corroboration requirements, and grant to an estate of an evidentiary benefit if a claimant is allowed to testify about a decedent's statements.

Indiana Code Ann. 34-45-2-4 Proceedings involving executor or administrator

(a) This section applies to suits or proceedings:

(1) in which an executor or administrator is a party;

(2) involving matters that occurred during the lifetime of the decedent; and

(3) where a judgment or allowance may be made or rendered for or against the estate represented by the executor or administrator.

(b) This section does not apply in a proceeding to contest the validity of a will or a proceeding to contest the validity of a trust.

(c) This section does not apply to a custodian or other qualified witness to the extent the witness seeks to introduce evidence that is otherwise admissible under Indiana Rule of Evidence 803(6).

(d) Except as provided in subsection (e), a person: (1) who is a necessary party to the issue or record; and (2) whose interest is adverse to the estate; is not a competent witness as to matters against the estate.

(e) In cases where: (1) a deposition of the decedent was taken; or (2) the decedent has previously testified as to the matter; and the decedent's testimony or deposition can be used as evidence for the executor or administrator, the adverse party is a competent witness as to any matters embraced in the deposition or testimony.

Colo. Rev. Stat. Ann. §13-90-102. Testimony concerning oral statements made by person incapable of testifying — when allowed

(1) Subject to the law of evidence, in any civil action or proceeding in which an oral statement of a person incapable of testifying is sought to be admitted into evidence, each party and person in interest with a party shall be allowed to testify regarding the oral statement if:

(a) The statement was made under oath at a time when such person was competent to testify;

(b) The testimony concerning the oral statement is corroborated by material evidence of a trustworthy nature;

(c) The opposing party introduces uncorroborated evidence of related communications through a party or person in interest with a party; or

(d) Such party or person testifies against his or her own interests.

(2) Questions of admissibility that arise under this section shall be determined by the court as a matter of law.

> **Va. Code. Ann. §8.01-397. Corroboration required and evidence receivable when one party incapable of testifying**
>
> In an action by or against a person who, from any cause, is incapable of testifying, or by or against the committee, trustee, executor, administrator, heir, or other representative of the person so incapable of testifying, no judgment or decree shall be rendered in favor of an adverse or interested party founded on his uncorroborated testimony. In any such action, whether such adverse party testifies or not, all entries, memoranda, and declarations by the party so incapable of testifying made while he was capable, relevant to the matter in issue, may be received as evidence in all proceedings including without limitation those to which a person under a disability is a party. The phrase "from any cause" as used in this section shall not include situations in which the party who is incapable of testifying has rendered himself unable to testify by an intentional self-inflicted injury.

QUESTION 13-4. You have been consulted by Harry Helper, a nurse's aide, who worked for Oliver Oldman as a live-in companion and housekeeper. Helper has told you that in June 2011 he was hurt in a fall in Oldman's house that was caused by a defective stair tread. Oldman died in September 2011. According to Helper, Oldman immediately apologized for the incident and said he had known the stair tread was broken. According to a handyman in the neighborhood, in May 2011 Oldman asked him how much he would charge to repair a broken stair tread. Oldman's son recalls a conversation in July 2011 in which Oldman told him he had recently seen Helper trip on his own feet and get hurt near the house's staircase. Helper would like to sue Oldman's estate, seeking damages for his injury. What evidence issues are raised by the information you have about this possible case, under the three statutes reproduced above?

> **GOOD TO REMEMBER**
>
> Dead Man's statutes nowadays reflect a range of views. They may fully prohibit a claimant from being a witness, may allow that testimony only with corroboration, or may balance that corroborated testimony by allowing introduction of the decedent's hearsay statements. Some jurisdictions have repealed these statutes entirely.

* * *

Can You Testify Against Your Spouse? — **Trammel.** In the following case, the United States Supreme Court scrutinized the spousal incompetency doctrine. This rule sometimes prevents a spouse from testifying against his or her spouse. It is sometimes confused with the well-known privilege for confidential marital communications. A privilege blocks someone from testifying about any confidential statements the privilege covers. The spousal incompetency concept blocks a spouse completely from being a witness. So, instead of just stopping a spouse from revealing confidential communications, the incompetency doctrine prevents a spouse from testifying about anything (confidential statements, nonconfidential statements, and knowledge acquired in any way).

TRAMMEL v. UNITED STATES
445 U.S. 40 (1980)

Mr. Chief Justice BURGER delivered the opinion of the Court.

We granted certiorari to consider whether an accused may invoke the privilege against adverse spousal testimony so as to exclude the voluntary testimony of his wife. This calls for a re-examination of *Hawkins* v. *United States*, 358 U.S. 74 (1958).

On March 10, 1976, petitioner Otis Trammel was indicted with two others, Edwin Lee Roberts and Joseph Freeman, for importing heroin into the United States from Thailand and the Philippine Islands and for conspiracy to import heroin. . . . The indictment also named six unindicted co-conspirators, including petitioner's wife Elizabeth Ann Trammel.

According to the indictment, petitioner and his wife flew from the Philippines to California in August 1975, carrying with them a quantity of heroin. Freeman and Roberts assisted them in its distribution. Elizabeth Trammel then traveled to Thailand where she purchased another supply of the drug. On November 3, 1975, with four ounces of heroin on her person, she boarded a plane for the United States. During a routine customs search in Hawaii, she was searched, the heroin was discovered, and she was arrested. After discussions with Drug Enforcement Administration agents, she agreed to cooperate with the Government.

Prior to trial on this indictment, petitioner moved to sever his case from that of Roberts and Freeman. He advised the court that the Government intended to call his wife as an adverse witness and asserted his claim to a privilege to prevent her from testifying against him. At a hearing on the motion, Mrs. Trammel was called as a Government witness under a grant of use immunity. She testified that she and petitioner were married in May 1975 and that they remained married. She explained that her cooperation with the Government was based on assurances that she would be given lenient treatment. She then described, in considerable detail, her role and that of her husband in the heroin distribution conspiracy.

After hearing this testimony, the District Court ruled that Mrs. Trammel could testify in support of the Government's case to any act she observed during the marriage and to any communication "made in the presence of a third person"; however, confidential communications between petitioner and his wife were held to be privileged and inadmissible. The motion to sever was denied.

At trial, Elizabeth Trammel testified within the limits of the court's pretrial ruling; her testimony, as the Government concedes, constituted virtually its entire case against petitioner. He was found guilty on both the substantive and conspiracy charges and sentenced to an indeterminate term of years pursuant to the Federal Youth Corrections Act.

In the Court of Appeals[,] petitioner's only claim of error was that the admission of the adverse testimony of his wife, over his objection, contravened this Court's teaching in *Hawkins* v. *United States*, and therefore constituted reversible error. The Court of Appeals rejected this contention. It concluded that *Hawkins* did not prohibit "the voluntary testimony of a spouse who appears as an unindicted co-conspirator under grant of immunity from the Government in return for her testimony."

The privilege claimed by petitioner has ancient roots. Writing in 1628, Lord Coke observed that "it hath been resolved by the Justices that a wife cannot be produced either against or for her husband." This spousal disqualification sprang from two canons of medieval jurisprudence: first, the rule that an accused was not permitted to testify in his own behalf because of his interest in the proceeding; second, the concept that husband and wife were one, and that since the woman had no recognized separate legal existence, the husband was that one. From those two now long-abandoned doctrines, it followed that what was inadmissible from the lips of the defendant-husband was also inadmissible from his wife.

Despite its medieval origins, this rule of spousal disqualification remained intact in most common-law jurisdictions well into the 19th century. It was applied by this Court in *Stein* v. *Bowman*, 13 Pet. 209, 220-223 (1839), in *Graves* v. *United States*, 150 U.S. 118 (1893), and again in *Jin Fuey Moy* v. *United States*, 254 U.S. 189, 195 (1920), where it was deemed so well established a proposition as to "hardly [require] mention." Indeed, it was not until 1933, in *Funk* v. *United States*, 290 U.S. 371, that this Court abolished the testimonial disqualification in the federal courts, so as to permit the spouse of a defendant to testify in the defendant's behalf. *Funk*, however, left undisturbed the rule that either spouse could prevent the other from giving adverse testimony. The rule thus evolved into one of privilege rather than one of absolute disqualification.

The modern justification for this privilege against adverse spousal testimony is its perceived role in fostering the harmony and sanctity of the marriage relationship. Notwithstanding this benign purpose, the rule was sharply criticized. Professor Wigmore termed it "the merest anachronism in legal theory and an indefensible obstruction to truth in practice." 8 Wigmore §2228, at 221. The Committee on Improvements in the Law of Evidence of the American Bar Association called for its abolition. 63 American Bar Association Reports 594-595 (1938). In its place, Wigmore and others suggested a privilege protecting only private marital communications, modeled on the privilege between priest and penitent, attorney and client, and physician and patient.

These criticisms influenced the American Law Institute, which, in its 1942 Model Code of Evidence, advocated a privilege for marital confidences, but expressly rejected a rule vesting in the defendant the right to exclude all adverse testimony of his spouse. In 1953 the Uniform Rules of Evidence, drafted by the

National Conference of Commissioners on Uniform State Laws, followed a similar course; it limited the privilege to confidential communications and "[abolished] the rule, still existing in some states, and largely a sentimental relic, of not requiring one spouse to testify against the other in a criminal action." See Rule 23 (2) and comments. Several state legislatures enacted similarly patterned provisions into law.

In *Hawkins* v. *United States*, 358 U.S. 74 (1958), this Court considered the continued vitality of the privilege against adverse spousal testimony in the federal courts. There the District Court had permitted petitioner's wife, over his objection, to testify against him. With one questioning concurring opinion, the Court held the wife's testimony inadmissible; it took note of the critical comments that the common-law rule had engendered, but chose not to abandon it. Also rejected was the Government's suggestion that the Court modify the privilege by vesting it in the witness-spouse, with freedom to testify or not independent of the defendant's control. The Court viewed this proposed modification as antithetical to the widespread belief, evidenced in the rules then in effect in a majority of the States and in England, "that the law should not force or encourage testimony which might alienate husband and wife, or further inflame existing domestic differences."

Hawkins, then, left the federal privilege for adverse spousal testimony where it found it, continuing "a rule which bars the testimony of one spouse against the other unless both consent."[7] However, in so doing, the Court made clear that its decision was not meant to "foreclose whatever changes in the rule may eventually be dictated by 'reason and experience.'"

The Federal Rules of Evidence acknowledge the authority of the federal courts to continue the evolutionary development of testimonial privileges in federal criminal trials "governed by the principles of the common law as they may be interpreted . . . in the light of reason and experience." Fed. Rule Evid. 501. The general mandate of Rule 501 was substituted by the Congress for a set of privilege rules drafted by the Judicial Conference Advisory Committee on Rules of Evidence and approved by the Judicial Conference of the United States and by this Court. That proposal defined nine specific privileges, including a husband-wife privilege which would have codified the *Hawkins* rule and eliminated the privilege for confidential marital communications. In rejecting the proposed Rules and enacting Rule 501, Congress manifested an affirmative intention not to freeze the law of privilege. Its purpose rather was to "provide the courts with the flexibility to develop rules of privilege on a case-by-case basis," and to leave the door open to change.

Although Rule 501 confirms the authority of the federal courts to reconsider the continued validity of the *Hawkins* rule, the long history of the privilege

---

7. The decision in *Wyatt* recognized an exception to *Hawkins* for cases in which one spouse commits a crime against the other. This exception, placed on the ground of necessity, was a longstanding one at common law. It has been expanded since then to include crimes against the spouse's property, and in recent years crimes against children of either spouse. Similar exceptions have been found to the confidential marital communications privilege.

suggests that it ought not to be casually cast aside. That the privilege is one affecting marriage, home, and family relationships — already subject to much erosion in our day — also counsels caution. At the same time, we cannot escape the reality that the law on occasion adheres to doctrinal concepts long after the reasons which gave them birth have disappeared and after experience suggests the need for change. . . .

Since 1958, when *Hawkins* was decided, support for the privilege against adverse spousal testimony has been eroded further. Thirty-one jurisdictions, including Alaska and Hawaii, then allowed an accused a privilege to prevent adverse spousal testimony. 358 U.S., at 81, n. 3 (Stewart, J., concurring). The number has now declined to 24.[9] In 1974, the National Conference on Uniform State Laws revised its Uniform Rules of Evidence, but again rejected the *Hawkins* rule in favor of a limited privilege for confidential communications. See Uniform Rules of Evidence, Rule 504. That proposed rule has been enacted in Arkansas, North Dakota, and Oklahoma — each of which in 1958 permitted an accused to exclude adverse spousal testimony. The trend in state law toward divesting the accused of the privilege to bar adverse spousal testimony has special relevance because the laws of marriage and domestic relations are concerns traditionally reserved to the states. Scholarly criticism of the *Hawkins* rule has also continued unabated.

Testimonial exclusionary rules and privileges contravene the fundamental principle that "'the public . . . has a right to every man's evidence.'" *United States v. Bryan*, 339 U.S. 323, 331 (1950). As such, they must be strictly construed and accepted "only to the very limited extent that permitting a refusal to testify or excluding relevant evidence has a public good transcending the normally predominant principle of utilizing all rational means for ascertaining truth." *Elkins v. United States*, 364 U.S. 206, 234 (1960) (Frankfurter, J., dissenting). Here we must decide whether the privilege against adverse spousal testimony promotes sufficiently important interests to outweigh the need for probative evidence in the administration of criminal justice.

It is essential to remember that the *Hawkins* privilege is not needed to protect information privately disclosed between husband and wife in the confidence of the marital relationship — once described by this Court as "the best solace of human existence." *Stein v. Bowman*, 13 Pet., at 223. Those confidences are privileged under the independent rule protecting confidential marital communications. The *Hawkins* privilege is invoked, not to exclude private marital communications, but rather to exclude evidence of criminal acts and of communications made in the presence of third persons.

---

9. Eight States provide that one spouse is incompetent to testify against the other in a criminal proceeding. . . .

Sixteen States provide a privilege against adverse spousal testimony and vest the privilege in both spouses or in the defendant-spouse alone. . . .

Nine States entitle the witness-spouse alone to assert a privilege against adverse spousal testimony. . . .

The remaining 17 States have abolished the privilege in criminal cases. . . .

No other testimonial privilege sweeps so broadly. The privileges between priest and penitent, attorney and client, and physician and patient limit protection to private communications. These privileges are rooted in the imperative need for confidence and trust. The priest-penitent privilege recognizes the human need to disclose to a spiritual counselor, in total and absolute confidence, what are believed to be flawed acts or thoughts and to receive priestly consolation and guidance in return. The lawyer-client privilege rests on the need for the advocate and counselor to know all that relates to the client's reasons for seeking representation if the professional mission is to be carried out. Similarly, the physician must know all that a patient can articulate in order to identify and to treat disease; barriers to full disclosure would impair diagnosis and treatment.

The *Hawkins* rule stands in marked contrast to these three privileges. Its protection is not limited to confidential communications; rather it permits an accused to exclude all adverse spousal testimony. As Jeremy Bentham observed more than a century and a half ago, such a privilege goes far beyond making "every man's house his castle," and permits a person to convert his house into "a den of thieves." 5 Rationale of Judicial Evidence 340 (1827). It "secures, to every man, one safe and unquestionable and ever ready accomplice for every imaginable crime." *Id.*, at 338.

The ancient foundations for so sweeping a privilege have long since disappeared. Nowhere in the common-law world — indeed in any modern society — is a woman regarded as chattel or demeaned by denial of a separate legal identity and the dignity associated with recognition as a whole human being. Chip by chip, over the years those archaic notions have been cast aside so that "[no] longer is the female destined solely for the home and the rearing of the family, and only the male for the marketplace and the world of ideas." *Stanton* v. *Stanton*, 421 U.S. 7, 14-15 (1975).

The contemporary justification for affording an accused such a privilege is also unpersuasive. When one spouse is willing to testify against the other in a criminal proceeding — whatever the motivation — their relationship is almost certainly in disrepair; there is probably little in the way of marital harmony for the privilege to preserve. In these circumstances, a rule of evidence that permits an accused to prevent adverse spousal testimony seems far more likely to frustrate justice than to foster family peace.[12] Indeed, there is reason to believe that vesting the privilege in the accused could actually undermine the marital relationship. For example, in a case such as this, the Government is unlikely to offer a wife immunity and lenient treatment if it knows that her husband can prevent her from giving adverse testimony. If the Government is dissuaded from making such an offer, the privilege can have the untoward effect of permitting one spouse to escape justice at the expense of the other. It hardly seems conducive

---

12. It is argued that abolishing the privilege will permit the Government to come between husband and wife, pitting one against the other. That, too, misses the mark. Neither *Hawkins*, nor any other privilege, prevents the Government from enlisting one spouse to give information concerning the other or to aid in the other's apprehension. It is only the spouse's testimony in the courtroom that is prohibited.

to the preservation of the marital relation to place a wife in jeopardy solely by virtue of her husband's control over her testimony.

Our consideration of the foundations for the privilege and its history satisfy us that "reason and experience" no longer justify so sweeping a rule as that found acceptable by the Court in *Hawkins*. Accordingly, we conclude that the existing rule should be modified so that the witness-spouse alone has a privilege to refuse to testify adversely; the witness may be neither compelled to testify nor foreclosed from testifying. This modification—vesting the privilege in the witness-spouse—furthers the important public interest in marital harmony without unduly burdening legitimate law enforcement needs.

Here, petitioner's spouse chose to testify against him. That she did so after a grant of immunity and assurances of lenient treatment does not render her testimony involuntary. Accordingly, the District Court and the Court of Appeals were correct in rejecting petitioner's claim of privilege, and the judgment of the Court of Appeals is *Affirmed*.

NOTES TO TRAMMEL v. UNITED STATES

1. *Married Life.* In terms of the possibility that involvement in a criminal investigation might place stress on a husband and wife, does the *Trammel* opinion argue that its result would lessen that stress? If so, are there arguments in the opposite direction? The Court wrote: "If the Government is dissuaded from making such an offer, the privilege can have the untoward effect of permitting one spouse to escape justice at the expense of the other." This analysis ignores the possibility that when the government makes an offer to a spouse to encourage that spouse to testify, the testifying spouse might "escape justice" in exchange for offering testimony.

2. *Range of Policy Choices.* Between maintaining the spousal incompetency doctrine in its common law form and, on the other hand, abrogating it completely, there are many middle choices. One is adopted in *Trammel*. As the *Trammel* opinion noted, states have adopted many approaches, as the following examples indicate.

Mississippi Rules of Evidence — Rule 601

Every person is competent to be a witness except as restricted by the following:

(a) In all instances where one spouse is a party litigant the other spouse shall not be competent as a witness without the consent of both, except as provided in Rule 601(a)(1) or Rule 601(a)(2):

(1) Husbands and wives may be introduced by each other in all cases, civil or criminal, and shall be competent witnesses in their own behalf, as against each other, in all controversies between them;

(2) Either spouse is a competent witness and may be compelled to testify against the other in any criminal prosecution of either husband or wife for a criminal act against any child, for contributing to the neglect or delinquency of a child, or desertion or nonsupport of children under the age of sixteen (16) years, or abandonment of children.

...

Colo. Rev. Stat. 13-90-107. Who may not testify without consent

(1) There are particular relations in which it is the policy of the law to encourage confidence and to preserve it inviolate; therefore, a person shall not be examined as a witness in the following cases:

(a)(I) Except as otherwise provided in section 14-13-310(4), C.R.S., a husband shall not be examined for or against his wife without her consent nor a wife for or against her husband without his consent; nor during the marriage or afterward shall either be examined without the consent of the other as to any communications made by one to the other during the marriage; but this exception does not apply to a civil action or proceeding by one against the other, a criminal action or proceeding for a crime committed by one against the other, or a criminal action or proceeding against one or both spouses when the alleged offense occurred prior to the date of the parties' marriage. However, this exception shall not attach if the otherwise privileged information is communicated after the marriage.

(II) The privilege described in this paragraph (a) does not apply to class 1, 2, or 3 felonies [with minimum punishments of four years of imprisonment]. In this instance, during the marriage or afterward, a husband shall not be examined for or against his wife as to any communications intended to be made in confidence and made by one to the other during the marriage without his consent, and a wife shall not be examined for or against her husband as to any communications intended to be made in confidence and made by one to the other without her consent.

■   ■   ■

Limited Topics for Testimony by Jurors — Kendrick. A judge may not be a witness at a trial over which he or she presides, as Rule 605 makes clear. Similarly, Rule 606 provides that a juror may not give testimony before his or her fellow jurors. These concepts are simple. Another aspect of control over jurors' competency is less straightforward. Rule 606(b) limits the type of testimony a juror may give in connection with an inquiry into the validity of a verdict.

Rule 605. Judge's Competency as a Witness

The presiding judge may not testify as a witness at the trial. A party need not object to preserve the issue.

Rule 606. Juror's Competency as a Witness

(a) **At the Trial.** A juror may not testify as a witness before the other jurors at the trial. If a juror is called to testify, the court must give a party an opportunity to object outside the jury's presence.

(b) **During an Inquiry into the Validity of a Verdict or Indictment.**

(1) *Prohibited Testimony or Other Evidence.* During an inquiry into the validity of a verdict or indictment, a juror may not testify about any statement made or incident that occurred during the jury's deliberations; the effect of anything on that juror's or another juror's vote; or any juror's mental processes concerning the verdict or indictment. The court may not receive a juror's affidavit or evidence of a juror's statement on these matters.

(2) *Exceptions.* A juror may testify about whether:

(A) extraneous prejudicial information was improperly brought to the jury's attention;

(B) an outside influence was improperly brought to bear on any juror; or

(C) a mistake was made in entering the verdict on the verdict form.

Kendrick examines Rule 606(b) and its exceptions. In particular, it considers what meaning to give to the rule's expression "extraneous prejudicial information." Ideally jurors would evaluate only the information presented at the trial. However, jurors necessarily use their own experiences to understand that information. In *Kendrick* one juror's personal knowledge was outside the range of information that typical jurors might be expected to have. The court applied Rule 606(b) to determine whether testimony or an affidavit about that was proper.

KENDRICK v. PIPPIN

252 P.3d 1052 (Colo. 2011)

BENDER, C. J.

This case arises out of an automobile accident that occurred in winter driving conditions. At trial, a jury found that the defendant, Holly Pippin, was not negligent in causing the accident in which her vehicle struck that of the plaintiff, Cheryl Kendrick. Kendrick appealed to the court of appeals, asserting that [the trial court erred in its] decision to deny Kendrick's motion for a new trial based on an allegation of juror misconduct. The court of appeals affirmed the trial court. . . .

The jury found that Kendrick incurred injuries, damages, or losses, but that Pippin was not negligent. Kendrick filed a motion for a new trial based on allegations that, during deliberations, the jury foreperson, a licensed engineer, performed calculations regarding Pippin's speed, distance, and reaction time which she shared with the other jurors. In support of the motion, Kendrick offered an affidavit from a jury consultant whom Kendrick had retained to interview the jurors following the verdict. The affidavit stated: (1) the foreperson had informed the other jurors that she was an engineer; (2) the foreperson had provided the consultant with the calculations, but the consultant had not written them down; (3) the foreperson had concluded that Pippin did not have enough time to avoid the collision; and (4) one juror said that the jurors had found the foreperson's calculations helpful. The trial court denied the motion for a new trial, declining to hold a hearing. . . .

Kendrick contends that, by sharing her calculations with the other jurors, the jury foreperson exposed the jury to extraneous prejudicial information and, therefore, the trial court should have ordered an evidentiary hearing on the allegations of juror misconduct. Supporting the court of appeals' decision, Pippin asserts that the foreperson did not introduce extraneous prejudicial information but, rather, applied her generally applicable, preexisting knowledge to the evidence admitted at trial. . . .

When a party seeks to impeach a verdict based on an allegation of juror misconduct, the party has a limited right to an evidentiary hearing on those allegations. Our law "strongly disfavors any juror testimony impeaching a verdict" but, rather, seeks to "promote finality of verdicts, shield verdicts from impeachment, and protect jurors from harassment and coercion." *People v. Harlan,* 109 P.3d 616, 624 (Colo. 2005). This policy is codified in CRE 606(b), which prohibits a juror from testifying or a court from receiving an "affidavit or evidence of any statement by [a] juror" about any "matter or statement occurring during the course of the jury's deliberations" or about "the effect of anything upon his or any other juror's mind or emotions." The rule allows juror testimony regarding a verdict only in three limited situations, to determine whether: (1) extraneous prejudicial information was improperly brought to the jurors' attention; (2) any outside influence was improperly brought to bear upon any juror; or (3) there was a mistake in entering the verdict onto the verdict form.

Of the three exceptions to CRE 606(b), Kendrick alleges only that extraneous prejudicial information was improperly before the jury. For a court to set aside a verdict on the basis of this type of juror misconduct, a party must show both that extraneous information was improperly before the jury and that the extraneous information posed the reasonable possibility of prejudice to the defendant. A trial court may hold a hearing to decide whether there is a reasonable possibility that the misconduct affected the jury's verdict. However, in order to satisfy CRE 606(b), before granting a hearing the court must first conclude that the party alleging misconduct has presented competent evidence that extraneous prejudicial information was before the jury. . . .

In previous cases, we considered what constitutes extraneous prejudicial information. We have instructed that "jurors are required to consider only the evidence admitted at trial and the law as given in the trial court's instructions" and, therefore, "any information that is not properly received into evidence or included in the court's instructions is extraneous to the case and improper for juror consideration." Applying this instruction, we have held that legal content and specific factual information learned from outside the record and relevant to the issues in a case constitute extraneous prejudicial information improperly before a jury.

For instance, in *Harlan,* we held it improper for jurors to consult a Bible for passages related to the death penalty. We reasoned that the passages constituted extraneous prejudicial information because "[t]he trial court had not admitted these materials into evidence, nor did the court's instructions allow their use." Similarly, in *Wiser* [*v. People*, 732 P.2d 1139 (Colo. 1987)], we held it improper for a juror to consult a dictionary for a definition of "burglary" because "[j]urors are required to follow only the law as it is given in the court's instructions."

While our prior decisions make clear that jurors may not consider legal content and specific factual information relevant to the case if they obtained that information outside of the judicial proceeding, this court has not considered whether jurors may use their own professional and educational experiences to inform their deliberations. The broader proposition that jurors may apply their general knowledge and everyday experience when deciding cases is generally undisputed.

Of the jurisdictions that have considered the particular issue of whether jurors may use their professional and educational expertise to inform their deliberations, courts have split over the issue. A minority of courts prohibit jurors from applying their specialized knowledge to deliberations and view a juror's professional or educational expertise as extraneous prejudicial information. . . .

By contrast, a majority of courts have held that a juror's intradeliberational statements, when based on personal knowledge and experience, do not constitute extraneous prejudicial information. Representative of this approach is *State v. Mann,* 131 N.M. 459 (2002). In *Mann,* a juror who possessed a background in engineering and physics used the evidence presented at trial to perform a "fairly simple five-step probability calculation" and, based on that calculation, informed the other jurors that there was only a one-in-twenty million chance the accident had occurred in the way the defendant claimed. The Supreme Court of New Mexico held that this was not juror misconduct, stating that "jurors may properly rely on their background, including professional and educational experience, in order to inform their deliberations" and may communicate their opinions to fellow jurors during deliberations.

To reach this conclusion, the Supreme Court of New Mexico reasoned that, "so long as the knowledge [shared with other jurors] is not imparted to them outside the judicial proceeding in which they sit as jurors," the jury deliberations do not deprive a defendant of his right to a fair and impartial jury and the juror's use of "[his] extrinsic knowledge in the deliberative process does not fall into the category of extrinsic influence." The court reasoned that the juror who performed the probability calculation, "albeit with greater understanding than the average person, was engaging in deliberation of the evidence presented at trial." Recognizing that the jury system intends for jurors to evaluate carefully evidence based on their background knowledge and life experiences, the court also stated that "[i]t would be inordinately bad policy to single out a juror who thoughtfully and conscientiously engaged in deliberation and presented his conclusion to the jury." [*S*]*ee also Hard v. Burlington N. R.R. Co.,* 870 F.2d 1454, 1460–62 (9th Cir. 1989) (holding that a juror's application of his knowledge of how to read an x-ray already admitted into evidence was not extraneous prejudicial information).

After reviewing the arguments on both sides, we agree with the majority of courts and determine that the correct approach is to allow jurors to rely on their professional and educational expertise to inform their deliberations so long as they do not bring in legal content or specific factual information learned from outside the record. First, allowing a juror's intradeliberational statements furthers the purposes of CRE 606(b) by promoting the finality of verdicts and protecting jurors from harassment. This approach prohibits a trial court from eliciting testimony that delves into "the [contents of the] jury's deliberations [or] a juror's mental processes leading to his or her decision" but still allows testimony regarding the jury's exposure to information or influences from outside the record. *Harlan,* 109 P.3d at 625.

Second, this approach better conforms to our previous cases requiring jurors to consider only the evidence developed at trial and the law given in the trial court's instructions. Allowing jurors to use their professional expertise and education to inform their deliberations does not introduce new evidence from outside the record but, rather, allows jurors to use their life experiences to engage the record evidence and to participate in thoughtful deliberations.

Finally, as other courts have noted, this approach recognizes the traditional role of the jury, that the jurors are expected to call on their personal experiences and common sense in reaching their verdict.

Applying this rule, we hold that, in this case, the juror's use of her background in engineering and mathematics to calculate Pippin's speed, distance, and reaction time and the sharing of those calculations with the other jurors did not constitute "extraneous" information within the meaning of CRE 606(b). The juror did not introduce any specific facts or law relevant to the case learned from outside of the judicial proceedings but, rather, merely applied her professional experience and preexisting knowledge of mathematics to the evidence admitted at trial.

The line between a juror's application of her background professional and educational experience to the record evidence and a juror's introduction of legal content or specific factual information learned from outside the record can be a fine one. The test requires that the experience used by the juror in deliberations be part of the juror's background, gained before the juror was selected to participate in the case and not as the result of independent investigation into a matter relevant to the case. Moreover, while our test allows a juror to use her personal experience or knowledge where that knowledge is relevant to the matter at hand, it does not allow the juror to introduce extra facts or law, not introduced at trial, that are specific to parties or an issue in the case.

Representative of a case that falls on the impermissible side of this line is *Destination Travel,* [*Inc. v. McElhanon,* 799 P.2d 454 (Colo. App. 1990)]. *Destination Travel* was a breach of contract case where the plaintiff claimed damages for compensation for work done by its employees, making the pay rate of the employees a primary issue in the case. The defendant claimed that juror misconduct occurred when one juror "provided members of the jury with estimates, based on prior business knowledge and experience, of what he assumed would have been the appropriate salaries for several of the plaintiff's employees." The jury used those estimates, rather than the numbers presented in evidence, to calculate damages. The court of appeals correctly determined that this amounted to extraneous prejudicial information improperly before the jury because the estimates constituted factual information specific to an issue in the case introduced from outside the record. Although the juror derived the estimates from his professional experience, the juror did not merely use his background experience to evaluate and form an opinion on the salary numbers introduced at trial. Rather, the juror reached outside the record to introduce a new fact into evidence, and the jury based its damages award on that new fact, ignoring the numbers introduced at trial.

The circumstances of this case are distinguishable from *Destination Travel.* Unlike *Destination Travel,* the juror in this case did not introduce a new, extra-record fact specific to the parties or an issue in the case. At trial, the parties introduced evidence concerning Pippin's speed and distance from the intersection when she began to slide. The jury consultant's affidavit stated that, because of the juror's background as an engineer, the juror "was able to do calculations of speed and distance and reaction time" and that, based on these calculations, the juror "provided the jury with an estimate of Ms. Pippin's reaction time, and they all discussed Ms. Pippin's conduct in relation to such reaction time."

In this case, the juror merely used her previously held knowledge regarding engineering and mathematics to evaluate the evidence introduced at trial and to derive an opinion regarding whether Pippin was at fault in causing the accident. Although her background in engineering was relevant to issues in the case, her statement to the other jurors did not introduce specific facts concerning the parties or issues in the case, but only showed her assessment of the evidence that had passed through the court's gatekeeping function.

Because the juror in this case did not introduce extraneous information into the jury deliberations, the affidavit used to support these allegations is inadmissible to impeach the verdict. Accordingly, the trial court did not abuse its discretion in denying Kendrick's motion for a new trial on the basis of juror misconduct.

While we agree with the court of appeals' decision on . . . juror misconduct, we hold that the trial court erred [on another issue and] we reverse the court of appeals on that issue. We remand this case to that court to return the case to the trial court for a new trial.

NOTES TO KENDRICK v. PIPPIN

1. *Juror Research and Experiments.* In many cases, applying Rule 606(b)'s exceptions is relatively easy. Testimony would be allowed to show that a juror did an investigation, such as visiting a crime scene or another place involved in the case. If a juror brings an unauthorized book into the jury room during deliberations, that could also be the subject of testimony.

2. *Proof of Event, Not Effect.* To comply with Rule 606(b), testimony about extraneous influences or information may state what influence or information reached the jury. It must not describe what effect an influence or information seemed to have on any juror. With regard to the rule's provision allowing testimony only about "extraneous prejudicial information," the possible prejudicial nature of the information is something that a court must decide in the abstract without inquiring into its actual effect on actual jurors.

3. *Bibles.* A number of jurisdictions have considered whether jurors' possession of or reading from a Bible during deliberations should constitute extraneous prejudicial information wrongly brought to a jury's attention. In many instances, courts have avoided the conclusion referred to in *Kendrick* that treats Bibles as extraneous prejudicial information. For example, in Fields v. Brown, 431 F.3d 1186 (9th Cir. 2005), the court held that some Bible verses may be considered common knowledge and are different from facts.

■ ■ ■

Can a Juror Testify about Another Juror's Bigoted Statements in Deliberations? — Peña-Rodriguez. Where a juror reveals ethnic or racial prejudices during deliberations, the juror's statements may show that they lied during voir dire, or may seem, to some, as equal to the introduction of impermissible outside influences. *Peña-Rodriguez* offers a detailed analysis of the issues related to this kind of testimony about juror conduct.

PEÑA-RODRIGUEZ v. COLORADO
137 S. Ct. 855 (2017)

Justice KENNEDY delivered the opinion of the Court. . . . State prosecutors in Colorado brought criminal charges against petitioner, Miguel Angel Peña-Rodriguez, based on the following allegations. In 2007, in the bathroom of a Colorado horse-racing facility, a man sexually assaulted two teenage sisters. The girls told their father and identified the man as an employee of the racetrack. The police located and arrested petitioner. Each girl separately identified petitioner as the man who had assaulted her.

The State charged petitioner with harassment, unlawful sexual contact, and attempted sexual assault on a child. Before the jury was empaneled, members of the venire were repeatedly asked whether they believed that they could be fair and impartial in the case. A written questionnaire asked if there was "anything about you that you feel would make it difficult for you to be a fair juror." The court repeated the question to the panel of prospective jurors and encouraged jurors to speak in private with the court if they had any concerns about their impartiality. Defense counsel likewise asked whether anyone felt that "this is simply not a good case" for them to be a fair juror. None of the empaneled jurors expressed any reservations based on racial or any other bias. And none asked to speak with the trial judge.

After a 3-day trial, the jury found petitioner guilty of unlawful sexual contact and harassment, but it failed to reach a verdict on the attempted sexual assault charge. . . .

Following the discharge of the jury, petitioner's counsel entered the jury room to discuss the trial with the jurors. As the room was emptying, two jurors remained to speak with counsel in private. They stated that, during deliberations, another juror had expressed anti-Hispanic bias toward petitioner and petitioner's alibi witness. Petitioner's counsel reported this to the court and, with the court's supervision, obtained sworn affidavits from the two jurors.

The affidavits by the two jurors described a number of biased statements made by another juror, identified as Juror H.C. According to the two jurors, H.C. told the other jurors that he "believed the defendant was guilty because, in [H.C.'s] experience as an ex-law enforcement officer, Mexican men had a bravado that caused them to believe they could do whatever they wanted with women." The jurors reported that H.C. stated his belief that Mexican men are physically controlling of women because of their sense of entitlement, and further stated, "I think he did it because he's Mexican and Mexican men take whatever they want." . . . Finally, the jurors recounted that Juror H.C. said that he did not find petitioner's alibi witness credible because, among other things, the witness was "an illegal." . . .

After reviewing the affidavits, the trial court acknowledged H.C.'s apparent bias. But the court denied petitioner's motion for a new trial, noting that "[t]he actual deliberations that occur among the jurors are protected from inquiry under [Colorado Rule of Evidence] 606(b)." . . .

The verdict deemed final, petitioner was sentenced to two years' probation and was required to register as a sex offender. A divided panel of the Colorado Court of Appeals affirmed petitioner's conviction, agreeing that H.C.'s alleged statements did not fall within an exception to Rule 606(b) and so were inadmissible to undermine the validity of the verdict.

The Colorado Supreme Court affirmed by a vote of 4 to 3. The prevailing opinion relied on two decisions of this Court rejecting constitutional challenges to the federal no-impeachment rule as applied to evidence of juror misconduct or bias. See *Tanner v. United States,* 483 U.S. 107 (1987); *Warger v. Shauers,* 135 S. Ct. 521 (2014).

After reviewing those precedents, the court could find no "dividing line between different *types* of juror bias or misconduct," and thus no basis for permitting impeachment of the verdicts in petitioner's trial, notwithstanding H.C.'s apparent racial bias. This Court granted certiorari to decide whether there is a constitutional exception to the no-impeachment rule for instances of racial bias.

[In *Warger,* the Court] rejected the argument that, in the circumstances there, the jury trial right required an exception to the no-impeachment rule. *Warger* involved a civil case where, after the verdict was entered, the losing party sought to proffer evidence that the jury forewoman had failed to disclose prodefendant bias during *voir dire.* As in *Tanner,* the Court put substantial reliance on existing safeguards for a fair trial. The Court stated: "Even if jurors lie in *voir dire* in a way that conceals bias, juror impartiality is adequately assured by the parties' ability to bring to the court's attention any evidence of bias before the verdict is rendered, and to employ nonjuror evidence even after the verdict is rendered.".

In *Warger,* however, the Court did reiterate that the no-impeachment rule may admit exceptions. [T]he Court warned of "juror bias so extreme that, almost by definition, the jury trial right has been abridged." "If and when such a case arises," the Court indicated it would "consider whether the usual safeguards are or are not sufficient to protect the integrity of the process."

Time and again, this Court has been called upon to enforce the Constitution's guarantee against state-sponsored racial discrimination in the jury system. Beginning in 1880, the Court interpreted the Fourteenth Amendment to prohibit the exclusion of jurors on the basis of race. The Court has repeatedly struck down laws and practices that systematically exclude racial minorities from juries. To guard against discrimination in jury selection, the Court has ruled that no litigant may exclude a prospective juror on the basis of race. In an effort to ensure that individuals who sit on juries are free of racial bias, the Court has held that the Constitution at times demands that defendants be permitted to ask questions about racial bias during *voir dire*.

The unmistakable principle underlying these precedents is that discrimination on the basis of race, "odious in all aspects, is especially pernicious in the administration of justice." Permitting racial prejudice in the jury system damages "both the fact and the perception" of the jury's role as "a vital check against the wrongful exercise of power by the State."

This case lies at the intersection of the Court's decisions endorsing the no-impeachment rule and its decisions seeking to eliminate racial bias in the jury system. The two lines of precedent, however, need not conflict.

Racial bias of the kind alleged in this case differs in critical ways from the compromise verdict in *McDonald* [*v. Pless*, 238 U.S. 264 (1915)], the drug and alcohol abuse in *Tanner,* or the pro-defendant bias in *Warger.* The behavior in those cases is troubling and unacceptable, but each involved anomalous behavior from a single jury — or juror — gone off course. Jurors are presumed to follow their oath, and neither history nor common experience show that the jury system is rife with mischief of these or similar kinds. To attempt to rid the jury of every irregularity of this sort would be to expose it to unrelenting scrutiny. "It is not at all clear . . . that the jury system could survive such efforts to perfect it."

The same cannot be said about racial bias, a familiar and recurring evil that, if left unaddressed, would risk systemic injury to the administration of justice. This Court's decisions demonstrate that racial bias implicates unique historical, constitutional, and institutional concerns. An effort to address the most grave and serious statements of racial bias is not an effort to perfect the jury but to ensure that our legal system remains capable of coming ever closer to the promise of equal treatment under the law that is so central to a functioning democracy.

Racial bias is distinct in a pragmatic sense as well. In past cases this Court has relied on other safeguards to protect the right to an impartial jury. Some of those safeguards, to be sure, can disclose racial bias. *Voir dire* at the outset of trial, observation of juror demeanor and conduct during trial, juror reports before the verdict, and nonjuror evidence after trial are important mechanisms for discovering bias. Yet their operation may be compromised, or they may prove insufficient. For instance, this Court has noted the dilemma faced by trial court judges and counsel in deciding whether to explore potential racial bias at *voir dire*. Generic questions about juror impartiality may not expose specific attitudes or biases that can poison jury deliberations. Yet more pointed questions "could well exacerbate whatever prejudice might exist without substantially aiding in exposing it."

The stigma that attends racial bias may make it difficult for a juror to report inappropriate statements during the course of juror deliberations. It is one thing to accuse a fellow juror of having a personal experience that improperly influences her consideration of the case, as would have been required in *Warger.* It is quite another to call her a bigot.

The recognition that certain ... safeguards may be less effective in rooting out racial bias than other kinds of bias is not dispositive. All forms of improper bias pose challenges to the trial process. But there is a sound basis to treat racial bias with added precaution. A constitutional rule that racial bias in the justice system must be addressed — including, in some instances, after the verdict has been entered — is necessary to prevent a systemic loss of confidence in jury verdicts, a confidence that is a central premise of the Sixth Amendment trial right.

For the reasons explained above, the Court now holds that where a juror makes a clear statement that indicates he or she relied on racial stereotypes or animus to convict a criminal defendant, the Sixth Amendment requires that the no-impeachment rule give way in order to permit the trial court to consider the evidence of the juror's statement and any resulting denial of the jury trial guarantee....

The practical mechanics of acquiring and presenting such evidence will no doubt be shaped and guided by state rules of professional ethics and local court rules, both of which often limit counsel's post-trial contact with jurors. These limits seek to provide jurors some protection when they return to their daily affairs after the verdict has been entered. But while a juror can always tell counsel they do not wish to discuss the case, jurors in some instances may come forward of their own accord.

That is what happened here. In this case the alleged statements by a juror were egregious and unmistakable in their reliance on racial bias. Not only did juror H.C. deploy a dangerous racial stereotype to conclude petitioner was guilty and his alibi witness should not be believed, but he also encouraged other jurors to join him in convicting on that basis....

While the trial court concluded that Colorado's Rule 606(b) did not permit it even to consider the resulting affidavits, the Court's holding today removes that bar. When jurors disclose an instance of racial bias as serious as the one involved in this case, the law must not wholly disregard its occurrence....

The Nation must continue to make strides to overcome race-based discrimination. The progress that has already been made underlies the Court's insistence that blatant racial prejudice is antithetical to the functioning of the jury system and must be confronted in egregious cases like this one despite the general bar of the no-impeachment rule. It is the mark of a maturing legal system that it seeks to understand and to implement the lessons of history. The Court now seeks to strengthen the broader principle that society can and must move forward by achieving the thoughtful, rational dialogue at the foundation of both the jury system and the free society that sustains our Constitution.

The judgment of the Supreme Court of Colorado is reversed, and the case is remanded for further proceedings not inconsistent with this opinion.

Justice ALITO, with whom THE CHIEF JUSTICE and Justice THOMAS join, dissenting.... The real thrust of the majority opinion is that the Constitution is less tolerant of racial bias than other forms of juror misconduct, but it is hard to square this argument with the nature of the Sixth Amendment right on which petitioner's argument and the Court's holding are based. What the Sixth Amendment protects is the right to an "impartial jury." Nothing in the text or history of the Amendment or in the inherent nature of the jury trial right suggests that the extent of the protection provided by the Amendment depends on the nature of a jury's partiality or bias. As the Colorado Supreme Court aptly put it, it is hard to "discern a dividing line between different *types* of juror bias or misconduct, whereby one form of partiality would implicate a party's Sixth Amendment right while another would not....

Imagine two cellmates serving lengthy prison terms. Both were convicted for homicides committed in unrelated barroom fights. At the trial of the first prisoner, a juror, during deliberations, expressed animosity toward the defendant because of his race. At the trial of the second prisoner, a juror, during deliberations, expressed animosity toward the defendant because he was wearing the jersey of a hated football team. In both cases, jurors come forward after the trial and reveal what the biased juror said in the jury room. The Court would say to the first prisoner: "You are entitled to introduce the jurors' testimony, because racial bias is damaging to our society." To the second, the Court would say: "Even if you did not have an impartial jury, you must stay in prison because sports rivalries are not a major societal issue."

This disparate treatment is unsupportable under the Sixth Amendment. If the Sixth Amendment requires the admission of juror testimony about statements or conduct during deliberations that show one type of juror partiality, then statements or conduct showing any type of partiality should be treated the same way....

Today's ruling will also prompt losing parties and their friends, supporters, and attorneys to contact and seek to question jurors, and this pestering may erode citizens' willingness to serve on juries. Many jurisdictions now have rules that prohibit or restrict post-verdict contact with jurors, but whether those rules will survive today's decision is an open question — as is the effect of this decision on privilege rules such as those noted at the outset of this opinion....

The Court's decision is well-intentioned. It seeks to remedy a flaw in the jury trial system, but as this Court said some years ago, it is questionable whether our system of trial by jury can endure this attempt to perfect it. [*Tanner.*]

NOTES TO PEÑA-RODRIGUEZ v. COLORADO

1. *Policy Reasons to Protect Jury Secrecy.* In United States v. Benally, 546 F.3d 1230 (10th Cir. 2008), the defendant, a Native American, sought to vacate a verdict and obtain a new trial by showing that a juror who had not answered affirmatively to voir dire questions about having prejudices against Native Americans nonetheless made statements during deliberations that showed he in fact was strongly prejudiced against them. The defendant sought to make that showing with an affidavit from another member of that jury, but the appellate court held that Rule 606(b) prevented the use of that information and that no new trial should be granted.

The court's opinion elaborates on the policy considerations inherent in deciding whether to interpret Rule 606(b) broadly or narrowly. The court wrote:

> Rule 606(b) is a rule of evidence, but its role in the criminal justice process is substantive: it insulates the deliberations of the jury from subsequent second-guessing by the judiciary. Jury decision-making is designed to be a black box: the inputs (evidence and argument) are carefully regulated by law[,] and the output (the verdict) is publicly announced, but the inner workings and deliberation of the jury are deliberately insulated from subsequent review. Judges instruct the jury as to the law, but have no way of knowing whether the jurors follow those instructions. Judges and lawyers speak to the jury about how to evaluate the evidence, but cannot tell how the jurors decide among conflicting testimony or facts. Juries are told to put aside their prejudices and preconceptions, but no one knows whether they do so. Juries provide no reasons, only verdicts. . . .
>
> If what went on in the jury room were judicially reviewable for reasonableness or fairness, trials would no longer truly be by jury, as the Constitution commands. Final authority would be exercised by whomever is empowered to decide whether the jury's decision was reasonable enough, or based on proper considerations. Judicial review of internal jury deliberations would have the result that "every jury verdict would either become the court's verdict or would be permitted to stand only by the court's leave." *Carson v. Polley*, 689 F.2d 562, 581 (5th Cir. 1982).
>
> Defendants undoubtedly have a powerful interest in ensuring that the jury carefully and impartially considers the evidence. This case presents that interest to the highest degree. But there are compelling interests for prohibiting testimony about what goes on in the jury room after a verdict has been rendered. The rule protects the finality of verdicts. It protects jurors from harassment by counsel seeking to nullify a verdict. It reduces the incentive for jury tampering. It promotes free and frank jury discussions that would be chilled if threatened by the prospect of later being called to the stand. Finally, it preserves the "community's trust in a system that relies on the decisions of laypeople [that] would all be undermined by a barrage of postverdict scrutiny." *Tanner* [*v. United States,* 483 U.S. 107, 121 (1987)].

2. *Narrower Prohibition.* The California Evidence Code prohibits only testimony about the mental processes of jurors.

California Evid. Code §1150. Evidence to test a verdict

(a) Upon an inquiry as to the validity of a verdict, any otherwise admissible evidence may be received as to statements made, or conduct, conditions, or events occurring, either within or without the jury room, of such a character as is likely to have influenced the verdict improperly. No evidence is admissible to show the effect of such statement, conduct, condition, or event upon a juror either in influencing him to assent to or dissent from the verdict or concerning the mental processes by which it was determined.

3. *Hearsay and Juror Affidavits.* An affidavit by an investigator stating that a juror told the investigator something about events in the jury room would be hearsay, if offered to prove that the events took place. Testimony by a juror about what another juror said might or might not be hearsay, depending on the purpose for which it was introduced. It would be inadmissible hearsay if offered to show that what the juror said was true (such as, "I went to the crime scene to observe it") but would not be hearsay if offered to prove something like an impermissible bias.

4. *Losses of Information.* Many evidence rules keep information out of trials to support particular social policies. The privilege for confidential spousal communications is an example, where we lose information that might be helpful at a trial in order to foster married couples' relationships. Rule 606(b) might offer a range of benefits, including encouraging jurors to deal with improper arguments when they occur, rather than to wait until after the trial to seek judicial redress.

QUESTION 13-5. After a judgment was entered for the defendant in a medical malpractice case, the plaintiff made a motion for a new trial based on information from a person who served on the jury. Which of the following items of information would most likely give proper support for that motion?

A. The juror will testify that two members of the jury did not pay attention during deliberations and spent almost all the time making jokes.

B. The juror will testify that one member of the jury compared what the defendant doctor was alleged to have done with what his own doctor had done with him for a similar health problem.

C. The juror will testify that one member of the jury printed out a Wikipedia article on the plaintiff's health problem, brought it to the jury room, and used it to argue that the defendant's conduct could not have caused the plaintiff's harm.

D. The juror will testify that a juror explained during deliberations that malpractice insurance premiums have increased greatly in recent years and that there are too many tort judgments against doctors.

E SUMMARY

Common law and the Federal Rules impose a number of requirements that a person must satisfy in order to be allowed to be a witness. These involve the person's knowledge, age and mental status, and other attributes such as whether the witness might testify about transactions with someone who is deceased, about his or her spouse in a criminal case, or in his or her role as a judge or juror.

Competency in General. Rule 601 states that every person is competent to be a witness, unless other rules contradict this. When children are proposed as witnesses, by tradition and under a separate federal statute, a competency inquiry is common. This inquiry involves the trial judge satisfying him or herself that the child understands the difference between truth and falsehood, and that the child is intelligent enough to be treated as a person who has personal knowledge of the subject of his or her testimony.

When a person has been hypnotized, special rules govern his or her competency as a witness. Per se treatment of this question, in either the always competent or always incompetent styles, has largely given way to a multifactor test for reliability of the testimony. Factors to be considered include whether the prehypnosis and posthypnosis facts remembered by the individual are similar or different, and whether the hypnotist had an investigative or therapeutic orientation.

Status-Based Competency Rules. Dead Man's statutes in many jurisdictions restrict a person's competence as a witness if the person is seeking damages against an estate and seeks to testify as to dealings with the decedent. In some places, an approach different from barring testimony is used: While testimony is allowed describing the decedent's conduct with or statements to the witness, the estate is given the benefit of a relaxation of the hearsay rule so that it can counter the witness's claims with additional information about the decedent's conduct or promises.

Spousal incompetency allows a husband or wife to refrain from being a witness against his or her spouse in a criminal case. In some states the choice to be a witness is controlled by either of the two spouses, while in others the choice is controlled only by the spouse whom prosecutors seek to have testify.

A judge is not competent to testify in a case the judge is trying, and a juror is similarly excluded from giving testimony in any case for which he or she is a juror.

For jurors, competency depends on the subject matter of possible testimony. The general rule prohibits jurors from testifying about deliberations, but they may testify about extraneous prejudicial information that may be present in the jury room, or about manifestations of racial prejudice by other jurors.

CHAPTER 14

Opinions

A. Introduction
B. Science-Based Opinions
C. Experience-Based Opinions
D. Topics for Expert Testimony
E. Inadmissible Evidence as a Basis for Expert Testimony
F. Lay Opinion
G. Summary

 INTRODUCTION

Topic Overview

Opinion testimony has a special status in evidence law. Ordinarily witnesses are required to testify about things they have observed, about which they have personal knowledge. In general terms, each witness at a trial can be classified as a "lay" witness or an "expert" witness. A lay witness ordinarily is limited to reporting facts about what he or she has perceived. But sometimes a topic may be outside the scope of a typical juror's knowledge. For those situations, an expert witness may state opinions.

Of course, practice is more complex. Lay witnesses sometimes are allowed to state opinions (such as whether a person seemed drunk). And experts usually give opinions, but they are allowed to state facts as well (such as descriptions of typical disease symptoms).

In deciding whether to allow someone to testify as an expert witness, courts have to evaluate the individual's qualifications and also have to evaluate whether the person's claimed expertise, as it will be applied to the issues at trial, is legitimate or bogus. This second inquiry could, in theory, be left to the jury that will hear that individual and also hear cross-examination and rival testimony. It could be left to the consensus of the

STEPS FOR...

Analyzing Opinion Evidence Issues

1. Is the topic appropriate for opinion testimony?
   - For an expert, it is outside typical jurors' knowledge?
   - For a lay witness, it is a fact the witness has observed that can best be conveyed by an opinion (such as "he was drunk")?
2. Is the witness qualified to give an opinion?
   - Does an **expert** have adequate training or experience in the field?
   - Does a **lay witness** allowed to state an opinion have personal knowledge?
3. Is an expert's methodology legitimate?
4. Is an expert's methodology a good fit for the topic to which the expert will apply it?
5. Is there an adequate factual basis for the expert's opinion?

expert's field, or it could be decided by the trial judge. Assigning this responsibility to the trial judge is the current choice under the federal rules and in most states.

The Federal Rules choice was developed in the context of epidemiology, which is clearly "scientific." Judges can use a variety of criteria to assess the quality of science-based expert testimony. Under the Federal Rules, judges are also required to assess an expert's nonscientific knowledge, such as knowledge gained by experience. Courts have applied a variety of criteria to evaluate experience-based expertise.

For certain frequent categories of expert testimony, special rules have developed. Some of these involve testimony about a person's credibility, testimony about typical patterns of conduct people exhibit in response to particular traumatic events, and whether "law" may or may not be an allowable topic for expert testimony.

Since experts are permitted to testify about things they have not seen in person, doctrines have developed to control their reliance on information that would ordinarily be inadmissible. If typical experts in a field would rely on a particular kind of data, a testifying expert may do the same, regardless of evidentiary problems (such as hearsay) that might otherwise restrict use of the data.

Basic Structure for Analysis

For issues about opinions evidence, it's helpful to differentiate between expert witnesses and lay witnesses. A lay witness may state an opinion only if that style of testimony is an efficient way for the witness to convey some fact the witness has observed. Opinion testimony by lay witnesses is rare. Opinion testimony by expert witnesses, on the other hand, is very common.

The topic must be appropriate for opinion testimony. The witness must be qualified as an expert with appropriate knowledge or as a lay witness with personal knowledge of whatever the lay witness will describe. And if the witness is an expert, the witness's methodology must be legitimate and it must have a rational relationship to the topic on which the expert will apply it. Also, the expert's testimony must be grounded in adequate factual data.

Chapter Organization

Most of the important issues about opinion testimony involve expert witnesses, so this chapter begins with the standards that control their testimony.

A landmark case, *Daubert*, introduces treatment of science-based expert testimony, and other cases consider the *Daubert* principles in a variety of contexts. The next major topic is the role of trial courts in controlling expert testimony that is not scientific but is rather based on the expert's experience.

The specific situations of expert testimony about credibility and alleged victims of abuse are treated next, along with the issues associated with expert testimony about law.

The chapter concludes with consideration of opinion testimony by lay witnesses.

 SCIENCE-BASED OPINIONS

Because expert witnesses play important roles in many trials, some specific practices have developed concerning (1) what topics are appropriate for expert testimony, (2) what people can properly be characterized as experts, and (3) allocating responsibility between the judge and jury for evaluating expert testimony. In federal courts, these issues are controlled by a 1993 Supreme Court decision, *Daubert,* and subsequent cases, as well as by detailed provisions of the Rule 702 that reflect the *Daubert* approach. Many states follow *Daubert* and the current Federal Rules. Some states reject *Daubert* and use rules that do not include specific provisions related to *Daubert.*

Rule 702. Testimony by Expert Witnesses

A witness who is qualified as an expert by knowledge, skill, experience, training, or education may testify in the form of an opinion or otherwise if:

(a) the expert's scientific, technical, or other specialized knowledge will help the trier of fact to understand the evidence or to determine a fact in issue;

(b) the testimony is based on sufficient facts or data;

(c) the testimony is the product of reliable principles and methods; and

(d) the expert has reliably applied the principles and methods to the facts of the case.

■   ■   ■

If a Scientific Analysis Is Generally Accepted in Its Field, Must That Analysis Be an Acceptable Basis for Expert Testimony?—**Daubert.** This opinion interprets words such as "scientific" and "knowledge," in Rule 702, to reject a test for admissibility of scientific evidence and replace it with a different test. The text of Rule 702, shown above, is different from the text of Rule 702 quoted in the *Daubert* opinion. The current text reflects an amendment adopted to conform the rule to *Daubert*'s holding. Consider how the opinion suggests trial courts should apply its new test, and how the results it might produce would compare with results likely under the former test.

DAUBERT v. MERRELL DOW PHARMACEUTICALS, INC.

509 U.S. 579 (1993)

Justice BLACKMUN delivered the opinion of the Court.

In this case we are called upon to determine the standard for admitting expert scientific testimony in a federal trial.

Petitioners Jason Daubert and Eric Schuller are minor children born with serious birth defects. They and their parents sued respondent . . . alleging that the birth defects had been caused by the mothers' ingestion of Bendectin, a prescription antinausea drug marketed by respondent. . . .

After extensive discovery, respondent moved for summary judgment, contending that Bendectin does not cause birth defects in humans and that petitioners would be unable to come forward with any admissible evidence that it does. In support of its motion, respondent submitted an affidavit of Steven H. Lamm, physician and epidemiologist, who is a well-credentialed expert on the risks from exposure to various chemical substances. Doctor Lamm stated that he had reviewed all the literature on Bendectin and human birth defects — more than 30 published studies involving over 130,000 patients. . . . On the basis of this review, Doctor Lamm concluded that maternal use of Bendectin during the first trimester of pregnancy has not been shown to be a risk factor for human birth defects.

Petitioners did not (and do not) contest this characterization of the published record regarding Bendectin. Instead, they responded to respondent's motion with the testimony of eight experts of their own, each of whom also possessed impressive credentials. These experts had concluded that Bendectin can cause birth defects. Their conclusions were based upon "in vitro" (test tube) and "in vivo" (live) animal studies that found a link between Bendectin and malformations; pharmacological studies of the chemical structure of Bendectin that purported to show similarities between the structure of the drug and that of other substances known to cause birth defects; and the "reanalysis" of previously published epidemiological (human statistical) studies.

The District Court granted respondent's motion for summary judgment. The court stated that scientific evidence is admissible only if the principle upon which it is based is "sufficiently established to have general acceptance in the field to which it belongs." The court concluded that petitioners' evidence did not meet this standard. Given the vast body of epidemiological data concerning Bendectin, the court held, expert opinion which is not based on epidemiological evidence is not admissible to establish causation.... Petitioners' epidemiological analyses, based as they were on recalculations of data in previously published studies that had found no causal link between the drug and birth defects, were ruled to be inadmissible because they had not been published or subjected to peer review.

The United States Court of Appeals for the Ninth Circuit affirmed. Citing *Frye v. United States,* 293 F. 1013, 1014 (1923), the court stated that expert opinion based on a scientific technique is inadmissible unless the technique is "generally accepted" as reliable in the relevant scientific community. The court declared that expert opinion based on a methodology that diverges "significantly from the procedures accepted by recognized authorities in the field . . . cannot be shown to be 'generally accepted as a reliable technique.'" . . .

We granted certiorari in light of sharp divisions among the courts regarding the proper standard for the admission of expert testimony.

In the 70 years since its formulation in the *Frye* case, the "general acceptance" test has been the dominant standard for determining the admissibility of novel scientific evidence at trial. Although under increasing attack of late, the rule continues to be followed by a majority of courts....

The *Frye* test has its origin in a short and citation-free 1923 decision concerning the admissibility of evidence derived from a systolic blood pressure deception test, a crude precursor to the polygraph machine. In what has become a famous (perhaps infamous) passage, the then Court of Appeals for the District of Columbia described the device and its operation and declared:

> "Just when a scientific principle or discovery crosses the line between the experimental and demonstrable stages is difficult to define. Somewhere in this twilight zone the evidential force of the principle must be recognized, and while courts will go a long way in admitting expert testimony deduced from a well-recognized scientific principle or discovery, *the thing from which the deduction is made must be sufficiently established to have gained general acceptance in the particular field in which it belongs.*" (emphasis added).

Because the deception test had "not yet gained such standing and scientific recognition among physiological and psychological authorities as would justify the courts in admitting expert testimony deduced from the discovery, development, and experiments thus far made," evidence of its results was ruled inadmissible.

The merits of the *Frye* test have been much debated, and scholarship on its proper scope and application is legion. Petitioners' primary attack, however, is not on the content but on the continuing authority of the rule. They contend that the *Frye* test was superseded by the adoption of the Federal Rules of Evidence. We agree. . . .

Here there is a specific Rule that speaks to the contested issue. Rule 702, governing expert testimony, provides:

> "If scientific, technical, or other specialized knowledge will assist the trier of fact to understand the evidence or to determine a fact in issue, a witness qualified as an expert by knowledge, skill, experience, training, or education, may testify thereto in the form of an opinion or otherwise."

Nothing in the text of this Rule establishes "general acceptance" as an absolute prerequisite to admissibility. Nor does respondent present any clear indication that Rule 702 or the Rules as a whole were intended to incorporate a "general acceptance" standard. . . . Given the Rules' permissive backdrop and their inclusion of a specific rule on expert testimony that does not mention "general acceptance," the assertion that the Rules somehow assimilated *Frye* is unconvincing. *Frye* made "general acceptance" the exclusive test for admitting expert scientific testimony. That austere standard, absent from, and incompatible with, the Federal Rules of Evidence, should not be applied in federal trials.

That the *Frye* test was displaced by the Rules of Evidence does not mean, however, that the Rules themselves place no limits on the admissibility of purportedly scientific evidence. Nor is the trial judge disabled from screening such evidence. To the contrary, under the Rules the trial judge must ensure that any and all scientific testimony or evidence admitted is not only relevant, but reliable.

The primary locus of this obligation is Rule 702, which clearly contemplates some degree of regulation of the subjects and theories about which an expert may testify. "*If scientific,* technical, or other specialized *knowledge will assist the trier of fact* to understand the evidence or to determine a fact in issue" an expert "may testify *thereto.*" (Emphasis added.) The subject of an expert's testimony must be "scientific . . . knowledge."[8] The adjective "scientific" implies a grounding in the methods and procedures of science. Similarly, the word "knowledge" connotes more than subjective belief or unsupported speculation. The term "applies to any body of known facts or to any body of ideas inferred from such facts or accepted as truths on good grounds." Webster's Third New International Dictionary 1252 (1986). Of course, it would be unreasonable to conclude that the subject of scientific testimony must be "known" to a certainty; arguably, there are no certainties in science. But, in order to qualify as "scientific knowledge," an inference or assertion must be derived by the scientific method. Proposed testimony must be supported by appropriate validation — *i.e.,* "good grounds," based

---

8. Rule 702 also applies to "technical, or other specialized knowledge." Our discussion is limited to the scientific context because that is the nature of the expertise offered here.

on what is known. In short, the requirement that an expert's testimony pertain to "scientific knowledge" establishes a standard of evidentiary reliability.[9]

Rule 702 further requires that the evidence or testimony "assist the trier of fact to understand the evidence or to determine a fact in issue." This condition goes primarily to relevance. . . . The consideration has been aptly described . . . as one of "fit." "Fit" is not always obvious, and scientific validity for one purpose is not necessarily scientific validity for other, unrelated purposes. The study of the phases of the moon, for example, may provide valid scientific "knowledge" about whether a certain night was dark, and if darkness is a fact in issue, the knowledge will assist the trier of fact. However (absent creditable grounds supporting such a link), evidence that the moon was full on a certain night will not assist the trier of fact in determining whether an individual was unusually likely to have behaved irrationally on that night. Rule 702's "helpfulness" standard requires a valid scientific connection to the pertinent inquiry as a precondition to admissibility.

That these requirements are embodied in Rule 702 is not surprising. Unlike an ordinary witness, see Rule 701, an expert is permitted wide latitude to offer opinions, including those that are not based on firsthand knowledge or observation. See Rules 702 and 703. Presumably, this relaxation of the usual requirement of firsthand knowledge . . . is premised on an assumption that the expert's opinion will have a reliable basis in the knowledge and experience of his discipline.

Faced with a proffer of expert scientific testimony, then, the trial judge must determine at the outset, pursuant to Rule 104(a), whether the expert is proposing to testify to (1) scientific knowledge that (2) will assist the trier of fact to understand or determine a fact in issue. This entails a preliminary assessment of whether the reasoning or methodology underlying the testimony is scientifically valid and of whether that reasoning or methodology properly can be applied to the facts in issue. We are confident that federal judges possess the capacity to undertake this review. Many factors will bear on the inquiry, and we do not presume to set out a definitive checklist or test. But some general observations are appropriate.

Ordinarily, a key question to be answered in determining whether a theory or technique is scientific knowledge that will assist the trier of fact will be whether it can be (and has been) tested. . . .

Another pertinent consideration is whether the theory or technique has been subjected to peer review and publication. Publication (which is but one element of peer review) is not a *sine qua non* of admissibility; it does not necessarily correlate with reliability, and in some instances well-grounded but innovative theories will not have been published. Some propositions, moreover, are too particular, too new, or of too limited interest to be published. But submission to the scrutiny

---

9. We note that scientists typically distinguish between "validity" (does the principle support what it purports to show?) and "reliability" (does application of the principle produce consistent results?). . . . In a case involving scientific evidence, *evidentiary reliability* will be based upon *scientific validity*.

of the scientific community is a component of "good science," in part because it increases the likelihood that substantive flaws in methodology will be detected. The fact of publication (or lack thereof) in a peer reviewed journal thus will be a relevant, though not dispositive, consideration in assessing the scientific validity of a particular technique or methodology on which an opinion is premised.

Additionally, in the case of a particular scientific technique, the court ordinarily should consider the known or potential rate of error, and the existence and maintenance of standards controlling the technique's operation.

Finally, "general acceptance" can yet have a bearing on the inquiry. A "reliability assessment does not require, although it does permit, explicit identification of a relevant scientific community and an express determination of a particular degree of acceptance within that community." *United States v. Downing,* 753 F.2d [1224, 1238 (3d Cir. 1985)]. Widespread acceptance can be an important factor in ruling particular evidence admissible, and "a known technique which has been able to attract only minimal support within the community," *Downing,* 753 F.2d, at 1238, may properly be viewed with skepticism. . . .

We conclude by briefly addressing what appear to be two underlying concerns of the parties and *amici* in this case. Respondent expresses apprehension that abandonment of "general acceptance" as the exclusive requirement for admission will result in a "free-for-all" in which befuddled juries are confounded by absurd and irrational pseudoscientific assertions. In this regard respondent seems to us to be overly pessimistic about the capabilities of the jury and of the adversary system generally. Vigorous cross-examination, presentation of contrary evidence, and careful instruction on the burden of proof are the traditional and appropriate means of attacking shaky but admissible evidence. Additionally, in the event the trial court concludes that the scintilla of evidence presented supporting a position is insufficient to allow a reasonable juror to conclude that the position more likely than not is true, the court remains free to direct a judgment. These conventional devices, rather than wholesale exclusion under an uncompromising "general acceptance" test, are the appropriate safeguards where the basis of scientific testimony meets the standards of Rule 702.

Petitioners and, to a greater extent, their *amici* exhibit a different concern. They suggest that recognition of a screening role for the judge that allows for the exclusion of "invalid" evidence will sanction a stifling and repressive scientific orthodoxy and will be inimical to the search for truth. It is true that open debate is an essential part of both legal and scientific analyses. Yet there are important differences between the quest for truth in the courtroom and the quest for truth in the laboratory. Scientific conclusions are subject to perpetual revision. Law, on the other hand, must resolve disputes finally and quickly. The scientific project is advanced by broad and wide-ranging consideration of a multitude of hypotheses, for those that are incorrect will eventually be shown to be so, and that in itself is an advance. Conjectures that are probably wrong are of little use, however, in the project of reaching a quick, final, and binding legal judgment — often of great consequence — about a particular set of events in the past. We recognize that, in practice, a gatekeeping role for the judge, no matter how flexible, inevitably on occasion will prevent the jury from learning of authentic insights and innovations. That, nevertheless, is the balance that is struck by Rules of Evidence designed not for the exhaustive search for cosmic understanding but for the particularized resolution of legal disputes.

To summarize: "General acceptance" is not a necessary precondition to the admissibility of scientific evidence under the Federal Rules of Evidence, but the Rules of Evidence — especially Rule 702 — do assign to the trial judge the task of ensuring that an expert's testimony both rests on a reliable foundation and is relevant to the task at hand. Pertinent evidence based on scientifically valid principles will satisfy those demands.

The inquiries of the District Court and the Court of Appeals focused almost exclusively on "general acceptance," as gauged by publication and the decisions of other courts. Accordingly, the judgment of the Court of Appeals is vacated, and the case is remanded for further proceedings consistent with this opinion.

Chief Justice REHNQUIST, with whom Justice STEVENS joins, concurring in part and dissenting in part. . . .

I do not doubt that Rule 702 confides to the judge some gatekeeping responsibility in deciding questions of the admissibility of proffered expert testimony. But I do not think it imposes on them either the obligation or the authority to become amateur scientists in order to perform that role. I think the Court would be far better advised in this case to decide only the questions presented, and to leave the further development of this important area of the law to future cases.

NOTES TO DAUBERT v. MERRELL DOW PHARMACEUTICALS, INC.

1. *Evaluation of Scientific Information.* Under the *Frye* test, the answer to the question of whether proposed expert testimony had an adequate scientific basis is provided by determining a consensus of scientists. Under *Daubert,* that consensus is one factor among others. The trial judge is assigned the task of evaluating the science to determine whether it is good enough to present to a jury.

A dissenting justice in a Mississippi Supreme Court decision criticized what might be thought of as a consequence of the evaluative role judges have under *Daubert,* writing:

> [In a recent case] we undertook to prescribe the methodology to be utilized by real estate appraisers. Now, we take on that same task in the field of economics. Is there no field of human endeavor in which this Court does not believe itself to know more than the real experts? Are there no limits upon the substitution of our judgment for that of the jurors who hear and observe the testifying experts for the parties to the disputes that juries exist to decide?

Rebelwood Apartments RP, LP v. English, 48 So. 3d 483, 498 (Miss. 2010).

2. *Rigidity, Flexibility,* **Daubert,** *and* Frye. Because the *Daubert* approach involves numerous factors, its application is likely to be more flexible than application of the *Frye* test. This flexibility may, in the opinion of some critics, allow courts to exclude evidence that a jury might consider worthwhile. On the other hand, the *Frye* test may prevent exclusion of evidence that once seemed reliable but that has begun to fail the test of time. For example, in Ibar v. State, 938 So. 2d 451, 467-468 (Fla. 2006), the court dealt with modern challenges to fingerprint and footprint evidence:

> Ibar also challenges the State's footwear impression expert. He argues that courts are reconsidering this type of identification testimony on the ground that it has no basis in science. Ibar cites federal and other state cases that follow Daubert v. Merrell Dow Pharmaceuticals, Inc., 509 U.S. 579 (1993), as the standard for the admissibility of experts' testimony. Florida courts do not follow *Daubert*, but instead follow the test set out in Frye v. United States, 293 F. 1013, 1014 (D.C. Cir. 1923). *Frye* sets forth the test to be utilized when a party seeks the admission of expert testimony concerning new or novel scientific evidence. In this case, however, there was no new or novel scientific theory being presented by the shoe print expert. Thus, neither *Daubert* nor *Frye* is applicable. This case is similar to Spann v. State, 857 So. 2d 845 (Fla. 2003), where this Court held that a *Frye* hearing was not necessary for the admission of an expert's testimony on handwriting analysis because handwriting analysis has been utilized by the courts for over 100 years and is not a new or novel science. Shoe print evidence has been utilized for at least as long. See, e.g., Whetston v. State, 31 Fla. 240, 12 So. 661 (1893) (explaining that footprints found at or near the scene of a crime which correspond to those of the accused can be admitted into evidence). The use and reliance on footprint evidence is not new or novel and is not subject to *Frye* analysis. Thus, there was no error in the trial court's admission of this testimony.

> **GOOD TO REMEMBER**
>
> If the trial judge believes scientific evidence fails to satisfy the *Daubert* standard, testimony based on it is forbidden. The jury, whose members might value the evidence differently than the judge did, will never hear the evidence.

3. *Review of Trial Court Expert Witness Decisions:* **Joiner.** A trial court's decision to admit or exclude expert testimony is reviewed only for an abuse of discretion. *See* General Electric Co. v. Joiner, 522 U.S. 136 (1997). In connection with the multifactor test established in *Daubert,* this standard suggests that reversals of these decisions will be infrequent.

■   ■   ■

Evaluating the **Daubert** *Approach* — Schafersman. This case presents one court's view on the relative merits of the *Frye* and *Daubert* frameworks. It also offers an example of application of *Daubert* to scientific testimony that may be outside the mainstream of its field.

SCHAFERSMAN v. AGLAND COOP

631 N.W.2d 862 (Neb. 2001)

GERRARD, J.

John Schafersman and Eileen Schafersman sued Agland Coop (Agland), a Nebraska cooperative corporation, and won a $120,000 jury verdict, based upon the jury's finding that contaminated hog feed, negligently delivered to the Schafersmans, caused illnesses and deaths among the Schafersmans' herd of dairy cows. Agland seeks further review of a decision of the Nebraska Court of Appeals affirming the district court's judgment. The primary question presented in this appeal is whether sufficient foundation was presented for the opinion of the Schafersmans' expert witness, Dr. Wallace Wass.

For the reasons that follow, we conclude that the district court abused its discretion in permitting Wass to testify regarding his theory that "multiple mineral toxicity" caused the injuries to the Schafersmans' cows and, therefore, reverse the judgment of the district court and remand the cause for a new trial. Furthermore, we conclude that the framework for evaluating expert opinion testimony in Nebraska should no longer be guided by *Frye v. United States* but should instead reflect the criteria set forth in *Daubert v. Merrell Dow Pharmaceuticals, Inc.* and its progeny.

The Schafersmans operate a commercial dairy farming operation in Washington County, Nebraska. Agland sells grain and feed for various agricultural endeavors....

The Schafersmans allege that in June 1994, they ordered 40 bushels of unadulterated commercial grade oats from Agland. On June 22, Agland delivered 3,260 pounds of product to the Schafersmans' grinder-mixer, to be mixed with other ingredients for the Schafersmans' dairy mix, and from which the mix was augered into a gravity bin to be fed directly to the cows.

Agland does not dispute that the oats were contaminated with "Envirolean 2.5L Swine Concentrate" (Envirolean), a hog premix concentrate that included high-protein minerals, vitamins, and other micronutrients....

The Schafersmans further allege that after the mixture was fed to the dairy herd, the cows went off their feed and milk production dropped....

The Schafersmans claimed damages for lost milk production, cows lost to natural death or slaughter, increased labor costs, and veterinary costs, for a total of $117,743.29 in special damages....

At trial, the Schafersmans presented the expert opinion testimony of Wass, who opined that the alleged damage to the Schafersmans' cows was caused by "multiple mineral toxicity," a condition that Wass said was the result of the aggregation of above-normal quantities of minerals potentially toxic to dairy cows. Agland filed a motion in limine seeking to prevent Wass'[s] testimony and objected at trial on foundational grounds, but both the motion in limine and the foundation objection were overruled.... Agland's expert witness testified that the Envirolean contained no minerals above tolerable levels and that the contaminated feed was nontoxic and did not harm the cows.

After the case was submitted, the jury returned a verdict finding for the Schafersmans on the negligence theory of recovery. . . . The district court entered judgment accordingly. . . .

Agland appealed to the Court of Appeals, which affirmed the judgment of the district court. . . . We granted Agland's petition for further review.

Agland [contends on appeal] that the Court of Appeals erred in determining that Wass'[s] expert testimony was properly admitted. . . .

The first argument to be addressed is Agland's claim that Wass' opinion lacked appropriate foundation. In connection with this claim, Agland argues on further review that this court should again consider adopting the standards for evaluating expert opinion testimony set forth in *Daubert v. Merrell Dow Pharmaceuticals, Inc.*

Wass is a professor at Iowa State University in the department of diagnostic and production animal medicine and was head of that department when it was known as the department of clinical sciences. Wass is board certified in veterinary internal medicine, and he specializes in diseases of metabolism, nutrition, and toxicology. . . .

Wass testified that in preparing his opinion, he physically went to the Schafersman farm, but only examined the Schafersmans' records relating to the cows. Wass admitted that he did not perform a clinical examination of any of the cows and did not treat the cows. Wass did not perform any tests on the cows to rule out other causes of the jaundice that had been observed in the cows by the Schafersmans' veterinarian, nor did he test for copper toxicity, which Wass opined was a contributing factor to the illness afflicting the cows. Wass performed no tests to rule out other potential causes for the alleged drop in milk production. Wass acknowledged that he should have tested for copper toxicity and performed other tests on the cows. . . .

Nonetheless, Wass testified that it was his opinion that the problems with the cows were caused by the Envirolean because the cows that had eaten the Envirolean-contaminated mix became sick. The basis for Wass'[s] opinion was his theory that the cows were afflicted with "multiple mineral toxicity," which Wass claimed could result when a number of potentially toxic minerals were simultaneously fed to cows in otherwise-tolerable quantities. Wass admitted that no minerals were present in the feed that were, singly, above scientifically accepted toxic or even tolerable levels.

With respect to the theory of multiple mineral toxicity, Wass testified that he had neither studied multiple mineral toxicity nor authored any publications concerning multiple mineral toxicity. Wass testified that he was aware of no controlled studies that related to multiple mineral toxicity, although he claimed that people in the field have observed it. Wass conceded that the theory he proposed set forth no standard for determining what levels of any given minerals could result in a toxic effect. . . . Wass conceded, in his deposition, that he had not conducted any tests that were intended to bear out his theory of multiple mineral toxicity.

In addition, Agland's expert witness, Dr. David Reed, a veterinarian who specializes in dairy cows and nutritional consulting for dairy producers, reviewed Wass'[s] deposition testimony and the attached exhibits. Reed testified that the scientific literature did not contain a theory of multiple mineral toxicity and that in his opinion, that theory did not apply to the instant case.

When a court is faced with an offer of a novel form of expertise which has not yet received judicial sanction, it must conduct an initial inquiry to determine whether the new technique or principle is sufficiently reliable to aid the jury in reaching accurate results. In this state, where the rules of evidence apply, the admissibility of an expert's testimony, including an opinion, which is based on a scientific principle or on a technique or process which utilizes or applies a scientific principle, depends on general acceptance of the principle, technique, or process in the relevant scientific community. Stated otherwise, Nebraska has adhered to the *Frye* test, under which the proponent of the evidence must prove general acceptance by surveying scientific publications, judicial decisions, or practical applications, or by presenting testimony from scientists as to the attitudes of their fellow scientists.

Under the standard of helpfulness required by Neb. Evid. R. 702, a court may exclude an expert's opinion which is nothing more than an expression of how the trier of fact should decide a case or what result should be reached on any issue to be resolved by the trier of fact. When an expert's opinion on a disputed issue is a conclusion which may be deduced equally as well by the trier of fact with sufficient evidence on the issue, the expert's opinion is superfluous and does not assist the trier in understanding the evidence or determining a factual issue.

The Schafersmans argue, and the Court of Appeals agreed, that Wass'[s] diagnosis of multiple mineral toxicity was not novel and, thus, that the *Frye* test does not apply. We disagree. The testimony of Wass and Reed clearly establishes the novelty of the theory underlying Wass'[s] conclusions regarding the cause of the illnesses afflicting the Schafersmans' cows. In originally promulgating the *Frye* test, the Court of Appeals of the District of Columbia stated that "while courts will go a long way in admitting expert testimony deduced from a well-recognized scientific principle or discovery, the thing from which the deduction is made must be sufficiently established to have gained general acceptance in the particular field in which it belongs."

The deduction at issue in this case, Wass'[s] opinion on the cause of the illnesses afflicting the Schafersmans' cows, is not derived from a principle or procedure that has gained general acceptance in the particular field in which it belongs. Wass'[s] opinion is dependent upon the underlying theory of multiple mineral toxicity, and the evidence at trial established that this theory is not generally accepted in any scientific field. . . .

In short, Wass'[s] theory of multiple mineral toxicity did not meet the requirements of the *Frye* test, and Wass offered no other reasoning or scientific analysis that would support his opinion on causation. The district court abused its discretion in permitting Wass to testify regarding multiple mineral toxicity and in allowing Wass to offer his opinion that any illnesses among the Schafersmans' cows were caused by the presence of Envirolean in the feed. As this error was clearly prejudicial to Agland, we conclude that the Court of Appeals erred in not reversing the judgment of the district court and remanding the cause for a new trial. That determination, however, does not end our analysis.

Agland urges this court to . . . consider adopting the test set forth in *Daubert v. Merrell Dow Pharmaceuticals, Inc.*, for the evaluation of expert opinion testimony. This issue is not necessary for our disposition of the present appeal. However, an appellate court may, at its discretion, discuss issues unnecessary to the disposition of an appeal where those issues are likely to recur during further proceedings . . . .

In [an earlier case] this court discussed two reasons for continued adherence to the *Frye* test: (1) that the *Daubert* standards were relatively undeveloped and uncertain and (2) that *Daubert* might fail to exclude unreliable "junk science." These concerns were, at the time, entirely reasonable. The experience of the intervening years, however, has put those concerns to rest. . . .

As one writer has noted:

> To say that *Daubert* is less restrictive of expert evidence, to say that it opens the door for the introduction of expert evidence that would not have been admissible under the *Frye* test, is not to say that *Daubert*'s test is an easier test. It may be more lenient in that it allows more — and more novel — science into evidence, but it can be much more difficult in that the *Daubert* test can require a more exacting, expensive, and time consuming foundation.
>
> . . . On the one hand, more science comes in. Science does not have to be generally accepted by other scientists to be admissible in court; the universe of admissible science is expanded by doing away with the general acceptance requirement. On the other hand, less science comes in. The trial judge is to act as gatekeeper and is to scrutinize carefully the proffered scientific evidence and to keep out what is not good science. . . . While it may be that most science generally accepted in the relevant scientific community will be good science, it is not necessarily so.

G. Michael Fenner, *The Daubert Handbook: The Case, Its Essential Dilemma, and Its Progeny*, 29 Creighton L. Rev. 939, 953 (1996). . . .

Moreover, the flexibility of *Daubert* does not require that the validity of a theory or technique be determined solely by the general acceptance of a particular field that may prove to be too accepting. As one writer has stated:

> Despite some dicta in *Daubert* stating that the test embodied by Rule 702 is a more liberal one than *Frye*, when compared to the general acceptance test, the *Daubert* test requires more from some fields and less from others depending on the state of the knowledge being offered. *Frye* asks whether something is generally accepted. *Daubert* asks whether it is dependable. These are different questions. Often they will produce the same answer. That happens when the basis of knowledge is weak and a field recognizes it is weak, or when the basis of knowledge is sound and a field

recognizes it is sound. But *Daubert* is more liberal when the expert evidence is solid, but on the cutting edge, and therefore not yet generally accepted. . . . On the other hand, *Frye* is more liberal when what is offered is unsound expert evidence that nevertheless has become "generally accepted" in its field. This is the category that judges have encountered in numerous cases in the wake of *Daubert*, and found themselves puzzled about why a supposedly more liberal standard was leading them toward exclusion of evidence that long had been admitted without question. . . .

David L. Faigman et al., *How Good is Good Enough?: Expert Evidence Under* Daubert *and* Kumho, 50 Case W. Res. L. Rev. 645, 656-57 (2000). . . .

We are convinced that by shifting the focus to the kind of reasoning required in science — empirically supported rational explanation — the *Daubert/Joiner/Kumho Tire Co.*[*] trilogy of cases greatly improves the reliability of the information upon which verdicts and other legal decisions are based. Because courts and juries cannot do justice in a factual vacuum, the better information the fact finders have, the more likely that verdicts will be just. Indeed, though the "scientific method" may not be an appropriate "standard" for all experts, the fundamental commonsense requirements of rational explanation and empirical support should apply to all experts.

We are persuaded that Nebraska should join the majority of jurisdictions that have already concluded that the *Daubert* standards provide a more effective and just means of evaluating the admissibility of expert opinion testimony. . . .

Specifically, we hold that in those limited situations in which a court is faced with a decision regarding the admissibility of expert opinion evidence, the trial judge must determine at the outset, pursuant to Neb. Evid. R. 702, whether the expert is proposing to testify to (1) scientific, technical, or other specialized knowledge that (2) will assist the trier of fact to understand or determine a fact in issue. This entails a preliminary assessment whether the reasoning or methodology underlying the testimony is valid and whether that reasoning or methodology properly can be applied to the facts in issue. . . .

In so holding, we also note that once the validity of the expert's reasoning or methodology has been satisfactorily established, any remaining questions regarding the manner in which that methodology was *applied* in a particular case will generally go to the weight of such evidence. Vigorous cross-examination, presentation of contrary evidence, and careful instruction on the burden of proof remain the traditional and appropriate means of attacking evidence that is admissible, but subject to debate.

We note that although Wass'[s] testimony did not meet the requirements of the *Frye* test at the first trial, this does not necessarily preclude the Schafersmans from offering such testimony at a second trial. As stated above, novel scientific theories can be reliable and thus admissible under *Daubert* even if not generally accepted in the scientific field, so long as foundation is presented to satisfy

---

[*] *Kumho Tire* is discussed in the next case, *Baines,* and in Section C of this chapter. — ED.

the court of the validity of the theory or methodology underlying the proffered opinion.

In evaluating expert opinion testimony under *Daubert*, where such testimony's factual basis, data, principles, methods, or their application are called sufficiently into question, the trial judge must determine whether the testimony has a reliable basis in the knowledge and experience of the relevant discipline. In determining the admissibility of an expert's testimony, a trial judge may consider several more specific factors that *Daubert* said might "bear on" a judge's gatekeeping determination. . . . These factors are, however, neither exclusive nor binding; different factors may prove more significant in different cases, and additional factors may prove relevant under particular circumstances.

In the instant case, the questions presented arise in the discipline of veterinary epidemiology. When epidemiology is used in legal disputes, the methodological soundness of a study and its implications for resolution of the question of causation require the assessment of whether the study reveals an association between an agent and disease, whether sources of error in the study may have contributed an inaccurate result, and whether any relationship between the agent and the disease is causal. A trial court must also consider whether an expert has accounted for other possible causes of disease; differential diagnosis — the process of eliminating other possible causes — can be an essential component in establishing specific causation.

Evidence of an association may be sufficient for formulation of a hypothesis that can later be tested and confirmed, but it is not proof of causation in the courtroom or the scientific community. A gatekeeping court must evaluate the reliability of the bridge the expert takes to the opinion, not the opinion itself.

Thus, in applying the *Daubert* standards, Nebraska courts should remember that the focus must be on the principles and methodology utilized by expert witnesses, and not on the conclusions that they generate. Reasonable differences in scientific evaluation are not a basis for exclusion of an expert witness' opinion....

We conclude that given the foundation presented, the district court abused its discretion in permitting Wass to testify regarding the theory of multiple mineral toxicity and his ultimate opinion as to causation in the instant case....

The judgment of the Court of Appeals is, therefore, reversed, and the cause is remanded to the Court of Appeals with directions to reverse the judgment of the district court and remand the cause for a new trial, including proceedings consistent with this opinion.

NOTES TO SCHAFERSMAN v. AGLAND COOP

1. *Purpose of the* Daubert *Test.* The court states that expert testimony should be based on reasoning that is empirically supported by rational explanation. It also states that the *Daubert* factors are not mandatory. Unless judges are better able than jurors to identify rational explanations and factual support, it could be argued that the *Schafersman* court's goals could be achieved by allowing jurors greater access to expert testimony.

2. *Blending Evidence Concepts and Substantive Doctrines.* The court states that evidence of association is not adequate to support a finding of causation "in the courtroom or scientific community." It would be possible for the law to define causation in a more plaintiff-friendly way than scientists do, given the different purposes of scientific and trial inquiries.

3. *Rejecting* Daubert. The Pennsylvania Supreme Court provided the following rationale for rejecting *Daubert*, in Grady v. Frito-Lay, Inc., 839 A.2d 1038, 1044-1045 (Pa. 2003):

> One of the primary reasons we embraced the *Frye* test . . . was its assurance that judges would be guided by scientists when assessing the reliability of a scientific method. Given the ever-increasing complexity of scientific advances, this assurance is at least as compelling today as it was in 1977, when we [adopted *Frye*]. We believe now, as we did then, that requiring judges to pay deference to the conclusions of those who are in the best position to evaluate the merits of scientific theory and technique when ruling on the admissibility of scientific proof, as the *Frye* rule requires, is the better way of insuring that only reliable expert scientific evidence is admitted at trial.
>
> We also believe that the *Frye* test, which is premised on a rule — that of "general acceptance" — is more likely to yield uniform, objective, and predictable results among the courts, than is the application of the *Daubert* standard, which calls for a balancing of several factors. Moreover, the decisions of individual judges, whose backgrounds in science may vary widely, will be similarly guided by the consensus that exists in the scientific community on such matters.

QUESTION 14-1. Walter Tranowski testified in defense of his brother Stanley who was on trial for passing counterfeit currency. He testified that he took a photograph (see below) of Stanley, their mother, and a dog in the backyard of their mother's home on a certain date between the hours of 2:00 and 3:00 P.M. If true, Walter's

testimony made it impossible for Stanley to have passed a counterfeit bill at the time the prosecution alleged. The jury rejected the alibi and found Stanley guilty.

Assume that a prosecutor is considering charging Walter with perjury. If the prosecutor sought to use the following evidence, discuss how it would likely be treated under *Frye* or *Daubert*:

> Larry Ciupik is an astronomer at a large museum's planetarium. He has worked as a consultant for a large map company and written astronomy articles for an encyclopedia. He can testify that if one knows the compass orientation of an object in a photograph it would be possible to date the photograph by: 1) measuring the directional angle of the shadow cast by that object to determine the azimuth of the sun; and 2) measuring the angle of elevation of a complete shadow cast by another object in the photograph to determine the altitude of the sun. He can state that the intersection of the altitude and azimuth define the sun's position in the sky and can correspond to only two dates per year.
>
> He could use the dog's shadow as the only complete shadow in the picture and measure the height of the dog and the length of the shadow in centimeters. Assuming the ground to be level he could use these two lengths as legs of a right triangle and could then find the angle of the sun's elevation. He could make other measurements on the photo and relate those to data on a "sun chart" usually used to measure the height of lunar mountains. He has performed lunar mountain height calculations many times, but has not used this technique to date photographs. He does not know of any published text detailing a method to use such calculations for that purpose.

■ ■ ■

Segment 14: gatekeeping for expert testimony

Fingerprints and Daubert — Baines. This excerpt shows a methodical application of the *Daubert* factors to fingerprint evidence. The unsurprising result is that the evidence passes the *Daubert* test, but the analysis could suggest that in additional settings that test should similarly be treated as a low threshold.

UNITED STATES v. BAINES

573 F.3d 979 (10th Cir. 2009)

HOLLOWAY, J.

. . . The first *Daubert* question is whether the technique can be and has been tested. We have seriously considered defendant's argument that the testing of fingerprint analysis that has been reported mostly falls short of the rigors demanded by the ideals of science. On the other hand, the core proposition — that reliable identifications may be made from comparison of latent prints with known prints — is testable. And unquestionably the technique has been subject to testing, albeit less rigorous than a scientific ideal, in the world of criminal investigation, court proceedings, and other practical applications, such as identification of victims of disasters.

Thus, while we must agree with defendant that this record does not show that the technique has been subject to testing that would meet all of the standards of science, it would be unrealistic in the extreme for us to ignore the countervailing evidence. Fingerprint identification has been used extensively by law enforcement agencies all over the world for almost a century. Fingerprint analysts such as Mr. Fullerton, who have been certified by the FBI, have undergone demanding training culminating in proficiency examinations, followed by further proficiency examinations at regular intervals during their careers. Although these proficiency examinations have been criticized on several grounds, most notably that they do not accurately represent conditions encountered in the field, we see no basis in this record for totally disregarding these proficiency tests.

In conclusion, on this record we believe that the first *Daubert* factor weighs somewhat in favor of admissibility, although not powerfully.

The second *Daubert* factor is whether the theory or process has been subject to peer review and publication. We find little in the record to guide us in consideration of this factor. Defendant argues persuasively that the verification stage of the ACE-V process [a four-step process for comparing prints] is not the independent peer review of true science. Agent Meagher's testimony included some references to professional publications, but these were too vague and sketchy to enable us to assess the nature of the professional dialogue offered. In short, the government did not show in this case that this factor favors admissibility.

The third *Daubert* factor is the known or potential error rate of the procedure. [T]esting has been done in training programs and other environments that are not shown to be accurate facsimiles of the tasks undertaken by fingerprint analysts in actual cases. Nevertheless, the accumulated data is impressive. Very few mistakes are reported in testing that trainees must complete before progressing to actual casework. Mr. Fullerton, who made the actual identification in this case, testified that he has always attained a perfect score in his proficiency tests.

More significantly, Agent Meagher testified to an error rate of one per every 11 million cases, and the defense did not — either in the evidentiary hearing or in the briefs on appeal — challenge that testimony. There may have been erroneous identifications that never came to light. Defense attorneys rarely have the resources to hire independent experts for trial, and in the interests of finality our system has created obstacles to post-conviction review. But even allowing for the likelihood that the actual error rate for FBI examiners may be higher than reflected in Mr. Meagher's testimony, the known error rate remains impressively low. We are not aware of any attempt to quantify the maximum error rate that could meet *Daubert* standards, but surely a rate considerably higher than one per 11 million could still pass the test. We conclude that the evidence of the error rate on this record strongly supported the judge's decision to admit the expert testimony.

The fourth *Daubert* factor is the existence and maintenance of standards controlling the technique's operation. On this point, we are persuaded by the analysis of the Third Circuit in *United States v. Mitchell,* 365 F.3d 215, 241 (3d Cir.

2004). The ACE-V system is a procedural standard but not a substantive one. Critical steps in the process depend on the subjective judgment of the analyst. We hasten to add that subjectivity does not, in itself, preclude a finding of reliability. But in searching this record for evidence of standards that guide and limit the analyst in exercise of these subjective judgments, we find very little. Because in the end determination of this factor is not critical to our decision, we will assume *arguendo* that this factor does not support admissibility.

The fifth *Daubert* factor is whether the technique has attained general acceptance in the relevant scientific or expert community. Conceding the general acceptance of fingerprint analysis by law enforcement officials nationwide and internationally, defendant contends that fingerprint analysis has not been accepted in "any unbiased scientific or technical community" and cites to the *Daubert* formulation of the standard, which was limited to the "relevant scientific community." This distinction is significant in this case because the field of fingerprint analysis is dominated by agents of law enforcement, with apparently little presence of disinterested experts such as academics.

But in *Kumho Tire,* the Court — dealing with proffered expert testimony that was characterized as technical rather than scientific — referred with apparent approval to a lower court's inquiry into general acceptance in the "relevant expert community," and then the Court discussed its own search in the record for evidence of acceptance of the controverted test by "other experts in the industry." Consequently, while we acknowledge that acceptance by a community of unbiased experts would carry greater weight, we believe that acceptance by other experts in the field should also be considered. And when we consider that factor with respect to fingerprint analysis, what we observe is overwhelming acceptance.

Defendant argues that many of the post-*Daubert* cases holding fingerprint analysis admissible placed so much weight on the general acceptance of the practice that they in effect applied the outdated standard of *Frye v. United States,* the standard that *Daubert* held had been displaced by Fed. R. Evid. 702. We need not either accept or reject this contention, as we have examined this issue on the record in this case and have found guidance from other courts primarily in their discussions of other factors. We have remained mindful of *Frye*'s displacement, but also mindful that the Court specifically said in *Daubert* that general acceptance "can yet have a bearing on the inquiry."

In reaching a conclusion after this process of focusing on each of the *Daubert* factors in turn, we must return to two overriding principles. The first is that our review here is deferential, limited to the question of whether the district judge abused her considerable discretion. The second is that the Rule 702 analysis is a flexible one, as both *Daubert* and *Kumho Tire* teach. The *Daubert* factors are "meant to be helpful, not definitive," and not all of the factors will be pertinent in every case. On the whole, it seems to us that the record supports the district judge's finding that fingerprint analysis is sufficiently reliable to be admissible. Thus, we find no abuse of discretion. . . .

In closing, we echo the thoughts of Judge Pollak, who said regarding the desirability of research to provide the scrutiny and independent verification of the scientific method to aid in assessing the reliability of fingerprint evidence, that such efforts would be "all to the good. But to postpone present in-court utilization of this 'bedrock forensic identifier' pending such research would be to make the best the enemy of the good." *United States v. Llera Plaza,* 188 F. Supp. 2d 549, 572 (E.D. Pa. 2002).

NOTES TO UNITED STATES v. BAINES

1. *Checklist, Definitive Test?* In *Daubert,* the Supreme Court wrote, "Many factors will bear on the inquiry, and we do not presume to set out a definitive checklist or test." Many opinions, like the one in *Baines,* seem to treat the Supreme Court's factors as required elements of the analysis.

2. *Handwriting Analysis.* Testimony by experts in handwriting analysis has long been accepted, but some scholars have asserted that its reliability has been overestimated. Courts applying both the *Frye* and *Daubert* tests have approved the continued use of this type of testimony. *See, e.g.,* Pettus v. U.S., 37 A.3d 213 (D.C. Cir. 2012) (*Frye* test), Williams v. State, 60 P.3d 151 (Wyo. 2002) (*Daubert* test). The issue is made more complicated by references in the FRE 901 "comparison by an expert witness" for the purpose of authenticating items.

QUESTION 14-2. Defendant is accused of conspiracy to produce an illegal drug, phencyclidine (PCP). The prosecution seeks to introduce testimony from a Drug Enforcement Agency (DEA) forensic chemist, A. Harman, about the actual yield of PCP that could be produced in a clandestine laboratory for purposes of establishing the fact that the conspiracy involved more than 100 grams of PCP. This quantity testimony is relevant with regard to sentencing under an applicable statute. Harman would testify to the following:

- The yield was likely 25 percent, based on an aggregate of data compiled by the DEA from seizures from clandestine laboratories. The DEA maintains an internal database, which contains data on the actual yield of PCP produced in clandestine laboratories. Harman has reviewed an e-mail from "headquarters," which indicated that the average yield from such laboratories was between 30 and 40 percent. Thus, she would testify to a 25 percent figure as a "conservative estimate" of actual yield in a clandestine laboratory.
- The 25 percent figure is "commonly used" by "forensic chemists throughout DEA." There are "an average of 30 chemists in each of the [DEA's] eight laboratories."
- A study has been published in the *Journal of Medicinal Chemistry* regarding actual yields of PCP in a laboratory.
- Harman has synthesized PCP in her laboratory and obtained an actual yield of about 55 percent. She synthesized PCP was to "mak[e] a determination on the issue of actual yield."

Should a trial court admit this testimony?

EXPERIENCE-BASED OPINIONS

Experience-Based Expertise: **Kumho Tire.** Sometimes a witness's claimed expertise is based on experience and training, rather than on the kind of science that was involved in *Daubert.* For example, an experienced mechanic might have valuable ideas about why a machine was working badly but might not be able to point to data or published research to support those conclusions. The Supreme Court has decided that the *Daubert* approach applies to all expert testimony, whether based on science or based on experience. *See* Kumho Tire Co. v. Carmichael, 526 U.S. 137 (1999).

Thus, federal courts and many state courts must apply the *Daubert* principles, extended by *Kumho Tire,* to all expert testimony, including testimony based on experience rather than on scientific training or scientific experiments. Translating the science-based *Daubert* inquiry to nonscience fields, however, can be difficult. Courts that are required to follow *Daubert* for experience-based testimony must face that problem directly. Courts that decline to apply the strict *Daubert* analysis to experience-based testimony may still seek to enforce some standards of reliability as a required foundation for expert testimony even when the testimony is based on experience rather than on science.

■ ■ ■

Determining Reliability of Something an Expert Knows from Experience — **Walker.** Should an experienced police officer be allowed to testify that some cocaine was imported into his state, rather than made there, on the basis of his experience in the market for cocaine? The Third Circuit considers a trial court's decision on that question in a way that differs from a standard *Daubert* multifactor analysis.

UNITED STATES v. WALKER

657 F.3d 160 (3d Cir. 2011)

POLLAK, J.

This consolidated criminal appeal arises from the conviction, in August 2008, of two brothers, Barron Walker and Barry Walker, for various federal drug trafficking, firearm, and robbery charges. The Walker brothers were each sentenced to prison terms of 47-1/2 years. They now appeal their convictions on several grounds.

[B]oth Walkers were charged with attempted robbery, in violation of the Hobbs Act, 18 U.S.C. §1951(a) [and numerous other crimes]. . . .

On August 6, 2008, five days before trial, the government disclosed to defense counsel its intention to prove the interstate commerce prong of the Hobbs Act robbery charge through the testimony of Chief John Goshert of the Dauphin County Criminal Investigation Division, a thirty-year veteran of cocaine trafficking investigations in Harrisburg and the region. The Walkers objected to . . . Chief Goshert's testimony regarding the interstate transportation of cocaine on the ground that it is possible to manufacture cocaine synthetically. The District Court rejected this argument and permitted Chief Goshert to testify as an expert that in his experience cocaine is manufactured outside of Pennsylvania. . . .

[T]he Walkers argue that Chief Goshert should not have been allowed to testify that cocaine is manufactured outside of Pennsylvania and transported into the state. Specifically, the Walkers argue that Goshert's testimony was unreliable because Wright could have possessed synthetic cocaine manufactured in Pennsylvania. The Walkers point out that recipes for synthetic cocaine are readily available on the Internet, and they also cite a series of court decisions from the 1970s and 1980s which recognized that cocaine could be manufactured domestically. The Walkers also note that Goshert admitted during his testimony that he is unable to distinguish synthetic cocaine from cocaine made from cocoa plants.

We review a district court's decision to admit expert testimony for abuse of discretion and exercise plenary review over a district court's legal interpretation of Rule 702 of the Federal Rules of Evidence. . . . In cases not involving scientific testimony, courts must still serve the gatekeeping function described in Daubert v. Merrell Dow Pharm., Inc., 509 U.S. 579, (1993), but "'the factors identified in Daubert may or may not be pertinent in assessing reliability, depending on the nature of the issue, the expert's particular expertise, and the subject of his testimony.'" Betterbox Commc'ns Ltd. v. BB Techs., Inc., 300 F.3d 325, 329 (3d Cir. 2002) (quoting Kumho Tire Co. v. Carmichael, 526 U.S. 137, 150 (1999)). In such cases "'the relevant reliability concerns may focus upon personal knowledge or experience.'" Id. (quoting *Kumho Tire*, 526 U.S. at 150).

The Walkers argue that Goshert, who acknowledged at trial that he is not a chemist and is unable to distinguish ordinary cocaine from synthetic cocaine, did not have the requisite expertise to testify about the geographic origins of the cocaine in Pennsylvania. We disagree. Goshert's testimony was based upon his thirty years of experience working as a narcotics investigator in Harrisburg, Pennsylvania. Goshert testified that during that time period he regularly participated in investigations involving the importation of cocaine into the Harrisburg area, that he spoke with drug traffickers on a daily basis, and that he had worked with a variety of other law enforcements agencies, including the Drug Enforcement Administration and New York Police Department. He also testified that he had taught courses and seminars on drug trafficking and drug identification to new and experienced police officers, to the Pennsylvania District Attorney's Association, and to community groups. Upon being qualified as an expert, Goshert identified New York City as the primary source for cocaine in the Harrisburg area, and testified that in his thirty years of investigating cocaine cases he had never had a single law enforcement agent, informant, drug trafficker, or other individual indicate that cocaine was manufactured inside Pennsylvania.

We agree with the District Court that Goshert's method for reaching these conclusions was reliable. Our court has previously recognized that law enforcement officials can rely upon their specialized knowledge or experience to offer expert testimony on various aspects of drug trafficking. See, e.g., United States v. Perez, 280 F.3d 318, 342 (3d Cir. 2002) (expert opinion on how drug traffickers use cellular telephones and pagers); United States v. Gibbs, 190 F.3d 188, 211 (3d Cir. 1999) (expert testimony on coded drug language). We have also recognized that law enforcement officers may, given the proper experience, testify in a Hobbs Act case regarding whether goods had originally been produced in another state. *See* United States v. Haywood, 363 F.3d 200, 210-11 (3d Cir. 2004) (holding that police officer who was a resident of the Virgin Islands had sufficient knowledge to testify that beer sold by bar originated in the mainland United States).

Goshert's expert opinions were based upon his personal experiences interacting with drug traffickers and law enforcement personnel over a period of decades. During that time, he had numerous opportunities to investigate the geographic origins of the cocaine sold in Harrisburg. Accordingly, he did not need to be a professional chemist in order to gather reliable information on whether cocaine was being produced inside Pennsylvania or instead being produced elsewhere and transported into Pennsylvania. See *Betterbox*, 300 F.3d at 328-29 (noting that specialized knowledge can be based upon "practical experience as well as academic training and credentials" (internal quotation marks omitted)).

We also hold that Goshert's expert testimony was not rendered unreliable by the evidence the defense presented regarding the possibility of manufacturing cocaine synthetically. Although it may be possible to find recipes for synthetic cocaine on the Internet, the defense presented no evidence that synthetic cocaine has, at any time in the recent past, actually been manufactured in Pennsylvania. Further, although the Walkers cite to a series of court decisions from the 1970s and 1980s which recognized that cocaine can be manufactured domestically, none of these cases involved conduct occurring in Pennsylvania, or conduct that occurred in the last twenty years. Indeed, more recent cases have suggested that it is common knowledge that cocaine is imported into the United States from Latin America. See United States v. Gomez, 580 F.3d 94, 102 (2d Cir. 2009) ("The importation and interstate transportation of cocaine, as well as the financial size of the cocaine trade, have been routinely and copiously discussed by public officials, candidates for office, and the news media for decades.").[14]

---

14. The parties assume, as do we for purposes of this appeal, that the place of origin of cocaine is sufficiently technical in nature to be the subject of expert testimony under Rule 702.

Accordingly, we agree with the government that the District Court did not abuse its discretion in determining that Chief Goshert's testimony regarding the interstate transportation of cocaine was reliable. . . .

For the foregoing reasons, the District Court's judgments of conviction and sentence will be affirmed in all respects.

NOTES TO UNITED STATES v. WALKER

1. *Echoes of* Frye? Two of the bases in *Walker* for approving admission of the expert's testimony are reminiscent of *Frye* jurisprudence. The court relies on precedents and relies on the expert's own testimony to suggest that conclusions of the type the expert offered are common and well accepted by courts and other police experts.

GOOD TO REMEMBER

Many of the suggested *Daubert* factors would fit badly with typical experience-based testimony, but courts are still required to scrutinize that testimony with some degree of rigor.

2. *Expert Opinion on Ultimate Issues.* At common law, an expert was barred from giving an opinion on an "ultimate issue." For example, in *Walker*, whether the cocaine was brought into Pennsylvania from another state would have been called an ultimate issue. Enforcing the common law rule required lots of difficult line-drawing. And the basis for it was never satisfactorily explained. Under the Federal Rules, that common law ban is almost completely eliminated. Rule 704 takes away the prohibition, except for issues about a criminal defendant's mental state.

> **Rule 704. Opinion on an Ultimate Issue**
>
> **(a) In General — Not Automatically Objectionable.** An opinion is not objectionable just because it embraces an ultimate issue.
>
> **(b) Exception.** In a criminal case, an expert witness must not state an opinion about whether the defendant did or did not have a mental state or condition that constitutes an element of the crime charged or of a defense. Those matters are for the trier of fact alone.

■ ■ ■

Distinguishing Tests for Scientific and Experience-Based Testimony — Torrez. In the context of nonscientific testimony, the court suggests that evaluating a nonscientific expert's credentials and evaluating that witness's proposed testimony for reliability are separate inquiries. It then applies that analysis to an expert on gang crime.

STATE v. TORREZ

210 P.3d 228 (N. Mex. 2009)

CHAVEZ, C.J.

Defendant Orlando Torrez directly appeals his convictions of first degree murder, shooting at a dwelling or occupied building resulting in injury, and tampering with evidence; charges arising from the shooting death of Danica Concha at a Halloween party in 2003....

On Halloween night in 2003, Defendant, his girlfriend, Samantha Sanchez, his friend, Alfredo Sanchez, and three others went to a house party near Taos, New Mexico. During the party, two unidentified men ... threatened the lives of Defendant and his family and instructed him and his friends to leave or they would be killed. Defendant and his companions got into his car, and while they were driving away, the two men fired gunshots at Defendant's vehicle, hitting it at least twice. No one was injured.

Defendant and his companions returned to his house. Defendant testified that he was scared that the assailants would come by his house and shoot at them again because they had told him they knew where he lived.... Defendant and Alfredo returned to the party in Defendant's car with ... firearms.

At trial, Defendant described the following events after he and Alfredo returned to the party. He parked the car near the edge of the property and, having noticed one of the two men who had threatened him earlier standing outside the house, Defendant approached the man. While talking to him, Defendant was hit on the head from behind, fell to the ground, and was kicked.... After getting back on his feet, Defendant was running to his car when he heard gunshots fired from behind him. Alfredo testified that when he saw Defendant running back toward the car, Defendant was unarmed and there was gunfire coming from the house. However, Alfredo could not state with certainty that Defendant had not been the first to shoot.

Once back at his car, Defendant testified that he grabbed [a] .303 caliber rifle and fired toward the house where he could see sparks of light that looked like gunfire....

[Concha was fatally wounded by an unidentified participant in the shooting.]

The jury convicted Defendant of first degree murder, shooting at a dwelling resulting in injury, and tampering with evidence....

At trial, the State called Detective Robert Martinez as an expert witness to testify about "gang-related law enforcement and gang culture." The trial court admitted his testimony over Defendant's objections. On appeal, Defendant [argues] that the trial court's admission of Detective Martinez's expert testimony was in error....

In our review of the record, we discern two distinct purposes of Detective Martinez's testimony: (1) to prove that Defendant was a member of the Barrio Small Town (BST) criminal street gang and (2) to explain Defendant's motive for returning to the party and shooting at the house. Prior to Detective Martinez's testimony, evidence had been introduced that Defendant had a tattoo that identified him as a BST member. Detective Martinez corroborated this testimony when he testified that BST was a "homegrown" gang in Taos and that the letters "BST" identified BST gang members. He emphasized that tattoos are prevalent in gang society and that tattoos of gang signs, symbols, and abbreviations are identifiers of who is a member of a particular gang. Thus, Detective Martinez offered circumstantial evidence that Defendant was a member of BST. However, no direct evidence was presented at trial that Defendant was a member of BST or any other gang at the time of the shooting.

The other, more significant purpose of Detective Martinez's testimony was to refute Defendant's claim of self-defense by offering another explanation of Defendant's motive for shooting at the house. The expert's testimony was significant because Defendant's intent was the primary focus of the parties' dispute. Defendant admitted that he shot at the house with a gun that could have fired the fatal bullet. However, he asked the jury to find that he did so in self-defense, in response to being shot at first by unidentified assailants. In contrast . . . the State asked the jury to conclude that Defendant, an alleged gang member, returned to the party that night seeking revenge or retribution for being threatened, shot at, and otherwise disrespected.

Detective Martinez testified that respect is the most important value in gang culture. . . .

Detective Martinez explained that gang members can be disrespected in a number of ways. For example, showing a gang-specific tattoo in public or to members of another gang would be disrespectful, as would "mad-dogging," a form of confrontation where two individuals aggressively stare at one another. Spoken threats are another form of disrespect, as are threats to a person's life and the destruction of a person's property. Detective Martinez further explained that disrespecting a gang member in front of other people demands retribution, especially if the member is disrespected in front of members of his or her own gang. Additionally, Detective Martinez repeatedly referred to gangs as "criminal[ ]." . . .

With these purposes for the expert's testimony in mind, we now turn to Defendant's arguments on appeal.

. . . Rule 11-702 permits a witness to be qualified based on his or her knowledge, skill, experience, training, or education, "but no set criteria can be laid down to test such qualifications." We have emphasized the use of the disjunctive "or" in Rule 11-702 in recognizing the wide discretion given the trial court in qualifying experts to testify.

The trial court qualified Detective Martinez to testify as an expert witness with respect to gang-related law enforcement and gang culture on the basis of his knowledge, skill, and experience in those fields. Defendant argues that Detective Martinez was not qualified to be an expert on these subjects because he (1) did not have personal knowledge of Taos area gangs; (2) did not have a college degree; (3) had not previously testified as an expert before a jury; (4) had never worked undercover in a gang unit; (5) had not published any materials that were subject to peer review; and (6) could not point to any recognized field of study that sought to determine why gang members assault one another. Defendant also argues that Detective Martinez was not qualified to predict the human behavior of gang members. The State contends that Detective Martinez was qualified to give expert testimony on gang culture and gang-related law enforcement because, among his other qualifications, he had thirteen years' experience as a police officer working with gang units, had spent approximately 2,000 hours instructing other law enforcement personnel about gang culture and investigation, and had written the Albuquerque, Bernalillo County Street Gang Manual. . . .

Based on these qualifications, we cannot say that the trial court abused its discretion in qualifying Detective Martinez as an expert on gang-related law enforcement and gang culture. Rule 11-702 expressly allows experts to be qualified based on their skills and experience, and Detective Martinez's experience with gangs was sufficient to allow his testimony on this subject. . . .

Although an expert may be qualified to give an opinion on a given subject, the expert's testimony may nevertheless be inadmissible under Rule 11-702, which requires that the testimony assist the trier of fact and be based on "scientific, technical or other specialized knowledge." *See* [State v. Alberico, 116 N.M. 156 (1993)] ("We discern three prerequisites in Rule [11-]702 for the admission of expert opinion testimony. The first requirement is that the expert be qualified. . . . The second consideration . . . is whether [the testimony] will assist the trier of fact. . . . The third requirement . . . is that an expert may testify only as to 'scientific, technical or other specialized knowledge.'"). We have already addressed the first of these three inquiries, whether the expert is qualified. We do not address whether the expert's testimony assisted the trier of fact because that argument was not raised by Defendant. In light of Defendant's remaining arguments, we now turn to whether Detective Martinez's testimony was based on his specialized knowledge.

Defendant argues that the trial court should have excluded Detective Martinez's testimony because it amounted to nothing more than "junk science" and an unscientific attempt to predict the behavior of gang members. Defendant also argues that the reliability of Detective Martinez's methodology could not be tested because there is no recognized field of scientific study that seeks to explain in a scientific manner why gang members assault one another. To the extent that Defendant is arguing that Detective Martinez's expert testimony should have been excluded because it is not the subject of a valid science and there are no means to test the reliability of his results, we disagree. Defendant confuses the standards applicable to determining the admissibility of expert scientific testimony with those for admitting expert testimony based on the specialized knowledge of the expert witness.

The requirements that scientific expert testimony be "grounded in valid, objective science" and "reliable enough to prove what it purports to prove," *Alberico*, 116 N.M. at 168, are inapplicable to expert testimony that is based on the expert's specialized knowledge. *See* State v. Torres, 1999 NMSC 10, P. 43, 127 N.M.

20, 976 P.2d 20 ("[A]pplication of the Daubert [v. Merrell Dow Pharmaceuticals, Inc., 509 U.S. 579 (1993)] factors is unwarranted in cases where expert testimony is based solely upon experience or training." . . . Nevertheless, "[i]t is the duty of our courts . . . to determine initially whether expert testimony is competent under Rule 702. . . . " *Alberico*, 116 N.M. at 164. In other words, even with non-scientific expert testimony, the trial court must exercise its gate-keeping function and ensure that the expert's testimony is reliable. However, when testing the reliability of non-scientific expert testimony, rather than testing an expert's scientific methodology as required under *Daubert* and *Alberico*, the court must evaluate a non-scientific expert's personal knowledge and experience to determine whether the expert's conclusions on a given subject may be trusted.

While this inquiry is similar to a determination of whether an expert is qualified to opine on a given subject, the two inquiries are not identical. The first inquiry, testing an expert's qualifications, requires that the trial court determine whether an expert's skills, experience, training, or education qualify him or her in the relevant subject. Although the second inquiry uses these same factors, the court uses them to test the validity of the expert's conclusions. In this way, an expert may be qualified to offer opinions on a subject, but those opinions may nevertheless be unreliable in that they do not prove what they purport to prove. We need not repeat Detective Martinez's qualifications here. We have already concluded that the trial court did not err in qualifying him as an expert on the subject of "gang-related law enforcement and gang culture." However, our inquiry does not stop with a determination of his specialized knowledge on these subjects. We must also determine whether his knowledge of gangs generally permitted him to offer an expert opinion regarding the motives of individual gang members.

It is widely held that expert opinion testimony is admissible to prove motive or intent of a gang member, subject to the balancing requirements of Rule 11-403 NMRA. . . . Here, Detective Martinez testified from his personal experience with gangs that gang members retaliate in violent ways when disrespected. He testified that being disrespected can occur in any number of ways, some of which could have been applicable in Defendant's situation if sufficient evidence of Defendant's gang affiliation had been presented to the jury. Based on his experience and knowledge, the trial court did not err in concluding that Detective Martinez's opinions were reliable and that his testimony regarding the motives of gang members proved what it was offered to prove. . . .

[In the absence of evidence showing that the defendant was a member of the gang at the time of the shooting, the evidence should have been excluded under the Rule 403 balancing test.]

For the reasons stated above, we hold that the trial court erred in admitting Detective Martinez's expert testimony on gang culture and gang-related law enforcement. We therefore vacate Defendant's convictions for first degree murder, shooting at a dwelling resulting in injury, and tampering with evidence, and remand to the district court for a new trial.

NOTES TO STATE v. TORREZ

1. *Required Precision for Experience-Based Testimony?* In United States v. Frazier, 387 F.3d 1244 (11th Cir. 2004), an experienced forensic investigator was prepared to testify in a sexual assault case that it would be expected that some transfer of either hairs or seminal fluid would occur if events alleged by the prosecution had occurred. The appellate court affirmed a trial court decision that rejected this testimony after attempting to apply *Daubert*-style scrutiny. A dissenter argued:

> The district court's rulings suggest that, if Tressel [the defendant's expert] had only been willing to testify with the careless grace of the government's witnesses, providing the court with slapdash, but facially numerical, guesstimations, his testimony may have been admitted. [See] Maj. Op. (characterizing Tressel's testimony as unreliable because he could not quantify the word "expect" or describe a sufficient number of sexual assault investigations to support his conclusions). To favor this brand of off-the-cuff approximations over well-settled, qualitative principles published in numerous editions of the field's leading textbook is hardly, to put it mildly, the hallmark of sound judicial practice. Not only does it create a perverse incentive for experts to fortify overstated conclusions in a manner largely unverifiable by the courts, it circumvents the spirit and letter of *Daubert*'s principles. As one court so tersely put it, "a number pulled out of the air is not 'scientific knowledge.'" Rather than resort to farcical solutions to difficult problems, courts should recognize that the contest between valid qualitative and quantitative data is properly one for the jury.

2. *Qualifications of Expert Witness.* Courts consider the relationship between a prospective witness's background and the topics of his or her proposed testimony in determining whether the individual is qualified to be an expert witness. For example, in Johnson v. Knebel, 485 S.E.2d 451 (Ga. 1997), the court held that a licensed professional engineer had expertise in the area of accident reconstruction that would allow him to give admissible opinions on topics like the course and rate of travel, and points of impact of the cars involved in the collisions. It rejected a claim that this witness could also be an expert on another topic, which of two separate collisions had caused a person's injuries, because he had no training, education, or experience about forces and stresses exerted by an automobile collision on a human body, such as training in physiology, anatomy, or biomechanics.

QUESTION 14-3. Defendant is on trial for robbing a convenience store. He was found about a mile from the store when a police officer tracked him down with the help of a bloodhound that had followed a track from the store to Defendant. The officer is prepared to testify that he has worked with this particular dog for about eight years and found him to be reliable at finding people. He can testify also that he has worked with other tracking dogs over a period of about 20 years and knows that they are reliable in finding people or things when they have been given a sample of their scents. If the prosecution offers this testimony as part of its proof that Defendant committed the charged crime, which response is best?

    A. Testimony is admissible because it likely satisfies a typical *Daubert* analysis including consideration of reliability, peer review, publication, and scientific principles.

    B. Testimony is admissible because it likely satisfies a typical experience-based expertise analysis including consideration of the police officer's lengthy practical experience with tracking dogs.

    C. Testimony is likely inadmissible because it contains hearsay for which there is no applicable exclusion or exception.

    D. Testimony is likely inadmissible because it is neither lay witness testimony nor adequately testable scientific testimony.

D TOPICS FOR EXPERT TESTIMONY

Expert testimony is allowed only if, in the words of Rule 702, it "will help the trier of fact to understand the evidence or to determine a fact in issue." This means that expert testimony is prohibited for topics within the usual understanding of typical members of a jury. Some complications have arisen in applying this idea to topics like the credibility of witnesses and shortcomings of eyewitness testimony. Testimony about law presents a variation on this problem. Details of statutes or legal doctrines are probably outside the knowledge of jurors, but it might not make sense to allow experts to testify about law when a judge is present who can give juries that information in the form of jury instructions.

■   ■   ■

Can an Expert Share Insights about a Person's Truthfulness? — **Spigarolo** *and* **Hobgood.** The plain language of Rule 702 could allow for admission of expert testimony about credibility, if a scientific basis was present for that kind of opinion. Tradition, however, sets up a supposedly absolute rule against expert testimony on this topic. It would, courts say, "invade the province of the jury." These two opinions explore this practice in the context of expert testimony about the credibility of alleged victims of crime. They show that expert testimony about a particular person's credibility is prohibited but that expert testimony about typical patterns of narration associated with truthfulness is allowed.

STATE v. SPIGAROLO

556 A.2d 112 (Conn. 1989)

GLASS, J.

The defendant, William M. Spigarolo, was charged with several criminal offenses in connection with allegations that he had sexually abused his girlfriend's children, B, a six year old male, and G, a nine year old female, on divers dates between October, 1984, and January 3, 1985. . . .

The defendant was found guilty by a jury of two counts of sexual assault in the second degree . . . and four counts of risk of injury to a minor. . . .

On appeal, the defendant . . . asserts that the trial court . . . denied the defendant due process by permitting expert testimony at trial on the testimonial credibility of the alleged victims. . . . We find no error. . . .

At the trial, the state offered the testimony of Brenda Woods, a social worker employed by Yale–New Haven Hospital. Over the defendant's objection, Woods was permitted to testify on direct examination that it is not unusual for alleged abuse victims to give apparently inconsistent stories. She testified: "It might sound like the child is being inconsistent, because they may give parts of the story initially, they may give part of the story then later more of it will come out as they begin to be able to talk about it more." The defendant contends that Woods was not qualified to testify as she did and that the admission of her testimony violated his constitutional right to a jury trial because it usurped the jury's function of assessing the credibility of witnesses. We disagree.

"'The trial court has wide discretion in ruling on the qualification of expert witnesses and the admissibility of their opinions.' *State v. Kemp,* 199 Conn. 473, 476, 507 A.2d 1387 (1986). 'Generally, expert testimony is admissible if (1) the witness has a special skill or knowledge directly applicable to a matter in issue, (2) that skill or knowledge is not common to the average person, and (3) the testimony would be helpful to the court or jury in considering the issues.' Id." *State v. Rodgers,* 207 Conn. 646, 651, 542 A.2d 1136 (1988).

Woods testified that she possessed a master's degree in social work, and had been a clinical social worker at Yale–New Haven Hospital for one and one-half years. At the hospital, she employed her skills both in pediatrics and in the emergency room, and had been involved in the evaluation or treatment of 100 to 150 cases of child sexual abuse. In addition, she was involved in the hospital's special Sexual Abuse Identification and Treatment program during the year prior to her testimony. In light of this evidence, we conclude that the trial court did not abuse its discretion in determining that Woods was qualified as an expert on the behavioral characteristics of child sexual abuse victims.

Prior to the introduction of Woods's testimony, counsel for the defendant sought to impeach the credibility of B and G. Specifically, defense counsel had queried B, G and J on the inconsistencies and incomplete disclosures the children had made to police and others prior to and during the official investigation of the alleged incidents. Under these circumstances, we hold that the trial court did not abuse its discretion in permitting Woods to testify that it is not unusual for sexually abused children to give inconsistent or incomplete accounts of the alleged incidents. [T]he overwhelming majority of courts have held that, where the defendant has sought to impeach the testimony of the minor victim based on inconsistencies, partial disclosures, or recantations relating to the alleged incidents, the state may present expert opinion evidence that such behavior by minor sexual abuse victims is common.

This variety of expert testimony is admissible because the consequences of the unique trauma experienced by minor victims of sexual abuse are matters beyond the understanding of the average person. Consequently, expert testimony that minor victims typically fail to provide complete or consistent disclosures of the alleged sexual abuse is of valuable assistance to the trier in assessing the minor victim's credibility. As the Oregon Supreme Court stated: "It would be useful to the jury to know that . . . many child victims are ambivalent about the forcefulness with which they want to pursue the complaint, and it is not uncommon for them to deny the act ever happened. Explaining this superficially bizarre behavior by identifying its emotional antecedents could help the jury better assess the witness's credibility." *State v. Middleton*, 657 P.2d 1215 (Or. 1983).

We disagree with the defendant's contention that Woods's testimony "usurped" the jury's function of assessing the credibility of witnesses. As noted above, Woods was not asked about the credibility of the particular victims in this case, nor did she testify as to their credibility. The cases that have considered this issue have noted the critical distinction between admissible expert testimony on general or typical behavior patterns of minor victims and inadmissible testimony directly concerning the particular victim's credibility.

We hold that, where defense counsel has sought to impeach the credibility of a complaining minor witness in a sexual abuse case, based on inconsistency, incompleteness or recantation of the victim's disclosures pertaining to the alleged incidents, the state may offer expert testimony that seeks to demonstrate or explain in general terms the behavioral characteristics of child abuse victims in disclosing alleged incidents. In the present case, Woods's testimony did not usurp the jury's function of assessing the credibility of B's and G's testimony, and was therefore admissible. We express no opinion on the state's use of such expert testimony in the absence of the defendant's impeachment of the victim's credibility. . . .

There is no error.

Segment 15: expert testimony on credibility

HOBGOOD v. STATE

926 So. 2d 847 (Miss. 2006)

Cobb, P. J.

On January 28, 2004, Richard Hobgood was convicted in the Hinds County Circuit Court, First Judicial District, of sexual battery of a child under the age of 14, pursuant to Miss. Code Ann. Section 97-3- 95(1)(d). He was sentenced to life in the custody of the Mississippi Department of Corrections. . . . Hobgood asserts the trial court erred by: . . . allowing the State's expert witness to vouch for the victim's credibility [and] allowing expert opinion testimony on child sexual abuse. . . . Finding no reversible error, we affirm the trial court.

From June 1, 2000, until June 27, 2001, Hobgood, then age 28, was living with his girlfriend in Jackson. Due to his girlfriend's emotional problems and difficulties with Hobgood, her two minor children lived with their maternal grandmother, Jane Doe. However, for a period of time, their mother regained custody, and the two children lived with her and Hobgood.

On June 28, 2001, Christina Cooke was baby-sitting the victim and his sister while staying at Doe's home. The victim, who was 5 years of age at that time, approached Cooke and asked if he could tell her a secret. He then proceeded to describe to Cooke how Hobgood forced him to lie on the bed and performed anal sex on him, something which the victim called "bad medicine." Cooke then called Doe and informed her that she needed to return home. When Doe arrived, Cooke asked the victim to tell Doe what he had told her, and he repeated the story "word-for-word."

Doe and Cooke took the victim to see psychotherapist Denise Detotto. Detotto spoke individually with each of them about the victim's allegations and then directly questioned the victim. . . .

Hobgood asserts it was error to allow Dettoto to make a direct comment on a child sex abuse victim's credibility. At trial Detotto's testimony was as follows:

Q: Okay. And during the disclosure that [the victim] made to you, did you find him credible?

A: Yes.

Q: Why?

A: Every time that —

By Mr. Wade: Your honor, I will object to her passing on the credibility of this witness. I believe the Supreme Court has spoken to this.

By The Court: She's making an observation. Overruled. It's subject to cross-examination.

By Ms. Purnell: (Continuing)

Q: Why did you find him credible?

A: Every time that [the victim] discuss(ed) the above with me the details never changed. They were consistent over an entire year's period. And in addition to that, there was also physical evidence which was found.

The State recognizes that such testimony has been held to be "of dubious competency" but asserts that here it is admissible because Detotto vigorously pursued the victim's credibility through an extensive developmental history study and administration of several tests, one of which, "showed that the victim had 'maladaptive behaviors'" encompassing cheating and lying.

This Court has never held that an expert's direct comment on a child sex abuse victim's credibility is per se reversible error, because in previous cases we reversed and remanded for several reasons including that error. . . .

This Court has, however, stated that under Rule 702 "experts called to testify about behavioral characteristics that may affect an alleged victim's credibility may not give an opinion of the credibility of a particular witness." *Goodson v. State,* 566 So. 2d 1142, 1153 (Miss. 1990). In *Goodson,* this Court first addressed the present issue. There a man was charged with sexual abuse of a young girl, when four years after the incident, the girl approached her family with the allegations. The family took her to see a physician. At trial, the physician testified that the victim had been telling the truth because the girl's statements were corroborated by physical evidence. This Court again held such testimony inadmissible. However, and again, *Goodson* was reversed on other grounds.

The Court of Appeals dealt with this issue in *Jackson v. State,* 743 So. 2d 1008 (Miss. Ct. App. 1999). In *Jackson,* a young girl reported being sexually abused by a neighbor. The child was taken to UMMC where she met with a therapist to describe the encounter. At trial the therapist testified that she assumed the child's statements were true unless they were disproved. In that case the Court of Appeals held that the statement was not reversible error because it was not a direct comment on the child's veracity.

In the present case, Dettoto never stated that the victim was telling the truth. Rather she explained the consistency of the accounts he made to individuals, at different times, not in the presence of the others, and found them to be credible. Hobgood contends that Detotto's testimony denied the jury its role as judge of credibility. We disagree. The jury heard Dettoto's testimony along with that of five other witnesses. The trial court thoroughly and correctly instructed the jurors regarding their role as the sole judges of the credibility of the witnesses and the weight their testimony deserved. He specifically stated they "should consider each expert opinion received in evidence in this case and give it such weight as you may think it deserves."

We hold that allowing Detotto's comment regarding the victim's credibility was not error, when viewed in the totality of her testimony. She did not cross the line and say that he was telling the truth. This issue is without merit. . . .

We hold that Hobgood's rights were not violated when Detotto commented on the victim's credibility, and we find no merit to the other issues raised. We affirm the judgment of the trial court.

NOTES TO STATE v. SPIGAROLO AND HOBGOOD v. STATE

1. *Distinguishing Testimony about Patterns of Narration and Specific Witnesses' Credibility.* In a prosecution for a sex crime against a child, a psychologist who had interviewed the alleged victim testified, in response to a question from the prosecution:

General attitudes, accepted attitudes as far as the literature concerning children is that children tend not to fabricate stories of sexual abuse and in giving reports tend to reproduce their experiences and your statement about children having had the erotic experience when young, in order to make these things up, there has to be a basis for that experience and unless it happened to them in this area, then in fact the description would be what had been done to them.

Classifying this testimony as general or specific might be difficult. *See* People v. Snook, 745 P.2d 647 (Colo. 1987).

2. *Protecting the "Province of the Jury."* Why might courts treat credibility as a dangerous topic for expert testimony? They often refer to protecting the "province of the jury" when explaining why credibility expertise should be barred. George Fisher, *The Jury's Rise as Lie Detector*, 107 Yale L. J. 576 (1997), suggests an explanation:

<table>
<tr>
<td>

GOOD TO REMEMBER

It is difficult to distinguish between alleged victims in general and an alleged victim in particular when witnesses are allowed to comment on general credibility factors but barred from commenting on a particular alleged victim. This may suggest that courts are ambivalent about the traditional "province of the jury" concept.

</td>
<td>

[A]lthough the jury does not guarantee accurate lie detecting, it does detect lies in a way that appears accurate, or at least in a way that hides the source of any inaccuracy from the public's gaze. By permitting the jury to resolve credibility conflicts in the black box of the jury room, the criminal justice system can present to the public an "answer" — a single verdict of guilty or not guilty — that resolves all questions of credibility in a way that is largely immune from challenge or review. By making the jury its lie detector, the system protects its own legitimacy.

</td>
</tr>
</table>

Segment 16: syndrome testimony

QUESTION 14-4. In a trial where the defendant was accused of a sex crime against a young child, a social worker who had interviewed the child gave the following testimony:

Q: After you interviewed [alleged victim], did you do anything else in relation to your investigation of this allegation?

A: Uh, just concluded my 311 and submitted that to my supervisor.

Q: And what's a 311?

A: A 311 is our final report when we receive a new report. A 311 report is basically our conclusion as to whether we found, uh, or whether we believe abuse or neglect occurred.

Q: And what are your options as far as conclusions . . . as far as abuse, alleged abuse?

[Defense Counsel:] I'm going to object. That invades the province of the jury, Your Honor.

[Prosecutor:] Judge, she can tell what her conclusion was as far as her report was and her duty and role as a case manager for the Department of Child Services. That wouldn't invade the province of the jury.

The Court: It was the witness's investigation. I think she's certainly allowed to give us her opinion and then, of course, that would be subject to cross. I'm going to allow the question.

A: Uh, when we receive a new report, we have to determine whether to substantiate abuse, which means that we believe that abuse and neglect occurred, or we can unsubstantiate it, which means we don't feel that there's enough evidence to say that abuse or neglect occurred. Regarding this report, I substantiated sexual abuse, meaning our office feels that there was enough evidence to conclude that sexual abuse occurred.

Should this testimony be characterized as prohibited testimony about the credibility of the alleged victim?

3. *Expert Testimony on Eyewitness Identification.* Many studies have shown that eyewitnesses' identification of wrongdoers may be less accurate than eyewitnesses or jurors are likely to think. Should experts be allowed to explain this research to jurors? *See* United States v. Langan, 263 F.3d 613, 621 (6th Cir. 2001):

The use of expert testimony in regard to eyewitness identification is a recurring and controversial subject. Trial courts have traditionally hesitated to admit expert testimony purporting to identify flaws in eyewitness identification. Among the reasons given to exclude such testimony are that the jury can decide the credibility issues itself, see United States v. Lumpkin, 192 F.3d 280, 289 (2d Cir. 1999) (determining that the "proposed testimony intrudes too much on the traditional province of the jury to assess witness credibility"); that experts in this area are not much help and largely offer rather obvious generalities, see United States v. Hudson, 884 F.2d 1016, 1024 (7th Cir. 1989) ("Such expert testimony will not aid the jury because it addresses an issue of which the jury already generally is aware, and it will not contribute to their understanding of the particular dispute."); that trials would be prolonged by a battle of experts, see United States v. Fosher, 590 F.2d 381, 383-84 (1st Cir. 1979) (adding "to the trial court's articulated concerns our own conviction that a trial court has the discretion to avoid imposing upon the parties the time and expense involved in a battle of experts"); and that such testimony creates undue opportunity for confusing and misleading the jury, see United States v. Rincon, 28 F.3d 921, 926 (9th Cir. 1994) ("Given the powerful nature of expert testimony, coupled with its potential to mislead the jury, we cannot say the district court erred in concluding that the proffered evidence would not assist the trier of fact and that it was likely to mislead the jury.").

Several courts, however, including our own, have suggested that such evidence warrants a more hospitable reception. See United States v. Smithers, 212 F.3d 306, 314 (6th Cir. 2000) (holding that "the district court abused its discretion in excluding [the eyewitness identification expert's] testimony, without first conducting a hearing pursuant to Daubert"); United States v. Smith, 156 F.3d 1046, 1053 (10th Cir. 1998) (agreeing that "expert testimony on eyewitness identification may properly be admitted under Daubert in certain circumstances"); United States v. Brien, 59 F.3d 274, 277 (1st Cir. 1995) (declining to adopt a blanket rule that qualified expert testimony on eyewitness identification must either be routinely admitted or excluded); United States v. Amador-Galvan, 9 F.3d 1414, 1417-18 (9th Cir. 1993) (declining to follow a per se rule excluding expert testimony regarding the credibility of eyewitness identification). Moreover, such testimony has been allowed in with increasing frequency where the circumstances include "cross-racial identification, identification after a long delay, identification after observation under stress, and [such] psychological phenomena as . . . unconscious transference." See United States v. Harris, 995 F.2d 532, 535 (4th Cir. 1993). Nonetheless, each court to examine this issue has held that the district court has broad discretion in, first, determining the reliability of the particular testimony, and, second, balancing its probative value against its prejudicial effect.

■   ■   ■

Since a Judge Is Present, Do Trials Need Expert Testimony on Law? — **Specht.** Should parties be permitted to introduce expert testimony about law? If application of legal doctrines is necessary for resolution of a case, could the trial judge determine the law and explain it to jurors through the medium of jury instructions? *Specht* analyzes this issue.

SPECHT v. JENSEN

853 F.2d 805 (10th Cir. 1988)

Moore, J.

This case is before the court for rehearing *en banc* of one issue. . . . The question considered is whether Fed. R. Evid. 702 will permit an attorney, called as an expert witness, to state his views of the law which governs the verdict and opine whether defendants' conduct violated that law. We conclude the testimony was beyond the scope of the rule and thus inadmissible.

This case is an action for damages pursuant to 42 U.S.C. §1983 grounded upon allegedly invalid searches of the plaintiffs' home and office. The underlying facts are set forth in the panel opinion and need not be restated here. What is germane for present consideration is whether defendants' conduct involved a "search" within the meaning of the Fourth Amendment and whether plaintiffs consented to the search were issues to be determined by the jury.

After testimony had been presented by the plaintiffs to establish the underlying facts, plaintiffs' counsel informed the court he wished to call an attorney who, after being given "a hypothetical of the facts that are in evidence in this case," would be asked if he believed that a search took place in the plaintiffs' home and business. Counsel stated that the witness would then be asked "based on the same facts in evidence whether he believed a consent search of either the business or the residence had been taken or undertaken." Finally, counsel proposed to ask the witness:

> [B]ased on his knowledge in these areas what would constitute a proper search, or the proper documents constituting or allowing a search and would expect that he would say as follows: That if there is no search warrant, if there is no consent, if

there are no exigent circumstances, that the search is illegal per se. And that would be the extent of his testimony.

Defense counsel objected to the propriety of the testimony, suggesting that the subject was beyond the scope of Rule 702. He argued, "here we have an issue involving whether or not this [testimony] intrudes on the province of this court in terms of the law." Counsel continued:

> [W]hat constitutes [a] reasonable or unreasonable search is a matter of law. How the jury applies that law to these facts is the province of the jury. But the law must be defined by the Court, not by an expert witness. . . . [I]n order for [the expert] to testify, he must first presume what the Court is going to instruct as to the law; and if he doesn't presume what he thinks the Court is going to instruct as to the law, he must . . . define his own definitions of the law; and that's where the intrusion of the Court is germane. . . .
>
> Now, is [the expert] going to tell the jury what the law is upon which he is going to apply a hypothetical set of facts, or is this court going to tell the jury what the standard is?

[T]he expert was allowed to testify, and he did so at length. On the basis of hypothetical questions tailored to reflect plaintiffs' view of the evidence, the expert concluded there had been no consent given, and illegal searches had occurred.

We begin our analysis with a careful look at the contents and purpose of Fed. R. Evid. 702. It states:

> If scientific, technical, or other specialized knowledge will assist the trier of fact to understand the evidence or to determine a fact in issue, a witness qualified as an expert by knowledge, skill, experience, training, or education, may testify thereto in the form of an opinion or otherwise. . . .

Our judgment must therefore be guided by consideration of whether the testimony of the attorney expert aided the jury in its determination of critical issues in this case. We must also consider, however, whether the expert encroached upon the trial court's authority to instruct the jury on the applicable law, for it is axiomatic that the judge is the sole arbiter of the law and its applicability. As one scholar noted:

> A witness cannot be allowed to give an opinion on a question of law. . . . In order to justify having courts resolve disputes between litigants, it must be posited as an a priori assumption that there is one, but only one, legal answer for every cognizable dispute. There being only one applicable legal rule for each dispute or issue, it requires only one spokesman of the law, who of course is the judge. . . . To allow anyone other than the judge to state the law would violate the basic concept. Reducing the proposition to a more practical level, it would be a waste of time if witnesses or counsel should duplicate the judge's statement of the law, and it would intolerably confound the jury to have it stated differently.

Stoebuck, *Opinions on Ultimate Facts: Status, Trends, and a Note of Caution,* 41 Den. L. Cent. J. 226, 237 (1964) (footnote omitted).

The concern that an expert should not be allowed to instruct the jury is also emphasized in Fed. R. Evid. 704, which allows witnesses to give their opinions on ultimate issues. In the advisory notes to this rule, the committee stated:

> The abolition of the ultimate issue rule does not lower the bars so as to admit all opinions. Under Rules 701 and 702, opinions must be helpful to the trier of fact, and Rule 403 provides for exclusion of evidence which wastes time. These provisions afford ample assurances against the admission of opinions which would merely tell the jury what result to reach, somewhat in the manner of the oath-helpers of an earlier day. They also stand ready to exclude opinions phrased in terms of inadequately explored legal criteria. Thus the question, "Did T have capacity to make a will?" would be excluded, while the question, "Did T have sufficient mental capacity to know the nature and extent of his property and the natural object of his bounty to formulate a rational scheme of distribution?" would be allowed.

The committee's illustration establishes the starting point for analysis of admissibility by distinguishing between testimony on issues of law and testimony on ultimate facts. While testimony on ultimate facts is authorized under Rule 704, the committee's comments emphasize that testimony on ultimate questions of law is not favored. The basis for this distinction is that testimony on the ultimate factual questions aids the jury in reaching a verdict; testimony which articulates and applies the relevant law, however, circumvents the jury's decision-making function by telling it how to decide the case.

Following the advisory committee's comments, a number of federal circuits have held that an expert witness may not give an opinion on ultimate issues of law. In *Marx & Co. v. Diners' Club, Inc.,* 550 F.2d 505 (2d Cir.), *cert. denied,* 434 U.S. 861, 98 S. Ct. 188, 54 L. Ed. 2d 134 (1977), for example, the Second Circuit held it was error for the trial court to allow a lawyer to render his opinions on the legal obligations arising from a contract and on the legal significance of various facts in evidence. The court stated, "legal opinions as to the meaning of the contract terms at issue . . . was testimony concerning matters outside [the witness's] area of expertise. [I]n *United States v. Zipkin,* 729 F.2d 384 (6th Cir. 1984), the Sixth Circuit reversed the trial court's decision to allow a bankruptcy judge to testify regarding his interpretation of the Bankruptcy Act and his own orders. "It is the function of the trial judge to determine the law of the case," the court stated. "It is impermissible to delegate that function to a jury through the submission of testimony on controlling legal principles."

The courts in these decisions draw a clear line between permissible testimony on issues of fact and testimony that articulates the ultimate principles of law governing the deliberations of the jury. These courts have decried the latter kind of testimony as directing a verdict, rather than assisting the jury's understanding and weighing of the evidence. In keeping with these decisions, we conclude the expert in this case was improperly allowed to instruct the jury on how it should decide the case. The expert's testimony painstakingly developed over an entire day the conclusion that defendants violated plaintiffs' constitutional rights. He told the jury that warrantless searches are unlawful, that defendants committed a warrantless search on plaintiffs' property, and that the only applicable exception to the warrant requirement, search by consent, should not vindicate the defendants because no authorized person voluntarily consented to allow a search of the premises. . . . By permitting the jury to hear this array of legal conclusions touching upon nearly every element of the plaintiffs' burden of proof under §1983, the trial court allowed the expert to supplant both the court's duty to set forth the law and the jury's ability to apply this law to the evidence.

Given the pervasive nature of this testimony, we cannot conclude its admission was harmless. There is a significant difference between an attorney who states his belief of what law should govern the case and any other expert witness. While other experts may aid a jury by rendering opinions on ultimate issues, our system reserves to the trial judge the role of adjudicating the law for the benefit of the jury. When an attorney is allowed to usurp that function, harm is manifest in at least two ways.

First, as articulated in *Marx & Co. v. Diners' Club, Inc.,* the jury may believe the attorney-witness, who is presented to them imbued with all the mystique inherent in the title "expert," is more knowledgeable than the judge in a given area of the law. *Marx,* 550 F.2d at 512. Indeed, in this case, the expert's knowledge and experience was made known to the jury by both the court and counsel in a manner which gave his testimony an aura of trustworthiness and reliability. Thus, there is a substantial danger the jury simply adopted the expert's conclusions rather than making its own decision. Notwithstanding any subsequent disclaimers by the witness that the court's instructions would govern, a practical and experienced view of the trial world strongly suggests the jury's deliberation was unduly prejudiced by the expert's testimony.

Second, testimony on ultimate issues of law by the legal expert is inadmissible because it is detrimental to the trial process. If one side is allowed the right to call an attorney to define and apply the law, one can reasonably expect the other side to do the same. Given the proclivity of our brothers and sisters at the bar, it can be expected that both legal experts will differ over the principles applicable to the case. The potential is great that jurors will be confused by these differing opinions, and that confusion may be compounded by different instructions given by the court.

The line we draw here is narrow. We do not exclude all testimony regarding legal issues. We recognize that a witness may refer to the law in expressing an opinion without that reference rendering the testimony inadmissible. Indeed, a witness may properly be called upon to aid the jury in understanding the facts in evidence even though reference to those facts is couched in legal terms. For example, we have previously held that a court may permit an expert to testify that a certain weapon had to be registered with the Bureau of Alcohol, Tobacco, and Firearms. *United States v. Buchanan,* 787 F.2d 477, 483 (10th Cir. 1986). In that case, however, the witness did not invade the court's authority by discoursing broadly over the entire range of the applicable law. Rather, the expert's opinion focused on a specific question of fact. *See also United States v. Garber,* 607 F.2d 92 (5th Cir. 1979) (trial court erred in refusing to let experts on income tax law testify regarding whether failure to report funds received for sale of blood plasma constituted income tax evasion).

These cases demonstrate that an expert's testimony is proper under Rule 702 if the expert does not attempt to define the legal parameters within which the jury must exercise its fact-finding function. However, when the purpose of testimony is to direct the jury's understanding of the legal standards upon which their verdict must be based, the testimony cannot be allowed. In no instance can a witness be permitted to define the law of the case.

Plaintiffs seek to avoid this conclusion by arguing the expert testimony here was no different from a medical expert testifying that specific conduct constitutes medical malpractice. We do not believe, however, there is an analog between the testimony of the medical expert and that of the legal expert because the former does not usurp the function of the court. The testimony of the medical expert in plaintiffs' hypothesis is more like that of the legal expert who explains a discrete point of law which is helpful to the jury's understanding of the facts.

[Remanded to panel for consideration of a cross appeal.]

[Dissenting opinion omitted.]

NOTES TO SPECHT v. JENSEN

1. *Line Drawing.* The court prohibits testimony that seeks "to direct the jury's understanding of the legal standards on which their verdict must be based," and seems to accept testimony that would "explain a discrete point of law which is helpful to the jury." These principles can be tested in these circumstances:

> Testimony on whether police officers' efforts in communicating with a deaf plaintiff satisfied federal disability statutes. *See* Burkhart v. Washington Metro. Area Transit Auth., 112 F.3d 1207, 1212-1214 (D.C. Cir. 1997).
>
> Testimony on whether, under securities laws, disclosure of a particular fact was required in the course of negotiating a transaction. *See* Adalman v. Baker, Watts & Co., 807 F.2d 359, 366 (4th Cir. 1986).

2. *Advisory Committee Example.* The court quotes the Advisory Committee suggestions that it would be wrong for an expert to testify that a person had lacked the capacity to make a will but that it would be proper for that witness to testify that the person knew enough about his property to devise a rational scheme to distribute it. The court also refers approvingly to admission of testimony that a certain weapon is required to be registered with a federal agency. This may contradict the Advisory Committee position, since a witness might otherwise have testified just about the identity of the weapon and left it to the trial judge to explain how a weapon of that description is treated under federal law.

GOOD TO REMEMBER

The judge is available to be a source of information about law in every trial. This decreases the need for expert testimony on it.

E INADMISSIBLE EVIDENCE AS A BASIS FOR EXPERT TESTIMONY

Rule 703 allows an expert to rely on inadmissible evidence in forming an opinion and necessarily allows the expert to convey some aspects of that information to the jury. *Sphere Drake Insurance* illustrates this process.

Rule 703. Bases of an Expert's Opinion Testimony

An expert may base an opinion on facts or data in the case that the expert has been made aware of or personally observed. If experts in the particular field would reasonably rely on those kinds of facts or data in forming an opinion on the subject, they need not be admissible for the opinion to be admitted. But if the facts or data would otherwise be inadmissible, the proponent of the opinion may disclose them to the jury only if their probative value in helping the jury evaluate the opinion substantially outweighs their prejudicial effect.

■   ■   ■

"My Informants Told Me Something" — **Sphere Drake Insurance.** Rule 703 allows an expert to base testimony on information that fails to satisfy evidence law's requirements for admissibility. It takes the position that if information is usually considered good enough to rely on by people in the expert's field, then it is good enough to be a basis for the expert's testimony. The rule obviously conflicts with evidence law's general prohibitions against hearsay evidence. It might also require very careful application if an expert's testimony were to be based on information that, in a criminal case, would be barred by the Confrontation Clause.

SPHERE DRAKE INSURANCE PLC v. TRISKO

226 F.3d 951 (8th Cir. 2000)

HEANEY, J.

Robert Trisko, doing business as Trisko Designer Jewelry and Trisko Jewelry Sculptures, Ltd., sustained a loss of jewelry that was insured collectively by Sphere Drake Insurance, PLC, UnionAmerica Insurance Company, Ltd., Copenhagen Reinsurance Company, St. Paul Reinsurance Company, and Terra Nova Insurance Company (the insurers). The insurers brought suit in the district court seeking a declaratory judgment that the loss was excluded from coverage. The jury found for Trisko, and following post-trial motions, judgment was entered accordingly. The insurers appeal, arguing that evidentiary errors mandate a new trial. . . . For the reasons articulated below, we affirm.

BACKGROUND

Trisko designs and sells unique pieces of jewelry. Trisko peddles these so-called "wearable sculptures" at art and jewelry shows throughout the country. He transports the jewelry from his home base in Waite Park, Minnesota, to various bazaars.

On the weekend of November 29 though December 1, 1996, Trisko and some of his employees were scheduled to attend shows in Florida. Because Trisko often frequents shows in Florida, he maintains a van there that he uses to transport the jewelry to shows. However, on this weekend, he had two shows to attend simultaneously, one in Miami and the other in Boca Raton. He decided that he and a fellow employee, Eric Liberacki, would work the Miami show, and other employees would work the Boca Raton show. He allowed the other employees to use the van, while he and Liberacki rented a car for the Miami show.

As dusk approached on Sunday, December 1, Trisko and Liberacki began to break down their display. They wrapped each piece of jewelry in its own plastic bag to avoid scuffing or scratching the pieces, and placed all the jewels in two small suitcases. The process of breaking down their display and preparing the jewelry for travel took roughly an hour.

After they finished breaking down the display, Trisko and Liberacki put the jewels in the trunk of their rented Buick, and waited for the other employees to join them following completion of the Boca Raton show. Trisko and Liberacki first waited outside the Buick, with their complete attention focused on the car. After about half an hour, they moved inside the vehicle. While inside the car, they played the radio, read the newspaper, and talked about hockey to pass the time. At no time while standing outside the car or sitting inside it did Trisko or Liberacki see or hear anything unusual.

Eventually the Boca Raton contingent arrived, and the caravan went to the airport to drop off the rental car. When Liberacki opened the Buick's trunk to transfer the jewelry to the van, he discovered both suitcases and all the jewelry they contained were gone.

Trisko had an insurance policy on his wares, often referred to as a "Jewelers Block" policy. The policy insured the jewelry against loss or damage. It did not, however, cover what it termed as any "unexplained loss" or "mysterious disappearance" of the jewelry. Neither did it cover a loss that occurred while the jewelry was within a vehicle, unless Trisko or his employees were also in the vehicle.

The insurers sought a declaratory judgment that Trisko's loss was excluded from coverage as a mysterious disappearance. The insurers further argued that while the loss may have been the result of a theft from the Buick, such loss was excluded because Trisko could not prove the theft took place while he or Liberacki were in the car.

A jury trial ensued, and the jury found in favor of Trisko in the amount of $275,554.99. The insurers appeal, contending that various evidentiary errors mandate a new trial. They alternatively argue that they are entitled to judgment as a matter of law because Trisko failed to prove his loss was covered by the policy. Trisko cross-appeals the district court's calculation of prejudgment interest.

The insurers' evidentiary objections center around the testimony of George Michael Crowley, a detective with the Miami-Dade Police Department. At trial, Trisko offered Crowley's deposition testimony as that of an expert witness who would assist the jury in understanding the jewelry's disappearance. Through Crowley, the jury heard evidence and viewed exhibits regarding crime in the Miami area. Crowley further testified that two informants, identified only as Hernando and Freddie, told him that two individuals had been paid $20,000 each to steal Trisko's jewelry. Crowley then expressed his opinion that Trisko's loss did not constitute a mysterious disappearance, but rather was likely a theft.

The district court is afforded substantial deference in its evidentiary rulings, and we review for an abuse of discretion.

We first consider whether the district court erred in permitting Crowley to opine that the loss was not a mysterious disappearance. The insurers seem to argue that Crowley was not qualified to offer such an opinion and that the basis for his opinion is unreliable.

Expert testimony should be admitted if the expert's specialized knowledge will assist the trier of fact in determining an issue in the case. "[D]oubts regarding whether an expert's testimony will be useful should generally be resolved in favor of admissibility." Attacks on the foundation for an expert's opinion, as well as the expert's conclusions, go to the weight rather than the admissibility of the expert's testimony.

There is no doubt that Crowley was qualified as an expert on theft in the Miami area. He investigated thefts in the area for several years, and has specialized knowledge of jewel thieves and their methods of operation. Further, his investigation of Trisko's theft afforded him distinct knowledge of this case outside of the jury's common experience. Although the insurers challenge the basis for his opinion, such a critique should be engendered through thorough cross-examination, and not through the wholesale exclusion of the expert's testimony.

The insurers next complain about the hearsay statements of Freddie and Hernando, introduced through the testimony of Crowley. Had these hearsay statements been introduced for their truth, they would be inadmissible. However, as an expert, Crowley was entitled to rely on otherwise inadmissible hearsay in forming the basis of his opinion, so long as the hearsay is of the type reasonably relied upon by experts in his field. *See* Fed. R. Evid. 703; *Brennan v. Reinhart Institutional Foods,* 211 F.3d 449, 450 (8th Cir. 2000). Crowley testified that he regularly relied on the statements of informants as an investigating officer. He likewise was permitted to do so in forming the basis of his expert opinion.

An expert may "testify about facts and data outside of the record for the limited purpose of exposing the factual basis of the expert's opinion." *Brennan*, 211 F.3d at 451. The district court specifically instructed the jury "to give no weight to the statements of Hernando or Freddie in the consideration of the issues in this case. You are to consider that testimony only in developing what Detective Crowley did in the course of his investigation." Because the hearsay statements were not admitted for their truth, but rather only to inform the jury of the factual basis of Crowley's expert opinion, they were properly admitted by the district court.

Lastly, we analyze whether evidence of similar crime in the Miami area was admissible. To be admissible, evidence must be relevant to some issue in the case. At trial, the insurers argued that the loss of the jewelry was excluded from coverage as a "mysterious disappearance" or "unexplained loss." In order to prove his case, Trisko was required to present some plausible explanation for the jewelry's disappearance. Accordingly, Trisko was permitted to show that, despite noticing nothing unusual while in the car, and despite not catching any thieves red-handed, a theft nevertheless may have occurred. The evidence complained of did just that: it provided the jury with information about jewel thieves at work in the Miami area around the same time period, whose stealthy methods made them difficult to detect. . . .

. . . Because Trisko did not present direct evidence of precisely what happened to the jewelry or precisely when it disappeared, the insurers contend that any verdict in Trisko's favor must have been based purely on speculation and conjecture. Long ago, the Supreme Court recognized the fallacy of the argument now espoused by the insurers:

> Whenever facts are in dispute or the evidence is such that fair-minded men may draw different inferences, a measure of speculation and conjecture is required on the part of those whose duty it is to settle the dispute by choosing what seems to them to be the most reasonable inference.

Lavender v. Kurn, 327 U.S. 645 at 653 (1946).

The jury was expected to draw inferences from the evidence and use reason to determine what happened. A reasonable inference from Trisko's evidence is that he is the victim of an unsolved theft that occurred while he was within the vehicle. The jury so found. . . .

For the above-stated reasons, we affirm the district court in all respects.

NOTES TO SPHERE DRAKE INSURANCE PLC v. TRISKO

1. *Expert's Quotation of Another Expert.* In a case where the prosecution accused a physician of writing prescriptions in violation of narcotics control laws, testimony by a Dr. MacIntosh was admitted in which Dr. MacIntosh described his own analysis of the defendant's records of his interactions with

patients. He also testified that his conclusions as to the defendant's actions were "essentially the same" as those of a Dr. Stevenson, who did not testify and whose report was not introduced into evidence. Dr. MacIntosh testified that he had examined the defendant's charts and the transcript of grand jury testimony of some of the patients and reviewed Dr. Stevenson's opinions on the same charts. He testified: "Dr. Stevenson is a general surgeon who is a close friend of mine. He is also a lawyer, and he is well thought of in Northern Virginia. He has been president of the Medical Society." When asked if his conclusions were contrary to those of Dr. Stevenson, the witness responded, "No. My findings were essentially the same." Was this testimony properly admitted? *See* U.S. v. Tran Trong Cuong, 18 F.3d 1132 (4th Cir. 1994).

Segment 17: allowable factual basis for expert testimony

2. *Counterexample.* The Texas Rules of Evidence are more detailed than Federal Rule 703 with regard to controlling the instances in which a jury might learn otherwise inadmissible data through the testimony of an expert witness:

> **Texas R. Evid. 705. Disclosure of Facts or Data Underlying Expert Opinion**
>
> . . .
>
> **(d) Balancing test; limiting instructions.** When the underlying facts or data would be inadmissible in evidence, the court shall exclude the underlying facts or data if the danger that they will be used for a purpose other than as explanation or support for the expert's opinion outweighs their value as explanation or support or are unfairly prejudicial. If otherwise inadmissible facts or data are disclosed before the jury, a limiting instruction by the court shall be given upon request.

3. *Limiting Instruction.* When an expert discloses otherwise inadmissible information as a basis for his or her opinion, the jury will be asked to rely on that information only to assess the strength of the expert's opinion. This is supposedly different from using the information as proof that what it conveys is accurate. For example, the jury in *Sphere Drake Insurance* was told "give no weight to the statements of Hernando or Freddie in the consideration of the issues in this case. You are to consider that testimony only in developing what Detective Crowley did in the course of his investigation." How could jurors reasonably follow that instruction, when the statements of Hernando and Freddie are equivalent to the conclusion of Detective Crowley?

4. *Limiting the Power of Inadmissible Evidence for Summary Judgment.* The supposedly narrow use of inadmissible evidence an expert relies on may be achieved in some special contexts. For example, if a plaintiff's case lacks evidence on a required element, the defendant would be entitled to summary judgment. In a situation of that type, summary judgment would still be granted even if otherwise inadmissible information on which an expert might rely would be offered in the plaintiff's case. Inadmissible evidence cannot protect against summary judgment or any other motion for judgment as a matter of law.

QUESTION 14-5. In a criminal case, the defendant sought to establish an insanity defense with testimony by experts. Those experts had not examined the defendant. They based their opinions on written reports from other mental health practitioners who had examined the defendant. Would it be proper for the trial judge to refuse to give a jury instruction on insanity, if the testimony by the defendant's experts was the only evidence of the defendant's mental state at the significant time?

F LAY OPINION

In line with the traditional practice that limits lay witnesses to testifying about facts, and not about opinions, Rule 701 describes the narrow range of circumstances in which opinion testimony by nonexpert witnesses may be allowed.

Rule 701. Opinion Testimony by Lay Witnesses

If a witness is not testifying as an expert, testimony in the form of an opinion is limited to one that is:
    (a) rationally based on the witness's perception;
    (b) helpful to clearly understanding the witness's testimony or to determining a fact in issue; and
    (c) not based on scientific, technical, or other specialized knowledge within the scope of Rule 702.

Rule 701 is more detailed in its current version than it was when first adopted, and some states continue to use a simpler form. Provision (c) in the current Federal Rule is the element that was added by amendment to the original rule.

■   ■   ■

A Knowledgeable Layperson — Davis. The *Davis* court interpreted a state version of Rule 701 that does not include the reference to "scientific, technical, or other specialized knowledge." It sets out many examples of typically permitted lay opinion testimony. In that context, it considers the propriety of admitting a lay witness's testimony based on unusual knowledge.

STATE v. DAVIS

351 Or. 35 (2011)

WALTERS, J.

In this criminal case . . . Defendant was charged with murder and manslaughter based on allegations that he shook the victim, his 15-month-old daughter, and inflicted fatal abdominal and brain injuries on the night that she died. Defendant contended that the victim's autopsy revealed that the victim had been injured at least several days before the night of her death and that nothing that he intentionally did to the victim on that evening caused the catastrophic brain hemorrhage that killed her. As relevant to this case, defendant attempted to introduce evidence that . . . a friend of the victim's mother saw the victim four days before her death and concluded that the victim looked like the friend's own daughter, who had suffered a brain injury as a baby. . . . [T]he trial court excluded the evidence. Defendant was convicted of one count of murder and one count of manslaughter. . . .

We turn to . . . whether the trial court erred in excluding . . . testimony [by Payne, a friend of the victim's mother], in which she explained her daughter's condition and stated that the victim looked like her daughter when she was the victim's age and when she was suffering from her brain injury or was dehydrated. Defendant argues that that testimony is admissible as lay opinion under OEC 701 and that the trial court erred in excluding it. For convenience, we set out that rule again here:

> "If the witness is not testifying as an expert, testimony of the witness in the form of opinions or inferences is limited to those opinions or inferences which are:
>   "(1) Rationally based on the perception of the witness; and
>   "(2) Helpful to a clear understanding of testimony of the witness or the determination of a fact in issue."

OEC 701 provides a "liberal standard for the admissibility of lay opinion" and permits a "shorthand" description of what the witness perceived, which is, in reality, an opinion. *State v. Lerch*, 296 Or. 377 (1984). As Justice Unis explained in his concurring opinion in *State v. Tucker*, 315 Or. 321, 340 (1993), the requirement in subsection (1) that lay opinion must be "rationally based on the perception of the witness" has two limitations. The first comes from OEC 602: the witness must have personal knowledge of the facts from which the opinion or inference is derived. The second is that

> "there must be a rational connection between the opinion or inference and the perceived factual basis from which it derives. The rational connection requirement means only that the opinion or inference advanced by the witness is one which a normal person could form on the basis of observed facts."

Id. Subsection (2) provides that, to be admissible, lay opinion must be "helpful" to the jury. As this court stated in *State v. Wright,* 323 Or. 8, 17 (1996), "[t]he concept of 'helpfulness' in OEC 701 subsumes a relevancy analysis." That is, as OEC 701 itself provides, lay opinion evidence is helpful only if it is relevant either to "clear understanding of testimony of the witness or the determination of a fact in issue."

As the court explained in *Lerch,*

> "[a]n essential difference between opinion testimony by a lay witness and an expert witness is that the lay witness is restricted to his personal perceptions while an expert witness may also testify from facts made known to him at or before the hearing."

Lay opinion is commonly admissible on a variety of topics. For example, the Commentary to the Oregon Evidence Code officially approves lay opinion on the following subjects: (1) the speed of an automobile, (2) the identity of a person, (3) the appearance of another person, (4) the sound of footsteps, (5) footprints, (6) distance, (7) uncomplicated illness or injury, and (8) apparent age. 1981 Conference Committee Commentary to the Oregon Evidence Code. In addition, Oregon case law recognizes that "lay witnesses are capable of offering an opinion as to whether a person is intoxicated." *State v. Wright,* 315 Or. 124, 132, 843 P.2d 436 (1992). Further, a lay witness may give an opinion that a stain on the floor was fecal matter. *Lerch,* 296 Or. at 384.

A lay witness and an expert may testify as to the same subject matter:

> "'The testimony of the chemist who has analyzed blood, and that of the observer who has merely recognized it by the use of the senses belong to the same legal grade of evidence, and though the one may be entitled to greater weight than the other with the jury, the exclusion of either is not sustainable.'"

Id., (quoting Clifford S. Fishman, 2 *Jones on Evidence,* §14:4, 591-592 (6th ed. 1972)). In fact, if the requirements of OEC 701 are met, lay opinion on subjects well outside the purview of most people is admissible. For example, in *Lerch,* a witness who had served in an infantry unit with the United States Army for 13 months during the Korean conflict was allowed to testify that he recognized the smell of decomposing human flesh in a dumpster, notwithstanding that that smell would be a "rare experience to the average person," because the witness's opinion was "rationally based on his perception in that he had previously experienced and recognized" that smell.

Applying those standards, we conclude that Payne's testimony that the victim looked like her own daughter when her daughter "had pressure on the brain or else she was dehydrated," as well as the background information about her daughter's condition, which explained the basis for her opinion testimony about the victim, satisfied the requirements of OEC 701.

At the outset, it is important to observe that defendant's offer of proof did not include testimony by Payne that, in her opinion, the victim actually was suffering from a brain injury on June 25. Only an expert could make that medical diagnosis. Rather, in the offer of proof, Payne was asked to describe what she saw when she arrived at Ecklund's home. In addition to describing the victim's physical appearance, Payne testified that her immediate thought was that the victim looked like her daughter when she was young and "had pressure on the brain or else she was dehydrated." Thus, Payne did not testify from the perspective of a physician who has diagnosed a patient, but from the perspective of an observer describing a person's appearance by associating it with a medical condition, much as a witness may describe a person's behavior and appearance by saying that the person looks intoxicated.

Although a person without Payne's prior experiences may not have been able to describe the victim's appearance in those terms, Payne was able to do so because, like someone who has seen blood or smelled decomposing human flesh, she often had observed the appearance of her child when she displayed the effects of pressure on the brain or dehydration. Payne's opinion that the victim resembled her daughter when her daughter was suffering from one of those two conditions was rationally based on her perceptions, in that she had a lifetime of previous experience with her own child suffering those conditions.

Payne's testimony also was "helpful to a clear understanding of testimony of the witness or the determination of a fact in issue." Payne's testimony was consistent with and helpful to corroborate the testimony of defendant's expert witnesses, based on their examination of the physical evidence, that the victim's brain and abdominal injuries occurred at least several days before she died. The state's experts testified that the fatal injuries had to have been inflicted on the night of her death. Payne's testimony that, on June 25, the victim resembled her child when her child displayed the effects of a brain injury or was dehydrated was relevant. It increased the probability, even if only slightly, that the defense experts were correct and the state's experts incorrect.

The state argues that, given that Payne was allowed to testify as to her observations of the victim's condition on June 25, the excluded evidence would not have made it any more probable that the victim had a brain injury on June 25. However, we think that Payne's opinion that, on that date, the victim resembled her own child when her child was suffering from pressure on the brain (or dehydration) is qualitatively different from a description of the victim's symptoms, in much the same way that a witness's opinion that a person looks intoxicated is qualitatively different from the simple observation that a person is disheveled or flushed or glassy-eyed. In both cases, the shorthand reference conveys a picture to the jury that is more complete than a mere list of physical characteristics. Payne's opinion, on June 25, that the victim resembled her child when she was suffering from a brain injury made it more probable that the victim did, in fact, have a brain injury on June 25. And, if the victim already was suffering from a brain injury on June 25, that fact, in turn, made it more probable that the victim died as a result of an injury inflicted on or before that date and not on June 29 or 30, as the state alleged.

In excluding Payne's lay opinion testimony, the trial court did not evaluate that testimony in light of the requirements of OEC 701. That is, the court did not consider whether that testimony was rationally based on Payne's perception or whether she had personal knowledge of the facts on which she based her opinion. Rather, the court excluded that testimony because "it really was speculative or conjecture or — and she was not certain."

We agree that Oregon's lay opinion rule precludes opinions based on conjecture or speculation, because opinions based on speculation or conjecture generally are not based on the perception of the witness or on the witness's personal knowledge. However, OEC 701 does not require certainty, as long as it is clear that the witness's opinion is based on personal knowledge and not guesswork.

Payne's opinion that the victim looked like her child when she "had pressure on the brain or else she was dehydrated" was not based on "speculation or conjecture." It was based on Payne's personal knowledge of her own daughter's appearance when suffering from one of those two conditions. Payne was offering her lay opinion concerning the victim's appearance as a mother of a brain-injured child; she did not purport to be an expert or to diagnose the victim's condition. Payne's opinion was rationally drawn from her perceptions, even though those perceptions were, as she herself acknowledged, susceptible to more than one plausible interpretation. . . .

As is evident from the foregoing, we conclude that the trial court erred in ruling that Payne's inability or unwillingness to state unequivocally that the victim looked like she was suffering only from a brain injury showed that she was simply guessing or speculating about the victim's condition. Because that was the sole reason that the trial court gave for excluding Payne's lay opinion testimony, and because Payne's opinion was relevant, rationally based on her perceptions, and helpful to the jury, we conclude that the trial court erred in excluding Payne's lay opinion in which she stated that the victim resembled her daughter when she was experiencing brain swelling. The trial court also erred in excluding Payne's testimony explaining her daughter's injury and resultant condition, because that testimony was essential to the jury's understanding of Payne's qualifications to offer her lay opinion. . . .

[Finding that the error was prejudicial,] we reverse the ruling of the trial court excluding Payne's lay opinion and the decision of the Court of Appeals affirming that ruling.

NOTES TO STATE v. DAVIS

1. *"Specialized Knowledge."* Federal Rule 701 has language not present in the state rule applied in *Davis*. The Federal Rule makes clear that testimony based on specialized knowledge of the type covered by Rule 702 (the general rule on experts) may not be given by a lay witness. Applying the Federal Rule might bar the testimony in *Davis*, since its topic (does an infant look like an infant with pressure on the brain or dehydration) might be characterized as something that requires expertise to really know.

In a recurring circumstance, police officers seek to testify about drugs, either to identify them or to describe quantities of drugs that in their experience are possessed by people who are dealing drugs and not merely using them. The *Walker* case in this chapter is an example of this. If testimony of this kind is treated as expert testimony, the witness must be qualified as an expert and the state must satisfy whatever procedural rules apply to anticipated use of expert testimony. *See, e.g.,* State v. Rothlisberger, 147 P.3d 1176 (Utah 2006).

2. *Helpfulness.* A lay witness may not give testimony that replicates what jurors could analyze for themselves. For example, if jurors could examine photographs of an accident scene and determine the relative size of the vehicles that were involved, testimony by a lay witness describing that would be improper.

QUESTION 14-6. Dan Driver was tried for driving while intoxicated. At the trial, Oscar Officer, a police officer, testified that he saw Dan Driver drive his car very slowly and then stop it in the middle of a street. Officer approached Driver, and then helped him get out of the car. Because Driver was very wobbly and unsteady on his feet, Officer leaned him against the car. Officer asked Driver to perform field sobriety tests, but Driver refused. Officer placed Driver under arrest and transported him to a police station. Driver collapsed while walking up the steps of the station. Two staff members assisted him the rest of the way to the processing room. Once they arrived, Officer asked Driver to take a breath test to determine his blood alcohol level, but Driver refused. After sitting at the processing table for about 15 minutes, Officer testified, Driver "vomited all over the processing room floor." Officer testified that Driver had "bloodshot, watery eyes" and "an odor of an alcoholic beverage." Officer also testified that Driver seemed confused and incoherent. Officer testified that, based on his experience, Driver was "highly impaired by alcohol."

If Officer was *not* qualified as an expert witness, was this testimony properly admitted?

G   SUMMARY

All witnesses are permitted to testify about facts they know, but only some witnesses may state opinions. The witnesses who may testify about opinions are expert witnesses. Nonexpert witnesses — lay witnesses — can give opinions only if the facts they know can best be articulated in that form.

Science-Based Opinions. Detailed jurisprudence has developed to control the use of science-based opinion testimony by experts. In federal courts and in most state courts, the *Daubert* framework applies. In that decision, the Supreme Court held that science-based testimony can be relevant, and therefore admissible, only if it is reliable. That means the proponent must show that it has an adequate basis, that its principles are legitimate, and that the principles and methods can reasonably be used for the purpose the expert intends to use them. The court suggested a range of inquiries that a trial court might use to probe these criteria, such as whether the science has been peer-reviewed and whether it can be tested. The *Daubert* court also recognized that general acceptance in a particular field can be part of the reliability inquiry. A rival approach, known as the *Frye* doctrine, continues to apply in some states. It allows science-based testimony only if the science has achieved general acceptance in a relevant scientific community.

Experience-Based Opinions. The Supreme Court decision in *Kumho Tire* requires that the same gate-keeping function a judge must carry out for science-based expert testimony is required for experience-based testimony. In various settings, courts have attempted to develop standards for nonscience expertise that can be similar in rigor and detail to those used for scientific testimony.

Topics for Expert Testimony. In general, expert testimony is permitted whenever it will "help the trier of fact to understand the evidence or to determine a fact in issue" (FRE 702). For some specific kinds of information, conventions have developed about whether the information satisfies this initial requirement. For example, experts are typically barred from testifying about someone's credibility. On the other hand, they are usually allowed to testify about patterns of narration, so long as they leave it up to the jury to compare the information about patterns of narration with information about how a particular witness or alleged victim has made statements. The field of law, as a topic for expert testimony, also involves typical rulings; usually testimony that would only describe legal doctrines to a jury is forbidden.

Inadmissible Evidence as a Basis for Expert Testimony. FRE 703 allows an expert to base his or her opinion on any data that experts in the field ordinarily would rely on, even if it is information that would ordinarily be inadmissible. This means that an expert might interview people who had seen an accident and then form an opinion about what caused the accident. If interviewing eyewitnesses is typically done by experts of this type, then the opinion would be admissible even though the eyewitnesses' statements would be hearsay. The information the expert has relied on can be revealed to the jury if the opposing party requests that it be revealed, or if revealing it is necessary for the jury's clear understanding of the testimony, so long as its probative value substantially exceeds its prejudicial effect.

Lay Opinion. Lay witnesses may testify about things they have perceived in any way. They are allowed to use opinions in some instances where using opinion language is clearer than restricting the narrative to objective facts. Testimony that someone seemed drunk is an example of opinion testimony that courts allow lay witnesses to give.

CHAPTER 15

Privileges

A. Introduction
B. Lawyers and Clients
C. Confidential Spousal Communications Privilege
D. Clergy-Penitent Communications
E. Mental Health Care Practitioners and Patients
F. Participants in Peer Review Processes
G. Summary

A   INTRODUCTION

Topic Overview

Testimonial privileges prohibit testimony about various kinds of confidential communications. In each instance, a court or legislature has decided that it is worth degrading the truth-seeking process of litigation in order to support some other social values. The most well-known privileges shield communications between a client and a lawyer, between spouses, and between a member of the clergy and a person seeking spiritual counseling from that member of the clergy. In addition to these, there are other privileges that protect a wide array of communications.

When the Federal Rules of Evidence were first developed, initial versions had detailed provisions for many kinds of privileges. Congress rejected all of them. Instead, a single rule was adopted that defers to the common law process (a somewhat unusual result, given that the Federal Rules of Evidence project meant to create clarity and uniformity by replacing the common law style of doctrinal development). Rule 501 articulates this "nonrule" position.

> **Rule 501. Privilege in General**
>
> The common law — as interpreted by United States courts in the light of reason and experience — governs a claim of privilege unless any of the following provides otherwise:
>
> - the United States Constitution;
> - a federal statute; or
> - rules prescribed by the Supreme Court.
>
> But in a civil case, state law governs privilege regarding a claim or defense for which state law supplies the rule of decision.

STEPS FOR...

Analyzing Privilege Issues

1. Aspects of the communication:
   - Did the people who communicated have one of the relationships protected by a privilege?
   - Did the people protect their confidentiality during the communication?
   - Was the topic of the communication consistent with application of the privilege?
2. Reasons to withdraw the privilege:
   - Did the holder of the privilege take some action that waives the privilege?
   - Would applying the privilege impair some important social value?

The Federal Rules contain one other privilege provision, FRE 502, which covers ways in which the holder of a privilege may waive its protection. For states, codes and statutes are a significant part of privilege law. All states recognize many privileges, under common law doctrines, statutes, or provisions of their state evidence codes.

For most privileges, certain basic issues are important. The proponent must establish that the communication was made in the exact relationship meant to be protected by the privilege. The communication must have been confidential when it was made. The issue of waiver is often important, since disclosing the privileged communication in any setting will void the privilege in a later judicial proceeding. Finally, if applying the privilege would hamper some very important social policy, usually the privilege will be withdrawn.

Chapter Organization

The chapter's cases confront the foundation issue for all privileges: Should any privilege be recognized for a particular kind of communication? The cases consider privileges for:

- Lawyers and clients
- Spousal communications
- Clergy and members of their religions

■ Mental health care practitioners and their patients
■ Participants in university tenure processes

The section on lawyer-client privilege considers some detailed aspects of that privilege in addition to the foundation question of whether such a privilege should ever be recognized. These issues are the application of the privilege in the corporate context, withdrawal of the privilege for communications in furtherance of crime or fraud, and the consequences (waiver or not) of inadvertent disclosures.

B LAWYERS AND CLIENTS

The lawyer-client privilege is usually justified with two rationales. First, encouraging people to obtain legal advice helps society because it can increase the prevalence of law-abiding behavior. Second, allowing secrecy for the communications between a lawyer and a client may represent society's desire to recognize a zone of privacy for particularly personal interactions. Of these two arguments, the first is most widely recognized. The cases in this section demonstrate the basic operation of the privilege. They also deal with applying the privilege to corporations and the concept of waiver.

■ ■ ■

Basic Rationale for Lawyer-Client Privilege, and Some Details About Its Waiver and Duration — Wesp. A husband and wife met with the husband's lawyer, and the husband met separately with that lawyer. After discussing the origins and values of the lawyer-client privilege, the court considers whether the wife's disclosure of communications during her and her husband's meeting with his lawyer should waive the husband's privilege with regard to statements made in his individual meeting with his lawyer. The court also considers whether the privilege should remain in force after the death of a client and whether a general "interests of justice" exception should operate in some situations to deny application of the privilege.

WESP v. EVERSON

33 P.3d 191 (Colo. 2001)

BENDER, J.

This original proceeding involves questions about the application of the attorney-client privilege. . . .

Plaintiff Heather Wesp, the respondent in this court, sought damages in tort against her mother and step-father, Cheryl and Frank Brewer, based on allegations that Frank Brewer had sexually abused her. Criminal charges were also filed based on the same allegations. After writing suicide letters to family and friends, both Brewers committed suicide. The criminal charges pending against Frank Brewer were dismissed and the personal representative of both Brewer estates was substituted as the party-defendant in the civil suit. Thereafter, the personal representative hired Frank Brewer's criminal defense attorneys to represent both estates on Wesp's claims....

In a series of rulings, the district court held that: (1) the attorney-client privilege was waived by the Brewers' suicide letters; (2) the attorney-client privilege did not survive the death of Frank Brewer; (3) the testamentary exception to the attorney-client privilege may apply; [and] (4) the privilege should be pierced because the exclusion at trial of testimony about communications between Frank Brewer and his criminal defense attorneys "would work a manifest injustice."...

Facts and Proceedings Below. In July of 1998, Heather Wesp reported to the police that her step-father, Frank Brewer, had sexually abused her during her childhood. Anticipating that criminal charges would be brought, Frank Brewer hired attorney Paul Prendergast and his associate, Janelle Oswald, to defend him.

Frank Brewer was charged with nineteen counts of aggravated incest and sexual assault. Prendergast discussed possible plea bargains with the district attorney's office but no agreement was reached.

The [estate] alleges that, during the course of Prendergast's representation of Frank Brewer, Frank Brewer spoke on the telephone and met privately with Prendergast ("private meetings"). Additionally, Prendergast met with both Frank and Cheryl Brewer on a Saturday in November ("joint meeting"). At the joint meeting, Prendergast told Frank Brewer of the criminal charges that had been filed against Frank Brewer, of the penalties associated with these charges, and of a possible plea agreement. According to Cheryl Brewer, Prendergast also recommended that Frank Brewer accept the plea bargain offered by the district attorney.

In the fall of 1998, Wesp brought civil claims seeking money damages against both Frank and Cheryl Brewer. Initially, Prendergast and Oswald did not represent either Frank or Cheryl Brewer in the civil case.

Approximately one week after the criminal charges were brought against Frank Brewer, the Brewers both prepared holographic wills. Additionally, the Brewers wrote letters containing denials that Frank Brewer had done the acts of which Wesp had accused him and provided explanations for their decisions to commit suicide. In giving these explanations, the Brewers related some of the information and advice about the criminal case that had been given to Frank Brewer by Prendergast at the joint meeting. For instance, in one letter to a friend, Cheryl Brewer wrote that "[t]he lawyer said with our record + Heather + Kerry

[to] testify . . . that it would be very, very hard to disprove this. The Lawyer wants Frank to plea + go to jail before Christmas." After writing these letters, the Brewers committed suicide.

The personal representative of the estates of Frank and Cheryl Brewer was then substituted as the defendant in the civil action. Several months later, Prendergast and Oswald entered their appearance as counsel for the defendant in this civil case. . . .

Wesp's counsel deposed Prendergast and Oswald. Both refused to answer almost all questions, citing attorney-client privilege and the work product doctrine. . . .

A second trial court judge [after the first judge's retirement] issued a second ruling which partially qualified the first judge's ruling that the attorney-client privilege did not survive the death of Frank Brewer, stating, "[T]he attorney-client privilege may survive the death of the client in some instances." However, the trial court ultimately concluded that "the exclusion of such testimony [about attorney-client communications] in this case would work a manifest injustice."

Thereafter, the defendant sought extraordinary relief from this court.

Attorney-Client Privilege. We begin our analysis by discussing the principles of the attorney-client privilege. This privilege is codified in Colorado by statute and operates to protect communications between attorney and client relating to legal advice.

In order to navigate within our legal system, lay people frequently require the assistance of attorneys. Attorneys are unable to provide clients with effective legal advice unless the clients reveal all pertinent facts, no matter how embarrassing or inculpating these facts may be. Open and honest communication between attorney and client thus furthers the attorney's ability to serve her client's interests. Absent assurances that communications will remain confidential, clients may be reluctant or unwilling to seek legal advice or to confide fully in their attorney. Thus, the right of parties within our justice system to consult professional legal experts is rendered meaningless unless communications between attorney and client are ordinarily protected from later disclosure without client consent. As early as 1833, courts extolled the virtues of protecting attorney-client communications because the privilege ultimately furthers the rule of law and the administration of justice:

> [S]o numerous and complex are the laws by which the rights and duties of citizens are governed, so important is it that they should be permitted to avail themselves of the superior skill and learning of those who are sanctioned by the law as its ministers and expounders . . . that the law has considered it the wisest policy to encourage and sanction this confidence [between attorney and client], by requiring that on such facts [communicated in confidence,] the mouth of the attorney shall be for ever [sic] sealed.

Hatton v. Robinson, 31 Mass. 416, 422 (1834).

Because the attorney-client privilege may frustrate the fact-finding process, it exists in constant tension with the judicial system's truth-seeking goals. However, that tension "is the price that society must pay for the availability of justice to every citizen, which is the value that the privilege is designed to ensure." *In re John Doe Grand Jury Investigation*, 408 Mass. 480 (1990). The overall social benefits of the privilege outweigh any harm that may result in a particular case from the privilege's application. Further, the harshness of the operation of the privilege is softened by a number of exceptions and by the doctrine of waiver, all of which are consistent with the goals of the privilege. . . .

Because the purpose of the privilege is to encourage clients to confide in their attorneys, it applies only "to statements made in circumstances giving rise to a reasonable expectation that the statements will be treated as confidential." *Lanari v. People*, 827 P.2d 495, 499 (Colo. 1992).

If a client communication is made to an attorney in the presence of a third party, then the communication is ordinarily not considered confidential. Since confidentiality is one of the elements that must be shown in order for the attorney-client privilege to attach, a communication made in the presence of a third party will not ordinarily receive the protection of the attorney-client privilege.[9] . . .

The client may impliedly or expressly waive the privilege that attaches to a protected communication. To prove an implied waiver, there must be evidence showing that the privilege holder, "by words or conduct, has impliedly forsaken his claim of confidentiality with respect to the communication in question." Waiver may occur in a variety of situations, including when a party places in issue a confidential communication going directly to a claim or defense, or when a witness testifies as to the communication without objection by the privilege-holder. The burden of establishing such a waiver rests with the party seeking to overcome the privilege.

As discussed, attorney-client communications made in the presence of a third party do not ordinarily receive the protection of the privilege, since they do not meet the confidentiality requirement. In contrast, if a communication to which the privilege has previously attached is subsequently disclosed to a third party, then the protection afforded by the privilege is impliedly waived. The rationale for this rule of waiver is that the subsequent disclosure of the communication is inconsistent with the confidentiality that must be maintained in order for the privilege to continue to apply.

The difference between situations where no privilege attaches and situations where a privilege is waived becomes important because some courts deem a waiver of the privilege with respect to a particular communication to operate as a waiver of the privilege with respect to all attorney-client communications on the same subject.

---

9. This rule is not absolute. The presence of certain employees or agents of the attorney does not defeat the privilege. Also, statements made in the presence of a co-defendant at a meeting with a joint attorney concerning a matter of common interest to a joint defense may be protected.

On the other hand, if the privilege never arises with respect to specific attorney-client communications, then we never reach the question of waiver. In such cases, as a matter of logic, there can be no waiver of the privilege because the statements disclosed were not privileged in the first instance.

In this case, the defendant argues that any statements made by Frank Brewer at the joint meeting are *not* privileged because these communications were made in the presence of a third party, Cheryl Brewer. Hence, the defendant contends that the subsequent disclosure of the statements made at the joint meeting did not constitute a waiver of the privilege attaching to any separate communications made between Frank Brewer and his criminal defense attorneys. The defendant argues that any confidential communications occurring between Frank Brewer and his attorneys at their private meetings, which happened outside the presence of a third party, remain privileged and protected despite the suicide letters.

Wesp does not dispute the defendant's contention that the statements made at the joint meeting are not protected by the attorney-client privilege. . . .

Wesp claims, however, that Frank Brewer expressly waived all protection of the attorney-client privilege because the suicide letters disclose communications made at the joint meeting. She argues that statements made in the Brewers' suicide letters operate as a waiver of other communications (such as those made between Frank Brewer and his attorneys at private meetings) which would have been privileged absent the suicide letters and the statements made therein. We disagree.

Wesp's argument omits the necessary first step of finding that a privilege exists for communications that occurred at the joint meeting and moves directly to the second step of finding that the privilege has been waived. As a matter of logic, one may not waive a privilege when a privilege does not exist. Wesp's concession that no privilege attached to statements made at the joint meeting defeats her ultimate argument that the suicide letters operate as a waiver of privileged communications.

Because the communications made at the joint meeting were not privileged, it follows that those communications are discoverable. Absent proof of another basis to pierce the protection of the attorney-client privilege, communications between Frank Brewer and his attorneys occurring at other times and places remain privileged so long as the party asserting the privilege can demonstrate that the requirements of the privilege are satisfied.

Having decided that the communications made at the joint meeting were not privileged and that the Brewers' suicide letters did not destroy any existing privilege applicable to other communications, we turn to the question of the effect of Frank Brewer's death on the attorney-client privilege.

The precedents uniformly hold or presume that the attorney-client privilege ordinarily survives the death of the client. The Supreme Court has noted that the very existence of the testamentary exception, discussed in greater detail below, presumes that the privilege must survive the death of the client. *Swidler & Berlin v. United States*, 524 U.S. 399 (1998). The *Swidler* Court reasoned that survival of the privilege is consistent with the privilege's policy, because "[k]nowing that communications will remain confidential even after death encourages the client to communicate fully and frankly with counsel. . . . Clients may be concerned about reputation, civil liability, or possible harm to friends or family. Posthumous disclosure of such communications may be as feared as disclosure during the client's lifetime." *Id.* These considerations led the *Swidler* Court to hold that the privilege survives death.

We find this reasoning to be persuasive. Therefore, we hold that any privileged communications between Frank Brewer and his attorneys remain privileged after his death.

There are several exceptions to the rule of attorney-client privilege, including the testamentary exception. In this case, the trial court suggested that the testamentary exception applies and that the attorney-client privilege may be pierced to prevent a "manifest injustice." We hold that the testamentary exception does not apply. We decline to create a manifest injustice exception to the rule of attorney-client privilege because precedent does not support such an exception and it would undermine the purposes of the privilege.

The testamentary exception permits an attorney to reveal certain types of communications in special circumstances. Specifically, the attorney who drafted the will of a deceased client may disclose attorney-client communications concerning the will and transactions leading to its execution in a suit between the testator's heirs, devisees, or other parties who claim by succession from the testator. The rationale for this exception is that it furthers the client's testamentary intent.

Wesp claims that the testamentary exception applies because this case involves litigation among the heirs and devisees of Prendergast's client. We are not persuaded. Prendergast and Oswald did not prepare the Brewers' wills. This case is not a will contest case and Wesp does not attempt to claim by succession. Instead, she stands as a potential tort claimant against her mother and stepfather's estates. Hence, the testamentary exception does not apply. . . .

The trial court ruled that the attorney-client privilege may be pierced if the application of the privilege results in a manifest injustice. Our research discloses neither legal precedent nor authority that supports the existence of any such exception to the rule of attorney-client privilege. Absent legislative direction to the contrary, we decline to read into the privilege such an exception which appears at odds with the purposes of the privilege.

The goal of the privilege is to encourage clients to confide all pertinent information in their attorneys to ensure the orderly administration of justice. Piercing the protection of the attorney-client privilege to prevent a manifest injustice could have far-reaching consequences to our judicial system. Such a rule would discourage clients from confiding in their attorneys or from seeking legal advice in the first instance. If clients lack the confidence in their attorneys to inform them of all relevant information, then attorneys may be unable to advise and assist clients effectively in a multitude of situations, including those where clients seek legal advice in order to ensure compliance with the law.

The Supreme Court pointed out the benefits of a privilege whose application is certain and predictable:

> [I]f the purpose of the attorney-client privilege is to be served, the attorney and client must be able to predict with some degree of certainty whether particular discussions will be protected. An uncertain privilege, or one which purports to be certain but results in widely varying applications by the courts, is little better than no privilege at all.

Upjohn Co. v. United States, 449 U.S. 383 (1981). The Supreme Court's concerns are relevant here.

If the attorney-client privilege could be pierced on the basis of an unpredictable manifest injustice standard, then this exception would swallow the protections of the privilege and undermine its purpose. Hence, we hold that the trial court erred to the extent that it recognized and applied a manifest injustice exception to this case. . . .

Because the parties agree that communications made at the joint meeting were not protected by the attorney-client privilege, we conclude that the Brewers' suicide letters did not waive any privilege that may apply to communications made between Frank Brewer and his attorneys at their private meetings. Frank Brewer's privilege survives his death and the testamentary exception does not apply in this case. Therefore, absent sufficient proof of an exception to the privilege or a waiver of the privilege, communications between Frank Brewer and his attorneys not occurring at the joint meeting remain privileged. . . .

We therefore make absolute both orders to show cause and vacate the trial court orders which hold that the privilege does not survive death, the testamentary exception applies, the suicide letters waived any privilege, and the privilege can be pierced to prevent a manifest injustice. . . .

NOTES TO WESP v. EVERSON

1. *Incentives for Consulting Lawyers.* If there were no privilege for confidential communications between lawyers and their clients, would people still seek legal advice in some situations? The answer to this question must be "yes." So the utilitarian rationale for the privilege must be based on instincts about how often people might consult lawyers and about how forthcoming they would likely be during those consultations. If the rate and completeness of consultations would decrease, most people would agree that this would represent a loss of some important values to society. Supporting the lawyer-client privilege requires a balancing of the benefits society would lose if people consulted lawyers less and the losses the privilege entails by making some information unavailable in trials.

2. *Third-Party Presence During Lawyer-Client Consultations.* In *Wesp,* the client's wife was present during one consultation between the client and the

lawyer. The court held that her presence meant that the conversation was not privileged. This led to the court's rejecting of the plaintiff's analysis (the plaintiff argued that when the client and the client's wife wrote to people about that meeting, they waived a privilege and the waiver should apply to information about that meeting and also information about related meetings between the client and the lawyer). Since the wife's presence precluded a finding of privilege, there was no waiver at all.

Courts typically tolerate the presence of some third parties during lawyer-client conversations and still treat those conversations as privileged, if the third party is someone like an interpreter or an investigator hired by the lawyer whose presence is necessary to assist in the providing of legal services.

The *Wesp* court holds that the presence of the client's wife precludes application of the privilege. There are not many cases deciding this issue, and courts are split on it. Since husband-wife communications can be privileged, it might seem that the presence of the client's wife should not negate the intended confidentiality of the lawyer-client communications. But on the other hand, the presence of the wife could be said to cancel the confidentiality required for lawyer-client communications, and the presence of the lawyer could be said to cancel the confidentiality required for the spousal communication privilege.

3. *Duration.* The conventional view is that the privilege is perpetual, continuing even after the end of the lawyer-client relationship and after the end of the client's life. On the other hand, some scholars have suggested that after a client's death, if information that client had given to a lawyer could be crucially important to someone, waiver of the privilege should be possible.

In one common circumstance, after the death of a client there is no privilege for statements made by the client relevant in litigation amongst the client's heirs, all of whom claim to have been the intended beneficiaries of the deceased client. It has been suggested that, in general, one who makes a will likely had no interest in statements about that will being kept secret after his or her death.

QUESTION 15-1. Lane Lawyer, a lawyer, and Cary Client, a client of Lawyer, had the following interactions. For which one is it most likely that lawyer-client privilege would be applied?

A. Client, a friend of Client's, and Lawyer met in Lawyer's office for a meeting in which Client asked Lawyer for advice about the tax consequences of giving money to the friend. In a lawsuit, a party seeks to question Lawyer about Client's intended gift.

B. Client met with Lawyer in a crowded fast-food restaurant and asked for advice about the tax consequences of giving money to a friend. In a lawsuit, a party seeks to question Lawyer about Client's intended gift.

C. Client met with Lawyer in Lawyer's office and asked for advice about the tax consequences of giving money to a friend. In a lawsuit, a party seeks to question Lawyer about Client's intended gift.

D. Client met with Lawyer to discuss a possible contract with someone, and he was wearing bloody clothing. In a lawsuit, a party seeks to question Lawyer about the condition of Client's clothing on that occasion.

■ ■ ■

Can an "Artificial Creature" Have a Privileged Communication? — Upjohn. Lawyer-client privilege in the corporate setting is heavily influenced by *Upjohn*. The Court states that "complications in the application of the privilege arise when the client is a corporation, which in theory is an artificial creature of the law, and not an individual," and offers solutions.

UPJOHN CO. v. UNITED STATES
449 U.S. 383 (1981)

Justice REHNQUIST delivered the opinion of the Court.

We granted certiorari in this case to address important questions concerning the scope of the attorney-client privilege in the corporate context. . . . [T]he parties and various *amici* have described our task as one of choosing between two "tests" which have gained adherents in the courts of appeals. We are acutely aware, however, that we sit to decide concrete cases and not abstract propositions of law. We decline to lay down a broad rule or series of rules to govern all conceivable future questions in this area, even were we able to do so. We can and do, however, conclude that the attorney-client privilege protects the communications involved in this case from compelled disclosure. . . .

Petitioner Upjohn Co. manufactures and sells pharmaceuticals here and abroad. In January 1976 independent accountants conducting an audit of one of Upjohn's foreign subsidiaries discovered that the subsidiary made payments to or for the benefit of foreign government officials in order to secure government business. The accountants, so informed petitioner, Mr. Gerard Thomas, Upjohn's Vice President, Secretary, and General Counsel. . . . He consulted with outside counsel and R.T. Parfet, Jr., Upjohn's Chairman of the Board. It was decided that the company would conduct an internal investigation of what were termed "questionable payments." As part of this investigation the attorneys prepared a letter containing a questionnaire which was sent to "All Foreign General and Area Managers" over the Chairman's signature. . . . The letter indicated that the Chairman had asked Thomas, identified as "the company's General Counsel," "to conduct an investigation for the purpose of determining the nature and magnitude of any payments made by the Upjohn Company or any of its subsidiaries to any employee or official of a foreign government." The questionnaire sought detailed information concerning such payments. Managers were instructed to treat the investigation as "highly confidential" and not to discuss it with anyone other than Upjohn employees who might be helpful in providing the requested information. Responses were to be sent directly to Thomas. Thomas and outside counsel also interviewed the recipients of the questionnaire and some 33 other Upjohn officers or employees as part of the investigation.

On March 26, 1976, the company voluntarily submitted a preliminary report to the Securities and Exchange Commission on Form 8-K disclosing certain questionable payments. A copy of the report was simultaneously submitted to the Internal Revenue Service, which immediately began an investigation to determine the tax consequences of the payments. Special agents conducting the investigation were given lists by Upjohn of all those interviewed and all who had responded to the questionnaire. On November 23, 1976, the Service issued a summons . . . demanding production of:

> "All files relative to the investigation conducted under the supervision of Gerard Thomas to identify payments to employees of foreign governments and any political contributions made by the Upjohn Company or any of its affiliates since January 1, 1971 and to determine whether any funds of the Upjohn Company had been improperly accounted for on the corporate books during the same period.
>
> "The records should include but not be limited to written questionnaires sent to managers of the Upjohn Company's foreign affiliates, and memorandums or notes of the interviews conducted in the United States and abroad with officers and employees of the Upjohn Company and its subsidiaries."

The company declined to produce the documents specified in the second paragraph on the grounds that they were protected from disclosure by the attorney-client privilege and constituted the work product of attorneys prepared in anticipation of litigation. [The Sixth Circuit Court of Appeals held] that the privilege did not apply "[t]o the extent that the communications were made by officers and agents not responsible for directing Upjohn's actions in response to legal advice . . . for the simple reason that the communications were not the 'client's.'" The court reasoned that accepting petitioners' claim for a broader application of the privilege would encourage upper-echelon management to ignore unpleasant facts and create too broad a "zone of silence." Noting that Upjohn's counsel had interviewed officials such as the Chairman and President, the Court of Appeals remanded to the District Court so that a determination of who was within the "control group" could be made. In a concluding footnote the court stated that the work-product doctrine "is not applicable to administrative summonses issued under 26 U.S.C. §7602."

Federal Rule of Evidence 501 provides that "the privilege of a witness . . . shall be governed by the principles of the common law as they may be interpreted by the courts of the United States in light of reason and experience." The attorney-client privilege is the oldest of the privileges for confidential communications known to the common law. 8 J. Wigmore, Evidence §2290 (McNaughton rev. 1961). Its purpose is to encourage full and frank communication between attorneys and their clients and thereby promote broader public interests in the observance of law and administration of justice. The privilege recognizes that sound legal advice or advocacy serves public ends and that such advice or advocacy depends upon the lawyer's being fully informed by the client. As we stated last Term in *Trammel v. United States*, 445 U.S. 40 (1980): "The lawyer-client privilege rests on the need for the advocate and counselor to know all that relates to the client's reasons for seeking representation if the professional mission is to be carried out." And in *Fisher v. United States*, 425 U.S. 391 (1976), we recognized the purpose of the privilege to be "to encourage clients to make full disclosure to their attorneys." This rationale for the privilege has long been recognized by the Court. Admittedly complications in the application of the privilege arise when the client is a corporation, which in theory is an artificial creature of the law, and not an individual; but this Court has assumed that the privilege applies when the client is a corporation, and the Government does not contest the general proposition.

The Court of Appeals, however, considered the application of the privilege in the corporate context to present a "different problem," since the client was an inanimate entity and "only the senior management, guiding and integrating the several operations, . . . can be said to possess an identity analogous to the corporation as a whole." The first case to articulate the so-called "control group test" adopted by the court below, *Philadelphia v. Westinghouse Electric Corp.*, 210 F. Supp. 483, 485 [(ED Pa. 1962)], reflected a similar conceptual approach:

> "Keeping in mind that the question is, Is it the corporation which is seeking the lawyer's advice when the asserted privileged communication is made?, the most satisfactory solution, I think, is that if the employee making the communication, of whatever rank he may be, is in a position to control or even to take a substantial part in a decision about any action which the corporation may take upon the advice of the attorney, . . . then, in effect, *he is (or personifies) the corporation* when he makes his disclosure to the lawyer[,] and the privilege would apply." (Emphasis supplied.)

Such a view, we think, overlooks the fact that the privilege exists to protect not only the giving of professional advice to those who can act on it but also the giving of information to the lawyer to enable him to give sound and informed advice. The first step in the resolution of any legal problem is ascertaining the factual background and sifting through the facts with an eye to the legally relevant. . . .

In the case of the individual client the provider of information and the person who acts on the lawyer's advice are one and the same. In the corporate context, however, it will frequently be employees beyond the control group as defined by the court below — "officers and agents . . . responsible for directing [the company's] actions in response to legal advice" — who will possess the information needed by the corporation's lawyers. Middle-level — and indeed lower-level — employees can, by actions within the scope of their employment, embroil the corporation in serious legal difficulties, and it is only natural that these employees would have the relevant information needed by corporate counsel if he is adequately to advise the client with respect to such actual or potential difficulties. . . .

The control group test adopted by the court below thus frustrates the very purpose of the privilege by discouraging the communication of relevant information by employees of the client to attorneys seeking to render legal advice to the client corporation. The attorney's advice will also frequently be more significant to noncontrol group members than to those who officially sanction the advice, and the control group test makes it more difficult to convey full and frank legal advice to the employees who will put into effect the client corporation's policy.

The narrow scope given the attorney-client privilege by the court below not only makes it difficult for corporate attorneys to formulate sound advice when their client is faced with a specific legal problem but also threatens to limit the valuable efforts of corporate counsel to ensure their client's compliance with the law. In light of the vast and complicated array of regulatory legislation confronting the modern corporation, corporations, unlike most individuals, "constantly go to lawyers to find out how to obey the law," Burnham, *The Attorney-Client Privilege in the Corporate Arena*, 24 Bus. Law. 901, 913 (1969), particularly since compliance with the law in this area is hardly an instinctive matter.[2] The test adopted by the court below is difficult to apply in practice, though no abstractly formulated and unvarying "test" will necessarily enable courts to decide questions such as this with mathematical precision. But if the purpose of the attorney-client privilege is to be served, the attorney and client must be able to predict with some degree of certainty whether particular discussions will be protected. An uncertain privilege, or one which purports to be certain but results in widely varying applications by the courts, is little better than no privilege at all. The very terms of the test adopted by the court below suggest the unpredictability of its application. The test restricts the availability of the privilege to those officers who play a "substantial role" in deciding and directing a corporation's legal response. Disparate decisions in cases applying this test illustrate its unpredictability. . . .

The communications at issue were made by Upjohn employees to counsel for Upjohn acting as such, at the direction of corporate superiors in order to secure legal advice from counsel. . . . Information, not available from upper-echelon management, was needed to supply a basis for legal advice concerning compliance with securities and tax laws, foreign laws, currency regulations, duties to

---

2. The Government argues that the risk of civil or criminal liability suffices to ensure that corporations will seek legal advice in the absence of the protection of the privilege. This response ignores the fact that the depth and quality of any investigations, to ensure compliance with the law[,] would suffer, even were they undertaken. The response also proves too much, since it applies to all communications covered by the privilege: an individual trying to comply with the law or faced with a legal problem also has strong incentive to disclose information to his lawyer, yet the common law has recognized the value of the privilege in further facilitating communications.

shareholders, and potential litigation in each of these areas. The communications concerned matters within the scope of the employees' corporate duties, and the employees themselves were sufficiently aware that they were being questioned in order that the corporation could obtain legal advice. The questionnaire identified Thomas as "the company's General Counsel" and referred in its opening sentence to the possible illegality of payments such as the ones on which information was sought. . . . Pursuant to explicit instructions from the Chairman of the Board, the communications were considered "highly confidential" when made, and have been kept confidential by the company. Consistent with the underlying purposes of the attorney-client privilege, these communications must be protected against compelled disclosure.

The Court of Appeals declined to extend the attorney-client privilege beyond the limits of the control group test for fear that doing so would entail severe burdens on discovery and create a broad "zone of silence" over corporate affairs. Application of the attorney-client privilege to communications such as those involved here, however, puts the adversary in no worse position than if the communications had never taken place. The privilege only protects disclosure of communications; it does not protect disclosure of the underlying facts by those who communicated with the attorney. . . .

Here the Government was free to question the employees who communicated with Thomas and outside counsel. Upjohn has provided the IRS with a list of such employees, and the IRS has already interviewed some 25 of them. While it would probably be more convenient for the Government to secure the results of petitioner's internal investigation by simply subpoenaing the questionnaires and notes taken by petitioner's attorneys, such considerations of convenience do not overcome the policies served by the attorney-client privilege. . . .

Needless to say, we decide only the case before us, and do not undertake to draft a set of rules which should govern challenges to investigatory subpoenas. Any such approach would violate the spirit of Federal Rule of Evidence 501. See S. Rep. (1974) ("the recognition of a privilege based on a confidential relationship . . . should be determined on a case-by-case basis"). While such a "case-by-case" basis may to some slight extent undermine desirable certainty in the boundaries of the attorney-client privilege, it obeys the spirit of the Rules. At the same time we conclude that the narrow "control group test" sanctioned by the Court of Appeals, in this case cannot, consistent with "the principles of the common law as . . . interpreted . . . in the light of reason and experience," Fed. Rule Evid. 501, govern the development of the law in this area.

Our decision that the communications by Upjohn employees to counsel are covered by the attorney-client privilege disposes of the case so far as the responses to the questionnaires and any notes reflecting responses to interview questions are concerned. . . .

Accordingly, the judgment of the Court of Appeals is reversed, and the case remanded for further proceedings.

NOTES TO UPJOHN CO. v. UNITED STATES

1. *Who's a Client?* A communication will only be protected by the lawyer-client privilege if it is between a lawyer and the lawyer's client. Outside the corporate setting, this requirement is straightforward. *Upjohn* makes it easy to satisfy this requirement, rejecting the "control group" test that had sought to identify individuals within a corporation who might have the most attributes in common with a single human client of a single human lawyer.

2. *Can a Corporation Have Motivations?* In footnote 2, the Court rejects the idea that avoiding criminal or civil liability would be a powerful motivator for the collection of information in a corporate setting. The Court points out that the same motivation exists in all aspects of life, and therefore ought not, logically, to be a rationale for treating lawyer-client privilege differently for corporations than for individuals. An additional factor may be present for corporations: vulnerability to shareholders' suits. A corporation that fails to make adequate efforts to comply with the law might be liable to shareholders for that failing. This risk does not have a parallel for ordinary individuals.

3. *The "Test" in* Upjohn. According to *Upjohn*, a worker's communication to a corporation's lawyer is most likely to be a privileged communication if it:

- was made for the purpose of considering a legal issue;
- was made because the worker's superior ordered the communication;
- related to a topic within the scope of the employee's duties;
- was considered confidential when it was made.

4. *Broad Application of the Privilege.* The demise of the control group test is illustrated in Baisley v. Missisquoi Cemetery Association, 708 A.2d 924 (Vt. 1998), which involved a suit against the legal entity that operated a cemetery. The cemetery caretaker's statements to the cemetery's lawyer were covered by privilege.

5. *Work Product.* Separate from the confidential communications privilege, the Federal Rules of Civil Procedure and Criminal Procedure offer a qualified privilege for attorney work product. The doctrine was developed by the Supreme Court in Hickman v. Taylor, 329 U.S. 495 (1947). The Court there considered "an attempt, without purported necessity or justification, to secure written statements, private memoranda and personal recollections prepared or formed by an adverse party's counsel in the course of his legal duties." The Court recognized a degree of privacy for information of this kind. Material that would reveal a lawyer's mental processes is particularly protected. Work product privilege can cover anything a lawyer collects for trial purposes, while the lawyer-client privilege covers only lawyer-client communications. The work product doctrine

protects items from discovery unless it would impose an "undue hardship," while the communications privilege is not subject to a balancing test.

QUESTION 15-2. XYZ Company occupies about 20 floors of a large office building, and it operates a cafeteria on one of those floors, for the use of employees and their guests. One day Frank Faller slipped and fell in the cafeteria, and suffered an injury. A week later, the manager of the cafeteria instructed the cafeteria's cashier and one of its cooks to send reports about the accident to XYZ's office of general counsel. The manager remembered that a delivery worker from a company that supplied vegetables to the cafeteria had seen the incident, and the manager asked that worker to send a report to XYZ's general counsel. If Faller sues XYZ Company, seeking damages for his injury, discuss the issues related to an attempt by Faller to obtain copies of the statements by the cashier, the cook, and the delivery worker.

> ## GOOD TO REMEMBER
>
> Lawyer-client privilege has a broad application in the corporate setting. Investigations that could produce discoverable records if they were carried out by nonlawyers will produce privileged communications if the corporate employee in charge of the investigation is the corporation's counsel.

■ ■ ■

Will Accidental Disclosure of a Communication Waive the Privilege? — **Harp.** The large volumes of data that are sometimes involved in satisfying discovery motions or answering Freedom of Information Act requests have led courts to consider whether "inadvertent" disclosures of occasional privileged communications should fairly be treated as causing a waiver of privilege. *Harp* treats that problem under the law of Connecticut. For federal cases, Rule 502 applies. It has been part of the Federal Rules only since 2008.

Rule 502. Attorney-Client Privilege and Work Product; Limitations on Waiver

The following provisions apply, in the circumstances set out, to disclosure of a communication or information covered by the attorney-client privilege or work-product protection.

    (a) Disclosure Made in a Federal Proceeding or to a Federal Office or Agency; Scope of a Waiver. When the disclosure is made in a federal proceeding or to a federal office or agency and waives the attorney-client privilege or work-product protection, the waiver extends to an undisclosed communication or information in a federal or state proceeding only if:

        (1) the waiver is intentional;

(2) the disclosed and undisclosed communications or information concern the same subject matter; and

(3) they ought in fairness to be considered together.

(b) Inadvertent Disclosure. When made in a federal proceeding or to a federal office or agency, the disclosure does not operate as a waiver in a federal or state proceeding if:

(1) the disclosure is inadvertent;

(2) the holder of the privilege or protection took reasonable steps to prevent disclosure; and

(3) the holder promptly took reasonable steps to rectify the error, including (if applicable) following Federal Rule of Civil Procedure 26(b)(5)(B).

(c) Disclosure Made in a State Proceeding. When the disclosure is made in a state proceeding and is not the subject of a state-court order concerning waiver, the disclosure does not operate as a waiver in a federal proceeding if the disclosure:

(1) would not be a waiver under this rule if it had been made in a federal proceeding; or

(2) is not a waiver under the law of the state where the disclosure occurred.

(d) Controlling Effect of a Court Order. A federal court may order that the privilege or protection is not waived by disclosure connected with the litigation pending before the court — in which event the disclosure is also not a waiver in any other federal or state proceeding.

(e) Controlling Effect of a Party Agreement. An agreement on the effect of disclosure in a federal proceeding is binding only on the parties to the agreement, unless it is incorporated into a court order.

(f) Controlling Effect of this Rule. Notwithstanding Rules 101 and 1101, this rule applies to state proceedings and to federal court-annexed and federal court-mandated arbitration proceedings, in the circumstances set out in the rule. And notwithstanding Rule 501, this rule applies even if state law provides the rule of decision.

(g) Definitions. In this rule:

(1) "attorney-client privilege" means the protection that applicable law provides for confidential attorney-client communications; and

(2) "work-product protection" means the protection that applicable law provides for tangible material (or its intangible equivalent) prepared in anticipation of litigation or for trial.

Rule 502 contains a number of provisions that raise complicated issues of the relationship between federal and state law. For example, part (d) asserts that a federal court's decisions that a party's conduct has not constituted a waiver of privilege will control treatment of that issue in a state proceeding (assumedly where the same issue is raised). Whether a state would be required to honor that outcome has not yet been tested.

HARP v. KING

835 A.2d 953 (Conn. 2003)

PALMER, J.

The plaintiff, Wendell C. Harp, an African-American real estate developer and architect who owns and manages seven low and moderate income housing developments financed by the Connecticut Housing Finance Authority (CHFA), appeals from the judgment of the trial court rendered in favor of the defendants, Gary E. King, Vincent J. Flynn, Lawrence C. Pilcher and Regina Rentz, who are all employees of CHFA. The plaintiff initiated this action against the defendants alleging, inter alia, that, during the course of the defendants' employment with CHFA, they jointly agreed: (1) to defame him; (2) to place him in a false light in violation of his right to privacy; (3) to interfere tortiously with his business expectancies; and (4) intentionally to cause him emotional distress. The trial court ... granted the defendants' motions for summary judgment....

The record reveals the following pertinent facts. The plaintiff owns seven low and moderate income housing developments (developments), six of which are located in New Haven and one of which is located in Ansonia. The developments are managed by Renaissance Management Company (Renaissance), an entity wholly owned by the plaintiff. From 1980 to 1991, CHFA loaned the plaintiff a total of approximately ten million dollars for the construction of those developments....

In January, 1995, the plaintiff requested that CHFA agree to restructure the financing of four of the seven developments....

On August 29, 1995, the board of directors of CHFA passed a resolution, in response to the plaintiff's request for loan restructuring, directing CHFA personnel to draft and implement a "supplemental management agreement" concerning the plaintiff's developments within thirty days. The resolution also directed CHFA's asset management staff to set performance standards for the developments. Finally, the resolution further required that Renaissance correct the maintenance deficiencies in the developments within seven months....

In response to concerns about the treatment he was receiving from CHFA, the plaintiff filed a request, in August, 1996, under the state Freedom of Information Act, to review all documents in the possession of CHFA that related to him or his developments. Those documents were made available for review by the plaintiff at CHFA's offices. During the course of his review of those documents with Renaissance's controller, Milton L. Jackson, the plaintiff came across two internal memoranda. One was labeled "litigation strategy" and the other was labeled "strategy." Both were stamped "privileged and confidential."

The memoranda, which were written by Flynn in June, 1996, at the direction of William A. Dickerson, CHFA's general counsel, were addressed to King, Pilcher and Rentz, among others, and discussed the written agreements between CHFA and the plaintiff concerning the plaintiff's CHFA-financed developments. According to the plaintiff, the legal strategies memoranda outline a scheme to remove Renaissance as the managing agent for the plaintiff's developments and, ultimately, to take those developments away from him, by falsely accusing him of financial improprieties and discrediting him publicly. Upon reading the legal strategies memoranda, the plaintiff summarized their contents in handwritten notes and, before leaving the CHFA office, requested a photocopy of each. His request was denied, however, when a CHFA staff member and Pilcher observed that the memoranda were marked privileged and confidential. . . .

In September, 1996, the plaintiff brought this action alleging, inter alia, defamation, invasion of privacy, tortious interference with business expectancies and intentional infliction of emotional distress. The plaintiff's claims are predicated on his contention that the defendants engaged in a plan to discredit him so that CHFA could declare his developments in default and ultimately force him to relinquish both his ownership and management of the developments. The plaintiff also alleged that the defendants had caused him to be subjected to reviews and audits that were "malicious and [racially] discriminatory. . . ."

During the course of discovery, the plaintiff sought copies of the legal strategies memoranda. The plaintiff asserted that the disclosure of the legal strategies memoranda to him in connection with his freedom of information request constituted a waiver of the attorney-client privilege with respect to those memoranda. The defendants refused to produce the legal strategies memoranda, claiming that the inadvertent disclosure of the memoranda did not constitute a waiver of the attorney-client privilege. The plaintiff then moved to compel disclosure of the memoranda. The trial court . . . denied the plaintiff's motion, concluding that, under the circumstances, there had been no waiver of the attorney-client privilege.

The defendants thereafter moved for summary judgment, claiming that, in the absence of the legal strategies memoranda, none of the plaintiff's claims was supported by admissible evidence. . . . The plaintiff reasserted his claim that the disclosure of the legal strategies memoranda in connection with the plaintiff's freedom of information request constituted a waiver of the attorney-client privilege with respect to those memoranda. The plaintiff also maintained that the evidence he had adduced in opposition of the defendants' motions for summary judgment was sufficient to defeat those motions. . . . The trial court . . . rejected the plaintiff's claims, granted the defendants' motions for summary judgment and rendered judgment thereon in favor of the defendants. This appeal followed.

The plaintiff first claims that the trial court . . . improperly denied his motion to compel production of the legal strategies memoranda. In particular, the plaintiff contends that the attorney-client privilege was waived when those documents were made available for his review in connection with his freedom of information request. . . .

After the plaintiff unsuccessfully sought production of the legal strategies memoranda during discovery, he filed a motion to compel their production. . . .

On February 11, 1999, the trial court . . . relying on Barnes/Science Associates Ltd. Partnership v. Barnes Engineering Co., Superior Court, judicial district of Ansonia-Milford, Docket No. CV89-02-77-64S (June 7, 1990) (1 Conn. L. Rptr. 724) (Barnes), denied the plaintiff's motion to compel. In so ruling, the court characterized the release of the legal strategies memoranda to the plaintiff as "a classic case of accidental, unintentional and inadvertent disclosure." Thereafter, on February 16, 2000, the trial court, . . . granted Flynn's motion for a protective order and precluded the plaintiff from asking questions relating to the legal strategies memoranda at Flynn's deposition. The trial court . . . also declined to consider that portion of the plaintiff's affidavit, which was submitted in opposition to the defendants' motions for summary judgment, that purported to summarize the statements that Flynn had made in the memoranda.

Our determination of the propriety of the ruling denying the plaintiff's motion to compel production of the legal strategies memoranda requires us to address a question of first impression for appellate review in this state, namely, what is the appropriate standard for determining whether the inadvertent disclosure of material that otherwise is protected by the attorney-client privilege constitutes a waiver of that privilege? "Generally [the voluntary] disclosure of confidential communications or attorney work product to a third party, such as an adversary in litigation, constitutes a waiver of [the] privilege as to those items. . . . Some courts, however, find an exception to the waiver of privilege when the disclosure is inadvertent." (Citations omitted; emphasis added; internal quotation marks omitted.) Genentech, Inc. v. International Trade Commission, 122 F.3d 1409, 1415 (Fed. Cir. 1997). We note that courts generally have followed one of three approaches in determining whether the attorney-client privilege has been waived as a result of the inadvertent disclosure of otherwise privileged material: (1) the lenient approach; (2) the strict approach; or (3) the "middle of the road" or moderate approach. E.g., Gray v. Bicknell, 86 F.3d 1472, 1483 (8th Cir. 1996).

> Under the lenient approach, [the] attorney-client privilege must be knowingly waived. [Under this approach], the determination of inadvertence is the end of the analysis. The attorney-client privilege exists for the benefit of the client and cannot be waived except by an intentional and knowing relinquishment. . . . The lenient test creates little incentive for lawyers to maintain tight control over privileged material. While the lenient test remains true to the core principle of [the] attorney-client privilege, which is that it exists to protect the client and must be waived by the client, it ignores the importance of confidentiality. To be privileged, attorney-client communications must remain confidential . . . and yet, under this test, the lack of confidentiality becomes meaningless so long as it occurred inadvertently.
>
> The second approach is known as the strict test. . . . Under the strict test, any document produced, either intentionally or otherwise, loses its privileged status with the possible exception of situations [in which] all precautions were taken. Once waiver has occurred, it extends to all other communications relating to the same subject matter. . . .

> While the strict test has some appeal in that it makes attorneys and clients accountable for their carelessness in handling privileged matters . . . [it] sacrifices the value of protecting client confidences for the sake of certainty of results. . . . There is an important societal need for people to be able to employ and fully consult with those trained in the law for advice and guidance. . . . The strict test would likely impede the ability of attorneys to fill this need by chilling communications between attorneys and clients. If, when a document stamped attorney-client privileged is inadvertently released, it and all related documents lose their privileged status, then clients will have much greater hesitancy to fully inform their attorney.
>
> Finally, there is the middle test. . . . Under [this] . . . test, the court undertakes a five-step analysis of the unintentionally disclosed document to determine the proper range of privilege to extend. These considerations are (1) the reasonableness of the precautions taken to prevent inadvertent disclosure in view of the extent of document production, (2) the number of inadvertent disclosures, (3) the extent of the disclosures, (4) the promptness of measures taken to rectify the disclosure, and (5) whether the overriding interest of justice would be served by relieving the party of its error. . . . If, "after completing this analysis, the court determines that waiver occurred, then those documents are no longer privileged."

(Citations omitted; internal quotation marks omitted.) Id., at 1483-84.

We conclude that the "middle of the road" or moderate approach strikes the fairest balance between the competing policy interests of preserving confidential attorney-client communications and encouraging the party seeking the benefit of the attorney-client privilege to take care in the handling of otherwise privileged material. This approach properly places a burden on that party to demonstrate that reasonable measures were taken to preserve the confidentiality of the material that inadvertently was disclosed notwithstanding those measures. Conversely, the approach allows for the recognition of waiver of the privilege when, in view of the totality of the circumstances, the party claiming the privilege has failed to take proper precautions to safeguard the confidentiality of the inadvertently disclosed material. Furthermore, this approach recognizes that the occasional inadvertent disclosure of privileged material is inevitable in the modern era of complex, document-intensive litigation. The moderate approach also recognizes that parties who seek legal advice reasonably may expect that the confidence of their communications with counsel will not be breached to their detriment by virtue of an excusable mistake or oversight in the handling of those communications.

Under the moderate approach, the trial court has discretion to determine if a waiver of the attorney-client privilege has occurred and the scope of that waiver. The determination of whether the privilege has been waived generally will require "a detailed court inquiry into the document practices of the party who inadvertently released the document." Furthermore, "as with all privileges, the [party] claiming the attorney-client privilege has the burden of establishing all essential elements." Because the party seeking to invoke the attorney-client privilege is responsible for maintaining the continued confidentiality of protected communications . . . that party also has the burden of showing that the inadvertent disclosure of those communications occurred even though reasonable precautions were taken to preserve the privilege.

Having identified the proper standard for determining whether a party's inadvertent disclosure of otherwise privileged material constitutes a waiver of the attorney-client privilege, we next must determine whether the trial court . . . applied that test. Despite the brevity of its ruling, we conclude that the trial court's express reliance on *Barnes* indicates that it used the correct test in determining that the disclosure of the legal strategies memoranda did not constitute a waiver of the attorney-client privilege in the present case. . . .

We now must determine whether the trial court . . . properly applied the moderate approach to the facts of the present case. . . .

The first factor, the reasonableness of the precautions taken by the holder of the privilege, weighs in the defendants' favor. The legal strategies memoranda were discovered by the plaintiff among the other documents that were maintained by Rentz in CHFA's general business files and made available to the plaintiff in connection with his freedom of information request. The memoranda were prominently stamped "privileged and confidential," and were included among the other documents requested by the plaintiff as a result of a clerk's filing error. Thus, the trial court reasonably could have inferred that the memoranda were made available to the plaintiff notwithstanding CHFA's policy and practice of maintaining the confidentiality of such documents by denoting them as privileged and confidential and segregating them from other, nonprivileged documents.

Under the approach that we have adopted today, "[t]he mere fact of disclosure does not establish that a party's precautions undertaken to protect the privilege[d] [material] were unreasonable." Thus, despite the inadvertent disclosure of the legal strategies memoranda, the record supports the conclusion that CHFA made reasonable efforts to preserve the confidentiality of privileged material.

The second factor to be considered is the ratio of the number of privileged documents inadvertently disclosed to the total number of documents disclosed in accordance with the request for production. Although the record is devoid of any precise indication as to the magnitude of the plaintiff's freedom of information request, the defendants have characterized the number of documents produced as "voluminous," and explained that these documents were contained in "quite a few" boxes that occupied about one half of a conference room. Moreover, even though the plaintiff now claims that "[t]he total volume of documents disclosed. . . . was not unusually large," Jacquelyn Hanhurst, the bookkeeper for Renaissance, stated in an affidavit filed with the trial court that, "[w]e were provided with a great number of files for review, so we proceeded to review the records in two teams . . . over a number of days." Thus, the magnitude of the document production in relation to the two privileged documents that inadvertently were disclosed is a factor that militates strongly against a finding of waiver.

The third and fourth factors, namely, the extent of the inadvertent disclosures and the time taken to rectify the error, provide further support for the defendants' position. Only two privileged documents inadvertently were disclosed. Moreover, CHFA did not delay upon learning that the legal strategies memoranda inadvertently had been made available to the plaintiff. As soon as CHFA personnel learned that the memoranda had been made available to the plaintiff, they explained to him that the memoranda were privileged and confidential and, consequently, not subject to disclosure. The employees therefore declined to fulfill the plaintiff's request for photocopies of the memoranda and would not permit the plaintiff to review the memoranda further. In addition, there is nothing in the record to suggest that the memoranda ever were made available to anyone else outside CHFA. Thus, once CHFA personnel learned of the unintended disclosure of the memoranda, they promptly took all steps necessary to minimize that disclosure.

Finally, we conclude that the fifth factor, namely, whether the overriding interest of fairness would be best served by relieving the party of its error, also favors the defendants. It is axiomatic that "[d]epriving a party of information in an otherwise privileged document is not prejudicial." Thus, "[t]he prejudice factor focuses only on whether the act of restoring immunity to an inadvertently disclosed document would be unfair, not whether the privilege itself deprives parties of pertinent information." In the present case, the legal strategies memoranda fall squarely within the attorney-client privilege. The disclosure of the memoranda clearly was inadvertent and was limited both in time and scope. Furthermore, CHFA rectified the error immediately upon learning of it. Although the plaintiff relied on the memoranda in deciding whether to bring this action against the defendants . . . he did so with full knowledge that, at the very least, the defendants had a strong claim that the inadvertent disclosure of the memoranda did not constitute a waiver of the attorney-client privilege.

Thus, the trial court's determination that, all relevant circumstances considered, the inadvertent disclosure of the legal strategies memoranda did not constitute a waiver of the attorney-client privilege is fully supported by the record. We therefore reject the plaintiff's claim that the memoranda are not protected by the attorney-client privilege. . . .

The judgment is affirmed.

NOTES TO HARP v. KING

1. *Policy Choice in FRE 502.* Rule 502(b) takes a position roughly equivalent to the moderate or "middle of the road" position described and adopted in *Harp.* The main factors associated with that position — reasonableness of precautions taken against inadvertent disclosure and reasonableness of actions taken after a disclosure — are explicitly stated in Rule 502(b). Note, though, that the federal rule does not specifically require an inquiry into the fairness of a waiver decision, although that concept is articulated in *Harp* and in precedents relied on by the *Harp* court.

2. *Waiver by Disclosure.* A client will lose the lawyer-client privilege if the client tells a third party about his or her communications with his or her lawyer.

Also, courts typically rule that there is no privilege if a client communicates something to a lawyer with the intention that the lawyer make it public.

If a client talks to a lawyer about some past event, for example a car crash, and also talks to other people about that crash, some courts would hold that there is no longer any lawyer-client privilege with regard to the client's communications with the lawyer because the underlying information has been made public. Other courts would take the more cautious position that a privilege is waived only when a client makes disclosures about the communications to the lawyer, as distinct from comments that happen to be on a topic that is the same as a topic that was discussed with the lawyer.

3. *Advice of Counsel Defense.* A commonsense limitation on privilege provides that the privilege is withdrawn if a client asserts a claim or defense based on alleged consultations with the client's lawyer. In that circumstance, the client and the lawyer may each be required to testify about the communications allegedly related to that claim or defense.

QUESTION 15-3. Terry Tutor was an associate director at a middle school operated by Genesis Foundation. Genesis terminated her employment in 2007 for failure to comply with an earlier written final warning and for negligence and inefficiency, as well as other grounds. Tutor sued Genesis in 2009, alleging that she was terminated in a discriminatory manner on the basis of a disability, and that her termination was retaliatory and thus violative of a state whistleblower protection statute. She alleged that Genesis had commenced a course of conduct to create a record sufficient to document its desire to terminate her.

Tutor was being deposed on February 13, 2010, when she testified that in June 2007 she was at the fax machine at the middle school receiving some papers on an insurance claim for her son. The fax machine was used from time to time by at a number of members of the teaching staff. Mixed in with some insurance company papers was a letter from Genesis's law firm to the director of the middle school. She read the letter, which stated that the university "did not have enough performance issues to fire me, and that it would have to be a business decision whether I was going to remain an employee." Counsel for Genesis said at the deposition that he was recording his objection to the letter as attorney-client privilege, noting that "it was obviously communicated accidentally." No letter was produced at the time of the deposition.

Genesis moved for a protective order in May 2010 to prevent Tutor from referring to the letter, because it was protected by attorney-client privilege. At a hearing, Genesis filed affidavits from the middle school director indicating that he did not intend for third persons to see the communication. Further underscoring the letter's confidentiality, counsel produced a cover sheet that had accompanied the faxed letter, which stated that the attached communication was protected by attorney-client privilege.

Tutor's attorney admitted that he had a copy of the letter provided to him by Tutor. He maintained that he had used the letter since "day one" to construct his strategy in the case. He claimed it would be unfair to prevent them from using it at this juncture because it showed that Genesis was being untruthful about its reasons for terminating Tutor.

Assuming this suit is being tried in a federal district court, discuss whether the judge should issue the requested protective order.

■   ■   ■

Applying the Exception for Communications about Crime and Fraud—In re Motion to Quash Bar Counsel Subpoena. There is universal agreement that the lawyer-client privilege has no application to communications for the purpose of committing or planning to commit a crime or fraud. As this opinion shows, however, for some important aspects of administering this doctrine, courts may choose from a range of options. In particular, they must decide what level of proof ought to be required to invoke the exception.

IN RE MOTION TO QUASH BAR COUNSEL SUBPOENA

982 A.3d 330 (Me. 2009)

MEAD, J.

The law firm of Verrill Dana LLP (the firm) appeals from an order entered by a single justice of this Court (Silver, J.) denying its motion to quash a subpoena issued to its former general counsel by Bar Counsel for the Board of Overseers of the Bar. The subpoena seeks records that the firm claims are protected from disclosure by the attorney-client privilege. Bar Counsel asserts that this interlocutory appeal should be dismissed, or, as he argued successfully to the single justice, that the crime-fraud exception created by M.R. Evid. 502(d)(1) acts to remove the firm's privilege claim. . . .

The origins of this matter lie in the misconduct of former attorney John Duncan, a former partner in the firm. Duncan's misconduct was detailed in this Court's order disbarring him for life. This case arises from Bar Counsel's investigation into the conduct of certain other attorneys at the firm in handling the discovery and reporting of Duncan's actions.

In June 2007, Duncan's former secretary reported to at least two attorneys at the firm that Duncan had stolen a significant amount of client funds. She eventually left Verrill Dana, retained counsel to represent her in a potential claim against the firm, and filed a grievance complaint against Duncan and several other Verrill Dana attorneys with the Board of Overseers of the Bar (Board). The firm engaged Attorney Gene Libby, then a Verrill Dana partner and its general counsel since 1996, to represent it in the matter. Libby undertook an investigation, during which he amassed numerous e-mails and other documents; he also wrote memos to others and to the file detailing both his conclusions and how he believed the evidence he had gathered supported them. Libby resigned from Verrill Dana on November 26, 2007.

Two days later, Libby wrote to Bar Counsel, reporting that "[d]uring the course of my investigation, I acquired what I believe is unprivileged knowledge of violations of the Maine Bar Rules that requires reporting." Because the firm claimed that the knowledge Libby referred to was privileged, he did not disclose any specifics. The firm eventually reached an agreement with Libby concerning the terms of his departure; under its provisions Libby agreed not to disclose any information conveyed to him as general counsel unless required to do so by court order.

On September 8, 2008, Bar Counsel issued a subpoena to Libby, compelling both his testimony and the production of any documents supporting his report made ten months earlier. The firm filed a motion to quash with the Board, asserting that the subpoena sought information protected by the attorney-client privilege and the work product doctrine. Bar Counsel's response to the motion asserted that the crime-fraud exception applied and acted to remove any privilege. The parties agreed to submit the dispute to a single justice of this Court. After reviewing the disputed documents *in camera*, the single justice found that:

> During Mr. Libby's investigation of the . . . complaint against the firm Mr. Libby may have uncovered criminal conduct by partners of Verrill Dana LLP. Pursuant to M.R. Evid. 502(d)(1) there is no privilege under Rule 502 pursuant to the furtherance of crime or fraud. This exception prevails here and all of the documents provided *in camera* to this Court fall under this exception.

The justice ordered that all of the disputed documents be turned over to Bar Counsel. This appeal followed. . . .

The attorney-client privilege claimed by the firm is "the oldest of the privileges for confidential communications known to the common law." *United States v. Zolin*, 491 U.S. 554, 562 (1989) (quotation marks omitted). Its purpose is "to encourage full and frank communication between attorneys and their clients and thereby promote broader public interests in the observance of law and administration of justice." *Zolin*, 491 U.S. at 562 (quotation marks omitted). To fulfill that purpose, clients must "be free to make full disclosure to their attorneys of *past* wrongdoings." (emphasis added).

When an attorney's advice is sought in order to commit or conceal *ongoing* or *future* wrongdoing, however, the "broader public interests in the observance of law and administration of justice" are not served, and the privilege does not protect those communications. In 1933, the Supreme Court said: "The privilege takes flight if the [attorney-client] relation is abused. A client who consults an attorney for advice that will serve him in the commission of a fraud will have no help from the law. He must let the truth be told." *Clark v. United States*, 289 U.S. 1 (1933). Fifty-six years later, the Court expounded on the rationale for a "crime-fraud" exception to the privilege:

[S]ince the privilege has the effect of withholding relevant information from the factfinder, it applies only where necessary to achieve its purpose. The attorney-client privilege must necessarily protect the confidences of wrongdoers, but the reason for that protection — the centrality of open client and attorney communication to the proper functioning of our adversary system of justice — ceas[es] to operate at a certain point, namely, where the desired advice refers *not to prior wrongdoing,* but to *future wrongdoing.* It is the purpose of the crime-fraud exception to the attorney-client privilege to assure that the "seal of secrecy" between lawyer and client does not extend to communications made for the purpose of getting advice for the commission of a fraud or crime.

Zolin, 491 U.S. at 562–63 (quotation marks omitted).

Maine law recognizes several exceptions to our rule of attorney-client privilege. *See* M.R. Evid. 502(d). Among them is a crime-fraud exception:

d) Exceptions.
There is no privilege under this rule:

> (1) *Furtherance of crime or fraud.* If the services of the lawyer were sought or obtained to enable or aid anyone to commit or plan to commit what the client knew or reasonably should have known to be a crime or fraud.

Because we have not had occasion to discuss the Maine crime-fraud exception previously, we take this opportunity to explain its requirements and the requisite burden for its application. Like its federal counterpart, the crime-fraud exception established by Rule 502(d)(1) applies to a continuing or future crime or fraud, not to purely past conduct that is not ongoing. The exception may apply, however, if the lawyer's services are used to actively conceal past wrongdoing.

Having defined the scope of the exception as including continuing or future conduct, but excluding past acts, we turn to the equally important question of the client's intent in employing the attorney. We agree with the First Circuit Court of Appeals when it said: "[I]t is not enough . . . that the client is guilty of crime or fraud. Forfeiture of the privilege requires the client's *use or aim to use* the lawyer to foster the crime or fraud." The applicability of the exception turns on whether the client intended to use the attorney's services, or advice, to commit or plan to commit an ongoing or future crime or fraud; the attorney's intent is irrelevant.

Combining these requirements of scope and intent, we adopt the test used by the First Circuit that must be satisfied before the crime-fraud exception can pierce a client's claim of attorney-client privilege: "(1) that the client was engaged in (or was planning) criminal or fraudulent activity when the attorney-client communications took place; *and* (2) that the communications were intended by the client to facilitate or conceal the criminal or fraudulent activity."

While the First Circuit has described the burden borne by the party seeking to invoke the crime-fraud exception as a requirement to make a "prima facie showing," or to establish a "reasonable basis" in order to find that the test for piercing the privilege has been satisfied, we conclude that the higher standard of proof by a preponderance of the evidence is necessary to protect this important evidentiary principle. We note with approval the reasoning of the Supreme Judicial Court of Massachusetts:

> [T]he crime-fraud exception is a narrow one. Unless the crime-fraud exception applies, the attorney-client privilege may not be invaded, even where the communication concerns possible future criminal conduct, because an informed lawyer may be able to dissuade the client from improper future conduct, and, if not, under the ethical rules may elect in the public interest to make a limited disclosure of the client's threatened conduct. The party invoking the crime-fraud exception must prove by a preponderance of the evidence that the exception applies.

In re A Grand Jury Investigation, 437 Mass. 340 (2002) (quotation marks omitted).

In order to decide the validity of the firm's argument on appeal, we must examine the single justice's order to see if the correct legal test was applied, and then examine the record to see whether it supports the single justice's conclusion that the crime-fraud exception applies on these facts to defeat the firm's claim of attorney-client privilege as to all of the documents at issue. We review the correctness of the Court's legal test de novo, and its findings of fact for clear error.

In discussing the crime-fraud exception, the single justice found that:

> During Mr. Libby's investigation of the . . . complaint against the firm Mr. Libby may have uncovered criminal conduct by partners of Verrill Dana LLP. Pursuant to M.R. Evid. 502(d)(1) there is no privilege under Rule 502 pursuant to the furtherance of crime or fraud. This exception prevails here and all of the documents provided *in camera* to this Court fall under this exception.

We are unable to determine from the Court's findings whether it was referring to only past potential criminal conduct, which would weigh against the applicability of the exception, or to ongoing wrongdoing; whether it found that the firm intended to use Libby's services or advice to facilitate or conceal criminal or fraudulent activity; or whether it found that the crime-fraud exception applied by a preponderance of the evidence. Accordingly, we must vacate the order of the single justice and remand for application of the appropriate standard as set forth in this opinion. On remand, the Court should consider for each of the firm's clients at issue whether documents concerning transactions with that client meet the test for application of the exception, or whether some or all of them remain privileged.

The entry is: Order denying motion to quash vacated; remanded to the single justice for further proceedings consistent with this opinion.

NOTES TO IN RE MOTION TO QUASH BAR COUNSEL SUBPOENA

1. *Considering Privileged Material to Apply the Crime-Fraud Exception.* In deciding whether to withdraw the privilege, a court may have an in camera review of documents or an in camera hearing. And the court is entitled to conclude that the crime-fraud exception applies, to withdraw the privilege, entirely on the basis of allegedly privileged material. It was once held that evidence separate from the allegedly privileged communications was required to apply the crime-fraud exception, but that position was rejected by the Supreme Court in United States v. Zolin, 491 U.S. 554 (1989).

2. *Communications About a Future Crime Not Seeking Advice About It.* A client might make a statement to a lawyer about a future crime without seeking advice about it, for example by saying, "I plan to kill the prosecutor who's working on my case." The crime-fraud exception would not apply to that statement, since it does not involve any effort to obtain the lawyer's cooperation or counsel in the killing. Some scholars have recommended that a test of "germaneness" be applied, so that a client's words would be outside the protection of privilege if the lawyer or client would reasonably have believed the words were not relevant to the subject of the consultation. This distinction has not been well received by courts, since it would make the availability of the privilege highly unpredictable.

GOOD TO REMEMBER

The crime-fraud exception prevents application of the lawyer-client privilege to communications intended to enlist the aid of the lawyer in a future crime or fraud; the privilege applies to communications related to past wrongdoing.

3. *Disclosure of Client's Statements to Prevent Likely Death or Substantial Bodily Harm.* Ethics rules allow and sometimes require a lawyer to violate a client's confidence if doing so would prevent a likely death or serious injury. When this kind of limited disclosure is made, the better view is that it does not render the privilege unavailable in other settings.

 ## CONFIDENTIAL SPOUSAL COMMUNICATIONS PRIVILEGE

Two doctrines related to marriage can restrict testimony. The privilege for confidential spousal communications prohibits testimony by either spouse that would reveal a confidential communication between them. A separate privilege allows a husband or wife to decline to be a witness against his or her spouse: this privilege, when exercised, keeps everything the nontestifying spouse knows out of the trial. It excludes information derived from confidential communications and also excludes additional information as well (that is, it excludes everything the nontestifying spouse knows about everything).

■   ■   ■

Reasons to Adopt a Spousal Communications Privilege—Christian. Even though the privilege for confidential spousal communications has been recognized at common law for at least 200 years, the state of Connecticut did not formally adopt it until 2004. Its decision recognizing the privilege provides a clear analysis of the rationale for the privilege and also introduces some of the controversial issues that may arise in applying it.

STATE v. CHRISTIAN
841 A.2d 1158 (Conn. 2004)

KATZ, J.

The defendant, Bruce R. Christian, Jr., appeals from the judgment of conviction, rendered after a jury trial, of manslaughter in the second degree with a motor vehicle . . . and reckless driving . . . The defendant claims that the trial court improperly. . .permitted the defendant's wife, Joan Christian, to testify, over the defendant's objection, regarding his confidential marital communications to her. . . .

[The defendant was involved in a car accident that killed someone who had been in the car.] At trial, the defendant did not contest that he was intoxicated on the evening of March 17, 2000. Rather, the defendant argued that the victim had been driving her car at the time of the accident and that he had been in the passenger seat. The state presented the testimony of [three witnesses], all of whom testified that the defendant repeatedly had told them that he had been driving at the time of the accident. The state also presented the testimony of the defendant's estranged wife, Joan Christian, who testified, over the defendant's objection, that the defendant had told her that he had been driving at the time of the accident. . . .

We first address the defendant's claim that the trial court improperly permitted the defendant's wife, Joan Christian, to testify, over his objection, regarding his confidential communications to her. The following facts and procedural history are relevant to our resolution of this claim. In the early hours of March 18, 2000, Joan Christian was finishing her shift as a waitress at a restaurant in Avon when she received a telephone call informing her of the defendant's accident. She immediately went to Hartford Hospital, where she was greeted by . . . a chaplain and several physicians, who told her that the victim had died in the accident and that they believed that the defendant had been the driver of the vehicle involved. After consulting with the physicians, Joan Christian went, by herself, to the defendant's hospital room to inform him that the victim had died. When she arrived, the defendant quietly told her that he had been driving the vehicle, and he then made motions with his hands as though he were operating a steering wheel. Joan Christian quickly covered the defendant's hands with her own and "hushed" him, ostensibly to prevent him from making any further incriminating statements. [The chaplain] and the physicians entered the room immediately thereafter. The defendant made no further incriminating remarks.

At trial, the state offered Joan Christian as a witness. She testified, upon voir dire, that at the time of trial, she and the defendant were separated and in the process of getting divorced. She further testified, however, that at the time of the accident in March, 2000, although she and the defendant still were living together, the marriage "was very rocky" and that it "went downhill" after the night of the accident. Finally, she testified that the marriage was over and that she did not feel that preserving the confidentiality of the defendant's statement would have any effect on repairing the marriage.

The defendant filed a motion in limine seeking to prevent Joan Christian from testifying about this communication on the ground that it was a privileged confidential marital communication. Specifically, the defendant argued that, although no Connecticut case expressly has recognized the existence of the marital communications privilege, the dictum of this court's opinion in State v. Littlejohn, 199 Conn. 631 (1986), indicates that the privilege "has seemingly been accepted" by the courts of this state. The defendant further argued that the marital communications privilege was applicable to the present case because the communication had been "made during [the] marriage, out of the presence of third parties. . . ." In response, the state argued that, regardless of whether the privilege was available, the communication was not confidential, and thus, not privileged, because the defendant previously had made similar communications . . . while riding in the ambulance to the hospital. The state further argued that application of the privilege would be inappropriate because the marriage between the defendant and his wife was "rocky" at the time of the communication, and that they were separated at the time of trial and in the process of getting divorced. The state argued, therefore, that any harm that disclosure might cause to the defendant's marital relationship was outweighed by the interest of the court and of society in "this judicial investigation of the truth."

The trial court denied the defendant's motion in limine. Although the court concluded that the marital communications privilege "may exist in certain circumstances," it determined that the privilege did not apply in the present case because the marriage irretrievably had broken down. . . . Consequently, Joan Christian testified concerning the communication. . . .

"[T]he rules of privilege, of which the most familiar are the rule protecting against self-incrimination and those shielding the confidentiality of communications between husband and wife, attorney and client, and physician and patient, are not designed or intended to facilitate the fact-finding process or to safeguard its integrity. Their effect instead is clearly inhibitive; rather than facilitating the illumination of truth, they shut out the light." 1 C. McCormick, Evidence (5th Ed.

1999), §72, p. 299. Privileges have "the effect of withholding relevant information from the factfinder. . . . Accordingly, although a . . . privilege must be applied so as to effectuate its purpose, it is to be applied cautiously and with circumspection because it impedes the truth-seeking function of the adjudicative process." (Internal quotation marks omitted.) State v. Montgomery, 254 Conn. 694 (2000). A privilege should be recognized, therefore, only if four essential conditions have been met: "(1) The communications must originate in a confidence that they will not be disclosed. (2) This element of confidentiality must be essential to the full and satisfactory maintenance of the relation between the parties. (3) The relation must be one which in the opinion of the community ought to be sedulously fostered. (4) The injury that would inure to the relation by the disclosure of the communications must be greater than the benefit thereby gained for the correct disposal of litigation." 8 J. Wigmore, Evidence (1961) §2285, p. 527.

The principles underlying the marital communications privilege are well recognized. "The basis of the immunity given to communications between husband and wife is the protection of marital confidences, regarded as so essential to the preservation of the marriage relationship as to outweigh the disadvantages to the administration of justice which the privilege entails. . . . Hence it is that the privilege with respect to communications extends to the testimony of husband or wife even though the different privilege, excluding the testimony of one against the other, is not involved." (Citations omitted.) Wolfle v. United States, 291 U.S. 7 (1934). The marital communications privilege protects "information privately disclosed between husband and wife in the confidence of the marital relationship-once described . . . as 'the best solace of human existence.'" Trammel v. United States, quoting Stein v. Bowman, 38 U.S. (13 Pet.) 209 (1839). The privilege has been described as "almost sacrosanct. . . ." Johnson v. United States, 616 A.2d 1216 (D.C. App. 1992), cert. denied, 507 U.S. 996 (1993). "[T]he primary purpose of the confidential marital communication privilege is to foster marital relationships by encouraging confidential communication between spouses. . . ." Curran v. Pasek, 886 P.2d 272, 276 (Wyo. 1994). The privilege "permit[s] a husband and wife to communicate freely with one another without fear that their communications will be used against them at some future date." G. Sodaro & P. Wilson, "Spousal Privileges," in 2 Testimonial Privileges (S. Stone & R. Taylor eds., 2d Ed. 1995) §5.07, p. 5-11. "We encourage married people to confide in each other by protecting their statements from later scrutiny in court." United States v. Lea, 249 F.3d 632, 641 (7th Cir. 2001).

It therefore is apparent that the purposes underlying the marital communications privilege asserted by the defendant are quite different from those supporting the separate and distinct privilege against adverse spousal testimony relied upon by the state. "The [adverse spousal testimony] privilege looks forward with reference to the particular marriage at hand: the privilege is meant to protect against the impact of the testimony on the marriage. The marital communications privilege in a sense, is broader and more abstract: it exists to insure that spouses generally, prior to any involvement in criminal activity or a trial, feel free to communicate their deepest feelings to each other without fear of eventual exposure in a court of law." United States v. Byrd, 750 F.2d 585 (7th Cir. 1984); see also State v. Adamson, 72 Ohio St. 3d 431 (1995) ("[s]pousal privilege and spousal competency are distinct legal concepts which interrelate and provide two different levels of protection for communications between spouses"). We therefore are not persuaded by the state's assertion that the privilege against adverse spousal testimony, codified at §54-84a, alone is sufficient to protect the interests of open communication in the marital relationship. Accordingly, we reaffirm our statement in State v. Littlejohn that the marital communications privilege "commends itself to judicial acceptance," and we expressly accept that privilege as a fixture of our common law.

Our conclusion, recognizing the existence of a privilege for confidential marital communications, aligns us with every other jurisdiction in the country. Connecticut is unique among its sister states, which each have a statute or a rule of evidence expressly providing for the privilege. Even when the marital communications privilege is a product of legislative fiat, however, courts have continued to recognize the strong common-law roots of the privilege. The federal courts, moreover, continue to recognize and apply the privilege as a matter of federal common law.

As we have stated, the marital communications privilege permits an individual to prevent his or her spouse or former spouse from testifying as to any confidential communication made by the individual to the spouse during their marriage. In the present case, it is uncontroverted that the statement made by the defendant to his wife, along with the accompanying gesticulations, were "communications." Accordingly, we must determine: 1) whether the defendant had made those communications to his wife during their marriage; and (2) whether those communications were confidential.

We begin our analysis by determining whether the defendant had made the communications to his wife while the couple were in a valid marital relationship. In the present case, the trial court determined that the marital communications privilege, if it existed, was inapplicable because "at the time the statement was made, but most importantly now, at the time of trial," the defendant's marriage irretrievably had broken down. The state contends that the trial court's decision was proper, because the defendant's marriage was "beyond repair" both at the time the statement was made and at the time of trial. The defendant claims that the trial court improperly refused to apply the privilege. Specifically, he claims that the trial court's focus was imprecise because the privilege attaches at the time that the confidential statement was made, and if made during the marriage, the privilege survives the dissolution of the marriage. We agree with the defendant....

For the marital communications privilege to apply, the communications must have been made in confidence during the marriage. Once the marital communications privilege has attached, moreover, it continues to survive even after the marriage has ended. See Pereira v. United States, 347 U.S. 1 (1954) ("divorce... does not terminate the privilege for confidential marital communications"); see also 1 C. McCormick, supra, §85, p. 339 ("about one-half of the statutes codifying the [marital communications] privilege explicitly provide that it continues after death or divorce"). In other words, the privilege focuses on the marital relationship between the spouses at the time that the communication was made, and not at the time of trial.

As we have noted, the marital communications privilege was founded upon the strong policy of preserving the marital relationship through the fostering of confidences between spouses. This policy applies with equal force to preserve all legally valid marriages, irrespective of marital difficulties. "Indeed, the reasons justifying the marital communications privilege — encourag[ing] marital partners to share their most closely guarded secrets and thoughts, thus adding an additional measure of intimacy and mutual support to the marriage — apply with equal force to married couples who, despite the appearance to outsiders of an irretrievably broken marriage, may still share hopes of reconciliation." (Internal quotation marks omitted.) Blazek v. Superior Court, 177 Ariz. 535 (Ct. App. 1994). We conclude, therefore, that the marital communications privilege applies to the present case.

Although the defendant's marriage may have been acrimonious at the time that he had made the communications to his wife, the marital communications privilege nonetheless was valid. Furthermore, because the focus is on the status of the marital relationship at the time of the communication, their marital status at the time of trial was immaterial. Accordingly, we conclude that the defendant's communications to his wife, made while the couple was living together as husband and wife, were subject to the marital communications privilege insofar as those communications were confidential.

We next focus our analysis on the question of whether the communications were confidential. The state contends that the trial court's denial of the defendant's motion in limine can be affirmed, nevertheless, because the marital communications were not confidential. Specifically, the state relies on the defendant's previous, similar statements [in the ambulance]. We disagree.

We note, at the outset, that the determination of the second factor, that is, whether a communication was confidential, depends on the facts of the particular case. It is axiomatic that the marital communications privilege protects only those communications that are confidential. . . .

We recognize that there is a split of authority concerning the test to be applied in determining whether a communication was confidential. Under the traditional view, a communication is confidential if the communicator, at the time of the communication, subjectively intended that the content of the communication not be disclosed to third parties or the public. Some jurisdictions, however, apply an objective test, wherein a communication is confidential if, at the time of the communication, the communicator could have had a reasonable expectation of confidentiality. We think that the latter standard is the better approach, because it is consistent with our prior case law construing the distinct, but analogous, privilege for attorney-client communications.

Under either test, however, the party offering the marital communication usually can overcome the presumption of confidentiality through evidence that the communication had been made in the presence of a third party. Even when no third party actually was present, the presumption of confidentiality may be rebutted by evidence that the communication was intended or expected to be disclosed to a third party or to the public.

In the present case, the trial court made no determination as to whether the defendant's communications to his wife were confidential. Rather than resolving the question of confidentiality, the trial court concluded that "the overriding factor" in its decision to admit the testimony was "that at the time the statement was made, but most importantly now, at the time of trial, the marriage relationship exists in name only, de jure, we might say, but not de facto." Thus, the trial court did not conclude that the state had overcome the presumption of confidentiality, nor did it conclude that the communication was not confidential. Similarly, the state has not presented any persuasive reason on appeal that would lead us to conclude that the communication was not confidential, that is, that the defendant did not have a reasonable expectation of confidentiality. Therefore, we do not agree with the state's contention that the trial court's decision to allow Joan Christian's testimony was proper.

[The court concluded that the error was harmless].

NOTES TO STATE v. CHRISTIAN

1. *Strengthening the Marital Relationship.* Many courts claim that the privilege for confidential marital communications can reinforce marriages because it facilitates communications between spouses. One way to test this idea would be to consider whether people who know the most about this privilege have better marriages than people who don't know its details. Do lawyers, who presumably are most likely to know about this privilege, typically have happier marriages than nonlawyers have?

2. *Noncommunicative Conduct.* If a husband shows his wife something distinctive, like a valuable ring, that turns out to be stolen property, would the privilege prevent the wife from testifying about that conduct? A minority of courts would prevent testimony about anything a spouse did in private with the other spouse if the conduct seemed to be in reliance on an expectation of privacy. Most courts limit the application of the marital communications privilege to statements and conduct meant to be the equivalent of a statement.

3. *Distinguishing Between the Communications Privilege and the Testimonial Privilege.* The communications privilege applies to confidential communications and remains effective even if the marriage in which those communications were made has ended. The testimonial privilege allows a spouse to decline to testify, so it applies to communications and anything else that spouse might know that would have been relevant at a trial. It ends when a marriage ends; there is no testimonial privilege for former spouses.

4. *Eavesdroppers.* For the privilege to apply, the communication must have been confidential. At common law, it was ordinarily ruled that an eavesdropper could testify about an overheard conversation between spouses. If the spouses did not protect themselves from being overheard, they must not have cared enough about confidentiality. Modern courts will apply the privilege if they are persuaded that the couple had a reasonable basis for believing that their conversation was private.

> ### GOOD TO REMEMBER
>
> The testimonial privilege keeps more information out of trials than the communications privilege keeps out. The communications privilege keeps out only testimony about confidential statements. The testimonial privilege keeps out everything a spouse knows, since it can prevent the spouse from being a witness.

5. *Spousal Communications and Intramarriage Wrongdoing.* When a civil or criminal case involves a claim that one spouse has committed a tort or a crime against the other or against the child or either of them, the privilege is withdrawn. Another circumstance in which the privilege is rejected is when spouses communicate with each other to carry out or plan a crime.

Segment 19: limits on spousal confidential communications privilege

QUESTION 15-4. Alan Able, held in a city's jail, spoke with his wife, Ann Able, in a phone conversation using a jail telephone. A sign next to the phone said calls may be monitored. No one actually monitored the call. Alan was later tried for the offense for which he had been held in the jail. Ann was willing to testify about statements Alan made during their phone conversation. If Alan objected to her testimony, the best response by the trial judge would be:

A. Prohibit Ann's testimony because of the spousal testimonial privilege.

B. Prohibit Ann's testimony because statements Alan made were covered by the spousal communications privilege.

C. Allow Ann's testimony only if the call was monitored.

D. Allow Ann's testimony because the call could have been monitored.

D CLERGY-PENITENT COMMUNICATIONS

A privilege for confidential communications made by individuals seeking "priestly consolation and guidance"* is recognized in federal courts and in all states. Some issues of variation among jurisdictions are the definition of clergyperson and the range of communications that might be included within the privilege.

■ ■ ■

---

* Trammel v. United States, 445 U.S. 40, 51 (1980) (The *Trammel* decision did not concern issues of clergy-communicant privilege, but referred to the privilege as context for its consideration of spousal incompetency).

May a Jurisdiction Recognize a Privilege for Statements to Clergy but Reject a Privilege for Statements to God? — **Varner.** As a matter of federal constitutional law, the court considers whether applying a privilege for communications based in religion only to communications with a clergyperson is legitimate. The opinion also offers background information on the history and typical characteristics of the usual clergy-penitent privilege.

VARNER v. STOVALL

500 F.3d 491 (6th Cir. 2007)

SUTTON, J.

A jury convicted Janniss Varner of assault with intent to commit murder after she hired a third party to shoot her abusive boyfriend. In her federal habeas petition, she claimed that the state courts . . . violated her rights under the Religion Clauses of the First and Fourteenth Amendments by admitting into evidence several journal entries that included prayers and an acknowledgment that she had tried to kill her boyfriend. . . . Because she has not shown that the state courts unreasonably applied relevant Supreme Court precedent, we affirm the district court's denial of the petition.

On November 27, 1995, Varner attempted to murder her abusive boyfriend, Alvin Knight, by hiring a third party to kill him. . . .

Two-and-a-half years later, someone shot and killed Knight outside of his apartment complex. Police searched Knight's apartment for clues to the murder and uncovered Varner's journals linking her to the 1995 shooting. The journals identified the gunman of the 1995 shooting and disclosed Varner's responsibility for arranging the attempted murder. The journals also revealed that Knight had raped, choked and abused her in the past. . . . Her entries also expressed her wish that Knight had died in 1995, her lack of remorse for her actions and her determination to kill him in the future. The entries often were addressed "Dear God," sometimes contained prayers of supplication and thanks ("Lord, give me guidance and insight concerning what I need to do. . ."); ("Lord I do thank you for helping me. God I thank you for saving me and keeping me in my right mind"), and in places expressed her disillusionment with organized religion and church services.

Varner was charged with and convicted of assault with intent to commit murder for her involvement in the 1995 shooting. At trial, the court admitted into evidence excerpts from her journals. . . . Varner received a sentence of 13 to 20 years' imprisonment for her conviction. The Michigan Court of Appeals affirmed her conviction and the Michigan Supreme Court denied leave to appeal.

After denying her federal habeas petition, the district court granted her a certificate of appealability on . . . whether her rights under the Religion Clauses of the First Amendment were violated when the state court admitted her private journal entries. . . .

Varner argues that the state courts' application of Michigan's clergy-penitent evidentiary privilege violated her rights under the Religion Clauses of the First (and Fourteenth) Amendment — "Congress shall make no law respecting an establishment of religion, or prohibiting the free exercise thereof." U.S. Const. amend. I. In doing so, she makes the following four-step argument. Step one: Michigan has created an evidentiary privilege for religious communications. Step two: the privilege applies only to religions that encourage their members to communicate with God through an intermediary. Step three: this limitation discriminates among religions because it disfavors belief systems in which individuals communicate directly with God. Step four: the solution to this First Amendment problem is not to strike the privilege (which would not benefit Varner) but to extend it to all religions, including those that do not use intermediaries, and thus to extend the privilege to any journal entry that might be construed as a prayer to God.

While we accept some of the premises of Varner's argument, we cannot accept her conclusion. A State, it is true, may not "enact [ ] laws that have the purpose or effect of advancing or inhibiting religion," *Zelman v. Simmons-Harris,* 536 U.S. 639 (2002) (internal quotation marks omitted). And a State, it is also true, may not "officially prefer [ ]" "one religious denomination . . . over another," *Larson v. Valente,* 456 U.S. 228 (1982), a requirement that has roots in the Establishment and Free Exercise Clauses. But the clergy-penitent privilege was never designed to apply to private journal entries, and the confinement of the privilege to its historic purposes does not offend these or any other requirements of the Religion Clauses of the First Amendment.

Recognized as early as the fifth century, the clergy-penitent privilege "originated" with the "Catholic sacrament of Penance," though it "fell into desuetude after the Reformation." *Cox v. Miller,* 296 F.3d 89 (2d Cir. 2002). In the earliest known American case concerning the privilege, a New York court recognized a nonstatutory privilege resting in the clergy person, who is caught "between Scylla and Charybdis": "If he tells the truth he violates his ecclesiastical oath — If he prevaricates he violates his judicial oath. . . . The only course is, for the court to declare that he shall not testify or act at all." *People v. Phillips* (N.Y. Ct. Gen. Sess. 1813). Today every State has enacted some form of the clergy-penitent privilege. 1 McCormick on Evid. §76.2 (6th ed.). Although the scope of the privilege varies from State to State, all States at a minimum "require that the communications be made in private, with an expectation of confidentiality, to a minister in his or her professional capacity as a member of the clergy." R. Michael Cassidy, *Sharing Sacred Secrets: Is it (Past) Time for a Dangerous Person Exception to the Clergy-Penitent Privilege?,* 44 Wm. & Mary L. Rev. 1627, 1645 (2003) (citations omitted).

Michigan has codified its clergy-penitent privilege, which appears in two statutes. One says: "Any communications between members of the clergy and the members of their respective churches are hereby declared to be privileged and confidential when those communications were necessary to enable the members of the clergy to serve as such member of the clergy. . . ." Mich. Comp. Laws §767.5a(2). The other says: "No minister of the gospel, or priest of any denomination whatsoever, or duly accredited Christian Science practitioner, shall be allowed to disclose any confessions made to him in his professional character, in the course of discipline enjoined by the rules or practice of such denomination." *Id.* §600.2156.

One of the two statutes, section 767.5a, does not apply just to religious communications. By its terms, it also applies to communications "between attorneys and their clients . . . and between physicians and their patients." The statute thus operates in secular and sectarian settings linked by a common purpose—the everlasting need of the individual to seek spiritual and worldly assistance from others on a confidential basis. *See Trammel v. United States,* 445 U.S. 40 (1980) ("The privileges between priest and penitent, attorney and client, and physician and patient . . . are rooted in the imperative need for confidence and trust.").

Just as the clergy-penitent privilege protects "the human need to disclose to a spiritual counselor, in total and absolute confidence, what are believed to be flawed acts or thoughts and to receive priestly consolation and guidance in return," *Trammel,* 445 U.S. at 51, so the "[t]he lawyer-client privilege rests on the need for the advocate and counselor to know all that relates to the client's reasons for seeking representation if the professional mission is to be carried out," *id.,* and so "the physician must know all that a patient can articulate in order to identify and to treat disease," *id.* "[B]arriers to full disclosure" in all three settings—including the barrier that would arise if the counselor could be called upon to testify against the counseled—would undermine the values served by these time-honored relationships. *Id.*

In view of this function of the privilege, neither Michigan nor any other State (to our knowledge) treats the clergy-penitent privilege as a broad cloak protecting *all* religious communications. *See* Mich. Comp. Laws §600.2156 (requiring the communication to be made to clergy in his or her "professional character"); *id.* §767.5a(2) (requiring a "communication [ ] between . . . members of the clergy and the members of their respective churches . . . when those communications were necessary to enable the . . . members of the clergy . . . to serve as" clergy). Because the objective of the privilege is to protect the "human need" to place "total and absolute confidence" in a spiritual counselor without risk that the law will extract those confidences from the counselor, the Michigan Court of Appeals had ample reason to hold that privilege does not apply to "private writings." *People v. Varner,* 2002 WL 741531 (Mich. Ct. App. Apr. 23, 2002). The privilege requires the communication to be directed to a member of the clergy—just as the other privileges require the communication to be directed to an attorney or doctor—because it is the clergy who may be subpoenaed to testify against the individual. The same possibility does not exist with private writings to God, who may be petitioned but never subpoenaed. . . .

Varner does not argue that a privilege for communications between a spiritual counselor and a congregant improperly advances religion, presumably because that argument would not help Varner. The prototypical way to remedy a law that unconstitutionally advances religion in general is to strike the law, not to *extend* it so that it advances other religions. What Varner argues is something different — that the law improperly favors religions that encourage their members to seek guidance through intermediaries, such as a pastor or priest, over faiths that have no such tradition.

The confinement of the privilege to its traditional function, however, does not favor some religions over others. No matter what form of faith an individual practices, the privilege does not protect journal entries, whether addressed to God or not. If a Catholic confesses to a priest *and* proceeds to repeat everything she said in confession in "Dear God" entries in her journal, the privilege protects only the first communication, not the second one.

Nor can Varner tenably maintain that this limitation on the privilege restricts her ability to practice her faith. Journal writings do not represent the *only* way she may communicate with God, even if she remains a skeptic when it comes to organized religion. Like members of any faith, she remains free to let life's challenges take her to her knees — and seek God's guidance and comfort in the most common and commonly accepted form of prayer. . . .

Varner does not alter this conclusion by invoking cases standing for the general proposition that the Establishment Clause mandates government neutrality in religious practice. The decision of Michigan not to extend the privilege to private writings, as we have shown, *is* neutral. Whether a Protestant, Muslim or Atheist pens the journal entries, the State does not protect them. Whether the content of the journal entries is deeply spiritual, agnostic or thoroughly nihilistic, the state does not protect them. Whether Mother Teresa, C.S. Lewis, Ayn Rand or Janniss Varner authors the entries, the State does not protect them. . . .

The Michigan Court of Appeals' decision therefore was not contrary to or an unreasonable application of clearly established Supreme Court precedent.

For these reasons, we affirm.

NOTES TO VARNER v. STOVALL

1. *Religious Purpose.* In order for the privilege to cover a communication, there must have been a religious purpose for the communication. For example, there would be no privilege if the topic of the communication was business or ideas for avoiding taxes. On the other hand, there is support for giving a broad definition to the concept of religious purpose. When a privilege for clergy-communicant communications was included in the draft Federal Rules, the Advisory Committee noted that many in the clergy nowadays are trained in marriage counseling and the handling of various personality problems, suggesting that conversations on those topics could be within the privilege.

2. *Involvement of a Recognized Clergyperson.* As *Varner* suggests, the privilege may be invoked only if there is a communication with a member of the clergy. Some state privilege provisions give detailed definitions of "clergy." Additionally, case law has considered whether people who have certain types of spiritual relationships with others may properly be characterized as clergy. In

particular, participants in Alcoholics Anonymous meetings have been evaluated in this context. In one prominent case, the court held that while the precepts of Alcoholics Anonymous include a spiritual dimension, a participant's statements in such a group are made for practical rather than spiritual purposes. *See* Cox v. Miller, 296 F.3d 89 (2d Cir. 2002).

3. *Range of Statutory Definitions.* State legislatures have taken widely different approaches to defining the individuals to whom communications may be made that will be covered by this privilege. The following examples represent a generous and broad definition and a detailed and therefore less broad definition.

> **Fla. St. A. §90.505(1)(A)**
>
> A "member of the clergy" is a priest, rabbi, practitioner of Christian Science, or minister of any religious organization or denomination usually referred to as a church, or an individual reasonably believed so to be by the person consulting him or her.

> **Kan. St. A. §60-129**
>
> **(a) Definitions.** As used in this section, (1) the term "duly ordained minister of religion" means a person who has been ordained, in accordance with the ceremonial ritual, or discipline of a church, religious sect, or organization established on the basis of a community of faith and belief, doctrines and practices of a religious character, to preach and to teach the doctrines of such church, sect, or organization and to administer the rites and ceremonies thereof in public worship, and who as his or her regular and customary vocation preaches and teaches the principles of religion and administers the ordinances of public worship as embodied in the creed or principles of such church, sect, or organization; (2) the term "regular minister of religion" means one who as his or her customary vocation preaches and teaches the principles of religion of a church, a religious sect, or organization of which he or she is a member, without having been formally ordained as a minister of religion, and who is recognized by such church, sect, or organization as a regular minister; (3) the term "regular or duly ordained minister of religion" does not include a person who irregularly or incidentally preaches and teaches the principles of religion of a church, religious sect, or organization and does not include any person who may have been duly ordained a minister in accordance with the ceremonial, rite, or discipline of a church, religious sect, or organization, but who does not regularly, as a vocation, teach and preach the principles of religion and administer the ordinances of public worship as embodied in the creed or principles of his or her church, sect, or organization. . . .

E   MENTAL HEALTH CARE PRACTITIONERS AND PATIENTS

The privilege for confidential communications between a mental health care practitioner and a patient has wide recognition in federal and state courts. A related privilege, for communications between a physician of any type and a patient, is recognized in most states but has so far not been adopted by federal courts. The physician-patient privilege usually has no effect in the class of cases where the information it covers might be the most useful — cases in which the health of a party is relevant. It is universally held that when a litigant places his or her health in issue (as in personal injury cases), the physician-patient privilege is waived.

■   ■   ■

Fostering Mental Health Care with a Privilege — Jaffee. The Supreme Court's analysis of whether to apply a privilege to confidential communications between a mental health care practitioner and a patient illustrates the general technique federal courts must use in complying with Rule 501's references to the common law, reason, and experience.

JAFFEE v. REDMOND

518 U.S. 1 (1996)

Justice STEVENS delivered the opinion of the Court.

After a traumatic incident in which she shot and killed a man, a police officer received extensive counseling from a licensed clinical social worker. The question we address is whether statements the officer made to her therapist during the counseling sessions are protected from compelled disclosure in a federal civil action brought by the family of the deceased. Stated otherwise, the question is whether it is appropriate for federal courts to recognize a "psychotherapist privilege" under Rule 501 of the Federal Rules of Evidence.

Petitioner is the administrator of the estate of Ricky Allen. Respondents are Mary Lu Redmond, a former police officer, and the Village of Hoffman Estates, Illinois, her employer during the time that she served on the police force. Petitioner commenced this action against respondents after Redmond shot and killed Allen while on patrol duty.

On June 27, 1991, Redmond was the first officer to respond to a "fight in progress" call at an apartment complex. . . . According to Redmond, Allen was brandishing a butcher knife and disregarded her repeated commands to drop the weapon. Redmond shot Allen when she believed he was about to stab [a] man he was chasing. Allen died at the scene....

Petitioner filed suit in Federal District Court alleging that Redmond had violated Allen's constitutional rights by using excessive force during the encounter at the apartment complex. The complaint sought damages under Rev. Stat. §1979, 42 U.S.C. §1983 and the Illinois wrongful death statute....

During pretrial discovery petitioner learned that after the shooting Redmond had participated in about 50 counseling sessions with Karen Beyer, a clinical social worker licensed by the State of Illinois and employed at that time by the Village of Hoffman Estates. Petitioner sought access to Beyer's notes concerning the sessions for use in cross-examining Redmond. Respondents vigorously resisted the discovery. They asserted that the contents of the conversations between Beyer and Redmond were protected against involuntary disclosure by a psychotherapist-patient privilege. The district judge rejected this argument. Neither Beyer nor Redmond, however, complied with his order to disclose the contents of Beyer's notes. At depositions and on the witness stand both either refused to answer certain questions or professed an inability to recall details of their conversations.

In his instructions at the end of the trial, the judge advised the jury that the refusal to turn over Beyer's notes had no "legal justification" and that the jury could therefore presume that the contents of the notes would have been unfavorable to respondents. The jury awarded petitioner $45,000 on the federal claim and $500,000 on her state-law claim.

The Court of Appeals for the Seventh Circuit reversed and remanded for a new trial. Addressing the issue for the first time, the court concluded that "reason and experience," the touchstones for acceptance of a privilege under Rule 501 of the Federal Rules of Evidence, compelled recognition of a psychotherapist-patient privilege....

Rule 501 of the Federal Rules of Evidence authorizes federal courts to define new privileges by interpreting "common law principles . . . in the light of reason and experience.". . . The Senate Report accompanying the 1975 adoption of the Rules indicates that Rule 501 "should be understood as reflecting the view that the recognition of a privilege based on a confidential relationship . . . should be determined on a case-by-case basis." The Rule thus did not freeze the law governing the privileges of witnesses in federal trials at a particular point in our history, but rather directed federal courts to "continue the evolutionary development of testimonial privileges." Trammel v. United States, 445 U.S. 40 (1980).

The common-law principles underlying the recognition of testimonial privileges can be stated simply. "'For more than three centuries it has now been recognized as a fundamental maxim that the public . . . has a right to every man's evidence. When we come to examine the various claims of exemption, we start with the primary assumption that there is a general duty to give what testimony one is capable of giving, and that any exemptions which may exist are distinctly exceptional, being so many derogations from a positive general rule.'" United States v. Bryan, 339 U.S. 323,(1950) (quoting 8 J. Wigmore, Evidence

§2192, p. 64 (3d ed. 1940)). Exceptions from the general rule disfavoring testimonial privileges may be justified, however, by a "'public good transcending the normally predominant principle of utilizing all rational means for ascertaining the truth.'" Trammel, 445 U.S. at 50 quoting Elkins v. United States, 364 U.S. 206 (1960) (Frankfurter, J., dissenting).

Guided by these principles, the question we address today is whether a privilege protecting confidential communications between a psychotherapist and her patient "promotes sufficiently important interests to outweigh the need for probative evidence. . . ." 445 U.S. at 51. Both "reason and experience" persuade us that it does.

Like the spousal and attorney-client privileges, the psychotherapist-patient privilege is "rooted in the imperative need for confidence and trust." Trammel, 445 U.S. at 51. Treatment by a physician for physical ailments can often proceed successfully on the basis of a physical examination, objective information supplied by the patient, and the results of diagnostic tests. Effective psychotherapy, by contrast, depends upon an atmosphere of confidence and trust in which the patient is willing to make a frank and complete disclosure of facts, emotions, memories, and fears. Because of the sensitive nature of the problems for which individuals consult psychotherapists, disclosure of confidential communications made during counseling sessions may cause embarrassment or disgrace. For this reason, the mere possibility of disclosure may impede development of the confidential relationship necessary for successful treatment. As the Judicial Conference Advisory Committee observed in 1972 when it recommended that Congress recognize a psychotherapist privilege as part of the Proposed Federal Rules of Evidence, a psychiatrist's ability to help her patients

> "is completely dependent upon [the patients'] willingness and ability to talk freely. This makes it difficult if not impossible for [a psychiatrist] to function without being able to assure . . . patients of confidentiality and, indeed, privileged communication. Where there may be exceptions to this general rule . . . , there is wide agreement that confidentiality is a sine qua non for successful psychiatric treatment."

By protecting confidential communications between a psychotherapist and her patient from involuntary disclosure, the proposed privilege thus serves important private interests.

Our cases make clear that an asserted privilege must also "serve public ends." Upjohn Co. v. United States, 449 U.S. 383 (1981). Thus, the purpose of the attorney-client privilege is to "encourage full and frank communication between attorneys and their clients and thereby promote broader public interests in the observance of law and administration of justice." Ibid. And the spousal privilege, as modified in Trammel, is justified because it "furthers the important public interest in marital harmony," The psychotherapist privilege serves the public interest by facilitating the provision of appropriate treatment for individuals suffering the effects of a mental or emotional problem. The mental health of our citizenry, no less than its physical health, is a public good of transcendent importance.

In contrast to the significant public and private interests supporting recognition of the privilege, the likely evidentiary benefit that would result from the denial of the privilege is modest. If the privilege were rejected, confidential conversations between psychotherapists and their patients would surely be chilled, particularly when it is obvious that the circumstances that give rise to the need for treatment will probably result in litigation. Without a privilege, much of the desirable evidence to which litigants such as petitioner seek access — for example, admissions against interest by a party — is unlikely to come into being. This unspoken "evidence" will therefore serve no greater truth-seeking function than if it had been spoken and privileged.

That it is appropriate for the federal courts to recognize a psychotherapist privilege under Rule 501 is confirmed by the fact that all 50 States and the District of Columbia have enacted into law some form of psychotherapist privilege. We have previously observed that the policy decisions of the States bear on the question whether federal courts should recognize a new privilege or amend the coverage of an existing one. Because state legislatures are fully aware of the need to protect the integrity of the factfinding functions of their courts, the existence of a consensus among the States indicates that "reason and experience" support recognition of the privilege. In addition, given the importance of the patient's understanding that her communications with her therapist will not be publicly disclosed, any State's promise of confidentiality would have little value if the patient were aware that the privilege would not be honored in a federal court. Denial of the federal privilege therefore would frustrate the purposes of the state legislation that was enacted to foster these confidential communications.

It is of no consequence that recognition of the privilege in the vast majority of States is the product of legislative action rather than judicial decision. Although common-law rulings may once have been the primary source of new developments in federal privilege law, that is no longer the case. . . . [O]nce a state legislature has enacted a privilege there is no longer an opportunity for common-law creation of the protection. The history of the psychotherapist privilege illustrates the latter point. In 1972 the members of the Judicial Conference Advisory Committee noted that the common law "had indicated a disposition to recognize a psychotherapist-patient privilege when legislatures began moving into the field." The present unanimous acceptance of the privilege shows that the state lawmakers moved quickly. That the privilege may have developed faster legislatively than it would have in the courts demonstrates only that the States rapidly recognized the wisdom of the rule as the field of psychotherapy developed. . . .

Because we agree with the judgment of the state legislatures and the Advisory Committee that a psychotherapist-patient privilege will serve a "public good transcending the normally predominant principle of utilizing all rational means for ascertaining truth," Trammel, 445 U.S. at 50, we hold that confidential communications between a licensed psychotherapist and her patients in the course of diagnosis or treatment are protected from compelled disclosure under Rule 501 of the Federal Rules of Evidence.

All agree that a psychotherapist privilege covers confidential communications made to licensed psychiatrists and psychologists. We have no hesitation in concluding in this case that the federal privilege should also extend to confidential communications made to licensed social workers in the course of psychotherapy. The reasons for recognizing a privilege for treatment by psychiatrists and psychologists apply with equal force to treatment by a clinical social worker such as Karen Beyer. Today, social workers provide a significant amount of mental health treatment. Their clients often include the poor and those of modest means who could not afford the assistance of a psychiatrist or psychologist, but whose counseling sessions serve the same public goals. Perhaps in recognition of these circumstances, the vast majority of States explicitly extend a testimonial privilege to licensed social workers. We therefore agree with the Court of Appeals that "drawing a distinction between the counseling provided by costly psychotherapists and the counseling provided by more readily accessible social workers serves no discernible public purpose."

We part company with the Court of Appeals on a separate point. We reject the balancing component of the privilege implemented by that court and a small number of States. Making the promise of confidentiality contingent upon a trial judge's later evaluation of the relative importance of the patient's interest in privacy and the evidentiary need for disclosure would eviscerate the effectiveness of the privilege. As we explained in Upjohn, if the purpose of the privilege is to be served, the participants in the confidential conversation "must be able to predict with some degree of certainty whether particular discussions will be protected. An uncertain privilege, or one which purports to be certain but results in widely varying applications by the courts, is little better than no privilege at all."

These considerations are all that is necessary for decision of this case. A rule that authorizes the recognition of new privileges on a case-by-case basis makes it appropriate to define the details of new privileges in a like manner. Because this is the first case in which we have recognized a psychotherapist privilege, it is neither necessary nor feasible to delineate its full contours in a way that would "govern all conceivable future questions in this area."

The conversations between Officer Redmond and Karen Beyer and the notes taken during their counseling sessions are protected from compelled disclosure under Rule 501 of the Federal Rules of Evidence. The judgment of the Court of Appeals is affirmed.

It is so ordered.

NOTES TO JAFFEE v. REDMOND

1. *Range of Views on the Value of Mental Health Care.* In a dissenting opinion not reproduced above, Justice Scalia wrote:

When is it, one must wonder, that the psychotherapist came to play such an indispensable role in the maintenance of the citizenry's mental health? For most of history, men and women have worked out their difficulties by talking to, inter alios, parents, siblings, best friends and bartenders — none of whom was awarded a privilege against testifying in court. Ask the average citizen: Would your mental health be more significantly impaired by preventing you from seeing a psychotherapist, or by preventing you from getting advice from your mom? I have little doubt what the answer would be. Yet there is no mother-child privilege. . . .

2. *Doctor-Patient Privilege.* Federal courts do not recognize a doctor-patient privilege. While virtually all states take the opposite position, they typically narrow the protection the privilege provides: They withdraw the privilege in criminal cases, will contests, any case in which a patient makes an issue of his or her health, and malpractice cases.

3. *Privilege and Confidentiality.* A privilege prevents disclosure of information in litigation. A confidentiality obligation, usually imposed by professional standards, might prevent disclosure in more contexts. For health care practitioners, many statutes require reporting of facts observed in treating patients, such as particular types of injuries or illnesses. A physician might comply with a reporting statute and thus be excused from honoring a confidentiality obligation, but a privilege might still block use of that information in litigation.

> **GOOD TO REMEMBER**
>
> The privilege for statements to a mental health care practitioner will be waived in cases where the patient puts his or her mental health into issue.

QUESTION 15-5. Patient One was attacked by Patient Two while One and Two were patients at a mental health care facility operated by HealthCo. Patient One suffered severe injuries and has sought damages from HealthCo, claiming that it did not act properly to prevent Patient Two from inflicting harm on other patients. Patient One has sought records of the psychiatric counseling sessions conducted by HealthCo physicians with Patient Two.

In the state where the facility is located, a statute creates a privilege against disclosure of "confidential communications, made for the purposes of diagnosis or treatment of the patient's mental or emotional condition among the patient, the patient's psychotherapist, and persons who are participating in the diagnosis or treatment under the direction of the psychotherapist." It recognizes limits on the privilege for commitment proceedings, court-ordered examinations of a party or a witness, criminal cases where the privilege claimant has asserted an insanity defense, and cases involving an asserted breach of the psychotherapist-patient duty owed to the patient.

Under this statute, or under the general principles articulated in *Jaffee*, should the records be protected by privilege?

F   PARTICIPANTS IN PEER REVIEW PROCESSES

In many organizations, peer review processes gather and evaluate information about the organizations' personnel. For example, many health care providers organize periodic reviews of the quality of care or make individual investigations of instances of substandard performance. In higher education, tenure committees solicit reviews of applicants' scholarship and teaching. In each of these instances, it could be argued that providing a privilege to keep statements made in these processes out of court would encourage these reviews and improve their quality. Most state legislatures have adopted a privilege for peer review in the medical setting. The academic parallel has typically been rejected.

■   ■   ■

When a Doctor's Hospital Hurts Her, Does Privilege Prevent All Uses of Peer Review Records? — Lowy. Courts sometimes state that privileges should be construed narrowly. In other words, while society seeks to benefit from creating a zone of privacy, society may sometimes keep that benefit and also get to use information in litigation if courts make it difficult for beneficiaries to use a privilege. In *Lowy*, peer review records were not sought for the purpose of introducing them into evidence, but the court had to consider whether those records could be used as a technique of identifying other records that, free from privilege, could be used in litigation.

LOWY v. PEACEHEALTH

280 P.3d 1078 (Wash. 2012)

CHAMBERS, J.

This case presents the issue of whether, in civil litigation, a party may decline to produce requested discoverable information on the basis that to locate the information would require consulting privileged documents. A hospital seeks a protective order to prevent it from being required to review its quality assurance records to identify discoverable medical records in a medical negligence suit....

Dr. Leasa Lowy, MD, a staff physician at St. Joseph's Hospital in Bellingham, Washington (a hospital owned and operated by PeaceHealth), was admitted to the hospital as a patient. While a patient, Lowy sustained ulna nerve damage causing serious permanent impairment to her left arm. She claims that she can no longer practice her specialties of obstetrics, gynecology, and surgery. Lowy contends her injury was the result of an improper intravenous (IV) infusion procedure.

Lowy testified that she became aware of about 170 IV injuries at the hospital when she saw a list on a computer screen giving details of IV injuries with the patient names replaced by identification numbers. Contending the hospital has a serious and systemic problem with IV infusion injuries, Lowy brought a medical negligence action alleging, among other things, corporate negligence on the part of the hospital.

In connection with her theory of corporate negligence, Lowy sought to obtain, through a deposition under CR 30(b)(6), information relating to instances of "IV infusion complications and/or injuries at St. Joseph's Hospital for the years 2000-2008." It is undisputed that the requested information is within the hospital's records and is relevant and otherwise discoverable. The patient records are maintained by the hospital electronically but the hospital does not have the capability to electronically search the records. The hospital moved for a protective order as to Lowy's request. It argued that the deponent requested by Lowy would have to locate the information by going through thousands of patient files by hand. The hospital contended, and Lowy conceded, that an individual search of all of the hospital records for a nine-year period would be unduly burdensome.

But Lowy pointed out the list she had seen, created for quality assurance purposes, identified instances of IV infusion injuries. Lowy suggested that it would not be unduly burdensome for the hospital to consult that list to locate the relevant patient files and produce only the relevant patient files after redacting sensitive patient information. The hospital acknowledged the existence of the list but argued that the list itself was created for PeaceHealth's "Cubes" database, which contains information derived from incident reports and maintained for the sole purpose of quality review. Because the list itself was prepared for purposes of quality assurance by its quality improvement committee and is thus protected from discovery, the hospital claimed it could not be required to use the list to locate items not protected from discovery. Lowy argued that the statutory protections for quality assurance information do not prevent the hospital from conducting an internal review of its quality improvement committee information in order to locate unprotected information. Because such a review would allow the hospital to produce relevant discoverable information without undue burden, Lowy argued that the hospital was required to produce the information. The trial court first agreed with Lowy but then granted the protective order on a motion for reconsideration by the hospital. The Court of Appeals reversed the protective order.

The legislature has established a comprehensive peer review schema to improve health care in Washington State. The general purpose of the peer review statute is to encourage health care providers to candidly review the work and behavior of their colleagues to improve health care. RCW 4.24.250 was the first of these peer review statutes; it was enacted in 1971 and prohibited discovery of records of internal proceedings where one member of the health care profession presents evidence of negligence or incompetence against another. Following the passage of the federal Health Care Quality Improvement Act of 1986, many more states passed peer review statutes in response. One such statute was RCW 70.41.200, enacted by the Washington legislature in 1986. More complex than the 1971 statute, it set forth a quality improvement scheme for hospitals, while at the same time protecting certain quality improvement records from discovery. Under this scheme, hospitals are required, among other things, to establish a coordinated quality improvement program, a quality improvement committee, and a medical malpractice prevention program; to collect information concerning negative health care outcomes; and to conduct periodic review of the competence in delivering health care services of all persons who are employed or associated with the hospital.

The legislature was concerned that if the data and other information generated by quality improvement committees could be used against a hospital, it would create a disincentive for hospitals to report effectively and evaluate candidly information concerning the hospital's experience. To ensure a candid discussion about the quality of health care by hospitals, the legislature shielded from discovery a hospital's quality review committee records. . . .

The hospital argues that the list or database falls within the statutory privilege extending to "[i]nformation and documents . . . created specifically for, and collected and maintained by, a quality improvement committee." St. Joseph's Hospital contends that it cannot be required to consult a privileged list of unfavorable IV infusion outcomes maintained by its quality improvement committee in order to identify and produce non quality improvement committee records it concedes are discoverable. Lowy counters that she is not seeking discovery of the IV injury list, but only the unprivileged records that could be located by the hospital's review of the list. Whether the scope of the statutory privilege prevents the hospital from consulting its undiscoverable list to locate discoverable information is a different question than whether the statute prohibits internal review. It is also a question of first impression in this court and, as far as we can tell, nationwide.

In enacting RCW 70.41.200, our legislature adopted a peer review approach to improve the quality of health care in Washington hospitals. To encourage frank and candid discussion, it struck a balance among policy concerns and granted hospitals a privilege from discovery. In essence, the legislature has granted quality improvement committees two privileges. The first shelters communications that take place within the confines of a quality improvement meeting. *See* RCW 70.41.200(3) ("no person who was in attendance at a meeting of [a quality improvement] committee . . . shall be permitted or required to testify in any civil action as to the content of such proceedings"). The second protects documents and information, much like the immunity granted an attorney's work product. *See id.* ("Information and documents . . . created specifically for . . . a quality improvement committee are not subject to . . . discovery.").

As a policy matter, because some relationships are deemed so important and cannot be effective without candid communication, courts and legislatures have granted them privilege. But inasmuch as privileges frustrate the search for truth, they are limited in scope so as to accomplish their intended purpose and no more. Thus, the attorney-client, physician-patient, and clergy-penitent privileges are all founded on the premise that communication in these relationships is so important that the law is willing to sacrifice its pursuit for the truth, the whole truth, and nothing but the truth. . . .

In addition to a privilege for the communications, the legislature has created what we have described as something akin to a work product immunity for the documents created specifically for quality improvement committees. . . .

The seminal case of *Hickman* is instructive. There the Court held the work product of an attorney was protected from discovery to the extent that it reflected the lawyer's thoughts, mental impressions, legal theories, planning, and strategy. *Hickman v. Taylor,* 329 U.S. 495 (1947) (holding statements taken from witnesses by a lawyer were not protected by attorney-client privilege, but were protected from discovery absent a showing of need). Importantly, *Hickman* holds that work product is not protected from discovery in all circumstances; the court notes that production might be justified if, among other things, documents "give clues as to the existence or location of relevant facts." The Court explained that "[w]ere production of written statements and documents to be precluded under such circumstances, the liberal ideals of the deposition-discovery portions of the Federal Rules of Civil Procedure would be stripped of much of their meaning." To hold otherwise would permit the lawyer's office to be more than a shield; instead, it would become a fortress wherein the keys to find and unlock all secrets would be secure.

Here, the hospital's database gives, not clues, but the actual location of relevant facts. It is true that, unlike the work product doctrine, the peer review statute at issue does not specifically list any exception to the protection from discovery. RCW 70.41.200(3) "[i]nformation and documents . . . created specifically for . . . a quality improvement committee are not subject to . . . discovery"). But Lowy is not asking the hospital to produce the database. She is asking the hospital to turn over relevant documents everyone agrees are easily locatable by the hospital's review of the database. The principles of liberal discovery are as important in construing statutory provisions as court-created protections, like the work product doctrine. Here the hospital can easily produce unprotected information without revealing any information protected by the statute. The requested information is completely external to the hospital's "careful self-assessment," and thus there is no reason the hospital should be permitted to deny the request.

[T]he purpose of RCW 70.41.200 is twofold: to encourage health care providers to report adverse medical outcomes and to allow them to freely discuss, debate, and analyze the competence and conduct of peers. The privilege does not protect what goes into or comes out of the quality improvement committees. But documents created as part of the inner workings of the committee are privileged and disclosure of those documents may not be compelled. Our legislature did not intend quality improvement committees to institutionalize a conspiracy of silence or to create unnecessary barriers to a patient's quest for the truth. Our rules of discovery are grounded upon the constitutional guaranty that justice will be administered openly. Our legislature did not intend that defendants could conceal discoverable documents not created specifically for a quality improvement committee and not privileged by moving electronic search and other identifying tools under a quality improvement committee's umbrella of secrecy. But this sort of hide and seek gamesmanship would be encouraged were we to adopt the hospital's position in this case.

As the Court of Appeals observed, the plain language of the statute prevents disclosure of the quality review committee records themselves. . . . But the statute is not a shield to obstruct access to records outside the scope of the privilege. The medical records Lowy seeks were not created specifically for the quality improvement committee and are undisputedly relevant and discoverable. The Court of Appeals correctly explains:

> In disclosing [the patient records], the hospital will not be required to disclose who participated in the review process concerning IV injuries, which incidents the hospital found relevant or important, or how it sorted, grouped, or otherwise organized those incidents. The hospital will not disclose any analysis, discussions, or communications that occurred during the proceedings of the quality assurance committee. The response to the discovery request will reveal no more than if the hospital had produced the medical records through a burdensome page-by-page search. . . .

We conclude the legislature did not intend RCW 70.41.200 to be a fortress where a hospital can hide the keys to locating discoverable information. Absent a protective order, a hospital is required to review its own privileged records to identify relevant discoverable records.

NOTES TO LOWY v. PEACEHEALTH

1. *Protecting Otherwise Discoverable Data by Communicating It in a Privileged Relationship.* The *Lowy* court offers a clear explanation of an important idea in privilege law. Information that would otherwise have been discoverable continues to be discoverable even if it has been delivered to someone in the context of a relationship covered by a privilege. The fact that the information, usually documents, had been stored in a lawyer's office, for example, could be kept from a jury, but the actual documents and questions about them would be outside the protection of a privilege.

2. *University Peer Review Materials.* In University of Pennsylvania v. Equal Employment Opportunity Commission [EEOC], 493 U.S. 182 (1990), the Court considered and rejected a privilege for peer review materials that were claimed to be relevant to charges of racial or sexual discrimination in tenure decisions. The Court rejected a privilege on a variety of grounds. The Court held that Congress had created equal employment statutes without including any privilege provisions. While this fact need not prevent a court from choosing to create a privilege, the Court found that it was persuasive in this case:

> Acceptance of petitioner's claim would also lead to a wave of similar privilege claims by other employers who play significant roles in furthering speech and

learning in society. What of writers, publishers, musicians, lawyers? It surely is not unreasonable to believe, for example, that confidential peer reviews play an important part in partnership determinations at some law firms. We perceive no limiting principle in petitioner's argument. Accordingly, we stand behind the breakwater Congress has established: unless specifically provided otherwise in the statute, the EEOC may obtain "relevant" evidence. Congress has made the choice. If it dislikes the result, it of course may revise the statute.

QUESTION 15-6. If you were in a position to decide whether to recognize a privilege for statements made by students to high school and college guidance counselors and academic advisors, what factors would you consider, and what choice would you make? Would your analysis vary according to whether you were a legislator or a judge on a state's highest court?

G   SUMMARY

Privileges in General and in the Federal Rules. Privileges prevent the introduction of evidence about certain confidential communications, and may prevent a person from being compelled to testify about them. They inhibit the search for truth in our trial process, but they have developed to facilitate certain relationships that have great value. Common privileges protect communications between a lawyer and a client, spouses, members of the clergy and those making confessions or other spiritual communications with them, and mental health professionals and their patients. Rule 501 of the Federal Rules specifies that federal courts shall refer to common law to determine privilege issues.

Lawyer-Client Privilege. The lawyer-client privilege shields communications between a lawyer and a client, provided several requirements are established. The communication must have been private, and must have been for the purpose of obtaining legal help. If the client discloses the substance of the communication, the privilege is waived. It is also rejected in any case where the purpose of the communication was to obtain assistance in a future crime or fraud.

Applying the privilege to corporate entities raises a conceptual problem because it is not always easy to define "client." Modern doctrines use an expansive definition, and apply a privilege to communications between a corporation's lawyer and anyone employed by the corporation so long as the communication is made because a supervisor of the worker required it, and it was understood to be confidential, for the purpose of legal work, and on a subject within the scope of the employee's work.

When a client accidentally discloses a privileged communication, the question of waiver arises. FRE 502 adopts the view of the majority of states on this issue. To decide whether the disclosure should affect a waiver, a court must consider whether the disclosure was inadvertent and whether the holder of the privilege took reasonable steps to avoid disclosure and to remedy disclosure after it occurred.

Spousal Communications Privilege. Confidential communications between spouses are covered by a privilege, during and after their marriage. This privilege for confidential communications is different from the spousal testimonial privilege that can keep a spouse off the witness stand completely at a trial of the spouse's husband or wife. The communications privilege can be lost if the spouse who seeks to claim it has previously disclosed the contents of the communication. It is also treated as withdrawn if a communication would be relevant in a trial concerning a crime against the spouse or a child of that spouse or the spouse's husband or wife.

Clergy-Penitent Privilege. Statements made in the context of religious practice, to a member of the clergy by someone seeking spiritual guidance or solace are privileged.

Mental Health Care Practitioners and Patients. Statements made in this relationship are privileged in federal court and in all states. A similar privilege, for statements made between patients and doctors, is recognized in all states but is subject to many limitations. It is waived when a patient puts his or her physical condition into issue at a trial, or in criminal cases, malpractice cases, and will contests.

Peer Review Processes. Most states recognize a privilege for statements made in medical peer review proceedings. These privileges have been recognized to encourage the development of these reviews, on the theory that participants in adverse medical outcomes will speak freely if they know that their statements will not be admissible in trials.

CHAPTER 16

Authentication and the Original Writing Rule

A. Introduction
B. Authentication
C. Original Writing Rule
D. Summary

 ## INTRODUCTION

Topic Overview

Authentication and the original writing rule are evidentiary requirements meant to increase the likelihood that information presented at a trial will be accurate. Rule 901(a) imposes the general authentication requirement. It requires that the proponent of any item of evidence must support it with evidence capable of supporting a finding that the item of evidence really is what its proponent claims it is.

The original writing rule is more specific. It restricts testimony that is introduced for the purpose of proving what a document, recording, or photograph says. According to Rule 1002, that type of testimony may be given only if the proponent also introduces the actual original document, recording, or photograph that the testimony describes, introduces a copy of it, or provides an acceptable excuse for the lack of an original or a copy.

Chapter Organization

The chapter explores authentication with several cases that consider the requirement in different contexts, such as documents, postings on social media, and videos. It treats the original writing rule similarly, with attention to the most basic question related to that rule: When should testimony be characterized as testimony that seeks to prove the contents of a document or recording or photograph?

B   AUTHENTICATION

Satisfying the authentication requirement is usually straightforward. All the rule requires is that the proponent offer a basis on which a finder of fact could conclude that something about which the witness is testifying really was or is what the witnesses says it was or is. Rule 901 provides illustrations of possible methods of establishing authenticity, such as proof of appearance and circumstances.

Rule 901. Authenticating or Identifying Evidence

(a) **In General.** To satisfy the requirement of authenticating or identifying an item of evidence, the proponent must produce evidence sufficient to support a finding that the item is what the proponent claims it is.

(b) **Examples.** The following are examples only — not a complete list — of evidence that satisfies the requirement:

(1) *Testimony of a Witness with Knowledge.* Testimony that an item is what it is claimed to be.

(2) *Nonexpert Opinion About Handwriting.* A nonexpert's opinion that handwriting is genuine, based on a familiarity with it that was not acquired for the current litigation.

(3) *Comparison by an Expert Witness or the Trier of Fact.* A comparison with an authenticated specimen by an expert witness or the trier of fact.

(4) *Distinctive Characteristics and the Like.* The appearance, contents, substance, internal patterns, or other distinctive characteristics of the item, taken together with all the circumstances.

(5) *Opinion About a Voice.* An opinion identifying a person's voice — whether heard firsthand or through mechanical or electronic transmission or recording — based on hearing the voice at any time under circumstances that connect it with the alleged speaker.

(6) *Evidence About a Telephone Conversation.* For a telephone conversation, evidence that a call was made to the number assigned at the time to:

(A) a particular person, if circumstances, including self-identification, show that the person answering was the one called; or

(B) a particular business, if the call was made to a business and the call related to business reasonably transacted over the telephone.

(7) *Evidence About Public Records.* Evidence that:

(A) a document was recorded or filed in a public office as authorized by law; or

(B) a purported public record or statement is from the office where items of this kind are kept.

(8) *Evidence About Ancient Documents or Data Compilations.* For a document or data compilation, evidence that it:

(A) is in a condition that creates no suspicion about its authenticity;

(B) was in a place where, if authentic, it would likely be; and

(C) is at least 20 years old when offered.

(9) *Evidence About a Process or System.* Evidence describing a process or system and showing that it produces an accurate result.

(10) *Methods Provided by a Statute or Rule.* Any method of authentication or identification allowed by a federal statute or a rule prescribed by the Supreme Court.

This rule states the basic requirement and then offers numerous examples of ways to meet it. Even though the current version of the Federal Rules has been "restyled" for clarity and conciseness, Rule 901(b) states that its paragraphs provide examples and then states redundantly that those examples are not a complete list of ways in which a litigant might satisfy the authentication requirement. This suggests that the drafters were concerned that the list of examples might be mistakenly construed as limiting authentication to only the methods described in the list.

■　■　■

Whose Swiss Bank Account Numbers Are These? — Newton. The court follows the distinctive characteristics and circumstances method to approve authentication of a document found on one person as a document that had been prepared by someone else.

UNITED STATES V. NEWTON
891 F.2d 944 (1st Cir. 1989)

BOWNES, J.

Stuart H. Newton (Newton) and Thomas W. Gilbert (Gilbert) were convicted by a jury in the District Court of Rhode Island of conspiring to import marijuana into the United States [and numerous other drug crimes]. All of the charges stem from the importation of 20,000 pounds of hashish from Pakistan into the United States near Jamestown, Rhode Island, on or about July 4, 1983. Appellants raise numerous errors with the trial including evidentiary rulings, governmental misconduct, and other issues. After reviewing the entire record, we find that none of the alleged errors fatally flawed the trial and therefore affirm. . . .

A Swiss police officer testified that Kenneth Bloomfield (an alleged participant) was arrested in Geneva in possession of two passports, both with his picture, one in his name and one in the name of an alias . . . and a three-page unsigned and undated typed document that provided instructions on handling financial affairs. The document included a list of names (additional aliases it was proven that Newton used), account numbers and the names of banking officers of various Swiss bank accounts. The government claimed that the document was written by Newton and urged that it be admitted as an admission by a party opponent. The defendants objected claiming that the document was not properly authenticated and was irrelevant.

The judge ruled that the document had enough indicia of trustworthiness to be authentic under Fed. R. Evid. 901(b)(4). He admitted the document pursuant to Fed. R. Evid. 801(d)(2)(A) as an admission of a party opponent. The government used the document in its closing to argue that some of the fruits of the crime were deposited into Swiss bank accounts.

Rule 901 of the Federal Rules of Evidence requires that documents be authenticated or identified before they can be admitted into evidence. Authentication can be achieved through appearance, contents, substance, internal patterns, or other distinctive patterns taken in connection with circumstances. Fed. R. Evid. 901(b)(4). There are statements in the Bloomfield List from which it could be inferred that Newton authored the document. In particular, the document: refers to "Laura Newton" (Newton's wife) and asks that in the event of the author's death any money should be split between his family and Laura; refers to various aliases proven to be used by Newton ("my lawyer Milton Shapiro . . . knows me as Joseph Jaffee"); states, call "Tom" at a telephone number that it was proven was registered in Gilbert's long-time girlfriend's name; and lists bank account numbers next to proven aliases of Newton. Although, as the defendants urge, it is possible that some of the information in the document was known by conspirators other than Newton, Newton was proven to have used the aliases in the Bloomfield list and it is unlikely that anyone would have split money with Laura except Newton.

In addition, despite the defendants' contentions to the contrary, external evidence of the truth of the statements in the document was introduced by the government. Other documents indicated that Milton Shapiro acted as a lawyer for Newton. One of the names and numbers of a Swiss bank account in the Bloomfield list was identical to a number on a piece of paper found in a search of Newton's house. Given the circumstantial evidence of authorship, we do not find that the judge erred in determining that the Bloomfield list was authentic. . . .

NOTES TO UNITED STATES v. NEWTON

1. *Distinguishing Between Authentication and Admissibility.* Satisfying the authentication requirement does not guarantee that a document will be admitted. To be admissible, a document must satisfy a range of other requirements, starting, for example, with relevancy.

2. *Intrinsic and Extrinsic Information.* A court may rely on both intrinsic and extrinsic information in considering authentication. For example, the *Newton* court noted the use of aliases in the document and related those aliases to the fact that other evidence had shown those aliases had been used by the defendant.

3. *Reply Doctrine.* A common kind of circumstantial proof of authentication is a showing that the document sought to be authenticated seems to be a reply to some earlier communication that a witness can testify was sent to the claimed writer of the item sought to be authenticated.

QUESTION 16-1. William Worker died due to a form of cancer often associated with workplace exposure to asbestos products. His estate sought damages from Builders Supply Company, a supplier of industrial insulation that is sometimes made with asbestos. To prove that Worker had been in contact with products sold by Builders Supply, Worker's estate seeks to introduce hundreds of documents. These documents were produced, in response to a discovery request seven years prior to trial, by a law firm that then represented Builders Supply. The documents purport to be invoices. They include the name Builders Supply and that company's address at the top; invoice numbers; the buyers' names and addresses; the date of the sales; the products sold; the quantities purchased; the costs per item; and the dates of the sales. Some of these documents show Worker's former employer as a purchaser of products that contained asbestos.

No witness is available who can explain how these documents were sent to the former lawyer. Should the trial court treat them as adequately authenticated?

■   ■   ■

Linking a Social Media Page to a Particular Author — **Tienda.** Since anyone can create a Facebook or MySpace page without providing identifying information, problems might arise in trying to link a particular social media page to any specific person. The *Tienda* court confronts this issue and explains the strength of circumstantial evidence.

TIENDA v. STATE

358 S.W.3d 633 (Tex. Crim. App. 2012)

PRICE, J.

The appellant was convicted of murder. He pled true to one enhancement count, and the jury assessed punishment at thirty-five years' imprisonment. In an unpublished opinion, the Fifth Court of Appeals affirmed the appellant's conviction, holding that the trial court did not abuse its discretion in admitting evidence from MySpace pages that the State believed were created by the appellant. We will affirm the judgment of the court of appeals.

David Valadez and his two passengers were the targets of a multiple car shootout while driving southbound in Dallas on I-35E towards I-30. The shooting was apparently the product of some tension displayed between two rival groups at a nightclub earlier that evening, where members of the appellant's group were "throwing" gang signs and "talking noise" to Valadez and his friends. . . .

During preparation of the State's case against the appellant, the deceased's sister, Priscilla Palomo, provided the State with information regarding three MySpace profile pages that she believed the appellant was responsible for registering and maintaining. After subpoenaing MySpace.com for the general "Subscriber Report" associated with each profile account, the State printed out images of each profile page directly from the MySpace.com website, and then marked the profile pages and related content as State's exhibits for trial. The State used Palomo as the sponsoring witness for these MySpace accounts at guilt/innocence, and, over the appellant's running objection as to the authenticity of the profile pages, the State was permitted to admit into evidence the names and account information associated with the profiles, photos posted on the profiles, comments and instant messages linked to the accounts, and two music links posted to the profile pages. . . .

According to the subscriber reports, two of the MySpace accounts were created by a "Ron Mr. T," and the third by "Smiley Face," which is the appellant's widely-known nickname. The account holder purported to live in "D TOWN," or "dallas," and registered the accounts with a "ronnietiendajr@" or "smileys_shit@" email address. The State introduced multiple photos "tagged" to these accounts because the person who appeared in the pictures at least resembled the appellant. The person is shown displaying gang-affiliated tattoos and making gang-related gestures with his hands.

The main profile pages of the MySpace accounts contained quotes boasting "You aint BLASTIN You aint Lastin" and "I live to stay fresh!! I kill to stay rich!!" Under the heading "RIP David Valadez" was a link to a song that was played by Valadez's cousin at Valadez's funeral. Another music link posted to one of the profiles was a song titled "I Still Kill." The instant messages exchanged between the account holder and other unidentified MySpace users included specific references to other passengers present during the shooting, circumstances surrounding the shooting, and details about the State's investigation following the shooting. The author of the messages made specific threats to those who had been "snitchin" and "dont run shit but they mouth," assigning blame to others for being the "only reason im on lock down and have this shit on my back." . . . Several of the instant messages also complained about the author's electronic monitor, which was a condition of the appellant's house arrest while awaiting trial. . . .

In his only issue for discretionary review, the appellant contends that the trial court erred in admitting into evidence the electronic content obtained from MySpace during both the guilt/innocence and punishment phases of his trial. The appellant broadly argues that the State failed to properly authenticate any of the evidence printed from the social networking website; and more specifically, that the "contents of a website cannot authenticate the website" itself. In other words, he complains that the State did not prove that he was responsible for creating and maintaining the content of the MySpace pages by merely presenting the photos and quotes from the website that tended to relate to him. Therefore, the appellant concludes, the trial court erred in overruling his running objections under Texas Rules of Evidence Rule 901, and the court of appeals should not have affirmed its ruling. . . .

Under Texas Rules of Evidence Rule 104(a), whether or not to admit evidence at trial is a preliminary question to be decided by the court. A bedrock condition of admissibility of evidence in any legal contest is its relevance to an issue in the case — that is to say, its tendency to make a fact of consequence to determination of the action more or less probable. Evidence has no relevance if it is not authentically what its proponent claims it to be. Rule 901(a) of the Rules of Evidence defines authentication as a "condition precedent" to admissibility of evidence that requires the proponent to make a threshold showing that would be "sufficient to support a finding that the matter in question is what its proponent claims." Whether the proponent has crossed this threshold as required by Rule 901 is one of the preliminary questions of admissibility contemplated by Rule 104(a). The trial court should admit proffered evidence "upon, or subject to the introduction of evidence sufficient to support a finding of" authenticity. The ultimate question whether an item of evidence is what its proponent claims then becomes a question for the fact-finder — the jury, in a jury trial. In performing its Rule 104 gate-keeping function, the trial court itself need not be persuaded that the proffered evidence is authentic. The preliminary question for the trial court to decide is simply whether the proponent of the evidence has supplied facts that are sufficient to support a reasonable jury determination that the evidence he has proffered is authentic. . . .

Evidence may be authenticated in a number of ways, including by direct testimony from a witness with personal knowledge, by comparison with other authenticated evidence, or by circumstantial evidence. Courts and legal commentators have reached a virtual consensus that, although rapidly developing electronic communications technology often presents new and protean issues with respect to the admissibility of electronically generated, transmitted and/or stored information, including information found on social networking websites, the rules of evidence already in place for determining authenticity are at least generally "adequate to the task." Widely regarded as the watershed opinion with respect to the admissibility of various forms of electronically stored and/or transmitted information is *Lorraine v. Markel American Insurance Co.*[24] There the federal magistrate judge observed that "any serious consideration of the requirement to authenticate electronic evidence needs to acknowledge that, given the wide diversity of such evidence, there is no single approach to authentication that will work in all instances." Rather, as with the authentication of any kind of proffered evidence, the best or most appropriate method for authenticating electronic evidence will often depend upon the nature of the evidence and the circumstances of the particular case.

Like our own courts of appeals here in Texas, jurisdictions across the country have recognized that electronic evidence may be authenticated in a number of different ways consistent with Federal Rule 901 and its various state analogs. Printouts of emails, internet chat room dialogues, and cellular phone text messages have all been admitted into evidence when found to be sufficiently linked to the purported author so as to justify submission to the jury for its ultimate determination of authenticity. Such prima facie authentication has taken various forms. In some cases, the purported sender actually admitted to authorship, either in whole or in part, or was seen composing it. In others, the business records of an internet service provider or a cell phone company have shown that the message originated with the purported sender's personal computer or cell phone under circumstances in which it is reasonable to believe that only the purported sender would have had access to the computer or cell phone. Sometimes the communication has contained information that only the purported sender could be expected to know. Sometimes the purported sender has responded to an exchange of electronic communications in such a way as to indicate circumstantially that he was in fact the author of the particular communication, the authentication of which is in issue. . . .

In this case, the internal content of the MySpace postings — photographs, comments, and music — was sufficient circumstantial evidence to establish a prima facie case such that a reasonable juror could have found that they were created and maintained by the appellant. That circumstantial evidence included:

. . .

- The Subscriber Report for MySpace User # 300574151 lists the owner as "First Name: ron; Last name: Mr. T" with an email address of "ronnietiendajr@." As with the first MySpace listing, the city for this listing is "D*Town." The zip code is 75212. . . .
- The first MySpace page of User # 120841341 offered into evidence contains a photograph of the appellant under the title "SMILEY FACE." The photograph shows the appellant pulling a shirt up over the bottom half of his face. The tattoos on his arms, however, are clearly visible. There is a date stamp on the photograph of "03/01/2007 17:09." . . .

---

24. 241 F.R.D. 534 (D. Md. 2007).

- Below the appellant's photograph and the caption on that MySpace page is the legend "RIP David Valadez" and a music button which, according to Priscilla Paloma, played the song that was played at David Valadez's funeral.
- On the MySpace page for User # 300574151, there is a photograph of the appellant, bare-chested, with his gang tattoos — including "Tango Blast" written across his chest.
- The MySpace page is titled "MR. SMILEY FACE" even though the Subscriber Report list the User's name as "ron Mr. T" and his email address as "ronnietiendajr@." . . .
- The MySpace User # 300574151 message page contains numerous messages to other MySpace users. Only the 53 messages sent between 2:00 P.M. and 9:44 P.M. on September 21, 2008, were introduced into evidence. The messages that indicate that it is the appellant himself who is the creator, owner, and user of this MySpace account include the following:
- At 2:09 P.M. the User sent a message to User # 73576314: "SHIT CAN U BELIEVE I ALREADY BEEN ON DIS MONITOR A YEAR NOW."[46] . . .
- At 2:22 P.M. the User sent a message to User # 73576314: "MAN JESSE BOY HECTOR SNITCHIN ON ME I AINT TRIPPIN ON BEEF BUT TELLIN A WHOLE NOTHER BALL GAME DAT I DONT PLAY." . . .
- At 2:50 P.M. the User sent another message to the same User: "YEA SHIT U KNO I KEEP GANGST EVEN AFTER HECTOR SHOT AT NEW AT RUMORS WE STILL DIDNT TELL AND I KNO JESSE TOLD HIM WE WAS THERE CUZ WE SAW THEM AT THA CLUB BUT ITS COO IF I GET OFF MAN@!!!!!"

This combination of facts — (1) the numerous photographs of the appellant with his unique arm, body, and neck tattoos, as well as his distinctive eyeglasses and earring; (2) the reference to David Valadez's death and the music from his funeral; (3) the references to the appellant's "Tango Blast" gang; and (4) the messages referring to (a) a shooting at "Rumors" with "Nu–Nu," (b) Hector as a "snitch," and (c) the user having been on a monitor for a year (coupled with the photograph of the appellant lounging in a chair displaying an ankle monitor) sent from the MySpace pages of "ron Mr. T" or "MR. SMILEY FACE" whose email address is "ronnie tiendajr@" — is sufficient to support a finding by a rational jury that the MySpace pages that the State offered into evidence were created by the appellant. This is ample circumstantial evidence — taken as a whole with all of the individual, particular details considered in combination — to support a finding that the MySpace pages belonged to the appellant and that he created and maintained them.

---

46. According to the Clerk's Record, the appellant was released on pretrial bond with an ankle monitor on October 24, 2007. One of the photographs on the MySpace page for User # 435499766 (registered to "SMILEY FACE" with an email address of "ronnietiendajr@") is of the appellant lounging in a chair with a gold chain hanging down his chest, wearing bright white sneakers and an ankle monitor. . . .

It is, of course, within the realm of possibility that the appellant was the victim of some elaborate and ongoing conspiracy. Conceivably some unknown malefactors somehow stole the appellant's numerous self-portrait photographs, concocted boastful messages about David Valadez's murder and the circumstances of that shooting, was aware of the music played at Valadez's funeral, knew when the appellant was released on pretrial bond with electronic monitoring and referred to that year-long event along with stealing the photograph of the grinning appellant lounging in his chair while wearing his ankle monitor. But that is an alternate scenario whose likelihood and weight the jury was entitled to assess once the State had produced a prima facie showing that it was the appellant, not some unidentified conspirators or fraud artists, who created and maintained these MySpace pages....

Because there was sufficient circumstantial evidence to support a finding that the exhibits were what they purported to be — MySpace pages the contents of which the appellant was responsible for — we affirm the trial judge and the court of appeals which had both concluded the same.

NOTES TO TIENDA v. STATE

1. *Adequate, Not Conclusive, Proof.* The proponent of an item sought to be authenticated is required to produce evidence sufficient to support a finding that it is what the proponent claims it is. This is different from evidence that requires such a finding. The *Tienda* court relies on this aspect of authentication when it acknowledges the risk of an "elaborate and ongoing conspiracy" to produce a false MySpace page. That risk is real but did not make the rest of the circumstantial evidence too weak to support the finding of authentication.

GOOD TO REMEMBER

The jury is the ultimate decision maker for the authentication concept; the judge determines only whether the proponent of evidence has produced information adequate to support a jury finding of authenticity.

2. *Judge and Jury.* For authentication, the judge must decide if the proponent of evidence has produced enough information to support a jury finding that the item is what the proponent claims it is. For many other findings related to admissibility, the judge personally decides whether the requirements for admission have been met. For example, if there is a hearsay objection to some evidence and the proponent argues that the evidence is admissible as a statement by a party opponent, the judge would decide all the facts related to applying the hearsay doctrine.

3. *Descriptions of Computer Systems.* Rule 901(b)(9) describes a common method of authenticating information stored in and produced from computer systems. The example's statement: "Evidence describing a process or system and showing that it produces an accurate result" was described by the Advisory Committee as intended to cover computer output. The Committee wrote that "[c]omputer output may be authenticated under Rule 901(b)(9). . . . When the

proponent relies on the provisions of Rule 901(b)(9) . . . it is common for the proponent to provide evidence of the input procedures and their accuracy, and evidence that the computer was regularly tested for programming errors. At a minimum, the proponent should present evidence sufficient to warrant a finding that the information is trustworthy and provide the opponent with an opportunity to inquire into the accuracy of the computer and of the input procedures."

4. *Videos and Photos.* Litigants often seek to introduce videos and still photos into evidence. They can be authenticated by a witness's testimony that the witness has personally seen whatever the video or photo shows and that the video or photo seems to the witness to be an accurate representation of what the witness has seen. Another way to authenticate these items is with testimony about the process by which the video or photo was made, as in testimony about the operation of an automatic surveillance camera.

QUESTION 16-2. To prove that Harry Homeowner had been aware that water would be shut off at his house for a two-day period needed for repair of a water main, a party in a suit seeks to introduce as an exhibit a card describing the shutoff that was placed on the doorknob of Homeowner's front door a week prior to the repair. For this evidence to be admitted, the proponent must show that:

A. The card is relevant.
B. The card is relevant and authentic.
C. The card is relevant, authentic, and covered by an exception to the rule against hearsay.
D. The card is relevant, authentic, and covered by an exception to the rule against hearsay, and its probative value is not substantially outweighed by its risk of unfair prejudice.

■   ■   ■

Must Chain of Custody Evidence Be Perfect? — Johnson. The *Johnson* court answers this question as one would expect, and it explains why "perfect" would be too demanding a standard on this issue.

UNITED STATES v. JOHNSON

977 F.2d 1360 (10th Cir. 1992)

TACHA, J.

This appeal arises from a joint trial of four defendants. The jury returned guilty verdicts against appellants Clay Dalton Johnson, Jerry Duane Spears, Harold Onee Behrens, and Edward Dale Summerlin for multiple counts related to the manufacturing, possession and distribution of drugs and possession of firearms. We . . . affirm in part, reverse in part, and remand for resentencing. . . .

Johnson . . . contends that the district court erred by admitting into evidence two thermos bottles containing amphetamine and a prescription bottle filled with white powder. He asserts that the government failed to establish an adequate chain of custody and failed to properly identify these items before they were admitted into evidence. We review a trial court's decision to admit or exclude evidence under an abuse of discretion standard. "The requirement of authentication or identification as a condition precedent to admissibility is satisfied by evidence sufficient to support a finding that the matter in question is what its proponent claims." Fed. R. Evid. 901(a).

When "evidence is unique, readily identifiable and relatively resistant to change, the foundation need only consist of testimony that the evidence is what its proponent claims." United States v. Cardenas, 864 F.2d 1528, 1531 (10th Cir.), *cert. denied*, 491 U.S. 909, 105 L. Ed. 2d 705, 109 S. Ct. 3197 (1989). On the other hand, when the evidence "is not readily identifiable and is susceptible to alteration by tampering or contamination, the trial court requires a more stringent foundation 'entailing a "chain of custody" of the item with sufficient completeness to render it improbable that the original item has either been exchanged with another or been contaminated or tampered with.'" Id. (quoting Edward W. Cleary, McCormick on Evidence §212, at 667 (3d ed. 1984)).

However, "the chain of custody need not be perfect for the evidence to be admissible." Id. If the trial court — after "considering the nature of the evidence, and the surrounding circumstances, including presentation, custody and probability of tampering or alteration" — "determines that the evidence is substantially in the same condition as when the crime was committed, the court may admit it." Id. Once the court properly decides that the evidence is admissible, "deficiencies in the chain of custody go to the weight of the evidence, not its admissibility; the jury evaluates the defects and, based on its evaluation, may accept or disregard the evidence." United States v. Brandon, 847 F.2d 625, 630 (10th Cir.), *cert. denied*, 488 U.S. 973 (1988).

At trial, FBI agent Jim Elliott testified regarding his participation in the search of several vehicles. He stated that he searched a GMC pickup truck — identified as Johnson's truck — and found two thermos bottles in the front seat that emitted an odor that he associated with "methamphetamine." He also found a prescription bottle in the truck that contained a white substance. He testified that the bottles were "turned over to the Oklahoma State Bureau of Investigation [OSBI] chemists at the scene." During the first day of his testimony, Elliott answered affirmatively when the prosecutor asked whether he had given the prescription bottle to another agent for the purpose of relaying them to a chemist for analysis. The next day, Elliott stated that he gave the thermos bottles "to the OSBI chemist." Defense counsel did not cross-examine Elliott with respect to whom Elliott gave the thermos bottles and the prescription bottle.

OSBI chemist Richard Dill later took the stand. He carried several sacks, two of which contained the thermos bottles and one of which contained the prescription bottle. He testified that these items were brought to him at the cabin lab site and that he then carried them from the cabin to the OSBI laboratory. He also testified that he could not recall who had given him the exhibits. Dill indicated that, except for entry into the bottles for testing, the exhibits were in the same sealed condition as when he received them at the lab site. Counsel for Johnson objected to the admission of the thermos bottles. The district court overruled the objection and admitted the exhibits into evidence. On appeal, Johnson contends that the district court abused its discretion by admitting the thermos bottles and the prescription bottle. He specifically points to inconsistencies in Agent Elliott's testimony regarding whether he gave the bottles to another agent or gave them directly to an OSBI chemist.

Although the chain of custody for the bottles may not be perfect, we conclude that the district court did not abuse its discretion in admitting this evidence. Johnson introduced no evidence that the bottles had been tampered with or altered in any way. Agent Elliott testified that he found two thermos bottles and a prescription bottle in the truck and that he either gave them to an OSBI chemist or to another agent who relayed them to a chemist. Defense counsel failed to cross-examine Elliott on this issue to determine whether this slight inconsistency was inadvertent or the result of a deliberate alteration. An OSBI chemist testified that he received the bottles at the lab site, that they remained in the same condition thereafter, and that they tested positive for amphetamine. In addition, another witness, Joe Pierce, testified that he had seen large thermos containers filled with "crank" (amphetamine) at Johnson's house. This evidence was sufficient to warrant the district court's admission of the bottles.

In Cardenas, we held that "[t]he trial court need not rule out every possibility that the evidence underwent alteration; it need only find that the reasonable probability is that the evidence has not been altered in any material respect." We have also held that "'absent some showing by the defendant that the exhibits have been tampered with, it will not be presumed that the investigators who had custody of them would do so.'" United States v. Lepanto, 817 F.2d 1463, 1465 (10th Cir. 1987). Because Johnson proffered no evidence of tampering, we hold that the district court did not abuse its discretion in admitting the bottles into evidence and that any imperfections in the chain of custody were to be weighed by the jury.

NOTES TO UNITED STATES v. JOHNSON

1. *Distinctive Items.* Courts may be more or less demanding with regard to chain of custody evidence depending on attributes of the item sought to be introduced. If an item of evidence has distinctive characteristics, such as a gun with a serial number, proof of where it has been prior to trial may be unimportant, if testimony can describe its characteristics and link those characteristics

to the events at issue in the trial. A fungible item, such as blood or drugs, will require greater detail to establish its link with the litigated circumstances.

2. *Same Standard for Civil and Criminal Cases.* The same standard for quality of chain of custody evidence applies in civil and criminal cases. The chain of custody version of authentication is essentially a relevance inquiry. While a prosecutor's burden of proof is greater than a civil litigant's preponderance burden, the degree to which the trier of fact must ultimately be persuaded does not affect the question of relevance for any particular items of evidence that might eventually support a finding under the governing standard.

 ## ORIGINAL WRITING RULE

The Federal Rules incorporate the "original writing rule," known sometimes at common law as the "best evidence rule," in Rules 1001-1004 set out the main provisions. If a party seeks to establish as a fact that a particular document or recording contained certain information, the rule allows a party to introduce testimony about the document or recording *only if the party also produces the document or recording* (or a copy or an excuse for its absence).

Rule 1001. Definitions That Apply to This Article

In this article:

(a) A "writing" consists of letters, words, numbers, or their equivalent set down in any form.

(b) A "recording" consists of letters, words, numbers, or their equivalent recorded in any manner.

(c) A "photograph" means a photographic image or its equivalent stored in any form.

(d) An "original" of a writing or recording means the writing or recording itself or any counterpart intended to have the same effect by the person who executed or issued it. For electronically stored information, "original" means any printout — or other output readable by sight — if it accurately reflects the information. An "original" of a photograph includes the negative or a print from it.

(e) A "duplicate" means a counterpart produced by a mechanical, photographic, chemical, electronic, or other equivalent process or technique that accurately reproduces the original.

Rule 1002. Requirement of the Original

An original writing, recording, or photograph is required in order to prove its content unless these rules or a federal statute provides otherwise.

Rule 1003. Admissibility of Duplicates

A duplicate is admissible to the same extent as the original unless a genuine question is raised about the original's authenticity or the circumstances make it unfair to admit the duplicate.

Rule 1004. Admissibility of Other Evidence of Content

An original is not required and other evidence of the content of a writing, recording, or photograph is admissible if:

    (a) all the originals are lost or destroyed, and not by the proponent acting in bad faith;

    (b) an original cannot be obtained by any available judicial process;

    (c) the party against whom the original would be offered had control of the original; was at that time put on notice, by pleadings or otherwise, that the original would be a subject of proof at the trial or hearing; and fails to produce it at the trial or hearing; or

    (d) the writing, recording, or photograph is not closely related to a controlling issue.

■ ■ ■

Is a Blurry Copy as Good as an Original?—**Alexander.** In this case, from an era when some copying machines did not work very well, the court considers application of the original writing rule to a copy used to prove that the defendant stole a particular check from the mail.

UNITED STATES v. ALEXANDER

326 F.2d 736 (4th Cir. 1964)

BOREMAN, J.

Appellant, Ernest Franklin Alexander, and one Robinson were charged in a two-count indictment with violations of the laws relating to the postal service. The first count charged that Alexander and Robinson had taken from an authorized depository for mail matter a letter addressed to Sammie W. Woodall, 205 North Franklin Road, Greenville, South Carolina, containing a United States Treasury check made payable to the addressee. The second count charged the possession of the particular Treasury check which was the 'contents' of the letter addressed to Sammie W. Woodall, with knowledge that the same had been stolen, taken or abstracted from an authorized depository for mail matter. Alexander entered a plea of not guilty as to both counts and alone was tried

BASIC EXAMPLES

Testimony about Streets. Could you testify about what streets run between your house and your law school, even though that information is recorded in maps that are published by map publishers? This testimony would be permitted, because it is an example of a person testifying about something he or she knows that is also, coincidentally, the subject of a writing. The testimony is not based on the writing and is not an effort to prove what the writing says.

Testimony about Maps. If you were suing the map publisher, claiming that its map had an error that had caused some injury, testimony and proof about the contents of the map would be governed by the original writing rule.

Testimony about a Book as an Object. If someone were on trial for stealing a book, the prosecution could introduce evidence showing that he or she had been seen taking a book from a store without paying for it without satisfying the requirements of the original writing rule, since the actual words in the book have no relevance to the prosecution's case.

before a jury. Upon his motion, the first count was dismissed as to him and the jury returned a verdict of guilty as charged in the second count. Defendant did not testify in his own defense. The admission, over objection, of certain evidence is challenged on appeal. We think that the defendant is entitled to a new trial. . . .

There was no direct evidence to show that the check, or a letter in which it was contained, had been stolen or taken from Mrs. Woodall's mailbox. Over timely objection by the defense, several government witnesses were permitted to testify as to the terms of the check and a copy of the check was admitted in evidence.

The first witness presented by the Government was C.V. McCall, Special Deputy Sheriff for Greenville County. In addition to his account of the circumstances of the arrest, McCall testified that when shown the check which he, McCall, had given the postal inspector, Alexander admitted having had it in his possession and throwing it from [a police car after he had been arrested]. Officer McCall described the check as follows: 'It was to Sammie W. Woodall, 205 North Franklin Road, Greenville, South Carolina.'

The postal inspector, Earl W. McClure, was the second government witness. He testified that after the defendant's arrest he went to the sheriff's office where he obtained from the arresting officers the check which Officer McCall had retrieved; that he showed the check, which he described as addressed to Sammie W. Woodall in the amount of $106.20, to Alexander who admitted having dropped the check out of the police car; that he subsequently caused the check to be delivered to the payee, Mrs. Sammie W. Woodall, with instructions to cash it; that while the check was in his possession he, McClure, attempted to have a copy made of it with a thermofax machine; that the machine did not reproduce the name and address of the payee and he typed those terms on the copy. The copy prepared by the postal inspector was admitted in evidence and the terms were read to the jury by the inspector. . . .

It is the defendant's contention that the admission of the copy and the parol evidence to show the terms of the check, without the production of the check itself or a reasonable explanation of the Government's failure to produce it, violated the 'best evidence rule' and constituted prejudicial error. The Government concedes that there was no sufficient foundation laid for the introduction of secondary evidence; it argues, however, that the evidence objected to was introduced to show the identity of a specific physical object, namely, the check, and hence its admission was not violative of the best evidence rule. . . .

It would seem that this case, involving as it does secondary evidence of a writing, without any explanation of the failure to produce the writing itself, is within the mandate of the best evidence rule. The Government argues, however, that the rule is not applicable here because the purpose of the Government in offering the evidence was only to identify the check found in Alexander's possession. With this contention we cannot agree. It is true, as the Government urges, that the best evidence rule is aimed only at excluding evidence which concerns the contents of a writing and testimony as to other facts about a writing, such as its existence or identity, may be admissible. As stated in IV Wigmore, Evidence §1242 (3d ed. 1940):

> "The rule applies only to the terms of the document, and not to any other facts about the document. In other words, the rule applies to exclude testimony designed to establish the terms of the document, and requires the document's production instead, but does not apply to exclude testimony which concerns the document without aiming to establish its terms: . . ."

Here, however, the very purpose of the evidence objected to was to establish the terms of the check. The identity of the check could be established only by proof of its terms; the check was not described merely in general terms as a physical object, such as 'a check' or 'a Government check,' but instead its terms were set forth with particularity; indeed the copy purported to include its every characteristic. It is clear that the Government's primary purpose was to prove the terms of the check in accordance with the indictment which set forth those terms in detail, including the serial number, symbol, amount and the name and address of the payee. Moreover, the terms of the check, if properly proved, would tend to establish that the check which Alexander had in his possession was the same check which Mrs. Woodall should have received and which should have been delivered to her mailbox. Without proof of its terms, there was virtually nothing in the record to connect the check with the mails or its possession with the offense charged. The terms of the check were vitally material to the Government's case.

A careful examination of certain cases cited by the Government convinces us that they do not support the Government's position. . . .

[I]n State v. Pappas, 195 Wash. 197, 80 P.2d 770 (1938), the evidence concerned a federal liquor license. In a prosecution for the unlawful possession of liquor, the raiding officers testified that they had seen a federal liquor license on defendant's premises but did not testify as to its contents. The court, holding that the testimony was properly admitted, stated:

> "The license, or stamp, was thus a part of the furnishings with which the place was equipped and, being a physical thing, was capable of identification and description by the officers and agents who saw it."

Thus, the court treated the license as a physical object not within the scope of the best evidence rule. Significantly, however, the court went on to state:

> "If the license be considered in the aspect of a written document, then it is to be noted that the testimony of the officers was not with respect to its terms, but only with respect to its existence or identity. The rule requiring the production of written instruments or documents applies only to the terms and not to the existence of such documents." . . .

Another case cited by the Government, United States v. Calamaro, 137 F. Supp. 816 (E.D. Pa. 1956), is of similar import. There the defendant, a pickup man in a numbers operation, was indicted and convicted of failing to pay the special gambler's tax imposed by the Internal Revenue Code. He moved for a judgment of acquittal and alternatively for a new trial, assigning as error, inter alia, the admission of testimony of police officers pertaining to the numbers slips taken from his possession, without the production of the slips themselves. The arresting officers had testified that they had taken from the possession of defendant 48 sheets of paper which were three inches wide and seven inches long, and that there were 1800 notations of three-digit numbers followed by dashes and other numbers on the papers. The officers characterized the sheets as 'banker slips.' The District Court found no error in the admission of the testimony. Significantly, however, the court emphasized that

> "*** The government was required to prove only that the slips had existed, that they were numbers slips, and that the defendant had been carrying them. The government had no burden and made no attempt to prove the specific contents of the slips. Consequently, the best evidence rule has no application to the problem presented by the failure to produce the numbers slips in the present case. ***" . . .

It is correct, as the Government asserts, that the cases cited support the proposition that oral testimony may be allowed to establish the existence or identity of a written document. But it is significant that each of those cases indicates that the testimony may not go so far as to include the terms of the writing. Such a conclusion is strengthened by a consideration of the purpose of the best evidence rule. . . .

Little reflection upon the reasons for the rule is required to note its applicability in the present case. Here the indictment alleged the terms of the check with particularity and the Government undertook to prove those terms as circumstantial evidence of the unlawful possession of the check as charged in the second count of the indictment. Any error in such proof could easily have been of significant legal consequence. Consider, for example, the effect of a witness's failure to notice, or a reproducing machine's failure to copy, an indorsement on the back of the check. We are convinced that it was for the purpose of avoiding the possibility of such errors as might have occurred here that the best evidence rule was formulated.

As pointed out by Wigmore, "where a document is referred to as identical with or the same as another document, or as helping to identify some transaction or some other physical object, the question is a difficult one; and the ruling will depend upon whether in the case in hand greater emphasis and importance is to be given to the detailed marks of peculiarity or to the document as a whole regarded as an ordinary describable thing." Here the emphasis was clearly and of necessity on the "detailed marks of peculiarity" which the check bore. The Government could not have sustained its burden by merely showing that the defendant had a Government check in his possession; proof was required to establish that the check which the defendant possessed was, to his knowledge, contained in a letter which had been stolen, taken or abstracted from the mail. The prosecution was obviously aware of the fact that in the absence of proof of the specific terms and contents of the check its case must fail. We believe the evidence went beyond that which is permissible for the purpose of identifying a physical object. As between a written instrument and a copy or parol description thereof, the rule operates to accept the former and exclude the latter. As to its contents, the writing is certain; any oral description thereof necessarily involves the frailties of human recollection and any copy, the hazards of faulty duplication. In addition, there exists the possibility of prejudice or interest influencing either the testimony of a witness or the accuracy of the copy. Given a choice between the two, the law accepts the certain and rejects the uncertain. The defendant is entitled to a new trial. . . .

Reversed and remanded.

NOTES TO UNITED STATES v. ALEXANDER

1. *Rationale for the Rule.* The original writing rule is derived from the common law's best evidence rule which generally required parties to produce the best available evidence to prove any point. We no longer impose that kind of general requirement, relying instead on the self-interest of parties to give them an incentive to produce persuasive evidence. But where writings (and photographs and recordings) are concerned, the Federal Rules of Evidence retain the common law's rule and do require — subject to many exceptions — production of originals. Where the terms or details of a writing are important, it makes sense to require that an original be brought into court instead of just allowing someone to testify about what he or she remembers the document said. *Alexander* highlights the value of the rule in a case where the precise contents of a writing were crucial.

2. *Copies and Excuses.* The current original writing rule, in FRE 1003 and 1004 allows the use of copies and other evidence when, for a good reason, an original or a copy is not available. The quality of a copy (or "duplicate") is subject to challenge.

3. *Furthering the Purpose of the Rule.* The *Alexander* court refers to cases where items with writing were permitted to be described without production of the originals or other compliance with the original writing rule. In cases of that type, for example involving testimony about a license posted at a location, courts attempt to distinguish between testimony describing the contents of a document and testimony that just describes the existence of the document. Obviously, to know that something was a liquor license, one would have to read it and understand its contents. So as a matter of logic, the original writing rule might apply. Courts tend to ignore this logic and restrict application of the rule to circumstances where there is a reasonable likelihood that the precise details of the writing might matter. In other instances, courts are likely to treat the writing as an object outside the coverage of the original writing rule.

> ## GOOD TO REMEMBER
>
> The original writing rule was created when forgeries were a significant problem and when documents may have been hard to read. Courts bear this history in mind when deciding whether to apply the rule.

■ ■ ■

Segment 2: application of original writing rule

Overlap Between Perceptions of Past Events and Records of Past Events — Howard. If someone who heard or participated in a conversation seeks to testify about the conversation, what should a court do if the conversation was recorded? Should a court treat the testimony as testimony that seeks to prove the contents of a recording, or should a court treat the recording as something that exists in the world but that is not the subject of the witness's testimony?

UNITED STATES v. HOWARD

953 F.2d 610 (11th Cir. 1992)

PER CURIAM.

In this appeal, we are presented with the following [issue]: whether the district court abused its discretion by allowing the government to introduce testimony to prove the contents of a recorded conversation, in addition to the inaudible recording itself. . . .

The appellant, Franklin David Howard ("Howard"), was indicted in a one-count indictment of attempting to possess with intent to distribute marijuana, in violation of 21 U.S.C. §846. After Howard's pretrial motion was denied as being untimely filed, the case was set for trial and tried before a jury. Howard was convicted and sentenced by the district court to a forty-one month period of confinement to be followed by a three-year period of supervised release. . . .

The record demonstrates that in April 1990, Howard approached his long-time friend and fellow resident of Cedartown, Georgia, Richard Landrum ("Landrum"), and asked him for help in obtaining fifty-one hundred pounds of marijuana. At the time of the inquiry, Howard was aware that Landrum had recently been arrested on narcotics charges in Alabama. Landrum referred this information to the Drug Enforcement Agency ("DEA"). Landrum was subsequently introduced to DEA agent Mike Dolan ("Dolan"). After debriefing Landrum with DEA agent Jack Harvey ("Harvey"), Dolan instructed Landrum to make a monitored telephone call to Howard later that same day to discuss the marijuana deal. Prior to making the call, Dolan told Landrum that the scenario would be that an individual by the name of "Mike" would be bringing the marijuana in from Texas. As originally planned, Dolan was to pose as "Mike."

Numerous monitored telephone conversations between Landrum and Howard were recorded. During one of the conversations, Howard stated that a portion of the purchase money would be provided by a third party. Howard's side of the taped conversation was only partially audible, so the district court, after having the tape played for the jury, permitted, over objection, the monitoring agent, Harvey, to testify as to its contents. According to Harvey, Howard made references during the call to an earlier attempt on his part to purchase marijuana and to the manner and price at which he planned to resell the marijuana about to be purchased. . . .

Howard argues that agent Harvey should not have been permitted to testify as to recorded statements made by Howard which he overheard, even though, as Howard concedes, the tape was only partially audible. Howard relies on the "best evidence rule" in support of his contention that Harvey's testimony was inadmissible. The best evidence rule, however, requires the introduction of original recordings, if at all, only when the content of the recording itself is a factual issue relevant to the use. Since the proffered testimony was offered not to prove the content of the tapes, but rather, the content of the conversations, the best evidence rule does not apply, and agent Harvey's testimonial recollection of the conversation was properly admitted.

The tape in issue concerned a May 7, 1990, conversation between Landrum and Howard, which was monitored by Harvey. Harvey testified that, although much of the tape was inaudible, he was able to hear both sides of the conversation while it was taking place as though he was participating in it. At trial, Howard did not contend that the transmitting equipment was not working properly, only that the tape recording was the best and only evidence of the conversation which should have been admitted. We disagree. . . .

[W]e are persuaded that, since the prosecution was attempting to prove the contents of the recorded conversation and not the contents of the disputed tape, the district court acted within its discretion in permitting the testimony of the listening agent. Accordingly, we affirm Howard's conviction.

NOTES TO UNITED STATES v. HOWARD

1. *Transcripts of Recordings.* After a recording has been made, sometimes someone writes a transcript of the recording. In this situation, the transcript would be barred from introduction into evidence unless the recording was first introduced. It is common, however, to allow a jury to read a transcript to help it understand a recording as it is played for them.

> ### GOOD TO REMEMBER
>
> Even if a record has been made of something, a person who knows that information in a way different from having seen the record may testify about the information. This testimony is *not* considered testimony about the contents of the record.

2. *Receipts and Licenses.* Receipts and licenses are examples of writings that have an overlap with some other aspect of reality. A receipt shows that one person gave something to another. A license shows that an entity has treated some person or other entity as entitled to do something. In each case there are actions separate from the writing that happened in the world, and about which it would be proper to allow testimony even in the absence of introduction of a document like a receipt or license.

QUESTION 16-3. Assume that an individual testified at a trial in 2005, that a transcript was made of that testimony, and that the individual was later tried in 2007 for having given perjured testimony at the 2005 trial. In the 2007 perjury trial, if the prosecution *did not* introduce the 2005 transcript, would a prosecution witness who had heard the 2005 testimony be permitted to give testimony describing it?

■   ■   ■

Is a Drawing a "Writing, Recording, or Photograph"? — Seiler. All courts would apply the original writing rule to writings or recordings of words and numbers, and no courts would apply it to tangible objects. *Seiler* explores whether the reasons behind the original writing rule should make the rule apply to a work of art.

The opinion also considers whether the judge or jury should decide if a substitute for an original may be introduced. FRE 1008 provides part of the analysis for this question.

> **Rule 1008. Functions of the Court and Jury**
>
> Ordinarily, the court determines whether the proponent has fulfilled the factual conditions for admitting other evidence of the content of a writing, recording, or photograph under Rule 1004 or 1005. But in a jury trial, the jury determines — in accordance with Rule 104(b) — any issue about whether:

(a) an asserted writing, recording, or photograph ever existed;

(b) another one produced at the trial or hearing is the original; or

(c) other evidence of content accurately reflects the content.

SEILER v. LUCASFILM, LTD.

808 F.2d 1316 (9th Cir. 1987)

FARRIS, J.

Lee Seiler, a graphic artist and creator of science fiction creatures, alleged copyright infringement by George Lucas and others who created and produced the science fiction movie "The Empire Strikes Back." Seiler claimed that creatures known as "Imperial Walkers" which appeared in The Empire Strikes Back infringed Seiler's copyright on his own creatures called "Garthian Striders." The Empire Strikes Back appeared in 1980; Seiler did not obtain his copyright until 1981. . . .

Seiler contends that he created and published in 1976 and 1977 science fiction creatures called Garthian Striders. In 1980, George Lucas released The Empire Strikes Back, a motion picture that contains a battle sequence depicting giant machines called Imperial Walkers. In 1981 Seiler obtained a copyright on his Striders, depositing with the Copyright Office "reconstructions" of the originals as they had appeared in 1976 and 1977.

Seiler contends that Lucas' Walkers were copied from Seiler's Striders which were allegedly published in 1976 and 1977. Lucas responds that Seiler did not obtain his copyright until one year after the release of The Empire Strikes Back and that Seiler can produce no documents that antedate The Empire Strikes Back.

Because Seiler proposed to exhibit his Striders in a blow-up comparison to Lucas' Walkers at opening statement, the district judge held an evidentiary hearing on the admissibility of the "reconstructions" of Seiler's Striders. Applying the "best evidence rule," Fed. R. Evid. 1001-1008, the district court found at the end of a seven-day hearing that Seiler lost or destroyed the originals in bad faith under Rule 1004(1) and that consequently no secondary evidence, such as the post-Empire Strikes Back reconstructions, was admissible. In its opinion the court found specifically that Seiler testified falsely, purposefully destroyed or withheld in bad faith the originals, and fabricated and misrepresented the nature of his reconstructions. The district court granted summary judgment to Lucas after the evidentiary hearing.

On appeal, Seiler contends that the best evidence rule does not apply to his works, [and] that if the best evidence rule does apply, Rule 1008 requires a jury determination of the existence and authenticity of his originals. . . .

The best evidence rule embodied in Rules 1001-1008 represented a codification of longstanding common law doctrine. Dating back to 1700, the rule requires not, as its common name implies, the best evidence in every case but rather the production of an original document instead of a copy. Many commentators refer to the rule not as the best evidence rule but as the original document rule.

Rule 1002 states: "To prove the content of a writing, recording, or photograph, the original writing, recording, or photograph is required, except as otherwise provided in these rules or by Act of Congress." Writings and recordings are defined in Rule 1001 as "letters, words, or numbers, or their equivalent, set down by handwriting, typewriting, printing, photostating, photographing, magnetic impulse, mechanical or electronic recording, or other form of data compilation."

The Advisory Committee Note supplies the following gloss:

> Traditionally the rule requiring the original centered upon accumulations of data and expressions affecting legal relations set forth in words and figures. This meant that the rule was one essentially related to writings. Present day techniques have expanded methods of storing data, yet the essential form which the information ultimately assumes for usable purposes is words and figures. Hence the considerations underlying the rule dictate its expansion to include computers, photographic systems, and other modern developments.

Some treatises, whose approach seems more historical than rigorously analytic, opine without support from any cases that the rule is limited to words and figures.

We hold that Seiler's drawings were "writings" within the meaning of Rule 1001(1); they consist not of "letters, words, or numbers" but of "their equivalent." To hold otherwise would frustrate the policies underlying the rule and introduce undesirable inconsistencies into the application of the rule.

In the days before liberal rules of discovery and modern techniques of electronic copying, the rule guarded against incomplete or fraudulent proof. By requiring the possessor of the original to produce it, the rule prevented the introduction of altered copies and the withholding of originals. The purpose of the rule was thus long thought to be one of fraud prevention, but Wigmore pointed out that the rule operated even in cases where fraud was not at issue, such as where secondary evidence is not admitted even though its proponent acts in utmost good faith. Wigmore also noted that if prevention of fraud were the foundation of the rule, it should apply to objects as well as writings, which it does not. 4 Wigmore, *Evidence* §1180 (Chadbourn rev. 1972).

The modern justification for the rule has expanded from prevention of fraud to a recognition that writings occupy a central position in the law. When the contents of a writing are at issue, oral testimony as to the terms of the writing is subject to a greater risk of error than oral testimony as to events or other situations. The human memory is not often capable of reciting the precise terms of a writing, and when the terms are in dispute only the writing itself, or a true copy, provides reliable evidence. To summarize then, we observe that the importance of the precise terms of writings in the world of legal relations, the fallibility of the human memory as reliable evidence of the terms, and the hazards of inaccurate or incomplete duplication are the concerns addressed by the best evidence rule.

Viewing the dispute in the context of the concerns underlying the best evidence rule, we conclude that the rule applies. . . .

The contents of Seiler's work are at issue. There can be no proof of "substantial similarity" and thus of copyright infringement unless Seiler's works are juxtaposed with Lucas' and their contents compared. Since the contents are material and must be proved, Seiler must either produce the original or show that it is unavailable through no fault of his own. Rule 1004(1). This he could not do.

The facts of this case implicate the very concerns that justify the best evidence rule. Seiler alleges infringement by The Empire Strikes Back, but he can produce no documentary evidence of any originals existing before the release of the movie. His secondary evidence does not consist of true copies or exact duplicates but of "reconstructions" made after The Empire Strikes Back. In short, Seiler claims that the movie infringed his originals, yet he has no proof of those originals.

The dangers of fraud in this situation are clear. The rule would ensure that proof of the infringement claim consists of the works alleged to be infringed. Otherwise, "reconstructions" which might have no resemblance to the purported original would suffice as proof for infringement of the original. Furthermore, application of the rule here defers to the rule's special concern for the contents of writings. Seiler's claim depends on the content of the originals, and the rule would exclude reconstituted proof of the originals' content. Under the circumstances here, no "reconstruction" can substitute for the original.

Seiler argues that the best evidence rule does not apply to his work, in that it is artwork rather than "writings, recordings, or photographs." He contends that the rule both historically and currently embraces only words or numbers. Neither party has cited us to cases which discuss the applicability of the rule to drawings.

To recognize Seiler's works as writings does not, as Seiler argues, run counter to the rule's preoccupation with the centrality of the written word in the world of legal relations. Just as a contract objectively manifests the subjective intent of the makers, so Seiler's drawings are objective manifestations of the creative mind. The copyright laws give legal protection to the objective manifestations of an artist's ideas, just as the law of contract protects through its multifarious principles the meeting of minds evidenced in the contract. Comparing Seiler's drawings with Lucas' drawings is no different in principle than evaluating a contract and the intent behind it. Seiler's "reconstructions" are "writings" that affect legal relations; their copyrightability attests to that.

A creative literary work, which is artwork, and a photograph whose contents are sought to be proved, as in copyright, defamation, or invasion of privacy, are both covered by the best evidence rule. We would be inconsistent to apply the rule to artwork which is literary or photographic but not to artwork of other forms. Furthermore, blueprints, engineering drawings, architectural designs may all lack words or numbers yet still be capable of copyright and susceptible to fraudulent alteration. In short, Seiler's argument would have us restrict the definitions of Rule 1001(1) to "words" and "numbers" but ignore "or their equivalent." We will not do so in the circumstances of this case.

Our holding is also supported by the policy served by the best evidence rule in protecting against faulty memory. Seiler's reconstructions were made four to seven years after the alleged originals; his memory as to specifications and dimensions may have dimmed significantly. Furthermore, reconstructions made after the release of the Empire Strikes Back may be tainted, even if unintentionally, by exposure to the movie. Our holding guards against these problems.

As we hold that the district court correctly concluded that the best evidence rule applies to Seiler's drawings, Seiler was required to produce his original drawings unless excused by the exceptions set forth in Rule 1004. The pertinent subsection is 1004(1), which provides:

> The original is not required, and other evidence of the contents of a writing, recording, or photograph is admissible if—
> (1) Originals lost or destroyed. All originals are lost or have been destroyed, unless the proponent lost or destroyed them in bad faith . . .

In the instant case, prior to opening statement, Seiler indicated that he planned to show to the jury reconstructions of his "Garthian Striders" during the opening statement. The trial judge would not allow items to be shown to the jury until they were admitted in evidence. Seiler's counsel reiterated that he needed to show the reconstructions to the jury during his opening statement. Hence, the court excused the jury and held a seven-day hearing on their admissibility. At the conclusion of the hearing, the trial judge found that the reconstructions were inadmissible under the best evidence rule as the originals were lost or destroyed in bad faith. This finding is amply supported by the record.

Seiler argues on appeal that regardless of Rule 1004(1), Rule 1008 requires a trial because a key issue would be whether the reconstructions correctly reflect the content of the originals. Rule 1008 provides:

> When the admissibility of other evidence of contents of writings, recordings, or photographs under these rules depends upon the fulfillment of a condition of fact, the question whether the condition has been fulfilled is ordinarily for the court to determine in accordance with the provisions of rule 104. However, when an issue is raised (a) whether the asserted writing ever existed, or (b) whether another writing, recording, or photograph produced at the trial is the original, or (c) whether other evidence of contents correctly reflects the contents, the issue is for the trier of facts to determine as in the case of other issues of fact.

Seiler's position confuses admissibility of the reconstructions with the weight, if any, the trier of fact should give them, after the judge has ruled that they are admissible. Rule 1008 states, in essence, that when the *admissibility* of evidence other than the original depends upon the fulfillment of a condition of fact, the trial judge generally makes the determination of that condition of fact. The notes of the Advisory Committee are consistent with this interpretation in stating: "Most preliminary questions of fact in connection with applying the rule preferring the original as evidence of contents are for the judge ... thus the question of ... fulfillment of other conditions specified in Rule 1004 ... is for the judge." In the instant case, the condition of fact which Seiler needed to prove was that the originals were not lost or destroyed in bad faith. Had he been able to prove this, his reconstructions would have been admissible and then their accuracy would have been a question for the jury. In sum, since admissibility of the reconstructions was dependent upon a finding that the originals were not lost or destroyed in bad faith, the trial judge properly held the hearing to determine their admissibility. . . .

Affirmed.

NOTES TO SEILER v. LUCASFILM, LTD.

1. *Only Words and Figures?* The court notes that treatises "opine without support from any cases" that the original writing rule is limited to words and figures. It may be that the treatises cite no cases because the question had not come up before. The rule states that it covers writings, recordings, and photographs, and defines "writing" and "recording" as consisting "of letters, words, numbers, or their equivalent set down in any form." The court reasons that drawings are equally subject to risks of falsification as are writings and recordings, and for that reason treats drawings as "equivalent" to writings that use letters.

2. *What Questions Are for the Judge?* Rule 1008 reserves some fact questions that can arise under the original writing rule for decision by the jury. They are questions that are highly likely to be outcome determinative and highly likely to involve disputes of fact. The Seiler court pays close attention to the import of Rule 104, however, and underscores that even for the questions treated in Rule 1008, some preliminary inquiries that may eliminate the need for resolving those questions are intended to be carried out by the judge.

QUESTION 16-4. Harry Homeowner had experienced some break-ins at his home. He mounted a motion-activated deer camera on top of his refrigerator. When Homeowner returned home from work at approximately 1:00 A.M. on October 28, 2010, he noticed someone or something had tampered with the window next to his back door. After going inside his home and checking the deer camera, he discovered photographs of someone in his kitchen that he did not recognize. He waited to contact the police until around 10 A.M. and then told them of the photographs.

Police Officer Rhonda Responder went that morning to Homeowner's residence on October 28, 2008. Homeowner showed her the photographs on the deer camera. Homeowner came to the police station with the deer camera to download and print the photographs. The equipment at the police station could not connect properly with the camera. Homeowner said that he could download the photographs at his place of business. He did that later that day, and brought the prints to the police.

Bob Burglar has been charged with committing the burglary of Homeowner's house. Would he likely have successful objections to admission of the prints from the deer camera on grounds of authentication or the original writing rule?

D SUMMARY

Authentication and the original writing rule are both particularized requirements that seek to increase the likelihood that information at a trial will be accurate.

Authentication. The authentication requirement simply imposes on the proponent of any evidence the burden of providing a basis for a jury finding that the item is what the proponent says it is. Often this can be accomplished with circumstantial evidence. For example, in the case of a writing this conclusion can be supported with the contents of the writing itself and by external circumstances as well. The trial judge decides if the information offered by the party is adequate to support a jury finding of authenticity. If that foundation is adequate, the authentication requirement is met and the jury can rely or not rely on the information, based on its own assessment of its legitimacy. FRE 901(b) provides a suggestive but not limiting list of examples of ways in which evidence may be authenticated.

Original Writing Rule. If a party wants to introduce testimony that describes the contents of a writing, recording, or photograph, the party must satisfy the original writing rule. This requires that the party introduce the original writing, recording, or photograph, or a copy. One other way to satisfy the rule is to show that the original was lost in good faith and that there is a reasonable excuse for failing to have substitute proof such as a copy.

The rule does not prohibit testimony about something a witness knows even if that information has independently been made into a record. The witness can testify from the witness's own knowledge. Because that is not considered proving what the record says (because it is not derived from the record), the testimony is outside the coverage of the original writing rule.

CHAPTER 17

Presumptions and Judicial Notice

A. Introduction
B. Presumptions: Federal Treatment
C. Presumptions: Range of State Treatments
D. Judicial Notice
E. Summary

A INTRODUCTION

Topic Overview

Presumptions and judicial notice each make it easier for parties to prove certain facts. A presumption is a legal device that treats proof of one fact as equivalent to proof of another fact. These facts are usually called the "basic fact" and the "presumed fact." When a presumption has its full effect, the jury will be instructed that if it is persuaded of the existence of the basic fact, it must find that the presumed fact is true. Jurisdictions differ on how the opponent of a presumption can limit its effect. Judicial notice is a technique that excuses a party from having proof of a fact. For the various kinds of facts that are defined as suitable for judicial notice, a jury instruction will require (in civil cases) or permit (in criminal cases) the jury to treat the judicially noticed facts as true.

Chapter Organization

The chapter begins with coverage of presumptions, giving attention to the Federal Rules of Evidence and also to various state choices. The state choices are important because they reflect a wide range in the power accorded to presumptions and because they will be used in federal court for matters where state substantive law applies. Judicial notice is the chapter's concluding topic.

B   PRESUMPTIONS: FEDERAL TREATMENT

Evidence codes that treat presumptions usually use expressions that refer to two concepts: the burden of production and the burden of persuasion. The burden of production requires a party that is required to introduce evidence on a specific issue in a case. The burden of persuasion identifies the party that is required to be ruled against on an issue unless it can persuade the trier of fact on that issue. The Federal Rules take a position on presumptions that limits their role to altering the burden of production.

Rule 301. Presumptions in Civil Cases Generally

In a civil case, unless a federal statute or these rules provide otherwise, the party against whom a presumption is directed has the burden of producing evidence to rebut the presumption. But this rule does not shift the burden of persuasion, which remains on the party who had it originally.

■   ■   ■

How Powerful Is a Presumption? — **Marr.** The Truth in Lending Act recognizes a presumption that a person who signs an acknowledgement stating that he or she has received certain documents actually did receive those documents. The *Marr* court considers how much benefit this presumption gives to the party that seeks to take advantage of it.

MARR v. BANK OF AMERICA, N.A.
662 F.3d 963 (7th Cir. 2011)

Wood, J.
In the world of the Truth-in-Lending Act (TILA), it often seems that no detail is too insignificant to matter. We have called TILA "hypertechnical" in the past, and this case provides yet another opportunity to see this level of precision in

operation. The case before us involves a borrower who alleges that he did not receive all of the documents to which he was entitled when he refinanced his mortgage. If he is correct, then he had not a measly three days, but a more generous three years in which to rescind the transaction. The district court ruled for the bank, but we conclude that the borrower presented enough evidence to defeat summary judgment, and so we reverse and remand for further proceedings.

One provision of TILA requires the creditor to provide the consumer with "clear[ ] and conspicuous[ ]" notice of his right to rescind this type of loan within three business days following the transaction. Regulation Z, issued by the Federal Reserve Board to implement TILA, elaborates on this rule by requiring the lender to give the consumer *two* copies of the notice of his three-day right to cancel at closing. . . . This case turns on whether the plaintiff, Richard G. Marr, received the obligatory two copies of his Notice, or if he received just one; the answer to that question dictates whether his effort to rescind a loan was timely.

In 2007, Marr decided to refinance his mortgage with Countrywide Bank, the predecessor in interest to defendant Bank of America, N.A. . . . Marr's story is depressingly familiar in the wake of the 2007 financial crisis. Marr, now a retired auto mechanic, purchased a home in Wauwatosa, Wisconsin, in 1973, using funds secured by a mortgage. He has refinanced that loan several times since then to help pay the bills. In early 2007, a mortgage broker called Alpine Financial contacted Marr about refinancing his mortgage. Marr decided that this was a good idea, and so he applied in February 2007 for a new loan to help with his credit card bills. Countrywide accepted Marr's application. Summit Title, the title insurance company that provided closing services for Countrywide, closed the loan with Marr on February 23, 2007.

The focus of this litigation is on what exactly happened at that closing. Marr testified that the closing agent put a duplicate of every document he signed in a pile next to him, but he did not have time to review them. One of those documents, which Marr signed, was an acknowledgment that he had been given the required two copies of the Notice. At the end of the closing, Summit's agent gave Marr a folder in which to put the documents. The agent stuffed everything into the folder, and then Marr left. When he returned home, Marr put the folder in a filing cabinet in his dining room where he keeps all of his important documents. As he put it, "I live by myself, so there's [*sic*] no children or anything there that would mess with [the filing cabinet] . . . and that's where it stayed." He maintained that he did not disturb the folder until two years later when his attorney inspected it in connection with an unrelated lawsuit. Only then, Marr testified, did they "discover[ ] that there was only one copy of that right to cancel in there." . . .

Debora Ann Smith, a Summit closing agent, submitted an affidavit stating that she was Marr's closing agent. She did not discuss the specific events that took place at Marr's closing, but she provided information on Summit's closing practices and procedures. Summit required its closing agents to review closing instructions and checklists with the borrower; to discuss all closing documents with the borrower to confirm the borrower's understanding of them; to present and review the Notice with the borrower at the end of the closing to ensure the borrower's understanding of his rights; and to put at least two copies of the Notice in the borrower's document pile. Smith was confident that she must have given Marr two copies of the Notice, because she could not recall a time when she did not follow these practices.

Marr submitted an affidavit in response to Smith's statement. He asserted that his closing did not follow the standard practices and procedures outlined by Smith in her affidavit. Instead, he said, "the closing agent did not review anything at the end of the closing." She "did not look through my documents, her documents, or anything else between the time when I finished signing the closing documents and when I left Summit Title's office." He also stated that Smith did not present the Notice at the end of the closing; rather, she presented it "somewhere near the beginning or in the middle of the closing."

Based on this record, the district court concluded that Countryside and Summit were entitled to summary judgment. Marr's signed acknowledgment that he had received *two* copies of the Notice created a rebuttable presumption that this was true. See 15 U.S.C. §1635(c). The court believed that Marr's testimony that he received only one copy, which he placed in the envelope furnished by Summit, and that he never withdrew anything from that envelope (even if he might have added an item or two) was not enough to rebut that presumption. Marr challenges those conclusions on appeal.

The standard of review from a grant of summary judgment is well known, but it is worth emphasizing that the non-moving party does not bear the burden of *proving* his case; the opponent of summary judgment need only point to evidence that can be put in an admissible form at trial, and that, if believed by the fact-finder, could support judgment in his favor. Our role, applying what is usually called *de novo* review, is to see if the opponent has identified such evidence in the record; in so doing, we draw all reasonable inferences and view all facts in favor of the non-moving party. The question in this case is whether Marr's testimony and affidavit is sufficient to allow a reasonable jury to find that Marr received only one copy of the Notice. . . .

To succeed in this case, Marr must overcome the fact that he signed a form at closing acknowledging that he received two copies of the Notice. . . . As we consider this issue, it is helpful to recall the precise weight that the statute gives to the written acknowledgment:

> Notwithstanding any rule of evidence, written acknowledgment of receipt of any disclosures required under this subchapter by a person to whom information, forms, and a statement is required to be given pursuant to this section does no more than create a rebuttable presumption of delivery thereof.

15 U.S.C. §1635(c). This phrasing strongly suggests that Congress was warning courts not to overrate the importance of the acknowledgment; that is why it cautions that the statement "does no more than" create the rebuttable presumption of delivery.

Although both parties have spent a great deal of time in their briefs talking about "bursting bubble" presumptions, the legislative history of Federal Rule of

Evidence 301, and the debate between Thayer and Morgan about what is left of a presumption after the bubble bursts, we do not need to take those detours. Although TILA and Regulation Z do not specify the quality or quantity of evidence needed to overcome the presumption, Rule 301 provides the default rule, and it states:

> In a civil case, unless a federal statute or these rules provide otherwise, the party against whom a presumption is directed has the burden of producing evidence to rebut the presumption. But this rule does not shift the burden of persuasion, which remains on the party who had it originally.

Here, to overcome the presumption created by his written acknowledgment and thus to raise a genuine fact that would make summary judgment inappropriate, Marr needed to produce enough evidence to permit a reasonable jury to find that he did not receive two copies. . . .

The district court focused on two pieces of evidence provided by Marr: (1) his testimony that his attorney found only one copy of the Notice in the folder in which the closing agent put Marr's copies of the closing documents, and (2) his allegation that the contents of the folder remained undisturbed — at least in the sense that nothing was removed — since the February 23 closing. The court did not incorporate in its analysis Marr's affidavit statement that his closing experience deviated from Summit's standard practices.

The court gave several reasons for its conclusion that Marr's showing fell short of what was needed:

> Even when viewed in a light most favorable to plaintiff, plaintiff's testimony as a whole actually suggests that he is unable to identify with any certainty which documents and how many of those documents he received at closing, rather than that he received only one notice.

The court was concerned that Marr did not note, read, or review the number of copies he was given during the closing. It deemed it "immaterial whether Marr was rushed through the closing" and thus unable to determine the number of copies he received. The court was also unpersuaded by Marr's argument that the full set of documents he had received from Summit had been preserved in the Redweld folder. It called this the "envelope theory" and rejected it, largely because several documents that post-dated the closing were found in the folder. It regarded this as evidence of tampering and thus inconsistent with Marr's testimony that the closing documents had remained undisturbed. It concluded that "[a]t best, this contradictory testimony, as well as the fact that the folder did not remain untouched, suggests that Marr cannot state with any certainty whether or not he removed any documents from the folder during the two years before the closing and the meeting with his attorney."

Both the court and the bank were understandably worried about the possibility that the presumption of delivery could be rebutted by nothing more than the borrower's say-so; if rebuttal were that easy, they say, section 1635(c) might as well not be in the statute. We need not take a position on that extreme case, although we note again that TILA is a remedial statute and it appears that the Third Circuit has decided that it indeed goes that far. *Cappuccio* [*v. Prime Capital Funding LLC,* 69 F.3d 180, 190 (3d Cir. 2011)] ("[W]e hold that the testimony of a borrower alone is sufficient to overcome TILA's presumption of receipt."). We also do not need to determine whether Marr's evidence that the envelope remained undisturbed (the so-called envelope theory) standing alone is sufficient, because Marr presented more than that. Marr stated in his affidavit that his experience at the February 23 closing deviated from the standard practices and procedures that Smith described in her affidavit. Taken as a whole, Marr's evidence is enough to permit a reasonable jury to find in his favor.

Marr left the closing agent's office on February 23 with the loan documents in the folder that the title company had given him. He put that folder into his filing cabinet. He added additional loan documents to the folder later on, but he never removed anything from the folder. When he took the folder to his attorney's office, he and the attorney discovered that there was only one copy of the Notice. If believed, this evidence is enough to rebut the presumption created by Marr's acknowledgment that he received two copies of the Notice. We note, finally, that although the difference between one and two copies may seem to be an empty formality, Regulation Z demands two copies. This is not a situation in which there is any room for some kind of substantial compliance rule. Two copies means two copies, not one. Marr is entitled to the opportunity to convince the trier of fact that he did not receive all that the Regulation promised him, and thus that he may proceed with his suit to rescind the loan. We reverse and remand for further proceedings consistent with this opinion.

NOTES TO MARR v. BANK OF AMERICA, N.A.

1. *Establishing the Applicability of a Presumption.* In order for the proponent of a presumption to obtain any benefit from it, the proponent must offer evidence adequate to support a finding that the presumption's basic fact exists. In *Marr,* the basic fact was the plaintiffs having signed an acknowledgement of receipt of the required notice. There was apparently no dispute about the existence of that fact.

2. *Consequences of Applicability of a Presumption.* Once the basic fact has been established, litigants must deal with the remaining question of what power the presumption may have. Under FRE 301, that power is slight. While invoking the presumption requires the opponent of the presumption to satisfy a production burden on the fact the presumption covers, *Marr* shows that the production burden can be satisfied easily.

3. *Rescission.* The doctrine of rescission allows a borrower to reverse a transaction. The borrow returns the lender's money and the lender refunds

interest payments. Usually borrowers cannot pay back the amount of the loan, but in this case (in a portion not reproduced above) apparently the loan had already been paid, so the borrower sought return of interest payments, some statutory damages for refusal to rescind, and attorney's fees.

QUESTION 17-1. Vince Victim was killed when his idling truck shifted into reverse and struck him as he stood behind it. His estate seeks damages from the truck's manufacturer, claiming that the defendant did not provide adequate warnings about the risk of "mis-shifting." Besides proving that the information provided by the manufacturer was deficient, the plaintiff must establish causation. To show that a better warning more likely than not would have prevented the injury, the plaintiff has relied on the "heeding presumption." This presumption allows a jury to infer that a product user would have complied with a warning if a warning had been given.

The defendant introduced evidence showing that the owner's manual for the truck cautioned that before the driver leaves the vehicle, "to reduce the risk of personal injury as a result of vehicle movement," the driver should apply the parking brake, shift to park, shut off the engine, and remove the key. Despite this warning, Victim apparently did not set the parking brake, turn off the engine, or remove the key immediately prior to the accident.

Discuss whether, under FRE 301, the trial judge should give this jury instruction:

> Where a warning is given, a seller may reasonably assume that it will be read and heeded. If you find the warning is adequate, then your verdict must be for Defendant on this claim. However, if you find the warning to be inadequate, then you must start with the presumption that an adequate warning would have been read and heeded. In those circumstances, the Defendant then has the burden of proving that it is more probably true than not that an adequate warning would not have been read or would not have been heeded.
>
> You may consider all the evidence presented in this case to make that determination. If you find the Defendant has proved that an adequate warning would not have been read or heeded, then your verdict must be for Defendant on this claim. If you find that Defendant has not proved that an adequate warning would not have been read or heeded, then you may return a verdict for Plaintiff on this claim if you find that Plaintiff has proved the other elements of this claim.

GOOD TO REMEMBER

Under FRE 301, presumptions do not have much power. They require a finding in favor of the proponent of a presumption only when the opponent of the presumption fails to produce evidence on the presumed fact.

PRESUMPTIONS: RANGE OF STATE TREATMENTS

In contrast to the slim power assigned to presumptions in the Federal Rules, some states treat presumptions as shifting the burden of persuasion in addition to shifting the burden of production. This reflects a debate among some famous evidence scholars: James Bradley Thayer and John Henry Wigmore were identified with the "bursting bubble" theory. This theory, adopted in FRE 301, gives a presumption the power to require the opponent to produce evidence, but once the opponent produces evidence the presumption has no further effect. The rival view, advocated by Edmund M. Morgan and Charles T. McCormick, would give the presumption the power of shifting the persuasion burden. Some states follow a compromise between these two positions, with some presumptions having only the power to shift the production burden and others having the power to shift the persuasion burden.

The state provisions apply in all state cases, and are also required to be used in some federal cases, under FRE 302.

Rule 302. Applying State Law to Presumptions in Civil Cases

In a civil case, state law governs the effect of a presumption regarding a claim or defense for which state law supplies the rule of decision.

Counterexamples. In many states, evidence rules identical in substance to FRE 301 have been adopted. But many states apply different rules. The following examples indicate the range of state choices.

Alaska Rules of Evidence
Rule 301. Presumptions in General in Civil Actions and Proceedings

(a) **Effect.** — In all civil actions and proceedings when not otherwise provided for by statute, by judicial decision or by these rules, a presumption imposes on the party against whom it is directed the burden of going forward with evidence to rebut or meet the presumption, but does not shift to such party the burden of proof in the sense of the risk of nonpersuasion, which remains throughout the trial upon the party on whom it was originally cast. The burden of going forward is satisfied by the introduction of evidence sufficient to permit reasonable minds to conclude that the presumed fact does not exist. If the party against whom a presumption operates fails to meet the burden of producing evidence, the presumed fact shall be deemed proved, and the court shall instruct the jury accordingly. When the burden of producing evidence to meet a presumption is satisfied, the court must instruct the jury that it may, but is not required to, infer the existence of the presumed fact from the proved fact, but no mention of the word "presumption" may be made to the jury. . . .

Wyoming Rules of Evidence
Rule 301. Presumptions in general in civil actions and proceedings.

(a) **Effect.** — In all civil actions and proceedings not otherwise provided for by statute or by these rules, a presumption imposes on the party against whom it is directed the burden of proving that the nonexistence of the presumed fact is more probable than its existence.

Hawaii Rules of Evidence
Rule 302. Presumptions in civil proceedings.

(a) **General rule.** In all civil proceedings not otherwise provided for by statute or by these rules, a presumption imposes on the party against whom it is directed either (1) the burden of producing evidence, or (2) the burden of proof. . . .

Rule 303. Presumptions imposing burden of producing evidence.

(a) **General rule.** A presumption established to implement no public policy other than to facilitate the determination of the particular action in which the presumption is applied imposes on the party against whom it is directed the burden of producing evidence.

(b) **Effect.** The effect of a presumption imposing the burden of producing evidence is to require the trier of fact to assume the existence of the presumed fact unless and until evidence is introduced which would support a finding of its nonexistence, in which case no instruction on presumption shall be given and the trier of fact shall determine the existence or nonexistence of the presumed fact from the evidence and without regard to the presumption. Nothing in this rule shall be construed to prevent the drawing of any inferences.

(c) **Presumptions.** The following presumptions, and all other presumptions established by law that fall within the criteria of subsection (a) of this rule, are presumptions imposing the burden of producing evidence:

(1) **Money delivered by one to another.** Money delivered by one to another is presumed to have been due to the latter. . . .

(10) Letter properly addressed and mailed. A letter correctly addressed and properly mailed is presumed to have been received in the ordinary course of mail....

(15) Continuation of a fact, condition, or state. A fact, condition, or state of things is presumed to continue....

Rule 304. Presumptions imposing burden of proof.

(a) General rule. A presumption established to implement a public policy other than, or in addition to, facilitating the determination of the particular action in which the presumption is applied imposes on the party against whom it is directed the burden of proof.

(b) Effect. The effect of a presumption imposing the burden of proof is to require the trier of fact to assume the existence of the presumed fact unless and until evidence is introduced sufficient to convince the trier of fact of the nonexistence of the presumed fact. Except as otherwise provided by law or by these rules, proof by a preponderance of the evidence is necessary and sufficient to rebut a presumption established under this rule.

(c) Presumptions. The following presumptions, and all other presumptions established by law that fall within the criteria of subsection (a) of this rule, are presumptions imposing the burden of proof....

(6) Ceremonial marriage. A ceremonial marriage is presumed to be valid.

(7) Death. A person who is absent for a continuous period of five years, during which the person has not been heard from, and whose absence is not satisfactorily explained after diligent search or inquiry, is presumed to be dead.

QUESTION 17-2. Consider a case where an insurance claimant sought to establish that an insured had died, and the claimant introduced evidence showing that the insured had been absent from his home and had not been heard from for seven years.

A. If the defendant insurance company offered no evidence to show that the insured was alive, how would the presumption of death from seven years' absence affect the case in Alaska, Wyoming, and Hawaii?

B. If the defendant insurance company offered evidence showing that the insured had been seen alive three years after his absence began, how would the presumption of death from seven years' absence affect the case in Alaska, Wyoming, and Hawaii?

Legislative Choices and the Policies They Advance — **Schultz.** Indicative of the wide variety among states concerning presumptions, this case interprets a state statute that specifies two concepts: (1) a presumption shifts the production burden but does not shift the persuasion burden, and (2) a presumption shall have continuing effect even though contrary evidence is received. In sorting this out, the court describes rival views on how much power it makes sense to give to presumptions.

SCHULTZ v. FORD MOTOR CO.

857 N.E.2d 977 (Ind. 2006)

SULLIVAN, J.

A jury rendered a defense verdict on plaintiffs' product liability and negligence claims relating to the collapse of the roof of a Ford Explorer in a rollover accident. The Court of Appeals found the trial court's giving of a jury instruction on a presumption to have been reversible error. We hold that Indiana Evidence Rule 301, which authorizes presumptions to be given "continuing effect even though contrary evidence is received," operated to authorize the jury instruction given here.

In December, 1997, Richard Schultz lost control of his 1995 Ford Explorer when it hit a patch of black ice on Indiana State Road 2. The Explorer slid off the road into a ditch, hit a sloped embankment, and rolled over, eventually coming to rest upright. Schultz was wearing his seatbelt, and experts testified that when the Explorer first left skid marks, it was traveling between 26 and 32 miles per hour.

During the accident, the roof on the Explorer collapsed on top of Schultz, snapping his neck and rendering him a quadriplegic. Schultz and Gail Schultz (the "Schultzes") sued Ford Motor Company, alleging defective roof design and negligence and seeking compensatory and punitive damages.

The jury returned a verdict in favor of Ford.

The Court of Appeals reversed and remanded for a new trial. It found that the trial court had committed reversible error when it gave the jury the following instruction:

> Ford Motor Company has alleged that the Plaintiffs' 1995 Ford Explorer complied with the Federal Motor Vehicle Safety Standard 216. Ford Motor Company has the burden of proving this allegation.
>
> If you find Ford Motor Company has proved by a preponderance of the evidence that before the 1995 Ford Explorer was sold by Ford Motor Company that it complied with Federal Motor Vehicle Standard 216 then you may presume that Ford Motor Company was not negligent in its design of the 1995 Ford Explorer and that the 1995 Ford Explorer was not defective.
>
> However, the Plaintiffs may rebut this presumption if they introduced evidence tending to show that the 1995 Ford Explorer was defective.

We granted transfer.

Effective January 1, 1994, this Court adopted Rules of Evidence to govern proceedings in Indiana courts. We first appointed a Rules of Evidence Drafting Committee, which proposed a draft of the Rules. After a public comment period, we promulgated a final version of the Rules. In doing so, we made a number of changes from the draft. One rule that we changed from the draft is Indiana Evidence Rule 301, which, as adopted, provides:

> In all civil actions and proceedings not otherwise provided for by constitution, statute, judicial decision or by these rules, a presumption imposes on the party against whom it is directed the burden of going forward with evidence to rebut or meet the presumption, but does not shift to such party the burden of proof in the sense of the risk of nonpersuasion, which remains throughout the trial upon the party on whom it was originally cast. A presumption shall have continuing effect even though contrary evidence is received.

The change was the addition of a second sentence: "A presumption shall have continuing effect even though contrary evidence is received." The rule proposed by our Drafting Committee consisted only of the first sentence, language that was consistent with prior Indiana law. Presumptions were now to have "continuing effect." Although commentators at the time viewed the addition of this sentence as a significant change, neither this Court nor the Court of Appeals has been called upon to apply it in the intervening 12 years.

In the year following that in which our Evidence Rules took effect, the Legislature amended the Indiana Product Liability Act (the "Act"), now codified at Indiana Code sections 34-20-1-1 to -9-1, to provide:

> In a product liability action, there is a rebuttable presumption that the product that caused the physical harm was not defective and that the manufacturer or seller of the product was not negligent if, before the sale by the manufacturer, the product ... complied with applicable codes, standards, regulations, or specifications established, adopted, promulgated, or approved by the United States or by Indiana, or by an agency of the United States or Indiana.

Ind. Code §34-20-5-1 (1998).

The claims brought by the Schultzes against Ford in this case — defective design of the roof of the Explorer and negligence — are governed by the Act. The disputed instruction advised the jury of the "rebuttable presumption" articulated in Indiana Code section 34-20-5-1. And so our decision as to whether the disputed instruction was properly given turns on the interrelationship of this statute that recognizes a "rebuttable presumption" with Indiana Evidence Rule 301 that gives presumptions "continuing effect."

The Schultzes argue on appeal that it was improper for the trial court to instruct the jury on Indiana Code section 34-20-5-1 because the statute "is a presumption that imposes a burden of production — not proof — and hence, is an improper subject of jury instruction altogether."

Ford's response is that the presumption created by the Legislature here is not a rule of law that shifts the burden of proof from the party that has it to the one that does not. . . .

The Schultzes vigorously oppose the notion that the statute creates an inference. . . .

The Court of Appeals adopted the Schultzes' analysis, and held that when the opponent of the presumption has met the burden of production, the purpose of the presumption has been fulfilled and the presumption should be dropped from the case. It held that the instruction, by using the language "may presume," created "a permissive inference" for the jury about the evidence in the case. However, the court said, this was an incorrect statement of law because the plain language of the statute created "a mandatory presumption of substantive law." "The rebuttable presumption of IC 34-20-5-1 is not evidence; instead, it should be used as guidance for the court and not as evidence for the jury."

We find both of these to be respectable arguments. But we think the answer is dictated by Indiana Evidence Rule 301.

As alluded to *supra,* prior to the adoption of the Rules of Evidence, the law of Indiana had been that:

> [A] presumption is not evidence and is not to be weighed by the trier of fact as though it had evidentiary value. When the party against whom the presumption operates introduces evidence that disputes the presumed fact, the presumption ceases to operate, disappears from the case, and no longer remains to assist any party.

12 Robert Lowell Miller, *Indiana Practice* §301.102 at 188-89 (2d ed. 1995) ("Miller") (citing cases).

This approach to presumptions has a century-old provenance in the work of Professor James Bradley Thayer, who taught evidence at Harvard in the late 19th century. Thayer's theory is popularly referred to as the "bursting bubble" theory because its sole effect is to force the opponent of the presumption to rebut it by producing enough evidence to avoid a directed verdict. It does not, in other words, shift the burden of persuasion, only the burden of production.

A different approach was taken a generation later by another Harvard professor, Edmund Morgan. Under his view, a presumption should shift not only the burden of producing evidence, but also the burden of persuasion. That is, the finder of fact would be required to find the presumed fact once the basic fact is established, unless the opponent of the presumption persuaded the factfinder of the nonexistence of the presumed fact.

Both rules, it has been noted, have in common giving the benefit of a "presumed fact" to a party who triggers a presumption by proving a "basic fact." In this respect, both approaches impose the same burden on the opponent to come forward with some evidence, or the presumption governs. The difference is in the rules' operation following the introduction of rebuttal evidence. Under Thayer's approach, once rebuttal evidence is produced by the opponent of the presumption, the presumption disappears and the case proceeds on the basis of evidence actually produced. But under Morgan's approach, the presumption shifts to the opponent of the presumption the burden of disproving the presumed fact.

Over time, both positions have attracted support. Wigmore is said to have sanctioned Thayer's bursting bubble theory, the Model Code of Evidence to have adopted it, and Federal Rule of Evidence 301 to embody it. Professor Morgan's burden-of-persuasion-shifting theory is said to have been endorsed by McCormick, included in the Uniform Rules of Evidence, and recommended by the Advisory Committee on the original Federal Rules of Evidence (though rejected by Congress in favor of the Thayer rule).

The rationale, it should be apparent, for choosing between Thayer's and Morgan's approaches will depend on one's view of how strong a role a presumption should play in dictating the course of litigation. Thayer's view gives presumptions relatively light weight; Morgan's heavy. Of course, one's view of whether presumptions should be given relatively light or relatively heavy weight will depend in turn on one's view of the significance of the policies giving rise to presumptions in the first place. Judge Miller makes this point as follows:

> The strongest criticism against the "bursting bubble" theory of presumptions is that it affords too little protection to the policies that give rise to presumptions. A presumption may have been created, for example, because the party it favors otherwise would be handicapped by lack of access to proof, or because the law favors a particular result. If the mere production of contrary evidence removes the presumption from the case entirely, the jury never will learn of the policies behind the presumption.

Miller §301.102 at 189-90.

Adding particular complexity to the subject is the obvious fact that policies of differing significance give rise to different presumptions. The original Uniform Rules of Evidence, for example, made a distinction between presumptions that were based on probability and presumptions that were based on social policy. But making such distinctions requires a hybrid approach somewhere between Thayer and Morgan, thereby eliminating one great advantage that both have in common: simplicity in their application.

Returning to our Indiana Evidence Rule 301, the first sentence clearly adopts the Thayer approach of allocating only the burden of production, not burden of persuasion, "which remains throughout the trial upon the party on whom it was originally cast." But Rule 301 clearly rejected a pure Thayer "bursting bubble" approach and changed prior Indiana law when we added the new second sentence: "A presumption shall have continuing effect even though contrary evidence is received."

As discussed *supra* . . . the problem with the Thayer "bursting bubble" rule is that it can operate to prevent juries from effectuating the policies that gave rise to the presumption. It is to overcome this problem that this Court modified the Thayer rule by adding the new "continuing effect" language when we adopted Indiana Evidence Rule 301. Judge Miller has well captured the intent of this Court:

Because the rule's second sentence appears to be a response to the commentators' concern that the "bursting bubble" approach too often prevents juries from effectuating the policies that gave rise to the presumption, it seems most likely that the rule's second sentence is intended primarily to affect the instructions given to the jury.

Miller §301.102 at 190.

We hold that a presumption is properly given "continuing effect" under the last sentence of Indiana Evidence Rule 301 by the trial court instructing the jury that when a basic fact is proven, the jury may infer the existence of a presumed fact. . . .

The judgment of the trial court is affirmed.

NOTES TO SCHULTZ v. FORD MOTOR CO.

1. *Ambiguity of Legislative Choice.* Since courts and scholars have debated and been confused by the concept of presumptions, it may be overly optimistic to use the word "presume" in a jury instruction in the hope that a jury will do something sensible with it.

The Indiana statutory choice can be understood by comparing it with other options. Suppose in a products liability suit, a plaintiff introduced evidence that the defendant's product violated applicable safety regulations. And suppose that the defendant introduced evidence that the design was reasonably safe. The following table suggests the consequences of that array of proof under various presumption regimes.

JURY INSTRUCTIONS WHERE PLAINTIFF SHOWS DANGEROUS DESIGN AND DEFENDANT SHOWS COMPLIANCE WITH REGULATIONS

PRESUMPTION RULE	JURY INSTRUCTION
FRE 301	Find for Plaintiff if Plaintiff has persuaded you that the design was defective.
Indiana statute	Find for Plaintiff if Plaintiff has persuaded you that the design was defective. You may presume that the design was defective if you believe the design violated applicable regulations, and the Defendant may rebut that presumption with evidence showing that its design was safe.
Wyoming statute (incorporating the persuasion burden shift advocated by McCormick and Morgan).	Find for Plaintiff unless the Defendant has persuaded you that the design was not defective.

2. *Presumptions in Criminal Cases.* Federal Rule of Evidence 301 applies only to civil cases. Supreme Court decisions have held that the use of presumptions in criminal cases violates the Due Process clause because they would relieve the prosecution of its obligation to establish every essential element of a crime beyond a reasonable doubt. Presumptions that support only an inference would be free from this prohibition.

D   JUDICIAL NOTICE

The federal rules authorize judicial notice of adjudicative facts. The rules omit a definition of adjudicative facts, but the term is generally understood to operate in contrast with the concept of legislative facts. Legislative facts are general aspects of life and society that courts might use in applying doctrines or creating them, such as the fact that privacy fosters clear communications when a court is considering adopting a privilege. Adjudicative facts are specific to the parties and transactions involved in any particular case.

Rule 201. Judicial Notice of Adjudicative Facts

(a) Scope. This rule governs judicial notice of an adjudicative fact only, not a legislative fact.

(b) Kinds of Facts That May Be Judicially Noticed. The court may judicially notice a fact that is not subject to reasonable dispute because it:

(1) is generally known within the trial court's territorial jurisdiction; or

(2) can be accurately and readily determined from sources whose accuracy cannot reasonably be questioned.

(c) Taking Notice. The court:

(1) may take judicial notice on its own; or

(2) must take judicial notice if a party requests it and the court is supplied with the necessary information.

(d) Timing. The court may take judicial notice at any stage of the proceeding.

(e) Opportunity to Be Heard. On timely request, a party is entitled to be heard on the propriety of taking judicial notice and the nature of the fact to be noticed. If the court takes judicial notice before notifying a party, the party, on request, is still entitled to be heard.

> **(f) Instructing the Jury.** In a civil case, the court must instruct the jury to accept the noticed fact as conclusive. In a criminal case, the court must instruct the jury that it may or may not accept the noticed fact as conclusive.

■ ■ ■

What Does Everybody Know? — Dippin' Dots, Inc. For an unfair competition case, it was relevant to establish whether the color of ice cream indicates its flavor. If the color had this functionality, the plaintiff's effort to protect its own colored ice cream pellets under a trade dress theory would be hampered. The court's analysis is straightforward; it also relies on a group of examples of types of facts that were properly subject to judicial notice.

DIPPIN' DOTS, INC. v. FROSTY BITES DISTRIBUTION, LLC

369 F.3d 1197 (11th Cir. 2004)

DUBINA, J.

Plaintiff-Appellant Dippin' Dots, Inc. ("DDI") brought suit against Defendant-Appellee Frosty Bites Distribution, LLC ("FBD") alleging trade dress infringement of DDI's product design and logo design, both in violation of the Lanham Act, 15 U.S.C. §1125. The district court granted summary judgment in favor of FBD on both claims. For the reasons that follow, we affirm the judgment of the district court.

Plaintiff DDI markets and sells a brightly-colored flash-frozen ice cream product, called "dippin' dots," consisting of free flowing small spheres or beads of ice cream. . . .

Defendant FBD makes and sells a competing brightly-colored flash-frozen ice cream product, called "frosty bites," consisting of mostly small popcorn-shaped, along with some spherical-shaped, ice cream bites. . . .

In the Fall of 1999, several of DDI's retail dealers secretly started the FBD business while still under contract with DDI to sell dippin' dots at various locations. On March 16, 2000, eight of these dealers terminated their contracts with DDI. The following day, without changing locations, they began selling their frosty bites under the "Frosty Bites" logo.

DDI filed suit against FBD alleging infringement of DDI's trade dress . . . in the form of its unique, flash-frozen ice cream product . . . in violation of the Lanham Act, 15 U.S.C. §1125. FBD moved for summary judgment.

The district court granted FBD's motion for summary judgment finding that (1) DDI's product design — small, predominantly separated colored beads or pieces of ice cream — is functional and therefore not subject to trade dress protection. . . . DDI timely filed this appeal.

This court reviews a grant of summary judgment *de novo*, applying the same legal standards that governed the district court. . . .

Section 43(a) of the Lanham Act [15 U.S.C.A. §1125] states that

> (1) Any person who, on or in connection with any goods or services, . . . uses in commerce any word, term, name, symbol, or device, . . . or any false designation of origin, . . . which (A) is likely to cause confusion, or to cause mistake, or to deceive as to the affiliation, . . . of such person with another person, . . . shall be liable in a civil action by any person who believes that he or she is or is likely to be damaged by such act.

Section 43(a) creates a federal cause of action for trade dress infringement. . . . In order to prevail on this claim for trade dress infringement under §43(a), DDI must prove that (1) the product design of the two products is confusingly similar; (2) the features of the product design are primarily non-functional; and (3) the product design is inherently distinctive or has acquired secondary meaning. Because we conclude that DDI has not met its burden of establishing the non-functionality of its product design, we decline to address the other two elements of the claim. . . .

The features of product design that we must analyze in this case are the size, color, and shape of dippin' dots. . . .

[T]he product design of dippin' dots in its individual elements and as a whole is functional under the traditional test. The color is functional because it indicates the flavor of the ice cream, for example, pink signifies strawberry, white signifies vanilla, brown signifies chocolate, etc. . . . The district court took judicial notice of the fact that color indicates flavor of ice cream. DDI argues that such judicial notice was improper. We disagree.

Judicial notice is a means by which adjudicative facts not seriously open to dispute are established as true without the normal requirement of proof by evidence. Fed. R. Evid. 201(a) and (b); *see also* Fed. R. Evid. 201(a) advisory committee's note (explaining that it is proper to take judicial notice of facts with a "high degree of indisputability" that are "outside the area of reasonable controversy"). Adjudicative facts are facts that are relevant to a determination of the claims presented in a case. *Id.*

One category of adjudicative facts subject to judicial notice (and the only category relevant in this case) is facts that are "generally known within the territorial jurisdiction of the trial court." Fed. R. Evid. 201(b). Such judicially-noticed facts are of breathtaking variety. *See, e.g., Friend v. Burnham & Morrill Co.*, 55 F.2d 150, 151-52 (1st Cir. 1932) (noting the method for canning baked beans in New England); *Seminole Tribe of Fla. v. Butterworth*, 491 F. Supp. 1015, 1019 (S.D. Fla. 1980), *aff'd*, 658 F.2d 310 (5th Cir. 1981) (noting that bingo is largely a senior citizen pastime); *First Nat'l Bank of South Carolina v. United States*, 413 F. Supp. 1107, 1110 (D.S.C. 1976), *aff'd*, 558 F.2d 721 (4th Cir. 1977) (noting that credit cards play a vital role in modern American society); *Carling Brewing Co. v. Philip Morris, Inc.*, 277 F. Supp. 326, 330 (N.D. Ga. 1967) (noting that most establishments that sell beer also sell tobacco products); *Colourpicture Publishers, Inc. v. Mike Roberts Color Prods., Inc.*, 272 F. Supp. 280, 281 (D. Mass. 1967), *vacated on other grounds*, 394 F.2d 431 (1st Cir. 1968) (noting that calendars have long been affixed to walls by means of a punched hole at the top of the calendar).

A court may take judicial notice of appropriate adjudicative facts at any stage in a proceeding, including at the summary judgment stage. While a court has wide discretion to take judicial notice of facts, *see* Fed. R. Evid. 201(c), the "taking of judicial notice of facts is, as a matter of evidence law, a highly limited process." *Shahar v. Bowers*, 120 F.3d 211, 214 (11th Cir. 1997). "The reason for this caution is that the taking of judicial notice bypasses the safeguards which are involved with the usual process of proving facts by competent evidence in district court." *Id.* In order to fulfill these safeguards, a "party is entitled . . . to an opportunity to be heard as to the propriety of taking judicial notice." Fed. R. Evid. 201(e).

In this case, the district court took judicial notice of the fact that color is indicative of flavor in ice cream. This fact is adjudicative in nature and is generally known among consumers. In addition, the district court specifically questioned DDI's counsel regarding the propriety of taking judicial notice of the fact:

The Court: — would you agree that I could take judicial notice that chocolate ice cream is, generally speaking, brown, vanilla is white, strawberry is pink?

[Counsel]: I think you could do that, I think you could, sir, but I think it would be appropriate to acknowledge that sometimes it's not. Chocolate can be white. I mean, that's not an uncommon occurrence. Certainly with M&M's, chocolate comes sometimes in a blue color.

The Court: I'm just talking about ice cream.

[Counsel]: Yes, sir.

The Court: Ice cream is, generally speaking, chocolate is brown, vanilla is white, and strawberry is pink.

[Counsel]: That's correct, sir, but it's not necessarily so.

Therefore, the district court properly took judicial notice of the fact that the color of ice cream is indicative of its flavor. Likewise, we, who also questioned DDI's counsel at oral argument regarding the propriety of taking judicial notice, take judicial notice of the fact that color of ice cream is indicative of flavor. Accordingly, we conclude that color is functional in this case because it is essential to the purpose of the product and affects its quality. . . .

Based on our review of the record and dippin' dots' individual elements, we conclude that the totality of the dippin' dots design is functional because any flash-frozen ice cream product will inherently have many of the same features as dippin' dots. Therefore, DDI's product design as a whole is essential to its purpose and affects its quality. Accordingly, it is functional under the traditional test, and not subject to trade dress protection. . . .

Accordingly, summary judgment in favor of FBD was proper. . . .

NOTES TO DIPPIN' DOTS, INC. v. FROSTY BITES DISTRIBUTION, LLC.

1. **Common Knowledge.** The court characterized the judicial notice in this instance as being justified under FRE 201(b)(1), covering facts that are generally known in the court's jurisdiction. This characterization has been applied to many different kinds of information, including the following:

- The North Platte River tends to run below the high water line. Davison v. Wyoming Game & Fish Commission, 238 P.3d 566 (Wyo. 2010).
- Locations of facilities where Workers' Compensation claimant could have sought assistance. Shirley v. J&S Dozer Services, Inc., 12 So. 3d 1109 (La. Ct. App. 2009).
- Lay-offs had been common at a particular industrial plant. Ritter v. Hughes Aircraft Co., 58 F.3d 454 (9th Cir. 1995).

2. **Verifiable Facts.** FRE 201(b)(2) refers to facts whose accuracy can easily and readily be determined from reliable sources. Examples of this category of facts include:

- *A party's prior conviction.* Kowalski v. Gagne, 914 F.2d 299 (1st Cir. 1990).
- *Time of sunrise on a certain day.* Davis v. Freels, 583 F.2d 337 (7th Cir. 1978).
- *Stock prices.* Greenhouse v. MCG Capital Corp., 392 F.3d 650 (4th Cir. 2004).

3. **Criminal Cases.** Note that FRE 201(f) requires that a jury instruction related to judicial notice in a criminal case may state only that the jury *may* accept the judicially noticed fact as conclusive.

QUESTION 17-3. Which of the following would be an *improper* basis for taking judicial notice that several blocks of a street in a large city are extremely curvy?

A. A map published by the city's department of street maintenance.
B. A trial judge's belief that most people in the city consider the street curvy.
C. A trial judge's knowledge that the street is curvy because the judge drives on the street many days a week.
D. An aerial photo from an Internet-based map service.

SUMMARY

Presumptions and judicial notice are both techniques that allow facts to be established without requiring litigants to have direct proof of those facts. A presumption allows a fact to be established when a litigant has persuasive proof of some other related fact. Judicial notice allows a fact to be established when a judge excuses the litigant from proving it because it is generally known or subject to easy and accurate determination from reliable sources.

Presumptions in General. A presumption gives its proponent a procedural benefit when the proponent introduces evidence sufficient to support a finding of a basic fact. To establish, for example, that someone has died, proof of a basic fact — that during seven years the person has not been seen in the places where the person had ordinarily been or been heard from by people with whom the person had ordinarily been in contact — will be treated as equivalent to proof of a presumed fact that the person is dead.

Specific Procedural Effect of Presumptions. In some places, assuming for clarity that the plaintiff is the proponent, the plaintiff gets the benefit of a shift in the persuasion burden, so that the defendant must persuade the jury of the nonexistence of the presumed fact. This is a contrast to the ordinary circumstance in which the plaintiff would have the persuasion burden on that fact.

In federal court and in many states, the benefit to the proponent of a presumption is much less. All that the presumption does is shift the production burden. This means that if the opponent of the presumption fails to introduce evidence on the topic of the presumed fact, that presumed fact will be treated as established. On the other hand, if the opponent of the presumed fact does introduce evidence adequate to support a conclusion that the presumed fact does not exist, then the presumption has no further role in the case.

Judicial Notice. Judicial notice treats facts as established, or (for criminal cases) as available for the jury to accept, if the court finds that they are well known in the court's jurisdiction or that they can be ascertained readily and accurately from reliable sources.

Scientific facts from reference works, geographical facts from maps, information from public records, the atmosphere of a city's neighborhoods, locations and characteristics of public places, and typical practices in professions like law are all examples of topics that might be subject to judicial notice.

Principal cases are indicated by italics.

A

Abel; United States v., 478, 483
Adalman v. Baker, Watts & Co., 594
Adamson; State v., 640
Adjutant; Commonwealth v., 93, 96, 124
Aguiar; United States v., 379
Aikman v. Kanda, 132, 135–136, 157
Alberico; State v., 580, 581
Alberts; State v., 151
Alberty v. United States, 19
Aldrich v. Railroad, 48
Alexander; United States v., 677, 681–682
Alexis; State v., 471
Alford v. United States, 480
Allen; United States v., 518, 521–522
Aloi v. Union Pac. R.R. Corp., 27, 31–32, 44
Amador-Galvan; United States v., 589
Application of. *See name of party*
Aramony; United States v., 108
Arias-Santana; United States v., 355
Armstrong v. State, 183
Ary; United States v., 341
Ault v. International Harvester Co., 49
Austad; State v., 89–91

B

Baines; United States v., 570, 573
Baisley v. Missisquoi Cemetery Ass'n, 622
Baker v. Kammerer, 489–491
Ballou v. Henri Studios, Inc., 114
B&K Rentals & Sales Co. v. Universal Leaf Tobacco Co., 217, 220–221, 226
Bank of Am., N.A. v. Barr, 344
Bank of Lexington & Trust Co. v. Vining-Sparks Sec., Inc., 352
Barnes/Science Assocs. LP v. Barnes Eng'g Co., 627, 629
Barnett v. Hidalgo, 213, 214, 216, 226
Beahm; United States v., 18
Becker v. ARCO Chem. Co., 131
Beech Aircraft Corp. v. Rainey, 353
Beechum; United States v., 109
Begin; State v., 471
Benally; United States v., 549
Beneficial Me., Inc. v. Carter, 343, 347
Bengali; United States v., 108

Best; United States v., 292
Bethel v. Peters, 51, *52*, 54–55, 72
Betterbox Commc'ns Ltd. v. BB Techs., Inc., 575, 576
Bevan v. Garrett, 190
Biegas v. Quickway Carriers, Inc., 172, 173–174, 197
Bill v. Farm Bureau Ins. Co., 212
Blake v. State, 298
Blakey; United States v., 264
Blazek v. Superior Court, 641
Blechman; United States v., 339, 342–343
Bob Jones Univ. v. United States, 356
Bonser v. Shainholtz, 492
Boyd v. United States (142 U.S. 450 (1892)), *76*, 78, 124
Boyd; United States v. (53 F.3d 631 (4th Cir. 1995)), 108
Bradford; State v., 278
Brandon; United States v., 674
Brennan v. Reinhart Institutional Foods, 597, 598
Brien; United States v., 589
Brink; United States v., 250
Briscoe; United States v., 334, 336
Broderick v. King's Way Assembly of God Church, 385, 388–389
Brouillette; State v., 474
Brown v. Hebb, 218
Brown; State v., 130, 132, 157
Brown; United States v., 355
Bryan; United States v., 535, 650
Buchanan; United States v., 593
Buckner; State v., 451
Bullcoming v. New Mexico, 431, 437, 439, 440, 442, 443
Burkhart v. Washington Metro. Area Transit Auth., 594
Byrd; United States v., 640

C

Cain; United States v., 264
Calamaro; United States v., 680
Caldwell; State v., 449, 450, 454
Camm v. State, 289, 291–292, 308
Cappuccio v. Prime Capital Funding LLC, 696
Cardenas; United States v., 674
Carling Brewing Co. v. Philip Morris, Inc., 709
Carlson; State v., 209, 212–213, 226
Carson v. Polley, 550
Carter v. State, 290
Cazares-Mendez; State v., 395, 402–403

713

Cerrillo v. Esparza, 147
Cestnik; United States v., 341, 342
Chambers v. Mississippi, 146, 395, 397–399, 401, 402
Chapman v. California, 487
Chomicki v. Wittekind, 132
Christian; State v., 637, 642–643
Christie v. New England Tel. & Tel. Co., 48
City of. *See name of city*
Clark v. United States, 633
Coca-Cola Co. v. Tropicana Prods., Inc., 283
Coe; State v., 104
Cohen; United States v., 290
Cole v. State, 183
Collins v. Wayne Corp., 495
Colourpicture Publishers, Inc. v. Mike Roberts Color
    Prods., Inc., 709
Colvard v. Commonwealth, 301, 304–306, 308
Commonwealth v. *See name of opposing party*
Conner v. State, 306
Conroy v. Abraham Chevrolet-Tampa, Inc., 313
Cookson v. Schwartz, 254
Cooper v. United States, 20
Cornell; State v., 221, 224–226
Cox v. Miller, 645, 648
Cox v. State, 33, 35–36, 44
Crane v. Kentucky, 402
Crawford v. Washington, 254, 378, 404, 405, 407–410,
    412–415, 417–421, 423–431, 433–438, 440, 442, 443,
    445
Creaghe v. Iowa Home Mut. Cas. Co., 179
Cruz; State v., 522
Culp v. State, 267
Curran v. Pasek, 639
Cyr v. J.I. Case Co., 47, 50–51, 72

D

Darden; State v., 146
Daubert v. Merrell Dow Pharms., Inc., 526, 555, *556,*
    561–564, 566–575, 577, 581–583, 605–606
Davis v. Alaska, 486
Davis v. Freels, 710
Davis; State v., 600, 601, 604–605
Davis; United States v., 250
Davis v. Washington, 405, 408–410, 413, 415–421,
    423–425, 428, 430, 431
Davison v. Wyoming Game & Fish Comm'n, 710
Dawkins v. Sawicki, 135
Day; United States v., 233, 234, 237, 256
Dazey; United States v., 317, 318, 320–321
Decker v. State, 20
Delaware v. Van Arsdall, 486, 487
Dent; United States v., 391
Destination Travel, Inc. v. McElhanon, 543

DiCaro; United States v., 232
Dierling; United States v., 508
DiFrancesco v. Excam, Inc., 25
Dillon; United States v., 16, 17, 19–20, 44
Dippin' Dots, Inc. v. Frosty Bites Distribution, LLC, 707,
    710
Distler; United States v., 232
DiZenzo; United States v., 110
Dollar v. Long Mfg., N.C., Inc., 115
Dowdell; United States v., 353, 356–357
Dowling v. United States, 115
Downing; United States v., 560
Dullard; State v., 191, 196, 198
Dunaway v. State, 290
Dupont Cellophane Co. v. Waxed Prods., 281
Duquette; State v., 516
Dykes v. Raymark Indus., Inc., 362

E

Eakins; State v., 85, 86
Ede v. Atrium S. OB-GYN, 489, 490
Edwards v. Commonwealth, 302, 304
Eickelberg v. Deere & Co., 22
Elkins v. United States, 535, 651
Espeaignnette v. Gene Tierney Co., 25, 26
Evans v. State, 268
Ex parte. *See name of party*

F

Fells v. State, 148, 149, 150–151, 157
Field v. Trigg Cnty. Hosp., Inc., 185, 187–188, 198
Fields v. Brown, 543
First Nat'l Bank of S.C. v. United States, 709
Fischer v. State, 261, 264–265, 307
Fisher v. United States, 619
Flaminio v. Honda Motor Co., 56, 58–60, 72
Flores; State v., 269, 270, 272, 307
Ford; United States v., 108
Fosher; United States v., 589
Foxhoven; State v., 102, 105–107, 125
Frazier; United States v., 582
Friend v. Burnham & Morrill Co., 708
Frye v. United States, 525, 557, 558, 561–563, 565–567,
    569, 570, 572, 573, 577, 606
Funk v. United States, 533

G

Gabe; United States v., 154, 155
Gajo; United States v., 230, 233, 256
Gamerdinger v. Schaefer, 136, 138–139, 157
Garber; United States v., 593
Gassler; State v., 474, 475
Genentech, Inc. v. International Trade Comm'n, 627

General Elec. Co. v. Joiner, 562
Germain v. State, 322, 326, 330
Geyer; State v., 472
Gibbs; United States v., 576
Giles v. California, 410, *411*, 414
Glover v. BIC Corp., 30
Goforth v. State, 252, 255–257
Gomez; United States v., 576
Goodson v. State, 587
Gordon v. Commonwealth, 172
Gordon v. United States, 459
Gowan; State v., 87, *88*, 91, 124
Grady v. Frito-Lay, Inc., 569
Grand Jury Investigation, In re, 635
Grandmont; United States v., 18
Grant v. State, 365, 367
Graure v. United States, 272, 274–275, 307
Graves v. United States, 533
Gray v. Bicknell, 627
Gray; United States v., 376, 379–381
Greenhouse v. MCG Capital Corp., 710
Gregory; State v., 146
Guenther; State v., 461, 465–466

H

Hadaway; United States v., 110
Hallmark v. Allied Prods. Corp., 59
Halsey v. Sinsebaugh, 316
Hammon v. Indiana, 405, *406*, 410, 416–418, 423, 424, 438
Hansen v. Heath, 293, 295–296, 308
Hard v. Burlington N. R.R. Co., 542
Harding v. State, 525, 527
Hardy; State v., 469, *470*, 472, 475–477
Harlan; People v., 540–542
Harp v. King, 623, *625*, 630–631
Harris; United States v., 355, 590
Hatton v. Robinson, 611
Haughton; United States v., 356
Hawkins v. United States, 532–537
Hayden; United States v., 108
Haywood; United States v., 576
Henderson, Ex parte, 19
Hernandez; State v., 184
Hickey v. Settlemier, 188, 190–191, 198
Hickman v. Taylor, 622, 658
Hill v. State, 277
Hilyer v. Howat Concrete Co., 264
Hobbs; State v., 451
Hobgood v. State, 583, *585*, 587–588
Hoffart v. Hodge, 135
Hollow Horn; United States v., 152, 156, 158
Holmes v. South Carolina, 401, 402
Hord v. Commonwealth, 19

Houston Oxygen Co. v. Davis, 262
Howard; United States v., 682, 684
HSBC Mortgage Servs. v. Murphy, 346
Huddleston v. United States, 109
Hudlow; State v., 146
Hudson; United States v., 589
Hudson Pulp & Paper Corp.; NLRB v., 312
Huff v. White Motor Corp., 388
Hurd; State v., 526, 527

I

Ibar v. State, 562
Ihnot; State v., 475
Inadi; United States v., 409
Ingram; State v., 20
In re. *See name of party*
Iron Shell; United States v., 298

J

J.A., In Interest of, 265
Jackson v. State, 587
Jaffee v. Redmond, 649, 653–654
James; State v., 285, 288–289, 291, 308
James v. Tucker, 492
Japanese Elec. Prods. Antitrust Litig., In re, 391
Jin Fuey Moy v. United States, 533
Joe; United States v., 298, 299
John A. Russell Corp. v. Bohlig, 78, *79*, 81–82, 124
John Doe Grand Jury Investigation, In re, 612
Johnson v. Knebel, 582
Johnson v. Lutz, 342–343
Johnson v. United States (616 A.2d 1216 (D.C.)), 639
Johnson v. United States (980 A.2d 1174 (D.C.)), 273
Johnson; United States v. (977 F.2d 1360 (10th Cir. 1992)), *673*, 675–676
Jones v. Pak-Mor Mfg. Co., 25, 26
Jones; State v. (271 N.W.2d 534 (Minn. 1978)), 474–476
Jones; State v. (101 Wash. 2d 113 (1984)), 470–472, 476
Jones; State v. (625 So. 2d 821 (Fla. 1993)), 303
Jones; State v. (230 P.3d 576 (Wash. 2010)), *145*, 148, 157
Jones; United States v., 311, 313–314

K

Kaechele v. Kenyon Oil Co., 12, 15, 44
Kaquatosh; United States v., 250
Katt; People v., 390, 394
Keeter; United States v., 254
Kelly; State v., 85, 86
Kemp; State v., 584
Kendrick v. Pippin, 539, *540*, 544
Kennewick, City of v. Day, 83, *84*, 86–87, 124
Kenny v. Southeastern Pa. Transp. Auth., 56, *57*, 58–60, 72
Kentucky v. Stincer, 253

Kenyon v. State, 181, 184, 198
Kowalski v. Gagne, 710
Kronisch v. United States, 31
Kumho Tire Co. v. Carmichael, 567, 572, 574, 575, 606

L

Lambert; State v., 207, 209, 226
Lanari v. People, 612
Langan; United States v., 589
Langness v. Fencil Urethane Sys., Inc., 498, *499*, 501
Larson v. Valente, 645
Lavender v. Kurn, 598
Lea; United States v., 639
LeCompte; United States v., 154
Lepanto; United States v., 675
Lerch; State v., 601, 602
Lerner; State v., 208
Lewis; United States v., 245, 248, 256
Leyva v. State, 115, *116*, 118–119, 125
Littlejohn; State v., 638, 640
Livingston; United States v., 236
Llera Plaza; United States v., 573
Long; State v. (656 A.2d 1228 (Me. 1995)), *514*, 516–517
Long; State v. (140 S.W.3d 27 (Mo. 2004)), 465
Lopez; United States v., 250
Lord Morley's Case, 412
Lorraine v. Markel Am. Ins. Co., 670
Lovick v. Wil-Rich, 20, 23, 44
Lowy v. PeaceHealth, 655, 659–660
Luce v. United States, 476
Lumpkin; United States v., 589
Lust v. Sealy, Inc., 336, 338

M

Mack; State v., 525
Manfre; United States v., 264
Mann; State v., 542
Marchand; United States v., 247
Mark; United States v., 110
Marr v. Bank of Am., N.A., 692, 696–697
Martin v. Savage Truck Line, 220
Martin v. United States, 236
Marx & Co. v. Diners' Club, Inc., 592, 593
Massengill; State v., 271
Matsushita Elec. Indus. Co. v. Zenith Radio Corp., 391
Matter of. *See name of party*
Mattson; State v., 9
McDonald v. Pless, 547
McGinnis; State v., 113, 114
McIntyre; United States v., 341
McKee v. State, 501, 503–504
Melendez-Diaz v. Massachusetts, 427, 431–437, 439–443
Michelson v. United States, 89, 90

Michigan v. Bryant, 414, *415*, 421, 424, 426, 439
Middleton; State v., 585
Midwest Fireworks Mfg. Co.; United States v., 351, 352–353
Miller v. Crown Amusements, Inc., 265
Miller; State v., 121, 122
Miller; United States v., 240
Mitchell v. State, 156
Mitchell; United States v., 571
Moats Trucking Co. v. Gallatin Dairies, 164, 165
Moccia; United States v., 39
Moen v. Thomas, 177, 180, 198
Montague; United States v., 380
Montgomery; State v., 639
Morgan v. Foretich, 303
Morsley; United States v., 108
Moskowitz; United States v., 167
Motion to Quash Bar Counsel Subpoena, In re, 632, 636
Mueller v. Abdnor, 176
Mutual Life Ins. Co. v. Hillmon, 286–291
Myers; United States v., 17, 19

N

Neadeau; United States v., 230, 233, 256
New Hope, Village of v. Duplessie, 212
Newton; United States v., 665, 667
New York City Application re Lincoln Square Slum Clearance Project, 204, *205*, 206, 225
Nick; United States v., 387
NLRB v. *See name of opposing party*
Novak v. McEldowney, 10

O

O'Banion v. Owens-Corning Fiberglas Corp., 361, 363
Odom; State v., 265
Ohio v. Clark, 422, 426
Ohio v. Roberts, 404, 421, 423, 425, 428, 434
Ohler v. United States, 476
Oken v. State, 324
Old Chief v. United States, 37, 43, 44
Olden v. Kentucky, 483, *484*, 487
Oldman v. State, 296, 299–300, 308
Orkin Exterminating Co. v. McIntosy, 483
Orlando v. Herco, Inc., 25
Ormsby v. Emil Frankel, Comm'r of Transp., 23
Ortega; People v., 347, 348, 349
Ortiz; United States v., 472
Owens; United States v., 253–255

P

Palinkas v. Bennett, 139
Palmer v. Hoffman, 429
Pannu, In re, 144

Pappas; State v., 679
Paredes; State v., 369, 374–375
Patterson; State v., 166, 168–169, 197
Peck v. Valentine, 316
Peede v. State, 277
Peña-Rodriguez v. Colorado, 545, 549–551
People v. *See name of opposing party*
Pereira v. United States, 640
Perez; United States v., 576
Perrin v. Anderson, 131
Peterson v. State, 472
Pettus v. United States, 573
Philadelphia v. Westinghouse Elec. Corp., 619
Phillips; People v., 645
Pierce v. Underwood, 15
Pietranton; State v., 120
Pinnell; State v., 105
Pointer v. Texas, 486
Pressey v. State, 266, 268–269, *307*

Q

Queen; United States v., 107, 111, 119, 125
Queen's Case, 508
Quezada; United States v., 356
Quinto v. City & Borough of Juneau, 85
Quirion v. Forcier, 66, 69, 72

R

Rabe; State v., 85
Ragghianti; United States v., 236
Rahman; United States v., 483
Raleigh's Case, 409
Rappy; United States v., 325
Rattenborg v. Montgomery Elevator Co., 22
Rebelwood Apartments RP, LP v. English, 561
Renville; United States v., 296, 298, 299, 302, 304, 387
Reyes v. United States, 274
Reyes Contreras v. United States, 273–274
Reyes-Sanchez; State v., 399, 402
Reynolds v. United States, 378, 379
Rich v. Fuller, 13
Rincon; United States v., 589
Ritter v. Hughes Aircraft Co., 710
Rivera v. Anilesh, 135
Rivers; State v., 184, 473
Roach; United States v., 176
Roark v. Commonwealth, 523, 528
Robbins v. Farmers Union Grain Terminal Ass'n, 49
Robert S., Matter of, 96
Robinson; United States v., 176
Rock v. Arkansas, 402, 525
Rodgers; State v., 584
Rodriguez v. Commonwealth, 19

Romero; People v., 527
Ross v. State, 117
Rothlisberger; State v., 605
Roucoulet; Commonwealth v., 472
Rowbottom v. State, 503
Rowland v. Commonwealth, 524, 527
Rush v. Illinois-Central R.R. Co., 326, 330–333
Russell; United States v., 108
Russo; United States v., 335

S

Saada; United States v., 510
Samaniego; United States v., 341
Sampson v. Karpinski, 68
Sanchez; United States v., 108
Sanders; United States v., 335
Sandoval; People v., 143
Sandry v. John Deere Co., 22
Saunders; United States v., 142
Schafersman v. Agland Coop, 562, 563, 568–569
Schaffer v. State, 169, 171–172, 197
Scheerer v. Hardee's Food Sys., Inc., 338
Schering Corp. v. Pfizer, Inc., 279, 280, 283–284, 307
Schnapp; United States v., 504, 505, 508–509
Schultz v. Ford Motor Co., 701, 705–706
Schultz v. Schultz, 180
Segovia; People v., 455, 456, 460–461
Seiler v. Lucasfilm, Ltd., 684, 685, 689
Seminole Tribe of Fla. v. Butterworth, 708
Shahar v. Bowers, 709
Shaw; State v., 248, 249, 251, 257
Sheets; State v., 147
Shell Oil Co. v. Industrial Comm'n, 295
Shields v. Reddo, 203, 204, 225
Shirley v. J&S Dozer Servs., Inc., 710
Shoultz; People v., 184
Shoupe; United States v., 327–329
Siebert; People v., 472
Simonelli; United States v., 244
Simplex Inc. v. Diversified Energy Sys., Inc., 134
Slayton v. Ford Motor Co., 67, 68
Smith v. United States (583 A.2d 975 (D.C. 1990)), 133, 134
Smith v. United States (666 A.2d 1216 (D.C. 1995)), 274
Smith; United States v. (156 F.3d 1046 (10th Cir. 1998)), 589
Smith; United States v. (197 F.3d 225 (6th Cir. 1999)), 329
Smithers; United States v., 589
Snook; People v., 588
Snyder; United States v., 341
Spann v. State, 562
Specht v. Jensen, 590, 594

Sphere Drake Ins., PLC v. Trisko, *595*, 598–600
Spigarolo; State v., 583, *584*, 587–588
Spino v. John S. Tilley Ladder Co., 20, *23*, 27, 44
Spoonhunter; United States v., 519, 520
Sprick; United States v., *201*, 203, 225
Stanton v. Stanton, 536
State v. *See name of opposing party*
Stein v. Bowman, 533, 535, 639
Stoll v. State, *276*, 278–279, 307
Supreme Pork, Inc. v. Masterblaster, Inc., 5, *6*, 10–11, 44
Sutton; United States v., 508
Swidler & Berlin v. United States, 613–614

T

Tague v. Richards, 143
Taken Alive; United States v., *97*, 100–101, 124
Tanner v. United States (483 U.S. 107 (1987)), 546, 547, 549, 550
Tanner; United States v. (61 F.3d 231 (4th Cir. 1995)), 108
Taylor; State v. (598 N.E.2d 693 (N.Y. 1992)), *314*, 317
Taylor v. State (659 N.E.2d 535 (Ind. 1995)), 290
Taylor v. State (268 S.W.3d 571 (Tex. 2008)), 299
Tenerelli; United States v., *175*, 177, 198
Thomas; United States v., 250
Thompson; State v., 472
Tibbetts; State v., 19
Tienda v. State, 667, *668*, 672–673
Tome v. United States, *239*, 243–244
Torres; State v., 580
Torrez; State v., 577, *578*, 582
Trammel v. United States, 531, *532*, 537–538, 619, 639, 643, 646, 650–652
Tran Trong Cuong; United States v., 599
Trenkler; United States v., 355
Trower v. Jones, 494, 495
Truby v. Seybert, 204
Tucker; State v., 87, 500, 601

U

Union Nacional de Trabajadores; United States v., 355
University of Pa. v. Equal Emp't Opportunity Comm'n, 659
Upjohn Co. v. United States, 615, *617*, 622–623, 651
Utley v. City of Independence, 189

V

Varner; People v., 646
Varner v. Stovall, *644*, 647–648
Vick v. Texas Emp't Comm'n, 29
Vick v. United States, 20
Vigneau; United States v., 342
Village of. *See name of village*

Vincelette v. Metropolitan Life Ins. Co., 162, *163*, 165, 197
Vodusek v. Bayliner Marine Corp., 30

W

Walker; United States v., *574*, 577
Wallace v. Leedhanachoke, 490
Wal-Mart Stores, Inc. v. Londagin, 61, *62*, 64–65, 72
Walsh v. Chan, 43
Walton; State v., 466
Warger v. Shauers, 546, 547
Washington v. Texas, 146
Weatherspoon; United States v., 335
Wesp v. Everson, *609*, 615–616
Wheeler v. United States, 519, 520
Whetston v. State, 562
Whitman; State v., 483
Whittemore v. Lockheed Aircraft Corp., 132
Willett; State v., *119*, 122–123, 125
Williams v. Alexander, 349
Williams v. Illinois, *437*, 443, 469
Williams v. State (681 N.E.2d 195 (Ind. 1997)), 140, *141*, 144
Williams v. State (60 P.3d 151 (Wyo. 2002)), 157, 573
Williams; State v. (771 N.W.2d 514 (Minn. 2009)), *473*, 475–477
Williams; United States v., 232
Williamson v. United States, 371
Willingham v. Crooke, 303
Wilson; State v., 472
Wilson v. Volkswagen of Am., Inc., 133
Winebarger; State v., *112*, 115
Wiser v. People, 541
Wolfle v. United States, 639
Wong Sun v. United States, 20
Wong Wing Foo v. McGrath, 352
Woods v. State, 277
Woolum v. Hillman, 487, *488*, 492
Wright; State v., 602
Wright v. Tatham, 193
Wrobleski v. deLara, *492*, 496–497

Y

Yazzie; United States v., 131
Yellow; United States v., 155
Yoho v. Thompson, 592
Young v. Commonwealth, 264

Z

Zaehringer; State v., 150, 472
Zelman v. Simmons-Harris, 645
Zipkin; United States v., 592
Zippo Mfg. Co. v. Rogers Imps., Inc., 282
Zolin; United States v., 633, 634, 636

Federal Rules of Evidence (FRE)

103(a)	319
103(c)	328, 329
104	32, 689
104(a)	33, 559
104(b)	32–34, 516
106	233
201	706
201(a)	708
201(b)	708
201(b)(1)	710
201(b)(2)	710
201(c)	709
201(e)	709
201(f)	710
301	692, 695–698, 704–706
302	698
401–403	50
401	4, 5, 7, 8, 10, 15, 16, 38, 39, 43–45, 71, 480, 482
402	4, 5, 8, 38, 45, 480
403	5, 9, 15, 36, 38, 39, 42, 44, 45, 50, 55, 66, 68, 74, 98–100, 108–111, 114, 115, 142, 151, 154, 155, 201, 202, 282, 468, 481–483, 527, 592
404–415	16
404	76, 79, 82, 83, 87, 92, 95–97, 101, 124, 127, 131, 144, 152, 156, 449, 454
404(a)	73, 75, 78, 79, 127
404(a)(1)	82, 86, 101
404(a)(2)	98
404(a)(2)(A)	83, 86
404(a)(2)(B)(ii)	93, 100
404(a)(3)	449
404(b)	39, 73, 98, 102–105, 107–109, 111–114, 120–122, 127, 143, 154, 457
404(b)(1)	101
404(b)(2)	101, 102, 105, 111, 115, 141
405	81, 82, 91, 95, 98, 454
405(a)	98
405(b)	82
406	127–129, 131, 139
407	46, 47, 50–52, 54, 55, 57, 59–61, 71, 72
408	61, 64, 65, 68, 69, 72
409	70, 71
410	70, 71
411	70, 71
412	92, 128, 139, 141–144, 157, 487
412(b)	140, 143
413	128, 151–156, 158
413(a)	154
413(d)	154
414	128, 151, 152, 154–156, 158
415	128, 151, 152, 158
501	534, 607, 608, 618, 621, 649, 650, 652, 653, 660
502	608, 623, 624, 630, 660
502(b)	630
502(d)(1)	634
601	513, 517–519, 521, 522, 551
602	513, 514, 517, 528
603	520, 522
605	513, 539
606	513, 539
606(b)	539, 540, 544, 549–551
607	447, 449, 480
608	449, 454–456, 461, 480, 509
608(b)	457, 482
609	142, 449, 467, 469, 476, 480, 482, 509
609(a)	468
609(a)(1)	469
609(a)(2)	469
609(b)	468
610	480
611	330, 498, 501
611(b)	481
612	321, 322, 327–329, 333
613	504, 508, 509
613(b)	332, 506–509
614(b)	327
701	559, 600, 604
702	526, 555, 556, 558–561, 566, 572, 575, 576, 583, 587, 590, 591, 594, 604, 606
703	559, 595, 597, 599, 606
704	577, 592
801	162, 168, 190, 200, 228, 232, 241, 247, 386
801(a)	167, 195
801(c)	173, 176, 227, 283
801(d)	229, 246
801(d)(1)	228, 232, 248, 252, 255, 257
801(d)(1)(A)	230, 232, 233, 235–237, 331, 332
801(d)(1)(B)	238–240, 242, 331, 332
801(d)(1)(B)(i)	239, 243
801(d)(1)(B)(ii)	243, 244

801(d)(1)(C)	247–251
801(d)(2)	200, 207, 216, 374, 504, 509
801(d)(2)(A)–(E)	200
801(d)(2)(A)	203, 666
801(d)(2)(B)	209
801(d)(2)(C)	216
801(d)(2)(D)	218–220
802	162, 281
803	260, 275, 292, 310, 311, 334, 350, 359, 387, 388
803(1)–(3)	337
803(1)–(2)	271
803(1)	262–264, 269
803(2)	416
803(3)	282–285, 288–291
803(4)	292, 293, 296, 298–301, 303
803(5)	311–313, 317, 319, 329, 332
803(6)	334–338, 340, 342, 350, 351, 429
803(8)	351–356
803(8)(A)(ii)	353, 354
803(8)(A)(iii)	351–353
803(8)(B)	263, 264, 351, 353–356
803(8)(C)	351, 352
803(21)	454
803(23)	386–388
803(24)	384
804	359, 360, 364, 365, 368, 376, 381, 388
804(a)	362, 363
804(a)(5)	362
804(b)(1)	312, 360–362
804(b)(1)(B)	363
804(b)(2)	365, 368, 382
804(b)(3)	312, 368, 370, 374, 375
804(b)(5)	384, 386
804(b)(6)	375, 376, 378–380, 410, 413
805	341, 343
806	509, 510
807	384, 385, 389, 391
901	573, 664, 666, 670
901(a)	663, 674
901(b)	665, 690
901(b)(4)	666
901(b)(9)	672, 673
1001–1008	685
1001–1004	676, 677
1001	686
1001(1)	686, 688
1002	663, 686
1003	681
1004	681, 688, 689
1004(1)	685, 687, 688
1008	684, 685, 688, 689

Books and Articles

Broun, Kenneth, *McCormick on Evidence* (6th ed. 2006), 290, 645

Burnham, *The Attorney-Client Privilege in the Corporate Arena*, 24 Bus. Law. 901 (1969), 620

Cassidy, Michael, *Sharing Sacred Secrets: Is it (Past) Time for a Dangerous Person Exception to the Clergy-Penitent Privilege?*, 44 Wm. & Mary L. Rev. 1627 (2003), 645

Cole, Simon A., & Rachel Dioso-Villa, *Investigating the "CSI Effect" Effect: Media and Litigation Crisis in Criminal Law*, 61 Stan. L. Rev. 1335 (2009), 43

Faigman, David L., *How Good is Good Enough?: Expert Evidence Under* Daubert *and* Kumho, 50 Case W. Res. L. Rev. 645 (2000), 567

Fenner, G. Michael, *The* Daubert *Handbook: The Case, Its Essential Dilemma, and Its Progeny*, 29 Creighton L. Rev. 939 (1996), 566

Fisher, George, *The Jury's Rise as Lie Detector*, 107 Yale L.J. 576 (1997), 588

Fishman, Clifford S., *Jones on Evidence* (6th ed. 1972), 602

Graham, Michael H., *The Confrontation Clause, the Hearsay Rule, and Child Sexual Abuse Prosecutions: The State of the Relationship*, 72 Minn. L. Rev. 523 (1988), 304

Hare, Jr., Francis H., *Admissibility of Evidence Concerning Other Similar Incidents in a Defective Design Product Case: Courts Should Determine "Similarity" by Reference to the Defect Involved*, 21 Am. J. Trial Advoc. 491 (1998), 21

Hornstein, Alan D., *Between Rock and a Hard Place: The Right to Testify and Impeachment by Prior Conviction*, 42 Vill. L. Rev. 1 (1997), 472

McFarland, Douglas D., "Present Sense Impressions Cannot Live in the Past," 28 Fla. St. U.L. Rev. 907 (2001), 337

Miller, Robert Lowell, *Indiana Practice* (2d ed. 1995), 703

Mosteller, Robert P., *Child Sexual Abuse and Statements for the Purpose of Medical Diagnosis or Treatment*, 67 N.C. L. Rev. 257 (1989), 304

Murray, P., *Maine Evidence* (3d ed.. 1992), 516

Note, Toups v. Sears, Roebuck & Co.: *Re-Assessing Admissibility of Subsequent Remedial Measures Evidence in a Products Liability Suit*, 48 La. L. Rev. 985 (1988), 49

Powell, E., *The Practice of the Law of Evidence* (1st ed. 1858), 412

Saltzburg, *A Special Aspect of Relevance: Countering Negative Inferences Associated with the Absence of Evidence*, 66 Calif. L. Rev. 1011 (1978), 41

Sodaro, G. & P. Wilson, "Spousal Privileges," in *Testimonial Privileges* (S. Stone & R. Taylor eds., 2d ed. 1995), 639

Stoebuck, *Opinions on Ultimate Facts: Status, Trends, and a Note of Caution,* 41 Den. L. Cent. J. 226 (1964), 592

Strong, John W., *McCormick on Evidence* (5th ed. 1999), 63, 85, 102, 138, 298

Waltz, Jon R., "Judicial Discretion in the Admission of Evidence Under the Federal Rules of Evidence," 79 N.W.U. L. Rev. 1097 (1984), 121

Weinstein, Jack B. & Margaret A. Berger, *Weinstein's Federal Evidence* (2d ed. 1998), 35

Weinstein, Jack B. & Margaret A. Berger, *Weinstein's Federal Evidence* (Joseph M. McLaughlin, ed., 2d ed. 2004), 303, 327

Weinstein, Jack B. & Margaret A. Berger, *Weinstein's Federal Evidence* (Joseph M. McLaughlin, ed., Matthew Bender 2d ed. 2008), 8

Wigmore, J., *Wigmore on Evidence* (3d ed. 1940), 95, 96, 349, 650–651, 679

Wigmore, J., *Wigmore on Evidence* (Chadbourn rev. 1972), 686

Wigmore, J., *Wigmore on Evidence* (Chadbourn rev. 1974), 451

Wigmore, J., *Wigmore on Evidence* (Chadbourn rev. 1979), 109

Wigmore, J., *Wigmore on Evidence* (McNaughton rev. 1961), 619, 639

Wigmore, J., *Wigmore on Evidence* (Tiller rev. 1983), 89

Wright, Charles A. & Victor J. Gold, *Fed. Prac. & Proc. Evid.* (West 1990), 525, 527

A

Abuse of discretion. *See* Standards for review

Accident reports, 32, 51–55, 338, 429. *See also* Business records exception

Adjudicative facts, 706–727. *See also* Judicial notice

"Admission against interest," 205. *See also* Opponents' statements; Statements against interest

Admissions. *See* Opponents' statements

Adoptive statements, 200, 207–213, 225–226

Advice of counsel defense, 631. *See also* Lawyer-client privilege

Affidavits

  business records, integrating outsiders' information, 343–347

  Confrontation Clause and, 437–444

  defined, 428

  forensic analysis, regarding, 427–431

  of forgery, 347

  hearsay, and juror affidavits, 551

  juror, extraneous prejudicial information from, 539–541

  juror misconduct, 545–551

  medical malpractice case, 213–216

  purpose of, 427–428

  "testimonial" concept and, 404–405, 406–407, 427, 428, 429

  "trial by affidavit," 404

Animals, information from, 168

Appeals, generally, 2. *See also* Standards for review

Artwork, original writing rule, 684–690

Attorney-client privilege. *See* Lawyer-client privilege

Authentication of evidence, 664–676

  admissibility vs., 667

  chain of custody, 673–676

  circumstantial proof, 667–673, 690

  computer systems, information in and from, 672–673

  distinctive characteristics and circumstances method, 665–667

  examples of ways to meet requirement, 664–665

  extrinsic information, 667

  intrinsic information, 667

  judge and jury roles, 672

  methods of establishing authenticity, 664–665

  original writing rule, 663

  photos, 673

  reply doctrine, 667

  social media page, linking to particular author, 667–673

  videos, 673

Authorized speakers

  authorized but not controlled, 213–216

  proof of authorization, 216

B

Bench trial, 1

Best evidence rule. *See* Original writing rule

Bias, 478–497

  balancing jurors' racial biases with witness's romantic bias, 483–487

  discretion of court, 492

  due process rights of defendant, 484

  expert witnesses, income earned by, 492–497

  extrinsic evidence, 483

  financial interest in outcome of case, 487–492

  impeachment, 448, 509, 511–512

  insurance, commonality of, 487–492

  membership in prison gang, 478–483

  mutual assured destruction, 496

  nonsettling parties, toward or against, 66

  professional witnesses, 492–497

  proof of, 496

  sources of, 483

  substantial connection test, 492

Bible

  flight, references to, 19–20

  juror's possession or reading from, 544

Bootstrapping, 216

Burden of proof, 700. *See also* Presumptions

  burden of persuasion, 2, 692

  burden of production, 2, 692

"Bursting bubble" theory of presumptions, 694–695, 698, 703, 704, 705

Business records exception, 333–350

  absence of record of regularly conducted activity, 350

  accident reports, 338. *See also* Accident reports

  computer records, 336

  customer's actions, records of, 334–336

  foundational requirements, 344–345

  hospital records, 347–349

  integrating outsiders' information in operation of business, 343–347

  medical records, 295

nonliability, evidence of, 336–339
omissions in records, 349
outside sources of information, 339–343, 358
rationale for, 310, 333, 358
recipients' incentives, 347
recorded recollection exception, 310
regularly conducted activity, 333–350

C

Chain of custody, 673–676
civil vs. criminal cases, 676
distinctive items, 675–676
fungible items, 676
Character evidence, 73–125
aggressive character of defendant, 97
aggressive character of victim, 92–101
analysis of, 75
balancing test, 74
character as relevant fact itself, 81
conduct vs. character, proof of, 81
crimes or other acts, 101–102
cross-examination of character witness, 91
deferential appellate review, 115
essential element of claim or defense,
     character as, 82
foundation requirements, 454
good character of defendant, 87
habit evidence distinguished, 127, 129–132. *See also*
     Habit evidence
identity, proof of, 102–105
inconsistent statements to police, 118–119
intent, proof of, 107–112
lying to police officer, 118–119
modus operandi, proof of, 102–105
noncharacter use of evidence that could show
     character, 105
noncharacter vs. character uses of evidence,
     106–107
"opening the door" for, 87–92
opinion testimony, proof by, 82, 91
"other acts" evidence, doctrinal frameworks, 119
past acts evidence
     appellate litigation on, 122
     charged act vs. past act, similarity between, 111
     charged crime vs. past crime, similarity between,
          102–105
     drug sales in past as context for alleged drug
          sales, 119–123
     intent as well as traits shown by past conduct,
          111–115
     "part" of charged acts, past acts that are,
          115–119
     relevance of, 105

trial and acquittal on past acts, 115
     unlawful acts not resulting in conviction, 111
peaceful character of victim, 92, 93, 97
pertinent trait, 83–86, 87
propensity inference. *See* Propensity evidence
reasonable fear, 96
relevance, 10–11
reputation evidence, 87
reputation testimony, proof by, 82, 91
self-defense cases, 92, 93–96, 97–100
sex crimes cases, 92
sexual conduct
     of perpetrator, 128, 156
     of victim, 128, 139, 140–141
social policy rules, 46
specific acts, proof of, 82
style of proof, 81–82
of victim, 92–101, 124
Child abuse cases, 298–299, 302–306, 387–388, 585–589
Child competency statute, 521–522
Child hearsay statutes, 305
Child molestation cases, 33–34, 74, 152, 154–155
Child sexual assault cases, 456–460
Child witnesses
     competency, 518–523
     Confrontation Clause, 422–427
     hearsay, 390–394
     oath or affirmation requirement, 522
Circumstantial evidence
     authentication of evidence, 667–673, 690
     intent, proof of, 107
Class bias, 19
Clear error. *See* Standards for review
Clergy-penitent privilege, 643–648
     generally, 660
     clergyperson, defined, 647–648
     function of, 646
     God, statements to, 644–648
     history of, 645
     religious purpose for communication, 647
Clergyperson, defined, 647–648
Closing argument, 2
Coconspirators' statements
     "during course of" requirement, 223
     "in furtherance" requirement, 223–224
     membership requirement, 223
     opponents' statements, 200, 221–225, 226
     preponderance standard, 225
Collateral matter
     cross-examination on, 498, 504
     defined, 504
     extrinsic evidence relating to, prohibition against,
          498–499, 501–504, 512

Common knowledge, 710. *See also* Judicial notice
Competency, 517–551
    child witnesses, 518–523
    civil cases, 518
    criminal cases, 518
    Dead Man's statutes, 529–531, 552
    defined, 517
    everyone treated as competent, 518, 522, 551
    general rule, 518, 523, 551–552
    hypnotized witnesses, 517, 523–529, 552
    impaired witnesses, 522
    of judge as witness, 529, 539, 551
    of juror as witness, 529, 539–544, 551, 552
    low intelligence, 522
    mental illness, 517, 529
    personal traits, 517–529, 551–552
    spousal incompetency, 513, 529, 531–538, 551, 552
    status-based rules, 529–551, 552
    witnesses, 513
Completeness rule, 233
Compromise offers, 61–65
Computer records, business records exception, 336
Computer systems, authentication of evidence,
        672–673
Conditional relevance, 35–36, 516. *See also* Relevance
Confidentiality, privilege and, 654
Confrontation Clause, 403–444
    child's statements, 422–427
    continuing emergency, 407, 408, 414–427, 445
    Crawford analysis, 404–414
    crime lab reports, 427–444, 445
    cross-examination, 252–256
    domestic violence cases, 410–414, 416
    expert witnesses, 595
    hearsay claims and, 380–381
    interrogation, primary purpose of, 416–420, 438, 445
    ongoing emergency, existence of, 407, 408, 414–421,
        438, 445
    opponents' statements, 213
    pre-2004 treatment of hearsay, 403–404
    public records exception, 356
    recent criminal conduct, statements to police
        about, 414–427
    routine documents in criminal investigation pro-
        cess, 427–444
    testimonial statements. *See* Testimonial statements
Conspiracy
    coconspirators' statements. *See* Coconspirators'
        statements
    defined, 223
Continuing emergency, 414–427
Contract law, objective standards in, 180
Contradiction, 448, 497–509, 512

Control group test, 622
Convictions. *See* Criminal convictions, impeachment by
Copies
    blurry copies, 677–682
    original writing rule, 677–682
Corporate setting
    control group test, demise of, 622
    lawyer-client privilege, 617–623, 660
Corroboration
    present sense impression, 265
    statements against interest, 372, 373, 374
Credibility of witness. *See* Truth telling, character for
Crime-fraud exception, 632–636, 660. *See also*
        Lawyer-client privilege
Crime lab reports, 427–444, 445. *See also*
        Confrontation Clause; Testimonial statements
Criminal cases
    chain of custody, 676
    character evidence, 101–102
    competency, 518
    dying declarations, 367, 381–382
    former testimony, 363, 381–382
    gang crime, 577–583
    judicial notice, 710, 711
    juror expectations regarding proof, 43
    lab reports, 427–444, 445
    no doctor-patient privilege in, 654, 661
    past acts vs. charged acts, 102–105
    presumptions, 706
    reputation evidence, 87
    sex crimes. *See* Sex crimes
    statements against interest, 374, 382
    words that are part of crime, 175–177
Criminal convictions, impeachment by, 467–478
    generally, 448
    appeal, limitations on, 476
    balancing test, 469, 470
    conviction more than ten years old, 469, 511
    counterexamples, 476–477
    criminal defendant vs. other witness to be
        discredited, 469, 511
    defendants' strategy, 476
    drug dealing and truthfulness, 469–478
    hearsay, 509–510
    truth-telling vs. non-truth-telling crime, 469, 511
Cross-examination
    availability of witness, 252–256
    collateral matters, 498–504
    direct, scope of, 501
    memory impairment, 252–256, 257
    nonrelevant topics, 498–501, 512
    prior inconsistent statements, 252–256, 257, 504–509
    relevance, 2

scope of, 498–501
voluntary refusal to testify, 255–256
wide-open rules, 501
witnesses' prior statements, 252–256, 257
"CSI effect," 43

D

Daubert framework, 562–570. *See also* Science-based
    opinions
    experience-based opinions, 605
    experience-based testimony and, 574
    fingerprint evidence, 570–573
    gatekeeping function of court, 544, 568, 570, 575
    nonscience fields and, 574
    opinion testimony, 555
    science-based opinions, 556–562
Dead Man's statutes, 529–531, 552
Death, presumption of, 700, 710
Decedent, transactions with. *See* Dead Man's statutes
Declarant rendered unavailable, 375–381
    deterring threats and harm to witnesses, 376–381
    motive for causing unavailability, 376–381
    ways to render declarant unavailable, 379–380
Defamation cases, 82, 188–191
Definitions
    affidavit, 428
    clergyperson, 647–648
    collateral matter, 504
    competency, 517
    conspiracy, 223
    duplicate, 676–677
    feasibility, 58–59
    habit evidence, 133, 138, 157
    hearsay, 162
    judicial notice, 691
    lawyer-client privilege, 624
    original, 676–677
    "original writing rule" definitions, 676
    photograph, 676
    presumptions, 691
    recording, 676
    relevance, 4–11, 43–44
    sexual assault, 152
    work product, 624
    writing, 676
De novo. See Standards for review
Destruction of evidence, 16, 27–32
Direct examination, 2, 501
Dissociative identity disorder, 528–529
Doctors
    doctor-patient privilege, 649, 654, 661
    malpractice. *See* Medical malpractice cases
    reporting statute, 654

Domestic violence cases, 410–414, 416
Donative intent, 180
Double jeopardy, 115, 255, 456, 457, 460
Drawings, original writing rule, 684–690
Drug dealing convictions, truthfulness and, 469–478
Due process
    bias evidence that might violate defendant's
        rights, 484
    prior act to show common plan or intent,
        admissibility of, 115
Due Process Clause
    hearsay rules vs., 395–403
    presumptions in criminal cases, 706
    residual exception, 444–445
    statements against interest, 395–403
Duplicates, admissibility of, 676–677, 681. *See also*
        Original writing rule
Dying declarations, 365–368
    civil cases, 367, 381–382
    counterexample, 367
    criminal cases, 367, 381–382
    excited utterance exception, overlap with, 367
    facts supporting application of rule, 367
    failure to die, 367
    last words, 367
    surviving declarants, 367
    testimonial setting, 421

E

Eavesdroppers, 643. *See also* Privileges
Elderly, hearsay treatment for, 306
E-mails between workers, 220
Employee of party, statements by, 200, 216–221, 226.
        See also Opponents' statements
Equal Protection Clause, 156
Excited utterance exception, 260–275
    answers as, 272–275
    child abuse prosecution, 305
    contents of statement, 269
    continuous excitement, 268
    dying declarations, overlap with, 367
    "excited," meaning of, 269–272
    foundational requirements, 267–268, 273
    kind of event, 269
    present sense impression vs., 268–269
    rekindled excitement, 268
    responses to questions, 272–275
    state-of-mind exception, 307
    textbook case, 272
    timing of statement, 268–269
Exclusionary rules
    accident reports, 55
    character evidence, 107, 121

compromise offers, 63
excited utterance exception, 260
party's own statement, 203
products liability cases, 50
relevance, 72
spousal incompetency, 535
Experience-based opinions, 574–583. *See also* Expert witnesses; Opinion testimony
generally, 554
Daubert analysis and, 574
Daubert framework, 605
on gang crime, 577–583
precision required for, 582
reliability of testimony, 575–577
science-based testimony distinguished, 577–583
Expert witnesses, 553
bias of, 492–497
credibility of victim, testimony on, 583–589, 606
experience-based opinions. *See* Experience-based opinions
eyewitness identification, testimony on, 589–590
finances of, 492–497
inadmissible evidence as basis for testimony, 595–600, 606
income earned by, 492–497
law, testimony about, 583, 590–594, 606
nonscientific knowledge, 554. *See also* Experience-based opinions
opinion testimony. *See* Experience-based opinions; Opinion testimony; Science-based opinions
patterns of narration, 583, 587–588, 606
professional, 492–497
"province of the jury," 588
qualifications of, 582
quoting another expert, 598–599
review of decision to admit or exclude, 562
review of trial court decisions, 562
science-based opinions. *See* Science-based opinions
topics for testimony, 554, 583–594, 606
ultimate issues, opinion on, 577
Extrinsic evidence
of bias, 483
collateral matter, relating to, 498–499, 501–504, 512
of contradiction, 504–509
of prior inconsistent statements, 504–509
of specific past lies, 461–467

F

False accusations, 461–467
False advertising cases, 83
False statements
about nonrelevant topics, 498–501
relevance and, 165

Feasibility
defined, 58–59
of greater safety, 55–60. *See also* Subsequent remedial measures
Financial interest in outcome of case, 487–492. *See also* Bias
Fingerprint evidence, 570–573
Flight, evidence of
absence from trial, 20
Bible references to, 19–20
class bias and, 19
inferring guilt from, 17–20
relevance, 16–32
Former testimony exception, 360–364
civil cases, 360–361, 363, 381–382
criminal cases, 363, 381–382
predecessor in interest, 360–364, 382
unavailability of declarant, 363–364, 382
Freedom of Information Act, 623
Frye test, 562–570, 573, 577, 606. *See also Daubert* framework; Science-based opinions

G

Gang crime, experience-based opinions on, 577–583
"General acceptance" test, 556–570, 605–606. *See also* Science-based opinions

H

Habit evidence, 127–139. *See also* Character evidence
business habits. *See* Routine practices of businesses
complexity and, 132–136
consistency, 138–139
defined, 133, 138, 157
due care, 135
negligence, 136–139
post-injury, 135–136
ratio of reactions to situations, 135
specificity of habit, 131, 132
traits distinguished, 127, 129–132
volition and, 132–136
Handwriting analysis, 573
Harmless error analysis, 2, 122, 363, 487
Health care providers
doctor-patient communications. *See* Doctors
mental health. *See* Mental health care
peer review records, 655
reporting statute, 654
Health care statements. *See* Medical statements exception
Hearsay
admission of statements barred by hearsay doctrine. *See* Due Process Clause
analysis of, 160, 165, 168

animals, information from, 168
child's, 390–394
confronting an absent declarant. *See* Confrontation Clause
constitutional issues, 213. *See also* Confrontation Clause; Due Process Clause
cross-examination, value of, 187–188
defined, 162
donative intent, 180
exceptions vs. exemptions, 203. *See also* Hearsay exceptions
exclusion of statements admissible under hearsay rules. *See* Confrontation Clause
exemptions, 161
foundations of doctrine, 159–198
hearsay within hearsay, 172–174
identifying hearsay, 320
identifying statements, 197
impeachment of declarants, 448, 509–510
implied quotation, 169–172
juror affidavits and, 551
juror testimony, 551
levels of, 174, 197–198, 217, 220–221, 295, 347–349, 374
machines, information from, 168
modifications of basic rules, 383–445
multiple hearsay, 172–174
nonhearsay compared, 162
nonverbal statements, 166–169
overview, 159–161
policy foundation, 197
quoting statements to explain police actions, 172
rationale of, 168
rule against, 162
self-quotation as, 173–174, 227
statements quoting statements, 172–174
subpoena power of defendants, 443
surveillance videos, 169
testimonial statements. *See* Testimonial statements
things are not statements, 168–169
"truth content" of statements, 174
witness's own out-of-court statements, 227–257
Hearsay exceptions
"availability immaterial" exceptions, 260
business records. *See* Business records exception
catchall, 384. *See also* Residual exception
child hearsay statutes, 305
confronting an absent declarant. *See* Confrontation Clause
declarant rendered unavailable, statement by, 375–381, 382
dying declarations. *See* Dying declarations
elderly, treatment for, 306

excited utterance. *See* Excited utterance exception
former testimony. *See* Former testimony exception
medical diagnosis or treatment, statements for. *See* Medical statements exception
present sense impression. *See* Present sense impression
public records. *See* Public records exception
recorded recollection. *See* Recorded recollection exception
refreshing present recollection. *See* Refreshing present recollection
regularly conducted activity, records of. *See* Business records exception
reputation concerning character, 454
residual exception. *See* Residual exception
statements against interest. *See* Statements against interest
state-of-mind exception. *See* State-of-mind exception
"tender years" exception, 394
then-existing mental, emotional, or physical condition, 260, 275–292, 307–308
unavailability required exceptions, 359–382, 402–403
establishing unavailability, 359
Hearsay exemptions
admission by party-opponent. *See* Opponents' statements
hearsay compared, 161. *See also* Hearsay
opponents' statements. *See* Opponents' statements
witnesses' prior statements. *See* Witnesses
Higher education, peer review materials, 655
Hospital records, business records exception, 347–349
Hypnotized witnesses
competency, 514, 517, 523–529, 552
exclusion of posthypnosis evidence, 528
scientific acceptance of hypnotically refreshed testimony, 528

I

Identifying person after perceiving person
cross-examination requirement, 252–256, 257
prior statements, 245–251
witness's own out-of-court statements, 228
Impaired witnesses, 522. *See also* Competency
Impeachment, 447–512
bias, by evidence of. *See* Bias
character-based propensity inference, 448, 449, 511. *See also* Propensity evidence
contradiction, 448, 497–509, 512
criminal conviction. *See* Criminal convictions, impeachment by

deceitfulness as character trait. *See* Criminal convictions, impeachment by
false accusations of rape, 463–466
false statements about nonrelevant topics, 498–501
of hearsay declarants, 448, 509–510
irrelevant information in witness testimony, 497–498
opinion evidence, 449
prior inconsistent statements, 448, 497–509, 512
prior statements, 229
propensity inference, 448, 449, 511. *See also* Propensity evidence
reputation evidence, 449–455
techniques for impeaching party, 447–448
witness's own past statements, 331–332
Inadmissible evidence as basis for testimony, 595–600, 606
Insurance, commonality of, 487–492
Intelligence of witness, 522. *See also* Competency
Intrinsic evidence
authentication of evidence, 667
of personal knowledge, 516
Investigative reports, 263, 357

J

Judge and jury roles
authentication of evidence, 672
mistakes by judges, 460
original writing rule, 684–685, 689
personal knowledge, 516–517
statements against interest, 369–375
Judge as witness, 529, 539, 551
Judicial admissions, 216
Judicial notice, 706–710
adjudicative facts, 706–727
common knowledge, 710
criminal case, 710, 711
defined, 691
jury instruction in criminal case, 710
legislative facts, 706–727
topics subject to, 711
verifiable facts, 710
Jury trials
generally, 1–2
Bible, juror possession or reading from, 544
bigoted statements during deliberations, 545–551
competency of juror as witness, 529, 539–544, 551, 552
criminal cases, juror expectations regarding proof in, 43
extraneous prejudicial information in jury room, 539–552

juror affidavits
hearsay and, 551
to show racial bias, 551
juror research and experiments, 544
jury instructions, 2, 111
judicial notice, 710
limiting instructions, 69, 599
racially biased statements during deliberations, 545–551
verdict, inquiry into validity of, 539–551
voir dire, 2, 451, 545–551, 638

L

Lawyer-client privilege, 609–636
accidental disclosures, 623–632
advice of counsel defense, 631
artificial creatures, 617–623
confidentiality requirement, 607, 608, 615–616, 617
control group test, demise of, 622
corporate setting, 617–623, 660
crime-fraud exception, 632–636, 660
death of client, effect of, 616
defined, 624
duration, 609, 616
inadvertent disclosure, 623–632
incentives for consulting lawyers, 615
preventing likely death or substantial bodily harm, 636
rationale for, 609
third-party presence during consultations, 615–616
waiver, 608, 609, 615–616, 623–624, 630–631, 660
Lay witnesses
helpfulness of opinion testimony to jury, 605
knowledgeable layperson, 600–605
opinion testimony by, 553, 554, 600–605, 606
specialized knowledge, 604–605
topics appropriate for opinion testimony, 553, 554, 606
Leading questions, 2, 330
Legislative facts, 706–727
Liability insurance, evidence of, 46, 70, 71, 72
Licenses, original writing rule, 684
Lineups, identification in, 194, 247, 251, 257
Losses of information, 551
"Lustful disposition" doctrine, 156

M

Malpractice cases
lawyer malpractice, 177
medical malpractice, 492–497
affidavits, 213–216
bias, 487–492
expert witnesses, 594

habit evidence, 132–136
hearsay, 551
out-of-court statements, 185–188
privileges, 654, 661
rape shield laws, 466
settlements, 66–70
Marriage
domestic violence. *See* Domestic violence cases
intramarriage wrongdoing, 643
range of policy choices, 537–538
spousal communications privilege. *See* Spousal communications privilege
spousal incompetency, 513, 529, 531–538, 551, 552
spousal testimonial privilege. *See* Spousal testimonial privilege
McCormick, Charles T., 698
Medical diagnosis or treatment, statements for. *See* Medical statements exception
Medical expenses after injury, payment of, 46, 70, 72
Medical malpractice cases, 487–497
experts' financial interest in case, 492–497
expert witnesses, 594
financial interest in outcome of case, 487–492
habit evidence, 132–136
hearsay, 551
medical malpractice, 213–216
out-of-court statements, 185–188
privileges, 654, 661
rape shield laws, 466
settlements, 66–70
Medical statements exception, 292–306
business records, 295
excited utterance exception, 260
medical records, hearsay in, 295
mental health practitioners, statements to, 299–300
naming assailant in statement to doctor, 296–301
patients' incentives for accurate health care statements, 301–306
state-of-mind exception, 308
Memory impairment, cross-examination of witness, 252–256, 257
Mental health care
practitioner-patient privilege, 649–654, 661
views on, 654
waiver of privilege when patient puts mental health at issue, 654
Mental illness, 517, 522. *See also* Competency
Modus operandi, proof of, 102–105
Morgan, Edmund M., 698
Motion for judgment as a matter of law, 599–600
Motion for summary judgment. *See* Summary judgment

Motion in limine
bias, 485
character evidence, 97–100, 108
habit evidence, 137
hearsay, 163
medical malpractice cases, 488
medical statements exception, 293
relevance, 7, 11, 24
science-based opinions, 563
settlements, 63
spousal communications privilege, 638, 641
statements against interest, 370
trial structure, 1
Motion to dismiss, 2, 456, 457
Multiple personality disorder, 514, 528–529

N

Negligent entrustment, 82
911 calls, interrogation in, 405–410, 419. *See also* Confrontation Clause; Testimonial statements
Nonhearsay
crime, words that are part of, 175–177
defamatory words, 188–191
impression made on person who hears words, 181–185
legally operative words, 175
legal power, words with, 177–180
verbal acts, 175, 177
Nonverbal statements, 166–169. *See also* Hearsay
"No prior claims" evidence, 24, 26–27

O

Oath or affirmation to testify truthfully, 513, 522
Opening statement, 2
Opinion testimony, 553–606
analysis of, 554
counterexample, 599
experience-based opinions. *See* Experience-based opinions
expert testimony, topics for, 554, 583–594, 605–606. *See also* Expert witnesses
impeachment, 449
inadmissible evidence as basis for expert testimony, 595–600, 606
lay opinion, 554, 600–605, 606. *See also* Lay witnesses
propensity evidence, 82, 91
science-based opinions. *See* Science-based opinions
on ultimate issue, 577
Opponents' statements, 199–226. *See also* Nonhearsay
adoptive statements, 200, 207–213, 225–226
"against the party" requirement, 204
agents' statements, 200, 216–221
authorized speakers, 200, 213–216, 226

coconspirators' statements, 200, 221–225, 226
e-mails between workers, 220
employees' statements, 200, 216–221, 226
of guilt, 201–203
motive when making statement, 204–206
party's own statement, 200, 201–206, 225
reasons for admission of, 204
silence as statement, 207–213
spokesperson's statement, 200, 213–216
Original writing rule, 676–690
artwork, 684–690
authentication of evidence, 663, 690
blurry copies, 677–682
copies and excuses, 681
definitions, 676
drawings, 684–690
duplicates, admissibility of, 676–677, 681
judge and jury roles, 684–685, 689
licenses, 684
rationale for, 681
receipts, 684
recordings of past events, 682–684
transcripts of recordings, 684
Out-of-court statements
characterization as relevant, 185–188
cross-examination, value of, 187–188
defamatory words, 188–191
implied assertions, 196
limiting instruction, clarity of, 188
media defendants, 191
relevant only if what they assert is true.
See Hearsay
unintended assertions, 191–196, 198
unintended inference from conduct, 191
videotape, 190
witness's own past statements, 227, 331–333

P

Past false charges, 461–467
Past injuries, 20–23. *See also* Relevance
Past recollection recorded. *See* Recorded recollection
exception
Past sexual conduct of victim. *See* Rape shield laws
Peaceful character of victim, 92, 93, 97
Peer review processes, privilege for, 655–660, 661
purpose of quality improvement committee, 656
use of privileged records to identify discoverable
records, 655–660
Peremptory challenges, 2
Personal knowledge
competency, 513
hypnotized witnesses, 528
intrinsic evidence of, 516

judge and jury roles, 516–517
proof of, 514–517
Photos, authentication of, 673
Physicians. *See* Doctors
Plans
probative value of, 288–289
state-of-mind exception, 285–292, 307
Pleadings, 216
Pleas and plea discussions, relevance, 70–71
Postaccident reports. *See* Accident reports
Predecessor in interest, former testimony exception,
360–364, 382
Prejudice vs. unfair prejudice, 15–16
Present memory refreshed. *See* Refreshing present
recollection
Present recollection revived. *See* Refreshing present
recollection
Present sense impression, 260–275
contents of statement, 269
corroboration, 265
counterexamples, 268–269
excited utterance exception vs., 268–269
kind of event, 269
state-of-mind exception, 306
time passage and reflection, 264–265
timing of statement, 268–269
Presumptions
burden of proof imposed, 700
"bursting bubble" theory, 694–695, 698, 703, 704, 705
ceremonial marriage, 700
civil cases, 692, 698
consequences of applicability of, 696
counterexamples, 698–700
criminal cases, 706
death, 700, 710
defined, 691
establishing applicability of, 696
federal treatment, 692–697
jury instructions, 705
legislative choices and policies advanced, 701–706
power of, 692–697, 698, 701, 711
procedural effects, 711
state treatments, 698–706
Prior consistent statements
counterexample, 243–244
cross-examination requirement, 252–256, 257
meaning of "prior," 239–244
substantive vs. nonsubstantive use of, 243–244
timing of statement, 239–244, 256
Prior inconsistent statements, 228–238
categories of, 237
counterexamples, 237
cross-examination, 252–256, 257, 504–509

current-trial requirement, 230, 233
detention hearing, testimony at, 230
extrinsic evidence of, 504–509
false testimony vs. different testimony, 233
hearsay declarants, 509
impeachment use, 331–332, 448, 497–509, 512
lack of memory of event, 230–233
legislative history, 233–237
partly inconsistent statements, 233
setting in which statement is made, 233–237
substantive use, 244, 331–332
Privileges, 607–661
analysis of, 608
clergy-penitent, 643–648, 661
common law, deference to, 607, 608
confidentiality and, 615–616, 617, 654
doctor-patient, 649, 654, 661
lawyer-client, 609–636, 660–661
mental health care practitioners and patients, 649–654, 661
peer review processes, 655–660, 661
reasons for, 660
social policy and, 608
spousal communications, 531, 539, 551, 636–643, 661
testimonial, 607
waiver, 608
work product of attorney, 622–623
Probative value. *See also* Relevance
measurement of, 43
subsequent remedial measures, 47
unfair prejudice, balancing with, 55
balancing test, 12, 15–16, 36–43
character evidence, 10–11
relevance, 3, 5, 9, 10, 44
Products liability cases, 20–27, 47–51, 55, 60. *See also* Safety record of product
Professional witnesses, 492–497. *See also* Expert witnesses
Propensity evidence
alternative basis for admissibility, 78
barring the inference, 83, 124
basic rule against, 75–83
character evidence, 73–74
"character" vs. "noncharacter" use in case, 78–82
circumstantial evidence, 81
defendant's introduction of defendant's propensity, 87–92, 124
evolving confidence in inference, 100–101
exceptions to prohibition against, 100–101
identifying the inference, 86
impeachment, 511

nonpropensity evidence that may show propensity, 101–123
permitted inferences, 83–101, 124
prohibition against, reasons for, 83
rationales for, 93–96
sexual conduct of defendant, 156
style of proof, 124–125
victim's character, 92–101, 124
Prostitution, 140–144, 157
Psychotherapist-patient privilege, 649–654, 661
Public records exception, 350–357
factual findings, 350–353
information and analysis, blends of, 353
investigative reports, 357
law-enforcement limitation, 353–357
opinions, 352–353
recorded recollection exception, 310
trustworthiness factor, 353

R

Rape shield laws, 139–140
balancing tests, 151
bias evidence and, 487
conduct ambiguously related to sexual acts, 148–151
defendant's need for evidence, 148
false claims of rape, 151, 466
past charges related to sexual conduct, 466
past false allegations of rape, 466
propensity evidence, 158
purpose of, 151
rationale for, 148
recent conduct, 145–148
sanctions for violation of, 144
sexual behavior, defining, 151
Rational relationship test, 156
Receipts, original writing rule, 684
Recorded recollection exception, 310–321
accuracy, 314
affirmance at trial, 313
foundation, 311
inability to testify fully and accurately, 317–321
leading questions, 330
more than one person, records created by, 314–317
public records exception, 357
read or played to jury, not given to jury as exhibit, 320–321
videotaped interrogation, 311–314
Recross examination, 2, 137
Redirect examination, 2, 137, 231, 361
Refreshing present recollection, 321–333
foundation for, 331, 333
insufficient memory of topic, 330

leading questions, 330
public records exception, 310
recorded recollection vs. refreshed recollection, 326
stimulating in-court testimony, 332
what can be used to refresh recollection, 330–333
with witness's own statements, 326–333
Regularly conducted activity, business records exception, 333–350. *See also* Business records exception
Rehabilitation of witness, 448
Relevance, 1–44
admissibility distinguished, 4–11
admissibility vs., 7–8, 9
analysis of, 3–4
bad character for truthfulness, 454
balancing test
probative value, 3, 5, 9, 12–16, 36–43, 44
unfair prejudice, 10–11, 15–16, 55
character, evidence of. *See* Character evidence
compromises. *See* Settlements
conditional, 3, 32–36, 44, 516
defined, 4–11, 43–44
destruction of evidence, 16, 27–32
discretion to exclude relevant evidence, 36–43
exclusion of relevant evidence, 5
false statements, 165
flight, 16–32
liability insurance, evidence of, 46, 70, 71, 72
medical expenses after injury, payment of, 46, 70, 72
missing witnesses, 31–32
"no prior claims" evidence, 24, 26–27
of out-of-court statements. *See* Out-of-court statements
overview, 2–4
past injuries, 20–23
pleas and plea discussions, 70–71, 72
policy concerns, 10
probative value vs. unfair prejudice
balancing test, 3, 5, 12–16, 36–43
character evidence, 10–11
subsequent remedial measures, 55
unfair prejudice, 9, 10
prohibited rational connections, 10–11
remedial measures. *See* Subsequent remedial measures
safety record of product, 16–32
settlements. *See* Settlements
sexual misconduct, 46
social policy rules, 45–72
standards of review, 12, 15
substantive legal theory, 12–16
test for, 4

unfair prejudice
analysis, 3
balancing test, 10–11, 12–16, 36–43
prejudice vs., 15–16
probative value, 5, 9, 44
subsequent remedial measures, 55
Remedial measures. *See* Subsequent remedial measures
Repairs, evidence of. *See* Subsequent remedial measures
Reply doctrine, 667
Reputation evidence
common law, 87
impeachment with, 449–455
foundational requirements, 451
general cross-section of community, 451–453
representativeness requirement, 450, 451–453
standards for, 449–455
propensity evidence, 82, 91
prosecutors vs. criminal defendants, 87
Rescission, 696–697
Res gestae, 218, 272
Residual exception, 384–394. *See also* Hearsay exceptions
circumstantial guarantees of trustworthiness, 385–389, 444
"near misses" under other exceptions, 384, 390–394, 399, 444
notice to opponent of intent to use exception, 385, 390
repetition of contents of initial statement, 389
requirements for admissibility, 386–387
Routine practices of businesses, 128, 129, 132–136, 137, 139. *See also* Business records exception; Habit evidence

S
Safety record of product
good vs. bad safety records, 27
"no prior claims" evidence, 24, 27
past injuries, evidence of, 20–23
relevance, 16–32
Science-based opinions, 555–573
Daubert framework, 555, 556–573, 605–606
evaluation of scientific information, 561
experience-based testimony distinguished, 577–583
fingerprint evidence, 570–573
Frye test, 562–570, 573, 577, 606
gatekeeping function of court, 544, 568, 570, 575
"general acceptance" test, 556–570, 605–606
handwriting analysis, 573
Self-defense cases, character evidence in, 92, 93–96, 97–101

Self-quotation as hearsay, 173–174, 227
Settlements
    bias toward or against parties not settling, 65–66
    impeachment use of settlement talk statements, 69
    relevance, 46, 72
    unfair prejudice, risk of, 68
    use to prove something different from conduct in
        dispute, 66–70
    validity of claim in dispute, use to show, 61–70, 72
Sex crimes
    character evidence, 92
    child molestation cases, 152
    defendants accused of, 151–157, 158
    "lustful disposition" doctrine, 156
    past conduct of victim. *See* Rape shield laws
    past false charges, impeachment and, 463–466, 511
    propensity inference in, 156, 158
    prostitute, victim's work as, 140–144, 157
    sexual assault cases, 152
    victims of, 128, 139–151
Sexual abuse, past false charges, 461–467
Sexual assault
    character evidence, 74
    defendants accused of, 152
    defined, 152
    experience-based opinions, 582
    past sexual wrongdoing vs. charged sexual
        wrongdoing, 152–156, 158
    similar crimes evidence, 152
Sexual conduct
    automatic assumptions, 144
    counterexample, 144
    of perpetrator, 128, 156
    of victim, 128, 139, 140–141. *See also* Rape shield
        laws
Sexual misconduct, 46
Shoplifting, 455–461
Sixth Amendment, 403, 404. *See also* Confrontation
    Clause
Social media page, authentication of evidence, 667–673
Spokesperson's statement, 200, 213–216
Spoliation of evidence, 27–32
Spousal abuse cases, 410–414, 416
Spousal communications privilege, 636–643
    competency, 531, 539, 551
    eavesdroppers, 643
    intramarriage wrongdoing, 643, 661
    lawyer-client privilege, 615–616
    noncommunicative conduct, 642
    rationale for, 637–643
Spousal incompetency, 513, 529, 531–538, 551, 552
    range of policy choices, 537–538
Spousal testimonial privilege, 636, 642, 643, 661

Standards for review
    abuse of discretion
        authentication, 674
        bias, 481
        business records exception, 344
        child witnesses, 392–393
        competency, 518
        Daubert framework, 562
        opinion testimony, 597
        public records exception, 355
        recorded recollection exception, 313
        relevance, 9, 15, 35
        settlements, 68
        sexual assault, 154
        statements quoting statements, 173
        unfair prejudice, 13
    balancing test, 15
    clear error, 15, 313, 344, 528, 635
    de novo, 15, 173, 344, 355, 635, 694, 708
Statements against interest, 368–375
    corroboration requirement, 372, 373, 374
    counterexample, 375
    criminal cases, 374, 381–382
    Due Process Clause and, 395–403
    implied adverseness to speaker's interest, 369–375
    judge and jury roles, 369–375
    partial adverseness to speaker's interest, 369–375
    statement by party opponent vs., 373, 375
State-of-mind exception, 275–292
    belief, statements of, to show belief, 279–285, 307
    excited utterance exception, 260
    fear, victim's statements of, 276–279
    plans, 285–292, 307
        planning for someone else to act, 289–292, 307
        planning to be someplace with somebody,
            285–289, 307
    surveys, 279–285, 307
    then-existing mental, emotional, or physical
        condition, 307–308
Strict liability cases, 20–27, 47, 60
Style of proof, 124–125
Subpoena power of defendants, 443
Subsequent remedial measures, 46–55
    allowed uses of, 59–60
    counterexample, 50–51
    "feasibility" rationale, 55–60, 72
    forbidden uses of, 59–60
    postaccident reports, 51–55
    "remedial," meaning of, 51–55
    "subsequent," meaning of, 51–55
Summary judgment
    business records exception, 343–347
    defamatory words, 188–191

judicial notice, 707–710
opinion testimony, 599–600
presumptions, 693–695
privileges, 625–628
relevance, 31
residual exception, 385–389
science-based opinions, 556–557
Supreme Court, U.S., composition of, 426
Surveillance videos, 169
Surveys, 279–285, 307

T

"Tender years" hearsay exception, 394
Tenure committees, peer review materials, 655, 659
Testimonial statements, 404–444
    911 calls, interrogation in, 405–410, 419
    affidavits regarding forensic analysis, 427–431
    crime lab reports, 427–444, 445
    grammar choice of speaker, 405, 408, 445
    interrogation in investigating possibly criminal past
        conduct, 408–410
    law enforcement personnel, statements to, 405–410
    meaning of "testimonial," 407–408, 445
    motivation of speaker, 405–410
    nontestimonial vs., 407, 408, 410
    statements not specifically about particular person,
        431
Thayer, James Bradley, 698
Trade dress infringement, 707–710
Transcripts of recordings, original writing rule, 684
Trial by affidavit, 404
Trial structure, 1–2
Truth in Lending Act, 692–697
Truth telling, character for, 454. *See also* Impeachment
    bad character for truthfulness, relevance of, 454
    counterexample, 460–461
        extrinsic proof of specific past lies, 461–467
        false accusations, 461–467
        probative value of, 460
        reasons for exclusion of, 462–463
        taking the answer, 460
    deceitfulness as character trait. *See* Criminal con-
        victions, impeachment by
    drug dealing convictions, 469–478
    extrinsic proof of false allegations, 461–467
    past acts evidence, 448, 455–461
    past convictions, proof of. *See* Criminal convictions,
        impeachment by
    shoplifting and, 455–461

U

Unavailability of declarant, 359–382, 402–403
Unfair competition case, 707–710

Unfair prejudice. *See also* Relevance
    balancing test, 10–11, 12–16, 36–43
    character evidence, 100, 114–115
    measurement of, 43
    prejudice vs., 15–16
    probative value, 5, 9, 10, 44
    relevance, 3
    subsequent remedial measures, 55
University peer review materials, 655, 659–660

V

Verdict, validity of. *See also* Jury trials
    juror testimony, 551
    mental processes of jurors, 550
Victims
    character evidence, 92–101, 124
    fear, statements of, 276–279
    prostitute, past work as, 140–144, 157
    of sex crimes, 128, 139–151
    sexual conduct of, 128, 139, 140–141. *See also* Rape
        shield laws
Videos
    authentication of evidence, 673
    of interrogation, 311–314
    out-of-court statements, 190
Voir dire, 2, 451, 545–551, 638

W

Waiver
    doctor-patient privilege, 654, 661
    lawyer-client privilege, 608, 609, 615–616, 623–624,
        630–631, 660
    mental health care practitioner-patient privilege,
        654
    privilege, 608
    work product privilege, 623–624
Wigmore, John Henry, 698
Will contests, no doctor-patient privilege in, 654, 661
Witnesses, 513–552
    competency of. *See* Competency
    experts. *See* Expert witnesses
    hypnosis, and competency, 517, 523–529, 552
    impaired, 522
    lay. *See* Lay witnesses
    low intelligence, 522
    mental illness, 517
    multiple personalities, 514
    oath or affirmation to testify truthfully, 513, 522
    opinion testimony. *See* Opinion testimony
    own out-of-court statements, 227–257
    personal knowledge, 514–517
    prior statements
        cross-examination requirement, 252–256, 257

identifying person after perceiving person, 228, 245–251, 256–257
impeachment of witness, 229
lack of memory of event, 230–233
prior consistent statements, 228, 238–245, 256
prior inconsistent statements, 228–238, 256
substantive vs. nonsubstantive use of, 229, 256
professional witnesses, 492–497
rehabilitation of, 448

scrutinizing witness's testimony, 331–332
stimulating in-court testimony, 332
substitutions for in-court testimony, 331, 332–333
truthfulness of. *See* Impeachment
Work product privilege, 622–623
definition of work product, 624
inadvertent disclosure, 623–624
waiver, 623–624